The Rough

D0362044

Switzerland

written and researched by

Matthew Teller

with additional contributions by

Kev Reynolds

ROUGH
GUIDES

We set out to do something different when the first Rough Guide was published in 1982. Mark Ellingham, just out of university, was travelling in Greece. He brought along the popular guides of the day, but found they were all lacking in some way. They were either strong on ruins and museums but went on for pages without mentioning a beach or taverna. Or they were so conscious of the need to save money that they lost sight of Greece's cultural and historical significance. Also, none of the books told him anything about Greece's contemporary life – its politics, its culture, its people, and how they lived.

So with no job in prospect, Mark decided to write his own guidebook, one which aimed to provide practical information that was second to none, detailing the best beaches and the hottest clubs and restaurants, while also giving hard-hitting accounts of every sight, both famous and obscure, and providing up-to-the-minute information on contemporary culture. It was a guide that encouraged independent travellers to find the best of Greece, and was a great success, getting shortlisted for the Thomas Cook travel guide award, and encouraging Mark, along with three friends, to expand the series.

The Rough Guide list grew rapidly and the letters flooded in, indicating a much broader readership than had been anticipated, but one which uniformly appreciated the Rough Guide mix of practical detail and humour, irreverence and enthusiasm. Things haven't changed. The same four friends who began the series are still the caretakers of the Rough Guide mission today: to provide the most reliable, up-to-date and entertaining information to independent-minded travellers of all ages, on all budgets.

We now publish more than 150 titles and have offices in London and New York. The travel guides are written and researched by a dedicated team of more than 100 authors, based in Britain, Europe, the USA and Australia. We have also created a unique series of phrasebooks to accompany the travel series, along with an acclaimed series of music guides, and a best-selling pocket guide to the Internet and World Wide Web. We also publish comprehensive travel information on our Web site:

www.roughguides.com

HELP US UPDATE

We've gone to a lot of effort to ensure that the first edition of *The Rough Guide to Switzerland* is accurate and up to date. However, things change – places get "discovered", opening hours are notoriously fickle, restaurants and rooms raise prices or lower standards. If you feel we've got it wrong or left something out, we'd like to know, and if you can remember the address, the price, the time, the phone number, so much the better.

We'll credit all contributions, and send a copy of the next edition (or any other Rough Guide if you prefer) for the best letters. Please mark letters: "Rough Guide Switzerland Update" and send to:
Rough Guides, 62–70 Shorts Gardens, London WC2H 9AB, or Rough Guides, 345 Hudson St, New York NY 10014.
Or send email to: mail@roughguides.co.uk
Online updates about this book can be found on Rough Guides' Web site at www.roughguides.com

THE AUTHOR

After graduating in 1991, **Matthew Teller** took off to spend most of the 1990s anywhere but London, enjoying extended periods in Europe, North America and the Middle East, where he sustained himself with writing work in between odd jobs milking cows, picking fruit and washing dishes. He worked on the Rough Guide to Amsterdam, and spent 1997–98 in Amman researching and writing the Rough Guide to Jordan.

ACKNOWLEDGEMENTS

At **Rough Guides**, Claire Saunders' patient, enthusiastic and skilful editing made the book much better than it might have been. Big thanks also to Mark Rogers and Camille Obering; Paul Gray; Sean Harvey and Alistair McDermott for extra Basics research; Helen Ostick for typesetting; Nichola Goodliffe for cartography; and Susannah Wight for proof-reading.

Helpful and efficient tourist office staff in towns big and small around Switzerland were invariably willing to go way beyond the call of duty. Space precludes listing them all, but extra-special thanks go, in no particular order, to Nicole Pandiscia (Ticino), Reto Küng (Chur), Isabelle Hesse and Gianna Mestermann (Geneva), Trudi Adank (Baden), Paul-Michel Bagnoud (Sierre), Martina Michel-Hoch (Liechtenstein), and Heidi Reisz, Evelyn Lafone and Russell Palmer in London. Elke Seccafico at Swissair New York patiently untangled bureaucratic knots aplenty. Mrs Aeschlimann, Cultural Attaché at the Swiss Embassy in London, provided valuable research materials, as did Pro Helvetia; the Swiss National Museum in Zürich; the Forum of Swiss History in Schwyz; Hugo Furrer of SBB in Bern; and Frau Caduff at the Lia Rumantscha in Chur. The Teatro Dimitri, Verscio, were kind in putting me up one memorable night, as were staff at the University of Geneva in taking time to explain some of the broader issues to me. Kev Reynolds was an inspiration.

Many thanks to Rough Guide readers Karen Head (Leighton Buzzard, UK) and Olga Obregón (Miami) who wrote in with suggestions for inclusion before the book had even been written.

Friends around Switzerland went out of their way for me during the hectic research period: in Luzern, Heidi Vogt, Chloizy, Beat, Naama, Brigitte and Thomas; in Zürich, Gisela, Philipp, Peter and Jeanette; in Lausanne, Constantin and Eugène; and in Bern, Ursula and Lily. Their support, warmth and generosity made a huge difference, and is greatly appreciated. Special gratitude to Anna and to Christian, without whose openhearted friendship, enthusiasm and insight, this book would be much less than it is. Thanks, too, to Richard and Janet Adams, and Alistair Adams, for an offer not taken up; to Hannah for support tangible and intangible; and, as ever, to Neville and Sheila Teller.

CONTENTS

Introduction x

● CHAPTER 9: ZÜRICH AND AROUND   369

● CHAPTER 10: THE NORTHEAST AND LIECHTENSTEIN   409

● CHAPTER 11: GRAUBÜNDEN   442

● CHAPTER 12: TICINO   480

PART THREE   CONTEXTS   511

LIST OF MAPS

MAP SYMBOLS

▬▬▬	Motorway	☈	View point
═══	Major road	✈	Airport
═══	Minor road	◆	Point of interest
‥‥‥	Tunnel	⌣	Bridge
-----	Footpath	⌣⌣	Viaduct
▥▥▥	Steps	⚐	Campsite
▪▪▪▪▪	Wall	▓	Vineyard
▬▬	Railway	Ⓗ	Hospital
───	Metro line	⊙	Statue
∙∙∙∙∙∙	Funicular railway	ⓘ	Tourist information
●‑‑‑‑●	Cable car	⊠	Post office
— —	Ferry route	Ⓜ	Metro station
∙∙∙∙∙	River	▬	Building
▬ ▬ ▬	National boundary	◯	Stadium
▬∙∙∙	Canton boundary	✚	Church/cathedral
▬ ▬ ▬	Chapter boundary	▓	Built-up-area
▲	Mountain peak	▒	Park
⊰	Mountain pass	▒	National Park
⋔	Cliffs	▒	Forest
/ʹ\	Hill shading	▒	Cemetery
⚱	Waterfall	▒	Glacier
⌇	Gorge		

INTRODUCTION

In Italy for thirty years under the Borgias they had warfare, terror, murder, bloodshed, but they produced Michelangelo, Leonardo da Vinci and the Renaissance. In Switzerland they had brotherly love; they had 500 years of democracy and peace. And what did that produce? The cuckoo clock.

Orson Welles as Harry Lime, in *The Third Man* (1949)

Never has one throwaway movie line done so much to damage the reputation of a whole country. Even now, despite being one of the most visited countries in Europe, Switzerland remains one of the least understood. The facts are that until national reconciliation in 1848, Switzerland was the most consistently turbulent, war-torn area of Europe (so much for brotherly love), and yet, both before and after it found stability, it brought forth such literary and artistic pioneers as Hans Holbein, Jean-Jacques Rousseau, Paul Klee, Hermann Hesse and Alberto Giacometti (so much for the cuckoo clock).

Nonetheless, two centuries of tourism have left their mark: faced by an ever-increasing onslaught of visitors, these days the Swiss are content to abide by a quaint stereotype of Switzerland that's easily packaged and sold – the familiar Alpine idyll of cheese and chocolate, Heidi and the Matterhorn – while keeping the best bits for themselves. Come for a "Lakes and Mountains" package, or a week of skiing, or a short city-break, and you'll get all the pristine beauty, genteel calm and well-oiled efficiency of the Switzerland that the locals deem suitable for public consumption. The other Switzerland – the one the Swiss inhabit – needs time and patience to winkle out of its shell, but can be an infinitely more rewarding place to explore.

The **mountains** are what bring most visitors to Switzerland, and their drama does not disappoint. The Alps, which form a barrier across Europe stretching from Lyon to Vienna, were named from the Swiss-German word *Alp*, which refers to the high sloping summer meadows where Swiss farmers to this day pasture their herds. The rocky, snowy peaks, their ridges, crests and foothills, form a stark natural wilderness which presses in on the densely populated valleys of the centre of the country. Jagged views from between the houses in almost any town in the country bring the presence of the mountains into the rhythm of everyday life, reminding the Swiss of their origins and, both with their fixity and their austerity, shaping the national character more than any other single influence.

Within this rugged environment, **community spirit** is perhaps stronger in Switzerland than anywhere else in Europe. Since the country is not an ethnic, linguistic or religious unity, it has survived – so the Swiss are fond of saying – simply through the will of its people to resolve their differences. Today, a unique style of "bottom-up" democracy ensures real power still rests with the people, who seem to vote almost weekly on a series of referenda affecting all aspects of life from local recycling projects to national economic policy. The constitution devolves power upwards from the people to municipal governments and up again to the regions (known as **cantons**), only as a last resort granting certain powers to the federal government.

This kind of decentralized structure means that the cantons – which are, in essence, tiny self-governing republics who have volunteered to join together – have mostly held onto their own, unique flavours. Although Swiss people value their shared Swissness above all, they also cherish their own home-town identity and their

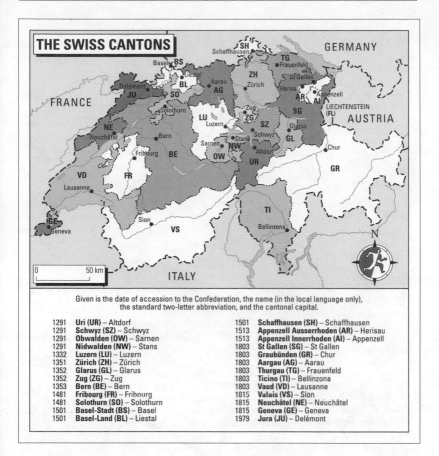

THE SWISS CANTONS

GERMANY

FRANCE

LIECHTENSTEIN (FL)

AUSTRIA

ITALY

0   50 km

Given is the date of accession to the Confederation, the name (in the local language only),
the standard two-letter abbreviation, and the cantonal capital.

1291	**Uri (UR)** – Altdorf	
1291	**Schwyz (SZ)** – Schwyz	
1291	**Obwalden (OW)** – Sarnen	
1291	**Nidwalden (NW)** – Stans	
1332	**Luzern (LU)** – Luzern	
1351	**Zürich (ZH)** – Zürich	
1352	**Glarus (GL)** – Glarus	
1352	**Zug (ZG)** – Zug	
1353	**Bern (BE)** – Bern	
1481	**Fribourg (FR)** – Fribourg	
1481	**Solothurn (SO)** – Solothurn	
1501	**Basel-Stadt (BS)** – Basel	
1501	**Basel-Land (BL)** – Liestal	

1501	**Schaffhausen (SH)** – Schaffhausen
1513	**Appenzell Ausserrhoden (AR)** – Herisau
1513	**Appenzell Innerrhoden (AI)** – Appenzell
1803	**St Gallen (SG)** – St Gallen
1803	**Graubünden (GR)** – Chur
1803	**Aargau (AG)** – Aarau
1803	**Thurgau (TG)** – Frauenfeld
1803	**Ticino (TI)** – Bellinzona
1803	**Vaud (VD)** – Lausanne
1815	**Valais (VS)** – Sion
1815	**Neuchâtel (NE)** – Neuchâtel
1815	**Geneva (GE)** – Geneva
1979	**Jura (JU)** – Delémont

differences from their neighbours. Tensions exist between the **four language communities** – French, German, Italian and Romansh (the last a direct descendant of Latin which has survived in pockets of the mountainous southeast), as they do between Catholic and Protestant, or between urban and rural areas – while **regional characteristics** remain sharply defined and diverse. In the centre and the east, the old isolation of the close-knit mountain communities lingers on in Swiss-German *Kantönligeist* ("little cantonal spirit"), a stubborn parochialism that's leavened by a heartwarming, down-to-earth rumbustiousness. In the west, across the **Röstigraben** (a comical but slightly discomfiting name given to the invisible language border – a *Graben* is a military trench – between French-speaking Switzerland where they don't eat the traditional potato dish *Rösti*, and German-speaking Switzerland where they do), the less severe landscape has encouraged cultural interchange with neighbouring France, imbuing the people of *Suisse-Romande* with more than a whiff of Gallic hauteur as well as a much greater willingness to end traditional Swiss neutrality in favour of joining the EU. On the south side of the Alpine chain,

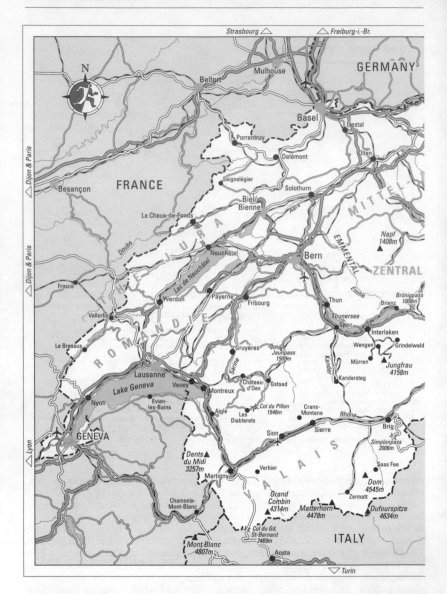

Swiss Italian-speakers have tended to feel cut off, both from the rest of Switzerland by the lack of shared language and culture, and from the economic powerhouse of northern Italy by the implacable presence of the international border.

Local pride and community spirit are fuelled by traditional **folkloric customs**, most of which stem from pagan or medieval Christian festivals. Most prominent of

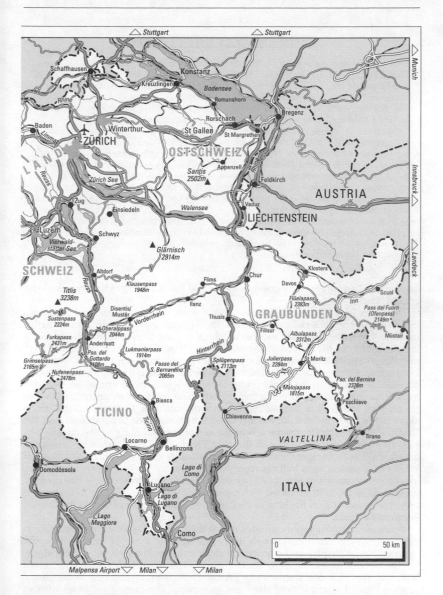

these is **carnival**, held around the country on or around Mardi Gras, the last day before Lent. The most exuberant celebrations, held in Luzern, Bern and Basel, feature bands, masked parades, street dancing and spontaneous partying that belie the stereotype of a placid, unadventurous Switzerland. A host of smaller events fills out the calendar and it's still easily possible to stumble on a village festival devoted to,

FACTS AND FIGURES

Switzerland covers an **area** of 41,285 square kilometres (roughly the size of Wales or West Virginia), and borders France to the west, Germany to the north, Liechtenstein and Austria to the east, and Italy to the south. At the most it is 220km from north to south, and 348km from west to east. The highest point is the Dufourspitze peak at 4634m above sea level, the lowest is Lago Maggiore at 193m. The total **population** is around 7 million, of whom about 5.7 million are Swiss citizens.

Switzerland – known officially as the Swiss Confederation – is ruled by a seven-member government called the **Federal Council**, with the Presidency rotating annually between all seven members. This Federal Council and the **Supreme Court** are both elected by the bicameral **Parliament**. Constitutional amendments can be proposed either by Parliament or by popular initiative, the latter requiring 100,000 signatures; in either case a referendum ensues, and a double majority – of votes cast both nationally and canton-by-canton – sees the proposal becoming law. 50,000 signatures can also put any existing law to a referendum.

Each **canton** has its own constitution, parliament, government and courts, and there is also a considerable degree of autonomy vested in the **communes**, of which there are 2942 nationwide, varying in size from small, crowded city districts up to vast, thinly populated tracts of mountain terrain.

say, harvest-time or the banishment of winter that has been staged by local people for centuries past.

This sense of cultural continuity sits oddly with the fact that Switzerland has grown into one of the world's **richest** countries. Its economy is small-scale but thoroughly modern: traditional industries such as watchmaking and textiles now thrive by focusing closely on the luxury end of the market and have ceded prime position to engineering, pharmaceuticals and service industries galore, including **tourism**, which has been a high earner since the mid-nineteenth century, when the Alps became both a fashionable destination for wealthy travellers and a prescribed retreat for sufferers from respiratory diseases needing curative sunshine and fresh mountain air. And yet the country, seized by an increasingly anachronistic national *Kantönligeist*, still stands alone. In the 1940s, Switzerland was surrounded by hostile Axis powers; these days, the "friendly" EU encircles the country. With the end of the Cold War, recent damaging revelations of Swiss collaboration with the Nazi Third Reich, and increasingly close ties amongst Western European nations, Swiss **neutrality** rings ever more hollow – and yet, far from embracing a wider perspective, the country has collectively taken a step into conservatism, with a new breed of extreme rightwing Eurosceptic politicians gaining ground in the 1999 elections. Commentators are noting sadly that Switzerland is only now embarking on the kind of multiethnic social integration that its neighbours began in the 1950s.

Nonetheless, having taken centuries to bolt their country together from diverse elements, the Swiss seem instinctively to return to their sense of community spirit, expressed most tangibly in the order and cleanliness you'll see on show everywhere. Yet the sterility so decried by Graham Greene (who wrote Harry Lime's jibe about brotherly love), if it characterizes any part of the country, applies only to the glossy, neatly packaged tourist idyll of lakes and mountains. The three great Swiss cities of Geneva, Zürich and Basel are crammed with world-class **museums** and galleries and, in Zürich and Geneva's neighbour Lausanne, a humming arts scene and underground club culture that feeds **nightlife** as vibrant as anything you'll find in much larger European cities. The **landscapes** are dominated by the Alps and their foothills, but mountains aren't the only story. In the north and centre are lush, rolling grasslands epitomized by the velvety green hills of the Emmental, traditional dairy-farming country. Vineyards rise tiered above Lake Geneva and the broad valley of the young Rhône in the southwest, and above the Rhine in the east. The fairy-tale southeast is cut through by wild, high-sided valleys, lonely, dark and thickly forested. Most surprisingly of all, bordering Italy in the south you'll find subtropical Mediterranean-style flower gardens, sugarloaf hills and sunny, palm-fringed lakes. For a small, little-regarded mid-continental country with a deeply ingrained image problem, Switzerland has plenty more to offer than most visitors suspect.

Where to go – and when

Although Switzerland is best known for its mountain scenery, there are any number of hooks on which to hang a visit, whether you choose to stay in one city or resort, take in the hiking or cycling possibilities of a single region, or make a tour of exploration around the whole country. In the space of a short holiday and without moving far from a central base, you could easily take in a dizzying diversity of landscapes and cultures. Getting about is easy, with an unrivalled network of trains, buses and boats cutting journey times between the regions to an hour or two in most cases. You'll find places to stay and get a hearty meal wherever you end up, even in the wildest of mountain valleys. English is widely spoken, and highly organized tourist offices mean that information is readily accessible wherever you go.

Thankfully, Switzerland has no big metropolises on the scale of Paris or London. Swiss towns and cities were preserved from bombing in World War II, and all of them have at their core explorable networks of medieval alleys and old houses and churches. **Geneva** is positioned at the tip of the idyllic **Lake Geneva** in the southwest, a short distance from the graceful lakeside city of **Lausanne**. In the northeast, **Zürich** too is set on its own lake, within striking distance of the peaceful **Bodensee** (Lake Constance). The diminutive Swiss capital **Bern** has a UNESCO-protected Old Town of sandstone arcades and cobbled alleys, while equally attractive **Luzern** (Lucerne) lies in the centre of the country on its own, famously beautiful lake. Two much-overlooked urban centres are in the extreme north and south of the country respectively: **Basel** is located on the Rhine at the point where France, Germany and Switzerland meet, while sunny **Lugano** basks on the shores of an azure lake a few kilometres from the Italian border. Any of these – or smaller but no less characterful cantonal capitals such as St Gallen, Schaffhausen, Neuchâtel, Chur, Fribourg, Sion or Bellinzona – could serve as a base for a relaxing short break, especially during the temperate summer months (June–Sept). At other times they can get distinctly chilly, although most receive generous dumps of snow in the winter, which, combined with glittering sunshine and frozen lakes and rivers, paints the most romantic of urban pictures.

Switzerland is ideal if you're looking to get out into nature, and whether it's for hiking, skiing or simply relaxation, there are almost limitless possibilities. The Alps run in a band across the centre and south of the country, with resorts big and small along with stunning scenery guaranteed wherever you head for. The two main **seasons** run from late May to October, and from mid-December to mid-April; between these times, mountain resorts close down altogether. The best-known Alpine region is the **Bernese Oberland**, focused around the tourist hub of **Interlaken** and boasting such famous names as **Wengen** and **Gstaad**; just to the south, in Canton Valais, sit **Verbier**, **Crans Montana** and, at the foot of the shark's-tooth Matterhorn, **Zermatt**. Occupying the southeast of the country is Canton Graubünden, holding **Davos**, **Klosters** and – perhaps most famous of all – **St Moritz**. Justifiably popular, all these places boast some of the best skiing in Europe but can draw stifling crowds. Although it's relatively easy in even the busiest centres (which are still nothing like the mega-resorts of the French and Italian Alps) to head off the beaten path and explore alone, or to aim for smaller, more manageable satellite resorts in adjacent side valleys, you may prefer to shun the big names altogether and seek peace and quiet in the less frenetic hinterlands. Two regions stand out: in the northwest, the scrubby, windswept **Jura** mountains hugging the French border are an ideal landscape for long lonely walks and bike rides; while in the south, the wild valleys of **Alto Ticino** lace the southern foothills of the Alps with little-known hiking trails, a world away from the super-chic lakeside resort of **Locarno** nearby.

SWITZERLAND'S CLIMATE

The table shows average monthly minimum and maximum temperatures (in °C), and average monthly precipitation (in mm). Precipitation patterns vary widely, with the northern cities (Bern, Zürich) experiencing more overcast skies than, for instance, Lugano, which tends to have long periods of sunshine punctuated by sudden summer downpours.

	Jan	Feb	Mar	Apr	May	Jun	Jul	Aug	Sep	Oct	Nov	Dec
BERN												
Min °C	-5	-3	-1	3	8	10	11	11	8	4	-2	-5
Max °C	0	4	9	13	18	20	21	20	17	11	5	0
Precipitation, mm	56	49	62	77	97	120	118	114	96	71	68	65
DAVOS												
Min °C	-11	-11	-8	-4	1	4	8	7	4	0	-4	-8
Max °C	-1	-1	3	8	10	14	18	18	14	10	7	1
Precipitation, mm	71	60	57	60	66	121	140	135	90	69	63	70
GENEVA												
Min °C	-2	-1	0	4	8	10	12	13	11	7	3	0
Max °C	3	5	10	14	19	20	22	22	21	15	9	5
Precipitation, mm	63	57	55	50	67	92	64	98	102	77	84	59
LUGANO												
Min °C	-2	-1	2	6	9	11	14	14	11	9	5	0
Max °C	6	8	11	17	20	23	28	29	25	19	13	8
Precipitation, mm	61	64	96	148	217	199	183	196	160	172	158	95
SION												
Min °C	-6	-3	1	3	8	10	11	10	9	4	0	-3
Max °C	3	6	9	14	20	21	25	24	21	15	9	5
Precipitation, mm	51	45	40	37	39	46	50	64	45	50	53	62
ZÜRICH												
Min °C	-5	-2	0	3	9	11	13	13	11	8	2	-2
Max °C	0	4	9	15	20	22	25	23	20	14	9	3
Precipitation, mm	75	70	64	81	108	137	144	135	110	80	76	64

PART ONE

THE

BASICS

GETTING THERE FROM BRITAIN

Flying is by far the easiest, cheapest and most convenient way to get from Britain to Switzerland. Travelling by train is comfortable and scenic, but is both more expensive than flying and can take the best part of a full day. Both trains and long-distance buses are only really worth considering if you incorporate a trip to Switzerland into a longer jaunt around Europe.

BY AIR

A **scheduled flight** is the most obvious way to go: Geneva and Zürich are Switzerland's main international gateways, but Basel, Bern and Lugano also handle international flights. Milan's second airport at Malpensa is only 25km south of the Swiss border: it's quite feasible to fly there and catch a bus straight from the airport to Lugano without spending any time or money in Italy. Direct winter flights from London to Sion, in the heart of the Swiss Alps, are a godsend for skiers and snowboarders wanting to maximize their time on the slopes.

Flight time to Switzerland from London is around 1hr 30min, from the north of England and Scotland 2–3hr. Principal **carriers** are Swissair (code SR), its subsidiary Crossair (LX), British Airways (BA) and the ticketless airline EasyJet (EZY), all of which offer nonstop flights from a handful of UK airports. Flights operated by KLM (KL) and Air France (AF) require you to make at least one stop on the ground at their hubs (Amsterdam or Paris respectively), but can – along with BA – offer enormous flexibility of UK departure points.

RAIL BAGGAGE

The Swiss have come up with one of the greatest, and simplest, ideas around for easing the stress of air travel. For a relatively small fee, you can send your bags direct from the **check-in desk** at your home airport through to pretty much any train station in Switzerland for collection later the same day, entirely eliminating the hassle of reclaiming your bags at the airport carousel and then lugging them around while you find your hotel. Whoever you're flying with (it doesn't have to be Swissair, and it can be from any airport in the world), all you need to do is to fill out a special green **customs label** and attach one to each item of baggage. Each label costs £10, but you can get them only from the Swissair ticket desk in Terminal 2 at Heathrow, or from the Swissair office at Leicester Square in central London (☎020/7434 7300). If you're not flying out of Heathrow, or if you can't get into London, you'll need to send a guaranteed cheque covering the cost of however many labels you need to Swissair Tickets, Swiss Court, London W1V 4BJ, including an SAE.

On arrival, your bags are spirited away to the train station you specified on the label, via the super-efficient **Swiss Federal Railways** network. Bags are normally available for pick-up three to seven hours after you land, depending on how far away you end up from the airport you flew into. **Baggage counters** at larger Swiss train stations are open long hours for collection, often 7am to 11pm or so daily, but note that counters at smaller stations quite often close at 7 or 8pm. You don't have to pick up your bags in person, since the station staff only need to see ID and your label-stub: check with your hotel whether or not they'll charge for sending a porter to collect your bags for you.

For more **information**, and a pamphlet with a complete list of processing times at all Swiss stations served, call the Swiss Federal Railways office in London (☎020/7734 1921). The homeward-bound version of "Rail Baggage" is "Fly Baggage", covered on p.36.

AIRLINES IN BRITAIN

Air Engiadina, *www.airengiadina.ch* – book via KLM. Small Swiss airline partnered by KLM, flying nonstop London City to Bern daily.

Air France, *www.airfrance.fr* – ☎0845/084 5111. Flights from London and around the UK via Paris.

British Airways, *www.british-airways.com* – ☎0845/722 2111. Nonstop flights into Geneva from Heathrow, Gatwick, Birmingham and Manchester; into Zürich from Heathrow and Gatwick; and into Basel from Heathrow. Connections link in to these flights from many UK airports.

Crossair, *www.crossair.ch* – ☎020/7434 7300. Subsidiary of Swissair with a host of nonstop or one-stop direct flights from London City, Manchester, Edinburgh, Birmingham, Jersey and Guernsey to all Swiss airports. Their Saturday morning winter (Dec–April) flights Heathrow to Sion can have you swishing down the slopes at Verbier or Crans-Montana by lunchtime.

EasyJet, *www.easyjet.com* – ☎0870/600 0000. Nonstop flights from Luton, Gatwick, Stansted and Liverpool to Geneva, and Luton to Zürich.

Booking by phone or Internet only, ticketless travel, unnumbered seating on the plane, and no inflight meals slashes fares to half the cost of a "normal" airline.

Go, *www.go-fly.com* – ☎0845/605 4321. Nonstop Stansted to Milan Malpensa, a short distance from Lugano; as with EasyJet, there are no tickets, you book direct by phone or Internet, and prices are competitive. Owned by British Airways, but run as a separate company.

KLM Direct, *www.klmuk.com* – ☎0870/507 4074. Flights from virtually all UK airports (22 of them) to Amsterdam, with easy connections there on to Geneva, Zürich and Bern.

Lufthansa, *www.lufthansa.co.uk* – ☎0845/773 7747. Heathrow, London City, Stansted, Birmingham and Manchester to Frankfurt, with onward flights to Geneva, Basel or Zürich.

Swissair, *www.swissair.com* – ☎020/7434 7300. Nonstop flights into Zürich from Heathrow, Stansted and Manchester, and into Geneva from Heathrow. Also plenty of one-stop flights from around the UK to all Swiss airports, often code-sharing with Crossair or Sabena (Belgian).

High **seasons** apply from July to September, around Christmas and New Year, and again in February, with shoulder seasons operating either side of these, and low season at all other times. The following indication of fares – which should be taken only as a guideline – applies to return tickets, booked two weeks in advance and spanning at least a Saturday night away in the high season.

Oddly enough for a world-renowned airline with such quietly efficient, gold-plated service (padded leather seats in all classes, organic food as standard, fresh-baked bread, free chocolate) Swissair generally offers the best deals on **fares** of the big European carriers from wherever you fly in the UK, and it's not hard to find their prices for flights between Heathrow and **Geneva** or **Zürich** dropping below £100. Flying nonstop from other London airports rarely pushes prices above £120, while fares from other airports in the UK are only slightly higher; flying nonstop with, for example, Crossair from Birmingham or Manchester to Zürich, or with BA from Birmingham to Geneva, will set you back around £140–150. If you're prepared to sacrifice some creature comforts (such as an inflight meal), you could quite literally halve

costs by flying with EasyJet; booking three months ahead can turn up a fare to Geneva (from Luton, Gatwick, Stansted or Liverpool) of just £48 return, or to Zürich (from Luton only) of £58.

As for other destinations in Switzerland, **Basel**'s super-slick EuroAirport – actually on French territory, and shared between the neighbouring towns of Mulhouse (France) and Freiburg (Germany) – can be reached most cheaply on Crossair's flights out of Heathrow or London City for around £120. **Bern** is served by regular shuttles from London City operated by Air Engiadina under the wing of KLM – under-26s can take advantage of a fare of £112 with Usit Campus. **Lugano** is too small and too far off the beaten track to be competitive, with fares as high as £195 midweek from London; instead, you should book with Go from Stansted to Milan Malpensa nearby for just £100 return. The tiny airfield at **Sion** sees international traffic only in winter, when Crossair has nonstop Saturday-morning flights from Heathrow for around £160, geared towards week-long ski packages.

Finding the best fare involves ringing round a few of the discount flight agents listed in the box

FLIGHT AGENTS IN BRITAIN

As well as the agents listed below, it's worth checking in the newspapers – the weekend travel sections, or in London *Time Out*, the *Evening Standard*, and free giveaways like *TNT* – and, of course, with any of the hundreds of agents who advertise flights on the Internet: *www.cheapflights.co.uk* and *www.lastminute.co.uk* are good places to begin.

Flightbookers, 177 Tottenham Court Rd, London W1 (☎020/7757 2000). Low fares on an extensive offering of scheduled flights. Extended opening hours at their branch at Gatwick train station (☎01293/568300).

London Flight Centre, 131 Earls Court Rd, London SW5 (☎020/7244 6411); 47 Notting Hill Gate, London W11 (☎020/7727 4290); 33 Broadway Centre, Hammersmith tube, London W6 (☎020/8748 6777). Long-established agent dealing in discount flights.

North South Travel, Moulsham Mill Centre, Parkway, Chelmsford (☎01245/608291). Friendly, competitive travel agency, offering discounted fares – profits are used to support projects in the developing world, especially the promotion of sustainable tourism.

STA Travel, *www.statravel.co.uk* – 86 Old Brompton Rd, London SW7; 117 Euston Rd, London NW1; 38 Store St, London WC1; 11 Goodge St, London W1 (all ☎020/7361 6161); 30 Upper Kirkgate, Aberdeen (☎01224/658222); 38 North St, Brighton (☎01273/728282); 25 Queens Rd, Bristol (☎0117/929 4399); 38 Sidney St, Cambridge (☎01223/366966); 27 Forrest Rd, Edinburgh (☎0131/226 7747); 184 Byres Rd, Glasgow (☎0141/338 6000); 88 Vicar Lane, Leeds (☎0113/244 9212); 78 Bold St, Liverpool (☎0151/707 1123); 75 Deansgate, Manchester (☎0161/834 0668); 9 St Mary's Place, Newcastle-upon-Tyne (☎0191/233 2111); 36 George St, Oxford (☎01865/792800); and branches on university campuses in Birmingham, Bristol, Canterbury, Cardiff, Coventry, Durham, Glasgow, Leeds, London, Loughborough, Nottingham, Sheffield and Warwick. Worldwide specialists in low-cost flights and tours for students and under-26s, though other customers welcome. Also over 200 offices abroad.

Trailfinders, *www.trailfinders.co.uk* – 215 Kensington High St, London W6 (☎020/7937 5400); 1 Threadneedle St, London EC2 (☎020/7628 7628); 22 The Priory Queensway, Birmingham (☎0121/236 1234); 48 Corn St, Bristol (☎0117/929 9000); 254 Sauchiehall St, Glasgow (☎0141/353 2224); 58 Deansgate, Manchester (☎0161/839 6969). One of the best-informed and most efficient agents for independent travellers.

Travel Cuts, *www.travelcuts.co.uk* – 295a Regent St, London W1 (☎020/7255 1944). Specialists in budget, student and youth travel, with offices in London and abroad.

Usit Campus, *www.usitcampus.co.uk* – nationwide ☎0870/240 1010; 52 Grosvenor Gdns, London SW1 (☎020/7730 3402); 541 Bristol Rd, Selly Oak, Birmingham (☎0121/414 1848); 61 Ditchling Rd, Brighton (☎01273/570226); 37 Queen's Rd, Clifton, Bristol (☎0117/929 2494); 5 Emmanuel St, Cambridge (☎01223/324283); 53 Forest Rd, Edinburgh (☎0131/225 6111, telesales 668 3303); 122 George St, Glasgow (☎0141/553 1818); 166 Deansgate, Manchester (☎0161/833 2046); 105 St Aldates, Oxford (☎01865/242067). Student/youth travel specialists, with branches also in YHA shops and on university campuses all over Britain.

opposite, comparing prices and routings, or consulting EasyJet by phone or Internet (they don't deal with agents, thus cutting out the middleman's commission). Students and those under 26 can take advantage of **discounted tickets** – STA Travel and Usit Campus are your best bet for these, and they're worth calling even if you're not a student, since they also offer highly competitive budget fares to all-comers. What **charter flights** exist are usually block booked by package holiday firms, but even in the height of the summer and winter seasons spare seats are often sold off at a discount. For an idea of current prices and availability, contact any high-street travel agent or call some of the larger package operators listed on p.6. The major disadvantage with charter flights is the fixed return date – often a maximum of four weeks from the outward journey.

PACKAGES AND CITY BREAKS

Most high-street travel agents stock brochures for **package holidays** to Swiss destinations, but you may find that the standard "Lakes and Mountains" umbrella title used by dozens of companies may cover only one or two Swiss resorts –

TOUR OPERATORS IN BRITAIN

Airtours, Wavell House, Holcombe Road, Helmshore, Lancs BB4 4NB (☎01706/260000). Standard summer packages to Interlaken and Luzern, winter packages to Verbier.

British Airways Holidays, Astral Towers, Betts Way, London Rd, Crawley, W. Sussex RH10 (☎0870/242 4243, www.baholidays.co.uk). Year-round city-break packages to Geneva or Luzern.

Crystal Holidays, Crystal House, Arlington Rd, Surbiton, Surrey KT6 6BW (☎0870/848 7000). Well-respected winter sports specialists, with a range of Swiss destinations including all the top names plus less well-known resorts such as Engelberg and Villars/Les Diablerets. Also standard summer city-breaks and "Lakes and Mountains" deals.

Exodus, 9 Weir Rd, London SW12 0LT (☎020/8675 5550, www.exodustravels.co.uk). Experienced adventure tour operator running excellent small-group walking tours in the Swiss Alps.

Inghams, 10–18 Putney Hill, London SW15 6AX (☎020/8780 4444, www.inghams.co.uk). Major operator with summer and winter packages of all kinds, competitive prices and plenty of experience.

Kuoni Travel, Kuoni House, Dorking, Surrey RH5 4AZ (☎01306/742500); 33 Maddox St, London W1R (☎020/7499 8636); 2a Barton Square (off St Anne's Sq), Manchester M2 7LW (☎0161/832 0667). A wealth of flexible summer and winter package holidays around Switzerland with good family offers.

Naturetrek, Chautara, Bighton, nr Alresford, Hants SO24 9RB (☎01962/733051, www.naturetrek.co.uk). Acknowledged leaders in birdwatching and botanical holidays worldwide, offering sympathetic, expert guidance for small-group summer tours to Wengen and the Bernese Alps.

Martin Randall Travel, 10 Barley Mow Passage, London W4 4PH (☎020/8742 3355). Small group cultural tours: experts on art or music lead travellers on week-long summer packages taking in art collections throughout Switzerland.

Plus Travel, 9 Eccleston St, London SW1W 9LX (☎020/7259 0199). Dedicated Switzerland specialists, Swiss-owned and Swiss-run, with winter and summer brochures, including city-breaks, fly-drives, tailor-mades and combination possibilities around the country. Options include train itineraries, bike or adventure holidays and gourmet tours, as well as plenty of more orthodox packages and skiing at resorts big and small.

Swiss Travel Service, Bridge House, 55–59 High Rd, Broxbourne, Herts EN10 7DT (☎01992/456123). The oldest Swiss specialist tour operators, founded in 1949, with a wealth of experience and local knowledge. Almost limitless choices around the country, covering one-centre and two-centre packages, city-breaks, train tours, walking weeks, golf holidays, adventure excursions and biking, farmhouse stays, health and beauty holidays, even open-air painting tuition for budding Alpine artists. Winter skiing possibilities are equally comprehensive.

---

principally Interlaken and Luzern. Seven nights in a two- or three-star hotel, with flights and transfers included, costs from around £400–450 per person; prices drop if you choose self-catering accommodation, or stay in less famous resorts such as Meiringen or Flims.

A few operators offer short **city-breaks** in summer or winter, and for a quick getaway and guaranteed accommodation with minimum hassle, these can represent excellent value (especially in the low seasons). Depending on the location, three nights sharing in three- or four-star hotels starts from around £330 per person, with breakfasts, flights, transfers and – handily – a half-fare travel card (see p.35) included. Adding extra nights is always possible. Favoured destinations are Geneva, Lausanne, Bern, Luzern and Zürich, but

the specialist operators can come up with deals to Lugano or Basel, as well as resorts such as Zermatt, Wengen or Mürren, and even all-in weekends in St Moritz, Davos or Klosters.

Several companies do summer **walking tours**, mostly following the high Alpine routes around and between Mont Blanc and the Matterhorn, and also in the Bernese Oberland. These can be a great way for experienced hikers and novices alike to get well off the beaten path and out into nature, without having to worry about the practicalities of bed and board or getting lost in the snows. Some put you up in campsites, others use mountain huts and refuges, and a few may include vehicle support and/or porterage. All stick to small groups of around 10–15 people. Prices can vary dramatically, but £700 is a very rough average, covering about a week's hut-to-hut walking or a two-week camping tour (including flights).

The main focus of packages to Switzerland, though, is of course **skiing**, and any brochure offering winter holidays in the Alps will have at least one or two Swiss destinations. Skiing packages tend to include flights, transfers and half-board accommodation (breakfast and dinner), but exclude lift passes. Prices vary tremendously depending on the operator, the resort, the style of accommodation, and the time of the season. Nothing happens much before December 20; Christmas and New Year weeks are premium priced; February slightly less so; and the best deals are to be had in mid-January and mid-March. The absolute minimum for a seven-night deal at a popular resort is around £350; a more realistic average might be £500, while £650 allows you considerable freedom of choice. Choosing more out-of-the-way places such as Les Diablerets or Flims can bring prices down noticeably.

Switzerland managed to escape the worst of the 1960s boom in resort construction which afflicted many parts of the Alps, and benefits today from resorts which are generally small in scale and which retain a good deal of character compared to the concrete monstrosities just over the borders in France or Italy. The **best skiing** is to be had at the classic destinations, a selection (or all) of which are offered by most operators. These take in Davos, Verbier, Zermatt, Saas-Fee, Wengen, Mürren and Grindelwald. Resorts which turn up less often (and so are less pricey) include Kandersteg, Engelberg, Klosters, Villars/Les Diablerets, Leysin, Arosa and Flims. **Beginners** are perhaps best served at Arosa, Kandersteg or Mürren; dedicated **family** resorts like Villars, and even small, tucked-away places not in any brochures such as St Cergue or Meiringen, are great for **kids** finding their feet; sporty thrills and spills on the slopes followed by buzzing après-ski **nightlife** is best sampled at Davos or Verbier; while Zermatt, Wengen and Klosters offer top-notch skiing amidst quiet village-style surroundings. Big-name resorts such as Crans-Montana, Gstaad and St Moritz deliver more prestige and designer-label shops than on-piste satisfaction. **Summer skiing** is possible at resorts with access to glacier slopes above 3000m – these include Verbier, Zermatt, Les Diablerets, Crans-Montana and Saas-Fee.

Accommodation is almost always of high quality, if not exactly inventive – standard two- and three-star resort hotels abound, although deals in Verbier, for instance (which doesn't have a great range of hotels), or Zermatt, tend to include a choice of **catered chalets**, which can sleep anything from two people to a group of fifteen or more; obviously, the more people sharing a chalet, the less expensive it works out for everyone. Free or discounted **extras** to look out for, which can turn a mediocre-value deal into a bargain, include lift passes, rental of skis or snowboards and other gear, lessons, train passes to allow you to get around from resort to resort, and reductions for children. Most operators also offer self-drive car-rental that can cut well over £100 per person off a package price, if you choose to forego flights altogether and drive from the UK to Switzerland and back.

BY TRAIN

Travelling by train still has much of its old leisurely romance and can be a pleasant, scenic and relaxing way to travel to Switzerland. However, you won't save much on the airfare; indeed, you may end up paying quite a bit more.

There are two main options on **point-to-point routings**. The first involves making the sea crossing, taking a train from the coast and changing again, probably at Paris or Brussels, for transport on to Switzerland – all of which lengthens the journey out to a numbing fifteen hours and is really not worth your while. The better and faster option, which might only take eight hours London–Geneva, is to travel through the Channel Tunnel and change trains in Paris. Preferable to either option is to slot Switzerland into a longer **tour** around Western and/or Central Europe, for which a host of tickets and passes are available.

CHANNEL TUNNEL ROUTES

Eurostar trains depart more or less hourly from London Waterloo through the Channel Tunnel direct to **Paris Gare du Nord** (journey time 3hr). From Paris, many trains serve Switzerland, but unfortunately not from the Gare du Nord, and also not from one single station, meaning you have to plan your route in advance and be prepared to lug your bags through the Paris metro. From the **Gare de Lyon**, high-speed TGV trains – for which you must pay a small supplement – depart throughout the day on three different routes: to Geneva (3hr

40min); to Lausanne (3hr 50min); and, once a day, to Bern (4hr 30min) and Zürich (6hr). The **Gare de l'Est**, handily situated right beside the Gare du Nord, has non-TGV trains departing frequently to Bâle/Basel (5hr 30min), as well as daily overnight sleeper services delivering you to Zürich or Chur for breakfast.

Eurostar quotes **fares** only between London and Paris; to book through to Switzerland, your best bet is the Swiss Federal Railways office in London (see box). Their top offer, and the best-value way to get to Switzerland by train, is £109 for a second-class return between London and Basel; you must book seven days in advance, and include a Saturday night.

EUROPEAN TRAIN PASSES

If Switzerland is only part of your itinerary, and you plan to travel further afield in Western or Central Europe, a **train pass** represents much better value than point-to-point tickets. All varieties are available from Rail Europe, Usit Campus and Wasteels (see box). However, you should note that the pan-European train passes tend to be less good value for travel within Switzerland than the various Swiss passes detailed on p.35. The latter, as well as being more flexible, can offer substantial discounts on mountain railways and cable-cars (for which the various European passes quite often aren't valid) while also throwing in free transport on Swiss buses and boats. If you're on a train tour of Europe it may therefore be better to get a European pass for travel outside

Switzerland, and some kind of Swiss pass for travel within Switzerland.

EU nationals, and non-EU nationals resident in Europe for at least six months, have a few choices – which you go for depends on how far afield you're planning on travelling. The **Inter-Rail pass** groups together 28 European countries in zones: Switzerland is located in Zone C, along with Germany, Austria and Denmark; France is in Zone E, along with the Benelux countries; Italy is in G, along with Slovenia, Greece and Turkey. This means that a one-zone pass for Zone E covers travel from the Channel ports north to Amsterdam, south to Marseilles, and as far as the Swiss border, from where a Swiss pass can take over coverage. A two-zone pass for Zones E and G, plus a Swiss pass, gives you the run of Western and Southern Europe from Brussels to Istanbul. **Prices** are good value. A one-zone 22-day pass costs £159 for those under 26, or £229 for those over 26. A two-zone monthly pass is £209/279, three-zone monthly £229/309, or all zones monthly £259/349. Note that Inter-Rail passes don't include boat-train travel between Britain and the continent, although pass holders are eligible for discounts on the London–Paris Eurostar service, on rail travel within Britain, and on some mountain railways and cable-car lines in Switzerland.

Another option is the **Eurodomino Freedom Pass**, which gives unlimited train travel for anything between three and eight days' travel in a one-month period within any one of 27 European countries. Sample under-26 prices for Switzerland, for three/six/eight days are £59/79/89; over-26 equivalents are £79/99/109. You can buy as many separate country passes as you want, but bear in mind that for travel inside Switzerland, Swiss train passes (see p.35) can be much better value. For those over 60, the **Rail Europe Senior Card** costs £5, and gives a thirty percent discount on rail travel between – but not within – 25 European countries, including Eurostar and rail-connected sea crossings. However, before you can purchase this card you must have a British Rail Senior Card (£18); both are valid for a year.

BY BUS

Switzerland is not well served by **international buses**. Fares from the UK are also higher than the cheapest flights, making the agonizingly long overnight road journey – via the Dover–Calais ferry – hard to justify. **Eurolines** have buses from London to Geneva (journey time 17hr) daily in summer or four times weekly the rest of the year, with a change in Lyon; for a one-month return ticket, under-26s/over-26s pay £95/105 in July and August, or £88/97 at other times. From London direct to Basel (14hr 30min) and Zürich (16hr 15min) buses run four times weekly in summer or twice weekly otherwise; under-26s/over-26s pay £84/94 to either city, or a flat £69 if you book fourteen days in advance.

If you're planning a pan-European jaunt, Eurolines offers a **pass** covering 48 European cities (including Basel and Zürich). In summer (mid-June to Sept), a 30-day pass for under/over-26s costs £199/229, or a 60-day one costs £249/279; at all other times, a 30-day pass is £159/199, a 60-day pass is £199/249. Another option is **Busabout**, which runs buses every two or three days on five circuits around Europe in summer, fewer in winter, taking in the major cities of thirteen countries (touching down in Switzerland at Luzern and Interlaken), with add-on connections to more countries, plus a link to London and through

BUS INFORMATION

Busabout, *www.busabout.com* – ☎020/7950 1661; 258 Vauxhall Bridge Rd, London SW1.
Eurolines, *www.eurolines.co.uk* – ☎0870/514 3219; 52 Grosvenor Gardens, London SW1. You can also get tickets from any National Express agent (☎0870/580 8080).

tickets from elsewhere in Britain and Ireland. Fifteen-day tickets are £139 for youth or student card-holders, £155 for others, rising to £259/289 for a month or £499/549 for three months. There are also special deals on set itineraries. Everything is bookable through their Web site (see box).

BY CAR

Switzerland is just about within reach of the UK on a day's drive: the Swiss border is very roughly 850km from the Channel coast and, given an early start and a clear *autoroute* run through northeastern France or Belgium, you could be in Basel, or even Bern or Lausanne, for dinner.

It's fifty-fifty whether Calais or Oostende are better ports to aim for. The Oostende route suffers from traffic around both Brussels and Luxembourg, but then has much better *autoroute* access to eastern Switzerland. The Calais route – benefiting also from rapid Eurotunnel access – is shorter as the crow flies, and avoids large cities, but the *autoroute* runs out as you approach the Jura mountains, giving only minor roads or long detours by which to cross into Switzerland.

CHANNEL TUNNEL ROUTES

Eurotunnel runs shuttle trains between Folkestone and Coquelles, near Calais, via the **Channel Tunnel**, which are reserved solely for vehicles and their passengers. There are up to four departures per hour (only one per hour midnight–6am), and the journey takes 35–45 minutes. **Fares** depend on the time of year, time of day and length of stay; travelling between 10pm and 6am can cut costs considerably, while travelling at weekends, or in July and August, adds a premium. As an example, a standard return at an off-peak time costs £240 (passengers included) in the low season and goes up to £270 in the high season.

Once you emerge in France, you need to aim for the A26 to Reims, and thereafter to Mulhouse or Besançon, taking care to avoid Paris like the plague.

OTHER CROSS-CHANNEL SERVICES

Eurotunnel's appeal notwithstanding, there are a host of other ways to cross the Channel with your vehicle. Hoverspeed, P&O Stena Line and Sea France all currently operate hovercraft or catamaran services between **Dover and Calais**. Although Sea France have slightly less frequent

USEFUL CROSS-CHANNEL SERVICES

Brittany Ferries, *www.brittany-ferries.com* –
☎0870/536 0360. Poole to Cherbourg; Plymouth
to Roscoff.

DFDS Seaways, *www.scansea.com* –
☎0870/533 3000. Newcastle to Amsterdam, and
in summer to Hamburg. Also Harwich to Hamburg.

Eurotunnel, *www.eurotunnel.com* – ☎0870/535
3535. 24hr recorded info ☎0891/555566.
Folkestone to Calais.

Hoverspeed, *www.hoverspeed.co.uk* –
☎0870/524 0241. Dover to Calais or Oostende;
Folkestone to Boulogne; Newhaven to Dieppe.

P&O European Ferries, *www.poef.com* –
☎0870/242 4999. Portsmouth to Le Havre.

P&O Stena Line, *www.ferry.co.uk* – ☎0870/600
0600. Dover to Calais.

P&O North Sea Ferries, *www.ponsf.com* –
☎01482/377177. Hull to Rotterdam or Zeebrugge.

Sea France, *www.seafrance.com* – ☎0870/571
1711. Dover to Calais.

sailings than the other two, they're noticeably less expensive: a car and up to five people costs £165 return. Fares on Hoverspeed and P&O Stena are more or less identical: a car with two people costs £210–290 for a year's return. Boats in summer can get very crowded, and booking ahead is strongly advised. Hoverspeed's rapid Sea-Cats take two hours to cross between **Dover and Oostende**; an open-dated return for a car plus five people costs £245–270.

If you live in the north of England, you'd probably do better to take advantage of the direct ferry services from Hull and Newcastle to the Belgian and Dutch coasts, even though the drive from there to Switzerland is longer. P&O North Sea Ferries have daily overnight services **from Hull** to both Rotterdam and Zeebrugge (the latter is slightly more convenient for onward travel to Switzerland), which both take fourteen hours or so, giving you a full night's sleep on board. Year-round prices are the same for either destination: a car costs £130 for an open return, plus £84 per person, with fifty percent discounts for students and under 26s. A reclining seat is included in these prices; a bed in a cabin costs from £26 per person extra. **From North Shields**, near Newcastle, DFDS (formerly Scandinavian Seaways) have services to Amsterdam (14hr), costing in summer/winter £120/64 for the car plus £95/52 per person; these prices include a berth in a cabin.

LIFT-SHARING AND HITCHING

There is currently **no organized lift share agency** in the UK. The best option is to consult the notice boards of specialist travellers' bookshops or put up your own notice; Nomad Books at 781 Fulham Rd, London SW6 (☎020/7736 4000) has a particularly good notice board downstairs. The travel magazine *Wanderlust* has a useful "Connections" page worth consulting for possible lift shares or travel companions, or for placing your own ad. Pick up a copy of the magazine, or check out *www.wanderlust.co.uk* for more.

Hitching is a genuinely viable means of getting to Switzerland. In most of northern and central Europe the locals are much more favourably inclined towards the practice than in Britain or America (as long as you don't look *too* outlandish on the roadside). As anywhere, though, hitching alone is inadvisable, and hitching after dark doubly so. Although there are certain notorious blackspots for hitching – Oostende port is one of them – in general it's relatively easy to get lifts. Fares on Eurotunnel cover the car and whoever's inside it, meaning that if you're filling an empty space it costs you (and the driver) nothing. If you opt to shell out for the crossing, be prepared for £25 one-way on Hoverspeed and P&O Stena, regardless of the routing; or a bargain £15 Dover–Calais on Sea France.

GETTING THERE FROM IRELAND

The only nonstop flights from Ireland are daily from Dublin to Zürich on either Crossair or Aer Lingus; you should be able to pick up fares on either for around IR£170–190. To reach another Swiss airport – or if you want to fly out of Belfast, Cork, Shannon or elsewhere in

---

AIRLINES

Aer Lingus, N. Ireland ☎0845/973 7747; 40 O'Connell St, Dublin; 13 St Stephen's Green, Dublin; 12 Upper St George's St, Dun Laoghaire (all ☎01/886 3333); 2 Academy St, Cork (☎021/327155); 136 O'Connell St, Limerick (☎061/474239).

British Airways, 1 Fountain Centre, College St, Belfast (☎0845/722 2111 or 028/9032 6566). From the Republic, call ☎1800/626747.

KLM UK, N. Ireland ☎0870/507 4074.

Lufthansa, N. Ireland ☎0845/773 7747; Republic ☎01/844 5544.

Swissair and Crossair, 3rd floor, 54 Dawson St, Dublin (☎01/677 8173).

FLIGHT AGENTS

Fahy Travel, 3 Bridge St, Galway (☎091/563055).

Joe Walsh Tours, 69 Upper O'Connell St, Dublin (☎01/872 2555); 8 Baggot St, Dublin (☎01/676 3053); 117 St Patrick St, Cork (☎021/277959). General budget fares agent.

Liffey Travel, 12 Upper O'Connell St, Dublin (☎01/878 8322). Package tour specialists.

Neenan Travel, 12 South Leinster St, Dublin (☎01/676 5181). Specialists in European city breaks.

Thomas Cook, 11 Donegal Place, Belfast (☎028/9055 0232 or 9055 4455); 118 Grafton St, Dublin (☎01/677 0469). Package holiday and flight agent, with occasional discount offers.

Trailfinders, 4 Dawson St, Dublin (☎01/677 7888). Competitive fares out of all Irish airports, as well as deals on hotels, insurance, tours and car rental worldwide.

Usit NOW, Fountain Centre, College St, Belfast (☎028/9032 7111); 33 Ferryquay St, Derry (☎028/7137 1888); 19 Aston Quay, Dublin (☎01/602 1600); 10 Market Parade, Patrick St, Cork (☎021/270900); Victoria Place, Eyre Square, Galway (☎091/565177); Central Buildings, O'Connell St, Limerick (☎061/415064); 36 Georges St, Waterford (☎051/872601). Student and youth specialists for flights and trains.

TRAIN INFORMATION

Continental Rail Desk, 35 Lower Abbey St, Dublin (☎01/836 6222).

NIR Travel, 28 Great Victoria St Station, Belfast (☎028/9023 0671).

FERRY COMPANIES

Brittany Ferries, 42 Grand Parade, Cork (☎021/277705). Cork to Roscoff (March–Oct only).

Irish Ferries N. Ireland booking centre (☎0870/517 1717); 2 Merrion Row, Dublin (☎01/638 3333). Larne to Cairnryan; Dublin to Holyhead; Rosslare to Pembroke, Cherbourg or Roscoff. French services operate March to September only.

Norse-Irish Ferries, Victoria Terminal 2, Westbank Rd, Belfast (☎028/9077 9090). Belfast to Liverpool.

Stena Sealink Line, Dun Laoghaire (☎01/204 7777); Rosslare Harbour, Wexford (☎053/33115). Dun Laoghaire to Holyhead; Rosslare to Fishguard.

Swansea Cork Ferries, 52 South Mall, Cork (☎021/276000). Cork to Swansea (March–Dec only).

Ireland – you're looking at a change of plane, most commonly in London, Amsterdam or Brussels. **If you have to get to Geneva, Crossair/Swissair combinations which fly you to Zürich and then double back might seem counterproductive, but in fact connection times at Zürich are so well co-ordinated that they can save time on routings via European hubs. Fares to any Swiss airport on BA via London, KLM via Amsterdam, Lufthansa via Frankfurt, and so on, fall in the IR£220–250 bracket.**

Students and anyone under 31 should contact Usit (see p.11), which generally has the best discount deals on flights and **train** tickets. Otherwise, NIR Travel and Continental Rail Desk (see box on p.11) both offer the range of European train passes covered on p.35.

If you want to take the **car**, you can either cross to Britain and then drive to the Channel ports for another ferry or the Eurotunnel shuttle; or you might prefer to put your feet up for the extra-long crossings direct from Cork or Rosslare to the French coast – fourteen hours to Roscoff or seventeen to Cherbourg, the latter leaving you within a (very long) day's drive of the Alps. Prices vary tremendously according to the day of travel; in the low season (March–May & Sept), you could pay roughly IR£120 for a car plus two people one-way to Cherbourg, but in the high season (June–Aug) the same thing costs IR£300. A basic cabin costs from IR£35 extra.

GETTING THERE FROM NORTH AMERICA

Several airlines fly direct to Zürich from North America, and many other airlines have flights to Zürich via other major European cities. If Switzerland is part of a longer European trip, you'll also want to check out details of the Eurail pass, which must be purchased in advance of your arrival and can get you by train from anywhere in Europe to Switzerland.

SHOPPING FOR TICKETS

Leaving aside discounted tickets, special promotional offers or courier flights, the cheapest way to go is with an **APEX** (Advance Purchase Excursion) ticket, although these carry certain restrictions: you generally have to book – and pay – up to 21 days before departure, spend at least seven days abroad (maximum stay of three months), and you tend to get penalized if you change your schedule. Some airlines also issue **Special APEX** tickets to youth/student travellers, often with fewer restrictions on the period of stay. There are also winter **Super APEX** tickets, sometimes known as "Eurosavers", which are slightly cheaper than an ordinary APEX, but limit your stay to between 7 and 21 days.

However, discount outlets can often do better than an APEX fare. They come in several forms. **Consolidators** buy up large blocks of tickets that airlines don't think they'll be able to sell at their published fares, and sell them at a discount. Besides being cheap, consolidators normally don't impose advance purchase requirements (although in busy times you'll want to book ahead just to be sure of getting a ticket), but they do often charge very stiff fees for date changes. Also, these companies' margins are pretty slim, so they make their money by dealing in volume – don't expect them to entertain lots of questions.

Discount agents – such as STA, Council Travel, or others listed on p.14 – also wheel and deal in blocks of tickets offloaded by the air-

AIRLINES IN THE US AND CANADA

Air Canada, *www.aircanada.ca* – ☎1-888/247-2262 in Canada; ☎1-800/776-3000 in US. Daily nonstop flights to Zürich from Toronto plus connections (with a change of planes) from Calgary, Montréal and Vancouver.

Air France, *www.airfrance.fr* – ☎1-800/237-2747 in US; ☎1-800/667-2747 in Canada. They fly from many North American cities to Paris, then a change of planes and onward to Zürich, Geneva and Basel.

Alitalia, *www.alitalia.com* – ☎1-800/223-5730 in US; in New York, ☎1-800/442-5860; in Canada, ☎1-800/361-8336. Flights to Rome and Milan from several major North American cities, with onward connections to Geneva and Zürich. The Milan connections are a bit more economical for North American travellers.

American Airlines, *www.americanair.com* – ☎1-800/433-7300 in US. Runs a daily nonstop flight from Chicago to Zürich, with connections from their other American gateways to Chicago.

Balair/CTA, ☎1-800/322-5247 in US. Weekly charter flights to Zürich May–November, departing from Miami, Orlando and Ft Myers and heading nonstop to Zürich.

British Airways, *www.british-airways.com* – ☎1-800/247-9297 in US; ☎1-800/668-1059 in Canada. Nonstop flights to London from various North American cities, with onward connections to Zürich and Geneva.

Continental Airlines, *www.flycontinental.com* – ☎1-800/231-0856 in US. Nonstop daily flights to Zürich from New York, with connecting flights from most US cities. One of the most reasonably priced Zürich nonstops, running around US$400 in low season.

Delta Airlines, *www.delta-air.com* – ☎1-800/241-4141 in US; ☎1-800/221-1212 in

Canada. The most comprehensive selection of nonstop flights from the US, including daily nonstops from Atlanta, New York and Washington DC; six times weekly nonstops from Boston, Chicago and Los Angeles; five times weekly nonstops from San Francisco; and a five times weekly direct from Cincinnati (with a stopover in either Chicago, New York or Brussels, Belgium).

Finnair, *www.finnair.fi* – ☎1-800/950-5000 in US and Canada. Daily nonstops from New York to Helsinki, with connecting flights to Zürich.

Iberia, *www.iberia.com* – ☎1-800/772-4642 in US and Canada. Daily nonstops from New York to Barcelona and Madrid, with onward connections to Zürich and Geneva. Their special offers are often particularly good value.

Pakistan International Airlines, *www.piac.com* – ☎1-800/221-2552 in US. Three times weekly nonstop flights from New York to Zürich.

SAS (Scandinavian Airlines), *www.flysas.com* – ☎1-800/221-2350 in US and Canada. Daily nonstops from Chicago, New York City and Seattle to Copenhagen with onward connections to both Geneva and Zürich. From the Pacific Northwest, this is by far the easiest way to get there.

Swissair, *www.swissair.com* – ☎1-800/221-4750 in US; ☎1-800/267-9477 in Canada. Their comprehensive list of connections includes daily nonstops to Zürich, Geneva and Basel from New York, plus daily nonstops to Zürich from Atlanta, Boston, Chicago, Cincinnati, Los Angeles, San Francisco and Washington DC. From Canada they offer a five times weekly nonstop to Zürich from Montréal, with connections available from Toronto and Vancouver. Generally one notch more expensive than most competitors, but with near-constant special offers available.

lines, but they typically offer a range of other travel-related services such as insurance, rail passes, youth and student ID cards, car rentals, tours and the like. These agencies tend to be most worthwhile to students and under-26s, who can often benefit from special fares and deals. Some agents specialize in **charter flights**, which may be cheaper than anything available on a scheduled flight, but departure dates are fixed, withdrawal penalties high (check the refund policy) and not all North American cities are serviced by Swiss-bound

charters. **Travel clubs** are another option for those who travel a lot – most charge an annual membership fee, which may be worth it for discounts on air tickets, car rental and the like.

You should also stay on the lookout for any **special promotional offers** the airlines might have. These crop up throughout the year and, for the flexible traveller, can deliver substantial savings. A further possibility for those with a flexible schedule is a **courier flight** to Zürich or Geneva, though these don't turn up as often as they do for other major European cities like London and Paris.

DISCOUNT TRAVEL COMPANIES IN THE US AND CANADA

Air Courier Association, *www.aircourier.org* – 15000 W 6th Ave, Suite 203, Golden, CO 80401 (☎1-800/282-1202 or 303/278-8810). Courier flight broker with occasional Zürich deals. Annual fee $64.

Airhitch, *www.airhitch.org* – 2641 Broadway, New York, NY 10025 (☎1-800/326-2009 or 212/864-2000). Standby-seat broker that charges an initial set price and guarantees to get you on a flight as close to your preferred destination as possible within a week. Keep in mind that you're almost certain to wind up with a ticket to Zürich, regardless of which Swiss city you request.

Council Travel, *www.counciltravel.com* – 205 E 42nd St, New York, NY 10017 (☎1-888-COUN-CIL), and branches in many other US cities. Student/budget travel agency offering a wide array of services, including travel insurance, discounted airfares, Eurail passes, Europasses and bus passes.

Discount Airfares Worldwide On-Line, *www.etn.nl/discount.htm*. Web site maintained by the non-profit European Travel Network and listing dozens of Web links for consolidators and discount agents who can get you a rock-bottom priced ticket to Zürich or Geneva.

High Adventure Travel, *www.highadv.com* – 442 Post St, Suite 400, San Francisco, CA 94102 (☎1-800/350-0612 or 415/912-5600). Round-the-world tickets, including over 100 pre-packaged RTW itineraries that include Zürich.

International Association of Air Travel Couriers, *www.courier.org* – 220 S Dixie Hwy, #3, Lake Worth, FL 33460 (☎561/582-8320). Courier flight broker with occasional discounted flights to Zürich. Annual fee $45.

Skylink, 265 Madison Ave, 5th Fl, New York, NY 10016 (☎1-800/AIR-ONLY or 212/599-0430) with branches in Chicago, Los Angeles, Montréal, Toronto, and Washington DC. Major North American consolidator that can usually get you a good deal on a direct flight to Zürich or Geneva.

STA Travel, *www.sta-travel.com* – 5900 Wilshire Blvd, Suite 2110, Los Angeles, CA 90036 (☎1-800/777-0112), and other branches in New York, San Francisco, Boston, Miami, Chicago, Seattle, Philadelphia and Washington DC. Worldwide discount travel firm specializing in student/youth fares, and also offering travel insurance, car rental discounts, plus Busabout, Europass, Eurail and Swiss rail passes.

Travel CUTS, *www.travelcuts.com* – 187 College St, Toronto, ON M5T 1P7 (☎1-800/667-2887 or 416/979-2406), and other branches all over Canada, also with an office in San Francisco (☎415/247-1800). Organization specializing in student and youth fares and the standard array of travel services, including bus and rail passes.

Travelocity, *www.travelocity.com*. Online consolidator with a handy Web tool that offers you the cheapest airfares to Zürich, Geneva or Basel for any given time period.

In return for shepherding a parcel through customs, and possibly giving up your baggage allowance, you can expect to get a heavily discounted ticket, anything between US$150 and US$500, depending on season. A couple of courier outfits are listed in the box above.

Regardless of where you buy your ticket, the fare will depend on **season**. As a general rule, you can expect fares to Switzerland to be highest from around June to mid-September; they drop during the "shoulder" seasons, April to mid-May, and mid-September to October; and you'll get the best deals during the low season, which extends from November through March (excluding the weeks around Christmas and New Year when prices are hiked up and seats are at a premium). The high season fare can be more than double that of the low season. Note

that flying on weekends ordinarily adds around US$60/C$90 to the round-trip fare; prices quoted in the following sections assume mid-week travel in the low season, exclude tax and are subject to change.

If Switzerland is only one stop on a longer journey, you might want to consider buying a **Round-the-World** (RTW) ticket. Some travel agents can sell you any of a hundred or more "off-the-shelf" RTW tickets which include Zürich on their itineraries; prices range from US$1200/C$1770 all the way up to US$5000/C$7400.

FROM THE US

Zürich is the destination for almost all direct flights from the US to Switzerland: Swissair and Delta are the major carriers, both offering non-stop or direct flights from their gateway cities.

These flights are supplemented by American Airlines' nonstop flights from Chicago, and Continental Airlines and Pakistan International Airlines' nonstop flights from New York. Swissair also has daily nonstop flights to **Geneva** and **Basel**, but these depart from New York only.

You may also find good occasional deals on routings **via other major European cities** with the airlines of those countries: Air France via Paris, British Airways via London, Finnair via Helsinki, or Alitalia via Rome or Milan, for example. (Milan's Malpensa airport is just 25km south of the Swiss border.) Iberia often has particularly cheap special offers on flights from New York to Zürich, with a change of planes in Barcelona or Madrid.

At the time of writing, the major carriers were offering the following APEX round-trip **fares** direct to Zürich: Atlanta $600–700; Boston $450–550; Chicago $425–550; Cincinnati $500–570; Los Angeles $880–930; New York $400–475; San Francisco $880–930; and Washington DC $425–500.

TOUR OPERATORS IN THE US AND CANADA

Abercrombie & Kent, www.abercrombiekent.com – ☎1-800/323-7308. Five-star guided sightseeing tours and customized tours with a heavy accent on resort towns like St Moritz and the scenery of the Alpine rail routes. One- and two-week tours available, plus a tour that combines Switzerland with northern Italy and Lake Como. Rates run between $5500 and $7500.

Above the Clouds Trekking, ☎1-800/233-4499. One- and two-week trekking tours through the Swiss Alps during the summer for around $1000 excluding flights.

Adventure Center, ☎1-800/227-8747. Fifteen-day treks along the Mont Blanc circuit, taking in Switzerland plus the French and Italian Alps; be prepared to camp the whole way. Tours run from July through September, and cost around $1000 excluding flights.

Alphorn Tours, ☎1-800/ALP-HORN or 215/794-5653. Quality hiking trips during the summer, and ski trips to all the major resorts January through April. Prices run between $1000 and $2000 excluding flights.

Austro Tours, ☎1-800/333-5533 or 713/960-0090. Ski packages (December through March) that include airfare, transfers and accommodation with meal plan. Prices are good at around $730–1200 per week, though ski lift passes are not included. Sightseeing tours are offered the rest of the year.

Backroads, www.backroads.com – ☎1-800/462-2848. Terrific independent tour company that offers one- and two-week mountain hiking and biking trips throughout July and August, costing around $2600 excluding flights.

CBT Bicycle Tours, ☎1-800/736-BIKE. A variety of mountain biking tours, some that also include hiking, designed on an individual basis and costing about $1200 excluding flights. Also worth checking out is their winter trekking trip, which involves several days of hiking and several days of sledding through the Alps (also around $1200).

Ciao Travel, ☎1-800/942-2426. Festival tours to the Montreux Jazz Festival for between $1440 and $2100.

Collette Tours, www.collettetours.com – ☎1-800/832-4656, in Canada ☎1-800/468-5955. Luxury, leisurely paced sightseeing tours of Switzerland ($1000–1200), plus a couple of two-week tours that take in Switzerland plus Austria and northern Italy ($1800–2000).

European Journeys, ☎1-800/337-3057. Week-long ski vacations to all the major Swiss resorts, plus golf-oriented vacations around Lucerne, both running to around $2500.

Europeds, ☎1-800/321-9552 or 831/646-4920. Family-oriented sightseeing tours that run to around $2800 per person, with a discount for kids.

Globus and Cosmos www.cosmostours.com – ☎1-800/221-0090. Half a dozen different sightseeing tours of Switzerland, one including a jaunt into Austria as well. Tours run between $1200 and $2400, depending on the length of your stay. To request brochures only, call 1-800/338-7092.

Red Seal, in Canada ☎1-800/668-4224 or from US ☎416/503-2233. Five-star sightseeing tours to Zürich and Geneva, running from April through October and costing around C$2400 per week.

Wild Women Adventures, ☎1-800/992-1322 or 707/829-3670. Women-only ski trips, summer culture tours and annual trips to carnival in Lucerne. Expect to pay around $3500.

World Expeditions, www.worldexpeditions.com – ☎613/241-2700. Canadian-run bicycling trips to Ticino, running May-September and costing around C$700–900 for a week excluding flights.

With special promotional offers, round-trip fares can drop as low as $300 from New York and $500 from LA. Note that Swissair's published fares are generally US$50–75 higher than that of their competitors, but if you have some flexibility in your schedule you'd do well to wait for one of their many special offers, which can bring the price tag down by as much as US$150.

Another option worth investigating is Balair/CTA – a wholly owned subsidiary of Swissair – who offer Sunday **charter flights** from May through November, departing from Miami ($600), Orlando and Ft Myers ($800) and heading nonstop to Zürich.

FROM CANADA

All direct flights from Canada to Switzerland are bound for Zürich. **Air Canada** offers daily nonstop flights from Toronto, with connections available from Calgary, Montréal and Vancouver. **Swissair** offers nonstop flights from Montréal, with connections from Toronto and Vancouver. At the time of writing, low-season round-trip APEX fares to Zürich were around C$850–950 from Montréal, C$880–930 from Toronto and C$1100–1260 from Vancouver. Both Air Canada and Swissair run **special promotional offers** to Zürich regularly, so keep checking and you'll probably turn up some sort of discounted flight.

Travel CUTS is the most reliable student/youth agency, with some deals for non-students, too; alternatively, check the travel ads in your local newspaper and consult a good travel agent.

PACKAGE TOURS

Package tours may not sound like your kind of travel, but don't dismiss the idea out of hand. In addition to the fully escorted variety, many agents can put together very flexible deals, sometimes amounting to no more than a flight plus car or rail pass and accommodation; if you're planning to travel in moderate or luxury style, and especially if your trip is geared around special interests, such packages can work out cheaper than the same arrangements made on arrival. A package can also be great for your peace of mind, if only to ensure a worry-free first week while you're finding your feet on a longer tour (of course, you can jump off the itinerary any time you like). Most companies will expect you to book through a local travel agent, and since it costs the same you might as well.

RAIL BAGGAGE

Switzerland's "rail baggage" service is covered on p.3. Labels cost US$15/C$22, and are available from Swissair ticket desks and offices throughout North America. The homeward-bound version of "Rail Baggage" is "Fly Baggage" (see p.36).

EUROPEAN RAIL AND BUS PASSES

If you're planning to do much **train** travel in Europe, then consider buying a **Eurail pass**, which comes in various forms, all of which must be bought before you leave home. The pass allows unlimited free train travel in sixteen other countries and can translate into a pretty good bargain. However, if you're planning to stick mainly to Switzerland, you're much better off buying one of the **Swiss rail passes** outlined on p.35, since Eurail passes are not valid on many smaller mountain railways or on any post-bus journeys. We've flagged Eurail discounts in the guide text where relevant.

The **Eurail Youthpass** (for under-26s) costs US$388/C$570 for 15 consecutive days, US$499/C$733 for 21 days, US$623/C$915 for one month, US$882/C$1296 for two months or US$1089/C$1600 for three months; if you're 26 or over you'll have to buy a **first-class pass**, available in 15-day (US$554/C$814), 21-day (US$718/C$1055), one-month (US$890/C$1308), two-month (US$1260/C$1852) and three-month (US$1558/C$2290) increments. For groups of two to five (three to five in summer), the **Eurail**

RAIL CONTACTS IN NORTH AMERICA

CIT Rail, 15 W 44th St, 10th Floor, New York, NY 10136 (☎1-800/248-7245 or 212/730-2400).
Council Travel, see p.14.
Online Travel, 9501 W Devon Ave, Suite 1E, Rosemont, IL 60018 (☎1-800/660-5300, *www.online@eurorail.com*).
Rail Europe, 226 Westchester Ave, White Plains, NY 10604 (☎1-800/438-7245 in US; ☎1-800/361-7245 in Canada, *www.raileurope.com*). Official Eurail Pass agent in North America.
ScanTours, 3439 Wade St, Los Angeles, CA 90066 (☎1-800/223-7226 or 310/636-4656, *www.scantours.com*).
STA Travel, see p.14.
Travel CUTS, see p.14.

Saverpass (first class only) can knock 15 percent off the cost of the standard Eurail offerings.

You stand a better chance of getting your money's worth out of a **Eurail Flexipass**, which is good for a certain number of travel days in a two-month period. This, too, comes in both under-26 and first-class versions: 10 days costs US$444/C$652 or US$654/C$961 respectively; 15 days, US$585/C$860 or US$862/C$1267. Again, parties of two to five can save 15 percent with the **Eurail Saver Flexipass**.

The **EurailDrive Pass** is valid for any six days in a two month period and allows four days free rail travel and two days free car hire; the price for two adults travelling together in an economy car is US$339/C$498; an additional day with the car costs US$61/C$89.

A scaled-down version of the Flexipass, the **Europass**, allows first-class travel in Switzerland, France, Germany, Italy and Spain for any five days in two months for US$348/C$511, with the option of adding up to ten additional rail days at US$42/C$61 each. Up to four "associate" countries (Austria, Hungary, Belgium, Netherlands, Luxembourg, Greece and Portugal) can be included

for an additional fee. For under-26s, the **Europass Youth** costs US$233/C$342 for any five days of second-class travel in two months, with extra rail days costing US$29/C$42 each. Groups of two to five can save fifteen percent with the **Europass Saverpass**. The **Europass Drive** allows travel for any five days within a two-month period (three by rail and two by car); the price for two adults in an economy car is US$284/C$417; each additional car day costs US$59/C$86.

All these passes can be **reserved** through Rail Europe (in US ☎1-877/456-RAIL, in Canada ☎1-800/361-RAIL, www.raileurope.com), or travel agents (see box opposite). Note that both Eurail and Europass holders are often eligible for discounts on the fares of privately run mountain railways and cable-cars in Switzerland that are not covered for free travel.

North Americans considering travelling through Europe by bus should check out the **Busabout passes** (for more, see p.9), available from STA Travel, Council Travel or Travel CUTS (see box p.14); fifteen-day passes are $395 ($285 for youth or student card-holders); a month's pass costs $635/465.

GETTING THERE FROM AUSTRALIA AND NEW ZEALAND

There's a good selection of airlines that can get you to Switzerland from Australia and New Zealand, but there are no direct flights. Given the high cost of flights in general from Australasia, however, a "Round the World" fare is a good option. Destinations in south-

ern Switzerland are also served by flights to Milan, from where you can continue your journey by land. Various rail and bus passes can be bought before you leave should you wish to extend your trip into Europe.

Fares vary significantly with the **season**: low season runs from mid-January to the end of February and during October and November; high season runs from mid-May to the end of August and from December to mid-January; the rest of the year is counted as "shoulder season".

Tickets purchased direct from the airlines tend to be expensive – travel agents offer better deals and have the latest information on special deals, such as free stopovers en route and fly-drive-accommodation packages. Flight Centres and STA (see box p.19) generally offer the best discounts, especially for students and those under 26.

Most airlines have a set fare ("common rated") from major eastern Australian cities, while from Perth and Darwin you'll pay between A$100 and

AIRLINES IN AUSTRALIA AND NEW ZEALAND

Air New Zealand, *www.airnz.co.nz* – in Australia ☎13 2476; in New Zealand ☎0800/737 000. Daily flights from major Australian and New Zealand cities via LA to London or Frankfurt, with connecting flights on to Switzerland.

Alitalia, *www.alitalia.it* – in Australia ☎1300/653 757; in New Zealand ☎09/379 4457. Six times a week (from Sydney, with Ansett connections from Australian and New Zealand major cities) to Amsterdam (code sharing with KLM) or Milan. Connect in these cities for flights to Switzerland or go overland from Milan.

Britannia Airways, book through UK Flight Shop in Sydney (☎02/9247 4833, *www.ukflightshop.com.au*) or World Aviation in Auckland (☎09/308 3355). Charter flights from Sydney and Auckland to London via Indonesia and Abu Dhabi (both stops for refuelling). Change in London for connections to Switzerland.

British Airways, *www.britishairways.com.au* – in Australia ☎03/9603 1133 or 02/8904 8800; *www.britishairways.co.nz* in New Zealand ☎09/356 8690. Daily to London from Sydney, Perth or Brisbane, with onward connections to Swiss cities.

KLM, *www.klm.com.au* – in Australia ☎03/9654 5222, 02/9231 6333 or 1800/500 747; in New Zealand ☎09/309 1782. Six times a week (from Sydney, with Ansett connections from Australian and New Zealand major cities) to Amsterdam or Milan (code sharing with Alitalia). Connect in these cities for flights to Switzerland or go overland from Milan.

Lauda Air, *www.laudaair.com* – in Australia ☎03/9600 4000, 02/9251 6155 or 1800/642 438. Four departures a week from Melbourne and Sydney to Geneva via Vienna, or with a code-share on to Zürich, Basel or Bern.

Lufthansa, *www.lufthansa.com* – in Australia ☎1300/655 727; in New Zealand ☎0800/945 220. Daily flights from Sydney, Melbourne and Auckland via Bangkok or Singapore and Frankfurt, to Zürich. Code share with Thai or Singapore Airlines for the first leg.

Qantas, *www.qantas.com.au* – in Australia ☎13 1313; in New Zealand ☎09/357 8900 or 0800/808 767. Daily from Australian and New Zealand major cities with code-sharing arrangements via Asian or European cities to Switzerland.

Singapore Airlines, *www.singaporeair.com* – in Australia ☎13 1011; in New Zealand ☎09/303 2129 or 0800/808 909. Daily flights to Zürich via Singapore from Australian and New Zealand major cities.

Swissair, *www.swissair.com* – in Australia ☎03/9670 2191, 02/9232 1744 or 1800/221 339; in New Zealand ☎09/358 3216. Code share with Qantas to Singapore three times a week with onward flights to Zürich and connections to Geneva and Basel. Air New Zealand or Singapore Airlines can arrange connections from Auckland to the Swissair flights starting in Singapore.

Thai Airways, *www.thaiairways.com* – in Australia ☎1300/651 960; in New Zealand ☎09/377 3886. Daily flights to Zürich from Auckland and Sydney via Bangkok.

A$200 less via Asia, or A$200–400 more via Canada and the US. Fares from Christchurch and Wellington are around NZ$150–300 more than those from Auckland.

For a **scheduled flight** from the Australian east coast or Auckland, count on paying A$1500–2260/NZ$1900–2800 on Alitalia or KLM; A$1900–2500/NZ$2280–3000 on Thai Airways, Lauda Air, Lufthansa or Swissair; A$2400–2850/NZ$2700–3400 on British Airways, Qantas, Singapore Airlines and Air New Zealand, depending on the season. See the box above for a full rundown of airlines and routes.

If you want to fly to **another European gateway** and then travel overland to Switzerland, you'll find lowest fares are with Britannia

Airways to London during their limited charter season (Nov–March), when you can expect to pay A$1000–1600/NZ$1200–1900.

For extended trips, a **Round-the-World** (RTW) ticket, valid for up to a year, can be good value. Tickets that take in Switzerland include the One World Alliance "Global Explorer" (Qantas, British Airways, American, Canadian, Cathay, Finnair, Iberia) which starts at A$2400–2900/NZ$2900–3400, and the Star Alliance's RTW option (Ansett, Air Canada, Air New Zealand, Lufthansa, SAS, Thai, United Airlines) which starts at A$2800/NZ$3350. These are mileage-based tickets (backtracking permitted) and can be booked through any of the partner airlines, so you should use whichever is the most convenient.

DISCOUNT AGENTS AND SPECIALIST OPERATORS IN AUSTRALIA AND NEW ZEALAND

DISCOUNT AGENTS

Anywhere Travel, *www.anywheretravel.com.au* – 345 Anzac Parade, Kingsford, Sydney (☎02/9663 0411).

Budget Travel, *www.budgettravel.co.nz* – 16 Fort St, Auckland (☎09/366 0061 or 0800/808 040).

CIT, *www.cittravel.com.au* – 422 Collins St, Melbourne (☎03/9650 5510); 263 Clarence St, Sydney (☎02/9267 1255), with branches in Brisbane, Adelaide and Perth. One of the main agents for Eurail and Swiss passes.

Destinations Unlimited, 3 Milford Rd, Milford, Auckland (☎09/373 4033).

European Travel Office (ETO), *www.eto.com.au* – 122 Rosslyn St, West Melbourne (☎03/9329 8844); 20th Floor, 133 Castlereagh St, Sydney (☎02/9267 7727).

Flight Centre, *www.flightcentre.com* – in Australia call ☎13 1600 for your nearest branch; in New Zealand, National Bank Towers, 205–225 Queen St (☎0800/354 448), plus branches nationwide.

Harvey World Travel, *www.harveyworld.com.au* – 631 Princes Highway, Kogarah, Sydney (☎02/9567 6099 or13 2757), with branches nationwide.

Northern Gateway, 22 Cavenagh St, Darwin (☎08/8941 1394).

STA Travel, in Australia: 256 Flinders St, Melbourne (☎03/9654 7266), 855 George St, Sydney (☎02/9212 1255 or 1800/637 444), other offices in state capitals and major universities (Australia-wide ☎1300/360 960, *www.statravelaus.com.au*); in New Zealand: 10 High St, Auckland (☎09/309 0458), 90 Cashel St, Christchurch (☎03/379 9098), 130 Cuba St, Wellington (☎04/385 0561), plus branches in Dunedin, Palmerston North, Hamilton and major universities (*www.statravel.co.nz*).

Suntravel, in New Zealand: 407 Great South Road, Penrose (☎09/525 3074).

Thomas Cook, in Australia: 257 Collins St, Melbourne (☎03/9282 0222 or 13 1771), 175 Pitt St, Sydney (☎02/9231 2877 or 1800/801 002), plus branches in other state capitals; in New Zealand: 159 Queen St, Auckland (☎09/379 3924 or 0800/353535). Sells Eurail and Busabout passes and Swiss passes.

Topdeck Travel, 65 Glenfell St, Adelaide (☎08/8232 7222).

Trailfinders, *www.trailfinders.com.au* – 8 Spring St, Sydney (☎02/9247 7666).

Travel.com, *www.travel.com.au* – 80 Clarence St, Sydney (☎02/9249 5444).

Tymtro Travel, 428 George St, Sydney (☎02/9223 2211).

USIT Beyond (formerly YHA Travel), *www.usitbeyond.co.nz* – cnr Shortland St & Jean Batten Pl, Auckland (☎09/379 4224), plus branches in Hamilton, Palmerston North, Wellington and Christchurch.

UTAG Travel, *www.utag.com.au* – 122 Walker St, North Sydney (☎02/9956 8399 or 13 1398), plus branches throughout Australia.

SPECIALIST OPERATORS

Adventure World, in Australia: 73 Walker St, North Sydney (☎02/9956 7766 or 1800/221 931, *www.adventureworld.com.au*), plus branches in Brisbane and Perth; in New Zealand: 101 Gt South Rd Remuera Auckland (☎09/524 5118, *www.adventureworld.co.nz*). Fifteen-day tours of the Swiss mountains, involving five days of walking, for A\$1285/NZ\$1600 excluding airfares.

CIT, (see above). City tours and accommodation packages in Zürich, Geneva, Interlaken and Luzern.

National World Travel, *www.natworldtravel.com.au* – 1 O'Connell St, Sydney (02/9251 1977 or 13 1435). Swiss travel experts, with tons of information on hiking, cycling and skiing tours, plus rail tickets.

Snow Bookings Only, 1141 Toorak Rd, Camberwell, Melbourne (☎03/9809 2699 or 1800/623 266). Ski tour specialists.

Swiss Travel Centre, *www.sydneytravel.com.au/swiss/* – Level 8, 75 King St Sydney (☎02/9299 8000). Specialist operator for escorted tours and ski packages. Can also book car rental, train passes and inexpensive accommodation. Eight-day itinerary covering the major sights in Switzerland starts at A\$560 per person for two-star accommodation.

Travel Plan, *www.travelplan.com.au* – 118 Edinburgh St, Castlecraig, Sydney (☎02/9438 1333). Ski packages in St Moritz, Verbier and Davos, starting at around A\$900 for twin-share accommodation.

PACKAGE TOURS

If you're interested in activities like skiing or hiking, and prefer to have all the arrangements made for you before you leave, then seeking the help of a specialist agent is a good way to plan your trip. Unfortunately, there are few pre-packaged tours that include airfares from Australasia, but most specialist agents will be able to assist with flight arrangements as well. In turn, many of the tours we've listed (see box on p.19) can also be arranged through your local travel agent.

RAIL BAGGAGE

Switzerland's "rail baggage" service is covered on p.3. Labels cost A$20/NZ$25, and are available from Swissair offices in Australia and New Zealand. The homeward-bound version of "Rail Baggage" is "Fly Baggage" (see p.36).

EUROPEAN RAIL AND BUS PASSES

If you're planning to visit Switzerland as part of a wider European trip, it's worth looking into the various rail and bus passes on offer, though if you're planning to stick mainly to Switzerland, you're considerably better off buying one of the **Swiss rail passes** outlined on p.35 – these are available from travel agents or from Rail Plus (in Australia: ☎03/9642 8644 or 1300/555 003, fax 03/9642 8403, *info@railplus.com.au*; in New Zealand: 09/303 2484). Eurail passes are not valid on many smaller mountain railways or on any postbus journeys. We've flagged Eurail discounts in the guide text where relevant.

The **Eurail Youthpass** (for under-26s) allows unlimited free train travel in Switzerland and sixteen other countries and costs A$615/NZ$765 for 15 days, A$790/NZ$990 for 21 days, A$990/NZ$1225 for one month, A$1400/NZ$1750 for two months and A$1730/NZ$2135 for three months. If you're 26 or over you'll have to buy a **first-class pass**, available in 15-day A$880/NZ$1090, 21-day A$1140/NZ$1415, one-month A$1410/NZ$1750, two-month A$1995/NZ$2460 and three-month A$2470/NZ$3055 increments. For groups of two to five, the first-class **Eurail Saverpass** can knock around fifteen percent off the price of the standard pass.

The **Eurail Flexipass** is good for a certain number of travel days in a two-month period and also comes in youth/first-class versions: 10 days cost A$725/1040 or NZ$900/1285; and 15 days, A$950/1370 or NZ$1175/1700. Again, parties of two to five can save fifteen percent with the **Eurail Saver Flexipass**.

A scaled-down version of the Flexipass, the **Europass**, allows travel in France, Germany, Italy, Spain and Switzerland for (youth/first-class) A$370/550 or NZ$460/675 for five days in a two-month period, on up to A$815/1155 or NZ$1020/1435 for 15 days in two months; there's also the option of adding "associate" countries (Austria, Hungary, Belgium, Netherlands, Luxembourg, Portugal and Greece) for an additional fee. Groups of two to five can save fifteen percent with the **Euro Saverpass**.

Those considering travelling through Europe by bus should check out the **Busabout passes** (for more, see p.9); 15-day passes are A$400/NZ$500; 21-day passes are A$570/NZ$710; and a month's pass costs A$750/NZ$940. There is a discount of roughly ten percent for students.

All these passes can be **reserved** through your travel agent (see box below).

TRAVELLERS WITH DISABILITIES

Switzerland is one of the most enlightened European countries with regard to travellers with disabilities. There's a wealth of information available in advance to help in planning your trip, and once you arrive you'll find most tourist facilities have been designed with everybody, not just the able-bodied, in mind.

There are many organized tours and holidays specifically put together for **people with disabilities** – the contacts in the box will be able to put you touch with any specialists for trips to Switzerland. Switzerland Tourism (see p.30 for worldwide addresses) publishes a very useful **hotel guide** specifically for visitors with dis-

abilities, listing and assessing hotels around the country according to their access for people with limited mobility or in wheelchairs. Mobility International Switzerland (see box on p.22) have their own list, and also publish **city guides** for 26 localities around the country written with people with disabilities in mind (Fr.5 each). Swiss Federal Railways publish a brochure covering **train-travel** around the country: all fast trains, many regional trains and the Zürich double-decker S-Bahn trains have spaces within second-class carriages to park wheelchairs, identified by a wheelchair pictogram. Once alerted that you'll be turning up at a specific time, station staff will give you a hand getting

---

CONTACTS FOR TRAVELLERS WITH DISABILITIES

IN BRITAIN

Access Travel, 6 The Hillock, Astley, Lancs M29 7GW (☎01942/888844, fax 891811). The sole licensed UK tour operator dealing specifically with travellers with disabilities, but only able to sell flights to Switzerland.

Holiday Care Service, 2nd floor, Imperial Building, Victoria Rd, Horley, Surrey RH6 7PZ (☎01293/774535, fax 784647, Minicom 776943, *holiday.care@virgin.net*). Provides a free list of accessible accommodation in Switzerland. Information on financial help for holidays available.

RADAR (Royal Association for Disability and Rehabilitation), 12 City Forum, 250 City Rd, London EC1V 8AF (☎020/7250 3222, Minicom 7250 4119). A good source of advice on holidays and travel abroad. They produce *Getting There* on travel abroad (£5).

Tripscope, The Courtyard, Evelyn Rd, London W4 5JL (☎020/8994 9294, fax 8994 3618; Minicom, and from around the UK ☎0845/758 5641, *tripscope@cableinet.co.uk*). This registered charity provides a national telephone information service offering free advice on UK and international transport for those with limited mobility.

IN IRELAND

Disability Action Group, 2 Annadale Ave, Belfast BT7 3JH (☎028/9049 1011).

Irish Wheelchair Association, Blackheath Drive, Clontarf, Dublin (☎01/833 8241, fax 833 3873, *iwa@iol.ie*).

IN NORTH AMERICA

Mobility International USA, PO Box 10767, Eugene, OR 97440 (Voice and TDD: ☎541/343-1284, *www.miusa.org*). Travel tips and listings of disabled-friendly hotels and sights, plus information on foreign exchange programs for the disabled. $35 annual membership fee.

Society for the Advancement of Travel for the Handicapped (SATH), 347 5th Ave, Suite 610, New York, NY 10016 (☎212/447-7284, *www.sath.org*). Non-profit-making travel industry referral service that passes queries on to its

members as appropriate; allow plenty of time for a response.

Travel Information Service (☎215/456-9603). Telephone-only information and referral service.

Twin Peaks Press, Box 129, Vancouver, WA 98666 (☎360/694-2462 or 1-800/637-2256). Publisher of the *Directory of Travel Agencies for the Disabled*, listing more than 370 agencies worldwide; *Travel for the Disabled*; the *Directory of Accessible Van Rentals* and *Wheelchair Vagabond*, loaded with personal tips.

on and off if you need it. Contact Swiss Federal Railways in London (see p.8) for more information before you leave. The Swiss Invalid Association (see box) also sells a **map and brochure** in four languages covering travel in Switzerland for people with disabilities.

CONTACTS FOR TRAVELLERS WITH DISABILITIES

IN AUSTRALIA AND NEW ZEALAND

Barrier Free Travel, 36 Wheatley St, North Bellingen, NSW 2454 (☎02/66551 733).
DPA (Disabled Persons Assembly), Wellington Trade Centre, 173–175 Victoria St, Wellington (☎04/801 9100).
Wheelchair Travel, 29 Ranelagh Dr, Mt Eliza VIC 3930 (☎1800/674 468 or 03/97878861, *www.travelability.com*).

IN SWITZERLAND

Mobility International Switzerland, Postfach 129, Feldeggstrasse 77, CH-8032 Zürich (☎01/383 04 97).
Swiss Invalid Association, *www.siv.ch* – German-speaking: Schweizerischer Invalidenverband, Froburgstrasse 4, CH-4600 Olten (☎062/206 88 88, fax 206 88 89, *siv-info@bluewin.ch*). French-speaking: Association suisse des Invalides, Flore 30, CH-2502 Bienne (☎032/322 84 86, fax 323 82 94, *asiromand@bluewin.ch*). Italian-speaking: Associazione Svizzera degli Invalidi, Via Ciseri 6, CH-6900 Lugano (☎ & fax 091/921 07 67).

RED TAPE AND VISAS

All EU nationals and citizens of the US, Canada, Australia and New Zealand require only a valid passport to visit Switzerland and Liechtenstein. In theory, stays are limited to a three-month maximum per trip, and six months total per year, but in practice border officials never stamp passports unless asked.

Duty-free allowances for visitors arriving from Europe are 200 cigarettes or 50 cigars or 250g of tobacco (doubled if you're arriving from outside Europe), 2 litres of wine under 15 percent, 1 litre of alcohol over 15 percent, plus, should you want to carry coals to Newcastle, 125g of butter and 1kg of ham or sausages. There are no restrictions on the import of currency.

WORK PERMITS AND RESIDENCY

Switzerland is one of the wealthiest countries in Europe, and so short-term employment can bring rich rewards: serving in a fast-food restaurant could net you £7/$11 per hour; working as a manual labourer half as much again. The problem is getting the right **permits**. With Switzerland being outside the EU, rules elsewhere in Europe about the free movement of labour don't apply. A massive and controversial influx throughout the 1990s of asylum seekers from the Balkan states has

SWISS EMBASSIES AND CONSULATES ABROAD

Australia 7 Melbourne Avenue, Forrest, Canberra, ACT 2603 (☎02/6273 3977, fax 6273 3428, *swiemcan@dynamite.com.au*); 7th floor, 420 St Kilda Rd, Melbourne, VIC 3004 (☎03/9867 2266, fax 9866 5907, *swisscgmelb@ozemail.com.au*); Plaza II #2301, 500 Oxford St, Bondi Junction, Sydney NSW 2022 (☎02/9369 4244, fax 9369 1334, *swicgsyd@ozemail.com.au*).

Canada 5 Avenue Marlborough, Ottawa, ON, K1N 8E6 (☎613/235-1837, fax 563-1394, *swissemott@compuserve.com*); 1572 Avenue Dr Penfield, Montréal, PQ, H3G 1C4 (☎514/932-7181, fax 932-9028); 154 University Avenue #601, Toronto, ON, N5H 3Y9 (☎416/593-5371, fax 593-5083); World Trade Center 790-999 Canada Place, Vancouver, BC, V6C 3E1 (☎604/684-2231, fax 684-2806).

Ireland 6 Ailesbury Rd, Ballsbridge, Dublin 4 (☎01/218 6380, fax 283 0344, *100634.3625@compuserve.com*).

New Zealand 22 Panama St, Wellington (☎04/472 1593, fax 499 6302); 40 Drake St, Auckland (☎09/366 0403).

UK *www.swissembassy.org.uk* – 16–18 Montagu Place, London W1H 2BQ (☎020/7616 6000, fax 7724 7001; recorded info ☎0891/331313); Portland Tower 6th floor, Portland St, Manchester M1 3LD (☎0161/236 2933, fax 236 4689).

USA *www.swissemb.org* – 2900 Cathedral Ave NW, Washington DC 20008 (☎202/745-7900, fax 387-2564); 633 Third Ave 30th floor, New York, NY 10017 (☎212/599-5700, fax 599-4266); Olympia Center #2301, 737 N Michigan Ave, Chicago, IL 60611 (☎312/915-0061, fax 915-0388); 11766 Wilshire Blvd #1400, Los Angeles, CA 90025 (☎310/575-1145, fax 575-1982); also in Atlanta, Houston and San Francisco.

---

prompted recent, draconian revision of immigration procedures, and without the backing of a zero-rich bank account and/or some unique work skills, if you try for legal work – especially if you're not an EU national – you'll have a sticky time of it in the dense web woven by Swiss bureaucrats.

The official line is that, firstly, only those foreigners who have skills not shared by any Swiss people will be considered for a work permit; and, secondly, that applications for permits will only be considered from people outside the country at the time of application (ie you can't enter as a tourist and then take up work). This also applies to au pairs.

However, even in Switzerland, rigid rules tend to flex in the face of real life, and if you go out looking for seasonal work in a ski resort or on a building site (see p.76), you may find employers willing and able to get you issued with permits within a few weeks.

There are several kinds of permits. The **A Permit** (Saisonbewilligung, permis saisonnier) – valid for the duration of a particular seasonal work project, or for a maximum nine months – is the best you can hope for, and generally covers work through the summer or winter tourist seasons only. The renewable **B Permit** (Aufenthaltsbewilligung, permis de séjour) is valid for a year, but is issued either to skilled professionals with a job already set up, or to big-time investors, or if your bank balance happens to show a £1 million credit. Hold a B Permit for five years, and you automatically get a **C Permit** (Niederlassungsbewilligung, permis d'établissement), conferring the right of permanent residence. All these are issued in accordance with an annual quota system in each canton.

Without a permit, you can't stay more than six months per year in Switzerland. All foreigners living in Switzerland for more than three months must also register with the authorities of the commune (not the canton) in which they reside.

For complete information, contact the nearest Swiss embassy, or – for plainer answers – get *Living and Working in Switzerland* by David Hampshire, published by Survival Books in London (*www.survivalbooks.net*).

INSURANCE

Even for travel in a supposedly "safe" country such as Switzerland, it is advisable to have good travel insurance. Aside from absorbing the horrendous costs of medical emergencies and treatment (break an ankle on a mountain path and you might need a £15,000 helicopter rescue), insurance also covers the loss or theft of your property, flight tickets and money. Many companies will also tailor policies for you if you plan on going skiing, or if you want to take part in other "dangerous" sports or adventure activities.

Note that very few insurers will arrange on-the-spot payments in the event of a major expense or loss; you will usually be reimbursed only after going home. In all cases of loss or even minor theft of goods, you *must* contact the local police to have a report made out so that your insurer can process the claim.

If you plan to participate in water sports or adventure activities, or do some hiking or skiing, you'll probably have to pay an extra premium; check carefully that any insurance policy you are considering will cover you in case of an accident.

Debit, credit and charge cards (particularly American Express) often have certain levels of medical or other insurance included, especially if you use them to pay for your trip – although this isn't meant to take the place of normal travel insurance. Coverage can be quite comprehensive, anticipating anything from lost or stolen baggage and missed connections to charter companies going bankrupt.

BRITISH AND IRISH COVER

Most travel agents and tour operators will offer you **insurance** when you book your flight or holiday, and some will insist you take it. The government has acted to ban packages which compel you to take out travel agents' own policies, but agents may get round this by offering it "free" – you should be wary of this "special offer" since the quality of cover may not be so good. As ever, you should check the small print: if you feel the insurance is inadequate, or if you want to shop around, any travel agent, insurance broker or bank should be able to give you advice and a quote. If you have a good "all risks" home insurance policy it may well cover your possessions against loss or theft even when overseas, or you can extend cover through your household contents insurer. Many private medical schemes also cover you when abroad – make sure you know the procedure and the helpline number.

In **Britain**, travel insurance starts from around £26 a month for Europe. Good-value policies are issued by Usit Campus and STA Travel (see p.5 for addresses), and by the travel insurance companies listed in the box opposite. Some insurance companies refuse to cover travellers over 65, or stop at 69 or 74 years of age, and most charge hefty premiums. The best policies for **older travellers**, with no upper age limit, are offered by Age Concern (☎01883/346964). Worldwide sets no upper age limit on single trips in Europe.

In **Ireland**, travel insurance is best obtained through a travel specialist such as Usit NOW (see p.11). Their policies cost IR£23 for 6–10 days in Europe (£29 for one month). Discounts are offered to students of any age and anyone under 35.

NORTH AMERICAN COVER

Before buying an insurance policy, check that you're not already covered. **Canadian provincial health plans** typically provide some overseas medical coverage. Holders of official **student/teacher/youth cards** are entitled to accident coverage and hospital in-patient benefits – the annual membership is far less than the cost of comparable insurance. **Students** may also

TRAVEL INSURANCE COMPANIES

IN BRITAIN AND IRELAND

Columbus Direct Insurance, 17 Devonshire Sq, London EC2M 4SQ (☎020/7375 0011, *www.columbusdirect.co.uk*).

Endsleigh Insurance, Cranfield House, 97–107 Southampton Row, London WC1B 4AG (☎020/7436 4451).

Marcus Hearne & Co, 65 Shoreditch High St, London E1 6JL (☎020/7739 3444).

Snowcard, Owl End Lane, Lower Boddington, Daventry, Northants NN11 6BR (☎01327/262805, *www.snowcard.co.uk*). Specializes in mountaineering and activity holiday travel insurance.

Worldwide Travel Insurance Services, The Business Centre, 1–7 Commercial Rd, Tonbridge, Kent TN12 6YT (☎01892/833338).

IN NORTH AMERICA

Access America ☎1-800/284-8300
Carefree Travel Insurance ☎1-800/323-3149
Desjardins Travel Insurance ☎1-800/463-7830 (Canada only)

STA Travel Insurance – see p.5.
Travel Insurance Services ☎1-800/937-1387
Worldwide Assistance ☎1-800/821-2828

IN AUSTRALIA AND NEW ZEALAND

AFTA ☎02/9956 4800 in Sydney.
Cover More ☎02/9202 8000 in Sydney, *www.covermore.com.au*

Ready Plan ☎03/9771 4000 or 1300/555 018 in Melbourne; ☎09/300 5333 in Auckland.
Travel.com 76-80 Clarence St, Sydney ☎02/9249 5444, *www.travel.com.au*

---

find that their student health coverage extends during the vacations and for one term beyond the date of last enrolment. **Homeowners' or renters'** insurance often covers theft or loss of documents, money and valuables while overseas.

After exhausting the possibilities above, you might want to take out a specialized travel insurance policy; your travel agent can usually recommend one, or see the box above.

Travel insurance **policies** vary: some are comprehensive while others cover only certain risks (accidents, illnesses, delayed or lost luggage, cancelled flights, etc). Note that most North American policies will only cover items lost, stolen or damaged while in the custody of an identifiable, responsible third party – hotel porter, airline, luggage consignment, etc.

The best **premiums** are usually to be had through student/youth travel agencies; STA Travel Insurance's worldwide coverage comes in packages covering 7 days ($35), 15 days ($55), 1 month ($115), 45 days ($155), 2 months ($180), and 1 year ($730) – add an extra $30–40 for each additional month of longer stays. You'll pay slightly more for shorter stays if you go through one of the other travel insurance companies listed in the box above; with these, expect to pay around $65 for a week, $75 for 2 weeks, and $105 for a month, with an additional charge of around $65 for each additional month.

AUSTRALIAN & NEW ZEALAND COVER

Travel insurance is available from most travel agents (see p.19) or direct from insurance companies (see box), for periods ranging from a few days to a year or even longer. Most **policies** are similar in premium and coverage. A typical policy covering medical costs, lost baggage and personal liability will start at about: A$100/NZ$110 for two weeks, A$170/NZ$190 for one month. These are over-the-Internet prices; add about A$30/NZ$40 for over-the-counter insurance. Most policies cover recreational skiing and snowboarding, rafting and bungee jumping, but check the fine print first. If you intend to partake in "**high-risk activities**" such as paragliding, abseiling or rock climbing, expect to pay an added premium of around A$90–150/NZ$110–190, depending on the activity. Note that some insurers no long cover canyoning.

HEALTH

If you're arriving from Europe, North America or Australasia, you don't need any jabs for Switzerland, and a visit is unlikely to present significant health problems. Virtually all travellers' afflictions arise from a lack of awareness of the impact of the high Alpine environment on those used to lowland life.

The best readily accessible source of **information** about travel health matters is *www.cdc.gov* operated by the US government's Centers for Disease Control. In Britain, pick up the Department of Health's free booklet *Health Advice for Travellers*, available at post offices, by phone on ☎0800/555777, or at *www.open.gov.uk/doh/hat*. The booklet includes an application for Form E111, which entitles all EU citizens to free medical care across the EU and EEA, including Liechtenstein but not including Switzerland.

The Swiss have no public, state-run health service, and also no reciprocal arrangements for healthcare with other countries, so you must pay upfront for all medical services – none of which comes cheap – and claim the costs back from your insurers later; make very sure you hang onto full doctors' reports, prescription details and all receipts to back up your claim. A quick chat with a doctor is likely to cost in the order of £20–30/$30–50 inside normal business hours, perhaps double at other times; lengthier consultations and any kind of procedures or treatments will cost substantially more.

Virtually every **hospital** (*Spital*, *hôpital*, *ospedale*) has some kind of 24-hour service: ask tourist-office staff and/or your embassy for details of the nearest (or least expensive) one. Every district has a rota system whereby one local **pharmacy** (*Apotheke*, *pharmacie*, *farmacia*) stays open outside normal shopping hours: each pharmacy will have a sign in the window telling you where the nearest open one is. Local newspapers also have details.

WATER

Water is safe to drink all over Switzerland, whether from taps or from the ubiquitous public street-fountains. These fountains, even though they may look manky, almost always gush with

> The nationwide ambulance emergency number is ☎144.

pure spring water: the bottled water which is sold around Europe as Passugger, for instance, flows from every tap and street-fountain in Chur. There are a few exceptions to the fountain rule, always marked "kein Trinkwasser", "eau non potable" or "acqua non potabile" – also with a pictogram of a crossed-out drinking glass.

Take care with mountain streams, which look crystal-clear but which may be hosting a herd of happily splashing cows just upstream. Contaminated water can bring on a list of diseases as long as your arm – raging diarrhoea is the best of the bunch. If you're planning to head off the beaten track, you should consider taking a **water purifier** with you. Boiling water for ten minutes kills most micro-organisms, but it's not the most convenient method, and you should be aware that the higher you are in altitude, the lower the temperature at which water boils (ineffective boiling allows some of the bugs to survive). Sterilization with iodine tablets is effective, but the resulting liquid doesn't taste very pleasant and you'll probably want to filter the water as well. (Iodine is unsafe for pregnant women, babies and people with thyroid complaints.) Portable water purifiers, which sterilize and filter the water, give the most complete treatment. A low-cost and highly recommended range made by Pre-Mac (*www.pre-mac.com*) is available in the UK from British Airways Travel Clinics (for details of your nearest branch call ☎01276/685040, or visit *www.british-airways.com*) and specialist outdoor equipment retailers. In Ireland contact All Water Systems in Faggart, Co. Dublin (☎01/466 0133).

SUNBURN AND HYPOTHERMIA

Otherwise, the sun and the cold are your worst enemies. You can get **sunburnt** very quickly in the mountains, due to the combination of a thin atmosphere and reflection off snow, ice and/or water. High-factor sunscreen, a hat, and total sunblock for sensitive areas such as lips, nose and ears are essential. Reflection of the sun's glare can also damage your eyes after a time, so UV-protective sunglasses or ski visors are a must.

You can buy good pre-packed **travellers' first-aid kits** from ordinary pharmacies or travel clinics. Particularly useful if you're planning to go trekking are: antiseptic cream; insect repellent; plasters/band aids; water sterilization tablets or water purifier; lint and sealed bandages; knee supports; a course of Flagyl antibiotics; paracetamol or aspirin (useful for combating the effects of altitude); multi-vitamin and mineral tablets; hypodermic needles and sterilized skin wipes (more for the security of knowing you have them, than any fear that a Swiss hospital would fail to observe basic sanitary precautions).

There are no rules about judging weather in the mountains. Conditions can change from calm to stormy in minutes, and if you're heading into the snows you should be prepared for the worst at all times. **Layered all-weather gear** is essential equipment for Alpine hikers at any time of year, and you'd do well to consult a travel clinic and/or one of the specialist Alpine tour operators (see p.6) in advance for advice both on what to take for your particular trip and on how to keep yourself and others alive in emergency situations. **Hypothermia**, when the body loses heat faster than it can conserve it, is most often brought on by a combination of cold, wind and driving rain, with hunger and fatigue also playing their part. Symptoms include exhaustion, lethargy or dizziness, shivering, numbness in the extremities and slurring of speech. In these initial stages, you must get the sufferer out of the elements and under cover, replace any clothing of theirs that is wet (with your own dry garments if necessary), give them hot liquids and high-calorie sugary foods such as chocolate, and encourage and reassure them by talking. Despite the Alpine heroics of brandy-laden St Bernard dogs in the past, alcohol is a bad idea at such a critical time. Prompt action will head off acute hypothermia which, if allowed to develop, can be fatal.

Virtually all high-altitude walks in Switzerland stay below 3000m, the rough cut-off point above which **altitude sickness** can rear its head. Headaches, dizziness and breathlessness are the main symptoms, all of which should pass after a day or two at altitude. If they don't, the only treatment is to head down.

TICKS AND SNAKES

If you're hiking in woodland below 1200m, there's a slight risk of receiving attention from **ticks**. These can occasionally carry nasty diseases such as encephalitis, so they're worth avoiding – proper hiking boots and socks significantly cut down your chances of a bite. The medically favoured way of extracting them, contrary to tales of dabbing them with alcohol or heating them with a match-flame, is to pull them out carefully with small tweezers. Switzerland also has a couple of species of non-fatal **snakes**, but to find them you'll have to creep stealthily: they're frightened of humans.

INFORMATION AND MAPS

Information on Switzerland is not hard to come by: the Swiss tourist industry has had 150 years or so to refine its approach to visitors, and the efficient, super-helpful tourist offices in Switzerland and abroad are only too happy to regale you with more details on any particular city, region or the whole country than you could possibly ever get to grips with.

All cities, virtually all towns, and a sizeable number of villages in Switzerland have a **tourist office** (*Verkehrsverein, Verkehrsbüro* or *Tourismus; Office du Tourisme; Ente Turistico*),

pretty much always located next to, opposite, or within five minutes' walk of, the train station. Most staff speak English and are scrupulously helpful. They can provide you with free city or town maps, lists of hotels, campsites and apartment rentals, and information on local sights and events, as well as detailed hiking maps and guides to the surrounding area and transport information. Beware, though, of the long Swiss lunch break: outside a handful of the larger cities and resorts, offices **close** between noon and 2pm during the week and all day Sunday,

---

MAP OUTLETS

BRITAIN

Blackwell's Map and Travel Shop, 53 Broad St, Oxford (☎01865/792792, *bookshop@blackwell.co.uk*).

Daunt Books, 83 Marylebone High St, W1 (☎020/7224 2295, fax 7224 6893); 193 Haverstock Hill, NW3 (☎020/7794 4006).

Heffers Map and Travel, 3rd floor, 19 Sidney St, Cambridge (☎01223/568467, *www.heffers.co.uk*). Mail order available from here; more maps and travel literature at their excellent shop at 20 Trinity Street.

James Thin Melven's Bookshop, 29 Union St, Inverness (☎01463/233500, *www.jthin.co.uk*). Established 1849; map department with all foreign maps; mail order specialist.

John Smith and Sons, 57 St Vincent St, Glasgow (☎0141/221 7472, *www.johnsmith.co.uk*). Specialist map department in long-established booksellers; full range of foreign maps; mail order service.

The Map Shop, 30a Belvoir St, Leicester (☎0116/247 1400). Mail order available.

National Map Centre, 22 Caxton St, SW1 (☎020/7222 2466, *www.mapsworld.com*).

Newcastle Map Centre, 55 Grey St, Newcastle upon Tyne (☎0191/261 5622, *nmc@enterprise.net*).

Stanfords, 12 Long Acre, WC2 (☎020/7836 1321, *sales@stanfords.co.uk*). The UK's largest map sellers, with orders taken by post, phone or email. Other London branches are within Campus Travel at 52 Grosvenor Gardens, SW1 (☎020/7730 1314), and within British Airways at 156 Regent St, W1 (☎020/7434 4744). Also in Bristol at 29 Corn Street (☎0117/929 9966).

The Travel Bookshop, 13 Blenheim Crescent, W11 (☎020/7229 5260, *www.thetravelbookshop.co.uk*).

Waterstone's, 91 Deansgate, Manchester (☎0161/837 3000, *www.waterstones-manchester-deansgate.co.uk*). Particularly good map department in this branch of the UK-wide chain of bookshops; mail order service. In Belfast at Queens Bldg, 8 Royal Ave (☎028/9024 7355).

IRELAND

Easons Bookshop, 40 O'Connell St, Dublin (☎01/873 3811).

Fred Hanna's Bookshop, 27 Nassau St, Dublin (☎01/677 1255).

Hodges Figgis Bookshop, 56 Dawson St, Dublin (☎01/677 4754).

Waterstone's, 7 Dawson St, Dublin (☎01/679 1415); 69 Patrick St, Cork (☎021/276522).

USA

Adventurous Traveler Bookstore, PO Box 1468, Williston, VT 05495 (☎1-800/282-3963, *www.AdventurousTraveler.com*).

Book Passage, 51 Tamal Vista Blvd, Corte Madera, CA 94925 (☎415/927-0960, *www.bookpassage.com*).

and may be closed for most of Saturday as well. Outside opening hours, ask at the train station, where staff generally keep a small stock of maps and information leaflets behind the counter. If you're really stuck, Anglophone (☎157 50 14) has general information in English, although geared mostly towards expat residents.

THE INTERNET

There's a vast quantity of useful information on the **Internet**. Switzerland Tourism, the national tourist organization, has a vast interactive homepage at *www.myswitzerland.com* that has virtual tours around every resort, weather and snow forecasts, live pictures, stacks of background information, booking details, special offers and tons more. The Swiss Hotel Association at *www.swisshotels.ch* has a full listing of their thousands of quality-controlled hotels nationwide, and – more significantly – plenty of last-minute offers for cut-price multi-night deals. Most individual cities and resorts run efficient and informative sites geared towards tourists, which we've flagged in the guide text where relevant. Unsurprisingly, there's stacks of other online information devoted to Switzerland, official and unofficial, from individuals and organizations big and small; what follows is a selection.

The Complete Traveler Bookstore, 199 Madison Ave, New York, NY 10016 (☎212/685-9007); 3207 Fillmore St, San Francisco, CA 92123 (☎415/923-1511).
Map Link, 30 S La Petera Lane, Unit #5, Santa Barbara, CA 93117 (☎805/692-6777, *www.maplink.com*).
The Map Store Inc., 1636 1st St NW/Farragut, Washington, DC 20006 (☎202/628 2608).
Phileas Fogg's Books & Maps, #87 Stanford Shopping Center, Palo Alto, CA 94304 (☎1-800/533-FOGG, *www.foggs.com*).

Rand McNally, 444 N Michigan Ave, Chicago, IL 60611 (☎312/321-1751); 150 E 52nd St, New York, NY 10022 (☎212/758-7488); 595 Market St, San Francisco, CA 94105 (☎415/777-3131), etc. Rand McNally now has more than twenty stores across the US; call ☎1-800/333-0136 (ext 2111) for the address of your nearest store, or mail order from *www.randmcnallystore.com*.
Sierra Club Bookstore, 6014 College Ave, Oakland, CA 94618 (☎510/658-7470, *www.sierraclub.org*).
Travel Books & Language Center, 4437 Wisconsin Ave NW, Washington, DC 20016 (☎1-800/220-2665).

CANADA

International Travel Maps and Books, 552 Seymour St, Vancouver V6Z 1G3 (☎604/687-3320, *www.itmb.com*).

Open Air Books and Maps, 25 Toronto St, Toronto, ON M5R 2C1 (☎416/363-0719).
Ulysses Travel Bookshop, 4176 St-Denis, Montréal PQ H2W 2M5 (☎514/843-9447).

AUSTRALIA

Map Land, 372 Little Bourke St, Melbourne (☎03/9670 4383, *mapland@lexicon.net*).
The Map Shop, 16a Peel St, Adelaide (☎08/8231 2033, *www.mapshop.net.au*).
Map World, 371 Pitt St, Sydney (☎02/9261 3601).
Perth Map Centre, 884 Hay St, Perth

(☎08/9322 5733, *www.perthmap.co.au*).
Travel Bookshop, Shop 3, 175 Liverpool St, Sydney (☎02/9261 8200).
Worldwide Maps and Guides, 187 George St, Brisbane (☎07/3221 4330, *www.powerup.com.au/~wwmaps*).

NEW ZEALAND

Mapworld, 173 Gloucester Street, Christchurch (☎03/374 5399, *www.mapworld.co.nz*).

Speciality Maps, 58 Albert St, Auckland (☎09/307 2217).

SWISS TOURIST OFFICES ABROAD

Australia & NZ 33 Pitt St, Level 8, Sydney, NSW 2000 (☎02/9231 3744, fax 9251 6531, *swissair@tiasnet.com.au*).

UK & Ireland Swiss Court, London W1V 8EE (☎020/7734 1921, fax 7437 4577, *stc@stlondon.com*).

USA & Canada 608 Fifth Ave, New York, NY 10020 (☎212/757-5944, fax 262-6116, *stnewyork@ switzerlandtourism.com*). Local numbers in Chicago (☎312/332-9900), Los Angeles (☎310/640-8900), Montréal (☎514/333-9526), San Francisco (☎415/362-2260) and Toronto (☎416/695-2090) all get routed to the New York call-centre.

www.nzz.ch/online/04_english/english.htm
Daily stories and weekly digest of Swiss news and comment from the *Neue Zürcher Zeitung*, the country's best-respected newspaper.

www.swissinfo.org/eng
Continuously updated ticker of news and features from Swiss Radio International.

www.sma.ch
Detailed weather forecasts for the whole country.

www.slf.ch/slf/avalanche/avalanche.html
Continuously updated year-round avalanche warnings and snow forecasts.

www.topin.ch
Webcams with live pictures from dozens of locations.

www.rail.ch
Comprehensive and massively useful English-language homepage of Swiss Federal Railways, with information and booking possibilities for trains, buses, boats and cable-cars nationwide, including fare information and exact connection times.

www.rail-info.ch
Lovingly detailed site for buffs devoted to the many Swiss narrow-gauge railways.

www.post.ch
Full details of postbus excursions and fares.

www.tcs.ch
Homepage of the Swiss Touring Club, with information for drivers.

www.search.ch/index.html.en
sear.ch/hosien.tbw?lang=e
Two Swiss search engines in English.

www.LOL.li
Liechtenstein Online – but in German only.

www.111.com/e_etv.asp
www.branchenbuch.ch
Two searchable versions of the Swiss phone directory – but not in English.

www.expo2001.ch
Official site of the 2002 Swiss Expo (see p.158).

www.liarumantscha.ch
Fascinating homepage of the Lia Rumantscha, a Chur-based cultural organization devoted to documenting, supporting and promoting Romansh, Switzerland's fourth language.

www.arte24.ch/english
Cultural activities and organizations around the country.

www.museums.ch
Catalogue of Switzerland's hundreds of museums.

www.swisscastles.ch
As it says, a look at Switzerland's many medieval castles.

www.swisswine.ch/anglais
Umbrella site puffing the merits of Swiss wine and detailing notable regions and vignerons; *www.walliswine.ch* is a subsidiary site devoted solely to the wines of Valais/Wallis, while *www.vins-vaudois.com* is for the wines of Vaud.

www.swiss-alpine-cheese.com
No surprises, given the name.

www.topevents.ch
Tourist-office rundown of the glitziest and chicest of Switzerland's annual festivals and events.

www.fastbox.ch
Premier site to book tickets for just about any forthcoming show, gig, club or happening around Switzerland.

www.hugo.ch
Underground club culture.

www.admin.ch
Dourly titled official site of the Federal Government, with some reasonable information on the organization of government and some other bits and pieces, but (as it points out) you'll find better and more engaging information in English about the country and its politics at the homepages of the Swiss embassies in London (*www.swissembassy.org.uk*) and Washington (*www.swissemb.org*). All 26 cantons maintain local-info homepages, most of them accessed with the two-letter abbreviation (eg the

homepage of Vaud is *www.vd.ch*); exceptions to this rule are noted in the text.

MAPS

Our **maps** of town centres and regions should be fine for most purposes; otherwise tourist offices always have town maps to give out, either free or for a franc or two. Kümmerly & Frey and Hallwag are both major cartographic publishers with worldwide distribution and a host of products covering Swiss cities and countryside on many different scales; the Freytag & Berndt 1:460,000 and Bartholomew 1:300,000 also cover the country. The Federal Office of Topography (Bundesamt für Landestopographie, Office fédérale de topographie, Ufficio federale di topografia) publishes a full range starting at 1:1 million, including detailed 1:100,000 regional maps and 1:50,000 and 1:25,000 hikers' maps, as well as specialist maps on different scales for cyclists and inline-skaters, skiers, maps pinpointing historic sites, cultural attractions and more. Kümmerly & Frey's walkers's maps (*Wanderkarte*) are based on the LS sheets and usually have main walking routes and mountain huts highlighted. These are all widely available in Swiss bookshops, in some specialist map shops abroad, from *www.swisstopo.ch* or from the publishers at Seftigenstrasse 264, Postfach, CH-3084 Wabern.

MONEY AND COSTS

Switzerland is the wealthiest country in the world, nursing an average per-capita income bordering on £28,000 a year – and that's *after* paying taxes of some thirty percent. The country is famous – or infamous – as one of the safest and most discreet places to stash a fortune, hard-earned or otherwise, and it's been estimated that there's about £1,000,000,000,000 squirrelled away in the anonymous numbered accounts of the various Swiss banks. The Swiss franc is renowned for its stability and is one of the benchmarks against which international standards are set, and Zürich is one of the world's principal financial centres. The main impact of all this on visiting foreigners is to make the place rather pricey to travel in, unless you're careful to watch those pennies.

CURRENCY

Prices in both Switzerland and Liechtenstein are in **Swiss francs** (*Schweizer Franken, francs suisses* or *franchi svizzeri*). The most common abbreviation, which we've adopted, is "Fr." – but you may also see "fr", "sFr", "Sfr", "SF", "FS", or the official bank abbreviation "CHF". Each franc is divided into 100; these are called *Rappen* (Rp.) in German-speaking areas, *centimes* (c) in francophone areas, and *centisimi* (also c) in Italian-speaking areas. There are coins of 5c, 10c, 20c, 50c, Fr.1, Fr.2 and Fr.5, and notes of Fr.10, Fr.20, Fr.50, Fr.100, Fr.200 and Fr.1000.

Approximate **exchange rates** at the time of writing were Fr.2.60 to the British pound, Fr.1.65 to the US dollar, and Fr.1.60 to the euro.

CARRYING AND CHANGING MONEY

Switzerland has a healthy mix of small rural communities where cash is the sole method of payment, and international cities dedicated to the art of high finance, where anything will do nicely as long as it's money. You'll never be caught short – either for purchases or for cash withdrawals – if you **carry your money** in the

WIRING MONEY FROM ABROAD

Wiring money is a fast but expensive way to send and receive money abroad, and should be considered only in emergency situations. The sum wired should be available for collection in Swiss francs from the company's agent within a few minutes of being sent via Western Union or Moneygram; both charge on a sliding scale, but sending larger amounts of cash is better value. Thomas Cook has a much cheaper flat rate but it takes 1–2 days for the money to arrive. You should also check with your bank before you depart to see if they have reciprocal arrangements with any banks in Switzerland.

Agents vary from city to city; in Britain, for instance, Western Union is at Going Places trav-

el agents and some newsagents and chemists, while Moneygram is at Thomas Cook offices, Eurochange and all post offices. In Switzerland, Western Union is far more accessible, represented at all Swiss train-station change desks. Rates with both are broadly similar: £12–14 to send £100 or £33–37 for £500, for example, while from the US, wiring $500 will cost about $30. Thomas Cook's Telegraphic Transfer service from the UK costs £15 plus one percent of the amount to be sent (with a minimum charge of £25). Cook's can also credit foreign bank accounts for the same fee (2–3 days). UBS bank are the Thomas Cook agents throughout Switzerland.

Moneygram International toll-free ☎00800/8971 8971; US ☎1-800/926-9400; Canada ☎1-800/933-3276; Australia ☎1800/230 100; New Zealand ☎0800/262 263. Switzerland ☎0800/895973.

Thomas Cook UK ☎01733/318922; Rep. of Ireland ☎01/677 1721; US & Canada ☎416/359-

3764; Australia ☎02/9248 6100; NZ ☎09/379 3920. Switzerland – call collect to ☎00441733/318949.

Western Union UK ☎0800/833833; Rep. of Ireland ☎1800/395395; US & Canada ☎1-800/325-6000; Australia ☎1800/649565; NZ ☎09/270 0050. Switzerland ☎0512/223358.

form of only debit and/or credit cards, although the now rather pedantic travellers' cheque still holds good. Switzerland is generally much safer than elsewhere in Europe, but carrying large wads of cash about is still not advisable.

Most banks in the West keep Swiss francs on hand for over-the-counter **exchange**, and it's a good idea to bring a small supply with you to cover first-night expenses in case of difficulties.

PLASTIC MONEY

Plastic is the most convenient way to carry your money. Every corner of Switzerland is plastered with banks, most of which have English-language **ATMs** (cash-machines) which accept foreign debit and credit cards. The only significant exceptions are the various cantonal banks (for example, Luzerner Kantonalbank or Banque Cantonale Vaudoise or Banca dello Stato del Cantone Ticino), and small local banks such as Raiffeisenbank. Otherwise, ATMs attached to branches of the ubiquitous Big Two – UBS and Crédit Suisse, which are present in every town and together control sixty percent of the domestic market – accept a panoply of brands including Visa, MasterCard, EC, Maestro, Cirrus, Plus and plenty more. You can also pay for most goods and

services around the country using a card, although there may be a lower limit of Fr.20 or Fr.30. Bank charges on plastic transactions can often work out less than commissions on purchases of travellers' cheques.

As usual, **charge cards** such as Amex or Diners Club are not as widely accepted as debit/credit cards, and tend to be restricted to top-end purchases.

CASH AND CHEQUES

If you're carrying foreign **cash or travellers' cheques**, the best places to change them are invariably the desks to be found next to the ticket counters at virtually all train stations around the country – rates are identical with the banks, no commission is charged (except at some airport locations), and they're usually open seven days a week for long hours. Otherwise, bank opening times vary, but are generally Monday to Friday 8.30am–4.30pm, sometimes with a break for lunch. Some city and tourist-resort banks also open on Saturday, often 9am–4pm. If you choose to take travellers' cheques, you'd do best sticking to major brands such as American Express, Visa or Thomas Cook. The exchange rate is about one percent better than for cash.

If you have a bank account in the EU, you can ask your bank for a **Eurocheque** book and card before you depart – these work the same as ordinary cheques, drawn on your current account, but you write them out in Swiss francs (up to a Fr.300 maximum). However, with an annual fee, plus a handling charge per cheque, plus a bank commission on the franc-to-pound exchange, they're no bargain.

SOME BASIC COSTS

It'll come as no surprise to learn that Switzerland is **expensive**. In one recent survey, Zürich (which even the Swiss shake their heads at) was assessed to be twenty percent more expensive than London across the board and almost double the UK average, while another survey found it to be pricier even than Tokyo. However, this gives a somewhat slanted view, since you're unlikely to be spending like a local, and most places in the rest of Switzerland aren't very much more expensive than you'd expect for Western Europe. However, Swiss **food** prices are notoriously high, for no readily apparent reason, and this translates into higher-than-normal restaurant prices. **Accommodation** costs can go through the roof, but careful choices will keep per-night rates affordable.

At the very lowest end of the scale, if you're prepared to cut all corners by walking or cycling your own bike around the country, staying in hostels or campsites, and never eating out, you could scrape by on Fr.40–50 (£18/$30) a day; add in one cheap meal and a beer, and Fr.60–65 (£26/$42) is more realistic, while budgeting something for visiting a few sights or museums (average Fr.5–7 (£2.50/$4) per place) would mean you might actu-

ally enjoy your trip too. If you don't have a bike, you'd have to factor in transport costs on top of this (see p.34 for more).

Staying at simple inns or guesthouses in one or two rural areas, avoiding cities altogether, and spending your days hiking or just relaxing in reasonable comfort is unlikely to set you back more than Fr.100/day (£42/$67), but going up mountains – which may be the whole point of your visiting Switzerland in the first place – can wipe out a day's budget in one cable-car ride. Journeys up the Jungfraujoch, for instance, are roughly Fr.120 (£50/$81), even taking discounts into consideration. Hiking part or all of the way up or down can bring big savings. If you're planning a skiing holiday, you should definitely book an all-in package from home, which cost a fraction of the equivalent over-the-counter rates.

A comfortable double room in a two- or maybe three-star city hotel is on average Fr.130–160 (£62/$100), depending on the season and the city. Using this kind of accommodation, eating lunch and dinner in moderate restaurants, taking in a scattering of sights, the odd boat trip or train ride, and a luxury or two, amounts to a rough daily average of Fr.160 (£67/$108) per person.

Students (with ID) can benefit from a raft of discounts, principally on admission prices to larger museums and attractions, but also on some resorts' ski passes – crucially, however, not on public transport within Switzerland. Similarly, **children** get in half-price or less to many museums, and can travel free with their parents on a Family Card, issued free alongside any kind of Swiss travel pass (see p.35).

GETTING AROUND

The efficiency of the massively comprehensive Swiss public transport system remains one of the wonders of the modern world. It's hard to overstate just how good it is: you can get anywhere you want quickly, easily and relatively cheaply; everybody relies on it as a matter of course; and it's clean, safe and pleasant.

Services always depart on the dot, and train timetables are well integrated with those of the postbus system, which operates on routes not covered by rail, including the more remote villages and valleys. Switzerland's many lakes – and some of its rivers – feature plenty of opportunities to enjoy some relaxing views from the deck of a boat, and there's an array of discount travel passes to take advantage of. Cyclists are well served by the Swiss instinct for encouraging green thinking in all things.

There are plenty of **domestic flights** shuttling daily between Zürich, Geneva, Basel, Bern and Lugano, most of them operated solely by Crossair. Prices are absurdly high: the half-hour Zürich–Geneva route, for instance, represents pretty much the most expensive air travel, in cost per kilometre, in the world. With the smooth, efficient and rapid nationwide train service, planes simply aren't worth the expense.

TRAINS

Travelling through Switzerland by **train** is invariably comfortable, hassle-free and extremely scenic, with many mountain routes an attraction in their own right. Swiss Federal Railways or

SBB-CFF-FFS (*Schweizerische Bundesbahnen, Chemins de fer fédéraux suisses, Ferrovie federali svizzere*) has long been heavily subsidized by the state: maintaining a modern, integrated, ecologically sound transport system has been a top priority of successive Swiss governments and today fares are affordable, equipment and rolling stock are state-of-the-art, and staff motivation is high. SBB was privatized in 1999, but corner-cutting in the near future seems unlikely.

SBB covers virtually the whole country, but there are a few routes, especially Alpine lines, which are operated by the individual rail companies which constructed them often a century or more ago. Two of the largest of these are BLS, which runs the pivotal Bern–Lötschberg–Simplon route between the Swiss capital and Italy; and RhB, the Rhätische Bahn, which operates services within Canton Graubünden. There are dozens more of these private lines, often tiny concerns used by local people to get to and from their nearest town, sometimes massive enterprises ferrying thousands of tourists from valley to summit and back again.

Ticketing systems are well integrated, though, and you don't really need to know which company is which, since each route has only one company providing services: you never have to shop around between competing offers. Swiss travel passes always get **discounts** on these smaller lines, normally of between 25 and 50 percent; the only difficulties come with pan-European rail passes, since different companies give different levels of discount, or no discount at all, to Inter-Rail and Eurail passholders. These are mentioned in the text where relevant.

FARES AND SEASON TICKETS

One-way **fares**, if you buy ordinary tickets for each journey, work out at a very reasonable Fr.31 per 100km in second class. However, it's unlikely you'll need to buy ordinary tickets, since there's a plethora of ways to save money using passes and season tickets, some geared towards foreigners (see the box "Swiss Travel Passes" on p.35), others taken advantage of by the locals to get around their own country.

The Swiss are the most frequent train users in Europe – not surprising, given both the quality of the network and the astonishingly good-value **half-fare travel card** (*Halbtax-Abo, Abonnement*

SWISS TRAVEL PASSES

	£	US$	Fr.
Swiss Pass – 4 days	90	188	216
Swiss Pass – 8 days	112	238	270
Swiss Pass – 15 days	130	288	314
Swiss Pass – 30 days	180	400	430
Swiss Flexi-Pass	90	188	216
Swiss Card	60	128	144
Swiss Transfer Ticket	42	71	—
Swiss Half-Fare Card	38	—	90

There's a confusing array of different travel passes for Switzerland, although all are good value – it just takes some untangling to see which is best suited for your trip. All the nation-wide passes bring a discount on bike rental from train stations (see p.40).

Top of the pile is the **Swiss Pass**, available from Swiss tourist offices at home (see p.30) or from airport and city stations in Geneva and Zürich (in francs only, and on production of a foreign passport). This gives free unlimited travel *on consecutive days* on all SBB and most private trains, as well as on all boats and postbuses and most city tram-and-bus networks. Where travel isn't free (eg on cable-cars and mountain railways), discounts of 25 percent apply.

The **Swiss Flexi-Pass** gives free travel on any three days in 15, with the same privileges as the Swiss Pass. The **Swiss Card** gives a month's travel by train, postbus and boat at fifty percent discount (plus partially reduced fares on most mountain railways), and one free return journey between the airport or border and your home- or hotel-base in Switzerland. The **Swiss Transfer Ticket** is geared towards winter-sports visitors, and is only available outside Switzerland: valid for a month, it's limited to giving one free journey from the airport or border

to your resort, and back again. The **Swiss Half-Fare Card**, also valid for a month, is supposedly designed for motorists who might use public transport only occasionally within cities or on scenic routes. It lets you buy any number of individual tickets – in first or second class – for trains, buses, boats and most city networks at a fifty percent discount (most mountain railways also give half price). There are also offers for families travelling together: see p.76.

If you're planning to concentrate on one area of the country, but still want the flexibility to visit local sights, it might be more economical to get a **regional pass** for your particular region. These vary across the country in both price and validity, but normally give 5 days' free travel in 15 within a limited region, often including discounts for the other 10 days. Regional passes are most popular in the Berner Oberland, the Gstaad–Château d'Oex region, Central Switzerland around Lake Luzern, and the Lake Geneva shoreline, but are also offered by many other regional tourist offices. It would be pointless to list every one, and you'd do best to contact the Swiss tourist office in your home country for details of a pass covering your chosen region or regions before you depart.

demi-tarif, Abbonamento metà prezzo), which costs Fr.150 for a year and lets you buy unlimited first- or second-class tickets at a fifty percent discount across virtually the entire network. This is such a popular way to go for the locals that most published offers, and all automatic ticket machines, are marked for full price (1/1) and half price (1/2); if you intend being in Switzerland for more than a month, the card is certain to repay itself, not least because it also gives discounts on bike rental from train stations (see p.40). You need a passport-sized photo in order to buy it. Once you have one, you can then buy day-card add-ons for Fr.52 (first class Fr.86) to give free unlimited travel

nationwide for that day; multi-day add-ons, valid for any six days, cost Fr.260/430. If you're under 25, you can pay Fr.99 for a **Track 7** card which gives a year's free travel nationwide after 7pm; unlimited half-price travel before 7pm plus free travel after 7pm costs Fr.249.

With no barriers on the platforms, inspectors on the trains are the sole method of **fare-enforcement**, and they'll move through the whole train more or less between every station: get caught without a valid ticket or pass for your journey and they'll blithely slap a Fr.50 **fine** on you, which rises to Fr.60 if you can't pay on the spot. Quite a few of the regional and local trains

FLY BAGGAGE

This is the outward-bound flipside of the "Rail Baggage" incoming service (see box p.3), and is just as useful. If you're flying out of Geneva, Zürich or Basel, you can check your bags in ahead of time for Fr.20 per item at any one of 116 Swiss train stations all over the country, from where they're transported independently to your departure airport and loaded onto your flight; you don't have to lay a finger on them until the baggage-reclaim carousel in your home airport.

Excluded from the service are bulky items such as bicycles, but you can register up to 32kg of baggage in total. You'll need to show to the station staff your flight ticket (with an "OK" reservation), and – most importantly – a train ticket or pass to prove that you'll be travelling to the airport by train; otherwise, you pay a surcharge of Fr.30 extra per item. Virtually all airline companies let you use the service, but all American Airlines flights, Delta flights DL067 and 123, Swissair flights SR8012 and 8022, and all US charter flights are **excluded**, as are all flights out of Bern, Lugano and Sion. If you're flying out

of Basel, check with the station staff or call ☎0900/300 300 beforehand.

At the same time, and for no extra cost, some airlines also allow you to make a seat reservation and pick up a **boarding card**, cutting out all hassle and queuing at the airport and letting you proceed directly to your departure gate. This service is available – on production of your passport – **only** if you're flying with Austrian, Balair, Crossair, Delta (except flights DL067 and 123), Sabena, Singapore Airlines or Swissair (except flights SR8012 and 8022); and it's **only** available at 23 stations in Switzerland, including Arosa, Basel SBB, Bern, Biel/Bienne, Davos Dorf and Platz, Fribourg, Geneva, Interlaken Ost and West, Lausanne, Locarno, Lugano, Luzern, Montreux, Neuchâtel, St Gallen, St Moritz and Zürich HB.

You can do a station check-in at the **earliest** 24 hours before your flight departure. A booklet "Fly-Rail Baggage", available from most stations, has a list showing the **latest** possible check-in times for all 116 stations, which vary depending on which airport you're flying out of.

are marked with a prominent **swirly eye pictogram**: this means that there's no conductor and that you're trusted to buy a ticket, either from the station staff or from a platform ticket machine. Roving bands of inspectors may board at any point to check tickets. If you intend using any kind of multi-day pass or undated ticket, you must stamp it before you board in the little boxes marked with the same swirly eye pictogram on platforms or near escalators.

TIMETABLES AND INFORMATION

The national three-volume **timetable** (*Kursbuch* or *Fahrplan*, *indicateur* or *horaire*, *orario*), covering all rail, bus, boat and cable-car services, costs Fr.16; most main stations keep a public copy to consult. There's also an abridged single-volume version called *Reka* for Fr.12. Both are available to buy at just about all stations, where you'll also find piles of leaflets and free pocket timetables covering the local region. Check times carefully if you're travelling in the last week of May, when the timetable is revamped each year. The national train **enquiry number** is ☎0900/300 300, or you can ask ticket-office staff how to get from any station to any other and they'll print out an itinerary for you showing exact connection times. At

larger city stations (Zürich, Geneva and others) you'll find a stand-up Internet terminal where you can surf the SBB Web site, book tickets, and get fare quotes and timetable information for free.

On all train and bus station notice boards, timetables are colour coded: the **yellow timetable always shows departures** (*Abfahrt*, *départ*, *partenza*), while the white one always indicates arrivals (*Ankunft*, *arrivée*, *arrivo*). Trains are identified by an alphabet soup of initials denoting where, when and how fast they go. **CIS** are tilting express "Pendolino" trains run by Cisalpino between Switzerland and Italy; **ICE** are Inter-City Express services between Switzerland and Germany; **TGV** are high-speed trains between Switzerland and France. Sleeper services are either **CNL** (CityNightLine) or **EN** (EuroNight). Day trains between major European cities – that may stop at only two or three places in Switzerland – are denoted **EC** (EuroCity). If you're holding an ordinary ticket or train pass, all of these are free of any surcharges within Swiss borders; you must pay **supplements** only if you cross an international frontier, or if the train is marked in the timetable with an R in a square box. In these cases, seat reservations cost Fr.4 per person.

Within Switzerland, **IC** InterCity expresses cross the country stopping at larger cities only. **IR** InterRegio trains ply between regions, stopping at a few more places in between; **RX** RegioExpress services are one step slower. Something described as a *Schnellzug*, *train direct* or *treno diretto* goes from village to village; while a *Regionalzug*, *train régional* or *treno regionale* stops at every tiny halt on the way.

Platforms are marked out in **sectors**, from A to D. For mainline services, the PA announcement (and a list next to the timetable boards) tells you which sectors the first- and second-class carriages will arrive at, saving you running up and down the train. Beware of truncated one- or two-carriage local trains departing from Platform 3 Sector A while you're standing at Platform 3 Sector D tapping your watch. Sometimes two short trains will depart in opposite directions from different sectors of the same platform.

STATIONS AND SERVICES

It takes something of a leap of faith to realize, but in Switzerland a **train station** (*Bahnhof*, *gare*, *stazione*) isn't the dregs-of-the-earth place it might be in another country. In fact, many Swiss stations harbour genuinely good restaurants next to their formica-table buffets – going out for a nice meal at the station is a new experience for most visitors – and many also shelter the only shops and supermarkets in their town open after 6pm. Where supermarkets and kiosks stop, large 24-hour vending machines take over, quite often dispensing loaves of bread, salami and cartons of milk in addition to Coke and chocolate.

You can find many convenient facilities at just about all train stations. **Luggage lockers** are universal, found at all but the tiniest country halts, and normally come in two or three sizes: average prices are Fr.3 for a small one (into which you can just about stuff a full rucksack), Fr.5 for a large and – only at main stations – Fr.8 for an extra-large. Once they're locked, you can open them only once. Your gear is safe in them for several days without a problem, but – especially at the large city stations – after a week or two staff may open the locker, impound your property at the left-luggage office, and require you to pay through the nose to get it back. Ask at the information counters beforehand what the time limit is. Access to lockers may also be prohibited between midnight and 5am.

Virtually every station also has a staffed **left-luggage office** (Fr.5 per item per day), invariably

open daily for long hours, and often combined with a **lost-property office**, a **bike-rental counter** (see p.40), and the **fly-baggage check-in** service (see box, opposite).

Just about the only people you'll see lugging suitcases or rucksacks through train compartments are foreigners: most Swiss register their heavy bags at the baggage counter before they board (for around Fr.10 per item per journey) and let SBB's team of baggage-handlers take the strain, picking up their stuff from their destination station later that day. This is a great service to take advantage of if you want to see a lot of things in a day but don't fancy carting your gear from locker to locker.

Train-station **lost property** offices are linked by computer, so they can all run a nationwide check for you; it costs Fr.5 to retrieve a small item, Fr.20 for a large or heavy piece. Other services you'll find in all stations are **bureau de change** and money-wiring facilities (see p.32), invariably spotless toilets (free or Fr.1–1.50) and, in city stations, equally spotless shower cubicles (Fr.10).

BUSES

Backing up the already comprehensive train network is a yet more comprehensive system of **buses**, which get to every single village and hamlet in the country, covering ground – such as in the high mountains or deep countryside – left untouched by the trains. Many travellers don't even consider using the buses, imagining them to be too slow or too much hassle to figure out, but this is a shame since buses are not there to compete with the trains but to complement them, and they can get you to all kinds of out-of-the-way places – and some essential ones – quickly and easily. In addition, all Swiss travel passes are valid for travel on buses as well as trains (a plus-point over the limited-validity European train passes).

With Swiss pragmatism, bus stations are nearly always located in the forecourt of train stations. Even more handily, the bus and train **timetables** are co-ordinated together, ensuring watertight connections from one to the other. Perhaps uniquely in Europe, Swiss buses stick to their schedules with utter reliability – another leap of faith for many visitors is to learn to trust what a bus timetable says.

Most bus-lines in Switzerland are operated, in an endearing remnant of pioneer times, by the post office. These yellow **postbuses** – with *Die*

EXCURSIONS BY PUBLIC TRANSPORT

Although few Swiss journeys are short on scenery, there are a handful of exceptionally beautiful routes around the country which are marketed as unified single journeys. On most – after having **reserved** a seat the day before for a few francs – you just sit back, flash your travel pass and drink in the views. Some require you to change from train to boat, or bus to train, but you never have to walk more than the length of a station platform, and timetables always allow enough leeway that you're never in a hurry. Plus, of course, you can always send your heavy bags ahead. Some of the more spectacular routings run special **panoramic** train carriages, either with partial or total glass roofs, or (in first class) with some raised seating inside a transparent bubble in the roof giving 360-degree views, but for these – and for extras such as onboard lunches – you always pay a **supplement**. For information, timings and routings, you should check well in advance, either at train stations or at larger tourist offices anywhere in the country. Note, too, that it's easy to follow the same routes on ordinary trains and pay no extras, or to get on or off at intermediate points: the Centovalli line, for instance (see p.500), is worth exploring regardless of its marketed Lötschberg add-on. And, it should be added, these are only the trips in the spotlight: equally spectacular shorter rides such as Chur to Arosa, or the tiny Lauterbrunnen-to-Mürren line, don't get the glossy-brochure treatment.

We've described the journeys roughly north-to-south, but all make the return trip as well. Most need advance reservation, and some cross international borders (passport needed). Note that some tour operators will let you add these excursions to a package holiday (at the time of booking) for bargain rates.

Bernina Express or **Heidiland Bernina Express** Various routes from Chur, St Moritz or Davos over the high Bernina Pass and through the gorgeous Val Poschiavo to Tirano (Italy), where you switch onto a postbus and skirt Lake Como to Lugano. Total, including a couple of hours in Tirano, 8hr. June–Oct daily. Reserve at any train station. Panorama carriages.

Glacier Express A spectacular and understandably popular route, and – given its ups and downs – the slowest express in the world (average speed 30kph). From St Moritz (1775m) or Davos down to Chur (585m), then up the Rhine valley to the high Alps, crossing the Oberalp Pass (2033m) to Andermatt, through the tunnel beneath the Furka Pass and down the Rhône valley to Brig (671m), before climbing to Zermatt (1604m). Total 8hr, 291 bridges and 91 tunnels. Daily. Reserve at any train station (also reserve for the dining car). Panorama carriages.

Golden Pass Flagship panorama route from Luzern to Geneva, running via Interlaken, the expansive countryside around Gstaad, Montreux, and the Léman lakeshore, with a variety of different panoramic carriages on various legs of the journey. Total 6hr. Daily. Reservations needed for some stretches; ask at any station.

Lötschberg–Centovalli South from Bern beneath both great Alpine ranges, courtesy of the Lötschberg tunnel into Canton Valais, and the Simplon tunnel from Brig to Domodossola (Italy), where you switch to the tiny, rackety trains which ply the wild and gorgeous Centovalli east

to Locarno. Total 4hr. Daily. No reservations needed.

Palm Express Postbus from St Moritz over the Maloja Pass into the dreamy Val Bregaglia, crossing the border to Chiavenna (Italy) and the shores of Lake Como, then crossing back into Switzerland before ending at Lugano. No train-track exists on this route. Total 4hr 15min. June–Oct daily; Nov–June Fri–Sun only. Reserve at St Moritz bus station (☎081/837 67 64), or Lugano bus station (☎091/807 85 20).

Rhône Express Memorably diverse scenery, with a boat ride from Geneva to Montreux, and a train running the length of the Rhône valley up to Brig, changing again for the rack railway to Zermatt. If you take the whole package (with a hefty supplement), you get the boat ride on an old-time paddle steamer with three-course lunch included and first-class transport all the way; otherwise, it's easy to link ordinary boat and train services together to form the same ride without supplements. Total 9hr. June–Sept daily. Reserve at ☎022/741 52 30.

William Tell Express Another incredibly beautiful journey, from Luzern by boat across the whole of Lake Luzern to Flüelen, then a train south, corkscrewing its way up into the Gotthard Tunnel beneath the Alps and then down again through the Ticino to Lugano. If you go for the whole package, you get a three-course lunch in a lake paddle steamer, plus first-class panorama seating on the train. Avoid the supplement by making your own way. Total 6hr. May–Oct daily. Reserve at ☎041/367 67 67.

Post, *La Poste* or *La Posta* on the side – once brought the mail to remote rural communities, but nowadays concentrate solely on transporting people and their goods. Various regions have their own local bus companies, either instead of or as well as postbuses, but all are equally reliable. The largest postbus stations in Switzerland are at Sion and Chur, both set amidst mountainous but populated landscapes too difficult for trains to access. Note that some longer, more difficult or direct bus-routes – such as over the Alpine passes – require either advance **seat reservation** and/or a small supplement of Fr.5–10 to be paid: check in the timetables or with bus-station staff ahead of time.

For a flat fee of Fr.12 you can send **unaccompanied baggage** ahead by postbus to a post office for picking up later – a particularly handy service for hikers using buses to reach remote countryside trails and wanting to walk unencumbered.

BOATS

All of Switzerland's bigger lakes, and a sizeable proportion of its smaller ones, are crossed by regular **ferry services** of one sort or another. Most run only during the summer season – which can vary, but at its broadest covers the period from April to October – and are primarily pleasure-oriented, duplicating routes which can be covered more cheaply and quickly by rail. However, if you have the time, a leisurely cruise through the Alpine foothills to Interlaken, for example, or between the three lakes of Neuchâtel, Morat and Biel/Bienne, or from shore to shore along the length of Lake Geneva, beat the equivalent train journeys hands down. Apart from on Lago Maggiore (which is mostly in Italy), travel by boat is covered by the Swiss travel passes detailed on p.35, and there's also a **Swiss Boat Pass** (Fr.35) available, which is valid for a year and knocks fifty percent off fares on fourteen of Switzerland's bigger lakes.

Two lakes are worth a special mention, since it would be a crying shame to miss experiencing them from the water. Luzern's **Vierwaldstättersee** plumb in the heart of Switzerland and the setting for the William Tell legend, offers some of the most dramatic vistas imaginable – forested slopes emerging from dark, mist-laden waters and crowned by the snowy peaks of the high Alps behind. And the azure **Lago di Lugano**, on the Italian border flanked by its larger and better-known

siblings Maggiore and Como, is in a magically beautiful setting of palm trees and lush, sugar-loaf hills. Both have plenty of boats in summer, while in winter Luzern is one of the few lakes to maintain a skeleton boat service (Geneva is another), mostly for the residents of lakeshore villages hemmed in by the mountains who would otherwise face long and difficult road or rail journeys.

Most of Switzerland's **rivers** are too young and fast flowing to be navigable, but three that are offer wonderful riverboat cruises that are well worth going out of your way for. West of Geneva, boats ply the short, wooded section of the **Rhône** before the French border. Northeast of Biel/Bienne, there's a lovely stretch of the **Aare** – which runs past an island stork colony – navigable until Solothurn. But best of all, and one of Europe's great river journeys, is the uniquely peaceful part of the **Rhine** between Konstanz (Kreuzlingen) and the falls at Schaffhausen, the sole stretch of that river that is free from any kind of bankside industry. The falls merit a journey in themselves.

MOUNTAIN TRANSPORT

It's inevitable that at some point during your stay you'll use transport to get to the top of a mountain. There are few areas or ranges that have no means of getting to the top of at least one local peak – the train timetable lists them all – and even relatively unsung Swiss summits can be breathtakingly beautiful. Few peaks that can be accessed by public transport don't also feature at least one mountain-top restaurant or terrace café for refreshment and relaxation; if you need solitude and tranquillity you generally have to hike away from the summit station.

There are six principal means of transport in the mountains: **funicular** (*Standseilbahn*, *funiculaire*, *funicolare*); **cable-car** (*Luftseilbahn*, *téléphérique*, *funivia*) and the (more or less interchangeable) **gondola** (*Gondelbahn*, *télécabine*, *cabinovia*); **chairlift** (*Sesselbahn*, *télésiège*, *seggiovia*); and T-bar skilift or **draglift** (*Schlepplift*, *téléski*, *sciovia*). The lack of security on draglifts, as well as accidents caused by skiers letting go too soon or forgetting to let go at all, means that they're being replaced almost everywhere. You'll also come across **mountain railways**, also called rack, rack-and-pinion, or cog railways.

All of these various systems around the country are operated by small local transport companies, not the SBB. Fares – except on the flagship tourist routes such as to the Jungfraujoch or the Titlis – aren't excessive, and are usually discounted a little (25 percent is common) if you hold a travel pass. Where timetables don't show exact timings (often because departures may be continuous), they at least note the first **ascent** (*Bergfahrt, montée, salita*) of the day; the frequency of service in between; and the final **descent** (*Talfahrt, descente, discesa*) from the mountain in the evening. On the high peaks you may have to leave the top station in mid-afternoon, say 3–4pm, if you want to reach the valley without hiking or skiing part or all of the way down.

CITY TRANSPORT

The most common form of transport within cities is **buses**, whether the ordinary petrol-driven kind, or the more ecologically sound electricity powered **trolleybuses**. Many cities also have **trams**, and a few hillside ones have a **funicular** or two, but the only true **metro** system is in and around Lausanne. Zürich has a dense network of suburban commuter trains called the **S-Bahn**, which run out to neighbouring towns and along the lakeshore.

Within each city or local area, all transport is integrated under one **ticketing system**, with no limitations on changing from buses to trams or even some boats within the time validity of your ticket. The Swiss Pass and Swiss Flexi-Pass cover free travel within 35 cities across the country (listed on the card); tourist-oriented regional passes give free travel within their allotted area; and city tourist offices sell various **day passes** of their own giving free or discounted travel, which can be excellent value. Otherwise, you must buy a ticket *before boarding* from the machines located at every stop. These are fairly self-explanatory, in whichever language they're labelled: you choose your destination; adult or child; single or return journey; full fare (1/1) or, if you hold a relevant travel pass, half fare (1/2); and pay what it says. Machines in the larger cities have options to sell day passes.

Ticket inspections are common within cities, and if your ticket is found wanting, you'll be **fined** Fr.50 on the spot, or Fr.60 if you need to pay later.

There are plenty of metered **taxis** sharking around every town and city in the country, but given the density of public transport they're pretty much unnecessary, and besides you need to be on a Swiss salary to afford them: flagfalls of Fr.6, plus per-kilometre rates of up to Fr.3, are common.

BIKES

Given the nature of the landscape, **cycling** is not the easiest way of exploring the country, but the scenery more than compensates for the extra effort required. It's a very popular Swiss pursuit, and the locals don't restrict themselves to flat lakeside or valley-floor routes: summer weekends see any number of lycra-clad, sinewy characters pumping their way slowly up the long 12 or 14 percent gradients of the high Alpine passes. Cycle routes – in the cities too – are plentiful.

Getting around on two wheels is made significantly more feasible by the ease of bike access. You can **rent** a seven-gear country bike or a quality 21-gear mountain bike from Rent-A-Bike (*www.rent-a-bike.ch*), located at 200 SBB-CFF-FFS train stations nationwide, and a majority of the smaller train companies: it's a rare train station that *doesn't* offer bike rental. Each year, Rent-a-Bike sell off their entire national stock of 4000 bikes and buy in completely new supplies, ensuring that you never get a clapped-out squeaker. If there's no dedicated bike office in the station, you normally rent from left-luggage counters, which are generally open long hours (often from 6 or 7am until 10 or 11pm). At the time of writing, **prices** were, for a country bike, Fr.19 for a half-day (return by 1pm, or rent no earlier than noon), Fr.25 for a full day and Fr.100 for seven days; for a mountain bike, equivalents are Fr.24/31/124. Note that if you hold any kind of Swiss travel pass, all these prices **drop** by about a quarter. Kids' bikes and seats for children which you can attach to an adult's bike are also available.

It's well worth knowing that if you rent for a full day or more, you don't have to return the bike to the same station you rented from. If you tell them where and when you want to drop your bike, you pay a surcharge of Fr.6. Station bike rental is massively popular, especially throughout the summer months, and if you're planning to rent from the larger city stations in particular you should always **reserve** as far as possible in advance (normally, a day or two is OK). Even so, on summer weekends, stations like Bern and Zürich that hold hundreds of bikes for rent can be completely cleaned out: in these cases, you may have to take a train (or call ahead) to a smaller town and try there, or try looking for other companies in the phone-book under *Mietvelos*, *vélos à louer* or *à location*, or *bicicletta a noleggio*.

As a way to teach local unemployed people new skills and get them back to work, Zürich, Bern and a handful of other cities run **free bike-rental** schemes year-round, invariably from depots beside or opposite the train station. All you do is pay a Fr.20 deposit and leave some ID, and you're free to cycle off for as long as you like.

Another option is to take advantage of a cut-price offer whereby you can rent a brand-new 24-gear mountain bike from certain **HI hostels** for just Fr.15 a day (or Fr.10 for a four-hour half-day) – you don't have to be staying overnight to be able to rent. Currently seventeen hostels nationwide provide this service: major ones are Brienz, Château d'Oex, Figino (near Lugano), Grindelwald, Interlaken, Kreuzlingen, Locarno, Pontresina, Saanen-Gstaad, Sainte-Croix, St Moritz, Schaffhausen, Solothurn and Zermatt. Most keep only limited supplies of bikes in stock, so you need to reserve ahead. To rent, you must show ID, leave a Fr.100 deposit (cash or credit-card slip) and return the bike to the same hostel you rented from.

In 1998, under the banner of *Veloland Schweiz*, *La Suisse à vélo*, the tourist authorities opened up nine national **long-distance** cycle routes that crisscross the country on 3300km of dedicated signposted paths mostly well away from traffic. These vary between, say, the Rhône Route (Andermatt to Geneva, 324km), the Alpine Panorama Route (Rorschach to Aigle, 483km) and the North-South Route (Basel to Chiasso, 363km). Tourist offices can give you a map of all nine routes, and information in English on each one, as well as maps showing other cycle routes within their region or city. If you're already in the country, Eurotrek will rent you a bike, book hotels in any class at towns along each of the nine national routes, and will also transport your gear from hotel to hotel for a supplement of Fr.18/day: contact them at Freischützgasse 3, CH-8021 Zürich (☎01/295 55 55, fax 295 56 40, *eurotrek@rbm.ch*). Otherwise, check with specialist tour operators at home about adding these services to a package holiday before you book.

If you're arriving in Switzerland with **your own bike**, you have to buy a **vignette** from post offices for around Fr.5, which covers road tax and third-party insurance for a year. You can transport a bike between any two train stations in Switzerland for Fr.6 in regional trains, or Fr.12 in InterCity trains;

some EC trains and the Zürich S-Bahn are prohibited during rush hours. You have to load and unload it yourself using the special carriage marked with a big bicycle pictogram, and you must have a ticket or pass for the same destination. Yellow train timetables mark those trains on which bikes cannot be transported with a crossed-out pictogram next to the destination name, and SBB also have a booklet of the best bike-train connections.

DRIVING

Getting around on public transport is easy enough, but **driving** obviously gives you extra freedom to explore nooks and crannies that others zip past without stopping. However, the consciously green Swiss transport policy means that cars are slowly being given the squeeze, with tough city parking regulations and strict law enforcement. Nonetheless, Switzerland's road network is comprehensive and well-planned, and although the mountainous terrain can make for some circuitous routes there is, of course, the compensation of impressively scenic – if sometimes hair-raising – mountain drives.

DRIVING YOUR OWN VEHICLE

Despite Switzerland being outside the EU, there's very little extra **bureaucracy** needed for foreigners to drive in the country. Minimum driving age is 18, British licences are recognized for one year's driving in Switzerland and, as across the rest of Europe, **third-party insurance** is compulsory. In the UK, most normal third-party insurance policies don't cover foreign travel, so you should contact your insurer in advance to extend your policy: look into the RAC's European Cover (☎0800/550055, *www.rac.co.uk*) or the AA's Five-Star Europe cover (☎0800/444500, *www.theaa.co.uk*). It's compulsory within Switzerland to carry both a red warning triangle and the registration documents of the vehicle.

If you intend driving on Swiss motorways, you have to stick a **vignette** inside your windscreen. These cost Fr.40 for any vehicle up to 3.5 tonnes, are bought most easily from the customs officials when you first cross the border (also at post offices and petrol stations), and remain valid until January 31 of the following year. Trailers or caravans must have their own, additional vignette. Getting caught without one lays you open to a Fr.100 fine. If you prefer, it's quite easy to avoid Swiss motorways altogether and stick to ordinary main roads, which are free and – outside urban centres at least – reasonably fast.

PRINCIPAL SWISS ALPINE PASSES

There are 72 **Alpine passes** in Switzerland that are open to motor traffic, and hundreds more that are for hikers or bikers only. We've given the names (in alternative languages where necessary) of the most important ones; their altitude above sea level; period during which the pass road, and any tunnel road, is open to traffic,barring significant weather disruption; the gradient (in percent) of the pass road; and the main towns on either side of the pass. Approach roads to all passes have large signboards displaying whether the pass, and the high-altitude towns or resorts on the way, are **open** (offen, ouvert, aperto) or **closed** (geschlossen, fermé, chiuso).

Albula/Alvra (2312m; June–Oct; 12) Tiefencastel GR–La Punt GR

Bernina (2328m; all year; 12) St Moritz GR–Poschiavo GR

Brünig (1008m; all year; 13) Sarnen OW–Brienz BE

Croix (1778m; all year; 12) Villars VD–Les Diablerets VD

Flüela (2383m; all year; 12) Davos GR–Zernez GR

Forclaz (1526m; all year; 9) Martigny VS–Chamonix, France

Fuorn/Ofen (2149m; all year; 12) Zernez GR–Val Müstair GR

Furka (2431m; June–Oct; 11) Gletsch VS–Andermatt UR

Grand-St-Bernard (2469m; pass June–Oct, tunnel all year; 11) Martigny VS–Aosta, Italy

Grimsel (2165m; June–Oct; 11) Gletsch VS–Meiringen BE

Jaun (1509m; all year; 14) Bulle FR–Simmental BE

Julier/Güglia (2284m; all year; 13) Tiefencastel GR–St Moritz GR

Klausen (1948m; June–Oct; 10) Altdorf UR–Glarus GL

Lukmanier/Lucomagno (1914m; May–Nov; 10) Disentis/Mustér GR–Biasca TI

Maloja (1815m; all year; 11) St Moritz GR–Val Bregaglia GR

Mosses (1445m; all year; 10) Aigle VD–Château d'Oex VD

Nufenen/Novena (2478m; June–Sept; 11) Ulrichen VS–Airolo TI

Oberalp (2044m; June–Oct; 10) Andermatt UR–Disentis/Mustér GR

Pillon (1546m; all year; 11) Les Diablerets VD–Gstaad BE

San Bernadino (2065m; pass June–Oct, tunnel all year; 12) Thusis GR–Bellinzona TI

St Gotthard/San Gottardo (2109m; pass May–Oct, tunnel all year; 11) Göschenen UR–Airolo TI

Simplon/Sempione (2005m; all year; 10) Brig VS–Domodossola, Italy

Splügen (2113m; May–Oct; 13) Thusis GR–Chiavenna, Italy

Susten (2224m; June–Oct; 9) Meiringen BE–Andermatt UR

RENTING A CAR

Car rental in Switzerland is nastily expensive, double the cost of neighbouring European countries and up to three times as expensive as in the US. For unlimited kilometrage on the smallest car, you're looking at a minimum of Fr.130 a day. Prices are much lower if you include a Saturday night; Budget, for example, has a three-day weekend deal at Fr.190. However, it's significantly cheaper to rent in advance from offices of the international agencies in your home country (see box opposite). If you're already in Switzerland, you can save money by renting via the Internet or by shelling out a franc or two to call the US offices of the big agencies and rent from them direct with a credit card.

The big agencies comprehensively cover Switzerland, with offices in all major towns, most minor ones, and at all airports. **One-way rentals** are simple to arrange, although they usually attract a handling fee. Hertz has a deal with SBB whereby you can reserve, pick up or drop off cars at any of 700 train stations across the country, also for a surcharge. There are dozens of smaller local rental companies in most towns, usually operating out of ordinary petrol stations or garages, with mostly trustworthy cars at prices that undercut the big agencies' walk-in rates: find them in the phonebook under *Autovermietungen* or *Mietwagen*, *location des voitures*, or *noleggio di automobili*.

Another way to cut costs and still get mobile is to **rent a Smart car**: these tiny, fuel-efficient, extremely reliable (Mercedes-built) two-person runarounds are comfortable, speedy and cheap to rent – as little as Fr.49/day gets you on the road. At the time of writing, only a handful of big agency outlets have them and even fewer local

CAR RENTAL AGENCIES

Avis *www.avis.com – www.avis.co.uk*
Budget *www.budgetrentacar.com – www.budgetrentacar.co.uk*

Europcar *www.europcar.com*
Hertz *www.hertz.com – www.hertz.co.uk*
Holiday Autos *www.holidayautos.co.uk*

UK AND IRELAND

Avis UK ☎0870/590 0500; Rep. of Ireland ☎01/874 5844

Budget UK ☎0800/181181; Rep. of Ireland ☎0800/973159

Europcar UK ☎0845/722 2525; Rep. of Ireland ☎01/874 5844

Hertz UK ☎0870/848 4848; Rep. of Ireland ☎01/676 7476

Holiday Autos UK ☎0870/530 0400; Rep. of Ireland ☎01/872 9366

NORTH AMERICA, AUSTRALIA AND NEW ZEALAND

Avis USA and Canada ☎1-800/331-1084; Australia ☎1800/225 533; New Zealand ☎09/526 2847

Budget USA and Canada ☎1-800/527-0700; Australia ☎1300/362 848; New Zealand ☎09/375 2222

Hertz USA ☎1-800/654-3001; Canada ☎1-800/263-0600; Australia ☎13 3039; New Zealand ☎09/309 0989

SWITZERLAND

Avis ☎0848/811 818
Budget ☎01/838 58 88

Europcar ☎01/813 65 66
Hertz ☎0848/822 020

---

outfits. Try Smart Rent, Riva Paradiso 26, in Lugano (☎091/993 13 13, *www.smartrent.ch*), or Bantiger, Bernstrasse 37, Ostermundigen near Bern (☎031/932 28 88).

To rent a car, you need a valid, clean British, European or international **driving licence** that you've held for more than a year. Minimum driver's age is 20 or 21, occasionally 25, depending on the rental company. All rental cars – identifiable by a V after the licence-plate number – have the annual motorway vignette prepaid and, in winter, are fitted with snow tyres, and supplied with snow-chains (and even a ski rack) for free.

Although it's no problem to drive across borders in Swiss rental cars, leaving them in EU countries (on one-way rentals, for instance) invokes tides of byzantine export regulations; larger Swiss rental agencies keep a supply of vehicles with German, French or Italian plates for this purpose, which you should ask for specifically if this is what you're planning.

ON THE ROAD

You can find fuel in just about every village in the country. **Unleaded fuel** (*Bleifrei, sans plomb,*

senza piombo) is currently around Fr.1.20 per litre of standard 95 octane, good for all rental cars. Petrol stations in more remote places, such as mountain resorts, charge much more than those on routes easily accessible by tankers. Unstaffed automatic dispensers – where you feed cash or a credit card into a machine – are cheapest of all. Super-plus unleaded, 98 octane, is also widely available for a few cents more, as is diesel. Leaded fuel, also 98 octane, is less common.

Swiss **motorways are signed in green**, while main roads are signed in blue. **Speed limits** are 120kph (75mph) on motorways, 80kph (50mph) on main roads, 50kph (30mph) in urban areas, and 30kph (18mph) on speed-bumped residential streets. The Swiss are a law-abiding lot, and tend to stay inside the limit, partly because there are dozens of cameras, radars and laser traps around the country to catch offenders. If you're caught doing 5kph above, expect a **spot-fine** of Fr.40; if you were 20kph above, expect Fr.200; any more and you'll be taken to court. Most motorways have two or more lanes in each direction; some, though, have only one and ban overtaking. In **tunnels**, of which there are hundreds all over the country, it's

The nationwide breakdown number is ☎140.

forbidden to overtake and obligatory to use dipped headlights.

You'll see **roadsigns** to "places" such as Gotthard or Grand-St-Bernard as far away as Zürich or Montreux: you're supposed to recognize automatically that these aren't towns but Alpine pass routes. Although Switzerland has four languages, you'll rarely have to struggle with multilingual roadsigns. Signs to specific towns are always in the language of that town: on motorways and main roads, Geneva is always "Genève", never "Genf" or "Ginevra". As for crossing the language border, there'll just come a point speeding between Fribourg and Bern when you'll notice that the exits, previously marked "Sortie", suddenly become "Ausfahrt". Difficulties come on the backroads, with signs marked for locals who instinctively know, when looking for the route to the Lukmanier Pass, that they should follow signs for the Passo del Lucomagno. We've given place names in three languages at the end of guide chapters.

Other road rules offer no surprises. Switzerland drives on the **right**, **seatbelts** are compulsory for all, and penalties for **drink driving** are tough (one glass of beer has you on the limit). At junctions, yellow diamonds painted on the road show who has **priority**; if in doubt, always give way to trams, buses and traffic coming from your right. On gradients, vehicles heading **uphill** have priority over those coming down, and some narrow mountain lanes have controlled times for ascent and descent. If you hear an outrageously loud triple-tone klaxon sounding on country lanes or twisting mountain roads, it means that a **postbus** is approaching: it always has priority, up or down, so get out of the way. In cities, it's forbidden to overtake **trams** when they're at their stops. In the winter, signs indicate where **snow chains** are necessary (it's a good idea to practise fitting and removing them beforehand).

PARKING

Parking in Switzerland is hellish, and can be very limited and prohibitively expensive. In cities across the country, full car parks will quite often harbour queues of cars, their engines off, drivers waiting – sometimes for over an hour – for the next person to finish their shopping and so liberate a space.

The easiest options are covered or open **parking garages**, signposted in all cities. Prices can be outrageous – Fr.30 a day or more in central Geneva and Zürich, an average Fr.15/day around the country, and rarely less than Fr.1/hr anywhere. Out of town car parks, often located near motorway exits and tagged P+R (Park and Ride), are sometimes free or discounted; they always have a bus or a tram heading into the town centre, though, for which you must pay.

Otherwise, **onstreet parking** is colour coded, as in much of the rest of Europe. Spaces delineated with white lines – the **White Zone** – are free, unless there's a sign reserving them for a particular company (as in *nur für Kunden*, "only for customers") or a particular licence-plate number. You can park in the **Blue Zone** if you have a special parking disc (available for free from tourist offices, car rental agencies, police stations and banks). Spin the wheel round to show your time of arrival and leave it on your dashboard: this gives you 90 minutes' free parking if you arrive between 8am and 11.30am or between 1.30pm and 6pm; if you arrive between 11.30am and 1.30pm, you're safe until 2.30pm. If you arrive after 6pm, you're OK until 9am next day. As long as you keep returning to your car to spin the wheel, you're entitled to stay in the same space all day. **Red Zone** spaces are free for up to 15 hours. There are also Pay-and-Display car parks and on-street meters; again, feeding them throughout the day isn't forbidden.

Illegal parking of any kind is much less tolerated in Switzerland than in its neighbours, and fines of Fr.50–100 for minor transgressions are common.

ACCOMMODATION

As a general rule, it's no problem to turn up in any Swiss town at any time of the year and find a room. With the popularity of the bigger cities and resorts, though, booking ahead – especially in the summer and winter high seasons – is strongly advised. Aside from anything else, it saves you the effort of searching for a place once you arrive, and also guarantees that you won't be forced into spending over budget in order to rest your head. Despite the fact that Geneva and Zürich suffer from exceptionally high hotel prices, Fr.90–120 will buy you some kind of double room in any town in the country.

Compared with other European countries, Swiss accommodation is expensive but nearly always excellent, conscientiously run and hospitable. Tourist offices always have lists of hotels, hostels, campsites and apartments in their area, and outside office hours they normally have a display board on the street with details of the local hotels, often with a courtesy phone. In many cases you'll find these boards at train stations as well. Swiss hoteliers, campsite managers and hostel staff invariably speak English, but in the unlikely event that you can't make yourself understood, most tourist offices will make a booking for you, either for free or for a small fee. It's rare to be able to negotiate **multi-night bargain rates** over the counter, but many tourist offices run deals throughout the year that can save plenty if you book three or seven nights in a row. Wherever you check in, you should always ask for a free **guest card** (*Gästekarte, carte des visiteurs, tessera di soggiorno*), as this perk for overnight visitors can give substantial discounts for local attractions and transport.

The main thing to take into account when planning your trip are the high and low seasons, since hotel prices, pressure on rooms and even periods of opening – especially in the resorts – can fluctuate dramatically. Problems come in trying to pin down the seasons, since they vary according to the town. Across the country, July and August are peak-season **summer** months, when everything is open but everything costs the most. Accommodation in the major cities and lakeside resorts follows a summer season which extends from at the earliest mid-May until at the latest mid-October. However, the higher in altitude you go, the more the season is truncated: snow may not melt on the Alpine pass roads until mid-June, and may fall again in late September, limiting the opening times of the highest huts and mountain refuges to ten or twelve crowded weeks. Countrywide, the **low seasons** are April, May, and mid-October to early December: cities and lowland towns still welcome tourists at these times (and, indeed, offer cut-price deals on accommodation), but many mountain resorts –

ACCOMMODATION PRICE CODES

All the hostels and hotels in this book have been graded according to the following price codes, which indicate the price for the cheapest double room available during the high season. For dormitories in hostels or mountain inns, the price per bed in Swiss francs has been quoted. Single rooms generally cost between sixty and eighty percent of the double-room rate. Bear in mind that an establishment graded as a ②, for example, may also have a range of more comfortable rooms at ③-level prices.

① under Fr.100	④ Fr.200–250	⑦ Fr.350–400
② Fr.100–150	⑤ Fr.250–300	⑧ Fr.400–500
③ Fr.150–200	⑥ Fr.300–350	⑨ over Fr.500

Most hotels in the country (and some hostels) are regulated by the **Swiss Hotel Association**, which awards stars (between zero and five) according to strict guidelines on everything from room size to the presence or absence of bubble bath. *The Swiss Hotel Guide* (Fr.15) is its annual directory of all quality-controlled hotels across Switzerland, with photos, prices, contact details, facilities and assessment of each one. Contact the SHA at Monbijoustrasse 130, Postfach, CH-3001 Bern (☎031/370 41 11, fax 370 44 44), or surf to *www.swisshotels.ch* for the full directory and – more significantly – for plenty of last-minute offers for cut-price multi-night deals.

including all hotels and shops – close down altogether and use the time for renovations. The **ski season** traditionally opens in the week before Christmas and lasts until April; cities and lakeside resorts are bitterly cold for general street wanderings at these times, and (unless they offer direct access to the mountains) flog accommodation at rock-bottom prices.

Note that in the accommodation listings throughout the guide, rooms in each hotel listed are en suite unless mentioned otherwise.

HOTELS

Swiss **hotels** are among the best in the world, with renowned high standards of service. Value-for-money is the motive force behind the hotel industry, rather than cost-cutting, so you'll find that even ① and ② hotels offer rooms that are perfectly comfortable, clean and respectable, if a little expensive compared to dingier bottom-end establishments in other countries.

At the least expensive level, what makes a difference in price is whether a room contains a shower or an **en-suite bathroom**, since these can add Fr.20 or more to the bill as compared with rooms where the shared shower and toilet are down the corridor (*sur l'étage*, often translated bizarrely as "shower and WC on the floor").

Breakfast is included in the room price at virtually all hotels apart from the very cheapest and the most expensive; what you get varies with the hotel's classification. One thing to watch out for is that in most resorts, hotel prices quoted for the summer season are **bed and breakfast**, while those quoted for the winter season tend to be **half board** (ie bed plus two meals – normally breakfast and an evening meal après-ski); we've marked this differentiation clearly in the guide text where relevant, but to be certain you should check what you're paying for at the time of reservation. Note that a hotel advertising itself as "**garni**" has no restaurant, and serves only breakfast to its overnight guests. Confusingly enough, some towns quote hotel prices *per person*, while others quote prices *per room*; our code system standardizes them across the board, but you'd do well to bear this in mind if you ask for prices direct from a hotel or tourist office.

There are a number of Swiss **hotel groups** which, if you can fight your way through the marketing blurb, can be useful for seeking out hotels

E&G Swiss Budget Hotels, CP 160, CH-1884 Villars (☎024/495 11 11, fax 495 75 14, *www.rooms.ch*). Zero- to three-star places (150 of them), most with character, ranging from small city hotels to dorms and mountain lodges. E&G stands for *einfach und gemütlich*, roughly "simple and cosy".

Idyll Hotels, Postfach 133, Seestrasse 231, CH-8820 Wädenswil (☎01/680 22 28, fax 780 65 64, *idyllhotels@chardon.ch*). Fifteen peaceful country hotels, two- to four-star, run on ecologically sound lines.

Relais du Silence, CH-1923 Les Marécottes (☎027/761 16 67, fax 761 16 00, *www.relais-du-silence.com*). Local arm of a swanky international chain, concentrating on providing tranquillity, leisure and relaxation in its 37 Swiss hotels, all in countryside locations far from traffic and towns.

Romantik Hotels and Restaurants, c/o Romantik Hotel Beau-Site, CH-3906 Saas-Fee (☎027/958 15 60, fax 958 15 65, *www.romantikhotels.com*). Eighteen top-end hotels in historic surroundings, with the focus squarely on pamperment.

around Switzerland with particular features that appeal to you, whether they be complete peace and quiet (Relais du Silence), historic buildings and locations (Romantik Hotels) or just plain, good-value inexpensive accommodation (E&G Hotels). See the box opposite for contact details of some more interesting hotel groups.

MOUNTAIN INNS

Whole books have been written about the joys of staying in a Swiss **mountain inn** (*Berghaus, Berggasthaus, Berggasthof, Berghotel, auberge de montagne*). The term is a tricky one to pin down, since it can refer to varying styles of simple rustic accommodation in a mountain setting. All, though, possess unique character, by dint both of their often spectacular isolated location (generally only accessible by foot, and then often involving hard long hikes) and of their history – many are old Alpine farmhouses converted more than a century ago to meet the needs of the first holidaying British gentlemen and ladies on their summer tours of the Swiss Alps. Most have undergone some renovation over the intervening decades, but often not much: in general, you can expect an all-wood building in the local architectural style, with rustic decor throughout (window boxes, antiques on the sideboard, ticking grandfather clocks) and a uniquely relaxed, informal atmosphere of cosy communality. Hikers are the main clientele, and Swiss families may return season after season to hike their favourite paths, stay at their favourite *Berghaus*, and catch up on news from the family who owns and runs the place.

Nature, not amenities, are the focus: most *Berghäuser* maintain charmingly old-style bedrooms, with chunky old beds smothered under plump duvets, but very few offer private bathrooms, some may not have showers, and a handful have no hot water, or must generate their own electricity. Most have plenty of **dorm** places. Food is universally good: a *Berghaus* that skimps on sustenance is a contradiction in terms. Prices are not that much higher than elsewhere – an average Fr.130 for a double, or Fr.45 for a dorm place, both including dinner and breakfast – but you invariably have to pay in cash. It's customary to settle your bill the night before you depart.

HOSTELS

If you're travelling on a budget, a **youth hostel** (*Jugendherberge, auberge de jeunesse, alber-go/ostello della gioventù*) is likely to be your accommodation of choice, whether you're youthful or not. They can often be extremely good value, and offer clean and comfortable dorms as well as a choice of rooms (doubles and sometimes singles) that can often undercut normal hotel prices. Both city and country locations can get very full between June and September, when you should book in advance.

There are two main hostel associations in Switzerland. The 70-odd "official" hostels of **Swiss Youth Hostels** are affiliated to the Hostelling International network (aka International Youth Hostel Federation) and are refered to throughout this guide as "HI hostels". These places are of a universally high standard, although they tend to be better choices in countryside and mountain locations than in cities, where they are quite often located awkwardly far from town centres and can suffer from an atmosphere of institutionality. The old habits of early breakfasts and daytime and late night curfews have survived – most are closed for cleaning between roughly 10am and 6pm, and also lock their doors sometime between 10pm and midnight. Almost all close down in the low seasons: spring and autumn in the mountains, winter in the cities. Bed prices depend on the season and the individual hostel, covering the range Fr.19–32 for a dorm bed including breakfast and bedding (average roughly Fr.25). Extras such as kitchens for guest use, TV rooms, and so on are common, and evening meals, where available, are around a bargain Fr.10. If you're not already an HI member in your home country (see box on p.48), you pay Fr.5 extra per night, or you can get annual membership while in Switzerland at any affiliated hostel for Fr.25 (membership is also automatic after any six nights of paying the supplement). Under-25s tend to be given priority and there's usually a three-night maximum stay during summer in city hostels. Note that you can reserve by fax but not phone, but since all hostels worldwide are linked by an International Booking Network, you can also ask the Swiss hostel you're already staying in to reserve a bed for you at your next port of call – this costs Fr.1 (plus a Fr.9 deposit).

Many new hostels have opened in the last few years to supplement the "official" ones, and there's now a rival, and very popular, grouping of thirty called **Swiss Backpackers**. Their lively hostels are less institutional than the HI ones, often in prime locations in the centres of town

YOUTH HOSTEL ASSOCIATIONS

*Membership fees shown are for over-18s –
substantial discounts apply to those under 18 at the time of joining.*

Australia Level 3, 10 Mallett St, Camperdown, NSW 2050 (☎02/9565 1699, fax 9565 1325, *www.yha.org.au*). A$47 to join; A$29 annual membership renewal.

Canada 205 Catherine St #400, Ottawa, ON, K2P 1C3 (☎1-800/663-5777 or 613/237-7884, fax 237-7868, *www.hostellingintl.ca*). Annual membership C$26.75.

England & Wales Trevelyan House, 8 St Stephen's Hill, St Albans, Herts AL1 2DY (☎01727/845047, fax 844126, *www.yha.org.uk*). Also 14 Southampton St, London WC2 (☎020/7836 8541). Annual membership £11.

New Zealand PO Box 436, Christchurch 1 (☎03/379 9970, fax 365 4476, *www.yha.org.nz*). Annual membership NZ$40.

Northern Ireland 22 Donegall Rd, Belfast BT12 5JN (☎028/9032 4733, fax 9043 9699, *www.hini.org.uk*). Annual membership £8.

Republic of Ireland An Óige, 61 Mountjoy St, Dublin 7 (☎01/830 4555, fax 830 5808, *www.irelandyha.org*). Annual membership IR£10.

Scotland 7 Glebe Crescent, Stirling FK8 2JA (☎01786/891400, fax 891333, *www.syha.org.uk*). Annual membership £6.

USA 733 15th St NW #840, Washington DC 20005 (☎202/783-6161, fax 783-6171, *www.hiayh.org*). Annual membership $25.

SWITZERLAND

Naturfreunde Schweiz/Fédération suisse des Amis de la Nature, Pavillonweg 3, Postfach, CH-3001 Bern (☎031/301 60 88, fax 301 61 18, *www.naturfreunde.ch*). No membership needed.

Swiss Backpackers, Postfach 530, CH-8027 Zürich (fax 01/201 70 72, *www.backpacker.ch*). No membership needed.

Swiss Youth Hostels, Schaffhauserstrasse 14, CH-8042 Zürich (☎01/360 14 14, fax 360 14 60, *www.youthhostel.ch*). Annual membership Fr.25.

and cities, and priced to compete. No membership is required. You'll almost certainly spot their informative and very useful *Swiss Backpacker* newspaper while in Switzerland, available free in all their hostels and other prominent touristed places around the country.

Comparatively priced **Naturfreunde** hotels, run by the Swiss Federation of the Friends of Nature, are an alternative to youth hostels if you prefer a little more peace and quiet, and something of a personal touch. Their 97 hotels, well away from beaten tracks and often historic buildings lovingly restored and maintained, are all run by individuals with a passion for nature and the environment.

Otherwise, pretty much all ski resorts have places offering **dormitory** accommodation, quite often hotels putting a converted annexe to good use. Such a dorm (*Touristenlager, Massenlager* or *Matratzenlager, dortoir, dormitorio*) may simply comprise one room with as many mattresses as

possible squeezed into it side-by-side, each "bed" sold at bargain-basement prices. This is also the style of dorm accommodation in the 150 or so **Alpine huts** (see p.72) dotted around higher altitudes on or close to hiking trails (some of the more isolated ones may only be accessible to full-blown mountaineers), although bed prices tend to rise according to how remote the place is.

FARM-STAYS, B&BS AND PRIVATE ROOMS

Schlaf im Stroh, Aventure sur la paille, or **Sleeping in the Hay**, is a great way to get a feel for countryside life while guaranteeing accommodation at a fixed price wherever you are. Hundreds of farming families from every canton in the country (bar Glarus) have collaborated in the scheme, which runs from May to October only, each offering 10–15 places to sleep on straw in a barn (but as fresh and pristine a barn as you could wish for), sometimes also offering a handful of bed spaces within the farmhouse, and occasionally a place to pitch a tent or two if you prefer. An overnight stay costs a flat Fr.18 including breakfast (Fr.11 for under-12s) at all farms. You must bring your own sleeping bag if you want to sleep on straw, and a shower – available at most farms – costs Fr.2 per person. Your host family can also offer a range of services, including putting together a picnic (Fr.9), serving a home-cooked dinner for Fr.18, providing horses (Fr.21–26 per day), renting bikes, and offering guided tours of the countryside around and about. A booklet giving details of every farm in the scheme, including whether the family speaks English or not, is available from Cécile Sciboz, Le Pratzet, CH-1733 Treyvaux (include a C5-sized SAE), but all bookings must be made directly with the farm or farms you choose. You can get more information at *www.agri.ch/stroh* and from the organizer Christian Stähli-Fehr, Bois du Fey, CH-1430 Orges (☎024/445 16 31).

A slightly less raw option for farm-stays are the 250 **Swiss Holiday Farms**, which offer fullblown apartments and rooms for daily or weekly rent on the farm, year-round. You can get a catalogue from Schweizer Reisekasse (Reka), Neuengasse 15, CH-3001 Bern (☎031/329 66 33, fax 329 66 01, *www.reka.ch*).

Bed and breakfasts, where you normally lodge in a room in someone's private house or farmhouse, are something of an innovation in Switzerland, but are becoming steadily more popular. Many tourist offices can give you details of B&Bs in their area, or you can request an excellent illustrated catalogue of B&Bs all over the country from Rolf Suter, Bernstrasse 6, CH-3067 Boll (☎ & fax 031/839 74 84, *www.homestay.ch*). Prices can vary quite a bit, depending on the house and the location, but a rough average is a bargain Fr.30–40 per person. You may also come across signs in rural and Alpine resort areas offering **rooms** in private houses (*Zimmer frei, chambres à louer, affitasi camere*). Again, these aren't as widespread as in other parts of Europe, but still can be less expensive, and much more welcoming, than hostel accommodation.

CHALETS AND APARTMENTS

Self-catering accommodation in holiday **chalets**, bungalows and apartments tends to be booked solid for entire summer and winter seasons. For chalets in places like Zermatt, Verbier, Gstaad and so on, you may have to book six months or more

ahead. Most are only let for a week at a time (Saturday to Saturday).

Interhome is one of the largest and most efficient **international agencies**, dealing with more than 5000 chalets and apartments all over Switzerland, sleeping from two to twelve people. Prices vary tremendously depending on the property and the season, but start from a bargain Fr.16–18 per person per night. High-season bookings are for a minimum of seven nights, Saturday to Saturday, but in the low season you may be able to find properties available for three or four nights only. Booking months in advance ensures you get a full choice of places to stay, but if you leave things to a week before departure, some chalet owners will knock up to a third off their usual prices. Contact details are: 383 Richmond Rd, Twickenham, TW1 2EF, UK (☎020/8891 1294, fax 8891 5331, *www.interhome.co.uk*); 1990 NE 163 Rd #110, N Miami, FL 33162, USA (☎305/940-2299, fax 940-2911, *www.interhome.com*); Level 5, 22 Darley Rd, Manly, Sydney, Australia (☎02/9976 2155 or 1800/257 171, fax 02/9976 2208, *www.interhome.com.au*); Buckhauserstrasse 26, CH-8048 Zürich (☎01/497 22 22, fax 497 27 23, *www.interhome.ch*).

CAMPING

The typical Swiss **campsite** is shiny, clean and well equipped, although the higher the altitude the more limited the opening times: many close altogether outside the summer season (May–Sept). Just about every town and village in the country has a site or two. Campsites are classified according to facilities, from one to five stars, and tourist offices in every region in the country have a camping map showing the locations, contact details and facilities of campsites in the locality. The TCS is a particularly useful source of information, with a national map showing every campsite in the country, and their own Camping Guidebook (*Campingführer, Guide Camping, Guida dei Campeggi*), available in Swiss bookshops or from the TCS camping office, CP 176, CH-1217 Meyrin 1 (☎022/785 13 33).

Bear in mind, though, that most campsites are located well away from cities (and often well away from transport facilities too), so they're not ideal if you're planning to see the sights of the country on the cheap – in fact, once you factor in transport costs to reach the site, you won't pay much less than you would in a hostel. Average campsite **charges** are Fr.6–8 per person, plus

Fr.5–8 for a tent, and Fr.4–5 for a car. Eight TCS-run campsites around the country offer two- and four-person **tents to rent** on site: a two-person "Canadian Tent" plus bedrolls costs Fr.26 per night in high season. Booking ahead is recommended at all times of the year.

If you're planning to do a lot of camping, an **international camping carnet** (Camping Card International or CCI; £4.50) is a good investment. It's available in the UK from the AA, the RAC or the Camping and Caravanning Club, Greenfields House, Westwood Way, Coventry CV4 8JH (☎024/7669 4995); and in the US and Canada from Family Campers and Rvers, 4804 Transit Rd, Building 2, Depew, NY 14043 (☎1-800/245-9755), or from home motoring organizations like the American Automobile Association and the Canadian Automobile Association. The carnet serves as useful identification, and many campsites will accept it instead of making you surrender your passport during your stay. It covers you for third-party insurance when camping, and sometimes helps you get ten percent reductions or other incentives at the nine campsites listed in the CCI Information booklet which comes with your carnet.

Camping rough, outside authorized sites, is formally prohibited by law, and you may well find yourself with a fine or worse if you try it in populated or cultivated areas, but in the mountain wilds – as long as you take care to clean up properly after yourself – it's hard to envisage how anyone could complain. Discretion and environmental respect are everything.

FOOD AND DRINK

Switzerland is overshadowed by its near neighbours when it comes to food and drink, and yet the country nurtures a wide and absorbing range of local cuisines, taking in influences and styles from the surrounding diversity of French, German and Italian cooking while sticking close to its rural and Alpine roots. Extreme cultural decentralization means that if you dig below the surface of the national staples, you'll consistently come across delicious regional dishes relying on local ingredients and idiosyncratic styles of preparation that are unknown in the next canton, let alone elsewhere in Europe.

The Swiss take the joy of communal eating to heart, and many eateries rely on old-style rustic decor, wood beams, plenty of Swiss kitsch (cowbells, alphorns and the like) and a cosy, hearty, family-like atmosphere – and that may just be for a diner in Zürich's financial district. For the Swiss, much as for the Italians or the French, eating is an expression of local culture, and many people have no time or patience for **foreign cuisines**. High levels of immigration over the 1980s and 1990s has resulted in a host of Turkish, Arabic and, to a

	I am a vegetarian (m/f)	Have you got any special dishes for vegetarians?
German	– Ich bin Vegetarier/-in	– Haben Sie spezielle Menus für Vegetarier?
French	– Je suis végétarien/-ne	– Avez-vous des menus spéciaux pour les végétariens?
Italian	– Sono vegetariano/-a	– Avete menù speciali per vegetariani?

EATING ON THE CHEAP

Budget travellers should head for the often surprisingly good, and always packed, **self-service restaurants** in chain department stores in town-centres nationwide: Manora is almost always best (also known as Placette in Romandie and Inova in Ticino), but Migros, EPA, and Coop are all worth checking out. The best of these places offer a wide variety of fresh-cooked generic dishes – soups, casseroles, pasta and the like – with by far the best bargains coming on the large buffets of fresh salads and chicken-and-rice staples. Veggie and vegan ranges help non-carnivores to gorge. With pricing generally going by the size of the plate rather than by the amount you actually pile onto it, you can easily get a full meal for Fr.10–13 at these places, and with all-day opening they're ideal mid-afternoon stand-bys for when most other eateries are closed. Watch out for the places which allow you to pile the food on, but then charge you by weight (say Fr.2.20 per 100g), which can work out quite a bit more expensive.

Another option is a **student dining hall**, or *mensa*, attached to a university, often open to everyone and serving cut-price meals at limited lunch- and (early) dinner-times.

Migros is also the largest national chain of **supermarkets**, with outlets in almost all towns which are marked by a big orange initial: a single M indicates a small shop, while a triple MMM is a giant hypermarket. Denner is another chain, and Aperto are small deli-style outlets with usefully long opening hours found at main train stations. Range of products is normally excellent, but prices – if you do the comparison to equivalents at home – are high. The tradition of individually owned specialist food shops survives in most places, with a baker (*Bäckerei, boulangerie, panetteria*), a grocer (*Lebensmittelgeschäft, épicerie, negozio alimentari*), a cheese shop (*Käserei, fromagerie, bottega del formaggio*) and a health-food shop (*Reformhaus, magasin diététique, erboristeria*) offering high-quality **picnic supplies** in most town centres.

lesser extent, East Asian eateries opening up in towns and cities across the country, but they tend to be fast-food joints for wolfing down kebabs or chow mein on the hoof rather than musing on the subtle flavours of the orient – you'll only find quality international cooking in Geneva, Zürich and possibly Bern.

Every town and village market groans with top-quality farm produce, much of it organically produced, and you're very likely to stumble on unpretentious family-run restaurants around the country that serve up inexpensive village fare to the locals. That's not to say that you can't eat like a gourmet in Switzerland – you can, and very easily – but your most memorable meals may well come from the simplest of kitchens and the most ordinary-looking of restaurants.

Unsurprisingly, Swiss cooking is firmly rooted in **dairy products** – cheese, milk, cream, butter and/or yoghurt find their way into most dishes. It's far from impossible to find good-quality, interesting and varied **vegetarian** options, and all but a handful of places offer vegetarian set menus alongside the standard meaty ones, but veggies should be aware that most restaurants default onto **meat-based** dishes: innocent-looking tomato soup may have bits of bacon added, and fresh salads may come layered with ham or salami. Switzerland must be the only place in the world

where you can order a *Fitness Teller* ("healthy meal") and be presented with a thick slab of veal in a cream sauce. **Vegans** will no doubt come prepared to cook their own food at least some of the time but, with careful choices, you should be able to pick your way through a menu with the help of accommodating restaurant staff. Alternative-style co-operative-run diners, many in squats in the major cities, offer budget vegetarian and vegan meals as standard.

See p.75 for advice on **tipping**.

CHEESE

Cheese is an institution in Switzerland. Everyone eats it, morning noon and night; some is still made in the traditional way by hand on summer mountain pastures (and so represents the very core of Swissness to the Swiss themselves); it's a lucrative pillar of industry and is exported to serve as an ambassador for Switzerland to the world; and it bears about as much resemblance to a shrink-wrapped Mild Cheddar or Monterey Jack as a muddy brick does to a wedge of black forest gateau.

Cheese has been around in Switzerland at least since the Romans, for whom *caseus helveticus* ("Swiss cheese") was popular enough to catch the eye of the historian Pliny. For cen-

SWISS CHEESE – A HIT LIST

Unlike in France, Switzerland has no system of control over use of the names of its cheeses, and nowadays only 2.5 percent of world Emmental production actually comes from Switzerland, most originating in France and Germany instead. However, aficionados – and your own taste buds – will confirm that the best Emmental comes from Emmental. Cheese shops and supermarket chill-cabinets are crammed with dozens of cheeses, of which the following are best known:

Appenzeller Family name for some of the world's smelliest cheeses. The most pungent, known as *Räss*, gains its odour from being brushed with a herb-and-brine marinade throughout the ripening process; it's hugely popular within Switzerland but unknown outside.

Emmental The holey mousetrap classic, known simply as "swiss" in the US. King of Swiss cheeses, with a massive 55,000 tonnes produced annually, in Emmental and across the German-speaking lowlands. Although coming in various grades, it tends to be mild, and has a subtle, nutty flavour.

Gruyère Smooth, rich and creamy-tasting hard cheese, with a distinctive salty-dry sharpness that makes it the favourite of the Swiss themselves, and a prime ingredient in fondue.

Sbrinz Originating in Brienz, but now produced in and around Luzern, this is Switzerland's Parmesan, matured over three years, crumbly, grainy and powerful.

Schabziger aka Sapsago. Distinctive green conical cheese made in Glarus for centuries according to the same recipe, using an intensely strong herb known as melilot that was originally imported from the Middle East by returning Crusaders.

Tête de Moine aka Bellelay. First made at Bellelay monastery in the Jura in the twelfth century, but gleefully renamed "Monk's Head" following widespread guillotining during the French Revolution. Only made in Canton Jura and the northern reaches of Canton Bern. The small cylinders of aromatic, spicy cheese are spiked and then shaved by hand into tissuey rosettes at the table with a special revolving blade.

Tilsiter Creamy, semi-hard cheese developed by Swiss emigrés in Tilsit in eastern Prussia in the late nineteenth century, and brought back to Switzerland shortly after. Produced in the eastern cantons bordering the Bodensee.

Vacherin Fribourgeois A recipe reputed to have been brought back from Catalonia by a Swiss monk in the thirteenth century, and produced only in Canton Fribourg since then to serve primarily as the fondue cheese *par excellence*.

Vacherin Mont d'Or A delectably smooth, creamy soft cheese only made in winter in the Vaud Jura.

Valais cheese and Raclette Spicy, easily meltable cheese in high demand, now produced throughout Switzerland for the winter speciality raclette.

turies, cheesemaking was a skill confined to mountain farmers, sequestered for months with their herds in summer pastures. After the opening of the Gotthard Pass in the thirteenth century, farmers would travel to Italy to trade their cheese for luxury goods such as wine and spices, a tradition which continued virtually into the modern era.

These days, some 1200 village dairies are in daily operation, processing fresh, mostly raw, milk from local cows. (Pasteurization is frowned upon by most cheesemakers, who claim it undermines the full body and aroma of the cheese; helpfully, Swiss hygiene regulations on the matter are much less stringent than those of the EU. All Swiss cheese is made from raw milk unless otherwise stated.) Locally produced cheeses are savoured much as local beers are in Britain or local wines in France.

Most cheese is now produced in the valleys, but the tradition of making **Alpine cheese** (*Bergkäse, Alpkäse; fromage des alpes; formaggio alpe*) over the short summers on high pastures is very much alive. The ceremonies driving cattle up to the lush alps in June, and down again in October, are festive celebrations in rural areas (Appenzell, and around Gruyères in Canton Fribourg, for instance). Only cheese which has been made on the alp from raw milk processed from cows fed on fresh grass, wildflowers and clover can qualify for the *Bergkäse* name. The cheeses are produced by hand, allowed to ripen for a few months, and then at the end of the summer are handed out to the farmers proportionately, according to the number of cattle they own. Many are sold on to specialist cheese shops around the country, where they are much in demand for their richness and individual nuances of flavour.

BREAKFAST AND SNACKS

Most Swiss eat their **breakfast** at home, and it's not that much different in essence from the kind of fare served up in hotels (above the very cheapest establishments anyway). Hotel breakfasts tend to take the form of substantial **buffets** of juices, butter croissants, fresh-baked crusty bread, a choice of hard and soft cheeses, boiled eggs, an array of cold meats and salamis, and tea or coffee. At more expensive places you'll also find a range of **muesli** and cereals with lashings of fresh milk, but despite marketing techniques across most of the world extolling the Alpine virtues of Swiss muesli – Dr Bircher-Benner of Zürich invented muesli at the end of the nineteenth century to serve to patients at his health clinic – the Swiss themselves seem to steer clear of the stuff at breakfast, a few older mountain folk instead indulging in a bowl of cold Birchermuesli (a stomach-lining porridge with plenty of fruit and rich yoghurt already mixed in) in the afternoon or even at night with bread and milk.

Bread is different from canton to canton, but as a rule you'll find light, white breads in the French- and Italian-speaking regions, and more substantial loaves in the German-speaking cantons: Basel's double loaf is thick and doughy, Zürich's drier and oval shaped, and so on. Rye bread abounds in Graubünden (Poschiavo's is flavoured with aniseed) and in the Valais, where nuts are often added. The Emmental has its own delectable *Züpfe*, a plaited white loaf rich with milk.

In the towns and larger resorts, you'll have no trouble finding chances to **snack** on the universal standbys of burgers, pizza slices, kebabs and falafels. You'll also find various different kinds of sausage (*Wurst, saucisse, salsiccia*) around the country served as chargrilled fast food in a warmed breadroll with mustard; the similarity with limp US-style hotdogs is purely cosmetic. The most popular are pork *Bratwürste*, but you may also find smoked *Frankfurterli* and *Wienerli*, *Blutwurst* made from black pudding (blood), and *Leberwurst* or liver sausage. One seasonal treat, in late autumn and winter, are delicious and filling roast chestnuts (*Marroni, marrons, marroni*) sold by street vendors countrywide.

MAIN MEALS

The line between a **café** and a **restaurant** is blurred: either can normally do you a meal,

although generally only at set times (mostly noon–2pm & 6–10pm), with only snacks available in between. A *Restaurant, restaurant, ristorante*, is more or less the same as an **inn** (*Beiz, Gasthof, Gaststätte, Gasthaus; auberge; grotto, osteria*), although somewhere with the latter name probably serves more traditional local cuisine. Both generally take at least one day a week off as a holiday (*Ruhetag, jour de repos, giorno di chiusura*). Also watch out for *alkohol-frei* or *sinalco* establishments, as well as the noticeably tiny number of places with smoking restrictions.

Eating out can knock a big hole in your budget. The key to avoiding excessive **expense** is to make lunch your main meal, and always to plump for the dish of the day or *menu* (*Tagesmenu, Tagesteller, Tageshit; plat/assiette du jour, piatto del giorno*) – often comprising two or even three courses of substantial, quality nosh, whether in a café or a proper restaurant, for around Fr.15. The English term can be confusing: note that in all eating-places the **menu** is the particular dish or dishes on offer that day, while the house list from which you select individual courses is called the *Karte* or *Speisekarte, carte, carta*. Lunch *menus* are by far the least expensive way to sample the best of Swiss cuisine, and even Michelin-starred gourmet restaurants will have exquisite multi-course lunches for Fr.25–40 (not including wine). The same meal in the evening, or choosing à la carte anytime, can easily cost double, although beerhalls in the German-speaking cities often serve hearty inexpensive evening meals, and – depending on where you are – pizza-pasta joints and simple informal eateries can fill your stomach for Fr.15–20.

FONDUE

These days, you'll find **cheese fondue** all over the country, but it's really a speciality of Suisse-Romande. The word "fondue" refers to the broad, shallow earthenware or cast-iron pot used to heat the cheese ... but that's where agreement runs out, and you'll find myriad varieties served across the country. The classic style, mainstay of eateries in the fondue heartland of Fribourg and the Vaud countryside, is a *moitié-moitié*, or half-and-half, using either Gruyère and Vacherin Fribourgeois, or Gruyère and Emmental. Others may use several grades of Gruyère, or mix in some local Alpine cheese, Valaisian raclette cheese or Appenzeller. Whichever, it's a winter dish designed to be sampled with friends: a restaurant

SWISS GERMAN FOOD AND DRINK TERMS

THE BASICS

knife	Messer	tapwater	Hahnenwasser
fork	Gabel	mineral water	Mineralwasser
spoon	Löffel	juice	Saft
plate	Teller	ice	Eis
napkin	Serviette	a beer	Stange
bottle	Flasche	red wine	Rotwein
glass	Glas	white wine	Weisswein
cup	Tasse	dry	trocken
menu	Speisekarte	sweet	süss
bread	Brot	sugar	Zucker
butter	Butter, Anke	salt	Salz
ham	Schinken	pepper	Pfeffer
bacon	Speck	oil	Öl
cheese	Käse	mustard	Senf
milk	Milch	"waiter!"	"Bedienung!"
whole milk	Vollmilch	"I'd like…"	"Ich nehme…"
skimmed milk	Magermilch	with	mit
buttermilk	Buttermilch	without	ohne
yoghurt	Joghurt	to eat	essen
cream	Rahm	to drink	trinken
curd cheese	Quark	non-smoking area	Nichtraucherzone
fromage frais	Frischkäse	breakfast	Frühstück, Zmorge
egg	Ei	lunch	Mittagessen, Zmittag
jam	Konfitüre	dinner, supper	Abendessen, Znacht
honey	Honig	the bill	die Rechnung

SNACKS AND STARTERS (*VORSPEISEN*)

sandwich	Sandwich	soup	Suppe
chips (french fries)	Pommes frites	prawn cocktail	Krevetten Cocktail
crisps (potato chips)	Pommes Chips	green salad	Grüner Salat
omelette	Omelett	mixed salad	Gemischte Salat
olives	Oliven		

MAIN COURSES (*SPEISEN*)

meat	Fleisch	horse	Pferde
veal	Kalb	fillet	Filet
beef	Rind	a chop	Kotelett
pork	Schwein	diced meat	Geschnetzelte
lamb	Lamm	mincemeat	Hackfleisch
chicken	Poulet	liver	Leber

offering it in the summer is a restaurant to be avoided.

The cheeses are melted together behind the scenes, generally with a shot of some kind of alcohol (cider in the orchard-rich east, Kirsch in the cherry-growing central regions, white wine in Neuchâtel and Vaud), and small cubes of bread (or in some places boiled potato) are speared with a

long fork and swirled through the cheese. Lose your bread in the pot, and traditionally the drinks are on you.

With roughly 250g of molten cheese consumed per person, a fondue can be quite a heavy load on your system: the Swiss-German remedy is to gulp plenty of hot herbal tea throughout, making sure the cheese doesn't solidify in your innards, but the

kidney	Niere	mushrooms	Pilze
sausage	Wurst	fish	Fisch
rice	Reis	salmon	Lachs
boiled potatoes	Salzkartoffeln	trout	Forelle
pasta	Teigwaren	tuna	Thunfisch
noodles	Nudeln		

VEGETABLES (GEMÜSE)

tomato	Tomate	peas	Erbse
carrot	Rüebli	sweet pepper	Peperoni
cabbage	Chabis	spinach	Spinat
cauliflower	Blumenkohl	fennel	Fenchel
corn	Mais	broccoli	Broccoli
cucumber	Gurke	onion	Zwiebel
asparagus	Spargel	garlic	Knoblauch
beans	Bohnen		

USEFUL WORDS

hot	heiss	baked	gebacken
cold	kalt	fried	gebraten, fritiert
smoked	geräuchert	spices	Gewürze
roast	gebraten	traditional cooking	gutbürgerliche Küche
rare	bluetig	Swiss-German cooking	Schweizer Küche
well done	gar	Swiss-French cooking	Welsche Küche
boiled	gekochte	Ticinese cooking	Tessiner Küche
steamed	gedämpft	Romansh cooking	Romanische Küche
stuffed	gefüllt	in the style of	art
grilled	gegrillt	home-made	Hausgemacht
raw	roh		

FRUIT (FRÜCHTE) AND DESSERTS (DESSERT)

apple	Apfel	banana	Banane
pear	Birne	orange	Orange
plum	Zwetschge	grapefruit	Grapefruit
apricot	Aprikose	lemon	Zitrone
peach	Pfirsich	mandarin	Mandarine
cherry	Kirsche	fig	Feige
grape	Trauben	cake	Kuchen, Torte
raspberry	Himbeere	chocolate	Schokolade
blackberry	Brombeere	ice cream	Glace
strawberry	Erdbeere	chestnut purée	Vermicelles

fearless Romands go the other way and favour plenty of chilled white wine. Their *coup de milieu* of a shot of Kirsch halfway through supposedly helps things settle.

You'll also see **fondue chinoise**, an entirely different thing where you dip slivers of meat into spicy bouillon; **fondue bourguignonne**, only for the stoutest of constitutions since it involves dous-ing lumps of red meat in hot spitting oil; **fish** fondues, Valaisian **fondue Bacchus** using mulled wine, and even novelty **chocolate** fondues.

Since they're never eaten alone, fondues are rarely priced per person; you're more likely to see them listed as a two-person (or more) deal and as "fondue à discrétion" or "fondue à gogo" (both of which mean "all you can eat").

FRENCH FOOD AND DRINK TERMS

THE BASICS

knife	couteau	tapwater	eau de robinet
fork	fourchette	mineral water	eau minérale
spoon	cuillère	juice	jus
plate	assiette	ice	glace
napkin	serviette	a beer	une pression
bottle	bouteille	red wine	vin rouge
glass	verre	white wine	vin blanc
cup	tasse	dry	sec
menu	carte	sweet	doux
bread	pain	sugar	sucre
butter	beurre	salt	sel
ham	jambon	pepper	poivre
bacon	lardon	oil	huile
cheese	fromage	mustard	moutarde
milk	lait	"waiter!"	"Monsieur/Madame!"
whole milk	lait entier	"I'd like…"	"Je voudrais…"
skimmed milk	lait écrémé	with	avec
buttermilk	babeurre	without	sans
yoghurt	yogourt	to eat	manger
cream	crème	to drink	boire
curd cheese	fromage blanc	non-smoking area	espace non-fumeurs
fromage frais	fromage frais	breakfast	petit déjeuner
egg	oeuf	lunch	déjeuner
jam	confiture	dinner, supper	dîner
honey	miel	the bill	l'addition

SNACKS AND STARTERS (HORS D'OEUVRES)

sandwich	sandwich	soup	potage, consommé
chips (french fries)	frites	prawn cocktail	cocktail des crevettes
crisps (potato chips)	pommes chips	green salad	salade verte
omelette	omelette	mixed salad	salade mixte
olives	olives		

MAIN COURSES (PLATS PRINCIPAUX)

meat	viande	chicken	poulet
veal	veau	horse	cheval
beef	boeuf	fillet	filet
pork	porc	a chop	côtelette
lamb	agneau	diced meat	émincé

REGIONAL SPECIALITIES

Fondue is the prime speciality of **Suisse-Romande**, but there's a host of other cheesy dishes claiming their roots in the region, including **raclette**, known countrywide but born and best savoured in the Valais. A large half-round of special raclette cheese is held in front of a fire, and as it melts it's scraped (*raclé*) onto a plate, and served with boiled potatoes, pearl onions and pickles, often "à gogo". The **saucisson vaudois**, or mixed pork and beef Vaud sausage, is also famous for its delicately smoked flavour, served boiled or steamed, and accompanied by *papet vaudois*, a delicious purée of potatoes and leeks. Lakeside resorts prepare fresh fish in a hundred different ways, most deliciously as **truite meu-**

mincemeat	*hachée*	noodles	*nouilles*
liver	*foie*	mushrooms	*champignons*
kidney	*rognon*	fish	*poisson*
sausage	*saucisse*	salmon	*saumon*
rice	*riz*	trout	*truite*
boiled potatoes	*pommes nature*	tuna	*thon*
pasta	*pâtes*		

VEGETABLES (*LÉGUMES*)

tomato	*tomate*	peas	*poix*
carrot	*carotte*	sweet pepper	*poivron*
cabbage	*chou*	spinach	*épinards*
cauliflower	*choufleur*	fennel	*fenouil*
corn	*maïs*	broccoli	*brocoli*
cucumber	*concombre*	onion	*oignon*
asparagus	*asperge*	garlic	*ail*
beans	*haricots*		

USEFUL WORDS

hot	*chaud*	baked	*au four*
cold	*froid*	fried	*frite*
smoked	*fumé*	spices	*épices*
roast	*rôti*	traditional cooking	*cuisine bourgeoise*
rare	*saignant*	Swiss-German cooking	*cuisine suisse*
well done	*bien cuit*		*alémanique*
boiled	*bouilli*	Swiss-French cooking	*cuisine romande*
steamed	*à la vapeur*	Ticinese cooking	*cuisine tessinoise*
stuffed	*farci*	Romansh cooking	*cuisine romanche*
grilled	*grillé*	in the style of	*à la*
raw	*cru*	home-made	*fait à la maison*

FRUIT (*FRUITS*) AND DESSERTS (*DESSERTS*)

apple	*pomme*	banana	*banane*
pear	*poire*	orange	*orange*
plum	*prune*	grapefruit	*pamplemousse*
apricot	*abricot*	lemon	*citron*
peach	*pêche*	mandarin	*mandarine*
cherry	*cerise*	fig	*figue*
grape	*raisin*	cake	*gâteau, tarte*
raspberry	*framboise*	chocolate	*chocolat*
blackberry	*mûre*	ice cream	*glace*
strawberry	*fraise*	chestnut purée	*vermicelles*

nière, fresh trout floured and sautéd in butter. Autumn across Romandie (and across Ticino too) sees **wild mushrooms** (*Pilzen, champignons, funghi*) making an appearance on the menu, from simple *croûtes aux champignons* (creamy mushrooms on toast) up to flavourful game and mushroom casseroles. In high summer, Valais overflows with golden apricots and peaches,

while apples and plums thrive in the lowlands from Lake Geneva to Basel and across to the Bodensee.

All across **Deutschschweiz** you'll find plentiful variations of **Rösti** or *Röschti*, grated potato formed into a large patty and fried golden-brown on both sides. This can either be an accompaniment to a main course, or, with the embellishment

ITALIAN FOOD AND DRINK TERMS

THE BASICS

knife	*coltello*	tapwater	*acqua di rubinetto*
fork	*forchetta*	mineral water	*acqua minerale*
spoon	*cucchiaio*	juice	*succo*
plate	*piatto*	ice	*ghiaccio*
napkin	*tovagliolo*	a beer	*una birra*
bottle	*bottiglia*	red wine	*vino rosso*
glass	*bicchiere*	white wine	*vino blanco*
cup	*tazza*	dry	*secco*
menu	*carta*	sweet	*dolce*
bread	*pane*	sugar	*zucchero*
butter	*burro*	salt	*sale*
ham	*prosciutto*	pepper	*pepe*
bacon	*pancetta*	oil	*olio*
cheese	*formaggio*	mustard	*senape*
milk	*latte*	"waiter!"	*"Cameriere/-a!"*
whole milk	*latte intero*	"I'd like…"	*"Vorrei…"*
skimmed milk	*latte scremato*	with	*con*
buttermilk	*latticello*	without	*senza*
yoghurt	*joghurt*	to eat	*mangiare*
cream	*panna*	to drink	*bere*
curd cheese	*ricotta*	non-smoking area	*area non-fumatori*
fromage frais	*formaggio fresco*	breakfast	*prima colazione*
egg	*uovo*	lunch	*pranzo*
jam	*marmellata*	dinner, supper	*cena*
honey	*miele*	the bill	*il conto*

SNACKS AND STARTERS (*ANTIPASTI*)

sandwich	*panino*	soup	*zuppa, minestra*
chips (french fries)	*patate fritte*	prawn cocktail	*cocktail di gamberi*
crisps (potato chips)	*patatine*	green salad	*insalata verde*
omelette	*frittata*	mixed salad	*insalata mista*
olives	*olive*		

MAIN COURSES (*SECONDI PIATTI*)

meat	*carne*	chicken	*pollo*
veal	*vitello*	horse	*cavallo*
beef	*manzo*	fillet	*filetto*
pork	*maiale*	a chop	*cotoletta*
lamb	*agnello*	diced meat	*spezzatino*

of ham, melted cheese, a fried egg and/or bacon bits, be a comfortably affordable main course itself. An Alpine stomach-liner that has made its way into the lowlands is **Älpler Magrone**, essentially macaroni cheese with extra onion, bacon, potatoes and cream, often served with puréed apples with cinnamon. *Käseschnitten*, in different forms, is Welsh rarebit (toasted cheese),

while *Spätzli* and *Knöpfli* are tiny buttons of boiled dough drizzled with butter. In and around Bern, you'll find **Bernerteller** or *Bernerplatte*, a hefty pile of cold and hot meats including pork sausage, bacon, various hams, smoked pork, knuckles and beef tongue served with beans and plenty of *Sauerkraut*. Zürich has **Züri Gschnetzlets**, diced veal in a creamy mushroom

mincemeat	*carne macinata*	noodles	*tagliatelle*
liver	*fegato*	mushrooms	*funghi*
kidney	*rognone*	fish	*pesce*
sausage	*salsiccia*	salmon	*salmone*
rice	*riso*	trout	*trota*
boiled potatoes	*patate bollite*	tuna	*tonno*
pasta	*pasta*		

VEGETABLES (*VERDURE*)

tomato	*pomodoro*	peas	*piselli*
carrot	*carota*	sweet pepper	*peperone*
cabbage	*cavolo*	spinach	*spinaci*
cauliflower	*cavolfiore*	fennel	*finocchio*
corn	*mais*	broccoli	*broccolo*
cucumber	*cetriolo*	onion	*cipolla*
asparagus	*asparagi*	garlic	*aglio*
beans	*fagioli*		

USEFUL WORDS

hot	*caldo*	baked	*al forno*
cold	*freddo*	fried	*fritto*
smoked	*affumicato*	spices	*spezie*
roast	*arrosto*	traditional cooking	*cucina casalinga*
rare	*al sangue*	Swiss-German cooking	*cucina svizzero*
well done	*ben cotto*		*tedesca*
boiled	*bollito*	Swiss-French cooking	*cucina romanda*
steamed	*al vapore*	Ticinese cooking	*cucina ticinese*
stuffed	*farcito*	Romansh cooking	*cucina romancia*
grilled	*alla griglia*	in the style of	*al/alla*
raw	*crudo*	home-made	*fatto in casa*

FRUIT (*FRUTTA*) AND DESSERTS (*DOLCI*)

apple	*mela*	strawberry	*fragola*
pear	*pera*	banana	*banana*
plum	*prugna*	orange	*arancia*
apricot	*albicocca*	grapefruit	*pompelmo*
peach	*pesca*	lemon	*limone*
cherry	*ciliegia*	mandarin	*mandarino*
grape	*uva*	fig	*fico*
raspberry	*lampone*	cake	*torta*
blackberry	*mora*	chocolate	*cioccolata*
		ice cream	*gelato*

sauce, served with *Rösti*, while St Gallen revels in its own pale, milky veal sausages. In Basel, winter menus offer **Basler Mehlsuppe**, a heavy brown brew of onions, pork lard and cream, thickened with flour and topped with grated Sbrinz cheese. Graubünden is best known for **Bündnerfleisch**, prime beef air-dried in an attic and sliced paper-thin in an aromatic *Bündnerteller*, or as prime ingredient in **Bündner Gerstensuppe** (barley cream soup with vegetables). With hunting still very popular in Graubünden, you'll also see plenty of **game** on autumn menus, such as stews (*Pfeffer, fratem*) of chamois (*Gemse, chamutsch*) or deer (*Hirsch, tschierv*). Zug and Luzern are famous for their black cherries, while Basel has its own dark red variety. **Meringue** was invented in or near Meiringen, and most Emmental and Bernese Oberland villages offer their own spectacular super-rich, cream-laden meringue creations.

Italian-speaking **Ticino** has its own cuisine, entirely different from what's on offer in the rest of the country and more akin to the flavours and methods of neighbouring Piemonte and Lombardy. **Polenta** (cornmeal) and **risotto** are staples; leafy salads abound, dressed lightly with olive oil instead of the mayonnaise-based concoctions favoured further north; and fresh home-made pastas and **gnocchi** (bite-sized potato dumplings), with the familiar tomato- or pesto-based sauces, are delectable. **Pollo alla cacciatora** is a spicy chicken-and-tomato stew with mushrooms and white wine, served with polenta or boiled potatoes. The Ticinesi also love their sausages, with Mardi Gras in Lugano serving as an excuse for a public pig-out on risotto with **luganiga**, an extra-rich pork sausage. Spicy *mortadella* is unlike the Italian version, and can either be cooked or air-dried for eating raw.

CHOCOLATE

Chocolate (*Schokolade, chocolat, cioccolata*) is a way of life in Switzerland. The Swiss eat a world record ten and a half kilos of the stuff per person per annum – roughly one ordinary-sized bar for every single person, every day of the year. Conscripts in the Swiss army get free chocolate, wrapped in special foil bearing the Swiss flag, and adults bring each other chocolate as a dinner-party gift.

Swiss chocolate is held by many aficionados to be the best in the world, rich with scrupulously high levels of expensive cocoa butter, super-smooth, and above all creamy – the industry imports most ingredients except milk, which comes in fresh from the clover-munching Alpine herds.

Chocolate is **seasonal** in Switzerland, with the usual Easter bunnies padded out during the year with chocolate chestnuts and chocolate mushrooms in autumn, and chocolate flowers in spring. Chocolate is **regional**, too, with chocolatiers in the Jura making presentation boxes of chocolate watches, Bern producing elaborate chocolate bears, Geneva turning out stacks of little chocolate *marmites* (cauldrons full of marzipan "vegetables") for the Escalade festival each December, and Zürich making miniature chocolate *Bööggs* for the Sechseläuten spring festival.

Switzerland has had since 1819 to perfect its chocolate-making, and these days there are three big names: **Nestlé** is the biggest, having taken over most Swiss competitors (and many international ones too); **Suchard**, now owned by Philip Morris, remains well respected; but perhaps **Lindt** has the edge, still an independent concern with its own famous **Sprüngli** outlets in Zürich. Even if the chichi chocolatiers of Geneva, Basel and Zürich are beyond your means, a bar of two of Lindt is worth the indulgence.

DRINK

Swiss **cafés** – open from breakfast onwards – often sell alcohol and might also be called **bars**, although the latter tend to open their doors for late-afternoon and evening business only. Most people just pop in and pop out – a coffee in the morning, a quick beer – and tend not to while away hours in cafés (other than in Ticino, where relaxed afternoon people-watching is a favourite pastime). Around the country, daytime places for tea and cakes are dubbed **tearooms**, or left as nameless nooks attached to a *Konditorei, pâtisserie* or *confiserie, pasticceria*. Other than ordinary **pubs**, drinking venues vary according to region. A cosy *Bierstube* or *Stübli* – replete with wood beams and Swiss kitsch – is the evening meeting place of choice in both city and village in German-speaking Switzerland, while in Romandie and Ticino pavement cafés are more common.

As well as normal espresso, cappuccino and the rest, **coffee** has some local variations: in German-speaking areas *Kaffee creme*, coffee with sugar and cream, is popular, as is *Milchkaffee*, with fresh milk. Ask for *Kaffee fertig* and you'll get coffee with Schnapps. In Romandie, *café renversée* is the local name for a frothy French-style *café au lait*. **Tea** (*Tee, thé, tè*) has its usual variety of styles, with or without milk, or, most refreshingly, as iced tea (*Eistee, thé froid, tè freddo*) in summer. A herbal tea is a *Krautentee; tisane* or *infusion; tisana*. With most Swiss tap-water purer than the bottled stuff, **mineral water** (*Mineralwasser, eau minérale, acqua minerale*) is only worth paying for if you fancy it sparkling (*mit Kohlensäure, gazeuse, gassata*). **Soft drinks** comprise all the familiar brands, aside from a hugely popular flavoured fizzy soda called Rivella, that tastes quite pleasant until you discover that it's made from milk serum.

BEER AND SPIRITS

Beer (*Bier, bière, birra*) varies from region to region, with breweries such as Feldschlösschen in

Basel or Cardinal in Fribourg supplying their local area. Most local beers on draught (*vom Fass, à la pression, alla pressione*) are flavourful but unremarkable lager-type brews, always served with a sizeable head of foam. The standard measure (*Stange, pression, birra*) is three decilitres (3dl), which costs about Fr.3–4, or you can ask for a *Grosses Bier, demi, birra grande*, which will either turn up a half litre of the same, or possibly a 0.58-litre bottle. There's also a 2dl measure universally known, for some reason, as a *Herrgöttli*. A *panaché* is a mixed beer-lemonade shandy. Most bars also have a choice of familiar bottled beers from around Europe. Alcoholic **cider** is *suure Most, cidre, sidro* – but if you leave the "*suure*" off in Swiss-German you may end up with non-alcoholic apple-juice, or *Süssmost*, instead.

With extensive fruit cultivation in many areas, Switzerland has plenty of **distilled spirits** or liquor (*Schnapps, eau de vie, aquavite*) to choose from, king of which must be powerful *Kirsch* (cherry spirit) from Zug and around Lake Luzern. Plums and quetsches go to make *Zwetschgenwasser* or *eau de vie de quetsche*. A kind of mini-plum known as a *damassine*, which was reputedly brought back from Damascus by a crusading knight and which now grows only in the Ajoie region of Canton Jura, is distilled into a delectably fragrant *eau de vie* also called *Damassine*; it's sold only at the distillery itself and the Jura tourist office in Saignelégier, and is well worth making the journey for. Apple-spirits turn up as *Träsch, Gravensteiner* and many more, while Valaisian pears go to make aromatic *Williamine*. The Ticino nurtures its own, quite unique range of *grappa*, a heady firewater made from grape-skins.

WINE

Wine is often referred to as Switzerland's best-kept secret, since viticulture is flourishing, quality and standards are high, annual production regularly hits 200 million bottles, but – in the usual Swiss way – many wines don't get beyond the borders of their canton (just one percent goes for export).

Even the simplest restaurants and bars will have wine, both on a winelist (*Weinkarte, carte des vins, carta dei vini*) and – much more affordably – as *Offene Wein, vin ouvert, vino aperto*, a handful of house reds and whites chalked up on a board and sold by the decilitre. Standard measures are 1dl and 2dl, which come to you in glass-es; and 3dl and 5dl, which come in a small carafe. Around Fr.3–6 per decilitre is normal.

Switzerland's best-known wines come from the steeply terraced vineyards of the **Valais**. Of the whites, bright and floral *Fendant* is king, named for the ripeness of its golden Chasselas grapes, which, when pressed, *se fendre*, or split, rather than squish. Other Valais whites include fruity and alcoholic *Johannisberg*, sweeter *Ermitage*, and *Malvoisie* from the Pinot Gris grape (the late harvests, marked *flétrie*, or shrivelled, are particularly sought-after). Valais's reds, led by *Dôle*, a blend of Pinot Noir and Gamay grapes, are equally respected. Bottles of 100 percent Pinot Noir have recently begun to make an appearance, but the connoisseur's Valais red is a *Humagne Rouge*. *Dôle blanche* is one of Switzerland's few rosé wines.

Until the mid-twentieth century, **Vaud** was Switzerland's leading wine-growing canton, and the vineyards lining the **Côte** and **Lavaux** shores of Lake Geneva (see p.131) hold some of the most picturesque walks in the whole country. Chasselas is ubiquitous, and with their concentration on this one white grape to the exclusion of all others, Vaudois *vignerons*, particularly those at Dézaley, St Saphorin and Epesses, produce some of the best of all Swiss wines. In the **Chablais** region southeast of Montreux are the vineyards of Château d'Aigle, home to a wine museum, and Yvorne. Canton **Geneva** also has extensive Chasselas vines – the Genevois *Perlan* is more affordable than its Vaudois competitors – and low-priced Gamays have recently taken on imported French Beaujolais with some success.

Around **Neuchâtel** and Biel/Bienne, the combination of a plate of fresh lake fish and a bottle of local white is unbeatable; there are dozens of local producers, and each estate brings forth something different from the Chasselas grapes that still dominate. In the German-speaking north and east, though, Chasselas gives way to the Riesling-Sylvaner grape, perhaps best known on the "**Gold Coast**" of Lake Zürich's eastern shore that basks in the afternoon sunshine. The Rhine shores at **Schaffhausen** are mostly given over to Pinot Noir, while only the warm southern *Föhn* wind allows Pinot Noir grapes to flourish in an area known as the **Bündner Herrschaft** in Graubünden, around Maienfeld and particularly Fläsch in St Gallen, and Liechtenstein. **Ticino**'s vine growing is dominated by Merlot, and almost every village has its own brand of *Merlot del Ticino*. The Sopraceneri region, north of Bellinzona, is less successful than the

Sottoceneri, around Lugano and especially Mendrisio, but you'd have to struggle to find a truly bad specimen anywhere.

POST, PHONES AND EMAIL

Post offices – identified by a yellow logo and *Die Post, La Poste* or *La Posta* – generally open Monday to Friday 7.30am–noon & 1.30–6.30pm, and Saturday 8–11am, although watch out for slight regional variations and restricted hours in smaller branches. Some main offices stay open over the lunch break.

For both domestic and international post, there's a two-tier system. **A–Priority post** is delivered next day in Switzerland, within five days to Europe, and within ten days worldwide (both of the latter by airmail); **B–Economy post** takes three days domestic, up to ten days to Europe, and up to eight weeks by surface delivery worldwide. Currently sending a postcard or a 20g letter by A/B post costs Fr.1.10/0.90 to Europe, or Fr.1.80/1.10 worldwide. Liechtenstein has stamps which look different but cost the same. For all A post, you should write a prominent "A" with a box around it above the address, or ask for one of the blue stickers.

Poste restante is available at any post office: all you need to know is that town's four-figure postal code. We've given these in the guide chapters covering major cities and resorts, and they're displayed outside each post office, but Swiss phonebooks and *www.post.ch* list the lot. The correct format is, for example: Your Name, Poste Restante, CH-3920 Zermatt ("CH" is the standard postal designation for Switzerland). Liechtenstein shares the Swiss postal system, but uses its own prefix: Your Name, Poste Restante, FL-9490 Vaduz. To minimize confusion at pickup, you should ask anyone writing to you to print your surname in underlined capitals, and include only one initial. If you want to receive mail at a smaller countryside office in the German-speaking part of the country (where the term "Poste Restante" may be less understood), you should get your correspondents to add the German equivalent – *Postlagernde Briefe* – to the address. You need your passport to pick up your mail, and the service is always free. Uncollected mail is returned to sender after 30 days.

PHONES

Another first for Switzerland: the country has more public **phones** per square kilometre (some 60,000 of them) than anywhere else in the world. There are always at least one or two phones (sometimes ranks of them) outside post offices and at train stations, and invariably you'll find that the most remote mountain refuge or country cottage has a phone or two, maybe a fax as well. The former public utility **Swisscom** was privatized in 1998, and although it currently retains its monopoly over land-lines and local calls, and still owns and operates all the public phones, there is now rapidly increasing competition in the long-distance and international call markets, and prices are dropping.

Note that phoning direct from your **hotel room** to anywhere can add outrageous surcharges of 100 percent or more onto the cost of the call.

CALLING FROM SWITZERLAND

A few ancient **public phones** still accept coins, but the majority take only Swisscom phonecards ("**taxcards**"), available from post offices, many

TELEPHONE NUMBERS

Emergency numbers

Police	☎117
Fire, accidents and life-threatening situations	☎118
Ambulance	☎144
Helicopter rescue (REGA)	☎1414
Poisoning centre	☎01/251 51 51

Useful numbers

*Avalanche bulletins	☎187
*Weather forecast	☎162
*Speaking clock	☎161
International operator	☎1141
Alarm call	☎150
The Samaritans (crisis line)	☎143

in local languages only

DIALLING CODES

The dialling codes for individual Swiss towns and cities are provided throughout the guide. When dialling the codes below, don't include the initial zero that precedes a regional code.

To Switzerland

From Britain and New Zealand	☎00 + 41
From North America	☎011 + 41
From Australia	☎0011 + 41

To Liechtenstein

From Britain and New Zealand	☎00 + 423
From North America	☎011 + 423
From Australia	☎0011 + 423

From Switzerland and Liechtenstein

To Britain	☎00 + 44
To Ireland	☎00 + 353
To North America	☎00 + 1
To Australia	☎00 + 61
To New Zealand	☎00 + 64

hotels, newsagents, kiosks, train station ticket counters, and some vending machines in Fr.5, Fr.10, Fr.20 and Fr.50 denominations. Pressing button L on the phone switches the display to English.

For calls **within Switzerland**, note that numbers beginning ☎156, ☎157, ☎0900 and ☎0901 are more expensive than normal; ☎155 and ☎0800 are free; ☎0842 and ☎0848 are charged as local calls. Domestic rates are highest on weekdays between 8am and 5pm, and between 7pm and 9pm, but the minimum charge at any time is still a whopping 60c. For the domestic operator call ☎111 (minimum charge Fr.2), but you can search the complete Swiss phone directory in English on the self-explanatory *Teleguide* screens in phonebooths for free.

To call **internationally**, there's already a wide choice of carriers. It's no problem to use a Swisscom taxcard to dial internationally direct from phonebooths, but this ties you to Swisscom's prices, which are some of the highest in Europe. You'd do better to go for one of Swisscom's many competitors, who can give you equal service for a fraction of the cost. The two best carriers at the time of writing were **diAx** and **Teleline** – but you have to ask for their taxcards (in Fr.20, Fr.50 and Fr.100 denominations) by name, and even then they may take some sniffing out. Some kiosks may stock them but not know what they're for (beware of being sold cards intended for use in Swiss mobiles, which look the same, are produced by the same companies, but which are useless for public phones), while others may not stock anything other than Swisscom cards.

You can also use **credit cards** in public phones (Visa, Mastercard, Amex, etc), with no surcharges – you're charged only for the call cost, but have to put up with Swisscom's inflated rates. Slide the card in, then pull it out straightaway, and dial.

CALLING FROM LIECHTENSTEIN

In 1999, as part of a diplomatic and trade agreement, Swisscom lost the right to provide phone services in **Liechtenstein**, which now has its own phone company – Telecom FL – although all the public phones look and work the same as those in Switzerland, and you can still use Swisscom taxcards in them. Local calls within Liechtenstein are straightforward. However, whereas formerly the whole of Liechtenstein was covered by a Swiss area code (the now-defunct ☎075), these days dialling between Liechtenstein and Switzerland counts as an **international** call. Many of the pre-paid discount taxcards may not work from Liechtenstein.

FAX

You can type a short **fax** on the screens in public phonebooths, and send it within Switzerland for Fr.1, to Europe for Fr.1.50, or worldwide for Fr.2; you must insert a Swisscom taxcard into the phone in order for the cost to be deducted from it.

Otherwise, if your hotel can't help out, main post offices have phone sections where you can send a paper fax for about Fr.2 plus the cost of the call.

EMAIL AND THE INTERNET

Access to the **Internet** is everywhere, with cybercafés or public-access terminals in most towns and resorts, either free or roughly Fr.2–4 for 10mins. City train stations often have a public stand-up coin- or credit-card-operated Internet terminal, and you can even type in and send a short email from the screens in phonebooths for Fr.1.50 (Swisscom taxcard needed), although you can't pick up any email this way.

More difficulties arise if you're travelling with a **laptop** or palmtop, and have all the necessary paraphernalia to connect but just need a phoneline. Although some Swiss phones use the US-style RJ-11, most of them – and the majority in hotel rooms – use either an idiosyncratic chunky square jack or (rarely) an ancient four-pin plug. None uses the British-style design. Business hotels generally keep a supply of adaptors and leads for lending to guests; otherwise, you'll have to seek advice from an electronics store. Check out *www.kropla.com* for invaluable advice on how to proceed.

THE MEDIA

In general, the Swiss have a healthy disregard for the mass media, and watch much less TV than the European average – in fact, the German-speaking Swiss watch least of all. To make up for it they read more, and more locally oriented, newspapers than anyone else in Europe.

SWISS TV AND RADIO

Switzerland has at least six terrestrial **TV stations** available everywhere, two channels each from Schweizer Fernsehen (SF), Télévision Suisse Romande (TSR) and Televisione Svizzera Italiana (TSI), plus a handful of national channels from mostly German-speaking private operators, and plenty of local stations for each area. None is what you might call glittering, offering an undemanding diet of chat-shows, game-shows, made-

for-TV movies (dubbed) and lots of local news and local interest programming.

Each language area of the country has three broad-coverage regional **radio stations**, one channel devoted to each of news, classical music and popular music, although stations from neighbouring countries are easy to pick up as well. Aside from regular programmes of traditional Alpine music and alphorn recitals on the Swiss-German DRS-1, Romandie's Couleur-Trois is the most entertaining station by miles, playing consistently good cutting-edge dance music from France, the US and the UK. The German-language equivalent, DRS-3, has its moments, but is much less adventurous. Both are on varying frequencies depending on where you are, but generally stick around 104–107FM. Italian-language music stations are eurobland in the extreme. Switzerland also has more than forty local radio stations catering to various communities around the country. **Swiss Radio International** broadcasts news and analysis in English on short wave at 6.165MHz at breakfast time and the evening, and at 9.535MHz at lunchtime, and is also on cable.

THE SWISS PRESS

Switzerland has a clutch of **newspapers** – more than 200 nationwide – but almost without exception they're parochial local news-sheets, reporting cantonal and municipal affairs in some detail, but relegating the rest of Switzerland, let alone the world, to a few inside columns. It's a mark of differing attitudes within the country that whereas French-speaking Swiss regularly turn to Paris's *Le Monde* or *Libération* for opinion from beyond their own borders, and the Ticinesi are happy to jump on the coat-tails of Milan's *Corriere della Sera*, newspapers from Germany have barely any readers at all amongst the proudly Swiss-minded German-speakers south of the border.

Zürich's *Neue Zürcher Zeitung*, or *NZZ*, is the best known of Swiss newspapers. Conservative and highbrow in the extreme – you'll never see a photo on its close-printed front page – it nonetheless has gained its reputation by reporting Swiss and world events with scrupulously high journalistic standards. If the *NZZ* has a francophone equivalent, it's the much more dynamic *Le Temps*, published in Geneva and formed from the 1998 merger of the *Journal de Genève* (one of Switzerland's oldest newspapers) and the *Nouveau Quotidien* (one of its youngest). Fiercely pro-EU, with consistently progressive stances on social and political issues, it's the only Swiss newspaper that makes it onto Paris newsstands each morning. Otherwise, the field is thin, though Zürich's quality *Tages Anzeiger* offers a lively alternative to the NZZ's ponderousness. Switzerland's biggest-selling paper is *Blick*, a blaring, reactionary rag that regularly espouses anti-immigration and anti-asylum causes.

Of the **weeklies**, *Die Weltwoche* offers quality, left-leaning world news analysis, while the *Wochen Zeitung*, or *WOZ*, has a radical alternative agenda, pushing green issues particularly

strongly and packaging once a month the German translation of the highly respected journal of world affairs *Le Monde Diplomatique*. Lausanne's *L'Hebdo* leads the field of francophone weeklies, but lacks any kind of newsy bite.

The Arts Council of Switzerland *Pro Helvetia* twice a year publishes *Passages*, a heavily intellectual compendium of musings on Swiss culture and society, interviews with Swiss artists and short fiction, all translated into English. Subscriptions are free if you live outside Switzerland: contact Pro Helvetia, Information and Press, Postfach, CH-8024 Zürich (☎01/267 71 71, fax 267 71 06, *mlarre@pro-helvetia.ch*).

FOREIGN MEDIA

You'll find most British **newspapers** on sale the same day (from 3pm) in main train stations and some city kiosks in Geneva, Lausanne, Zürich, Basel and Bern, as well as in well-touristed resorts such as Zermatt, Gstaad and Interlaken, and a day late in some other towns. Prices for the normal papers are extraordinary – up to Fr.5.50 for the broadsheets – but you can find *The Guardian's* condensed European edition, the *International Herald Tribune*, *USA Today*, and a handful of financial heavyweights for less.

If a hotel room has a **TV** it's almost certain to be hooked up to cable or satellite, giving you the dubious pleasure of 30 or 40 channels covering the panoply of European languages, plus a few more exotic offerings such as Turkish or Arabic. CNN is the only English-language dead cert wherever you are, although many places have BBC Prime, showing British drama and comedy.

As for **radio**, the BBC World Service is on 648kHz medium wave more or less all day and most of the night, but in practice it seems that the mountains can quite often block reception, forcing you onto short wave instead (12.095, 9.760, 9.410, 7.325, 6.195, 5.975 or 3.955MHz). If your hotel has cable or satellite TV, it will also receive a host of crystal-clear radio stations, including one or all of BBC World Service, domestic Radios 1 to 4, various British music stations and Voice of America (although these may not be piped into every room).

BUSINESS HOURS, MUSEUMS AND PUBLIC HOLIDAYS

Switzerland's reputation for calmness and domesticity is borne out by its down-to-earth attitude to the consumer revolution: in contrast to most of the rest of the Western world, Swiss laws on strictly limited opening times reflect universal public concern to uphold the rights of serving staff at the expense of consumers. The classic example of this, which will raise the eyebrows of hard-nosed Londoners, New Yorkers and Sydneysiders alike, is that banks, post offices, shops, supermarkets – just about everything – in even quite large Swiss towns shut between noon and 2pm, to allow staff to go home for lunch.

Shop opening hours are customarily Mon–Fri 9am–noon & 2–6.30pm, Sat 8.30am–noon, although it's becoming more common in the bigger cities to ignore the lunch break and also stay open on Saturdays until 4pm; the flipside is that many places then take Monday morning off. Quiet Sundays are sacrosanct. Most towns operate universal late opening until 9pm for one day a week, generally Thursday (Friday in Graubünden). Shops and cafés in the subterranean malls at train stations stay open daily, and also close later.

Cafés fall into two broad categories. Those that open in the morning for coffee and breakfasts might then close when the shops shut, at about 6 or 6.30pm. Some, though, open for lunch or in mid-afternoon, and then metamorphose into **bars** until midnight or so. Those that serve full meals (which is most of them) will only do so at the customary mealtimes: roughly noon to 2pm and 6 to 10pm. Outside those hours, you'll generally be able to find only snacks. Formal **restaurants** keep to the same mealtimes, closing altogether in-between times. Closing times of all establishments are regulated by each individual municipality: Lausanne, for instance, carouses until 1am, Lugano insists on midnight, while Bern plumps for 12.30am. All places can stay open an hour later than normal on Friday and Saturday nights.

MUSEUM ADMISSION

Virtually every museum and public attraction in the country is open on Sundays and closed on Mondays; a few also take Tuesdays off.

If you're planning to visit even a handful of museums in Switzerland, you'd do well to pick up a **Swiss Museum Passport** (*Schweizer Museumspass, Passeport Musées suisses, Passaporto Musei svizzeri*) which gives free entry to some 250 museums, galleries and castles around the country. You can get one from Switzerland Tourism before you go, from larger tourist offices in Switzerland or over the counter from any of the museums in the scheme (all of which display a sticker). The pass, plus a little booklet giving addresses and opening days of all the places included, costs Fr.30 for a month (students Fr.25), or you can pay Fr.5 extra to have up to five children included on the same pass. Covering virtually every significant attraction in the country, it can easily pay for itself in a weekend of gallery-hopping; there are just a few unmissable institutions which aren't part of the scheme (Zürich's Kunsthaus and Basel's Fondation Beyeler stick out like a sore thumb by their absence). We've indicated those museums and attractions offering free admission with the museum pass as "SMP" in the guide. For more information, contact the administration at Hornbachstrasse 50, CH-8034 Zürich (☎01/389 84 56, *www.museums.ch/pass*).

PUBLIC HOLIDAYS

The **national** holidays – when almost everything is closed – are listed in the box, but they're only

SWISS PUBLIC HOLIDAYS

January 1 – New Year's Day, *Neujahr, Nouvel An, Capodanno*

March/April – Good Friday, *Karfreitag, Vendredi saint, Venerdì Santo*

– Easter Monday, *Ostermontag, lundi de Pâques, Lunedì di Pasqua*

May – Ascension Day, *Auffahrt/Christi Himmelfahrt, Ascension, Ascensione*

May/June – Whit Monday, *Pfingstmontag, lundi de Pentecôte, Lunedì di Pentecoste*

August 1 – Swiss National Day, *Nationalfeiertag, Fête Nationale, Festa nazionale* (public institutions, and some shops and banks, closed)

December 25 – Christmas Day, *Weihnachten, Noël, Natale*

December 26 – Boxing Day, *Stefanstag, Saint-Etienne, Santo Stefano*

part of the story. Most cantons supplement these with a handful of often religious holidays of their own, which can tie in with local festivals: various Catholic cantons, for instance, observe various saints' days, and Ticino manages to authorize 17 annual holidays for itself. Common ones include January 6 (Epiphany, *Dreikönigstag, Epiphanie, Epifania*), May 1 (Labour Day, *Tag der Arbeit, Fête du Travail, Festa del Lavoro*), Corpus Christi in late May, August 15 (Assumption, *Mariä Himmelsfahrt, Assomption, Assunzione*), and November 1 (All Saints' Day, *Allerheiligen, Toussaint, Ognissanti*).

Look out also for the seasonal pageants centred in various cities, and the often tumultuous celebrations of **carnival** on and around Mardi Gras in mid-February, which – amidst raucous partying in Luzern and Basel in particular – can often throw an unauthorized spanner in the works of shop opening times; for more, see p.68.

IN LIECHTENSTEIN

Liechtenstein keeps the same holidays as Switzerland, except that August 1 is a normal working day and the National Day is instead August 15. May 1 (Labour Day) is a full public holiday.

FESTIVALS AND ANNUAL EVENTS

Running counter to the dour national stereotype, Switzerland in fact has masses of festivals (*Feiertage, jours féries, festività*), held in towns and villages all over the country for the slightest excuse, from celebrating the joys of carrots up to St Moritz's inimitable horse-racing-on-ice extravaganza. Listing them all would be impossible, and anyway would ruin the experience – still well within the bounds of possibility – of stumbling by chance onto some small Swiss village's unadvertised annual knees-up of folk-dancing, street-barbecuing and general merriment. Switzerland Tourism's free annual "Events of Switzerland" brochure outlines hundreds of pageants big and small.

In Catholic areas – French-, German-, Italian- and Romansh-speaking – each town or region keeps one day a year to honour the local patron saint, and these are jovial local events, by, with and for the townspeople. Equally, the many local festivals celebrating food or wine are heartfelt community experiences, with not a thought of tourism in mind. Filling out the calendar are many large or international events, often themed around sport, music or art, which are primarily moneyspinners but which, with Switzerland's pulling power, can be graced by more than just a handful of world-class performers.

In **music**, the biggest show is July's famous Montreux Jazz Festival, televised around the world and these days featuring as much rock, dance and world music as jazz and blues. Massive open-air weekends in July at Bern and Nyon are regular stopoffs on the European festival circuit, and Bern's own orthodox jazz festival pulls in top artists year after year. Zürich's Street Parade attracts half a million techno revellers from all over Europe. In classical music, the Luzern International Festival each August is one of the premier events of its kind, with opera at Avenches and summer performance cycles at Verbier, Gstaad and Sion no less stellar. The Locarno International **Film** Festival is one of the top five in the world.

Of the more **traditional festivals**, carnival, in mid-February, features huge street parties in Luzern, Basel and Bern in particular, with Zürich,

JANUARY

early Basel – Vogel Gryff: *traditional costumed dance and drum festival*

mid Wengen – World Cup downhill ski-racing on the Lauberhorn

late Mürren – Inferno giant-slalom ski race

late Château d'Oex – international hot-air ballooning week

FEBRUARY

early Lötschental VS – Roitschäggättä: *elaborate masked parades.*

early St Moritz – horse-racing on the frozen lake

mid St Moritz – toboggan competitions on the Cresta Run

mid around Switzerland – Carnival: *the biggest events, which run contiguously, are in Luzern (six days, from the Thursday before Mardi Gras up to Mardi Gras night), Bern (two days, beginning on the Thursday evening after Mardi Gras), and Basel (three days, beginning at 4am on the Monday after Mardi Gras). Many towns and villages celebrate Carnival, at various times from mid-February until early March.*

APRIL

mid Visp VS – traditional Valaisian cow fights

mid Zürich – Sechseläuten: *traditional spring festival, with parades and fireworks*

mid Nyon – International Documentary Film Festival

late Appenzell – Landsgemeinde: *the annual session of public voting on local issues, with residents in traditional dress*

late Lausanne – Fête du Soleil: *live bands, open-air restaurants and markets*

MAY

early Glarus – Landsgemeinde: *the annual session of public voting on local issues, with residents in traditional dress*

early Bern International Jazz Festival

mid Aproz VS – the cantonal cow-fighting champions' meeting

JUNE

early Appenzell, Gruyères and many villages in central and eastern Switzerland – Celebration of the cattle's ascent to Alpine pastures

until Sept Interlaken – open-air performances of Schiller's play *William Tell*

until July Zürich Festival: *theatre, opera, music and art*

mid Tour de Suisse cycle race

late Ascona Jazz Festival

late Winterthur – Albanifäscht: *popular music festival*

JULY

all month Avenches Opera Festival: *performances in the Roman amphitheatre*

early Montreux Jazz Festival: *everyone from Alannis Morrisette to Femi Kuti*

early Lausanne – Festival de la Cité: *free open-air performances and music*

early Gstaad – Swiss Open tennis tournament

4 Geneva – US Independence Day celebrations: *the biggest outside the US*

Lugano and smaller towns also mounting parades. Spring festivals in Zürich and Lausanne, and autumn harvest festivals all round the country, keep alive traditions of costume and cuisine stretching back to the Middle Ages. Some of the moveable events worth looking out for include **Schwingen**, traditional Swiss wrestling that's hugely popular in rural areas and is generally accompanied by traditional markets, beer-quaffing and hearty sausage-

mid St Ursanne JU – Medieval Festival: *medieval costumes, music and food*

mid Bern – Gurten Festival: *mass hilltop rock festival*

late Nyon – Paléo Music Festival: *huge summer rock and dance happening*

late Verbier Festival and Academy: *world-renowned classical soloists and conductors*

until Sept Gstaad – Music Summer: *series of top classical performances*

until Sept Sion – Tibor Varga Music Festival: *classical, focused on the violin*

AUGUST

1st Swiss National Day: *fireworks, folkloric shows, parades and more, in every corner of the country*

early Geneva – Fêtes de Genève: *fireworks, parades and concerts*

early Zürich – Street Parade: *immense citywide techno/dance gathering*

early Locarno International Film Festival

early Saignelégier JU – Marché Concours: *horse-riding festival*

15 Liechtenstein National Day

mid Montreux – International Classical Music Festival

until mid-Sept Luzern – International Music Festival: *one of Europe's leading classical music events, with soloists and orchestras of world renown*

late Chur – City Festival

late Lausanne – International Rollerskate and Inline Championships

late Willisau (LU) Jazz Festival: *experimental and modern jazz groups from around the world, performing in the Luzern countryside*

SEPTEMBER

early Zürich – Theater Spektakel: *international open-air drama festival*

early Bern – Old Town Festival

mid Fribourg – La Bénichon: *traditional Thanksgiving festival*

late around Switzerland – Winegrowers' festivals: *local village and town celebrations of the grape harvest, especially in cantons Vaud, Valais, Neuchâtel, Bern, Schaffhausen and Ticino*

OCTOBER

early Charmey FR, Appenzell and many villages in central and eastern Switzerland – Celebration of the cattle's descent from Alpine pastures

late Basel Autumn Fair: *traditional food fair held since 1470*

NOVEMBER

early Vevey VD and Porrentruy JU – St Martin's market: *festivals devoted to sausages, ham and pork*

early Aarau – Rüeblimärt: *festival devoted to carrots*

late Bern – Zibelemärit (Onion Market): *festival devoted to onions*

late Luzern International Piano Festival

DECEMBER

10–12 Geneva – Fête de l'Escalade: *celebrating Geneva's independence*

mid Zürich – Lichterschwimmen: *candles floated down the River Limmat*

31 Urnäsch AR – masked parade for St Sylvester

feasting (see also p.74). Weekends devoted to *Schwingen* championships take place all over the centre and east of the country at various dates between April and September – either ask at tourist offices or keep your eyes peeled for posters and flyers. There are also many **yodelling** events through the springtime, culminating in the annual Swiss Alpine Yodelling Championships, held in early July in a different town each year.

TROUBLE AND THE POLICE

Compared to most Europeans, the Swiss are law-abiding to a fault, rendering even the minimal police presence superfluous. There's only a small force of plain-clothes federal police (*Polizei, police, polizia*), since most police duties are managed by the cantonal authorities, all of which maintain uniformed, armed police. Towns and cities also have their own armed police, operating in conjunction with the cantonal force.

It's very rare you'll even see a police officer in Switzerland, although you may come across one or two directing the traffic. Nonetheless, Swiss police are nothing of a soft touch, and have drawn recent approbation from Amnesty International for their heavy-handed approach to foreigners, asylum seekers and Swiss citizens of non-European descent in particular, with random

The nationwide police emergency number is ☎117.

street searches and "unjustified use of violence" cited.

If you do come into contact with the police, they'll want to see your **passport**, which you're obliged to carry at all times. Ordinary traffic offences will be dealt with swiftly and courteously – as long as you pay the fine – although police officers, especially outside the cities, may not speak any English and so, should there be any disputes, they may insist you accompany them to the nearest police station to have all the necessaries explained. As across Europe, urban Switzerland has a serious **hard-drug** problem. All drugs are illegal, but curiously, drug laws are enforced less rigorously in the German-speaking cities than elsewhere: limited personal cannabis smoking in Bern and Zürich is usually ignored (except when there's a blitz on), but anywhere else you can expect fines and major hassle. Possession of more than a joint or two's worth of cannabis, or of any other drug at all, will land you in serious trouble, involving either prison or deportation plus a criminal record. Expect no sympathy from your embassy.

If you're unfortunate enough to be **robbed** you should always go to the nearest police station to get a report filled out (you'll need it for your insurance if nothing else). It may take hours to complete all the paperwork required.

SPORTS AND OUTDOOR ACTIVITIES

Switzerland is heaven for indulging in sports and outdoorsiness of all kinds, and since the Swiss themselves are very active, this ensures that facilities abound in all areas of sport and exercise for literally all ages and abilities (the number of Swiss grandparents who spend their "declining years" hiking mountain trails is amazing). Safety is taken very seriously and standards are very high.

WALKING

Swiss mountains are among the most dramatic and challenging of all the Alpine ranges, but you don't have to be a skilled mountaineer or climber to enjoy an active holiday among them, for Switzerland contains some of Europe's finest **walking** terrain, with enough variety to suit every taste. In the northwest of the country, for example, the rolling Jura hills are heavily wooded, but with open meadows that provide long views across the lowlands to Alpine giants. The Bernese Alps, with notoriously savage peaks such as the Eiger, Schreckhorn and Finsteraarhorn, harbour a glacial heartland but they also feature gentle valleys, pastoral ridges and charming alp hamlets with well-marked trails weaving through. On the south side of the Rhône Valley the Pennine Alps are burdened with snow and glaciers, yet walkers' paths lead along their moraines to give a taste of adventure without overtly courting danger. By contrast the mountains of Canton Ticino projecting south into Italy are almost completely snow- and ice-free in summer, and you'll find a wonderland of trails among their modest, lake-jewelled peaks.

In major tourist areas walkers can use chairlifts, gondolas and cable-cars in summer and autumn to reach high and otherwise remote trails, while rustic inns and a network of **Alpine or mountain huts** (*Hütte; refuge; rifugio, cabane* or *capanna*) provide rudimentary dormitory accommodation, and often meals too, for those who plan to make multi-day walking tours.

Paths are well maintained, and always clearly marked with regular yellow signposts displaying the names of major landmark destinations, often with an estimate of the time it takes to walk to them. Most signposts also have a white plate giving the name and altitude of the spot you're standing on. There are two major types of path. A *Wanderweg, chemin de randonnée pédestre, sentiero escursionistico* remains either in the valley or travels the hillsides at a modest altitude, is sometimes surfaced and will be graded at a relatively gentle angle. **Yellow** diamonds or pointers show the continuation of the route. (You may also spot some cultural trails – old pilgrims' roads and the like – signposted in **brown**.) A *Bergweg, chemin de montagne, sentiero di montagna* is a mountain path which runs higher or steeper and can be quite demanding, often rough, narrow and sometimes fading if not in regular use. They're marked with the same yellow signposts, but with a **red and white** pointer instead of yellow. Waymarks along a mountain path are marked with similar white-red-white bars, and you may occasionally come across cairns directing the way across boulder slopes, or where poor visibility could create difficulties. Higher, extremely tough Alpine trails, marked in **blue**, are only for those accompanied by a mountain guide and carrying specialist equipment.

For more information, and general guidance about walking, contact the Swiss Hiking Federation, Im Hirshalm 49, CH-4125 Riehen (☎061/601 15 35). Switzerland Tourism publishes a brochure "Ways to Switzerland", introducing and mapping six major long-distance hiking routes of particular cultural interest, including the network of Roman roads in Switzerland, the

"Chemins de St Jacques", followed for centuries by pilgrims heading from Germany to Santiago de Compostela in Spain, and trans-Alpine mule-tracks used by traders in former ages.

PLANNING YOUR WALK

No one should venture among the mountains, whatever level of walking is proposed, without consulting a good **map** (see p.28). Local shops and tourist offices usually have a selection on offer, and the latter sometimes also publish their own walkers' maps with suggested routes and times given on the reverse. On occasion **guided walks** are arranged by tourist offices in mountain areas, which may be free of charge for guests staying in local hotels. A series of excellent English-language **guidebooks** for walkers covering the Bernese Alps, Central Switzerland, Engadine, Ticino, and the Valais, plus several long-distance Alpine walks, are published by Cicerone Press in the UK (2 Police Sq, Milnthorpe, Cumbria LA7 7PY; ☎01539/562069).

Always check the **weather** forecast before setting out. The local tourist office or mountain guides' bureau invariably displays a two- or three-day forecast. Needless to say, do not venture to high altitudes if bad weather is expected. In any case, though, it's sensible to take a pullover or fleece and a waterproof jacket as minimum protection even if you simply plan to take a cable-car ride followed by a short stroll. On more ambitious outings it is essential to be properly equipped with wind- and waterproof clothing and good footwear. Trainers may be adequate for short valley walks, but for tackling steep hillsides and mountain paths, walking boots with ankle support and hard-wearing soles are indispensable.

ONE-DAY WALKS

Never embark on a walk that under normal conditions cannot be completed **well before dark**. Reasonably fit walkers carrying a light rucksack should be able to manage 4.5kph (2mph) on the flat, plus an additional hour for every 350m of ascent. Carry food for the day, including emergency rations, and at least one litre of water per person. Take extra care when crossing snow patches, exposed rocks and mountain streams. On some *Bergweg* routes, fixed ropes are provided as safeguards. Elsewhere there may be sections of metal ladder fitted to enable walkers to overcome a short stretch of rock. Always check these first before committing your weight to them. Do not stray onto glaciers and snowfields unless accompanied by a mountaineer experienced in glacier travel and with the necessary equipment to deal with crevasse rescue. And, perhaps the best advice of all is don't be too proud to turn back should the weather deteriorate or the route become difficult or dangerous.

MULTI-DAY WALKS

When tackling **hut-to-hut walks** the list of what to take with you increases. It is prudent to carry a map and compass – and to know how to use them. You should also take a first-aid kit, whistle and torch (flashlight) in case of emergencies. Leave a note of your planned itinerary and expected time of return with a responsible person who's staying behind in a fixed location, and when staying in mountain huts enter your route details in the book provided. If for some reason you can't reach the destination where you're expected, try to send a message ahead to prevent the mountain rescue team being called out. In an emergency the **International Distress Signal** is six short blasts on a whistle (or flashes with a torch), followed by a minute's pause. Repeat until you receive an answer – the response is three signals followed by a minute's silence.

Switzerland has no free mountain rescue service, and the cost of an accident can be extremely high. Standard travel **insurance** policies do not cover such emergencies, so if you are devoting all or most of your holiday to serious walking in the mountains, it's sensible to choose a policy which specifically covers mountain activity and includes emergency rescue.

Mountain huts provide simple accommodation for climbers and walkers, are invariably situated in remote and scenically spectacular locations and are owned either by local groups of the Swiss Alpine Club (SAC), other clubs, or by private companies or individuals. Many are staffed by a guardian during the summer months – usually from mid-June to mid-September – who will prepare simple meals and drinks. Mixed-sex dormitories with large, side-by-side sleeping platforms are the norm. Blankets and pillows, but not sheets, are supplied, so it's a good idea to take a sleeping bag liner (sheet sleeping bag) with you if you plan to use huts. Prices vary, but hover around Fr.25–30 for a bed, plus about the same again if you include dinner and breakfast.

Most huts have a phone and as a matter of courtesy you should phone ahead to book a place; we've listed numbers of the more popular and accessible huts throughout the book, but local tourist offices will have details of all of them, and they're also listed in a very useful book, *Schweizer Hüttenverzeichnis*, available throughout bookshops in Switzerland. The **Swiss Alpine Club** is at Monbijoustrasse 61, CH-3007 Bern (☎031/370 18 18, fax 370 18 00, *www.sac-cas.ch*), and every year their journal runs a complete listing of the 600 or so huts throughout Switzerland, both their own and those belonging to other Swiss climbing associations. Membership of an Alpine club in your home country may entitle you to reduced overnight charges in SAC huts, or you can join the SAC itself (Fr.70–120 for a year). Members of the British Mountaineering Council (BMC, 177–179 Burton Rd, Manchester M20 2BB; ☎0161/445 4747), the New Zealand Alpine Club (☎03/377 7595, fax 03/377 7594, *www.nzalpine.org.nz*), the Australian Sport Climbing Federation (☎03/9894 7897, fax 03/9894 3023, *http://spelean.com.au/ASCF/index.html*) and the Alpine Club of Canada (☎403/678-3200 ext 108, *www.alpineclubofcanada.ca*) can purchase a Reciprocal Rights Pass (Fr.40) from the Swiss Alpine Club on arrival in the country. The US has no national Alpine club.

SKIING AND WINTER SPORTS

It goes without saying that Switzerland is one of the best **winter sports** destinations in the world. Ski resorts of all grades, facilities, atmospheres and costs cover the country. The best-known, such as Zermatt, Wengen, Crans-Montana, Verbier, St Moritz, Davos and Klosters, need no introduction, but although they're the best equipped they're far from the end of the story. It's quite possible – especially for first-timers or relative novices – that less renowned resorts will turn out to be more rewarding; cheaper and less crowded, to start with, but also with a greater emphasis on the personal touch, if you're looking for lessons, and less of a daunting competitive edge as well. The invaluable *Good Skiing and Snowboarding Guide*, edited by Peter Hardy and Felice Eyston (Which Books, UK) and updated annually, is highly recommended.

These days you can often get better value for money skiing in Switzerland than in France or Italy. The general tenor of Swiss ski resorts is much more cosy and village-based than elsewhere, and although Switzerland is only now starting to catch up on investment in cable-cars and gondolas to ease peak-time queues, the country's resorts benefit from peaceful, mostly entirely natural Alpine runs set against some of the greatest mountain vistas to be seen anywhere.

Skiing is generally split into two varieties. Alpine or **downhill skiing** (*skifahren, ski alpin, sci*) gets all the glamour, and tends to be most expensive, while Nordic or **cross-country skiing** (*Ski Langlauf, Ski Wandern; ski de fond, ski nordique; sci di fondo*) is seen as much harder work for much less thrill. However, cross-country eliminates all the queues, most of the expensive equipment and all the hassle, it allows you to get way out into the countryside, and – for your body – is much less punishing and a much better workout. Prepared trails, known as *Loipen* or *loipes*, are laid on signposted routes fanning out from most resorts, with the cream of the crop in the Engadine Valley in Graubünden. The Swiss Ski Federation has plenty of information in English on cross-country skiing in Switzerland, and can be contacted at Haus des Skisports, Worbstrasse 52, Postfach 478, CH-3074 Muri bei Bern (☎031/950 61 11). **Snowboarding** is massively popular throughout the country.

The **winter season** runs from December to April with the busiest times clustered together in early January and mid-February: these peak times are when you'll pay most for ski passes and accommodation. The last week of March and first week of April are when you can take advantage of late snow and snap up deals on resort accommodation, since winter skiing is finished across the board by mid-April – though at altitudes above 2000 or 2500m the season extends from November to May. Year-round summer skiing is possible in a few resorts on glaciers at around 3000m.

Ski passes vary hugely in price, but a rough average is around Fr.40–60 per day, decreasing for longer periods. Use of buses in and around resorts is usually included. You can always **rent** any amount of equipment after you arrive at a resort: one day's downhill gear is approximately Fr.45–50, cross-country gear around Fr.20–25. InterSport (*www.rentasport.ch*) and SwissRent (*www.swissrent.com*) have outlets in virtually every resort in the country, and both also allow you to reserve equipment via the Internet before you leave home.

If you're an absolute beginner, all Swiss resorts have **ski schools** attached, where you can, in most cases, just turn up and pay for a day's or a week's tuition in a group or one-to-one. Prices vary dramatically, from Fr.150 to Fr.200 for five mornings' tuition; for more information, contact the Swiss Ski School Federation, Oberalpstrasse, CH-6490 Andermatt (☎041/887 12 40, fax 887 13 69). Joining a **ski club** at home gives you access to plenty of information and impartial recommendations for resorts around Switzerland and the rest of the world that can be geared to your particular needs. Most can also provide details of tour operators which concentrate on ski- or winter-packages (or occasionally may offer such packages themselves). In the UK, contact the Ski Club of Great Britain, The White House, 57–63 Church Rd, London SW19 5SB (☎020/8410 2000, fax 8410 2001, *www.ski-club.co.uk*) – their Web site is particularly impressive.

There's any number of more or less crazed minor sports which tag along on the heels of skiing and snowboarding. **Mono-skiing**, like head-on snowboarding, uses a single extra-wide ski into which both feet are strapped side by side. **Ski-joring**, where you're pulled along by galloping horses, is one of the more exhilarating thrills in the snow, as is **snow-biking** or **snow-bobbing** – essentially cycling on snow. **Tobogganing** or sledding is hugely popular, and many places have pistes reserved for it; **bob-sleighing** (for instance at St Moritz's death-defying Cresta Run), is the pro's version, while **luge** – a one-person tea-tray, on which you shoot feet-first down a bob-run – is for nutters. If you're getting bored with all those black runs, try **heli-skiing**, where you pay a helicopter pilot to dump you in an inaccessible spot at 4000m and fly off, or **ski hang-gliding**, where you float to earth out of an aeroplane, and then ski back to the pub. **Zorbing**, which can count as a winter or a summer "sport", has gained new devotees in the classier "been-there done-that" resorts of the Valais in particular, and involves being strapped immobile inside a giant plastic sphere, arms and legs spread, and then rolled down a mountainside.

OTHER SPORTS AND ACTIVITIES

Cycling is massively popular, covered in some detail on pp40–41. To complement the country's many cycle routes, there are also currently three long-distance **inline skating** routes of around 200km each, from Geneva to Brig, Zürich to Yverdon, and Bad Ragaz to Schaffhausen. Eurotrek (see p.41) can take care of your gear, and provide more information.

Swimming and watersports have big followings at all the lakeside resorts, and almost everywhere is clean enough (signs are posted otherwise). Boats and equipment for windsurfing are available for rent on almost all lakes, but getting enough of a breeze can be a problem. Rowing and canoeing are also popular, especially on the Rotsee near Luzern.

The boom in **adventure sports** has arrived in Switzerland with a vengeance, and places like Interlaken and the Ticino have dozens of companies offering canyoning and bungee-jumping, as well as **aerial sports** such as paragliding, hang-gliding and a host of others. Hot-air ballooning is headquartered in Château d'Oex, nerve centre of the 1998 record-breaking balloon flight around the world.

On a more pedestrian level, the Swiss have a host of their own sports, rooted in celebrations of Alpine brawn. **Schwingen** is an idiosyncratic kind of sumo-wrestling, in which both participants wear leather or canvas over-shorts; you've got to keep at least one hand on your opponent's shorts at all times, and still manage to heave him onto his back within a laid-out circle of sawdust. **Steintossen** involves flinging a massive rock as far as possible. **Hornussen** isn't much like any other sport at all: one person hits the *hornuss*, a puck, along a curved track with a long cane, while other people stand well back and try to knock the *hornuss* aside with large wooden bats before it hits the ground. All of these tend to be indulged in by local communities – often in traditional dress – on open field sites during spring and summer months, along with much festivity and carousing. *Schwingen* is taken particularly seriously, and champs become rural folk-heroes.

DIRECTORY

CONTRACEPTIVES You can buy condoms (*Kondoms* or *präservatives, préservatifs, preservativi*) over-the-counter at all pharmacies and most supermarkets. If you use other forms of contraception, you should bring enough supplies to last the duration of your trip. Oddly enough, Switzerland has one of the highest per capita occurrences of AIDS in Europe.

ELECTRICITY 220v, 50Hz (the same as in the rest of continental Europe). Plug sockets are generally of the round or flat two-pin type. British appliances will need a plug adaptor, while North American appliances will also need a 220-to-110v transformer.

GAY AND LESBIAN LIFE You'll find Switzerland to be generally very tolerant towards gay (*schwul, gai, gay*) and lesbian (*lesbisch, lesbien, lesbico*) lifestyles – in 1992, the age of consent was unified at 16 and equality of treatment under the law is guaranteed. All major urban areas have organizations lobbying local and cantonal governments on gay issues which serve as a focus for the local scene, while the Pink Cross in Bern (see p.231) is a national mouthpiece. Nightlife is varied and welcoming, with Zürich and Geneva enjoying the lion's share of the action. You'll find some bars and contacts in Geneva, Lausanne, Basel, Bern and Zürich listed in the relevant guide chapters. There's plenty of information online, with the co-ordinating site *www.swissgay.ch* as good a place as any to start surfing.

LAUNDRY Public coin-op laundries aren't a very common sight, since all Swiss apartment blocks have their own washing machines for residents' use in the cellar. University towns such as Geneva, Lausanne and Zürich have a few coin-ops for students living without such facilities, or otherwise you may have to resort to the many places offering specialist service washes, which are hideously expensive.

JEWISH TRAVELLERS The *Jüdischer Almanach der Schweiz* newspaper puts out the free "Jewish City Guide of Switzerland" four times a year, a pocket booklet with information on Jewish communities, synagogues, kosher hotels and restaurants, and so on. Contact the publisher Spectrum Press International, Raphael Bollag, Im Tannegg 1, CH-8055 Zürich (☎01/462 64 11, fax 462 64 62, *www.jewishguide.ch*).

RACISM Racism is perhaps the biggest current social issue in Switzerland, with ongoing, none-too-civil debates raging about the absorption of foreigners into Swiss society, and the high levels of asylum seekers arriving from conflict-torn parts of Europe and the world. Small-town Switzerland is hopping from foot to foot, forced to address the issue but unable to reconcile traditional Swiss hospitality and respect for others with the equally traditional mistrust and rejection of outsiders. While society is in flux, the fact remains that outside certain parts of Geneva, Lausanne, Bern and Zürich, non-white faces are a rare sight on the street. Across the country there's some antagonism directed towards both refugees from the former Yugoslavia, who are commonly perceived as gangsters, and, on a different level altogether, tourists from East Asia, who are often seen as an irritant. Luzern is infamous as the major recruiting ground for Switzerland's newly expanding extreme-rightwing political parties. Despite all this, you're very unlikely to actually encounter any trouble, but some neanderthal attitudes – stares or condescension – may persist in out-of-the-way corners.

TIME Switzerland is on Central European Time (CET): for most of the year one hour ahead of the UK, six hours ahead of US Eastern, nine hours ahead of US Pacific, and nine hours behind Sydney.

TIPPING All bar, restaurant and hotel bills are calculated with fifteen percent service included, and tipping is officially abolished. Nonetheless, unless service was truly diabolical, everyone rounds things up at least to the nearest franc; in restaurants, it's common to add a few francs.

TRAVELLING WITH CHILDREN is extremely easy and very rewarding, with facilities galore for kids of all ages, and endless opportunities for diversions and fun. Locals regularly travel in family groups for outdoor holidays in various parts of the country, family skiing is well established in almost all resorts, and there's a host of perks to take advantage of. An add-on to the Swiss Half-Fare Card (see p.35) to cover partners and children costs Fr.20, while parents can also request a free Family Card, which lets your own kids (up to the age of 16) travel with you for free, and knocks fifty percent off the fares for Swiss Passes or Flexi-Passes for other children travelling with you.

WORK Permits are your first headache (see pp.22–3); being expected to work like the Swiss – hard, and for long hours – is your second; and having at least a smattering of the local lingo is your third. The rewards are salaries and per-hour wages way above anything you'll be able to get at home. The following are some pointers for seasonal jobs; longer-term work or permanent contracts are a whole other book. Key hunting-grounds are ski resorts, although you should note that you get no unemployment insurance: if the snow is bad and tourist levels are down, you may be summarily fired. Chalet-rental companies need staff to cook in and clean their hundreds of chalets. Qualified ski instructors and unqualified ski guides for foreign tour operators are always in demand, as are technicians for maintaining ski equipment and fitting skis and boots in resort shops, large hotels and for tour companies. In addition, of course, people are needed at big hotels as kitchen assistants, porters, messengers, dishwashers, cleaners and so on, summer and winter. All of these jobs can, if you're lucky, result in a permit being organized by your employer within a few weeks, allowing you to start work on the spot. It's more prudent, but not necessarily any more guaranteed, to write to potential employers months ahead of the season: August for winter jobs, March for summer ones. Resorts seeing a lot of English and American tourists (and so more likely to hire an English speaker) include Arosa, Crans-Montana, Davos, Grindelwald, Klosters, Saas-Fee, St Moritz, Verbier, Wengen and Zermatt, but smaller resorts than these have the advantage of less competition from jobseekers. *Working in Ski Resorts – Europe* by Victoria Pybus and Charles James (Vacation Work, UK) is especially helpful.

The main other form of work in Switzerland is voluntary work, or work for nominal pay, mostly on farms. The Swiss Farm Work Association can place unskilled French- or German-speakers under 30 on farms around the country – long, hard hours pay you Fr.20 a day, plus board and lodging. Contact Landdienst Zentralstelle, Postfach 728, CH-8025 Zürich (☎01/261 44 88, *www.landdienst.ch*) well ahead of time. Otherwise, WWOOF (Willing Workers on Organic Farms) can organize placements at 45 farms around the country, for which you get the experience but no wages. Contact WWOOF Switzerland, Postfach 59, CH-8124 Maur (*www.welcome.to/wwoof*).

PART TWO

THE

GUIDE

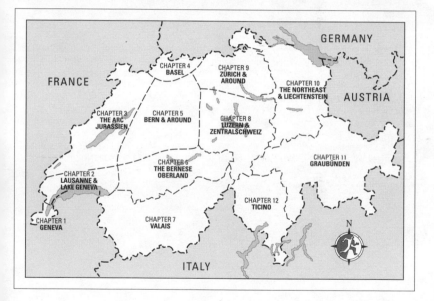

CHAPTER ONE

GENEVA

G ENEVA is an anomaly, the nearest thing the world has to a truly international city, and yet with nothing of the pizzazz such a description might suggest. From its profile in world events, you'd imagine a megalopolis on the scale of London or New York, but Geneva is little more than town-sized. From its demographic diversity – 38 percent of the population are foreigners – you'd imagine its streets to be thronged with the nationalities of the world, but across most of the city centre you'd be hard pushed to spot a non-white face or eavesdrop on a conversation that wasn't in either French or US-accented English. It's in the most beautiful of locations, centred around the point where the River Rhône flows out of Lake Geneva (*Lac Léman* in French, *Genfersee* in German) flanked on one side by the Jura ridges and on the other by the first peaks of the Savoy Alps, but for all that, it's a curiously unsatisfying place to spend more than a few days.

The spiritual father of the city is the Reformer Jean (or John) Calvin, the inspiration behind Puritanism and Presbyterianism, who turned Geneva into what was dubbed a "Protestant Rome" in the sixteenth century. His parsimonious spirit – paradoxically enough – remains the motive force behind this wealthiest of city-states today. What's officially still known as "The Republic and Canton of Geneva" is only nominally within Switzerland's borders, squeezed into a bulge of land that shares just 4km of internal border with its Swiss neighbour but 108km with France all around. Some thirty thousand French *frontaliers* commute daily to their workplaces in Geneva from dormitory towns just over the border, benefiting from both a high Swiss salary and relatively low French living expenses, and equally high numbers of Genevois save money by doing their shopping in France. The Gallic influence is what defines the city, and yet this is tempered by a streak of Calvinism so ingrained that the conservative Genevois – surrounded as they are by some of the world's most expensive shops and most exquisite restaurants – can't quite bring themselves to indulge, and leave most of the high living to the jetset glitterati who've taken up residence on the lakeside hills.

Instead, Geneva has become the businessperson's city *par excellence*, unrufflable, efficient and packed with hotels. The cobbled **Old Town**, high on its central hill, is atmospheric but strangely austere, with abiding impressions of high, grey walls and the stern tap-tap of passing footsteps. At the heart of the city is the huge **Cathédrale St-Pierre**, and packed in all around are an array of top-class **museums**, including the giant Musée d'Art et d'Histoire and an impressive gallery of East Asian art, the

---

ACCOMMODATION PRICE CODES

All the hostels, pensions and hotels in this book have been graded according to the following price codes, which indicate the price for the cheapest double room available during the high season. Single rooms can cost anything between sixty and eighty percent of the double-room rate. For hostels with dormitories, the price per bed has been quoted. See p.45 for more details.

① under Fr.100	④ Fr.200–250	⑦ Fr.350–400
② Fr.100–150	⑤ Fr.250–300	⑧ Fr.400–500
③ Fr.150–200	⑥ Fr.300–350	⑨ over Fr.500

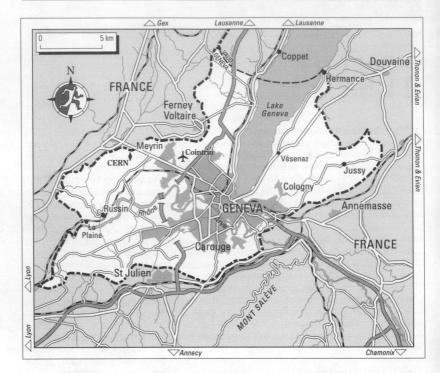

Collections Baur. Livelier residential neighbourhoods on both banks of the Rhône, such as **Les Pâquis** and **Plainpalais**, offer more appealing wandering, and a short way south of the centre is **Carouge**, an attractive eighteenth-century suburb built in Sardinian style to be a place of decadence and freedom beyond Geneva's control; its reputation lives on in its population of artists and designers.

Last but not least, Geneva is home to dozens of international organizations. Two of them – the **United Nations'** European headquarters and the International Committee of the **Red Cross**, the latter with an award-winning museum – allow visitors a glimpse of the unseen lifeblood of the city, the diplomatic and administrative confidence that have made Geneva world capital of bureaucracy.

Some history

Pile dwellings have been unearthed on the lakeshore dating back to 3000 BC, but Geneva's high ground wasn't inhabited until 500 BC, when the Celtic Allobroges tribe settled. By 58 BC, **Rome** had taken over: the first recorded use of the name *Genua* was by Julius Caesar. The town grew rapidly, and was a bishopric by 400 AD but, located on the turbulent mid-line of Europe, Geneva was continually conquered and reconquered, by Burgundians, Franks, Merovingians, Carolingians and more, until the fifteenth century, when the famous **Geneva Fairs** gave the city a reputation as a trading capital. The dukes of **Savoy** retained their grip on the town's affairs up until 1530, when citizens took matters into their own hands and formed a pact with Bern and Fribourg. The Savoyards granted Geneva independence shortly after.

In 1535, the Genevois accepted the **Reformation**; the following year, the preacher **Jean Calvin** visited the city for the first time. Born in Picardy in 1509, Calvin was expelled from the University of Paris in 1533 for his heterodox views, and arrived by chance in Geneva three years later, where he was called upon by the leader of the religious community in the city, Guillaume Farel, to help consolidate the Reformation. After two years of opposition from city politicians, both were expelled, only to return in 1541 with Calvin at the helm. From a position of authority, Calvin was able to institute sweeping social and political reforms within a strict, uncompromising Protestant theocracy. Geneva became a beacon of **refuge** for the persecuted of Europe, and French Huguenots and Italian Protestants in particular flooded to the city, which also rapidly became a centre of academic excellence. The Geneva Bible of 1560 was the first English translation to be organized methodically, with numbered verses, and the city's printing presses turned out hundreds of radical texts, unprintable elsewhere.

In 1602, forces of the Duke of Savoy tried to retake Geneva, but were repulsed in an event that is still commemorated today, in a celebration of the city's independent, patriotic spirit, as **L'Escalade** (see p.83). Wave after wave of refugees flowed into the city, shaping a cosmopolitanism and religious liberality which continue today. Commerce, banking and watchmaking all flourished, and in 1792 the aristocratic rulers of the city were overthrown and a **Republic** was declared with political equality for all. Geneva was annexed by France in 1798, and following the defeat of Napoleon in 1813, threw in its lot with the Swiss Confederation in 1815. A Genevan businessman, Henri Dunant, shaped the **Geneva Convention** of 1864, setting down for the first time rules for soldiers' conduct in war. This led to the creation of the International Red Cross, designed to help soldiers or civilians caught up in war or natural disasters. After World War I, Geneva was chosen as seat of the League of Nations and later as the European headquarters of the **United Nations**. Since then, the city has looked outwards for inspiration, away from the rest of Switzerland and towards the international community. Only in the last few years, with the ongoing proposals to join the cantons of Geneva and neighbouring Vaud into a single Canton Léman, have the Genevois begun to look to their Swiss partners.

Arrival

Geneva's international **airport**, just 5km northwest of the city on the French border at Cointrin, has to be one of the best-designed in the world. With just 200m walking distance from plane to train, it needn't take more than half-an-hour from touchdown for you to be done with all the formalities and heading into the city.

There's only one terminal, replete with English-language signing. The **tourist information** and airport information desks (both daily 6am–midnight) are in plain view, offering free maps and advice and hotel reservations boards (with complimentary phone). To the left of tourist information is a revolving door giving access into the adjacent CFF train station.

For transport on from the airport, the simplest and cheapest way to go is by city **bus** #10, which departs from the top of the escalators just inside the train station's revolving door. A fifteen-minute drive can drop you directly on the Rue du Mont-Blanc (for the Rive Droite) or Place Bel-Air (for the Rive Gauche) in the centre of town – buy a Fr.2.20 ticket from the machine before you board. The airport **train** station is the beginning of the line, and all trains from here pass through Geneva at the start of their journeys (Fr.4.80; 6min; last 11.55pm) – if you're heading straight for the mountains you can generally get to where you want to be directly from the airport, avoiding train-changes in Geneva. If the ticket desks (daily 6am–8.30pm) are closed, use the self-explanatory ticket machines nearby. The train station is the best place in the airport to **change** money (daily 6.20am–8pm), and the concourse also has luggage lockers (Fr.3/5) and a staffed left-luggage office (daily 6.40am–8.40pm; Fr.5/day). **Taxis** gather just outside the terminal, but charge a steep Fr.25–35 into the city.

By train

The city's main **train** station – the **Gare de Cornavin** – couldn't be more central, barely 400m north of the lake. The station is also a terminus of the French rail network: if you're arriving on an intercity SNCF train (TGV or not), from Paris, Lyon or Grenoble – which come in on platforms 7 and 8, separate from the rest – you'll be directed to pass through both French and Swiss customs and passport control before joining the throng within the station proper. The station has the usual array of facilities, including a change bureau (daily April–Oct 6.45am–9.30pm; Nov–March 6.45am–8pm) and bike rental (Mon–Fri 6.50am–6.45pm, Sat & Sun 7am–12.30pm & 1.30–5.45pm). There's also a city transport office, giving out tram and bus maps and selling tickets (daily 6.15am–8pm).

Sporadic French SNCF local trains from Evian, Chamonix and Annecy, connecting at Annemasse and La Roche, arrive at the tiny **Gare des Eaux-Vives**, well to the east of the centre. Opposite the station is a terrace of houses, to the right of which is the Rue de Savoie heading 50m up to the main road, from where trams #12 and #16 head right into the centre.

By bus

All international **buses** into Geneva arrive at the Gare Routière, on Place Dorcière (☎022/732 02 30, *www.gare-routiere.ch*), just off Rue du Mont-Blanc in the heart of town. Most are massive overland hauls from the far corners of Europe, although there are also plenty of more useful arrivals from nearby points in France, such as Chamonix, Grenoble, Lyon, Annecy and Evian, and a daily service from Turin.

By car

Geneva is in an odd position for drivers, surrounded on all sides by France – the only Swiss motorway into the city is the N1 from Lausanne and Nyon. In addition, parking in the city centre is a nightmare, and you'd do well to get rid of your vehicle as soon as possible on the city limits. The long-term car park at the airport train station offers a discount to train users, bringing the price down to a bargain Fr.9 for the first 24hr, and Fr.6 per day following. Otherwise, the long-term car park P51, next to World Trade Centre-2 at the airport, 300m from the terminal building (bus #10 stops outside the adjacent WTC-1), costs Fr.15 for the first 24hr, with every 4hr following adding Fr.1. On-street parking in the centre is metered, with heavily restricted hours. There are plenty of garages – the ones under Place Cornavin (☎022/731 66 61) and beneath the south side of the Pont du Mont-Blanc (☎022/310 01 30) are two biggies that allow you to reserve a place in advance – but you'll be paying Fr.25 or more per day.

By boat

By far the most romantic way to arrive in Geneva is by **boat**, on one of the many services (April–Oct only) from towns on both shores of the lake. Boats operated by the Compagnie Générale de Navigation sur le Lac Léman (CGN; ☎0848/811 848) village-hop along the French shore (Rive Gauche) from Thonon and Yvoire, and along the Swiss shore (Rive Droite) from Lausanne and Nyon, stopping at one or all of the CGN jetties within Geneva itself: Eaux-Vives, east of the Jet d'Eau; Les Pâquis, near the Casino; and the Jardin Anglais and Mont-Blanc, at each end of the Pont du Mont-Blanc.

Orientation and information

Genevans orient the city centre around the Rhône, which flows from the lake west into France. The **Rive Gauche**, on the south bank, takes in a grid of waterfront streets which comprise the main shopping district (Les Rues-Basses) and the adjacent high ground of the Old Town. Just south is the university, spilling over into the Plainpalais district, and a little northeast is the populous working neighbourhood of Eaux-Vives. Six bridges, including the main Pont du Mont-Blanc, link the Rive Gauche to the **Rive Droite** waterfront, where most of Geneva's grand hotels sit. Behind them lies the main station, alongside the cosmopolitan and occasionally rough Les Pâquis district, filled with cheap restaurants and much seediness. The international organizations are clustered together a kilometre or two north.

Information

Geneva's **tourist office** (☎022/909 70 00, *www.geneva-tourism.ch*) is one of the best-equipped and managed in the country, a mine of information on everything to do with the city and canton. The main branch is in the central post office at 18 Rue du Mont-Blanc (Mon–Sat 9am–6pm), and there's also a desk within the information office of the Municipality of Geneva, situated on the Pont de la Machine (Mon noon–6pm, Tues–Fri 9am–6pm, Sat 10am–5pm; *www.ville-ge.ch*). Either office can give you an adequate street- and transport-map of the city for free, or sell you a detailed one for Fr.3. They also have endless stacks of material in English, including the useful *Guide Pratique*, along with lists of budget hotels, museums, restaurants, galleries, excursions and more – the *Young People* brochure is particularly comprehensive. During the summer, a bus parked at the station end of the Rue du Mont-Blanc houses "CAR" (Centre d'Accueil et de Renseignements) – they can help with accommodation and transport information (mid-June–early Sept daily 8am–11pm).

Genève Agenda, a French/English weekly publication, is a useful source of information on sightseeing, the latest exhibitions and other bits and bobs, available free from the tourist office and most hotels. Also handy is the monthly *Genève: Le Guide* which has good maps and trustworthy information (Fr.3; *www.le-guide.ch*). The quarterly *La Clef* is an alternative-leaning cultural agenda (Fr.5; *www.laclef.ch*), but most authoritative

---

GENEVA'S FESTIVALS

Geneva's biggest celebration is **L'Escalade** (*www.escalade.ch*), commemorating the failed attempt by the Duke of Savoy to seize the town by surprise on the night of December 11–12, 1602. Locals dress up in costume and parade by torchlight around the streets with drums and fifes, groups of kids sing in city-centre cafés, and confectioner's sell the *Marmite d'Escalade*, a small pot made of chocolate and filled with marzipan "vegetables" to commemorate a Genevan housewife who dispatched a Savoyard soldier by tipping her boiling soup over his head from a high window. A few days before is the Course d'Escalade, a fun-run through town.

Geneva's **Fourth-of-July** celebrations for US Independence Day are the biggest in the world outside the States, and its **Swiss National Day** festivities, every August 1, are equally spectacular. The **Fêtes de Genève** (Geneva Festival) is the city's premier annual pageant, held in early August on the waterfront, with music of all kinds, lovemobiles and techno floats on the lake, theatre, funfairs, street entertainers, stalls selling food from around the world, and an enormous lakeside musical fireworks display. During the last week of August and early September, **La Bâtie Festival de Genève** features live music and theatrical performances. Finally, Geneva's famous **Motor Show**, held every March in the Palexpo arena, is the largest and most prestigious in Europe.

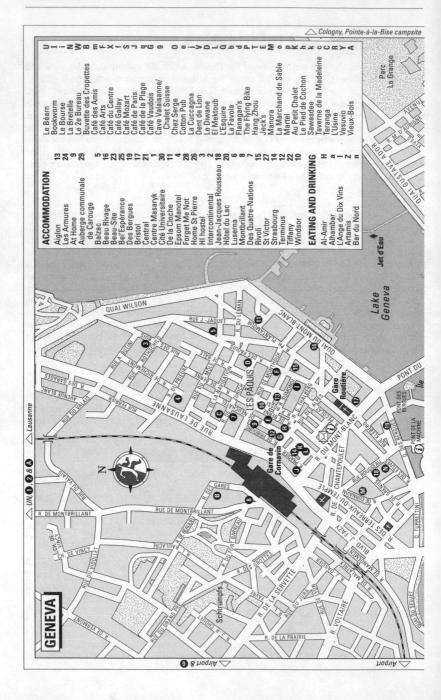

△ Cologny, Pointe-à-la-Bise campsite

GENEVA

ACCOMMODATION

Aiglon	13
Les Armures	24
At Home	9
Auberge communale de Carouge	29
Balzac	5
Beau Rivage	16
Beau-Site	23
Bel Espérance	25
Des Bergues	19
Bristol	21
Central	17
Centre Masaryk	1
Cité Universitaire	30
De la Cloche	11
Epsom Manotel	4
Forget Me Not	28
Home St Pierre	26
HI hostel	3
Intercontinental	2
Jean-Jacques Rousseau	18
Hôtel du Lac	20
Luserna	6
Montbrillant	8
Des Quatre-Nations	7
Rivoli	15
St Victor	27
Strasbourg	14
Terminus	12
Tiffany	22
Windsor	10

Le Béarn	U
Bookworm	I
Le Bourse	N
La Bretelle	i
Le 2e Bureau	W
Buvette des Cropettes	B
Café des Amis	m
Café Arts	F
Café du Centre	X
Café Gallay	f
Café Mozart	S
Café de Paris	J
Café de la Plage	G
Café Vaudois	g
Cave Valaisane/ Chalet Suisse	O
Chez Serge	e
Cotton Pub	j
La Cuccagna	V
Dent de Lion	D
Le Diwane	L
El Mektoub	b
L'Esquire	d
La Favola	b
Flanagan's	P
The Flying Bike	T
Hang Zhou	E
Jeck's	M
Manora	o
La Marchand de Sable	p
Martel	K
Au Petit Chalet	h
Le Pied de Cochon	k
Sawasdee	C
Taverne de la Madeleine	R
Teranga	Y
L'Usine	A
Vesuvio	
Vieux-Bois	

EATING AND DRINKING

Al-Amir	H
Alhambar	a
L'Ange du Dix Vins	l
Artamis	Z
Bar du Nord	n

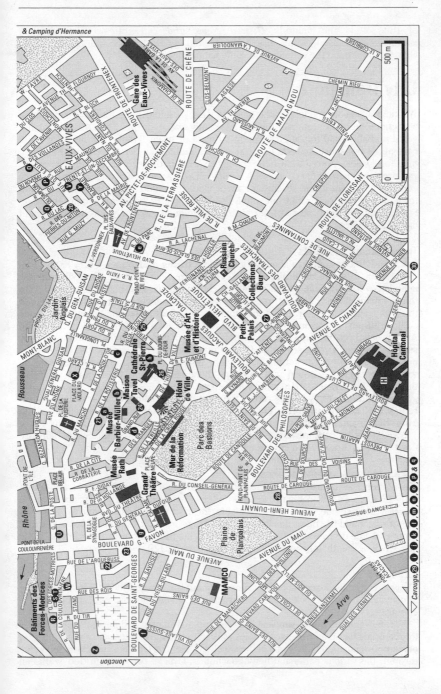

of the lot is the monthly *Geneva News and International Report* (Fr.6; *www.genevanews.com*), which has business and political news and features from Geneva and around the country, and some listings information.

City transport

Walking is feasible enough for the heart of Geneva, and even getting to further-flung attractions such as Carouge or the UN takes only twenty or thirty minutes on foot, but you'll probably want to use **city transport** once or twice. Trams and buses form the core of the transport network, with a few boats linking the two lakeshores. Renting a bike (or even a powered two-wheeler) makes sense, both to get around the city and to explore the generally flat countryside around. Taxis are only for the rich and famous: you can hail them in the street, take them from the station and other ranks around town, or call ☎022/331 41 33, but with a Fr.6.30 flagfall, Fr.2.70 per kilometre (more on Sundays and at night) plus Fr.1 per piece of luggage, they're only a ski-mask short of daylight robbery.

Trams, buses and boats

You'll find little to complain about with Geneva's **trams and buses** – they're fast, efficient, clean, safe, affordable and they go everywhere. The entire city, including the airport, is covered by Zone 10, tickets for which must be bought before you board the machines at every stop. A three-stop ticket, which can get you from the station onto the Rive Gauche, costs Fr.1.50. A full city pass is Fr.2.20 (valid one hour) or Fr.5 (one day). Transport offices in the station or at the large Rive interchange near the Jardin Anglais sell three-day city passes (Fr.19), as well as useful discounted multifare tickets, such as six one-hour passes for Fr.12. You must validate day and multifare tickets by punching them in the ticket machine before boarding. All trams and buses running within the city are identified with numbers; those running into the suburbs, or across the border into France, are marked with letters.

Tiny **mouettes** ferry people across the mouth of the lake (April–Oct only), on two routes, both covered by normal city tickets: M1 runs between the Pâquis jetty (Quai du Mont-Blanc) and Place du Molard (Rues-Basses); M2 between Pâquis and Eaux-Vives.

Swiss Pass holders travel free, but Eurail, InterRail and even the Swiss Half-Fare Card bring no discounts on city transport.

Bikes, mopeds and motorbikes

The station has the usual **bike-rental** facilities (Mon–Fri 6.50am–6.45pm, Sat & Sun 7am–12.30pm & 1.30–5.45pm) or, as an alternative, you can take advantage of the *Genèv'Roule* scheme, with bikes available for rent at Fr.5/day from 17 Place de Montbrillant and the Bains des Pâquis (both May–Oct daily 7.30am–9.30pm). Horizon Motos, 51 Rue de Lausanne (☎022/731 23 39) rents **mopeds and motorbikes** by the day, week or month: long-weekend deals start from Fr.120.

City tours

There are literally dozens of **tours** offered around the city and its environs, and all the information centres stock plenty of brochures giving details, and can help with enquiries.

For **self-guided tours**, simplest is to pick up a Walkman and headphones from the tourist office for an informative 26-point walk in the Old Town at your own pace (Fr.10, plus Fr.50 deposit), or follow one of the excellent "Geneva On Foot" brochure-led walks through the various parks and neighbourhoods. Official two-hour **guided walks** all depart from the Hôtel-de-Ville and cost Fr.12: a walk through the Old Town runs year-round (June–Oct Wed & Sat 11am, Nov–May Sat 11am), while other regular tours outline Historic Geneva, The Red Cross, and Medieval Geneva (June–Oct alternating Mondays 2.30pm). Other walks, highlighting International Geneva, parks and gardens, Carouge, Geneva by night, and more, run on fixed dates from various points around town – ask at the tourist office for details.

Opportunities for getting onto the **water** also abound: the CGN has plenty of cruises long and short from their Mont-Blanc jetty, including *Les Belles Rives Genevoises* – a circular tour of both lakeshores (April–Sept daily 11.05am & hourly 1.05–5.05pm; 55min; Fr.11) – and dozens of eat-aboard brunch, lunch and evening cruises. However, note that the smaller companies ranged along the Quai du Mont-Blanc tend to offer better value and more regular departures for much the same thing. One of them, Mouettes Genevoises Navigation, 8 Quai du Mont-Blanc (☎022/732 29 44), has an excellent 2hr 45min return trip down the Rhône, from the Pont de l'Ile (Quai des Moulins) past cliffs and densely wooded shores to Verbois dam near the French border (May–Sept daily 2.15pm, also Wed, Thurs, Sat & Sun 10am; April daily 2.15pm only; Fr.22, reserve ahead).

Accommodation

For a city with such a jet set reputation, Geneva has a good selection of budget and mid-range **accommodation**, adding to the swathe of jaw-droppingly expensive palaces catering to diplomats and the international glitterati. However, booking ahead is essential, since all affordable rooms in the city can get snapped up by delegates to the continuous round of congresses, conferences and international events that are the lifeblood of the city.

The tourist office's dedicated **hotel reservation service** (☎022/909 70 20, fax 909 70 21, or over-the-counter) can book a room in the hotel of your choice for an unnecessarily high Fr.5, but it's worth asking them about any weekend or off-season deals the city happens to be running, which can often slash walk-in rates to bargain levels.

Camping and hostels

There are two **campsites** easily accessible from the city, both northeast on the Rive Gauche lakefront and both accessible on bus #E in Zone 31 (Fr.4). The first – 7km from town – is *Pointe-à-la-Bise*, on Chemin de la Bise in Vésanaz (☎022/752 12 96; April–Oct). Another 7km on, a short walk beyond the terminus of bus #E in Hermance and a few metres before the French frontier, is *Camping d'Hermance*, Rue du Nord 44 (☎022/751 14 83; April–Sept), which has free access to the lake.

There are plenty of **hostel** beds in Geneva, partly because so many student dorms open their doors to visitors out of term-time. The tourist office brochure *Young People* lists 24 places (including six women-only hostels). The brand-new *City Hostel* is due to open in the year 2000 at 2 Rue Ferrier (☎022/789 22 93, *info@cityhotel.ch*, *www.cityhostel.ch*), with dorms from Fr.24, Internet access, washing facilities and more.

Centre Masaryk, 11 Avenue de la Paix (☎022/733 07 72). Some 2km north of town and a little institutional, with Fr.27 dorms and inexpensive rooms. ①.

Cité Universitaire, 46 Avenue Miremont (☎022/839 22 22, fax 839 22 23). Gigantic 500-bed behemoth nearly 3km south of the centre. Dorm beds for individuals are Fr.16 in July & August only (Sept–June groups only), but there are plenty of cut-price singles, doubles and studios year-round. Breakfast is extra. Bus #3 to Champel. ①.

Forget Me Not, 8 Rue Vignier (☎022/320 93 55, fax 781 46 45). Rock-bottom backpackers' hostel, with dorms from Fr.25 and doubles from Fr.80. Tram #13 to Plainpalais. ①.

HI hostel, 30 Rue Rothschild (☎022/732 62 60, fax 738 39 87). Open year-round in a good location in the north of the Pâquis, with dorm beds Fr.23 including breakfast. Big, bustling and well maintained. Bus #1 to Wilson. ①.

Home St Pierre, 4 Cour St Pierre (☎022/310 37 07). Women-only hostel in the heart of the Old Town next to the cathedral, with dorm beds from Fr.22 excluding breakfast, and a few rooms. Reception closed noon–4pm. ①.

Inexpensive hotels

There are plenty of **inexpensive** hotels dotted around town. The *Young People* brochure lists 21 establishments offering en-suite doubles for Fr.83–120, some of them with cheaper rooms too, and most slap in the centre of town.

Station area and Les Pâquis

Aiglon, 16 Rue Sismondi (☎022/732 97 60, fax 732 87 71). Very large well-worn doubles – en suite and not – that aren't spotlessly clean, but are perfectly OK, inexpensive and good value. Ask in the street-level bar. ②.

At Home, 16 Rue de Fribourg (☎022/906 19 00, fax 738 44 30, *athome@bluewin.ch*, *www.kis.ch/at-home*). Clean, modern Pâquis rooms, convenient for the location, but small, soulless and, despite the name, thoroughly unhomely. ②.

Balzac, 14 Rue de l'Ancien-Port (☎022/731 01 60, fax 738 38 47). Quiet and very spacious rooms – unrenovated but still comfortable – just off the Place de la Navigation. Good value. ③.

De la Cloche, 6 Rue de la Cloche (☎022/732 94 81, fax 738 16 12). Very clean, characterful, high-ceilinged rooms in what was formerly a private apartment in a quiet area of the Pâquis 50m from the lake. The pleasant atmosphere is enhanced by the ministerings of the *patronne*. Regularly full. ①.

Jean-Jacques Rousseau, 13 Rue Rousseau (☎022/731 55 70, fax 738 41 05). Odd little place, seemingly a basic city-centre cheapie – but not so cheap. Spartan outdated rooms, all en suite, are overpriced but handily located. ②.

Luserna, 12 Avenue de Luserna (☎022/345 46 76, fax 344 49 36, *hotel.luserna@span.ch*). Very quiet and friendly family-run place north of the centre, with pleasantly renovated wood-floor chalet-style rooms (most en suite – ask for the attic) and great breakfasts. Super-attentive management lifts it well out of the ordinary. Bus #3, #9 or #10 to Servette, then walk via Avenue Wendt. ①–②.

Des Quatre-Nations, 43 Rue de Zurich (☎022/732 02 24, fax 731 21 41). Divey little Pâquis den above a lowlife Portuguese bar, with blithely unhelpful staff (if you can find them) and dead cheap shower-free rooms. ①.

Rivoli, 6 Rue des Pâquis (☎022/731 85 50, fax 738 41 17). Good, quiet central location, but a little gloomy inside – unrenovated rooms are nothing to write home about, but their studios are slightly better value. ③.

Terminus, 20 Rue des Alpes (☎022/732 80 95, fax 732 18 43). Clean and comfortable, a stone's throw from the station but off the main traffic street. ③.

Windsor, 31 Rue de Berne (☎022/731 71 30, fax 731 93 25). Simple, unadorned rooms, adequate and not without character – higher floors avoid the Pâquis street-noise. Formal, friendly staff. ③.

Old Town, Plainpalais, Eaux-Vives and Carouge

Auberge communale de Carouge, 39 Rue Ancienne, Carouge (☎022/342 22 88, fax 342 22 05). Characterful old building unfortunately gutted and renovated inside, with spotless modern, floral-style rooms – the best are under the eaves. The most appealing choice in Carouge. Reception closed Mon eve & Tues. Tram #13 to Ancienne. ③.

Beau-Site, 3 Place du Cirque (☎022/328 10 08, fax 329 23 64). Creaky wood-floor rooms perched out of range of the Plainpalais street-noise, with nice decor and understanding staff. ①.

Bel'Espérance, 1 Rue de la Vallée (☎022/818 37 37, fax 818 37 73). Formerly Salvation Army, now completely renovated into an excellent modern hotel on a steep Old Town alley. Exceptionally quiet rooms are bright and plasticky, with free use of kitchen and great views. A renowned dentist nearby attracts toothache sufferers from all over Europe, making for quirky, cosmopolitan breakfast-times. One no-smoking floor. ②.

Central, 2 Rue de la Rôtisserie (☎022/818 8100, fax 818 8101). Quiet, comfortable, renovated top-floor rooms seconds below the Old Town, all with balcony. Prices depend on the room size, but are all good value. ②.

Hôtel du Lac, 15 Rue des Eaux-Vives (☎022/735 45 80, fax 735 45 82). Top-notch cheapie, possibly best value in town, with no-fuss management and plain rooms up on the sixth & seventh floors all with balcony but none en suite. Street-side rooms are no noisier this high up. ①.

St Victor, 1 Rue François-LeFort (☎022/346 17 18, fax 346 10 46, *stvictor@iprolink.ch*, *www.saint-victor.ch*). Marvellous old chandelier-and-wood-floor pension steps from the Old Town, justifiably popular, with 14 characterful, individually decorated, basin-only rooms, some with super-romantic views of the Russian Church. Internet access Fr.1. ①.

Mid-range and expensive hotels

As you might expect from a city which plays regular host to top-level suits on unlimited expense accounts, Geneva has no shortage of stratospherically **expensive** hotels – the Quai des Bergues and Quai du Mont-Blanc in particular are shoulder-to-shoulder with them. There's also a wealth of choice in **mid-range** rooms, with some bargains still available from hotels which haven't yet updated to the slick, generic style that tends to prevail. Many of these renovated places are poor value: often you'll find that characterful old buildings and/or swish reception areas prelude boxy, soullessly impersonal little rooms. The line of shabbier mid-range places opposite the station are much of a muchness, but occasional price wars between them can slash rates.

Les Armures, 1 Rue du Puits St-Pierre (☎022/310 91 72, fax 310 98 46, *armures@span.ch*, *www.hotel-les-armures.ch*). Seventeenth-century building in the heart of the Old Town; uniquely characterful rooms with wood beams and frescoed decor that are the height of tasteful luxury. ⑧.

Beau Rivage, 13 Quai du Mont-Blanc (☎022/716 66 66, fax 716 60 60, *reservation@beau-rivage.ch*, *www.beau-rivage.ch*). Dreamy classical-style palace, drenched in luxury redolent of its 1865 foundation. The same family tends to the hotel's guests now as then, and a farther cry from international business-class anonymity you couldn't find. If Paco Rabanne enjoyed it here, so can you. ⑨.

Des Bergues, 33 Quai des Bergues (☎022/731 50 50, fax 732 19 89). Oldest of Geneva's palace-style hotels, this much-loved 1834 landmark was recently renovated to glittering international standards, yet retains its atmosphere of discreet and unassailable opulence. Its history, which takes in – quite literally – the crowned heads of Europe, seeps from the tastefully draped walls. ⑨.

Bristol, 10 Rue du Mont-Blanc (☎022/732 38 00, fax 738 90 39, *bristol@bristol.ch*, *www.bristol.ch*). A venerable city-centre institution, dating from 1896, with subtle modern decor and quality service. ⑧.

Epsom Manotel, 18 Rue Richemont (☎022/732 08 35, fax 738 85 47, *info@manotel.com*, *www.manotel.com*). One of the seven Manotel hotels (all in Geneva), with hundreds of reasonably affordable, spacious and well-appointed business rooms off the Rue de Lausanne, less expensive ones on lower floors. ④.

Intercontinental, 7 Chemin du Petit-Saconnex (☎022/919 39 39, fax 919 38 38, *geneva@interconti.com*, *www.interconti.com*). A vast Sixties high-rise out near the UN, some rooms boasting spectacular lake-views, that is the favoured choice of politicos and visiting international delegations. Cosy decor softens the generic interior, but sombre, world-affairs formality is the tone. The visitors' book reads like a rollcall of history, running through the last half-dozen US presidents, King Hussein, Fidel Castro and Nelson Mandela, to name a few. ⑦–⑨.

Montbrillant, 2 Rue du Montbrillant (☎022/733 77 84, fax 733 25 11). Overlooking the station, with quiet and atmospheric modern rooms under the sloping roof in particular. ③–④.

Strasbourg, 10 Rue Pradier (☎022/906 58 00, fax 738 42 08, *info@hotel-strasbourg-geneva.ch*, *www.hotel-strasbourg-geneva.ch*). Top station-area choice, on a quiet backstreet, renovated in classic style, with good service and cosy rooms. ④.

Tiffany, 1 Rue des Marbriers (☎022/329 33 11, fax 320 89 91, *hoteltiffany@swissonline.ch*). Attractive, cosy and homely Art Deco-style place near Plainpalais, with efficient, helpful staff. ⑤.

The Rive Gauche

Geneva's **Rive Gauche** (Left Bank, or southern bank) is lined with the tall, blank, almost disapproving facades of dozens of bank buildings. Behind the banks, the arrow-straight Rue du Rhône – principal thoroughfare of **Les Rues-Basses**, once a dockside slum and now Geneva's fanciest shopping district – stretches a kilometre or more east, crammed with jewellers, department stores and designer boutiques of all kinds. A throng of traffic streams over the **Pont du Mont-Blanc** beneath the spectacular view of Europe's highest mountain (4807m), which stands some 80km distant amidst the Savoy Alps beside the immense, shimmering blue lake and its extraordinary water-spout. At the foot of the bridge is the charming lakeside **Jardin Anglais**, focused around a double statue celebrating Geneva's joining the Confederation in 1815, a fountain, bandstand and famous Flower Clock. The **Jet d'Eau** spouts only 400m along the lakeshore (see box), while **Parc La Grange**, 1km further east along the lakeshore, is a landscaped expanse of some forty thousand rose bushes which drench the air with scent for most of the year.

West of the Pont du Mont-Blanc, past the bustling Place du Molard with its medieval tower, is the **Pont des Bergues**, with a footpath midway along it linking to a tiny island, the **Île Rousseau**, formerly a bastion and now a minuscule public garden graced with a statue of the Genevan philosopher. With such controversy surrounding Rousseau, even half a century after his death the city authorities were grudging in honouring him, and the statue, behind its sheltering camouflage of trees, originally faced the empty lake – to all intents and purposes cut off from view until the Pont du Mont-Blanc was built alongside in 1861.

Place Neuve and around

At its western end, the Rue du Rhône feeds into hectic Place Bel-Air, sliced across by tramlines and bus-wires. The Pont de l'Île spans the river here across an island, which boasts the diminutive **Tour de l'Île**, last remaining tower of a thirteenth-century

---

LIQUID ASSET

The **Jet d'Eau** fountain, icon of Geneva, is inescapable – emblazoned on every piece of tourist literature and every book about the city, it's the logo of the tourist office and Geneva's prime photo-op. Even if you happen to visit off season when it's switched off, you'll be in no doubt what you're missing.

Its predecessor dated from 1886, when the new hydraulic turbines on the Rhône built up excessive water pressure after the city's craftsmen had closed the valves in their workshops and gone home. An engineer created a temporary outlet which spurted a 30m fountain to release the pressure while a reservoir system was developed, but by the time the fountain became unnecessary a few wily Genevois had caught on to its power as a tourist attraction. Then purely decorative, it was moved from the river to an exposed lakeside location, and furnished with more and more powerful pumps. Today, the height of the jet is an incredible 140m, with 500 litres of water forced out of the nozzle every second at about 200kph. Each drop takes sixteen seconds to complete the round-trip from nozzle to lake and, on windy days, the plume can rapidly drench the surroundings (they tend to turn it off if the wind picks up). It's worth risking a dousing by walking out onto the jetty to appreciate the force and noise of the thing close up.

The Jet d'Eau operates in summer (May–mid-Sept daily 9.30am–11.15pm; late-March–April & mid-Sept–Oct Mon–Fri 10am–sunset, Sat & Sun 10am–10.30pm), and also during the Motor Show in early March. It's illuminated after dark.

château. Grandiose Rue de la Corraterie heads south to yet more grandiose **Place Neuve**, dominated by the high retaining wall of the Old Town and a host of Neoclassical temples. The street joins the square beside the **Musée Rath**, Geneva's first art museum, opened in 1826, and still holding a changing series of world-class art shows (Tues & Thurs–Sun 10am–5pm, Wed noon–9pm; admission varies). Adjacent is the **Grand-Théâtre**, Geneva's opera house and principal theatre stage, which only just clung onto its facade after the devastating fire of 1951, when a rehearsal of the last act of Wagner's *Walkyrie*, in which Brunhilde is encircled by flames, got out of hand. Further round the square is the equally ornate Conservatoire de Musique (see p.104).

Heading south from Place Neuve through the enormous gates brings you into the **Parc des Bastions**, a tranquil patch of green below the Old Town ramparts that's much beloved of students (the university buildings are all around) and oldtimers playing giant chess. At the east edge of the park, in a dramatic location propping up the Old Town, is the gigantic **Mur de la Réformation**, a 100m-long wall erected in 1917 and dominated by forbidding, 5m-high statues of the four major Genevan reformers: Guillaume Farel, first to preach the Reformation in Geneva; Jean Calvin, leader of the Reform movement and spiritual father of the city; Théodore de Bèze, successor to Calvin; and John Knox, friend of Calvin and founder of Scottish Presbyterianism. Behind runs the motto of the city and the Reformation, *Post Tenebras Lux* ("After the Darkness, Light"). Various figures and bas-reliefs show scenes from Protestant history: just to the right of the main statues is Roger Williams, a Calvinist Puritan who sailed on the *Mayflower* and founded the city of Providence, Rhode Island. The English Parliament's 1689 Bill of Rights – which established a constitutional monarchy under the Protestant king William of Orange, and barred Catholics from the throne – is also depicted, but Luther and Zwingli (see p.385), whom Calvin came to disagree with, are relegated to blocks carved with their surnames flanking the wall.

The Old Town

A gate at the back of the Parc des Bastions brings you up to a small junction and Rue St-Léger, which winds further up into the atmospheric **Old Town**, characterized by quiet, cobbled streets and tall, shuttered, grey-stone houses that give nothing away. Rue St-Léger curls up into the oddly split-level **Place du Bourg-de-Four**, a marketplace since medieval times that was probably built over the Roman forum, these days adorned with a fountain and lined with relaxed terrace cafés. From here, Rue Fontaine descends to the north to Temple de la Madeleine, a Gothic church that has clung on to its Romanesque tower, but if you head up the other way on Rue de l'Hôtel-de-Ville, you'll come to **Place de la Taconnerie**, dominated by the cathedral. Tucked on your right is the **Auditoire de Calvin**, a small thirteenth-century chapel built over a fifth-century predecessor. Following Geneva's acceptance of the Reformation, refugees flooded into the city from all over Europe and, in the knowledge that most of them spoke no French, Calvin gave this chapel over for the refugees to worship in their own languages – Geneva's first international building. John Knox preached here in the 1550s (there's still a Church of Scotland service every Sunday at 11am, slotted between Dutch and Italian), and the austere building also doubled as Calvin's lecture hall.

Cathédrale St-Pierre

Geneva's **Cathédrale St-Pierre** (June–Sept Mon–Sat 9am–7pm, Sun 11am–7pm; Oct–May Mon–Sat 10am–noon & 2–5pm, Sun 11am–12.30pm & 1.30–5pm) is a rather odd building, a mishmash of architectural elements that doesn't really inspire. Begun in 1160, the original building took some 72 years to complete and has had a multitude of bits and pieces stuck on over the centuries. A small side-chapel, the Chapelle des Macchabées, was added in 1397; an incongruous Neoclassical portico – more reminiscent of a museum than a church – was tacked onto the main west front of the building in 1752, facing onto Cour St-Pierre; the two square towers above the east end are totally dissimilar, and between them rises a curious greenish steeple added in the late nineteenth century.

As you enter, though, all confusion is stripped away and you're left with the clean lines of dour, severely austere stonework. In 1535, spurred on by Bern, the people of Geneva accepted the Reformation and embarked on an iconoclastic rampage – all the altars in the cathedral, as well as every statue and icon, were destroyed, the organs were smashed and the painted decoration on the interior walls was whitewashed. Only the great **pulpit** and, by chance, the stained glass of the chancel, survived. As you wander through the soaring interior, the architecture, and the austerity, draw your gaze upwards; almost the only decoration to survive is on the capitals of the nave's clustered pillars, grotesque monsters and a bare-breasted double-tailed mermaid. What is purportedly **Calvin's chair** sits at the back of the church on the left, near the door to the North Tower, climbable for spectacular views over the city (Fr.3). You shouldn't leave without spending time in the delightful **Maccabean Chapel**, last on the left before you leave. Used as a warehouse and later as a lecture hall, it was rededicated as a place of worship in 1878 and is filled with lavish and beautiful decoration dating from then. Copies of the only fifteenth-century frescoes to survive the Reformation – angels playing musical instruments – are on the ornamented vaults of the chancel within the chapel.

The cathedral is built on the remains of occupation going back to the Romans: the first church, just north of the present cathedral, has been dated to around 350 AD. From then on, the hill on which the cathedral stands was the site of almost continuous building and rebuilding. Since 1976, archeologists have been working to expose walls, rooms and mosaic floors beneath the cathedral, and the huge **archeological site** is open to the public (June–Sept Tues–Sat 11am–5pm, Sun 10am–5pm; Oct–May Tues–Sat 2–5pm, Sun 10am–noon & 2–5pm; Fr.5), pretty rarefied stuff but exceptionally well presented and labelled, subterranean catwalks weaving around and over the crumbling remains. With more than 200 levels of building work so far discovered in eleven zones, it's necessarily difficult to tweeze out exactly what's going on, but the free audioguide helps.

Maison Tavel

From the cathedral portico, an alley leads you on to the Rue du Puits-St-Pierre. A few metres left, at no. 6, is the distinctive grey-blue sandstone facade – etched with *trompe l'oeil* mortar-lines – of Geneva's oldest house, now the **Maison Tavel** museum (Tues–Sat noon–5pm, Sun 10am–5pm; permanent collection free). Built by the Tavel family in the twelfth century, the house was renovated after a fire in 1334, but in the sixteenth century the Tavel line died out. The house was maintained by various noble families until it was bought by the city in 1963 to display items from the history and urban life of Geneva. The vast cellars, which survived the fire intact, are the oldest part of the house, and they and the three upper floors are filled with moderately diverting items – massive carved doors, painted inn-signs and a complete twelve-room apartment showing everyday life in the seventeenth century – but the highlight of the museum is in the attic, a giant **relief map of Geneva** dating from 1850, showing the city complete with its fortifications, before the Pont du Mont-Blanc or the railway had been built. There's a sound-and-light show talking you through points of interest on the map; ask the staff to play the English version for you.

Around the Old Town

It's a few steps west from the Maison Tavel to a cobbled crossroads. To the right is Grand-Rue, birthplace of Rousseau, and parallel to it **Rue des Granges**, named "Street of Barns" but in fact graced by huge mansions built in the eighteenth century in French style to house Geneva's wealthiest residents. Looming over the junction is the **Hôtel-de-Ville** with an atmospheric internal arcaded courtyard, from where it's easy to spot the different styles of the building – going counterclockwise, the sixteenth, seventeenth and eighteenth centuries. Ahead is the Alabama Room, where the Geneva Convention on the humanitarian rules of war was signed by sixteen countries in 1864, and where, in 1872, conflict between two states was solved in a neutral state for the first time, when Britain and the US settled their differences over British support for the Confederacy during the Civil War. The League of Nations also assembled here for the first time in 1920. This is one of only three buildings in Europe to have a sloping ramp inside instead of stairs (the others are on the Loire and at Schaffhausen), both to facilitate cannons being pulled up to the ramparts and, so it's said, to enable councillors to arrive at meetings on horseback or in their sedan chair. You can work your way up to the top – feeling like an Escher drawing come to life – but the doors are all firmly locked. Behind the building is the lovely **Promenade de la Treille**, with the longest wooden bench in the world, at 126m, and a view over the city framed by chestnut trees. The last tree on the left, bent forward, is the official tree of Geneva – tradition has it that the chief city councillor must record the day its first bud blossoms as being the first day of spring. A board of dates has been kept in the Town Hall since 1818 and is added to annually.

Back along the Rue du Puits-St-Pierre, you'll come to a set of stairs leading down towards the Rues-Basses. Off to the left is Rue Calvin, with, at no. 10, the **Musée Barbier-Müller** (daily 11am–5pm; Fr.5; SMP), housing a striking and beautifully displayed collection of non-European sculpture and artwork. Notes are copious, guiding you from an incredible room filled with antique gold from Africa to huge carved masks from Oceania, and more.

Musée d'Art et d'Histoire

A few metres east of the Old Town at 2 Rue Charles Galland is the **Musée d'Art et d'Histoire** (Tues–Sun 10am–5pm; free), Geneva's biggest and most important museum and Switzerland's unofficial national collection. It's a gigantic place, that covers in encyclopedic fashion the whole sweep of Western culture from antiquity to the present; to do it justice would take days, but you could spend a worthwhile few hours absorbing the different areas.

For the marvellous **fine-art** collection, head up the grand staircase. What confronts you at the top is perhaps the highlight of the museum, a graceful and heart-stoppingly romantic sculpture in marble of Venus and Adonis, standing alone and lit by a skylight. Antonio Canova, a pre-eminent but now little-known Neoclassical sculptor, has given Venus the fingers of a pianist. Also at the head of the stairs are two powerful Rodins, *The Thinker* and *The Tragic Muse*. The collection begins in Hall 401 to the right of Venus and Adonis and, although it more or less keeps a chronological thread, don't be surprised if you come across photography, concrete installations or even video art scattered in amongst the painting. In room 402 you'll find Konrad Witz's famous altarpiece, made for the cathedral in 1444, which shows Christ and the fisherman transposed onto Lake Geneva. As you work your way around the perimeter rooms, Rembrandt and other Dutch and Flemish artists are in room 406, nineteenth-century Swiss in 408–9; the inner ring of smaller rooms features work by the eighteenth-century Genevois painter Liotard in 419–20. Perimeter rooms 412–14 are devoted to Vallotton, Pissarro, Cézanne, Renoir and Modigliani, with some striking Hodlers on the inner ring, including a mystical *Lac de Thoune* (1909) in room 425.

Back downstairs, the **applied arts** collection is on the mezzanine gallery and the ground floor, a wealth of silverware, pewter, armour and costume. The Cartigny room, with 1805 wood panelling by the Genevois craftsman Jean Jaquet, shows exquisitely elegant Louis XV and XVI furniture. The ground floor also often features temporary exhibits (admission charged).

The lower floor is given over to the massive **archeological** collection. Turn right for the breathtaking Egyptian rooms, including sections from the Book of the Dead, a complete ninth-century BC mummy, and a beautiful granite statue of the goddess Sekhmet, with the body of a woman and the head of a lioness, from the fourteenth century BC. There's also an excellent display on hieroglyphics. The halls devoted to Ancient Greece and Rome are no less impressive, filled with statuary, glassware and good historical notes.

South and west of the Old Town

Within sight of the Musée d'Art, on the high ground opposite, rise the gilded onion domes of the **Russian Church** (open sporadically), built in 1863 on the remains of a sixteenth-century Benedictine priory – at that time isolated on an empty hilltop – with money donated by Grand Duchess Anna Feodorovna Constancia, aunt of Queen Victoria and a longtime Geneva resident. A gridlike neighbourhood of long, straight boulevards lined with solid town houses rapidly grew up around the church at the end of the nineteenth century, and the area, known as Les Tranchées, is still grand and quiet today. Five minutes from the church, at 8 Rue Munier-Romilly, is the astonishing **Collections Baur** (Tues–Sun 2–6pm; Fr.5), the country's premier collection of East Asian art. Start at the top floor, with a bright-lit display, complete with paper-screen doors, of nineteenth-century Japanese ceramics. One floor down is the Chinese collection: aim for room 8, featuring some delicately luminescent yellow Yongzhang ceramics. The ground floor has some older Chinese work, including beautifully simple white bowls from the ninth century, a little interior garden and fountain in room 3 surrounded by Ming porcelain, and other rooms with brilliant cobalt-blue ceramics and spectacular Qing jade, almost translucent.

Barely five minutes' walk northwest, at 2 Terrasse St-Victor, is a grand mansion, its doorway flanked by torch-holding figures. This is the **Petit Palais** (Mon–Fri 10am–noon & 2–6pm, Sat & Sun 10am–1pm & 2–5pm; Fr.10), housing yet another art museum, this time devoted solely to French modernism 1870–1930. A wide selection of works trace the period's evolution of style but, despite the presence of a few big names, there are no major works and it's probably more for buffs than general passers-by. A broad Impressionist and Neo-Impressionist collection is scattered across four floors, aided by examples of Nabi, Fauvist and Naïf style, and plenty of works from the schools of Montmartre and Montparnasse.

Plainpalais

The broad Boulevard des Philosophes traces a path around the Parc des Bastions and the university district to the Rond-Point de Plainpalais, on the eastern tip of a diamond of open space known as the **Plaine de Plainpalais**. If Geneva still has a village green or a marketplace, this is it – a little oasis of humanity ringed around by buzzing traffic. Most days see a market of one kind or another, whether fruit and veg or the famous Wednesday and Saturday flea markets, and the space is always bustling with people walking their dogs, students reading on the benches or kids testing their skills on the skateboarding ramps.

Just off the western angle of the diamond is **MAMCO**, the Musée d'Art Moderne et Contemporain, housed in an old industrial space at 10 Rue des Vieux-Grenadiers (Tues noon–9pm, Wed–Sun noon–6pm; Fr.9). The museum has kept the former factory's concrete floors and overhead strip lighting to display its often stark but high-quality collection, covering installations, video art, photographs, sculptures and painting produced since the 1960s, both permanent acquisitions and a running series of temporary exhibits. Next door, the Centre d'Art Contemporain also holds many temporary shows of young Genevois and Swiss artists in all fields (Fr.4).

From the Place du Cirque at Plainpalais' northern tip, Boulevard de St Georges heads due west through one of Geneva's funkiest and most engaging young neighbourhoods. A short way along, a brick wall conceals the beautiful **Cimitière de Plainpalais**, permanent home to, among others, Sir Humphry Davy, who invented the miners' lamp. Gravestone #707, close to the wall and the object of much recent care, is marked only with a faint "J.C.": this is presumed to be the last resting place of Calvin. Adjacent to the cemetery's western wall is an area of what look like derelict, graffitied warehouses, but which are in fact the studios and workshops of Artamis (as in *art-amis*, "friends of art"), an artists' collective. Behind, Rue de la Coulouvrenière feeds into the atmospheric **Place des Volontaires**, with a scattering of cafés and the L'Usine squat, Geneva's biggest alternative arts venue, with galleries, a theatre space, music venue, café and more (see p.103). The riverfront Quai des Forces Motrices, also with cafés and clubs, is dominated by the arched windows of the **Bâtiments des Forces Motrices**, which once housed gigantic hydraulic turbines supplying the city with water and which has now been converted into a massive space for opera and drama (see p.104). Further along Boulevard de St-Georges is the rundown district of **Jonction**, at the point where the Arve meets the Rhône; residents have a tradition, in the torrid days of summer, of flinging themselves off the Pont de Sous-Terre for a refreshing float downstream in the cool water.

Carouge

Some 2km south of the city centre, the suburb of **Carouge** is a quite different experience from Geneva proper. Practically deserted until 1754, the township, now as then beyond the city limits, was granted to Victor Amideus, King of Sardinia (ruling from Turin). The king envisioned Carouge as a trading competitor to Geneva – one day possibly overtaking it – and turned it into a refuge for Catholics, Protestants unable to stomach Geneva's puritanical ways and, uniquely in Europe for the time, even Jews. Turinese architects developed a chessboard design of crisscrossing streets planted with trees, and low houses with wooden, Mediterranean-style galleries looking into internal gardens. From 1774 to 1792, this hamlet of a hundred people grew to a bustling town of four thousand and, although Carouge never did overtake Geneva, it's still something of a refuge from the city, its quiet, attractive streets packed with artists' workshops, old-style cafés and some of the city's best small-scale nightlife. Its tourist-office tag is the "Greenwich Village of Geneva", and although the streetlife is considerably less thrilling than that might suggest, it's still worth a half-day wander.

Trams #12 or #13 from the city centre can drop you at the **Place du Marché** in the heart of Carouge, still used as a marketplace and starting point for random exploration of the quarter. **Rue St-Joseph** is shoulder-to-shoulder artisans, from carpenters to milliners – check out the elegant exposed-mechanism clocks of Jean Kazes at no. 21, Anne-Claude Virchaux's linen-cotton clothes at no. 13, and the delicate artworks of the florist Les Cinq Sens round the corner on **Place du Temple**. A major feature of Carouge are the delightful internal galleried gardens which lurk behind almost every gate: most are open, so feel free to explore.

The Rive Droite

Geneva's **Rive Droite** (Right Bank), north of the Rhône, is less engaging for general exploration, and features only a couple of moderately interesting neighbourhoods – the

Pâquis for café life, and Les Grottes for architecture – on the way north to the **Place des Nations**, heart of the international area and dominated by the Red Cross Museum and the United Nations building.

Around the station

Rue du Mont-Blanc is Geneva's landmark street, a broad boulevard lined with airline offices and souvenir shops that slopes up the hill towards the train station and stands at the heart of the commercial shopping district. As with most such streets, though, it's what happens either side that's much more interesting. The **St Gervais** quarter, just west, was formerly the preserve of watchmakers, jewellers, engravers and goldsmiths. These days it has lost virtually all its character to traffic and modern commerce, although its old Gothic church survives on Rue du Temple.

Spreading east of Rue du Mont-Blanc is the cosmopolitan, rough-edged district of **Les Pâquis** centred on the long Rue de Berne – not a pretty place but crammed with restaurants and cafés devoted to every conceivable cuisine from Senegalese to Filipino. An equally visible feature of the Pâquis are the numerous sex shops and street prostitutes of Geneva's flourishing red-light trade. The further north you go, the quieter it gets; conversely, you could head out to the lakeside Quai du Mont-Blanc for a stroll north, past the marina and ranks of luxury hotels, to the beautiful Parc Mon Repos, first of five adjoining parks which lead you into the international area.

Immediately behind the station is a small residential area known as **Les Grottes**, a web of twisting lanes and mostly unrenovated nineteenth-century houses. In sharp contrast, on Rue Louis Favre, just off the main Rue de la Servette, you couldn't fail to spot the public-housing estate which looks as though it's been thrown together from plasticine. This is the **Schtrumpfs** (generic Euro-speak for the "Smurfs"), an exercise in Gaudi-esque fantasy which is worth a half-hour detour of anyone's time. All the estate's high-rises have lumps and blobs everywhere, giant mushrooms holding up balconies with cobweb railings, whimsical spiral staircases and twisted-liquorice columns, everything in a riot of primary colours. Pointless decoration in mosaics or arabesques covers the place. Designed by Robert Frei, Christian Hunziker and Georges Berthoud in the early 1980s for the municipality, it's a mad exercise in architectural whim ... but by all accounts the residents, who inevitably have come to be called Smurfs themselves, love it.

Place des Nations

A little over a kilometre north of the station is the **Place des Nations**, surrounded by offices of the dozens of international organizations headquartered in Geneva – everything from the World Council of Churches to Eurovision. Gates on the square open to the Palais des Nations, now occupied by UNOG, the United Nations Office at Geneva; the huge monolith just off the square to the west (like a bent playing card on its edge) is WIPO, the World Intellectual Property Organization; the high-rise to the south is ITU, the International Telecommunications Union; just to the east is UNHCR, United Nations High Commissioner for Refugees ... and so the alphabet soup continues. Most of these are just ordinary office buildings filled with working people; only the ICRC (International Committee of the Red Cross) and the UN are open to visitors.

The square itself, though, is an obvious gathering place for those who wish to make a point, and the little patch of grass in the middle is consistently trampled flat by the many demonstrators who march here. The giant **Broken Chair** which looms over it was installed in 1997 for the international conference at Ottawa banning the use of land mines, a graphic commemoration of the victims of such weapons. The square's an easy walk north from the station, or you can take any of an array of buses

– #8, #18, #F, #V or #Z – all of which go past the square to Appia, the best stop for the museums.

Musée International de la Croix-Rouge et du Croissant-Rouge

Housed within the headquarters of the International Committee of the Red Cross (ICRC), on a hill overlooking the UN at 17 Avenue de la Paix, the **Musée International de la Croix-Rouge et du Croissant-Rouge** (International Red Cross and Red Crescent Museum: Mon & Wed–Sun 10am–5pm; Fr.10; SMP; *www.icrc.ch*) is acclaimed as one of the best museums in Europe. Using highly effective video displays, slide-shows and interactive technology (always with an English-language option), it chronicles in detail the history of conflict in the twentieth century, and the role the Red Cross has played in providing aid to combatants and civilians caught up in both war and natural disasters. The displays are strikingly affecting, always using clear single images to tell a story instead of swamping you with facts and figures, and always avoiding judgement or ideological point-scoring. You shouldn't miss it on even the shortest trip to Geneva.

You enter through a trench in the hillside opposite the UN, emerging into an enclosed glass courtyard, surrounded by reflected images of yourself beside a group of stone figures, bound and blindfolded, representing the continual worldwide violation of human rights. Inside, above the ticket desk, is a quotation from Dostoievsky – "Everyone is responsible to everyone else for everything." The museum's very useful audioguide (Fr.5) takes you through the eleven undemarcated sections, all packed into a small floor area, which piece together in chronological order the history of kindness, from the Good Samaritan and Saladin to the experiences of Genevan businessman **Henry Dunant** which prompted him to found the Red Cross. Travelling in northern Italy in June 1859, Dunant found himself caught up in the Battle of Solferino, and was shocked to be brought face to face with the reality of the battlefield. With little or no provision to help the wounded, thousands perished where they fell, and Dunant returned to Geneva determined to take action. His tireless campaigning over five years resulted in the signing by the major powers of the first Geneva Convention in 1864, which, for the first time laid down guidelines for the conduct of war, and which led directly to international co-operation in the creation of the Red Cross.

In one area of the museum are ranged aisle after aisle of **record cards** from World War I – an astonishing seven million of them – detailing prisoners' particulars in order that they could be traced and reunited with their families. In another is a **reconstructed cell**, 3m by 2m, which an ICRC delegate reported housed seventeen prisoners – 34 footprints on the cell floor only go some way towards helping imagine the conditions. Also memorable is the eye-opening **Wall of Time**, an ingenious representation of those wars and natural disasters which have killed more than 100,000 people, year by year since the Red Cross's foundation: as you reach the second half of the century, the dizzyingly long lists of wars around the world tell their own, sombre story.

A final note of achievement: despite its skill and artistry, the museum's construction didn't use a penny of Red Cross funds, relying solely on outside donors.

The United Nations

Geneva is home to UNOG, the unattractively titled European headquarters of the **United Nations**, housed in a complex of buildings off Place des Nations. Some areas are open to the public for official guided tours (July–Aug daily 9am–6pm; April–June & Sept–Oct daily 10am–noon & 2–4pm; Jan–March & Nov–mid-Dec Mon–Fri 10am–noon & 2–4pm; Fr.8.50; *www.un.org*). The tours – in any of the UN's fifteen official languages – are only moderately interesting in themselves, but are packed with star quality for those who want to hobnob with history. This is the world's single largest conference centre for multilateral diplomacy and top-level international politicking – when the news has reports of "negotiating taking place in Geneva", they mean here. If this impresses, then you'll enjoy the visit; if it signals only the dreary prospect of traipsing along corridors and standing in empty conference halls, you should probably take your francs elsewhere.

The **Palais des Nations** was built from 1929 to 1936 to serve as the headquarters of the League of Nations, set up to prevent a recurrence of war on the scale of World War I but stymied soon after its birth by the outbreak of World War II. When the organization was re-founded as the United Nations in 1945, headquartered at New York, the Geneva office became European HQ. Since then it has burgeoned, and now encompasses offices administering a vast array of economic and social UN development work, as well as bodies dealing with the negotiation and signing of treaties and conventions of all kinds. It's also the hub of UN operations to deliver humanitarian aid and uphold human rights around the world.

The UN tour

The main entrance of the Palais des Nations, facing onto Place des Nations, is for UN staff only; the public entrance is up Avenue de la Paix opposite the Red Cross Museum. To enter, you'll have to hand in your **passport** and go through airport-style security procedures (you're effectively leaving Switzerland and entering international territory). You should then walk down the hill to the left, towards *Porte 39* in the new wing, from where tours depart. Note that you may have to wait fifteen or twenty minutes for the next tour in English (there's a bookshop for browsing), and also not only are there no lockers to leave your stuff, but the tour, which takes an hour, ends at a different exit closer to the passport-control gate.

Once you get going, you're regaled with a potted history of the UN and its philosophy, and odd factoids such as the UN is currently owed more than $2 billion by the US in unpaid subscriptions, or that when the US denied Yasser Arafat a visa to address the UN in New York in 1988, the entire General Assembly had to fly to Geneva to hear him speak in the great **Assembly Hall**, visitable today more or less in the same condition as when it was inaugurated in 1937. The **Council Chamber**, which hosted the negotiations to end the 1991 Gulf War, is decorated with gold-and-sepia murals painted in 1934 by the Catalan artist José Maria Sert, depicting the progress of humankind through health, technology, freedom and peace, all very heroic. Indeed, the whole architectural style of the main wing – granted to an international consortium after Le Corbusier's visionary modernist visions had been rejected – is, rather ironically, a prime example of 1930s fascist, complete with cold marble floors, gigantic bronze doors and the hard lines of Neoclassicist Art Deco. That the building's rear extension, built in the late Sixties, today resembles the worst of London or Paris's inner-city office blocks, merely adds insult to injury.

Musée Ariana

Just down the hill from the UN, in a distinctive Neo-Baroque mansion set in the same park, is the **Musée Ariana** (Mon & Wed–Sat 11am–5pm, Sun 10am–5pm; free), devoted solely to seven centuries of glass and ceramics from Europe and the East. Unless you're a fan, though, the building – semicircular galleries overlooking an internal atrium – is likely to be as inspiring as its contents. Highlights of the lavish collection include beautiful and intricately decorated European faience and porcelain from the sixteenth to eighteenth centuries, the earth tones of Spanish ware contrasting with deep creamy French colours and light Italian pastels. There are plenty of English notes to mug up on as you go around.

Eating and drinking

With more than a thousand restaurants in the city, you can **eat and drink** your way around the world in Geneva – at a price. The most visible establishments might give you the impression that you could afford nothing more adventurous than a baguette, but Genevois café culture is alive and well, and inexpensive diners do exist. If you're prepared to splash, you could dine as grandly in Geneva as in Paris, London or New York.

The city's excellent Swiss restaurants are somewhat overshadowed by a plethora of French places, drawing on influences from *haute-cuisine* Lyon just 160km away, but the Old Town in particular (around the Place du Bourg-de-Four) has a host of atmospheric Swiss eateries. Carouge is a foodie's paradise, with plenty of sometimes pricey choices. Eaux-Vives is much more down-to-earth and features many quality inexpensive Italian joints. Cosmopolitan – and occasionally tense – Pâquis has dozens of low-priced, authentic Arabic, East Asian, South American and African cafés and restaurants.

Cafés and café-bars

Almost every corner has its **café**, and the following list is highly selective, serving as much to give pointers as to what to expect in each neighbourhood as to recommend these particular establishments over others. The Old Town's Place du Bourg-de-Four, for instance, is lined with busy terrace cafés offering coffees, *apéros* and snacks to fuel hours of reading and people-watching, and there's little point picking one out to recommend. Wherever you end up, you'll have no trouble finding somewhere congenial to rest your feet and sample a little something.

Station area and Les Pâquis

Bookworm, 5 Rue Sismondi. Mini teashop within a crammed secondhand English bookshop, with tootling Thirties music and a faultless "pot of tea for two with biscuits". Closed Mon.

La Bretelle, 15 Rue des Etuves. Tiny kitsch tavern just off the Rive Droite, a glitz-drenched haven from the mean streets outside, that pulls in plenty of camp, alternative young-at-hearts, especially for the live accordion and/or drag cabaret (Thurs–Sat nights).

Buvette des Cropettes, Place Gruet, off Rue de Montbrillant. Tiny atmospheric six-table wood-floor café-bar tucked behind the station, opposite the sunny Cropettes park. Closed Sun & Mon.

Café Arts, 17 Rue des Pâquis. Bright café-bar with a young, excited clientele. A pleasant slice of sleaze-free Pâquis. Daily 5pm–midnight.

Café de Paris, 26 Rue du Mont-Blanc. Very central café that does one meal only, but does it spectacularly well – entrecôte steak in a herb-and-butter sauce with golden chips and salad, for Fr.35. Otherwise, it's a perfect place for down-time seconds from the station.

Café Vaudois, Rue des Alpes corner Rue de Neuchâtel. Simple plain tables in a simple plain room, with a bar at one end and big windows at the other for staring out of.

Cotton Pub, 4 Rue Louis-Duchosal. Small bar in the business district with more whiskies than beer – grab one of the comfy sofas for a long night in.

Old Town area and Plainpalais

Alhambar, 10 Rue Rôtisserie. Relaxed glittery bar behind a Rues-Basses cinema, with a yuppyish tone, plenty of tapas and evening DJs. Sunday's laidback piano-brunch is worth checking out.

Café du Centre, 5 Place du Molard (☎022/311 85 86). A very handy Rues-Basses pitstop with terrace seating in summer. The smell of the sea hits you as you push the door and that's really what this plain, very popular café-restaurant is all about, offering everything from 100g of periwinkles up to a dozen fresh oysters, aided by a huge wine list. Not cheap for dining, at Fr.30–50, but worth a coffee just to sample the old-style atmosphere.

Café Gallay, 42 Boulevard St Georges. Friendly neighbourhood café-bar opposite Plainpalais cemetery, attracting an arty young crowd of students and theatre people. Inexpensive food and shared tables add to the appeal. Closed Sun.

Café Mozart, 4 Quai des Forces Motrices. Cool split-level designer wine bar on the riverfront, regularly featuring live classical and jazz quartets (Thurs–Sat). An expensive menu promotes quaffing over scoffing. Closed Sun & Mon.

Le 2e Bureau, 9 Rue du Stand. Sleek postmodern bar, with sleek postmodern people draped over the sofas as deep beats rattle the glasses. Occasionally features live music or readings.

Flanagan's, Rue du Cheval-Blanc. Top-rated Irish pub, hidden on an Old Town alley and generally packed with expats and Genevois alike.

Le Vespetro in L'Usine squat, Place des Volontaires. Graffitied upstairs bar-café, sporting a rough-edged clientele puffing clouds of sweet smoke to a background of heavy noise. A prominent notice bans the presence of mobile phones in no uncertain terms. Solid meals for Fr.10 or so. Closed Sun & Mon.

Eaux-Vives

Chez Serge, Rue des Eaux-Vives, corner Rue des Vollandes. Quirky, snug little local bar, crammed with bric-à-brac, plants, candles and a fishtank.

The Flying Bike, 61 Rue des Eaux-Vives. Boisterous local drinking den, worth heading for if you're in the neighbourhood and fancy joining ordinary working Genevois for a jar or two.

Carouge

Bar du Nord, 66 Rue Ancienne. Dark, plasticky and filled with young designerish Carougeois carousing beneath murals by a local cartoonist.

Café des Amis, 23 Rue Ancienne. Oldest of the traditional cafés on Ancienne, full of atmosphere from an age now past. Join the locals for a trip down memory lane.

Café de la Plage, 10 Rue Vautier. Trendy alternative hangout, with long carved wooden benches and a homely, talkative ambience, regularly spilling drinkers out onto the street. It's a long way from the *plage*, though.

La Marchand de Sable, 4 Rue Vautier. Loud, graffitied little nook with a rough edge, packed most nights.

Martel Tea Room, 4 Rue du Marché. Perfect spot to punctuate an afternoon walk around Carouge, founded in 1818 and still offering exquisite chocolates and pastries as well as good, inexpensive meals. Closed Mon.

Inexpensive and mid-range restaurants

There's almost limitless choice in **inexpensive and mid-range** dining, with good-value, characterful places just off the main streets in all corners of the city. Excellent self-service dining is to be had at the huge Manora, 4 Rue de Cornavin: with such a fast customer turnover, its food is actually very fresh as well as rock-bottom cheap and you can easily stuff yourself for Fr.11.

Station area and Les Pâquis

Al-Amir, 12 Rue des Alpes. Excellent Lebanese place, its stool-and-counter area favoured by falafel-munching locals over the sit-down table section. Quality range of *mezze* (Fr.8–14 each), plus chicken or lamb *shwarmas* (Fr.10) as good as they should be. Top choice of the many Pâquis kebab dens.

Le Diwane, 6 Rue de Zurich (☎022/732 73 91). Excellent, authentically prepared Arabic cuisine. A meal of classy *mezze* is about Fr.25, or you can blowout and order the entire menu for Fr.160 – either way, don't miss the delicious *maamoul* afterwards. July–Sept daily noon–12.30am; Oct–June Mon–Fri noon–2.30pm & 7–10.30pm, Sat 7–10.30pm.

El Mektoub, 5 Rue Chaponnière (☎022/738 70 31). Discreet central hideaway for quality North African cooking in a pleasant ambience. Excellent couscous and a wealth of *tajines* are Fr.30–35, with a handful of veggie options too. Closed Sun.

Jeck's, 14 Rue de Neuchâtel (☎022/731 33 03). Small Thai place, with nice wood-and-rattan decor and surprisingly affordable quality cooking (Fr.25–30, or Fr.15 at lunch). House speciality is a range of Singaporean dishes, mixing influences from Malaysia, China and India. Closed Sat lunch.

Au Petit Chalet, 6 Rue Chaponnière. Unpretentious city-centre Swiss place for fondues, Rösti and pizza (Fr.20–25) in a refreshingly untouristic dark-wood setting. Closed Mon.

Teranga, 38bis Rue de Zurich (☎022/731 15 22). Tiny backstreet Senegalese place, attractively decorated, with good service and great food, including plantains, yassa (braised chicken in onion sauce) and fresh ginger juice. Around Fr.25. Closed Sat lunch & Sun.

Old Town area and Plainpalais

Les Armures, 1 Rue du Puits-St-Pierre (☎022/310 34 42). Traditional stone-floored Old Town institution on three storeys, refreshingly kitsch-free and once graced by the Clintons (with a plaque by the door to prove it). A full range of perfectly prepared Swiss dishes cost from Fr.30.

Cave Valaisanne/Chalet Suisse, Place du Cirque. Touristically minded place for those seeking that authentic fondue experience. The chalet side is all dim lights, dark wood-beamed interior and endless Swiss kitsch; the *cave* side less contrived and so slightly less grating. The food is fine at both, and affordable (Fr.20 or so), but neither is what you might call heart-warming.

La Favola, 15 Rue Jean Calvin (☎022/311 74 37). Charming little family-run restaurant on a cobbled Old Town alley, with a small menu of choice Ticinese specialities to dally over in an atmospheric setting. A romantic evening tête-à-tête could touch Fr.45 each; lunches much less. Closed Sat lunch & Sun.

Hang Zhou, 19 Rue de la Coulouvrenière (☎022/781 41 47). Excellent inexpensive Chinese, with a full vegetarian menu and *dim sum* galore (Fr.13–23). Closed Sun.

Kantine, in Artamis squat community, off Boulevard de St-Georges. On the far left side, tucked among the graffitied warehouses and studios of Artamis, divey *Kantine* offers one of the cheapest meals in Geneva, home-made food in big portions for Fr.10. Roughly Mon–Fri 11am–4pm, maybe later, maybe earlier.

Le Pied de Cochon, 4 Place du Bourg-de-Four (☎022/310 47 97). Bow-tied waiters bustle their way between the tinkling cutlery of one of Geneva's best-loved bistros, serving meaty Genevois and Lyonnais gutliners (Fr.35), including the namesake grilled pigs' trotters, to a clientele not short of a *centime* or two.

Taverne de la Madeleine, 20 Rue Toutes-Âmes. Quite possibly the oldest restaurant in the city, now an alcohol-free café-bistro, serving only lunches – unreconstructed home-made fare (Fr.15) – in a tiny old dining room below the Old Town. Closed Sun.

Eaux-Vives

Dent de Lion, 14 Rue des Eaux-Vives. Small, rather shabby vegetarian place that nonetheless serves up good wholesome food for Fr.22–25. Closed Sat & Sun.

Vesuvio, 7 Rue Cherbuliez (☎022/736 30 40). Eaux-Vives is full of Italian restaurants, but this is one of the best, boasting fresh-made pasta, a wood-fired pizza oven, relaxed open decor and friendly service. Meals are not expensive, mostly under Fr.20. Closed Sat lunch, Sun & Mon.

Carouge

Le Bourse, 7 Place du Marché, Carouge. Celebrated café-brasserie in the heart of Carouge, with a wide, heavily fishy menu, taking in *moules* and *huitres* as well as a protein-packed *marmite du pêcheur* (Fisherman's Pot; Fr.35). Fondue, salads and steak help out less briny diners, and a quality lunch *menu* can be had for Fr.15. Closed Sun & Mon.

La Cuccagna, Place du Temple, Carouge. Quality among Carouge's high-class cuisine that won't break the bank, with simple, delicious pizza and pasta dishes for Fr.25 or so.

Sawasdee, 24 Avenue Cardinal Mermillod, Carouge (☎022/300 08 42). Best Thai in Geneva, with calm, attentive service, simply exquisite food and a bill at the end of it to lighten your spirits: a mere Fr.15–18 for lunch, twice that in the evening. Definitely worth the tram ride.

Expensive restaurants

Geneva has dozens of top-drawer **expensive** restaurants, where you can find cuisine to match the best in the world. Dining within the top hotels is nearly always superb – *Le Cygne* in the Noga Hilton, *Le Chat Botté* in the Beau Rivage and *Les Continents* in the Intercontinental stand out, with the first two offering spectacular views and terrace seating in addition to top-quality food. The following is a tiny trawl through accessible non-hotel places; all require pockets deep enough to absorb a Fr.60–100 per-head bill.

L'Ange du Dix Vins, 31 Rue Jacques Dalphin, Carouge (☎022/342 03 18). Much-loved little place, with warm Provençale ochre-and-sky-blue decor and cuisine to match. A convivial atmosphere in both the restaurant and less formal bistro adjacent fits precisely the relaxed appreciation of good food and wine, overseen by a chef "qui oppose au snobisme de la gastro les magies chaleureuses du restau". Daily specials around Fr.23, full menu Fr.60, truffle menu Fr.110. Closed Sat & Sun.

Le Béarn, 4 Quai de la Poste (☎022/321 00 28). Geneva's premier establishment, supremely elegant and with lavish and inventive cuisine earning plaudits from those in the know. *Menus* are from Fr.50, but most meals probably won't remain in mere double figures. Closed Sat & Sun & mid-July–Aug.

L'Esquire, 7 Rue du Lac (☎022/786 50 44). Gourmet French cuisine in the unlikely surroundings of an Eaux-Vives backstreet. The place is also a gallery for local artists, and pleasant decor and respectful service aids peaceful digestion of the *foie gras* and *filet mignon de veau*. Lunch is Fr.35, evening *menus* Fr.65–85. Closed Sat lunch & Sun.

Vieux-Bois, 12 Avenue de la Paix (☎022/919 24 26). High-quality showcase of the world-famous catering school *L'École Hôtelière de Genève*: all the chefs and waiting staff are students, which means you'll get sharp, attentive service and an *haute cuisine* lunch – French, with light, inventive touches and veggie options – for a fraction of prices elsewhere. Scoff a four-course *menu* for as little as Fr.45, or choose from the daily specials for half that, and then retire to the garden for coffee. Mon–Sat noon–2.30pm; garden May–Sept Mon–Sat noon–6pm. Closed Easter, mid-July–mid-Aug, Christmas & New Year.

Nightlife and entertainment

Geneva's **nightlife** is unlikely to set your pulse racing. As far as popular culture goes, the city suffers from a major image problem both abroad and inside Switzerland, and few bands or DJs come visiting. There are endless venues catering to visiting businesspeople and wealthy locals – formal dinner-dance, yawnworthy cabaret, and vast quantities of strip-shows and hostess bars – but aside from checking out the handful of alternative arts venues, it's not easy to find what young Genevois get up to … often because they've vanished up the road to the cutting-edge clubs in and around Lausanne instead.

The flipside of that image problem is that you can find top-notch classical music and opera, with a world-famous orchestra dividing its time between Geneva and Lausanne, as well as major international performers. Dance and drama are also well accounted for. The Fêtes de Genève is the city's premier annual arts festival, held in early August on the waterfront, with music of all kinds, theatre, funfairs and street entertainers.

What's on **listings** are published weekly in *Genève-Agenda*, the free city guide available from the tourist office and hotels, but *La Clef* tends to have a better idea of where to go (Fr.5 quarterly). You can get **tickets** for most shows from either City-Disc at the station (☎022/900 18 50), or UBS Ticket Corner, 5 Rue de la Corraterie (☎022/376 62 65). Prices are not cheap: Fr.10–15 for ordinary live bands and clubs, Fr.25–30 for special events, Fr.15–60 for classical concerts, and Fr.24–200 for the opera.

Note that bars are open all night during March's Motor Show weekend, August's Fêtes de Genève, and L'Escalade in December.

Live music

Geneva is not exactly heart of the European music industry, and even Suisse-Romande bands prefer Lausanne, but there are a few venues around town for **live music**. Friday

GAY AND LESBIAN GENEVA

Geneva's **gay** scene is centred around Dialogai, 11 Rue de la Navigation (Mon, Tues & Fri 3–6pm, Wed 3–10pm; ☎022/906 40 40, *www.hivnet.ch/dialogai*), which, as well as being a library and resource centre for the whole of Romandie, has news about one-offs around the city as well as a regular programme of on-site events. The adjacent café metamorphoses between being the *Chez Rosy* tearoom (Sun–Thurs 9am–5pm) and the *Sunset* tapas bar (Wed–Sun 5–10pm). Every week, they put on a mass candlelit dinner in a back room, guys crowding at long tables for the home-made food (Wed 7–10pm; Fr.12; maximum 80 – arrive early). Every other Friday is *Genfshaft*, best macho jeans/leather night in the city (11pm–5am; Fr.10). The *Rêve d'O* techno club has occasional gay nights, while *Le Loft*, 20 Quai de Seujet, is a big, glitzy campy disco, with top-quality drag shows during the week. *La Bretelle* (see p.99) and *L'Evidence*, 13 Rue des Grottes (Mon–Fri 6am–1am, Sat & Sun 11am–1am), are gay-friendly café-bars, while *Thermos*, 10 Rue Goetz-Monin, is a gay night-café with bars and a darkroom (Wed–Sun 8pm–2am). You'll find no shortage of cruising possibilities among the Pâquis sex-shops – *Le Garage*, 14 Rue de Neuchâtel, is king. The Gay International Group (☎022/789 18 69) meets every fortnight and welcomes newcomers.

Dialogai can help out with **lesbian**-oriented information, or you should call the Centre femmes Natalie Barney, 19 Château-Bloch in Vernier (☎022/797 27 14), or La Clef, 3 bis Rue du Stand (☎022/781 71 30). The latter has regular lesbian dance nights (Fri & Sat 10pm–3am). *L'Inédite* is a bookshop and resource centre for women – lesbian and not – at 15 Rue St Joseph, Carouge. There are no lesbian-only clubs.

Check out *www.gay-geneva.ch* and *www.swissgay.ch* for more.

and Saturday nights are when the bars and clubs lining Rue Vautier in Carouge come into their own. There's a festival of rock, jazz and folk in July & August at Parc La Grange in Eaux-Vives, but if you're around in the summer you should aim for the big Paleo festival at Nyon just around the lake (see p.136).

Le Chat Noir, 13 Rue Vautier, Carouge. Bar and cellar venue dedicated to live performance, with two or three concerts a week, everything from *chansons* to drum'n'bass, acid jazz and acoustic blues. Mon–Thurs 6pm–4am, Fri 6pm–5am, Sat & Sun 9pm–5am.

Forumeyrin, 1 Place des Cinq-Continents, Meyrin. Main arena venue for Geneva, on the border near the airport, hosting anyone and anything.

Les Halles de l'Île, Place de l'Île. River-view restaurant with jazz that won't upset the purists. Live music Fri & Sat 8.30pm.

Sud des Alpes, 10 Rue des Alpes. Jazz-buffs' mecca, with live music that sometimes pushes the boat out a fraction. Generally Thurs–Sat at 9.30pm.

L'Usine, Place des Volontaires (☎022/328 08 18). Alternative arts squat venue, featuring live bands at the Salle PTR ("Post Tenebras Rock"), experimental dance and drama at the Théâtre de l'Usine and non-commercial movies at the Cinéma Spoutnik.

Clubs

There's a handful of dance **clubs** worth dipping a toe into, but nothing to get very excited about – Lausanne and Zürich are where top DJs tout their wares. Geneva suffers from a surfeit of expense accounts, and often you'll find that places billing themselves as *discothèques* turn out to enforce a smart-casual door policy for entry to a deeply depressing floorshow (occasionally nude dancing girls) and/or Top 40 disco. The following are the best of an uninspiring bunch. Note that although a few places open during the week, weekend nights (generally 10pm–5am) are more likely to be worthwhile. Entry is usually Fr.10–15.

L'Abag, 10 Rue des Vieux-Grenadiers. Salsa club in the courtyard of MAMCO.

L'Interdit, 18 Quai de Seujet. Pumping and hugely popular disco cavern, sharing its clientele and energy with the Loft next door (see "Gay and Lesbian" box).

La Pirogue, 4 Ruelle des Templiers. Reggae and African beats.

Power, 12 bis Passage Malbuisson. Techno-free funk, house and jungle.

Rêve d'O, 19 Rue de la Coulouvrenière. Exposed-metal interior of an old riverfront warehouse vibrates nightly to hardcore techno, with occasional forays into drum'n'bass and triphop. Free entry.

Classical music, theatre and film

There's plenty of **classical music** in Geneva. The Orchestre de la Suisse Romande, which shuttles between Geneva and Lausanne, is one of Europe's best, and often performs – in amongst big-name visiting orchestras and soloists – at the glittering Victoria Hall, 14 Rue Général-Dufour (☎022/328 81 21). The Grand Théâtre on Place Neuve (☎022/311 23 11) has a continuous programme of classical concerts and chamber music, and both it and the Grand Casino, 19 Quai du Mont-Blanc (☎022/732 06 00), stage plenty of **opera**. There are free classical concerts in many of Geneva's churches year-round, and open-air concerts at the Hôtel-de-Ville in July and August. The Conservatoire de Musique, also on Place Neuve (☎022/311 76 33), hosts a prestigious annual international competition for young soloists in late September.

You may come across high-quality amateur **theatre** companies performing in English: TIE (Theatre in English; ☎022/341 51 90) has details of productions by GEDS (Geneva English Drama Society), LTG (Little Theater of Geneva) and GAOS (Geneva Amateur Operatic Society). However, most theatre is in French. The Comédie de Genève, 6 Boulevard des Philosophes (☎022/320 50 01), is the main stage for classic drama, and the huge Bâtiments des Forces Motrices (BFM), formerly housing hydro-electric machinery on the Rhône, has been converted into a gigantic, lofty space for contemporary theatre and occasional opera (Quai des Forces Motrices; ☎022/322 12 20). There are also dozens of smaller, more experimental theatres, including Théâtre La Poche, 7 Rue du Cheval Blanc (☎022/310 37 59), and Théâtre du Grütli, 16 Rue Général-Dufour (☎022/328 98 78). Kids will love Les Marionettes de Genève, 3 Rue Rodo (☎022/329 67 67). The Théâtre de l'Usine on Place des Volontaires often features avant-garde dance and music-drama.

As for **film**, you'll find dozens of city-centre cinemas showing Hollywood releases (often ahead of London), but you should check in the listings for "v.o." (*version originale*), which indicates original dialogue with French subtitles – many prime-time showings are dubbed. The tiny handful of non-commercial movies you might be able to discover rarely feature English subtitles. Every summer there are big open-air screenings of all kinds of movies on the waterfront at Port Noir. The **Geneva Film Festival**, every October, is devoted to airing the work of unknowns from around Europe.

Listings

Boat rental For a taste of freedom, you can rent boats by the hour or the day from a handful of quayside operators, including Les Corsaires (33 Quai Gustave-Ador; ☎022/735 43 00) and Marti Marine (31 Quai du Mont-Blanc; ☎022/732 88 21).

Books The best place for English-language media is Elm Books, 5 Rue Versonnex, near Rive. L'Inédite, 15 Rue St-Joseph in Carouge, has a quirky selection of English and French books by, for and about women. *Bookworm* (see p.99) is piled high with secondhand English books of all kinds. English-language newspapers are widely available from kiosks all over the city centre.

Car rental Avis, 44 Rue de Lausanne (☎022/731 90 00) and airport (☎022/929 03 30); Budget, 36 Rue de Zurich (☎022/900 24 00) and airport (☎022/798 22 53); Europcar, 37 Rue de Lausanne (☎022/732 52 52) and airport (☎022/798 11 10); Hertz, 60 Rue de Berne (☎022/731 12 00) and airport (☎022/798 22 02).

Changing money The best place to change cash or cheques or get an advance on a debit/credit card is the change bureau in the station (April–Oct daily 6.45am–9.30pm; Nov–March daily 6.45am–8pm). This is also the place to pick up money wired by Western Union.

Consulates Australia, 56 Rue Moillebeau (☎022/918 29 00); Canada, 1 Chemin du Pré-de-la-Bichette (☎022/919 92 00); New Zealand, 28a Chemin du Petit-Saconnex (☎022/734 95 30); UK, 37 Rue de Vermont (☎022/918 24 00); USA, 29 Route de Pré-Bois (☎022/798 16 15).

Email and Internet In the shopping area below the station, directly beneath the change bureau, is Café Video ROM (Mon–Thurs 11am–8.30pm, Fri & Sat 11am–10pm, Sun 1–8.30pm), with 5 PCs at Fr.5/hr. Charly's, 7 Rue Fribourg (Mon–Sat 10am–10pm), has a room full of Macs at Fr.2/10min. Out of town, CERN (see p.107) offers free unlimited access.

Flights For all domestic and international flight enquiries from Geneva-Cointrin, call ☎157 15 00. Leopair, based at the airport (☎022/798 21 10), is one of nine firms offering sightseeing flights.

Laundry Lavseul, 29 Rue de Monthoux (daily 7am–midnight).

Libraries and cultural centres There are dozens of cultural organizations and libraries serving Geneva's sizeable English-speaking expat communities – the tourist office has details, but the American Library, 3 Rue de Monthoux (Tues & Fri 12.30–5pm, Wed 2–7pm, Thurs 2–5pm, Sat 10am–4pm, Sun 11am–12.30pm; ☎022/732 80 97), is an excellent place to start, with stacks of books, community information and a well-used notice board.

Lost property If you lost something on a plane, call ☎022/799 33 35; if you lost it in the airport, call ☎022/788 22 26; if you lost it in a train station or on a train, call ☎022/715 22 13. The main CFF lost property office is on platform 1B of Gare Cornavin (Mon–Fri 6am–9pm, Sat & Sun 9am–7.45pm), and the city's lost property office is at 7 Glacis-de-Rive (Mon–Fri 8am–4pm; ☎022/787 60 00).

Markets The best markets in the city are the venerable old fleamarket on the Plaine de Plainpalais (Wed & Sat 8am–5pm); the general market on Place de la Madeleine (Mon–Sat 10am–6pm); and crafts (Thurs 8am–7pm) and books (April–Oct Fri 8am–7pm), both on Place de la Fusterie. Plainpalais also has big fruit & veg markets (Tues, Fri & Sun).

Medical facilities The Cantonal Hospital, 24 Rue Micheli-du-Crest (☎022/372 33 11), has a 24-hour emergency room, as do the Permanances medical centres dotted around town (21 Rue Chantepoulet, ☎022/731 21 20; 1 Rue du Jura, ☎022/345 45 50; 17 Rue de Carouge, ☎022/329 56 56). For emergency dental treatment, call ☎022/791 04 30 (Old Town area) or ☎022/320 31 22 (station area). Call ☎022/748 49 50 if you need a doctor.

Post Geneva's most convenient large post office is at 18 Rue du Mont-Blanc. You can collect mail sent to you at Poste Restante, Mont-Blanc, CH-1211 Geneva 1, from windows 3–7 with your passport.

Radio WRG (World Radio Geneva), on 88.4FM, is an English-language expat station, with MOR music, phone-ins and news. Family Radio 74, at 88.8FM, is, if anything, even more wishy-washy, with regular BBC/VOA news padded out with wholesome Christian programming, some in French.

Sport Two large outdoor swimming complexes have pools and access to the lake waters: Genève Plage is on the Rive Gauche at Port-Noir (daily: June–Aug 9am–8pm, May & Sept 9am–7pm; Fr.5; bus #2), with a heated pool and waterslide, basketball, volleyball, waterskiing and windsurfing; the Bains des Pâquis at 30 Quai du Mont-Blanc (daily: late-May–Aug 9am–8pm, May & Sept 10am–6pm; Fr.1), dating from the 1930s, is more popular but has fewer facilities. For details and to reserve places on the canoeing, rafting and kayaking trips on the Arve's 7km of rapids, contact the tourist office; departures are from the Gare Routière (July & Aug daily 1.30 & 5pm; May, June & Sept on request; ☎022/784 02 05). On a more sedate note, the America pool hall, 3 Rue Fribourg (Sun–Thurs 10am–1am, Fri & Sat 10am–2am) has tables at Fr.16/hr.

Travel agents Discount flight agents SRR Voyages are at 3 Rue Vignier (Mon–Fri 9am–6pm, Sat 9am–noon; ☎022/329 97 33). Plenty of travel agents crowd Rue du Mont-Blanc and Rue Chantepoulet

Around Geneva

If you're on an unhurried visit, there's plenty of opportunity to get out into the beautiful countryside of **Canton Geneva**, Switzerland's smallest. The tourist office brochure *Sites naturels et cours d'eau de la campagne genevoise* features eight two- or three-hour walks in the Genevese countryside, easily manageable from the city itself, but it's also simple to strike out alone and discover bucolic villages, châteaux, views of the mountains or the lake for yourself. In general, the slopes of the Rive Droite (north bank) are winegrowing territory, those of the Rive Gauche (south bank) devoted to farmland. Public transport of all kinds – from boats to buses – extends to every corner, but you'd do just as well renting a bike (see p.40) or on foot.

As well as the nearest high mountain to Geneva, **Mont Salève**, which is a perfect place for sunshine when the lake is foggy, the Rive Gauche village of **Cologny** is worth a jaunt, both for its atmosphere and ease of access. In an entirely different vein, **CERN**, Europe's leading particle physics laboratory and the place where the World Wide Web was born, straddles the French border at **Meyrin** to the northwest.

Mont Salève

First ridge of the Alps rising southeast of Geneva is **Mont Salève** (1380m), the Genevois' principal retreat into nature, with wide-open countryside for walking or skiing, and views over the city, the whole canton and the Jura hills opposite. There are footpaths galore on top (which become cross-country skiing trails in winter), both through woodland and, higher up, across expansive green meadows dotted with wildflowers in season. In contrast to the sheer face presented to Geneva, the other, southern side of the mountain is a gentle slope, looking out onto Mont Blanc and the Savoy Alps.

Bear in mind that Salève is actually in France, so if you're going to need a visa (either to get into France, or to get back into Switzerland), you'll probably do best to give it a miss. Bus #8 terminates on the border at Veyrier, from where it's a short walk through customs to the cable-car, which rises to a crest of the ridge (Fr.15 return).

Cologny and Hermance

The Rive Gauche lakeside slopes, all the way from Geneva to the French border, are dotted with peaceful, attractive villages that can offer some of the most beautiful and relaxing walking in the vicinity. The first of these, **COLOGNY**, some 6km northeast of Geneva, has long been known as an exclusive and somewhat refined suburb, and the difference from Geneva is striking, with country lanes weaving between fields and open woods, and many large detached houses set back behind walls. From central Geneva, you can either follow the Rive Gauche road past the Parc des Eaux-Vives, and take a turn-off to the right, Rampe de Cologny, up the hillside into the village; or grab bus #A, which takes a different route through Frontenex up to Cologny, remaining within Zone 10.

Byron wrote the third canto of *Childe Harold* in 1816 while staying in Cologny at the Villa Deodati at 9 Chemin de Ruth, and waxed lyrical about the rarity of seeing Mont Blanc reflected in the lake from up here. Milton, too, came visiting in 1639. If you follow Chemin de Ruth north, you'll come to the district of Montalègre, and the Maison Chapuis, where Shelley and Clairmont stayed in 1816 with Mary Godwin, who began writing *Frankenstein* here. The association with fame has stayed rock solid over the centuries, and Cologny has its fair share of resident big-names, including Isabelle Adjani, Charles Aznavour, various sheikhs and Petula Clark. True to form, the tourist office has obligingly dubbed the place the "Beverly Hills of Geneva".

Cologny also has an esoteric museum attraction, the **Bibliotheca Bodmeriana**, at 19 Route de Guignard next to the bus stop (Thurs 2–6pm, also first Tues in month 6–8pm; Fr.5). One of the greatest private libraries ever assembled, it takes in 160,000 works of literature, many of unique historical value, including illuminated medieval manuscripts, one of the few copies of the Gutenberg Bible and the oldest surviving text of the Gospel of St John.

Some 10km further along the lakeshore on a minor road, the tiny village of **HERMANCE**, last before you cross into France and reachable on bus #E (or summertime boats), is even more tranquil, with a gorgeous lakeside location, remnants of its thirteenth-century walls and many medieval houses. Its charming *Auberge d'Hermance*, at 12 Rue du Midi, has five cosy and attractive rooms, and is also celebrated for its French cuisine (☎022/751 1368, fax 751 16 31, *auberge.dhermance@infomaniak.ch*, *www.kis.ch/hermance*; ③)).

CERN
Northwest of Geneva, the suburbs dribble on either side of the main autoroute to Lyon, beyond the airport to the French border at **Meyrin**. The only reason to come out here – aside from possibly catching a concert at the huge *Forumeyrin* (see p.103) – is to visit the European Laboratory for Particle Physics, known by its old initials of **CERN** (☎022/767 84 84, *www.cern.ch/public*; bus #9). This awe-inspiring place is one of the world's largest scientific laboratories, dedicated to pure research into the tiniest building-blocks of nature. A joint venture by a welter of European countries, which between them provide the near-Fr.1 billion annual budget, it's truly international, with scientists from eighty countries conducting mammoth months- or years-long experiments. CERN's – and the world's – largest particle accelerator, a circular tunnel around which electrons are fired at just under the speed of light to see what happens when they hit their antimatter counterparts, is an incredible 27km around, buried 100m below the French-Swiss border here.

CERN has an exceptionally well-organized public visits office, which runs regular **free tours** of the entire site (Mon–Sat 9am & 2pm; 3hr), for which you should book ahead; if you visit between October and March, you'll also get to stand inside the accelerator tunnel (it's switched off in winter). There's also a less engaging schools-oriented exhibition, Microcosm, explaining some of the work at the centre (Mon–Sat 9am–5pm; free) and providing free Internet access. It was a scientist working at CERN in 1989, Tim Berners-Lee, who began to realize the limitations of the data-only Internet at that time, and the need for electronic transmission of texts, images and references to other data files; to fill the gap, he created the **World Wide Web**. CERN's website is suitably encyclopedic on this and other matters.

travel details

TRAINS

Geneva to: Aigle (hourly; 1hr 20min); Basel (hourly; 2hr 50min); Bern (hourly; 1hr 45min); Bex (every 2hr; 1hr 35min); Biel/Bienne (hourly; 1hr 40min); Brig (twice hourly; 2hr 20min); Delémont (hourly; 2hr 15min); Fribourg (twice hourly; 1hr 20min); Geneva airport (5 times hourly; 10min); Lausanne (3 times hourly; 35min); Martigny (hourly; 1hr 35min); Montreux (hourly; 1hr 5min); Neuchâtel (hourly; 1hr 20min); Nyon (3 times hourly; 15min); St Gallen (hourly; 4hr 20min); Sierre (hourly; 2hr); Sion (twice hourly; 1hr 50min); Solothurn (hourly; 2hr); Vevey (hourly; 1hr); Yverdon (hourly; 55min); Zürich (hourly; 3hr).

BOATS

(following is a summary of May–Sept summer services; fewer boats run in other months, generally Sat & Sun only if at all)

Geneva (Quai du Mont-Blanc or Jardin Anglais) to: Evian, France (2 daily; 2hr 45min); Hermance (1 or 2 daily; 45min); Lausanne (3 daily; 3hr 30min); Montreux (3 daily; 5hr); Nyon (4–7 daily; 1hr–1hr 30min); Vevey (3 daily; 4hr 30min).

FLIGHTS

Geneva to: Basel (3–5 daily; 40min); Bern (3 weekly; 40min); Lugano (3–5 daily; 50min); Zurich (15 daily; 50min).

INTERNATIONAL TRAINS

Geneva to: Barcelona (1 daily; 9hr 30min); Grenoble (4 daily; 2hr 10min); Lyon (6 daily; 1hr 40min); Marseille (1 daily; 5hr 45min); Milan (5 daily; 3hr 45min); Montpellier (1 daily; 4hr 20min); Paris (5 daily; 3hr 40min); Venice (1 daily; 7hr 40min).

Geneva (Gare des Eaux-Vives) to: Annemasse for Evian (9 daily; 10min); La Roche-sur-Foron for Chamonix (7 daily; 35min).

INTERNATIONAL BUSES

Geneva (Gare Routière) to: Annecy (2–6 daily; 1hr 15min); Chamonix (1–4 daily; 1hr 35min); **Evian** (3 daily; 1hr 25min); London (4 weekly; 17hr); Thonon (4–6 daily; 50min); **Turin** (6 weekly; 4hr 30min).

PLACE NAMES IN THIS CHAPTER		
German	**French**	**Italian**
Genf	Genève	Ginevra
Genfersee	Lac Léman	Lago Ginevra

CHAPTER TWO

LAUSANNE AND LAKE GENEVA

Y ou can find the whole of Switzerland on the shores of **Lake Geneva** –
    snowy mountains, bucolic wine-villages, city nightlife, the sound of cow-
    bells in rolling pastureland, castles, cathedrals and the dreamily beautiful,
    cerulean blue lake itself (*Lac Léman* in French, *Genfersee* in German). The
southern shore of the lake is in France, taking in the mighty Savoy Alps as well as
Mont-Blanc a little further south. The northern, Swiss, shore forms the economic
and cultural focus of Suisse Romande, centred around **Lausanne**, an energetic,
endearing city that's too often skimmed over in favour of Geneva's more limited
pleasures.

Aside from Geneva in the southwest and a fragment of Canton Valais in the southeast, this is all **Canton Vaud** (pronounced *voh*). In 1536, Bern's army swept down
from the north, implanting the Reformation and placing the whole area under bailiffs;
just over two centuries later, in a 1798 revolution backed by France, Vaudois freedom-
fighters won control of the Bernese lakeside estates and agricultural heartland.
Napoleon put his seal on the deed by formally creating a new canton out of the territory, which duly joined the Swiss Confederation in 1803 under a green-and-white flag
which still flies in towns and villages to this day bearing the words "Liberté et Patrie".
The ambience of the region is thoroughly Gallic: historical animosity towards
Catholic France has given way to a yearning on the part of most urban francophone
Swiss to abandon their heel-dragging compatriots in the more stolid east and
embrace the EU. The short train-ride from the Swiss-German cities of the *Mittelland*
crosses more than just a linguistic boundary – it seems to span a whole continent of
attitude.

ACCOMMODATION PRICE CODES

All the hostels, pensions and hotels in this book have been graded according to the following price codes, which indicate the price for the cheapest double room available during the high season. Single rooms can cost anything between sixty and eighty percent of
the double-room rate. For hostels with dormitories, the price per bed has been quoted.
See p.45 for more details.

① under Fr.100 ④ Fr.200–250 ⑦ Fr.350–400
② Fr.100–150 ⑤ Fr.250–300 ⑧ Fr.400–500
③ Fr.150–200 ⑥ Fr.300–350 ⑨ over Fr.500

EXPLORING VAUD

Main-line CFF **trains** describe an arc around the northern lakeshore, from Geneva via Nyon, Lausanne and Vevey to Montreux and on into the Valais. Smaller lines branch off at various points into the hills which cup the lake on both sides – the Jura foothills in the west and the Prealps in the east. However, you shouldn't miss the chance to take a **boat trip** on the lake. The CGN links all the towns and villages on both the Swiss and French shores in a web of routings, some of which run year-round. Tourist offices in all towns stock their timetable brochures, which are also posted at every *débarcadère* (jetty). The lake is divided into three: the Petit-Lac in the southwest, between Geneva and Nyon; the Grand-Lac between Nyon and Lausanne; and the Haut-Lac in the east around Vevey and Montreux. Boats run on short and long tours within and between all three areas, as well as hopping along the shoreline villages. Some also cross the lake, from Nyon and Rolle to Yvoire (France); from Lausanne to Evian (France); and from Vevey to St Gingolph (a divided village on the French–Swiss border) – for all of which you need your passport. Eurail and Swiss Pass holders travel free on CGN boats, but InterRailers get no discounts.

The Office du Tourisme du Canton de Vaud (*www.lake-geneva-region.ch*) offers an excellent **regional pass**, sold through all local tourist offices. The pass costs Fr.135 (or Fr.108 if you hold a Swiss Pass, Swiss Card or Half-Fare Card), for which you get seven consecutive days of validity – any three days of free travel, plus the other four days of travel at a discount of 25 to 50 percent. **Coverage** is extremely wide, taking in buses, trains and cable-cars throughout the whole of Canton Vaud (everywhere mentioned in this chapter, and also Yverdon, the Vallée de Joux, Payerne and Avenches, covered in Chapter 3; the Pays d'Enhaut, covered in Chapter 6; and the Alpes Vaudoises, covered in Chapter 7), as well as journeys to but not within Geneva, and, in the other direction, as far as Gstaad and south to Aigle and St-Maurice. Note, though, that CGN boats are only covered for a fifty percent discount on all days.

LAUSANNE

[From] the terrace of the cathedral, I saw the lake above the roofs, the mountains above the lake, the clouds above the mountains, and the stars above the clouds. It was like a staircase where my thoughts climbed up step by step and broadened at each new height.

Victor Hugo

LAUSANNE tends to inspire hyperbole. In a country of spectacular natural beauty it is the most beautiful of cities, Switzerland's San Francisco, a city of incredibly steep hills that has developed tiered above the lake on a succession of compact, south-facing terraces. Vistas of blue water, glittering sunlight and the purple and grey of the looming, whitecapped Savoy Alps peep through between gaps in buildings or at the ends of steeply dropping alleys. Much of the city is still wooded, there are plenty of parks, and the tree-lined lakefront promenades spill over with lush, beds of vibrantly colourful flowers. Attractive, interesting, worldly, and well aware of how to have a good time, it's simply Switzerland's sexiest city.

The comparisons with San Francisco don't stop at the gorgeous setting. If Switzerland has a counterculture, it lives in the clubs and cafés of Lausanne, a fact which – odd though it seems – lies broadly within the city's long tradition of fostering intellectual and cultural innovation. From medieval times, Lausanne has stood at the Swiss cultural avant-garde. Back then, the **cathedral** crowned the city the most influential of the region; it still sits resplendent on an Old Town hill, the country's most impressive Gothic monument. After the Reformation, students flocked to Lausanne's

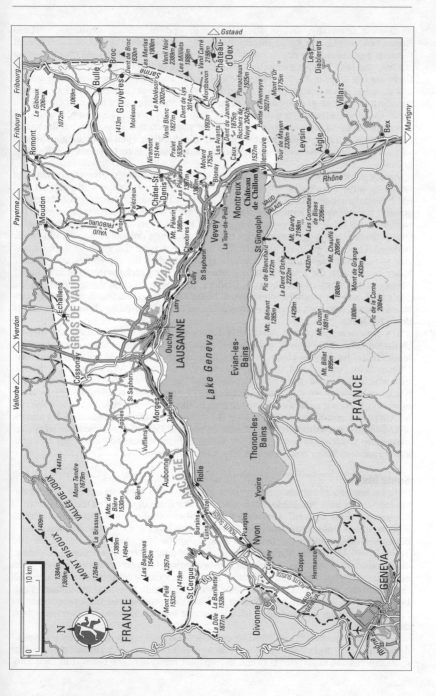

pioneering university, and in the eighteenth and nineteenth centuries, restless Romantics sought and found inspiration in the setting and the life of Lausanne. It remains a grand-looking city, full of shuttered foursquare mansions and ritzy shopping streets, and with its own glamorous lakeside resort of Ouchy; but, despite the looks, there are few cities in Europe that so actively value and support the pleasure principle. For decades, the municipality has generously subsidized art and culture of all shades, resulting in a range of festivals, live music, clubs, theatre, opera and dance to rival a more sluggish metropolis ten times bigger than 300,000-strong Lausanne. It would be an exaggeration to say you could find anything you wanted in Lausanne, but the happy combination of a long tradition of cultural experimentation, open and willing audiences and chunky public subsidies gives the city's arts and entertainment a refreshing breadth.

Aiding the dynamism, a defining feature of the city is its international population of students, attracted to the prestigious University of Lausanne, Switzerland's biggest, and the French-language arm of the Federal Institute of Technology. Hundreds of language schools and private academies enhance the city's reputation for learning, along with the world-famous École Hotelière, training ground for top chefs and hotel staff. An array of international study programmes helps to feed Lausanne's uniquely diverse multi-ethnic makeup. This youthful spirit, and the city's hilly aspect, have also given Lausanne a new role as European blading and skateboarding capital: when the sun shines, every public space hisses with the spinning of tiny wheels, and the Ouchy waterfront in summer echoes to the clack of skateboards. Bladers have been clocked doing 90kph on the city's hills, and in the winter, after days of heavy snow when blading is necessarily curtailed, it's not unknown to see the same intrepid characters skiing through the streets down to Ouchy.

On a more orthodox line, since 1874 Lausanne has been the home of the highest Swiss federal court of appeal, and has also attracted many multinational companies, not least Philip Morris, who chose Lausanne as a base from which to sell their Marlboro, Chesterfield, Suchard and Toblerone brands to Europe and Africa. However, the feature which the tourist office has lit upon is that the International Olympic Committee has been headquartered in Lausanne since 1915, and has attracted to the city an array of world governing bodies in sports ranging from chess to volleyball; they tout the city as "Olympic Capital" and endlessly plug the rather vapid Olympic Museum. It's a mark of Lausannois spirit that given the chance to host the 1994 winter games, the locals dismayed the municipality and the IOC by voting the idea down and embracing the annual International Roller and Skateboarding Contest instead.

Some history

Vidy, on the waterfront immediately west of Ouchy, was the focus of settlement in the Lausanne area from **Neolithic** times onwards. The **Romans** founded the small town of Lousonna at Vidy in 15 BC. Lousonna flourished as a trading town, but during increasingly troubled times in the fourth century AD, the lakefront site was abandoned for a better-defended spot on the heights overlooking the lake, today the site of the Old Town. In 590 AD, Bishop Marius transferred his bishopric from Avenches to Lausanne, confirming the city's rising influence. Succeeding bishops gathered power, even becoming imperial princes in 1125, until by the thirteenth century they were overseeing one of the largest cities in the region, with some nine thousand inhabitants. Both Pope Gregory X and Emperor Rudolf of Habsburg considered the consecration of Lausanne's fabulous **cathedral** in 1275 important enough to grace the ceremony with their presence.

During the fourteenth and fifteenth centuries, Lausanne was buffeted by a series of devastating fires and plague epidemics, as well as increasing social disorder stemming from the division of the city between the opulent lifestyle of the bishops in their lofty palace and the poverty of the people in the *Ville Basse*, or lower town. (Meanwhile, far below, the last remaining stragglers and fisherfolk had finally abandoned the lakeside ruins at Vidy, and decamped eastwards to the area around the Château d'Ouchy, protecting a small port.) In 1525, in an attempt to lift the yoke of the bishops from their neck, the Lausannois made a pact of mutual military assistance with Bern and Fribourg; eleven years later when the **Bernese** army, fired with the zeal of the **Reformation**, swept down towards Lake Geneva, the Lausannois were finally able to eject the bishops. Their independence was shortlived, though, since no sooner had the bishops departed (founding a new see in Catholic Fribourg) than the Bernese installed bailiffs of their own and reduced Lausanne to the status of a subject city.

Lausanne's university was founded in 1540 as the first French-language centre of Protestant theology, but the city remained a Bernese-run backwater until, in 1803, **Napoleon** hived Canton Vaud away from Bern and granted Lausanne the status of Vaudois capital. Shortly after, the modernizing municipality filled in the rivers Flon and Louve, which wound between the city's summits, and threw grand arching bridges over the ditch to link disparate neighbourhoods for the first time. Foreigners had already spotted Lausanne, and artists, romantics and adventurers soon flocked to both the city and the adjacent *commune libre et indépendante* of Ouchy, turning the place into a rather genteel stop on the Grand Tour of Europe (see box on p.133). By the turn of the century, Lausanne was hosting a thriving community of expats – including forty retired British colonels – and boasted four English churches, a hundred English boarding schools, a cricket pitch, a football (soccer) field and an English library serving afternoon tea. Lausanne has had a quiet twentieth century, flourishing commercially, socially and culturally while happy to remain in the shadow of its over-illustrious, sober and considerably less desirable neighbour Geneva.

Orientation, arrival and information

Lausanne's topography looks confusing on a map, but isn't actually too hard to grasp. At the top is the Old Town, in the middle are the train station and commercial districts, and at the bottom is the one-time fishing village of **Ouchy**, now prime territory for waterfront strolling and café-lounging. But the gradients between them all are no joke: the peak of Mont Jorat, only 10km northeast of the city, rises to 927m; just north of the Old Town is a viewpoint at 643m; the central districts are ranged around 475m; while residential neighbourhoods slide on down for another kilometre to the lakeshore at 372m.

Focus of the city centre is the grand **Place St-François**, hub of bus routes and heart of the shopping district. Gilt-edged **Rue de Bourg** entices shoppers uphill from St-François, while beside it Rue St-François drops down north into the valley and up the other side to the cobbled **Place de la Palud**, an ancient, fountained square plum in the heart of the Old Town and flanked by the arcades of the Renaissance town hall. The elegant Gothic turrets of the **Cathedral** rise loftily above, while the foursquare **Château** stands even further up, at the highest and most northerly tip of the Old Town. Beyond rise the Jorat forests and open parkland, alongside the peaceful village of Cugy.

Northwest of St-Francois, the giant Grand Pont soars over the warehouse district of **Le Flon**, hotbed of Lausanne's burgeoning club culture, to **Place Bel-Air** and on to Place Chauderon at the head of the Pont Chauderon, which also rises above Le Flon. The steep slope south of St-François ends at the main **train station**, south of which a succession of opulent and elegant residential districts around the Montriond and Jordils metro stations trickle down to **Place de la Navigation** on the Ouchy waterfront. Lakeside promenades lead in both directions from Ouchy, east to the gentle villages of **Pully** and **Lutry**, west to the parkland of **Vidy** and the lakeside campuses of the **University of Lausanne** and adjacent Federal Institute of Technology at Dorigny.

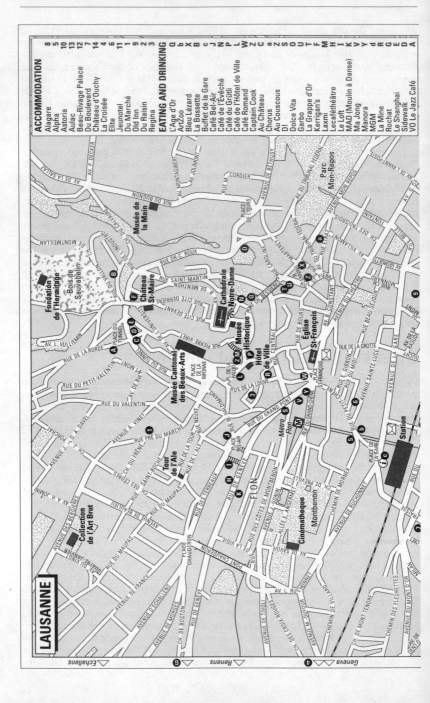

LAUSANNE

ACCOMMODATION

Alagare	8
Alpha	5
Astoria	10
Aulac	13
Beau-Rivage Palace	12
Du Boulevard	7
Château d'Ouchy	14
La Croisée	4
Elite	6
Jeunotel	11
Du Marché	1
Old Inn	9
Du Raisin	2
Regina	3

EATING AND DRINKING

L'Age d'Or	Q
ArtZoo	b
Bleu Lézard	B
La Bossette	c
Buffet de la Gare	J
Café Bel-Air	N
Café de l'Evêché	P
Café du Grütli	L
Café de l'Hôtel de Ville	W
Café Romand	Z
Captain Cook	C
Au Château	a
Chorus	Z
Au Couscous	S
DI	O
Dolce Vita	U
Garbo	T
La Grappe d'Or	F
Kerrigan's	M
Laxmi	H
Lecaféthéâtre	I
Le Loft	K
MAD (Moulin à Danse)	V
Ma Jong	Y
Manora	R
La Mine	d
Rochat	G
Le Shanghai	E
Sidewalk	D
VO Le Jazz Café	A

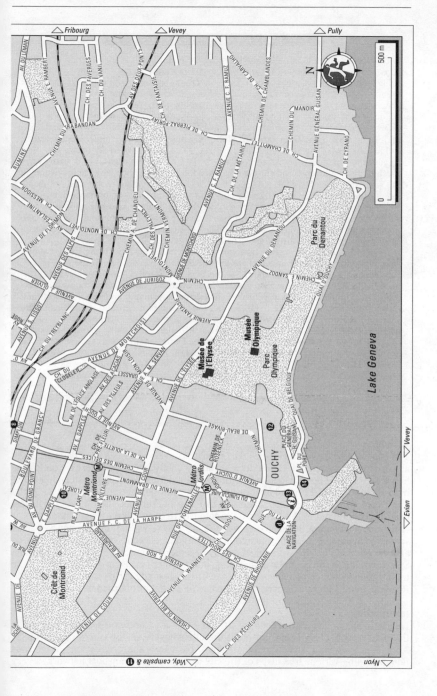

LAUSANNE'S FESTIVALS

With such a vibrant – and healthily subsidized – cultural scene, aided by an energetic population of young people, it can seem like there's always some celebration or other happening in Lausanne. All summer long, the **Ouchy waterfront** hosts informal music events – from techno to chamber music to African dance – just about every weekend, and always free. *Entrée libre pour un été* is a summer-long programme of free music, dance and culture at various locations around the city (see *www.lausanne.ch*), taking in such diversities as Friday evening organ concerts in the Cathedral and hip-hop/DJ acts staged during the late-August **International Roller Contest**, Europe's premier skateboarding and inline event of the year, attracting over 100,000 skaters (*www.roller-contest.ch*).

Lausanne's biggest party is the **Festival de la Cité** held in early July, in many ways much more spontaneous and cutting edge than the Montreux Jazz Festival happening at the same time just down the road, not least because everything is free and out in the streets: the whole of the Old Town (*la cité*) is given over to live performance of all kinds – music, dance, drama, mime, and more. Both the best in their field and student novices vie for the promenading audiences, with performances starting at dusk and running continuously until the small hours on more than half-a-dozen open-air stages, with stalls all around selling beer and food to the crowds.

If you're in town at the wrong time for that, try and coincide with the **Cully-Lavaux Jazz Festival**, held in the wine cellars and medieval alleys of Cully village (see p.140), 8km east of Lausanne, in late March; or the **Fête du Soleil**, Lausanne's version of carnival held each April; or the Flon's **Atlantis Festival** in May, devoted to leading electronic music and dance; or the **Fête de la Musique**, impromptu music in the streets and bars in mid-June; or the **Fête à Lausanne**, a weekend of fairground attractions in late June; or the **Paleo Rock Festival** (*www.paleo.ch*), a mammoth event held every July in a field outside Nyon (see p.135), which draws top-name artists and a crowd of a quarter of a million; or the **Festival of Contemporary Dance**, held in late September at the Sévelin 36 arts centre; or the **Bach Festival**, held throughout Lausanne over two weeks in early November. Finally, chilly January hosts both an **International Circus Festival** on the Place de Bellerive (held for the first time in 1999), and the acclaimed **Prix de Lausanne** competition and workshop for young dancers, an annual fixture since 1970 inspired by world-famous choreographer Maurice Béjart and his resident company, the Béjart Ballet Lausanne.

Arrival

The imposing **train station** is served by regular main-line services from Paris and from all corners of Switzerland. **Boats** dock at the CGN jetty in Ouchy. There's a metro station more or less opposite the dock, with regular shuttles climbing the steep hill to the train station (Gare CFF), and further up to Flon. Alternatively, bus #2 from the Ouchy waterfront (direction Désert) snakes up to Place St-François, then heads northwest over the Grand-Pont to Bel-Air, and on to Rue Neuve beside Place de la Riponne.

By **car**, negotiating the approaches to the city centre without finding yourself inadvertently bypassing Lausanne altogether is difficult enough, but then once you do arrive, you're left to cope with objectionably expensive or awkward city-centre parking. Street parking in the centre is a dead loss, but it's worth cruising around south of the train station in search of a blue-zone space. The largest city car park is under Place du Riponne, but it's more expensive than the one on the lakefront road in Ouchy.

Information

Lausanne has two **tourist offices** (☎021/613 73 73, *www.lausanne-tourisme.ch*), one in the train station (daily 9am–7pm), and the other beside Ouchy metro station (daily: April–Sept 9am–9pm, Oct–March 9am–6pm). Both have the usual stacks of information, including various free maps of the city and the public transport network, a very handy *Bienvenue/Welcome* booklet crammed with useful background material on the city and its surroundings, a guide to the city's museums, timetables for the boats, and so on. Their *Lausanne Promenade* brochure series, all of which include maps and notes on subjects such as "Gracious Houses", "Parks and Gardens" and "Family Activities" are especially good. If you're looking for more focused infomation on cultural happenings and the life of the city, or if you want to buy tickets for local shows, it's worth dropping into the municipality's **information office**, in the Old Town at 2 Escaliers du Marché (Mon–Fri 8am–noon & 1.15–5pm; ☎021/315 25 55, *www.lausanne.ch*). They have a booklet, *Allons-y!* ("Let's go!"), outlining the city's budget restaurants, museums and excursions that are either free or cost less than Fr.15.

"Tempo", the Saturday supplement of Geneva's *Le Temps* newspaper, is the best source of **listings** and reviews of film openings, performances and cultural events throughout Romandie (although all in French). Lausanne's own *24 Heures* tabloid has cinema reviews but only a handful of other events listed. The tourist office puts out its own bimonthly offering.

City transport and tours

Although the Old Town is compact, and flying crow distances across the city don't look too bad, maps can only give half the story: in practice, days on end negotiating Lausanne's mountainous gradients and cat's cradle of valleys and bridges can get wearying. It's likely that you'll resort to the city's excellent **public transport** sooner or later. A short journey of up to three stops costs Fr.1.30, while unlimited journeys across the whole network cost Fr.2.20 (one hour) or Fr.6.50 (24hr). A two-day Lausanne Card costs Fr.15, and gives free city transport as well as many discounts at shops and attractions around town, including twenty percent off museums, the opera and all meals at *Manora* (see p.126) on Place St-François, plus reduced entry to the huge indoor skate park on Rue Sévelin and free entry to municipal swimming pools.

You'll mostly be using the **buses**, many of them electric, which fan out from the centre to cover all corners of the city, routes extending to neighbouring towns such as St-Sulpice in the west and Pully (see p.124) in the east. Most lines skirt the Old Town from St-François to Bel-Air to Riponne – only bus #16 winds through it. There's also a **metro**: the steep Métro-Ouchy line (known fondly as *la Ficelle*, the String) links the Ouchy waterfront with Flon in the city centre, via the train station; the Métro-Gare shuttles continuously to and fro between Flon and the train station; and Métro-Ouest runs from Flon out to the university and Renens. At the time of writing, a tunnel was under construction to link Flon to the suburban train station under Place Chauderon, from where LEB operates commuter trains to Echallens (see p.131). For details of the commercial **boat** services on the lake, see p.110.

The station has **bikes** for rent as normal (daily 6.40am–7.40pm), but even the locals have to get off and wheel them up and down the city's hills. Where they score is if you fancy a leisurely day cycling through the lakeshore vineyards either side of Lausanne, dropping your bike off in Nyon or Vevey and getting the train back to the city in the evening; or, conversely, taking it up into the hilly forests above Lausanne and then free-wheeling down again. To blend in imperceptibly with the locals, rent some **blades** or a **skateboard** from the kiosk at 6 Place de la Navigation in Ouchy (July & Aug daily 1.30–7pm, April–June & Sept–Oct Sat & Sun 1.30–7pm; Fr.8 for the first hour, Fr.4/hr thereafter).

If you have heavy bags and a equally heavy wallet, **taxis** are a good standby for conquering those hills. Most of Lausanne's cabs come under the umbrella of the Taxi Services' central computerized network; call ☎0800/810 810.

Tours

The tourist office sponsors two-hour multilingual **walking tours** of the Old Town, which start from the Place de la Palud (May–Sept Mon–Sat 10am & 3pm; Fr.10). You can request tours at other times, and during the low season, from ☎021/321 77 66. During the *Entrée libre pour un été* season of summer cultural activities, there are a handful of literary and historical walking tours of Lausanne guided in English – check with the tourist office or the municipality information office for dates and details.

Accommodation

Lausanne has plenty of **accommodation** to suit all budgets and aspirations, from simple hostels and pensions up to luxury palaces no less opulent than those in Geneva or Zürich. There's only a couple of hotels within the Old Town, although a few more are dotted on its outskirts – if you're looking to get into the life of the city, these obviously have a good deal going for them, and you're unlikely to be troubled by street noise anywhere. Hotels on the Ouchy lakefront have an entirely different, graceful ambience, perfect if your aim is to soak up the views, although the lakefront road sees plenty of traffic. Between the two are a handful of places around the train station, something of a bargain compared with their competitors.

Camping and hostels

The closest **campsite** to town is lakeside *Vidy* (☎021/624 20 31), sandwiched between the Roman ruins and the International Olympic Committee headquarters – it's a five-star site, with plenty of facilities and high prices. From St-François take bus #2 (direction Bourdonette) to Bois de Vaux, or from the station take bus #1 to Maladière and walk five minutes.

Lausanne's huge, charm-free HI **hostel**, dubbed *Jeunotel*, is at 36 Chemin du Bois-de-Vaux (☎021/626 02 22, fax 626 02 26), right beside the *Vidy* campsite. A night in its quality four-bed dorms, plus breakfast, costs Fr.24. It also has a range of private rooms (①). *La Croisée*, 15 Avenue Marc Dufour (☎021/321 09 09, fax 321 09 08) is a small guesthouse a few minutes' uphill walk from the train station (or bus #3 to Cécil), with clean, well-kept dorms for Fr.25, and some pleasant rooms (①).

Inexpensive hotels

There's a fair spread of **inexpensive hotels** across the city centre, but unfortunately one of the only bastions of affordable lodging in Ouchy, the formerly one-star *Hôtel du Port*, is undergoing extensive renovation to bring it up to three-star standard (scheduled to reopen in 2001).

Alpha, 34 Rue du Petit-Chêne (☎021/323 01 31, fax 323 01 45, *alpha@pingnet.ch*). Handily central on a busy pedestrian street, boasting lurid 1970s-style carpets and ordinary rooms. Walk-in prices plummet after 8pm. ②–③.

Astoria, 17 Avenue Dapples (☎ & fax 021/616 51 55). Rather depressing boarding house 100m from Métro Montriond, with plastic sheeting taped to the carpets but low prices. ①.

Du Boulevard, 51 Boulevard de Grancy (☎021/617 28 11, fax 617 28 72). Respectable little city hotel that has managed to retain and nurture a hint of a weekend romantic getaway. All doubles with kitchenette, pleasantly done up (many with bathtub). ③.

Elite, 1 Avenue St-Luce (☎021/320 23 61, fax 320 39 63, *elite@worldcom.ch, http://home.worldcom. ch/elite*). Extremely pleasant, very quiet and well-run hotel, surrounded by greenery and centrally located between the train station and St-François. Top-floor balconied rooms perch you above the roofs for views over the lake. ②.

Du Marché, 42 Rue Pré-du-Marché (☎021/647 99 00, fax 646 47 23, *ikucera@worldcom.ch*). Plain and comfortable small hotel, with spacious and very clean rooms, both with and without en-suite bathrooms. Usefully placed near Riponne, with some parking spaces. ②.

Old Inn, 11 Avenue de la Gare (☎021/323 62 21). Quiet, spartan and lived-in little pension, with a friendly *patronne* and three large doubles. ①.

Du Raisin, 19 Place de la Palud (☎021/312 27 56). A handful of rooms above an old café in the heart of the Old Town, with character and atmosphere but not much else. ①.

Mid-range and expensive hotels

Any number of **upmarket** château-style hotels capitalize on Lausanne's unique topography to offer romantic lake views along with their more or less tasteful line in opulent pamperment – but none offers outstanding value for money. The stately old *Hôtel d'Angleterre* on the lakefront, where Byron is reputed to have written *The Prisoner of Chillon*, has closed off its rooms for the foreseeable future for much-needed redevelopment, although its terrace café remains in service.

Alagare, 14 Rue du Simplon (☎021/617 92 52, fax 617 92 55, *alagare@vtx.ch*, *www.alagare.com*). Small serviceable hotel in a quiet pedestrian zone just below the station. ③.

Aulac, 4 Place de la Navigation (☎021/617 14 51, fax 617 11 30, *aulac@cdmgroup.ch*, *www.aulac.ch*). Large, comfortable rooms, balconied ones at the front with lake views (but more expensive, and exposed to street noise), those at the back cheaper and perfectly quiet. ③–④.

Beau-Rivage Palace, 17 Place du Port (☎021/613 33 33, fax 613 33 34, *reservation@beau-rivage-palace.ch*, *www.beau-rivage-palace.ch*). Lausanne's – and one of Switzerland's – top establishments, set in its own waterside garden estate and recently sparklingly resorted to its original 1861 grandeur. You could want for nothing more. ⑨.

Château d'Ouchy, 2 Place du Port (☎021/616 74 51, fax 617 51 37). Grandiose old pile put up in the 1890s on the ruins of a twelfth-century keep. This is the only hotel situated on the lake-side of the main road, separated from the water by lush gardens. Stout, woody decor, open fireplaces and some surprisingly affordable rooms add to the charm. Romantics will relish the lofty tower room, its Romanesque windows framing dreamy lake views. ⑥.

Regina, 18 Rue Grand St-Jean (☎021/320 24 41, fax 320 25 29, *hotel-regina@gve.ch*, *www.hotel-regina.ch*). Steps from the central Place de la Palud, quality renovated rooms in modern style, with marvellous top-floor views. ④.

The City

Lausanne's **city centre** spans several hilltops, linked by bridges spanning deep, riverless gorges. **Place St-François** dominates the hilltop district known as the **Bourg**, formerly the wealthiest part of the city and still known for its upmarket shops and boutiques. To the north, the hill of the **Old Town**, crowned by the **Cathedral**, dominates the city, while expansion during the nineteenth century roped in more heights to the west and east. The whole of Lausanne's explorable centre lies north of and above the train station, with Place St-François at the edge of a pedestrian-only zone covering virtually the entire Old Town. Walking is the best, and often the only, way to explore.

St-François and the Bourg

The train station looks over the unprepossessing Place de la Gare, continuously hectic with human and motorized traffic. A gap between buildings directly ahead marks the steep **Rue du Petit-Chêne** which winds up to **Place St-François** on the terrace above. Bedecked with bus-wires, buskers and shoppers, with traffic surging through, St-François – given the adenoidal nickname *Sainf* by the locals – is the heart of Lausanne's modern commercial centre, dominated by the giant bulk of the post office and, opposite, the considerably more attractive **Église St-François**, one of the city's landmarks. Bishop Jean de Cossonay invited the Franciscans to found a community in Lausanne in 1258; by 1272, they had completed their new church, which then stood at the centre of a monastic complex hard up against the southern city walls. However, various medieval fires took their toll, and in 1536 the Reformation arrived, the monastery was dissolved, and the building was cleared of religious imagery to become the parish church of Lausanne's *Ville Basse* (lower town). Further renovations, not all in especially good taste, disfigured the interior during later centuries, and although the church remains an atmospheric retreat from the bustle outside, today not a great deal is left of St-François' illustrious past.

The quarter in which the church stands, the **Bourg**, spreads over a narrow ridge between two gorges, and before the nineteenth century stood alone as a separate community, rather wealthier than those all around: the **Rue de Bourg**, today a somewhat glitzy shopping street rising steeply from behind the church, had much the same style in the past too, lined then with restaurants, inns and luxury shops. In the 1780s, the English historian Edward Gibbon lived in a house on the site of the St-François post office, right at the heart of the high society of the day.

A massive expansion of the city in the early nineteenth century included the razing of many of the old slums, the filling in of the Flon river – which followed the course of the present Rue Centrale – and the construction of grand bridges unifying the disparate neighbourhoods of the city. Most dramatic of these is the **Pont Bessières**, spanning the yawning Flon gorge from the eastern top end of the Rue de Bourg over to the Old Town. In recent years this has become the favoured spot for suicidal Lausannois to shake off this mortal coil, so much so that every New Year's Eve the city posts guardians halfway along the bridge to make sure no melodramatic revellers decide to test out their theories of flight; it's a tradition for locals to stop by sometime during the evening, warm their hands over the fire, share a tot or two and wish each one *"Bonne Année!"* A walk over the **Grand-Pont**, first of the bridges to be built in 1844, from Place St-François northwest to **Place Bel-Air**, can also highlight Lausanne's extraordinary topography – stairs and alleys running off at odd angles, traffic surging along the valley road way beneath, the lake glittering below on one side and the Cathedral crowning the hill above on the other. Below the Grand-Pont, and also accessed by stairs leading down from beside the distinctive Bel-Air tower (Switzerland's modest first skyscraper, dating from the 1930s), is the **Flon** district; once full of merchants and traders, today its warehouses have been converted into dance clubs, alternative cafés, galleries and theatre spaces.

The Collection de l'Art Brut

A fifteen-minute walk northwest of Bel-Air (or bus #2 from St-François or Bel-Air to Beaulieu) brings you to one of the most original art galleries in the country, the **Collection de l'Art Brut**, 11 Avenue des Bergières (Tues–Sun 11am–1pm & 2–6pm; Fr.6; SMP). This quite unique collection is devoted to what's been called "outsider art", the creative output of ordinary people with no artistic training at all – often loners, psychotics or the criminally insane – who for some reason suddenly began making their own art, on many occasions in middle or old age. What results is art entirely free from any conception of formal artistic rules or conventions, which challenges both how we tend to view such "outsiders" in our own communities, and our expectations of what art should be about. Without really doing or saying anything, the gallery and its collection forces you to be open minded; even though short biographies of the artists alongside each piece tell some heart-rendingly sad or disturbing stories. The gallery displays art by Henry Darger, a hospital porter in Chicago, who died alone, an old man unknown by his neighbours; it was only after his death that his 19,000-page novel, illustrated with dozens of detailed watercolours up to three metres long, came to light. Scottie Wilson, an illiterate Glaswegian junk dealer, began at the age of 40 to produce whimsical and incredibly intricate Escheresque drawings; while a London art gallery was selling his drawings for hundreds of pounds, Wilson was found outside in the street hawking others to passers-by for a pound or two. There's art on show from a factory worker whose talent was only discovered because he pinned his drawings up in his workshop, from a medium imprisoned in the 1930s for her interest in spirituality, from a postman who believed his hand was being directed by an external force, and so on.

As well as its permanent collection, founded by the late Jean Dubuffet, the gallery has regular temporary exhibitions of *art brut* from artists around the world. Whatever is showing, it's worth going some distance out of your way to see.

The Old Town

Located in the tranquil core of Lausanne's **Old Town**, the cobbled **Place de la Palud** is a perfect spot for people-watching: with shopping streets cascading through the square from all sides, plenty of pavement cafés and the handy **Fontaine de la Justice** usually ringed with promenaders perching on its wide rim, it's a tempting place to take a break for a reviving *café renversée*, especially if the Wednesday and Saturday morning markets are in full swing. Every hour on the hour, mechanical figures emerge on the wall behind the fountain for a little chiming display. Dominating the south side of the square is the arcaded **Hôtel de Ville** (Town Hall), built in 1675 on the site of a covered marketplace dating back to the fourteenth century.

Place de la Riponne and around

From the Place de la Palud, Rue Madeleine leads up to the huge **Place de la Riponne**, a plain of concrete usually dotted with students hanging out or sitting on the steps of the overbearing **Palais de Rumine** on the far side – an absurdly grandiose late nineteenth-century neo-Renaissance structure adorned with lions, angels and pink marble, named after a local philanthropist and designed by a Parisian architect who hadn't actually bothered to visit Lausanne beforehand. The palace is now home to a clutch of museums, most interesting of which is the **Musée cantonal des Beaux-Arts** (Tues & Wed 11am–6pm, Thurs 11am–8pm, Fri & Sat 11am–5pm; Fr.6; SMP). A huge percentage of its works, including those from the medieval and Baroque periods, and all its Renoirs, are currently in storage in the basement; instead it displays three rooms of Swiss art from the eighteenth to twentieth centuries (including many Vaudois artists), and devotes most of its time and energy to high-quality exhibitions of contemporary art hung in the brighter, less fussy rooms at the back.

From Riponne, Rue Haldimand heads down to the church of **St Laurent**, in the heart of the old quarter also known as St-Laurent. The Rue de l'Ale and Rue de la Tour bring you further west – past the crooked *Pinte Besson*, the city's oldest tavern, to the stout, circular **Tour de l'Ale** atop the hill, built in 1340 during a reorganization of the city's defences. The traffic hub of Place Chauderon is a few metres south and downhill, at the head of the **Pont Chauderon**, third of the major bridges spanning the Flon valley. On the south side of the bridge is the Montbenon park with, tucked into the trees, the Swiss film archives, housed in the *fin-de-siècle* casino building now transformed into the Cinémathèque Suisse (see p.127).

The Cathedral

Stairs lead up from both Place de la Palud and Place de la Riponne to the higher points of the Old Town. The atmospheric **Escaliers du Marché**, covered wooden stairs heading up from Palud, deliver you to Rue Viret, circling around the pinnacle of the hill,

THE NIGHTWATCH

Lausanne suffered from many devastating medieval fires, and is the last city in Europe to keep alive the tradition of the **nightwatch** (*le guet*). If you install yourself on the cathedral terrace, every night between 10pm and 2am, after the bells have struck the hour, you'll hear – and possibly spot – a sonorous-voiced civil servant calling out from all sides of the cathedral tower *"C'est le guet; il a sonné l'heure"* ("This is the nightwatch; the hour has struck"), assuring the lovers and assorted drunks sprawled under the trees that all is well. Having fulfilled his civic duty, he then retreats to a comfortable little room within the tower for the next 59 minutes. For some years past, this post has been filled by a cartoonist on Lausanne's weekly *L'Hebdo*, who is reported as appreciating the four hours of peace and quiet this nice little earner brings him each night to concentrate on drawing his strips. As yet, though, he's had no fires to report.

from where more stairs bring you up to the **Cathédrale Notre-Dame** (daily 8am–7pm), generally acclaimed as Switzerland's finest Gothic building, on a par with the greatest of French Gothic architecture. A short tour around the walls brings such a claim home. Elegant and proportioned towers, turrets and spires claw their way up stage by stage into the sky, the south facade is studded with a spectacular giant Gothic rose window of stained glass, and flying buttresses encircle the exterior of the choir and ambulatory. The foundations of the current building were probably laid in the mid-twelfth century, with construction continuing from 1190 through to the cathedral's consecration in 1275. Despite extensive renovations and alterations just before the Reformation, and the loss of the altars, screens, and most of the statuary, paintings and glass during and after it, the cathedral has lost none of its grace and poise.

You enter through the west portal, bedecked with figures and dubbed the **Montfalcon portal** after a sixteenth-century bishop. The interior **Great Porch**, an unusual lofty open arcade with its recessed doorway and two tiers of columns, echoes similar setups in English cathedrals such as Lincoln and Canterbury, and it's been suggested that Notre-Dame's main architect, Jean de Cotereel, may have been Norman or part English himself. Just beyond, a squarish vestibule gives into the vast, broad **Great Bay** which, prior to 1504, was actually an open thoroughfare which connected the Rue Cité-Devant (to your left) with the Rue St-Étienne (to your right) under a vaulted gallery and beneath arches which seem extra large now that they have been enclosed within the building.

The interior of the cathedral is stunning, every line and detail drawing your eye dizzily up to the lofty vaulted heights. On the south wall of the nave is the impressive **Painted Portal**, dating from 1215–30; its exterior is still encrusted with original statues, but has suffered badly from weathering in recent years, and may well still be covered for protection. The crossing and transept, a few steps up from the nave and filled with light, are endowed on the south side with the glowing thirteenth-century **rose window**. Opposite is the doorway to the former cloister, above which columns in front of the rectangular windows have been snapped off to allow more light to enter the building. A few steps up again is the **choir**, housing some exceptionally beautiful thirteenth-century carved choir stalls; on the left is the tomb of Otto of Grandson, a rather diminutive figure for such a celebrated medieval knight (see pp.171–2). You'll find more, extremely worn tombs ranged around the **ambulatory** running under the walls, and also in the **crypt** beneath the choir. With a truly spectacular view over the whole of the city and most of Lake Geneva too, climbing the southwest **tower** (Mon–Sat 8.30–11.30am & 1.30–5.30pm, Sun 2–5.30pm; Fr.2) is one of the highlights of visiting Lausanne.

Right next to the cathedral building is the Ancien Évêché, the old Bishop's Palace, which has been converted into the **Musée Historique** (Tues–Sun 11am–6pm, Thurs until 8pm; Fr.7, audioguide Fr.4; SMP). Crammed with all kinds of displays illustrating the history of Lausanne, its highlight is the giant scale-model of the city in the basement, with an excellent accompanying commentary (in English) detailing the history of the various neighbourhoods since medieval times – the least of it is that you can finally get a clear, bird's-eye view of how the city's hills and valleys lie in relation to each other.

North of the Cathedral

Two parallel streets, Rue Cité-Devant and Rue Cité-Derrière, lead up from the cathedral to the top of the Old Town. Oldtimers bemoan the fact that the **Ancienne Académie** at 7 Rue Cité-Devant, built in the 1580s as Lausanne's first university, formerly lay at the heart of a bustling student quarter, but that since the new out-of-town campus opened, the students have all departed. It's true that the alleyways are now tranquil, but they're also uniquely atmospheric, the blank old facades giving away little of their long history. A number of tiny cellar theatres, as well as mouthwatering smells wafting from the dark interiors of small bistros, hint that the quarter is far from dead. At the very top of the Old Town sits the unshakeable **Château St-Maire**, begun in the fourteenth-century and completed in brick by northern Italian masons a century later. The structure symbolizes political power: in former times it was the residence of the Bernese bailiffs, and today it is the seat of the cantonal government of Vaud.

Rue de la Barre continues north, rising over the workaday district known as **Tunnel**, busy with traffic and home to many students, accessed by stairs down to the left (west) of the street. Place du Tunnel is ringed by bars, cafés and music venues, while the eponymous tunnel itself – a major traffic route – cuts beneath Rue de la Barre and the whole Old Town hill through to the eastern districts of the city, which hold another of the city's groundbreaking museums, the **Fondation Claude Verdan** (Tues, Wed & Fri noon–6pm, Thurs noon–8pm, Sat 11am–6pm; Fr.6; SMP), 21 Rue du Bugnon, accessed also by bus #5 and #6 (to Montagibert). Otherwise known as the Musée de la Main (Museum of the Hand), it's dedicated to Professor Verdan, a specialist in reconstructive hand surgery, and is a surprisingly engaging tour through how we use our hands – to communicate, to shape our environment, and to kill – mostly avoiding the preachy and the overly scientific.

The open **Bois de Sauvabelin**, the beginnings of the Jorat forests, flanks Rue de la Barre northwards. Set into the park some way up (and this is no mean hill) is an expansive nineteenth-century villa housing the **Fondation de l'Hermitage** art gallery (2 Route du Signal; Tues–Sun 11am–6pm, Thurs until 9pm; admission varies; SMP; bus #16). The foundation owns a permanent collection taking in Degas, Sisley and Magritte, but displays only portions of it to complement the two or three high-quality temporary shows it mounts each year. The park, and the bus, continue further up the hill to the Signal viewpoint (643m), and on past lawns and copses to the pretty Lac de Sauvabelin, encircled by pines and oaks.

Ouchy and the lakefront

As if Lausanne weren't relaxed enough already, it has **Ouchy** as a lakeside terrace on which to stroll, chill out, and enjoy the mountain views and fresh breezes. Officially – and proudly – a separate commune from Lausanne, Ouchy for years survived as a fishing port, but these days, although some fishing continues, it's become one of the more chic of the Swiss lakeside resorts, with waterfront cafés abounding.

Some 500m west of Ouchy's neo-Gothic château, now a hotel, and beyond the majestically opulent *Hôtel Beau-Rivage* set in its own grounds, you'll come to the Parc Olympique, home of Lausanne's much-touted flagship **Musée Olympique** (May–Sept daily 9am–7pm, Thurs until 8pm; Oct–April Tues–Sun 10am–6pm, Thurs until 8pm;

Fr.14, audioguide Fr.3; SMP; *www.olympic.org*). Opened in 1994, it's a very grand affair, with formal gardens and fountains preluding the sweeping pomp of the interior design, but it's rather unsatisfying nonetheless. Displays on the Olympics of ancient Greece and the restoration of the games in modern times are moderately engaging, but the main focus of the museum – banks of video screens replaying events from past summer and winter games, to the accompaniment of suitably stirring music – is handy for recalling the triumphs of Daley Thompson or Florence Griffith but ends up, unfortunately, as little more than glorified TV. Rows and rows of medals, sheets of Olympic postage-stamps, and cases of objects from athletes past (discuses, speed bikes, and Carl Lewis's old running shoes) do nothing to help tell any special stories. The computerized **video library**, which lets you select and view any of several hundred past events from the Olympics, the soccer World Cup, European championships, the NBA, Wimbledon or the Tour de France, *would* make the museum unmissable but for the fact that you're only allowed to choose two events, and they tend to comprise, for instance, three or four minutes of goal action, or one single track event. Even for sports fans, it's a washout.

In the same park, set slightly back from the Olympic Museum, you'll find the much more worthwhile **Musée de l'Elysée** (Tues–Sun 10am–6pm, Thurs until 9pm; Fr.5; SMP), dedicated to photography from the earliest daguerrotypes up to contemporary photojournalism. Its continuous cycle of temporary exhibitions are generally outstanding, and the museum has a range of shows on different subject matter running concurrently, so even if Czech avant-garde photography from the 1920s isn't your thing, a retrospective of David Hockney's photos might be.

The shady and flowered lakeside promenades (and bus #8) continue east for a couple of kilometres to the old fishing port of **PULLY** (pronounced *pwee*), now an extremely ordered and monied suburb of gentility and discretion – but no less beautiful for that.

Vidy

A kilometre or so west of Ouchy is **VIDY**, and one of the first indications that you're approaching the place is a boxy building on stilts in a lakeside park: this is the Théâtre de Vidy (see p.127), Switzerland's leading contemporary drama venue. The parkland just beyond the theatre was the location of the first settlements in the Lausanne area, in Neolithic times, and then later under the Romans. Approaching through the park, you'll stumble onto remnants and ruins of the Roman town of Lousonna, an assembly of low walls and tumbled stones with an explanatory board nearby. A short distance beyond, at 24 Chemin du Bois-de-Vaux, is the modern and well laid out **Musée Romain** (Tues–Sun 11am–6pm, Thurs until 8pm; Fr.6; SMP). Finds are displayed with explanatory boards mostly in French (although they do have a leaflet in English), with particularly impressive glassware, some mosaic work and interesting displays of artefacts and other bits and bobs.

Eating and drinking

If all you want is a reviving drink and somewhere to take the weight off your feet, the city centre and the Old Town can offer dozens of **cafés and café-bars** – almost every corner of every quarter has its local haunt, most of which offer food as well. Ouchy is a little less straightforward, since the cafés lining the waterfront are universally over-priced and under-quality, and although there's no shortage of portside **restaurants** offering fresh lake fish, none stands out as particularly noteworthy.

Aside from the city's reasonable choice of ethnic eateries, there are plenty of haunts offering Vaudois specialities. A *tomme* is a round soft cheese baked to melting point within its white Brie-like rind, and often served on a bed of leafy salad. A local speciality of the La Côte region just west of Lausanne is a *malakoff*, a hot, rich fried round of cheese served on a bread or pastry base; the nearby villages of Vinzel and Luins (see p.137) compete for whose *malakoff* is the best, but you can also easily find Lausannois versions in the city's more traditional diners. The mighty *saucisson vaudois*, a smoked pork and beef sausage, is served hot, accompanied by *papet vaudois*, a puree of leek and potato, and graded according to quality, with the best labelled reverentially with the green cantonal flag.

Cafés and café-bars

ArtZoo, 27 Rue du Petit-Chêne. Bright modern café attached to a cinema, popular with turtleneck urbanites.

Bleu Lézard, 10 Rue Enning. Fashionable and lively café-bar on a busy corner, with a windowful of gnomes and a comfy colourful interior. The mood mutates into restaurant territory in the evenings, when food (including veggie options) is pricey – but you don't have to eat and the atmosphere is free.

La Bossette, 4 Place du Nord, east of Tunnel. Comfortable and uniquely friendly local café on a patch of green beneath the château, serving a range of speciality beers along with excellent food.

Buffet de la Gare, train station. Deeply atmospheric station buffet, with high ceilings, wood-panelled walls, white-aproned waiters and more than a hint of the age of steam. If your eye's on the minute hand, ask for the *assiette express* (Fr.13.50).

Café Bel-Air, Place Bel-Air. The place to be seen, with the gentle tinkle of teaspoons accompanying the most discreet of gossip behind plate-glass windows.

Café de l'Évêché, 4 Rue Curtat. Atmospheric little haunt of talkative students and local old-timers just below the cathedral – perfect for morning coffee, authentic fondue, or beer and dominoes.

Café de l'Hôtel de Ville, 10 Place de la Palud. Wonderful little intimate wood-floor café, with excellent Vaudois specialities – including hot and cold goats' cheeses with salad – quality service and especially fancy desserts. The cellar features small-scale shows of *chansons*, jazz and comedians.

Café Romand, Place St-François (under *Pizza Hut*). Unmissable and much-loved city-centre retreat, a heartwarming place with parquet floor and cosy alcoves for beer, coffee or Swiss gutliners.

Lecaféthéâtre, 10 Rue de Genève. Appealing café-bar in the Flon, with a cellar atmosphere, fantasy art on the walls and nightly live sessions of piano, guitar or French *chansons* for entertainment. Food is excellent, home-cooked style, and not expensive. Closed Sun & Mon.

MGM, 14 Rue du Lac. Café-bar in Ouchy, the best of the bunch, with tunes and rather tacky decor which aim for Miami Beach and miss.

Du Raisin, 19 Place de la Palud. Prime people-watching terrace café in the Old Town.

Sidewalk, 7 Place du Tunnel. Popular local joint in a little-visited area.

Restaurants

L'Age d'Or, 3 Pont Bessières (☎021/323 73 14). The city's top vegetarian restaurant (and one of its best in any category), with a spectacular terrace tucked beneath the bridge. *Menus* range from Fr.28 to Fr.100 or more, with mains on their own hovering around Fr.21. Exquisite fresh fish is a highlight. Closed Mon eve and Sun.

Café du Grütli, 4 Rue de la Mercerie. Venerable old tile-and-darkwood brasserie in the heart of the Old Town, with very affordable *menus* (Fr.16 or so), or idiosyncratic options like a dozen snails (Fr.19). Head past the pavement tables and make for the hum of conversation within. Closed Sun.

Au Couscous, 2 Rue Enning (☎021/321 38 40). Long-standing Arabic restaurant in a lively part of town, lacking some atmosphere but making up for it with excellent couscous and tajine (Fr.22+) and mezze (Fr.25), with veggie and macrobiotic dishes too. *Menus* from Fr.15. Closed Sat & Sun lunchtimes.

Da Geppetto, in *Hôtel Boulevard*, 51 Boulevard de Grancy (☎021/617 28 11). *Menus* for Fr.16, or fresh pasta dishes for Fr.25–30, in a lively, pleasant ambience away from the city-centre hubbub. Closed Sun.

La Grappe d'Or, 3 Cheneau-de-Bourg (☎021/323 07 60). Top gourmet temple for classic and modern French cuisine, benefiting from attentive service and a warm ambience. Expect no change from Fr.100. Closed Sat lunch & Sun.

Laxmi, 5 Escaliers du Marché. Excellent authentic Indian/veggie food, well prepared and cooked. Budget all-you-can-eat buffet lunches are Fr.15, or Fr.11 for veggies, or Fr.10 for cold dishes; evening *menus* cost no more. Students get a ten percent discount. Closed Mon lunch and Sun.

Ma Jong, 3 Escaliers du Grand-Pont. Just down from *Manora*, with excellent-value freshly wok-fried meals, piled high for Fr.14. Sushi too. Closed Sun.

Manora, 17 Place St-François. Self-service place with a wide range of excellent cheap food. Daily 9am–10.30pm.

Rochat, 1 Rue d'Yverdon, Crissier (☎021/634 05 05). Formerly the domain of the legendary Frédy Girardet, said to be the greatest chef in the world in his day, and now taken over by Philippe Rochat, an underling for some seventeen years. This is considered to be Switzerland's best restaurant – Michelin give it three stars. The style is classic, the presentation and service are impeccable. Reserve two months ahead for dinner, two weeks ahead for lunch. Closed Sun & Mon, and early Aug.

Le Shanghai, 6 Place du Tunnel. Rock-bottom cheap Chinese, plain and serviceable. Lunches for less than Fr.15. Closed Sun.

Nightlife and entertainment

Lausanne's **nightlife** and cultural offerings are second to none in Switzerland, with a vast range of music and performance to check out aside from the swathe of festivals listed in the box on p.116.

Bars, clubs and live music

Bars and clubby nightlife abound. First place to look is Le Flon, a low-lying warehouse district bounded by Bel-Air, Grand-Pont and the metro station, where following your ears after dark will bring you to the happening joints of the moment. Otherwise, good areas for concentrations of bars and night-people are Rue Enning; Le Tunnel, around Place du Tunnel; and, on a more sedate note, the streets immediately behind the château. The bars listed here all close at 1–2am, the clubs at 4–5am.

Café Freeport, train station. Quite a pleasant, if tackily neon, bar, with an intriguingly random clientele and the longest opening hours in town (Sun–Thurs 5am–1am, Fri & Sat 5am–2am).

Café de l'Hôtel de Ville, 10 Place de la Palud. Wonderful little wood-floor café with *chansons* and jazz quartets in the cellar.

Captain Cook, 2 Rue Enning. Crammed and smoky pub in the heart of the action, offering English TV football.

Au Château, 1 Place du Tunnel. Funky music bar serving flavourful home-brewed beers – pale, dark and red – to an excited, talkative crowd.

Chorus, 3 Avenue Mon-Repos. Prime basement spot for live jazz. Closed Mon & Tues.

D!, Place Centrale. Highly respected Flon basement club, close and sweaty, playing house some nights, jungle other nights, and able to pull in some international DJs. Entry Fri & Sat Fr.15. Closed Mon–Wed.

Dolce Vita, 30 Rue César-Roux. Excellent live venue and club, a Swiss institution since 1985, with a regular programme covering all musical genres. Admission varies. Closed Mon & Tues.

Garbo, 3 Rue Caroline. One of the better Caroline bars, split between a hectic downstairs and quieter upstairs. Open nightly.

Kerrigan's, 8 Rue de la Barre. Hilltop Irish pub in a peaceful spot behind the château. Closed Sun.

Lecaféthéâtre, 10 Rue de Genève. Flon café-bar with live entertainments most nights. Closed Sun & Mon.

Le Loft, 1 Escaliers Bel-Air. A techno club on the stairs up from the Flon, which has a rather tougher reputation than its near neighbours, but has free Friday night admission (Sat Fr.15). Occasional live acts. Closed Mon & Tues.

MAD (Moulin à Danse), 23 Rue de Genève. Infamous and hugely popular Flon dance club with adjoining theatre, galleries and alternative-style café. The club is open from 11pm, and comprises a basement "parlour", dancefloor, bar and chillout room. Entry Fri & Sat Fr.20. Gay night Sun. Closed Mon & Tues.

La Mine, 2 Place Pépinet. All-day techno bar. Closed Sun.

VO Le Jazz Café, 11 Place du Tunnel. Café-bar plus live venue, also with regular DJ nights featuring British and European big names. Open nightly.

Classical music, dance, opera, film, and theatre

Contemporary and classical dance, theatre and music are all represented in Lausanne by some of Switzerland's best performers. The Théâtre de Beaulieu, 10 Avenue des Bergières (☎021/643 21 11), is the main venue for full-scale **classical music** productions – the Orchestre de la Suisse Romande performs here regularly when not in Geneva – and is also famous as the place where the highly acclaimed **Béjart Ballet** presents new material every June and November. The **Opéra de Lausanne** performs at Beaulieu too, as well as at its home at 12 Avenue du Théâtre (☎021/310 16 00), while the Orchestre de Chambre de Lausanne stages concerts at the Salle Métropole (☎021/311 11 22), also the venue for many Béjart productions. The arts centre at Rue Sevelin 36 is the home of **contemporary dance**, with continuous seasons of productions year-round. Don't miss the cycle of free concerts – mostly, but not exclusively, organ recitals – in the **Cathedral**, every Friday evening from June to September, with extra concerts around Easter, Whitsun and Christmas.

Plenty of **cinemas** around town show latest releases, often with afternoon shows in the original language (v.o., or *version originale*) and evening shows dubbed into French. The Cinémathèque Suisse, housed in the casino in Montbenon park (☎021/331 01 01) has a continually changing programme of non-commercial movies from Europe and around the world, sometimes (but rarely) with English subtitles.

The Théâtre de Vidy, 5 Avenue É-Jacques-Dalcroze (☎021/619 45 45) is one of Europe's premier **theatres**, with innovative productions and extremely high standards – but universally in French. The city also has dozens of smaller spaces for classical and contemporary drama, and cabaret: L'Atelier Volant, 12 Rue des Côtes-de-Montbenon (☎021/311 52 80) and Le Lapin Vert, 2 Ruelle du Lapin-Vert (☎021/320 09 94) are renowned, while Théâtre de l'Arsenic, 57 Rue de Genève (☎021/625 11 36) is a Flon-based alternative theatre venue.

Tickets can be had direct from the venue; from the centralized Service Culturel Migros-Vaud, 12 Passage St-François (☎021/318 71 71); or from tourist offices or the city information office.

Listings

Boat rental Rowing boats and pedalos are available to rent from opposite the *Hôtel d'Angleterre* for Fr.19/hr, motorboats for Fr.45/hr.

Books Librairie Payot, 4 Place Pépinet, has a sizeable selection.

Car rental Avis, 50 Avenue de la Gare (☎021/340 72 00); Budget, 18 Rue du Maupas (☎021/683 30 50); Europcar, 2 Avenue Ruchonnet (☎021/323 91 52); Hertz, 17 Place du Tunnel (☎021/312 53 11).

Changing money The best place to change money is in the station (daily 6.20am–7.30pm).

Email and Internet There's one PC for free Internet access in the cantonal library within Palais de Rumine on Place de la Riponne (Mon–Fri 8am–10pm, Sat 8am–5pm). Otherwise, you can surf in the Sega video arcade next to *McDonald's* opposite the station for Fr.8/hr (Mon–Thurs 11am–midnight, Fri 11am–1am, Sat 10am–1am, Sun noon–midnight).

Flights La Blécherette, 123 Avenue du Grey (☎021/646 15 51) operates sightseeing flights from Lausanne's tiny airfield over the Alps: a 45-minute tour costs Fr.360 for three people.

Gay and lesbian life VoGay, 13 Avenue des Oiseaux (☎021/646 25 35) is the local gay association for Canton Vaud, with get-togethers and a telephone helpline. *ML16*, 16 Avenue Mon Loisir, is a gay bar open daily, while Sunday is gay night at the MAD club (see opposite). Lilith, 60 Route Aloys-Fauquez (☎021/646 26 18) is a lesbian organization which hosts parties and events.

Laundry At the top of town, 24 Rue de l'Université (Mon & Wed–Sun 9am–9pm, Tues noon–9pm); and behind the station, 15 Rue Simplon (daily 8am–9pm).

Lost property The city office is at 7 Place Chauderon (Mon–Fri 8am–noon & 1.45–5.45pm, Sat 8am–noon; ☎021/315 33 85), or try in the train station (Mon–Fri 8am–noon & 2–6pm; ☎0512/242 707).

Markets The Place de la Palud and the town centre host a regular lively food market (Wed & Sat 8am–1pm) as does the Petit-Chêne (Fri 8am–1pm). Palud also has a crafts market (March–Dec first Fri of month 10am–7pm), and Place Chauderon's flea market is renowned (Thurs 8am–7pm). Riponne is the focus for Lausanne's Christmas celebrations, with a market of mulled wine, candles and roasted chestnuts from mid-December.

Medical facilities The Centre hospitalier universitaire vaudois (CHUV) is at 46 Rue du Bugnon (☎021/314 11 11). The Centre médical d'urgences at 32 Avenue Ruchonnet (☎021/320 19 61) is more central. If you need a doctor, call ☎021/652 99 32. The train station has a pharmacy (daily 6am–9pm).

Post Main office (CH-1000) is beside the station, but the most convenient large office is at Place St-François (CH-1001).

Sport Prime arena for Lausanne's passion, blading and skateboarding, is the giant indoor La Fièvre skatepark, also called HS36 (36 Avenue Sévelin), open daily – you'll also find dance companies, artists' ateliers and music rehearsal rooms in the same complex. For summer swimming, pricey Plage de Bellerive, 23 Avenue de Rhodanie, offers an Olympic-sized pool as well as access to the lake, but the beach is free at Vidy. The open-air ice rink Patinoire de la Pontaise (11 Route des Plaines-du-Loup) is one of five in the city open from October to March. Waterskiing on the lake happens only in fine summer weather.

Travel agents Discount flight agents Voyages SSR are at 20 Boulevard de Grancy (Mon–Fri 9.15am–6pm, Sat 9am–noon; ☎021/617 56 27).

Around Lausanne

Past the hills **northeast of Lausanne**, beyond the Bois de Sauvabelin, you leave the tourist trails behind and enter the classic scenery of Switzerland's rural heartland – rolling emerald-green hills backed by distant peaks and tinkling with the neck-bells of cows happily munching their way across the slopes. Vaud's cantonal boundary is only about 20km northeast of Lausanne, and most of the sights in this region fall inside Canton Fribourg; however, unless you have your own transport, Fribourg's famous cheese-making centre of **Gruyères** is most easily accessible by train from Lausanne. **Romont's** Gothic church and thirteenth-century town centre make a particularly beautiful detour on the journey to or from Fribourg itself (see p.239), while the untouristed **Gros de Vaud** region north of Lausanne is perfect for countryside cycling tours. The northern stretches of Canton Vaud – Yverdon, Payerne and Avenches, as well as the Vallée de Joux – are covered in Chapter 3.

La Gruyère region

The walls and turrets of **Gruyères's** fairytale castle, 50km northeast of Lausanne, bristle atop a single crag rising above the gorgeous rolling lowlands of Canton Fribourg. The whole region – of which Gruyères village is the best-known attraction – is known as **LA GRUYÈRE**, taking in the long Lac de la Gruyère and the Sarine valley south of Fribourg, the market town and regional transport hub of **Bulle**, and a handful of resorts clinging to the slopes of the Prealpine peaks which prelude the Pays d'Enhaut (see p.284) further south. Dominating the landscape is the great towering wedge of the **Moléson**, a jutting chunk of mountain rising to 2000m with plenty of hiking possibilities and some gentle skiing in winter. This is dairy country, the most famous product by far being Gruyère cheese, run a close second by the local butterfat-rich double cream, served with forest fruits in Gruyères's heavenly, artery-clogging version of afternoon tea.

Some 30km northeast of Lausanne, **BULLE** isn't lacking in charm, but there's little reason to visit other than to switch transport. Its medieval town centre features a solid castle, housing the **Musée Gruérien** (Tues–Sat 10am–noon & 2–5pm, Sun 2–5pm; Fr.4; SMP) with a collection devoted to traditional costumes and farm implements. On the road to Gruyères, you'll pass through **LA-TOUR-DE-TRÊME**, its eponymous thir-teenth-century tower plum in the middle of the village, but you might easily find your-self diverted by the luscious scent emanating from the Nestlé **chocolate factory** at **BROC**, 4km east of La Trême (May–Oct Mon–Fri 9–11am & 1.30–4pm; free; reserva-tions essential on ☎026/921 51 51), which offers free samples if you can sit through the rather technical video screened beforehand. East of Broc, the road passes through the tiny resort of **Charmey** on its way to the Jaunpass into Canton Bern.

At the foot of Gruyères village in the adjacent village of **PRINGY** (the actual location of Gruyères train station), you'll find a working **dairy** (daily 8am–7pm; free) where you can watch the cheesemaking process close up, helped by an informative slide-show in English. The best times to visit are during production hours (9–11.30am & 1–3.30pm).

Gruyères

A perfectly preserved old castle-village, isolated on its crag but within easy reach of Lake Geneva, **GRUYÈRES** is one of Switzerland's most photogenic sights and attracts hordes of daytrippers throughout the summer season, come to stroll on the village's only street and explore the impressive château. By 10am in season, the village can get uncomfortably crowded, and can stay so until late afternoon. Cars are banned, but you'll find several large parking areas on the hillside just below.

The **château** was formerly the regional seat of power, occupied from 1080 to 1554 by the nineteen counts of Gruyères, but was decimated by a fire in 1493 which destroyed virtually everything but the dungeons. The last occupants reconstructed the living quarters in a lavish Savoyard style; Michael, the final Count of Gruyères, ran up huge debts doing this and then fled, leaving his creditors – the governments of Fribourg and Bern – to divide up his lands between them. A rich Geneva dynasty, the Bovy and Balland families, bought the castle in 1848 and supported a number of artists in resi-dence, including the French landscape painter Corot, before the cantonal government of Fribourg took over maintenance of the castle in 1938. To approach it, you must walk the length of Gruyères's dipping, picturesque main street with its central fountain and quaint old houses on either side bedecked with hanging signs. A huge gate at the end affords **entry** to the castle grounds (June–Sept daily 9am–7pm; March–May & Oct daily 9am–noon & 1–5pm; Nov–Feb Mon–Fri 9.30am–noon & 1.30–4pm, Sat & Sun 10.30am–noon & 1.30–5pm; Fr.5; SMP). Highlights include Flemish tapestries decorat-ing the count's bedchamber, Corot's room with landscapes painted by him, and other rooms throughout the castle with grand fireplaces, heraldic stained glass, often featur-ing the dynastic symbol of a crane (*grue* in French), and booty from the Battle of Murten (see p.179) where Louis II, Count of Gruyère, fought on the Swiss side. The wood-panelled Knights' Hall is impressive, as is the small formal garden at the very back, on the tip of the hill. Beside the castle, Gruyères's **church** is in an exceptionally beautiful location, backed by valley vistas.

In a couple of extremely odd counterpoints to the grandeur of the castle, you'll find at the gate of the castle and covered by the same entrance fee and opening hours, the **Centre International de l'Art Fantastique**, a small gallery devoted to modern fan-tasy art – which is fine if you like that kind of thing but has no connection whatsoever with the cobbled quaintness all around. This, though, is as nothing compared with the truly nasty **H.R. Giger Museum** adjacent (Tues–Sun 10am–6.30pm; Fr.8; SMP; *www.hrgiger.com*). Giger is a graphic artist, born in Chur, who is most famous for designing the special effects for the movie *Alien* – for which he won an Oscar – as well as *Poltergeist II*, *Alien 3* and others. Flushed with success he took a shine to Gruyères, bought one of the old houses, and has turned it into a showcase for his unique brand of grotesque art, sexualized surrealist visions of machine-like humanoids, nightmarish cityscapes and fantasy-porn gynaecological obsessions crowding over three dark and unpleasant floors. "Giger," enthused Timothy Leary, 1960s acid-guru, after the success of *Alien*, "you razor-shave sections of my brain and plaster them still pulsing across your canvas; [you] give us courage to say hello to our insectoid selves." Giger's now planning an *Alien*-style bar in the castle grounds as well as a Castle Train Ride. Heaven help Gruyères.

PRACTICALITIES

Trains from Lausanne to Fribourg pass through **Palézieux**, where you must change for the local GFM trains that wind slowly through the gorgeous countryside to **Bulle**, and then further on to **Gruyères-gare** at the foot of the village; it's a short but stiff walk from the station up the hill to Gruyères, or you could time your arrival to coincide with one of the half-dozen buses a day shuttling between Gruyères-gare and Gruyères-ville. The Palézieux–Gruyères trains trundle on to terminate at **Montbovon**, on the MOB line between Montreux and Gstaad. If you're approaching from Fribourg, take a GFM express bus to Bulle and switch onto a train there. One lunch-time bus a day goes direct to Gruyères-ville from Bulle station.

Everything in Gruyères is on the village's single street. The **tourist office** is at the car park end (mid-May to mid-Oct daily 9am–noon & 1.30–5.45pm; mid-Oct to mid-May Mon–Fri 10am–noon & 1.30–5pm; ☎026/921 10 30, *www.gruyeres.ch* and *www.lyoba.ch*). There are only a few **hotels**, all of which take one or two days a week off in the winter, so turning up without a booking is a risky business. Whichever side of the street you're on, getting a room at the back gives you a view over the valley. The *Hôtel de Ville* (☎026/921 24 24, fax 921 36 28, *hoteldeville-gruyeres@swissonline.ch*; ②) is perfectly serviceable, while the pinewood *Fleur de Lys* (☎026/921 21 08, fax 921 36 05; ③) is a step up in comfort and cuisine. Best of the bunch is the idyllic *Hostellerie des Chevaliers* (☎026/921 19 33, fax 921 25 52; ③–④), just outside the village above the parking area.

Finding a place to **eat** is a case of strolling until you spot something or somewhere that takes your fancy. Everywhere offers terraces on both the village-side and the valley-side on which to partake of a substantial range of cheesy delights, as well as bowls of berries slathered in the village's silky *crème-double*. The *Auberge de la Halle* is one of the least pretentious places to get a proper meal, with Fr.17 *menus* incorporating the house speciality – thick cheesy-vegetable soup. Otherwise, all the hotels offer quality traditional Gruyères and French cuisine, with the *Hostellerie St-Georges* (☎026/921 83 00) top choice within the village.

Moléson

Ten minutes on the bus past Gruyères-gare is **MOLÉSON** village, a small, bucolic resort giving access to the heights of **Le Moléson** mountain, via a funicular and gondola. The village square has as its focus a **dairy** dating from 1686 (May–Oct daily 9.30am–10pm), where cheese is made according to the old mountain ways. To view the cheesemaking process, you must reserve ahead with the Moléson tourist office (☎026/921 24 34, *www.moleson.ch*). Panoramic views from the summit of the Moléson, at 2002m, take in Lake Geneva, the Prealps and even Mont Blanc, and there are plenty of ridge-top walks and, in winter, easy-to-medium ski runs.

Romont and the Gros de Vaud

Train-tracks and the minor roads from Lausanne to Fribourg bypass **RUE**, 7km southeast of **Moudon** and supposedly the smallest "town" in Switzerland (population 600) before reaching **ROMONT**, a small medieval town perched atop an isolated round hill, with lofty 360-degree views over the surroundings. From the train station, below the hill, the town's wall and two distinctive round towers stand out against the sky. It's a steep ten-minute walk up from the train station.

Thirteenth-century ramparts surround the town, which consists of little more than two broad streets with a round tower at each end. The **castle** dominates, with one tower converted into the **Musée du Vitrail** (Museum of Stained Glass; April–Oct Tues–Sun 10am–noon & 2–6pm; Nov–March Sat & Sun same times; Fr.6; SMP), holding mostly modern examples along with an informative slide-show. Nearby is the town's beautiful Gothic *Collégiale* **church** of Our Lady of the Assumption, also dating from the thirteenth century, replete with original woodcarving from a rebuilding in 1434 and some wonderfully detailed stonework. The **tourist office** is at 112 Rue du Château (Mon–Fri 10am–noon & 2–4pm, April–Oct also Sat 10am–noon; ☎026/652 31 52, *www.romont.ch*).

The Gros de Vaud

The peaceful country between Lausanne and Yverdon is known as the **Gros de Vaud**, rural heart of the canton and breadbasket for the region. **ECHALLENS**, some 20km north of Lausanne, is the main centre, formerly an important market town which earned the right to be called a city in the fourteenth century but has now metamorphosed into a popular retreat for young families looking to escape big-city life. Despite its sometimes twee touches of renovation, it's still a picturesque place, with a thirteenth-century château and many eighteenth-century buildings testifying to past grandeur. Arrive on a Thursday in high summer and you might run into one of the regular crafts markets held in the town centre. The **tourist office**, 5 Place de la Gare (☎021/881 11 15), has details of the dozens of especially good walking and cycling routes through the fields round about.

The ancient LEB narrow-gauge **railway** – Switzerland's oldest, opened in 1873 – runs from Lausanne's Place Chauderon station north to Echallens and, in summer especially, is one of the more scenic rides in the country. One or two steam trains a day make the run, for no supplement above the ordinary fare.

LAKE GENEVA

The croissant-shaped **LAKE GENEVA**, bluest of the Swiss lakes, is ringed with villages, castles and gorgeous walks that demand attention. This is wine country, with vineyards spread around the full sweep of the lakeshore and carpeting the first slopes of the hills which rise behind. Genteel, calming small towns such as **Nyon** and **Vevey**, either side of Lausanne, have made a living recharging the batteries of frazzled urbanites for generations. Over the decades, the lake has also attracted the world's wealthiest people, and the shores around the jetset playground of **Montreux** in particular are lined with opulent villas – although a lakeside stroll can still let you taste the unspoilt beauty which drew Byron and the Romantic poets in a former age. Relaxing on one of the boats which crisscross the lake beneath the looming presence of the Savoy Alps and the Dents-du-Midi mountains on the French side helps bring home the full grandeur of the setting.

The lake has had various names over the centuries. The Romans called it *Lacus Lemanus*. In the Middle Ages it was known as the *Lac de Lausanne*, reflecting that city's importance. Between the sixteenth and nineteenth centuries, when Geneva rose to world fame, its title changed to the *Lac de Genève*, although a few maps stubbornly named it the *Lac d'Ouchy*. These days it's reverted to its Roman name of *Lac Léman*, despite still being called Lake Geneva in English, and *Genfersee*, a direct translation, in German.

FACTS AND FIGURES

Lake Geneva is the largest freshwater lake in Western Europe, holding some 89 trillion litres. It's really just a big bulge in the course of the River Rhône, which rises at the Furkapass and flows westwards between the mountains of Canton Valais to enter the lake near Villeneuve. Its water takes an estimated seventeen years to cover the 73km to Geneva before flowing on through France to an outlet into the Mediterranean near Marseille. Although the lake is only 14km wide at its broadest point, it plunges to 310m maximum depth and is subject to heavy winds which rip across the surface, causing stormy conditions not unlike an inland sea.

Aside from the people working on the lake's ferries, some 150 French and Swiss families currently earn their living on the water by fishing for perch, pike, trout and more, selling the majority of their catch directly to restaurants and supermarkets in the shoreside towns. A new trend for whitefish smoked over beechwood has given them a much-needed shot in the arm of late.

From Geneva to Lausanne

The gently curving northwestern shore of the lake from Geneva to Lausanne (some 65km) is known as **La Côte**, and is characterized by a succession of hamlets and small villages, almost without exception gorgeously pretty, well kept and pristinely picturesque. Those along the minor shoreline road, the *Route Suisse*, are less numerous and more visited than those placed back behind the main *autoroute* on the first slopes of the Jura foothills, amongst vineyards tilted towards the sun which produce some of the highest-prized wine in Vaud. Things are much less developed here for **wine-tasting tours** than in the Lavaux region east of Lausanne. However, if you rent a bike from larger train stations for a day's gentle exploration along the narrow *Route des Vignerons*, which winds from vineyard to vineyard along the gentle slope, you'll find plenty of *caveaux* (wine cellars) offering *dégustations* (tastings) of local products. You have to pay for the tasting – generally two, three or four choices of wine, in 1dl glasses – but can then turn up a bargain if you choose to buy a bottle or two. Countless *auberges* and *pintes* (country taverns) along the way offer local home-cooked specialities.

Whether down by the lake or up among the vines, you'll be passing dozens of **châteaux**, evidence both of the region's key strategic significance in medieval times, and its attraction to Europe's nobility in more recent centuries. Some are now museums, but most remain in private hands. Major stopoffs include the historic **Château de Coppet**, close to Geneva, the attractive little harbour-town of **Nyon** with its own château and Roman museum, and the nearby **Château de Prangins**, housing an excellent museum devoted to Swiss history.

Coppet and Céligny

COPPET is only a couple of kilometres over the Geneva–Vaud cantonal boundary. Just across the narrow strait of the Petit Lac opposite the village is Hermance (see p.107), south of which the shores narrow to Geneva, only 12km away, while the bulge of low hills to the north is French territory, culminating in the thickly wooded headland of Yvoire. The village sits plum astride the lakeshore *Route Suisse* and has an attractive arcaded main street but is otherwise unremarkable except for its lavish **chateau**, which in the turbulent years around the French Revolution was dubbed "the Parliament of

THE LAKESIDE HALL OF FAME

Hundreds of notable writers, artists, musicians and poets have visited Lake Geneva over the centuries. For cultured nineteenth-century sophisticates, the lakeside was as important a stop on the Grand Tour of Europe as Paris, Florence or Vienna, and where one artist settled others inevitably followed, drawn – depending on individual circumstance – by the fresh air, the Château de Chillon, political neutrality, or the numbered bank-accounts.

Edward Gibbon spent long periods in Lausanne, meeting **Voltaire** there in the 1750s, and completing his monumental *Decline and Fall of the Roman Empire* during an eleven-year stay between 1783 and 1793. Jean-Jacques **Rousseau**, a native of Geneva, set his *La Nouvelle Héloïse*, completed in 1761, in Clarens near Montreux. **Wordsworth** came through Lausanne in 1790 and 1820. The English artist **Turner** first visited the area in 1802, painting watercolours of the landscape around Chillon. In 1816, while **Mary Shelley** stayed in Geneva to write *Frankenstein*, **Lord Byron** and **Percy Bysshe Shelley** set off on an eight-day boat tour of the lake; they both almost drowned off St Gingolph, then toured the Château de Chillon, which inspired Byron to dash off *The Prisoner of Chillon* in his Ouchy hotel room. **Robert Southey** waxed lyrical about Lausanne following a visit in 1817, as did **Victor Hugo** in 1839. The famous English actor **John Kemble** died and was buried in Lausanne in 1823. **Alexandre Dumas**, on one of his many Swiss journeys, wrote of a visit to Chillon in 1832. **Tennyson**, **Thackeray** and others dropped in to visit **Charles Dickens**, who began *Dombey and Son* while staying in Lausanne in 1846; Thackeray himself worked on *The Newcomes* in Vevey in 1853. **George Eliot** spent nine months writing in Geneva over the winter of 1849–50. In 1861, **Hans Christian Andersen** wrote *The Ice Maiden* in Montreux. **Tolstoy** and **Dostoievsky** both passed through Lausanne, the latter spending two years in Geneva writing *The Idiot*, followed by a summer writing *The Gambler* in Vevey; **Gogol** began *Dead Souls* in Vevey, which was the setting for **Henry James**'s *Daisy Miller* and which was also where **Arnold Bennett** spent 1908–09 writing *The Card*. **Tchaikovsky** composed his Violin Concerto in F major (Op.35), and also began *Eugène Onegin* while in Clarens in 1877–78. **Stravinsky** spent 1911–14 in the same town, where he composed his revolutionary *The Rite of Spring*; he spent the World War I years working in Lausanne. **T.S. Eliot** convalesced in Lausanne in 1921 and 1922 while writing his equally revolutionary *The Waste Land*. In 1952, at the age of 63, **Charlie Chaplin** moved to Vevey to escape Hollywood's McCarthyism, and died there 25 years later. **Noël Coward** lived in Les Avants, above Montreux, from 1958, while **Audrey Hepburn** lived in Tolochenaz, near Morges, from 1963. **Vladimir Nabokov** spent the last sixteen years of his life in Montreux (after 1961); and **Graham Greene** died in Vevey in 1991. Of the dozens of pop musicians who've dabbled with second, third or fourth houses on the lake, **Freddie Mercury** had a particularly soft spot for Montreux, and returned many times during the last ten years of his life.

European Opinion" for the glittering and controversial *salon* hosted by Madame de Staël (see box, overleaf) and attended by the leading figures of the day.

The approach to the château – a rather diminutive edifice if you're expecting Versailles – is beneath a vaulted arch into a peaceful interior courtyard, open on one side to the gardens behind a wrought-iron gate surmounted with the elaborate initials "N.C.", demonstrating the partnership between Jacques Necker and his wife Suzanne Curchod. **Entry** (daily: Easter–Oct 2–6pm, July & Aug also 10am–noon; Fr.10) is only on the multilingual guided tours given by the extremely knowledgeable staff: these run every half-hour or so, according to demand, and last about half-an-hour. Some nine rooms are open to the public, including the grand library, formerly the main reception room and filled with Empire and Directoire furniture; Madame de Staël's bedroom, with her Louis XVI bed draped in Lyon silk; Juliette Récamier's bedroom next door,

CHÂTEAU DE COPPET

The Château de Coppet was built by **Jacques Necker**, a Genevois banker and Minister of Finance to the French king Louis XVI from 1776 until the Revolution in 1789. He seems to have been more liberal than his masters, and was rather disgusted by the ostentatious excesses of the regime he was publicly responsible for: in a uniquely privileged position, he built up a dossier carefully documenting the full extent of the financial corruption of the regime, eventually publishing the accounts in full. The revelations, it's said, helped to initiate the Revolution.

In 1784, perhaps sensing the upheavals to come in France, Necker had bought the barony of Coppet to serve as a safe haven. His only daughter **Germaine**, then eighteen, was already gaining a reputation in the Paris *salons* for her intellect and vivacity, and had an array of suitors from whom she picked the man "she least disliked", the stolid and self-important Baron de Staël Holstein, chamberlain to the Queen of Sweden. The marriage seems to have proved unsatisfactory for both of them, and the Baron took very much the back seat, overshadowed by his wife's high profile and her passionate *joie de vivre*.

Necker retired to Coppet in 1790 after the Revolution, from when Germaine's (now **Madame de Staël's**) literary and philosophical *salon* began to attract the leading intellects of the day. The Swiss author Benjamin Constant (with whom de Staël may have conducted a long-lasting affair) was a regular visitor, as were the philosopher Schlegel, Chateaubriand, Lord Byron, and others. Madame de Staël organized life at the château around her constant flow of guests: lunch, it is said, was served at 5pm, dinner at 11pm, with musical *soirées* and lavishly staged playlets presented in the library in between, and debates and discussions afterwards which continued late into the night.

In 1804 Necker died, and the château passed into the hands of Madame de Staël, who was forced to remain there in permanent exile after 1806 following her persistent public denunciation of Napoleon. She died a celebrated writer and commentator in 1817, at the age of 51, and the château is still in her family to this day. The renowned portraitist Ingres painted Madame de Staël's granddaughter Louise de Broglie, Countess of Haussonville, and proceeds from the recent sale of this masterpiece to a gallery in New York enabled the current Count to retain ownership of the château. The Haussonvilles now stay in Coppet for just a couple of weeks each summer, but still maintain the house in its original eighteenth-century grandeur.

hung with exquisite eighteenth-century Chinese wallpaper; and, upstairs, a drawing-room and a gallery of family portraits.

In addition to a scattering of plain **eating** places along the main street, Coppet boasts the glorious **hotel** *Du Lac*, 51 Grand'Rue (☎022/776 15 21, fax 776 53 46; ④). This wood-beamed inn was classified as a *grand logis* in 1628, granting it "the exclusive right to receive and lodge people arriving by coach or on horseback"; the atmosphere hasn't changed much, and after ducking in off the busy road, you trail through grand dining-rooms and antique-laden drawing rooms until you reach the shady, perfectly calm lakeside terrace at the back. Common foot travellers in days of yore presumably stayed at simpler places like the *Hôtel d'Orange* (☎022/776 10 37, fax 776 25 40; ②), a few doors down at no. 61.

Céligny

Tucked in a tiny enclave of Canton Geneva, surrounded by Vaud and also no more than a few kilometres from the French border, gentle **CÉLIGNY** is about as endearing a rural gem as you could hope to find, enjoying waterside lawns, vineyards all around and through the village, an atmospheric church and château (not open to the public) and an air of undisturbed tranquillity hanging over its fountained square that proved particularly balming for the actor Richard Burton, who spent the last few years of his life here.

If you walk up into the village from the tiny station, across the square and then head left, cutting around a parking area, you'll eventually stumble on the Vieux Cimitière, a damp and mossy grove on the bank of a little stream (the other bank is Vaudois territory) that is Burton's final resting place.

Céligny's real treasure is the *Hôtel du Soleil* on the village square (☎022/960 96 33, fax 776 08 00; closed Mon eve & Tues), a characterful country *auberge* with friendly staff that has a wide choice of light, imaginatively prepared food, including delicious fresh perch; *menus* are Fr.25 or so. You'd do well to reserve a table to **eat**, especially in summer – the place is well known to the locals and to La Côte's many expat families – although you might just as well savour the atmosphere over a glass or two of wine on the terrace. A handful of comfortable **rooms** on the upper floor (②) add to the appeal.

Nyon

Some 9km north of Coppet, **NYON** – a major town under the Romans which has mellowed into a laconic and attractive little port – is a perfect stopover on a leisurely tour of the lake. The town, on a flattish plain sandwiched between the Jura and the lake, is spread out among verdant fields and lawns which reach down to the water, and is backed by acres of vineyards on the gentle slopes behind. There's a château and an excellent Roman museum, and the nearby **Château de Prangins** houses the regional branch of the National Museum. And if museums aren't your thing, there's the option of riding a mountain railway up to the little Jura resort of **St Cergue**.

Some history

After Julius Caesar had finally conquered Gallia Comata (Long-Haired Gaul) in 52 BC, he retired his cavalry veterans to the **Colonia Julia Equestris**, founded on the shores of the lake over the Helvetian settlement of **Noviodunum** which had stood there previously. For two centuries, the town flourished, becoming an urban centre of 3000 people (the population didn't reach such heights again until the mid-nineteenth century). The second half of the third century AD saw increasing attacks from Alemans and Franks, who succeeded in breaking through Roman defences; stones from the ruined buildings were carted off to make a defensive wall around Geneva, and by the mid-fifth century the grand colony was virtually deserted. Only its Roman name survived, the Latin "Colonia" compressed into the single nasal syllable "Nyon". The region was integrated into the Kingdom of **Burgundy** after 443, then was passed from lord to lord until the Bernese conquered Vaud in 1536. In 1781, a French entrepreneur Jacques Dortu opened a **porcelain** workshop in the town, staffed by local artisans who produced work of exceptionally high quality, rapidly establishing Nyon as a centre of the craft: museums in Switzerland and around Europe now display Nyon porcelain alongside the best of Limoges china as some of the highest-prized ceramic art of the period.

The Town

Heading southeast from the train station towards the lake will bring you in a couple of minutes into the compact Old Town, centred on **Place du Château**, a shady, charmingly laid-back square with terrace cafés that is backed by the **château** itself, a mighty twelfth-century turreted fortress looking out over the lake. Closed for renovations throughout 1999, it's due to reopen in 2000 with the town's **Musée Historique** occupying all six floors, displaying silver, fine art, photographs, and a comprehensive collection of Nyon porcelain. Opposite the chateau at 4 Place du Château is the headquarters of Focale, one of the most important associations of Swiss photographers; their cramped **bookshop** is excellent, as is the gallery downstairs showing contemporary photography. The Rue du Vieux Marché leading west off the square brings you

---

PALEO ROCK FESTIVAL

Nyon's biggest party is also one of Europe's biggest – the giant **Paleo Rock Festival** (infomation and tickets ☎022/365 10 10, *www.paleo.ch*), which takes place over a week in late July in a field outside town, with a consistently excellent line-up of musicians attracting hundreds of thousands of revellers. Acts in 1999 were as diverse as Bryan Adams and Ruben Gonzalez, the Fun Lovin' Criminals and Cesaria Evora, Garbage and Charles Aznavour. If you buy early, you can snap up a day ticket for as little as Fr.38, or a full six-day pass for Fr.180; transport from Nyon to the site and back is free. The tourist office also has festival-plus-hotel packages, which again rise in price the later you book.

---

past a statue of Julius Caesar to the impressive **Musée Romain** on Rue Maupertuis (Tues–Sun: April–Oct 10am–noon & 2–6pm; Nov–March 2–6pm; Fr.6 ticket covers all of Nyon's museums; SMP). The museum is housed in a Roman basilica, originally part of Nyon's forum; a giant trompe l'oeil fresco of the original basilica's interior on the wall outside, as well as a model in the museum, give an idea of the size of Nyon's public buildings in its Roman heyday. The museum's extensive collection is very well laid out, but with notes only in French – you pass first into the central area (the nave of the basilica) which houses inscriptions, statues and architectural details, and from there move around the walls of the room through zones devoted to daily life, crafts and religion.

The street ends at the small but atmospheric **Église Notre-Dame**, dating from 1110 and of unusual asymmetrical design, endowed with new, glowing stained glass. The arched **Porte Ste Marie** round the corner gives onto the **Esplanade des Marronniers** (chestnut trees), exposed to fresh lake breezes and dominated by two-and-a-half impressively sited Roman columns silhouetted against the blue. Walking along the city walls east and down some steps to the lakefront delivers you to the small, diverting **Musée du Léman**, 8 Quai Louis-Bonnard (April–Oct Tues–Sat 10am–noon & 2–5pm, Sun 10am–5pm; Nov–March Tues–Sat 2–5pm, Sun 10am–5pm; combined ticket with Musée Romain; SMP). The ground floor has informative displays on the lake fauna, with large aquariums, while up above are paintings, models of ships and disquisitions (in French) on how to protect the lake's natural resources. From the **Place de Savoie**, 150 metres to the east, with its jetty from which you can make out the plume of Geneva's Jet d'Eau some 20km away, atmospheric Rue de Rive heads slightly uphill, lined with antique shops and some very odd murals on sidewalls of cartoonish figures peeping out of painted windows. At the end, Rue de la Colombière continues uphill, and where it meets Rue de la Porcelaine you should spot Nyon's **Roman amphitheatre** half hidden in the grass a little east, virtually the same size as the one at Avenches (see pp.177–8) but much more ruined and unfortunately now hemmed in by modern housing developments.

Practicalities

Plenty of **trains** serve Nyon from both directions, although note that not all those heading east go to Lausanne – some branch off at Morges on their way to Yverdon. Regular **boats** serve Nyon from both Geneva and Lausanne. The **tourist office** is one minute's walk from the station, at 7 Avenue Viollier (June–Sept daily 8.30am–noon & 1.30–5.30pm; Oct–May Mon–Fri same times; ☎022/361 62 61, *www.nyon.ch*), and offers a free **guided walk** around the town, starting from the Place du Château (June–Sept Thurs–Sat 10am).

Nyon's best **hotel** is the *Beau-Rivage*, 49 Rue de Rive (☎022/365 41 41, fax 365 41 65; ⑥), a fabulous pile below the castle that's been in business since 1481 and boasts large, traditionally furnished rooms, most looking lakewards. The charming *Hostellerie du XVIe Siècle*, 2 Place du Marché (☎022/361 24 41, fax 362 85 66; ①–②) is an atmospheric arcaded building in the cobbled Old Town, renovated throughout; some rooms are en suite, others not. Rue de Rive has any number of places to **eat** fresh fish, but the fillet of perch (Fr.30) served at *Au Cheval Blanc* at no. 62 must rank with the best. More affordable pizzas and pasta *menus* (Fr.16–18) can be munched at *Le Léman*, 28 Rue de Rive.

Château de Prangins

A kilometre or two east of Nyon is the idyllic village of **PRANGINS**, in the midst of which, set in its own formal English gardens, is the **Château de Prangins**, built in the 1730s in the French style and now an arm of the Swiss National Museum especially devoted to the history of Switzerland in the eighteenth and nineteenth centuries. The museum (Tues–Sun 10am–5pm; Fr.5; SMP) is a huge place holding an imaginative and engaging collection that's well worth a couple of hours; all the rooms are numbered sequentially, but the layout can be very confusing and you may find yourself back-tracking more than once.

The ground floor, outlining the ideals of aristocrats and the bourgeoisie around 1800, and the cellars, exploring Switzerland's pre-industrial rural economy, are less engaging than the two upper floors, both of which are devoted to Swiss cultural history from 1750 into the twentieth century. Each room ("From Birth to Death", "The Display of Power", "Travellers and Tourists") has detailed English notes, with items from everyday life displayed next to historically significant objects. The multimedia stations that are dotted around enhance wanderings tremendously by letting you play period music while you're examining the cases and, for instance, as well as selecting readings from contemporary accounts of history, you can listen to original songs from the Swiss Revolution. Reconstructed interiors, such as that of a late-nineteenth century schoolroom, have uncanny attention to detail. Outside, an extensive kitchen garden has been planted with fruit and vegetables according to eighteenth-century literary accounts of horticulture.

Bus #5 runs hourly from Nyon's train station on a circular route through Prangins, stopping either at the post office three minutes from the château (Mon–Sat) or at the château itself (Sun).

Above Nyon

Rising above Nyon are the final stretches of the Jura range within Switzerland, known as the **Pied du Jura**, sliced across by the international border which separates the French Pays de Gex above Geneva from the Swiss mountain resort of **ST CERGUE**. This quiet, unassuming town is set in some wild countryside with hiking trails that don't see the quantity of ramblers you might be sharing the paths with elsewhere in the Jura. In winter, the town concentrates on providing safe, quality downhill **skiing** for families, and plenty of excellent cross-country routes. The *desalpe*, or annual descent of cattle from the high pastures to winter quarters in the valley, accompanied by much floral decoration and folkloric celebrations is a highlight of St Cergue's calendar, taking place on a Saturday in late September. Riding on the little red NStCM **trains** (InterRail not valid) which depart from the forecourt of Nyon station on a winding narrow-gauge route up into the green hills is worth an afternoon in itself, whether you get off at St Cergue or shuttle on over the **Col de la Givrine** (1228m) to the hamlet of **La Cure** on the border.

Some 10km northeast of Nyon on the *Route des Vignerons* are the neighbouring communes of **LUINS** and **VINZEL**, both of them wine villages, and both famous for their *malakoffs*. These little gastronomic heartwarmers – a fried cheese-and-egg mixture served hot and rich on a round bread base – were renamed following the triumphant return of a band of Vaudois mercenaries under the Russian General Malakoff from the

1855 siege of Sebastopol; the two villages, which are no more than ten minutes' walk apart, have competed since then for whose *malakoff* is better. Take the taste test at the *Auberge Communale* in Luins (☎021/824 11 59), then wander down the road past the vineyards to *Au Coeur de la Côte* in Vinzel (☎021/824 11 41) – both are open daily, serving *malakoffs* for around Fr.6 each, and you can grab the opportunity while you're at it to compare and contrast the excellent village wines. Wander on to **Bursins**, a few kilometres east, and you may bump into Peter Ustinov, who's lived in the village for many years; or, instead, hike above Luins to a tiny church-with-a-view, dating from 1393, and on up past the vineyards into thick woodland – beech, chestnut and oak – eventually emerging into the open pasture and cultivated fields of the plateau above.

From Rolle to Lausanne

ROLLE is a little-visited place roughly midway between Nyon and Lausanne which lies at the heart of the La Côte wine country. Its huge lakeside château, plum in the heart of town, dates from 1270 but is not open to the public. Just offshore – crowned by an obelisk – is the tiny **Île de la Harpe**, built up in 1835 from earth dumping during construction of the town's harbour; unfortunately for posterity, the harbour works incorporated a quantity of pre-hewn oak posts which had stood just offshore for as long as anyone could remember – remnants, no doubt, of prehistoric stilt dwellings, destroyed in the name of progress. It's a tragic irony that shortly afterwards the railway arrived, negating the whole point of building a harbour in the first place. The island, named after local revolutionary and statesman Frédéric-César de la Harpe (see box), is now the focus for Rolle's active community of yachties, who regularly organize sailing festivals and races around it, often tying up for a fortifying dram or two at the handy midway point.

Five kilometres east of Rolle on the lakeshore road you'll find the massive **Château d'Allaman** built in the twelfth century, torched in 1530, rebuilt in 1723 and now serving as one of the most impressive furniture showrooms you're likely to see – twenty antique dealers rent space within the castle to display their wares (Wed–Sun 2–6pm), which suit the grand halls and corridors perfectly, although the price tags might give you indigestion. The cellar (Wed–Fri 1–8pm, Sat & Sun 11am–7pm) features tasting of wines from La Côte and around Vaud – swilling four samples will set you back Fr.22, and you can throw in a tasting of five cheeses for another Fr.14. Local bottles are also on sale for Fr.18 and up.

FRÉDÉRIC-CÉSAR DE LA HARPE

Frédéric-César de la Harpe was a key Swiss and Vaudois patriot in the turbulent times around the end of the eighteenth century. He was born in Rolle in 1754, but hardly spent any time there, instead becoming a major in the Bernese army at an early age. As his awareness of Bernese domination over his homeland grew, he left the army, eventually becoming tutor in St Petersburg to Catherine the Great's grandson, Alexander. While at the Russian court during the French Revolution, he wrote many pamphlets urging the Vaudois people to liberate themselves from the Bernese, and he eventually travelled to Paris in 1797 to urge the revolutionary French government to intervene in Vaud. The following year, due largely to de la Harpe's petitioning, the Bernese were ejected and Vaud won its independence.

In the years following, Bern made various attempts to regain power in Vaud; de la Harpe stepped in again, this time persuading his former charge Alexander, now Czar of Russia, to take the side of Vaud. De la Harpe died at Lausanne during construction of Rolle's new harbour, and his home town decided to name their little offshore island after him, planting on it an obelisk and a plaque bearing his portrait facing the Vaudois shore.

A SHAGGY DOG STORY

The château of **St-Saphorin-sur-Morges** (not to be confused with St-Saphorin near Vevey) was built in the eighteenth century. Elisabeth Upton-Eichenberger, in her excellent book on Vaud (see "Books", p.531), tells the story of a twentieth-century occupant, one **Georges de Mestral**, who had studied engineering in Lausanne and returned to live in the château. Mestral was on a shooting trip one day in the Jura foothills when, as usual, he found himself spending ages extracting burrs that had got caught in his dog's soft furry ears. The legend goes that it was here, on his knees in the forest, that de Mestral had the idea to copy nature and invent a fabric using sharp little burr-like hooks to stick to soft furry material. Thus, he thought, could rackety unreliable zips be consigned to history. He patented his idea and started production in nearby Aubonne. Although his **Velcro** has survived, and is now manufactured under licence around the world with all sorts of earnestly practical uses (in the clothing of US astronauts, for instance), it has indisputably lost the zip wars. With an indefinable grace that leave Velcro's horrible ripping noise way behind, zips are still the thing and, adding insult to injury, St-Saphorin-sur-Morges has largely forgotten its most famous son.

The lakeside road winds on to Lausanne through **MORGES**, another peaceful little harbour town famed for its kilometre-long Quais du Dahlia and the Fête de la Tulipe held during April and May in the lakefront Parc de l'Indépendance. Its huge château holds a military museum, but the main reason to come is to take the bus from the train station a kilometre or two west to **TOLOCHENAZ**, where the commune and local volunteers have set up the **Pavillon Audrey Hepburn** (Tues–Sun 1.30–5.30pm; Fr.10; bus-stop La Plantaz), honouring the actress who lived in the village from 1963 until her death in 1993 and who was, according to Billy Wilder, "what the Latin calls *sui generis* – the original, and there are no more examples, and there never will be". The exhibition offers a chronological tour through Hepburn's career, including her first contract, dated 1948 (paying £9 a week as a chorus girl), both her Oscars, a fan letter from Samuel Goldwyn and dozens of photos and film posters. Buffs will be thrilled, not least because proceeds go to the Audrey Hepburn Foundation for Children, supporting an orphanage in Romania, UNICEF schools in Somalia and Ethiopia and other worthy causes.

Just 3km west of Lausanne is the ancient village of **ST-SULPICE**, featuring a well-preserved Romanesque church. This impressive triple-apsed building was built by Cluniac monks in the eleventh century amidst grounds which include a priory, formerly housing some forty monks but converted after the Reformation into a private residence. The church is now famous for its series of year-round classical music concerts.

From Lausanne to Vevey

The compact stretch of Lake Geneva coastline east from Lausanne to Vevey – the **Lavaux** – is one of the most alluring regions of the country, its lush floral waterside promenades flanked on one side by wide expanses of vines and on the other by vistas across to the Savoy Alps rising behind the Dents-du-Midi on the far shore. Trains heading to Montreux and beyond hug the shoreline, the tracks passing within a few metres of the water, seeming to whisk you along inches above the glittering lake itself. Some of the country's best **wines** come from the dozens of vineyards clustered cheek by jowl along the steep Lavaux slopes: this is perfect country for gentle walks and bike rides punctuated by samplings of the local nectar. Cafés and *pintes* abound, set in the cobbled streets of the region's gloriously picturesque villages.

EXPLORING THE LAVAUX

The best path to follow through the Lavaux is termed the **Corniche**, winding scenically through the vineyards between the main lakefront traffic road and the *autoroute* and Lausanne–Bern train tracks on a terrace higher up. The **Grande Traversée** route, marked with a "GT" signpost, starts in Ouchy, follows the lakefront to Lutry, then snakes up to the Corniche, ending 32km away in Chillon. You can follow any number of shorter trails on and around the Corniche, marked with **Parcours Viticole** (Vineyard Trail) signposts. Local **trains** are plentiful, meaning you can hop on and off at will. Another option is to rent a **bike** in Lausanne, dropping it off in the evening in Vevey or Montreux, or taking it back to Lausanne on the train. **Boats** stop at Lutry, Cully and Rivaz.

The Lavaux wine villages

Tourist offices in towns around the lake offer plenty of information guiding you through the **Lavaux wine villages**, a line of hamlets strung along the slopes between Lausanne and Vevey devoted for centuries past to the art of viticulture. Pick up a pamphlet entitled *À la decouverte des terrasses de Lavaux*, which has routes throughout the area. Between May and October, most reliably on weekends (Thurs–Sun), you'll find *caveaux* (cellars) and *carnotzets* (cellars with rough benches and tables for extended wine- and food-sampling sessions) open in every village, some of them belonging to that commune's *vignerons* association, others attached to private châteaux or independent *vignobles*. Contact the Vevey tourist office (see opposite) for a full list of phone numbers to make reservations.

The shuttered village of **CULLY** (pronounced *kwee*), 8km east of Lausanne, is crammed full of *caveaux* and *carnotzets* offering the rich, forest-fruity wines of nearby Epesses, Calamin, Riex, Villette and Lutry. The village also boasts the extraordinary *Auberge du Raisin*, 1 Place de l'Hôtel de Ville (☎021/799 21 31, fax 799 25 01; ③–⑧), the old thirteenth-century town hall which has been converted into a uniquely characterful hotel, filled with period furniture, original Old Masters and ten individually decorated rooms which vary tremendously in price. Its creative cuisine is outstanding, acclaimed by Michelin, Gault & Millau and others, but not cheap (*menus* from Fr.50). If you're around on the last Friday in November, stop in Cully for the *Nuit du vin cuit*, or Night of Cooked Wine – a festive all-night masked musical parade accompanied by quaffing of must (new unfermented wine) mulled on open fires. Some 3km east are the open vineyards of **DÉZALEY**, producing some of the highest-rated *grand cru* wines in Switzerland; the lakeside *Auberge* in next-door **RIVAZ** (☎021/946 10 55, fax 946 38 82; ②) has a dozen or so clean, comfortable rooms.

A kilometre east of Rivaz is **ST-SAPHORIN**, about as romantic and photogenic a waterside hamlet as you could ever hope for, piled up on steep slopes above the lake, with an old church, skinny cobbled alleys that crook their way up between crumbling old cottages, and superb flinty, smoke-perfumed wines best sampled at the village's central *Auberge de l'Onde*. This atmospheric old inn, once a major halt for stagecoaches plying between Geneva and Italy, is simply bewitching – you could easily find its languorous combination of wood-beamed quaintness, day-fresh perch sautéed delectably in herb-butter and a heady carafe or three of the village wine charming you into abandoning whatever plans you had for the rest of the day. The seven comfortable rooms at *Le Castel* (☎021/921 47 51; ③) are on hand for just such a turn of events.

If your legs haven't already turned to spaghetti, you could try strolling 2km up the hill from St-Saphorin to picturesque **CHEXBRES**, a minor resort clinging to a terrace with views over the lake and mountains and a choice of hotels and restaurants, and then 4km further east to **CHARDONNE** on the slopes of towering Mont Pèlerin, home of the consistently excellent *Cure d'Attalens* wine. An amble under the funicular tracks and through uninspiring **Jongny** brings you down to Corsier, on the western edges of Vevey.

Vevey

At the little town of Vevey, in Switzerland, there is a particularly comfortable hotel ... The entertainment of tourists is the business of the place, which, as many travellers will remember, is seated upon the edge of a remarkably blue lake – a lake that it behoves every tourist to visit.

Henry James, from *Daisy Miller* (1878)

Whereas brassy Montreux, a few kilometres down the road, has over the decades embraced with abandon all that glisters – gold, paper or otherwise – its old-fashioned neighbour **VEVEY** is more discriminating. Vevey quietly cleans its streets, tends its flowerbeds, makes sure it has enough, but not too many, hotels and then waits for visitors of a certain style to find the town for themselves, become enchanted, and stay. It's a hard place to quantify, neither prim, nor stuffy, nor sophisticated, nor especially graceful ... yet it somehow manages to incorporate strands of all of them in an ambience of tasteful, restrained gentility which seeps out of its modest facades. It *is* enchanting, a world apart (or a remnant of a world now past), and you may well find yourself lulled into staying.

Henry James set his *Daisy Miller* – the story of a headstrong young woman on the Grand Tour who broke the rules of propriety by visiting the Château de Chillon unchaperoned, and so got her comeuppance – in Vevey, specifically at the *Hôtel des Trois Couronnes*, which is much the same now as it seems it must have been in James's day. And, in a similar vein, **Anita Brookner** set her Booker Prize-winning novel *Hotel du Lac* in a reserved, taciturn but anonymous lakeside town opposite the Dent d'Oche (the huge 2222m mountain on the French shore facing Vevey). Vevey breathes the decorous Brookner style: generations of tourists return to stroll the flowered promenades, muse on the Dent d'Oche, venture across the water on the Belle Epoque ships of the Lake Geneva fleet, and take high tea in grand hotels. Yet there's plenty more to do than this suggests. Vevey's shops, museums and local life are far more engaging than Montreux's, and if big cities such as Lausanne or Geneva don't appeal, you could easily use smalltown Vevey as a comfortable base for a couple of days or weeks from which to explore the whole lake and surrounding region.

Arrival, orientation and information

Vevey's **train station**, on the main line between Lausanne and Montreux, is 300m north of the lakeshore on a busy east–west main road: cross over and head towards the lake on the Rue de Lausanne, and within a minute or two you'll come to the gigantic central square of Grande-Place, also known as Place du Marché, which fronts directly onto the lake. The Old Town alleys are clustered to the east. The town has three **ferry-stops** – Vevey-Plan is to the west, behind the Nestlé building; Vevey-Marché is metres from Place du Marché in the town centre; and Vevey-La Tour is east, close to La Tour-de-Peilz.

The **tourist offices** of Vevey and Montreux have joined forces, meaning that you can get exactly the same information from both on their whole stretch of coast, often dubbed the "**Swiss Riviera**". Vevey's office is in the pillared Grenette building, the old town granary, on Grande-Place (July–Sept Mon–Sat 8.30am–7pm, Sun 10am–7pm; Oct–June Mon–Fri 8.30am–noon & 1.30–6pm, Sat 8.30am–noon; ☎021/922 20 20,

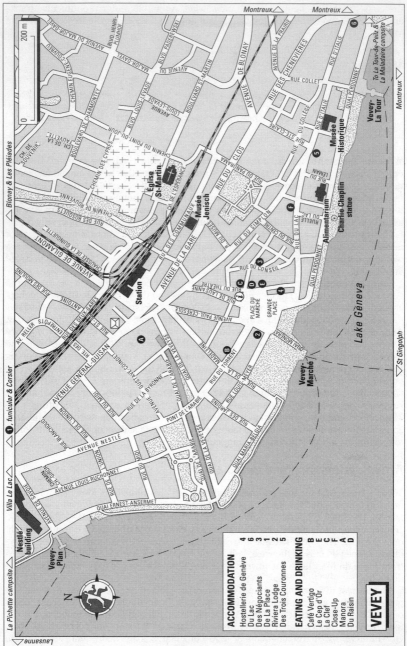

ACCOMMODATION

Hostellerie de Genève	4
Du Lac	6
Des Négociants	3
De La Place	1
Riviera Lodge	2
Des Trois Couronnes	5

EATING AND DRINKING

Café Vertigo	B
Le Cep d'Or	E
La Clef	C
Close-Up	F
Manora	A
Du Raisin	D

VEVEY

www.vevey.ch). They offer a two-hour **guided walk** around the town (April–Sept Wed–Fri 10am; Fr.10), starting from the train station, but you should check in advance about the availability of an English-speaking guide. Otherwise, the excellent brochure "On The Trail of Hemingway" pinpoints a welter of sites in the area with famous-name associations. The local **museum passport** covers entry to ten museums in Vevey and Montreux (including the Château de Chillon) for Fr.15. If you're staying around Vevey or Montreux for any length of time, you should splash out on the 75-page **magazine** Tourist Info Pass (Fr.8), which is crammed with useful information about the whole region and discount offers. If you happen to be around in July, you might want to check out the **International Festival of Comedy Films**, held annually in memory of the town's adopted son Charlie Chaplin.

One of the most pleasant long walks in the area is the **Chemin Fleuri**, or Flowered Path, covering the sumptuous 9km lakefront promenade between Vevey and Villeneuve (aside from a short stretch east of La Tour-de-Peilz, where private lakefront properties force you back into the town). The tourist office has a brochure describing the walk and its various highlights.

Accommodation

Vevey has a limited, but high-quality, range of **accommodation** options. The pristine Swiss Backpackers *Riviera Lodge* **hostel**, 5 Place du Marché (☎021/923 80 40, fax 923 80 41, *rivieralodge@bluewin.ch*, *www.rivieralodge.ch*; ①) has excellent dorms in the centre of town for Fr.25, while you can **camp** on the lakeside at either *La Pichette* (☎021/921 09 97, fax 925 53 35), 2km west of Vevey, or *La Maladaire* (☎021/944 31 37), 3km east of La Tour-de-Peilz. Of the **hotels**, *Des Négociants*, 27 Rue du Conseil (☎021/922 70 11, fax 921 34 24; ②) and *Hostellerie de Genève*, 11 Place du Marché (☎021/921 45 77, fax 921 30 15; ③) are both simple family-run places in the centre; while rustic *De La Place*, 5 Place du Temple in the nearby village of Corsier (☎ & fax 021/921 12 87; ②) is a building dating from 1692 overlooking Corsier's ancient church on the slopes above Vevey, with spartan but thoroughly atmospheric rooms. At the top end of the scale, the heavenly *Hôtel du Lac*, 1 Rue d'Italie (☎021/921 10 41, fax 921 75 08; ⑤) offers small-scale, understated grandeur, with inevitable associations with Anita Brookner; while *Des Trois Couronnes*, 49 Rue d'Italie (☎021/921 30 05, fax 922 72 80; ⑦) – the original setting for Henry James's *Daisy Miller* – retains all its period style, stuffy but utterly charming. Both lap up the lakeside panoramas.

The Town

The best way to get the flavour of Vevey is simply to wander: its narrow Old Town alleys, enclosing the huge **Grande-Place** – or **Place du Marché** – in a cat's cradle of

FORMULA ONE

Henri Nestlé was born in Frankfurt in 1814, and moved to Vevey in his twenties, a merchant and small-scale inventor. He slowly gravitated towards foods and foodstuffs, experimenting with various recipes for baby-food to help mothers who were unable to breastfeed, and eventually came up with a concoction he called *farine lactée*, based, as he put it, on "wholesome Swiss milk [and a] cereal component baked by a special process of my invention". In 1867, he fed this to a premature baby boy whose mother was dangerously ill herself; the boy survived, and Nestlé's reputation skyrocketed. The following year he opened an office in London to cope with the quantity of orders, and within five years was exporting to South America and Australia. In 1874 he sold his company for a million francs. Nestlé bought out Anglo-Swiss Condensed Milk in 1905, and chocolatemakers Peter, Cailler and Kohler – pioneers in making milk chocolate – in 1929; although it had always concentrated on milk alone, it started to diversify. Benefiting from massive surpluses of coffee beans in the 1930s, Nestlé launched the world's first instant coffee – *Nescafé* – in 1938. More takeovers followed, of processed-food manufacturer Maggi in 1947, Crosse & Blackwell in 1950, and frozen-food giant Findus in 1963, broadening the range even further. By the mid-1960s, Nestlé was Switzerland's biggest company, a huge multinational incorporating over 200 factories around the world, with global management still based in Vevey.

Today, having swallowed up cosmetic company L'Oréal in 1974 and British confectioner Rowntree's in 1991, Nestlé employs almost a quarter of a million people, and buys up more than ten percent of the world's entire crop of coffee and cacao beans. However, its most controversial product is, strangely, its original one: baby formula. With a marketing policy in developing-world countries that has been deemed by many to be aggressively profit driven at the expense of consumer health, Nestlé has been riding a storm of anger in recent years from children's organizations and health watchdogs in both the developed and the developing world. Many of these groups continue to lobby for boycotts of Nestlé products unless the company takes a role in helping educate mothers in developing-world countries to breastfeed whenever possible, and to buy formula only as a last resort. The company maintains its ads don't dissuade mothers from breastfeeding, and are merely offering them a choice. The dispute shows few signs of resolution and, frankly, little chance of toppling such a mighty global industrial entity as Nestlé.

arcades and shuttered facades, are alive with people, shops and activity. Arrive on a Tuesday or Saturday and you'll find the marketplace packed with stalls – food, crafts, wine or all three. The huge pillared building dominating the square is the Grenette, or town granary, dating from 1808 and now housing the tourist office.

Vevey's excellent fine-art museum is the **Musée Jenisch**, 2 Rue de la Gare (Tues–Sun: March–Oct 11am–5.30pm, Nov–Feb 2–5.30pm; Fr.10; SMP), an impressive Neoclassical-style temple built in 1897 with a donation from a Hamburg émigré family named Jenisch – despite the tide of Swiss who apparently make the long journey from Graubünden expecting a museum devoted to the Jenisch gypsy people (see p.454), there's no connection. The museum, now about ten times too small for its massive collection, stages changing exhibitions of Swiss art on various themes, while its Cabinet cantonal des Estampes (Cantonal Museum of Prints) holds the largest collection of Rembrandt lithographs in Europe, as well as hundreds of graphic works by Dürer, Corot, Le Corbusier and others. Not least, the museum is also the repository of the Oskar Kokoschka Foundation, owning and displaying examples of work from this expressionist Austrian painter and graphic artist who spent the last 26 years of his life in Villeneuve.

Some 500m west of the centre you can't miss the giant green building on the waterfront, Nestlé's world HQ (see box). A little uphill on the Chemin de Meruz is the atmospheric village of **CORSIER**; on the right of the road you'll find a small cemetery, location of the graves of Oona and Charlie Chaplin, who moved to Corsier in the 1950s as an escape from McCarthyite America, and never left. Further up the hill is Corsier's tiny church (also accessible on bus #11), watched over by graceful angels and holding inside some frescoes dating from 1420–30 which were plastered over during the Reformation and rediscovered in the nineteenth century. Back on the main lakefront Route de Lavaux some 200m west of the Nestlé building you'll find **Villa Le Lac**, an elegant low white bungalow designed by modernist architect Le Corbusier for his parents in 1924 (guided tours March–Oct Wed 1.30–5pm; free), and which features an 11-metre long south-facing window onto the water (effective shielding from the road noise), a roof garden and much original Corbusier-designed furniture.

To the east, Vevey merges imperceptibly with its neighbour, the colourful port village of La Tour-de-Peilz. Along the way, you'll pass a photogenic statue of a bowler-hatted Chaplin twirling his cane amidst the roses on the Quai Perdonnet just east of Place du Marché, followed shortly after by the **Alimentarium** (Tues–Sun 10am–noon & 2–5pm; Fr.6; SMP), a rather dull Nestlé-sponsored exhibition on food and nutrition, designed for French-speaking kids. Another 200m brings you to the **Musée Historique**, 2 Rue du Château (Tues–Sun: March–Oct 10.30am–noon & 2–5.30pm; Nov–Feb 2–5.30pm; Fr.4; SMP), with a large section devoted to Vevey's mammoth Fête des Vignerons (Wine-Growers' Festival), a Bacchic celebration in music, costume and dance of the region's viticulture that's traditionally held about every 25 years – most recently in 1999. The appropriately named Quai d'Entre Deux Villes leads you on into **LA TOUR-DE-PEILZ**, 1km east of Vevey and dominated by its white château (the towers of which were apparently once roofed with animal pelts – hence the odd name). Inside is the **Musée Suisse du Jeu** (Swiss Museum of Games; Tues–Sun 2–6pm; Fr.6; SMP), an absorbing run-through of diversions and entertainments down the millennia, from 2500-year-old ancient Egyptian dice to the latest video games. Plenty of the more modern exhibits are hands-on – you're encouraged to play and tinker as much as you like, and there are cupboards full of board games should you feel the urge for a quick session of Kerplunk! or Connect-4.

Eating and drinking

There are plenty of pavement **cafés and restaurants** throughout the centre. Excitable *Café Vertigo*, 6 Rue du Torrent, is expansive and friendly, with quality nosh for under Fr.15; *Close-Up*, 8 Rue du Lac, is smaller, peaceful and jazzy; *La Clef*, 1 Rue du Théâtre is an atmospheric little corner bistro serving up steaming Vaudois specialities; while the cafés all around Place du Marché, including *Du Raisin* and *Le Cep d'Or* on the east side of the square, offer terraces for people-watching and simple *menus* for under Fr.20. The boss of the *Hôtel Des Négociants* rolls up his sleeves of an evening and cooks solid, unpretentious fare in the hotel brasserie that'll bust no budgets. If you're saving every franc – or are just looking for a fast and uncomplicated salad – check out the self-service *Manora* in the St Antoine mall opposite the station.

Listings

Car rental Avis, 16 Rue du Clos (☎021/921 88 60); Hertz, 8 Rue Collet (☎021/922 21 18).
Changing money In the train station (daily 6.15am–8.45pm).
Email and Internet *Darkside*, 8 Rue du Torrent (daily 2–8pm; Fr.10/hr).
Post Main office (CH-1800 Vevey 1) is beside the train station.

Above Vevey

There are three routes for excursions by train into the hills **above Vevey**, all leading in different directions, and all with unique attractions.

From the Vevey-Plan station opposite the Nestlé building (at the terminus of bus #1), a **funicular** rises every twenty minutes through the wine village of Chardonne (see p.140) to a terrace on the slope of **Mont-Pèlerin** at 800m, where you'll find two luxury hotels and plenty of places to appreciate the views over a little something to whet the whistle. A twenty-minute hike (or a four-times-daily bus) up to the summit brings you to the TV tower, with its high-speed **Plein-Ciel** glass lift whisking you up to the even better views at 1100m (April–Oct daily 9am–6pm, July & Aug until 8pm; lift Fr.5; funicular, bus & lift Fr.16).

The **Train des Vignes** (Wine Train) runs hourly from Vevey's train station on a short but steep line northwest through the Lavaux vineyards that's especially scenic during the summer and harvest times. The whole ride is only fifteen minutes, through Corseaux to Chexbres (see p.140) and terminating at the village of **Puidoux** on the Vaud plateau, itself served by trains between Lausanne and Fribourg.

Much more dramatic is the curving train line from Vevey station up to the vantage point of **Les Pléiades**, perched in the hills way above the lake at 1364m. The section beyond **Blonay** village – a junction for the line down to Montreux as well as the old steam railway to **Chamby** (see p.153) – is rack and pinion to cope with the gradient, but the ride still takes an hour to the top. The penultimate station, **LALLY**, is situated next to the cosy old-world *Hôtel Les Sapins* (☎021/943 1395, fax 943 71 19; ②), a peaceful little place set amongst hiking trails with great food and a few simple rooms. From here, it's a quarter-hour climb (or the last six minutes of the train ride) to the summit, face to face with the mighty Dent de Jaman peak, only 1875m but prominent and pyramidal enough to earn the nickname of the Vaudois Matterhorn. Views yawn out in all directions, as do hiking trails – a long, leg-stretching one leads east across the exposed hill tops above the lake to Les Avants (see p.153), served by the MOB train line between Montreux and Gstaad.

Montreux

If you want your soul to find peace, go to Montreux.

Freddie Mercury

MONTREUX is a snooty place, full of money and not particularly exciting. It's spectacularly located, bathed in afternoon sunshine streaming across the lake and protected from chill northerlies by a wall of giant mountains, but once you've had your fill of window-shopping and strolling beneath the palm trees, it's really rather dull.

From the early nineteenth century, Montreux was one of the centres for pan-European – and particularly British – tourism to Switzerland, following on from the importance of the impressive medieval **Château de Chillon** 3km away as a controlling presence on the road over the Alps: an edict dated 1689 from the Bernese lords of Chillon authorized the building of inns in the area to accommodate travellers making their way to and from the Grand-St-Bernard pass, and since then travel and tourism have been mainstays of the region's economy. Up until the 1960s, the name Montreux referred to just one village in a loose affiliation of some 24 vineyard-communes spread around the neighbouring hills, including picturesque **Clarens** to the west, and **Territet** to the east. Both of these are now super-plush suburbs, their long and venerable visitors' books taking in the great and the good, crowned heads of Europe, Russia and elsewhere, and literary and artistic personages famous and struggling.

The main reasons to visit Montreux are to absorb the spectacular panorama of the Dents-du-Midi peaks across the lake, and to visit Chillon – the latter perhaps Romandie's only genuinely unmissable sightseeing excursion. The stellar annual **Jazz Festival**, which broadcasts Montreux's name worldwide, offers top-drawer performers in all areas

---

---

of music. In a gleeful case of truth being stranger than fiction, a century ago Montreux's hoteliers were casting about for a logo they could attach to the advertisements they placed in the English press each season. On a walk in the nearby hills they came across the perfect answer, growing in lush abundance all around; and so since 1897 the symbolic flower of Montreux has been, with ever-increasing aptness, a **narcissus**.

Arrival, orientation and information

Montreux occupies a bulge of land jutting out into the lake, with the landmark **Casino** on the tip of the bulge. The large **train station** is set on a terrace above and slightly west of the town centre; stairs and escalators within the station raise you up to the **Old Town** on the slopes above, while **Avenue des Alpes**, the street outside the station's ticket office, has stairs and a lift which shuttle you down a level to the main central boulevard, **Grand-Rue**. A patch of park sandwiched between Grand-Rue and the lakefront promenade has at its western end the **ferry** *débarcadère*, and at its eastern end the town's huge covered market, **Place du Marché**. East of here, Grand-Rue becomes the **Avenue du Casino** which heads out of town as Avenue de Chillon on its way along the lakefront to the château. **Bus #1** from Vevey runs along Grand-Rue, stopping below the train station, at the *débarcadère*, the covered market and the Casino, before heading on to Chillon.

The **tourist office** is next to the *débarcadère* in a lakefront hut (April–Sept Mon–Sat 9am–6pm, Sun 9am–noon; Oct–March Mon–Fri 9am–6pm, Sat 9am–noon; ☎021/962 84 84, *www.montreux.ch*). There's a two-hour **walking tour** of the town, which leaves from beside the *débarcadère* (April–Oct Wed–Sat 10am & 3pm; Fr.10); check in advance about the availability of an English-speaking guide, and beware too that the walk will take you up the mountainous slopes into the Old Town and down again. See p.143 for details of the local museum passport and Tourist Info Pass magazine.

Accommodation

As you might expect, when it comes to **accommodation** Montreux favours its high-rollers more than its backpackers. Adding insult to injury, prices rise across the board in summer. If you're arriving in late April (during the Golden Rose TV festival) or in early July (the Jazz Festival) you're likely to find the town booked solid.

Dorm space costs from Fr.29 at the sole **hostel**, an HI place 1.5km east of Montreux on Passage de l'Auberge in Territet (☎021/963 49 34, fax 963 27 29; ①) – beside Territet train station (slow trains only), or near the L'Eaudine stop on bus #1. There are a couple of **pensions** within Montreux, the best of which is the welcoming *Pension Wilhelm*, 13 Rue du Marché (☎021/963 14 31, fax 963 32 85; ①); otherwise you're looking at inflated prices for distinctly ordinary rooms. The least expensive **hotels** are *La*

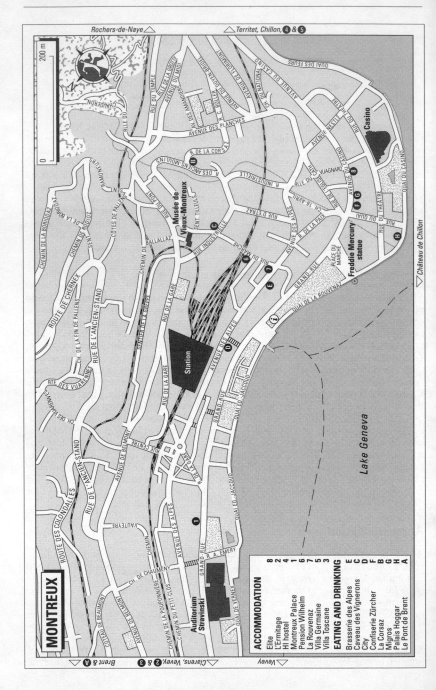

MONTREUX

Lake Geneva

Station

Casino

Auditorium
Stravinski

Musée de
Vieux-Montreux

Freddie Mercury
statue

200 m

Rochers-de-Naye △

△ Territet, Chillon, ❹ & ❺

Château de Chillon ▷

▽ Vevey

▽ Clarens, Vevey, ❷ & ❸

△ Brent & Ⓐ

ACCOMMODATION

Elite	8
L'Ermitage	2
HI hostel	4
Montreux Palace	1
Pension Wilhelm	6
La Rouvenaz	7
Villa Germaine	5
Villa Toscane	3

EATING AND DRINKING

Brasserie des Alpes	E
Caveau des Vignerons	C
City	D
Confiserie Zürcher	F
La Corsaz	B
Migros	G
Palais Hoggar	H
Le Pont de Brent	A

Rouvenaz, 1 Rue du Marché (☎021/963 27 36, fax 963 43 94; ②), six comfy enough rooms in a central but quiet family-run place with Italian restaurant, and *Elite*, 25 Avenue du Casino (☎021/966 03 03, fax 966 03 10, *hotel.elite@vtx.ch*; ②), small and generic but slap in the heart of town. Fin-de-siècle *Villa Germaine*, 3 Avenue Collonge in Territet (☎021/963 1528; ②) is considerably more characterful and well out of the hubbub. There are any number of pricier, sterile business-class options and run-of-the-mill holiday hotels; shunting round the lake to Vevey (see p.141) or up to Glion or Caux in the hills (see p.152), will turn up better value.

It's when you break through the Fr.300-a-night barrier that things get interesting again. *L'Ermitage*, 75 Rue du Lac in Clarens (☎021/964 44 11, fax 964 70 02; ⑥) a water-side villa set in its own grounds, has only seven rooms, all fresh and attractive, accompanied by spectacular gastronomic delights from the resident chef. *Villa Toscane*, 2 Rue du Lac (☎021/963 84 21, fax 963 84 26, *villatoscane@bluewin.ch*; ⑥; closed Jan) is a fabulous white, Art Nouveau creation on the Montreux waterfront, with balconies, meticulous service *et al*; it's a "garni" place (without restaurant), so prices are lower than they might otherwise be. For the full works, the only place to go is the legendary *Montreux Palace*, 100 Grand-Rue (☎021/962 12 12, fax 962 17 17, *www.montreux-palace.com*; ⑨), a gigantic Belle Epoque folly opened in 1906 that was home to Vladimir Nabokov for thirteen years and that still effortlessly draws in the platinum-card classes.

The Town

Aside from rubbing shoulders with the hoi polloi of international tourism amidst the thronging honky-tonk of Grand-Rue and Avenue de Casino – everyone looking at everyone else wondering where all the rich people are – there's actually precious little to do in Montreux, although it's worth taking time for the gorgeous lakeside stroll along the **flowered promenades**. Backing onto the Place du Marché, with impressive views across the water to the Dents-du-Midi, stands Montreux's newest and most popular photo-op – a flamboyant statue in bronze of long-time local resident **Freddie Mercury** which was unveiled in 1996, five years after his death. His group Queen first recorded an album in Montreux in 1978 and returned many times afterwards, Freddie eventually buying an apartment on the Territet waterfront (now private property), where he spent his last few months.

Associations with rock music continue when you reach the **Casino**, on Rue du Théâtre: this somewhat grating modern building replaced the grand original, which opened in 1883 and was burned to the ground on December 4, 1971, during a concert by Frank Zappa and the Mothers of Invention. During the show, someone in the audience thoughtfully let off a rocket-flare, which immediately set the ceiling on fire; everyone got out without injury, but the building continued to burn all night. Ian Gillan, lead singer of the band **Deep Purple**, who were holed up in a hotel nearby, watched the flames leaping into the sky and was thus inspired to write his seminal rock classic "Smoke On The Water".

The zigzagging streets and hillside terraces of the steep Old Town above the train station provide marginally more interest. A group of eighteenth-century buildings houses the modest **Musée de Vieux-Montreux**, 40 Rue de la Gare (April–Oct daily 10am–noon & 2–5pm; Fr.6; SMP), illustrating the town's history, with a particular focus on the impact of tourism.

Eating and drinking

There are plenty of inexpensive places to **eat and drink** around the station on Avenue des Alpes offering meals for Fr.12–14, including some with lake-view terraces:

Brasserie des Alpes, at no. 23, has pasta staples, while *Restaurant City*, at no. 37, and *Migros*, 49 Avenue du Casino, are both self-service. In the Old Town, check out the fondue and Swiss dishes at *Caveau des Vignerons*, 30 Rue Industrielle; or take a chance with the home-style fare – tripe, sauerkraut and all – at the local diner variously entitled *La Corsaz, La Petite Brasserie Alsacienne* or *Le Flamm's* on Rue de la Corsaz. *Confiserie Zürcher*, 45 Avenue du Casino (☎021/963 59 63), is Montreux's most venerable old tearoom (since 1894), perfectly situated with plate-glass windows for crowd-watching, a patisserie for exquisite cakey creations and a restaurant section with mid-priced *menus*. The most appealing place to eat is the oriental-fantasy *Palais Hoggar*, 14 Quai du Casino (☎021/963 12 71); Arabic meals start from Fr.25, with plenty for veggies, or you could just savour the lakeside views over a Moroccan mint tea. If you've got a spare Fr.150, and you've already tried out Lausanne's *Rochat* (see p.126), take a taxi to *Le Pont de Brent*, in the nearby suburb of Brent (☎021/964 52 30), another gourmet temple with three Michelin stars (closed Sun & Mon, late July, Christmas and New Year).

Listings

Car rental Europcar, *Montreax Palace Hotel* (☎021/963 72 41); Hertz, 233 Route de St Maurice, La Tour-de-Peilz (☎021/977 05 06).

Changing money In the train station (daily: May–Oct 5.50am–8.45pm, Nov–April 5.50am–8pm).

Email and Internet The luxury *Montreax Palace Hotel*, 100 Grand-Rue, has a café with stratospheric prices (Sun & Tues–Thurs noon–8pm, Fri & Sat noon–11pm; Fr.20/hr).

Laundry 30 Rue Industrielle (Mon–Fri 9am–6pm, Sat 10am–5pm).

Post Main post office (CH-1820 Montreux 1) is beside the train station, plus a smaller office next to *Confiserie Zürcher* on Avenue du Casino.

Château de Chillon

Lake Leman lies by Chillon's walls:
A thousand feet in depth below
Its massy waters meet and flow...
There are seven pillars of Gothic mould,
In Chillon's dungeons deep and old,
There are seven columns massy and grey,
Dim with a dull imprison'd ray,
A sunbeam which hath lost its way...

Lord Byron, *The Prisoner of Chillon*

The climax of a journey around Lake Geneva, and one of the highlights of a visit to Switzerland, is the stunning thirteenth-century **CHÂTEAU DE CHILLON** (daily: April–Sept 9am–7pm; March & Oct 9.30am–6pm; Jan, Feb, Nov & Dec 10am–5pm; last entry 1hr before closing; Fr.7; SMP; *www.chillon.ch*). This impressive specimen, among the best-preserved medieval castles in Europe, is in Veytaux, only about 3km south of Montreux; whether you opt for the 45-minute shoreline walk, bus #1 from Vevey or Montreux, a bike, or best of all a boat (which run year-round), your first glimpse of the castle is unforgettable – an elegant, turreted pile jutting out into the water, framed by trees and the craggy mountains. You could easily spend a half-day soaking up the atmosphere.

Some history
Although the scenery all around the castle is impressive enough, the **location** of the building is more impressive still – and is the key to its history. The mountains in

front of the castle fall directly into the lake, with only the narrowest of through-routes between the sheer rock wall and the water. Directly opposite the defile, a razor-edge, sheer-sided islet rises from the water, of which only the very top is visible. This is where Chillon sits: if you were to drain the lake, the castle would teeter above an incredible drop of over 300m, as high as the Eiffel Tower. Such depths are cold and the lake's weather is capricious, making attack from open water extremely unlikely. Equally, the road is narrow, the heights are virtually unscaleable, and there's no other way to pass, making it impossible to avoid the castle. Whoever controlled the castle could control the traffic, and exact tolls from a position of unassailable security.

In **Bronze Age** times, there was no path around the lake – travellers had to climb the steep, 200m slopes at Chillon to a village on the heights above, then drop back down to rejoin the path. The **Romans** cut a narrow ledge along the lakeshore, and also opened up the Grand-St-Bernard pass over the Alps further south, turning the road past the unfortified islet just offshore into the only route connecting northern and southern Europe through the mountains. By the **Middle Ages**, the quantity of traffic meant the road had to be widened and also that a form of toll could be set up. The village above was abandoned in favour of a new town (*ville neuve*, today's Villeneuve) built on open, accessible land a little way south on the valley floor. First surviving mention of a "guardian of the stronghold of Chillun" dates from 1150.

The Counts of **Savoy**, particularly Pierre (1203–68), made Chillon a princely residence, also developing Villeneuve into a major trading centre which poured tolls and customs duties into Chillon's coffers – in 1283, on average, one horse rider and perhaps a dozen foot travellers were crossing the Grand-St-Bernard pass every hour of daylight, on every day of the year. Pierre's architects and engineers transformed Chillon, rebuilding the half facing the shore as a fortress with three strong towers and a keep, and filling the half facing the water with grand halls and royal apartments.

As the Savoyards extended their influence north to the Aare and began to threaten the Habsburgs, Chillon became their military and naval headquarters. The castle was both the centre of court life and a much-feared prison: when **plague** broke out in Villeneuve in 1348, the town's Jews were accused of plotting with Christian accomplices to poison the water supply, and large numbers of both were tortured in Chillon's dungeons before being burned alive. By this time, the Gotthard Pass further east was in use, and the transfer of traffic away from Chillon and the Grand-St-Bernard led to the castle's terminal decline as a military fortress, although it remained handy as a secure jail. In 1530, the Savoyards imprisoned a Genevois scholar, **François Bonivard**, at Chillon for inciting the Genevois people to form an alliance with the Swiss against Savoy. They left him shackled to a pillar in the dungeons for six years, until his release in 1536, when the **Bernese** army swept down from the north, briefly bombarded the castle from above with their newfangled mobile artillery, and took control. The chief legacy of the Bernese bailiffs' 200-year residency at Chillon was an abundance of painted bears (the symbol of Bern).

Fortunately for posterity, Chillon became a quiet backwater. In 1816, after Vaud had won independence from Bern, **Byron** (aged 28) and **Shelley** (24) visited the castle on their tour of the lake. A guide took them into the dungeons where Bonivard had been shackled and wove enough of a tale around him, and around the castle's history, to catch the poets' imagination. While bad weather grounded them in a hotel in Ouchy, Byron scribbled out his *Prisoner of Chillon*, a long narrative poem supposedly spoken by Bonivard (but entirely fictitious throughout), which celebrates the cause of individual liberty, and which brought Chillon to the attention of the wealthy tourists who were starting to explore the Alps. Archeologists and historians launched renovations of the crumbling infrastructure in the late nineteenth century, which restored a great deal of the castle's original grandeur. Work to maintain the castle continues today.

The château

As throughout history, the **road** passes outside the castle walls – these days, it's the Montreux–Villeneuve highway, served by bus #1 (the *autoroute* clings to the hillside high above). The eighteenth-century **gatehouse** is supported on stilts, replacing the original drawbridge. At the ticket window you'll get a follow-the-numbers pamphlet, which plunges you straight down into the vaulted and atmospheric **dungeons** (rooms 4–7) where the Dukes of Savoy imprisoned François Bonivard – he was manacled to the fifth pillar along, which still bears a ring and a length of chain. Bonivard wrote that the dungeon was excavated to below the water-line, and Byron also wrote about the damp, but the room is in fact above the water and is quite an airy place. The Irish novelist Maria Edgeworth, visiting in 1820, perhaps missed the point when she brightly chipped in: "If I were to take lodgings in a dungeon I should prefer this to any I have ever seen because it is high and dry with beautiful groined arches and no bad smells." She also noted that Byron's name was cut into the third pillar of the dungeon, as it still is, and that the guide remembered his visit four years previously. A grille in the external wall gives onto the lake, facilitating a rapid exit by rowing boat should things have ever got nasty up above.

The real wonder of the castle, however, lies in the rooms upstairs, gloriously grand knights' halls, secret twisting passages between lavish bedchambers, gothic windows with dreamy views, a frescoed chapel, and more. The **Grand Kitchen** (room 8) still has its original wooden ceiling and two massive oak pillars, installed around 1260. The **Bernese Bedchamber** (room 10) has original bird and ribbon decorations dating from the 1580s, while the expansive **Hall of Arms** (room 12), complete with fireplace and windows over the lake, is covered with escutcheons of the Bernese bailiffs. The **Lord's Chamber** adjacent (room 13), incredibly enough, retains its original thirteenth- and fourteenth-century wall paintings, rustic scenes of animals in an orchard with St George slaying the dragon on the chimneypiece. The **chapel** (room 18) features an impression of the full glory of the fourteenth-century decoration, with slides projected onto the partly decorated walls. Next door, the breathtaking **Great Hall of the Count** (room 19) has slender black marble pillars, shimmering chequered wall decoration, a coffered ceiling dating from the fifteenth century, and four windows over the lake topped by a beautiful four-leafed clover design.

Above Montreux

Montreux's train station is served by three different gauges of track. As well as the main-line CFF trains running west along the lake and south into the Valais, there are two different narrow-gauge lines operated by **MOB (Montreux–Oberland-Bernois)** running up into the hills above Montreux that offer spectacular viewpoints, excellent hill walking, and panoramic rides through the countryside towards the high Alps of the Bernese Oberland.

The smaller line has creaking trains winding their laborious way northeast up to the giant Rochers-de-Naye summit (Eurail not valid, InterRail gets half-price, and the Swiss Pass is free to Caux, with a 25 percent discount from there to Rochers). Emerging from a series of corkscrew tunnels you come to **GLION**, an eyrie of a village perched amidst fields of narcissi directly above Montreux, with jaw-dropping views over the lake and the Rhône. There are a couple of luxury old-world hotels up here, but the more affordable *Des Alpes Vaudoises*, on Rue du Bugnon and with its own train station (☎021/963 20 76, fax 963 56 94, *hotelalp@montreux.ch*; ②–③; closed Jan) is just as characterful and tranquil a place to unwind. A steep funicular also serves Glion from Territet on the lakeside below. Further up on the train line is **CAUX**, home to the Conference Centre for Moral Re-Armament, the dramatically sited and turreted headquarters of a rather odd collective which seeks to ease global political and economic strife through personal religious reconciliation. Spiritual rebirth notwithstanding, you might prefer a quiet stroll and a night or two at the *Hôtel les Rosiers*, on Chemin de l'Impératrice (✆ & fax 021/963 61 73; ②), a tranquil, respectable little family hotel behind the village. After another half-hour, trains reach the vantage point of **ROCHERS-DE-NAYE** (2045m), with suitably incredible views, plenty of hiking trails over the grassy hilltops and the basic *Plein-Roc* restaurant.

The more important MOB narrow-gauge line above Montreux climbs northwest through the hills into Canton Bern (Eurail, InterRail and Swiss Pass all qualify for free travel). This is the route of the Crystal Panoramic Express, one of the showcase journeys of Swiss railways (see p.38) – you must pay a small supplement on the special panoramic trains, but not on the ordinary ones. A little above Montreux on this route is **CHAMBY**, one end of the Chemin de Fer-Musée (Museum Railway; May–Oct Sat & Sun 9am–6pm; Fr.12; SMP), which has steam trains running on a 3km stretch of track to and from **Blonay**, on the Vevey–Les Pléiades line (see p.146) as well as a depot full of old rolling stock. The MOB trains from Montreux continue through the village of **LES AVANTS** – starting point of a number of beautiful walks – to **Montbovon**, access point for trains north into the gorgeous countryside around **Gruyères** (see p.129). The MOB narrow-gauge line continues east to **Château d'Oex** and **Gstaad** (see p.281), but runs out at **Zweisimmen**, where you must change for connections to Interlaken and Bern.

travel details

TRAINS

Bulle to: Gruyères (hourly; 10min); Montbovon (for Montreux or Gstaad; hourly; 30min); Palézieux (for Lausanne; hourly; 40min).

Coppet to: Céligny (hourly; 5min); Geneva (hourly; 20min); Nyon (hourly; 10min).

Gruyères to: Bulle (for Fribourg; hourly; 10min); Montbovon (for Montreux or Gstaad; hourly; 20min); Palézieux (for Lausanne; hourly; 50min).

Lausanne to: Aigle (every 30min; 30min); Basel (twice hourly; 2hr 35min); Bern (hourly; 1hr 10min); Biel/Bienne (hourly; 1hr 10min); Brig (twice hourly; 1hr 40min); La Chaux-de-Fonds (hourly; 1hr 30min); Delémont (hourly; 1hr 50min); Echallens (every 30min; 20min); Fribourg (twice hourly; 45min); Geneva (4 times hourly; 35min); Interlaken Ost (hourly; 2hr 10min); Martigny (every 30min; 50min); Montreux (twice hourly; 20min); Neuchâtel (hourly; 50min); Nyon (every 30min; 25min); Palézieux (for Gruyères; hourly; 15min); St Gallen (hourly; 3hr 45min); Sierre/Siders (twice hourly; 1hr 15min); Sion (twice hourly; 1hr 5min); Vallorbe (hourly; 45min); Vevey (twice hourly; 15min); Winterthur (hourly; 3hr); Yverdon (hourly; 25min); Zürich (hourly; 2hr 25min).

Montreux to: Caux (hourly; 25min); Château d'Oex (hourly; 1hr); Geneva (every 30min; 1hr 10min); Gstaad (hourly; 1hr 20min); Lausanne (4 hourly; 20min); Martigny (every 30min; 30min); Montbovon (for Gruyères; hourly; 45min); Vevey (4 hourly; 7min); Zürich (hourly; 2hr 45min).

Morges to: Lausanne (every 30min; 10min); Nyon (3 hourly; 15min).

Nyon to: Céligny (hourly; 7min); Coppet (hourly; 10min); Geneva (3 hourly; 25min); Lausanne (every 30min; 25min); Morges (3 hourly; 15min); Neuchâtel (hourly; 1hr); St Cergue (every 30min; 35min); Yverdon (hourly; 25min).

Palézieux to: Bulle (hourly; 40min); Gruyères (hourly; 50min); Lausanne (hourly; 15min).

Vevey to: Geneva (every 30min; 1hr 5min); Lausanne (4 hourly; 10min); Martigny (every 30min; 25min); Montreux (4 hourly; 7min); Zürich (hourly; 2hr 40min).

BUSES

Bulle to: Fribourg (hourly; 30min); Gruyères (3 daily; 20min).

Chillon (Château) to: Montreux (every 10min; 10min); Vevey (every 10min; 20min).

Gruyères to: Bulle (3 daily; 20min); Moléson (every 2hr; 15min).

Montreux to: Chillon (every 10min; 10min); Vevey (every 10min; 20min).

Nyon to: Coppet (every 2hr; 40min).

Vevey to: Chillon (every 10min; 30min); Montreux (every 10min; 20min).

BOATS

(following is a summary of May–Sept summer services; fewer boats run in other months, generally Sat & Sun only if at all)

Céligny to: Geneva (1 daily; 1hr); Lausanne (1 daily; 2hr 30min).

Chillon (Château) to: Lausanne (3 daily; 1hr 45min); Montreux (4–5 daily; 20min); Vevey (3 daily; 35min).

Coppet to: Geneva (2–3 daily; 45min); Lausanne (2–3 daily; 2hr 45min).

Lausanne (Ouchy) to: Céligny (1 daily; 2hr 30min); Chillon (3 daily; 1hr 45min); Coppet (2–3 daily; 2hr 45min); Evian, France (10–15 daily; 40min); Geneva (3 daily; 3hr 30min); Montreux (5–6 daily; 1hr 20min); Morges (2–3 daily; 30min); Nyon (3–4 daily; 2hr 10min); Rolle (2–3 daily; 1hr 10min); Vevey (5–6 daily; 1hr).

Montreux to: Chillon (4–5 daily; 20min); Geneva (3 daily; 5hr); Lausanne (5–6 daily; 1hr 20min); St Gingolph (3–4 daily; 50min); Vevey (5–6 daily; 20min).

Morges to: Geneva (2–3 daily; 3hr); Lausanne (2–3 daily; 30min).

Nyon to: Geneva (4–7 daily; 1hr–1hr 30min); Lausanne (3–4 daily; 2hr 10min); Rolle (2–3 daily; 50min); Yvoire, France (6 daily; 20min).

Vevey to: Chillon (3 daily; 35min); Geneva (3 daily; 4hr 30min); Lausanne (5–6 daily; 1hr); Montreux (5–6 daily; 20min).

INTERNATIONAL TRAINS

Lausanne to: Barcelona (1 daily; 10hr 30min); Dijon (5 daily; 2hr 10min); Milan (5 daily; 3hr 10min); Paris (5 daily; 3hr 50min); Rome (1 daily; 11hr 30min); Venice (1 daily; 6hr 30min).

PLACE NAMES IN THIS CHAPTER		
German	**French**	**Italian**
Aare	Aar	Aar
Freiburg	Fribourg	Friborgo
Genf	Genève	Ginevra
Genfersee	Lac Léman	Lago Lemano
Greyerz	Gruyères	Gruyères
Kanton Waadt	Canton Vaud	Cantone Vaud
Lausanne	Lausanne	Losanna
Rotten	Rhône	Rodano
Saane	Sarine	Sarine

CHAPTER THREE

THE ARC JURASSIEN

The northwest frontier dividing Switzerland from France is the **Jura** mountain range – line after line of long, northeast-southwest ridges that trap between them a succession of sausage-shaped lakes. The Jura are nothing like the Alps: much lower to start with (rarely more than 1500m), with none of the majesty but all of the ruggedness. Scrubby rounded hilltops and deep, parallel valleys are dotted by windswept, privately minded villages nursing a weatherbeaten Gallic culture cut off for centuries from both France and Switzerland. The whole **Arc Jurassien**, which takes in the highlands of the Jura Vaudois, the region's three largest lakes – the Lac de Neuchâtel, Murtensee and Bielersee/Lac de Bienne, which lie clustered together at the foot of the Jura range – Canton Neuchâtel, and Canton Jura in the far northwest, is well off the beaten track of most visitors to Switzerland. Guidebooks and brochures tend to skimp on detail, since it doesn't easily fit into the usual Swiss pigeonholes. If you choose to venture out here, you'll find a minimum of tourist hype and few actual sights other than the main towns of **Neuchâtel** and **Biel/Bienne**, but what exists in abundance is virtually untouched nature – and this is why the Swiss know and love the place.

Once you leave the lakes and the lowlands, **public transport** isn't easy, and even main roads are a relatively recent innovation. If you don't have a car, the best way to get around is by bike, or even, if your legs can take it, on foot. Tourist offices in the area know their clientele and can direct you onto any number of cycling trails or footpaths that reach all scenic spots. On p.406, we've outlined a long, multi-day walk through the area, which starts near Zürich, winds through the whole Jura region and ends up at Lake Geneva.

The huge majority of the area covered by this chapter is **francophone**, and yet it straddles the linguistic divide, the *Röstigraben*, between French- and **German-speaking** Switzerland (see p.544). As many places or regions have two names, travelling to and fro across the language border can sometimes get confusing. For example, the German word **Seeland** ("Country of Lakes") has been adopted by francophones, although the area is also known as "La Région des Trois-Lacs" after the three largest lakes, Neuchâtel, Murten (Morat) and Biel/Bienne. **Neuchâtel**, the main town of the region, is entirely French speaking, but is known to German speakers as **Neuenburg**; the lake it sits on is either the Lac de Neuchâtel or the Neuenburgersee. Since local bus

---

ACCOMMODATION PRICE CODES

All the hostels, pensions and hotels in this book have been graded according to the following price codes, which indicate the price for the cheapest double room available during the high season. Single rooms can cost anything between sixty and eighty percent of the double-room rate. For hostels with dormitories, the price per bed has been quoted. See p.45 for more details.

① under Fr.100	④ Fr.200–250	⑦ Fr.350–400
② Fr.100–150	⑤ Fr.250–300	⑧ Fr.400–500
③ Fr.150–200	⑥ Fr.300–350	⑨ over Fr.500

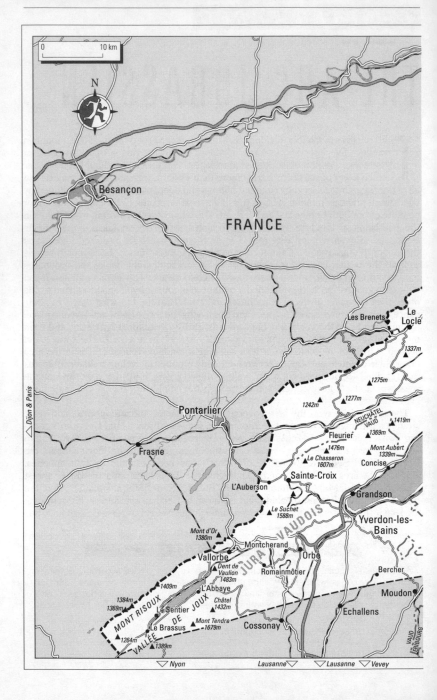

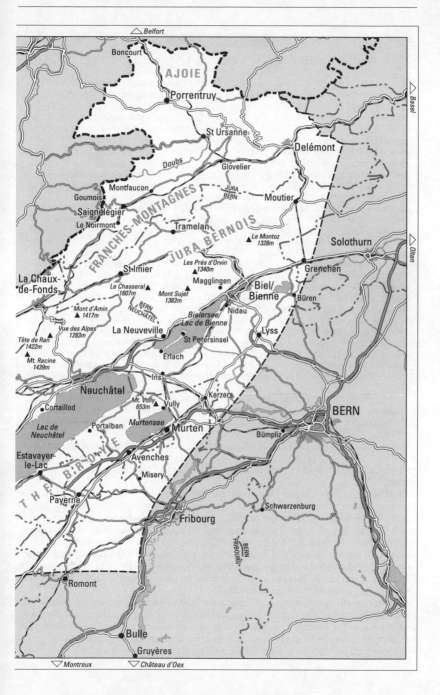

EXPO 02

For six months in 2002, the area of Seeland will be the location of the Swiss national **EXPO 02**, the first such event in the country for over 35 years. Rather than being a display of technical achievements in various fields, the Expo is planned to be a themed exhibition showcasing the culture and outlook of Switzerland at the turn of the millennium, investigating "the potential of a nation" (to quote the official blurb).

It will be focused on five temporary sites, or **"arteplages"**, which will each have a particular theme. **Neuchâtel**'s arteplage will have exhibitions and events on the theme of nature and artificiality; **Murten**'s on the moment and eternity; **Yverdon**'s on "the universe and I"; and **Biel/Bienne**'s on power and freedom. The arteplages, built of ecologically sound, recyclable materials, will be moored just offshore in each town, and exhibitions, displays and happenings will take place both on the arteplage itself and in waterfront parks. The fifth, **Jura** arteplage, with the theme of limits, will be mobile, trundling around the three lakes throughout the Expo summer. Organizers suggest that it'll take you three days to tour the five arteplages. Ecologically sound modular hotels and restaurants either within the arteplages or nearby are planned to boost existing tourist infrastructure, along with extra trains and package deals to the area.

That's the theory anyway. In practice, the whole project has been dogged by controversy from day one, with boardroom conflicts regularly finding their way into the newspapers, unpopular appointments and bitter resignations of organizing staff, along with a general puzzlement among the Swiss public as to exactly what the Expo is for, and what on earth is supposed to be happening in it. On October 4, 1999, the Federal Council officially pushed back the Expo from 2001 to 2002 amidst ongoing rows about funding. At the time of writing, although planning has been under way for two years or more, very little has been finalized and corporate sponsors – who provide four-fifths of the budget – are starting to get cold feet. It's impossible to say at the moment what you'll be faced with on the day, or whether the whole thing will be worth your hard-earned francs or not. In January 2000, the Expo organizers confirmed some Fr.300m of private pledges to boost the Fr.1.3bn of federal funds, and called for new artistic tenders for the relaunched Expo 02. The fiasco looks set to stumble on, with the public kept up to date via the Expo Web site.

Entry prices for the original Expo 01 were fixed at around Fr.120 for three days, or Fr.48 for one day, but with the postponement, prices could easily change again. For bookings and current **information**, contact Expo 01, 4 Place de la Gare, CH-2001 Neuchâtel (☎032/726 20 01, fax 726 20 05, *www.expo-01.ch*).

and boat timetables tend to stick to either French or German, it's useful to know both names.

Southeast of Neuchâtel is the small majority-German-speaking lakeside resort of **Murten**, known to French speakers as **Morat**. Its lake is the Murtensee or the Lac de Morat. On its southern shore the language border weaves between communities, and you'll find, for instance, the German-speaking village of Münchenwiler (Canton Bern) a kilometre or so from the francophone village of Cressier (Canton Fribourg). Tiny enclaves of Bern, Fribourg and Vaud jostle for position in this impossibly fragmented region. The lake to the north, almost surrounded by Canton Bern, is either called the Bielersee or the Lac de Bienne, with the town at its head known as **Biel/Bienne** – the only officially bilingual town in Switzerland.

Further north are German-speaking Canton **Solothurn** (known as **Soleure** in French), and francophile Canton **Jura**, established in 1979 on a wave of anti-Bern separatist feeling. For Canton Jura, taking pride in French language and culture is a political, almost nationalistic, matter, and little quarter is given to German-ness of any kind – even though strongly Germanic Basel lies next door.

Ferries around the region

The Lac de Neuchâtel, the Murtensee (Lac de Morat), and the Bielersee/Lac de Bienne are all connected by canals, and one of the scenic highlights of the area is taking a long **ferry cruise** (3–4hr one-way) between Biel/Bienne, Neuchatel and Murten (Morat). Point-to-point routings link the major towns of Neuchâtel, Estavayer, Yverdon, Murten (Morat) and Biel/Bienne, along with a host of smaller lakeside villages. It's also possible to take a peaceful river-cruise (2hr 40min) up the River Aare from Biel/Bienne to Solothurn (Soleure). As ever, there's only a handful of boats running outside the summer season (June–Sept), and then only on local routings – none of the long cruises operates in winter.

Two companies provide service: the Société de Navigation sur les Lacs de Neuchâtel et Morat (**LNM**; ☎032/725 40 12), and the Bielersee Schiffahrtsgesellschaft (**BSG**; ☎032/322 33 22, *www.bielersee.ch*). There's some overlap between them, but not much. Both advertise each other's routings and connections, and you can pick up timetables for both at all tourist offices. The BSG gives free travel to Eurail and Swiss Pass holders, and fifty percent off to InterRailers. The LNM gives free travel to Swiss Pass holders, but Eurailers and InterRailers pay full price.

Neuchâtel

Beam yourself down into **NEUCHÂTEL**, and for a while you might think you've landed up in France. The Neuchâtelois people are the most French-oriented in Switzerland, speaking a dialect of Swiss-French that is celebrated – by those for whom such a thing is significant – as the "purest" in Romandie (that's to say, the closest to the "true" French spoken over the border). The town's air of dignity and easy grace is fuelled by a profusion of French-influenced architecture: many of the seventeenth- and eighteenth-century buildings are made from local yellow sandstone, a fact which led Alexandre Dumas to describe Neuchâtel as looking "like a toytown carved out of butter". And the modern and disarmingly Gallic street life of pavement cafés and studenty night bars, upscale street markets and hip designer boutiques, has the slightly unreal flavour of a town actively seeking influences from beyond its own borders – a rare thing indeed in Switzerland.

The Neuchâtelois, for whom the issue of joining the EU is a matter of the plainest common sense, are perhaps the epitome of the Swiss mystery; they are about as far removed in attitude, values, style and language from the people of Luzern – with whom their future is inextricably linked – to the east, as they are closely related to the people of Dijon – the supposed foreigners – to the west. You get the feeling while in Neuchâtel that the locals have thrown up their hands in disbelief at such injustice, and – ensconced between their broad lake and the mountain border – have sought solace in a life of fine wines, rich foods and French TV while waiting for their compatriots to see sense.

The town's main attractions are its café-lounging Gallic atmosphere and its location, with **boats** weaving to and fro across the lake and the first ridges of the high **Jura** range standing poised over the town. However, the **Musée d'Art** is worth going out of your way to experience, both for its innovative fine-art collection, and for its set of charming eighteenth-century **mechanical figurines** which demonstrate in understated style the quite exceptional skills of the Neuchâtel watchmakers of the era.

Throughout the summer of 2002, Neuchâtel will be one of the principal focuses for **Expo 02**, the Swiss national exposition (see box opposite). All kinds of happenings may (or may not) take place, not least of which will be the mooring of a giant "arteplage" exhibition space on the lake just offshore and, rather more prosaically, extreme difficulty in booking a hotel room in or near the town throughout that summer.

Some history

In 1011, Rudolf III of Burgundy presented a new castle (*neu-châtel*) on the lakeshore to his wife Irmengarde. The first **counts** of Neuchâtel were named shortly afterwards, and in 1214 their domain was officially dubbed a city. For three centuries, the **Earldom of Neuchâtel** flourished, and in 1530, the people of Neuchâtel accepted the **Reformation**, and their city and territory were proclaimed to be indivisible from then on. Future rulers were required to seek investiture from the citizens.

With increasing power and prestige, Neuchâtel was raised to the level of a **principality** at the beginning of the seventeenth century. On the death in 1707 of Mary of Orléans, Duchess of Nemours and Princess of Neuchâtel, the people had to choose her successor from among fifteen claimants. They wanted their new prince first and foremost to be a Protestant, and also to be strong enough to protect their territory but based far enough away to leave them to their own devices. Louis XIV actively promoted the many French pretenders to the title, but the Neuchâtelois people passed them over in favour of Frederick I, King of Prussia, who claimed his entitlement in a rather complicated fashion through the Houses of Orange and Nassau. With the requisite stability assured, Neuchâtel entered its golden age, with commerce and industry (including watchmaking and lace) and banking undergoing steady expansion.

At the turn of the nineteenth century, the King of Prussia was defeated by Napoleon and was forced to give up Neuchâtel in order to keep Hanover. Napoleon's marshal, Berthier, became Prince of Neuchâtel, building roads and restoring infrastructure, but never actually setting foot in his domain. After the fall of Napoleon, Frederick III of Prussia reasserted his rights by proposing that Neuchâtel be linked with the other **Swiss** cantons (the better to exert influence over the lot of them). On September 12, 1814, Neuchâtel became the 21st canton, but also remained a Prussian principality. It took a bloodless revolution in the decades following for Neuchâtel to shake off its princely past and declare itself, in 1848, a **republic** within the Swiss Confederation. To this day, the Republic and Canton of Neuchâtel is the only one of the 26 to proudly fly a tricolour – green, white and red, with a minute Swiss cross hanging in the top corner.

Arrival, orientation and information

Neuchâtel's **train station** is perched above the town; it's a walk of about ten minutes, or a short hop on bus #6, down to the compact lakefront town centre focused around **Place Pury**, at the foot of the Old Town on a slender stretch of flat ground. A **funicular** from the station down to Avenue du Premier-Mars is planned for opening in 2001. Pury is 100m west of **Place du Port**, which backs onto the harbour and the *débarcadère*: **boats** arrive at Neuchâtel from all points around the three lakes, including Yverdon, Estavayer, Murten (Morat) and Biel/Bienne.

The **tourist office**, which has information on the city and the canton, is in the Hôtel des Postes building (main post office) on Place du Port (June–Aug Mon–Sat 9am–7pm, Sun 4–7pm; Sept–May Mon–Fri 9am–noon & 1.30–5.30pm, Sat 9am–noon; ☎032/889 68 90, *www.ne.ch*). They offer two **walking tours** – of the city (July & Aug Tues & Sat 9.30am) and of the nearby countryside (July & Aug Thurs 9.15am). Both cost Fr.8 and start from the tourist office. For Fr.30, a **Neuchâtel Museum Pass** gets you into eleven museums throughout the canton. There's also a host of good-value regional **packages**, with three nights half board plus one "activity" on each of four days (such as free museum entry, river-boat cruise, funicular ride, wine-tasting session, and so on) costing from Fr.199, or six nights from Fr.337. Whether you book a package or are travelling independently, dozens of attractions around the canton are free for under-16s – ask for the special "Families Welcome!" flyer, which you must get stamped by your hotel.

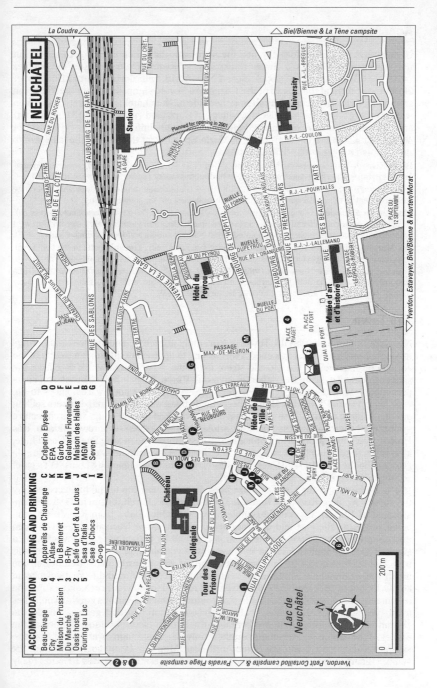

NEUCHÂTEL

La Coudre △   △ Biel/Bienne & La Tène campsite

△ Yverdon, Estavayer, Biel/Bienne & Murten/Morat ▽

Yverdon, Petit Cortaillod campsite & ▽   ▽ Paradis Plage campsite

ACCOMMODATION	
Beau-Rivage	6
City	4
Maison du Prussien	1
Du Marché	3
Oasis hostel	2
Touring au Lac	5

EATING AND DRINKING			
Appareils de Chauffage	K	Crêperie Elysée	D
L'Atlas	C	EPA	O
Du Banneret	H	Garbo	F
B-Fly	M	Gelateria Fiorentina	E
Café du Cerf & Le Lotus	J	Maison des Halles	L
Casa d'Italia	A	MGM	B
Case à Chocs	I	Seven	G
Co-op	N		

Station

Planned for opening in 2001

University

Hôtel du Peyrou

Musée d'art et d'histoire

PASSAGE MAX.-DE-MEURON

Hôtel de Ville

Château

Collégiale

Tour des Prisons

Lac de Neuchâtel

200 m

N

Accommodation

Neuchâtel is not a grandiose city, and the **accommodation** on offer is serviceable but not spectacular. There's a Swiss Backpackers **hostel**, *Oasis*, 35 Rue du Suchiez (☎032/731 31 90, fax 730 37 09; ①; closed Nov–April), with dorms from Fr.23; it's over 2km west of town at the mouth of the Gorges du Seyon, signposted from the Vauseyon stop on bus #1. The three **campsites** either side of Neuchâtel are all pretty good: 8km west are *Petit Cortaillod* in the nearby village of Cortaillod (☎032/841 40 31; April–Oct) and the better, but more expensive, *Paradis Plage* in adjoining Colombier (☎032/841 24 46, fax 841 43 05; March–Oct); while in Marin-Epagnier, at the head of the lake 5km to the east, is *La Tène* (☎032/753 73 40; April–Sept).

Beau-Rivage, 1 Esplanade du Mont-Blanc (☎032/723 15 15, fax 723 16 16, *www.beau-rivage-hotel.ch*). Top of the range lakefront palace, with double-swanky rooms and views to match. ⑦.

City, Place Piaget (☎032/725 55 77, fax 721 38 69). A traditionally minded, comfortable mid-range establishment in the city centre which has wisely splashed out on soundproofing. ②.

Maison du Prussien, Gor du Vauseyon (☎032/730 54 54, fax 730 21 43, *www.hotel-prussien.ch*). Neuchâtel's most characterful choice – a restored sixteenth-century mill beside a stream 2km west of town, with six comfortable, well-appointed wood-beamed rooms and four expensive suites. ③–④.

Du Marché, 4 Place des Halles (☎032/724 58 00, fax 721 47 42). The only hotel in the Old Town, with ten pleasant and spacious rooms (none en suite) overlooking a bustling café-lined square. ②.

Touring au Lac, Place Numa-Droz (☎032/725 55 01, fax 725 82 43, *www.touring-au-lac.ch*). Not a tranquil location beside both the harbour and the main road, but with some nice views. Its boxy rooms (some en suite) are nothing to write home about. ②–③.

The Town

Neuchâtel's atmospheric **Old Town** is extremely attractive, and random wanderings through its steep alleys are as good a way as any to appreciate the golden beauty of the architecture, as well as the 140-odd street fountains, a handful of which date from the sixteenth century. From the rather anonymous **Place Pury** – hub of buses and shoppers alike – with the main artery of Rue du Seyon leading northwards, alleys to the west bring you to **Place des Halles**, perpetually filled with talkers and drinkers spilling out of a handful of cafés. The square itself is overlooked by fine Louis XIV architecture – shuttered facades and the turreted orioles of the sixteenth-century **Maison des Halles**. You'll find informal lunchtime *boules* sessions on the nearby Rue du Coq d'Inde, a broad, tranquil courtyard away from the bustle. A two-minute walk east, on Rue de l'Hôpital, is the grand 1790 **Hôtel de Ville** (Town Hall), designed by Louis XVI's chief architect Pierre-Adrien Paris.

The highlights of the Old Town are poised on the very top of the hill, accessed by the steeply winding **Rue du Château**. The **Collégiale** church, begun in 1185 and consecrated in 1276, is a graceful example of early Gothic. Stairs from Rue du Château bring you up to the east end of the church, with its three Norman apses. The main **entrance** (daily 8am–6pm), to the west, is crowned by a giant rose window of stained glass. Within the vaulted interior, the nave draws you along to the glowing transept, lit by a lantern tower, and the unique **Cenotaph of the Counts of Neuchâtel** on the north wall of the choir (shielded for renovations since 1997, and due for re-display in 2000). Begun in 1372, and the only artwork of its kind to survive north of the Alps, the monument comprises fifteen near-life-size painted statues of various knights and ladies from Neuchâtel's past, framed by fifteenth-century arches and gables. Beside the church is the imposing **Château**, begun in the twelfth century and still in use as the offices of the cantonal government: **entry** is only on guided tours, which start from the signposted Door no. 1 (on the hour: April–Sept Mon–Fri 10am–noon & 2–4pm, Sat 10am, 11am & 2–4pm, Sun 2–4pm; free). The nearby turreted **Tour des Prisons** (daily

---

ABOVE NEUCHÂTEL

From the suburb of **La Coudre**, some 4km east of the town centre and reached on bus #7, a panoramic funicular rises through thick forests to the village of **CHAUMONT** (1087m). Set on a balcony above Neuchâtel, on the first of the Jura ridges, the viewpoint of Le Signal (1171m), a short walk from the funicular station, offers a vista over the three lakes of Neuchâtel, Murten and Biel/Bienne, with the plateau of Mont Vully rising opposite Murten and a patchwork of fields and forests stretching clear across the Swiss flatlands to the distant snowy fringe of the Bernese Alps. On the clearest of days, with such an unobstructed view across the whole country, it's claimed that you can even make out Mont Blanc and the Matterhorn.

Beside the top station is the *Hôtel Chaumont* (☎032/754 21 75, fax 753 27 22, *www.hotelchaumont.ch*; ③), a seminar and golfing hotel with very comfortable, if bland, rooms, great views and plenty of hilltop hiking routes fanning out on all sides.

8am–6pm; 50c), remains of a medieval bastion, has panoramic views over the town, along with interesting models of Neuchâtel in different eras.

Musée d'Art et d'Histoire

The flagship **Musée d'Art et d'Histoire**, Esplanade Léopold-Robert (Tues–Sun 10am–5pm, Thurs until 9pm; Fr.7, free on Thurs; SMP), and its star attractions, the astonishing Automates Jaquet-Droz (Jaquet-Droz Mechanical Figurines), is unmissable.

The ground floor is devoted to the **historical** collections, with absorbing rooms on the history of Neuchâtel aided by an excellent self-start slide show (in English). Upstairs are the rooms devoted to **fine art**, which have been organized radically differently from most other museums. Instead of displaying works by period, or artist, or genre, the collection is grouped by theme, with the various rooms labelled Nature, Civilization, The Sacred, and so on. In an inspired piece of creative design harking back to earlier centuries, the curators have crammed each room with art from floor to ceiling, with medieval still lifes, contemporary abstractions, Impressionistic indulgences and more all mounted higgledy-piggledy, thereby inducing you to make dynamic connections between utterly distinct works. In each room you can climb podia – each one hung all round with paintings – in order to get a better view of the works hung high on the four walls.

But the most extraordinary exhibits are kept in a room at the rear of the ground floor: the **Automates Jaquet-Droz**, three mechanical figurines built to the most exacting technical standards by a Neuchâtelois watchmaker in the 1770s (see box on p.164) and still in perfect working order today. The three – the Draughtsman, the Writer and the Musician – are displayed static behind glass, with a fascinating accompanying slideshow in English by way of explanation, but if you can you should really time your visit for the first Sunday of the month, when they are brought to life for a demonstration (2pm, 3pm & 4pm only). The **Draughtsman** is a child sitting at a mahogany desk and holding a piece of paper with his left hand; his right hand, holding a pencil, performs extraordinarily complex motions to produce intricate little pictures of a dog, the god Eros in a chariot pulled by a butterfly, or a noble profile of Louis XV. The **Writer**, a chubby-cheeked little boy, also sits at a mahogany desk, with a goose quill in his right hand and a tiny pot of ink nearby for dipping. He writes in a florid and chunky style, and staggeringly enough, can even be programmed to produce any text of up to forty characters. While he writes, his eyes follow the words across the page. But perhaps the most charming of the three is the **Musician**, a gracious young girl with slender and dextrous fingers who plays a small organ – a real instrument, not a disguised musical-

THE CELEBRATED MONSIEUR JAQUET-DROZ AND HIS AMAZING MECHANICAL FIGURINES

Pierre Jaquet-Droz (1721–90) was born in La Chaux-de-Fonds into a venerable and wealthy local family. After studying theology at university, he returned to Neuchâtel – by then already a centre for clock and watchmaking – and worked to combine his interest in mathematics with the skills of applied mechanics used by the artisans of the watch industry. By the age of 26, Jaquet-Droz had gained a reputation for technical brilliance, and in 1758 he and his father-in-law, a craftsman named Abram Sandoz, travelled to Madrid to show off the skill of Neuchâtelois clockmakers at the Spanish court (Jaquet-Droz's so-called "Shepherd's Clock" is still on display in one of the King of Spain's palace museums).

Jaquet-Droz was by now wealthy enough to retreat from business life and concentrate on problems of applied mathematics, exemplified in his construction of incredibly complex mechanical figurines – the earliest of computers – designed to do particular tasks. He trained his son, Henri-Louis, and a colleague, Jean-Frédéric Leschot, to work with him; together, they produced **the Writer**, **the Draughtsman** and **the Musician**, and presented all three for the first time to the public in La Chaux-de-Fonds in 1774. Writers of the day reported that people flocked from all over the country to see such extraordinary works of whimsy and technical skill. The same year, the three craftsmen showed their figurines in drawing rooms and royal palaces all across Europe, from London to Russia and Paris to Madrid, receiving high acclaim wherever they went. Perhaps aware of impending revolutionary violence in France and Switzerland, Jaquet-Droz sold the figurines to a collector in Spain in 1778. After the conflicts, in 1812, they reappeared in Paris and began touring again. Some twenty years later, they became the centrepiece of Martin and Bourquin's "Museum of Illusions", which toured Central Europe until the turn of the century. In 1906, helped by a grant from the Swiss federal government, Neuchâtel bought the figurines back, and they have been on display in the town's museum ever since, in virtually the same condition as when they were first made, almost 230 years ago.

box. As her fingers strike the keys to produce the notes and her eyes, head and body move subtly from side to side in time, her chest rises and falls delicately in an imitation of rhythmic breathing. Her melodies were composed in the early 1770s by Henri-Louis Jaquet-Droz, a fleeting and unique auditory time capsule from pre-Revolutionary Europe.

Eating and drinking

With such a heavy French influence, Neuchâtel takes **eating and drinking** seriously, with dozens of pavement cafés and relaxed bistros all over the centre. For **self-service** diners, check out both the EPA and Co-op department stores off Place Pury. Local specialities, best sampled at places like the *Hôtel du Marché* (see below) include tripe in wine, *tomme panée* (baked cheese) and fresh lake fish. A *fondue neuchâteloise* takes full advantage of the nearby vineyards, with local whites splashed liberally into the bubbling pot for an especially heady cheese-dipping experience.

Uniquely, Canton Neuchâtel permits all-night opening, and the resulting **restaurants de nuit** (generally open 9pm–6am or so) – most of them loud bars with small dining rooms attached, rather than true restaurants – keep the city's nightlife a-buzz.

Cafés, café-bars and clubs

Appareils de Chauffage et de Cuisine, 37 Rue des Moulins. Wonderful old place converted from a shop ("Heaters and Cookers") into a friendly, sociable Old Town bar.

B-Fly, 16 Faubourg de l'Hôpital. Very popular techno and house club. Thurs–Sun only.

Café du Cerf, 4 Rue de l'Ancien Hôtel-de-Ville. Lively central watering hole, serving beers from around the world.

Casa d'Italia, 1 Rue Prébarreau. Behind the château, one of the up-and-coming night cafés – avoid the *Cobra* cabaret in the same building. Closed Mon.

Case à Chocs, 16 Quai Godet. Top club in town, with innovative DJ nights of everything from ska to acid jazz and drum'n'bass, plus occasional live bands. Thurs–Sat only.

Garbo, 7 Rue des Chavannes. Classy night café in the Old Town, with dancefloor. Closed Mon.

Gelateria Fiorentina, 31 Rue des Moulins. In a quiet courtyard off the street, a perfect place to relax with an ice cream.

Hôtel Touring au Lac, Place Numa-Droz. Overlooking the harbour and the open lake, one of the best terraces for croissant-and-*renversée* breakfasts, mellow salad lunches and long sundowner *apéros*. Excellent fresh fish is an added attraction.

MGM, 45 Rue des Moulins. Posey night-bar. Closed Mon.

Seven, 15 Avenue de la Gare. Minor glitz at this disco/live-band venue. Fri & Sat only.

Restaurants

L'Atlas, 14 Rue Fleury (☎032/724 11 98). Tiny Moroccan restaurant tucked away on an Old Town alley, with Fr.13–15 *menus*, authentic couscous and *tajine*, Moroccan wine, and sweet mint tea as it should be.

Du Banneret, 1 Rue Fleury (☎032/725 28 61). Peaceful little spot in a crook of the Old Town's steep alleys, opposite a fountain at the foot of Rue du Château. The food is consistently good – regional specialities, lightly prepared, with fresh fish a staple. *Menus* around Fr.23. Closed Sun.

Crêperie Elysée, 26 Rue des Moulins. Old Town joint for *crêpes* with dozens of fillings to choose from, from a Fr.4 snack up to a Fr.13 meal. Closed Sun.

Hôtel du Marché, Place des Halles (☎032/723 23 30). Central Old Town landmark, serving hearty Swiss and French cuisine for Fr.20 or so. Closed Sun & Mon lunch.

Le Lotus, 4 Rue de l'Ancien Hôtel-de-Ville (☎032/724 27 44). Upper floor Thai restaurant, with high-quality Asian cuisine for Fr.20-odd (*menus*) or Fr.30 (à la carte). Closed Sun.

Maison des Halles, Place des Halles (☎032/724 31 41). Not to be confused with the *Hôtel du Marché*, this is in the fairy-tale turreted building next door – an excellent wood-fired pizzeria down below (from Fr.13), and perhaps the town's most refined *haute cuisine* restaurant (closed Mon, Sat lunch & Sun) up above.

Maison du Prussien, Gor du Vauseyon (☎032/730 54 54); see hotels. One of Neuchâtel's gourmet highlights, with characterful French-oriented *menus* for as little as Fr.30 or so. Closed Sun.

Listings

Bike rental In the station (Mon–Sat 6am–9pm, Sun 6.30am–9pm).

Car rental Avis, 2 Esplanade Robert (☎032/723 11 67); Europcar, 22 Rouges-Terres, Hauterive (☎032/753 11 47); Hertz, 25 Pierre-à-Mazel (☎032/725 17 60).

Changing money In the train station (Mon–Sat 5.45am–9.10pm, Sun 6.30am–9.10pm).

Email and Internet *Mouse Killer*, 6 Avenue du Premier-Mars (Mon–Thurs 10am–midnight, Fri & Sat 10am–2am; Fr.10/hr).

Laundry Salon Lavoir, 27 Rue des Moulins (Mon–Fri 7am–8pm, Sat & Sun 8am–8pm).

Post Main post office (CH-2001) is at Place du Port; another is way up opposite the train station (CH-2002 Neuchâtel 2).

Around Canton Neuchâtel

Above Neuchâtel, roads and train tracks rise steeply into the folds and ridges of the Jura range – known within the canton as the **Montagnes Neuchâteloises**. Like the continuation of the mountains to either side, this is wild and hilly country, not exactly mountainous compared with the high Alps further south but still characterized by remote, windswept settlements and deep, rugged valleys. It is also the heartland of the celebrated Swiss watchmaking industry, centred on the once-famous towns of **La Chaux-de-Fonds** and **Le Locle**, which both rely heavily on their horological past to draw in visitors. The Doubs river marks the border with France, set down in a gorge and forming along its path an impressive waterfall, the **Saut du Doubs**, and lake, the **Lac des Brenets**, both of them together making a pleasant day out.

La Chaux-de-Fonds

LA CHAUX-DE-FONDS is an oddity. To start with, more people live there than in Neuchâtel, although you'd never guess it from the sparsity of street life. Then it touts itself as Switzerland's highest city, though at 1000m that's no great shakes, and with just 37,000 people it would barely qualify as a town in most countries. Strangest of all, however, is the fact that this rather unprepossessing place was once a household name across Europe and the world, the humming centre of the Swiss watchmaking industry, which in its heyday of the late eighteenth and nineteenth centuries was largely responsible for establishing Switzerland's reputation – which survives today – for producing refined luxury goods of the highest quality. The town was burned to the ground in 1794, and was rebuilt shortly after on a strict grid system, characterized by enormously long, very broad parallel boulevards. Over the decades, the authorities have placed a high value on modern and postmodern architecture, with glass-built towers featuring prominently. This combination has given La Chaux-de-Fonds today the rather unfortunate air – very odd for Switzerland, and frankly bizarre for such an historic place – of a new town transported from somewhere in anonymous Middle America. It's rather an exhausting place to walk around, even though its museums definitely merit a visit.

Arrival, information and city transport

If you have your own transport and are approaching from Neuchâtel (whether on the winding minor road or through the climbing motorway tunnels), make sure you stop for a while at the **Vue des Alpes** (1283m), a magnificent viewpoint just short of La Chaux-de-Fonds, giving a broad panorama of the Swiss plateau backed by the snowy Bernese Alps.

The **train station** (with change counter daily 5.45am–8.30pm, and bike rental) is reasonably central, set back 100m from the main **Avenue Robert**, which cuts a perfectly straight northeast–southwest groove through the centre of town. In the tall Espacité cylindrical glass tower on the north side of Avenue Robert some 500m east of the station you'll find the **tourist office** (May–Oct Mon–Fri 8am–5.30pm, Sat 10am–2pm; Nov–April Mon–Fri 8am–noon & 1.30–5.30pm, Sat 9am–noon; ☎032/919 68 95). In front of the tower is a monumental nineteenth-century **fountain**, central landmark of the town.

The town's **buses** run on circular routes, and all pass in front of the train station. A day ticket is Fr.5. After 7pm daily, and before 11am on Sundays, some route numbers don't operate and others combine in a very un-Swiss way to make completely new route numbers.

Accommodation

The *Bois du Couvent* four-star **campsite** (☎032/913 25 55) is in a nice forest setting about 1.5km southeast of the station, but no buses stop nearby. There's an HI **hostel** at 34 Rue du Doubs (☎032/968 43 15, fax 968 25 18; ①; closed Nov & Dec), with dorms from Fr.24; take bus #4 (direction Hôpital). The *France* **hotel** is next to the station (☎032/913 11 16, fax 913 18 49; ①–②), a garni place with slightly shabby rooms both en suite and not; almost a kilometre east near the market square is the *Balance*, 8 Rue de la Balance (☎032/968 26 21, fax 968 05 66; ①), a better bottom-end choice. The *Fleur-de-Lys*, 13 Avenue Robert by the fountain (☎032/913 37 31, fax 913 58 51; ②), is modest and pleasant. Moving slightly upscale, *Moreau*, 45 Avenue Robert (☎032/913 22 22, fax 913 22 45; ③) has comfortably furnished rooms in a very central location.

The Town

La Chaux-de-Fonds' main draw is the admittedly impressive **Musée international d'horlogerie**, 29 Rue des Musées (Tues–Sun: June–Sept 10am–5pm; Oct–May 10am–noon & 2–5pm; Fr.8; SMP), about 500m east of the station, set back 150m from Avenue Robert. Even if you don't find clocks and watches the height of inspiration, there'll be something in this award-winning subterranean museum to divert you for an hour or two. There are hundreds of items on display, tracing the art of keeping time from the very beginnings up to the most recent models, with a concentration of exceptionally beautiful pieces from La Chaux's heyday in the eighteenth and nineteenth centuries. Upstairs you'll find various atomic and electronic clocks, including one with all the design flair of a disk drive that is accurate to a millionth of a second per day. Even this kind of technology is now of course ancient history – a more modern piece beside it keeps time to within 0.000,000,000,0001 of a second per year. There are also various videos which show the history and technical side of horology, as well as a few diversions such as a machine which tests reaction times in fractions of a second. In one corner local watchmaking firms, which are also the world market leaders, put their latest bejewelled creations on display – without price tags, however. In the park outside is a giant tubular-steel **carillon** with digital readout (all the rage when it was built in 1980) that chimes every quarter-hour.

Immediately adjacent is the **Musée des Beaux-Arts**, 33 Rue des Musées (Tues–Sun 10am–noon & 2–5pm; Fr.8, or Fr.6 for the permanent collection only; free on Sun morning; SMP), housed in an impressive neoclassical building with an annexe for temporary exhibits that's refreshingly light, open and airy. The permanent collection takes in a Modigliani, a couple of Van Goghs, Delacroix and Renoir among a selection of mostly little-known early modern works. The troubled face of local artist Léopold Robert in a portrait by his son Aurèle, hints at his disturbing fate: Robert cut his own throat in 1835 at the age of 41 after the failure of an unhappy relationship with Charlotte Bonaparte. Plenty of Robert's own romantic images of Venetian sailors, exotic peasant women and rogueish mountain bandits – as well as mawkish works on death and impending mortality – cover the walls.

Perhaps La Chaux's most famous son was the modernist architect Charles-Edouard Jeanneret, known as **Le Corbusier**. He was born in 1887 at 38 Rue de la Serre; dotted around the town are several examples of his work, including the Villa Jeanneret, 12 Chemin de Pouillerel (not open to the public), built in white following a journey aged 25 to Eastern and Southern Europe. The Mediterranean-style Villa Schwob, also known as **Villa Turque**, 167 Rue du Doubs, is a private house open for public visits, though only by prior arrangement on ☎032/912 31 31. The tourist office has a brochure outlining an 11-point Le Corbusier itinerary through the town.

Eating, drinking and nightlife

For **eating and drinking**, a few pavement cafés are dotted along Avenue Robert offering standard brasserie fare – the *Trattoria Toscana* at no. 13 is typical. Tiny *Café du Musée*, 7 Rue Daniel Jeanrichard, has a couscous *menu* for Fr.10, while the *Croix d'Or*, 15 Rue de la Balance, has pizzas for Fr.14 and quality fish for under Fr.20. The *Hôtel Moreau* (see above) has higher standards for not much higher prices: *menus* from Fr.20 or so. The best view in La Chaux is from the *Citérama* café, on the 14th floor of the Espacité tower; aside from ice cream, coffee and light snacks, they have a spectacular outside terrace with bird's-eye views over the whole town and, most dramatically, along the full, arrow-straight length of Avenue Robert – best after dark, when with a beer or two inside you, you might just imagine yourself in LA for a brief second. There's an Internet café, *Global Café*, at 18 Rue Jaquet-Droz (Tues–Thurs 6–10pm, Sat 2–6pm; Fr.10/hr).

The town's best **live music** and arts venue, the *Bikini Test* at 3 Rue Joux-Perret, was gutted by fire in January 1999 and is undergoing a refit until mid-2000. Until then, the vaulted *P'tit Paris*, 4 Rue du Progrès, has the market to itself, serving good inexpensive food as well as staging live music sessions in the cellar on weekend nights.

Le Locle and around

Eight kilometres west of La Chaux is the small town of **LE LOCLE**, where Swiss watchmaking was born. Daniel Jeanrichard, a native of Neuchâtel (where he made his first watch in 1681, aged 16) settled in Le Locle in 1705 and taught the trade to his family and a small group of apprentices, who then took the skill on to La Chaux and elsewhere in the Jura. Today, there's not an awful lot to see in the town, although if the watch bug has bitten you, you'll enjoy the **Musée d'horlogerie** in the grand Château de Monts above the town (Tues–Sun: May–Oct 10am–5pm; Nov–April 2–5pm; Fr.6; SMP), its rooms furnished in eighteenth-century style crammed with ticking timepieces of all kinds, including a roomful of whimsical and intricate mechanical figures by Maurice Sandoz.

The **Col-des-Roches underground mills** (daily: mid-June to mid-Sept 10am–5.30pm; May to mid-June & mid-Sept to Oct 10am–noon & 1.30–5.30pm; Fr.7; SMP) are 2km west of Le Locle on the French border. These vast, dank chambers were chiselled out of the rock little by little in the seventeenth century in order to take advantage of the flow of water heading down to the Doubs basin: there are two mills for grinding flour, a saw mill, and various other bits of heavy machinery down there, none of it particularly gripping.

A sideroad branches 3km north from the Col-des-Roches down to the small riverside village of **LES BRENETS**, where the Doubs broadens slightly to form a long bulge, optimistically called the **Lac des Brenets** (or, to the French on the other bank, the Lac de Chaillexon), which freezes over in winter to form the largest natural icerink in Europe. At its eastern end, through an impressive craggy gorge, the lake terminates in the impressive, 27m-high **Saut du Doubs** waterfall.

Practicalities

From La Chaux, it's easiest to get the regular **buses** #60 or #61 to Le Locle, which stop at the central Place du Marché. Hourly postbuses from Le Locle to La Brévine stop at the Col-des-Roches mills. There are CMN buses and narrow-gauge trains from Le Locle down to Les Brenets, where you can take a **boat** on the lake as far as the falls (20min journey; service provided by NLB; ☎032/932 14 14, *www.nlb.ch*). The bus drops you at the NLB jetty; from the train station walk left down through the village for twenty minutes to the river bank.

Yverdon-les-Bains and around

A busy, attractive market town on the southern tip of Lac de Neuchâtel, **YVERDON-LES-BAINS**, is best known for its thermal springs – celebrated at least since Roman times – and is handy as a jumping-off point both for the terrific old castle at nearby **Grandson**, and for trips into the Vaudois hinterland around **Vallorbe** and into the little-visited **Vallée de Joux**.

The town was founded in 1260 when Pierre of Savoy, who worked on the Château de Chillon (see p.150), built a castle on what was then the lakefront to defend against attack from the east (the lake has since silted up so that the fortress is now the best part of a kilometre inland). However, the presence of prehistoric standing stones, and also of Roman remains scattered throughout the area, indicates that the Savoyards were not the first to see the strategic importance of Yverdon's location. In fact, Yverdon – known as Eburodunum (the Fortress of the Yew Tree) in Gallo-Roman times – lies on one of Europe's most significant ancient crossroads. The shortest routes from central France to Italy, and from southern France to Middle Europe and Germany, not to mention the vital water route linking the Rhône and the Rhine, all passed through Yverdon.

These days, though, Yverdon lies second in Vaud to Lausanne, and is a gentle place, with its solid castle, a pleasant and compact Old Town with many baroque and neoclassical facades, 5km of sandy beaches, and a marshland nature reserve stretching along the lakeshore northeast of town. It's also one of the main locations for the much-fêted Swiss national expo in 2002 (see box p.158).

Arrival, information and accommodation

Yverdon's **train station** (with change counter Mon–Sat 5.20am–8.40pm, Sun 5.50am–8.40pm, and bike hire) is 100m northeast of the Old Town, and about 600m southwest of the lakeshore; the **post office** (CH-1400 Yverdon 1) is next door. **Boats** dock at the *débarcadère* on Quai de Nogent near the racecourse; it's a fifteen-minute walk south along the River Thièle and under the train tracks (or take bus #2) to reach the Old Town. The focus of the Old Town is **Place Pestalozzi**, in front of the castle walls; on the south side of the square is the **tourist office** (July & Aug Mon–Fri 8.30am–6pm, Sat 9am–noon; June & Sept Mon–Fri 8.30am–noon & 1.30–6pm, Sat 9am–noon; Oct–May Mon–Fri 8.30am–noon & 1.30–5.30pm; ☎024/423 62 90, *www. yverdon-les-bains.ch*). Their free guided tours of the town are in French and German only (July & Aug Mon 4pm), unless you book as a group, in which case they cost a standard group rate of Fr.100 for up to twenty people.

Accommodation

Accommodation is thin on the ground. The only **hotel** within the town proper is *L'Ecusson Vaudois*, 29 Rue de la Plaine (☎024/425 40 15, fax 425 44 85; ①–②), a pretty good option featuring rooms en suite and not, and pleasant staff. Fifteen minutes east of town is the rather charming *Hôtel de l'Ange*, 25 Rue de Clendy (☎024/425 25 85, fax 426 31 20; ①), on a busy traffic street but also with a mix of rooms and a wisp of character too. Clustering around the Centre Thermal on Avenue des Bains, you'll find the generic *Motel des Bains* (☎024/426 92 81, fax 426 14 94; ③), *Hôtel La Prairie* (☎024/425 19 19, fax 425 00 79; ③) and, cream of the crop boasting its own thermal pools, *Grand Hôtel des Bains* (☎024/425 70 21, fax 425 21 90; ④). Otherwise, plump for the tranquil riverside HI **hostel**, 14 Rue du Parc (☎024/425 12 33, fax 426 00 96; ①; April–Oct), with dorms at Fr.20.50; or *De Iris* **campsite**, on the lakefront northeast of the station (☎024/425 10 89; April–Sept).

The Town

The central **Place Pestalozzi** is dominated by the broad-fronted Louis XV-style Hôtel de Ville and, next to it, the foursquare turreted **château**, built after 1260 by Pierre II of Savoy, occupied by the Bernese in 1536, and taken by force during the Vaudois revolution in 1798. From 1805 to 1825 the château housed an educational institute set up by

JOHANN HEINRICH PESTALOZZI

Johann Heinrich (Henri) Pestalozzi, born in Zürich in 1746, was a visionary educationalist, who devoted his life's work – twenty years of it in Yverdon – to giving poor and underprivileged children from around Europe the chance to have a decent education and so to realize life opportunities otherwise denied them. Pestalozzi married at 23, and first lived with his wife Anna Schulthess in Birr (Canton Aargau), where they tried to organize help for local abandoned children and from where Pestalozzi wrote books and newspaper articles to bring the problem of children in poverty to wider attention.

After four years as a schoolteacher in Bern, Pestalozzi was invited in 1804 by the Yverdon municipality to come and set up an educational institute for underprivileged children in the château. Pestalozzi took in up to 150 boys aged 7 to 15 who would otherwise have been begging on the streets, fed and clothed them, and organized a flexible school curriculum suited to each child's abilities, covering mathematics, languages, music, gymnastics, biology, astronomy and more, thus gaining worldwide attention from social scientists of the day. Two years later, he set up a similar school for girls, followed in 1813 by Switzerland's – and one of the world's – first schools for children with hearing and/or speech disabilities.

His wife died in 1815, but Pestalozzi continued his work in Yverdon for another ten years, eventually returning to Birr where he died in 1827. To this day there remains a great deal of interest in his methodology, documented in sheaves of letters and articles written during his lifetime. His vision of education for all was seized upon by Victorian reformers in Britain and elsewhere as a cornerstone of the development of welfare policy through the nineteenth and into the twentieth centuries. If anything, Pestalozzi's legacy is only beginning to be fully realized today, with the UN acknowledging education to be a human right and recognizing that children have a right to be treated with the same respect as adults. When Pestalozzi wrote, "Development of a child's mind should be made continuously relevant to that child's personality and everyday life," such an idea was laughable; today it seems obvious, largely due to his inspiration.

the visionary reformer Heinrich Pestalozzi (see box) – Yverdon's schoolchildren continued to be taught within the castle walls right up until 1974. Today it's the home of the moderately interesting town **museum** (Tues–Sun: June–Sept 10am–noon & 2–5pm; Oct–May 2–5pm; Fr.6; SMP), for which you can get extensive English notes when you enter. Highlights include the castle chapel (room 2), modernized and now used for marriage services; a couple of impressive Gallo-Roman dugout canoes, on display in a high-tech setting below the doughty keep (room 4); a rather homesick Egyptian mummy in the Jew's Tower (room 6); and a costume collection in room 7. Room 10 beside the exit is filled with Pestalozzi memorabilia.

Far more engaging, however, is the **Maison d'Ailleurs** opposite the chateau ("House of Elsewhere"; Wed–Sun 2–5pm; Fr.6; SMP; *www.ailleurs.ch*). This self-billed "museum of science-fiction, utopia and extraordinary journeys", housed in the old prison, holds a massive collection of some 80,000 items, with several hundred antiquarian books from as early as the fifteenth century (notably a 1631 Amsterdam edition of Thomas More's *Utopia* in Latin), and several thousand paperbacks including an array of Asimovs in what seems like all the languages of the world. Recently under new direction, the museum is currently staging a series of changing exhibits on various futuristic themes, combining all kinds of posters, old sci-fi magazines, videos, Web-based material, sketches and unpublished drawings from Hollywood movie designers, and samples from its amazing collection of toys (1950s ray-guns, original Superman dolls, Star Trek and Star Wars figures, and more). You're welcome to browse through their huge English library, and kick back in their "Giger Cell" – a room kitted out by *Alien* designer H.R. Giger (see p.129) – for a spot of solo literary journeying during the afternoon.

THE CLENDY STONES

About 1.5km northeast of Yverdon, in a wood between the suburb of **Clendy** and the lakeshore, are **standing stones**, or menhirs, some five thousand years old. Take bus #1 to Clendy, walk left (north) under the railway bridge, and then head straight along a footpath beside a wood for about 50m. Cut right on paths through the trees, and you'll emerge into a neatly mown clearing set with the stones.

The Clendy stones were reset in their original positions in 1986, just one of many significant clusters of **Neolithic** stone circles and dolmens on the north shore of Lac de Neuchâtel – the greatest concentration of them in Switzerland (more are on Lake Geneva and around Sion). The pitted and blotchy Clendy stones – big, but no Stonehenge – form a rough rhomboid shape, with a line extending out from one corner; their purpose is unknown, but may have been connected with worship and/or ley-lines (Yverdon sits at a conjunction of ancient roads). The atmosphere of the place is tangible, but unfortunately today the stones lie beside a main road, shielded by trees from all but the sound of modern traffic.

Yverdon is suffixed "-les-Bains" for its **spa waters**, 14,000-year-old mineral springs bubbling up from 500m below ground and rich with all kinds of curative properties, most notably easing joint pain and helping with respiratory problems. The water emerges at between 28 and 34°C, and is these days corralled into various indoor and outdoor pools about 1km southeast of the Old Town at the **Centre Thermal**, a state-of-the-art complex off Avenue des Bains (Mon–Fri 8am–10pm, Sat & Sun 9am–8pm; Fr.13). Over a thousand people come here every day to take the waters. Extras include a sauna to yourself (Fr.30), or use of the collective sauna and hammam (Fr.9), as well as massages (from Fr.55) and any amount of physiotherapy and inhalation courses. You can even drink the stuff, bottled and sold around Switzerland as "Arkina".

Eating, drinking and entertainment

There's a good range of **eating and drinking** options in Yverdon, including the self-service diner at *Manora* on Rue de l'Ancienne Poste (Mon–Thurs & Sat 8am–7pm, Fri 8am–8pm, Sun 11.30am–7pm). Tunisian *Orient Express*, 22 Rue de la Plaine, has quality falafel and kebabs, while *Crêperie l'Ange Bleu*, 11 Rue du Collège has salads, crêpes and light *menus* for around Fr.10. *Don Camillo*, 10 Rue du Pré (closed Sun), has excellent pizza/pasta dishes; and *La Fourchette*, 8 Rue du Casino, offers simple but well-prepared French and Italian favourites. *Intemporel*, 8 Rue du Lac, is an upstairs **café-bar** popular with young people and open late nightly, with ten kinds of coffees and teas, plus salad meals. *Restaurant de Champ-Pittet* (☎024/425 65 14; March–Oct Wed–Sun only) is part of the Champ-Pittet marshland nature reserve 2km northeast of Yverdon on the lakeshore, and uses wild plants and herbs in its delectable organic creations that are beautiful as well as healthy.

The small *hippodrome* (racecourse) between the station and the lake sees low-key **horseracing** one or two weekends a month between March and October.

Grandson

A village on the lakeshore some 4km north of Yverdon, **GRANDSON** resonates in the mind of every Swiss schoolchild as the location of one of the three greatest victories ever won by a Swiss army. Its castle – focus of the battle (against Charles of Burgundy in 1476) – now houses one of the best **castle museums** in the country.

Although a tower was built by Adalbert of Grandson as early as 1050, the main buildings date from 1281, when **Otto I of Grandson** returned from the Eighth Crusade wealthy enough to build a new castle, a Franciscan cloister in the village and a Carthusian monastery further along the lake near Concise. Otto's tomb is prominent within Lausanne cathedral (see p.122).

In 1475, during clashes throughout western Switzerland and eastern France as **Charles the Bold**, Duke of Burgundy, expanded his territory and influence, the Swiss confederate army besieged the fortress at Grandson for the first time; after less than a month, the Burgundian garrison surrendered and was allowed to escape. Early the following year, on February 26, the Burgundian army under Charles retook the town of Grandson and, on the 28th, the castle. Treacherously, the Swiss garrison of 412 men were hanged from the apple trees in the castle orchard. Two days later, on March 2, the Swiss army marched against Charles, and met him in **battle** north of Grandson, lining up rank after rank of their feared fusiliers, pikemen and halberdiers. "The sun was opposite them," reports an eyewitness, "and their weapons sparkled like mirrors. At the same time, the raised bugles and battle-trumpets of Uri and the Luzerner battalion were bellowing, and the din was such that the Duke's men took fright and began to retreat." The Swiss had no cavalry to give chase, and so they let most of the Burgundians run away unscathed, only to discover that the Bold Duke had abandoned his vast riches on the battlefield: 400 decorated tents and precious tapestries, countless items of gold and silver, 400 cannon, 10,000 horses, 600 flags, 300 tons of powder ... booty totalling several hundred million pounds at today's value, much of which remains on display in Grandson and other Swiss museums.

Soon afterwards, the Swiss defeated Charles twice more, at Murten and conclusively at Nancy, thus in short order eliminating the principal threat to the French throne and, in at least a small way, permitting France instead of Burgundy to grow as a united imperial force in the centuries following. The château at Grandson, meanwhile, faded from central importance, passing between the governments of Bern, Fribourg and Canton Vaud until its rejuvenation as a museum in the 1980s.

The castle and village
Entry to the castle is from the main Place du Château (April–Oct daily 9am–6pm; Feb & March Mon–Sat 8.30–11.30am & 1.30–5pm, Sun 9am–5pm; Nov–Jan Sat 1–5pm, Sun 9am–5pm; Fr.8; SMP). You get a follow-the-numbers leaflet at the ticket desk, but it's worth pausing a while at the foot of the walls to look out over the lake and up at the massively strong turreted fortress above – Grandson sees a fraction of the visitors who cram into Chillon, and its past lingers more tangibly in the old stones. (Bear in mind, though, that Wednesday tends to be school-trip day.) Highlights inside include the Torture Chamber (room 3), with original wheel and executioners' axe; an exceptionally informative and watchable English-language **slide-show** on the history of Grandson and the Burgundian Wars in room 7; vast quantities of booty from 1476, as well as a lifesize mock-up of Charles the Bold's war tent (room 12); the understandably claustrophobic Prison (room 16); and a ramparts walk leading through the various towers and watchrooms. Accessed by stairs leading down from a corner of the Banqueting Hall (room 15) is an incongruous **Vintage Car Museum** (rooms 17–19), displaying a whole wealth of dream machines, including Greta Garbo's immaculate 1927 white Rolls-Royce Phantom, Winston Churchill's 1938 Austin Cambridge, a 1913 Bugatti, and various others.

Five minutes' walk southwest from Place du Château up ancient Rue Haute brings you to **Église St-Jean-Baptiste**, a beautiful and atmospheric Romanesque church renovated by the Crusader Otto I in the thirteenth century as part of an ecclesiastical complex in the village.

Grandson practicalities
Grandson's **train station**, 700m west of the château along Rue Basse, is only served by occasional *trains regionaux* between Yverdon and Neuchâtel. It's better to get the reg-

ular **postbus** from Yverdon to Gorgier-St-Aubin, which can drop you in Grandson's Place du Château (10min). The castle's ticket desk doubles as a souvenir shop and the town's **tourist office** (☎024/445 29 26, *www.memsa.ch/grandson*).

The Jura Vaudois

To the west of Yverdon is a stretch of hilly countryside known as the **Jura Vaudois**, characterized by rushing streams (and the remnants of iron-working industries which exploited their power), hidden valleys and ancient cobbled villages. The area lies wholly within Canton Vaud hard up against the French frontier – one of Europe's oldest borders, unchanged since 1186. Main town of the region is **Vallorbe**, of only passing interest in itself, but positioned at the southern end of a pass through the Jura mountains that has been used since antiquity as a route from France southeast to the Grand-St-Bernard pass, and thus into Italy. Railway engineers followed the old roads when they carved a tunnel from Vallorbe beneath the Jura early in the twentieth century, forming the last link in a chain that allowed the launch of the classic Orient-Express train journey from Paris to Venice and onto Istanbul. The Jura Vaudois was also a stopoff for medieval pilgrims following the Chemin de St-Jacques from Germany southwest to Santiago de Compostela in Spain: Romanesque and Gothic churches at **Orbe** and **Montcherand** and the huge priory at **Romainmôtier** fulfilled both spiritual and material needs on the mammoth journey. Behind parallel bands of hills, and guarded by high peaks at either end, the secluded **Vallée de Joux** has only a couple of roads, a handful of villages, and some great walking and cross-country skiing routes.

Sainte-Croix

A small village up in the Jura near the French border, 19km northwest of Yverdon on a steep and tortuous road, **SAINTE-CROIX**'s claim to fame is its 200-year history of making musical boxes, on show at the surprisingly diverting **Musée du CIMA** (Centre International de la Méchanique d'Art), 2 Rue de l'Industrie (guided tours June–Aug Mon 3pm, Tues–Sun 10.30am & 2–5pm; Sept–May Tues–Sun 2–5pm; Fr.9; SMP). The tours, which are in French with English notes available, last an hour and a quarter, and take in the full history, design and development of the art. As you go around, the guide starts up loads of intriguing musical figures, including an acrobat balancing on a chairback, a whimsical Pierrot writing with a long quill, pianos, orchestras and fairground musicians. Some 6km west of Sainte-Croix is the small village of **L'AUBERSON**, with – on much the same lines – the **Musée Baud**, 23 Grand-Rue (July to mid-Sept daily 2–5pm; mid-Sept to June Sat 2–4pm, Sun 10am–noon & 2–6pm; Fr.7; SMP), displaying a grand Parisian fair-organ from 1900 and various musical figurines.

Northeast of Sainte-Croix, a sharp-edged ridge culminates in **Mont Chasseron** (1607m), one of the highest of Jura peaks, commanding a majestic panorama across the whole sweep of the distant Alps. There's plenty of moderately taxing downhill skiing in winter, focused on the village of **Les Rasses** below the slopes at 1200m.

Practicalities

Hourly narrow-gauge trains climb from Yverdon to Sainte-Croix, terminating at the lower end of Rue de l'Industrie, 200m from the Musée du CIMA, which also houses the **tourist office** (☎024/454 27 02). Buses shuttle between Sainte-Croix and L'Auberson, and Sainte-Croix and Les Rasses.

Within Sainte-Croix, there's a good HI **hostel**, 18 Rue Centrale (☎024/454 18 10, fax 454 45 22; ①; April–Oct), with small dorms from Fr.25 and bikes for rent. Of the **hotels**,

Les Fleurettes, 3 Chemin des Fleurettes (☎ & fax 024/454 22 94; ①) has plain rooms and some dorm beds, while the pine-shaded *Grand Hôtel Résidence* in Les Rasses (☎024/454 19 61, fax 454 19 42; ③) lives up to its name, with spacious balconied rooms facing south to drink in the sunshine and gorgeous views.

Vallorbe

VALLORBE, right on the Franco-Swiss frontier, is known – if at all these days – simply as a stop on the TGV line between Paris and Lausanne, but in times past this small, rather austere town (loomed over from the southwest by the 700m-high Dent de Vaulion) was the centre of a thriving iron industry. This is commemorated in the riverside Grandes-Forges building, dating from 1495 and now housing the **Musée du Fer et du Chemin de Fer** (Iron and Railway Museum; March–Oct daily 9.30am–noon & 1.30–6pm; Nov–Feb Mon–Fri same times; Fr.9). The main draw is the working smithy, powered by waterwheels on the River Orbe outside and still turning out iron tools and implements much as the whole town did throughout the Middle Ages. Upstairs is the rather romantic railway section, where loads of memorabilia and old signboards from the Venice-Simplon Orient Express do well to resurrect the exoticism of early twentieth-century train travel. There's also a lengthy – and rather good – slide-show (in French only, but you can still enjoy the pictures) detailing the construction of the tunnel from Vallorbe through the Jura, and the expansion of rail travel.

Vallorbe's **train station** is perched on a terrace high above the town and offers bike rental; it's a ten-minute walk down to the **tourist office** (☎021/843 25 83, *www. vallorbetourisme.ch*), in the same building as the museum. The Fr.24 Carte Trèfle covers entry to the Musée du Fer, the Grottes and the Prè-Giroud fort (see below). Aside from the switched-on *Auberge Pour Tous* hostel, 11 Rue du Simplon (☎021/843 13 49, fax 843 13 89), with good dorms from Fr.21, the only **accommodation** in the town is *Hôtel de l'Orbe*, 41 Rue de Lausanne (☎021/843 12 41, fax 843 36 27; ①) with five serviceable rooms. The main street, Grand-Rue, has plenty of inexpensive **eating and drinking** options, including the pleasant *Le France* brasserie/pizzeria at no. 20, and cosy *Café de la Poste* on parallel Rue de l'Ancienne Poste. Several fast **buses** a day link Vallorbe with Yverdon, beating the tortuous train ride by more than an hour.

Around Vallorbe

Much more rewarding than Vallorbe itself is the rather wild and largely unvisited countryside around and about. Local trains and buses go everywhere but, with hourly schedules at best, they're rather less convenient than your own transport.

Just over 2km southwest of Vallorbe are some caves, **Les Grottes de Vallorbe** (daily: June–Aug 9.30am–5.30pm; April & May 9.30am–4.30pm; Fr.12), forming a tunnel over the River Orbe and replete with impressive stalactites and stalagmites, along with an exhibition of minerals dubbed Le Trésor des Fées (Fairy Treasure). Some forty minutes' walk from Le Day train station just outside Vallorbe is the **Fort de Pré-Giroud** (July & Aug daily noon–5.30pm; May, June, Sept & Oct Sat & Sun same times; Fr.9), an extensive military complex dug into a hillside in 1937 to defend against possible incursion by enemy forces over the nearby Col de Jougne from France. An innocuous chalet on the surface hides vertical shafts giving access to chilly labyrinthine tunnels and a whole subterranean bunker, complete with kitchen, dorms and a hospital, capable of supporting 130 people.

ROMAINMÔTIER, a small village in a secluded valley about 14km east of Vallorbe near **Croy**, has managed to preserve in near-mint condition its extraordinarily grand Romanesque **priory church**. Switzerland's oldest monastery was founded on the same site in about 450, and the current building was constructed by Cluniac monks in 990–1028. The church – approached from the picturesque village street beneath an even more picturesque fourteenth-century clock-tower – reopened in late 1999 after several years of renovations. As you **enter** (daily 7am–6pm), you pass into the impressive and harmonious **nave**, with its massive piers and a vividly painted thir-teenth-century vault overhead. On the left of the choir and chancel, with fourteenth-century frescoes, is the separate **Chapel of the Holy Virgin**, with a beautiful medieval statue of Mary. The remains of the **cloister** run along the outside of the south wall.

Continuing the ecclesiastical theme, **MONTCHERAND**, a tranquil village 8km northeast of Romainmotier with a view over the Orbe valley, shelters a small but notable tenth-century **church** (daily: May–Sept 8.30am–8.30pm; Oct–April 8.30am–6.30pm). Its most striking feature is a set of twelfth-century frescoes in the apse, depicting the saints Paulus, Ithos, Andreas, Jacobus, Matias and Filipus standing shoulder to shoulder in brilliantly restored colours.

ORBE, halfway between Vallorbe and Yverdon on the bus or train, is a picturesque old town up on a rock, with steep cobbled streets and another atmospheric **church**, a five-naved effort dating from the fifteenth century. Orbe was known to the Romans as *Urba*, and 2km north of the town, in a muddy field at the hamlet of **BOSCÉAZ** near the junction of the *autoroute* and highway, are some of the best **Roman mosaics** to be seen in Switzerland (Mon–Fri 9am–noon & 1.30–5pm, Sat & Sun 1.30–5.30pm; Fr.3; SMP). Nearest to the ticket hut is Pavillon IV, sheltering hexagonal mosaics of gods and god-desses, with the central medallions showing the deities of the seven days of the week. Further on, Pavillon III has a countryside procession, led by a trumpeter; and Pavillon II displays an intriguingly complex mosaic maze. Excavations of other areas are ongoing.

The Vallée de Joux

About 5km southwest of Vallorbe, the sharp Dent de Vaulion rises to 1483m, standing guard over the secluded **Vallée de Joux**, a long thin valley sandwiched at 1000m between the Grand Risoud pine forest, which conceals it from France, and the parallel Mont Tendre range, which cuts it off from Lake Geneva. It's perfect summer walking country, with many routes along the valley floor beside the **Lac de Joux**, while the thickly wooded valley sides turn into cross-country skiing heaven in winter. The valley has its own, bracing microclimate, reminiscent of Alpine areas 400m higher in altitude: temperatures of -20°C on the valley floor are not unknown in winter, and precipitation tops 1800mm a year. High winds can also rip their way along the valley. It's no surprise that the first people to consider settling in the valley were ascetic monks: even by 1700 there were still just 173 inhabitants, plus 22 bears.

Between the small **Lac Brenet** and Lac de Joux is **LE PONT** village. In front of the train station is what's left of a colossal hangar, used between 1880 and 1936 (before the age of fridges) to store ice which was hacked from the lakes and then transported by fast train to Paris, Lyon and Geneva. (In April 1927, the hangar was somehow gutted by fire.) Roads run west from Le Pont along both shores of the Lac de Joux: the south road passes through **L'ABBAYE** with ruins of a medieval abbey, meeting up at the end of the lake with the northern road and **LE SENTIER**, chief town of the valley and a one-time watchmaking centre to rival those in the Neuchâtel mountains (such prestigious names as Audemars Piguet, Blancpain and Breguet still make watches in the valley). **LE BRASSUS**, 4km southwest, is being developed as a resort, although you'd barely notice much actual development going on: the place is pretty, quiet and boasts nothing at all to divert you from the wilds of nature all around. From here all the way southwest to the Col de la Givrine is the huge **Parc Jurassien Vaudois** – Switzerland's second-largest protected natural environment.

Practicalities

Hourly **trains** from Vallorbe (connecting with services from Lausanne at Le Day) run along the north shore of the lake, terminating at Le Brassus. One **boat** a day in summer does a circular cruise of the lake, to and from Le Pont. A summer **road** from Le Brassus surfs over the mountains at Marchairuz before dropping down to Lake Geneva.

The **tourist office** for the valley is in the giant sports centre at the southern end of Le Sentier (daily 9am–noon & 1–6pm; ☎021/845 17 77, *www.valleedejoux.ch*). They have plenty of leaflets and brochures, as well as a useful 1:25,000 map and *guide touristique* (in French; Fr.15) detailing walks. You can hire ice skates here (Fr.5) for either the indoor ice stadium (Fr.6) or, when everyone is skating on it, the lake itself. They also have mountain bikes (Fr.40/day), cross-country skis (Fr.20), a climbing wall, tennis courts, and even plain dorms (Fr.15). Most amenable **hotels** are in Le Brassus: *De La Lande* (☎021/845 44 41, fax 845 45 40, *hotel.lalande@span.ch*; ②) is fresh and pleasant, as is the *De France* nearby (☎021/845 44 33, fax 845 44 31; ②) – but the former is family-owned, whereas the latter is a generic chain. *Hôtel du Cygne* in Les Charbonnières on the south side of the lake (☎021/841 12 81, fax 841 12 82; ①) wins no prizes for charm, but has plenty of dorm beds. **Camp** year-round at *Le Rocheray* in Le Sentier (☎021/845 51 74). **Eating and drinking** is a hotel experience, but for one or two small brasseries in Le Pont and Le Brassus.

The Broye

The mellow countryside between Yverdon and Bern is known as the **Broye**, after the River Broye which flows gently through the area. Not a great deal happens here, and it's perfect cycling country – reasonably flat, with plenty of small villages, a dearth of even middling-sized towns, and the shores of both the Lac de Neuchâtel and the Murtensee (Lac de Morat) to explore. **Estavayer-le-Lac** is a lakeside resort town with peace and quiet as its main attributes; nearby **Payerne** is home to a spectacular Romanesque abbey, while **Avenches** was once the capital of Roman Switzerland and has plenty for ruin-hunters to enjoy. **Murten** (Morat), on the line where French-speaking Western Europe meets German-speaking Central Europe, is a variation on the theme of attractive but staid lakeside resorts with well-preserved medieval centres.

Estavayer-le-Lac

ESTAVAYER-LE-LAC is a picturesque little yachties' town on the lakeside 19km northeast of Yverdon, with plenty of medieval architecture scattered throughout a centre which has remained largely unchanged since 1599. Today it occupies a little enclave of Canton Fribourg, surrounded on three sides by Vaud. It trades on two features: the town museum, which has a collection of stuffed frogs, and the climbing roses which cover its ancient stones throughout the summer, giving the place its nickname of the City of the Rose.

EXPLORING THE BROYE

Local tourist offices have a **package** to explore the region (April–Oct only). Two people sharing can have dinner, a three-star hotel room, breakfast, a drink, free entry to the church at Payerne and the Roman museum of Avenches, plus free lunch in Avenches, for Fr.150 per person. Throw in an extra night of half board, entry to the Estavayer museum, and a lunch of fresh fish in Estavayer as well, and you pay Fr.280 per person. You can book and get more information from tourist offices in Estavayer and Avenches.

Château de Chillon, Lake Geneva

UNESCO building, Geneva

Russian Church, Geneva

Rathaus on Marktplatz, Basel

Zytglogge, Bern

Chalets in the Bernese Oberland

Château d'Aigle, Haut-Léman

Hot Air Balloon Festival, Château d'Oex

Lauterbrunnen valley, Bernese Oberland

Jungfraujoch summit station

Grimsel Pass in summer

It's a ten-minute walk from the station northwest along Route de la Gare to **Place du Midi** on the edge of the Old Town. Heading east from here takes you past the Hôtel de Ville to the Gothic **Église St-Laurent**. Left (north) from here brings you to the open **Place de Moudon**, the medieval marketplace which formerly looked over the lakeshore. Over to the east is the solid **Château de Chenaux**, built and added to over 450 years, with towers and turrets sprouting all over. It's the seat of the local government, but you can wander around and through its courtyards. South of the church, Grand-Rue heads out of town via the mighty **Porte des Religieuses**. Partway down, Rue du Musée branches off to the medieval Maison de la Dîme, housing a diverting **museum** (July & Aug daily 9–11am & 2–5pm; March–June & Sept–Oct Tues–Sun same times; Nov–Feb Sat & Sun 2–5pm; Fr.3; SMP). A random collection of bits and bobs – ivory Chinese chesspieces from the eighteenth century, some old playing cards, assorted railway memorabilia – is filled out with 108 small frogs, stuffed in the 1860s by François Perrier, a retired captain of the Vatican's Swiss Guard, and arranged in glass cases in various poses to mimic the social life of the period. It's all utterly pointless, and more than a bit macabre: the frogs don't look impressed in the least.

Practicalities
The **train station** – on the slow Yverdon–Fribourg line – has bikes available for rent and is 600m southwest of Place du Midi, where the **tourist office** is situated (Mon–Fri 9am–noon & 2–6pm; July & Aug also Sat 10am–noon & 2–4pm; ☎026/663 12 37, *www.estavayer-le-lac.ch*). Plenty of **boats** serve Estavayer from both Yverdon and Neuchâtel. **Campsite** *Nouvelle Plage* (☎026/663 16 93; April–Sept) is on the lakeshore east of the harbour, about 1km north of the Old Town. The most appealing **hotel** is *My Lady's Manor*, Route de la Gare (☎026/663 23 16, fax 663 19 93; ③), a romantic manor house set in its own fragrant gardens, with very large, characterful rooms (none en suite); prices drop if you stay more than three nights. Otherwise, you're looking at the pleasant and quiet *Fleur-de-Lys* in town (☎026/663 42 63, fax 663 48 78; ②) or the similar *Hôtel de Ville* next door (☎ & fax 026/663 24 59; ②), the latter with a swishy Chinese **restaurant** upstairs and a plainer brasserie downstairs (closed Tues eve).

Payerne

Some 8km inland from Estavayer is the small market town of **PAYERNE**, highlight of which is the breathtaking **Église Abbatiale** (Mon–Fri 10.30am–noon & 2–5pm, Sat & Sun 10.30am–noon; Fr.3 or more, depending on exhibition; SMP), one of the most impressive examples of Romanesque architecture in the country. There's a wealth of detail in the five-naved church, which dates from the eleventh and twelfth centuries and which stands amidst the buildings of an abbey; its square, turreted **tower**, with a slender **twisted spire**, dominates the town. The lofty barrel-vaulted interior is impressive, with natural light reflecting off the variegated sandstone pillars of the nave to set the whole space glowing. Carved **capitals** in the transept and detailed **frescoes** from around 1200 on the vaultings of the porch and in the narthex are gorgeous. However, the church has not been used as a house of worship since 1562, and it's unfortunate that you may well find modern art exhibitions filling the nave and aisles with distractions and the hum of conversation.

Avenches

About 10km northeast of Payerne, **AVENCHES** was the capital of Roman Switzerland, at one time supporting a population of 20,000. These days, life in the town is more smugly suburban, but it's well worth visiting, both for the medieval town centre and the extensive Roman remains.

After a defeat at the hands of Julius Caesar, the **Helvetians** founded their new capital of Aventicum in the early first century BC (Aventia was the name of the local Celtic goddess of water). Emperor Vespasian granted it the status of colony in 72 AD, whereupon Aventicum entered its golden age. During the second and third centuries, the huge city wall boasted 73 watchtowers, and many of the public buildings of that period – a baths, temples, the amphitheatre, and more – have been excavated. The Aleman tribes raided the town around 277 AD, and sacked large parts of it; by 450, Aventicum's glory days were over.

Climbing the hill from the train station, the first thing you come to is the large oval **amphitheatre** crowning the eastern edge of the Old Town, well restored and now the scene of an annual summer opera festival (see box). The tower at the rear of the arena houses the excellent **Musée Romain** (Tues–Sun: April–Sept 10am–noon & 1–5pm; Oct–March 2–5pm; Fr.2; SMP). The ground floor is filled with statuary and mosaics, while up above are very impressive collections of Roman bits and bobs, sensibly organized and with English notes available. Fascinating details of ordinary life – such as the fact that a glass of wine cost a quarter of a sesterce, while commissioning a statue of the goddess Aventia with an inscription would set you back 5200 sesterces – are filled out with maps and figurines, including a copy of a spectacular gold bust of Emperor Marcus Aurelius (the original is in Lausanne). Dotted around the town are seven other Roman sites – the tourist office has a brochure – all of which are well signposted and free. One of the most impressive is the **Tour de la Cigogne**, a gnarled old column almost swamped by suburbia but still standing tall in a field: it once formed part of a giant temple sanctuary.

Practicalities

Avenches' **tourist office**, 3 Place de l'Église (Mon–Fri 8am–noon & 1.30–5pm, Sat 9am–noon; ☎026/676 99 22, *www.avenches.ch*), has plenty of books and brochures on the Roman and medieval town. An HI **hostel** is five minutes' walk south, at 5 Rue du Lavoir (☎026/675 26 66, fax 675 27 17; ①; mid-April to mid-Oct), with dorms from Fr.23. The nicest **hotel** is the grand *Couronne*, 20 Rue Centrale (☎026/675 54 14, fax 675 54 22; ③; closed Jan), which also has the poshest **brasserie** around (*menus* Fr.25). There are plenty more pavement cafés along Rue Centrale, or you could try inexpensive pizza/pasta in *Tearoom du Musée*, opposite the amphitheatre.

Avenches' **train station** (with bike hire facilities) is on the Murten–Payerne line. There are also plenty of **buses**: the ride from Fribourg is especially picturesque, and as a bonus passes through the intriguingly named village of Misery (which actually looks rather self-satisfied).

AVENCHES' FESTIVALS

Every July, little Avenches hosts a prestigious **opera festival**, with atmospheric open-air productions in the 8000-seat amphitheatre that draw world-class artists and thousands of promenading spectators. Performances start around 9pm and last until after midnight – many people stay overnight, booking the town's few hotels out months ahead of time. You can get tickets (Fr.40–150) and information through the tourist office's Web site.

Every August, the same amphitheatre sees the **Rock oz'Arènes** festival, running since 1992 with headliners like P.J. Harvey, the Wailers and Neneh Cherry, plus smaller stages with jugglers, acoustic sets and more. For tickets, contact CP 245, CH-1580 Avenches (*www.rockozarenes.ch*).

Murten (Morat)

Belying its deep historical resonance for the Swiss, **MURTEN**, 6km northeast of Avenches, has the air of a holiday town, its neat suburban streets and low-key waterfront promenade remniscent of the English south coast. It's bang on the *Röstigraben* (linguistic divide), though among its 5,000 inhabitants, German speakers far outnumber francophones (who call the place **Morat**). It's also one of the best preserved of Switzerland's medieval towns, and is still encircled by its fifteenth-century walls. These days, offering nothing much to do other than strolling on cobbled lanes, sipping drinks at lakeview terrace cafés and boating around the lakes, it's the perfect place for a lazy, romantic getaway. The Old Town's hotels oblige with a range of "honeymoon" suites.

The town's name is derived from the Celtic word *moriduno*, meaning "lakeside fortress". Fire in 1416 led to rebuilding in stone, a useful move since, shortly after, in June 1476, Murten allied itself with Bern and Fribourg against the Burgundians and found itself facing down a concerted siege from **Charles the Bold**. The town hung on for thirteen days, whereupon a Bernese force arrived from over the hills, weighed into the Burgundian army and massacred the lot – some 10,000 were slaughtered, and local legend tells of bones being washed up on the lakeshore even eighteen years later. A runner took news of the victory 17km to Fribourg, but expired after recounting his tale – his exploit is commemorated today by thousands who take part in a fun run between the two towns on the first Sunday in October.

Murten's **Old Town** is a simple three-street affair, full of picturesque medieval vaulted arcades and facades. You're most likely to enter at the **castle**, which, although closed to the public, has a peaceful internal courtyard with lake views. Rathausgasse leads east, packed with hotels whose rear terraces afford prime views across the lake to the Vully vineyards. Parallel to the south are Hauptgasse, crammed with bars and eateries; and tranquil Schulgasse/Deutsche Kirchgasse, providing some relief from the hubbub. One of the best ways to see Murten is from the **ramparts**, accessible at a number of points along Deutsche Kirchgasse. The main eastern gate is the **Berntor**, or Porte de Berne, with a distinctive clock face; paths lead from here downhill to the tiny **harbour**. Five minutes west along the lakefront promenade, just below the castle, is an old mill, now the town's **museum** (May–Sept Tues–Sun 10am–noon & 2–5pm; Oct–Dec & March–April Tues–Sun 2–5pm; Jan & Feb Sat & Sun 2–5pm; Fr.4), housing a diverting collection of archeological bits and pieces exposed when dredging of the marshes to the east lowered the water level in the lake to reveal evidence of Neolithic settlement.

Practicalities

The **station** – with trains from Fribourg and Payerne, as well as connections from Neuchâtel (via Ins) and Bern (via Kerzers) – is a five-minute walk west of the Old Town and has bikes for rent. **Boats** cruise in summer to and from Neuchâtel and Biel/Bienne. Of the **hotels**, *Murtenhof*, on Rathausgasse (☎026/672 90 30, fax 672 90 39; ②–④) is prime choice, a medieval house renovated throughout: there are some plain but attractive inexpensive rooms as well as spacious boudoirs boasting original beams, a round king-size bed, or a semi-circular bedside bathtub-for-two. A more refined option is *Weisses Kreuz*, Rathausgasse 31 (☎026/670 26 41, fax 670 28 66, *www.weisses-kreuz.ch*; ④), in the same family for eighty years; the modern rooms in its seaview wing are outdone by the jaw-dropping ones in the town-view annexe opposite, boasting antique beds and furnishings in broad, wood-panelled splendour (ask for room 33). *Ringmauer*, Deutsche Kirchgasse 2 (☎026/670 11 01, fax 672 20 83; ②) is a comfortable budget alternative.

Eating and drinking are well taken care of at the Hauptgasse cafés and hotel restaurants, although many cater for day-trippers and so can be overpriced; the

Murtenhof menu is long and inexpensive, with veggie options, and *Anatolia*, on Hauptgasse, can do pizza or kebabs for under Fr.20. The restaurant at *Weisses Kreuz* is one of the many gourmet options, with its excellent fish specialities starting at Fr.25, but for formal dining you won't get much better than *Le Vieux Manoir au Lac*, a romantic manor house set in its own gardens 1km west of town on Lausannestrasse (☎026/678 61 61): staying here overnight will cost you Fr.300 or more, but you can sample their top-rated French cuisine in a waterside dining room for just a little less (*menus are around Fr.80*).

Biel/Bienne and around

The double-barrelled town 32km northeast of Murten, and almost exactly halfway between Geneva and Zürich, can get a little confusing. German-speakers call it **BIEL**, French speakers know it as **BIENNE**, but it's Switzerland's only officially **bilingual** town and so all road signs, documents and public information must be in both languages. Train timetables, maps and books always call the place Biel/Bienne, and the locals cheerfully straddle the *Röstigraben* without a second thought – perhaps chatting with a friend in German whilst ordering lunch in French. In addition, some forty percent of the town's inhabitants originate from outside Switzerland, with particularly high populations of Italian and Spanish residents as well as Turks, people from the former Yugoslavia, Arabs and more. Eavesdropping can be an entertaining pastime, but it takes a certain shift in attitude in order to find your way around smoothly. Unless you're a linguist yourself, there's no reason why you should know that the street called Seevorstadt, for instance, is one and the same as Faubourg du Lac, or even that the body of water stretching southwest from the town is either the **Bielersee** or the **Lac de Bienne** depending on who you're talking to.

Aside from the town's continuous shifting between German- and French-speaking control, Biel/Bienne's **history** isn't particularly distinguished, and it was only when the railway arrived in the latter half of the nineteenth century that it began to expand beyond its old walls. Watchmaking had been a mainstay of the regional economy for a century or more, but had been suffering from the inefficiency of tiny cottage industries – there were some 350 enterprises throughout the Jura at one point, each employing a few artisans working by hand. Mechanization meant that production could be expanded and made more competitive, and Biel/Bienne took on the role of factory centre, initially for watchmaking and subsequently for precision machinery and other industries. To this day, such huge names as Omega, Rolex and Swatch maintain factories and headquarters here.

Biel/Bienne is a lively, modern town, utterly different in both style and mood from its near-neighbours Neuchâtel and Bern. The main attractions are strolling in the Old Town, dropping in on a couple of small museums and taking a boat ride on the lake or the river, but it's also a remarkable place to spend a day acclimatizing yourself to the language and culture prevailing on the other side of the *Röstigraben*.

Arrival, information and accommodation

The **train station** is between the town and the lakeshore: it's a 500m walk northeast along Bahnhofstrasse/Rue de la Gare to **Zentralplatz/Place Central**, heart of the modern shopping districts, from where the Old Town is the same distance again northwards. **Boats** dock at the *Schifflände/débarcadère*, some 500m southwest of the station. The **tourist office** is directly opposite the station (Mon–Fri 8am–12.30pm & 1.30–6pm; May–Oct also Sat 9am–noon & 2–5pm; ☎032/322 75 75, *www. bielnews.ch/tourism*).

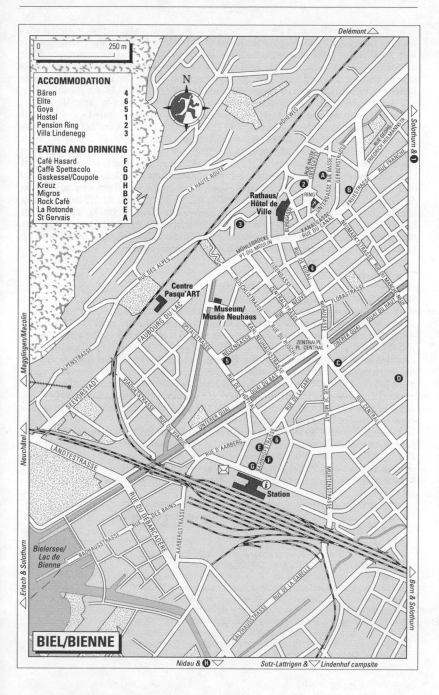

ACCOMMODATION

Bären	4
Elite	6
Goya	5
Hostel	2
Pension Ring	1
Villa Lindenegg	3

EATING AND DRINKING

Café Hasard	F
Caffè Spettacolo	G
Gaskessel/Coupole	D
Kreuz	H
Migros	B
Rock Café	C
La Rotonde	E
St Gervais	A

BIEL/BIENNE

Most **accommodation** in the town is geared towards business people – character tends to take a back seat. A pleasant Swiss Backpackers **hostel**, called *The Hostel*, is 4km northeast of town in an unromantic roadside location at Solothurnstrasse/Route de Soleure 137 (☎ & fax 032/341 29 65; ①; bus #3N to Renferstrasse) but is nonetheless welcoming and well equipped, with dorms from Fr.23. The nearest **campsite** is *Lindenhof* in Sutz-Lattrigen, a village 4km southwest (☎032/397 13 45, fax 397 10 77; mid-April to mid-Oct); take the little BTI train along the lakeshore to Sutz (10min).

Far and away the best **hotel** – tedious business-class chains included – is the beautiful *Villa Lindenegg*, Lindenegg 5 in the Old Town (☎032/322 94 66, fax 322 95 66; ②–③), a dreamy mansion built in 1831 in its own little park, bought by the city in 1985, renovated by three local women and reopened in 1996 as a bistro and hotel. All seven rooms are different, each of them fresh, light and wood-floored, the best (room 4) with a balcony over the garden. Alternatively, try *Pension Ring*, Ring 16 (☎032/322 81 08, fax 323 69 60; ①), a few airy but frill-free rooms above a café on the Old Town's central square; *Bären*, Nidaugasse/Rue de Nidau 22 (☎032/322 45 73, fax 322 91 57; ②), a creaky, shabby place in the centre; or *Goya*, Neuengasse/Rue Neuve 6 (☎032/322 61 61, fax 322 74 42; ②), which has slightly more going for it in terms of service and decor. *Elite*, Bahnhofstrasse/Rue de la Gare 14 (☎032/328 77 77, fax 328 77 70, *www.hotelelite.ch*; ④) boasts all the creature comforts but not a whiff of anything else.

The Town

Heading from the station along the main shopping streets of Bahnhofstrasse/Rue de la Gare, and on along Nidaugasse/Rue de Nidau, the bustle and high-street brand names suddenly fade painlessly away as you cross the line into the cobbled **Old Town**. Burggasse climbs past the old Zeughaus (arsenal), rejuvenated as the city's theatre, and the impressive 1676 step-gabled Rathaus (Town Hall), now police headquarters, into the open **Burgplatz/Place de Bourg**. Quaint shuttered old houses line the square, which centres on the Fountain of Justice, dating from 1714. Continue uphill, and head right to the **Ring**, core of the Old Town and named for the circle of head shakers who would sit here to deliberate on the fate of criminals brought for trial. Head east along arcaded Obergasse/Rue Haute, and then double back onto Untergasse/Rue Basse to stroll past the town's oldest houses.

A couple of the town's museums are worth a look. **Museum Neuhaus**, Schüsspromenade/Promenade de la Suze 26 (Tues–Sun 11am–5pm, Wed until 9pm; Fr.7; SMP) covers local art and history in a jumble of paintings, costumes, cinema posters and cameras, and also stages temporary exhibitions. The **Centre Pasqu'ART**, Seevorstadt/Faubourg du Lac 71 (Tues–Sat 11am–5pm, Wed until 9pm), devoted to

---

ABOVE THE CLOUDS

A favourite getaway for locals is to ride the funicular from Seevorstadt/Faubourg du Lac, west of the station, up through the forested slopes overlooking the town to the village of **MAGGLINGEN/MACOLIN** on the ridge, 400m above. Even when the town is swathed in fog (not such an unusual occurrence in autumn), the funicular can lift you above the clouds into sunshine. Once you're up there, there's not an awful lot to do, other than to head further up for some refreshing hikes around and about: you'll be in fit company, since Magglingen is known across the country as home of the Federal Institute of Sport. With strong legs, you can get 16km west to **Le Chasseral** (1607m), one of the highest summits in the Jura, where you'll find a simple hotel and mountain restaurant, *Chasseral* (☎032/751 24 51) along with spectacular views yawning out over the whole Swiss plateau towards the high Alps. Buses run between the hotel and St-Imier on the other side of the ridge.

contemporary art and photography, looks like it will be quite interesting whenever it finally opens after renovations.

Eating and drinking

There are inexpensive places to **eat** all through the centre, including self-service meals at the huge Migros supermarket at Freiestrasse 3. *Caffè Spettacolo* is opposite the station, with plenty of coffees and focaccia-style snacks, while round the corner at Bahnhofstrasse/Rue de la Gare 4 is *Café Hasard*, a small and attractive little daytime nook. The best place for restaurants, though, is in the Old Town: *St Gervais*, Untergasse/Rue Basse 21, is a lively, friendly, alternative-style joint with quality nosh, not the only choice on the street. *Kreuz*, Hauptstrasse/Rue Principale 23 in **Nidau**, a pleasant little town contiguous with Biel/Bienne to the south (☎032/331 93 03) is a wonderfully relaxed co-operative-run café and restaurant – old wood floors inside, garden terrace out back – serving excellent organic and veggie food (*menus* from Fr.15). The restaurant at the *Villa Lindenegg* hotel has gourmet evening *menus* (Fr.20) with or without meat using market-fresh produce inventively and attractively. *La Poissonière*, in the train station (☎032/322 33 11) is celebrated as an especially classy formal restaurant, but *L'Amphitryon*, in *Hôtel Elite* takes the biscuit as one of the highest star-rated restaurants in the country (*menus* from Fr.80; closed Sun).

Biel/Bienne's sizeable student population ensures plenty of **bars** around the centre, including the grungy *Rock Café* on Zentralstrasse/Rue Centrale and the trendy bar of the *La Rotonde* brasserie, Bahnhofstrasse/Rue de la Gare 11. Also check out the impromptu happenings and weekend dance nights at the *Gaskessel/Coupole*, a youth centre under a dome in a car park off Zentralstrasse.

Listings

Car rental Avis, Falkenstrasse 43 (☎032/341 12 61); Europcar, An der neuen Bernstrasse (☎032/366 51 80); Hertz, Bahnhofplatz 1 (☎032/322 33 43).

Changing money In the train station (Mon–Fri 6am–8pm, Sat & Sun 6am–7pm).

Email and Internet *Atomic Café*, Bahnhofplatz/Place de la Gare 5 (Mon–Sat 6am–12.30am, Sun 9am–12.30am; Fr.6/hr).

Laundry Salon Lavoir, 27 Rue des Moulins (Mon–Fri 7am–8pm, Sat & Sun 8am–8pm).

Post office Beside the station (CH-2500 Biel/Bienne 1).

Around Biel/Bienne

The northern shore of the Bielersee/Lac de Bienne is carpeted with **vineyards**, and wandering or cycling through the wine villages on the lakeshore can be a peaceful way to spend an afternoon. The tourist office in Biel/Bienne can give you a booklet detailing paths in and around the vineyards and places for sampling and buying the local wine.

From **Erlach/Cerlier**, opposite Biel/Bienne at the opposite, southwestern, end of the lake and served by plenty of boats, a footpath leads out for an hour-and-a-half's pleasant walk along a causeway to the wonderful **St Petersinsel/Île de St-Pierre**. No longer an island since the level of the lake dropped in the late nineteenth century during engineering work to control water flow throughout the Jura, this little dot of car-free, sun-dappled forest amidst the lake is well worth an afternoon. Cluniac monks were the first inhabitants, building a monastery here in 1127, but its most famous resident was the Genevois philosopher Jean-Jacques Rousseau, who spent two months here in 1765, later calling it the happiest time of his life. The renovated monastery buildings, idyllically set amidst vineyards, now house a gourmet **restaurant** (*menus* from Fr.20) and **hotel** (☎032/338 11 14, fax 338 25 82; ③; April–Oct), with eleven characterful and perfectly quiet rooms.

Northeast of Biel/Bienne is the **Taubenloch Gorge**, accessible on regular bus #1 or #3N (10min) or on foot from Magglingen (see p.182) above. Legend has it that a local young man fell in love with a young woman named Dove (Taube in German), and they agreed to marry. But the evil Lord of Rondchâtel wanted her for himself, and tried to force her to marry him instead. Rather than submit to his desires, she flung herself into the deep-set and fast-flowing **River Schüss/Suze**, and the gorge has been named after her ever since. There's a well-engineered path running through the dark and craggy defile for about 2km, and entry is free (although there's a donations box near the entrance). Canyoning Taubenlochschlucht in Biel/Bienne (☎079/357 92 57, *taubenloch@hotmail.com*) run guided canyoning adventures in the gorge (Fr.65; June–Sept only).

One of the best boat trips in the region is the river trip up the Aare from Biel/Bienne to Solothurn, which takes about two and a half hours and passes the stork colony at **Altreu** on the way.

Canton Jura

Ignored by most travellers, but well loved by the Swiss themselves, **Canton Jura**, in the far northwest corner of the country, is a rural gem, perfect if all you want from your holiday is to walk or cycle your way through gentle, rolling countryside and dark, fragrant forests, with only the smallest of villages and simplest of hotels (or campsites) to provide material comforts. This little bulge of land has over the centuries been shunted from pillar to post: from the Dukes of Burgundy to the bishops of Basel, seized by the Swiss, ruled by the French, handed to the Bernese, and finally in the 1970s – after decades of political turmoil that briefly threatened to ignite violent conflict (see box opposite) – granted independence and allowed to form its own government. Graffiti throughout the region showing the cantonal flag and the pro-separatist slogan "Jura libre" speak of a turbulent and politically active recent past. There's only a handful of towns, but most – including the cantonal capital **Delémont** – have spent the last centuries sidelined, well away from heavy industry and the major currents of European history, and so have retained a graceful, historic, Gallic air.

Delémont

An ancient town first mentioned in 737, **DELÉMONT** retains much of its medieval centre, and is an atmospheric place to stop over for an afternoon or a day. Its main historical claim to fame was as the summer residence of the prince-bishops of nearby Basel from the Middle Ages through to the Revolution. This century, the stirrings for Jurassien independence (see box) led to Delémont being named in 1976 as capital of

---

EXPLORING CANTON JURA

There are a couple of different deals on **transport** in and around Canton Jura. The *Carte journalière Region CJ* costs Fr.16 for a day (or Fr.8 with a half-fare card), and covers the train and bus network of CJ (Chemins de fer du Jura) only. The *Carte journalière Arc jurassien* costing Fr.25 (Fr.15) has a wider validity, including some mainline CFF trains. Train stations in the region have brochures showing the different ranges, and sell both cards.

DISCONTENT AND SECESSION

From the 1940s to the 1970s, Switzerland underwent serious political crisis, as a group of disaffected, historically marginalized people from the Jura pushed the flexibility of Swiss democracy to its limits. The origins of the conflict can be dated back to the 1815 Congress of Vienna which handed the area to Canton Bern. Bern welcomed the **Protestants** who lived in Biel/Bienne and the southern districts of the Jura around Moutier, and was powerful enough to ignore the destitute French-speaking **Catholic** peasants of the northern districts around Delémont and Porrentruy. Bernese moved into the area, bringing a new language and culture with them. Economic boom in the nineteenth century brought prosperity to Biel/Bienne, and largely passed Porrentruy by – but any rumblings of discontent in the north were quelled by the extreme hardship suffered by the whole region in the depression of the 1930s.

On September 20, 1947, a Jurassien member of Bern's parliament was refused election to the cantonal government because he spoke French. The outrage that followed led to the formation of a hardline anti-Bern grouping, which commanded popular support throughout the northern districts, and which got enough backing to force an extremely controversial **cantonal referendum** on splitting the Jura away from Bern. The voters of Canton Bern unsurprisingly rejected the proposal. However, it surprised the separatists that Jura too had voted against it: Porrentruy, Delémont and Saignelégier had supported separation two-to-one, but Moutier and its neighbours had rejected it by three-to-one. The francophone, separatist Catholics of the north, a minority both within Protestant, German-speaking Bern as a whole but also within the Jura itself, decided to resort to direct action.

The late 1960s were taken up with obscure and complex attempts by Canton Bern to solve the problem, none of which garnered any support in the Jura. Hardliners became more entrenched in their demands for out-and-out secession, and **paramilitaries** – with their slogan "Jura libre" – stepped up their campaigns, seizing a police station in Delémont, the Swiss Embassy in Paris, sabotaging Bern's trams, and, in a show of support for Walloon separatists, simultaneously storming the Belgian Embassy in Bern and the Swiss Embassy in Brussels. In 1973, Bern's cantonal government accepted terms for a **referendum on separation**, and on June 23, 1974, over ninety percent of eligible voters turned out, with a majority backing separation.

This shocked the Protestant southern districts of the Jura to the core, and immediately afterwards a pro-Bern, **anti-separatist bloc** formed, threatening violence against the Catholics of the north and demanding another referendum to allow the south to detach itself from the Jurassien independence movement and remain part of Bern. On March 16, 1975, this proposal was carried, but with a majority in Moutier of just 286 votes. Amidst the accusations of manipulation that followed, a pro-Jura demonstration turned into a full-scale riot, with 800 militants involved in an all-night running battle with police. Discontent simmered throughout the year, bursting into violence again in September.

Nonetheless, after a series of commune-by-commune referenda, popular opinion was shown to favour both the formation of a new canton in the north, and the adherence of the south to Bern. The split was inevitable. Moutier remained in Bern, and a new **Canton Jura** came into existence on January 1, 1979. Individual communes continued to shift over the next two decades: in 1989, the residents of Laufenthal voted to leave Bern and join Canton Basel-Land, and in 1995, Vellerat (population 70) voted to leave Bern and join Canton Jura.

As Jonathan Steinberg notes in his excellent book *Why Switzerland?* (see Books, p.532), it was this minute concentration on opinion within the tiniest linguistic, cultural or ethnic units, as well as a political structure able to take such micro-referenda into account, that meant that the Swiss could address Jurassien discontent, allow it to be expressed (with a minimum of violence and no casualties) and then have the flexibility to incorporate it into a new national order. Most countries facing similar discontent have neither the political structures nor the flexibility to effect similar solutions.

the new canton, but it retains a small-town charm – only around 12,000 people live here – and has good access into the rolling Jura countryside for walks and rides.

It takes five minutes to cross the river and stroll northwest from the station into the Old Town. The main street is Rue du 23-Juin, longer and more impressive than you might expect for a little town, and home to the eighteenth-century **Hôtel de Ville**, set skewed to the road and shaded by a huge tree. This ornate building was the scene, in 1947, of a historic demonstration which sparked the subsequent liberation movement. A few steps west is the **Église St-Marcel**, built in the 1770s in a mixture of the lavish decoration of Rococo and the formal lines of Neoclassical, and with some lovely dark oakwood stalls. Beside the church is the **château**, built in 1721.

At the western end of the road is the Porte de Porrentruy, one of the old city gates, with the Fontaine du Sauvage topped with a stature of a wild man of the woods and, adjacent, the **Musée Jurassien d'Art et d'Histoire** (Tues–Sun 2–5pm; Fr.6; SMP). This modest but interesting museum houses in the basement the treasures from the St-Marcel church. Prime exhibit, prominent and proudly spotlit, is the beautiful golden mitre of St Germain, first abbot of Moutier in the seventh century. It's a shame that his twisted old leather sandals, which are far more evocative, get rather shorter shrift.

A couple of kilometres northeast of Delémont is the atmospheric **Chapelle de Vorbourg**, a pilgrimage site tended by monks that's dramatically located up on a forested crag below the ruins of a medieval castle.

Practicalities

Delémont's tiny **tourist office**, 12 Place de la Gare (Mon–Fri 9am–noon & 2–6.30pm, Sat 9am–noon & 2–4pm; ☎032/422 97 78, *www.delemont.ch*) can help with local odds and ends, but the main cantonal office is in Saignelégier (see below). The train station has a **change counter** (Mon–Sat 5.45am–9.15pm, Sun 6.30am–9.15pm) and bike hire, with a **post office** (CH-2800) across the road.

A kilometre east of the centre is an excellent HI **hostel**, 185 Route de Bâle (☎032/422 20 54, fax 422 88 30; ①; March–Oct), with good facilities for families and quality food. Dorms are Fr.24. *Hôtel du Boeuf*, 17 Rue de la Préfecture (☎032/422 16 91, fax 422 20 91; ②) is a clean, well-run **hotel** within the Old Town. On the same street you'll find places to **eat**, including *La Cigogne* at no. 7 (closed Tues) serving home-made pasta and wood-fired pizzas. Place Roland-Béguelin, one street west, has plenty of shaded pavement cafés, and is also the scene of the town **market** (Wed & Sat morning).

Saignelégier and Franches-Montagnes

The stretch of the Jura range within Canton Jura itself is called **Franches-Montagnes**. Following wars between local lords in the twelfth and thirteenth centuries, Bishop Imier de Ramstein granted tax exemptions (*franchises* in French) to the whole area as a way to encourage repopulation, thus giving the area its name. It's a gorgeous landscape of rolling green hills and wide meadows flanked by fir trees, and is fiercely loved by the locals: one writer commented, "A Franc-Montagnard who sells off the land for profit is considered a traitor." In the 1960s, when the Swiss army proposed creating military installations and storehouses in the beloved hills, the locals got together and ensured (by voting) that such philistinism didn't get off the drawing board.

SAIGNELÉGIER is the main – indeed only – town in the region, just a shop or two larger than a village. The **tourist office** for the canton is opposite the train station (Mon–Fri 9am–noon & 2–6pm, Sat 9am–noon; July & Aug also Sun 9am–noon & 2–4pm; ☎032/952 19 52, *www.jura.ch* and *www.franchesmontagnes.ch*), and has an array of information, as well as local crafts and bottles of the delectable local firewater – a plum-based *eau-de-vie* called Damassine – for sale. Bikes are available for hire at the station. On the second weekend in August, the **Marché-Concours National de**

Chevaux rolls into town (*www.nti.ch/MarcheConcours*), a giant horse market and show occupying an arena south of town with parades, races and celebrations.

There are limitless possibilities for hikes and cycle routes through the countryside around and about: aim southeast to the idyllic **Étang de la Gruère** lake, or southwest along the ridge to the ancient village of **Le Noirmont**, or north, down into the Doubs valley for plenty of riverside forest trails around the border hamlet of **Goumois**.

You can **camp** at *Sous La Neuvevie* (☎032/951 10 82; May–Oct), 2km south of Saignelégier beyond the arena, or at the municipal site in Goumois (☎032/951 27 07; April–Sept) – both are basic, spartan sites; the Saignelégier–Goumois bus runs four times daily. **Hotels** and pensions abound, in every hamlet and scenic spot. The friendly *Café-Hôtel du Soleil*, two minutes south of the station in Saignelégier (☎032/951 16 88, fax 951 22 95, *www.cafe-du-soleil.ch*; ①) has seven rooms and a dorm (Fr.22), and doubles as a local arts centre, with some concerts and exhibitions. *Hôtel du Doubs*, 10m from the riverside border crossing in Goumois (☎032/951 13 23, fax 951 14 89; ②), offers comfortable, rustic rooms as well as excellent cuisine. For those with their own transport, *Le Theusseret* (☎032/951 14 51; closed Wed), just uphill from Goumois, is an outstanding **restaurant** in an idyllic old mill beside a weir, specializing in fresh local produce and melt-in-the-mouth fish (*menus* from Fr.17).

Porrentruy and around

In the heart of the **Ajoie** region – the bulge of Canton Jura that sticks out into France – is the rather attractive town of **PORRENTRUY**. Its graceful old centre is filled with eighteenth-century buildings, while a total of nine schools and colleges lend the cobbled streets a vivacity lacking in towns twice the size. Walking 500m west from the train station brings you onto the main Grand-Rue, dotted with medieval fountains and lined with ornate facades, including the **tourist office** housed in the old hospital at no. 5 (Mon–Fri 9am–noon & 2–6pm, July & Aug also Sat 10am–1pm; ☎032/466 59 59). Following the street down to the river leaves you a few metres west of the fourteenth-century **Porte de France** and at the foot of the impressive **château** towering above. Its mighty **Tour Refous** (daily 9–11.45am & 1.30–6pm; free) gives an expansive view.

Hotel De La Poste, 15 Rue Malvoisins (☎032/466 18 27; ①), is a tidy little **hotel** in the Old Town with pleasant, quiet rooms. The same street has many pavement **cafés**, including jolly *Aux Deux Clefs* at no. 7 and the *Monkey Bar* opposite, which serves inexpensive crêpes (Fr.5–10). *Au Faucon*, 15 Rue des Annonciades, is a lively student bar, with DJs and bands in the cellar. Don't miss *Guillaume Tell*, 36 Grand-Rue, a combination bistro (with terrific fondues) and patisserie: they make fresh cheesecake every Friday morning, which is as good a reason as any for spending Thursday night in Porrentruy. In November, the huge **Marché de St-Martin** is an excuse for scoffing vast quantities of the local pork *saucisse d'Ajoie* at stand-up stalls, along with plenty of local Tête-de-Moine cheese and Damassine to wash it down.

St-Ursanne

South of Porrentruy, the River Doubs loops into Swiss territory for the only time, enclosing a neck of land known as the **Clos de Doubs**: the scenic road from Saignelégier running alongside the valley is dubbed, romantically, the Corniche du Jura. **ST-URSANNE** is a picturesque old walled village on the river, 10km from Porrentruy, blessed with both a twelfth-century church and five small hotels. The 1km walk down from the station is gorgeous, and you approach the village through its eastern, sixteenth-century Porte de St-Pierre. The same road passes through to the Porte de St-Paul at the village's western end, while midway along, an alley branches south past the **tourist office**, 18 Rue du Quartier (March–Oct daily 10am–5pm; ☎032/461 37 16) through the Porte de St-Jean to an ancient, narrow bridge over the river. The beautiful **collégiale** church in the heart of the village, with its sculptured and painted south doorway, is airy and impressive inside, its Romanesque choir filled with fantastically lavish Baroque ornament. Above the nave, which has fifteenth-century frescoes, the vaulting is crowned with carved keystones giving the date 1301, and you'll find fewer more peaceful and attractive corners to spend a sunny hour or two than the Gothic **cloister** to the north.

Of the **places to stay**, the *Demi-Lune* (☎032/461 35 31, fax 461 37 87; ②) and *Hotel du Boeuf* (☎032/461 31 49, fax 461 38 92; ②) are both clean and serviceable. If you're in the area at the right time, don't miss St-Ursanne's fantastic **Fête Médiévale**, on a weekend in early July, with everyone in costume, medieval foods and beers on offer, minstrels and musicians, dancers, acrobats, jugglers and fire-eaters, and, to top it all, a grand Gregorian mass on Sunday morning.

travel details

TRAINS

Avenches to: Kerzers (for Bern; hourly; 30min); Murten (hourly; 5min); Payerne (hourly; 15min).

Biel/Bienne to: Basel (hourly; 1hr 10min); Bern (3 hourly; 30min); La Chaux-de-Fonds (hourly; 40min); Delémont (hourly; 30min); Lausanne (hourly; 1hr 10min); Neuchâtel (twice hourly; 20min); Solothurn (hourly; 20min); Yverdon (twice hourly; 45min).

Le Brassus to: Vallorbe (hourly; 45min).

La Chaux-de-Fonds to: Basel (hourly; 2hr); Bern (twice hourly; 1hr 20min); Biel/Bienne (hourly; 40min); Delémont (hourly; 1hr 20min); Lausanne (hourly; 1hr 30min); Le Locle (twice hourly; 7min); Neuchâtel (hourly; 30min); Saignelégier (hourly; 40min); Solothurn (hourly; 1hr 5min); Yverdon (hourly; 1hr).

Delémont to: Basel (hourly; 35min); Bern (hourly; 1hr); Biel/Bienne (hourly; 30min); Neuchâtel (hourly; 55min); Porrentruy (hourly; 30min); St-Ursanne (hourly; 20min); Solothurn (hourly; 40min).

Estavayer-le-Lac to: Fribourg (hourly; 35min); Payerne (hourly; 10min); Yverdon (hourly; 15min).

Murten (Morat) to: Avenches (hourly; 5min); Fribourg (hourly; 25min); Ins (for Neuchâtel; hourly; 40min); Kerzers (for Bern; hourly; 15min); Payerne (hourly; 20min).

Neuchâtel to: Basel (hourly; 1hr 35min); Bern (hourly; 35min); Biel/Bienne (twice hourly; 20min); La Chaux-de-Fonds (hourly; 35min); Delémont (hourly; 1hr); Geneva (hourly; 1hr 20min); Lausanne (hourly; 50min); Le Locle (hourly;

45min); Porrentruy (hourly; 1hr 35min); Solothurn (hourly; 40min); Yverdon (twice hourly; 25min); Zürich (hourly; 1hr 55min).

Orbe to: Chavornay (for Lausanne; hourly; 10min).

Payerne to: Avenches (hourly; 15min); Estavayer (hourly; 10min); Fribourg (hourly; 25min); Kerzers (for Bern; hourly; 45min); Murten (hourly; 20min); Palézieux (for Lausanne; hourly; 40min); Yverdon (hourly; 25min).

Porrentruy to: Delémont (hourly; 30min); St-Ursanne (hourly; 15min).

Saignelégier to: La Chaux-de-Fonds (hourly; 40min).

St-Ursanne to: Delémont (hourly; 20min); Porrentruy (hourly; 15min).

Vallorbe to: Le Brassus (hourly; 45min); Croy-Romainmôtier (hourly; 15min); Lausanne (hourly; 45min).

Yverdon to: Basel (hourly; 2hr); Bern (hourly; 1hr 10min); Biel/Bienne (hourly; 45min); La Chaux-de-Fonds (hourly; 1hr); Delémont (hourly; 1hr 20min); Estavayer (hourly; 15min); Fribourg (hourly; 50min); Geneva (hourly; 55min); Lausanne (hourly; 25min); Neuchâtel (twice hourly; 25min); Payerne (hourly; 25min); Sainte-Croix (hourly; 40min); Solothurn (hourly; 1hr 5min).

BUSES

Avenches to: Estavayer (4 daily; 45min); Fribourg (8 daily; 25min).

Le Brassus to: Nyon (June–Oct Sat & Sun 2 daily; 1hr 10min).

La Chaux-de-Fonds to: Le Locle (every 30min; 25min).

Estavayer-le-Lac to: Avenches (3 daily; 1hr 20min); Fribourg (3 daily; 2hr).

Orbe to: Croy-Romainmôtier (3 daily; 10min).

Le Pont to: Morges (June–Oct Sun 1 daily; 1hr 5min).

Saignelégier to: Glovelier (for Delémont; 6 daily; 35min).

Yverdon to: Orbe (hourly; 25min); Vallorbe (11 daily; 30min).

BOATS

(following is a summary of June–Sept summer services; fewer boats run in other months, generally Sat & Sun only if at all)

Biel/Bienne to: Erlach & St Petersinsel (at least 3 daily; 45min–1hr); Neuchâtel (2 daily except Mon; 2hr 20min); Murten (Morat; 1 daily; 2hr 50min); Solothurn (Soleure; at least 4 daily except Mon; 2hr 30min).

Erlach & St Petersinsel to: Biel/Bienne (at least

4 daily; 45min–1hr); Neuchâtel (2 daily except Mon; 1hr–1hr 30min).

Estavayer-le-Lac to: Neuchâtel (at least 3 daily except Mon; 1hr 30min); Yverdon (at least 3 daily except Mon; 1hr 25min).

Murten (Morat) to: Biel/Bienne (1 daily; 3hr 45min); Neuchâtel (at least 4 daily; 1hr 40min); Môtier/Vully (at least 3 daily year-round; 40min).

Neuchâtel to: Biel/Bienne (at least 1 daily; 2hr 20min); Estavayer (at least 3 daily except Mon; 1hr 35min); Erlach & St Petersinsel (at least 1 daily; 1hr–1hr 30min); Murten (Morat; at least 4 daily; 1hr 45min).

Yverdon to: Estavayer (at least 3 daily except Mon; 1hr 25min).

INTERNATIONAL TRAINS

Le Locle to: Besançon (3 daily; 1hr 50min).

Neuchâtel to: Dijon (3 daily; 2hr 20min); Paris (3 daily; 4hr).

Vallorbe to: Dijon (5 daily; 1hr 35min); Paris (5 daily; 3hr 15min).

PLACE NAMES IN THIS CHAPTER

German	French	Italian
Aare	Aar	Aar
Basel	Bâle	Basilea
Bielersee	Lac de Bienne	Lago di Bienne
Delsberg	Delémont	Delémont
Dreiseen	Trois Lacs	Tre Laghi
Freiburg	Fribourg	Friborgo
Jura	Jura	Giura
Münster	Moutier	Moutier
Murten	Morat	Morat
Murtensee	Lac de Morat	Lago di Morat
Neuenburg	Neuchâtel	Neuchâtel
Neuenburgersee	Lac de Neuchâtel	Lago di Neuchâtel
Pruntrut	Porrentruy	Porrentruy
Saane	Sarine	Sarine
Sankt Immer	St-Imier	San Imier
Schüss	Suze	Suze
Solothurn	Soleure	Soletta
Waadt	Vaud	Vaud
Zihl	Thièle	Thièle

CHAPTER FOUR

BASEL

You might expect **BASEL** (Bâle in French, and often anglicized to Basle), situated on the Rhine exactly where Switzerland, Germany and France touch noses, to be the focal point of the continent, humming with pan-European energy. It's true that Basel's voters are the most fervently pro-European of all Switzerland's German speakers but, somehow, the close proximity of foreign languages and cultures has introverted the city rather than energized it: Basel's a curiously measured place, where equilibrium is everything. You won't find anyone shouting about the new Europe here; in fact, you're unlikely to find anyone shouting about anything at all. Even the city's massive carnival is a rigorously organized set piece.

With both a gigantic river port – Switzerland's only outlet to the sea – and the research headquarters of several pharmaceutical multinationals (including Novartis, one of the principal players in global development of GM crops and foods), Basel nurtures its reputation as Switzerland's wealthiest and most discreet city. Its historic centre – dominated by the awe-inspiring **Münster** – is definitely worth seeing, and the city's long-standing patronage of the arts has resulted in a panoply of first-rate museums and galleries – 35 in all, including the stunning **Beyeler collection**, Basel's sole unmissable attraction. And yet, bequeathed a glittering medieval past endowed with some of the greatest minds of European history (Erasmus, Holbein and Nietzsche, to name just three) and centuries-long access to the best of three neighbouring worlds, it's almost as if Baslers lost the plot when it came to defining their city for today. Most people seem to back the standard Swiss default option of gathering wealth in a discreet and orderly fashion, saving money shopping in France and having a better time partying in Germany. Which is all very well, but it tends to leave their own city rather bereft in the process.

Another fly in the ointment has been the recent Nazi gold controversy (see Contexts, p.524), in which it was indicated that venerable Basel – and, more specifically, the little-known but extremely powerful Bank for International Settlements headquartered in the city – spent the 1930s and '40s quietly laundering the Nazis' ill-gotten gains under a cloak of neutrality. Evidence of such murky banking practice was received with shock, anger and disbelief in Basel and around the country, and has yet to be fully accepted. Unaccustomed to being faced with pointing fingers, Baslers may take some decades to assess and absorb the accusations.

ACCOMMODATION PRICE CODES

All the hostels, pensions and hotels in this book have been graded according to the following price codes, which indicate the price for the cheapest double room available during the high season. Single rooms can cost anything between sixty and eighty percent of the double-room rate. For hostels with dormitories, the price per bed has been quoted. See p.45 for more details.

① under Fr.100   ④ Fr.200–250   ⑦ Fr.350–400
② Fr.100–150   ⑤ Fr.250–300   ⑧ Fr.400–500
③ Fr.150–200   ⑥ Fr.300–350   ⑨ over Fr.500

Some history

A **Celtic** town stood on the hill now occupied by Basel's Cathedral in the first century BC, but the city is traditionally dated to 44 BC, when the nearby Roman city of **Augusta Raurica** (see p.206) was also founded. By 374 AD, **Basilia** was a fort, and seat of a bishopric following the Alemans' destruction of Augusta Raurica in the fifth century. In 917, the **Huns** swept through, sacking the town and destroying the Carolingian cathedral,

---

DR HOFMANN'S PROBLEM CHILD

It was a Friday afternoon, April 16, 1943, in the laboratories of one of Basel's major pharmaceutical companies, Sandoz. The 37-year-old **Dr Albert Hofmann**, who had worked for Sandoz for fourteen years, was doing research into the various properties of rye fungus, in a search for a cure for migraine. During the afternoon he began to feel peculiar, and went home to lie down. "With eyes closed," he wrote, "I perceived an uninterrupted stream of fantastic pictures, extraordinary shapes with intense, kaleidoscopic play of colours." Unwittingly, Dr Hofmann had taken the first-ever acid trip – he had synthesized lysergic acid diethylamide, or **LSD**, from the fungus and had absorbed the drug through his fingertips.

After the weekend, he decided to experiment on himself with more scientific precision, and so dosed himself with some more LSD. This time, though, his apprehension at exploring an untested area of pharmacology led to unforeseen paranoias. While cycling home, "a demon had invaded me," he later wrote. Thinking that milk would act as an antidote to the drug, he knocked on his neighbour's door to ask for some, only to discover that "she was no longer Mrs R., but rather a malevolent, insidious witch with a coloured mask." He took to his bed, and woke up next morning exhilarated. "Breakfast tasted delicious and gave me extraordinary pleasure. When I later walked out into the garden, in which the sun shone after a spring rain, everything glistened and sparkled in a fresh light."

Dr Hofmann continued his quiet work into the psychoactive properties of both LSD and other **hallucinogens**, such as magic mushrooms, in Basel while the drug itself – his so-called "problem child" – escaped the confines of the laboratory. A small band of writers were attracted to LSD as a way of unlocking the secrets of the mind: Aldous Huxley's *Doors of Perception* (1954) is probably the most famous creative work to stem from experiments with mescalin, an LSD derivative. Underground tests on volunteers by the British and American military were so dramatic that subsequent top secret reports suggested that if LSD could be deployed in a missile fired at the Soviet Union, it could at a stroke put the entire Red Army out of action. The drug hit the headlines through its role at the core of the 1960s hippy counterculture: the turmoil it appeared to be causing to US society, with teenagers dropping out of college and discovering alternative lifestyles, unnerved the establishment to such an extent that the US Congress passed a bill criminalizing LSD in 1966. Worldwide governments followed suit shortly afterwards. In the late 1980s and 1990s, illegality notwithstanding, a whole new generation of partygoers rediscovered LSD, on a wave which popularized a variant hallucinogen, Ecstasy, and gave rise to "club culture".

Massive controversy persists as to the medical uses of LSD and hallucinogens in general (such as cannabis) – but any meaningful research is hampered by the drug's continuing outlawed status. Dr Hofmann himself, in an interview given in 1993 at the age of 87 to the British *Independent* newspaper, said: "LSD is not addictive, it is not toxic. The danger with LSD is this very deep change in consciousness: it can be beautiful, it can be terrifying. We have integrated alcohol and tobacco, but we've not integrated the hallucinogens. The next step is that it should be put into the hands of the psychiatrists. Fifty years' experience is nothing. For a substance which exhibits such new and extraordinary properties you must have much longer. It should be possible to study this substance properly."

but nonetheless by the thirteenth century, Basel had become a prominent town in the region. In 1225, Bishop Heinrich II of Thun built the first **bridge** across the Rhine – ancestor of today's Mittlere Brücke – which coincided with the opening of a road over the Gotthard Pass into Italy, thus ensuring Basel's continuing growth as a natural focus for trade. Plague ravaged the population in 1349, killing some 14,000, and just seven years later a major earthquake and subsequent fire razed much of the city. Shortly after, the two communities on either side of the Rhine – Grossbasel and Kleinbasel – united as a single city. For almost 20 years (1431–49), the ecumenical **Council of Basel** pushed the city into the European limelight as the church set about reforming itself; Pope Felix V was crowned in Basel during the council's deliberations in 1440, and merchants, philosophers, emperors, princes and bishops flocked to the city, spurring the growth of papermaking, printing, and the development of ideas and trade in the region.

Responding to the impetus of the Renaissance, in 1460 Pope Pius II founded Basel's **university**, Switzerland's oldest and a major centre for humanism which was home to the philosopher **Erasmus of Rotterdam** throughout the 1520s and 1530s. During the sixteenth and seventeenth centuries, Protestant refugees from France, Flanders and Italy expanded Basel's industries but, since the city remained under the thumb of both noble families and the church, most were not accepted as citizens. In 1831, disaffected residents in the rural communities around Basel launched a **rebellion** against the city oligarchs and after a brief civil war managed to secede, forming their own half-canton of Basel-Land (countryside), separate to this day from Basel-Stadt (city).

Throughout the nineteenth century, a massive growth in industry led to the construction of the gigantic **port** facilities on the Rhine at the turn of the twentieth century, which still handle a large proportion of Swiss import/export trade a century later. But Basel is best known these days as a centre of both banking and chemical industry: the companies which started out dyeing silk ribbons woven by Huguenot refugees centuries ago are now the world's largest **pharmaceutical** companies, with their headquarters and laboratory facilities still in Basel. The Bank for International Settlements (BIS) – a kind of supranational controlling body used by governments and national banks – was founded in Basel in 1929.

Arrival and information

Basel has two **train stations** straddling three countries. The huge **Basel SBB** is the main one, most of it in Switzerland, although all trains from France terminate in an area known as **Bâle SNCF** which is in French territory; you'll have to go through passport control to reach the station proper. Trams #1 and #8 from outside connect to Barfüsserplatz. Many fast trains from Germany serve Basel SBB, but plenty – including local trains from Freiburg-im-Breisgau – stop short at Basel Badischer Bahnhof (**Basel Bad.** for short), run by Deutsche Bahn (DB; ☎061/690 11 11) in an enclave of German territory within Kleinbasel. Again, passport control separates the platforms from the ticket hall. Tram #6 from outside runs to Barfüsserplatz.

The **airport** – cringingly dubbed EuroAirport – is actually in French territory 5km north of the city, shared between Basel (Switzerland), Mulhouse (France) and Freiburg (Germany). A special customs-free fenced road links the Swiss terminal with Switzerland proper, along which bus #50 runs every twenty minutes, connecting the airport and Basel SBB station (daily 5am–midnight; Fr.2.80; journey time 15min).

By **car**, the N1 from Bern or Zürich and the N2 from Luzern all feed into Basel from the southeast; the Basel-City exit delivers you directly to parking facilities at the SBB station, but those in Basel-Nord at the Messe and beneath Basel Bad. station are less outrageously priced. The same highway goes on to form the French A35 (direction Mulhouse) and the German A5 (direction Freiburg).

BASEL'S FESTIVALS

Basel's most famous festival, attracting attention from all over Switzerland and Europe, is **carnival**, held over three days from the Monday following Mardi Gras (see p.198). Just as venerable, though, is January's **Vogel Gryff** festival, centred specifically on Kleinbasel (see p.201). In March, the Swiss Trade Fair, or **MUBA**, is held in Basel's Messe conference centre – a giant event serving as a showcase for Swiss accomplishments in trade and industry which is of little general interest in itself but which books the city out. The annual World Watch, Clock and Jewellery Fair does the same thing in April, while in June Basel's **ART International Contemporary Art Fair** (*www.art.ch*) is the largest event of its kind in the world, generally very interesting to attend and inspiring many associated arty happenings throughout the city. The night before the Swiss National Day – July 31 – sees a festival of folk music on the Rhine, with stalls, traditional foods and a huge fireworks display. TEFAF, or the International Art and Antiques Show, is a movable Messe feast in the early autumn. The last Saturday in October marks the start of Basel's two-week **Autumn Fair**, Europe's longest-running traditional fair, held without a break since 1471 and now metamorphosed into sub-carnival festivities centred on funfairs and street jollity.

Information

The two branches of Basel **tourist office** (☎061/268 68 68, *www.baseltourismus.ch*) are at Schifflände 5 (Mon–Fri 8.30am–6pm, Sat 10am–4pm), and inside the main SBB train station (June–Sept Mon–Fri 8.30am–7pm, Sat 8.30am–12.30pm & 1.30–6pm, Sun 10am–2pm; Oct–May Mon–Fri 8.30am–6pm, Sat 8.30am–12.30pm). They both have tons of information, free maps and brochures, as well as more detailed maps and books to buy. If you're planning to be in the city longer than a day or two, pick up the invaluable pocket-sized Tourist's Companion (Fr.5), crammed with all kinds of useful background. Don't, though, ask the tourist office to make a hotel reservation for you, since you'll get stung for Fr.5 at the main office, or Fr.10 at the SBB branch. Instead, you could ask about their good-value **weekend package** deal, which offers one night (either Fri or Sat) in a hotel, plus free museum entry, and discounts on car-rental, a boat trip, a sightseeing tour and more, from Fr.76 per person sharing a double in the lowest grade of hotel, up to Fr.138 for more upmarket accommodation. The **Basler Museumspass** (Fr.32) covers free entry to all the city's 35 museums (including the the Roman remains at Augusta Raurica and the Vitra museum in Weil-am-Rhein, Germany), and is valid on any four days within a one-month period. Also available from the tourist office, the **Basel Card** gives a range of discounts throughout the city, including free entry to all museums, free sightseeing tours, free rides on the river ferries which cross from bank to bank and discounts on river cruises, taxis and car rental and in some shops, restaurants and theatres; the card costs Fr.25/33/45 for 1/2/3 days.

You'll find **listings** and cultural information in the *Basler Zeitung* newspaper, and also in the tourist office's free *Basel Live*, published fortnightly.

City transport and tours

Stay overnight in Basel and you are automatically entitled to a **Mobility Card**, giving free tram and bus travel throughout the city; the card is available from your hotel at check-in. Basel runs on **trams**, with **buses** serving outlying neighbourhoods only. The whole of the city centre, as far north as the German border, is in Zone 10. Tickets for a four-stop journey cost Fr.1.80, for a longer journey within one zone Fr.2.80, across two zones (valid for the Vitra museum in Germany) Fr.3.60. There's little point shelling out Fr.7.80 for a day pass. Eurailers and InterRailers get no reductions on

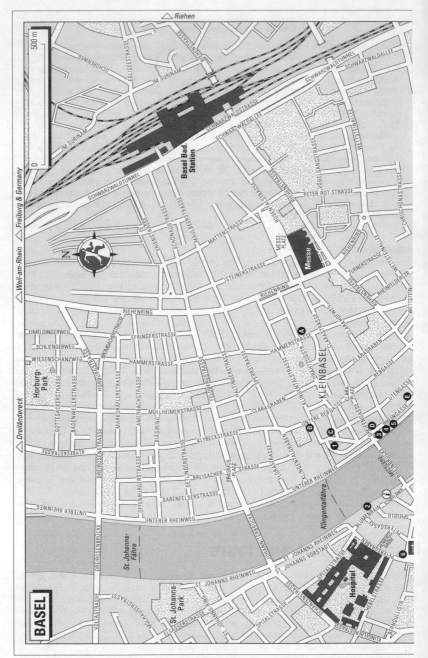

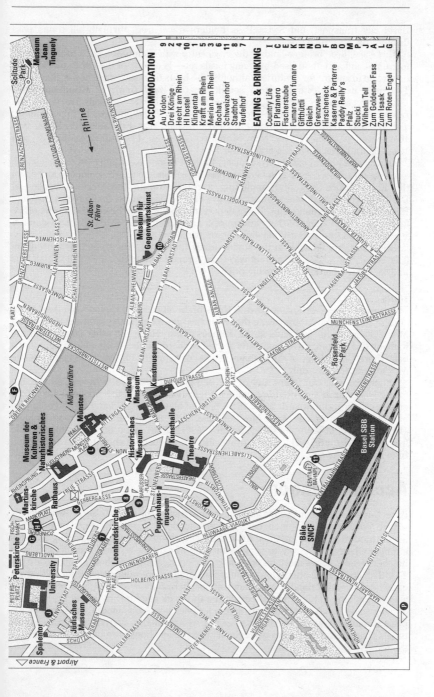

ACCOMMODATION

Au Violon	9
Drei Könige	2
Hecht am Rhein	4
Hl hostel	10
Klingental	1
Krafft am Rhein	5
Merian am Rhein	3
Rochat	6
Schweizerhof	11
Stadthof	8
Teufelhof	7

EATING & DRINKING

Country Life	I
El Platanero	C
Fischerstube	E
Fumare non fumare	K
Gifthüttli	N
Gleich	H
Grenzwert	D
Hirscheneck	F
Kaserne & Parterre	B
Paddy Reilly's	O
Pfalz	M
Stucki	P
Wilhelm Tell	J
Zum Goldenen Fass	L
Zum Isaak	A
Zum Roten Engel	G

Basel city transport, but Swiss Pass holders travel free. Virtually all trams pass through Barfüsserplatz.

There are three bridges linking the city centre with Kleinbasel, but a more fun way to cross – and a method used by many locals too – is on one of the **cable-ferries** that have plied to and fro for centuries (although the boats themselves are newer than that). The most useful, from north to south, are the *Vogel Gryff*, or **Klingentalfähre** (March–Oct Mon–Fri 7am–7pm, Sat & Sun 9am–7pm; Feb & Nov daily 9am–7pm); the *Leu*, or **Münsterfähre** (March–Oct daily 9am–noon & 1–7pm, except Fri morning); and the *Wild Maa*, or **St Alban-Fähre** (April–Sept Mon–Fri 7am–7pm, Sat & Sun 10am–7pm; March, Oct & Nov Mon–Fri 7–8am & 11.30am–6pm, Sat & Sun 10am–6pm). Fares are in the order of Fr.1.

As well as a host of eat-aboard cruises, Basler Personenschiffahrt (☎061/639 95 00, *www.bpg.ch*) runs a couple of scheduled passenger **boats** to nearby points up and down the Rhine (May–Oct only), including a round trip to the German border at Dreiländereck (Fr.13), and a longer journey east to Kaiseraugst (Fr.35 round trip) and Rheinfelden (Fr.44 round trip). Boats depart from Schifflände beside the tourist office in the city centre, next to their information and ticket booth (Mon–Fri 9am–noon & 1–5pm; April–Oct also Sat 11am–6pm & Sun 8am–3pm).

Bike rental is available at the station (daily 7am–9pm). **Taxis**, such as those from 33er (☎061/633 33 33), are a great way to get around if you think a Fr.5.30 flagfall plus Fr.2.65/km is a fair and reasonable price.

Tours

The tourist office co-ordinates **guided tours** of the city and the region – but they're not cheap. "Basel on foot" tours divide the city in two: one meets at the Münster (Cathedral; Mon 2.30pm; Fr.10) and ends at the Rathaus (Town Hall); the other starts from the Rathaus (Fri 2.30pm; Fr.10) and ends at the Leonhardskirche. Both take an hour and a half. There's also a tour of the Rathaus itself (Tues 3pm; Fr.10). All these run from late May to early October only.

Otherwise, you can follow any of five **self-guided** historical wanders, all starting from Marktplatz and marked by small blue information signs: the Erasmus Stroll (red on blue; 30min); Burckhardt Stroll (light blue on blue; 45min); Platter Stroll (yellow on blue; 45min); Paracelsus Stroll (grey on blue; 1hr); or Holbein Stroll (green on blue; 1hr 30min). All of them are described in a leaflet (free) and a book (Fr.26) available from the tourist office. The tourist office also has a brochure showing two self-guided **bike tours** of the city.

Accommodation

Basel thrives on the conference and convention trade – the vast Messe is Switzerland's largest conference/exhibition centre, and attendees to major events often fill all **accommodation** in the city (and most in neighbouring cities too). Reserving ahead is strongly advised. As a way to service the tide of expense-account travellers, Basel's hoteliers tend to focus more on providing comforting extras, such as minibars and big TVs, than on keeping prices down, and are generally more willing than their colleagues elsewhere in Switzerland to surrender atmosphere for the sake of features. They're also very willing to hike their prices during the week and/or throughout the duration of a big trade fair. A few of the city's grander piles break this mould, but if you pick a place at random you're more likely to end up with a generic, overpriced business hotel than a characterful Old Town gem. Small, inexpensive hotels are rarer than sharks in the Rhine.

Camping and hostels

The nearest **campsite** is *Waldhort*, Heideweg 16 in Reinach (☎061/711 64 29, fax 711 48 33; March–Oct), about 10km south of town (tram #11 to Landhof). Basel's pleasant riverside HI **hostel**, St Alban-Kirchrain 10 (☎061/272 05 72, fax 272 08 33; ①; closed Christmas & New Year), is quiet, spotless and well run, but pricey – dorms are Fr.29.

Inexpensive hotels

Although staying in the Old Town has obvious attractions – and there are a couple of **inexpensive hotels** to oblige – Kleinbasel, with its easygoing, everyday atmosphere, is by no means a second best. Atmospheric Rheingasse, one street back from the river, is lined with hotels and bars.

Hecht am Rhein, Rheingasse 8 (☎061/691 22 20, fax 681 07 88). Plain, unfussy "garni" place, with some pricier rooms overlooking the river and both en-suite and shared-bath options. ②–③.

Klingental, Klingental 20 (☎061/681 62 48, 681 97 26). Over in Kleinbasel, newly renovated shared-bath "garni" rooms above a cosy restaurant. ②.

Rochat, Petersgraben 23 (☎061/261 81 40, fax 261 64 92). Centrally placed beside the Peterskirche, with pleasant, if generic, rooms and a modestly cosy atmosphere. ③.

Stadthof, Gerbergasse 84 (☎061/261 87 11, fax 261 25 84). Plain and simple, and bang on the main shopping drag. No en-suite rooms. ②.

Au Violon, Im Lohnhof 4 (☎061/269 87 11, fax 269 87 12, *auviolon@iprolink.ch*, *www.au-violon.com*). Once a convent, then a women's prison, now beautifully renovated to offer comfortable, stylish rooms above a quiet Old Town courtyard. Service is faultless, and they offer discounts for entry to the nearby *Bird's Eye Jazz Club*. ②.

Mid-range and expensive hotels

As you might expect, there are plenty of outrageously **expensive hotels** in Basel, filled most weekday nights with happily pampered businesspeople. If you're searching for something a little more characterful, the following have style to recommend them over the rest.

Drei Könige/Trois Rois, Blumenrain 8 (☎061/261 52 52, fax 261 21 53, *www.drei-koenige-basel.ch*). Venerable Basel institution which began life as a small inn in 1026, and that year hosted Emperor Conrad II, his son Heinrich (later Heinrich III) and Rudolf III of Burgundy – the three kings of the title – who met to thrash out the details of Switzerland's absorption into the German Empire. These days, having received most of the crowned heads of Europe over the past millennium, it's still the haunt of presidents and royalty – who of course occupy the more expensive Rhineside rooms. ⑧–⑨.

Krafft am Rhein, Rheingasse 12 (☎061/690 91 30, fax 690 91 31, *hotel-krafft@datacomm.ch*). Atmospheric old pile on the Kleinbasel waterfront, with ornate and elegant rooms – shared-bath and en-suite – plus friendly service to go with them. Riverside rooms are pricier. ③–④.

Merian am Rhein, Rheingasse 2 (☎061/681 00 00, fax 681 11 01). Affordable quality above the renowned *Café Spitz* on the riverfront, with spacious rooms furnished in a pleasant, non-traditional style. ④.

Schweizerhof, Centralbahnplatz 1 (☎061/271 28 33, fax 271 29 19). Faded grandeur near the SBB station, once the absolute bee's knees but these days merely calm, cosy, tasteful, welcoming and expertly run. ④–⑤.

Teufelhof, Leonhardsgraben 47 (☎061/261 10 10, fax 261 10 04). The small "Kunsthotel" section has eight rooms, each of them a work of art, redecorated every two years by a different local artist and always uniquely comfortable. The "Galeriehotel" bit, with 25 rooms, is less lavishly done up, and so less expensive, but still reworked annually by a local artist. A breath of fresh air compared with Basel's standard trade-fair hotels, not least because – unless requested otherwise – rooms are TV-free. ⑤–⑥.

The City

The **Rhine** describes an elegant right-angled curve through the centre of Basel, flowing from east to north and dividing the city in two. On the south/west bank is **Grossbasel** (Greater Basel), focused on the historic Old Town. Glitzy shopping streets connect **Barfüsserplatz** and **Marktplatz**, the two main Old Town squares, while medieval charm is retained in the steep lanes leading off to either side, where you'll find peaceful leafy courtyards surrounded by sixteenth-century townhouses, a host of medieval churches, and the majestic steepled **Münster** dominating the skyline from its

CARNIVAL

Basel is famous around Switzerland and Europe for its ancient masked **carnival**, or *Fasnacht*, a three-day affair starting on the Monday after Mardi Gras. The earliest documented record of carnival is from 1376, although celebrations undoubtedly date back to well before that (earlier city records were destroyed in a fire in 1356): it's said that *Fasnacht*, originally spelled *Fastnacht*, is related to an old word *faseln*, meaning fruitfulness. In the fourteenth century, carnival took the form of knightly tournaments held on Münsterplatz, events which may have had an origin in pagan ancestor worship since noble families had been buried in and around the Cathedral for generations. Through the Middle Ages, theologians railed against both excessive drinking at carnival time and the use of devilish masks and disguises – it's no coincidence that the iconoclasm which marked the beginning of Basel's Reformation broke out on Mardi Gras, 1529. For some unexplained reason, over time celebrations were shifted one week later to after the beginning of Lent (Basel still celebrated carnival despite its embrace of Protestantism after the Reformation), and were transformed into a series of processions organized by the city's guilds and associations. Drum-and-pipe bands accompanied the display of weaponry, dancing and fancy-dress revelry. Greater organization throughout the nineteenth and early twentieth century resulted in the carnival of today, where some 12,000 people take part under the auspices of several hundred *Cliques*, groups or musical bands, all of which must apply in advance to the Fasnachts-Comité for permission to march. It's a feature of Basel's carnival that, unless you're part of a performing *Clique*, you have to stay as an observer – unlike, for instance, in Luzern, where carnival is an all-in street-party welcoming participation from anyone and everyone.

On the Sunday night after Mardi Gras, Basel's carnival-goers kick off their celebrations at the nearby town of Liestal's spectacular bonfire parade, which lasts until after midnight (see p.207). Everyone decamps back to Basel in preparation for the **Morgestraich**, a magical and unmissable parade of huge illuminated lanterns through the city centre which begins in invariably freezing darkness at 4am on the Monday morning; the ornately decorated lanterns are left on display in Münsterplatz from Monday evening through to Wednesday morning. From lunch time, the various masked *Cliques* parade through the city in a **Cortège**, with much music, dancing and jollity, followed in the evening by masked bands and small groups with fifes and drums roving through the Old Town. Baslers take their costumes seriously (half-masks and face paint are taboo), and many people spend weeks in advance making huge, cartoonish papier-mâché heads and sewing lavish jester-like costumes. It's a tradition for locals to recite **Schnitzelbängg**, satirical verses directed at local bigwigs, in the city's taverns and restaurants during the Monday and Wednesday evenings. Tuesday night sees **Guggemusige** concerts of comical oompah, played on old and dented brass instruments by bands gathered in Barfüsser-, Clara- and Marktplatz, and musical groups and masked *Cliques* continue to prowl through the Old Town during Wednesday afternoon until nightfall – whereupon everybody turns in for some restorative sleep. Throughout the celebrations, you'll come across places selling *Fasnachtsküchli*, a light, thin round cake covered in icing sugar, and *Fastenwähe*, a kind of caraway-seed pretzel.

lofty Rhineside terrace. The Old Town and surrounding districts comprise the main business, shopping and nightlife areas of the city. The university, off Petersgraben, overlooks the Old Town from the west, while the main Swiss and French train stations are about a kilometre south. On the north/east bank of the Rhine is down-to-earth **Kleinbasel** (Lesser Basel), more residential and less weightily historical than its neighbour, with some laidback nightlife and the German train station near the giant Messe conference centre some 500m east of Kleinbasel's central Claraplatz.

The **international border** with France is on the west bank of the Rhine, about 2km north of the city centre; that with Germany is on the east bank, about 3km north.

Barfüsserplatz and the Historisches Museum

The focus of the Old Town is hectic **Barfüsserplatz**, crisscrossed by trams and overlooked by the soaring pointed-arch windows of the **Barfüsserkirche**. This elegant white church, built by and named after the bare-footed Franciscans, dates from the fourteenth century, was deconsecrated in the eighteenth, and is now home to the impressive **Historisches Museum** (Mon & Wed–Sun 10am–5pm; Fr.5, free on first Sun of month), devoted to documenting Basel's cultural pre-eminence during the Middle Ages. Once you've absorbed the stunning detail of the monumental **choir stall** (1598) facing into the church, the highlight of the ground floor is the collection of sumptuous fifteenth-century **tapestries** (press the button to raise the protective blind shielding each one) – these vivid, wall-sized pieces were woven to decorate private houses and churches, specifically in Basel and Strasbourg, and are exceptionally rare, both for their artistic quality and their excellent condition. Their imagery frequently concentrates on woodsmen, fabulous animals and courtly lovers – only three of the sixteen pieces show religious imagery – and one of the best is no. 235 (from 1490), the allegorical *Garden of Love*, showing two lovers playing cards inside a summer pavilion: the man has just slapped down a card with the words, "That last play of yours was a good one," while the woman nods in anticipatory triumph: "And it's won me the game!" Downstairs you'll find an excellent detailed survey of Basel's history, including a board locating ancient buildings, maps and globes galore, the original 1640 **Lällekeenig** (see p.200), and bedchambers and elaborate wood-panelled rooms from the seventeenth century. Don't miss the touching tapestry no. 237, a cushion cover from Strasbourg (1510) showing a revealingly dressed woman of the forest who's been abandoned by a lover and now nurses a unicorn on her lap with the words "I've given the world my time, now I must live here in misery." Head to the back, and you'll come across a side room displaying the **treasure of Basel cathedral**, including two stunning silver-and-copper busts dating from 1270–1325, of St Pantalus (no. 251) and, with an even, almond-eyed gaze, a Buddhic St Ursula (no. 253). On a new upstairs level is a series of paintings showing the **Dance of Death**. The sequence originally formed part of a sixty-metre-long mural, which covered the inside of the cemetery wall of Basel's Dominican convent, until its demolition in 1805. The mural depicts, in a graphic reminder of human mortality, an array of people of all different ages and professions on a macabre procession, which leads, eventually, to the cemetery's charnel house.

West of Barfüsserplatz, lanes wind up to the beautiful **Leonhardskirche**, a Gothic construction built after the great 1356 earthquake with attractive portholed windows and an elaborate cat's cradle of vaulting within. The gallery is accessible, but only up the tightest, narrowest spiral staircase imaginable.

Marktplatz and around

Shop-lined Gerbergasse and Freiestrasse, as well as a dense network of narrow, sloping medieval alleys – such as Schneidergasse (Tailor Street), Sattelgasse (Saddle

Street) and Imbergässlein (Ginger Alley) – run north from Barfüsserplatz to **Marktplatz**, the Old Town's other main square and still crowded every morning with fruit-and-veg stalls. Lighting up the broad rectangular space with a splash of eye-catching colour is the elaborate scarlet facade of the **Rathaus** (Town Hall), the central arcaded section sixteenth century, the tower and side annexe both late nineteenth century. Feel free to wander into the frescoed interior courtyard – or take one of the tourist office's guided tours (Tues 3pm; Fr.10) of the interior. At the northern end of the square is the small Fischmarkt, with its central fountain, just beyond which is the tourist office at the southern end of the **Mittlere Brücke**, a modern construction at the site of what was for centuries the only bridge over the Rhine between the Bodensee and the North Sea.

On the facade of *Churrasco* restaurant, looking along the bridge, you'll spot an odd little bust of a bearded man: this is the **Lällekeenig**, or Tongue King. The original Lällekeenig adorned the gate of the bridge from the mid-seventeenth century, greeting all arrivals to the city until the gate's demolition in 1839, and had a clockwork motor so that he rolled his eyes and stuck out his tongue in time with the ticking. He was probably made to demonstrate what Grossbaslers thought of their down-at-heel Kleinbasel neighbours, but these days the city is united, the clockwork original is in the Historisches Museum, and the Lällekeenig still staring along the bridge is a static copy.

From Marktplatz and Fischmarkt, quiet old lanes climb steeply west towards the former city walls; up here are the Gothic **Peterskirche** (Tues–Sun 10am–5pm) on Petersgraben, the plain exterior of which harbours late-medieval frescoes, and more or less opposite, Basel's **university** campus. Among many famous names connected with the university, Nietzsche taught classical philosophy here from 1869 to 1879. The narrow Spalenvorstadt leads west from here to the **Spalentor**, most elaborate of the surviving city gates, with massive wooden doors and a huge portcullis. Nietzsche lived round the corner, at Schützengraben 47. The small **Jüdisches Museum der Schweiz**, Kornhausgasse 8 (Jewish Museum; Mon & Wed 2–5pm, Sun 11am–5pm; free; *www.igb.ch*) displays gravestone fragments with Hebrew inscriptions which date back to 1222 as well as plenty of interesting historical items from religious and everyday Jewish life. Their short video (in English) on the history of the Jews in Basel is excellent.

South and east of Barfüsserplatz

From Barfüsserplatz, Steinenberg climbs east. On the corner is the **Puppenhausmuseum** (Doll's House Museum; daily 11am–5pm, Thurs until 8pm; Fr.7; *www.puppenhausmuseum.ch*), with rather fun displays and audioguides telling the story of the teddy – including plenty of venerable old bears – as well as glass-case displays of some gigantic doll's-houses. Further up, past the sputtering Tinguely fountain in the grounds of the theatre, is the **Kunsthalle** (Tues–Sun 11am–5pm, Wed until 8.30pm; Fr.9), its big white rooms staging a continual flow of cutting-edge contemporary art shows.

At the top of the hill, St Alban-Graben heads northeast to the river. The venerable **Antikenmuseum** is at no. 5 (Tues–Sun 10am–5pm; Fr.5, free on first Sun of month), with detailed English notes available at the desk. Chronological displays begin on the top floor and work downwards, with superb Greek and Etruscan pottery, decorated in beautiful detail, standing out on every floor. The upper-floor vestibule of House B has a set of fourth-century BC floor-standing funerary vases, from Apulia in southern Italy, one of which is painted with an entertaining scene of three men stealing honey and being chased by a swarm of bees. The basement of the museum holds temporary exhibitions, often of Egyptian or Middle Eastern antiquities.

The Kunstmuseum and around

Basel's world-famous **Kunstmuseum** is at St Alban-Graben 16 (Tues–Sun 10am–5pm; Fr.7, also gives entry to Museum für Gegenwartskunst; free on first Sun of month; *www.kunstmuseumbasel.ch*). It's a rather stern Neoclassical building – all marble floors, high ceilings and grand staircases – which tends to do its absorbing collection down a bit, but don't let yourself be put off. Thorough renovations until 2001 mean that some areas may be closed for work. There's a dazzling array of **twentieth-century art**, including Dali's nightmarish *Perspectives*, roomfuls of paintings by Arp, Klee, Léger, Munch, Braque and the Impressionists, a fantastically attenuated cat by Giacometti, and fluid sculptures in wood by Kirchner and Scherer. Two of the Picassos – *Arlequin assis* and *Les deux frères* – were purchased in 1967 using Fr.6 million that had been voted for that purpose by the Basel electorate plus another Fr.2.4 million in donations: Picasso himself was so impressed by this popular enthusiasm that he personally donated four more works. However, the gallery's modern art, and its large collection of nineteenth-century German, French and Swiss painting, is in fact overshadowed by its vast and absorbing **medieval** collection. Dozens of rooms are devoted to works by the prolific Holbein family, including the extraordinary two-metre long *Body of the Dead Christ in the Tomb* (1521), a painting which obsessed Dostoievsky when he visited Basel on August 23, 1867. He climbed on a chair to get a better view of it, and then started to shout "Holbein was a great painter and a poet!" – his wife, who thought he was about to have a fit, had to usher him from the room. The painting resurfaces in Dostoievsky's novel *The Idiot*, when a character's recollections of it lead him to question the existence of God.

A five-minute walk away is the **Museum für Gegenwartskunst**, St Alban-Rheinweg 60 (Contemporary Art; Tues–Sun 11am–5pm; joint admission with Kunstmuseum), its installations by Frank Stella, Joseph Beuys and others sharing space with recent German painting.

Museum Jean Tinguely

On the north bank, in Solitude Park under the Wettsteinbrücke, is the glorious **Museum Jean Tinguely** (Wed–Sun 11am–7pm; Fr.7; *www.tinguely.ch*), beautifully designed by the celebrated Swiss architect Mario Botta and well worth a visit. Tinguely, who was born in Fribourg in 1925 and died in Bern in 1991, is perhaps Switzerland's

---

VOGEL GRYFF

Dating back to the thirteenth century or so, Kleinbasel's **Vogel Gryff** festival incorporates pagan rituals and customs in the guise of fêting the head of one of the three guild associations of Kleinbasel. It takes place on January 13, 20 or 27, depending on which association holds the baton that year. At 11am, a raft carries the **Wild Maa** (a hairy figure symbolizing fertility) down the Rhine to the Mittlere Brücke; he holds an uprooted pine sapling and dances – with his back always turned to Grossbasel – to an ancient drum march. The **Leu** (lion) and **Vogel Gryff** (griffon) meet him on the bank to the accompaniment of booming cannon, and at noon the three of them stand at the midpoint of the Mittlere Brücke and dance a traditional, highly ritualized dance to the sound of a drum, every precise step documented from the origins of the festival in the Middle Ages. This is as close as the party gets to Grossbasel, since everyone then proceeds back to Kleinbasel for the **Gryffemähli**, a luncheon for the members of the three guilds (where the symbolic dance is repeated), and a procession through the streets accompanied by four jingling jesters who collect money for Kleinbasel's poor. During the evening, the party enters full swing, with much drinking and merrymaking, while the three figures continue to dance their odd and mysterious dance in the older Kleinbasel restaurants.

best-loved artist, a maverick postmodernist who broadened the confines of static sculpture to incorporate mechanical motion. Living for years on a farm in the Swiss countryside with his long-time partner and fellow artist Niki de St-Phalle, Tinguely used scrap metal, plastic and bits of everyday junk to create room-sized Monty-Pythonesque machines that – with the touch of a foot-button – judder into life, squeaking, clanking and scraping in entertaining parody of the slickness of our modern performance-driven world. Most are imbued with an irreverent sense of humour (*Klamauk*, or Din, is a moving tractor complete with banging bells and cymbals, smoke, smells and fireworks), but some, such as *Mengele Dance of Death*, are darkly apocalyptic. Elsewhere in the city, a Tinguely fountain spits and burbles outside the Kunsthalle.

The Münster

Sixteenth-century Rittergasse leads from the Kunstmuseum to Basel's cathedral, the impressive **Münster**, built of red sandstone with a patterned roof in the thirteenth century and rebuilt following an earthquake in 1356. The tower of St George, on the left of the main frontage, has some white stonework dating from the original church (consecrated in 1019), as well as a thirteenth-century statue of the saint impaling a dragon. Stone carving from 1280 above the main portal shows the cathedral's founder, Emperor Heinrich II, holding a model of the church, with his wife Kunigunde to the left. To the right is a Foolish Virgin, with her Satanic seducer.

Inside (Easter–Oct Mon–Fri 10am–5pm, Sat 10am–4pm, Sun 1–5pm; Oct–Easter Mon–Sat 11am–4pm, Sun 2–4pm), in the north aisle, is the tomb of the Renaissance humanist Erasmus. Close by is the **St Vincent panel**, a Romanesque relief from around 1100 telling the story of the martyr who was killed in 312 AD: on the top left, Vincent speaks up for his bishop and is flogged for it; to the right he is tortured and led into a furnace; below, angels carry his soul to heaven while ravens protect his body before it is dumped at sea, retrieved and buried in a proper tomb. The lacy **pulpit** was carved – incredibly – from a single block of stone in 1486. On the north side of the choir, which has some intricate capitals, is the **tomb of Queen Anna**, wife of Rudolf of Habsburg, who chose to be buried in Basel, alongside her three-year-old son Karl, in an attempt to make up for her husband's cruelty whilst ruling the town during the 1270s. In the **crypt** you'll find ninth-century remains of an earlier cathedral along with some late-Romanesque frescoes.

One of the highlights of Basel is a wander through the memorably atmospheric **cloisters** adjoining the cathedral to the south, filled to bursting point with timeworn tombs and memorial stones. You emerge onto the **Pfalz**, an open, tree-lined terraced bastion behind the cathedral choir which overlooks the Rhine and gives views as far as the Black Forest. Carved elephants and grotesque creatures support the arches of the choir, and round the corner, on the north side of the church, is the spectacular **St Gallus Doorway**, a rich piece of Romanesque carving, with Christ at top centre, Wise and Foolish Virgins below him, and John the Baptist on the extreme left below a kneeling angel sounding a trumpet to wake the dead. Above is a round window depicting the wheel of fortune.

Tranquil alleys run northwest from Münsterplatz – amongst them Augustinergasse, with, at no. 2, the **Museum der Kulturen** (Museum of Civilizations; Tues–Sun 10am–5pm; Fr.6; *www.mkb.ch*) housing an overwhelmingly massive anthropological collection, and, separately in the same building, the equally daunting **Naturhistorisches Museum** (same times and price). The narrow Rheinsprung lane leads on to the **St Martinskirche** with, beside it, the little Elftausendjungfern-Gasse, or Alley of the Eleven Thousand Virgins; its curious name commemorates the martyrdom in Cologne of St Ursula, who refused to marry a pagan prince, and her legendary company of female supporters. The tiny lane – otherwise unremarkable – feeds down to the Mittlere Brücke.

Out of the centre

Perhaps your one single reason for coming to Basel at all, and certainly the city's sole unmissable attraction, is the astonishing gallery run by **Fondation Beyeler** at Baselstrasse 101 in the northeastern suburb of Riehen (daily 10am–6pm, Wed until 8pm; Fr.8; tram #6 to Riehen Dorf; *www.beyeler.com*). A masterfully soothing building, sympathetically designed by Renzo Piano, architect of Paris's Pompidou Centre, houses a small but exceptionally high-quality art collection featuring some of the best works by some of the twentieth century's best artists – Picasso, Giacometti, Warhol, Rodin, Klee, Kandinsky, Bacon, Miró and more. Both Matisse's paper cutouts (*Nu bleu* and others) and Mondrian's geometric abstractions – familiar from innumerable posters and T-shirts – still have the power to startle as full-size originals. Mark Tobey's crazed *White Journey* and *Oncoming White* are hypnotic. For some gentle relief, sink into a huge white sofa opposite a giant Monet, where piped Debussy (daily 1pm) fuels dreamy contemplation of the waterlilies in front of you and, through a floor-to-ceiling window, the watery gardens outside. Continue your reverie in front of a massive Rothko canvas with minimalist music by the American composer Morton Feldman (daily 2.15pm).

Across the border in Germany, 10km north of Basel, is the small town of **WEIL-AM-RHEIN**, unremarkable but for being the location of Vitra, a famous design company which collaborates with top international designers to produce office and home furniture, and whose premises – on an out-of-town green-field site – are the work of some of the world's leading contemporary architects. If you're halfway interested in design, the **Vitra Museum** is well worth a visit (Charles Eames Strasse 2, Weil-am-Rhein; Tues–Sun 11am–6pm; DM10, or a Fr.10 banknote only; *www.design-museum.de*). Bus #55 from the forecourt of Basel Bad. station takes twenty minutes to drop you outside the museum (passport needed; a two-zone Basel bus ticket is valid, but Swiss Pass and other Swiss transport tickets are not). The building itself is engaging enough to start with, a teetering, almost Cubist concoction by American architect Frank O. Gehry, while inside you'll find a changing series of exhibitions on various themes of design, concentrating on furniture: it's interesting to be able to see the originals of chairs which are now ubiquitous, such as the fold-up moulded plastic chair (Giancarlo Pirette, 1968), as well as classic designs by Frank Lloyd Wright, Charles and Ray Eames, Philippe Starck and others. It's also possible to join a two-hour guided tour of architecture on the Vitra site (Tues–Sun 2pm; DM13; in German only), which includes a factory designed by Nicholas Grimshaw and the supremely elegant, award-winning fire station by Zaha Hadid.

THREE-IN-ONE

One of Basel's curiosities is its location at the meeting point of France, Germany and Switzerland, and there are few places in the world where you can stand at the exact point where three countries meet. If you take tram #8 to its terminus amongst the massive warehouses and shipping cranes at Kleinhüningen, cross to the north bank of the River Wiese, head left 200m to the Rhine, then right (north) along a spit of land beside more warehouses and train sidings for 300m, you'll come to **Dreiländereck** (Three Countries' Corner), marked by a futuristic rounded steel-and-glass building. This is the *Restaurant Dreiländereck* (☎061/639 95 40), a pricey and rather soulless place for eating, but not bad for a riverside coffee and bun. Just beyond the restaurant, on the very nose of the spit of land is a tall, slender sculpture pointing the way west across the Rhine (the other bank is France), north to the German customs shed 50m away, and south into Switzerland. Unfortunately, as you might have predicted, everything looks more or less the same on all shores. Boats depart from beside the restaurant to take you back to Basel Schifflände.

Eating and drinking

Drawing influences from the neighbouring cuisines of France and Germany into its native Swiss culinary tradition, Basel manages deftly to sit on the fence as far as **eating and drinking** go. Beer and sausages is the snack of choice, but it's equally possible to find venues to savour classic French cuisine and, if the city could be said to have a local speciality, it's salmon (originally plucked from the Rhine but these days more likely to be imported) marinaded in the fruity local white wine and topped with fried onions.

Cafés and café-bars

There are plenty of **cafés** and *Bierstuben* around Marktplatz and Barfüsserplatz, with nearby Steinenvorstadt also core snacking territory. Perfect accompaniment to a Basel teatime is the local speciality *Leckerli* – a melt-in-the-mouth ginger biscuit made with honey, spices, almonds and candied orange- and lemon-peel: buy over-the-counter at the Läckerli-huus patisserie at Gerbergasse 57 or in *Café Spitz* (see "Restaurants", below).

Grossbasel

Fumare non fumare, Gerbergasse 38. Cool, high-ceilinged espresso bar on a people-watching junction, also with its own beer – one side is smoking, one non-smoking (hence the name). Open late.

Kunsthalle, Steinenberg 7. Gallery with a leafy terrace-café favoured by Basel's sizeable crowd of arty literati.

Paddy Reilly's, Steinentorstrasse 45. Standard Irish pub, Guinness and all, also serving up fish and chips and shepherd's pie for around Fr.16.

Pfalz, Münsterberg 11. Tiny, bright nook, with excellent fresh juices, sandwiches, quiches and a salad buffet. Closed Sat & Sun.

Zum Isaak, Münsterplatz 16. A tranquil, much-loved tea-drinkers' café and cellar-theatre that knows its darjeeling from its lapsang-souchong, and also offers lovingly prepared snacks and full meals. Also with a courtyard terrace. Closed Mon.

Zum Roten Engel, Andreasplatz. Cosy den on a secluded Old Town courtyard, with trestle tables outside and amiable, alternatively minded regulars scoffing veggie snacks, fresh juices and full meals (Fr.14).

Kleinbasel

El Platanero, Webergasse 21. Incongruously exuberant little corner deli-café, with two or three tables for *chorizo picante con arroz* and fried bananas, with red-hot salsa bottled on the tables and playing on the stereo.

Fischerstube, Rheingasse 45. Excellent backstreet beerhall, full of atmosphere, that brews its own beers as a snub to the big-name breweries and so attracts dedicated, single-minded drinkers. Salted pretzels hanging from wooden stands on every table, a dark, smoky interior, rich, powerful beer plus a uniquely hearty clientele make for a memorably convivial evening.

Grenzwert, Rheingasse 3. Cool, jazzy, spotlit little bar, attracting black-clad Kleinbaslers by the score.

Hirscheneck, Lindenberg 23. Graffitied budget café-bar-restaurant, co-op owned and popular with a rough-edged crowd, with loud music and simple food in generous portions (Fr.15).

Kaserne, Klybeckstrasse 1. An alternative-style hangout, with shady outdoor trestle tables and benches, offering veggie *menus* from Fr.16 and a very popular weekend brunch buffet that exemplifies the difference between laid-back Kleinbaslers and their more traditional neighbours across the river. The evening bar section (closed Mon) retains much the same atmosphere, on Tuesdays becoming Basel's premier gay and lesbian meeting place.

Parterre, Klybeckstrasse 1. A friendly, atmospheric café-bar next to *Kaserne* with Tom Waits on the stereo and light bulbs hanging on strings. Excellent food from Fr.10. Closed Sun.

Zum Goldenen Fass, Hammerstrasse 108. Small but very popular bar attached to a restaurant (see below), regularly packed.

Restaurants

The host of international visitors to Basel with access to high-end expense accounts means that eating costs can be inflated, but it's also not hard to uncover cosy local cafés for home-cooked fare in all corners of the city centre. For **self-service** food, there's a restaurant in the *Manora* department store on Greifengasse; otherwise *Mr Wong*, Steinenvorstadt 3, piles your dish high with fresh-cooked Asian fare for Fr.12. *Café Damas*, beside the Puppenhausmuseum off Barfüsserplatz, offers Arabic takeaways such as falafel and kebabs, as well as sit-down dishes like *magloubah* (chicken with rice); while *Pinar*, Herbergsgasse 1, is a plain Turkish neighbourhood diner, with a big choice of inexpensive *pide* (Turkish pizza).

Café Spitz, Rheingasse 2 (✆061/681 00 00). Historic building in the Kleinbasel district, with a riverside terrace and the best fish in Basel, if not Switzerland. Fr.30 upwards.

Country Life, Sattelgasse 3. Small veggie and wholefood diner off Marktplatz, with *menus* around Fr.17–20.

Gifthüttli, Schneidergasse 11 (✆061/261 16 56). The best place for traditional local cooking (even the menu is in Basel dialect), whether in the standard *Stube* downstairs or the more formal restaurant upstairs. They specialize in *cordon bleus* – slabs of cheese-slathered meat – with thirteen choices (around Fr.33), as well as plenty of other Swiss belt-bulgers.

Gleich, Steinenvorstadt 23. Upscale, very genteel vegetarian restaurant, with nothing but the tinkling of cutlery to disturb the low hum of discreet chat. Closed Sat & Sun.

Stucki, Bruderholzallee 42 (✆061/361 82 22). One of Switzerland's best restaurants, awarded two Michelin stars for its classic style and inventive touches. Expect *menus* starting from Fr.50 – if you can book far enough ahead to find a place. Closed Sun & Mon.

Au Violon, Im Lohnhof 4 (✆061/269 87 11). Very pleasant gourmet brasserie in a renovated old building near the Leonhardskirche, offering seasonal specialities prepared with care. *Menus* from Fr.20. Closed Sun & Mon.

Wilhelm Tell, Spalenvorstadt 38. Cosy, quiet den for solid Swiss fare, *rösti*, sausages and all, from Fr.15. Closed Sun.

Zum Goldenen Fass, Hammerstrasse 108 (✆061/693 11 11). Quality formal restaurant with an informal air in a Kleinbasel residential neighbourhood. Excellent, top-quality organic food, lightly prepared (plus veggie options), with lunchtime *menus* around Fr.20, evening ones double that.

Nightlife and entertainment

You wouldn't really come to Basel for the **nightlife**, and even the locals tend quite often to prefer skipping across the border to nearby towns in Germany or France to let their hair down. Even the presence of university students doesn't lighten the tone tremendously, and it's a common moan of students stuck in Basel for the duration that there's not much to do. Get full information on gigs and dance-nights from *Downtown*, a free leaflet put out monthly by the Basler Kantonalbank, available from the tourist office and at *www.bkb.ch* online.

As far as more refined entertainments go, the Basel Symphony and Basel Chamber **orchestras** both perform at the central Stadtcasino (✆061/272 66 57), along with a host of guest performers. The city's Musik-Akademie (Leonhardsgraben 4) has a rock-solid reputation, and also often presents concerts and recitals from students and visiting soloists. Basel's main draw is its burgeoning **theatre** scene (universally in German), with the Stadttheater (Theaterstrasse 7) and the Komödie (Steinenvorstadt 63) leading the field; book for both on ✆061/295 11 33. Of the dozens of smaller theatres, Theater Fauteuil (Spalenberg 12; ✆061/261 26 10) stands out for the quality of its productions, while the Baseldytschi Bihni (Im Lohnhof; ✆061/261 33 12) offers a truly incomprehensible evening of drama in the local Baseldytsch dialect. Steinenvorstadt is lined with first-run **cinemas**.

Clubs and live music

Atlantis, Klosterberg 13 (*www.atlan-tis.ch*). Universally known as "Tis", and the most popular venue in Basel, hosting live bands and dance nights, generally with a Fr.15 entrance.

Babalabar, Gerbergasse 4. City-centre club, with plenty of variation in dance styles (nightly), and famed all-nighters (Sat). Fr.10–15.

Bird's Eye, Kohlenberg 20 (*www.jsb.ch*). Live jazz every weekend (Thurs–Sun), jazz DJ-ing the rest of the week – very popular, very lively. Around Fr.15.

Hirscheneck, Lindenberg 23. Grungy hardcore, metal and ska acts in this café-bar venue, generally on weekends.

Kaserne, Klybeckstrasse 1b. Focus of Kleinbasel nightlife, a café-bar with adjacent venue for live bands, DJs, readings and happenings. Fr.10–15.

Parterre, Klybeckstrasse 1b (*www.eye.ch/schlappe*). Folky, jazz-trio music nights, often midweek.

Listings

Books Bider & Tanner, Aeschenvorstadt 2, have a large and diverse English-language section.

Car rental Avis, Hilton Hotel (☎061/206 95 45 or airport 325 28 40); Budget, airport only (☎061/325 47 35); Europcar, Hauptstrasse 35, Binningen (☎061/422 10 70 or airport 325 29 03); Hertz, Nauenstrasse 33 (☎061/205 92 22 or airport 325 27 80).

Changing money In the SBB train station (daily 6am–9pm).

Disabled access Taxi 22er (☎061/271 22 22) can take wheelchairs. Pro Infirmis (Birsigstrasse 45, CH-4054 Basel; ☎061/281 80 08) publishes a *Stadtplan für Rollstuhlfahrer/innen* (City Map for Wheelchair Users; also available from the tourist office), with information on wheelchair-accessible facilities, restaurants, museums and hotels.

Email and Internet *Domino* video arcade, Steinenvorstadt 52 (Mon–Thurs 9am–midnight, Fri & Sat 9am–1am, Sun 1pm–midnight; Fr.10/hr before 6pm, Fr.12/hr after 6pm).

Flights For all domestic and international flight enquiries from Basel-Mulhouse airport, call ☎061/325 31 11. MFG, at Basel airport (☎061/921 36 75) offers pricey sightseeing flights over the Jura, the Black Forest, Seeland, the Rhine or the Alps. Airport Helicopter (☎061/325 48 88) has a range of chopper flights, including one over the city for Fr.150 per person.

Gay and lesbian life You'll generally find livelier scenes in nearby Freiburg and Mulhouse, but there are still a few places to check out. *Kaserne*, Klybeckstrasse 1, is the place to start, with its popular Tuesday evening gathering named *Zisch*. Rebgasse, near Claraplatz, has *Dupf* at no. 43, and *Elle et Lui* at no. 39 – both bars open nightly. HABS, Homosexuelle Arbeitsgruppen Basel, runs a helpline (Wed 8–10pm & Fri 3–9pm; ☎061/692 66 55). Libs is a local lesbian organization (☎061/681 33 45).

Lost property The city office is ☎061/267 70 34; the SBB office is ☎0512/292 467; the Deutsche Bahn office is ☎061/690 12 51.

Markets Basel's main fruit and veg market is in Marktplatz (Mon–Sat mornings); otherwise, check out the flea markets in Barfüsserplatz (2nd & 4th Wed in month) and Petersplatz near the university (Sat).

Medical facilities 24-hour emergency room at Kantonsspital Basel Universitätsklinik, Hebelstrasse 30 (☎061/265 25 25). If you need a doctor, call ☎061/261 15 15.

Post Most central office (CH-4001) is on Rüdengasse. Near the station is another large office (CH-4002).

Travel agents Discount flight agents SSR Reisen are at Steinenberg 19 (Mon–Fri 10am–6pm, Sat 10am–2pm; ☎061/284 90 60).

Augusta Raurica

In its heyday, **AUGUSTA RAURICA** – a Roman Rhineside provincial capital about 20km east of Basel near the modern village of **Kaiseraugst** – was home to some twenty thousand people. These days it comprises the largest set of Roman ruins in Switzerland, and is an easy day trip from Basel.

Augusta was founded at the same time as Basel, 44 BC, in the territory of the Gallic Raurici tribe. During the first and second centuries AD it was a prosperous city, but was virtually destroyed by an invasion of the Alemanni tribes around 260 AD. Many of its stones were pilfered during the Middle Ages, but exploration of the site and excavations have been continuous for more than a century, and have uncovered the best-preserved classical theatre north of the Alps, temples, a forum, taverns, many public buildings and more. Focus of the site, well signposted from all over the village, is the **Römermuseum** (Roman Museum; Glebenacherstrasse 17; Mon 1–5pm, Tues–Sun 10am–5pm; Nov–Feb closed noon–1.30pm; Fr.5; *www.augusta-raurica.ch*). If you can fight your way through the stream of school parties, you'll find a well-laid out display of finds from the site, including a full reconstruction of a Roman house. The ticket desk can give you a leaflet showing a map of the whole site and recommended walks through the ruins (which are open and free), spreading out across a wide area all around the museum and down to the river. The impressive 10,000-seat **theatre** is directly opposite the museum, still under excavation and renovation, with a small sculpture garden to one side. Schönbuhl Hill in front of the theatre is topped by a **temple**. Some 200m south of the theatre is a large **amphitheatre**, with to the east of the theatre the **forum** and an exhibition of mosaics in the basement of the **curia** (Town Hall). Further east are taverns, potteries and houses in varying states of crumble. Down on the riverbank beside the boat jetty, 500m north, is an enclosed **fortress**, housing an extensive baths complex. Excellent signboards and displays all over the site ensure that you're never short of information.

There are two or three slow **boats** a day (May–Oct only) from Basel to Rheinfelden, stopping at the jetty at Kaiseraugst, about fifteen minutes' walk below the Roman Museum. Otherwise, regular local **trains** take about ten minutes to Kaiseraugst, or **bus** #70 from Basel's Aeschenplatz goes every twenty minutes to Augst village, some ten minutes' walk from the museum.

LIESTAL'S BURNING

Some 17km south of Basel, and 6km south of Augst, **LIESTAL** – capital of the half-canton Basel-Land – is a small, industrial town with a pretty, cobbled Old Town centred on Rathausgasse. It's along this street that Liestal's extraordinary and truly spectacular **carnival** celebrations take place. On the Sunday night after Mardi Gras, thousands turn out for the **Chienbesen** parade, giant bonfires dragged through the medieval town on floats with onlookers brandishing flaming torches of pine branches above their heads in a dramatic, ancient spectacle. The tradition is a long-standing one, described as far back as the sixteenth century, but it's been dogged by controversy, at one time from the church, which regarded it (with some justification) as diabolic in origin, and in more recent times from the fire brigade which regards it (also with justification) as being dangerous to life and property. Despite the raging inferno dragged through Liestal's narrow streets each year, flames as high as the houses and people crammed shoulder to shoulder throughout the Old Town amidst the flying cinders and scorching heat, no harm has yet been done. Neighbouring **SISSACH** has similar fiery revels, with the torching of a 10m-high effigy, the Chluris; while in **BIEL-BENKEN**, to the west, locals fling burning wooden discs into the night sky in an equally mesmeric fire-orgy termed the Reedlischigge. If you're in the area at the right time, these are all events to catch.

travel details

TRAINS

Basel SBB to: Baden (hourly; 50min); Bellinzona (hourly; 3hr 35min); Bern (twice hourly; 1hr 10min); Biel/Bienne (hourly; 1hr 10min); Brig (hourly; 3hr); Chur (hourly; 2hr 40min); Geneva (hourly; 2hr 50min); Interlaken Ost (hourly; 2hr 10min); Kaiseraugst (twice hourly; 10min); Lausanne (hourly; 2hr 30min); Lugano (hourly; 3hr 45min); Luzern (hourly; 1hr 10min); Neuchâtel (hourly; 1hr 30min); Olten (3 hourly; 25min); Zürich (3 hourly; 1hr 5min).

BOATS

Basel (Schifflände) to: Kaiseraugst (May–Oct 1–3 daily; 2hr 10min); Dreiländereck (May–Oct Mon–Sat 1 daily; 1hr 45min).

INTERNATIONAL TRAINS

Basel Bad. to: Berlin (hourly; 7hr); Frankfurt (hourly; 2hr 50min); Freiburg-im-Breisgau (3 hourly; 30min–1hr); München (hourly; 5hr); Schaffhausen via Germany (hourly; 1hr 10min); Stuttgart (hourly; 2hr 30min).

Basel SBB to: Amsterdam (2 daily; 7hr 40min); Berlin (2 daily; 7hr); Brussels (5 daily; 6hr 15min); Frankfurt (every 2hr; 2hr 50min); Freiburg-im-Breisgau (twice hourly; 40min); Hamburg (every 2hr; 6hr 30min); Köln (hourly; 4hr 45min); Milan (every 2hr; 5hr 20min); München (every 2hr; 5hr); Paris (6 daily; 5hr); Rome (1 daily; 12hr); Strasbourg (hourly; 1hr 15min); Stuttgart (every 2hr; 2hr 40min).

PLACE NAMES IN THIS CHAPTER

German	French	Italian
Aare	Aar	Aar
Aargau	Argovie	Argovia
Basel	Bâle	Basilea
Basel-Land	Bâle-Campagne	Basilea campagna
Basel-Stadt	Bâle-Ville	Basilea città
Deutschland	Allemagne	Germania
Frankreich	France	Francia
Rhein	Rhin	Reno

CHAPTER FIVE

BERN AND AROUND

The giant Canton Bern is one of the country's largest, taking in a swathe of diverse countryside from snowy Alpine peaks to gently rolling farmland. The north of the canton is focused around the small city of **Bern** itself, Switzerland's low-key and attractive federal capital. With a grand and glorious history at the fulcrum of Swiss history, Bern has often dominated the economic and political fortunes of the populated west-central heartland – or **Mittelland** – of the country. This arc of territory stretching from the Lake Geneva shores to Zürich holds, and has always held, the most fertile country, the densest population, and the greatest wealth of all the diverse areas of Switzerland. The Reformation may have begun in Zürich, and flourished in Geneva, but it was the Bernese army that seized hearts and minds in the countryside between the two. For centuries after the Burgundian wars, the patrician nobility of Bern controlled a wealthy city-state covering the entire Mittelland; it was only a French-backed revolution in 1798 that saw Bern stripped both of its Lake Geneva breadbasket (carved out to form Canton Vaud) and the rolling farmland of the north (Canton Aargau). Nonetheless, Bern was a natural choice for Swiss federal capital under the 1848 constitution, and with overwhelming economic and political clought, Bern can still to this day call the shots in its home region.

Every Swiss values his or her home canton above all the others, but the Bernese seem to be able to draw on a particularly deep wellspring of nationalistic pride in celebrating their own identity, culture and language. They're famous around the country for their slow, deliberate manner, and you'll pick up a sing-song tone in the lethargic Bernese dialect of Swiss-German that sparks inevitable associations with Welsh or Texan accents of English. Parallels with Wales or Texas don't stop at language: like them, Bern – once an independent state – is now bound into a larger polity but has a relatively static, self-assured population who tend to feel little affinity with the people over the border. Luzerners and Fribourgeois are strangers, with whom the Bernese share a nationality but neither a cultural nor a religious identity. The slow-talking Bernese traditionally decry Zürchers for being big-city hotheads, and Baslers and Genfers for being snobs – and the compliment is returned, with the Bernese dismissed as hair-splitting dullards.

Around Bern, the lush hills and tidy, picturesque farming communities of the **Berner Mittelland** hold plenty of rustic charm, not least in the **Emmental** region to

---

ACCOMMODATION PRICE CODES

All the hostels, pensions and hotels in this book have been graded according to the following price codes, which indicate the price for the cheapest double room available during the high season. Single rooms can cost anything between sixty and eighty percent of the double-room rate. For hostels with dormitories, the price per bed has been quoted. See p.45 for more details.

① under Fr.100	④ Fr.200–250	⑦ Fr.350–400
② Fr.100–150	⑤ Fr.250–300	⑧ Fr.400–500
③ Fr.150–200	⑥ Fr.300–350	⑨ over Fr.500

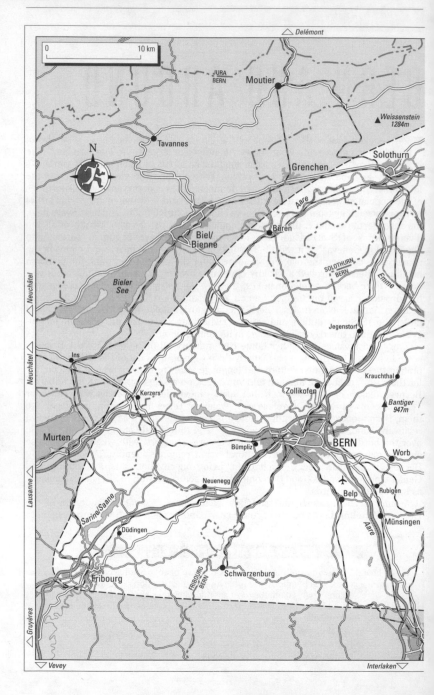

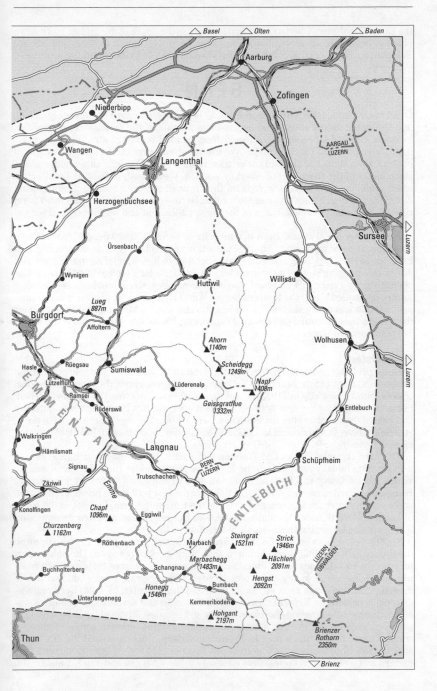

the east. (The Berner Oberland, or Bernese Alps, in the south of the canton, has its own chapter, beginning on p.248.) Two cities near Bern well worth making time for are **Solothurn** to the north, and the much-overlooked town of **Fribourg** to the southwest.

BERN

Of all Swiss cities, **BERN** (Berne in French) is perhaps the most immediately charming. Crammed onto a steep-sided peninsula in a crook of the fast-flowing River Aare, its quiet, cobbled lanes, lined with sandstone arcaded buildings straddling the pavement, have changed barely at all in over five hundred years but for the adornment of modern shop signs and the odd car or tram rattling past. The hills all around, and the steep banks of the river, are still liberally wooded. Views, both of the Old Town's clustered roofs and of the majestic Alps on the horizon, are breathtaking. Coming from Zürich or Geneva, it's hard to remember that Bern – once voted Europe's most floral city – is the nation's capital, home of the Swiss parliament and wielder of final federal authority.

For all its political status, Bern is a tiny city of barely 130,000 people and retains a small town's easy approach to life. The attraction of the place is its ambience; traffic is kept out of the Old Town and you could spend days just wandering the streets and alleys, café-hopping and – if it's warm – joining the locals for a plunge into the river. The perfectly preserved medieval street plan, with its arcades, street fountains and doughty towers persuaded UNESCO to deem Bern a World Heritage Site, placing it in the company of such legendary sites as Florence, Petra and the Taj Mahal. In a competition for the world's most beautiful and relaxing capital city, it's hard to think what could knock Bern into second place.

Some history

A castle probably stood at **Nydegg**, on the eastern tip of Bern's peninsula, from the eleventh century, before Berchtold V, Duke of Zähringen, chose the strategically ideal spot to found a new city in 1191. He had the oak forests covering the peninsula felled, using the timber for the first houses, and then – legend has it – went hunting nearby and named the new city after his first kill, a **bear** (*Bär* in German). Bern's coat of arms, sporting a bear, first appeared in 1224, and to this day bears remain indelibly associated with the city.

The Aare encircles Bern's Old Town on three sides; Berchtold's fourth defence was a wall, which initially ran through the Zytglogge tower. Under the Zähringens, and by virtue too of being in close proximity to the wealthy and powerful kingdom of **Burgundy**, Bern expanded rapidly. By 1256 it had a new wall at the present Käfigturm, and a century later the city reached as far as the Christoffelturm. In 1339, at the battle of Laupen, Bern defeated the united nobility of Burgundy, and asserted its newfound independence by joining the Swiss Confederation in 1353.

Shortly before 5pm on May 14, 1405, **fire** broke out in Brunngasse and tore through the timber-built city, killing one hundred and razing most of the town. The subsequent programme of rebuilding (this time in the local sandstone) gave the city much of its present character, including the street arcades, the surviving town plan, and monumental public buildings such as the Rathaus and the Münster. In 1528, Bern enthusiastically accepted the **Reformation**, and the sixteenth and seventeenth centuries saw a programme of upgrading the city's streets and arcades. Meanwhile Bern's nobility gathered greater and greater power, successfully putting down a series of citizens' revolts before finally falling prey to **French invaders**, who ransacked the city's treasury in 1798. Shortly after, the Congress of Vienna in 1814 forced Bern to surrender its eastern and western territories, thus creating Cantons Aargau and Vaud, donating the

Swiss Jura to Bern as a consolation prize. Nonetheless, the city retained its old prestige enough to be a popular choice for **federal capital** in 1848.

In 1864, after six years of fierce controversy, the communal authorities voted by 415 to 411 to demolish the medieval Christoffelturm to make way for construction of Bern's new railway station (the tower's foundations survive on display in the train station's lower level). **Einstein** published his Special Theory of Relativity in Bern in 1905, and **Hermann Hesse** spent the World War I years in Bern, when the city was already known as a hub of politically progressive ideas, hosting the anarchists Kropotkin and Bakunin.

During the twentieth century Bern continued to expand enormously, its new, arching bridges linking suburbs over the Aare such as **Kirchenfeld**, a planned district to the south characterized by many grand 1920s–30s mansions, a lot of which are now used as foreign embassies. To the west, **Bümpliz** has mushroomed to accommodate most of the city's rapid new growth, its low-income housing and high proportion of Arab, South Asian and Slavic immigrants contrasting dramatically with the settled affluence and ethnic homogeneity of the city centre.

Orientation, arrival and information

The huge **train station** is centrally situated at the western edge of the Old Town, within a few minutes' walk of practically all the hotels and sights. Trains arrive at the lower level, postbuses on the uppermost level. The **Old Town** stretches to the east, occupying the central high ground of a thin finger-like peninsula: three long, parallel cobbled streets (which all change their names along their length) define the Old Town area: Aarbergergasse/Zeughausgasse/Rathausgasse/Postgasse is the northernmost; Spitalgasse/Marktgasse/Kramgasse/Gerechtigkeitsgasse is in the centre; Schauplatzgasse/Amthausgasse/Münstergasse/Junkerngasse is to the south. The Zytglogge clocktower is bang in the centre of the Old Town; the Bärengraben (bear pits) are to the east; and the main museums are clustered around Helvetiaplatz to the south.

If you're on one of the few **flights** to operate into Bern's tiny airport, 9km southeast of the city in Belp, you can take the shuttle to nearby Belp station, from where trains cover the twenty minutes to Bern every half-hour (Fr.10.40 for shuttle and train). It's far easier, however, to take the airport bus (often just a roomy car), which meets all incoming flights to ferry passengers into town (Fr.14), dropping you in front of the tourist office at the train station. A taxi into Bern shouldn't cost more than Fr.35.

With your own transport, you'd do well to take advantage of the free **"park-and-ride"** facilities on the fringes of the city – parking in the centre is very expensive (Fr.30/day). Coming from Fribourg on the N12, take the Bümpliz exit for the P+R at Ausserholligen (bus #12 or #13 into the city); coming from Neuchâtel or Basel/Zürich on the N1, head for the P+R at Neufeld (bus #11); or coming from Interlaken on the N6, exit at Wankdorf for the P+R at Guisanplatz (tram #9).

Information

Bern's super-friendly **tourist office** is on the upper level of the train station (June–Sept daily 9am–8.30pm; Oct–May Mon–Sat 9am–6.30pm, Sun 10am–5pm; ☎031/328 12 12, *www.bernetourism.ch*). They have information on everything, including free maps of both the Old Town and the whole city (including a street-index), and they can reserve hotel rooms for a Fr.3 commission (even though there's a complimentary hotel-phone just outside). Pick up a free copy of the fortnightly *Bern aktuell*, which has English listings of mainstream cultural events in the city and some useful information on the city's attractions. There's also a smaller tourist information booth at the Bärengraben (daily: June–Sept 9am–5pm, March–May & Oct 10am–4pm).

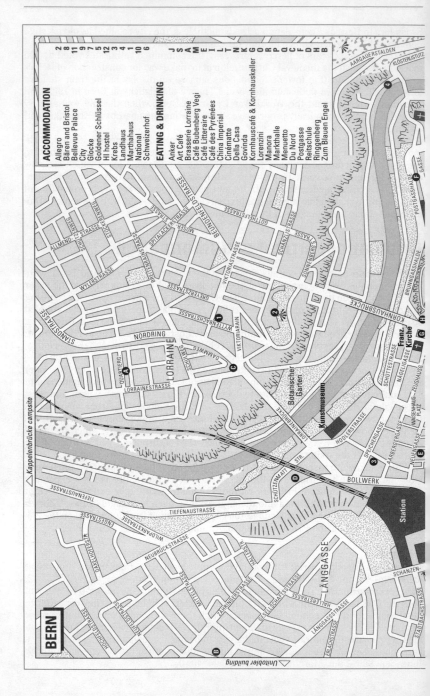

BERN

ACCOMMODATION

Allegro	2
Bären and Bristol	8
Bellevue Palace	11
City	9
Glocke	7
Goldener Schlüssel	12
HI hostel	5
Krebs	3
Landhaus	4
Marthahaus	1
National	10
Schweizerhof	6

EATING & DRINKING

Anker	J
Art Café	S
Brasserie Lorraine	A
Café Bubenberg Vegi	M
Café Litteraire	E
Café des Pyrénées	I
China Imperial	L
Cinématte	T
Della Casa	N
Govinda	K
Kornhauscafé & Kornhauskeller	G
Lorenzini	O
Manora	R
Markthalle	P
Menuetto	Q
Du Nord	C
Postgasse	F
Reitschule	D
Ringgenberg	H
Zum Blauen Engel	B

△ Kappelenbrücke campsite

▽ Unitobler building

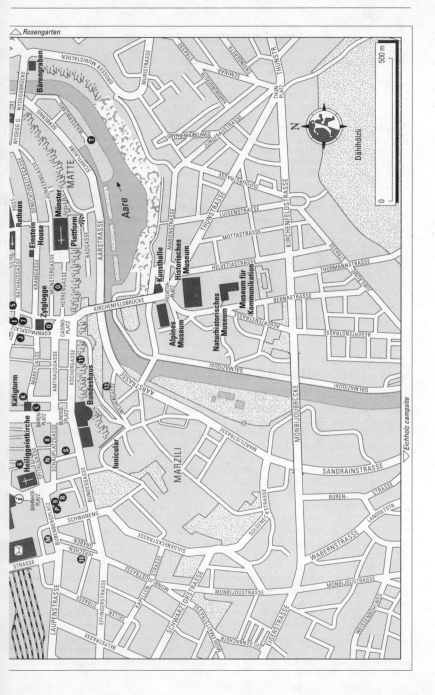

BERN'S FESTIVALS

The famous **Zibelemärit** (Onion Market) – held on the fourth Monday in November – is Bern's major annual festival, an excuse, despite the food stalls and the rustic-sounding name, for people to run around Spitalgasse throwing confetti, spraying silly-string and brandishing blow-up bananas. It is claimed that the spectacle originated after the fire of 1405, when people from nearby Fribourg helped Bern clean up the mess and, in gratitude, the Bernese granted the Fribourgeois the right to sell their onions every autumn in the city (down the centuries, the onions developing into blow-up bananas). In fact, Bern's Zibelemärit began – much more mundanely – in the mid-nineteenth century, when rural women, selling onions and other vegetables, began to turn up in Bern on the first day of the city's Martinmas Fairs – celebrated since the Middle Ages as marking the transition to winter. The quality of the produce, and the engaging demeanour of the vendors, meant that news of the women's market spread rapidly, until the newspapers got hold of the story in 1860 and proclaimed the Onion Market to be the "traditional" start of Martinmas. The tale quickly wove its way into popular thinking, somehow getting muddled with the 1405 fire and the Fribourgeois along the way. Linkage to a defining event in Bern's history guaranteed the event's survival into the modern age, even though today the Martinmas Fairs, the transition into winter and the farmers' wives themselves are long forgotten.

Zibelemärit aside, Bern's biggest party is probably its **Fasnacht/carnival**, spread over a weekend conveniently slotted in between the massive celebrations in Luzern (before) and Basel (after). From mid-May onwards, following a fragrant **Geranium Market** on Bundesplatz, the city is bedecked with flowers. Spring and summer see a host of cultural events, including an international **jazz festival** in May (Bern is home to one of Switzerland's best jazz schools), a **rock and folk festival** in July on the Gurten hilltop, and a **modern dance festival** over late August and early September.

City transport and tours

Bern's city centre is small enough that you can easily **walk** everywhere – the stroll from the train station to the Bärengraben is only around fifteen minutes and takes in the length of the Old Town on the way. Walking is the only way you're going to be able to get a sense of the atmosphere of the arcades and it's the principal delight of Bern, but a close second best comes in the form of **horse-drawn carriages**, which ply for trade in the central squares during the summer months.

Bern's network of **buses and trams** is comprehensive and efficient. Pretty much all lines run through Bahnhofplatz, which is bedecked with signs pointing the way to each individual stop. A ride of up to six stops costs Fr.1.50 (valid in one direction for 45min), of seven or more stops Fr.2.40 (valid 1hr 30min), or you can get a day ticket for Fr.7.50 which covers the entire city and suburban network (excluding night buses, which cost a flat Fr.5). Make sure you have a ticket before you start your journey, since you can't get one on board and the fine for travelling without one is Fr.50. Eurailers, InterRailers and Swiss Half-Fare Card holders get no reductions on Bern city transport, but Swiss Pass holders travel free.

If you need any information or timetables, check with the **public transport office** (Mon–Fri 6.30am–7.30pm, Thurs until 9pm, Sat & Sun 7.30am–6.30pm), just off Bahnhofplatz next to *Manora* restaurant. The routes that are most likely to be of use to visitors are tram #9 (direction Wabern) for Gurten, bus #12 (direction Länggasse) for the university, and bus #20 (direction Wyler) for Lorraine, although the last two destinations are no more than ten minutes' walk from the train station anyway.

The station has the usual **bike-rental** facilities (daily 7am–9pm). During the summer months (May–Oct), the municipality runs a free bike-rental scheme to get unemployed people into work. There are two pickup points, one outside the Loeb department store opposite the station, the other on Kasinoplatz (both daily 9am–8pm). For a Fr.20 deposit plus your passport, you can ride away for free; keep the bike longer than a day, and you're charged Fr.20/day.

With a Fr.6.50 flagfall, plus Fr.2.70 per kilometre (more at nights and Sundays), Bern's **taxis** are a luxury, and there's little need to use them. Plenty hang around at the train station, and also at Casinoplatz and Waisenhausplatz, but if you need to call, try Bären (☎031/371 11 11) or Nova (☎031/301 11 11).

Tours

The tourist office has a wide range of organized **tours** of Bern and the surrounding area. They offer a two-hour **guided walk** through the Old Town, starting from the station tourist office (June–Sept daily 11am; Fr.12); and a slightly shorter guided tour of "Hidden Bern", starting from the Bärengraben tourist information booth (July & Aug daily 11am; Fr.12). One of the more interesting ways to see the city is from a **river raft** (you're likely to get at least a bit wet, so sportsgear or a swimming costume is advisable) – ask at the tourist office for details of where to meet (June–Sept daily 5pm; Fr.30). Otherwise, there are plenty of **bus tours** of the city and various **boat trips** on the river (Fr.23–30), as well as full-blown day trips to the Thunersee (Fr.41; see p.260) and even the Jungfraujoch (Fr.164; see pp.278–9). Beware that most of the tours run in the summer season only.

Accommodation

Bern's **accommodation** is good value, especially considering that it's easy to choose an inexpensive place and still find yourself in an utterly tranquil room overlooking historic cobbled streets, with only voices and church bells as background. Standards, even within historic buildings, are as high as ever – the only drawback is the need always to book ahead.

Camping and hostels

There are two **campsites** near Bern. *Eichholz* is by far the nicer (Strandweg 49; ☎031/961 26 02, fax 961 35 26, *mueller.family.eichholz@swissonline.ch*; mid-April to Sept), on the riverbank a few minutes by tram (#9 to Gurten) south of the city. *Kappelenbrücke* (☎031/901 10 07, fax 901 25 91) is open year-round except for the first two weeks of February, and is on the river 5km northwest of town – take a postbus to Eymatt in Hinterkappelen village (20min).

Bern's HI **hostel**, Weihergasse 4 (☎031/311 63 16, fax 312 52 40; ➀; closed late Jan) is well run, with good facilities and a nice riverside location in Marzili – it's regularly chock-full, and imposes a three-day maximum stay in summer. Dorm beds are Fr.24, and they do good solid lunches and evening meals for around Fr.12. Walk down from the Bundesterrace, or take the funicular and then the lowest of three left-hand streets when you emerge. Otherwise *Landhaus* (see "Inexpensive hotels" below) has beds in quiet, super-clean partitioned dorms for Fr.30; you can use the kitchen for free, there's a café downstairs and Internet access. Take bus #12 to Bärengraben (direction Schosshalde).

Inexpensive hotels

You'd be fortunate to find a double room at any of the **inexpensive hotels** listed below for less than Fr.100 a night, and decent places start from around Fr.140. Location is only an issue around the train station, which can get a little noisy in the morning rush hour; elsewhere, the only sounds likely to disturb you are footsteps and the occasional tram bell. None of these is more than ten minutes' walk from the train station, or a couple of stops on a tram.

City, Bahnhofplatz (☎031/311 53 77, fax 311 06 36, *ambassador@mail.pingnet.ch*). Geared towards a hurried business clientele, with slick, futuristic designer interiors. Seconds from the train station and not at all bad. Street-side rooms are marginally noisier. ③.

Glocke, Rathausgasse 75 (☎031/311 37 71, fax 311 10 08). Simple, inexpensive rooms benefiting – like the *Goldener Schlüssel* nearby – from a perfect location. Slightly the cheaper of the two, though, and marginally worse value. Rooms with en-suite bath or shared facilities are adequate, but small and unremarkable. ②.

Goldener Schlüssel, Rathausgasse 72 (☎031/311 02 16, fax 311 56 88, *hotel-goldener-schluessel@bluewin.ch*). Comfortable place on a quiet Old Town street, with efficient, pleasant service. Simple, spacious rooms are very clean, mostly en-suite but with some good-value shared-bath rooms up under the eaves. ②.

Krebs, Genfergasse 8 (☎031/320 15 15, fax 311 10 35, *hotel-krebs@thenet.ch*, *www.hotelonline.de*). Clean, plain, solid-value option within spitting distance of the station; comfortable and welcoming. Recommended over the unappealing *Mövenpick* next door, which charges much the same. ②–③.

Landhaus, Altenbergstrasse 4 (☎031/331 41 66, fax 332 69 04, *landhaus@spectraweb.ch*). The most attractive budget rooms in town, in an historic, renovated building (with spiralling wooden stairs but no lift) overlooking a curve in the river. Spacious, modern design prevails throughout, with en suite or shared facilities, and some rooms have floor-to-ceiling windows and balcony. ①–②.

Marthahaus, Wyttenbachstrasse 22A (☎031/332 41 35, fax 333 33 86, *pension.marthahaus@bluewin.ch*). Best all-round value. A characterful building on a quiet cul-de-sac a few minutes out of the Old Town, friendly, well run and cosy. The few shared-bath rooms have sinks, and both the en-suite and hallway bathrooms are newly renovated and spotless. Free kitchen use, and winter and long-stay discounts. If it's full, negotiate crashing out in the TV room (around Fr.35). Bus #20 to Gewerbeschule (direction Wyler). ①–②.

National, Hirschengraben 24 (☎031/381 19 88, fax 381 68 78). Something of an institution, with a restaurant, theatre and – up above – a hotel occupying a lovely old building on an atmospheric tree-and tram-lined street. The ancient wooden lift rattles you up to characterful, renovated rooms with big windows and wood floors; some are en suite, all have modern facilities. ②.

Mid-range and expensive hotels

Bern has at least a couple of truly grand, characterful **expensive hotels**, but unless money is no object you'd probably do better to hang on to your francs until you get up to one of the better mountain resorts, where you'll probably get more for your card-swipe.

Allegro, in the Kursaal, Kornhausstrasse 3 (☎031/339 55 00, fax 339 55 10, *allegro@kursaal-bern.ch*, *www.allegro-hotel.ch*). Innovative business hotel set in the ultra-modern renovated Kursaal building (which also boasts Switzerland's largest casino). Super-slick postmodern design swishes you into stylish rooms – go for the Warhol ones – featuring widescreen TVs which also let you play Nintendo and surf the Internet. Top-floor balconies with Alpine vistas cost more. Weekend discounts can make this the best value, and least traditional, top-end accommodation anywhere in the country. ④.

Bären and **Bristol**, within 50m of each other on Schauplatzgasse (☎031/311 33 67, fax 311 69 83, *reception@baerenbern.ch*, *www.baerenbern.ch*). Two identical hotels seconds from the Bundeshaus, with different owners but shared management. Both underwent complete renovation in 1998–99, and rooms are now very modern, well designed and comfortable, though rather soulless. ④–⑤.

Bellevue Palace, Kochergasse 3 (☎031/320 45 45, fax 311 47 43, *reservation@bellevue-palace.ch*, *www.bellevue-palace.ch*). Top hotel in the city, right next to the Bundeshaus and the haunt of presidents, diplomats and billionaires, with as much palatial grandeur as you'd expect plus the added bonus of views of the river winding far below the hotel walls and, in the distance, the snow-capped Alps. Rooms are spacious, sumptuous, traditionally styled and horribly expensive. ⑧–⑨.

Schweizerhof, Bahnhofplatz 11 (☎031/326 80 80, fax 326 80 90, *info@schweizerhof-bern.ch*, *www.schweizerhof-bern.ch*). Opposite the train station, this is one of Bern's grandest piles, 140 years old and still family run with a personal touch. Traditional rooms are individually decorated and uniquely characterful, with some ordinary doubles boasting wood panelling, deep sofas and marble bathrooms. Gourmet dining completes the picture. ⑧.

The City

Wandering through Bern's UNESCO-protected **Old Town** can be a magical experience – few cities in the world are so visibly wedded to their distant past, with architecture and a street plan essentially unchanged since medieval times. The most hectic shopping goes on in the **western half** of the Old Town, on Marktgasse and Spitalgasse in particular; the older, **eastern half** is slow paced and tranquil. However, not for nothing does the tourist office tout the famous arcades, lining both sides of every street in the Old Town, as being "the longest covered shopping promenade in the world". In a strange turnaround of expectations, it's when you walk under the crowded arcades that you get a full-on blast of modern consumerism, with music, shop windows and advertising vying for your attention. Step a few metres to the side to walk in the open air and – with a little imagination – it's easy to picture yourself in the Bern of the sixteenth century.

The Zytglogge

An imposing presence at the centre of the old town, the **Zytglogge** (*tseet-klok-uh*), Zeitglockenturm or Clock Tower, is as much the symbol of Bern as the bear. The focal point of public transport and walking routes within the Old Town – and both the benchmark of official Bern time and the point from which all distances in the canton are measured – its squat shape, over-sized spired roof and giant, gilded clock face will imprint themselves on your memory of the city.

The tower was originally constructed partly in wood as the westernmost city gate in 1218–20, but by 1256 the city walls had moved west to the Käfigturm; the stranded tower was then converted into a prison for those prostitutes who made a living servicing the clergy. The devastating fire of 1405 razed the tower and it was rebuilt in stone with a new, squat design, a turreted staircase to one side (still used today) and a clock mechanism. The clock soon broke and stayed broken for 122 years until one Caspar Brunner designed an intricate and elegant new mechanism which has functioned since he installed it in 1530, and which is still complete with nearly all its original parts. Below the main east face of the clock is an intricate astronomical and astrological device, which, in one small diameter, displays a 24-hour clock, the twelve hours of daylight, the position of the sun in the zodiac, the day of the week, the date and the month, the phases of the moon and the elevation of the sun above the horizon throughout the year, everything kept accurate by linkage to the main clock mechanism. The external appearance of the Zytglogge as it is today dates from Baroque embellishments of 1770–71.

The main draw of the thing is generally touted to be a rather underwhelming little **display** of mechanical figures – a crowing cock, a parade of bears, Chronos with his hourglass and a dancing jester – which is set into motion four minutes before every hour on the clock's east face. What's far more interesting is to see close-up (and have explained) the actual inner workings of the mechanism as the pendulum swings and linked cogs turn gracefully. It's possible to go inside only as part of the tourist office's exemplary and fascinating one-hour **guided tour** (May–Oct daily 4.30pm; late Dec to early Jan daily 11.30am; Fr.6), which also lets you explore the rooms inside the spire and take in the romantic rooftop view.

The eastern Old Town

From the Zytglogge, the atmospheric lanes of the old town branch out in all directions. The meandering walking tour outlined below covers notable sights, but what's just as appealing is to follow your nose and explore unremarkable alleys and passageways that cut through and around the main routes.

The impressively wide main cobbled thoroughfare of the old town stretches away on both sides of the Zytglogge – Marktgasse (the heart of Bern's shopping district) is to the west, while elegant **Kramgasse** runs east, also with its fair share of commerce, and featuring many Baroque facades stuck on to the medieval arcaded buildings early in the eighteenth century. At no. 49 is the **Einstein House** (Tues–Fri 1–5pm, Sat noon–4pm; closed Dec & Jan; Fr.2), the apartment and workplace of the famous scientist, who developed his Theory of Relativity in 1905 while working in the Bern Patent Office, having graduated fom the Zürich Institute of Technology a few years before. It's also on Kramgasse that you'll come across the first of Bern's many ornamented **fountains**, an armoured bear holding the standard of the city's founder, Berchtold von Zähringen (dating from 1535). Halfway along the street is another, with a copy of a 1545 statue of Samson, and just before the Kreuzgasse junction is a statue-less fountain dating from 1779. At this eastern end of Kramgasse, and above head height, you'll also spot several eighteenth-century oversized figures mounted on pedestals, which indicated the location of Bern's various craft guilds: the Moor represented the clothworkers, the ape stonemasons and bricklayers, and the axe-wielding carpenter graphically demonstrates his own trade.

While the main street continues ahead, changing its name to Gerechtigkeitsgasse, the small **Kreuzgasse** heads left (north), past a quaint little shop which has been a pharmacy since 1571, to **Rathausplatz**, dominated by the double-staircased **Rathaus**. Although the building dates from 1406–17, it's been much altered over the centuries – not least in 1939–42, when the ground floor was entirely rebuilt. Opposite is a 1542 fountain sporting a Bernese standard-bearer in full armour. Next to the Rathaus is the

---

THE OLD (CHRIST) CATHOLIC CHURCH

In 1870, the **First Vatican Council** confirmed the rule of the Pope over the whole of the Catholic Church and asserted the doctrine of papal infallibility. At the same time, political unification in Italy, and Bismarck's *Kulturkampf*, or Culture Struggle, in Germany – a thinly veiled assault on church authority – drew Switzerland inexorably into the broader conflicts between church and state that were beginning to rage across Europe. Swiss liberals in particular saw the Vatican's dogmatism as challenging the basic principles of the church and the right to individual freedoms in decision making. In a meeting in Olten in 1872, they were troubled enough to form a separate church hierarchy. When the Bishop of Basel began to excommunicate priests who refused to accept the notion of papal infallibility, cantonal authorities in the north of Switzerland deposed him, and the dissenting priests formed their new church.

Known in Germany, Austria and the Netherlands as "Old Catholic" but generally in Switzerland as **"Christ Catholic"**, the church flourishes today in the areas of the north of the country influenced by political liberalism, principally cantons Bern, Basel, Aargau and Solothurn, with scattered communities as far apart as Geneva and St Gallen. About 140,000 Swiss consider themselves Christ Catholics, as opposed to Roman Catholics (of which there are 3.2m), following a church which holds that there is a priesthood of all believers, that priests are allowed to marry, that women can be ordained as deacons, and that services should always be performed in the language of the congregation. This has brought it closer in spirit to Anglicanism than to Roman Catholicism, with which relations have often been bitter and strained over the decades.

St Peter und St Paul-Kirche, built in 1858 as the first Catholic parish church to go up in the city since the Reformation. It's a cool, musty place in a mock-Gothic style which since 1875 has belonged to the heterodox Old Catholic church (see box).

This is one of the most peaceful and atmospheric corners in the Old Town. **Rathausgasse** to the west retains its facades, but has seen much cautious interior redevelopment in recent years for conversion of the old upper floors into luxury apartments, while to the east, tiny **Postgasse**, with a handful of endearing little cafés and antiquarian booksellers, trickles its way down the slope towards the oldest part of the city around Nydegg.

Nydegg

The three quietest and most characterful streets in the Old Town – Postgasse, Gerechtigkeitsgasse and Junkerngasse – all meet at the **Nydeggbrücke** (*nee-dek*), the easternmost point of Bern's peninsula and the location of Nydegg Castle, built probably before the 1191 founding of Bern and the spur to the city's construction. It was destroyed in the mid-thirteenth century and its location is now marked by the **Nydeggkirche**, although parts of its massive stone foundations survive here and there. The church is a mishmash of elements added to an original 1341 building, and it's worth stopping to savour the tranquil atmosphere of the courtyard outside, with a well which originally stood within the precincts of the twelfth-century castle and a picturesque view of the medieval houses clustering on the slopes all around. The covered Burgtreppe steps lead down from the courtyard to **Gerberngasse**; at the bottom, if you cross the street and walk 20m or so left, you'll find more steps leading down to the riverside, through a thirteenth-century arch which originally belonged to the **Ländtetor**, landing stage for the first ferry across the river. The wall fresco beneath the arch shows the neighbourhood in the early nineteenth century.

Matte

Emerging back onto Gerberngasse, to the right (northeast) is Läuferplatz, its fountain-statue of the city herald standing at the head of the low **Untertorbrücke**, one of the oldest bridges in Switzerland (1468). To the left (southwest), Gerberngasse follows the bend of the river down into one of the most appealing districts of the Old Town, **Matte**. For many centuries this was a self-contained district of craftspeople and dockworkers which long retained its own dialect, related to the Jenisch language of the Swiss gypsies (see pp.454–5) and dubbed *Mattenenglisch* by the other Bernese, to whom it was an incomprehensible language (as obscure as *Englisch*) spoken in a meadow (*Matte*). Gentrification of the neighbourhood in the 1970s brought sweeping social changes. The river is still channelled into an open canal along the main street, and there are plenty of crooked half-timbered houses all around, but a look at wall plaques will turn up more software companies, Internet consultancies and design partnerships than you could shake a stick at. The fact that the district now has its own Web site (*www.matte.ch*) speaks volumes. You'll find a great deal of graffiti down here too, a legacy no doubt of the presence of the *Wasserwerk*, Bern's premier techno club (see p.230). During the disastrous floods of 1999, Matte spent several weeks underwater, and you may still see evidence of high-water marks here and there.

From Matte, the least energetic way to get back to the Old Town is to continue southwest along the riverside Schifflaube until Badgasse, where there is a **lift** (Mon–Sat 6am–8.30pm, Sun 7am–8.30pm; Fr.1) to whisk you up to the Münsterplattform overhead. Many flights of steps wend their way up the hillside all around too. Otherwise, you could continue a riverside stroll under the Kirchenfeldbrücke into **Marzili**, a peaceful residential district with a handful of old industrial buildings on the riverbank now converted into music venues and arts centres. The Aare is particularly fast at Bern, and the locals have come up with a novel idea to go with the flow. Summer sees hordes crowding the riverbank lawns, and many people leave their possessions at the pool complexes at Marzili or Lorraine and walk or take public transport south to a convenient jumping-in point to let the strong current float them back north again. Cheapskates wrap their clothes up in a plastic bag and tie it to their wrist as they float along.

Across the Nydeggbrücke

There are few attractions on the eastern bank of the Aare. At the bridgehead across the river is the rather sad **Bärengraben** (bear pits; daily May–Sept 8am–6pm, Oct–April 9am–4pm; free), two large sunken dens which have housed a collection of shaggy brown bears – the symbol of Bern – since the early sixteenth century. The current occupants may look as if they're struggling to find a reason to go on with life, but don't be fooled; late one night in 1998, an unfortunate beer-happy individual fell into the pit, was welcomed by its occupants and didn't survive to tell the tale. The tourist complex adjacent has a restaurant-bar and city information booth. Heading left up the steep hill next to the Bärengraben will bring you to the **Rosengarten** (Rose Garden), with a marvellous collection of flora and breathtaking morning views of the town.

The Münster

Bern's late-Gothic **Münster** is unmistakeable, its feathery spire – the highest in Switzerland – towering over the Old Town and its sonorous bells dominating the quiet city. It's a reverential and quite awe-inspiring place, both for its lofty, gloomy interior and the terrific views from its tower.

The first chapel on the site – recorded in 1224 – probably dated from the founding of the city. On March 11, 1421, when just five thousand people lived in Bern, Matthäus Ensinger, a master builder from Strasbourg who already had three cathedrals under his belt, started construction on the new minster using the greenish local sandstone. Work continued according to his original plans until the mid-sixteenth century and, after a gap of three centuries or so, was finally completed in 1893 with the addition of the spire. Bern was a rapid convert to the Reformation and most of the church's treasures were destroyed in or soon after 1528, although some notable pieces such as the portal sculpture, choir stalls and stained-glass windows survived.

Outside the cathedral, cobbled **Münsterplatz** features the imposing Baroque facades of, among other buildings, the chapterhouse, and a 1790 fountain showing Moses, fired with the zeal of the Reformation, pointing to the Second Commandment (the one forbidding idolatry). It's worth stopping at the **central portal** of the cathedral before heading inside – this spectacular depiction of the **Last Judgement** is one of the only remaining unified examples of such late-Gothic sculpture in Europe. The 170 smaller figures are the fifteenth-century originals, but the 47 larger freestanding pieces were replaced by copies in 1964 and the originals now sit in the Bernisches Historisches Museum (see p.226). The left half of the portal depicts the saved, the right half the damned: you can imagine that the graphic, didactic counterpoint between the beatific smiles of one side and the naked, screaming torment of the other would have appealed even to the iconoclastic Reformers, who chose to spare it from destruction. In the very centre is Justice, flanked by angels, the Wise and Foolish Virgins and, above, the Archangel Michael wielding a sword and scales.

Entry to the cathedral (Easter–Oct Tues–Sat 10am–5pm, Sun 11am–5pm; Nov–Easter Tues–Fri 10am–noon & 2–4pm, Sat until 5pm, Sun 11am–2pm) is through the right-hand gate, and the hushed interior is immediately impressive. The immense roof span is laced around with vaulting (1572–3), the aisles are flanked by rows of porches and small chapels, and the nave, with square pillars placed diagonally and the original 1470 pulpit, channels attention towards the stained glass of the choir. Keystone busts of saints, Mary, Christ and others were left untouched by the Reformers (possibly because they were too high to reach). The 1520s **choir stalls** are marvellous, carved with faces of the prophets and much intricate detail of ordinary life. The gorgeous **stained-glass windows** of the choir date from 1441–50, although a hailstorm in 1520 damaged the right-hand windows (two replacements were installed in 1868).

If you have even a dram of energy, you shouldn't spurn the chance to climb the **tower**, the tallest in Switzerland. The way up is just inside the church door (same times as church, but closes 30min earlier; Fr.3), but be warned: this is a 100m climb up a steep and narrow spiral of 254 stone stairs. (You might want to ask in the church when the bells will be rung and make your ascent to coincide, since the experience of standing literally right next to a gigantic, tolling ten-and-a-half tonne bell – the largest in the country, cast in 1611 – is one you and your ribcage will remember.) The 360-degree vistas over the whole city, most of the surrounding countryside, and out towards the Alps, are dreamy.

On the south side of the church is the **Münsterplattform**, a buttressed terrace above the Aare which took about a hundred years from 1334 to build. Abandoned icons were dumped here during the Reformation, but later it was planted with lime and chestnut trees and given elegant Baroque corner turrets in order to serve as an open promenade, which is how it has remained. The views of the Aare and of silhouetted trams creeping along the soaring Kirchenfeldbrücke are spectacular. The net below the parapet was added a few years ago as a disincentive to desperate Bernese who chose this rather dramatic and beautiful spot to end it all.

The western Old Town

Some 100m west of the Münster is Casinoplatz – the actual Casino sees more concert-goers than gamblers – from where trams head south to the Helvetiaplatz museums (see below). The Zytglogge is a few steps north, and just beyond it is the nightmarish **Kindlifresserbrunnen**, or Ogre Fountain (1544), which shows a man devouring a struggling baby. The Bernese authorities would have you believe it's a light-hearted carnival scene, but the statue was once painted yellow (the colour used to vilify Jews) and may possibly be an unusually graphic representation of the suspicion held throughout medieval Europe that Jewish religious ritual involved the murder of children. Whichever, Bern's happy shoppers of today seem unfazed by images of cannibalistic infanticide in their midst.

A little north is the large **Kornhaus**, or Granary, now occupied by offices and a chic bar. Just behind is the **Französische Kirche** (French Church), the city's oldest, which originally formed part of a thirteenth-century Dominican monastery. The compact but beautiful interior (Mon–Sat 9–11am & 2–5pm) has been much renovated, but retains its stalls (1302) and a rare frescoed rood screen (1495).

From the main **Kornhausplatz**, trams weave their way west along Marktgasse, heart of the city-centre shopping district, neatly avoiding the fountain statues of a musketeer in full armour and Anna Seiler, founder of Bern's first hospital, who's been set up to serve as an allegory of moderation. Just beyond the Seilerbrunnen is the **Käfigturm**, an early city gate (1256–1344) which was used as a prison from 1642 until 1897. The broad, sunny marketplace of **Bärenplatz** opens beyond, and a little further west along hectic Spitalgasse, with its bagpiper fountain, lies the late-1720s **Heiliggeistkirche** (Holy Spirit Church; Easter–Oct daily 11am–3pm), acclaimed as Switzerland's finest example of Protestant church building, boasting a gorgeous Baroque pillared-and-galleried interior. It stands alone, trams, buses and people weaving a cat's cradle all around it. The train station – metres away – marks the limit of the medieval city, with several sections of excavated city wall on display on the lower concourse.

NASTY, BRUTISH AND SHORT?

There was much social unrest in Switzerland in 1980, most noticeably among radical leftists. Zürich's Autonomous Youth Centre (AJZ) – intended as a police-no-go building where young people could run their own entertainment free from mainstream commercial and social pressures – was violently suppressed, and a similar AJZ movement in Bern which took over the **Reitschule** (an abandoned city-owned former riding school near the train station, also known as the **Reithalle**) was also evicted by the police. The situation simmered until late 1987 when, following the eviction of the riverside Zaffaraya community, thousands demonstrated in the city centre, a large group re-squatted the Reitschule and, perhaps most significantly, retailers reported a ten-percent loss in profits over the Christmas shopping season. In the face of such a groundswell of discontent, the police and city council adopted a damage-limitation policy, and left the Reitschule squatters to their own devices.

Despite problems with violent anarchist gangs in the early 1990s, the Reitschule – now an arts centre and activist collective – has come to be highly valued by alternatively minded Bernese, and has even gained a certain official legitimacy while remaining in a curious legal grey area. Its cinema, for instance, is licensed with the council but the bar next to it is illegal; the concert venue pays its taxes, while the adjacent café is packed with dope-smokers. Unlike the similar *Rote Fabrik* movement in Zürich (see p.371), the Reitschule co-operative has consistently rejected proposals to accept funding from the city council, sticking tight to its counter-cultural principles ("No violence, no sexism, no commercial exploitation") by raising its own money through ticket sales, bar profits and an extremely popular annual fundraising party. Through effective word-of-mouth networking, it's been able to stage gigs by British, European and American bands and DJs, raising its profile still further, yet to this day, the police don't venture into the complex, turning a deliberate blind eye to such a self-contained concentration of – mostly very innocuous – lawbreaking. It's a rundown, heavily lived-in place and an obvious honeypot for drug dealers (who are barred from entry, but nonetheless gather outside), yet these days is quite safe. More to the point, it's become an icon of opposition to the city council, which has been trying for years to turn it into a multistorey car park and supermarket. A huge graffito as you approach reads *Reitschule bleibt autonom* ("Reitschule still rules itself"). In a remarkably effective and purposeful demonstration of communal self-government, virtually unknown in other European countries and running entirely counter to the Swiss stereotype, it's true.

The Bundeshaus

Immediately south of Bärenplatz is Bundesplatz, dominated by the **Bundeshaus**, or Federal Assembly building, built in Renaissance style in 1902 and inscribed *Curia Confoederationis Helveticae* (Assembly Building of the Swiss Confederation). When the parliamentarians are not in session, you can join a free 45-minute guided tour (on the hour Mon–Sat 9–11am & 2–4pm, Sun 10am, 11am, 2pm & 3pm; ☎031/322 85 22), which takes you through the various chambers, decorated with coats of arms, statues and paintings commemorating events in Swiss history. When the assembly is sitting (the flag overhead will be flying), you can watch proceedings from the public gallery. The building sits on a cliff edge above the Aare, and the **Bundesterrasse** behind rests on a massive retaining wall; this promenade has rather ironically become the heart of Bern's flourishing drug market, and is often scattered with glazed-eyed characters shooting up literally under the noses of the lawmakers. On one side, a quirky funicular runs down to the riverside district of Marzili (daily 6.30am–9pm; Fr.1).

The Kunstmuseum

Bern's marvellous **Kunstmuseum** is barely five minutes' walk northeast of the train station, in an impressively well-designed and newly renovated building at Hodlerstrasse

8–12 (Tues 10am–9pm, Wed–Sun 10am–5pm; Fr.8 for the permanent collection only, or more to include temporary exhibits; SMP; *www.kunstmuseumbern.ch*). Aside from often excellent changing shows, the main draw, and reason enough to stump up the admission fee, is the **Paul Klee** collection, the largest in the world with over two thousand works, most of them drawings and, unfortunately, the greater part in storage in the vaults. Nonetheless, the permanent collection, comprising large numbers of works by Klee and **Kandinsky**, along with plenty by Picasso, Modigliani, Giacometti, Cézanne, Matisse, Rothko, Miró, Pollock and more, makes this a magical and easy-to-digest experience. There's also an interesting smattering of works by contemporary artists – Willy Weber's piece in chrome entitled *My dentist has hidden my toothbrush again!* will stop you in your tracks – and a wide selection from **Swiss artists** such as Anker and Hodler.

It's a fifty-metre stroll from the Kunstmuseum down an alley on the west side of the building to the **Frauen-Kunstforum** (Women's Art Forum; Hodlerstrasse 16; Tues 10am–9pm, Wed–Sat 10am–5pm; free; *www.frauenkunstforum.ch*). A single room with changing exhibitions of contemporary art made by Swiss women, also with a small café and selection of books, it's a labour of love kept going by donations alone, and is worth your moral, and even financial, support.

PAUL KLEE

Born in Münchenbuchsee, just north of Bern, on December 18, 1879, **Paul Klee** is perhaps the best known of all Swiss artists, his attractive, dream-like works filled with allusions to music and poetry and suffused with an endearing humour and humanity. Art historians have a great deal of difficulty classifying his work, since his unique style takes in elements of primitive art, cubism, surrealism, naïve art and expressionism. Klee was a major influence on the abstract expressionist movement and on non-figurative painting of all kinds in the second half of the century.

His family was very musical, and it was only after a great deal of hesitation that Klee gave up developing his early proficiency on the violin to enrol in the Munich Academy of Art in 1900. There he met the pianist Lily Stumpf, playing duets on violin and piano with her. Shortly afterwards Klee toured Italy, finding particular pleasure and inspiration in Byzantine and early Christian art. He made many sketches, ink drawings and etchings during this period, two of the most famous of which, from 1903, are *Virgin in a Tree* and *Two Men Meet, Each Believing the Other to Be of Higher Rank*.

In 1906 Klee and Stumpf married and settled in Munich, at that time a dynamic centre for avant-garde art. There, Klee met the painter Wassily Kandinsky, starting a lasting friendship; on Kandinsky's urging, Klee joined the expressionist circle Der Blaue Reiter (The Blue Rider), and in 1914 journeyed to Tunisia on a trip which was to change his life. "Colour has taken possession of me," he wrote. "No longer do I have to chase after it, I know that it has hold of me forever. Colour and I are one. I am a painter." The same year, the Sturm gallery in Berlin staged a joint exhibition of Klee and Chagall.

After the Great War, Klee taught at the famous Bauhaus school in Germany, alongside Kandinsky and the architect Walter Gropius. In 1931 he moved to the Düsseldorf Academy, but after Hitler's rise to power, the Nazis condemned Klee's art – which by now was using delicate, ethereal colour harmonies in subtle, semi-abstract figurative compositions – as "degenerate". Klee fled back to Bern just before Christmas 1933, continuing both his painting and his elaborate ink drawings based on fantasy imagery. He soon, however, developed a crippling disease of the skin and muscles, which affected his ability to work and would eventually kill him. After 1935, his style changed to incorporate thick, crayonish lines and blocks of muted colour in a set of increasingly gloomy musings on war and death. Picasso visited the sick artist late in 1937, as did Braque. Following a giant retrospective of 213 later works at the Zürich Kunsthaus early in 1940, Klee died on June 29, in hospital in Locarno.

The Helvetiaplatz museums

Most of Bern's museums are clustered together around **Helvetiaplatz**, on the south side of the Kirchenfeldbrücke. Some, like the Bernisches Historisches Museum, shouldn't really be missed; others have less going for them. Trams #3 (direction Saali) and #5 (direction Ostring) shuttle from the train station and the Zytglogge to Helvetiaplatz.

Bernisches Historisches Museum

You could spend a long time exploring the fascinating **Bernisches Historisches Museum** (Bernese Historical Museum; Tues–Sun 10am–5pm; Fr.5, free on Sat; SMP), a grandiose turreted castle purpose-built in 1894. With seven floors of diverse bits and pieces, it's a good idea to pick up a floor plan before you start. Information is generally very good, with the scholarly German labelling nearly always given in English and French translation in leaflets kept in wall racks.

The ground floor is given over to temporary exhibitions, which tend not to have English explanations, and it's worth heading straight down to the basement (taking in, if you've time, the extensive porcelain and silver collection on the lower mezzanine on the way). At the bottom, to the left side of the staircase, is perhaps the highlight of the whole museum, a collection of extraordinary and macabre paintings showing "**The Dance of Death**"; these are 1649 copies of originals painted in 1516–17 on the wall of Bern's Dominican monastery and now lost. The sequence of 24 vivid images, showing a hideously grinning and fooling skeleton leading kings, prostitutes, nuns and lawyers alike to their inevitable fate, is enough to send a chill down your spine – as, no doubt, it was intended to. Equally impressive is the pillared room directly opposite, filled with the original sandstone figures from the **Last Judgement** portal of the Münster and fascinating for the chance to view their details up close. Through in another part of the basement are several rooms featuring rural and urban interiors from the seventeenth and eighteenth centuries, reconstructed down to the chamber pots and creaky floors.

From the ground floor all the way up the main staircase is a series of rather unflattering **portraits** of 280 Swiss peasants and craftspeople in traditional dress, made late in the eighteenth century as a kind of ethnographic record. The mezzanine is devoted to a spectacular **Islamic collection**, with daggers galore, a mounted Turkestan warrior in full armour, jewellery, ceramics and a reconstructed Persian sitting room. Stairs to the first upper floor bring you to an intricate **scale model of Bern** in 1800 (made in 1850). Nearby in the same room, for some unknown reason, sits a bust of Brigitte Bardot. Halls left and right display extremely impressive wall-sized medieval **Flemish tapestries**; the Burgundian Hall holds the Caesar Tapestries, telling the story of Caesar's life in Burgundian-style dress, and, highlight of the collection, the **Thousand Flowers Tapestry**, the only one surviving of a set of eight made in Brussels in 1466, which was looted by Bern during the Burgundian wars of 1474–77. Rooms further on with coins and medals include a mesmerising 1828 three-way portrait of Calvin, Luther and Zwingli. On the other side of the stairs is the **Trajan Hall**, with suits of armour, weapons, cavalry standards and heraldic tapestries galore.

The second upper floor features more military uniforms from different periods, and a series of overwhelmingly meticulous rooms devoted to "**Changes in Daily Life**", covering everything from reconstructed shops and schoolrooms from different periods to ephemera, old vending machines and musical instruments. The top floor has a small **archeological collection**, and above is a belvedere offering bird's-eye views of the Bundeshaus and the Alps.

Schweizerisches Alpines Museum

Beside the Historical Museum, the **Schweizerisches Alpines Museum** (Swiss Alpine Museum; May–Oct Mon 2–5pm, Tues–Sun 10am–5pm; Nov–April Mon 2–5pm,

Tues–Sun 10am–noon & 2–5pm; Fr.5; SMP) is surprisingly good, taking an intelligent, sensitive look at all aspects of life in the mountains, from tourism, the history of mountaineering and the social identity of mountain dwellers to surveys of Alpine flora and fauna and the impact of industry on the mountain environment. There's plenty to play with and read up on (in English). Crowded all over the museum are dozens of examples of relief mapmaking gone berserk, with mountains, whole valley systems and complete Swiss ranges rendered in perfect scale detail, almost rock by rock, by enthusiasts whose energy and patience can only be imagined.

Other museums

There are plenty of other museums on or very close to Helvetiaplatz. The porticoed **Kunsthalle** (Art Gallery; Helvetiaplatz 1; Tues 10am–9pm, Wed–Sun 10am–5pm; Fr.6) has changing exhibits of contemporary art, usually of very high quality. Behind the Historisches Museum, the **Naturhistorisches Museum** (Natural History Museum; Bernastrasse 15; Mon 2–5pm, Tues, Thurs & Fri 9am–5pm, Wed 9am–8pm, Sat & Sun 10am–5pm; Fr.5; SMP) has the largest diorama exhibit in Europe – a somewhat fancy way to describe an array of stuffed animals behind glass, including a rather threadbare "Barry", the famous St Bernard mountain-rescue dog. Its mineralogical displays are more engaging, with meteorites and cut diamonds, but they're scant recompense for fighting the tide of schoolkids. The **Museum für Kommunikation** (Helvetiastrasse 16; Tues–Sun 10am–5pm; Fr.5; SMP) surveys media and communication from postagestamps and early telephones to the Internet and beyond.

Outer districts

If you're on an extended visit to Bern, or if you just fancy something a bit different from medieval history at every turn, more modern districts slightly out from the Old Town can provide a little urban realism.

Easiest to reach – just a short walk north of the train station across the river – is **Lorraine**. Late in the nineteenth century a dyed-in-the-wool working-class district, in the last decades Lorraine has attracted a growing population of students and young people who have created a funky, relaxed community atmosphere which nonetheless doesn't exclude the many oldtimers still in the neighbourhood. Developers caught on to the appeal of the place in the 1990s, and more and more glass-and-steel architecture is appearing in amongst the old houses, but Lorrainestrasse and the streets around still retain much charm.

If you follow Schanzenstrasse up behind the train station, a short climb will bring you to Länggassstrasse, heart of the bustling university district of **Länggasse**. The

---

ABOVE BERN

A favourite Bernese getaway – if one were needed from such a gentle, slow-paced capital – is to the hill of **Gurten**, which towers over the city from the south. Take tram #9 to Gurtenbahn, in the neat suburb of Wabern, and walk 100m along Dorfstrasse to the funicular (daily, every 20min: May–Sept 8am–10pm, Oct–April 8am–6.30pm; Fr.7 return; Fr.7.50 city transport pass valid). The whole journey from the train station to the summit only takes about half-an-hour. On top you'll find a kids' play-area, a lavish folly of a castle (currently under renovation, but due to open in 2000 as a hotel and restaurant) and wide expanses of countryside laced with hiking trails that give views over Bern, out towards the Jura, and across the peaks of the Bernese Oberland. In winter the hill and snowy slopes are crowded with sledding families; in summer, you might have difficulty escaping the hikers and picnickers. Every year, for a weekend in mid-July, Gurten plays host to a very popular rock music festival; ask for details at the tourist office.

Unitobler building, at no. 49a, 300m along on the left (bus #12 stops outside), was formerly the factory where, for most of the twentieth century, the famous Toblerone chocolate was produced. In the 1980s, production moved to a more modern site outside Bern, and the building was renovated for use by the university (hence the Unitobler name), subsequently receiving numerous architectural awards for sensitivity of renovation. You're basically free to explore: the student café spills onto a sunny plaza behind the building, and the library occupies an extraordinary below-ground site between two wings of the building that has been converted into an impressive three-storey atrium space. Just behind Unitobler, on Freiestrasse, is the elegant **Pauluskirche**, dating from 1905 and one of the best examples of Art Nouveau in the country.

Eating and drinking

Bern's compact Old Town groans with **eating and drinking** possibilities, and you'll have no trouble finding something to suit your palate and your budget. The broad Bärenplatz, always busy with people, performers and market stalls, is shoulder to shoulder with cafés and is top choice for cappuccinos in the sunshine, but there's a host of places all through the cobbled lanes offering *al fresco* consumption during the summer and firelit warmth in winter.

Cafés and café-bars

Art Café, Gurtengasse 3. Bright, trendy café just off the main shopping streets that discovers a new line in studied urban dissipation after the shops shut.

Brasserie Lorraine, Quartiergasse 17. Just about the last café in Bern still owned by a co-operative, with excellent, inexpensive food, a great location high above the river, wood floors and a summer terrace. Games galore fill the cupboards for free use, and the Sunday brunch is the best in Bern. A cosy, calm meeting place for alternative types and politicos. Bus #20 to Lorraine (direction Wyler) – Quartiergasse is a little ahead on the left. Closed Mon.

Café Litteraire, in Stauffacher bookshop, Neuengasse 25. Cosy espresso bar in Bern's largest bookshop, with snacks and newspapers. Closed Sun.

Café des Pyrénées, Kornhausplatz 17. Jovial and unpretentious meeting place for artists, alcoholics and others with loud voices. Equal quantities of twenty- and forty-somethings crowd the place out nightly, with the *Ringgenberg* next door catching the overflow. Closed Sun.

Kornhauscafé, in the Kornhaus. The vaulted and renovated interior of the city's former granary is now home to a starkly postmodern-style café, with coiffed customers and pricey desserts and sandwiches. A cool contrast to the raucous *Pyrénées* opposite.

Kornhauskeller, below the Kornhaus. An atmospheric subterranean frescoed beerhall that was under renovation at the time of writing – perhaps the change of ownership will improve the waiters' tempers. Formerly, it offered live music nightly, a folkloric show on summer Mondays and solid Berner fare to soak up the alcohol.

Du Nord, Lorrainestrasse 2 (☎031/332 23 38). A quality Lorraine café-bar and eaterie, offering a nice mixture between heavy meat-and-potatoes dishes and lighter veggie options. A meal might only come to Fr.23 in the evening, or as little as Fr.13 at lunchtime. All the food is organic and comes from small local producers ensuring freshness, and monthly dance events and occasional concerts add to the allure. Bus #20 to Gewerbeschule (direction Wyler). Closed Wed.

Reitschule (aka Reithalle), graffitied buildings next to the railway bridge 5min north of the train station. See also box p.224. Co-operative-run bastion of Bernese counterculture. The hash-smoky café-bar (named *Sous Le Pont*) is uniquely amiable; however, if sharing a scratched-up table with a green-haired character in a holey sweater rolling a joint isn't your idea of fun, you should head elsewhere. A red traffic light means table service, green means bar service. Note that dope smoking is forbidden noon–2pm & 7–10pm. Open Mon & Sat 5pm–1am, Tues–Fri 11am–1am.

CHEAP EATS

It's not hard to find good, filling food in Bern for Fr.10–15, and the best way to cut costs is to take advantage of lunchtime specials and daily *menus – Café Bubenberg Vegi, Brasserie Lorraine* and *Cinématte* stand out as places where you can get great food for bargain prices. *Sous Le Pont* in the Reitschule has consistently appealing fare, and a feature of their social policy is to offer one square meal a day for a rock-bottom Fr.5. Bern's branch of the cheapo **self-service** *Manora* (Bubenbergplatz 5a; Mon–Sat 7am–10.30pm, Sun 9am–10.30pm) is a good one, offering some of the least bad Fr.10 meals in the centre.

Another good option is to head for the **university**; the *Unitobler* café at Länggassstrasse 49a (side entrance on Lerchenweg; Mon–Fri 8.30am–4pm; food 11.30am–1.45pm) is a self-service student dining hall, with the added attraction of a sunny terrace for lounging or playing *boules*. Opposite is *Mappamondo*, a self-service Italian with an echoing exam hall for a dining area; or check out the Fr.11 lunch *menu* at the cosy *Länggassträff* café at nearby Lerchenweg 33.

Zum Blauen Engel, Seidenweg 9b. Cosy student café near the university, with *objets trouvés*, worn gilt mirrors, hosts of candles and a crowd of young, arty regulars creating a pleasantly seductive atmosphere in which to while away the evening. Eat before you come, though, since the food is disappointing. Bus #12 to Mittelstrasse (direction Länggasse) – Seidenweg is first right. Closed Mon.

Restaurants

Anker, Kornhausplatz 16. Cosy, smoky pub, with a restaurant section in the back where you can eat Swiss stomach-liners such as fondue, *Röschti* and a meat-laden Berner-Teller (around Fr.20) without embarrassment, since the place is invariably full of hearty locals tucking in too.

Café Bubenberg Vegi, Bubenbergplatz 8 (Migros entrance). An escalator leads you up to superb and affordable veggie food within metres of the train station; don't let the depressingly bland surroundings put you off. The varied and interesting food has an Indian slant to it (the midweek evening Fr.30 Indian buffets are excellent), but the daily *menu* – balanced meals in sizeable portions – will fill you up for Fr.15.

China Imperial, Bärenplatz. Moderately good Chinese, worth mentioning only for its unique "Tellerservice": for Fr.17.50, choose from a large buffet of uncooked ingredients and marinades, and present the lot to the chef who will wok-fry it all on the spot for piling over rice. They also have à-la-carte options, but at a premium. Tellerservice Mon–Fri 11am–2.30pm & 10–11.30pm only.

Cinématte, Wasserwerkgasse 7 (☎031/312 45 46). Pleasant riverside nook attached to Bern's premier arthouse cinema. Weekday two-course lunch *menus* (meat or veggie) are great value at Fr.15, while the à-la-carte evening menu is varied and also not expensive. Only seven tables though, so book ahead. Closed Tues eve, and Sat & Sun lunch.

Della Casa, Schauplatzgasse 16 (☎031/311 21 42). An unprepossessing exterior preludes high-quality Swiss cooking. The Bernerplatte – a plateful of half-a-dozen varieties of meats with potatoes and sauerkraut – is a house speciality, but doesn't come cheap: you'd be lucky to walk out with change from Fr.50. Closed Sun.

Govinda, Marktgasse 7, 3rd floor. Tiny Krishna-run diner, serving pristinely healthy vegetarian food in an unlikely location above a menswear store. Lunch (Mon–Fri only) is a reasonable Fr.18, and the weekly dinner (Thurs) Fr.28. Closed Sat & Sun.

Lorenzini, Hotelgasse 8. High-flying young professionals flock here both for the café-bar and the top-drawer Tuscan cuisine, although you'll be looking at over Fr.30 for a meal. Closed Sun.

Markthalle, Bubenbergplatz 9. A slick indoor mall devoted to food from around the world – espressos, tapas, cheese, wine, bread, chocolates, and more. In the back is a full-blown restaurant (around Fr.30), but you could easily satisfy munchies at counters for sushi, Thai food or Mediterranean *mezze*. Despite the contrivance, it works rather well. Closed Sun.

Menuetto, Münstergasse 47. Chic veggie place, with delectable, imaginative dishes and lots of choice (Fr.25 and up). Daily specials can drop as low as Fr.13. Closed Sun.

Postgasse, Postgasse 48. Tiny old den on the quietest of alleys, with wood tables and an intimate, cosy atmosphere. The *menu* is good and not expensive (Fr.18), but the joy of the place is its dark, convivial ambience. Closed Mon & Tues.

Ringgenberg, Kornhausplatz 19. Warm and comfortable place that's as much a bar as an eaterie – although, unlike the *Pyrénées* next door, it's actually worth coming here for the food (around Fr.30). Closed Mon.

Nightlife and entertainment

Bern's **nightlife** is surprisingly vibrant, with live music (contemporary and classical), dance nights, theatre, opera and film all getting a substantial look-in. Posters all over town advertise events, or otherwise you can find complete city nightlife **listings** in *Agenda*, the Thursday supplement of *Berner Zeitung* newspaper, available free from many cinemas. For cutting-edge news about clubs and music events (in German), pick up the free *Bewegungsmelder* from the tourist office and elsewhere. The free fortnightly *Bern aktuell* has English listings of major cultural events, but nothing out of the mainstream. You can buy **tickets** for most big events from Konzertkasse Casino, Herrengasse 25 (Mon 3–6.30pm, Tues–Fri 10am–12.30pm & 3–6.30pm, Sat 10am–12.30pm; ☎031/311 42 42 Mon–Fri 12.30–3pm only).

Bars, clubs and live music

Aside from its **bars**, Bern's nightlife tends to be concentrated in a handful of large, multipurpose venues which offer a changing diet of live bands, DJs and other bits and pieces, mostly for Fr.15–20 entry. There's also a fair smattering of decent **clubs**, which charge more or less the same.

Babalu, Gurtengasse 3. Brash, city-centre club booming glitzy techno and house.

Dampfzentrale, Marzilistrasse 47 (*www.dampfzentrale.ch*). An old steam factory down on the riverbank, now hosting hugely popular nights featuring jazz, drum'n'bass, dance, theatre and film, as well as a daytime café-bar. Either walk, or take evening bus #30 (8.45–11.55pm only).

Drei Eidgenossen, Rathausgasse 69. A small, noisy bar in the Old Town, its wooden benches very popular with a loquacious, alternative young crowd.

ISC, Neubrückstrasse 10. Premier student venue and club.

Mühle Hunzigen, 13km south of town near Rubigen. An old wooden mill out in the countryside that has, over the years, hosted a jaw-dropping array of top-flight international jazz, blues and soul performers in an intimate, raucous setting more reminiscent of a delta juke-joint than the Swiss capital. If you see a gig advertised here, it's worth the taxi ride. Make friends quickly in order to nab a lift back to town after the show.

Reitschule (aka Reithalle; see also box p.224). Heart of the city's underground. Facilities include a cinema, concert venue, disco, women-only area and the *Sous Le Pont* café-bar.

Schwarz & Trionfini's Cocktail Club, Brunngasshalde 63. An unmarked wooden facade gives into an atmospheric bar, with a bare-rock cellar chiselled out of the hillside furnished with sagging red sofas and candelabra. The chic clientele are rather less dramatic than the space, sipping sidecars at each other like it was coming back into fashion, but the late-night blend of Jack Daniels and Miles Davis is a heady (if expensive) one nonetheless. Closed Sun.

Shakira, Hirschengraben 24. Mainstream Latino DJ-bar with salsa and regular Cuban nights.

Tübeli, Rathausgasse 50. A barfly's dream tucked away on a cobbled street in the Old Town, with lino on the floor, a long greasy counter and sad songs playing into the small hours.

U1, Junkerngasse 1. Atmospheric subterranean DJ-bar near Nydegg.

Wasserwerk, Wasserwerkgasse 5, below Nydeggbrücke. Bern's big techno joint, also hosting regular live bands.

Classical music, opera, theatre and film

Classical music is well served by the Bern Symphony Orchestra, which performs regularly at the Casino (Herrengasse 25) and the Stadttheater (Kornhausplatz 20), the latter also staging occasional **opera**.

Aside from major **theatre** productions at the Stadttheater, most nights of the week see a host of fringe shows in the many Old Town cellar studios. The Käfigturm theatre (Marktgasse 67) is the best known, with experimental drama, cabaret, pantos and comedy, and the Puppentheater (Gerechtigkeitsgasse 31) has striking and funny puppet shows, but there are literally dozens more – drop into the Stadttheater ticket office at Kornhausplatz 18 (Mon–Sat 10am–6.30pm, Sun 10am–12.30pm) for details.

All **cinemas** in the city cut their prices on Mondays to Fr.12 from the usual Fr.16, and there's plenty of mainstream choice. Both the Cinématte (Wasserwerkgasse 7; *www.cinematte.ch*) and the Kunstmuseum (Hodlerstrasse 8; *www.kunstmuseumbern.ch*) run programmes of non-commercial films.

Listings

Books Bern's biggest bookstore, and the only one with a sizeable quality range in English, is Stauffacher, Neuengasse 25 (Mon–Sat 8am–6.30pm, Thurs until 9pm). You'll find travel accessories and books – including Rough Guides – at Atlas, Schauplatzgasse 21. For English-language newspapers, your best bet is the large kiosk next to platforms U1–4 in the train station.

Car rental Avis, Egghölzlistrasse 1 (☎031/352 63 66) or Wabernstrasse 41 (☎031/378 15 15); Budget, Gewerbezone Ey 5, Ittigen (☎031/928 24 24); Europcar, Laupenstrasse 22 (☎031/381 75 55) or Wankdorffeldstrasse 60 (☎031/337 57 57); Hertz, Kasinoplatz (☎031/318 21 60). Bantiger, Bernstrasse 37 in Ostermundigen (☎031/932 28 88), rents cut-price two-seater Smart cars.

Changing money The best place is the change bureau on the lower level of the train station (June to mid-Oct daily 6.15am–9.45pm; mid-Oct to May daily 6.15am–8.45pm).

Email and Internet In the basement of the Loeb department store opposite the train station (Mon–Fri 9am–6.30pm, Thurs until 9pm, Sat 8am–4pm) is a Jäggi bookshop, with four PCs under the escalators. Two of them are first-come-first-served, limited to 20min per person but free of charge; the other two are bookable in advance, but cost Fr.10/hr. The train station's Internet terminal, in the same room as the Crédit Suisse ATMs (daily 24hr) costs Fr.1 for 6min.

Embassies Australia, Alpenstrasse 29 (☎031/351 01 43); Canada, Kirchenfeldstrasse 88 (☎031/352 63 81); Ireland, Kirchenfeldstrasse 68 (☎031/352 14 41); South Africa, Jungfraustrasse 1 (☎031/352 20 11); UK, Thunstrasse 50 (☎031/352 50 21); USA, Jubiläumstrasse 93 (☎031/357 70 11). New Zealand has no full embassy in Switzerland, and is represented only by its UN mission in Geneva (p.105).

Flights For all domestic and international flight enquiries from Bern-Belp airport, call ☎031/960 21 11. Alpar (☎031/960 22 22, *www.alpar.ch*) flies light aircraft on nine sightseeing routes over the surrounding landscapes, ranging from a short overfly of Bern (Fr.65pp), or a one-hour circuit over the mountains (Fr.160pp), to flights as far afield as Mont Blanc (Fr.265pp).

Gay and lesbian life *Anderland*, Mühleplatz 11, is the most popular gay café-bar, also home to HAB, the Homosexuelle Arbeitsgruppen Bern (☎031/311 63 53). Both the Reithalle (see p.224) and the ISC (see opposite) have reasonably regular gay and lesbian nights (and the Reithalle café is gay-and lesbian-friendly at all times). Schwulenbüro Schweiz, nicknamed The Pink Cross, is a national gay pressure group based in Bern at Zinggstrasse 16 – they have an information Rainbowline on ☎0848/805 080 (*office@pinkcross.ch*). LesBi-ruf is an information line for lesbians and bisexual women (Mon 7.30–9.30pm; ☎031/311 07 73).

Language schools Bern is not a bad place to study the idiosyncracies of *Schwyzertüetsch* – both the Volkshochschule (Kornhausplatz 7, Postfach, CH-3000 Bern 7; ☎031/311 41 92, fax 312 40 02) and the Migros Klubschule (Marktgasse 46, Postfach, CH-3000 Bern 7; ☎031/310 36 36, fax 310 36 01) run part-time courses over several months in Bernese Swiss-German, from around Fr.220, although you'll need to know some High German to start with.

Libraries The Schweizerische Landesbibliothek (Swiss National Library; Hallwylstrasse 15; Mon–Fri 9am–6pm, Wed until 8pm, Sat 9am–4pm) has a massive collection documenting the cultural, scientific and economic past and present of Switzerland. The central library of the University of Bern (Münstergasse 61; Mon–Fri 8am–9pm, Sat 8am–noon) is no less huge, and includes the attraction of English-language books and newspapers.

Lost property If you've lost something in town, head for the police Fundbüro (Zeughausgasse 18; Mon–Fri 8am–noon & 1–4.30pm, Thurs until 6pm; ☎031/321 50 50). For enquiries about tracking property lost on the trains, head for the train station's Fundbüro (Mon–Fri 8am–noon & 2–6pm; ☎0512/202 337).

Markets Bern has a wealth of markets, both year-round and annual one-off events. There are general markets on Tuesdays and Saturdays all year on Waisenhausplatz, Bundesplatz and Bärenplatz, with Bärenplatz in particular turned into a daily open-air jumble of stalls throughout the summer. Münsterplatz has a handicrafts market on the first Saturday of every month, and there's a wonderful riverside flea market on Mühlerplatz in Matte on the third Saturday of the month (May–Oct only). In December Münsterplatz and Waisenhausplatz both have Christmas markets, featuring scented candles and mulled wine. Bern's famous Onion Market (see p.216) is more of an excuse for a street party than anything else.

Medical facilities The Inselspital university hospital on Freiburgstrasse (☎031/632 21 11) has a 24-hour emergency room. Dial ☎031/311 22 11 if you need a doctor or dentist, or for details of night pharmacies. Pharmacy Hörning, on the upper level of the train station, is open daily 6.30am to 10pm.

Parks and gardens The glorious Botanischer Garten (Altenbergrain 21; Mon–Fri 7am–6pm, Sat & Sun 8am–5pm; free), has a host of Alpine flora in open-air cultivation, as well as hothouses (daily 8–11.30am & 2–5pm). To the south, Tierpark Dählhölzi (Tierparkweg 1; daily 24hr) is an open-access riverside park, with a section devoted to local fauna such as wolves, chamois and bears and a vivarium (daily: April–Sept 8am–6.30pm, Oct–March 9am–5pm; Fr.7) housing reptiles and fish.

Police Headquarters is at Waisenhausplatz 32 (☎031/321 21 21), but a more convenient office is in the change bureau in the train station lower level (daily 7am–9.15pm).

Post Bern's main post office (CH-3001 Bern 1) is the Schanzenpost on Schanzenstrasse just behind the train station. You can collect poste restante mail from counter 16 with your passport.

Radio One of Switzerland's more engaging radio stations is Radio Bern (known as RaBe), at 91.1FM, with diverse, multicultural programming by everyone from Brazilian expats spinning salsa to Reithalle activists condemning the city council to a soundtrack of deep ambient beats.

Travel agents Discount flight agents SSR Reisen's Old Town office is at Rathausgasse 64 (Mon–Fri 9.30am–6pm, Thurs until 8pm, Sat 10am–1pm; ☎031/312 07 24). Compare prices at Jugitours, Belpstrasse 49 (☎031/380 68 68).

AROUND BERN

To the east of Bern, a blissfully bucolic region of farmhouses and dairies, undulating hills and peaceful villages, spreads through and around the **Emmental**, the valley (*tal*) of the River Emme. Somehow or other, despite the presence of a show dairy and the

---

EXPLORING THE MITTELLAND

You can get information on the whole Mittelland region from the **Schweizer Mittelland tourist office**, which is based in the same offices as Bern tourist office, in Bern's main train station (☎031/328 12 28, *www.smit.ch*). They have plenty of contacts with companies running multi-day adventure packages in the area, and can put together any kind of itinerary covering hikes or long-distance cycling or inline skating on the hundreds of trails through the Mittelland, often throwing in extras to tempt you, such as canoeing on the Aare. A two-day package including riding, hiking and a night in a farmhouse costs from Fr.223, a canoe weekend from Fr.159, and a five-day cycling trip through the Emmental from Fr.535, including half board for four nights.

CUSTOMS AND FESTIVALS IN THE MITTELLAND

The Mittelland is one of the more traditional areas of the country, and has hundreds of **folk customs and festivals** surviving in various forms, many of them dating back to the pre-Christian pagan religions of the Celts. **"Chilbi"** is the generic name given to the summer highland festivals of the Emmental, raucous events taking in folk singers and dancers, yodellers, flag-throwers, alphorn blowers and more. The **Lüderenchilbi** is one of the most famous, held on the Lüderenalp meadow every second Sunday in August and centred on a **Schwingfest**, a traditional Swiss wrestling contest held in a sawdust ring. The winner gets to take home a heifer decked out in garlands. The **Schafsheid**, or sheep-sorting, held in Riffenmatt, 20km south of Bern, on the first Thursday in September, is a colourful event, when the sheep, after spending the summer on the alp, are sorted out by owner, amidst market stalls and celebrations. The **Sichlete** is a communal autumn meal, where in years gone by everyone who'd worked to bring in the harvest would sit down to gorge on stew, sausages, hams and fresh garden produce, helped down by huge meringues and local apple Schnapps; these days, with increasing farm mechanization (and so fewer seasonal farmhands taken on), the Sichlete has become merely an excuse for two or three villages to get together for a feast and a knees-up. In Burgdorf, the last Monday in June sees the **Solennität**, a 250-year-old festival for children, featuring contests, games and traditional costumes.

Many pagan New Year's Eve rituals survive in the villages of the Mittelland. Laupen's **Achetringele** stems from a Celtic exorcising of evil spirits and demons on the winter solstice; now shifted to December 31, it involves all the boys in the village chasing away the old year either as one of the masked Bäsemänner (broom-sweepers) or as a noisy, cowbell-swinging Tringeler (bell-ringer). One of the most bizarre customs, however, survives in Schwarzenburg, 8km north of Rittenmatt, where the **Altjahresel** (Old-Year Donkey) – these days a man dressed in a donkey suit – is whipped and beaten before being led away by a grim figure representing death. As well as the group of exorcists, various other characters take part in the ritual, including a bride and groom, representing joy in the year to come, the devil, a priest, and, most chillingly of all, a two-faced woman, the Hinnefürfraueli, whose beautiful front face looks forward to the new year, while her hideous rear face despatches the old year to memory.

region's prominent place in the hearts of the rurally minded, cheese-loving Swiss, the Emmental has managed to escape heavy tourist development. It's a wonderful place for long country walks or bike rides. To the north, generic suburban prosperity quietly covers the land as far as the dignified old city of **Solothurn**, capital of its own canton – a fact which rather awkwardly forced tourist offices to recently rename the Berner Mittelland as the "Schweizer Mittelland", in deference to non-Bernese sensibilities.

To the west and south, the Mittelland merges into the lakeside country of Canton Fribourg and the Broye (see p.176), with the extremely attractive and much overlooked city of **Fribourg** set in gorgeous countryside southwest of Bern on the French–German language border.

The Emmental

Just outside the eastern city limits of Bern rises the Bantiger mountain (947m); behind it stretches the **EMMENTAL**, a quintessentially Swiss landscape of peaceful, vibrantly green hills dotted with happily munching brown cows, sleepy rustic hamlets and isolated timber-built dairies. This is where Emmental cheese (the one with the holes) originates. A local nineteenth-century clergyman-writer celebrated the sturdiness and moral rectitude of Emmentaler dairy farmers in a series of famous novels under the pseudonym Jeremias Gotthelf; since then the place has gathered to itself an atmos-

phere of earnest rural stability and honesty. The salt-of-the-earth locals have the reputation of being the most reliable, the most sensible, the most Swiss of all the Swiss – a
reputation which, in a distasteful modern turnaround, has been exploited by politicians:
the extreme right-wing SVP party has recently begun to expand out of its traditional
base in Luzern to make significant gains in the Emmental countryside on a tide of anti-
immigration, anti-foreigner, anti-EU rhetoric.

Emmentaler **architecture** is distinctive, the local timber-built inns and dairies
crowned by huge roofs with overarching eaves, ringed by wooden balconies, and
encrusted with rows of tiny windows, each with its window box and neatly tied-back set
of net curtains. Emmentaler **cooking**, featuring cheese or cream with everything, is
renowned around the country, and in 1999, some forty local inns and restaurants got
together to regulate the quality of cuisine on offer in the region. All forty of these establishments now offer – among other dishes – the *Ämmitaler Ruschtig Menü*, a gut-bust-
ing four-course blowout for a standard Fr.46: from *Beeri Schämpis* (sparkling berry
wine), and a cheese salad served with the local *Züpfe* plaited bread, it takes in soup with
whipped cream, and *Chlepfer Ännis Schwynsschnitzu* (pork escalope in cream sauce,
with creamy mashed potatoes and vegetables), then moves on to *Meielis Merängge
Gschlaber* (fresh meringue with whipped cream, ice cream and caramelized cream),
before rounding it (and you) off with Schnapps-laced coffee. Consult the Bäregg association, CH-3552 Bärau (☎034/409 37 11), or local tourist offices, for details of the full
list of *Ämmitaler Ruschtig* establishments.

Burgdorf and the northern Emmental

On a pleasant road 19km northeast of Bern through Krauchthal village, the picturesque
old town of **BURGDORF** is built on a prominence above the Emme. From the train station, follow Bahnhofstrasse south and then head east on Oberstadtweg to meander up
into the Old Town, an atmospheric quarter characterized by steep cobbled streets. At
the top, the **Schlossmuseum** (Castle Museum; April–Oct Mon–Sat 2–5pm, Sun
11am–5pm; Fr.5) occupies the Zähringens' largest castle, begun in the seventh century and expanded in the twelfth. Several rooms grouped around an attractive courtyard
outline the history of Burgdorf and the Emmental, but the castle and the Old Town are
just as appealing for atmospheric wanderings as for the historical displays. Below, the
late-Gothic **Stadtkirche** features an elaborate choir screen that looks rather too big
and grand for the church housing it. Every Thursday, the Old Town hosts Burgdorf's
weekly **market**.

Roads climb northeast from Burgdorf to a viewpoint at **Lueg** (887m), offering classic panoramas over the rolling countryside. Nearby is **AFFOLTERN**, a pleasant village that's home to the Emmental's flagship **Schaukäserei** (Show Dairy; daily
8.30am–6.30pm; free), a rather hectic place that seems always to be full of busloads
of excitable Swiss-German old ladies. As well as being able to watch the various
cheesemaking processes – the dairy gets through some seven billion litres of milk a
year – you can take in plenty of English-language videos on the cheese industry. A
noisy and rather pricey café adjacent serves the *Ämmitaler Ruschtig Menü*. Plus, of
course, you can buy any amount of cheese, ranging from a bag of "Schnouserli" (bite-
sized cubes of different strengths of Emmental, for Fr.2) up to a full 9kg round of
Emmental shipped direct to your door (Fr.240). A booth also has tourist information
on the area.

Hasle-Rüegsau and Lützelflüh

Roads drop back down from Affoltern into the Emme valley at **HASLE-RÜEGSAU**,
two small villages which, over the years, have grown to hate each other like only next-
door neighbours can. Pressured by economic hardship over the last century or so, the

rough-and-ready farmers of Rüegsau have been forced to move down from their original hillside village (near-deserted Rüegsbach) through an intermediate community
(Rüegsau itself) to a village down on the Emme (Rüegsauschachen) right next to Hasle;
as the bumpkins approached, the ire of the settled, prosperous folk of Hasle grew and
grew. To this day, the two villages merely tolerate each other – Hasle has carefully tended gardens, modern houses and an air of suburban pride, while its neighbour is still
rustic, traditional and rundown – and this stretch of the river has become known locally as the Jordan, exemplifying the depth of warlike passion aroused on both sides. Just
west of the two, a five-minute walk away in a hard-to-spot woodsy location behind the
train tracks, is the largest arched wooden bridge in Europe, **Holzbrücke**, a mightily
impressive 69m-long construction built in 1839, damaged by cars in 1955 and so moved
800m downstream to its current position.

Along the valley floor 8km is a turning for **LÜTZELFLÜH**, a captivatingly charming
village at the heart of the Emmental that was home to the local novelist Gotthelf from
1831 to 1854. On the outskirts of the village you'll pass the **Kulturmühle**, an old mill
from 1821 that has been turned into a cultural centre (☎034/461 36 23), staging everything from the Emmentaler Cock-Crowing Contest to monthly classical music concerts
which attract the Bern cognoscenti out into the sticks. The oddly formal small Baroque
garden nearby, laid out in classic French style, isn't out of place: you can find similar
examples outside farmhouses throughout the Emmental – a legacy of French influence
over Bern following the 1798 revolution – though today the formal squares and circle
patterns are just as likely to be planted with carrots and lettuces. From Lützelflüh, back
roads climb to Affoltern, while the main valley road runs on south beside the Emme.

Langnau and the southern Emmental

Some 17km southeast of Bern, the tranquil town of **Konolfingen** marks the start of a
scenic road along the Kiese valley through Zäziwil to **LANGNAU**, the main town of the
Emmental, but a singularly sleepy place nonetheless, with not much traffic and less
than 10,000 people. A small **tourist office** in a travel agent off the main square
(Dorfmühle 22; Mon–Fri 8am–noon & 1–6pm, Fri until 9pm, Sat 9am–4pm) has information on the region, including details of the dozens of local walking routes. Look out
for the Friday morning **market** on Viehmarktplatz.

East of Langnau, the main road passes through the extremely picturesque village of
TRUBSCHACHEN, with big old wooden Emmentaler houses lining the street and a
demonstration **pottery** turning out examples of the pretty local ornamental ware. To
the north rises the **Napf** (1408m), the most famous of the Emmental's hills and a mecca
for hikers and Sunday hill walkers. East of Trubschachen, the road crosses briefly into
Canton Luzern and an area known as the **Entlebuch**, with its small countryside resort
of **Marbach** boasting a couple of ski lifts serving the Marbachegg (1483m) overlooking the town. Less than 5km southwest, and back in Canton Bern again, is **Schangnau**
village, at the upper end of the Emme valley. A minor road southeast from here winds
dramatically between the cliffs, which rise to 2000m on both sides, through tiny
BUMBACH (with lifts up to the giant wedge-shaped Hohgant, towering overhead at
2197m) and on to **KEMMERIBODEN** (976m). This end-of-the-road hamlet, sliced
through by the rushing, tumbling Emme – a mountain torrent at this stage – is the
place to get the single best **meringue** in Switzerland, and is also the trailhead for many
wilderness hikes, principally the tough path through the mountains to the 2350m
Brienzer Rothorn (7hr), from where a rack railway can take you down to Brienz (see
p.263).

From Schangnau, the main road crosses the Emme and heads north, through
Eggiwil to Langnau crossing nine picturesque wooden covered bridges that are typical
of the area. From Eggiwil, you can also reach Langnau by a parallel road further west

over the crest of **Chuderhüsi** (1103m), which offers spectacular views over the Emmentaler hills and valleys backed by the snowy Alps.

Emmental practicalities

The best way to get around in the Emmental is **by bike** or **on foot**, both of which allow you to set your own itinerary and pace, and explore as much or as little as you want; stations at Bern, Langnau and Burgdorf have bikes for rent. A scenic **train** line between Bern and Luzern passes through Konolfingen and Langnau, while a branch line runs north from Langnau through Hasle to Burgdorf, shadowing the Emme through verdant countryside. Hourly **postbuses** from Marbach run through Schangnau to Kemmeriboden.

The umbrella **tourist organization** Pro Emmental is at Schlossstrasse 3 in Langnau (☎034/402 42 52, *www.emmental.ch*); they, and tourist offices in Bern and Langnau, heavily tout the **hiking** possibilities of the area, with maps and route suggestions galore. Walking through hillside pastureland from Burgdorf to Affoltern, for instance, takes about three hours; from Burgdorf along the riverbank to Hasle, or Walkringen (above Konolfingen) to Lützelflüh, a little less. For a ramble down the Emme from Langnau to Burgdorf, or a stiffer hike from Langnau up to the Napf, reckon on a leisurely six hours or more. For Fr.10 per person, and with 24 hours' notice, Gepäck-Express (☎031/701 38 27) will pick up your bags from anywhere in the region and drive them up anywhere to 30km away, enabling you to spend the day unencumbered.

One of the more unusual ways to see the Emmental is from the back of a **llama** – Pro Emmental can set up a minimum of four people with a two-day llama trek for Fr.190 each, and can also put you in touch with companies running multi-day cycling or hiking adventure holidays in the area.

Accommodation and restaurants

The best **campsite** is *Mettlen* at Gohl, 2km north of Langnau (☎034/402 36 58), a modest place with goodish facilities; there's another, wilder option at Bumbach (☎034/493 47 00). The spartan HI **hostel** at Mooseggstrasse 32 in Langnau (☎034/402 45 26; closed Feb & Oct) has dorms at Fr.14 per person excluding breakfast, while the Berghotels on the summits of the Napf (☎034/495 54 08, fax 495 60 02; ①; closed Mon in winter) and the Marbachegg (☎034/493 32 66, fax 493 47 94) have dorm places for Fr.30–35.

Otherwise, every hamlet has its choice of small-scale country inns which double as **hotel** and **restaurant**, virtually all of which, big and small, use farm-fresh produce and ingredients brought straight into the kitchen from that morning's market – bad Emmentaler cooking is a contradiction in terms. Affoltern, for instance, has the impressive *Sonne* (☎034/435 80 00, fax 435 80 19; ②), with a few pleasantly renovated rooms above a good local restaurant; while the *Hirschen* (☎034/402 15 17, fax 402 56 23; ②), a huge inn in typical Emmentaler style, dominates the centre of Langnau. Kemmeriboden rejoices in the wonderful *Kemmeriboden-Bad* hotel (☎034/493 77 77, fax 493 77 70, *www.kemmeriboden.com*; ③), with comfortable rooms, dorm places (Fr.28) a superb *Ämmitaler Ruschtig Menü* and simply dreamy home-made meringues.

Solothurn

SOLOTHURN (Soleure in French), some 35km north of Bern, is touted as the most beautiful Baroque city in Switzerland – with justification. Its compact but very characterful Old Town is crammed with an odd architectural mix of Swiss-German sturdiness and lavish Italianate excess dating from the town's heyday in the seventeenth and eighteenth centuries.

In Celtic times, Salodurum was a fortified town, but it was only in the tenth century – after Roman domination and Alemannic invasion – that Solothurn rediscovered some stability. With the demise of the Zähringen dynasty in 1218, the city's finest expanded their territory to form a buffer zone sitting comfortably between the mighty Bern on one side and equally mighty Basel on the other. As a separate canton, Solothurn joined the Swiss Confederation in 1481. In the decades following, despite the turmoil of the Reformation all around, Solothurn remained Catholic and so, in 1530, was chosen by the Catholic ambassadors of the King of France as their place of residence. For more than 250 years, the **French ambassadors** lived in Solothurn, overseeing the town's redevelopment in the contemporary **Baroque** style. Some destruction followed the 1798 revolution, but a great deal of Solothurn's graceful Old Town has survived. These days it's a lively, cosmopolitan place, with thriving industry (watchmaking and precision manufacturing figure large) and a curiously varied mixture of ethnicities on its streets. It's an easy day trip – or overnight stay – from Bern, with a couple of spectacular Baroque churches, a very worthwhile art gallery, and a high viewpoint nearby for breezy walks.

Arrival, orientation and information

Solothurn is on the main SBB **train** line between Biel/Bienne and the big rail junction at Olten. It's also served by regular mini-trains from Bern operated by RBS, but these don't appear on the big departures board in Bern station; aim instead for platforms U1–4 down to the right. Solothurn's oddly huge **train station** is a few minutes' walk south of the river, with a **change** bureau and bike rental (both daily 5am–8.50pm) and, just to one side, the main **post office** (CH-4501 Solothurn 1).

Rötistrasse is the highway heading north from in front of the station, but quieter Hauptbahnhofstrasse, one street to the left, will deliver you to the pedestrian-only Kreuzackerbrücke, leading into the heart of the Old Town. **River boats** from Biel/Bienne dock at the Romandie jetty beside the railway bridge, two west of the Kreuzackerbrücke. The **tourist office** is at the foot of the cathedral steps, Hauptgasse 69 (Mon–Fri 8.30am–noon & 1.30–6pm, Sat 9am–noon; ☎032/626 46 46, *www.solothurn.ch/tourism*), and runs excellent ninety-minute **walking tours** of the town beginning from the Baseltor (May–Sept Sat 2.30pm; Fr.5).

Accommodation

Solothurn's HI **hostel**, on the Old Town bank just west of the Kreuzackerbrücke at Landhausquai 23 (☎032/623 17 06, fax 623 16 39; ①), is one of the country's best – modern steel-and-glass decor inside a seventeenth-century building. There's a wide choice of dorms (from Fr.26) and rooms with and without river views, and as well as all the usual services, including bike rental, they'll put together a packed lunch for you for Fr.11.50.

Of the **hotels**, rough-and-ready *Kreuz*, at Kreuzgasse 4 (☎032/622 20 20, fax 621 52 32; ①) has top value shared-bath rooms, spartan and wood-floor creaky (newer rooms are upstairs), with discounts for stays beyond one night and free kitchen use. *Zunfthaus zur Wirthen*, Hauptgasse 41 (☎032/626 28 48, fax 626 28 58, *www.wirthen.ch*; ②), is an all-wood guildhouse with plasticky but spacious rooms, some en suite, some not. The popular and friendly *Baseltor* brasserie, Hauptgasse 79 (☎032/622 34 22, fax 622 18 79, *www.baseltor.ch*; ③), has just six en suite rooms, all appealingly simple and fresh, and so generally snapped up well in advance. Top choice in town goes to *Krone*, Hauptgasse 64 (☎032/622 44 12, fax 622 37 24, *www.hotelkrone-solothurn.ch*; ⑤), its Baroque decor preluding solidly comfortable old-style rooms, with stout, tasteful furnishings and rooms at the back looking over the cathedral steps.

The Town

Jewel of the town is the massive **St Ursen Kathedrale**, an Italianate vision in local grey-white stone that seems to float above the main Hauptgasse. It's crowned by a greenish tower which rises to 62m. (Incongruously, the steps leading up to the entrance are a favourite smoking spot for the local kids – not all the fragrant odours drifting about are ecclesiastical incense.) Overhead, the Latin inscription in gold running around the building refers to Solothurn's patron saints, Ursus and Victor, who refused to worship Roman gods and were martyred. The bright, soaring **interior** (daily 8am–noon & 2–7pm; Oct–Easter until 6pm) is reminiscent of a wedding cake, with a riot of intricate stucco covering the white stone walls that is typical of the lavish late-Baroque era in which the church was built (1762–73).

Barely 100m along Hauptgasse is the atmospheric **Jesuit church**, sandwiched between shop-fronts – push the unremarkable door to gain entry to the extremely remarkable interior, dating from the 1680s and encrusted with a dizzying amount of lacy stuccowork. Halfway along Hauptgasse, overlooking the central Marktplatz, is the **Zytglogge**, Solothurn's oldest building, the lower part dating from the twelfth century, the upper part from 1467, and the astronomical device in the centre from 1545. The hour hand on the giant clock face is longer than the minute hand.

A few steps north of the cathedral is the doughty **Altes Zeughaus** (Old Arsenal), housing a moderately interesting museum of militaria (May–Oct Tues–Sun 10am–noon & 2–5pm; Nov–April Tues–Fri 2–5pm, Sat & Sun 10am–noon & 2–5pm; Fr.6; SMP). This massive collection documents Solothurn's history of battles and booty, most impressively with a gigantic hall full of suits of armour and more swords than you could shake a stick at. Some 50m east is the **Baseltor**, an old city gate dating from 1508. Hug the walls north to the corner bastion of the Old Town and you'll come to the circular **Riedholz** tower, now the location of a summer cycle of prestigious classical concerts.

Across the lawns to the north lies the impressive **Kunstmuseum** (Tues–Sat 10am–noon & 2–5pm, Thurs until 9pm, Sun 10am–5pm; free). Highlights of this surprisingly good collection are Holbein's *Solothurner Madonna* (1522), on a panel backed by the gorgeous *Madonna in the Strawberries* (1425), painted by the anonymous Master of the Garden of Paradise. Some spectacular Alpine canvases are led by Ferdinand Hodler's awesome and much-reproduced portrait of a Herculean William Tell emerging from a break in the clouds. One of Hodler's famous sequences of larger-than-life moving bodies decorates the stairs, while Klimt's luscious *Goldfish* is another highlight.

Last but not least, way on the other side of town, on the southern bank near the Romandie landing stage, is the highly odd **Krummer Turm**, or Twisted Tower, a fortification of the town dating from the 1460s. Looked at from any point other than its axis

---

ABOVE SOLOTHURN

One of the best viewpoints in the Swiss Jura is the **Weissenstein**, a ridge rising to 1284m with a breathtaking panorama over the entire Mittelland and out to the Bernese Alps. Local **trains** from Solothurn to Moutier stop at Oberdorf, from where you can either hike up or take the **chairlift** to the summit (April–Oct Mon–Fri 8.30am–6pm, Sat & Sun 8am–6pm; July & Aug Fri until 9.30pm; Nov–March Mon–Fri 9am–5pm, Sat 8am–5pm; Fr.19 return). On top is the super-slick *Weissenstein Hotel* (☎032/622 02 64, fax 623 89 47; ②–③), complete with gourmet restaurant, modern conference facilities and, alongside, a lovely garden planted with Jura flowers and plants, best in June and July. Plenty of walks branch out from the hotel, mostly along the crest of the ridge – you could also do a chunk of the long-distance Jura Höhenweg walk from here (see box p.406).

of symmetry, it appears to be hopelessly lopsided; in fact, though, its base is an irregular pentagon (due to the tower's original location at the sharp corner of a bastion of entrenchments). The spire on its scalene-pentagonal roof, although it seems about to topple off any minute, has been safe and secure these past five centuries. From the tower, you can cross to the northern bank and hike the riverside road for two hours west to the stork colony at **Altreu**.

Eating and drinking

Of all the many Old Town terrace **cafés**, *Rust* on Marktplatz has the edge, overlooked by the Zytglogge and facing the cathedral along the length of Hauptgasse. Look out for the local delicacy *Solothurner Kuchen*, a tart of nut fondant and whipped cream piled on a biscuit base, supplied by the slice in cafés and whole – in many sizes – by any of the *confiseries* in the centre.

Manora, the self-service **restaurant** in the Tardis-like Manor department store just off Marktplatz, has a rooftop terrace and a range of fresh-cooked dishes at rock-bottom prices (Mon–Fri 9am–6.30pm, Thurs until 9pm, Sat 8am–5pm). Both *Kreuz* and *Baseltor* hotels have co-operative café-bar-restaurants, both of them serving up delectable organic food in gargantuan portions; *Kreuz* is less expensive (*menus* from Fr.12, day and night), while *Baseltor* has the slight edge on quality (both closed Sun lunch). Otherwise, reflecting Solothurn's cultural mix, *Taverna Amphora*, Hauptgasse 51, offers Greek specialities for well under Fr.20; *Trattoria Alfredo*, Goldgasse 15, the same with an Italian bent; and tiny *Pittaria*, Kreuzgasse 12, has cut-price, but authentic, Arabic snacks – wash down your falafel (Fr.7.50) with delicious cardamom-spiced coffee.

Fribourg

Some 34km southwest of Bern, **FRIBOURG** (Freiburg in German) is one of Switzerland's best-kept secrets. Its winningly attractive medieval Old Town, almost perfectly preserved, is set on a forested peninsula in a meander of the River Sarine. Steep, cobbled streets, bedecked with wrought-iron lamp standards and ornate inn signs, are picturesque and characterful. Six bridges, from medieval wooden fords to lofty modern valley spans, provide woodcut-pretty views back across the town of the old houses piled up together on the slopes.

But the views only scratch the surface of Fribourg. For, behind its visual charm, Fribourg is perhaps Switzerland's most amiable and easygoing town, thoroughly modern at heart despite the medieval appearance of some quarters. It's small enough to have kept most of its city centre residential, but large enough to have attracted a lively, cosmopolitan mix of people to fuel the community atmosphere. One of the country's most prestigious universities – and its sole Catholic one – attracts a massive student body to Fribourg from all over the country, and especially from Italian-speaking Ticino, thereby generating a social dynamism that is tangible on the streets. In addition, the Sarine (Saane in German), which carves a path through the town, is the local defining line of the *Röstigraben*: Fribourg is split roughly 70:30 between French speakers, who call their town *free-boor* and are a majority on the western bank; and Swiss-German speakers, to whom the place is *fry-berg* and who form a majority on the eastern bank. The town's radio station has two separate channels, many streets have two names, and almost everyone is instinctively bilingual. Some of Fribourg's older folk even cling on to the ancient Bolze dialect, a mixture, unsurprisingly, of French and German which you might be able to catch in the taverns and public squares of the Basse-Ville (Lower Town): in Bolze, the town is *Frybùrg*, and you'll hear people calling each other *Ggopäingj* ("friend").

Fribourg is an understated place. For the time-pressed must-see visitor, it merits barely an hour or two – which is all the better for those on a long, slow journey of familiarity around Switzerland, who could spend a week in the place and not see it all.

Some history

Bertold IV of Zähringen founded Fribourg in 1157 as part of his consolidation of regional power, which also saw the establishment of Bern, Burgdorf, Thun and Murten, as well as Freiburg-im-Breisgau northeast of Basel in Germany. After 1218, the Zähringens were succeeded by the Counts of Kyburg, who were themselves bought out by the Austrian Habsburgs in 1277, Fribourg passing from hand to hand with each succession. In 1452, Savoy took over, although in the Burgundian Wars shortly afterwards Fribourg backed the victorious Swiss against Savoy, and so became a free city. In 1481, it joined the Swiss Confederation.

For reasons which haven't been fully explained, Fribourg remained Catholic throughout the Reformation (and is still determinedly Catholic today): virtually surrounded by Protestant Bern, it became a place of refuge for the exiled bishops of Geneva and Lausanne. The oligarchic ruling families retained their grip on power even throughout the 1798 upheavals, and in 1846 Fribourg joined the reactionary Sonderbund, fighting against Protestant liberalism all around. It lost, and suffered expulsion of its Jesuits as revenge. Intolerance was short-lived, though: Jews were allowed to return to Fribourg in 1866 after almost 400 years of banishment from the city, and a local entrepreneur, Georges Python, founded the Catholic university in 1889. Fribourg stagnated for much of the twentieth century, stymied by economic depression, but the boom of the last third of the century has brought new wealth and energy to the city.

Arrival, orientation and information

Fribourg's **train station** is high on the hill overlooking the Old Town from the northwest, with the brand-new **bus** terminal beneath. As you emerge, **Avenue de la Gare** heads at an angled left down to the central **Place Python** (pronouced *pee-tohh*). From here, the various districts of the Old Town cover the hill in front of you. **Rue de Lausanne** is the main thoroughfare, heading east and down to the **Bourg** district, centred on Place Notre-Dame (aka Place Tilleul) and the Cathedral. From the Bourg, steep

---

FRIBOURG'S FESTIVALS

In February, Fribourg's **carnival** is focused on the ritual mass torching of the Grand Rabadou effigy, bearer of the winter and of all evil. However, the event to watch out for is **Bénichon** (Kilbi in German), a kind of harvest feast held in the first half of September similar to the Emmental's Sichlete (see p.233). In former years, this would take the form of huge communal meals – lamb stews and hams and meringues and all kinds of seasonal specialities, such as a special mild mustard spread on oven-hot bread; *poires à botzi*, a sweet pear compote not found anywhere else; and paper-thin *beignets de Bénichon*, pastry leaves sprinkled with icing sugar, served elsewhere in the country only at carnival time. These days, the celebrations have lost their communal, seasonal edge, and tend to be more public affairs, with food stalls and tastings in the street.

In the first week of October, there's a **fun run** over the 17km between Murten/Morat and Fribourg, to commemorate the messenger who brought news of victory at the Battle of Murten in 1476 to Fribourg (see p.179). **St Nicholas Day**, in the first week of December, sees an evening parade headed by a jolly old man with a long white beard, who rides in on a donkey distributing *biscômes* (spicy cake squares), to the children of the town amid much revelry.

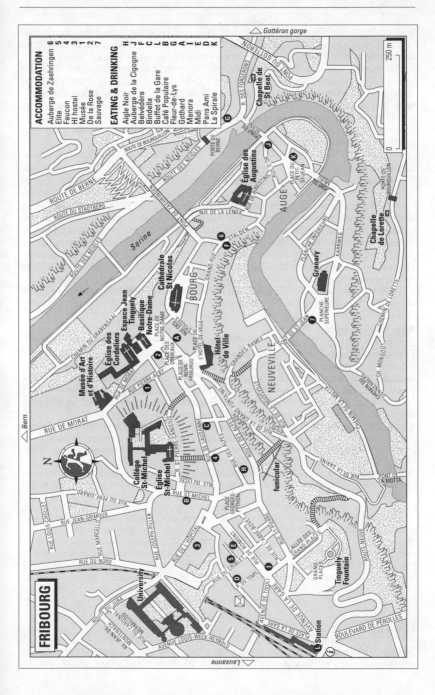

FRIBOURG

ACCOMMODATION	
Auberge de Zaehringen	6
Elite	5
Faucon	4
HI hostel	3
Musée	1
De la Rose	2
Sauvage	7

EATING & DRINKING	
Aigle Noir	H
Auberge de la Cigogne	J
Belvédère	F
Bindella	C
Buffet de la Gare	L
Café Populaire	B
Fleur-de-Lys	G
Gothard	A
Manora	I
Midi	E
Pans Ami	D
La Spirale	K

Gottéron gorge

Chapelle de St Beat

Église des Augustins

Chapelle de Lorette

Granary

BOURG

AUGE

NEUVEVILLE

Cathédrale St Nicolas

Hôtel de Ville

Espace Jean Tinguely

Basilique Notre-Dame

Église des Cordeliers

Musée d'Art et d'Histoire

Collège St-Michel

Église St-Michel

University

Station

Tinguely Fountain

funicular

Sarine

Bern

Lausanne

N

250 m

lanes cascade south down the hillside into **Neuveville**, while **Grand'Rue** heads east down to **Auge**, the oldest part of the Old Town at the tip of Fribourg's peninsula. It's a walk of about 1.5km – downhill all the way – from the station to Auge.

The **tourist office** is beside the station – turn right as you come out (Mon–Fri 9am–12.30pm & 1.30–6pm, Sat 9am–noon; June–Sept also Sat 1.30–4pm; ☎026/321 31 75, *www.fribourgtourism.ch* and *www.pays-de-fribourg.ch*). Cheery and efficient staff can book rooms and provide a wealth of information on the city and the whole canton, which extends as far south as Gruyères (covered in Chapter 2) and also takes in Murten/Morat and Estavayer-le-Lac (in Chapter 3). Ask for details on the many easy **countryside walks** which start from the city centre.

City transport

Fribourg is definitely a **walking** city, but the hills are steep enough that you may want to take advantage of at least one **bus** line: bus #4 runs every fifteen minutes on a very handy circular route, starting at the station, running down to Place Tilleul, then down all the way through the Old Town to Place du Petit-St-Jean, then over the Pont de Berne to beneath the Pont de Zaehringen, before turning round and crossing the Pont de Berne and Pont de Milieu to the Planche-Supérieure and the Pont de St-Jean, and running through Neuveville on its way back up to the station again. Individual **tickets** are Fr.2; or you can buy a general **city pass** for one day (Fr.5) or three days (Fr.10). **Bike rental** is available from the station (Mon–Sat 6am–8.45pm, Sun 7am–8.45pm).

For more information, and to buy these passes, head for the **public transport office** beside the train station (Mon–Sat 6am–7pm, Sun 6.40am–3pm & 3.45–7pm).

Accommodation

Fribourg's HI **hostel** occupies part of the old city hospital a few minutes' walk north of the station, 2 Rue de l'Hôpital (☎026/323 19 16, fax 323 19 40; ①; March–Oct), with clean dorms that are a tad institutional, from Fr.24. The nearest **campsite** is *La Follaz*, a basic riverside site in Marly, 5km south of Fribourg (☎026/436 24 95; April–Sept).

Otherwise, there's only a handful of **hotel** options, but they're all well located in or next to the Old Town, and cover a range of budgets.

Auberge de Zaehringen, 13 Rue de Zaehringen (☎026/322 42 36, fax 322 69 08). Fribourg's oldest patrician mansion is now a venerable and beautiful gourmet restaurant with just two guest rooms – spacious, luxurious and characterful like five-star hotels can never be. For once, you can splash out on a hotel and be quite certain that it will be a room to remember. ④.

Elite, 7 Rue du Criblet (☎026/322 38 36, fax 322 40 36). Plain, unremarkable, but perfectly adequate rooms within a couple of minutes of the station. Discounts apply for weekend stays. Cheaper attic rooms. ①–②.

Faucon, 76 Rue de Lausanne (☎026/347 16 70, fax 347 16 75). Lino on the floor and primary colours on the walls, but don't be put off – this is excellent value for money, simple, friendly and clean, with a choice of en-suite or shared-bath rooms. Prices drop for stays over three nights. ①.

Musée, 11 Rue Pierre Aeby (☎ & fax 026/322 32 09). Large-ish, spartan rooms seconds from the cathedral and the Musée d'Art, with both en-suite and shared-bath options. Reception closed Sun. ①.

De la Rose, 1 Rue de Morat (☎026/351 01 01, fax 351 01 00, *hotelrose@vtx.ch*, *www.minotel.com/hotel/ch231*). Cosy and very central, with efficient and friendly staff, but a little gloomy inside. ③.

Sauvage, 12 Planche-Supérieure (☎026/347 30 60, fax 347 30 61). Stylish renovated rooms in an old Neuveville house, spacious and individually decorated. Free parking, and bus #4 stops outside. ④.

The Town

Just south of the train station, the grassy, open **Grands-Places** marks an entry into the commercial heart of the city, overlooked both by department stores galore and the intensely ugly *Golden Tulip* hotel skyscraper – shown to be even uglier by its proximity to a beautiful shuttered medieval house on the square, now a café. The ensemble is mocked by one of Jean Tinguely's famous **fountains**, a spouting, spitting affair installed in 1984 and described by one critic as "a firework in iron and water".

Shopping streets lead east to the busy **Place Python**, at the centre of the modern city. From here, three routes lead you into the Old Town. To the south, the trafficky **Route des Alpes** is supported on pillars above Neuveville, but its valley-side railings offer wonderful views of the river and of Fribourg's rustic location. The central **Rue de Lausanne**, a picturesque cobbled thoroughfare of pavement cafés and bookshops, heads directly downhill from Place Python. It's worth, though, cutting north from Python on the narrow, steeply rising **Ruelle de Lycée** up to the atmospheric medieval **Collège St-Michel**, for most of its history a Jesuit seminary and now part of Fribourg University; the shaded grounds of the academy are utterly peaceful, and there's a terrace from where you can look out over the city. Ancient covered steps, the **Escaliers du Collège**, lead down from the terrace to join the lower end of Rue de Lausanne.

The Bourg

All routes from the new town converge in the Old Town's most historically important and prestigious district, known as the **Bourg**, home to churches, the cathedral, the town hall and an array of mansions and patrician townhouses. The Bourg's central square is a small space actually comprising four separate areas. At the foot of Rue de Lausanne is **Place de Nova-Friburgo** with, opposite it, **Place de l'Hôtel de Ville**; next to it is a tree-lined square known either as Place des Ormeaux (Square of the Elm Trees) or **Place de Tilleul** (Square of the Lime Tree); and next to that is **Place de Notre-Dame**. Just to confuse matters, the indeterminate, 50m-long Rue du Pont-Muré connects them all.

An impressive presence to one side is the late-Gothic **Hôtel de Ville** (Town Hall), a highly photogenic building dating from 1501–22, whose double exterior staircase was added in 1663. St George spears the dragon on a fountain statue dating from 1525 in the square in front of the building. A regular Saturday morning market spills over into the streets around, one of which, Rue des Épouses (Street of Spouses), is spanned by a decorative old sign attesting to the fidelity of the couples who once lived there. The dourly impressive **Grand'Rue** heads off down the hill, a virtually intact example of a seventeenth-to-eighteenth century street, complete with Baroque, Regency, Rococo and Louis-XVI facades jostling for position all the way down.

Fribourg's highlight is the towering, High Gothic **Cathédrale St-Nicolas**, just off Place Notre-Dame. Take a moment to absorb the breathtaking, soaring, buttressed **tower**, exposed to view for its entire 73m height clear to the ring of feathery spires on top. Built over a church dating from the city's foundation in 1157, the present building was begun in 1283, and took two centuries to complete. Traffic swishes past the elaborate main portal, featuring a tympanum with the Last Judgement. The vast **interior** (Mon–Sat 7.30am–7pm, Sun 8.30am–9.30pm) is immediately impressive, its mustiness and gloominess redolent with old incense. The **pulpit** (1516) and, opposite it, the octagonal **font** (1499) are both particularly ornate and beautiful, and the tracery **choir screen** (1466) is dazzlingly intricate. Virtually all the stained glass in the cathedral is modern Art Nouveau. Don't miss the tiny **Chapel of the Holy Sepulchre**, to the left of the door as you head out, beside a plaque commemorating the mass celebrated here by Pope John Paul II in 1984: inside you'll find a group of 13 figures, sculpted from sandstone in about 1430. Christ is being laid in the tomb by Nicodemus and Joseph of Arimathea; behind, Mary is supported by John the Baptist, Mary Magdalene, two other women and two angels, while in front are three sleeping soldiers. The life-sized ensemble, drenched in a blueish submarine light from modern stained-glass windows, is extraordinarily moving, every stony figure conveying an intense emotion that effortlessly spans the six centuries it has stood here.

About fifty metres north of the cathedral is the porticoed **Basilique Notre-Dame**, under renovation at the time of writing, with white-and-gold stucco work dating from the late eighteenth century adorning the spacious, airy interior. Samson prises apart the lion's jaws on a fountain statue in front (1547), copied from a design by Dürer. Adjacent on Rue de Morat is the Espace Jean Tinguely museum (see below), with beside it the Franciscan **Église des Cordeliers**. Originally part of a friary founded in 1256, the church was renovated in the eighteenth and nineteenth centuries, but retains its impressive medieval decor, including a vast altar painting (1480) showing the crucifixion and, on the opened wings, the adoration. High Gothic oak choir stalls (1300), the oldest in Switzerland, and a larger-than-life 1438 statue of Christ at the whipping post also stand out.

THE BOURG MUSEUMS

Between Notre-Dame and the Église des Cordeliers is the highly recommended **Espace Jean Tinguely**, 2 Rue de Morat (Wed–Sun 10am–5pm, Thurs also 8–10pm; Fr.5), devoted to the twentieth-century Swiss kinetic artist who was born in Fribourg. Housed in an old transport depot, this new museum complements the more famous one in Basel (see p.201), documenting Tinguely's whimsical but also trenchantly purposeful sculptural machines. Old rusty wheels, bits of iron and *objets trouvés* are all recycled in extraordinary constructions which use a lot of energy and demonstrate great skill and ingenuity – but which go absolutely nowhere. One of the most spectacular on display is the grand *Retable de l'Abondance occidentale et du Mercantilisme totalitaire* – press the foot button to set things in eccentric but somehow poetic motion.

About 150m north, within sight of the medieval Porte de Morat, is the **Musée d'Art et d'Histoire**, 12 Rue de Morat (Tues–Sun 10am–5pm, Thurs also 8–10pm; permanent collection free, temporary exhibits Fr.5–10 combined ticket with Espace Tinguely). This broad collection is housed in an elegant sixteenth-century patrician mansion and, bizarrely, an adjacent slaughterhouse. Begin on the left in the Ratzé mansion, filled with medieval art and reliquaries with, upstairs, a particularly striking series of fourteen intricate biblical scenes carved in relief from panels of lime wood (1600). Upstairs again is the especially revolting jewel-bedecked skeleton of St Felix, dating from 1755, with glitter for lips and a phial of dried blood resting beside the bones. From the ticket desk, a subterranean tunnel runs through to the old abattoir, whose sombre stones now shelter a line of fourteen saints taken from the cathedral portal alongside a particularly mournful Tinguely sculpture. Upstairs is a collection of Swiss art from the nineteenth and twentieth centuries.

Neuveville and Planche-Supérieure

From the Hôtel de Ville, the ancient cobbled Rue de la Grand-Fontaine heads sharply downhill into **Neuveville** – if you're male walking here, you're likely to be whistled and clicked at by women hanging from the top windows of the old buildings, since this street amounts to Fribourg's red-light district. Neuveville is, nonetheless, perhaps the most peaceful and picturesque area of the city, exemplified by the Escaliers du Court-Chemin (Short-Cut Stairs), which clatter down the hill through a triangular open square adorned with the tinkling Fountain of Strength (1550) onto **Rue de la Neuveville**, boasting whole rows of original Gothic buildings overlooked by the Hôtel de Ville on high. A quirky **funicular** runs down from St-Pierre, beside Place Python, to Place du Pertuis at the western end of Rue de la Neuveville (daily 9.30am–7pm; Fr.1, city passes valid) – it works by tapping the city's sewers and diverting raw sewage into a chamber beneath the car at the top to make it heavy enough to be able to haul its partner up the slope. It's without doubt the smelliest ride in Switzerland.

From Neuveville, the triple-arched Pont de St-Jean leads you past a tiny church up into the huge open **Planche-Supérieure**, overlooked by a fountain statue of John the

Baptist (1547) and these days used as a car park. Dominating the square is the old **granary** (1708), in shimmering white with dizzily zigzagging step gables and equally dizzy chevron-design shutters. At some point, the building is due to open as a museum of archeology. Cafés on the square offer incredible afternoon panoramas across the valley to the backs of the Grand'Rue mansions, all of which are supported on foundations that plunge as far down to the bedrock as the house is built above: they may show seven or more storeys of windows to the valley, but only the uppermost three or four are above the level of the street.

Stepped paths from the square climb south up to the ridgeside **Porte de Bourguillon** and, beside it on a lofty terrace, the **Loretto Chapel**, an ornate little building built in 1648 that offers spectacular vistas out over the whole city.

Auge

From the cathedral, Grand'Rue and its parallel neighbours channel traffic down to cross the lofty Pont de Zaehringen, leaving the lower quarter of the Basse-Ville (Lower Town) – known as **Auge** – mostly to pedestrians. This district, absorbed into the city as early as the 1160s, is the oldest in Fribourg outside the Zähringens' original fortress (which stood on the site of the current Hôtel de Ville). It's full of atmosphere, with its cobbled streets and crumbling old Gothic houses and inns still very much lived-in; the sense of community surviving in such ancient surroundings is what really marks Fribourg out as being special. The **Place du Petit-St-Jean** is the local hub, ringed by cafés overlooked from the fountain by St Anne, the patron saint of the tanners who used to live here. A little northwest is the **Église des Augustins**, part of a monastery founded in the mid-thirteenth century, with impressive later Baroque decoration. The **Pont de Milieu** beetles southwest from the square to Planche-Supérieure, below the mighty precipices cut by the Sarine.

Northeast from the Place du Petit-St-Jean is the covered wooden **Pont de Berne**, leading to the ancient **Rue des Forgerons** (Street of the Blacksmiths) on the east bank of the river. The little bridgehead square, one of Fribourg's prettiest, holds the celebrated **Loyalty Fountain** (1553), decorated with angels. To the left (northwest) is the **Porte de Berne**, a city gate dating from 1270 that has somehow clung on to its original doors. Rue des Forgerons itself – a narrow, medieval track – heads east into the **Gottéron gorge**, beneath the immensely graceful modern Pont de Gottéron some 60m up. On the south side of the stream, a footpath leads up to the minuscule Chapel de St-Beat hugging the rocky walls of the gorge, but the road itself leads along the northern bank of the stream. You can follow it into the forest for as long as you like, past old mills and cottages. The romantic riverside trail is well marked and maintained, drawing you into the cool, mossy gorge for an hour or so east to a crossing point at **Ameismühle**; from here, high-level routes to both left and right bring you back to the Pont de Berne in a bit over an hour.

Eating and drinking

Fribourg has plenty of quality places for **eating and drinking**. Fondue is a local speciality, and you can find some of the best fondues in the country in Fribourg's cafés and brasseries. The giant Cardinal brewery, which sends its palatable beers out across Switzerland, is located in the town.

The Placette department store overlooking Grands-Places (closed Sun) houses an excellent *Manora* **self-service** restaurant, with fifth-floor views, while *Fou Food*, 27 Rue de Lausanne, is a Lebanese hole in the wall offering a kebab and a drink for Fr.7.50.

Cafés and café-bars

Belvédère, 36 Grand'Rue. Uniquely amiable and atmospheric old student café, tucked away virtually out of sight at the head of the precipitous street Stalden. The mood is warm, the service friendly, but the joy of the place is its comfy old armchairs, saggy sofas and bookcase-lined walls. An outside terrace is true to the café's name, giving eagle-eye views over the river.

Café Populaire, 9 Rue St-Michel. As it says, a popular student café-bar, also offering simple stomach-fillers like bagels, baked potatoes, and fish and chips. Closed Sun.

Gothard, 18 Rue du Pont-Muré. A Fribourg institution, beloved of Jean Tinguely, that's equally full of old-timers at their regular seats sipping at their beer and excitable students downing an espresso before heading off to a party. Posters, ephemera and intriguing bits and pieces cover the walls under a riot of fairy-light decoration, but the food is solid quality – excellent fondues, and daily *menus* for Fr.15 or so. Unmissable.

Maison du Peuple, 76 Rue de Lausanne. Cheapest of cheap bars, big, rough and loud, with cut-price beer and plenty of student life. Also has simple veggie food – often Indian – for Fr.13 or less.

Midi, Rue de Romont. One of the best pavement cafés along this central street, in prime Fribourgeois-watching territory.

Pans Ami, 5 Rue du Temple. Smoky, friendly café-bar near the station open until 3am Friday and Saturday. Closed Sun.

La Spirale, 39 Place du Petit-St-Jean (*www.laspirale.ch*). Cellar bar and major venue for live music, with small-scale gigs on Wednesdays (Fr.10), very cool DJ-ing on Thursdays (free) and a range of jazzy, folky, worldish performers at the weekends (Fr.15–25). Wed–Sun 8.30pm–2am.

Restaurants

Aigle Noir, 10 Rue des Alpes (☎026/322 49 77). Quality French cuisine (from Fr.30) in the heart of the Old Town, with an attractive modern interior and warmly efficient service. Closed Sun & Mon.

Auberge de la Cigogne, 24 Rue d'Or (☎026/322 68 34). Beautiful little bistro in a medieval house opposite the Pont de Berne, using market-fresh produce to produce subtle, inventive dishes. Perfect for a romantic tête-à-tête. *Menus* around Fr.25. Closed Sun.

Auberge de Zaehringen, 13 Rue de Zaehringen (☎026/322 42 36). Fribourg's finest eatery, housed in an old patrician mansion, with a cosy brasserie that serves up fresh and interesting gourmet *menus* from Fr.20 or so at lunch time, a little more in the evenings, and an adjacent formal restaurant where prices – and *haute-cuisine* quality – rise dramatically. Closed Sun & Mon.

Bindella, 38 Rue de Lausanne (☎026/322 49 05). Classy Italian in the centre, with cosy, warm decor and excellent fresh pastas (*menus* around Fr.23). Closed Sun.

Buffet de la Gare, in the station. Three different areas – a shabby café-bar, a slightly more upmarket brasserie section and, upstairs, one of the city's better restaurants (☎026/322 28 16), specializing in exquisite fish dishes – although it's not cheap (*menus* from Fr.50).

Fleur-de-Lys, 18 Rue Forgerons (☎026/322 79 61). A gastronome's delight on a medieval lane by the river. A tumbledown exterior preludes a cosy, atmospheric interior and fresh seasonal dishes of the highest quality (*menus* from Fr.30). Locals love the place, which is a high recommendation. Closed Sun & Mon.

Musée, 11 Rue Pierre-Aeby. A spartan, very uncomplicated Chinese, offering exceptional value – quality *menus* from Fr.16.

Listings

Car rental Avis, 13 Route du Jura (☎026/322 75 55); Budget, 81 Rue de Vevey, Bulle (☎026/912 73 81); Europcar, 103 Route de Villars (☎026/402 38 88).

Changing money In the train station (daily 6am–8.30pm).

Markets Vegetable and flower markets occupy Place Python (Wed morning) and the area around the Hôtel de Ville (Sat morning) all year round. The Place du Petit-St-Jean features a traditional flea market on the first Saturday of the month (April–Nov), while there's a crafts market on Rue de Lausanne on the last Saturday of the month (March–Dec).

Post Main office in the large high-rise just east of the station (CH-1700 Fribourg 1).

travel details

TRAINS

Bern to: Baden (hourly; 1hr 25min); Basel (every 30min; 1hr); Biel/Bienne (hourly; 25min); Brig (hourly; 1hr 40min); Burgdorf (3 hourly; 15min); Fribourg (every 30min; 20min); Geneva (every 30min; 1hr 45min); Interlaken West & Ost (hourly; 45min); Langnau (every 30min; 40min); Lausanne (every 30min; 1hr 10min); Luzern (hourly; 1hr 15min); Neuchâtel (hourly; 35min); Solothurn (every 30min; 35min); Thun (twice hourly; 20min); Zürich (every 30min; 1hr 10min).

Burgdorf to: Bern (3 hourly; 15min); Fribourg (every 30min; 45min); Hasle-Rüegsau (3 hourly; 10min); Lützelflüh (twice hourly; 10min); Konolfingen (every 30min; 30min); Langnau (hourly; 25min); Luzern (every 30min; 1hr 25min).

Fribourg to: Bern (every 30min; 20min); Estavayer (hourly; 40min); Geneva (every 30min; 1hr 20min); Lausanne (twice hourly; 45min); Murten/Morat (hourly; 25min); Payerne (hourly; 25min); Yverdon (hourly; 1hr); Zürich (every 30min; 1hr 40min).

Langnau to: Bern (every 30min; 40min); Burgdorf (hourly; 25min); Hasle-Rüegsau (hourly; 15min); Lützelflüh (hourly; 10min); Luzern (every 30min; 1hr).

Solothurn to: Bern (every 30min; 35min); Biel/Bienne (twice hourly; 20min); Burgdorf (hourly; 30min); Moutier (hourly; 30min); Neuchâtel (hourly; 40min); Yverdon (hourly; 1hr 10min); Zürich (hourly; 1hr 10min).

BUSES

Fribourg to: Avenches (8 daily; 25min); Bulle (for Gruyères; hourly; 30min).

Kemmeriboden to: Schangnau (hourly; 15min).

BOATS

Solothurn to: Biel/Bienne (at least 4 daily except Mon; 2hr 30min).

INTERNATIONAL TRAINS

Bern to: Amsterdam (2 daily; 9hr); Barcelona (1 daily; 12hr); Berlin (1 daily; 9hr 30min); Dijon (1 daily; 3hr); Frankfurt (1 daily; 4hr); Köln (3 daily; 6hr); Milan (7 daily; 3hr 20min); Paris (1 daily; 4hr 40min); Strasbourg (1 daily; 2hr 20min).

PLACE NAMES IN THIS CHAPTER		
German	**French**	**Italian**
Aare	Aar	Aar
Bern	Berne	Berna
Freiburg	Fribourg	Friborgo
Saane	Sarine	Sarine
Solothurn	Soleure	Soletta

CHAPTER SIX

THE BERNESE
OBERLAND

South of Bern and Luzern lies the grand Alpine heart of Switzerland, a massively impressive region of classic Swiss scenery – high peaks, sheer valleys and cool lakes – that makes for great hiking and gentle walking, not to mention world-class winter sports. The **BERNESE OBERLAND** is the most accessible

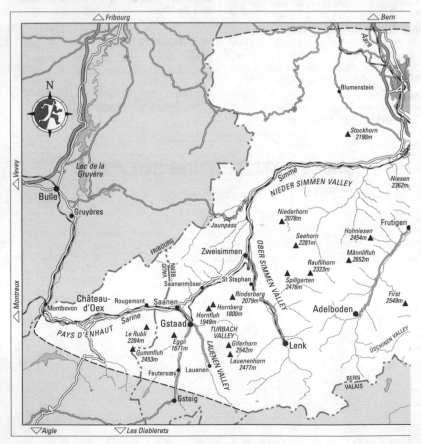

and touristed area, and also the most spectacular, best known for a grand triple-peaked ridge of Alpine giants at its core – the Eiger, Mönch and Jungfrau, cresting 4000m. However, the Oberland takes in a vast tract of territory, and the approaches to the high mountains have their own, less daunting pleasures: the twin lakes of the **Thunersee** (with the atmospheric old town of **Thun** at its head) and the **Brienzersee** (with **Brienz**) offer Alpine horizons and beauty enough to merit a stop of their own. Between the two, the bustling town of **Interlaken** is the main transport hub for the region, but the sheer volume of tourist traffic passing through can make it a less than restful place to stay. Coming from the big cities, many people aim for Interlaken as a supposed necessary stop, but it truthfully has little to offer beyond dozens of hotels and a handful of souvenir shops, and you'd do better to head straight for the mountains.

On a visit to the region, and stunned by the natural drama all around, the composer Felix Mendelssohn wrote: "Anyone who has not seen the scenery which surrounds Interlaken does not know Switzerland." Once you've seen it, you'll know what he means. Arguably the single most captivating place in the entire Alps lies just a short way south of Interlaken – the gorgeous **Lauterbrunnen valley**, with the resorts of **Wengen** and **Mürren** perched on plateaux above providing excellent winter skiing and summer hik-

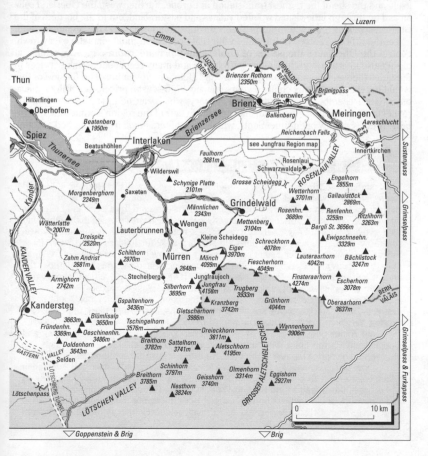

ing. **Grindelwald** is another bustling resort in its own valley slightly to the east. Both offer access to one of Switzerland's top excursions, the amazing rack-railway journey winding up through spectacular mountain scenery to the snow- and ice-bound **Jungfraujoch**, a windswept col nestling at 3454m just below the peak of the Jungfrau itself, and the site of the highest train station in Europe. Further west, the Oberland rolls on and on through little-visited wooded valleys and pastureland, out to the borders of the German-speaking area, where sits probably the most famous name in the region: **Gstaad**.

Tourist offices, centred in Interlaken but scattered throughout virtually every town, control the Oberland's thousands of **chalets and private rooms**, most of which, at higher altitudes anyway, close along with hotels and many resort shops and services in the quiet "between-seasons" of April–May and October–November. The flipside of this is that hoteliers and many chalet owners concoct high-season prices, generally applicable in late December and throughout February, which can be much higher than the rest of the year. Tourist offices can also provide details of the region's numerous **mountain huts** (generally open June–Sept), which offer hikers or ski trekkers a bed and sim-

EXPLORING THE BERNESE OBERLAND

Train stations and tourist offices throughout the region sell the Bernese Oberland **Regional Pass**, which has a vast area of validity well beyond the borders of Canton Bern, from Montreux in the west to Andermatt in the east, and from Bern and Luzern as far south as Zermatt. It's pricey but eminently worthwhile if you're based in the Oberland for a week or two's holiday. There are two passes, both available only in the summer season (May–Oct). The **seven-day pass** (Fr.165, or Fr.132 for holders of the Swiss Pass, Swiss Card, Swiss Transfer Ticket or Half-Fare Card) covers any three days of free travel in the core region (see below), plus the remaining four days' travel throughout the area at half-price. The **fifteen-day pass** (Fr.205/164) covers any five days' core-region travel for free, plus the remaining ten days at half-price across the area.

The **core region** extends from Gstaad to Meiringen, and includes boats and trains between Thun, Interlaken and Brienz, as well as trains, buses, funiculars and cable-cars serving Schynige Platte, Lauterbrunnen, Mürren, Stechelberg, Wengen, Grindelwald, First and Kleine Scheidegg, and even the car-carrying train between Kandersteg and Goppenstein via the Lötschbergtunnel. Core-region transport is free on the days you choose, and half-price the rest of the time. **All other transport** in the region is half-price throughout the pass's validity (aside from a few cable-cars around Gstaad and Adelboden which offer only a 25 percent discount): this includes the rides up to the Jungfraujoch and the Schilthorn; trains from Bern to Thun, Luzern to Brienz, and Montreux to Gstaad; and a network of connections outside Canton Bern, including those from Meiringen to Engelberg, from Brig to Andermatt or Zermatt, and even the mountain climb from Zermatt to the Gornergrat.

ple comforts in the wilds of nature. The co-ordinating **Bernese Oberland tourist office** has administrative offices at Jungfraustrasse 38, CH-3800 Interlaken (☎033/823 03 03, *www.berneroberland.com* & *www.berneroberland-hotels.ch*).

THE LAKES

The two lakes in the heart of the Bernese Oberland – the **Thunersee** and the **Brienzersee**, with the major resort of **Interlaken** lying between them – form the gateway to the region. Sidelined by more famous lakes such as Geneva and Luzern, the two are often overlooked by visitors in a hurry to get into the mountains, but there's something very peaceful about them, poised between the big cities of the north and the high Alps further south. In even the most hurried of Oberland tours, you could easily devote a day or two to enjoying the beauty of the lakes, set amidst cliffs and forested hillsides, dotted with quiet villages, and backed by a long chain of dramatic snowy heights.

Transport

Both the Thunersee and the Brienzersee are well served by transport, with mainline **trains** running between Thun, Spiez, Interlaken West & Ost, Brienz and on to Luzern, quite often swishing along within metres of the water, plunging in and out of tunnels cut beneath the mountains which ring the shoreline.

Unless speed is of the essence, though, you'd do well to take at least one trip by **boat**: the BLS train company (Bern-Lötschberg-Simplon; ☎033/334 52 11, *www.bls.ch*) provides service on both lakes, stopping at a host of towns and villages all along both shorelines. The Thunersee is the more picturesque of the two lakes, overlooked by the Niesen and the Stockhorn on the west, the wooded slopes of the Beatenberg on the east, and with the snowy peaks of the Eiger, Mönch and Jungfrau always in view to the south. There are at least half-a-dozen boats a day in summer (June–Sept) between **Thun and Interlaken West** (2hr), stopping at – among other places – Hilterfingen, Oberhofen, Spiez and the Beatushöhlen. Service is just as regular on the Brienzersee between **Brienz and Interlaken Ost** (1hr 15min). If you're visiting out of season, note that boats run on both lakes at least daily from April to October. In November and March, there's one boat a day between Thun and Interlaken only; from December to February the Thunersee service is reduced to weekends only. Boats on both lakes are free to Eurail and Swiss Pass holders, and half-price to InterRailers.

There's also a host of eat-aboard **cruises**, some on vintage steamships, generally running three times a day throughout the summer. Special evening cruises run on Friday and Saturday evenings all summer long departing from Thun, and once a month departing from Interlaken Ost (Fr.22). The paddle steamer *Blümlisalp* makes a six-hour meander from Thun to Interlaken West, while its sister ship the *Lötschberg* does a similar three-hour round trip from Interlaken Ost (both daily mid-June to mid-Sept, ordinary tickets valid).

Interlaken

Don't be ashamed of being a tourist in **INTERLAKEN** – that's what the place exists for. Interlaken is all that many visitors ever see of Switzerland, whisked through the country on a rapid lakes-and-mountains tour. The town is perfectly positioned as the gateway into the Oberland, linked into main train routes to and from Bern and Zürich, with branch lines feeding out in all directions into the high Alps nearby. It's a pleasant enough place, even if bustling and commercial and packed with Swiss-kitsch souvenir shops, and it's useful for its proximity to the mountains.

The town is situated on the Bödeli, a small alluvial neck of land between the Thunersee and Brienzersee. It's one of the oldest resorts in the country, famed for its superb **views** towards the Jungfrau massif, which lies perfectly framed between two hills to the south of town. And that's pretty much the whole story – history, character and tradition take a back seat to the necessities of providing for the hundreds of thousands of trippers who pass through on their way to more dramatic backdrops. One thing you can't fail to notice is that many of the shops which cram the centre of town have prominent signs in Japanese – of Interlaken's tourists, fully a quarter are from Japan, as many as from around Switzerland.

Arrival, orientation and information

The town hasn't much more to offer than its long main street, **Höheweg,** with a train station at each end. Mainline trains from Bern and Luzern terminate at **Interlaken Ost** station, 1km east of the centre, but those coming from the Bern direction pass first through **Interlaken West** station, a much more useful place to get off since it's right beside the centre. (Be aware that branch-line trains into the mountains depart only from Ost station.) **Boats** from the Brienzersee dock directly behind Ost station, those from the Thunersee behind West station. Ost and West stations are linked by trains and city buses, running roughly every ten minutes from one to the other. With **your own vehicle,** Interlaken is well signposted from Bern and Thun; approaching from the south, use the car-carrying train through the Lötschbergtunnel (see p.280), signposted between Brig and Sierre, to bring you through to Kandersteg, from where a spur road joins the Thun–Interlaken highway at Spiez.

Strictly speaking, Interlaken is only one of five communities on the neck of land between the two lakes: to the west is **Unterseen**; to the south are **Matten** and, a little further out, **Wilderswil**; to the east is **Böningen**. Although Interlaken overshadows them all, and the built-up area is contiguous from one to another, all five retain their individual identity and postal codes: if you go looking for something on Hauptstrasse, you should know that Unterseen's Hauptstrasse is a long way from Matten's Hauptstrasse.

Information

The **tourist office** is in the heart of town, at Höheweg 37 (Mon–Fri 8am–noon & 1.30–6pm, Sat 8am–noon; June & Sept also Sat noon–5pm; July & Aug also Sat noon–5pm & Sun 5–7pm; ☎033/822 21 21, *www.interlakentourism.ch*). Faced by such an onslaught of business, they remain surprisingly cheerful and helpful, and can load you down with more maps, brochures and information about Interlaken and the whole Jungfrau region than you could ever possibly want, including details on the hundreds of hiking trails around and about and the useful *Jungfrau Magazine* with ideas for excursions. They also have a guided **walking tour** of the town (June–Sept daily 6pm; Fr.10, or free if you hold a ticket for the Jungfraujoch). **Radio Berner Oberland** broadcasts a half-hour of tourist information and weather reports in English (Mon–Fri 8am, Sat 9am; Interlaken 96.8FM, Lauterbrunnen & Grindelwald 95.9FM).

With Interlaken as one of the country's premier tourist resorts, there's a host of **packages** available through the tourist office. As a sample, you can book a night in a two-star hotel with breakfast, plus a return ticket to Jungfraujoch and a walking tour of Interlaken for Fr.171 per person sharing a double in the summer high season – a bargain since the Jungfraujoch ticket alone will set you back Fr.159 each. Many of the town's hotels also have cut-price deals for **multi-night stays** – if you're planning to stay more than a couple of days, it's always worth asking for any discounts, especially in the low seasons.

Interlaken is famous throughout Switzerland for its annual staging of Schiller's play **William Tell**, performed every summer since 1912 in an open-air theatre (with covered seating) in the Rugen woods near Matten. The stage is framed by old wooden houses in thirteenth-century style, and backed by the forest – the perfect backdrop for the cast of 250, all sporting Swiss national dress and authentic medieval uniforms, and the several dozen horses, cattle and farm animals which wander around bringing a festive air to the show. The dialogue is in German only, but it's really pretty obvious what the plot is.

Evening performances run twice weekly throughout July and August. **Tickets** (Fr.12–32) are available from the West station ticket office and from the Tellbüro, Bahnhofstrasse 5a, CH-3800 Interlaken (July & Aug daily 8–11.30am & 2–5pm; ☎033/822 37 22, *www.tellspiele.ch*). The tourist office has packages comprising one or two nights' accommodation, plus tickets for the show, from Fr.164 upwards.

Accommodation

Almost everyone who ventures into the Oberland stays for at least a short while in Interlaken, and the town is well geared up for visitors: there are literally dozens of **accommodation** options. The downside of the popularity is that breakfasts can be skimpier, corners dusted less assiduously, and personal service less expansive than in less touristic towns. Beware that hotels fill up very quickly at the frantic height of the summer season; in winter, when most people stay in the mountains, many places close altogether for a month or two.

The tourist office runs a free **hotel reservation service**: call toll-free ☎0800/558 555 within Switzerland (or ☎033/822 21 54, fax 822 52 21). Otherwise, to relieve pressure on the overcrowded tourist office, make use of the hotel information boards and complimentary phones outside both train stations.

Camping and hostels

There are thirteen **campsites** within 4km of town. The closest is the rather simple *Sackgut* (☎033/822 44 34; May–Oct) behind Ost station. Less than a kilometre south of the centre is *Jungfraublick* (☎033/822 44 14, fax 822 16 19; May–Sept), a much more comfortable family choice. Five sites are clustered together in Unterseen: *Manor Farm* (☎033/822 22 64, fax 823 29 91) is the only one open all year, but it's also the most expensive, while *Lazy Rancho* (☎033/822 87 16, fax 823 19 20, *www.lazyrancho.ch*; April to mid-Oct) offers best value.

The best **hostel** in Interlaken is the inimitable *Balmer's Herberge*, fifteen minutes south of town at Hauptstrasse 23, Matten (☎033/822 19 61, fax 823 32 61, *www.balmers.com*; ①). This is the oldest privately run hostel in the country with fifty years' experience of catering to backpackers, offering kitchen access, laundry, and spartan comforts in well-tended pinewood dorms (from Fr.20, plus Fr.1 for a shower), quads, triples and doubles. The atmosphere is brash and convivial, a perfect place to hook up with other travellers for trips into the mountains; you can get discounts on Adventure World's extreme sports and activity excursions (see box, p.257) if you book direct through the hostel. In summer, when the frat-party atmosphere and queues for the shower and for breakfast get too much, they set up a giant tent in a field 800m south (☎033/822 96 97; May–Oct), with bunks sleeping over a hundred at Fr.19.

There are less frenetic hostels in town, led by the quality *Backpackers Villa Sonnenhof*, Alpenstrasse 16 (☎033/826 71 71, fax 826 71 72, *www.villa.ch*; ①), an attractive chalet with comfortable, spotless rooms, a good shared kitchen, and dorm beds from Fr.29; rooms at the back, with stunning views of the Jungfrau, command a Fr.3 sur-

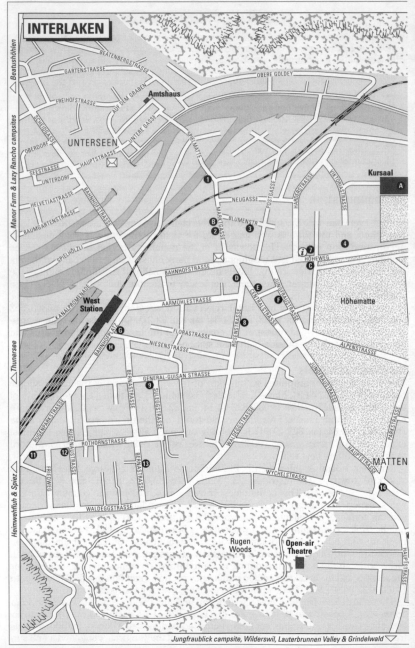

INTERLAKEN

Beatushöhlen

Manor Farm & Lazy Rancho campsites

Thunersee

Heimwehfluh & Spiez

BEATENBERGSTRASSE

GARTENSTRASSE

FREIHOFSTRASSE

AUF DEM GRABEN

Amtshaus

OBERE GOLDEY

SCHEUGASSE

OBERDORF

UNTERSEEN

UNTERE GASSE

SPIELMATTE

HAUPTSTRASSE

SEESTRASSE

UNTERDORF

HELVETIASTRASSE

BAHNHOFSTRASSE

BAUMGARTENSTRASSE

SPIELHÖLZLI

NEUGASSE

POSTGASSE

HARDERSTRASSE

VIKTORIASTRASSE

Kursaal

A

MARKTGASSE

BLUMENSTR.

1

B

2

3

4

7

HÖHEWEG

C

KANALPROMENADE

BAHNHOFSTRASSE

West
Station

AARMÜHLESTRASSE

D

E

F

JUNGFRAUSTRASSE

ZENTRALSTRASSE

Höhematte

BAHNHOFPLATZ

G

FLORASTRASSE

ROSENSTRASSE

8

ALPENSTRASSE

H

NIESENSTRASSE

RUGENPARKSTRASSE

BERNASTRASSE

GENERAL-GUISAN STRASSE

9

SULEGGSTRASSE

WALDEGGSTRASSE

JUNGFRAUSTRASSE

PARKSTRASSE

RUGENAUSTRASSE

ROTHORNSTRASSE

FRIEDWEG

11

12

BERNASTRASSE

13

MATTEN

WYCHELSTRASSE

HAUPTSTRASSE

14

WALDEGGSTRASSE

Rugen
Woods

Open-air
Theatre

HAUPTSTRASSE

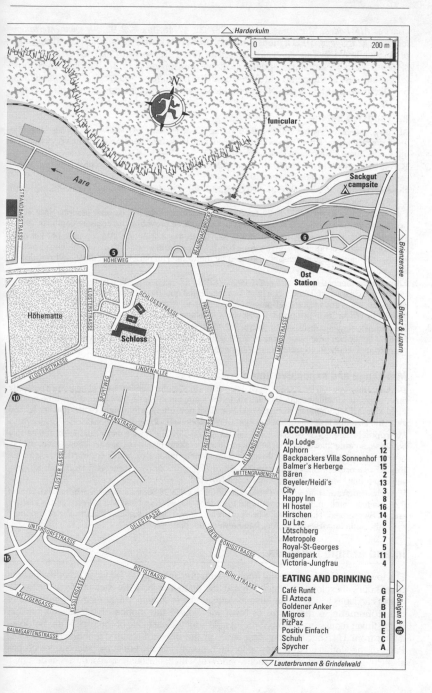

Harderkulm

0   200 m

N

funicular

Aare

Sackgut
campsite

STRANDBADSTRASSE

5
HÖHEWEG

6

Ost
Station

Brienzersee

Brienz & Luzern

KLOSTERSTRASSE

SCHLOSSSTRASSE

FREIESTRASSE

ALLMENDSTRASSE

Höhematte

Schloss

LINDENALLEE

KLOSTERSTRASSE

7

10

SPILMATTE

ALPENSTRASSE

FREIESTRASSE

ALLMENDSTRASSE

MITTENGRABENSTR

KLOSTER GÄSSLI

UNTERDORFSTRASSE

OELESTRASSE

ÜBERE BÖNIGSTRASSE

Du Lac

15

METZGERGASSE

KESSLERGASSE

RUTISTRASSE

BÜHLSTRASSE

Böningen &

BAUMGARTENSTRASSE

ACCOMMODATION

Alp Lodge	1
Alphorn	12
Backpackers Villa Sonnenhof	10
Balmer's Herberge	15
Bären	2
Beyeler/Heidi's	13
City	3
Happy Inn	8
HI hostel	16
Hirschen	14
Du Lac	6
Lötschberg	9
Metropole	7
Royal-St-Georges	5
Rugenpark	11
Victoria-Jungfrau	4

EATING AND DRINKING

Café Runft	G
El Azteca	F
Goldener Anker	B
Migros	H
PizPaz	D
Positiv Einfach	E
Schuh	C
Spycher	A

Lauterbrunnen & Grindelwald

charge. *Alp Lodge*, Marktgasse 59 (☎033/822 47 48, fax 822 92 50, *www.interlaken-tourism.ch/alplodge*; ①) is a modest place with dorms from Fr.27 and rock-bottom room prices, while *Happy Inn*, centrally located at Rosenstrasse 17 (☎033/822 32 25, fax 822 32 68; ①), is a backup dorm option, clean but uninspiring at Fr.27. Interlaken's HI hostel is 2km east of the centre, at Aareweg 21 in Böningen (☎033/822 43 53, fax 823 20 58; ①; closed mid-Jan & mid-Nov to mid-Dec), with dorms from Fr.25 and bike rental.

Inexpensive hotels

Alphorn, Rugenaustrasse 8 (☎033/822 30 51, fax 823 30 69, *www.hotel-alphorn.ch*). Charming little place (formerly named the *Pilgerruhe*) on a residential backstreet near West station, very clean and quiet, with some giant triples. Parking is easy. ②.

Bären, Marktgasse 19 (☎033/822 76 76, fax 822 28 55). Huge unrenovated old dive, with low prices, especially on the shared-bath rooms. ①–②.

Beyeler/Heidi's, Bernastrasse 37 (☎033/822 90 30). Comfortable enough garni stopgap, with some OK rooms (and some not-OK ones). ①.

City, Marktgasse 6 (☎033/822 10 22, fax 823 10 18, *www.city-hotel.ch*). Generic modern place in the heart of town, a little characterless but efficient enough on providing the creature comforts. ③.

Hirschen, Hauptstrasse 11, Matten (☎033/822 15 45, fax 823 37 45). Atmospheric old inn on a crossroads south of the centre, in the same hands for some 300 years, with freshly redone pinewood rooms – comfortable and pleasant – boosted by the wonderful dark-beamed *Stübli* and restaurant. Also with plenty of parking. Closed Nov. ③.

Lötschberg, General-Guisanstrasse 31 (☎033/822 25 45, fax 822 25 79, *www.interlakentourism.ch/lotschberg*). Characterful family-run hotel in a residential quarter, with excellent-value attic rooms in particular and a good-value B&B guesthouse attached. Apartments also available (Fr.100 for two people, Fr.175 for up to five people). Discounts for stays over six nights. Closed Jan. ②–③.

Rugenpark, Rugenparkstrasse 19 (☎033/822 36 61, fax 823 36 61, *rugenpark@tcnet.ch*). Quiet, very friendly family-run little place close to West station, with modest, attractive rooms that are cosily unrenovated – only some are en suite. Also with a non-smoking floor. ②.

Mid-range and expensive hotels

Du Lac, Höheweg 225 (☎033/822 29 22, fax 822 29 15). Comfortable, stylish old house in a perfectly quiet riverside location beside Ost station. In the same family since 1888 (and at one time hosting Field Marshal Montgomery during World War II), it now offers bright, light rooms that are far and away the best mid-range bargains in town. Closed Dec–Feb. ③–④.

Metropole, Höheweg 37 (☎033/828 66 66, fax 828 66 33). The town's major landmark, and its sole high-rise, soaring above the tourist office. Utterly generic business-class facilities inside, memorable only for the stunning upper-floor views (the fourteenth is top), which are worth paying for. ⑤.

Royal-St-Georges, Höheweg 139 (☎033/822 75 75, fax 823 30 75). Gorgeously stuffy palace, renovated to prime condition throughout. Closed Nov–Jan. ④–⑤.

Victoria-Jungfrau, Höheweg 41 (☎033/828 28 28, fax 828 28 80, *www.victoria-jungfrau.ch*). One of the grandest hotels in the country, dating from 1864–65, which hosted Mark Twain on his journey around Switzerland. These days it's been entirely restored, with its pricier front rooms overlooking the Höhematte for views of the Jungfrau between the hills. ⑥–⑦.

In and around the town

The town itself is only of passing interest, with precious little to see or do other than a couple of hours of exploratory wanderings, either on foot or from the back of one of the horse-drawn carriages which ply for business outside West station. The large grassy parkland of the **Höhematte** in the centre of town was where the monks of Interlaken's ancient Augustinian monastery pastured their cattle – on the east side of the park is the **Schloss**, dating from 1747 but incorporating some of the fifteenth-century monastical buildings. Parts of the Gothic church survive in the renovated **Schlosskirche** adjacent, which has also clung onto its old cloister, each window of which, curiously, is of a different design.

INTERLAKEN ACTIVITIES

At the heart of Switzerland's **adventure activity** scene, Interlaken is crammed with companies offering all kinds of extreme sports, including river-rafting, canyoning, paragliding, abseiling, skydiving, bungee jumping and more. **Safety** is obviously of paramount importance: the Brienzersee was the scene of a canyoning accident in 1999 when 18 tourists were killed by a flash flood, and although an inquiry is currently under way, safety standards – already scrupulously high – may well be tightened even more.

The following list of operators doesn't attempt to be exhaustive, and is intended only to give a sample of what's on offer. If you have any doubts, check with the tourist office for up-to-date information and guidance. Most travel **insurance** policies specifically exclude "dangerous" sports – check your policy carefully in advance, and make sure you're covered before you book anything. Alternatively, ask at the tourist office for details of local companies offering insurance cover.

Adventure World (☎033/826 77 11, fax 826 77 15, *www.adventureworld.ch*). Probably the best and most accomplished operator in Interlaken, with a vast range of activities on offer: river rafting (Fr.90), paragliding (Fr.150), canyoning (Fr.90–150), bungee jumping (100m Fr.100; 180m Fr.220), skydiving from 4000m (Fr.380), flying fox (Fr.75) and more.

Alpin Center (☎033/823 55 23, fax 823 07 19, *www.alpincenter.ch*). Branch of the Swiss Ski and Snowboard School, with a full range of ski equipment for rent, all levels of classes, and carving and snowblading on offer.

Alpin Raft (☎033/823 41 00, fax 823 41 01, *www.alpinraft.ch*). Half-day programmes rafting on rivers around Interlaken for under Fr.100 and plenty of canyoning options. As with Adventure World, skydiving, paragliding and hang-gliding can be done alone or in tandem with an instructor, leaving you free to relax and enjoy the experience. They also offer horse trekking (Fr.75/2hr) and "house-running", where you hook a rope round yourself and run full-tilt down the side of a tall building (Fr.68).

Skydive Interlaken (☎033/222 58 48, fax 222 58 80, *www.skydiveinterlaken.ch*). As it says, skydive specialists, with flights to 3500m (Fr.380) and the chance to photograph and video your jump (Fr.200).

Swiss Alpine Guides (☎033/822 60 00, fax 822 61 51, *www.swissalpineguides.ch*). Professional guide team offering a full day of climbing on walls of rock (Fr.95) or ice (Fr.125), with all equipment provided, as well as glacier walks (Fr.110 and up), heliskiing from 3900m (from Fr.250), snowshoeing and more.

Xtreme World (☎033/654 97 37, *www.xtremeworld.ch*). Among a wealth of canyoning, rafting and bungeeing choices, you can indulge in zorbing (Fr.50), where you're strapped immobile inside a giant plastic sphere and rolled down a mountainside.

Otherwise, you're just as well served by strolling along the Aare beneath the looming cliffs west into pretty **Unterseen**, adjoining Interlaken north of West station. This atmospheric village houses some of the area's oldest buildings, and the square in front of the **Amtshaus** off Untere Gasse is particularly picturesque.

Interlaken starts to reveal its secrets when you explore further afield. Before you even venture into the mountains, there are three viewpoints above the town to enjoy, all of them laced around with hiking trails galore. A funicular (May–Oct) rises from behind Ost station through the woods to the **Harderkulm** (1310m), offering vistas over the town, both lakes and a panorama of snowy peaks close enough to touch. Friday evening sees folk music and dancing at the summit restaurant, with special late trains laid on; book through the tourist office. On the other side of town, some 500m south of West station, is the vintage red funicular (May–Oct) serving the **Heimwehfluh** (669m), a more touristic venture, with the summit often crowded with parents taking the kids round the model-train exhibition and the miniature bob-run.

The best excursion from Interlaken, though, is the breathtaking **Schynige Platte** (2000m), acclaimed as offering one of the best views in the entire Alps. The peaceful village of **Wilderswil** is a few kilometres south of Interlaken, reachable by train (from Ost station) or bus #5 from West station; an attractive little place, full of traditional wooden houses, it serves as the base station for a cog-wheel train winding up for almost an hour to Schynige Platte (Fr.32 one way, Fr.54 return; Eurail and Swiss Pass 25 percent discount, InterRail not valid; late-May to mid-Oct only). Trails lead out in all directions from the top station – including a two-hour panorama route circling the summit – or you can just relax with a short stroll around the **Alpine Botanical Gardens** (Fr.3), filled with luscious examples of the local flora, and one of the few places where you can be guaranteed to see a genuine living edelweiss. Every Wednesday in July and August, trains depart Wilderswil at 5.40am to catch the **sunrise**, with the optional extra of breakfast at the summit hotel (Fr.15).

One of the most attractive **walks** in the whole Oberland region is from Schynige Platte along the crest to the Faulhorn (2681m), on to First and then down to Grindelwald (roughly 6hr). This is worth doing at any time, but if you're around in July and August, grab the unique opportunity to walk the route **by moonlight**: on the two Saturday nights with the fullest moon, trains leave Interlaken Ost at 10.30pm, bringing you to Schynige Platte by midnight, from where a local guide leads you along the six-hour trail. Ask the Interlaken tourist office for more details.

St Beatus Höhlen

Some 3km northwest of Interlaken, tucked into the cliffs on the shore of the Thunersee, are the **ST BEATUS HÖHLEN** (St Beatus Caves; *www.beatushoehlen.ch*), an impressive set of drippy subterranean chambers filled with stalactites and stalagmites that were formerly the residence of the early Christian ascetic St Beatus. It's a **walk** of about 2hr from Interlaken to the caves, or you can take hourly **bus** #21 from both Ost and West stations (journey time 15min). In the summer, about half-a-dozen **boats** a day between Interlaken West and Thun stop ten minutes' walk south of the cave entrance at Beatushöhlen.

Beatus himself reputedly came from Britain. The story goes that having given all his wealth to the poor to follow Christ, he was baptized in Rome by St Peter and sent with a companion, **Justus**, into the Alps as the first apostle to the heathen Helvetians. (In all probability, though, Beatus was one of the Irish followers of St Columba who brought Christianity to Switzerland in the sixth century.) When Beatus and Justus came to the lake, local people told them of a terrible dragon who occupied a cave overlooking the water. Beatus climbed up to the cave alone, and when the dragon emerged, raised his cross and spoke the name of the Holy Trinity, thereby sending the monster over the cliff edge into the water below. Beatus took over its cave, praying and working miracles until his death at the age of 90. A cult of pilgrimage rapidly grew up around him and the cave, which, after being walled up during the Reformation, was restored for public visits in the nineteenth century.

Today, you can visit only on **guided tours**, which depart every half-hour (April–Oct daily 10.30am–5pm; Fr.14; duration 50min) from the ticket office a short climb above the lakeside road. Note that a visit involves a full 2km walk through the caves (1km each way), which are chilly year-round. You can leave bags at the ticket desk for Fr.1. The guides lead you past the grotto where Beatus reputedly passed his days, and then on into the cool gloom of the cave interior, filled with the noise of rushing underground streams – the best time to visit is springtime, when a wet winter and snowmelt conspire to shoot torrents of water through the tortuous corkscrewing channels.

Eating and drinking

Food is not an especially high priority in Interlaken, and much of what's on offer is fairly basic, unadventurous fare. *Migros* restaurant opposite West station has self-service staples (closed Sun).

Cafés and café-bars

Balmer's Herberge (see "Camping and hostels"). The sociable travellers' bar attached to this busy hostel serves up cheap beer nightly to its backpacking clientele.

Brasserie 17, Rosenstrasse 17. Loud central bar, beneath the *Happy Inn* hostel, with cheap food and big beers.

Café Runft, opposite West station. A cosy tearoom, snackerie and bar open daily until 3am.

Goldener Anker, Marktgasse 57. Local pub crammed most nights with young people hanging out and shooting pool. The food is cheap and simple (*menu* Fr.14), and occasional live bands fill out the atmosphere a bit.

Panoramic Café, top floor of *Hotel Metropole*, Höheweg 37. Fifteenth-floor views out over the town and lakes, with an outdoor terrace.

Positiv Einfach, Centralstrasse 11. Popular crowded little DJ-bar in the centre of town.

Schuh, Höheweg 56. A tearoom-cum-restaurant on the corner of the Höhematte, refinement in the midst of kitsch-souvenir hell. The supremely elegant interior preludes equally elegant tea-and-cakes, or Swiss cuisine (plus veggie options), helped down by the cocktail pianist tinkling away in the corner.

Restaurants

El Azteca, Jungfraustrasse 30 (☎033/822 71 31). Attractive little Mexican place on a side street, with *menus* from Fr.13 and live mariachi (Fri & Sat). Closed Wed in winter.

Hirschen, Hauptstrasse 11, Matten (☎033/822 15 45). Traditional, rustic old wood-beamed inn serving up huge portions of steaming Swiss fare, with *menus* from Fr.25 or so. Closed Tues.

Matahari, in *Hotel Lötschberg*, General-Guisanstrasse 31 (☎033/822 25 45). Quality Indonesian cuisine, including *rijsttafel*, a sample of many Indonesian dishes, filled out with a range of Indian dishes, with plenty for vegetarians. *Menus* around Fr.22. Closed Tues.

PizPaz, Centralplatz (☎033/822 25 33). Pleasant but generic pasta, pizza and fish dishes for Fr.16 upwards, on a central crossroads. Closed Mon.

Spycher, in Casino Kursaal, Strandbadstrasse 44 (☎033/827 61 00). Just one part of this entertainment complex, housing a casino, bars, cafés and a formal garden, this restaurant is dedicated to touristic dinner-plus-folklore shows. They run three to six nights a week (May–Oct), and you can just watch the dancing and alphorn blowing for Fr.16, or choose from five *menus* of typical Swiss fare for Fr.40–60, which include the show.

Listings

Bike and skate rental A host of operators in town have mountain and city bikes for rent, including both train stations, the HI hostel, and Adventure World and Alpin Raft (see box on p.257). Many also offer guided mountain-bike tours of the countryside around Interlaken, for around Fr.65/day. Action Sport Landolt, Gsteigstrasse 12, Matten (☎033/821 10 03) have inline skates for rent (Fr.20/day).

Car rental Avis, Waldeggstrasse 34a (☎033/822 19 39); Budget, Wychelstrasse 38, Matten (☎033/823 13 00); Europcar, Untere Bönigstrasse 21 (☎033/822 04 94); Hertz, Harderstrasse 44 (☎033/822 61 72).

Changing money In Ost station (daily 5.20am–8.40pm) and in West station (daily 8am–noon & 2–6pm).

Email and Internet *Weltraum*, Rosenstrasse 5, is full of lava lamps, streetwear and trancey beats, along with a few PCs for pricey access (Fr.16/hr; closed Sun & Mon). Otherwise, go for *Buddy's Pub* round the corner, open daily until late (Fr.20/hr).

Flights Bohag (☎033/828 90 00) runs helicopter sightseeing flights over the high mountains. For a minimum of four people, they cost from Fr.150 per person, taking off from their base in Gsteigwiler; in winter, flights from a take-off spot at Männlichen cost from Fr.80. Air Glaciers (☎033/856 05 60) does the same thing from their Lauterbrunnen base.

Laundry Beatenbergstrasse 5, Unterseen (open 24hrs daily for self-service washes).

Post office Junction of Bahnhofstrasse and Marktgasse (CH-3800).

Around the Thunersee

The **Thunersee** (Lake Thun) is one of the prettiest in the country, a tranquil patch of misty blue loomed over by high shoreline mountains. The presence of the snowy Bernese Alps to the south, ranged above the water in a breathtaking panorama, constantly beckons you on. **Thun**, at the northernmost tip of the lake where the Aare flows out towards Bern, is an attractive overnight stop on the way into the mountains – much more relaxing than Interlaken – and small, rather twee little lakeside resorts such as **Spiez** can pleasantly break a slow journey south.

Thun

Set astride the River Aare on the lake which bears its name, **THUN** (pronounced *toon*) is much overlooked by visitors pressing on to Interlaken. This is a shame, since with its picturesque castle and quaint medieval centre, it's well worth a visit; views of the Eiger, Mönch and Jungfrau and, closer at hand, the giant pyramidal Niesen (2362m) and flat-topped Stockhorn (2190m) are a gentle prelude to the Alpine vistas further south.

The town has an odd secret, however. After World War II, the authorities decided that in the event of a future invasion, the whole of Switzerland south to Thun was to be abandoned, and the entire population was to assemble here for dispersal into mountain retreats. Switzerland's largest hospital was hollowed out of the Niesen, but despite constant upkeep, has never been used; it remains pristine and fully equipped, and there are probably dozens of other major military and civil emergency installations hidden in the mountains nearby.

Across the river from the station, Thun's low-lying Old Town – disastrously flooded in May 1999 – is renowned for the arcading both of the main street, split-level **Obere Hauptgasse**, and the tranquil, cobbled **Rathausplatz** at its northwestern end. Steps lead up from various points along the picturesque street to the fairy-tale turreted **castle** which looms above, built in 1190 and occupied by the Bernese in 1386. Its lofty halls now contains a historical **museum** (daily: June–Sept 9am–6pm; April, May & Oct 10am–5pm; Feb & March 1–4pm; Fr.5; SMP), with the usual period furniture and militaria.

At the lakeshore but on the station side of the river is the lush **Schadau Park**, home to perfectly tended flowerbeds, stunning views across the water to the mountains, and a lavish nineteenth-century folly planted majestically on the waterside. Beside it is an odd cylindrical building housing the **Wocher Panorama** (Tues–Sun: July & Aug 10am–6pm; May, June, Sept & Oct 10am–5pm; free), a giant painting – the oldest of its kind in the world – running all the way around the interior wall, which depicts the daily life of Thun circa 1810.

Practicalities

The **train station** is five minutes southwest of the centre, with bikes for rent; adjacent is the town **tourist office** (July & Aug Mon–Fri 9am–7pm, Sat 9am–4pm; Sept–June Mon–Fri 9am–noon & 1–6pm, Sat 9am–noon; ☎033/222 23 40). There's a weekly walking tour of the town, starting from Rathausplatz (July & Aug Wed 6.30pm; Fr.8). For information on the whole lakeside region, consult Thunersee tourist office (☎033/251 00 00, *www.thunersee.ch*). **Boats** around the lake, and to Interlaken, depart from outside the station.

For **accommodation**, walk right from the station for the spotless *Herberge zur Schadau* **hostel**, Seestrasse 22 (☎033/222 52 22, *www.herberge.ch*; ①), an old house in a quiet location, newly renovated but pricey at Fr.35 for a dorm bed; or you could plump

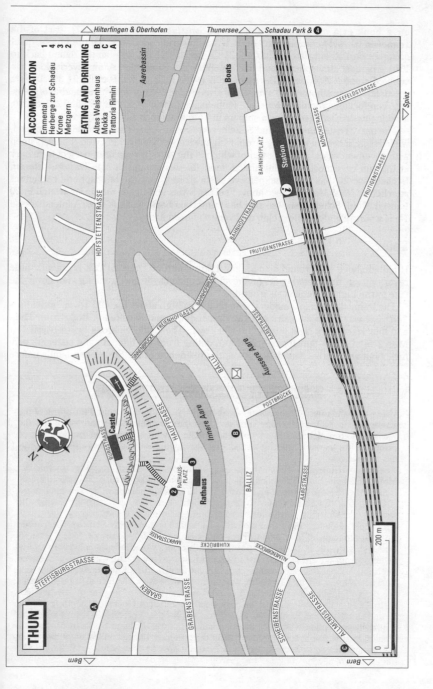

THUN

△ Hilterfingen & Oberhofen   Thunersee △△ Schadau Park & ④

Aarebassin

Boats

Station

ACCOMMODATION
Emmental   1
Herberge zur Schadau   4
Krone   3
Metzgern   2

EATING AND DRINKING
Altes Waisenhaus   B
Mokka   C
Trattoria Rimini   A

Aussere Aare

Innere Aare

Castle

Rathaus

▽ Spiez

▽ Bern

▽ Bern

200 m

for a bunk in a metal tubular module at *Swisstube* (☎033/336 40 67), part of the *Younotent* lakeside **campsite** at Gwatt, a 3km bus-ride southwest. Of the **hotels**, quiet *Metzgern* on Rathausplatz (☎033/222 21 41, fax 222 21 82; ②) – an inn dating back to 1361 – is most atmospheric, and has exceptionally good-value rooms overlooking the cobbled square. *Emmental*, Bernstrasse 2 (☎033/222 01 20, fax 222 01 30; ②) is a colourful old guesthouse that's now also a venue for live music, with a handful of pleasant, comfortable rooms. *Krone* on Rathausplatz (☎033/227 88 88, fax 227 88 90, *www.hauensteinhotels.ch*; ③) is a step up in both ambience and quality.

The many **restaurants** around Scheibenstrasse are varied and competitively priced, while Bälliz, a central shopping street with a twice-weekly market (Wed & Sat), is lined with pavement cafés, most relaxed of which is the *Altes Waisenhaus*, perfect for a beer in the sun or a meal of quality Italian food (*menus* around Fr.25). *Trattoria Rimini*, Bernstrasse 26, has good inexpensive pasta dishes, and the atmospheric restaurant attached to *Hotel Metzgern* (see above) serves Swiss and Italian *menus* for around Fr.20 (closed Mon). Scheibenstrasse also has numerous **bars**, while *Mokka*, Allmendstrasse 14, is a surprisingly exciting club and venue (closed Mon).

Spiez

Huddled above and around a small bay 11km south of Thun, **SPIEZ** is a gentle little resort village, dominated by its medieval waterside castle and stunning views over the lake to the high mountains all around.

The train station is in a modern shopping area high above the Old Town, or Städtli - find your way down on stairs and the descending main Seestrasse. Boats from Thun and Interlaken dock right beside the Old Town. The castle, **Schloss Spiez** (April–Oct Mon 2–5pm, Tues–Sun 10am–5pm; Fr.4), dating from the fifteenth and sixteenth centuries but with earlier foundations, was the residence of the Stretlingen family before

---

CASTLES ON THE THUNERSEE

There's a handful of visitable castles and stately homes dotted around the shore of the Thunersee aside from the fine medieval specimens within Thun and Spiez and the Victorian folly at Schadau, all of which are in fact less impressive than the two outlined below. All are served – and best visited – by boats which stop at or very close to the castles themselves.

Schloss Hünegg at Hilterfingen, 2km southeast of Thun (mid-May to mid-Oct Mon–Sat 2–5pm, Sun 10am–noon & 2–5pm; *www.schlosshuenegg.ch*; Fr.5) is worth a visit. Built in the 1860s in the style of a Loire château, Hünegg houses an interior unchanged since 1900, extraordinarily lavish bedchambers, boudoirs and halls displaying the wealthiest of lifestyles (the owner was a former officer in the Prussian army).

A couple of kilometres further along the lakeshore is the mighty **Schloss Oberhofen** (mid-May to mid-Oct Mon 2–5pm, Tues–Sun 10am–noon & 2–5pm; Fr.4; SMP), set in its own lush gardens. It dates from the thirteenth century, and houses collections of furnishings from the Bernisches Historisches Museum (see p.226) – a range of restored interiors, a stone-flagged knights' hall, salons furnished in Empire style and even a Turkish *selamlik*, or smoking room, way up under the eaves. The formal waterside parks are delightful, shaded by trees and planted with all kinds of flowers. A few hundred metres east of the castle, also in the park, you'll find the **Im Obersteg** gallery (mid-May to mid-Oct Tues–Sat 10am–noon & 2–5pm, Sun 2–5pm; Fr.5; SMP), with a small but impressive collection of modern painting and sculpture, taking in works by Modigliani, Hodler, Maillol, Rodin and more, including the touching Chagall *Jew in Black and White* (1914) and Picasso's piercingly well-observed *Absinthe Drinker* (1901).

passing to the Bernese noble dynasties of Von Bubenberg and, from 1516 to 1875, Von Erlach. You can visit several of the grand halls within, including the Baroque Banqueting Hall of 1614. The Romanesque **church** adjacent, with its seventeenth-century spire, has original frescoes in the apse and the crypt. Wandering through the tiny lanes around the castle, and around the bay filled with yachts (Spiez is home to a renowned sailing school) is a good way to get a feel for the town.

Practicalities

Spiez's friendly **tourist office** is on platform 1 of the station (May–Sept Mon–Fri 8am–6.30pm, Sat 9am–noon & 2–4pm; Oct–April Mon–Fri 8am–noon & 2–6pm; ☎033/654 21 38). There's a computer for **Internet** access in the office (Fr.12/hr), and bike hire facilities in the station.

The town's popularity with holidaying German and Swiss-German families means that there are plenty of **hotels**, but conservatism is the watchword. *Krone*, on Seestrasse (☎033/654 41 31, fax 654 94 31; ①) is an old, lived-in place with shared bathrooms near the station with parking. Down a bit further on the same street, past the junction, is *Bellevue* (☎033/654 84 64, fax 654 84 48; ②), a slightly cosier place with more modern rooms. Beside the bay is *Aqua Welle* (☎033/654 40 44, fax 654 76 75; ③) with more material comforts, better views, but less character. The nearest HI **hostel** is a few kilometres south, at Leissingen: *La Nichée* (☎033/847 12 14, fax 847 14 97; ①; May–Oct) is a pleasant, peaceful place with only a few dorm places (Fr.30).

Next to Spiez station is a self-service *Migros* **restaurant**, with views over the castle and the lake, while Seestrasse holds a clutch of inexpensive tearooms and pizzerias, including the popular *Brasserie 66* up near the station.

Around the Brienzersee

Stretching east of Interlaken, the **Brienzersee** (Lake Brienz) is much vaunted as the cleanest lake in Switzerland, beautifully set in a bowl amidst forested slopes, streams tumbling down from on high, overlooked to the south by the Faulhorn (2681m) and to the northeast by the Brienzer Rothorn (2350m), the latter served by a nostalgic old rack railway from the main town of the lake, **Brienz**. East of Brienz, a tortuous road crosses the Brünigpass into Canton Obwalden, heading for Luzern, while the main road scoots along the valley floor, beside the youthful Aare, to **Meiringen**, scene of the "death" of Sherlock Holmes and final staging post before the major trans-Alpine routes over the Grimsel and Susten passes.

Brienz

At the easternmost tip of the lake, **BRIENZ** has a quiet, community feel – not many people come visiting, and those that do mostly stop for just an hour or two before catching the boat back to Interlaken. The town is known as the most accomplished centre for **woodcarving** in Switzerland, and has many low-key workshops and souvenir shops hawking everything from mass-produced tat to quality hand-tooled busts, figurines and nativity scenes in limewood. Brienz also boasts the last **steam-driven rack railway** in Switzerland, with a fine old beast puffing its way up the flower-strewn slopes for an hour to the Rothorn summit (daily June–October; Fr.66 return, Eurail and InterRail not valid, Swiss Pass 25 percent discount). There are plenty of strolls around and about on the top, as well as a tough trail heading northwest through the mountains to Kemmeriboden (see p.235).

The major draw of Brienz is its proximity to the **Freilichtmuseum Ballenberg** (Open-Air Museum; April–Oct daily 10am–5pm; *www.ballenberg.ch*; Fr.14; SMP), 3km or so east of the town, a huge area of rolling parkland which serves as a living show-case for traditional Swiss architecture and crafts. There are two entrances, the West nearest Brienz and, some 4km away, the East entrance near Brienzwiler; regular post-buses from outside Brienz station serve both. In-between are thirteen separate areas, each containing several examples of traditional houses from different parts of Switzerland, transported here piece by piece from their original settings, reassembled and restored. Within each building are held daily demonstrations of traditional crafts, everything from needlework to faggot binding. The museum can be a little heavy going and the whole place is really too big to absorb in one go; you'd do well to select a few areas from the museum map (Fr.2) and aim for them alone. There are four restaurants on site, as well as groceries where you can buy provisions for a barbecue (free firewood provided).

Practicalities

The **tourist office**, Hauptstrasse 143 (July & Aug Mon–Fri 8am–6.30pm, Sat 8am–noon & 4–6pm; Sept–June Mon–Fri 8am–noon & 2–6pm; April–June & Sept also Sat 8am–noon; ☎033/952 80 80) is metres from the jetty where **boats** dock from Interlaken Ost and directly opposite the **train station**. A stone's throw away is the **Rothornbahn** station, departure point of the vintage locos.

Brienz's comfortable HI **hostel** is at Strandweg 10, a fifteen-minute walk east around the head of the lake (☎033/951 11 52, fax 951 22 60; ①; mid-April to mid-Oct), with dorms from Fr.24 and bike rental. A little further east is the *Aaregg* **campsite** (☎033/951 18 43, fax 951 43 24, *www.aaregg.ch*; April–Oct). **Hotels** within Brienz include the pleasant *Schützen*, Hauptstrasse 156 (☎ & fax 033/951 16 91; ②), within minutes of the train station, with OK doubles, en suite and not. There are a couple more generic hotels in the ② range along the lakefront, but a better choice is up on a slope above the town: the *Schönegg*, Talstrasse 6 (☎033/951 11 13, fax 951 38 13; ②) is a rus-tic chalet, carefully managed by an attentive owner, and providing neat, pretty rooms, also en suite and not. On the Rothorn summit is the *Rothorn Kulm* hotel (☎ & fax 033/951 12 21; ②) with plain, unremarkable rooms. All along the waterfront Hauptstrasse are any number of **restaurants**, all offering fresh lake fish: the best by a long streak is the *Steinbock* chalet, at no. 123 (☎033/951 40 55; closed Tues), a rather fussy place but with the best fish in town (*menus* from Fr.20).

Meiringen and around

The creation of meringue and the death of Sherlock Holmes are the two claims to fame of the old town of **MEIRINGEN**. From the way visitors approach the place, though, it seems that many have difficulty deciding which story is real and which invented.

Set at the heart of the Hasliberg hiking region, the town has long been a favourite mountain-walking resort of the English. Sir Arthur Conan Doyle, creator of Sherlock Holmes, stayed in genteel Meiringen many times, and the town's sole attraction is the **Sherlock Holmes Museum** in Conan Doyle Place (May–Sept daily 10am–6pm; Oct–April Wed–Sun 3–6pm; Fr.3.80, or Fr.8.50 combined ticket with Reichenbach falls funicular; SMP). This interesting little den is in the cellar of the English Church, and includes a life-size replica of the detective's study at 221b Baker Street, complete with taped commentary. The town **church**, north of the centre on Kirchgasse, has a free-standing Romanesque tower with a wooden spire, some fourteenth-century interior frescoes, and interesting archeological investigations below the crypt of the eleventh-century predecessor. Meiringen was popular enough with English visitors of a bygone age to attract not only Conan Doyle, but also semi-official trinket hunters: ancient bits and pieces from Meiringen's old church now sit in the vaults of the British Museum in London.

THE "DEATH" OF SHERLOCK HOLMES

The novelist **Sir Arthur Conan Doyle** chose the Reichenbach falls as the setting for the death of his character Sherlock Holmes. In *The Final Problem* (1891), Conan Doyle wrote of Reichenbach:

> *It is, indeed, a fearful place. The torrent, swollen by the melting snow, plunges into a tremendous abyss, from which the spray rolls up like the smoke from a burning house. The shaft into which the river hurls itself is an immense chasm, lined by glistening coal-black rock, and narrowing into a creaming, boiling pit of incalculable depth, which brims over and shoots the stream onward over its jagged lip.*

The story goes on to tell of the death of Holmes. On May 4, 1891, the detective met his archenemy Professor Moriarty on a ledge above the falls; the two became locked in a titanic hand-to-hand struggle before both tumbled over the precipice, presumably to their deaths. This neat device was Conan Doyle's way to free himself of the burden of constantly churning out pulpy detective stories and was intended to give himself the freedom to write more elevated literature instead. But he didn't reckon on public opinion. The outcry against the death of such a popular character as Holmes was so great that in 1903 Conan Doyle was forced to give in to the pressure of his fan mail. He resurrected his nemesis by claiming that Holmes had managed to grab a tuft of grass during the fall into the "dreadful cauldron" and so had lived to solve another mystery. Much to Conan Doyle's chagrin, the author was far more celebrated during his lifetime for his detective stories than for his various expeditions and good works; these days his numerous elevated writings have largely been forgotten, while his 45 Holmes novels are world famous.

Every year on May 4, members of the international Sherlock Holmes Society make a pilgrimage to the falls to commemorate the "death" of their beloved hero.

Practicalities

Meiringen's **train station** is in the town centre, with the **tourist office** opposite (July & Aug Mon–Fri 8am–6pm, Sat 8am–noon & 4–6pm; Sept–June Mon–Fri 8am–noon & 2–6pm, Sat 8am–noon; ☎033/972 50 50, *www.meiringenhasliberg.ch*). Innertkirchen, 1km beyond the Aare gorge and served by regular buses, has four **campsites**, best of which is the year-round *Aareschlucht* (☎033/971 53 32). **Hotels** within Meiringen include the *Victoria* on Bahnhofplatz (☎033/972 10 40, fax 972 10 45; ②), under new management, entirely renovated, and excellent value, although undercut in price by the appealing old *Hirschen*, 300m east on Rudenz (☎033/971 18 12, fax 971 47 12; ①), with shared bath old-style rooms. Conan Doyle's old haunt, the *Parkhotel du Sauvage* (☎033/971 41 41, fax 971 43 00; ④) is still around: the management undoubtedly benefits by a few francs from associations with fame, but can still come up with the appropriate atmosphere and comforts. **Eating and drinking** is a case of follow-your-nose: the *Victoria* has a decent-ish restaurant, with some veggie options, as does the *Alpin Sherpa* hotel opposite. The best **meringue** in Meiringen, by all accounts, is served at the low-key *Café Brunner*, Bahnhofstrasse 8 – but on careful analysis you may feel that the ones whipped up over the mountains at Kemmeriboden (see p.235) steal a march.

Around Meiringen

Meiringen itself is much less appealing than the countryside all around. The tourist office can supply details of the many hikes in and around the Hasli valley and Hasliberg region, but the most accessible excursion is to the dramatic **Reichenbach falls**. A wonderful old funicular (May–Oct; Fr.8.50 combined ticket with Sherlock Holmes Museum) runs from the south of town up to a vantage point below the roaring falls, best visited in spring laden with snowmelt from the glaciers further upstream.

A STICKY END

Odd though it seems for such a delicate creation, **meringue** originated in the rural Bernese Oberland. At some unknown time in the pre-Revolutionary eighteenth century, an Italian baker by the name of Gasparini invented a baked concoction of egg whites, sugar and cream, and named it after Meiringen, the scene of his inspiration. Documented names of the rich dessert include *meiring* (plural *meiringe*) and *meirinken* – until Louis XV took a liking to Gasparini's creation, whereupon the French name "meringue" took over.

Unfortunately, the documentary evidence for Meiringen's noble patrimony went up in smoke long ago during two disastrous town fires. Undaunted, researchers in Frankfurt's Culinary Museum early in the twentieth century turned up further solid evidence. Meiringen's bigwigs thought their claim to fame was now secure ... but Allied fighter-pilots during World War II had other ideas, and bombed Frankfurt – and the museum – into dust. Nonetheless, the locals are sticking to their story, and patisseries in Meiringen still churn out 1500 top-quality meringues a day to fuel the legend.

Stepped paths lead up beside the falls through the mossy forests to **Zwirgi** village, at the foot of the deep and dramatic Reichenbach valley. Trails lead on southwest up the valley past the hamlet of Kaltenbrunnen to **ROSENLAUI**, where a grand four-storey pile, the atmospheric *Rosenlaui Hotel* (☎ & fax 033/971 29 12; ②, dorms Fr.38; mid-May to Oct), sits overlooking a stream. The hotel was built a hundred years ago to service tourists come to explore the Rosenlaui valley and its mighty glacier, and to bathe in the valley's mineral springs, and its public rooms are a breath of elegance from a former age. From Rosenlaui, trails head on up to Schwarzwaldalp (beyond which private cars are forbidden) and over the **Grosse Scheidegg** pass to Grindelwald. This route through the Reichenbach valley to Grindelwald is also served by hourly postbuses from Meiringen (June–Sept).

A couple of kilometres east of Meiringen, served by buses to Innertkirchen, is the **Aareschlucht** (Aare gorge; daily: July & Aug 8am–6pm; April–June & Sept–Oct 9am–5pm; Fr.6), with a path snaking for 1.4km into the deep and dramatic sheer-sided gorge, which is floodlit on summer nights (July & Aug Wed & Fri 9–11pm).

THE ALPINE PASSES
Meiringen is one of the starting points for the excellent **Three- and Four-Passes** tours by **postbus**, which run once or twice a week in the summer months (June–Sept) – you must, though, reserve a seat in advance at any bus station. The route from Meiringen crosses the **Susten** (2224m) to Andermatt (another possible starting point; see p.364), then goes on to the **Furka** (2431m; see p.367) and **Grimsel** (2165m; see p.325) before returning to Meiringen in the late afternoon. Add a fourth pass (the **Grosse Scheidegg**, 1962m) if you start from Grindelwald. With your own transport you can add a long extra midway loop, cutting south from Andermatt over the **Gotthard** (2108m; see p.366), then to the **Nufenen** (2478m; see p.325), then back north over the Grimsel to Meiringen again – this way, though, you miss the Furka pass. Needless to say, riding around on the highest roads in Europe brings with it marvellous scenery from every angle. Every one of these passes has at least a restaurant on top, and most have some form of inn accommodation as well, making it easy to break your journey.

THE JUNGFRAU REGION

The **JUNGFRAU REGION** south of Interlaken is the rather uninspiring title foisted on what is perhaps the most dramatic, certainly the most memorable, mountain

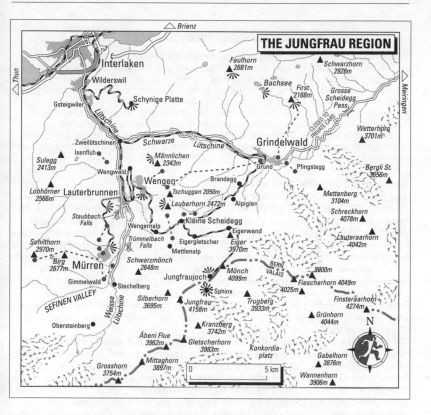

scenery in the whole of Switzerland. The Matterhorn may be more recognizable, Davos and St Moritz may be flashier, but the quantity and sheer scale of the awesome giants on offer here at close quarters takes your breath away.

The area is dominated by the mighty triple crest of the **Eiger, Mönch and Jungfrau** (Ogre, Monk and Virgin) – three giant peaks rising side-by-side to 4000m and seemingly always mentioned in the same breath. The Jungfrau is the focus, partly because it's the highest (at 4158m), and partly because the network of mountain trains from Interlaken Ost culminates at the **Jungfraujoch**, a saddle below the Jungfrau peak that claims the honour of being the site of the highest train station in Europe. The ride up to the summit – dubbed the "Top of Europe" – is touted endlessly in Interlaken and beyond as being the highlight of a Swiss visit and, despite the hype, it's not far wrong. However, plenty of equally stunning scenery is also to be had at lower altitudes. The region is focused on two valleys, which divide a few kilometres south of Interlaken. To the west is the famous **Lauterbrunnen valley**, celebrated with justification as the loveliest mountain valley in Europe, with its alluring resorts of Wengen and Mürren. To the east, the narrow Lütschen valley widens out on its way to the bustling town of **Grindelwald**, perfectly placed for its many visitors to take advantage of the hiking and skiing possibilities all around. Excellent transport around all these places – mostly trains, but also taking in cable-cars, funiculars and the odd bus – means that you can roam to your heart's content, which, with the quality of natural scenery on offer, may take a while.

EXPLORING THE JUNGFRAU REGION

Mountain trains throughout the Jungfrau region are operated by the Jungfraubahnen (☎033/828 71 11, *www.jungfraubahn.ch*). They have a **Jungfraubahnen Pass**, valid for free travel on their entire network apart from the Kleine Scheidegg–Jungfraujoch section (on which passholders travel for half the full fare). The pass, valid for five consecutive days, costs Fr.133, or Fr.85 to holders of the Swiss Half-Fare Card.

Eurailers get a 25 percent discount on all Jungfraubahnen trains, except where mentioned in the guide text. Swiss Pass holders get free travel on trains to Mürren, Wengen and Grindelwald, and a 25 percent discount on journeys higher up. InterRail brings no discount at all, apart from on the few occasions mentioned in the guide text.

Skiing in the Jungfrau Region

The Jungfrau Region is the heart of **skiing** in the Bernese Oberland, and its trio of resorts – Wengen (1274m), Mürren (1650m) and Grindelwald (1034m) – have long been a favourite of the British. They still offer some of the best skiing to be had in the Alps. The three areas are linked in the **Jungfrau Top Ski Region**, with a single pass covering the whole vast spread (2 days Fr.105, 7 days Fr.267), or individual passes valid for each area (1 day Fr.52, 2 days Fr.95). Various deals are offered for longer periods and for off-peak skiing – contact the Interlaken tourist office for more details. All the resorts have **schools** offering both daily classes and private lessons in skiing, snowboarding and other, wackier techniques for all proficiencies; class lessons tend to cost from around Fr.45 for three hours. All of them also lay on various diversions for skiers taking a break, including curling, ice-skating, sledging and adventure activities such as tandem paragliding.

Skiing and snowboarding pistes are open for all levels. Beginners are best served at Wengen and Grindelwald, both of which have nursery slopes and plenty of blue (easy) runs very close to the village centres. Red (intermediate) pistes run beneath the long Männlichen–Grindelwald gondola line, while there are long blue runs from Kleine Scheidegg down to Brandegg and Grindelwald-Grund. First (2168m), above Grindelwald, also has a host of leg-stretching blue and red runs. Mürren offers some of the most scenic skiing in the Alps, with a new chairlift accessing more than half-a-dozen routes down from the Schiltgrat (2145m), and the Allmendhubel funicular accessing lots more pistes-with-a-view.

There are thrilling red and black (advanced) runs from the Lauberhorn down to Wengen, following the course of the famous World Cup downhills and slaloms – at 4km, this is the world's longest competition piste (the downhill record is currently held by Kristian Ghedina at an amazing 2min 24.23 seconds) and, aside from skiing it yourself, if you're around in mid-January you should try and catch a glimpse of the professionals.

Black runs in the region are satisfyingly testing, most notably those down to Wengen from the Eigergletscher (2320m). The incredibly steep "Inferno" piste from the Schilthorn summit (2970m), through difficult mogul fields and the infamous "Gun Barrel" down to Mürren covers 11km.

The Lauterbrunnen valley

It's hard to overstate just how stunning the **LAUTERBRUNNEN VALLEY** is – even hardened Alpinists shrug their shoulders and call it the most beautiful valley in Europe, bar none. An immense U-shaped valley (the world's deepest) with bluffs on either side rising 1000m sheer, doused by some 72 waterfalls, it is utterly spectacular. Staying in Interlaken or Grindelwald comes a very poor second to basing yourself in or above

Lauterbrunnen for your time in the Oberland. However long you stay, two hours or two weeks, you won't want to leave.

Lauterbrunnen village itself lies on the valley floor, while the slopes above nurture two of Switzerland's most appealing little resorts. **Mürren** to the west is the transfer point for the dramatic cable-car ride up to the **Schilthorn** peak, while **Wengen** to the east is a stop on the train line up to Kleine Scheidegg and the **Jungfraujoch**. Both of them are car-free, perched on narrow shelves of pasture way above the world below, and both offer some of the best hiking and skiing to be had in the Alps.

Lauterbrunnen

The road south from Interlaken shadows the train tracks and the Lütschine river through Wilderswil and on into the deep countryside. Cliffs close in either side as you reach **Zweilütschinen**: the Schwarze Lütschine tumbles in from Grindelwald further east, while the road and railway continue south alongside the rushing Weisse Lütschine (named "white" for its foaminess) through a charming wooded gorge. At the point where the valley opens up, airily broad, sunlit and impossibly picturesque, you enter the busy little village of **LAUTERBRUNNEN**. The train station here is the junction point for journeys up to **Wengen** and on up to the **Jungfraujoch**.

The wealth of opportunity for sightseeing and exploring around and about is virtually limitless. At the entrance to the village is a funicular cresting the west wall of the valley: this serves **Grütschalp**, from where a cliff-edge train – one of the most scenic rides in Switzerland – trundles its way to **Mürren**. You might, however, prefer to follow the steep path up to Grütschalp (rising 690m in 2hr), to take advantage of the panoramic stroll alongside the tracks to Mürren (1hr 10min).

Just before Lauterbrunnen, precipitous roads and footpaths wind up west to **Isenfluh**, an isolated little hamlet on a tiny patch of green alp, from where little-trod hiking trails fan out and a cable-car rises to the Sulwald alp, at the foot of the distinctively jagged **Lobhörner** crag (2566m).

Just beyond the southern end of Lauterbrunnen village, the delicate **Staubbach falls** – at nearly 300m, the highest in Switzerland – gush out of a sheer cliff, like a lacy decoration on the rugged precipice. It's a scenic half-hour walk, or an hourly postbus, 3km up the valley to the **Trümmelbach falls** (daily: July & Aug 8am–6pm; Sept–June 9am–5pm; Fr.10). These impressively thunderous waterfalls – the runoff from the high mountains – have carved corkscrew channels through the valley walls: a stepped catwalk leads you over and around the enclosed, boiling cauldrons of rushing water (up to 20,000 litres a second), which throw up plenty of spray and have gradually eroded the rock into weird and wonderful shapes. From the top, trails from **Mettlenalp** connect to paths leading to Wengen and Wengernalp.

Practicalities

Lauterbrunnen's **train station** is at the northernmost end of the village, directly opposite the Mürrenbahn station. A 200m walk up into the village brings you to the **tourist office** on the main street (Mon–Fri 8am–noon & 2–6pm; July & Aug also Sat & Sun 8am–3pm; ☎033/855 19 55, *www.lauterbrunnen.ch*).

Lots of places offer dorm **accommodation**. If you go behind the station, cross the river on a tiny bridge and turn right, you'll come to *Matratzenlager Stocki* (☎033/855 17 54; Fr.13) with good dorms in a converted farmhouse and kitchen use. A little before the tourist office and down by the tracks is cosy *Valley Hostel* (☎ & fax 033/855 20 08; Fr.20), most rooms with a balcony. There are two **campsites**, both at the southern end of the village: *Jungfrau* (☎033/856 20 10) is on the west bank, while quieter *Schützenbach* (☎033/855 12 68) is on the other side, alongside the road to Stechelberg – both also have dorms (Fr.15–20) and rooms (①). Among the **hotels** are jovial, back-

---

LOSING YOUR WHEELS

Since both Wengen and Mürren are car-free, Lauterbrunnen has built for itself a huge multistorey **car park** directly behind the train station at the northernmost edge of the village – horrendous though that sounds, the community knows the value of its views, and has ensured both that the car park doesn't disturb the eye, and that it filters most of the traffic away from the village centre. Parking for a 24-hour day costs Fr.9 (July to mid-Sept), Fr.11/15 (mid-Dec to mid-April weekdays/weekends) and Fr.7 at other times; eight-day equivalents are Fr.59, Fr.76 and Fr.56. Two other small open-air parking areas within the village cost Fr.5–7 per day. Stechelberg has another large parking area at the foot of the Schilthornbahn cable-car (Fr.5/day, Fr.21/week).

---

packer-ish *Horner* (☎033/855 16 73, fax 855 46 07; ①), just beyond the tourist office, whose staff may slash rates to Fr.10 per person for post-9pm check-in if they have space. Beside the station is the *Bahnhof* (☎033/855 17 23, fax 855 18 47; ②), with cosy, uncomplicated rooms and cooking to match. *Silberhorn* (☎033/855 14 71, fax 855 42 13; ②–③) is up off the main drag but only a minute from the station, with pristinely quiet rooms – slightly pricier ones with a view. **Eating and drinking** are best done in the various hotels along the main street: the *Horner* has bargain pizza/pasta meals for under Fr.13, while the *Oberland* and *Schützen*, either side of the tourist office, are solid places for solid fare, both also specializing in afternoon tea with fresh apple strudel. The *Horner* has **Internet** access (Fr.12/hr).

Stechelberg and beyond

The bus from Lauterbrunnen to the Trümmelbach falls continues on to **STECHEL-BERG**, a peaceful hamlet at the end of the road. It has a minuscule **tourist office** (☎033/855 10 32, *www.stechelberg.ch*), open limited hours. Stechelberg is famous for being the starting point for the **cable-car ride** (see opposite) up to Gimmelwald and Mürren, and on to the Schilthorn; the huge base station complex is 1km before the hamlet. This is where Interlaken's thrill merchants (see box p.257) do their bungee-jumping – a quality spectator sport in itself. Buses terminate at the end of the road in front of the *Hotel Stechelberg* (☎033/855 29 21, fax 855 44 38; ①), a fine old hikers' inn with creaky rooms upstairs. Round the corner are dorm beds in the *Naturfreundehaus* (☎033/855 12 02; Fr.26; bring your own sleeping bag), also with some spartan rooms (①).

Beyond Stechelberg, trails continue into the undeveloped and unpopulated upper part of the valley, which forms part of the hiking circuit described in the box on p.273. Only the hardiest outdoorsy types venture here, but the trails aren't difficult and can offer some of the most rewarding hikes in the region, both for the spectacular views and for the isolation. There are no roads, and a short distance beyond Stechelberg begins a large area of land protected as a **nature reserve**. Three comfortable old **inns** along the main trail, all open May to October only and all requiring advance reservation, might persuade you to stay a night or two. An hour beyond Stechelberg is the *Berghaus Trachsellauenen* (☎033/855 12 35, fax 855 23 65; ①), a pretty half-timbered house set in the woods; an hour and a half further is the atmospheric and characterful *Hotel Tschingelhorn* (☎033/855 13 43; ①), while twenty minutes on up the trail is the *Obersteinberg* (☎033/855 20 33, fax 855 15 85; ①), a working farm that relies on candlelight after dark and has no showers. Both the *Tschingelhorn* and the *Obersteinberg* also have dorm places, and both are above the treeline, giving spectacular views.

Mürren and the Schilthorn

The Schilthorn cable-car from Stechelberg leaps the valley's west wall to reach the idyllically quiet hamlet of **GIMMELWALD**, a little-visited spot set among meadows ablaze with spring and summer wildflowers. You have to switch cable-cars to rise further to car-free **MÜRREN**, an eyrie of a village set on an elevated shelf of pasture which has managed to retain its endearing desert-island atmosphere (in the off season at least).

It's worth the journey for the views. From Mürren, the valley floor is 800m straight down, and the panorama of snowy peaks filling the sky is dazzling: you gaze across at the blank wall of the Schwarzmönch, with the great Trümmelbach gorge slicing a wedge of light into the dark rock, while the awesome trio of the Eiger, Mönch and Jungfrau are ranged above and behind in picture-perfect formation. From Mürren, the cable-car continues its breathtaking ride up to **Birg** and on to the **Schilthorn** summit (2970m; *www.schilthorn.ch*), where you can enjoy exceptional panoramic views and sip cocktails in the revolving *Piz Gloria* summit restaurant, featured in the James Bond film *On Her Majesty's Secret Service*. The trip's less expensive than that to the Jungfraujoch, and also less of a tourist merry-go-round, but just as memorable. The exposed terrace on the top is, if anything, even more dramatic than the Jungfraujoch, with a wraparound vista of icy peaks all around, from the Eiger to the Matterhorn to Mont Blanc, also offering a clear sight down to Thun and Bern. **Fares** on the Schilthornbahn are steep, but not outrageous. From Stechelberg to the top is currently Fr.85 round trip, from Mürren Fr.57. Eurailers pay 75 percent and Swiss Pass holders travel free to Mürren and pay 75 percent from there upwards.

Mürren itself was "discovered" by the British in the 1840s, and has a long tradition both of winter sports (see p.268) and of hospitable gentility – some of the first competition **skiing** in Switzerland was done on the slopes around Mürren. An Englishman, Arnold Lunn, claims to have invented the slalom here in 1922, while the famous "Inferno" amateur downhill race from the Schilthorn peak to Mürren (a descent of 2170m) was held for the first time in 1928, and is still an annual fixture in February.

The Schilthorn cable-car station is at the southern end of the village; at the opposite, northern, end is Mürrenbahn train station, starting point for the cliff-edge train (see p.269) to Grütschalp. Between the two a vintage funicular (Fr.23 return, Interrailers full fare, Eurailers pay 75 percent, Swiss Pass holders 75 percent) rises from between the chalets up to the **Allmendhubel** meadow. From here, hiking trails connect to the Blumen valley (see overleaf) and another 3hr 15min trail leads up to Marchegg, then down into the rugged Saus valley and through the Sprissenwald forest to Grütschalp.

Practicalities

Mürren's sports centre houses the **tourist office** (Mon–Fri 9am–noon & 1–6.30pm, Thurs until 8.30pm; July–Sept & Dec–April also Sat & Sun 1–5.30pm; ☎033/856 86 86, *www.muerren.ch*), with plenty of information on hiking and skiing routes around the area and listings of the many chalets and apartments. A **holiday pass** for Fr.130 (May–Nov only) buys unlimited journeys over six consecutive days on all transport on the Mürren side of the valley, including the buses between Lauterbrunnen and Stechelberg.

Accommodation in the village is excellent, and service is unreservedly good wherever you go. Almost all places close for April and November. Most hotels will arrange to pick you and your bags up from either the cable-car or the train station, if you've reserved in advance. *Belmont* (☎033/855 35 35, fax 855 35 31; ③) is outside the train station, a modern, well-equipped guesthouse also with some dorm beds (Fr.39), but for cut-price sleeping head for the popular self-catering *Mountain Hostel* in Gimmelwald

(☎033/855 17 04, fax 855 26 88; Fr.16). In Mürren, the *Regina* (☎033/855 42 42, fax 855 20 71; ①; closed May, June & Sept) has well-appointed, Art-Deco-style rooms; the *Alpenblick* (☎033/855 13 27, fax 855 13 91; ②) is comfortable with yawning balconies; while the *Alpenruh*, beside the Schilthorn cable-car (☎033/856 88 00, fax 856 88 88; ③), is simply one of the most appealing little hotels in the whole region – cosy, attractive, friendly and with dreamy views.

Eating, as ever, is a hotel affair, with top billing going to the *Alpenruh*'s excellent fare. *Snacks and Drinks*, on the main street, has – incongruously enough – authentic Japanese and Thai food done to order for around Fr.16. For an early morning excursion, many hotels allow you to defer your breakfast until you reach the Schilthorn summit restaurant – and the food's actually not that bad once you get there.

Above Mürren, a short half-hour hike east brings you up to the *Sonnenberg* (☎ & fax 033/855 11 27; Fr.40), a cosy and atmospheric modern inn in the **Blumen valley** (so-called for its carpet of wildflowers) with, a little further on, the *Suppenalp* (☎033/855 17 26; Fr.40), a much older building with simple comforts and simpler rooms.

Wengen

On the opposite side of the valley from Mürren, trains bound for Kleine Scheidegg grind up from Lauterbrunnen to **WENGEN**, another gorgeous, car-free haven perched on a shelf of tranquil southwest-facing meadow. Wengen is one of Switzerland's best-known ski resorts (see p.268), most famous for hosting World Cup downhill and slalom races on the Lauberhorn every January. It's slightly bigger and livelier than Mürren but still no more than a chalet-style village, with as long a tradition of hospitality as its competitor. The resort stays bustling with skiers well into April. Once the snows have receded, Wengen sits amidst ideal hiking country, overlooked by the Jungfrau and the distinctive creamy cone of the Silberhorn. Its lofty outlook means it enjoys unrivalled valley sunsets.

Walks of varying degrees of toughness from simple strolls to taxing hikes thread through the countryside around and above Wengen. Even simple little excursions such as down to **Wengwald** below the village can reveal flower-strewn meadows, romantic footpaths and stunning views out over the great chasm of the Lauterbrunnen valley. Opposite, the horse's tail of the Staubbach falls is clearly visible, while the jagged Lobhörner peak stands out, silhouetted against the sky. The cliff-edge **Mönchblick** viewpoint beyond Wengwald is less than an hour's stroll (120m down) from Wengen. Longer walks lead up to **Wengernalp** (also with a useful train station) and on up to the rail junction at Kleine Scheidegg (3hr total). A cable-car from Wengen formerly crested the bluff overlooking the village to the beautiful plateau of **Männlichen** before 1999's avalanches swept the whole thing away; until it's replaced, you can hike the steep three-hour trail, which rises a testing 1070m.

Practicalities

Heading out of the **train station**, and up onto Wengen's main street brings you to the **tourist office** (Mon–Fri 8am–noon & 2–6pm, Sat 8.30–11.30am; July–Sept & Dec–April also Sat & Sun 4–6pm; ☎033/855 14 14, *www.wengen.com*). Trains from Lauterbrunnen to Wengen are free to Swiss Pass holders, a quarter off to Eurailers and full price for InterRailers, but beware that they can be crowded even in the between-seasons; during the summer and winter peak periods, you'll be unlikely to get a seat. Kaderli Tours (☎033/855 36 81) offer guided **winter walks** for non-skiers.

Accommodation is plentiful, but watch out for between-season closures (as at Mürren) and also for the international skiing in January, which is great to watch but which can book the village, and the valley, out. Several **hotels** offer dorm beds: best is

WALKING IN THE BERNESE ALPS

Making a loop around the Lauterbrunnen valley, the week-long **Grindelwald Circuit** enjoys magnificent big-mountain scenery without treading glaciers or major screes, and is ideally suited to keen walkers. The paths are mostly good, but with some very long and steep slopes to negotiate – both in ascent and descent – and you'll need to be fit. With an abundance of accommodation along the route, each stage could be shortened or lengthened to suit personal preference, and there's the option of staying either in major resorts or in more peaceful lodgings in idyllic surroundings. The map LS 5004 (1:50,000), and the paperback *The Bernese Alps, a Walking Guide* by Kev Reynolds (see "Books", p.531), are both essential companions.

Start by riding the rack railway from **Wilderswil** outside Interlaken to the tremendous viewpoint of **Schynige Platte** (see p.258) and set out on what many consider to be *the* classic walk of the area, the high route to Grindelwald by way of the Faulhorn and Bachsee. Instead of going all the way to Grindelwald though, it's better to spend the first night at the hotel on the summit of the **Faulhorn** (see p.277) in order to enjoy sunset and sunrise over the mountains. On day two descend past the tranquil Bachsee lake before the crowds gather – there are stunning views directly ahead to the Wetterhorn, Schreckhorn and witch's-peak Finsteraarhorn (4274m) – and from there continue down to **Grindelwald**.

Below Grindelwald head southwest up steep meadows at the foot of the notorious North Face of the Eiger to **Kleine Scheidegg** and one of the nearby inns (see p.274). Crossing the saddle on day three a track leads down to Wengernalp and Mettlenalp from whose meadows you can safely watch avalanches pour down the face of the Mönch and Jungfrau. Either take the easy way to **Wengen**, and steeply down from there to **Lauterbrunnen**, or for preference tackle a knee-testingly steep path via the little alp of Preech which descends through the **Trümmelbach Gorge** into the Lauterbrunnen valley. Wherever you reach the valley, wander upstream to **Stechelberg** and continue on into the secluded upper valley where several rustic mountain inns provide peaceful lodging with romantic views from every window (see p.270).

On day four take the path which climbs steeply above the *Berghotel Obersteinberg* to gain the crown of the **Busengrat** at an astonishing little meadow known as the Tanzbödeli (the dancefloor). The pasture plunges dizzyingly to great depths on two sides, but a 360° panorama will hold you in its spell. On the north side of the Busengrat the path descends to the wild Sefinen valley (also with accommodation), then climbs to **Gimmelwald** and **Mürren**. Next day go up into the Blumen valley and follow a gentle trail across pastures to Grütschalp, and then through forest to the Soustal before tackling a final climb that leads to the **Lobhorn Hut** (☎033/855 30 85). The hut enjoys a privileged view of the Jungfrau – unforgettable at sunset. Day six is spent climbing to the Ballehochst viewpoint, then descending to **Saxeten** and finally all the way down to **Wilderswil** to complete the circuit.

the Christian-run *Bergheim* (☎033/855 27 55, fax 855 27 26; ②; dorms Fr.22), part of *Hotel Jungfraublick* at the top of the village, which is itself not a bad budget choice (②). Lower down the street, *Eddy's Hostel* (☎033/855 16 34, fax 855 39 50; Fr.27) has comfortable clean dorms, but charges extra for breakfast. The popular *Hot Chili Peppers Café* (☎ & fax 033/855 50 20; ①), on the main street, has simple, lively dorms (Fr.24) and rooms. Smoke-free *Edelweiss* (☎033/855 23 88, fax 855 42 88; ②) is a cosy choice overlooking the valley. The *Belvédère* (☎033/855 24 12, fax 855 37 30; ③) is a beautiful old Jugendstil house from 1912 in a quiet location above the village centre. A handful of grand old palaces, including the *Victoria-Lauberhorn* (☎033/856 51 51, fax 855 33 77, *www.hovic.ch*; ④) and the stunning *Regina* (☎033/855 15 12, fax 855 15 74; ⑤) have got the rooms-with-a-view-plus-all-the-luxury-trimmings service down to perfection. There's not much to **eat** outside the hotel restaurants – the *Hot Chili Peppers* does plenty of budget food (*menus* from Fr.14), while *Da Sina's* is a pleasant and similarly priced pizzeria and pasta joint at the end of the main street, also with a pub attached.

Kleine Scheidegg

Above Wengen, the train line curls over the Wengernalp, breaking through the tree line before arriving at **KLEINE SCHEIDEGG** (2061m) – four buildings huddled in the most dramatic of locations directly below the soaring **North Face of the Eiger** (*www.eiger-live.ch*), a sheer wall of rock 2300m high. The settlement (it doesn't even count as a hamlet) throngs with daytime crowds switching trains for the **Jungfraujoch** (see p.267), but sees virtually nobody staying overnight, although the "Good Morning" return to Jungfraujoch from here is a moderate Fr.58 (first train 8am), a significant saving on the full fare. Kleine Scheidegg is also the terminus for trains arriving from Grindelwald, over the hill to the east.

The station buffet (☎033/855 11 51, fax 855 11 52; ①) has spartan, comfortable **dorms** (Fr.38) and rooms, while the grand old *Scheidegg Hotel* – the two large chalets beside the station, focus of the Clint Eastwood film *The Eiger Sanction* (☎033/855 12 12, fax 855 12 94; ④–⑤; closed Easter–June & Oct–Dec) – has historically been the base station for worried relatives scanning the Eiger wall to track the progress of loved ones engaged in what's become known as one of the most difficult mountaineering ascents in the world. The hotel decor, all chintzy pelmets, wood panelling and armchairs by the fire, is from another world, and is an odd counterpoint to the muddy-boot hiking fraternity who tramp the area. Within view behind the hotel is the *Grindelwaldblick* (☎033/855 13 74, fax 855 42 05; Fr.35), a serviceable restaurant with dorms.

Kleine Scheidegg is the trailhead for a wealth of **high-country walks**. Hikes down to Wengen (roughly 2hr) or Grindelwald (roughly 4hr), or up the "back" of the nearby Lauberhorn (1hr), are relatively easy-going. There's also a tougher one-hour trail up to Eigergletscher train station (2320m), overlooking the massive sheet of ice sliding down from the high peaks. In the other direction, a picturesque route to **MÄNNLICHEN**, perched on a ridge and with one of the best mountain refuges in the region (☎033/853 10 68, fax 853 35 32; Fr.35), is particularly lovely (1hr 30min) and virtually flat the whole way. The Männlichen–Wengen cable-car suffered avalanche damage in 1999 and is under repair at the time of writing; instead, take the amazing half-hour gondola ride in the other direction to Grindelwald-Grund (InterRailers pay half price), and either hike back to Kleine Scheidegg (3hr 50min) or take the train.

Grindelwald and around

At Zweilütschinen south of Wilderswil, the road and the train tracks divide: one branch heads south to Lauterbrunnen, while the other follows the course of the Schwarze Lütschine torrent east through the Lütschental valley into broad open uplands and the hugely popular resort of **GRINDELWALD**. Unlike Wengen and Mürren over the ridge, Grindelwald *is* accessible by car and bus, and thus sees a great deal more tourist traffic than the Lauterbrunnen resorts. Although there are many ways to escape the crush, the village's main drag comes as a jarring blast of commercial reality.

Rural character is to be found out of the village. Nestling under the craggy trio of the Wetterhorn, Mettenberg and Eiger, Grindelwald offers easy access to explore some large glaciers close-to, and has a network of cable-cars leading up to numerous short- and long-distance trails throughout the region and beyond. Skiing is excellent (see p.268), but there are also plenty of hiking trails which stay as such all winter, making this a top choice for non-skiers on a winter holiday.

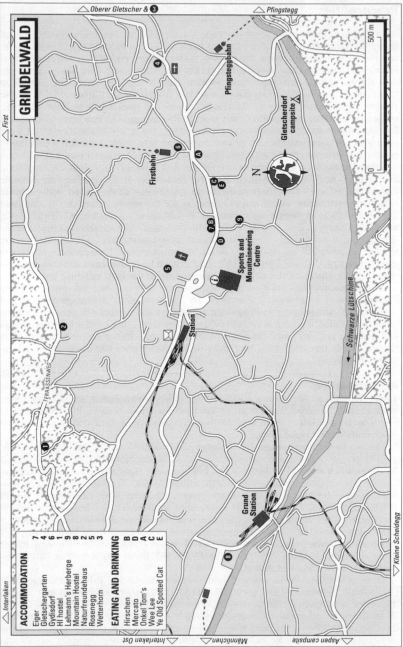

GRINDELWALD

△ Interlaken

△ First

△ Oberer Gletscher & ③

△ Pfingstegg

TERRASSENWEG

Firstbahn

Pfingsteggbahn

Station

Sports and
Mountaineering
Centre

Gletscherdorf
campsite

N

Schwarze Lütschine

Grund
Station

△ Interlaken Ost

△ Männlichen

△ Aspen campsite

▽ Kleine Scheidegg

0 — 500 m

ACCOMMODATION

Eiger	7
Gletschergarten	4
Gydisdorf	6
HI hostel	1
Lehmann's Herberge	9
Mountain Hostel	8
Naturfreundehaus	2
Rosenegg	5
Wetterhorn	3

EATING AND DRINKING

Hirschen	B
Mercato	D
Onkel Tom's	A
Wee Lee	C
Ye Old Spotted Cat	E

Practicalities

It's not always easy to make sense of where you are in Grindelwald. The village is tiered above the valley floor on a series of long terraces. Trains to and from Interlaken Ost and Kleine Scheidegg arrive at the **station**, at the western end of the centre, with most facilities strung east from here along the 1km-long main street. The Männlichen gondola arrives at **Grindelwald-Grund station** (also a stop for the Kleine Scheidegg trains), way down on the valley floor – it's a stiff hike (or a shuttle-bus ride) up to the village. At the eastern edge of the village, a cable-car rises north to **First** (2168m); while a little further east, another rises south to **Pfingstegg**. The **road** into Grindelwald from Interlaken continues east through the village, but a few kilometres on (at a car park near the Oberergletscher) private cars must turn back, although a handful of **postbuses** go on to cross the Grosse Scheidegg pass to Meiringen (see p.264).

Grindelwald's friendly **tourist office** (July & Aug Mon–Fri 8am–7pm, Sat 8am–5pm, Sun 9–11am & 3–5pm; Sept–June Mon–Fri 8am–noon & 2–6pm, Sat 8am–noon & 2–5pm; ☎033/854 12 12, *www.grindelwald.ch*) is 200m east of the station, with reams of information on hiking, skiing and practicalities for the whole region. It sits alongside the Oberland's main **Bergsteigerzentrum** (Mountaineering Centre; ☎033/853 52 00), which offers easy guided ascents (Fr.75 to the 2928-metre Schwarzhorn), canyon jumps (Fr.95), the much-touted "Kiss the Glacier" abseil adventure (Fr.180), and more. Contact Tandem Flights (☎033/853 55 53) for accompanied paragliding – no experience necessary – off the First (Fr.140), Lauberhorn or Männlichen (Fr.170). You can surf or check **email** at the Compeg copyshop, close to the First cable-car station.

InterRailers pay half-price on the Männlichen cable-car, and full price to First, Pfingstegg and Jungfraujoch. Eurailers pay 75 percent to Männlichen, First and Jungfraujoch, and full price to Pfingstegg. Swiss Pass holders get a 25 percent discount on all four routes. If you're in Grindelwald for a few days, check out the **Erlebnispass** (Adventure Pass; Fr.70 for 3 days or Fr.128 for 7 days) – this covers free transport on the local cable-cars and buses, free entry to the glacier sites and discounts on adventure activities.

Accommodation

To suit its high profile, there's a wider range of **accommodation** – and kitschy souvenir shops – in Grindelwald than in the Lauterbrunnen resorts, but unfortunately prices aren't any lower. Note that the between-seasons of April and November see much of the resort close down.

The two nearest **campsites** are *Gletschendorf* (☎033/853 14 29, fax 853 31 29) near the Pfingstegg cable-car and *Aspen* (☎033/853 11 24, fax 853 41 57) beyond Grund on the Männlichen slopes. For dorms, a bus from opposite *Hotel Bernerhof* outside the station, or a steep fifteen-minute walk north, will get you to Terrassenweg, a quiet lane running on a terrace above the village proper. Up here is an excellent HI **hostel** (☎033/853 10 09, fax 853 50 29; ①) with a cosy atmosphere, spotless dorms (Fr.30), good facilities and amazing views; they also rent out bikes and, in winter, *Velogemel*, or snow bikes – wooden bikes with runners instead of wheels (Fr. 15/day). Nearby is a less studenty *Naturfreundehaus* (☎033/853 13 33, fax 853 43 33; ①). The new, rather soulless *Mountain Hostel* (☎033/853 39 00, fax 853 47 30; ①) is on the valley floor beside Grindelwald-Grund station.

There are dozens of **hotels** and hundreds of chalets and private apartments in Grindelwald. *Lehmann's Herberge* (☎033/853 31 41; ①) is a popular family-run place in the centre, with spotless, spartan rooms, while the *Wetterhorn* (☎033/853 12 18, fax 853 58 18; ②) is a comfortable old roadside inn an hour's walk east of the village opposite the Oberergletscher at the point where private cars must park or turn back; it attracts plenty of hikers not only for its location but also for the hearty portions of Swiss cooking on offer in the restaurant. The *Rosenegg* (☎033/853 12 82, fax 853 50 59; ②–③) is in an excellent location, poised above the main street opposite the tourist office, with spacious rooms, a sun-drenched south-facing terrace and friendly service. At the foot of the First cable-car, *Gydisdorf* (☎033/853 13 03, fax 853 13 11; ②–③) has a reputation for fine service to complement its serviceably comfortable rooms. The road climbing to the east from here brings you to the rustic, window-box-laden *Gletschergarten* (☎033/853 17 21, fax 853 29 57; ③–④), a wonderful old pension with a loyal clientele who return year after year. In the heart of the bustle, but with rooms well off the street that remain quiet, *Eiger* (☎033/853 21 21, fax 853 21 01; ④–⑤) delivers the kind of generic comforts reminiscent of a city business hotel.

Eating and drinking

Eating and drinking, again, can be limited to your hotel, but there are a few places to sniff out. On the main street, *Mercato* has reasonably good pizzas and pasta for Fr.16, or a little more in the evenings, while the fish at *Hirschen* is rightly celebrated (Fr.20–25). The latter also has good veggie dishes for Fr.14 or so. *Onkel Tom's* is a tiny chalet at the east of town (closed Mon) serving up excellent (and enormous) wood-fired pizzas in a cosy ambience. For authentic, quality Chinese cuisine, try *Wee Lee*, on the main drag beneath *Hotel Spinne* (closed Mon), though it's not cheap (Fr.35 and up); they do equally good Japanese specialities, with veggie options.

There are a couple of obvious **bars** up and down the main street – including the misleadingly titled *Espresso Bar* – but the back terrace of *Ye Old Spotted Cat* in the *Hotel Bellevue* (closed Sun) is the quietest and most atmospheric place to enjoy a tipple as the sunset fades on the Eiger.

Around Grindelwald

The possibilities for exploring the area are endless. The area around **First** (2168m) has some particularly lovely hiking trails (for skiing, see p.268): the gondola rises in three stages, and from the top relatively easy routes lead off in all directions – to the Schwarzhorn summit (3hr) passing through Schilt, renowned for its population of marmots; on a high-level route over the Grosse Scheidegg pass (2hr or so); back down to Grindelwald (2hr 30min); or, best of all, on a breathtakingly expansive ridge-top walk to the gorgeous Bachsee lake and on to the **Faulhorn** summit (2hr 30min) with its atmospheric *Berghaus* (☎033/853 27 13, fax 853 10 25; Fr.34); the stunning sunset and sunrise views from here are one of the high points of a walking tour of Switzerland. Schynige Platte (see p.258) is about the same distance again further on.

The cable-car up to **Pfingstegg** and the little café at the top station with its giant views, make for a pleasant excursion for non-athletic types; an interesting trail leads for a little over an hour from Pfingstegg through varying geological formations on the slopes of the Mettenberg (the **Breitlouwina** terrace is celebrated for its evidence of glacial action), to the Oberergletscher (see p.278), from where an easy valley-floor hour's stroll brings you back into Grindelwald.

Grund station is the start for several fine walks, including a two-hour ramble up the sloping pastureland through Brandegg to **Alpiglen**, a stop on the Kleine Scheidegg train line (this can help cut costs if you're aiming for the Jungfraujoch). The gorgeous five-hour trail from Grund beneath the gondola up to Männlichen brings you through meadows and rolling open countryside, with the towering Eiger a constant presence. From Grund, if you cross the river and head southeast for a few minutes, you'll come to the **Gletscherschlucht** (Glacier gorge; May–Oct daily 9am–6pm; Fr.5), catwalks leading you for 1km or more into a narrow defile above the Lütschine river, with evidence of glacial erosion everywhere, including polished valley walls, corkscrew potholes and lumps of green and pinkish marble in the river bed.

An hourly bus from Grindlewald station (or an hour's walk east) leads you close to the icy caverns of the **Obererergletscher** – from the *Hotel Wetterhorn* bus stop follow the leafy trail down to the river and, on the other side, climb the 890 stairs to the nose of the glacier. There's a missable ice-grotto up there (May–Oct daily 9am–6pm; Fr.5), and, a ten-minute walk further up, a much more dramatic path which runs alongside the glacier itself, giving spectacular views.

The Jungfraujoch railway

Switzerland's most popular (and expensive) mountain railway excursion is unmissable. Trains trundle through lush countryside south from Interlaken before coiling spectacularly up across either Wengen or Grindlewald's mountain pastures, breaking the treeline at Kleine Scheidegg and tunnelling clean through the Eiger to emerge at the **JUNGFRAUJOCH**, an icy, windswept col at 3454m, just beneath the Jungfrau summit. It's the site of the highest train station in Europe, and offers an unforgettable experience of the mountains. You'd be missing out if you decided against shelling out the exorbitant sums necessary to reach the place.

However, **good weather** is essential – if there's a hint of cloud you'd be wasting your time heading up. Check the pictures from the summit, broadcast live on cable TV throughout the region, for an idea of the weather conditions, call the Jungfraujoch weather line (☎033/855 10 22) or ask your hotel or nearest tourist office for the latest forecasts. Remember, too, that it takes two and a half hours to reach the summit from Interlaken, and weather conditions can change rapidly. Coy though it sounds, even if you plan nothing more adventurous than looking out of the summit station window you should still bring **sunglasses** with you: the snows never melt up here, and if the sky is blue, the sun's glare and glitter can be painful.

There are two **routes** to the top. Trains head southwest from Interlaken Ost along the valley floor to Lauterbrunnen, from where you pick up the mountain line which climbs through Wengen to Kleine Scheidegg; different trains head southeast from Interlaken Ost to Grindelwald, where you change for the climb, arriving at Kleine Scheidegg from the other direction. All trains terminate at Kleine Scheidegg, where you must change for the final pull to Jungfraujoch – the popular practice is to go up one way and down the other.

Currently, the adult round-trip **fare** to Jungfraujoch from Interlaken is a budget-crunching Fr.159 – the Jungfraubahnen Pass (see p.268), and the broader Bernese Oberland Regional Pass (see p.250), both pointlessly stop short at Kleine Scheidegg, requiring passholders to shell out an extra Fr.50 to reach the summit. One way to cut costs is to take advantage of the discounted **Good Morning ticket** (Fr.120; Eurail Fr.105; Swiss Pass Fr.94), valid if you travel up on the first train of the day (6.35am from Interlaken), and leave the summit by noon (or Nov–April: first or second train plus later departure permitted).

Walking some sections of the journey, up or down, is perfectly feasible in summer, and can also save plenty, with fares from intermediate points along the route considerably lower. The undiscounted Good Morning ticket from Grindelwald is Fr.103, from Lauterbrunnen Fr.102, from Wengen Fr.91, and from Kleine Scheidegg Fr.58. Excellent transport networks and vista-rich footpaths linking all stations mean that with judicious use of a hiking map and timetable you can see and do a great deal in a day and still get back to Interlaken, or even Bern or Zürich, by bedtime.

The Jungfraujoch

The **summit station**, inevitably, is a tourist circus of ice sculptures, huskie sleigh rides, glacier walks, a short ski run, dismal restaurants and a post office, all invariably overflowing with tour groups. Nonetheless, panoramic views from the open-air 3571m

Sphinx Terrace to Germany's Black Forest in one direction and across a gleaming wasteland to the Italian Alps in the other are heart-thumping. Yawning away below the silver-domed weather station on top is the mighty Jungfraufirn glacier, which joins up with several others (including the Aletschgletscher, largest in the Alps) at the resonantly named **Konkordiaplatz** ice plain 3km southeast.

The best way to avoid being smothered by snap-happy crowds is to travel up on the first train of the day, and on arrival follow the signs quickly straight to the Sphinx Terrace – that way, you can snatch five or ten minutes of crisp, undisturbed silence at the loftiest point of all, and be the first of the day to sweep the snow off the railings. At other times, you may have to queue for an hour or more just to get your nose into the fresh air. Once you've finished at the terrace, it's easy to leave the bustling summit station behind and head out across the snows into solitude and silence, although you must stick to the marked trails (crevasses give no warning).

If you've had experience of snow hiking in the mountains, and you have good boots, a map, sunglasses and proper clothing, let the tourist office in Interlaken know that you want to head out on the simple one-hour trail from the Jungfraujoch around the base of the Mönch to the **Mönchsjochhütte** at 3629m (☎033/971 34 72; April–May & July–Sept; dorms Fr.26) – the isolation of the hut offers a night to remember. You should walk at half pace, or you'll find yourself dizzy and labouring to catch your breath in the thin atmosphere. A handful of other glacier-bound huts are dotted around the area, but you need a mountain guide and all the professional gear to reach them.

THE WESTERN VALLEYS

The section of the Bernese Oberland west of the Thunersee – which holds the only route through the mountains towards Lake Geneva – stands in sharp contrast to the rock and ice of the Jungfrau region. Broad, leafy valleys reach between the peaks, sheltering a handful of resorts and quiet country towns which see much less tourism than their hectic counterparts around Interlaken. The especially lovely Kander valley runs south from Spiez, climbing to the old-style resort village of **Kandersteg**, while the forested, picture-pretty gorge of the River Simme heads west through a succession of old villages filled with examples of the local heavy-eaved ornate darkwood chalets, some dating from as early as the 1750s. The valley of the **Simmental** curves south into the rural, hilly **Saanenland**, focused around the world-famous ski resort of **Gstaad**. Continuing west, you cross into an outpost of French-speaking Canton Vaud, whereupon the same rolling hills and broad, quiet valleys are re-titled the **Pays d'Enhaut**.

The Kander valley

South of Spiez, the Niesen stands sentinel over the peaceful **Kander valley**, a narrow finger pointing the way south to the wall of high peaks around the mighty Blümlisalp massif (which rises to 3663m). Nestling at the very end of the sharply ascending valley, hard up against the mountains in the most idyllic of locations, is the laid-back resort of **Kandersteg**, terminus for the Lötschbergtunnel. Further south, beyond the point where trains disappear into the valley wall on their way to Italy, are the remote and little-visited Üschinen and Gastern valleys, which offer hikers fantastic opportunities to get out in the wild.

Kandersteg

Long a centre for mountaineering, the picturesque, chalet-strewn village of **KANDERSTEG** was for centuries the trailhead for travellers crossing the high moun-

DRIVING BENEATH THE ALPS

For drivers, the **Lötschbergtunnel** is a very handy link between Bern and the north of Switzerland, and Valais and the south – especially since you would otherwise be forced to aim for the Grimselpass or make a detour to Montreux. Regular shuttle trains through the tunnel between Kandersteg and Goppenstein in Valais are dedicated to transporting motor traffic. Departures run year-round, every half-hour between 5am and midnight; in July only, there are hourly shuttles throughout Friday nights. Both termini have drive-on drive-off facilities, and journey time is only fifteen minutes. You can buy your ticket on the spot – Fr.25 for a car holding up to nine people or a motorbike. For more information, call ☎033/675 83 83.

tain passes into Canton Valais. In 1912, though, Kandersteg was changed forever by the completion of the **Lötschbergtunnel** (see box) just south of the village, a crucially important rail link between northern and southern Europe – the only one between Geneva and the Gotthard – which created a through route from Bern to Milan. Although the small valley road into the village can get heavy with trans-Alpine traffic, most people are heading for the car-train terminus, situated on the outskirts; once you arrive in Kandersteg itself, all is tranquil.

The main reason to visit Kandersteg is to explore the surrounding area – attractions are all rural and scenic. Kandersteg is also one of the best places in Switzerland to learn how to ski: beginners can test out their snowplough techniques on the easiest and least daunting of slopes, with other beginners all around and not a trace of big-resort swagger. The village itself is strung out along the valley floor for several kilometres, loomed over by the massive bulk of the Doldenhorn to the southeast and the First massif to the northwest. Prime hiking and recreation spot above the village is the dramatically crag-ringed **Oeschinensee**, a small lake accessed by a chairlift from the eastern edge of the village. From the top station, it's a twenty-minute stroll to the lake itself, warm and glittering in summer and iced over for cross-country skiing in winter. A handful of trails fan out around the area, dotted with mountain refuges (the tourist office in Kandersteg has a complete list, with hiking routes), and the walk back down to Kandersteg is only about an hour. Another lift on the opposite side of the valley accesses the **Allmenalp**.

A ten-minute drive north of Kandersteg, just off the main valley-floor road, is the underwhelming **Blausee** (Fr.4.50; *www.blausee.ch*), a privately owned area of land surrounding a tiny boating lake. It's all a bit overblown, since once you stroll through the trees to the lakelet itself, there's not much to do other than order a plate of fresh trout on the restaurant terrace, and watch kids boating around the lake. Even the views are hemmed in by thick pine woods.

Practicalities

Kandersteg's **tourist office** is on the main street, just ahead from the train station (July & Aug Mon–Fri 8am–6pm, Sat 8–11.30am & 2.30–6pm; Sept–June Mon–Fri 8am–noon & 2–6pm; ☎033/675 80 80, *www.kandersteg.ch*). This is also the office of the **Mountaineering School** (☎033/675 80 89). Even before the Lötschbergtunnel put Kandersteg on the map, the village had a tradition of hospitality, and **accommodation** is of universally good quality. Plenty of places offer **dorms**: the *Rendezvous*, near the Oeschinen chairlift (☎033/675 13 54; Fr.15), the International Scout Centre at the southern edge of the village (☎033/675 82 82, fax 675 82 89, *www.kisc.ch*, Fr.15), and *Hotel National*, near the turning for the Allmenalp chairlift and with some cheap rooms too (☎033/675 10 85, fax 675 22 85; ①; Fr.27). Breakfast for dorm sleepers at all these places is an extra Fr.6–10. There's a good **campsite** next to the *Rendezvous* (☎033/675 15 34, fax 675 17 37).

Hotels are led by the amazing *Ruedihus*, in a meadow off the road south of the *National* (☎033/675 81 82, fax 675 81 85; ③). A beautifully restored chalet from 1753, its nine characterful rooms display minute attention to detail, with original rustic furniture and fittings set off by the most spotless of modern en-suite bathrooms. The *Zur Post* (☎033/675 12 58, fax 675 22 58; ②), in the centre, is a quality lower-end choice, as is the comfortable *Alpina* (☎033/675 12 46, fax 675 12 33; ②), at the northern entrance to the village. There's a welter of luxury pads, best of which is the *Victoria Ritter* in the centre (☎033/675 80 00, fax 675 81 00, *www.hotel-victoria.ch*; ③–④), a stout old building drenched in tradition. The *Waldhotel Doldenhorn* (☎033/675 81 81, fax 675 81 85; ③) is out in the countryside, boasting comfort and quiet but not much else.

Eating and drinking covers the gamut from the simple but palatable dishes (some veggie) in the *Bahnhofbuffet* train station diner, up to the gourmet spreads at the luxury hotels. Meals at the *Ruedihus* (see above) are spectacularly good, with a choice between the formal restaurant above and the wonderfully atmospheric *Stübli* below, serving a range of inexpensive Swiss specialities (from Fr.20). Most of the hotels along the main street serve food, but the *Victoria-Ritter* prides itself on its kitchen – justifiably so, with the menu of intricately well-presented international cuisine changing every two or three months (from Fr.25).

Beyond Kandersteg

At the end of Kandersteg village, beside the rushing Kander torrent, is a small crossroads. To the southwest a tortuous path climbs into the bleak **Üschinen valley**, which penetrates for 4 or 5km between the summits, and is the scene for some tough mountain-bike trails and tougher hikes up to the Gemmipass above the town of Leukerbad.

Southeast from the same crossroads, a private road (Fr.10, pay at tourist office) allows cars to access the wild **Gastern valley**; beware that the road is narrow and rocky, and runs on an alternate one-way system (into the valley between 30 and 50mins past each hour; out of the valley between the hour and 20 past). Nobody comes down here apart from local hikers in the know, but this was formerly the main route by foot into the Valais: about an hour and a half's walk from the crossroads into the forgotten valley – the walls of which are laced with dramatically spouting waterfalls – you'll come to the hamlet of **Selden** (1535m) with a couple of inns, including cosy *Gasthaus Selden* (☎033/675 11 63, fax 675 21 44; ①). From here, a path cuts south four hours up to the Lötschenpass (2690m), passing another inn, the *Gfelalp* (☎033/675 11 61; ①), on the ascent. From the basic *Lötschenpasshütte* (☎027/939 19 81, *www.loetschental.ch/loetschenpass*; Fr.22) on the summit, three more paths lead down to the villages on the other side. A little east of Selden, the Gastern valley is blocked by the huge Kanderfirn glacier. Check with the Kandersteg tourist office before embarking on exploration in these remote areas.

Gstaad

GSTAAD – twinned expertly with Cannes – is an odd place. You'd think, from the high profile of its name, that it would be some kind of glittering Geneva-in-the-Alps, a fantastically expensive mountain paradise. Yet although its instant name recognition may effortlessly attract Europe's royal households, celebrities galore and countless lesser hangers-on, Gstaad is in fact just a one-street village, a rather charming, attractively located place full of restored weathered-wood chalets – even if there is an overabundance of jewellery shops and furriers. Nonetheless, its high-roller status makes it a village like no other. If you fancy being snubbed by the world's richest people, come here for Christmas week, scene of a heady round of sparkling soirées and lavish banquet-style dinner parties all but barred to ordinary mortals.

GSTAAD EVENTS

Gstaad hosts two of Switzerland's most glittering events, in two very different fields. The first ten days of July see the world's sporting media – and sports celebs galore – descend on the village for the **Swiss Open** tennis tournament, a principal fixture on the international ATP tour drawing the best players in the world. **Tickets** cost around Fr.80 for the final, or Fr.400 for the week, and are available from Rado Swiss Open, Postfach, CH-3780 Gstaad (☎033/748 83 83, *www.swissopen.ch*).

The **Gstaad Music Summer** runs from mid-July until early September each year. Founded by the famous violinist Yehudi Menuhin to serve as a showcase for young talent, it has developed into a cycle of major classical concerts – with stellar performers – staged at a variety of locations, principally the church at Saanen, but also at venues in Gstaad and the nearby villages of Lauenen, Zweisimmen and Gsteig. Individual tickets (Fr.20–125) and various passes are available from Musiksommer Gstaad, Postfach 65, CH-3780 Gstaad (☎033/748 83 38, *www.musiksommer.ch*).

Lesser events, both still with enough pulling power to book the area out, are the Polo Silver Cup in mid-August, and an international country music weekend in mid-September.

Glossy magazines may advertise the town as some kind of winter wonderland, but St Moritz steals its luxury-class thunder on this score: Gstaad is really more of a place to spend the odd ten grand renting a hillside chalet and sipping champagne around town than it is somewhere you can get stuck into any serious skiing. Where Gstaad really enters into its own, prosaically enough, is as a centre from which to **hike** the little-known Saanenland during the summer months.

The village and around

Gstaad's main pedestrian-only street, running north–south through the village, is dubbed **Promenade** – no more than five minutes' walk end to end. Focus of the village centre is an open area just at the point cars are barred, which in July is the location for the highly prestigious **Swiss Open** tennis tournament, and which becomes an ice rink all winter.

There's plenty of hiking in the four main valleys surrounding Gstaad. A cable-car, and trails, run up to the nearby **Eggli** (1557m), favoured excursion from the village, with plenty of paths from there across the plateau, and a long high-level route winding past the tranquil Arnensee and down to **Feutersoey**, some 9km further up the Saane. On the opposite, eastern side of Gstaad looms the **Wispile** (1911m), also served by a cable-car, with trails of about two and a half hours leading back to Gstaad. It's equally easy to head due east from the village along the **Turbach** valley, through a hamlet or two on the banks of the stream, and then keep heading straight over the low pass at Reulissen to the busy resorts of **Lenk** or **St Stephan**, both on the Simme some 12km east (4hr 30min total) and linked to Zweisimmen by train.

The **skiing**, however, might be a disappointment. None of the lifts around the village rises above 2200m, which means that even snow cover is unreliable, although some lifts just about within feasible reach beyond Gsteig do serve the Diablerets glacier, at 2979m. Gstaad's **ski pass** is valid for the Gstaad Super Ski region – six different areas incorporating 69 lifts rising from Château d'Oex, Rougemont, Saanen, Schönried, Saanenmöser, Zweisimmen, St Stephan, Lauenen and Gsteig. Roughly half the pistes in the whole area are rated blue or easy red.

Practicalities

Gstaad is on the MOB narrow-gauge **train** line between Montreux and Zweisimmen; approaching from Bern or Interlaken, you must change trains in Spiez and again in Zweisimmen. Arriving by car, a turning from **SAANEN** – the village on the main Simmental road some 45km west of Spiez – heads south for 3km to Gstaad. Cars are diverted away from Gstaad centre, although if you head straight on at the first round-about – where you can see the main street stretching out ahead of you – just before the barrier is a covered parking garage; otherwise, turn right at that roundabout and head through the Gstaad Tunnel west of the centre for more parking.

The village's tiny **station** is just off the main Promenade. Some 100m further south on Promenade, after the railway bridge, is the **tourist office** (July, August & Dec–March Mon–Fri 8am–6.30pm, Sat 9am–6pm, Sun 11am–3pm; rest of year Mon–Fri 8am–noon & 1.30–6pm, Sat 9am–noon; ☎033/748 81 81, *www.gstaad.ch*). Staff need no prompting to come up with ideas for excursions and are well tuned to the requirements of customer service, doing everything for you save leading you by the hand out to the trail. Swissraft (☎033/744 50 80, *www.swissraft.ch*) offers mountain-bike rental (Fr.39/day) and a host of **adventure activities**, including rafting (Fr.140) and canyoning (Fr.90). Alpinzentrum (☎033/744 60 01, *www.gstaad.ch/alpinzentrum*) do many of the same things, throwing in extreme winter sports as well.

Accommodation

As you might expect, the sky's the limit if you choose to **stay** in Gstaad. However, it's not impossible to find inexpensive accommodation, either in the village or nearby. The *Bellerive* **campsite** is 1km north of Gstaad (☎033/744 63 30, fax 744 63 45), well equipped but a tad pricey. *Beim Kappeli*, a more spartan option, is just south of Saanen on the outskirts of Gstaad (☎033/744 61 91, fax 744 60 42; closed early May), while ten minutes' walk northwest of Saanen is a comfortable, rustic HI **hostel** in the old-style Chalet Rüblihorn (☎033/744 13 43, fax 744 55 42; ①; closed Nov), with quality dorms from Fr.26 and bike rental.

Saanen, and neighbouring villages such as Saanenmöser, also have the least expensive **hotels**, including the *Bahnhof* in Saanen (☎033/744 14 22; ②), with parking and a choice of en-suite or shared-bath rooms. Within Gstaad, *Posthotel Rössli* is a cosy lower-end choice (☎033/748 42 42, fax 748 42 43; ④), the oldest hotel in the village with renovated pine-decor rooms, while *Olden* (☎033/744 34 44, fax 744 61 64; ⑥) is a fresher and slicker choice but still with plenty of atmosphere. Steps from the station is the *Bernerhof* (☎033/748 88 44, fax 748 88 40; ⑤–⑥), a huge place with generous rooms and an indoor pool. Towering over the village and visible from all points is the fantasy *Palace Hotel* (☎033/748 50 00, fax 748 50 01, *www.palace.ch*; ⑨), laughingly calling itself a "family pension" as it asks Fr.1000 for a ski season double room – but then again, with underwater music in the pool, giant rooms and lavish dinners on the south-facing terrace, they know their clientele well.

Eating and drinking

Eating and drinking is least expensive at the *Co-op* self-service restaurant near the station. Otherwise, you can check out where the champagne set are gathering in any of half-a-dozen terrace cafés and restaurants along Promenade. *Charly's* is perhaps the most famous, followed up by *Rialto* and *Pernet* facing each other near the chapel. The restaurant in *Posthotel Rössli* has good, plain Swiss meals without the fuss (*menus* Fr.20 or so), while *Sporthotel Rütti*, ten minutes' walk south of town, is acclaimed for its tasty Swiss and Italian-ish cooking, from Fr.15. At the other end of the scale, *Chesery*

(☎033/744 24 51) is the place to see and be seen, a lively late-night gourmet eatery and piano-bar, with the prices as high as the stilettos; not less than Fr.150 for dinner.

The Pays d'Enhaut

Barely 3km west of Saanen you cross the border from Canton Bern into Canton Vaud, and with it the linguistic *Röstigraben* – not a kilometre further on is the francophone resort of **Rougemont**, a charming little place full of character that is, so far, reasonably successfully fending off the encroachment of Gstaad's high-rollers. This area is known as the **PAYS D'ENHAUT**, or Highlands, a sliver of mountain territory originally owned by Gruyères, then seized by Bern, before forming part of the new Vaudois territory after the 1798 revolution. The main valley, with its succession of broad, enclosed side valleys set amidst gentle peaks carpeted by lush summer pasture, is separated from Vaud's better-known resorts such as Leysin and Les Diablerets by the Col des Mosses pass (1445m) further south. West of Rougemont is the largest town of the region, **Château d'Oex**, best known as a centre for hot-air ballooning.

The MOB narrow-gauge **train** line runs along the valley floor from Gstaad through Château d'Oex, shortly afterwards winding its way down alongside the Dent de Jaman to Montreux (see p.153). A branch line from **Montbovon**, some 11km west of Château d'Oex, runs north to Gruyères (see p.129).

Rougemont

Seven kilometres west of Gstaad, **ROUGEMONT** is an attractive historic village full of the traditional broad-eaved wooden chalets that characterize the region. Its late eleventh-century Romanesque **church** is especially picturesque, as is the sixteenth-century **château** behind, although the latter is privately owned.

Rougemont is a quiet and attractive place to base yourself if you're hiking or skiing in the area; the village is included in the Gstaad ski pass and, as well as hosting its own blue and red runs, it's only a short train ride from access to the pistes above Gstaad. Amidst the village's handful of simple **hotels**, *La Sapinière* (☎026/925 81 18, fax 079/0449 0486, *www.sapiniere.ch*; ①) is a cosy and friendly little place with appealingly home-cooked meals, while the *Hôtel de Commune* (☎026/925 81 42, fax 925 86 58; ②) on the main street is only slightly more generic. The Videmanette **cable-car** runs from the village up to a trailhead for high-country walks at 2186m, where you'll find a restaurant and, round the corner, a mountain inn with dorms (☎026/924 64 65; Fr.26). The pleasant and very scenic stroll along the valley floor from Rougemont to Saanen only takes about an hour and a half.

Château d'Oex

A family ski and sports resort located where the road from the Col des Mosses joins the valley, **CHÂTEAU D'OEX** (pronounced *day*) doesn't have a great deal to offer, although it is nonetheless spectacularly sited. The wide, sloping valley bowl in which it sits generates exactly the right kinds of thermal air currents for perfect **hot-air ballooning**, and the town is acclaimed as one of the world centres for the sport. When Bertrand Piccard, from Lausanne, and the Briton Brian Jones made their record-breaking 45,000km round-the-world balloon flight in 1999, which ended on March 21 after 19 days, 21 hours and 55 minutes, the take-off point, and nerve centre of the whole operation, was Château d'Oex. Every January, the town hosts perhaps the most beautiful sports event in the Swiss calendar, the annual **Hot-Air Ballooning Week**, when eighty or more colourful giants catch the dawn thermals to float peaceably over the hills and valleys round about.

For speedier thrills, the town and its slopes are linked in to the Gstaad Super Ski Region (see p.282): as well as easy and intermediate pistes all around the town, there are a few testing runs down from the La Braye cable-car, spanning the valley up to a height of 1630m.

Practicalities

The **station** is in the centre, right opposite the cable-car station. About 100m west is the **tourist office** (Mon–Fri 8am–noon & 2–6pm, Sat 9am–noon & 2–5pm; ☎026/924 25 25, *www.chateau-doex.ch*). They can set you up with a balloon flight, or you should contact Swissraft in Gstaad direct (☎033/744 50 80, *www.swissraft.ch*), who charge Fr.360 for an hour's silent floating. Château d'Oex is also one of the few places where you can try ski-joring – being towed on skis behind a horse. It costs about Fr.50 to hire a horse for an hour; contact the tourist office for more details.

There's a **campsite**, *Au Berceau* (☎026/924 62 34), on the riverside a ten-minute walk west of town, and an HI **hostel** a few minutes' walk downhill from the centre (☎026/924 64 04, fax 924 58 43; ①; closed Nov & Dec), with dorms from Fr.24 and bikes for rent. Of the **hotels**, the *Buffet de la Gare* beside the station (☎026/924 77 17, fax 924 79 52; ①), as well as offering casual, uncomplicated meals in its café and **restaurant**, has a few shared-bath rooms. *La Printanière*, right beside the Catholic church (☎ & fax 026/924 61 13; ①) is an old characterful house, with plain shared-bath rooms that are kept spotlessly clean. On the other side of the church is *Richemont* (☎026/924 52 52, fax 924 53 84; ②), a big chunky weatherbeaten chalet with comfortable, old-style rooms. One kilometre further west, set in its own grounds, is the *Bon Acceuil* (☎026/924 63 20, fax 924 51 26; ③), bargain of the region, a small, utterly charming hotel in a restored eighteenth-century light-wood chalet overlooking the valley; attention to detail – and spectacularly good lightly prepared cuisine in the atmospheric restaurant – mark it out as extra special.

travel details

TRAINS

Brienz to: Interlaken Ost (hourly; 15min); Luzern (hourly; 1hr 15min); Meiringen (hourly; 10min).

Château d'Oex to: Gstaad (hourly; 20min); Interlaken West & Ost (hourly; 2hr 15min; change at Zweisimmen & Spiez); Montreux (hourly; 1hr).

Grindelwald to: Interlaken Ost (hourly; 20min); Kleine Scheidegg (every 30min; 35min).

Gstaad to: Château d'Oex (hourly; 20min); Interlaken West & Ost (hourly; 1hr 50min; change at Zweisimmen & Spiez); Montreux (hourly; 1hr 20min).

Interlaken Ost to: Bern (hourly; 50min); Brienz (hourly; 15min); Grindelwald (hourly; 40min); Gstaad (hourly; 1hr 50min; change at Spiez & Zweisimmen); Jungfraujoch (at least hourly; 2hr 30min; change at Grindelwald or Lauterbrunnen, and Kleine Scheidegg); Lauterbrunnen (hourly; 20min); Luzern (hourly; 1hr 55min); Meiringen (hourly; 30min); Thun (hourly; 30min); Wilderswil (at least hourly; 5min); Zürich (hourly; 2hr 15min).

Interlaken West to: Bern (hourly; 45min); Gstaad (hourly; 1hr 45min; change at Spiez & Zweisimmen); Thun (hourly; 25min); Zürich (hourly; 2hr 10min).

Kandersteg to: Bern (hourly; 1hr 5min); Brig (hourly; 35min); Interlaken West & Ost (hourly; 50min; change at Spiez); Spiez (hourly; 30min); Thun (hourly; 40min).

Kleine Scheidegg to: Grindelwald (every 30min; 35min); Jungfraujoch (every 30min; 50min); Lauterbrunnen (every 30min; 1hr); Wengen (every 30min; 30min).

Lauterbrunnen to: Interlaken Ost (hourly; 20min); Kleine Scheidegg (every 20min; 45min); Mürren (every 15min; 30min); Wengen (every 20min; 15min).

Meiringen to: Brienz (hourly; 10min); Interlaken Ost (hourly; 30min); Luzern (hourly; 1hr 25min).

Mürren to: Lauterbrunnen (every 15min; 30min).

Spiez to: Bern (twice hourly; 30min); Gstaad (hourly; 1hr 10min; change at Zweisimmen); Interlaken West & Ost (hourly; 20min); Kandersteg (hourly; 30min); Thun (3 hourly; 10min).

Thun to: Bern (twice hourly; 20min); Burgdorf (hourly; 45min); Interlaken West & Ost (hourly; 25min); Spiez (3 hourly; 10min).

Wengen to: Kleine Scheidegg (every 30min; 30min); Lauterbrunnen (every 20min; 15min).

BUSES

Château d'Oex to: Leysin (3 daily; 1hr 30min; change at Le Sépey).

Grindelwald to: Meiringen (June–Oct hourly; 1hr 35min; change at Schwarzwaldalp).

Gstaad to: Les Diablerets (5 daily; 50min).

Interlaken Ost & West to: Beatushöhlen (hourly; 25min).

Interlaken West to: Wilderswil (every 30min; 10min).

Lauterbrunnen to: Stechelberg (hourly; 20min).

Meiringen to: Göschenen via Sustenpass (July–Sept 2 daily; 1hr 45min); Grindelwald (June–Oct hourly; 1hr 55min; change at Schwarzwaldalp).

BOATS

(following is a summary of June–Sept summer services; fewer boats run in other months, generally Sat & Sun only if at all)

Brienz to: Interlaken Ost (hourly; 1hr 20min).

Interlaken Ost to: Brienz (hourly; 1hr 20min).

Interlaken West to: Beatushöhlen (6 daily; 30min); Spiez (hourly; 1hr 20min); Thun (hourly; 2hr 5min).

Thun to: Beatushöhlen (5 daily; 1hr 30min); Hilterfingen (hourly; 15min); Interlaken West (hourly; 2hr 5min); Oberhofen (hourly; 20min); Spiez (hourly; 45min).

CHAPTER SEVEN

VALAIS

The **VALAIS** (Wallis in German; Vallese in Italian) is Switzerland's third-largest canton, a diverse swathe of country occupying the valley – hence the name – of the River Rhône, from its source in the glaciers of the central Alps all the way to its inflow to Lake Geneva. Fully twenty percent of the canton is covered by glaciers, and yet the region has the driest climate, with the lowest rainfall and the most sunshine, of the whole country. The artificial irrigation system set in place by the valley dwellers in the Middle Ages – a vast network of channels, called *bisses* in French and *Suonen* in Swiss-German – still weaves a cat's cradle over the foothills of the high mountains, supplemented these days by half-a-dozen of the tallest and highest-altitude dams in the world. For the Swiss, the Valais somehow represents a piece of common heritage all but lost elsewhere in the country: in the most unlikely corners of Geneva or Zürich, you can find restaurants done up as traditional Valaisian-style darkwood chalets, complete with windowboxes full of geraniums and farm tools as decoration on the walls, serving up the local speciality **raclette** (see p.56) under a nameboard "Chalet Valaisanne" or "Walliser Stube". The dryness and sunshine of the valley are ideal vine-growing conditions, and the canton's 22,000 vineyard owners are famous for producing some of the finest **wine** in the country.

Cut off on all sides by mountains, the Valais has always been a world apart. On a push to conquer the Celtic peoples of the valley in the first century BC, a Roman army under **Julius Caesar** ventured the crossing of the Grand-St-Bernard Pass from Italy and then spread out through the valley. They got as far as modern-day Sierre, and left behind them a legacy of Latin – even today, Sierre is the easternmost **French-speaking** town in the canton, while beyond it the mother tongue is **Swiss-German**, descended from the language of the Aleman tribes who remained unconquered. Indeed, once the Romans retreated, few outsiders had much success in challenging the peoples of the valley. **Christianity** arrived before the fourth century, with the travel of clerics and merchants over the Grand-St-Bernard pass, but the Reformation never made it any further into the valley than Aigle, in neighbouring Canton Vaud, and Valais remains majority Catholic to this day. Even the mighty **Bernese** army was stopped by the mountains and the wildness of the terrain. At times of severe hardship during the Middle Ages and later, however, many **Walsers** have voluntarily chosen to depart, forced to leave their

---

ACCOMMODATION PRICE CODES

All the hostels, pensions and hotels in this book have been graded according to the following price codes, which indicate the price for the cheapest double room available during the high season. Single rooms can cost anything between sixty and eighty percent of the double-room rate. For hostels with dormitories, the price per bed has been quoted. See p.45 for more details.

① under Fr.100	④ Fr.200–250	⑦ Fr.350–400
② Fr.100–150	⑤ Fr.250–300	⑧ Fr.400–500
③ Fr.150–200	⑥ Fr.300–350	⑨ over Fr.500

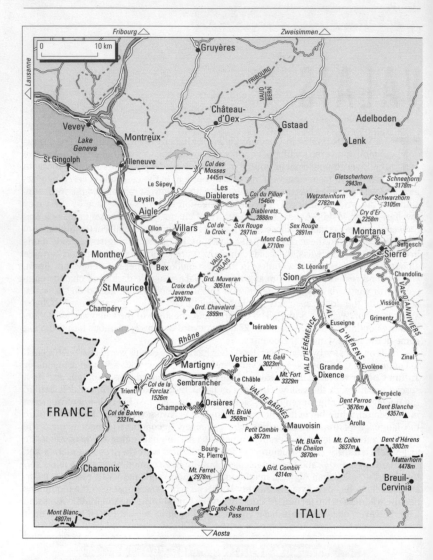

home villages and travel over the mountains to seek a better life elsewhere. Walser communities survive in places as far apart as Argentina and Liechtenstein, still nurturing their distinctive dialect and culture.

The Valais remained independent until 1815 when, following a brief period of French governorship, it joined the Swiss Confederation as a new canton. It's a mark of the social changes taking place over recent years that German speakers in the east of the canton are now starting to worry about the encroachment of French up the valley: with the economic power and prestige of the French-speaking lower valley, German speakers are increasingly finding employment in francophone areas, while francophone firms

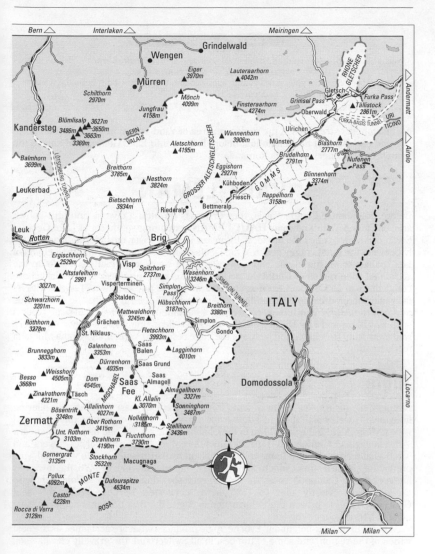

are expanding their bases of operation into German-speaking communities. Locals in Brig in particular shake their head at the quantity of French now being heard in the town, but there seems little they can do about it.

The Valais is still a wild and little-known place outside the trio of famous resorts bred by the mountains: **Zermatt**, **Verbier** and **Crans-Montana**. Few outsiders bother to penetrate the deep rural side valleys either side of the single road and rail line that runs along the valley floor – though those who do make the effort find plenty of long-distance hiking and adventure sports of all kinds. The only town of any size is the cantonal capital **Sion**, with a low-key, easygoing atmosphere and a handful of sights. In the northernmost extremities of the region, an area of Vaud known as **Haut-Léman** occupies the east bank of the Rhône just before it flows into Lake Geneva and shares the mountainous scenery of Valais Romand.

HAUT-LÉMAN

Before trains enter Canton Valais, they first pass through a diverse and little-known area of Canton Vaud known as **HAUT-LÉMAN**, extending southeast of Lake Geneva. South of Montreux lies the broad, flat Rhône valley, the river meandering languorously between the great craggy peaks of the Dents-du-Midi on one side, and the heights of Les Diablerets on the other. The valley floor and west-facing foothills make up the acclaimed wine region of **Chablais**, no less prestigious a producer than its lakeshore competitors of La Côte and Lavaux, and centred on the fine old town of **Aigle**, with its fairy-tale turreted castle surrounded by vineyards. Above Aigle rise the 3000m-plus peaks of the **Alpes Vaudoises**, centred on a handful of attractive, small-scale resorts such as **Villars** and **Les Diablerets** that offer excellent skiing and a cosy atmosphere well away from the clutter and bustle of the huge resorts of Verbier and Crans-Montana further south.

Aigle

Although the main valley highway south from Montreux bypasses **AIGLE**, this alluring little town is well worth the small detour for a lazy afternoon of castle exploration and wine tasting. Aigle is the main town of the Chablais wine region, and its prime landmark – the fantastical **Château d'Aigle**, a fifteenth-century folly with corner towers and witch's-hat turrets – is now home to two excellent **museums** devoted to wine and wine production. Aigle's other claim to fame is five hundred years old: in 1476, the town was integrated into Canton Bern as the first French-speaking territory to join the Swiss Confederation. Shortly after, in 1526, newly converted Bernese Protestants sent Guillaume Farel to preach the Reformation in Aigle, the first time this had ever been done in a francophone region.

Along with its near-neighbour Yvorne, Aigle produces what are acclaimed as the best **wines** of the region, and some of the best in all Switzerland, the gravelly clay-like soil nurturing especially good dustily elegant, fruity whites ("It's difficult to find a bad white Aigle," commented wine writer John C. Sloan). *Les Murailles*, from the Badoux winery, is one of the very few Swiss wines to be marketed in North America – it and the *Crosex Grillé* Grand Cru are the two best names to ask for. Further south, the nearby towns of Bex and Ollon produce their own tangy, flowery whites, largely for local consumption only: *Philos* is probably the best of them.

Arrival, orientation and accommodation

Aigle's **train station**, with **change** facilities (daily 5.15am–10.10pm), is west of the centre, at one end of the 300m-long Rue de la Gare. At the other end you'll find the small **tourist office**, 4 Rue de la Gare (Mon–Fri 8am–noon & 2–5pm; ☎024/466 30 00); they stock photocopied maps and few bits and pieces about the town. Just outside the office is **Place du Centre**, from where the pedestrianized café-street of **Rue de Bourg** leads north. Parallel to it is the remarkable little cobbled alley **Rue de Jérusalem**, the upper floors of its old wooden houses spanning the street in a style which reminded one nineteenth-century observer of the shaded residential quarters of Middle Eastern cities. The main Rue de Colomb heads southeast from the Place du Centre to adjacent **Place du Marché**, from where Avenue du Cloître leads you further southeast towards the château.

Aigle has only a couple of central **hotels**: *Les Messageries*, 19 Rue du Midi (☎024/466 20 60, fax 466 62 58; ①) offers the simplest of comforts, with a choice of en-suite and shared-bath rooms; *Hôtel du Nord*, 2 Rue Colomb (☎024/466 10 55, fax 466 42 48; ②) is more upmarket. Otherwise, you can **camp** at *Les Glariers* (☎024/466 26 60; April–Sept), about 1km west of town.

Château d'Aigle

Barely ten minutes' walk southeast of the town centre loom the fabulous turrets of **Château d'Aigle**. Ranged beneath is an attractive little quarter of old houses, among which lies the ancient **Église St-Maurice** or **Église du Cloître**, founded in 1143 and renovated over the centuries in a mixture of styles.

Atmospheric cobbled lanes wind up from here to the **château** (July & Aug daily 10am–6pm; April–June & Sept–Oct Tues–Sun 10am–noon & 2–6pm; last entry one hour before closing; *www.swisscastles.ch/vaud/aigle*). The main castle building houses the Musée de la Vigne et du Vin (Vine and Wine Museum; Fr.7; SMP); opposite the gates, in the stout Maison de la Dîme, is the Musée de l'Étiquette (Wine-Labels Museum; Fr.4; SMP) – a combined entry ticket for both museums is Fr.9.

The château is an impressive example of medieval castle building, founded and expanded by the advancing Savoyards in the thirteenth century. The Bernese burnt the place to the ground in 1475, rebuilding and redesigning it to serve both a defensive function on the fringes of Bernese power and as a residence for the installed bailiffs. Following the Vaudois revolution of 1798, the castle reverted to local hands, and remained the town's prison right up until 1972, when nobody could be found to take on the job of jailer and so all the resident convicts had to be transferred to Vevey. As you enter, you're given a follow-the-numbers pamphlet, which leads you through the various rooms around the courtyard which house the permanent and temporary exhibits of the **Musée de la Vigne et du Vin**. Look out for the old shop signs in the vestibule of the main dwelling (room 9) and the mighty barrels and winepress in the cellar below (room 10). The ramparts walk is especially spectacular, with frescoes in the various watchtowers and romantic views out over the sea of vines all around. The **Musée de l'Étiquette** opposite the castle gates is, by necessity, a rather sedate affair, with the generally very ornate labels from bottles around the world displayed on placards in a grand, wood-beamed attic.

THE SALT MINES OF BEX

Some 9km south of Aigle and connected by hourly train is the small town of **BEX** (pronounced *bay*), unremarkable but for the fact that it sits beside the only working **salt mine** in Switzerland, named *Le Bouillet*. All through the Middle Ages Switzerland had to rely on importing salt, mainly from Franche-Comté – an expensive business, not least because of the transportation costs. Then, in the fifteenth century, legend has it that a shepherd pasturing his flocks above Bex noticed that the animals preferred drinking from two particular springs. Tasting the water himself, he discovered that it was salty and this led to further investigation, principally by the Bernese authorities, who began to mine the hills around Bex. The mines have been worked ever since, and today a labyrinthine network of galleries burrows for some 50km beneath the mountains, still producing salt for domestic consumption.

You can **visit** some portions of the mines on guided tours (April–Oct daily every 90mins 9.45am–3.45pm; reservations essential on ☎024/463 03 30; Fr.17, cash only). Tours (available in English) last for over two hours, beginning with an audiovisual show and including a long underground narrow-gauge train ride and plenty of subterranean walking. There's no public transport to the mine entrance. Irregular **buses** run from Bex station to the village of Les Dévens, twenty minutes' walk away, or you can walk from Bex itself in about 45 minutes.

Eating and drinking

Rue de Bourg is lined with pleasant **restaurants** – check out popular *La Croix Blanche*, serving reasonably priced pizzas and simple *menus* (Fr.15), and *Le Mediéval*, a slightly more upmarket establishment on the same street. An unnamed shady courtyard-café at the southern end of Rue de Jérusalem offers an array of fresh salads along with seven kinds of *Rösti* (Fr.15–20). The streets around the château offer plenty of places to buy and sample **wine**, but most atmospheric of all is the *Pinte du Paradis* within the Maison de la Dîme (Sun, Tues & Wed 10am–6pm, Thurs–Sat 10am–11pm).

The Alpes Vaudoises

The huge peaks east of Aigle and the Rhône Valley are collectively dubbed the **Alpes Vaudoises**, sheltering a few attractive, quite isolated little ski villages – all specifically family-oriented – that offer some of the best facilities outside the huge Valaisian resorts further south. Friendly **Villars** leads the bunch, connected by a system of lifts both with its neighbour, Gryon, and with the separate resort of **Les Diablerets**. Tiny **Leysin**, tucked away in a valley above Aigle, completes the picture. In summer, all these villages slumber quietly in the sunshine, hosting walkers and those seeking the kind of undisturbed Alpine retreat money can't buy. **Transport** between all three is sporadic; they serve better as places to base yourself for a few days or a couple of weeks rather than as stepping stones around the region. **Lift passes** for Villars-Gryon and Les Diablerets (excluding the glacier) cost Fr.42 for one day or Fr.117 for three days; a five-day pass for the Alpes Vaudoises, which includes the Diablerets glacier and Leysin, and is also valid for Gstaad, costs Fr.201.

Villars

The neat, unpretentious little resort of **VILLARS** is linked to Bex, down in the valley, by a quaint Edwardian train, and to Aigle by a rather less romantic postbus. It wins no awards for grace or stylishness, but where it does score (and where it has won awards) is for its family-oriented service. Winter after winter Villars, and its neighbouring community of **Gryon**, 4km away on the Bex–Villars train line, attract scores of families on skiing breaks, while still remaining virtually unknown to a wider clientele. The skiing around the town is actually pretty good, with the added bonuses of direct lift linkage to Les Diablerets for glacier pistes up to 3000m, and a deal whereby multi-day lift passes are also valid in the Gstaad Super Ski Region (see p.282) a bus ride away.

A gondola rises from the edge of the village up to the **Roc d'Orsay** (2000m), from where a long blue run delivers you to the hub of the skiing at **Bretaye**, set in a broad bowl and also served by a rack railway from Villars centre. Gentle red pistes abound, and from **Barboleuse** a gondola heads up to Les Chaux (1750m), offering a long and rewarding blue run, as well as a red or two and a long steep black down to Sodoleuvre. It's also easy to work your way over to Les Diablerets (see below), from where lifts serve the Scex Rouge and Diablerets Glacier – although beware that if the snow at Villars and especially Gstaad isn't that great, everybody heads up to the glacier, which can make things uncomfortably overcrowded.

Practicalities

Villars' **station** is in the heart of the village; 50m to the right on the main Avenue Central is the **tourist office** (Christmas, New Year, Feb, July & Aug daily 8am–7pm; rest of year Mon–Sat 8am–noon & 1.30–6pm, Sun 10am–4pm; ☎024/495 32 32, *www. villars.ch*). For **accommodation**, *Hôtel du Cerf* (☎024/495 27 15, fax 495 14 37; ②) is cosy enough, with good meals, while the huge *Elite* (☎024/496 39 00, fax 496 39 01; ③) is conveniently located right beside the Roc d'Orsay gondola, with brand-new renovated rooms. *Alpe Fleurie* (☎024/495 34 64, fax 496 30 77; ③) and *Ecureuil* (☎024/495 27 95, fax 495 42 05; ③) are old-style chalet-hotels with a long history of catering to families, both conveniently central. A low-end option is the charming *Chalet Martin* **hostel** five minutes' walk above Gryon station (☎024/498 33 21; ①), a cosy, friendly place run by a Swiss-Australian couple, with dorm space for Fr.18. *Le Vieux-Villars*, on the Route des Hôtels, is a three-storey **restaurant** known for its fondues and raclettes.

Les Diablerets

Snoozing quietly in its peaceful backwater valley, **LES DIABLERETS** really deserves to be left well alone. It's so tranquil that it's almost a shame to mark it on a map – indeed, less than a century ago, it wasn't on any maps, and it was only with the arrival of the railway in 1914 that outsiders noticed the place. These days Les Diablerets has a small but loyal band of guests, who return each year to enjoy the valley's charm.

The **skiing** is good, marked out by close access to the Col de Pillon gondola serving the **Diablerets Glacier**, which slides down from the peaks of Scex Rouge (2970m) and Les Diablerets itself (3209m). Most of the pistes up here are blue and red, even way on top around the Quille du Diable – a jutting natural obelisk up at 3000m. A single hair-raising black run plunges beneath the gondola cables from **Pierres-Pointes** (2217m) down to the Col du Pillon. From the village itself, another gondola serves the slopes of **Isenau** to the north, laced with blue and red runs, while a third rises to Les Mazots, in the direction of Villars. Les Diablerets prides itself on its **summer skiing**, with good snow assured year-round on the glacier.

Practicalities

Regular **trains** run to Les Diablerets from Aigle; **buses** also connect the village with Gstaad via a dramatically steep road which winds over the Col du Pillon (1546m), 4km east of Les Diablerets. The tiny switchback road over the Col de la Croix (1778m) 4km south of Les Diablerets leads to Villars; three buses a day (July–Sept only) shuttle between the two resorts.

THE DEVILS OF LES DIABLERETS

The mountain communities of the Alpes Vaudoises are replete with legends and **folk tales**, and Les Diablerets – its name meaning "abode of devils" – is no exception. To the south and east of the village rise the heights of Les Diablerets themselves, with their two huge glaciers, Diablerets and **Tsanfleuron**. Legend has it that in ancient times the latter ("Field of Flowers" in the local dialect) was a beautiful sunny meadow until the arrival, long ago, of demons and devils in the mountains. Soon after, the shepherds of Tsanfleuron and the Ormont Valley began to be troubled by boulders bouncing down from on high, as the devils played their games of skill, trying to hit a huge tower of rock – the **Quille du Diable** (Devil's Skittle) – sticking up from the heights of the mountain. The shepherds, fearing for the safety of their flocks and themselves, moved away from the area, which lost its vitality and beauty and turned into the icy wasteland it remains today. The Quille du Diable still stands atop the mountain, close to the peak of the **Scex Rouge** (Ruby Mountain), so named after a local shepherdess discovered a fabulous cave studded with rubies and amethysts, home of the mountain spirit. In return for not telling a soul about the cave, the shepherdess was allowed to take away three large rubies; she kept her promise and left the valley. Since then, no one has been able to discover the entrance to the cave, but the story goes that when people have gone looking, the spirit has become angry and has started to shake the whole mountain.

Other tales abound of **lost souls** seen at night, drifting with lanterns alone or in groups through the woods, pastures and rocky defiles of the mountain; local people attested to seeing their lantern lights and hearing their moans just before the two terrible landslides of 1714 and 1740. The meadows and hills all around are also said to be inhabited by elves, goblins and a local brand of **imp** named a *servan*, one of whom, it is said, once mischievously turned himself into a fox and was seen sitting at night in a hay loft knitting with the hair of his own tail.

The **station** is in the village beside the river, about 100m north of the **tourist office** (July, Aug & Dec–April daily 8.30am–6.30pm; rest of year Mon–Sat 8.30am–12.30pm & 2–6pm, Sun 9am–12.30pm; ☎024/492 33 58, *www.alpes.ch/diablerets*). Every September, Les Diablerets hosts the International Alpine Film Festival. Mountain Evasion (☎024/492 12 32) and Centre Par Adventure (☎024/492 23 82) are two companies in the village organizing **adventure activities**, including canyoning, zorbing, luge, mud biking, rappelling and more.

Most accommodation is in chalets, but of the **hotels**, the *Auberge de la Poste* (☎024/492 31 24, fax 492 12 68; ②), a 200-year old inn that claims to have hosted Victor Hugo, Stravinsky and Lenin in years gone by, is pleasantly rustic. A little out of town on the Route de Pillon is *Les Diablotins* (☎024/492 36 33, fax 492 23 55; ①), a more basic choice with shared-bath rooms. Two comfortable places facing each other north of the station are *Le Chamois* (☎024/492 26 53, fax 492 26 06; ③), a "garni" hotel, and *Les Lilas* (☎024/492 31 34, fax 492 31 57; ①–②), the latter with some cheaper shared-bath rooms. There are two mountain inns with **dorms** above the village – one at Isenau (☎ & fax 024/492 32 93; Fr.34; June–Sept & Dec–April), and the other, the *Cabane des Diablerets* (☎024/492 21 02; Fr.29; mid-June to mid-Sept), overlooking the glacier at 2525m. **Eating** is mainly a hotel option, with the inexpensive restaurants at the *Auberge de la Poste* and especially *Les Lilas* worth checking out.

Leysin

The road from Aigle up into the mountains divides at Le Sépey – Les Diablerets is east, the Col des Mosses leading to Château d'Oex is north, while buses follow a tiny winding road west to the beautifully located little village of **LEYSIN**, once a high-altitude centre for the treatment of respiratory diseases, but now metamorphosed into a popular and well-maintained ski resort. Lifts and gondolas from the village serve a host of red and blue pistes, as well as a half-pipe for snowboarders below the peak of **La Berneuse** (2048m), where there's a panoramic revolving restaurant. Summer hiking in this mountain hideaway is excellent.

The best **accommodation** in the village can be found in the friendly *Hiking Sheep Guesthouse* in Villa La Joux (☎ & fax 024/494 35 35, *www.leysin.net/hikingsheep*; ①), with some twin rooms and space in small dorms (Fr.28); satellite TV, a large cosy lounge, dining rooms with log fires, kitchen use, balconies with perfect views and switched-on multilingual staff add to the attraction (as do reductions for long stays). Hotels – the *Orchidées* (☎024/494 14 21, fax 494 18 10; ②) or the *Mont-Riant* (☎024/494 27 01, fax 494 27 04; ②–③) for example – are comfortable enough but just can't compare.

Leysin was once famous around Switzerland for its giant August **rock festival** – that is, until they ran into major difficulties a few years back with crowd control and financing. Until they can sort things out again, a low-key Alpine Music Festival has taken its place – check with the **tourist office** (☎024/494 22 44) for more details.

VALAIS ROMAND

Tacked seamlessly south of Haut-Léman, **VALAIS ROMAND**, or the French-speaking part of Valais, comprises the westernmost portions of the canton. Occupying the broad Rhône valley floor and the most accessible foothills just above, it's more populated and livelier than the wilder German-speaking east. Mountain passes aside, the road and train line from Montreux is the sole route in and out; the mountains flanking the Rhône are cut through with a handful of dead-end valleys, wonderful for long-distance hiking, but only the high pass roads over the **Grand-St-Bernard** to Italy and the Col de la Forclaz to Chamonix in France give access from outside. These two roads join the valley at **Martigny**, a rather unprepossessing place much overshadowed in both style and appeal by its near neighbours, the cantonal capital **Sion** and, on the French–German language border, **Sierre**. The vapid resort towns of **Verbier** near Martigny, and **Crans-Montana** above Sierre, are two of the best-known ski resorts in the world, offering the combination of groomed pistes and chic après-ski that Switzerland is famous for.

South to Martigny

Roads and train tracks cross the broad Rhône at Aigle and Bex to a slice of Valais to the west and the small resorts of **Champéry** and **Morgins**, where you can ski the vast **Portes du Soleil** ski area in the shadow of the Dents du Midi range, shared with a number of French resorts just over the border (*www.portesdusoleil.com*). Main roads head on south towards Martigny, crossing the Vaud–Valais frontier at the ancient town of **St-Maurice**.

St-Maurice

About 3km south of Bex, at the point where the narrowing of the Rhône prompted the Romans to build a bridge, is **ST-MAURICE**, named after the warrior-saint Maurice who is purported to have been martyred nearby. Maurice was ordered in 287 AD by Emperor Maximian to serve against his fellow Christians on campaigns in Gaul, but refused, according to a later chronicler with the words: "We are your soldiers, O Emperor, but we freely acknowledge that we are also the servants of God ... To you is due military obedience, but to God, justice … We cannot take up arms to strike pious men, civilians … We are ready to submit to torture. We declare ourselves Christians." The Emperor duly had the whole legion slaughtered. Today, of course, mighty Maximian is forgotten, while there are apparently 4 cathedrals, 598 churches and 74 towns around the world named after Maurice, not counting two entire countries (Mauritius and Mauritania).

A shrine grew up around the supposed tomb of the saint, hard up against a rocky cliff on the banks of the Rhône, as early as 390, replaced by a monastery in 515; this is still in existence as the oldest surviving abbey north of the Alps. Pilgrims have come to the **abbey church** for over 1500 years, bringing with them items of gold and silver as homage, and the church **treasury** holds some exquisitely beautiful pieces, including a Roman sardonyx vase, the intricate gold cloisonné Casket of Teuderic, a breathtaking embossed silver bust of St Candidus and filigreed silver Arm of St Bernard, and other medieval golden caskets and reliquaries of the highest workmanship. Note that although the church is open at any time, you can only visit the treasury on **guided tours** (in English; Tues–Sun: July & Aug 10.30am, 2pm, 3.15pm & 4.30pm; Easter–June, Sept & Oct 10.30am, 3pm & 4.30pm; Nov–Easter 3pm; Fr.2).

Practicalities

Heading straight ahead out of the **train station** along Avenue de la Gare will bring you in a hundred metres to the friendly, English-speaking **tourist office** (July & Aug Mon–Fri 9am–7pm, Sat 9am–5pm; Sept–June Mon 3–6pm, Tues–Fri 9am–noon & 3–6pm, Sat 9am–noon; ☎024/485 40 40, *www.st-maurice.ch*). They run a walking tour of the town in English (April–Sept Wed–Sat 2pm; Fr.8), including the church more or less opposite, and the ancient Grand-Rue running through the centre of town, bedecked with wrought-iron inn signs and home to the few **hotels** and eating options. *Hotel Ecu du Valais*, 39 Grand-Rue (☎024/485 24 74, fax 485 33 05; ③) has been partly renovated, but also retains some older, more characterful rooms, while the small *Dent-du-Midi*, set in gardens at 1 Avenue du Simplon (☎024/485 12 09; ②) is comfortable and modern. For **eating**, the *Ecu du Valais* is known for its Valaisian specialities, while the best place for fondue is *La Croix Fédérale*, 45 Grand-Rue (closed Sun). *Manoir Rhodanien*, 84 Grand-Rue, has an eclectic menu taking in ostrich, barbecued kangaroo, crocodile steaks and more. There's a **campsite** at *Bois Noir* just south of town (☎027/767 11 76; April–Oct).

Martigny

There are few more dramatically sited cities in Switzerland than **MARTIGNY**. Set down on the broad valley floor, with wooded heights soaring on all sides, it's positioned at a natural crossroads. The Rhône, having flowed almost arrow straight along its valley for over 100km, suddenly makes a sharp right-angled turn at Martigny, heading off between the mountains to Lake Geneva; elevated points within the town give yawning views along both valleys, east and north. The major draw to the town is the **Fondation Pierre Gianadda**, one of the country's most prestigious art galleries. A handful of Roman ruins add a further smidgen of interest.

And yet Martigny is a curiously unsatisfying place to spend more than an afternoon. It's not an unpleasant town, but there's just not much going on, and – even worse – not many characterful places to sit and watch life go by. Stay overnight and make the best of it, or cut your losses and look elsewhere: St-Maurice has held onto its history better than Martigny; atmospheric Sion is close by; or you might prefer to plump for a "been-there-seen-it" night way up on the Grand-St-Bernard.

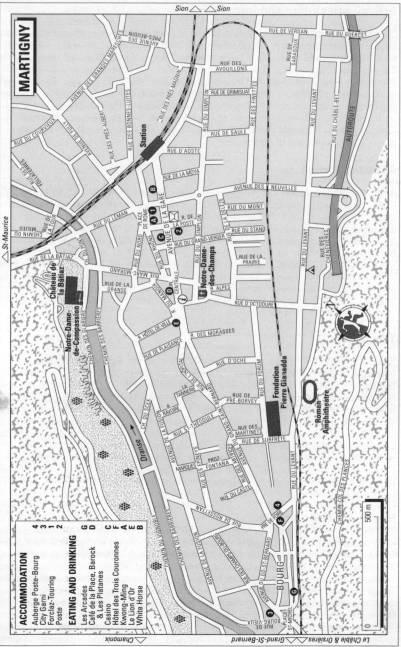

MARTIGNY

ACCOMMODATION
Auberge Poste-Bourg   4
City Garni   3
Forclaz-Touring   1
Poste   2

EATING AND DRINKING
Les Arcades   G
Café de la Place, Barock
 & Les Platanes   D
Casino   C
Hôtel des Trois Couronnes   F
Kwong-Ming   A
Le Lion d'Or   E
White Horse   B

Arrival, orientation and information

Martigny's **station** is at the northeastern end of Avenue de la Gare, which cuts a broad swathe through the centre. At the other end, 500m away, is the main Place Centrale, with the **tourist office** on one side (July & Aug Mon–Fri 9am–6pm, Sat 9am–noon & 2–6pm, Sun 10am–noon & 4–6pm; Sept–June Mon–Fri 9am–noon & 1.30–6pm, Sat 9am–noon; May, June, Sept & Oct also Sat 2–5pm; ☎027/721 22 20). They're well equipped with information and maps for the whole area, including the routes up to the Grand-St-Bernard pass and Verbier, and the Val de Bagnes. The Fondation Gianadda is on Rue du Forum about 500m south of Place Centrale, well signposted. The small Old Town, or Bourg, is a world apart, with cobbled lanes, old auberges and a villagey atmosphere, 1.5km southwest of the centre.

Accommodation

Aside from the **campsite** *Les Neuvilles*, 68 Route du Levant (☎027/722 45 44, fax 722 35 44; closed Jan), a quality place with four-person tents to rent (Fr.60–85) and dorms (Fr.20), there are a handful of town **hotels**, many unromantically planted on the busy Avenue du Grand-St-Bernard as sleepover motels to catch the traffic heading for the Alpine passes. Least expensive are the spartan shared-bath rooms of the old *Auberge Poste-Bourg*, 81 Avenue du Grand-St-Bernard (☎027/722 25 17; ①). *City Garni*, 7 Place St-Michel (☎027/723 36 00, fax 723 36 01; ①) is similarly priced, but modern and generic. The bland *Forclaz-Touring*, 15 Rue du Léman (☎027/722 27 01, fax 722 41 79; ②), has comfortable en-suite rooms near the station, whereas the *Poste*, 8 Rue de la Poste (☎027/722 14 44, fax 722 04 45; ②), is in the heart of town but could do with some renovation work and a good spring-clean.

The Town

Just behind Place Centrale and the tourist office is the **Église Notre-Dame-des-Champs**, completed in 1687, with magnificent carved doors but a modest interior. From Place Centrale, if you follow Rue Marc-Morand north, you'll come to an old covered wooden bridge over the Dranse river; this is an 1818 replacement of the 1350 original, and leads to a winding path climbing to the semi-ruined thirteenth-century **Château de la Bâtiaz**, its lofty round tower visible from all parts of the town, and especially dramatic when floodlit at night beside the meandering tail-lights of cars on the tortuous switchback road to Chamonix. The château is rarely open, but the views are worth the climb. Below the château is the small **Chapelle de Notre-Dame-de-Compassion**, built in the 1620s with a Rococo altar added more than a century later. Its most remarkable feature is a huge collection of ex voto paintings dating back 200 years and more.

Fondation Pierre Gianadda

The main reason for coming to Martigny at all is to visit the galleries and museums of the **Fondation Pierre Gianadda**, located on a patch of parkland off Rue du Forum (daily: June–Oct 9am–7pm; Feb–May 10am–6pm; Nov–Jan 10am–noon & 1.30–6pm; Fr.12; ☎027/722 39 78; *www.gianadda.ch*). Established in 1978 by a local philanthropist, Léonard Gianadda, and named after his brother, the complex takes in several areas within a single museum. Note that the Foundation offers various special deals, such as a twenty-percent discount on your train fare to Martigny and museum entry if you book the two together at any Swiss train station.

The main focus is the changing series of top-flight art exhibitions staged in the **main gallery** area – recent major shows have included Chagall and Modigliani retrospectives, an overview of Kandinsky's work and, until November 2000, a Van Gogh exhibition. The gallery space itself is not huge, but the quality of works brought in from around the world is always very high. The upper level of the gallery is given over to the **Musée Archéologique Gallo-Romain**, an interesting collection of statues, coins, pottery, jewellery and other bits and bobs garnered from digs around Martigny. Prime exhibit, which serves as the Foundation's mascot, is an impressive bronze head of a bull, dating from the first or second century AD. The whole building is built around the remains of a Gallo-Roman temple dedicated to Mercury, the inner-sanctum walls of which have been left intact in the middle of the museum's floorspace. In a back area off the gallery is the small permanent exhibition of fine art, the **Salle Franck**, ten modernist works donated from a private collection, including Picasso's *Nu aux jambes croisées* (1903), produced at the height of the artist's blue period. The smell of motor oil and rubber prelude the subterranean **Musée de l'Auto**, displaying fifty-odd vintage cars including a Model T Ford (1912), and a dashingly elegant Lagonda (1936). Outside is the **Parc des Sculptures**, an open area of green overlooked by Martigny's wooded slopes and dotted with works by Rodin, Moore, Miró and Brancusi's celebrated *Le Grand Coq* (1949), a striking zigzag of gleaming metal, amongst many more. Alongside the café at the rear of the park is the **Vieil Arsenal**, which stages temporary shows of photography or modern art.

Finally, you should call the Foundation – or check its Web site – for details of its cycle of **classical concerts**, twelve or fifteen a year, which give the unique opportunity to see stellar world-class artists performing at close quarters in the intimate gallery space: tickets (Fr.20–100) are very limited.

Within a few hundred metres of the museum, to the south beyond the train tracks, lies Martigny's Roman **amphitheatre**, dating from the second-to-fourth centuries AD

VALAISIAN COWFIGHTING

The Valais is known for a host of peculiar local traditions, one of the oddest of which must be **cowfighting**. Utterly unlike Spanish bullfighting – an altogether gorier spectacle – Valaisian cowfighting stems from village get-togethers to see whose cow was best suited to lead the herds up to the summer Alpine pastures. The cattle all come from the local Hérens breed, bright-eyed with short legs and powerful chests, and known for their aggressiveness, who would naturally pick fights with each other in the open meadows: in the beginnings, farmers merely corralled them together to see who would win. These days, the contests have become rather more important – breeding means big money for the Valaisian cattle farmers, and the winner of the annual round of cowfighting championships can be assured both a head price in the tens of thousands of francs plus the prestigious title Queen of the Herd.

Farmers feed up the most bullish of their cows on a special extra-rich diet to improve (or worsen) her temper, occasionally allowing her the odd bucket of wine as a tonic and coaching her in sparring contests amongst the herd. Come the day of battle, farmers tie a huge cowbell around their champion's neck, lead her into the "arena" (generally just a meadow), and introduce her to her opponent. Hérens cows rarely need any encouragement to provoke each other into aggression, and they happily lock horns to fight it out. There's never any bloodiness, and the winner is generally deemed to be the cow who has shoved or intimidated her opponent into submission.

Local contests are held on Sundays once or twice a month in various towns from late March through to September, accompanied by much revelry and the consumption of gallons of local wine. Two events stand out: the **cantonal championships** are held in Aproz, a small town just outside Sion, in mid-May, with the winners going on to Martigny for the **Combats des Reines**, a huge show held in the 5000-seater Roman amphitheatre in early October. It's here that the supreme champion is crowned Queen of the Herd.

and now restored to seat 5000 spectators. It comes into its own as the venue for the annual cowfighting championships in early October (see box p.299), but otherwise it's a quiet, grassy corner from which to survey the wooded slopes all around.

Eating and drinking

Place Centrale is where it happens in Martigny – though "it" covers little more than sitting around under the trees at pleasant terrace cafés **eating** plates of chips and drinking beer. Ranged along one side are bustling *Café de la Place*, specializing in fondues and raclettes (Fr.15–20), and adjacent *Barock* and *Les Platanes*, all of which get crammed on summer evenings churning out meals, beers and coffees to all and sundry. You'd do better down in the Bourg: the *Auberge Poste-Bourg* (see "Accommodation") offers inexpensive Valaisian dishes (Fr.16 or so), while the *Hôtel des Trois Couronnes*, 8 Place du Bourg (☎027/723 21 14; closed Sun & Mon) is an old traditional-style *auberge* from 1609, no longer offering lodging, but still serving up quality French cuisine, with *menus* at Fr.20 and up – go for the house speciality of kidneys in garlic. Back up near Place Centrale, *Le Lion d'Or*, 1 Avenue du Grand-St-Bernard, makes its own fresh pasta, and has quality pizzas and other Italian favourites such as *osso bucco* (closed Sun & Mon). The Gault & Millau recommmended *Kwong-Ming*, Place de Rome (☎027/722 45 15; closed June), serves up perfect Chinese dishes in a calm, darkwood interior or *al fresco* beside the interior garden; lunch *menus* can be Fr.20, rising to double that in the evening, or you could go for a cheaper takeaway instead. Nearby, the tearoom on the seventh floor of the *Forclaz-Touring* hotel has panoramic views over the town and along both valleys.

As for **drinking**, there's a string of divey pubs along Avenue de la Gare, including the rough-and-ready *White Horse*. Otherwise, the bar in the nearby *Casino* cinema, open daily until midnight, is a more civilized joint. Alternatively you could head down to *Les Arcades*, an atmospheric bar in a vaulted cellar at 31 Rue du Bourg, one of a handful of sociable taverns in the area.

Listings

Bike rental In the station (Mon–Sat 5.45am–8.45pm, Sun 6.15am–8.45pm).

Car rental Avis, Garage de la Forclaz, Rue du Simplon (☎027/722 23 33); Europcar, 43 Rue du Léman (☎027/722 12 27).

Changing money In the station (Mon–Sat 5.45am–8.45pm, Sun 6.15am–8.45pm).

Email and Internet The *Casino* cinema/bar/café, 17 Avenue de la Gare, open daily until midnight, offers Internet access (Fr.20/hr).

Post office Junction of Avenue de la Gare and Rue de la Poste (CH-1920 Martigny 1).

Pays du Grand-St-Bernard

South of Martigny is the **Pays du Grand-St-Bernard**, wild valleys hemmed in by the giant Pennine Alps marking the Italian border. Branch-line trains from Martigny station follow the Dranse valley and divide; one branch serves **Le Châble**, tucked beneath the famous ski resort of Verbier (see p.304), while the other is the gateway to the Val d'Entremont, leading south to the **Grand-St-Bernard Pass**, beyond which is Italy. If you plan to explore in the area, you'd do well to pick up the excellent 1:40,000 map and English guidebook *Au Pays du Grand-St-Bernard* (Fr.20), which recommends some good walking routes and is available from the Martigny tourist office.

WALKING FROM CHAMONIX TO ZERMATT

The snowy Pennine Alps of Canton Valais drain north to the Rhône through a series of spectacular valleys walled by high and craggy ridges. The **Walker's Haute Route** makes a traverse of these on a west-to-east journey which begins in **Chamonix** (France) below Mont Blanc, and ends in Zermatt at the foot of the Matterhorn, one of the most beautiful and scenically rewarding of Europe's long walks. It's a demanding two-week trek, but there are no glaciers or permanent snowfields to cross, and overnight accommodation is plentiful in huts, mountain inns or valley hotels. You can also easily join the route partway along at strategically accessible points for a few days' hiking – the Val de Bagnes, Arolla and Zinal, for instance, are all served by public transport from main Valais towns. Along with the **maps** LS 5003 Mont Blanc–Grand Combin, and 5006 Matterhorn–Mischabel (both 1:50,000), you'll need to pack *Chamonix to Zermatt, the Walker's Haute Route* by Kev Reynolds (see "Books", p.531).

With a long climb out of the Chamonix valley, the Haute Route enters Switzerland by way of Col de Balme and descends to **Trient**. On day three there are two routes to choose from: either the formidable but non-technical Fenêtre d'Arpette alongside the Trient Glacier, or the more pedestrian Alp Bovine route to **Champex** (see p.302) – the former is tough but visually exciting, the latter an energetic alternative, also with fine views. From Champex an easy valley walk leads to **Le Châble** in Val de Bagnes (see box, p.306), from where the route on day five makes a 1600m climb to the **Cabane du Mont-Fort** (☎027/778 13 84), a mountain hut with stunning views across to Mont Blanc. Leaving the hut next day an airy balcony walk takes you along the Sentier des Chamois, with the Grand Combin (4314m) a mighty presence across the valley, then over Col de Louvie to skirt below the Grand Désert glacier, and across Col de Prafleuri to **Cabane de Prafleuri** (☎027/207 30 67). Views from this hut are restricted, but a short climb to Col des Roux reveals the tranquil Lac des Dix below, with Mont Blanc de Cheilon (3870m) at the head of the valley. Beyond the lake, the way traces old moraines alongside a rubble-strewn glacier, then crosses either Col de Riedmatten (2919m) or the neighbouring Pas de Chèvres – the latter by way of two long and very steep ladders. Once you've crossed this ridge, there's a very pleasant descent through pastures to **Arolla** (see p.311).

Day eight is an easy one, taking you from Arolla down to Les Haudères and up to **La Sage**, while on day nine Col de Torrent (2919m) leads you into the Moiry glen, near the head of which **Cabane de Moiry** (☎027/475 45 34) overlooks a cascading icefall and the glacier easing from it. Col de Sorebois is next, with the descent from there to **Zinal** in Val d'Anniviers allowing you to make the acquaintance of the hugely impressive **Weisshorn** (4505m) and its attendant peaks on the far side. On day eleven, you leave Zinal on another balcony path, this time heading north for about four hours to the *Weisshorn* (☎027/475 11 06), a Victorian hotel perched high above the valley looking to the sunset from its glass-fronted dining room. Next day you cross the Meidpass (2790m) to **Gruben** in the Turtmann valley, the first German-speaking valley and a truly forgotten little corner. The penultimate stage (day thirteen) is the setting for another high-level crossing – the 2894m **Augstbordpass**. This brings you into the Mattertal, the valley which leads to Zermatt and the Matterhorn; an hour and a half below the pass the trail turns a spur to confront you with the most amazing of panoramas. Across the unseen depths of the Matter valley soars the **Dom** (4545m, the highest mountain entirely in Switzerland); at the head of the valley far away a long crest of snow and ice stretches from Monte Rosa to the Breithorn (the Matterhorn is just hidden from view), while the Weisshorn dominates the right-hand wall. An hour below that viewpoint lies Jungen, a summer alp hamlet clinging to the near-vertical hillside. The path then plunges steeply to **St Niklaus** in the bed of the valley. The last stretch (day fourteen) offers no passes to cross, but a mere wander up the valley to **Zermatt** (see p.317), in order to make your final pilgrimage to the **Matterhorn**.

The Grand-St-Bernard road

Trains, and the road, from Martigny divide at **SEMBRANCHER**, long a staging post on the route up to the Grand-St-Bernard. It's an attractive, medieval village, with a Baroque church and street fountains flowing with water that is unusually high in natural fluoride. About 6km south – and up – is **ORSIÈRES**, where trains terminate and buses take over. Orsières is notable for the exquisitely beautiful Gothic bell-tower alongside its relatively modern church, featuring double- and triple-arched windows and grotesque gargoyles. A branch road from here penetrates the lonesome **Val Ferret**, extending for some 20km between towering peaks and acclaimed as an excellent birdwatching area, where you might spot the rare red-billed chough, along with yellowhammers, kestrels and more. As one visitor wrote in 1876, the valley has "infernal beauties which are well worth seeing... There are few valleys in the Alps so fearsomely wild, where the sombre grey of the rocks, the white of the snow and the blue of the sky merge."

On a zigzagging road above Orsières lies the tranquil little resort of **CHAMPEX**, ranged around its tiny lakelet and well known as a mountaineering centre and trailhead for a host of mountain walks, including the famous Circuit of Mont-Blanc. Two **hotels** stand out, both country inns in idyllic woodland settings: down-to-earth *Belvédère* (☎027/783 11 14, fax 783 25 76; ②) is renowned for its organic, home-produced cuisine, while *Au Vieux-Champex* (☎ & fax 027/783 12 16; ②) is more up-market, with a gourmet edge and five comfortable apartments.

The main road from Orsières continues to climb amidst increasingly spectacular scenery up to the village of **BOURG-ST-PIERRE**, residence from the eighth century onwards of the guardians of the pass; the old church, rebuilt in 1739, has at its northeastern corner a Roman milestone dating from about 310 AD. Above the village, the main road is roofed over to limit problems with driving snow in winter. Shortly afterwards, traffic shoots into the Grand-St-Bernard tunnel, emerging 5.9km on in Italy, but a tiny winding road to one side continues up the mountainside, past a ski lift serving the small Super-St-Bernard peak (part of the Four Valleys ski area – see p.305 – with a couple of red runs and a wild and lonesome black), before it eventually arrives at the dramatic **Grand-St-Bernard Pass** itself, at 2470m.

The Grand-St-Bernard Pass

The Grand-St-Bernard Pass is the oldest Alpine pass route (see box opposite), protected by monks inhabiting the **hospice** on top for almost a millennium. The views aren't outstanding, and the souvenir stalls are an eyesore, but the sense of history is what draws you in – for centuries, this was the only road between northern Europe and southern Europe for hundreds of miles on either flank, and countless travellers have arrived to the same view of the little summit lake backed by the same mountain panorama. The interesting **museum** (daily: July & Aug 8am–6.30pm; June & Sept 9am–6pm; Fr.6) documents the history of the pass, and includes several quaking accounts of fatal or near-fatal crossings. The two buildings which make up the hospice, exposed to winter storms which have been known to bring 25m of snow with them and temperatures of -30°C, date from 1560 and 1898; the older one contains a Baroque **church**. If you walk down from the hospice, the Italian frontier guards will let you cross the **international border** to explore the rocky area behind the customs post and Italian hospice; around the **statue of St Bernard** atop its round pillar (1905) you'll find traces of the Roman road cut into the bedrock.

In summer, it's possible to **stay** in the hospice, which is still a functioning religious community (☎027/787 12 36, fax 787 11 07; ①), either in plain, cosy rooms, or dorms (Fr.17); the cooking is suitable hearty and warming and the atmosphere jovial. During the winter months (Nov–June) and over Easter, you can arrange an individual retreat,

HISTORY OF THE GRAND-ST-BERNARD

The **Grand-St-Bernard Pass** is the oldest of Alpine pass routes, in use at least since the Bronze Age (about 800 BC). Tribes and armies have tramped their way to and fro for millennia – in 390 BC, a Gaulish army crossed to defeat Rome – and from the earliest times ordinary people used the pass to trade goods between northern Europe and Italy. **Hannibal's** famous crossing of the Alps in 217 BC, reputedly with elephants, is indelibly associated with the Grand-St-Bernard, though there's little actual evidence of it. In 57 BC, **Julius Caesar** crossed the *Summa Poenina*, as it was known, to conquer the pagan peoples of Martigny, who worshipped the Celtic god Poenn (the chain of great peaks on the Swiss–Italian frontier is still called the Pennine Alps). Shortly after, Emperor Augustus built a road across the pass; on the top he left a temple to Jupiter, which subsequently lent its name to the area (*Mons Iovis*, or Mont Joux). The temple was sacked with the fall of Rome, but a refuge may well have remained on the pass, since the great and the good continued to tramp the road: Pope Stephen II crossed in November 753 to meet with Pepin the Short, King of France; while in 800 **Charlemagne** crossed back following his coronation in Milan.

In the early 900s, Huns and Saracens swept through the region, raping, pillaging and destroying churches: to keep them quiet, Hugh of Provence, King of Italy, granted them guardianship of the Mont Joux pass, whereupon they began to terrorize travellers and demand payment. Deeply concerned at the disruption caused to merchants and pilgrims Europe-wide, King Canute of Denmark took King Rudolf III of Burgundy to one side to have a quiet word. They ejected the heathens in short order, whereupon the archdeacon of Aosta, one **Bernard of Menthon**, who'd spent years tending to travellers coming down off the pass stripped of all their belongings, oversaw the construction of a hospice on the pass. Bernard himself travelled around the area, spreading the word of God, and was beatified shortly after his death in the 1080s. Pope Pius XI confirmed him as patron saint of the Alps in 1923.

The hospice immediately became a welcome point of safety on an extremely dangerous route, attracting favours and gifts from royal and noble households, and by 1177, a papal bull confirmed that the monks owned some 78 properties in Vaud, Valais, Savoy, Italy, France and England, including Hornchurch in Essex. Throughout the Middle Ages, the hospice provided free shelter and food to pilgrims, clerics and travellers, many crossing to and from Rome. By 1817 some 20,000 people were using the road annually. During the wars of the 1790s, entire armies crossed the pass: in May 1800, **Napoleon** led 40,000 troops over the pass into Italy, on the way consuming 21,724 bottles of wine, a tonne and a half of cheese, 800kg of meat, and more, running up a bill with the hospice of Fr.40,000 before departing with a wave of his hand. Fifty years later, the monks received Fr.18,500 towards payment, and had to wait until May 1984 for a token gesture of account settling from French president François Mitterrand.

First mention of the famous **St Bernard dogs** – product of an unknown cross between a mastiff, Great Dane and/or Newfoundland – was in 1708. Since then, these heavy-set, jowly beasts, with a little flask of reviving brandy tied round their collars, have come to stand as icons of the mountains. With the advent of skis, phone lines, radios, and now helicopters, the rescue services of the dogs have faded, but the hospice still keeps a kennel for them on the pass. (Some fifteen pure-bred St Bernard puppies are born every year, each with a tidy price-tag of Fr.1700.) With the construction of the Simplon Tunnel further east in 1905, trains rapidly superseded the St Bernard road, and in 1964 a motorway tunnel opened beneath the pass in order to safeguard traffic flow year-round. These days the hospice spends the summer crowded with visitors and hikers, and the winter receiving people climbing up from below to spend a few days or weeks on a solitary snow-bound retreat.

to take advantage of the solitude for personal reflection. The hospice also runs mountaineering courses and weekend hiking and skiing excursions.

Verbier

It's the skiing that put **VERBIER** on the map: few places in the world offer such breadth of possibilities with such awe-inspiring scenery as a backdrop. Before 1910, the plateau on which Verbier sits was an empty summer pasture; the first hotel opened in 1934, and even by 1950 the place was still a tiny village. No more. Following the 1960s ski boom, Verbier now sprawls, characterized by unattractive apartment blocks and modern housing. It's not particularly charming or endearing, but with this quality of skiing on offer, it doesn't have to be. European high society flocks to the resort in season, and the mood of the place can get tediously brash and trendy, but still the slopes hold sway. Fully half of the million annual visitors are Swiss, many scooting over from Lausanne and Geneva for a weekend in their apartments or chalets; it's a feature of Verbier that chalet accommodation outnumbers hotel beds ten-to-one, making it much more advisable to visit on a ski-chalet package booked from home than to arrive without a hotel reservation.

Arrival, orientation and information

Branch-line trains from Martigny split at Sembrancher, with one portion going on to terminate at Le Châble, the valley community at the foot of the hill. From Le Châble, a cable-car runs every fifteen minutes up to Verbier, arriving at the huge Médran cable-car station at the east end of the resort. Postbuses also do the run from Le Châble, climbing first through "Verbier-Village" (the locals' town) before terminating in "Verbier-Station", the resort, at the central post office just off Place Centrale.

Orientation around the resort can be a little confusing. The Rue de Médran climbs southeast from Place Centrale to the **Médran** lift station, from where gondolas and a chairlift rise to Les Ruinettes, main access point for the pistes. It's along this street, and in the surrounding area, that most of the resort's après-ski happens. The resort's other gondola rises from the **Savoleyres** station, best part of a kilometre north of Place Centrale. West of Place Centrale is the massive Sports Centre with, below and south of it, workaday Verbier-Village. **Free buses** link all of these throughout the summer and winter seasons (July, Aug & Dec–April daily 8am–7pm).

The highly organized **tourist office** is on Place Centrale (July, Aug & Dec–April Mon–Sat 8.30am–12.30pm & 2–6.30pm, Sun 9am–noon & 4–6.30pm; rest of year Mon–Fri 8.30am–noon & 2–6.30pm, Sat 9am–noon & 4–6pm, Sun 9am–noon; ☎027/775 38 88, *www.verbier.ch*). They have maps galore, and plenty of information on the resort and its pistes. The lift company, Téléverbier, provides a daily snow report on its Web site (*www.televerbier.ch*). Late July sees Verbier staging one of Switzerland's most prestigious classical music events, the **Verbier Festival and Academy**. For two weeks, the resort plays host to top-flight international names, who come to perform and also lead masterclasses and discussions. Tickets range from Fr.30 to Fr.120 for individual concerts, Fr.300 for a weekend pass, or Fr.1000-plus for a universal pass. Contact the festival administration for more details (☎021/922 40 10, *www.verbierfestival.com*).

Adventure sports

Verbier is a mecca for **adventure** addicts, with a host of companies competing with each other to come up with the newest and most exciting extreme thrill of the season. The Maison du Sport (Sports Centre; ☎027/775 33 63, *verbier-sportcenter.ch*) is home to ski and snowboarding schools, the mountain guides office, Centre Parapente offering tandem paragliding and hang-gliding flights, and No Limits with luge, snow-carting, snow-scooting and plenty more. Bureau de la Fantastique (☎027/771 41 41, *www.lafantastique.com*) offer heli-skiing, qualified guides for off-piste (Fr.390/day for one person) and long-distance ski safaris.

EXTREME EVENTS

Verbier comes into its own as testing ground for extreme sports. One of the best annual events is the **Xtreme Freeride Snowboarding Contest** (*www.xtreme-snowboard.com*), one of the top international showcases of the sport, held each March. Bec des Rosses, way up on the mountainside at Gentianes, is the scene for twenty of the world's best boarders to do their thing, competing by invitation only in the most dramatic of locations, with 55 degree gradients, broad expanses of powder and plenty of obstacles.

The **Patrouille des Glaciers** (Glacier Patrol; *www.pdg.ch*) is a long-distance endurance test across the 53km of glaciers, summits and passes between Zermatt and Verbier. Dubbed "Paris–Dakar on skis", it was halted in 1949 after three deaths, and restarted in 1984 with more than six hundred participants; since then it has taken place every other year (next in May 2002), with the current record standing at 7 hours 13 minutes. Not to be outdone, **mountain biking** has its own world championship at Verbier, an exceptionally tough one-day race over 131km to Grimentz, completed in 1997 in an amazing 6 hours 26 minutes.

Accommodation

Verbier is tricky when it comes to **hotels**: there just aren't that many of them, and you may find they won't accept bookings for less than seven days in season. Many places close in the April–May and October–November between-seasons. Accommodation is least expensive in the handful of private rooms on offer through the tourist office, or in any of the thousands of chalets, which must be booked months in advance. Note that there is no central parking garage.

Hôtel Les Touristes (☎ & fax 027/771 21 47; ①) offers one of the best ways to duck beneath Verbier's high prices and uninspiring anonymity: it's on a street corner in Verbier-Village, linked to the lifts by a bus, with spartan, shared-bath rooms. Its quiet restaurant and chic-free atmosphere are a breath of fresh air. Otherwise, you're looking at through-the-roof prices for the winter high season (summer and between-season prices can be up to a third cheaper). The least expensive hotel in the resort open year-round is the *Mont-Gelé* (☎027/771 30 53, fax 771 13 16; ③), beside the Médran lift station, with just fifteen comfortable, balconied rooms. The basic rooms in the *Rosablanche* (☎027/771 55 55, fax 771 70 55; ①) are only available June to October, booked out all winter by a tour operator. A good, quiet place for skiers willing to skip resort nightlife is *Le Relais de Pachou* (☎027/771 63 49, fax 771 77 34, *www.thealps.com*; ③), 1.5km west of Place Centrale, at the end station of one of the resort bus routes. The central *Garbo*, midway between Place Centrale and the Médran lifts (☎027/771 62 72, fax 771 62 71, *www.garbo.ch*; ⑤), represents OK value, except around the New Year and in February, when it tacks an outrageous Fr.100 onto its double-room prices. *Rois Mages* is a modern choice by the church (☎027/771 63 64, fax 771 33 19; ⑤), while the *Ermitage*, on Place Centrale (☎027/771 64 77, fax 771 52 64; ④), is well run and very convenient, delivering unexpected value for money. The *Bristol* (☎027/771 65 77, fax 771 51 50; ⑤) is friendly, cosy and quiet, and very central, but watch out for that peak-time price hike.

The skiing

For years, Verbier has suffered from notoriously long queues and poorly planned lift transport, but these days, with the opening of new gondolas almost every season, things are getting better. Verbier is the main resort of the **Four Valleys ski area**, covering a vast swathe of some 400km of piste at all levels of difficulty, stretching from

THE VAL DE BAGNES

The long **Val de Bagnes** runs southeast from **Le Châble**, a peaceful, entirely rural community tucked beneath the famous ski resort of Verbier. Le Châble is in fact the capital of the Bagnes commune, Switzerland's largest, and at 295 kilometres square larger than the cantons of Geneva, Schaffhausen or Zug (although about a third of the Bagnes is covered by glaciers). Buses run twice a day (July–Sept only) from Le Châble to the impressive **Mauvoisin Dam**, a giant wall 250m high blocking the end of the valley. At 1961m, it's one of the highest-altitude dams in the world. A **hotel** at the base (✆ & fax 027/778 11 30; ①) has rooms and dorms (Fr.20) allowing you to stay overnight, either after a walk up from Fionnay or Lourtier villages in the valley, or before taking a full day to hike back to Le Châble.

Thyon, Veysonnaz and Nendaz in the west, through the central Savoleyres and Mont-Fort areas, out to far-flung corners like the Super-St-Bernard. The **lift-pass** system is complicated: a Verbier pass (Fr.50/day, Fr.283/week) covers the Ruinettes, Mont Gelé and La Chaux runs, as well as Tortin, Thyon and Savoleyres, but isn't valid up to the high pistes on Mont-Fort. For that you need a full Four Valleys pass (Fr.56/day, Fr.318/week, Fr.509/two weeks).

Beginners would do better to look elsewhere: a handful of blues at **Bruson** are all there is, really. There is a host of red runs from **Savoleyres**, and the Medran lifts take you up to **Les Ruinettes**, with its own cat's cradle of reds and a scarily vertiginous black run. New, large-capacity gondolas connect to **Attelas** (2727m), with blacks and reds, and either on to the **Mont Gelé** summit (3023m), or by chairlift over to **Tortin** from where reds or a fiendishly difficult black to connect to the Siviez and Thyon ski areas. From **La Chaux** (2260m) above Ruinettes, one of Switzerland's largest cablecars, the Jumbo, swooshes 150 people at a time up to the glacier slopes of **Mont-Fort** (3330m), also one of the best places in the country for **summer skiing**. Boarders are well served by half-pipes at Gentianes on Mont-Fort, La Chaux and Savoleyres.

Eating and drinking

Eating options aren't very inspiring. Aside from supermarket fare, or burgers from *Harold's* on Place Centrale, food is generally poor value. Wander your way up Rue de Médran from Place Centrale until you see something you fancy. There is a handful of pizzerias: the *Fer à Cheval* is one of the better ones, with a reasonably lively après-ski scene to boot, or there's the *Garbo* close at hand, which also shakes a leg. *Al Capone* is another friendly pizza joint, west of the centre towards the Savoleyres lift. As you emerge from the Medran station, *Au Vieux Valais* is within view, a cosy traditional-style place for raclette, fondue and other belly-warmers; similar fare can be found at *Les Touristes* (see "Accommodation"), a quiet, pleasant place down in Verbier-Village that's well worth making the journey for. *Le Bouchon Gourmand* (✆027/771 72 96) makes a change, a relatively good French bistro west of the post office, specializing in rich *foie gras* and duck, but also with fresh pastas and salads (*menus* Fr.22 and up). The gourmet choice is the *Rosalp* (✆027/771 63 23), a staggeringly expensive place to savour what's been called the best cuisine in the country. The restaurant, and the chef Roland Pierroz, have been showered with awards. Even choosing from the wine list is likely to be quite an event: the cellar runs to 50,000 bottles. *Rosalp*'s ground-floor brasserie is slightly more affordable (around Fr.40).

Of a number of places to **drink** around the resort, the one with most colour is the raucous *Pub Monto Fort*, near the Médran station. The *Nelson*, off Place Centrale, near the *Marshal's* techno joint, is another good option, while the snobby *Farm Club*, west of the centre, is the best place for a spot of celeb- and royal-watching.

Sion

SION (pronounced *see-ohh*), known as Sitten in German, is the capital of Canton Valais, an alluring and attractive town of just 27,000 with an exceptionally long history: archeological evidence points to the site having been inhabited during Neolithic times. What attracted settlement, no doubt, was the incongruous presence, on the otherwise pancake-flat valley floor, of two jutting rocky hills, visible from afar not least for the medieval castles **Valère** and **Tourbillon**, which now adorn the crests of both. They're an odd and slightly sinister sight, which matches the belief seemingly held around the country that people from Sion – named Sédunois after the town's Latin name *Sedunum*, meaning Place of Castles – are themselves a bit odd, impenetrably taciturn and clannish.

For the entire decade of the 1990s, the municipality and the people exerted extraordinary efforts to attract the Winter Olympics to Sion, stressing the presence nearby of

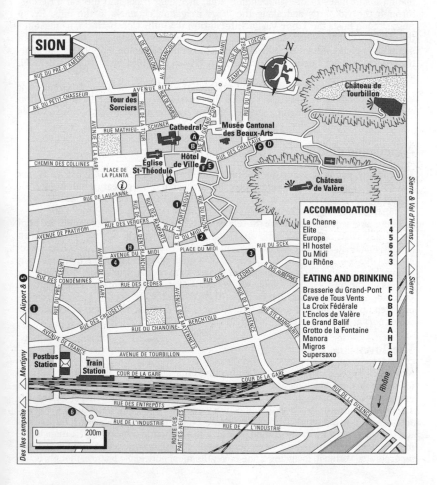

well-equipped Verbier, Crans-Montana and Zermatt – and yet they were rejected, both for the 2002 and (amidst profound controversy) the 2006 games, the latter awarded by the IOC without much clarity of purpose to Turin. For now, the Sédunois have lapsed into a shocked and sulky silence, while the town itself remains refreshingly down-to-earth after the grinding glitz of the big resorts.

Arrival, orientation and information

Sion's **train station** is at the southern end of the long, straight Avenue de la Gare, with the giant **postbus station** to one side. Some 500m north along Avenue de la Gare is the wide open concrete of the **Place de la Planta**, with a shack housing the **tourist office** (July & Aug Mon–Sat 8am–6pm; Sept–June Mon–Fri 8.30am–noon & 2–5.30pm, Sat 8.30am–noon; ☎027/322 85 86, *www.siontourism.ch*). They offer a good two-hour guided **walking tour** of the town (July & Aug Tues & Thurs 4pm; Fr.8), as well as information about hikes in the surrounding area, including treks into the Val d'Hérens, through the vineyards and along the *bisses* irrigation channels in the hills. Every August, Sion hosts the **Tibor Varga International Violin Competition**, named after the virtuoso violinist who settled in Sion for the health of his son, and centrepiece of a summer-long classical music festival at venues around the canton. For tickets and information, contact the **Festival Tibor Varga**, CP 1429, CH-1951 Sion (☎027/323 43 30, *www.nouvelliste.ch/varga*).

From Place de la Planta, the Rue de Lausanne heads east to meet Rue du Grand-Pont in the heart of the **Old Town**, clustered at the base of the two castle hills of **Tourbillon** and **Valère**. Sion's tiny **airport** – used regularly by international flights only in winter – is 5km west of the centre.

Accommodation

The nearest, and best, **campsite** to Sion is the five-star *Des Iles* (☎027/346 43 47, fax 346 68 47), 4km west of the centre near the airport and open year-round. A good HI **hostel** is just behind the station, at 2 Rue de l'Industrie (☎027/323 74 70, fax 323 74 38; ①; closed Jan, Nov & Dec) – modern, clean and well run, with dorms for Fr.26.

There are a few inexpensive **hotels** within Sion. The *Elite*, 6 Avenue du Midi (☎027/322 03 27, fax 322 23 61; ②), doesn't look like much, but it's recently been redone inside and is quite serviceable. In the Old Town, *La Channe*, at 9 Rue Porte-Neuve (☎027/322 32 71, fax 322 32 89; ②), is a quiet unassuming place that's pleasant and well kept, with a choice of en-suite or shared-bath rooms. The luridly decorated *Du Midi* is on the busy Place du Midi (☎027/323 13 31, fax 323 61 73; ②), while nearby is the cinder-block *Du Rhône*, Rue du Scex 10 (☎027/322 82 91, fax 323 11 88; ③), a definite step up in quality and service. Sion's best is the *Europa*, a business hotel out near the airport at 19 Rue de l'Envoi (☎027/322 24 23, fax 322 25 35; ③).

The Town

Sion's Old Town is interesting, and embarking on a slow wander through the cobbled alleys, with their old inns and sixteenth-century shuttered townhouses, can fill an atmospheric afternoon. Just northeast of Place de la Planta is the small **Église St-Théodule**, dating from the sixteenth century and with some fine vaulting in the choir. Just beside it is the atmospheric **Cathédrale Notre-Dame du Glarier** (Our Lady of the Gravel – referring to the ground on which the cathedral was built). The main building is fifteenth century, with elements of earlier Romanesque and Gothic structures incorporated within it, including a fine belfry. Its most noticeable feature, though, is the bells, which strike every quarter-hour in a near-exact copy of the sound of Big Ben in London, although the bass bell's slightly higher pitch gives the ensemble an inescapably mournful tone. A hundred metres to the south is Rue Supersaxo, with the **Maison Supersaxo** tucked into an alley off the street. This lavish residence (Mon–Fri 8am–noon & 2–6pm; free) was built in 1505 by the local governor, Georges Supersaxo, to show the town's bishop, Matthias Schinner, who was boss: climb the Gothic staircase inside to a hall on the upper floor with a magnificent carved and painted ceiling. Two minutes north on Rue de la Tour brings you to the witch's-hat **Tour des Sorciers**, part of the town's medieval fortifications and now used for housing various temporary exhibitions.

Beside the imposing **Hôtel de Ville** on Rue du Grand-Pont (visitable only on the tourist office's walking tour), lanes and back alleys cut east to Rue des Châteaux, which climbs steeply up towards the twin hills of Tourbillon and Valère looming over the town. Before you get there, though, after 150m you'll pass on the left the modest **Musée Cantonal des Beaux-Arts**, Place de la Majorie (Tues–Sun 10am–noon & 2–6pm; Fr.5; SMP), in an attractive fifteenth-century house. There are few outstanding works, although the section on Valaisian identity holds some interesting pieces. Opposite is the **Musée Cantonal d'Archéologie** (Tues–Sun 10am–noon & 2–6pm; Fr.4; SMP), with an impressive collection of mainly Roman bits and pieces gathered from digs around the canton, as well as massive steles, carved 2800–2300 BC, and a display of prehistoric dolmens.

Valère and Tourbillon

Rue des Châteaux climbs to a parking area in the groove between the twin castles of Sion. From here, paths divide up the dry, scrubby hillsides – left (north) to Tourbillon, right (south) to Valère.

Château de Valère is the more interesting of the two, and the more complete. The hike up brings you past the tiny Chapelle de Tous-les-Saints (dating from 1310 but unfortunately kept locked) and massive Roman foundation walls to the castle-church. As it stands, the château dates from the thirteenth century, but elements survive of earlier buildings, and the whole thing may well stand on the ruins of a Roman temple. A climb up rickety stairs brings you into the church interior (Tues–Sat 10am–noon & 2–6pm, Sun 2–6pm; Fr.3), where the most notable feature, high on the back wall, is the **oldest playable organ** in the world, dating from 1390. It's still in use, played every Saturday during July and August as part of the International Festival of Ancient Music.

The **Château de Tourbillon** on the opposite hill dates from 1294, but was ruined by fire in 1788 and today, aside from the external walls, little is left. These days, it's open for scramblings and yields excellent views along the valley and over the town (mid-March to mid-Nov Tues–Sun 10am–6pm; free).

Eating and drinking

There are a surprising number of good places to **eat and drink** for such a small city as Sion. The basics are taken care of at the various **self-service** places including a *Manora* within the Placette department store on Avenue du Midi, and a huge *Migros* supermarket and diner west of the station on Avenue de France.

Rue du Grand-Pont in the Old Town is lined with attractive, pleasant little corners to sample something nice. *Grotto de la Fontaine*, at no. 21 (closed Tues & Wed), is a Ticinese-style inn serving fresh pastas, pizzas and Ticinese stews and risottos (*menus* Fr.15); *La Croix Fédérale*, at no. 13 (☎027/322 16 95; closed Mon), specializes in mouthwatering fish dishes; while the *Brasserie du Grand-Pont*, at no. 6 (☎027/322 20 96; closed Sun), is a solid, down-to-earth place to have a good square meal and a carafe of local wine. Tucked away through a back door at 10 Rue du Grand-Pont and up some stairs is *Le Grand Ballif* (☎027/322 65 70; daily 6–11pm), a white-tablecloth place serving delectable Greek specialities (*menus* Fr.25).

To the east, and well out of the hubbub on steep, cobbled Rue des Châteaux, there are two excellent places very close to each other: *L'Enclos de Valère*, at no. 18 (☎027/323 32 30; Oct–April closed Sun & Mon), has a big shaded terrace on which to enjoy its classic gourmet cuisine (*menus* Fr.25), while just about next door is the *Cave de Tous Vents* (☎027/322 46 84; May & June closed Mon & Tues), an atmospheric vaulted cellar in a thirteenth-century building that opens in the evenings only for quality raclettes, fondues (including an alcoholic Fondue Bacchus) and sampling of local wines; *menus* are Fr.25. The best restaurant in Sion is the *Supersaxo*, Passage Supersaxo (☎027/323 85 50; closed Tues), serving refined nouvelle cuisine at a premium.

Listings

Bike rental In the station (Mon–Sat 6am–8pm, Sun 6.50am–8pm).

Car rental Avis, 23 Avenue de Tourbillon (☎027/322 20 77); Budget, Elf station, Route du Val d'Hérens (☎027/203 58 66); Europcar, 148 Rue de Lausanne (☎027/323 86 86); Hertz, Garage du Nord, Avenue Ritz (☎027/322 37 42).

Changing money In the station (Mon–Sat 6am–8.45pm, Sun 6.50am–8.45pm).

Email and Internet Quanta Virtual Fun, above the station, offers access (Fr.10/hr).

Medical facilities Hôpital de Champsec, 80 Avenue Grand-Champsec (☎027/324 41 11), has a 24-hour emergency room.

Post office Opposite the station (CH-1950 Sion 1).

Around Sion

The hills south of Sion are pierced by two long valleys, which are worth a detour if you fancy getting out into the hinterlands of the Valais. To the southwest a minor road winds into the **Val d'Hérémence**, culminating in the giant **Barrage de la Grande Dixence**, the largest and one of the highest-altitude dams in the world.

Of more interest, though, is the valley branching southeast from Sion. This is the **Val d'Hérens**, a world apart even from the main valley, dotted with mountain farms and high-altitude hamlets, and giving fascinating glimpses of traditional rural life. Even people from Sion can barely understand the thick valley patois, which rings with odd guttural sounds and strikes city folk as being a little like Arabic. Unsubstantiated supposition brings out the idea that the generally dark-skinned, dark-eyed people of the Val d'Hérens may somehow be descended from the conquering Saracen armies who invaded the valley in the eighth century. Having planted that idea, Sédunois will then tell you about the people of Isérables, a town west of Sion, who have had the nickname of *Les Bedjuis* for as long as anyone can remember – and "bedjuis" is remarkably close to "bedouin", Arabic for "people of the desert". The Allalinhorn peak near Saas-Fee is another clue, apparently stemming somehow from the Arabic word for God (Allah).

One of the sights of the valley can be found near the village of Euseigne, where the road passes beneath the **Pyramides d'Euseigne**, an extremely bizarre geological outcrop of glacial moraines. Whereas erosion flattened the area all around, these stone jags were protected from smoothing by hard rock caps. Today, they're hard to believe – a wall of unnaturally pointed stalagmites in the open wooded valley, each crag crowned by a dark boulder balanced on a needle point. A stall at the base lets you stop to gawp, and then buy a souvenir postcard.

Some 15km south of Euseigne is the village of **EVOLÈNE**, the scene of one of the worst avalanches in Switzerland in living memory, which killed ten people in February

1999. The quaint little village is now bypassed by the main road, and has preserved along its main street traditional wooden houses and an air of rural tranquillity. The locals have cheerfully capitalized on this by wearing traditional dress – plausibly enough, only partly in a self-conscious bid for tourist appeal. A handful of cafés and simple inns cater to hikers and day-trippers.

Arolla

South of the tiny hamlet of **Les Haudères** beyond Evolène, you begin to penetrate the wild countryside. One road branches east over the crest to Ferpècle, while another climbs west up and over into the tranquil hidden **Val d'Arolla**, terminating some 12km south after a series of nerve-racking tunnels at the hamlet of **AROLLA** (1998m). This tiny, outdoorsy place is one of the stops on the walkers' Haute Route between Chamonix and Zermatt (see p.317), and offers a wealth of half- and full-day hikes all around, including a testing one up to the Col de Riedmatten (2919m), three hours away. There's a handful of blue and red ski-pistes served by lifts rising from the village; passes are Fr.27/day, Fr.145/week. Four or five **hotels** offer quality retreats, including the *Grand Hôtel Kurhaus* (☎027/283 11 61, fax 283 11 63; ②; July, Aug & Dec–April only), a huge old place with renovated light-pine rooms, some ensuite. Half-a-dozen places offers dorms, and the **tourist office** (☎027/283 10 83, *www.arolla.com*) has information on these and chalets for rent. Hotels tend to cut their rates to half-price in January, meaning Fr.300 can buy you a week of Arolla comfort amidst the deep snow.

Sierre and around

Hardly any foreigners come to **SIERRE** (Siders in German) unless they're catching the funicular up to the ski resorts of Crans and Montana on the hillside above. Which is all to the good, because it leaves this idyllic little valley-floor town quiet, perfect for a day or two of strolling and winetasting in the vineyards all around. Sierre lies almost exactly on the French–German language border, which is marked by the tiny Raspille stream a couple of kilometres east of the town. The road east from Sierre to the sleepy village of **Salgesch** (Salquenen in French) begins as the Rue de la Gemmi and ends five minutes later as the Gemmistrasse; Sierre sits alongside the Rhône, while in Salgesch the same river is dubbed the Rotten.

Wine is what fuels both communities, and there are plenty of trails through and between the vineyards, with equally numerous opportunities to stop and sample a glass or two. Sierre is the driest town in Switzerland, and gets an average of almost seven and a half hours of sunshine daily from May to October (and a total of 330 sunny days a year), helping it to produce excellent Fendant whites; Salgesch, meanwhile, is renowned for its excellent Pinot Noir reds. Not for nothing did the Romans call the place *Sirrum amoenum*, Sierre the agreeable.

The Town

There's not an awful lot to see or do in Sierre, although if you turn left (west) from the train station and then aim northwest up Avenue du Marché, you'll come into the little-visited old quarters of town. The Rue de Villa, alongside a vineyard, marks the eponymous quarter of Villa, with, at the very top, the **Château de Villa**, one half of Sierre-Salgesch's modest **Musée de la Vigne et du Vin** (March–Oct Tues–Sun 2–5pm; Nov–Feb Fri–Sun 2–5pm; Fr.5 for both museums; SMP). The Sierre half focuses on the wine itself, with interesting displays (in French and German) on grape varieties and the history of cultivation and some old presses. From here, a *Sentier Viticole/Rebweg* (Wine

The people and history of Sierre are inextricably linked with the culture of the communities in the **Val d'Anniviers**, which opens at a narrow chink in the mountain high up opposite Sierre to the south but broadens out to extend southwards for some 40km, terminating in the hiking trailhead of **Zinal**.

The residents of the Anniviers (the name itself means "seasonal") are the last people left in Switzerland to follow a genuinely **nomadic** lifestyle, although modern ease of transport and economic pressures are making inroads. Up until a few decades ago, people would arrive in Sierre from the Anniviers in March or April: those from the village of **Grimentz** occupied the Villa quarter of Sierre, alongside people from **Vissoie**, while the Viouc quarter was for villagers from **Chandolin**, the Muraz quarter for those from **St Luc**, and so on. Each community had its own slightly distinct dialect, brought with it flocks, a schoolteacher and a priest, and celebrated Sunday mass in its own tiny chapel. For a few months, everyone would stay and work on the vineyards around Sierre, before departing in mid-June to pasture their flocks on the heights above the town. In mid-September, everybody would drift down again to Sierre for the grape harvest, which would continue for a few weeks, before dispersing back to their villages in the Anniviers valley for the winter. This kind of nomadism still carries on today, although these days families don't have to bring bag and baggage with them from their village when they come to work in Sierre, and tend also to keep their children in school in one place or the other.

Curiously, the patois of the Val d'Anniviers is very similar to that of the rural Val d'Aosta on the southern side of the Grand-St-Bernard Pass in Italy, even though the main language of Sierre is French and the main language of Aosta is Italian. Linguists, anthropologists and sociologists between them haven't yet come up with a theory as to why this should be.

Path) runs through the quiet shuttered lanes of old quarters of Sierre, such as Muraz and Veyras, for a couple of hours over to Salgesch and out through the open vineyards perched on hillside slopes above the town and the valley floor to the other half of the wine museum, in the creaky old **Zumofenhaus** in the heart of the village. Displays are yet more scholarly here, on the technical aspects of viticulture, cultivation methods and history, but the enthusiastic guardian will be happy to give you a rundown in English on what's what. Buses (every 2hr) can run you back to Sierre.

An interesting detour from the Wine Path is to the small **Musée Charles-Clos Olsommer**, signposted in Veyras (July–Sept Wed–Sun 3–7pm; Oct–June Sat & Sun 2–6pm; Fr.3). Olsommer, born in Neuchâtel in 1883, studied in Munich at the same time as Klee and Kandinsky, but unlike them became fixated with a Klimt-like style rooted in symbolism and mysticism. He lived in Veyras from 1912 until his death in 1966, painting moody scenes of women praying in the wilderness or surrounded by psychedelic patterns.

A fifteen-minute walk east of Sierre lie half-a-dozen low rounded hills, the result of alluvial deposits and an ancient landslide. The whole undulating area is one of the last remaining examples of undeveloped valley-floor ecology in the country. It's carpeted by a vast, pristine pine forest, dubbed **Forêt de Finges/Pfynwald**, and is fringed by swamps and marshland on the Rhône banks. Protected and maintained but not developed, it's perfect for long, shady hikes and peaceful picnics.

Practicalities

Sierre's **station** houses the **tourist office** (July, Aug & Dec–April daily 8am–7pm; rest of year Mon–Fri 8am–noon & 2–6pm, Sat 8am–noon; ☎027/455 85 35, *www.sierre-*

salgesch.ch). With Crans Montana close by, they have plenty of information about the skiing and hiking possibilities round and about, as well as on the Val d'Anniviers. Ask about their hotel deals, which offer three nights for the price of two in the low season. Opposite is the **post office** (CH-3960), while the station for **Montana** – base of the longest funicular in Switzerland (4.2km) – is two minutes' walk away, left onto the main Avenue Général-Guisan outside the station. Rhône Rafting (☎027/455 87 55) operate pleasant, easygoing **river rafting** on a 24km stretch to the west between Chippis and Riddes (May–Oct; Fr.80–100), as well as a tougher white-water 10km stretch upstream between Susten and Chippis (June–Aug; Fr.80).

There's **camping** in the Forêt de Finges (☎027/455 02 84; April–Oct). Of the **hotels**, basic *De La Poste*, east of the station (☎027/455 10 03, fax 455 86 35; ①), has a choice of en-suite and shared-bath rooms, while the unrenovated *Terminus* opposite the station (☎027/455 11 40, fax 455 23 14; ②–③) is comfortable (ask for the quieter back rooms) and has a good **restaurant** and bistro attached. If you head behind the station and down to the small Lac de Géronde, on the way you'll pass a handful of basic *auberges*, including the *Promenade* (☎027/456 34 04, fax 456 57 34; ①), with spartan shared-bath rooms. On the lake itself is the pleasant *La Grotte* (☎027/455 46 46, fax 455 14 37), a terrace restaurant known only to the locals, serving spectacularly good fish (*menus* Fr.25), with a handful of comfortable, characterful rooms upstairs (①–②).

St-Léonard

Almost midway between Sion and Sierre is the small village of **St-Léonard** with, as its sole draw, one of the largest **underground lakes** in Europe (March–Oct daily 9am–5pm; Fr.6). Regular buses between Sion and Sierre drop off either in the village or at the car park beneath the ticket office, which can get crowded with day-tripping families. Tours of the lake, by large rowing boats with everyone crowded in side by side, take about forty minutes – and it's cold down there, so bring a jumper. The cave entrance is just a gap in the mountainside, but as you launch off onto the inky water, the illuminated, other-worldly cavern stretching out ahead of you is very impressive. The guides, who do the rowing, have a nice line in multilingual patter, and regale you on the voyage with all kinds of stories and details about the lake and its geology.

Crans Montana

CRANS MONTANA is another of Switzerland's big, world-famous ski resorts, occupying what is claimed to be the sunniest plateau in the Alps, facing south over the Rhône valley with a spectacular panorama of peaks yawning beyond. Along with Verbier and St Moritz, it's also one of the glitziest, with what the tourist office like to call the finest shopping in the Alps.

The resort actually comprises three villages, Crans-sur-Sierre (pronounced *crawh*), Montana and, out on a limb, Aminona; the agglomeration sprawls for more than 2km between Crans, to the west, and Montana, to the east, with nothing to mark the shift from one to another. There's no restriction on cars at all and traffic is permanently heavy; in high season village-to-village gridlock is not unknown. The **skiing**, "irretrievably intermediate" according to those in the know, takes second place to the round of wining and dining embarked upon by fashionable aficionados of Crans Montana's affluent social life – although the resort does have the advantage of access to **year-round skiing** on the Plaine Morte glacier, way up above 3000m. Skiing aside, the place is best known for hosting the **European Masters golf** tournament every September, second only to the British Open for prestige and top names. Crans's scenic course – "by far the most spectacular tournament site in the world" according to Greg Norman – was redesigned in 1999 by Seve Ballesteros, and now boasts fiendishly complex upturned-saucer greens, which led one frustrated player to describe playing a round as "having eighteen teeth pulled one by one".

Arrival, information and accommodation

The **funicular** from Sierre arrives at **Vermala station** at the eastern end of Montana. **Buses** also run from Sierre on two different routes. The first (via Chermignon) passes through Crans, then Montana, then on to Aminona; the second (via Mollens) passes through Montana before terminating in Crans. There's also a bus running between Sion and Crans. All SMC buses shuttling to and fro on circular routes within the resort boundaries are free.

Montana's **tourist office** is 100m west (left) of the funicular station (mid-June to August & Dec–Easter Mon–Sat 8.30am–noon & 2–6.30pm, Sun 10am–noon & 4–6pm; rest of year Mon–Fri 8.30am–noon & 2–6pm, Sat 8.30am–noon; ☎027/485 04 04, *www.crans-montana.ch*). The village centre is another 200m west, focused around the Ycoor ice-skating rink. Just beyond is the small **Lac Grenon**. Running along the northern shore is the Route de Rawyl, always busy with cars. Some 800m west is Rue Centrale in Crans, home to the Crans **tourist office** (same times; ☎027/485 08 00) more or less opposite the **Étang Long** lakelet, which itself backs onto the championship golf course.

Information and **tickets** for the European Masters golf tournament (Fr.30–60 per day, Fr.90 for the weekend, or Fr.140 for five days), held in the first week in September, can be had from the Golf-Club Crans, CP 112, CH-3963 Crans-sur-Sierre (☎027/485 97 97).

Accommodation

Both tourist offices have **hotel boards** outside with free phones, and there's also a central **reservations** number for the resort (☎027/485 04 44; no commission). The *Lac Moubra* **campsite** in Montana (☎027/481 28 51, fax 481 05 51; closed mid-Oct to Dec) also has basic **dorms** (Fr.21). Otherwise, a host of basic **hotels** offer inexpensive rooms, normally with a choice of en-suite or not: *Pension Centrale* in Crans (☎ & fax 027/481 37 67; ②) and *Olympic* in Montana (☎027/481 29 85, fax 481 29 53; ②) are two examples, both in the centre of their villages, and both tidy and well-kept. The *Cisalpin* (☎027/481 24 25, fax 481 70 83; ②) is right beside the Violettes gondola, a pack-em-in kind of place, but perfectly OK, while the *Regina* in the centre of Montana (☎027/481 35 22, fax 480 18 68; ②) is another good option. *Robinson* (☎027/481 13 53, fax 481 13 14; ②) is beside the two Crans gondolas, an uncomplicated "garni" place.

The skiing

The major plus in recent years – for British skiers at least – is the introduction of a direct **flight** from London Heathrow to Sion every Saturday morning in the winter season. With rapid transfer from Sion direct to Crans, you can be on the slopes by lunchtime. **Passes** with/without access to the Plaine Morte glacier cost Fr.56/47 for a day, or Fr.161/129 for three days.

Access to the pistes, almost all of which are relatively straightforward blues and reds – if extremely scenic – is via five gondolas ranged along the base of the mountain. From west to east, these are **Chetseron** and **Crans** (both within Crans village), **Grand Signal** in Montana, **Violettes** near the Montana funicular station, and **Aminona**. The woods above Montana are crisscrossed by red runs winding between the trees, while **Cry d'Err** above Crans has a host of lifts serving blues galore down to the village. Violettes gives access to the **Plaine Morte** top station (3000m), with some exciting blues, and the start of a long meandering red back to the village.

Eating and drinking

Eating wins no prizes for invention or quality. Body and soul are kept together by simple diners such as *Crêperie Ma Bretagne* opposite Parking Victoria in Montana, *Café du Centre* beside the church, or *Le Bistrot* opposite Montana tourism. The *Auberge de la Diligence* (☎027/485 99 85), 500m east of Montana's Vermala station, is Lebanese-run, and serves up quality Middle Eastern food (*menus* Fr.20); it also has affordable rooms (②). Next door, the *Hôtel de la Forêt* (☎027/480 21 31) caters specifically for vegetarians.

Café-Bar 1900 is the place to hang out in the centre of Crans, just round the corner from the Rue du Prado with all the big glitzy designer names – Vuitton, Gucci, Hermès and all. *Pizzeria Le Prado* is a welcome burst of reality amidst the street's boutiques, serving inexpensive thin-crust pizza and some pasta dishes.

OBERWALLIS

East of Sierre stretches the German-speaking portion of Valais – or Wallis, as it officially becomes. To mark it out from the Lower Valais to the west, this is known as Upper Valais, or **Oberwallis**. The main town of the region, **Brig**, is an important road and rail junction, but is otherwise of limited interest. The reason that everybody passes through the area is to make a pilgrimage to the little mountain village of **Zermatt**, in order to lay eyes upon the **Matterhorn**, the most famous (if not actually the highest) of all Switzerland's mountains. In a side valley nearby sits the equally alluring resort of **Saas-Fee**, while east of Brig, the remote **Goms** region follows the Rhône to its glacial source.

Brig and around

By virtue of its location, you may find yourself spending a night in the graceful old town of **BRIG** (Brigue in French; Briga in Italian). It's the fulcrum for a dizzying series of major road and rail routes: southeast through the Simplon train tunnel into Italy; southwest to Zermatt at the foot of the Matterhorn; west to Lake Geneva; north through the Lötschbergtunnel towards Bern; and northeast to the high Alpine passes.

The huge train station stands at the northern edge of the town, connected to Brig's broad cobbled central square – the focus of the Old Town and called in its various sectors **Stadtplatz**, **Marktplatz** and **Sebastiansplatz** – by the main shopping street of Bahnhofstrasse. Overlooking the square is the tiny **Sebastianskapelle**, built by local bigwig Stockalper (see below) in 1637, with a network of picturesque alleys winding behind and around it.

Lanes off the southeast corner of the square lead along Alte Simplonstrasse past many fine patrician townhouses dating from the seventeenth and eighteenth centuries to the **Schloss Stockalper**. This grandiose Italianate palace – for much of its life the largest private residence in Switzerland – dominates the otherwise simple town. It was completed in 1678 to serve as the home of **Kaspar Jodok von Stockalper**, a merchant from Brig who first made a mint controlling the trade in silk over the Simplon Pass to Lyon, moved on to make another killing organizing mail transport between Milan and Geneva, and finally gained the monopoly in trading salt over the pass. At the height of his power, he was elected President of the Grand Council of Valais, the highest political office in the region. By 1658 he was wealthy enough to start building his own palace in Brig, the town through which all his goods passed, and which he himself had largely had built from scratch. After twenty years or more, it seems Stockalper finally got too big for his boots: his political colleagues plotted together to have him removed from office, and he was sent into exile into Domodossola, forfeiting part of his fortune on the way. Only six years later was he permitted to return to Brig, where he died a few years later at the grand old age of 82.

You can stroll from the street into the triple-arcaded **interior courtyard**, especially beautiful when it catches the sun. Rearing up overhead are three giant corner towers topped by the **onion domes** that are visible from much of the town. **Entry** to the few rooms open to the public is by guided tour only (May–Oct Tues–Sun 10am, 11am, 2, 3 & 4pm; June–Sept also 5pm; Fr.5) – unless you're confident in reading the German notes, though, or you have an English-speaking guide, you'd best save your money.

Brig practicalities

Brig's **tourist office** is in the train station up a spiral staircase (Mon–Fri 8.30am–noon & 1.30–6pm, Sat 8.30am–noon; July & Aug Sat also 2–5.30pm; ☎027/921 60 30, *www.brig-tourismus.ch*). They have information on the town, as well as on all the resorts around Brig, and also on the Goms region further east. Downstairs in the travel office, you can check **email** (Fr.11/hr).

As well as SBB trains, the forecourt of Brig station is a departure point for **BVZ** trains to Zermatt, and **FO Furka–Oberalp** trains northeast up the valley to Oberwald, through the tunnel beneath the Furka Pass, and on to Andermatt (see p.364). "Glacier Express" panoramic trains (see p.38) use this line to reach Chur, Davos and St Moritz. For details of the Lötschbergtunnel car-carrying train, which ducks beneath the mountains at nearby Goppenstein, see p.280.

Hotels in Brig are all moderately priced. The cheapest option is *La Poste*, Furkastrasse 23 (☎027/924 45 54, fax 924 45 53; ①), which has a few renovated rooms as well as some dorm places (Fr.30). The *Londres & Schweizerhof* on the central square (☎027/922 93 93, fax 922 93 94; ②) is a comfortable old place, with pleasant rooms overlooking the square. The quiet and graceful *Schlosshotel*, Kirchgasse 4 (☎027/923 64 55, fax 923 95 36; ②) directly overlooks the gardens and towers of the Schloss Stockalper, with bright and attractive rooms.

All the **cafés and restaurants** around the main square set tables outside during summer: pick of the bunch is *Zum Eidgenossen*, which offers fondues and meaty Walliser fare in a traditional atmosphere for around Fr.20. Nearby on Alte Simplonstrasse are two pleasant local bistros, *Matza* and *Angleterre*, both serving up pizzas and simple meals for Fr.13–18. Down by the station, as well as a self-service *Migros*, you'll find the *Hotel Victoria*, which offers good brasserie-style food, with some veggie options (Fr.15–20).

The Simplon Pass and Tunnel

The road over the **Simplon Pass** (2005m), southwest of Brig, was built by Napoleon as a military through route between 1800 and 1808, immediately after he'd successfully crossed the Grand-St-Bernard with an army (see p.303). These days the old pass road is a modern, Swiss-engineered highway, and the pass itself isn't really worth a specific journey, with views nowhere near as impressive as those from the other great Alpine passes. What *is* worthwhile, though, is to explore the cobbled alleys and picturesque old houses of Simplon-Dorf (village) on the other side – still in Switzerland – as well as, hard up against the Italian border, the impressive Gondo gorge. A long, energetic two- or three-day hike covers the 35km Stockalper Road, from Brig via the pass itself to the border hamlet of Gondo – this is the mule track completed by Stockalper (see above) for transport of goods between Italy and the Valais, and has inns aplenty dotted along its route, which is away from the highway for most of its route.

While you're standing on the pass heights, give a thought for those careering at speed on trains through the **Simplon Tunnel**, some 2400m beneath the Wasenhorn peak just to the east. This is the longest rail tunnel in the world, entered almost immediately after leaving Brig station and emerging 19.8km later in Italy for the short run to Domodossola (from where Swiss trains connect on the Centovalli line to Locarno; see p.500), and on south to Milan. The completion of the tunnel in 1905 opened up an entirely new train route from London and Paris to Istanbul – the so-called Venice–Simplon Orient Express – which in turn led to a whole new era in pan-European travel.

Zermatt

St Moritz may have the glamour, Verbier may have the cool, Wengen may have the pistes, but **ZERMATT** beats them all – Zermatt has the **Matterhorn**. No other natural or human structure in the whole country is so immediately recognizable; indeed, in most people's minds the Matterhorn stands for Switzerland, like the Eiffel Tower stands for France. Part of the reason it's so famous is that it stands alone, its impossibly pointy shape sticking up from an otherwise uncrowded horizon above Zermatt village. But you get the feeling that it would be famous even if it stood within a chain of peaks: there's just something about it that's bizarrely mesmerizing to see for real, and it may well be the most memorable part of your whole holiday.

Emerging from Zermatt station is an experience in itself: this one little village – which has managed, much to its credit, to cling on to its old brown chalets and atmospheric twisting alleys – welcomes everybody, regardless of financial status, and the station square is where all worlds collide. Backpackers and hikers rub shoulders with high society glitterati amidst a fluster of tour groups, electric taxis and horse-drawn carriages, but everyone has come to see the mountain. Zermatt has no off-season – it's crowded year-round – but the crowds never seem to matter. You may have to shoulder your way down the main street, but the terrain all around is expansive enough that with a little effort you could vanish into the wilderness, leaving everyone else behind.

The small area around Zermatt features 36 mountains over 4000m, a statistic as enticing to summer hikers as to winter skiers. As early as the 1820s, British climbers adopted the isolated hamlet as a base camp from which to scale the nearby peaks. The first hotel opened in 1838. All through the nineteenth century, word of the place spread, and the local community quickly saw the potential: grand hotels went up and public funds were diverted into construction of the Gornergrat rack railway at the turn of the century. The skiing boom of the 1960s saw the hamlet double in size, but today it's still acceptably small and low-key, rooted to the valley floor in a natural bowl open to the south. The Gornergrat railway lifts you up to a spectacular vantage point overlooking the **Monte Rosa** massif, with its summit the **Dufourspitze** (4634m) – the highest point in Switzerland. The skiing is good, but in many ways the hiking is better, with some of the most scenic mountain walks in the whole country within easy reach of the village.

Arrival, orientation and information

The **BVZ** company operates the trains from Brig and Visp to Zermatt. Although Brig is the starting point, mainline trains from the west (from Lake Geneva, Sion or Bern) are quite often timed to make the connection at Visp instead, which is also on the main Sion–Brig line; check the timetable carefully. At both Brig and Visp stations, BVZ trains run on tracks laid in the street outside the front of the station, not from the usual platforms. South of Visp, trains climb to **Stalden** (departure point for buses to Saas-Fee) and then enter the picturesque Matter valley, clinging precariously above the ravine as they rise higher and higher past a series of villages – as dramatic a prelude to the

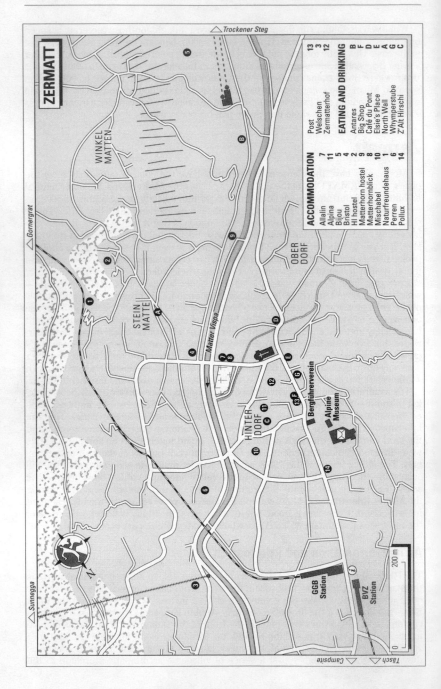

ZERMATT

△ Trockener Steg

WINKEL MATTEN

OBER DORF

STEIN MATTE

△ Gornergrat

Mattel Vispa

HINTER DORF

Bergführerverein

Alpine Museum

△ Sunnegga

N

GGB Station

BVZ Station

200 m

0

Campsite ▽   ▽ Täsch

ACCOMMODATION

Alalin	7
Alpina	11
Bijou	5
Bristol	4
HI hostel	2
Matterhorn hostel	9
Matterhornblick	8
Mischabel	10
Naturfreundehaus	1
Perren	6
Pollux	14

Post	13
Welschen	3
Zermatterhof	12

EATING AND DRINKING

Antares	B
Big Shop	F
Café du Pont	D
Elsie's Place	E
North Wall	A
Whymperstube	G
Z'Alt Hirschi	C

LOSING YOUR WHEELS

Zermatt is **car-free**, but it doesn't necessarily pay to drive all the way up the valley. Certain sections of the large parking garages at and near **Visp** station offer **free indefinite parking** if you ask for a permit at the train station ticket office when you buy your train ticket to Zermatt. However, free parking only applies if you've parked in the right place – look for the clearly-marked "BVZ park and ride" car parks to the east (covered) and west (open) of the station, and only use those areas marked with the **BVZ logo** (*not* the SBB one). Check with the train station staff that you're in the right place before you head off or you'll be charged when you return.

If you do choose to drive up the valley, all the villages along the way are well aware of tourists' desire to get something for nothing, and all of them either charge for parking, or happily ticket offenders for parking illegally. In **Täsch**, the end of the road, there are nine massive parking areas, none of them exorbitant, but all still charging more than the nothing you can get away with at Visp.

Matterhorn scenery as you could hope for. A minor **road** also runs along the valley: it's possible to drive as far as the village of **Täsch**, where vast car parks (see box) take care of all motorized transport, with everybody bundling onto trains, and extra Pendelzüge shuttles, for the final twelve-minute pull into Zermatt. BVZ trains are free to Swiss Pass holders, half-price to InterRailers, and full price to Eurailers.

Zermatt's **BVZ train station** is a large bustling place, with the usual left-luggage facilities, located at the northern end of the village's main street – Zermatt has no street-names. The square outside is generally full of little **electric taxis**, all of which run to a set tariff – Fr.12 for up to four people (or Fr.18 including luggage) to anywhere within the village, more to farther-flung places beyond the village, and an additional fifty percent for journeys between 10pm and 6am. The **GGB Gornergrat-Bahn** station is directly opposite the main station, while the underground funicular to **Sunnegga** leaves from the opposite bank (head east from the station beside the Gornergrat tracks and over the river, then cut left for 100m). Zermatt's narrow **main street**, although picturesque, is packed all the way down with shops, hotels, restaurants and – for much of the year – people. To the east, alleys run down into **Hinterdorf**, an attractive old quarter by the river with plenty of accommodation possibilities. Some 400m south of the station is the **church**, another main landmark, from where a street dog-legs east over the river past the famous **cemetery** to the district of **Steinmatte** on the opposite bank. The cable-car station up to **Trockener Steg** and Klein Matterhorn is 500m south of the church.

Information

Zermatt's super-friendly, helpful **tourist office** is right beside the station (mid-June to mid-Oct & mid-Dec to mid-April Mon–Fri 8.30am–6pm, Sat 8.30am–7pm, Sun 9.30am–noon & 4–7pm; rest of year Mon–Fri 8.30am–noon & 1.30–6pm, Sat 8.30am–noon; ☎027/967 01 81, *www.zermatt.ch*), and has everything you could possibly want to know about Zermatt, the Matterhorn, and hiking and skiing possibilities all around. A channel of cable TV within the village shows live pictures from three local summits – the Rothorn, Gornergrat and Trockener Steg – handy for viewing weather conditions. The travel agency Zermatt Tours (☎027/966 47 61) next to the tourist office can book any kind of excursion in the area. An individual who markets himself as "Jacques, your guide" (☎079/285 66 38, *www.rhone.ch/zermatt-mule-trekking*) runs short and long **mule treks** into the wilds; half-day excursions are Fr.35/hr per person and day-long rides, including a hearty picnic, are Fr.160 per person.

The **Bergführerverein** (Mountain Guides' Association; July–Sept & Dec–March Mon–Fri 8.30am–noon & 4–7pm, Sat 4–7pm, Sun 10am–noon & 4–7pm; ☎027/966 24

60), on the main street in the same building as the ski school, can offer advice on **climbing** some of the peaks nearby. The Matterhorn itself is out, unless you have plenty of experience, all the professional apparatus, a week for training, and about Fr.900 in fees. However, they do run daily guided excursions suitable for beginners, including a four-hour trek from Klein Matterhorn across glaciers to Trockener Steg (Fr.120), an ascent to a 4000m peak such as Weissmies or Allalin (Fr.200), or a basic climbing course on the Riffelhorn (Fr.180), as well as some quality canyoning (Fr.95).

Accommodation

Accommodation in Zermatt is almost always excellent. The village is so used to tourists – in fact, there *is* no village without the tourists – that service has been fine-tuned and facilities across all price brackets are good. There are literally dozens and dozens of hotels (the tourist office lists 63 just within the village), so you shouldn't have any problem finding somewhere to suit; high season is an exception, when you shouldn't arrive without a reservation. It must be said, too, that **Matterhorn views** from your balcony or window are truly worth paying for: the mountain is so magnificent that you won't get bored of opening your eyes to it each morning.

The favoured method of accommodation in the village, though, is renting an **apartment** or **chalet** – but you should do this well in advance (some places are booked a year ahead), and note that you almost certainly won't be able to get a chalet for less than a Saturday-to-Saturday week. Only a handful of owners are willing to rent for less, and then only in the low season for a minimum three days.

Camping and hostels

The *Matterhorn* **campsite** is just north of the train station (☎ & fax 027/967 39 21; June–Sept). The large HI **hostel**, way out in Winkelmatten beyond Steinmatte (☎027/967 23 20, fax 967 53 06; ①; mid-June to Oct & mid-Dec to May) has dorm beds, many with enticing Matterhorn views, for Fr.42 half board (breakfast plus a packed lunch or dinner), as well as bike rental. In the same quarter but on the riverbank, the Swiss Backpackers *Matterhorn* hostel (☎027/968 19 19, fax 968 19 15) has dorms from Fr.37 (breakfast only).

Inexpensive hotels

Alpina (☎027/967 10 50, fax 967 28 65). Down in the Hinterdorf, with amiable staff and a calm atmosphere. ③.

Mischabel (☎027/967 11 31, fax 967 65 07). Another quality choice in quiet Hinterdorf, an old creaky-floored building with fresh, sunny rooms (none en suite) and Matterhorn views. ②.

Naturfreundehaus (☎027/967 27 88, fax 967 60 29). Well-kept, cosy rooms (none en suite) far away from the bustle in Steinmatte, some with the views. ②.

Post (☎027/967 19 32, fax 967 41 14). Funky main-drag institution, with a popular bar, disco and youthful restaurant topped by a handful of comfortable, individually styled rooms. ③–④.

Welschen (☎027/967 54 22, fax 967 54 23). A real find, up on a hill beside the Sunnegga station, small, pleasant, spotless and atmospheric. ③.

Mid-range and expensive hotels

Allalin (☎027/966 82 66, fax 966 82 65). Down-the-line central "garni" hotel beside the church, with new decor and plenty of comforts, including balconies on all rooms (including ones facing south to the Matterhorn). ④.

Bijou (☎027/966 51 51, fax 966 51 55). Far away from the centre on a slope just next to the Matterhorn cable-car, a small family-run place with some nice, cosy touches in the rooms. ③–④.

Bristol (☎027/966 33 66, fax 966 33 65). Excellent mid-range choice, with efficient, friendly service and cosy rooms – those facing south with picture-postcard views (go for the upper floors). ④–⑤.

Matterhornblick (☎027/967 20 17, fax 967 50 93). Another modern place beside the church, drenched in light pine but living up to its name, with mountain views out back. ④.

Perren (☎027/967 01 45, fax 967 55 62). A graceful, modern hotel on the riverbank, with an appealing stylishness to its well-appointed rooms. A bargain. ③–④.

Pollux (☎027/966 40 00, fax 966 40 01). Modern glitzy place bang on the main drag, with plenty of style and comfortable rooms, some facing off the street. ④–⑤.

Zermatterhof (☎027/966 66 00, fax 966 66 99). The grandest hotel in the canton, and one of the finest in the country, built well over a century ago but glitteringly up to date inside, this manages to be effortlessly luxurious without a hint of tasteless resort swagger. ⑧–⑨.

In and around Zermatt

Uniquely for a mountain resort, a wander in Zermatt village is actually worth making time for. East of the main street is the **Hinterdorf** quarter, full of old weathered-wood chalets and traditional *mazots* (barns raised on stone discs to protect against mice). The town's burgeoning cemetery is down by the river, filled with memorials to attempts on the Matterhorn and other peaks gone wrong. The **Alpine Museum** beside the post office (May–Oct daily 10am–noon & 4–6pm; Nov–April Sun–Fri daily 4.30–6.30pm; Fr.5) is worth a visit, with an interesting collection of mountaineering bits and bobs, as well as a room devoted to Edward Whymper, the English climber, who led the first ascent of the Matterhorn on July 14, 1865, only for the rope to snap on the descent – four of his party of seven went over a precipice.

Above the village

Skiing aside, the reason for visiting Zermatt is to get out onto the slopes above the village to explore some of the country's most scenic hiking trails. The ever-popular **Gornergrat railway** (25 percent discount for Swiss Pass holders) leads up from the village across the meadows of the Riffelalp up to the Gornergrat itself (3130m) – get a seat on the right-hand side for magical Matterhorn vistas. The Gornergrat is the first point on a ridge that runs out to the Hohtälligrat (3286m) and, amidst a sea of ice, the Stockhorn (3407m), all linked by cable-car from Gornergrat. The view from any of these peaks is terrific, with the entire Monte Rosa massif laid out in front of you, the vast Gornergletscher carving along at your feet, and the Matterhorn itself in isolation away to one side, while at your back is the Rothorn (3103m), behind it the Dom (4545m), and behind the Dom the whole sweep of the Pennine Alps. As you might expect, the *Gornergrat Kulm* hotel (☎027/966 64 00, fax 966 64 04; ①) can get crowded, but it's a uniquely atmospheric place to spend the night. Hikes between the various stations on the Gornergrat railway are all immensely rewarding with, for example, three good trails leading out from the new hotel alongside the station at **Riffelalp** (☎027/966 46 46, fax 967 51 09; ②; mid-June to late Sept), easiest of which is the pleasant one-hour walk up to the **Riffelberg** hotel, on a spectacular exposed platform overlooking the valley (☎027/966 65 00, fax 966 65 05; ②; mid-June to mid-Oct), with dorm beds at Fr.75 half board. In summer, there are once-weekly dawn trains up to the Gornergrat so you can catch an awe-inspiring sunrise break on the Matterhorn.

Also from the village, an underground funicular tunnels up to **Sunnegga** (2300m), also on a plateau and linked to the **Rothorn** summit by gondola. Walks from Sunnegga are beautiful, weaving for a comfortable hour or two between the tiny lakelets of the Leisee, Moosjesee, Grindjisee and Stellisee out to **Fluhalp** (2616m). From the south end of Zermatt village, cable-cars run to Furi and on up to Trockener Steg (2939m), overlooking the gigantic Theodulgletscher, which slides over the Italian border at the foot of the Matterhorn. From Trockener Steg, another cable-car runs up to the crest of the Klein Matterhorn – at 3820m, this is the highest cable-car station in Europe, and there's an ice pavilion and other bits and bobs on top to bring the message home. From

Furi, though, the cable-car up to the little Schwarzsee gives what is commended as the most picture-perfect views of the Matterhorn, at close quarters *and* reflected in a pine-fringed lake. Again hikes abound round and about, including a long but easy walk (7hr) back down into Zermatt village.

For **skiing**, there are satisfying runs in all sectors, with a healthy dose of blues and manageable reds way up on the glacier above Trockener Steg and around Blauherd above Sunnegga, as well as plenty on the Gornergrat. Some of Zermatt's black runs are highly acclaimed, but as with all the pistes, are liable to overcrowding in the peak season. One exciting plus is that if you're happy with intermediate red runs, you can ski off the back of the Klein Matterhorn down to the Italian resort of **Cervinia** on the other side for a whole new perspective and a host of new runs (you'll need to show your passport). The **liftpass** system is complicated, with eight different bands of validity; a one-day pass for any of the ski sectors is around Fr.60, with a week's resort pass at Fr.314. A three-day pass covering lifts in Zermatt and Cervinia is Fr.206.

Eating and drinking

Considering the prices in some of Zermatt's hundred-plus **restaurants**, opting for picnic fare from the Co-op supermarket opposite the train station is a prudent move if you're on a tight budget. There are plenty of places where you can get diner-style fast food for under Fr.15: the *Hotel Post* is the best, incorporating a *Spaghetti Factory* and the *Broken* pizzeria, while also on the main street is the *Big Shop* takeaway. The popular *North Wall* bar, on the other side of the river south of the *Bristol*, has pizzas from Fr.10 and big beers for Fr.4.50. There are a few equally inexpensive cafés beyond the church – best is the peaceful and pleasant *Café du Pont* on a nice corner. *Z'Alt Hirschi*, down in Hinterdorf, is another, although it's more of a quiet place to savour a beer than anything else. *Elsie's Place*, opposite the church, is an unexpectedly cosy little nook, although a little over-glitzy in season; at least it offers light snacks to help your cocktail go down.

Moving up the scale, the *Antares*, on the other side of the river, serves quality fish dishes in its plush carved-wood dining room for around Fr.25. The *Rothornstube* in the *Hotel Perren* is another comfortable place where you can select from a range of different *menus*, from Fr.25 to Fr.60 or more. Needless to say, the atmosphere in the *Buffet Royal* at the *Zermatterhof Hotel*, or the glorious Edwardian-style *Whymperstube* in the central *Hotel Monte Rosa*, is formal and restrained, but if you can afford the three-figure sums required, a meal at either of these places is likely to be at least as memorable as your ride to the Gornergrat.

Listings

Car rental Zermatt is car-free, but two companies rent cars from (and allow drop-offs in) Täsch, the last village accessible on four wheels: Avis, Garage St Christophe, Täsch (☎027/967 35 35); Hertz, Garage Alphubel, Täsch (☎027/967 45 49).

Changing money Zermatt Tours beside the tourist office (Mon–Fri 8.30am–noon & 2–6pm; July–Sept & Dec–April also Sun 9am–noon & 3–6pm).

Email and Internet At the *Matterhorn* hostel (Fr.10/hr – book in advance); or the *Hotel de la Poste* (Fr.2 for the first 5min, then Fr.1.50 for 5min).

Emergencies Air Zermatt have helicopters based in Zermatt for mountain rescue (☎027/967 20 00).

Flights Air Zermatt (☎027/967 34 87) run scenic helicopter flights around the Matterhorn (Fr.170 per person – minimum four people – for a 20min round trip).

Laundry In the *Matterhorn* hostel (Fr.5).

Lost property Go to Haus Irène (Fremdenkontrolle), a little east of the church (Mon–Fri 8.30–11am & 2–4pm; ☎027/966 22 33).

Pharmacies Pharmacy Vital is at the station (call ☎027/967 67 77 outside business hours).
Police Beside the church (Mon–Fri 8–10am; ☎027/966 22 22).
Post office On the main street (CH-3920).

Saas-Fee

Lying in the next-door valley to Zermatt, **SAAS-FEE** is often overlooked, mostly because it doesn't have any train access. However, were it not for the Matterhorn next door, the array of peaks around Saas-Fee would be enough of a draw in themselves: the village is perched on a shelf of pasture at the base of a horseshoe of thirteen 4000m-plus peaks. Oozing out from between them is the giant Feegletscher – or Fairy Glacier – trickling its meltwater down through the village, and active enough in its various sectors to limit what would otherwise be spectacular skiing. The danger of falling down a glacial crevasse if you stray beyond piste-markings is more pronounced in Saas-Fee than in most other resorts.

Saas-Fee is one of four linked villages at the end of the Saas valley. **Buses** from Brig pass through Visp and then **Stalden** (both on the BVZ train line) before branching off into the valley, passing first through Saas Balen, then Saas Grund, the main village on the valley floor; from here, a road branches up to Saas-Fee – which is car-free – while a few kilometres on down the valley is Saas Almagell.

From the entrance to Saas-Fee, several quaint lanes lead down (southwest) into the heart of the village, full of shops and some boutiques, but still with much character and charm. In winter, several **lifts** serve a handful of good blue runs at the bottom of the glacial bowl towering all around, but the main route up the mountain is via the **Alpin Express**, the highest underground funicular system in the world, which emerges at the top of the **Mittelallalin** (3500m). From here there are some good red and blue runs on the Feegletscher, the longer ones winding all the way back down to the village; summer skiing is also possible up here. Passes cost Fr.58/day, Fr.152/three days or Fr.300 for a week. The top station also boasts a giant **ice pavilion** (Fr.7), with scholarly explications of the workings of glaciers. **Hiking** routes abound, both in summer, with long treks finding a way between the peaks into the Matter valley, and in winter, when some 30km of trails above the village remain open.

Throughout the village you may come across the name Zurbriggen on a number of shop signs; if the name sounds familar, it's because Pirmin Zurbriggen, a local boy made good, was a downhill skiing world champion in the 1980s. Today, he owns a hotel in tiny Saas Almagell up the valley, as well as another in Zermatt. Various branches of the family have kept their foothold in Saas-Fee.

Practicalities

Saas-Fee is car-free, and there is a huge – but expensive – **parking** area at the entrance to the village (Fr.13/day); you'd do better to take advantage of the cheaper deals in Visp, and catch the bus in. The **bus station** is beside the car park, as is the **post office** (CH-3906) and, just opposite, the **tourist office** (June–Sept & Dec–April Mon–Fri 8.30am–noon & 2–6.30pm, Sat 8am–7pm, Sun 9am–noon & 3–6pm; rest of year Mon–Sat 8.30am–noon & 2–6pm, Sun 10am–noon & 4–6pm; ☎027/958 18 58, *www.saas-fee.ch*).

Saas Grund has two **campsites**, but only the simple *Bergheimat*, alongside the village, stays open year-round (☎027/957 20 66). The cheapest **hotel** in Saas-Fee is the plain and simple *Happy Lodge* (☎027/957 15 55, fax 957 33 36; ①), 500m northeast of the tourist office. Following hard on its heels is the *Zur Mühle* (☎027/957 26 76, fax 957 26 77; ②), an excellent-value place in an old burnt-wood chalet, with all rooms facing south and balconied; it's 500m southwest of the tourist office, close to all the lifts and on the riverbank. Close by is the small, charming *Burgener* (☎027/957 15 22, fax 957 28 88; ③–④), beside the quiet *Ski Hütte* restaurant. The *Zurbriggen* (☎027/958 12 60, fax 958 12 65; ②–③), set in its own gardens, is another good mid-range choice, close to the tourist office, while more upmarket is the *Saaserhof* (☎027/957 35 51, fax 957 28 83; ⑤–⑦), a modern, extremely comfortable four-star place, very convenient for the lifts.

Eating and drinking is a case of keep wandering until your stomach, or your eyes, tell you to stop. Next door to each other in the centre are *Boccalino*, doing pizzas and the like for Fr.12–15, and *Pizzeria Philippe*, with quality Italian-inspired *menus* for Fr.22, along with steaks and pizzas from a wood oven. The restaurant attached to *Hotel Zur Mühle* is a reliable proposition for inexpensive Walliser cuisine – mainly fondues and raclettes. *La Ferme*, near the tourist office, is a step up in quality, with good *menus* from Fr.25 and brave attempts at rustic decor. The sky's the limit for gourmet cuisine, exemplified by two temples to the art: the *Fletschhorn* (☎027/957 21 31), out in the woods north of the village, and the restaurant within *Hotel Walliserhof* (☎027/958 19 00), in the centre.

The Goms

The upper part of the Rhône valley, stretching from Brig to the high Alpine passes, is known as **the Goms**. Winter sees thick snow covering the whole region, perfect for cross-country skiing at all levels. Traffic, at least in the warmer months, is always heavy on the valley road heading up to the Furka, Grimsel and Nufenen passes, but drivers generally prefer to plough on, zipping past the pine forests and wide-open meadows, and through picturesque little villages of traditional darkwood chalets. If you've got a car, it's worth stopping off at a couple of place on the long drive up the valley. Buses and local trains from Brig stop at all villages.

Seven or eight kilometres out of Brig you'll pass **Mörel**, with signs for cable-cars rising west to **RIEDERALP** and, a little further on, **Betten**, with cable-cars to **BETTMERALP**. Both these car-free resorts are perched on ridge-top plateaux, with lifts serving the huge and unspoilt **Aletschwald**, one of the highest pine forests in Europe, which in turn overlooks the gigantic **Aletsch Glacier**, a mammoth ice sheet – longest in the Alps – which winds its way down 23km from the base of the Jungfrau. There are hiking possibilities galore around here, and tourist offices in Riederalp (☎027/927 13 65) and Bettmeralp (☎027/927 12 91) can provide details of specific trails, as well as of the network of inns and mountain huts which can provide wilderness accommodation. **Fiesch**, the next main town along the valley, has lifts up to the vantage point of the **Eggishorn**, above the hamlet of Kuhboden, offering the finest views of the glacier.

Above Fiesch, the Rhône is little more than a fast-flowing mountain brook, and the villages become smaller and more rural. Six kilometres past Fiesch is the hamlet of **Niederwald**, which proudly announces its claim to fame with a US-style billboard – it was here, in 1850, that César Ritz, who went on to found the Ritz hotel chain, was born. Some 3km further on is the little community of **MÜNSTER**. Away from the main road, the tranquil village is characterized by the traditional Valaisian-style chalets, all clustered together higgledy-piggledy, burnt a rich dark brown and decorated with pretty geranium windowboxes. At their centre is a striking white church with a wood-panelled barrel-vault ceiling and florid Baroque interior – this is thought to be all that remains of a medieval monastery which once stood somewhere nearby. The handful of hotels in the village is worth passing over in favour of the extraordinary *Croix d'Or et Poste* beside the main road (☎027/974 15 15, fax 974 15 16; ②), a marvellous old building dating from 1620. Up to 1900 or so it was the residence of the noble family of prince-bishops Von Riedmatten; these days, it's every bit as atmospheric as that sounds, its public rooms draped with Victorian bric-à-brac, the few guest rooms more subdued but still characterful. Value for money extends to the cooking as well, with superb *menus* for Fr.20–25.

The high Alpine passes

Above Münster, you enter the Obergoms region (Upper Goms), and begin to approach the high Alpine passes. Ulrichen, 4km on, has a turning southeast along the Agene valley to the **Nufenen Pass**, or Passo della Novena (2478m), which crosses into Ticino and the Val Bedretto (see p.493). The main road continues through **Oberwald** (1368m), where the Obergoms tourist office is located (✆027/973 32 32), and then immediately begins to climb in a series of great looping switchbacks. If you're heading east and would prefer to avoid the Furka pass, note that **car-carrying trains** run daily year-round from Oberwald through the Furka-Basis Tunnel to Realp, at least every hour (6am–9pm) – a one-way fare is Fr.36, or Fr.27 between June and September.

Way above Oberwald, the junction point of **GLETSCH** (1759m) – not really even a hamlet, but with a hotel, *Glacier du Rhône* (✆027/973 15 15, fax 973 29 13; ①; June–Sept) from which to enjoy the spectacular views – is where roads divide. Northeast from Gletsch, heading up to the Furka pass, the road sidewinds its way up the cliffside, coiling around the landmark **Hotel Belvédère** on the way (2300m). In season, this once-grand edifice is swamped by the tide of traffic swarming up the road; it's not worth staying here, but it is worth stopping for the breathtaking views down into the valley, and also to explore the **Rhône Glacier**, which fills the head of the valley to the north. This is the source of the Rhône itself, which you can see spouting out as meltwater from beneath the glacier's eaves. Owners of a souvenir stall in the *Belvédère*'s car park have cashed in on the glacier's appeal – and its proximity to the road – by carving, fresh each year, a tunnel deep into the blueish ice for their many customers to walk along (June–Oct daily 8am–6pm; Fr.5). By the end of the summer, about a third of the tunnel's length has melted, as the glacier shifts by some 30m each year.

Grimsel Pass

The other road from Gletsch climbs west in ever tighter curves up to the **Grimsel Pass** (2165m), marking the border between Valais and Canton Bern. There are three hotels on the top, and it's an extraordinarily dramatic place to spend the night, with the bare, snow-patched rocks rising all around, the summit Totensee ("Dead Lake") icy all summer, and stunning sunset views down over the Grimselsee just below. The *Grimselblick* (✆027/973 11 77, fax 973 14 22; ①–②) is the best on offer, a cosy place once the daytime tour buses have departed, with one particularly enticing en-suite double room, complete with four-poster bed, that's worth asking for. On the other side of the lake is the simpler *Alpenrösli* (✆033/973 12 91, fax 973 12 90; ①). Three buses a day (July–Sept) run from Oberwald to Meiringen via the Grimselpass.

travel details

TRAINS

Aigle to: Bex (hourly; 5min); Champéry (hourly; 1hr 5min); Les Diablerets (hourly; 45min); Lausanne (every 30min; 30min); Leysin (hourly; 30min); Martigny (every 30min; 20min); Montreux (every 30min; 10min); St-Maurice (hourly; 10min); Sion (every 30min; 30min).

Bex to: Aigle (hourly; 5min); Villars (hourly; 45min).

Brig to: Andermatt (hourly; 1hr 45min); Basel (hourly; 2hr 55min); Bern (hourly; 1hr 40min); Chur ("Glacier Express" at least 1 daily via Furka–Oberalp; 4hr 10min); Geneva (twice hourly; 2hr 15min); Interlaken West & Ost (hourly; 1hr 25min; change at Spiez); Lausanne (twice hourly; 1hr 35min); Martigny (every 30min; 50min); Sierre (every 30min; 25min); Sion (every 30min; 35min); Zermatt (hourly; 1hr 20min); Zürich (hourly; 3hr).

Les Diablerets to: Aigle (hourly; 45min).

Leysin to: Aigle (hourly; 30min).

Martigny to: Aigle (every 30min; 20min); Brig (every 30min; 50min); Geneva (every 30min; 1hr 30min); Lausanne (every 30min; 50min); Orsières (hourly; 25min); St-Maurice (twice hourly; 10min); Sierre (every 30min; 25min); Sion (3 hourly; 15min); Verbier (hourly; 50min; change at Le Châble).

Montana to: Sierre (every 30min; 15min).

St-Maurice to: Aigle (hourly; 10min); Martigny (twice hourly; 10min).

Sierre to: Brig (every 30min; 25min); Lausanne (every 30min; 1hr 15min); Martigny (every 30min; 25min); Montana (every 30min; 15min); Sion (twice hourly; 10min); Zermatt (hourly; 1hr 30–50min; change at Visp).

Sion to: Aigle (every 30min; 30min); Brig (every 30min; 35min); Geneva (every 30min; 1hr 45min); Lausanne (every 30min; 1hr); Martigny (3 hourly; 15min); St-Maurice (hourly; 25min); Sierre (every 30min; 10min); Zermatt (hourly; 1hr 40min–2hr; change at Visp).

Villars to: Bex (hourly; 45min).

Visp to: Zermatt (hourly; 1hr 10min).

Zermatt to: Brig (hourly; 1hr 20min); Gornergrat (at least every 30min; 45min); Visp (hourly; 1hr 10min).

BUSES

Aigle to: Villars (every 2hr; 35min).

Arolla to: Sion (every 2hr; 1hr 20min; change at Les Haudères).

Brig to: Saas-Fee (hourly; 1hr 10min).

Le Châble to: Mauvoisin (July–Sept twice daily; 45min); Verbier (hourly; 25min).

Crans to: Montana (continuously; 5min); Sion (hourly; 45min); Sierre (every 30min; 40–50min).

Les Diablerets to: Gstaad (5 daily; 50min); Villars (July–Sept 3 daily; 35min).

Leysin to: Château d'Oex (3 daily; 1hr 30min; change at Le Sépey).

Martigny to: Grand-St-Bernard Pass (1 daily; 2hr; change at Orsières).

Montana to: Crans (continuously; 5min); Sierre (every 30min; 40–50min).

Oberwald to: Airolo via Nufenenpass (July–Sept 2 daily; 1hr 30min); Andermatt via Furkapass (July–Sept 2 daily; 1hr 30min); Meiringen via Grimselpass (July–Sept 3 daily; 1hr 20min).

Orsières to: Champex (every 2hr; 20min).

Saas-Fee to: Brig (hourly; 1hr 10min); Stalden (hourly; 40min).

Sierre to: Crans (every 30min; 40–50min); Montana (every 30min; 40–50min); Sion (hourly; 30min); Zinal (every 2hr; 1hr; change at Vissoie).

Sion to: Arolla (every 2hr; 1hr 20min; change at Les Haudères); Crans (hourly; 45min); Sierre (hourly; 30min).

Stalden to: Saas-Fee (hourly; 40min).

Villars to: Aigle (every 2hr; 35min); Les Diablerets (July–Sept 3 daily; 35min).

Visp to: Saas-Fee (hourly; 55min).

Zinal to: Sierre (every 2hr; 1hr; change at Vissoie).

INTERNATIONAL TRAINS

Brig to: Domodossola, Italy (hourly; 35min); Milan (every 2hr; 2hr 15min).

Martigny to: Chamonix, France (hourly; 1hr 30min).

INTERNATIONAL BUSES

Martigny to: Aosta, Italy (twice daily; 1hr 50min).

PLACE NAMES IN THIS CHAPTER

German	French	Italian
Alpen	Alpes	Alpi
Brig	Brigue	Briga
Matterhorn	Cervin	Cervino
Nufenen	Nufenen	Novena
Rotten	Rhône	Rodano
Salgesch	Salquenen	Salquenen
Siders	Sierre	Sierre
Simplon	Simplon	Sempione
Sitten	Sion	Sion
Tessin	Tessin	Ticino
Visp	Viège	Visp
Waadt	Vaud	Vaud
Wallis	Valais	Vallese

CHAPTER EIGHT

LUZERN AND ZENTRALSCHWEIZ

The oddly shaped **Vierwaldstättersee** ("Lake of the Four Forest Cantons") lies at the geographical and spiritual heart of Switzerland. It's the country's most beautiful and dramatic body of water by far, thickly wooded slopes rising sheer from misty wavelets, bays and peninsulas giving constantly changing views from vantage points on the decks of the steamers which ply to and fro. At the lake's western tip, **Luzern** (often anglicized to Lucerne) is an attractive town steeped in history that is a natural gateway to the diverse **Zentralschweiz** region all around.

Zentralschweiz – or, as it is often dubbed, Innerschweiz – is a land of tradition. Here, in the tidy little villages of Switzerland's inner core, is where the founding myths of the country are nurtured. In the Middle Ages, the communities of the four so-called "forest cantons" dotted around the lake – Uri, Schwyz, Nidwalden and Obwalden – guarded the approaches to the **Gotthard Pass**, key to the newly opened road between northern and southern Europe. When Habsburg overlords tried to encroach on their privileges, the communities formed an alliance at the lakeside Rütli Meadow in 1291 which was to prove the beginning of the **Swiss Confederation**. Luzern, as the principal market town for the region, was drawn into the bond shortly after, and tales soon began to circulate of a legendary figure from the Uri countryside named **William Tell**, who had pitted his wits against the local Habsburg tyrant and won. Today, the clifftop paths and shoreline trails of this region are trod less by foreigners than by a tide of Swiss tourists who make the journey from their suburban homes to walk in the footsteps of William Tell and the semi-mystical founders of the nation.

Transport links around the region are excellent, with the fleet of lake steamers from Luzern running throughout the year, serving shoreside villages and small resorts tucked against the sugarloaf cliffs that have little or no road access. In addition, a handful of rack railways serve mountain tops around the lake (most famously the **Pilatus** and the **Rigi**), and plenty of easy short- and long-distance hiking trails can get you well

---

ACCOMMODATION PRICE CODES

All the hostels, pensions and hotels in this book have been graded according to the following price codes, which indicate the price for the cheapest double room available during the high season. Single rooms can cost anything between sixty and eighty percent of the double-room rate. For hostels with dormitories, the price per bed has been quoted. See p.45 for more details.

① under Fr.100	④ Fr.200–250	⑦ Fr.350–400
② Fr.100–150	⑤ Fr.250–300	⑧ Fr.400–500
③ Fr.150–200	⑥ Fr.300–350	⑨ over Fr.500

WHAT'S IN A NAME?

The large lake lying at the centre of Switzerland has five very different names depending on the language you happen to be speaking. In German, it is the Vierwaldstättersee; in French, Le Lac des Quatre-Cantons; in Italian, Il Lago dei Quattro Cantoni; and in Romansh, Il Lai dals Quatter Chantuns – all of which translate as "The Lake of the Four (Forest) Cantons". Unfortunately, though, they are all way too much for most tourists to get their tongues around, and so for as long as foreigners have been coming to the lake, it's been retitled the **Lake of Lucerne** – a name you'll never hear Swiss people using to one another.

---

off the beaten path – although many also hop conveniently from one landing stage to the next. Central Switzerland's long-standing tradition of tourism means that every hamlet has its choice of hotels and restaurants. The array of sights, excursions, museums and activities makes this one of the densest, and most rewarding, areas of the country to explore.

LUZERN

An hour south of Basel and Zürich, and boasting invigorating mountain views, lake cruises and a picturesque old quarter, **LUZERN** (Lucerne in French and English, Lucerna in Italian) has long been one of Europe's most heavily touristed towns. When Queen Victoria came for a long holiday in August 1868 (checking in under a pseudonym), the town was already renowned, and a century of steady growth has resulted these days in five million admirers passing through each year. Tourism is the leading source of income, and yet the city has adeptly managed to retain all of its charm.

The River Reuss splits the town, flowing rapidly out of the northwestern end of the lake. River banks on both sides are clustered with medieval squares, frescoed houses, ancient guildhalls, churches and chapels, and filled with a liveliness that belies the city's age. Aside from using Luzern as a base from which to explore the region, it would be easy to spend at least a couple of days taking in some of its quality museums – a Picasso gallery, the impressive Verkehrshaus (Transport Museum) – in between walking on the medieval battlements, and exploring cobbled alleys and hidden garden courtyards.

But Luzern is no museum piece; café culture is treasured by the city's large population of young people, and at midnight on a weekend night, the main Pilatusstrasse boulevard has the feel of any European capital, with people bar-hopping, waiting for the last bus, or hanging out deciding where to go. Whether you're charmed by Luzern's sense of history and tradition, or by the misty lake at its doorstep and the snow-capped Pilatus rising above, or even by its nightlife, charmed is what you'll be.

Some history

Luzern's founding is lost in history. The town's name probably derives from the Celtic word *lozzeria*, meaning "a settlement on marshy ground", and that's more or less all Luzern was in the mid-eighth century when the small Benedictine **monastery** which existed here is thought to have come under the control of the Alsatian Abbey of Murbach. Nothing concrete is known about Luzern until 1178, when an abbot established a lay order at the Kapellkirche (now St Peter's Chapel), indicating that quite a substantial settlement must have existed in the area. Around 1220, the opening of the **Gotthard** pass further south created new impetus for growth, with merchants and

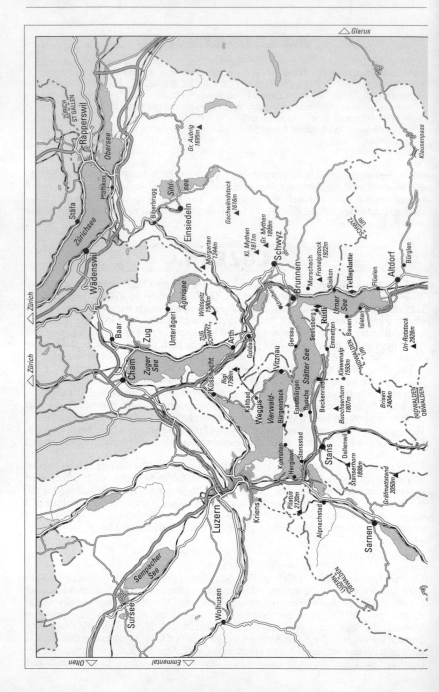

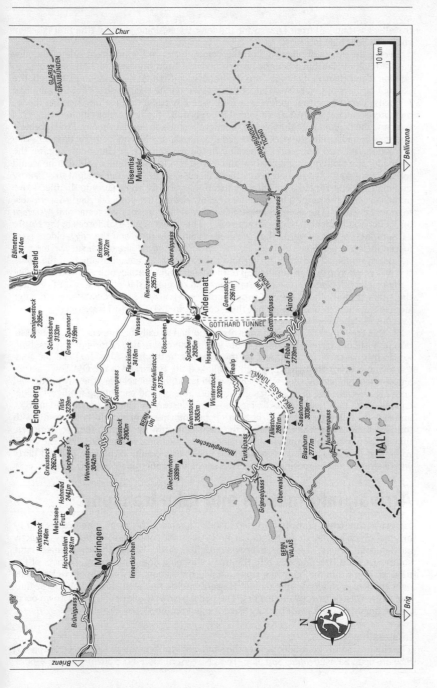

travellers setting sail from Luzern for the long trans-Alpine journey (the first lakeside road was built only in 1865).

Eyeing the prosperity flowing into the communities on the northern side of the new pass, Rudolf of Habsburg bought Luzern outright from Murbach in 1291, intending to subdue it and channel its profits into the imperial coffers. At the same time, though, the peasant farmers of Uri, Schwyz and Unterwalden on the eastern shores of the lake had formed a **pact of mutual defence** at Rütli (see box p.358) against the Austrian threat, and after some instability, Luzern joined them in 1332, the first major city to do so. This pact was the beginning of the Swiss Confederation, which survives today. Pro-Habsburg attempts to undermine the pact continued to flourish; one legend from the time tells of a boy who overheard conspirators meeting in the marketplace at Unter der Egg, on the riverside. The plotters caught the boy and forced him to swear under oath that he would tell no living soul what he had heard them discuss, so the boy ran straight to a nearby guildhall and interrupted a confederate meeting to tell his whole story to the tiled stove in the corner of the room. The confederates "overheard" the boy's tale, and so were able to thwart the plot. (The stove which stands today in the corner of the restaurant *Metzgern* on Weinmarkt is allegedly the self-same one). The defeat of Austrian forces in the **Battle of Sempach** in 1386 severed the Habsburg claim to Luzern, and the city's elders reinforced their independence by building the Musegg fortifications, which survive today.

Luzern remained Catholic throughout the Reformation and, like much of the country, was ruled by patrician families up until the late eighteenth-century revolutions. The early nineteenth-century quarrels in politics and religion led to civil war, with Luzern at the heart of the Catholic rebel **Sonderbund** (see p.518) – an association which, after Confederate forces had reasserted their control in 1847, led to Luzern being passed over for the choice of federal capital.

By this time, though, **tourism** to Switzerland had already begun, and with the cessation of hostilities Luzern became a focus for the increasing tide of foreign visitors, both for its own lakeside location, and as the gateway to the high Alps. In 1834, the mid-thirteenth-century **Hofbrücke**, which had linked the Hofkirche to the Old Town across a now-vanished marshy inlet, was torn down in favour of redeveloping the city centre and creating new lakeside promenades. Many old buildings and part of the medieval fortifications – with over forty towers and gates – were destroyed. The railway arrived in 1859, and over the following fifty years, Luzern's population quadrupled to forty thousand, with tourism, then as now, the mainstay of the city's economy. All through the twentieth century, Luzern has clung tight onto its conservative, traditional roots: these days, the city is renowned as the heartland of Switzerland's SVP, an extreme right-wing political party with a strident and increasingly successful set of anti-immigration, anti-EU policies.

Arrival, information and lake transport

Luzern's giant **train station** – opened in 1991 to replace the grand nineteenth-century original which burned to the ground in 1971 – is on the south bank of the Reuss, exactly at the point where the lake narrows into the river. Broad **Pilatusstrasse** runs southwest from Bahnhofplatz into the main shopping and commercial districts of the modern city. From the busy bus stops outside the station, the main **Seebrücke** heads over the Reuss alongside the ancient **Kapellbrücke**, the latter marked by the distinctive stone Wasserturm (water tower). The pedestrian-only alleys of the Old Town occupy the northern bank, with the city walls ranged on the slopes above.

Information

The city **tourist office** is 50m west of the station at Frankenstrasse 1 (May–Oct Mon–Fri 8.30am–6pm, Sat 9am–5pm, Sun 9am–1pm; Nov–April Mon–Fri 8.30am–noon & 2–6pm,

---

LUZERN'S FESTIVALS

Luzern's two biggest festivals come from opposite ends of the cultural spectrum. February's **carnival** features the biggest celebrations in the country (see box p.339), with six days and nights of continuous drinking and raucous partying throughout the city centre.

From mid-August to mid-September each year, the city also plays host to one of Europe's most prestigious classical music events, the **Internationale Musikfestwochen Luzern**, inaugurated in 1938 with a concert conducted by Arturo Toscanini in the grounds of Wagner's lakeside house at Tribschen. The cycle of concerts held in venues ranging from the stunning new Congress Centre beside the station, designed by architect Jean Nouvel, to churches around town and even the Lion Monument draw the world's finest soloists and orchestras. A newly established week-long **Osterfestspiele** has concerts on the theme of the Passiontide and Easter. Tickets (Fr.20–250) and programme details for both festivals can be had from IMF, Hirschmattstrasse 13, Postfach, CH-6002 Luzern (☎041/226 44 80, *www.lucernemusic.ch*).

The fourth Saturday in June sees the **Altstadtfest** – the Old Town filled with oompah bands and food and beer stalls – while that weekend and the two weekends following have international **rowing** regattas held on the Rotsee, a lake 2km north of town.

Sat 9am–1pm; ☎041/410 71 71, *www.luzern.org*). With the vast quantity of tourists tramping through the city, staff are well used to answering questions, and have stacks of information on the city and surrounding countryside. Luzern's **guest card** – which you must get stamped by your hotel – is especially good value, giving discounts on entry to most museums and 10–15 percent off car rental; it also allows you to purchase a Fr.8 three-day city bus pass (each journey normally costs Fr.1.70, although Swiss Pass holders travel free anyway). There's also a local **museum pass** (Fr.25), which gives free entry to all the city's attractions for a month. Luzern's tour guides are exceptionally good, and the official two-hour city **walking tour**, departing from the tourist office, is well worth taking (April–Oct Mon–Sat 9.45am; Nov–March Wed & Sat 9.45am; Fr.16).

The tourist office also runs a host of **guided excursions** to points nearby. The most popular are the half-day tours to the top of the Pilatus overlooking the city (see box p.342), the Rigi a short way east (see p.352) and the Titlis to the south (also p.352) – all of these run daily year-round for around Fr.85. They can also sell you the **regional travel pass** for Central Switzerland, the *Tellpass* (see box p.346), although this is only really worthwhile if you're planning a tour of the region – if you'll just be in and around Luzern itself, the free guest card is more than adequate.

Lake transport

A major reason for coming to Luzern at all is to explore the stunning Vierwaldstättersee, or **Lake Luzern**, crossed year-round by the fine old boats of the Schifffahrtsgesellschaft des Vierwaldstättersees (SGV; ☎041/367 67 67, *www.lakelucerne.ch*). All SGV boats – including their half-dozen paddle steamers (which incur no extra fare) – depart from the quay directly outside the station, and zigzag their way across the lake stopping at places on both shores: **Weggis** and **Vitznau** give access to Mount Rigi; **Kehrsiten** to Bürgenstock, and from there to the Hammetschwand summit; and **Beckenried** to Klewenalp. All of these have limited road and rail connections, but at the far, eastern end of the lake, **Brunnen** (close to Schwyz) and **Flüelen** (close to Altdorf) are both on the mainline route from Zürich to Ticino via the Gotthard Tunnel, and are less than an hour's train journey from Luzern.

In summer (June–Sept), at least seven boats daily make the full run from Luzern to Flüelen, with several more serving Brunnen, Vitznau and other intermediate points. In

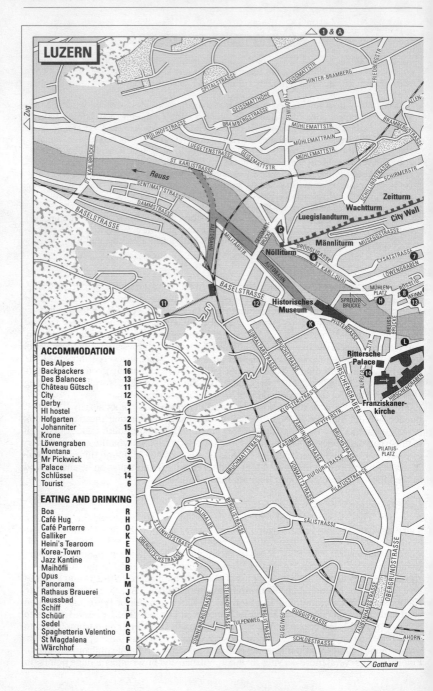

LUZERN

ACCOMMODATION

Des Alpes	10
Backpackers	16
Des Balances	13
Château Gütsch	11
City	12
Derby	5
HI hostel	1
Hofgarten	2
Johanniter	15
Krone	8
Löwengraben	7
Montana	3
Mr Pickwick	9
Palace	4
Schlüssel	14
Tourist	6

EATING AND DRINKING

Boa	R
Café Hug	H
Café Parterre	O
Galliker	K
Heini's Tearoom	E
Korea-Town	N
Jazz Kantine	D
Maihöfli	B
Opus	L
Panorama	M
Rathaus Brauerei	J
Reussbad	C
Schiff	I
Schüür	P
Sedel	A
Spaghetteria Valentino	G
St Magdalena	F
Wärchhof	Q

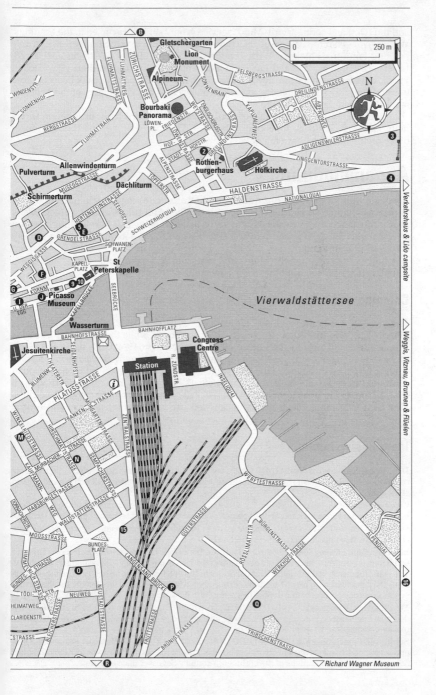

Gletschergarten
Lion Monument
Alpineum
Bourbaki Panorama
Allenwindenturm
Pulverturm
Dächliturm
Schirmerturm
Röthen-burgerhaus
Hofkirche
HALDENSTRASSE
NATIONALQUAI
St Peterskapelle
Picasso Museum
Wasserturm
Jesuitenkirche
Station
Congress Centre
BAHNHOFPLATZ
Vierwaldstättersee

B
2
3
4
5
D
E
F
G
9 10
15
M
N
O
P
Q
R

Verkehrshaus & Lido campsite

Weggis, Vitznau, Brunnen & Flüelen

Richard Wagner Museum

0   250 m

N

autumn (Oct) and spring (April–May), service is only slightly curtailed in the evenings. Winter (Nov–March) sees two boats a day as far as Brunnen, with Sunday services only running on to Flüelen. With round-trip **fares** Luzern–Vitznau at Fr.28, Luzern–Brunnen at Fr.38 and Luzern–Flüelen at Fr.42, the **Tagesbillett** (Day Ticket; Fr.42), valid for unlimited journeys on the whole lake, is a good deal. SGV boats are free to Eurail and Swiss Pass holders, as well as on selected days to holders of the Tellpass, and half-price to InterRailers.

In addition, SGV runs a wealth of **cruises** and eat-aboard trips, including a three-hour sunset cruise (daily June–Sept) for Fr.20. The tourist office, and the SGV ticket office on the quayside, have full details.

Accommodation

There's a wide range of **accommodation** in Luzern, covering the gamut from dorms to palaces. Summer is especially busy, with double-room prices in many hotels rising almost fifty percent – an establishment we've listed as being a ⑤ to reflect high-season prices might charge ③ prices between October and April. Booking ahead is a priority across all price brackets.

A hotel reservation booth (Mon–Sat 11am–2pm & 3–6pm), plus notice board and complimentary phone, is on the lower concourse of the station.

Camping and hostels

The nearest **campsite** is *Lido*, Lidostrasse 8 (☎041/370 21 46, fax 370 21 45; March–Oct), also with some non-reservable dorm beds, while the quality HI **hostel** is 1km northwest of town by the Rotsee, Sedelstrasse 12 (☎041/420 88 00, fax 420 56 16; ①; bus #18 to Jugendherberge), with dorms from Fr.31. Friendly *Backpackers*, a former student house on the shore of the Vierwaldstättersee, 800m southeast of the station at Alpenquai 42 (☎041/360 04 20, fax 360 04 42; ①; bus #6/7/8 to Weinbergli, then head left for 150m to the lakeshore promenade), has pleasant dorms for Fr.22, and basic doubles for a little more, along with free kitchen use and Internet access. The central *Tourist Hotel* (see below) has excellent dorms on the riverside for Fr.30.

Inexpensive hotels

Des Alpes, Rathausquai 5 (☎041/410 58 25, fax 410 74 51, *www.forum.ch/des-alpes*). Comfortable rooms, some with balconies, in an old building with a picturesque waterfront setting and a good restaurant. ③.

City, Baselstrasse 15 (☎041/410 40 40, fax 410 40 60). Very basic place a little west of the centre on a busy street (so ask for a back room), with poky rooms laid with lino that are nonetheless kept clean. ①.

Derby, Falkengasse 4 (☎041/410 26 62, fax 410 42 82). Plain, decent, generic "garni" place in the Old Town, with compact, characterless rooms. ②–③.

Löwengraben, Löwengraben 18 (☎041/417 12 12, fax 417 12 11, *hotel@loewengraben.ch*). Luzern's Old Town prison from 1862 to 1998, now converted into a surprisingly classy, comfortable hotel. The staff frogmarch you down the long corridors to the spotlessly refurbished cells, some with en-suite shower and all with barred windows. Prime choice is the panelled Director's Suite, the former prison governor's office, with a double bed where the desk used to be. ①–②.

Mr Pickwick, Rathausquai 6 (☎041/410 59 27, fax 410 51 08). In spartan contrast to *Des Alpes* next door, an English-style pub with rooms above, sharing the excellent views but not the welcoming management style of its neighbour. ①–②.

Schlüssel, Franziskanerplatz 12 (☎041/210 10 61, fax 210 10 21). By far the most characterful low-end accommodation in town, and the oldest hotel in Luzern to boot. Some rooms overlook the quiet square and the formal gardens of the eighteenth-century Segesser mansion. ①–②.

Tourist, St Karliquai 12 (☎041/410 24 74, fax 410 84 14, *info@touristhotel.ch*, *www.touristhotel.ch*). Clean, bright and very central, this has the atmosphere of a student dorm although the quality of the rooms (and the management) belies that. Some have suntrap balconies facing the river – peaceful, since the bankside road is quiet. ①–②.

Mid-range and expensive hotels

Des Balances, Weinmarkt (☎041/410 30 10, fax 410 64 51, *balances@tic.ch*, *www.balances.ch*). A reverentially white lobby preludes a super-chic Old Town choice, more reminiscent of midtown Manhattan than little Luzern. Back rooms overlook the water. ⑦.

Château Gütsch, Kanonenstrasse (☎041/249 41 00, fax 249 41 91, *info@chateau-guetsch.ch*, *www.chateau-guetsch.ch*). A nineteenth-century castle-folly perched on a wooded hill way above the town, lit up at night like a fairy-tale palace and with its own funicular for access. The gourmet restaurant downstairs (see "Eating and Drinking") has nothing on the grand romance of the rooms, all with huge baths and many with fourposter beds. Worthy of a splash. ⑤–⑧.

Hofgarten, Stadthofstrasse 14 (☎041/410 88 88, fax 410 83 33). The best-value hotel in Luzern, and one of the most attractive small city hotel in the country. A centuries-old protected building set in a quiet courtyard near the Hofkirche, with an excellent vegetarian terrace restaurant and eighteen modern, individually decorated rooms, all fresh, bright and carefully furnished. ⑤.

Johanniter, Bundesplatz 18 (☎041/210 18 55, fax 210 16 50, *info@johanniter.ch*, *www.johanniter.ch*). Standard, comfortable modern city hotel, with no surprises. ③–④.

Krone, Weinmarkt 12 (☎041/419 44 00, fax 419 44 90, *krone-luzern@tic.ch*, *www.krone-luzern.ch*). Friendly, bright family hotel in the heart of the Old Town, with all-modern fittings in spacious, pastel rooms. ⑤.

Montana, Adligenswilerstrasse 22 (☎041/410 65 65, fax 410 66 76, *info@hotel-montana.ch*, *www.hotel-montana.ch*). Exceptionally classy Art-Deco hotel on a hillside above the lake, reached by its own funicular. The 1920s-style decor is faultless, and rooms are generous and attractive. ⑤.

Palace, Haldenstrasse 10 (☎041/416 16 16, fax 416 10 00, *palace-luzern@bluewin.ch*, *www.palace-luzern.ch*). A giant Belle Epoque landmark catering for the ritziest of tastes, revelling both in wide-open views across the lake to Mount Pilatus, and the grandest of appointments to the broad, lofty guest rooms. With the huge *Kursaal* next door and the *Grand Hotel National* just beyond, these three edifices between them occupy half a kilometre of the city waterfront. ⑧–⑨.

The City

Evidence of Luzern's medieval prosperity is manifest in the frescoed facades of its Old Town and the two surviving covered wooden bridges spanning the River Reuss, both formerly part of the city's fortifications (and so with higher defensive side walls facing away from the town) and both boasting unique triangular paintings fixed to their roof-beams.

Any tour of Luzern must begin with the fourteenth-century covered **Kapellbrücke**, the oldest road bridge in Europe, angled around the octagonal mid-river **Wasserturm**. In deference to the fact that the city development arose largely from defence of this bridge, its highly distinctive Wasserturm (formerly a lighthouse, a prison, a treasury and today serving as a meeting house) has come to stand as the symbol of Luzern. In the early hours of August 18, 1993, a small boat moored alongside the bridge caught fire and, in one of the most dramatic spectacles in the city's recent history, the flames rapidly spread to engulf the whole structure. By dawn, virtually the entire bridge had been destroyed, with only the bridgeheads on both banks surviving. The authorities rapidly set about reconstruction, and an identical replacement was completed nine months later – though today it's still easy to see where the old wood meets the new.

The principal historical interest of the bridge lay in its collection of double-sided triangular **roof panels**, painted in the seventeenth century with scenes from the city's past and present – of the 111 panels, 65 were entirely ruined and had to be replaced with facsimiles, 30 were restored, and the remainder still remain charred and impossible to make out. Each is numbered, and captioned with rhyming couplets, the idiosyncratic local dialect written out in obscure medieval gothic script. The most distinctive image is panel no. 31, which shows **William Tell** shooting the apple from his son's head, but it's fun to work your way slowly along. Panel no. 1 shows a giant, the first Luzerner; no. 3 Luzern in the earliest times, with the Hofkirche separated from the town by a bridged inlet; no. 4 the foundation of Luzern's monastery; no. 6 the town around 1600; no. 15 St Beatus (see p.258); no. 16 Einsiedeln; no. 17 Luzern's Franciscan church; no. 26 local hero Winkelried slaying a dragon; no. 32 the Rütli oath; no. 38 the great fire of Luzern in 1340; and no. 58 the 1476 Battle of Grandson (see p.172).

Just downstream, the **Spreuerbrücke** is also worth a look for its macabre "Dance of Death" roof panels. These begin at the northern bankside with a little verse:

> *All living things that fly or leap*
> *Or crawl or swim or run or creep*
> *Fear Death, yet can they find no spot*
> *In all the world where Death is not.*

The succession of images shows a grinning skeleton leading kings, gallant princes, lawmen, nuns, merchants, prostitutes, peasants and maidens alike to their inevitable fate. The final panel, predictably enough, shows a majestic Christ vanquishing bony Death.

The Old Town

The **north bank** of the Reuss is home to the Old Town's compact cluster of medieval houses, with Mühlenplatz, Weinmarkt, Hirschenplatz and Kornmarkt forming an ensemble of cobbled, fountained squares ringed by colourful facades. Modern commerce is definitely the motive force of the place these days, and it takes some imagination to conjure up the Middle Ages amidst the welter of shoppers and high-street brandnames.

Kapellplatz, at the bridgehead of the Kapellbrücke, encircles the tiny eighteenth-century **St-Peterskapelle**, built over a predecessor dating from as early as 1178. Some 150m west is **Kornmarkt**, site of the medieval public marketplace. On one side, overlooking the riverside market area of Unter der Egg, is the huge **Rathaus**, completed in 1606 in Italian Renaissance style but crowned with an oddly incongruous Emmentaler-style roof. The market atmosphere survives today, with stalls selling vegetables, fish and flowers beneath the arcades along Unter der Egg doing a roaring trade every Tuesday and Saturday morning. Kornmarktgasse runs west to the atmospheric frescoed **Weinmarkt**, where Passion Plays were staged in the late Middle Ages.

Just off Kornmarkt, at Furrengasse 21, is Am Rhyn-Haus, an old restored building now housing the fascinating **Picasso Museum** (daily: April–Oct 10am–6pm; Nov–March 11am–1pm & 2–4pm; Fr.6; SMP). The whole collection was donated to the city by the Rosengart family, friends of the artist. The ground floor is given over to temporary exhibits, while the first upper floor displays a series of Picasso's paintings, including the wonderful *Femme et Chien Jouant* (1953) and *La Coiffure* (1954), as well as drawings, ceramics, sketches and etchings, one of the most striking of which is the tender *Portrait A.R. (Angela Rosengart)*. Upper floors hold the highlight of the museum, nearly two hundred intimate and often brilliant photographs of the artist's private life taken by American photographer David Douglas Duncan from 1956 until Picasso's death in 1973.

The battlements walk

A short stroll west from Weinmarkt along riverside St Karliquai past the sophisticated-looking hydroelectric turbines on the Reuss (which have had teething problems since

CARNIVAL!

Luzern's infamously raucous six-day all-in **carnival**, ending on Mardi Gras night, is the biggest and best in Switzerland, a genuinely participatory event which knocks Basel's stand-and-watch parades into a cocked hat. It's worth going a long way out of your way to visit, even though the streets of the Old Town get more and more crammed with revellers year-on-year.

Celebrations are focused around three "official" carnival days. The Thursday before Mardi Gras is dubbed **Schmotzig Donnschtig**, or Dirty Thursday; the following Monday is **Güdis Määntig**, or Fat Monday; while Mardi Gras itself (Fat Tuesday) is **Güdis Tseeschtig**. *Güdis* comes from the dialect word *Güdel*, meaning belly, while *Schmotzig*, or dirty, has its roots in the word for grease or fat: carnival was traditionally a time for excess, to lay in some high-calorie *Fasnachtsküechli*, fried sweet layered pastry, before Lenten fasting.

Luzern's carnival is centred on the figure of **Fritschi**, mentioned as early as 1443 and later subsumed into the legends surrounding a victory at the Battle of Ragaz on March 6, 1446. (March 6 was the day of Fridolin, patron saint of Glarus, and Fritschi is a diminutive of Fridolin.) Originally Fritschi was a lifesize straw doll carried through Luzern accompanied by **Fritschene**, his "wife"; these days a costumed couple take their place. Around the middle of the eighteenth century, the two were joined on parade by a nanny, a jester named Bajazzo and some musicians.

To this day, Fritschi begins Luzern's carnival, at 5am on the morning of Dirty Thursday, when he and his entourage lean out of an upper window of the **Rathaus** on Kornmarkt as a cannon signals the start of festivities. From breakfast time onwards, bands of masked and costumed musicians, dancers and acrobats roam the Old Town streets, some performing **Guggenmusig** – comical oompah played on a handful of dented trombones and percussion – while others set up stages to give impromptu gigs to the promenading costumed crowds. The highlight of the day is the evening **Fritschi parade**, where Fritschi, Fritschene and the rest are paraded through the Old Town and around Löwenplatz, all the while flinging oranges out to carousing onlookers.

Friday, Saturday and Sunday aren't official carnival days, but nonetheless see plenty of activity: there are parties around the town on Friday and Saturday nights, with bars open late and lots of live music in the streets and clubs. **Fat Monday** is when carnival really takes off, with strolling musicians and *commedia dell'arte* pantomime players roaming the cafés and restaurants, and all the Old Town squares taken over by exuberant mass dancing. Monday night's raucously chaotic parade is broadcast live on Swiss TV, and Old Town bars are given special all-night licences in preparation for **Fat Tuesday**, Mardi Gras itself. The climax of carnival is a **Monsterkonzert**, the grand finale of all the bands performing together throughout the Old Town on the Tuesday night, accompanied by plenty of eating, drinking and merrymaking, a mighty blowout which lasts until 4am. Two hours later, street cleaners arrive to restore order, and respectably groomed and suited business people return to Luzern's breakfast-time cafés to begin real life again, amidst the exhausted revellers of the night before, most of them nursing breakfast beers while still in their fancy dress and face paint.

they were installed, and still regularly clog up with silt) brings you to the **Nölliturm**, a fortified gate marking the southwestern extent of a lengthy stretch of the surviving fourteenth-century town walls. Pass through the gate and head right up the hill to gain access to the Musegg **battlements** (Easter–Sept daily 8am–7pm) and their impressive views. This is an oddly rustic corner of Luzern, cut off from the city behind the walls, and you may well come across a cow or two quietly grazing back here, resident of a part-time urban farm. Stairs rise to the top of both the **Männliturm** and, further along, the **Luegisland-Turm** (Countryside Viewpoint Tower), but the battlements walk proper starts at the **Wachtturm**. From here, you can follow the parapets along to the **Zytturm**, with the oldest clock in Luzern (granted the honour of chiming one minute before all the others in the town). The bizarrely ugly statue down below is *Urweib* by local artist Rudolf Blätter, such an unpopular fixture that the municipality had to unveil it in secret one evening. The rooftop walk continues to the **Schirmerturm** adjacent, gutted by an arsonist in January 1994 and still bearing smoke-blackened stones. This is where the battlements walk runs out, but you can descend to follow the road through the Schirmerturm gate and down tranquil Museggstrasse through another breach in the old wall to the traffic-choked Löwenplatz.

The Lion Monument and around

Just northeast of Löwenplatz is one of the highlights of Luzern, the terribly sad **Lion Monument**. This dying beast draped over his shield, with a broken spear sticking out of his flank, was hewn out of a cliff face in 1821 to commemorate the 700 Swiss mercenaries killed in Paris in 1792. On August 10 that year, French revolutionaries stormed the royal palace, the Tuileries; in the face of the mob, the Swiss palace guards were ordered to lay down their arms by Louis XVI and were subsequently massacred. This would be a movingly tranquil spot, with its foliage and gently rippling pool in front, were it not for the fact that it's the single most touristed place in the entire city.

Adjacent are a handful of nineteenth-century tourist attractions, quaint and rather old-fashioned today. The **Gletschergarten**, Denkmalstrasse 4 (Glacier Garden; May to mid-Oct daily 8am–6pm; March, April & mid-Oct to mid-Nov daily 9am–5pm; mid-Nov to Feb Tues–Sun 10.30am–4.30pm; Fr.8; SMP; *www.gletschergarten.ch*), holds within its grounds a rather fusty museum displaying old relief maps of Luzern and Switzerland; a fascinating Mirror Maze built for the Swiss National Expo in 1896 and recently restored in mock-Moorish style; and a set of geological potholes telling of the subtropical ocean beach that was Luzern twenty million years ago.

The **Alpineum** opposite (daily 9am–noon & 2–6pm; Fr.4; SMP) is a relic from a bygone age – static models of Alpine scenes behind glass no doubt sparked the imagination of our great-grandparents, but today they come across as a little dry. On Löwenplatz itself, a huge circular building houses the **Bourbaki Panorama**, due to reopen in 2000 after renovations. The panorama itself is a huge mural depicting the retreat of the French Eastern Army under General Bourbaki into Switzerland during the Franco-Prussian War of 1870–71.

The Hofkirche

Busy Löwenstrasse runs south from Löwenplatz to the riverside; just before you reach the Schweizerhofquai, the arrow-straight St-Leodegarstrasse cuts east to broad steps leading up to the **Hofkirche** (Sat–Thurs 10am–noon & 2–5pm). This grand structure sits on the site of the first monastery of Luzern, which dated from the mid-eighth century and was dedicated to St-Leodegar, or St Leger. The Romanesque church which replaced the monastery in the late twelfth century was burned to the ground on Easter Sunday 1633, the blaze reputedly sparked by the verger's careless shooting at birds. Only its twin **towers** escaped, and they survive today either side of a bizarrely incongruous Renaissance gable. The impressive main doors are carved with the two patron saints of Luzern: on the left is **St Leger**, a French bishop who was blinded with a drill (which he is holding), and on the right is **St Maurice**, the martyred Roman soldier-saint (see p.295).

The interior design and furniture are almost wholly original Renaissance from the 1630s and 1640s, a unity very rarely found in Swiss or European churches, a large proportion of which underwent renovation and embellishment during the later Baroque period. On the right, elaborate **pews** divided into individual seats were reserved for city councillors, while the plainer pews on the left were for the rank and file. Behind the exceptionally fine **choir screen** – one of the earliest examples of strong three-dimensional perspective used to draw the congregation's attention forward – is the **high altar** in black marble, flanked by statues of the two patron saints. Above the Italianate depiction of the Agony at Gethsemane is a half-length figure of God. The carved **choir stalls**, as well as the beautiful **pulpit**, are the work of Niklaus Geissler. Against the north wall (left) is the extraordinarily lavish **Death of the Virgin altar**, showing Mary on a bed surrounded by disciples: dating from around 1500, this was the only relic to survive the 1633 fire. The mighty **organ**, bedecked in ornament, features 2826 pipes, along with a machine to mimic the sound of rain and a special register for thunder and hail.

The church is set amidst a lovely Italianate **cloister**, lined with the graves of Luzerner patrician families (who continue to be buried here to this day). Old houses all around the church still serve as the homes for canons of the parish. Just west of the church is the ancient **Rothenburgerhaus**, a teetering pile that's generally held to be one of the oldest wooden townhouses in the country, dating from about 1500. On the slopes north of the church is the old cemetery, now a public park, while about 500m further north on the hilltop is the Capuchin monastery of **Wesemlin**, founded in 1584 and still functioning as the principal seat of the order in Switzerland.

The south bank

On the **south bank** of the Reuss is a triangular area known as the Kleinstadt, originally walled. Facing Unter der Egg is the huge **Jesuitenkirche**, dominating the riverside with its twin onion-domed towers. Completed in 1673, its astonishing interior is a frothy Rococo concoction of gilt stucco and marble. Among the profusion of frescoes is one on the ceiling that, intriguingly, depicts the church exterior as it was 300 years ago. A few steps west is the **Rittersche palace**, built in 1557 in Florentine Renaissance style as a private mansion but now the seat of Luzern's cantonal government. Behind it to the south is the **Franziskanerkirche** (Franciscan Church), the oldest building in Luzern, dating from 1270, though it has been much restored over the centuries. It's unusually richly decorated for a Franciscan church, with Renaissance choir stalls and battle standards lining the walls – copies of those looted from battlefields through the centuries. A marvellous Baroque side chapel is decorated with Italianate stucco and a host of kitschy, curly-haired angels.

Peaceful Pfistergasse curves to meet the south side of the Spreuerbrücke, where you'll also spot the stout old town arsenal, now home to the **Historisches Museum** (Tues–Fri 10am–noon & 2–5pm, Sat & Sun 10am–5pm; Fr.4; SMP; *www.hmluzern.ch*), filled with arms and armour, restored interiors, costumes and crafts telling the history of Luzern and the surrounding districts, unfortunately with notes in German only.

Due for reopening in 2000, Luzern's **Kunstmuseum** is right beside the station at Robert-Zünd Strasse 1, with plenty of works from Swiss artists of the nineteenth and twentieth centuries, as well as collections covering modernism and contemporary art.

Outside the centre

Although many of Luzern's sights are packed close together in the compact Old Town, there are a few incentives to venture further afield in the city. Facing each other across the lake roughly 2km out of the centre are the **Verkehrshaus** (Transport Museum) on the northern shore, and the former home of the composer **Richard Wagner**, now a museum, on the southern shore. Buses run close to both, but the way to get to either place in style is by **boat**.

The Verkehrshaus

One of the main draws of Luzern is the **Verkehrshaus**, 2km east of the centre at Lidostrasse 5 (Transport Museum; daily: April–Oct 9am–6pm; Nov–March 10am–5pm;

Fr.18, or various discounts available with rail passes or guest card; SMP; *www.verkehrshaus.org*); if you're not taking the boat, hop on bus #6 or #8, or else it's a pleasant fifteen-minute lakeside stroll. This vast complex is devoted to Swiss engineering skill and could keep you amused all day – you'll need the site plan handed out at the ticket desk to navigate your way around. It's divided into several large areas, taking in Road Transport, Rail Transport, Aviation and Astronautics, Cableways and Tourism, and so on. Everything is in English, and "hands-on" is a rule, not an exception. Kids will obviously be in seventh heaven.

Particular highlights include the train section, with dozens of giant locomotives on display (complete with evocative oily smell) and an exceptionally well presented walk-through account of the digging of the Gotthard tunnel, dramatized with slides and soundtrack. The airplane section has flight simulators, a mock-up of an airport control-tower and the Cosmorama, an interactive tour of the asteroid belt. The tourism bit has the endearingly dated Swissorama, a wraparound 360° movie of the delights of Switzerland circa 1977 projected onto the walls of a circular room. There's also a huge section devoted to communications, an excellent Planetarium and a separate, giant building housing Switzerland's only **IMAX cinema** (regular showings throughout the day for an extra Fr.14, or ask for the combination museum-plus-IMAX ticket at Fr.28).

In an entirely different vein altogether, a far-flung building on the edge of the site – overlooked by most visitors – houses a museum dedicated to the acclaimed twentieth-century Luzerner artist **Hans Erni**. Erni is barely known outside Switzerland, but has spent his long career producing art that is wonderfully warm and human, full of fluidity of figures and geometries that the museum blurb will try to convince you is linked in some spiritual way to the scientific prowess on display throughout the rest of the complex. Particularly outstanding are Erni's lithographs, made as illustrations for limited-edition books.

ABOVE LUZERN

The giant mountain looming above Luzern to the southwest is **Mount Pilatus** (2132m), an odd name supposedly deriving from the myth that the corpse of Pontius Pilate was flung into a small lake on the mountain, his spirit for ever after haunting the summit and bound to bring tempest and damnation down onto Luzern if disturbed. More prosaically, the name is probably derived from the Latin word *pileatus*, meaning "capped" (ie with clouds). There are two means of transport to the top, making it easy to do a half- or full-day round trip from Luzern – simpler than in 1868, when Queen Victoria made the excursion on muleback.

Boats and local trains run from Luzern to **Alpnachstad**, from where the steepest rack railway in the world runs at a gradient touching 48 percent directly to the top of the mountain – the journey up is half-an-hour, while the journey down takes a careful forty minutes. The second route up the mountain starts at **Kriens** (connected to Luzern's city centre by bus #1); from here a cable-car rises to Fräkmüntegg, itself connected to the summit by gondola. The Kriens–Fräkmüntegg–Pilatus route runs year-round, while the Alpnachstad–Pilatus railway is summer only (closed Dec to mid-May). Eurailers get a discount of 35 percent, Swiss Pass holders get a quarter off, while InterRailers pay full whack. Pilatus Railways have a weather line giving forecasts for the summit (☎041/329 11 29, *www.pilatus.com*).

On the top are a couple of hotels, but if you're looking for a mountain-top night, you'd do better on the Rigi instead (see p.352). The walk to the highest point of the mountain, the Tomlishorn, takes less than thirty minutes from the top station, with breathtakingly expansive views out over the lake the whole way along the clifftop path. It's also easy to walk back to Luzern from Fräkmüntegg (2hr 30min), or to make your way down from the summit to Alpnachstad or Hergiswil (3hr) or Kriens (3hr 30min).

The Richard Wagner Museum

Southeast of the centre, in an idyllic location on a headland named Tribschen projecting into the lake, is a villa that was Richard Wagner's home from 1866 to 1872, and is now a **museum** to him (March–Nov Tues–Sun 10am–noon & 2–5pm; Fr.5; SMP; boat to Tribschen, or bus #6/7/8 to Wartegg, then 5min walk). After many visits to Switzerland, the composer and his partner Cosima – Franz Liszt's daughter, who was still legally married to the pianist and conductor Hans von Bülow – spotted the derelict Tribschen villa in early 1866, made arrangements to rent it for an extended period, and moved in on April 15. "Nobody will get me out of here again," Wagner said, and it's generally agreed that this was the happiest and most productive time of his life, not least because Cosima's long-dead marriage was finally dissolved in 1870 and the couple were able to marry. The tranquillity of the house, in a gorgeous lakeside setting, is still tangible today, as you wander through the rooms laid out with Wagneriana of all kinds – letters, pictures, original furniture, instruments and even his death mask – with Wagner compositions playing in the background.

Eating and drinking

Luzern has a fine range of **eating and drinking** venues covering all budgets – the crowded, generic places that are in plain view tend to be least interesting, but a small amount of backstreet searching will turn up plenty of more rewarding places.

Local specialities to keep an eye out for are led by the celebrated Luzerner *Kügelipastete* – many Old Town restaurants spell it out in dialect along the lines of *Lozärner Chögalipaschtetli*, also often prefixed by *ächti* (authentic). This heartwarming, stomach-lining dish is a glorified vol-au-vent, a large puff-pastry shell filled with a super-rich concoction of diced veal and mushrooms in a creamy sauce – veggie versions omitting the veal aren't hard to find. Otherwise, fish is the thing, in endless varieties: you'll see *Forellen* (trout), *Egli* (perch), *Felchen* (a kind of white fish) and *Hecht* (pike) on most menus, virtually all of it plucked fresh from the lake – as witnessed by the stalls groaning with finny gogglers in the twice-weekly Old Town markets.

Wash it all down either with a *Kaffee fertig*, a coffee laced with Schnapps, or a *Kafi Luz*, traditionally seen in Canton Luzern outside the city but nowadays easy to find in the Old Town cafés. The right way to make one is to put a five-franc coin in a vase-shaped glass, pour hot coffee in until you can't see the coin, then add Schnapps until the coin becomes visible again. Stir in two large spoons of sugar, and you have the perfect farmers' pick-me-up.

Cafés and café-bars

Cafés and café-bars crowd the waterfront and the Old Town squares, and they do a roaring trade amongst the flood of tour groups passing through the town. Better places, frequented by locals, abound in less-trod corners.

Café Hug, Mühlenplatz. Superb breakfast café, open from 7am, with warm fresh bread and croissants, that also has quality inexpensive lunch *menus* (Fr.13–17). Closed Sun.

Café Parterre, Mythenstrasse 7. Relaxed and inexpensive locals' hangout, open daily from breakfast until after midnight, with quality lunchtime *menus* (Fr.14). Go ahead and try their English breakfast (Fr.14), but don't hold out too many hopes.

Heini's Tearoom, Falkenplatz. Perfect place for cakes and pastries on a broad, people-watching corner in the Old Town.

Jazz Kantine, Grabenstrasse 8. Buzzing Old Town hub, open during the day for coffee and beers, and on into the late night as a hopping bar and meeting point, with DJs and live music downstairs.

Löwengraben, Löwengraben 18. Chic postmodern café-bar in the old prison (see "Accommodation") that's the in-place of the moment.

Opus, Bahnhofstrasse 16. Pricey but excellent waterside café and wine-bar, with a bright warm interior and a huge salad buffet (Fr.15 buys a ton of the stuff).

Panorama, in the *Astoria* hotel, Pilatusstrasse 29. Rooftop bar with big views and bigger sofas.

Restaurants

There are hundreds of **restaurants** in Luzern, plenty of which need to do nothing more than occupy an old-style panelled dining room and churn out a handful of traditional dishes to gone-tomorrow tourists in order to make money. A little searching can turn up more worthwhile eateries.

If you're watching every franc, *EPA* on Mühlenplatz is top **self-service** choice, but also bear in mind the shabby *Bahnhof Buffet*, on the top floor of the station. This greasy-table diner – replete with down-and-outs, smoking schoolchildren and drunken businessmen – charges budget prices for food prepared next door in the kitchen of the Michelin-starred *Au Premier* gourmet restaurant. A meal which might cost you Fr.50 in *Au Premier* may set you back a third of that in the *Bahnhof Buffet* – if you can stand the ambience, that is.

Note that the venerable *Stadtkeller* on Sternenplatz is the eye of Luzern's tourist hurricane, a folklore restaurant which lays on alphorn, yodelling and traditional dancing for tour groups; perfect if you like that kind of thing, a screaming nightmare if you don't.

Château Gütsch, Kanonenstrasse (see "Accommodation"). Worth coming up here even if just for a cup of tea on the terrace, but if you can afford it, the restaurant is one of Luzern's finest (Fr.100-plus).

Galliker, Schützenstrasse 1 (☎041/240 10 02). Hearty Swiss specialities in a tavern-like setting crammed with people, noise and smoke. The food is consistently excellent, with quality *Chögelipastetli* standing at the top of the pile, joined by *Cordon Bleu* (veal steak stuffed with cheese and ham), and less palatable offerings such as *Kutteln* (tripe). Mains are Fr.30–40, not much more than lunchtime *menus*. Closed Sun & Mon.

Hofgarten, Stadthofstrasse 14 (see "Accommodation"). The city's best veggie food by miles, everything fresh and delicious whether from the buffet or ordered à la carte. A wonderful enclosed garden terrace and cheerful interior attract locals by the score. Fr.25 will see you satisfied.

Korea-Town, Hirschmattstrasse 23. Pleasant ambience and a good choice mark this place out as something a little more worthwhile than average, with midday buffets from Fr.17 and a range of *menus* (veggie and not) from Fr.21.

Maihöfli, Maihofstrasse 70 (☎041/420 60 60). Don't miss this marvellously relaxed and friendly little place 1km north of the centre – it's comfortable, cosy, and run by a twenty-something team who've put together a winning combination of the best service, the best atmosphere and some of the best food in town. The cuisine is fresh and modern, with a light, inventive touch, expertly presented, and servers are willing to help you decipher the menu with a recommendation or two, or take the time to talk you through the range of post-prandial grappas on offer. With an ambience-rich all-wood interior, this is somewhere you can lean back on your chair and feel good about your dinner. Highly memorable meals may set you back Fr.30–35. Closed Sun.

Reussbad, Brüggligasse 19 (☎041/240 54 23). Easygoing riverside joint to enjoy traditional cooking, relying on a renowned range of fresh fish dishes at around Fr.30. Otherwise, *menus* are Fr.15–18. Closed Sun & Mon.

Schiff, Unter der Egg 8 (☎041/418 52 52). Wonderful old wood-panelled hotel restaurant on the riverside, celebrated for three things: top-quality *Würst*, huge portions of *Chögelipastetli*, and twin Spanish waiters who've been serving in the place for twenty years. Summer sees tables set under the arcades directly on the waterfront. *Menus* are around Fr.25.

Schlüssel, Franziskanerplatz (see "Accommodation"). Tiny old hotel offering a bargain three-course lunch *menu* for just Fr.13.

Spaghetteria Valentino, Weinmarkt. Central pasta joint, with a range of risotto and other Italian dishes for under Fr.20. Closed Sun.

Nightlife and entertainment

Luzern's **nightlife** scene is active, with plenty of arts centres and music venues around the Old Town and the rest of the city. There are two places to check flyers: Doo-Bop, Brandgässli 8, is a dance music shop with plenty of information about events in Luzern; while Romp, Denkmalstrasse 17, is an "info-shop" at the centre of Luzern's squat culture, with music, flyers and contacts for all kinds of alternative activities around and about. The Stattkino, Baselstrasse 15, is an arthouse **cinema** with a varied daily programme of world cinema, plenty of it in English.

Look out for the monthly *Kultur Kalender* (Fr.4, if it's not free), available at the tourist office and cafés around town, with complete city listings. The *Luzerner Bar Guide* (*www.barfuehrer.ch*) is a free pocket appraisal of dozens of establishments.

Bars, clubs and live music

Boa, Geissensteinring 41. Arts centre with a range of interesting events and music nights.

Jazz Kantine, Grabenstrasse 8. Happening Old Town café-bar beside Luzern's jazz school, with DJs and live music (not only jazz) in the basement on weekends.

Rathaus Brauerei, Unter der Egg. Wonderful echoing cross-vaulted beerhall below the Rathaus, where young enthusiastic drinkers come to sample a range of self-brewed beers, all of which are pretty powerful.

Schüür, Tribschenstrasse 1. Daytime bar with cheap weekday lunches which after dark becomes a frenetic venue for excellent live music (Fri & Sat until 4am). Famous after-hours parties begin at 5am Sunday morning.

Sedel, near the HI hostel. A former women's prison outside the city, which now hosts noisy punkish/industrial bands and DJ nights at the weekend, with a kind of community-squat atmosphere during the week as bands practise in the graffitied cells.

St Magdalena, Eisengasse 5. Universally known as the Magdi-Bar, with a crowded ground-floor bar and a more sociable upstairs, although everything gets more and more raucous as the night veers wildly on.

Wärchhof, Werkhofstrasse 11 (*www.waerchhof.ch*). Tiny little co-op-run dive in an industrial area south of the station, with loud bands, DJs and alternative-style happenings. Open nightly until midnight only; Monday is women-only night.

Listings

Adventure sports Outventure, Hansmatt 5 in nearby Stans (☎041/611 14 41, *www.outventure.ch*), is the leading adventure operator in the region, with plenty to keep adrenalin junkies happy, including bungee jumping out of the Titlis cable-car (130m; Fr.149), flying fox (Fr.79), potholing (Fr.79), canyoning (from Fr.95), tandem paragliding, white-water rafting, mountaineering, abseiling and more. From May to October they offer a shuttle from Luzern to each location, many of which are in and around Engelberg (see p.349).

Bike rental In the station (June–Sept daily 7am–7.45pm; Oct–May Mon–Sat 7am–7.45pm, Sun 9.30am–7pm).

Boat rental SNG, Alpenquai 11 (☎041/368 08 08) has pedal boats (Fr.21/hr), rowing boats (Fr.22/hr) and motor boats (Fr.44/hr) for rent, all requiring a deposit (Fr.20–100). After 7pm, prices rise by Fr.6/hr. Bucher at Luzernerhof (☎041/410 20 55) and Herzog at Nationalquai (☎041/410 43 33) are two competitors.

Books Bücher Brocky, Güterstrasse 1, has second-hand books in English.

Car rental Avis, Schachenstrasse 38, Kriens (☎041/310 16 16) or Seetalstrasse 44, Emmenbrücke (☎041/260 66 46); Budget, Luzernerstrasse 57, Ebikon (☎041/420 75 00); Europcar, Luzernerstrasse 17, Ebikon (☎041/444 44 28); Hertz, Luzernerstrasse 33, Ebikon (☎041/420 02 77).

Changing money In the station (May–Oct Mon–Fri 7.30am–8.30pm, Sat & Sun 7.30am–7.30pm; Nov–April Mon–Sat 7.30am–7pm, Sun 9am–6pm).

Email and Internet *Café Parterre* (Mon–Sat 7am–12.30am, Sun 9am–12.30am; Fr.16/hr), and the *Löwengraben* (daily 7am–12.30am; Fr.15/hr) both offer access (see "Cafés and café-bars"). *Wärchhof* (see "Clubs and live music") offers free Internet access (Tues & Wed 7pm–midnight).

Flights Scenic Air, at Widi 3 in Alpnachstad (☎041/671 08 71, *www.scenicair.ch*), offers sightseeing flights – a 45-minute overfly of the lake and the Titlis (Fr.175) or a one-hour tour of the Bernese Oberland (Fr.220), with the extra option of a glacier landing.

Laundry Jet Wash, Bruchstrasse 28 (closed Sun); also in the *Tourist Hotel* (see "Accommodation").

Lost property The city office is at Hirschengraben 17b (☎041/208 78 08).

Markets Every Tuesday and Saturday morning, large and colourful food markets spill over both banks of the Reuss and under the arcades, with a supplementary fish market every Friday. There's a flea market every Saturday (May–Oct) on the south bank, and a monthly crafts market (April–Dec, first Sat of month) on Weinmarkt. In the modern part of town, Moosstrasse hosts a relaxed Saturday morning farmers' market of cheeses, organic vegetables, home-made jams and more.

Medical facilities 24-hour emergency room at the Kantonsspital, Spitalstrasse (☎041/205 11 11).

Post Main office is across from the station (Hauptpost, CH-6000 Luzern 1).

Travel agents Discount flight agents SSR Reisen are at Grabenstrasse 8 (Mon–Fri 10am–6pm, Thurs until 8pm, Sat 10am–1pm; ☎041/410 86 56).

Women's contacts Zefra, Vonmattstrasse 44 (☎041/240 71 40) is an alternative women's centre, with contacts and information. Monday night at the *Wärchhof* (see "Bars, clubs and live music") is women-only.

ZENTRALSCHWEIZ

Zentralschweiz, or Central Switzerland, is one of the most rewarding areas of the country in which to travel, with a host of different attractions to draw you off the beaten path. Routes around both shores of the lake give constantly changing perspectives, and even the shortest day trip in the area will turn up places of great natural beauty. For details of the boats which crisscross the lake year-round – often the most convenient method of transport – see p.333.

The southern shore is quiet, characterized by country towns such as **Stans**, and leg-stretching clifftop hikes above the glittering lake. The excursion south to the once-grand resort of **Engelberg**, base station for the trip up to the summit of the **Titlis**, is a journey to match the Bernese Oberland's more famous rides up the Jungfrau and the Schilthorn. The northern shore of the lake is studded by the lofty presence of the **Rigi**, with the old town of **Zug** behind, while its easternmost finger, oriented due north–south, is dubbed the **Urnersee**, or Lake Uri. One of the country's most historically resonant areas, its wild and rocky shores were the setting both for the legend of **William Tell**, and for an ancient pact of mutual defence signed on a lakeside meadow

---

EXPLORING ZENTRALSCHWIEZ

The Tellpass is the **regional pass** for Zentralschweiz – but you'll need to cover plenty of ground to make it pay. The core region covers all boats on the lake, all routes to the Rigi and Pilatus, the train from Luzern to Engelberg, and cable-cars from Engelberg up to Trübsee and the Jochpass. With a **seven-day** Tellpass (Fr.131), you get two days' free travel in the core region, with half-price travel on all other lines, including trains to Zug, Einsiedeln, Brienz, Meiringen and Andermatt; a **fifteen-day** Tellpass (Fr.179) buys five days' free travel in the core region, with the remaining ten days at half-price. You can buy the pass from tourist offices throughout the region.

The co-ordinating Zentralschweiz Tourist Office is at Postfach, CH-6002 Luzern (☎041/418 40 84, fax 418 40 81, *www.centralswitzerland.ch*).

– the **Rütli** – which laid the foundations for the Swiss Confederation as it survives today.

The southern lakeshore

The south shore of the lake – Vierwaldstättersee-Süd in German – is a land of broad green meadows and lush valleys interspersed with chunks of high forested plateau towering over the water. Once you gain some height, the views are magnificent, out across the whole shimmering expanse of blue. The shore forms part of the ancient canton of Unterwaldan, divided for as long as anyone can remember into two small half-cantons, **Nidwalden** (the Lower Forest) and **Obwalden** (the Upper Forest). It's a perfect area for hiking and cycling, and it's easy to base yourself either in Luzern or in the main town of the region, tiny **Stans**.

Stans

The highest peak in the area is the beautiful Stanserhorn, rising to 1900m above the old village of **STANS**, capital of Nidwalden and on a direct train link with Luzern. The centre of the village lies behind the station. The hub, Dorfplatz, is overlooked by the large **Pfarrkirche St Peter und Paul**. From the Middle Ages onwards this was the sole house of worship in the canton, and so was expanded time and time again to accommodate the increasing population until it was completely renovated in 1647 – the early Baroque building remains crowned by a Romanesque bell tower. Outside the church is an 1865 fountain dedicated to **Arnold von Winkelried**, a native of the town, who is celebrated for diverting the attention of the Austrian army during the Battle of Sempach in 1386, thereby committing suicide but opening a gap for his Swiss comrades to win their famous victory. The alleys surrounding Dorfplatz are worth a wander; Schmiedgasse to the east is a quiet and atmospheric back alley, while to the west is Altes Postplatz and the **Höfli**, or Rosenburg House, a medieval turreted building with a rear courtyard overlooked by beautiful Italianate loggias.

A couple of minutes beyond the Höfli is the station for the old-time cog railway up to the summit of the green and pleasant **Stanserhorn** (mid-April to Nov; Swiss Pass gets 25 percent off; Eurail & InterRail go for half-price; *www.stanserhorn.ch*), with views on a clear day from the sun-terrace restaurant and the many trails on the summit taking in ten lakes as well as the close-at-hand high mountains around the Titlis. The zigzag walk back down to Stans takes about three and a half hours, or alternatively, you can head down the side of the mountain to Wirzweli (in two and a half hours), from where a cable-car deposits you at the small village of **Dallenwil** for the bus ride back to Stans.

The **tourist office** for Stans and the Vierwaldstättersee-Süd region (Mon–Fri 9–11.30am & 2.30–5.30pm; ☎041/610 88 33, *www.vierwaldstaettersuesud.ch*) is above the train station, where there are bikes for rent. There are two pleasant, comfortable old **hotels** on Dorfplatz: the *Engel* (☎041/619 10 10, fax 619 10 11; ②) and the *Linde* (☎041/619 09 30, fax 619 09 48; ②–③). Both have good, traditional-style **restaurants**, or you could plump for the *Wilhelm Tell* restaurant just off the square (*menus* Fr.15). Stans's top eating choice is the fine restaurant within the Höfli (*menus* Fr.25; closed Mon & Tues).

From Hergiswil to Seelisberg

On the train line midway between Luzern and Stans is the small lakeside community of **HERGISWIL**, for centuries a fishing village until it rose to fame for the **Glasi Hergiswil** glassworks, founded in 1817. For over a hundred years, the glassworks was one of the busiest in the country, yet by 1975, it was hopelessly obsolete with no chance of matching the automated methods of more modern competitors. The Glasi would have closed altogether but for the move of Roberto Niederer, a Ticinese glass designer who, backed by local people, bought it up and changed its products and its target market. Niederer's rejuvenation, continued today by his son, enabled the plant – and the village economy – to survive: it's a remarkable success story. The "visitor-friendly" Glasi now employs a hundred people, producing hand-blown pieces for sale as well as serving as a workshop for artists from around the world to design and work with glass using traditional craft techniques.

The on-site **museum** (Mon–Fri 9am–noon & 1.30–5.30pm, Sat 9am–4pm; free) is excellent, focused around an engaging audiovisual walk-through history of glassmaking and the Glasi. The story ends as a door opens onto a gallery above the blazing-hot factory floor, where you can watch a team of glass-blowers do their stuff (although beware that they take a 4–4.30pm teabreak, and finish at noon on Saturdays).

Bürgenstock

West of Hergiswil on the lakeshore rises a grand plateau, atop which is the privately owned luxury business-resort of **BÜRGENSTOCK**. Buses from Stans stop short at Obbürgen (from where a private toll road serves the resort), and the only way to access the area directly is by **boat** from Luzern to Kehrsiten-Bürgenstock, way down on the lake; from there, a **funicular** rises to Bürgenstock itself. This odd little enclave is owned by the handful of business-class hotels who occupy it, themselves mostly owned by a single family. If you want to stay here, or eat here, or play golf here, you'll need a packet of money (double rooms start at Fr.300; *www.buergenstock-hotels.ch*; April–Oct only), but it doesn't cost anything to enjoy the views. Ignore the big cars and the well-cut suits clustering around the hotels, and instead strike out east on the Felsenweg path for a scenic twenty-minute clifftop walk to Europe's fastest outdoor elevator, which swishes you in seconds to the **Hammetschwand** summit (1128m), complete with a more affordable restaurant and stunning lake vistas. You can return to Bürgenstock via a steeper path zigzagging down the back of the Hammetschwand (35min), from where another path cuts down to the Kehrsiten boat station, or a four-hour trail heads east across the wooded hilltops down to Ennetbürgen and Beckenried, giving expansive views over the lake and towards the high mountains further south.

Beckenried and Klewenalp

Just round the lakeshore from Kehrsiten, and accessible by bus from Stans or lake boats, is **BECKENRIED**, from where a gondola rises to **Klewenalp** (1593m; *www.klewenalp.ch*) and a host of more walking routes. This is touted strongly as **mountain-bike** territory, and you can rent from Merkur outlets in Beckenried, Dallenwil and Seelisberg (see below) – Fr.31 for a full day, or Fr.24 for a half-day (7am–noon, or noon–5pm). Two easy bike routes link Dallenwil and Beckenried (10km), and Emmetten and Seelisberg (7km), with harder ones climbing to Klewenalp and beyond to various mountain inns. One option is to rent from Beckenried, cycle to Seelisberg (about 12km) and then catch a boat from Treib, Seelisberg's boat station, back to Beckenried. The same route on foot would take about four and a half hours.

Seelisberg and Treib

Beyond Beckenried, the main highway dips into a long tunnel beneath the cliffs and forests of the Seelisberg peninsula, emerging further south close to Flüelen (see p.362). Buses from Stans, however, follow a minor road up onto the plateau itself, through the village of **Emmetten**, and on, with ever-more spectacular panoramas over the glittering lake, until you round a corner to be met with a sign reading "Welcome to the International Capital of the Age of Enlightenment". This is little **SEELISBERG**,

The historically resonant Rütli meadow below Seelisberg (see box p.358) is the starting-point for the long-distance *Weg der Schweiz* (**Swiss Path**) walking route, inaugurated in 1991 as part of the celebrations for the 700th anniversary of the founding of the Swiss Confederation. The scenic path, which circumnavigates the Urnersee ending up in Brunnen, is almost 35km long, walkable in two days of roughly six hours each (with a mid-way overnight stop in Flüelen or Altdorf), or easily dividable into smaller chunks. Sections are: Rütli to Bauen (11km up and down; 3hr 30min); Bauen to Flüelen (a flat 10km; 2hr 45min); Flüelen to Sisikon (reasonably flat 8km; 2hr); and Sisikon to Brunnen (climbing and dropping 8km; 3hr). Distinctive yellow route markers – a Swiss cross incorporating an arrow – point the way. Boats shuttle between Rütli, Bauen, Isleten, Flüelen, Sisikon and Brunnen, and trains run between Flüelen, Sisikon and Brunnen, enabling you to pick and choose which sections you fancy. Tourist offices around the region have English guides to the route.

The idea behind the path is to provide a lasting reminder of the state of the nation in 1991. Each of the 26 cantons is represented by a length of the path proportionate to its population: impossibly meticulous attention to detail has calculated that every 5mm of the route represents a single Swiss citizen. So it takes 6.1km to cover populous Zürich, while sparser Luzern has 1.6km, and you can dispatch tiny Appenzell Inner-Rhodes in just 71m. Marked stones along the route identify the cantons in the order in which they joined the Confederation – the climb from the Rütli takes care of Uri, Schwyz, Nidwalden and Obwalden (all 1291), the section around Flüelen is labelled for Schaffhausen (1501), while the final walk into Brunnen covers Geneva (1815) and Jura (1979).

home to the Maharishi Ayur-Veda Health Centre, housed in a spectacularly sited Victorian hotel on the village outskirts (☎041/820 57 50), and offering everything from a one-day massage treatment for Fr.300, to a two-week residential cure for Fr.4000.

The village proper, a crow's nest of a place with expansive lake views, is as peaceful as you could hope for. A funicular from the northern end of the main street shadows the steep path coiling down the cliff to the quaint old lakeside inn and boat station of **Treib** below, directly opposite Brunnen. Below the top funicular station, on the short path which ends up at the Rütli meadow (see box p.358), you'll find an HI **hostel** (☎ & fax 041/820 17 84; ①; April–Oct), with simple dorms for Fr.21. Otherwise, Seelisberg has a handful of inexpensive **hotels**, including the comfortable, family-run *Montana* (☎041/820 12 68, fax 820 12 69; ①), and *Bellevue* (☎041/820 16 26, fax 820 16 17; ③), a rather plusher option with lake views. You can **camp** south of the village on the Seeli lakelet (☎041/820 35 96; May–Sept), or west of Beckenried near Buochs (☎041/620 34 74; April–Oct).

Engelberg

Situated at the southern end of the valley road and rail line from Stans in an enclave of Canton Obwalden, the modest ski resort of **ENGELBERG** boasts an excursion to the highest point in central Switzerland – a station at 3028m, just below the distinctive crest-of-a-wave summit of the **Titlis** mountain (3239m). This, along with the village's huge Benedictine **Kloster** (monastery) and the faded grandeur of its hotel architecture, make Engelberg well worth a visit.

Arrival, orientation and information

After a picturesque valley-floor ride, the Luzern–Stans–Engelberg (LSE) train pulls into the **station** in the middle of the village. Turn left on Bahnhofstrasse, and right onto the

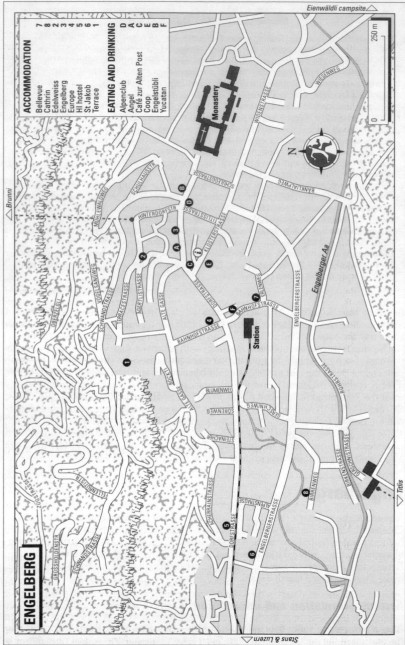

ENGELBERG

ACCOMMODATION

Bellevue	7
Cathrin	8
Edelweiss	2
Engelberg	3
Europe	4
HI hostel	5
St Jakob	6
Terrace	1

EATING AND DRINKING

Alpenclub	D
Angel	A
Café zur Alten Post	C
Coop	E
Engelstübli	B
Yucatan	F

Eienwäldli campsite

Monastery

Station

Brunni

Stans & Luzern

Titlis

main central Dorfstrasse for the **tourist office**, in a sports complex at Klosterstrasse 3 (mid-June to mid-Oct & mid-Dec to Easter Mon–Sat 8am–6.30pm, Sun 4–7pm; rest of year Mon–Fri 8am–noon & 2–6.30pm, Sat 8am–6.30pm; ☎041/637 37 37, *www.engelberg.ch*). Some 200m east of the tourist office rise the onion domes of the monastery, while the base station for the Titlis is 500m southwest of the station, well signposted on the south bank of the Engelberger-Aa stream. The **guest card** gives discounts on winter lift passes, which are otherwise Fr.48/55 per day (weekday/weekend), or Fr.123 for three days. Village ski buses are free. Plenty of places rent ski equipment all over the village, and most also have **mountain bikes** during the summer (also available to rent from the train station). Adventure Engelberg in the sports complex (☎041/637 20 30, *www.adventure-engelberg.ch*) organize extreme sports such as bungee jumping, abseiling and canyoning, mostly under the auspices of Stans-based Outventure (see p.345).

Accommodation

The five-star *Eienwäldli* **campsite** (☎041/637 19 49, fax 637 44 23; closed Nov) is on the southeastern edge of the village, about half-an-hour's walk from the centre. Otherwise, there's an HI **hostel** 500m west of the station, at Dorfstrasse 80 (☎041/637 12 92, fax 637 49 88; ①; June to mid-Oct & Dec to mid-April), with dorms from Fr.26 and excellent meals.

There are plenty of **hotels** big and small dotted throughout the centre and the surrounding slopes. All of them offer discounts for stays beyond three nights, and all have a winter high season.

Bellevue, Bahnhofplatz (☎041/637 12 13, fax 637 44 49). A grand lobby preludes characterful old-style rooms that are excellent value – most are en suite, and all have high ceilings and an air of faded grandeur. Many rooms are let to students during term time. ②.

Cathrin, Birrenweg (☎041/637 44 66, fax 637 43 28). Pleasant, quiet place near the Titlis cable-car, away from the bustle. ②–③.

Edelweiss, Terracestrasse (☎041/637 07 37, fax 637 39 00). Charming Art Nouveau hotel above the village, dating from 1901 and now in the hands of uniquely friendly and welcoming English-speaking owner/managers. Stylish, spotless rooms, and broad valley views bring it head and shoulders above its competitors. ④.

Engelberg, Dorfstrasse (☎041/637 11 68, fax 637 32 35). Comfortable place on the pedestrianized main street, with warm and cosy rooms. ③.

Europe, Dorfstrasse (☎041/637 00 94, fax 637 22 55). Grandiose village-centre pile dating from 1902, with some of the bright, attractive rooms boasting wrought-iron balconies, chandeliers and fittings from an age of tourism long past. ③.

St Jakob, Engelbergerstrasse (☎041/637 13 88). Small, simple family pension on the road west of the centre, also with dorms from Fr.36. ①.

Terrace, Terracestrasse (☎041/639 66 66, fax 639 66 99). Huge presence looming above the village, built in 1906 and newly renovated throughout, with a glorious sun terrace and comfortable rooms, accessible either by car or by its own tiny funicular. ③–④.

In and around the village

The major draw of the village is the huge Benedictine **monastery**. The first monks arrived in the valley around 1120, and during the Middle Ages, the monastery was central to the expansion of ascetic mysticism in Germany and Switzerland. The last of three major fires throughout the monastery's history, on August 29, 1729, razed the entire complex to the ground, with the buildings as they stand today dating from a subsequent rebuilding. Up until 1798, when French troops arrived in force, the monastery ruled the whole valley, which was independent of the Swiss Confederation and answered only to the Pope. The Revolution changed all that, and the monastery first joined Nidwalden in 1803, then changed its mind and switched to Obwalden twelve years later. These days, the sixty or so monks – over half of whom are priests – teach secondary school and further education courses, and have founded two affiliated monasteries in Missouri and Oregon. The Rococo **church**, dating from 1730, is stunning – a vast, elegant, light space complete with nine altars. A riot of ornamental stucco leads you through what would otherwise be an austere interior to the dramatic high altar, framing a luminescent painting of the Assumption. Guided **tours** of the whole complex, including the church and several impressive halls within the monastery, run year-round (Tues–Sat 10am & 4pm; Fr.2.50).

Above Engelberg

The monastery aside, Engelberg's attractions are all in the hills. The main excursion, well worthwhile if the weather's clear, is the four-stage journey to the **Titlis** (*www.titlis.ch*). The first ascent crests a plateau to **Gerschnialp**, from where walking routes depart on both sides around back to the village and another lift brings you to the ridge above the small picturesque **Trübsee**. From the Trübsee station, you can detour on an easy stroll around the lake to the base station of a different cable-car serving the **Jochpass** and **Engstlen**, a little-frequented corner – except in winter, when the whole lake area and slopes above hold the main cross-country and downhill skiing pistes (mostly red). Back at Trübsee, a gondola rises on a breathtakingly exposed journey over the lake to **Stand**, perched way above the valley at 2428m, with its own sun terrace and restaurant. From here, you switch onto the Rotair, the world's first revolving gondola; the broad cabin begins to rotate shortly after starting the ascent, and on the five-minute journey to the top station turns completely round once, giving you a 360° panorama of the ride over the vast and impressive Titlis Glacier. On top, you'll find the standard circus of souvenir shops, ice grottos and the highest karaoke bar in Europe, but the views beyond the Bernese Alps to the Pennine Alps of Valais and north as far as the Jura, more than compensate. The hike up to the very crest of the ice-bound Titlis itself takes a painstaking 45 minutes.

The full return **fare** Engelberg–Titlis is Fr.73, but as usual, walking some sections – notably from the Trübsee back down to the village (2hr) – can save plenty. The regional Tellpass brings a 50 percent discount, while Swiss Pass holders get 25 percent off. InterRailers and Eurailers get a 20 percent discount between May and mid-November only.

On the other side of the valley, a cable-car rises in two stages to **Brunni**, with a cat's cradle of idyllic walks along the hillside meadows and down through forests to the village. In winter, a handful of blue ski runs swish you down easily to the valley floor.

Eating and drinking

The *Coop* supermarket opposite the tourist office on Klosterstrasse has a budget self-service **restaurant** attached. Otherwise, there are plenty of places to fuel up along Dorfstrasse and through the centre. The *Engelstübli* has *saté* and other Indonesian specialities for around Fr.20, while across the road, the *Alpenclub* shelters several different eating places, including an inexpensive pizzeria, a *Käsestube* for fondue and the like, and a more formal restaurant with Swiss dishes for Fr.25 and up. Further east along Dorfstrasse, the *Café zur Alten Post* has basic stomach-filling *menus* for around Fr.15. Centre of the late-night après-ski scene is the *Yucatan* **bar**, which also offers good, filling evening meals for around Fr.18 or so. The English-style *Angel* pub on Dorfstrasse is another lively watering hole.

Routes to the Rigi

The titanic chunk of the **Rigi** (*www.rigi.ch*), which rises to 1798m plum between the lakes of Luzern and Zug, has long been famous as a majestic viewpoint. By itself, it's actually rather scrubby, a steep-scarped grassy ridge with several summits, but it stands alone dividing the two lakes, and offers wonderful views south to the Alps.

There are several transport options up the mountain, testifying to the scramble in the late nineteenth century to capitalize on burgeoning tourism to Luzern. Rival companies started laying track from **Vitznau** on Lake Luzern, and Arth-Goldau just south of the Zugersee, competing for who would be first to reach the summit. The Vitznau line – with the bonus of its accessibility from Luzern by boat – won out, but Arth-Goldau benefits from being a major junction point on the Zürich–Gotthard mainline train route. Tracks from both Vitznau and Goldau converge at Staffel near the summit for the final pull to **Rigi-Kulm** at the very top. A third route up the mountain, a cable-car from picturesque **Weggis**, also on Lake Luzern, rises to connect with the Vitznau trains at an intermediate stop named Rigi-Kaltbad. The popular method is to go up by one route and down by another, and the Swiss Pass, Eurail and InterRail all bring you a 25 percent discount. It's easy to make the Rigi a day trip from Luzern; or you could just as easily spend a night on the summit to enjoy the highly celebrated sunrise over the Alps. If you're set on hiking to the summit, reckon on four hours for the trek up from Weggis.

Weggis

On a sheltered, south-facing bay, protected from cold northerly weather by the Rigi itself, **WEGGIS** basks in its own subtropical microclimate – the palm trees, figs and magnolias grow naturally. It looks out over the lake and across to the Bürgenstock cliffs, and has been a popular summer resort for a couple of centuries, with a dedicated older clientele returning year after year to soak up the sun.

The **tourist office** for Weggis, the Rigi region and the whole north shore of the lake (taking in Brunnen and Schwyz as well) is right beside the boat station, at Seestrasse 5 (May–Sept Mon–Fri 8am–6pm, Sat & Sun 9am–2.30pm; Oct–April Mon–Fri 8am–5pm; ☎041/390 11 55, *www.weggis.ch*). There's no shortage of **accommodation**. Least pricey is the *Budget Hotel*, a plain, spartan place with en-suite and shared-bath rooms in a residential district a stiff walk uphill and west from the boat station (☎041/390 11 31, fax 390 14 80; ①); the eyesore of the *Victoria*, with shared-bath rooms over the promenade, is easier to reach (☎041/390 11 28, fax 390 01 09; ①). A couple of minutes east of the landing stage is the *Seehof Hotel du Lac* (☎041/390 11 51, fax 390 11 19; ②–③; mid-Jan to Oct), a charming, quiet family-run place of some quality – it's worth splashing out for the lakeview rooms with balcony. Just beside it is the classy *Beau-Rivage* (☎041/392 79 00, fax 390 19 81; ④–⑤; April–Oct), with plenty of creature comforts in the rooms and an enclosed lakeside lawn for sunny lounging. The cable-car station for Rigi-Kaltbad is northeast of the landing stage, well signposted.

Vitznau

A couple of hours' stroll east from Weggis is the small village of **VITZNAU**, base station for Europe's oldest rack railway (inaugurated in 1871) running up to the Rigi-Kulm. Whereas Weggis can seem a trifle twee or over pretty, tranquil Vitznau – set in a sheltered west-facing bay close to the narrowest strait of the lake – has plenty of character, despite the hordes of day-trippers in the village centre. The train station for the Rigi is right opposite the boat station, with the **tourist office** beside it (Mon–Fri 8am–noon & 1–6.30pm, Sat 9am–noon; ☎041/398 00 35, *www.vitznau.ch*). The best-value **accommodation** is the *Schiff*, 300m west of the centre in a quiet location (☎041/397 13 57, fax 397 24 98; ①; closed Nov), with six plain, old-style rooms above the most pleasant of lakeside restaurants. A few hundred metres beyond is Vitznau's landmark *Park Hotel* (☎041/399 60 60, fax 399 60 70; ⑧–⑨), a palatial Belle Epoque vision, with vast rooms, two gourmet restaurants, sauna, tennis courts and more. In the village itself, the *Rigi* (☎041/397 21 21, fax 397 18 25; ②–③) is an attractive shuttered old house with renovated rooms.

Less than two hours' walk east from Vitznau is tiny **GERSAU**, a patch of sloping meadow that was, from 1390 until the French invasion of 1798, the smallest independent free republic in Europe, with all of two thousand inhabitants. Midway between Gersau and Vitznau there's a handy HI **hostel** at Rotschuo (☎041/828 12 77, fax 828 12 63; ①; closed Dec–Feb). Hourly buses connect Weggis, Vitznau and Gersau, while different buses run from Gersau on to Brunnen and Schwyz.

The Rigi

There are hiking routes all over the Rigi, most starting from **Rigi-Kaltbad** or **Rigi-Klösterli**, the first accessible from both Weggis and Vitznau, the second a midway stop, barely a hamlet, on the Arth-Goldau train. Kaltbad is a peaceful traffic-free resort on a terrace of pastureland high above Weggis; there's a handful of hotels here, as well as relatively easy two- or three-hour hiking routes through the pine trees out to the Känzeli viewpoint, up onto the ridge at First, or to the Rotstock peak above Kaltbad (1659m). The Vitznau and Arth-Goldau train lines meet at Staffel for the final stretch to **Rigi-Kulm**, home of the *Hotel Rigi-Kulm* (☎041/855 03 03, fax 855 00 55, *www.forum.ch/rigi-kulm*; ③; closed Oct & Nov), a bald 1950s creation replacing earlier incarnations dating back more than a hundred years. It's a rather dull place in itself, but has the incomparable selling point of offering a highly memorable sunrise over the Alps. The summit is a 200m stroll from the hotel, and gives bird's-eye views over Luzern and the Vierwaldstättersee on one side, and Zug and the Zugersee on the other.

Zug

The town of **ZUG** (pronounced *tsoogk*), 22km from Luzern on the north side of the Rigi, is the richest place in Switzerland, which makes it very rich indeed. Tiny Canton Zug has the lowest tax rates in the country – about half the national average – which attracts flocks of multinational corporations, which in turn pushes average *per capita* net income up to an incredible Fr.70,000 (£30,500) a year. Zug's modern, business-driven existence proceeds without pomp amidst the glittering offices and malls of the new town, a world away from the picturesque medieval churches and cobbled waterfront lanes of the compact Old Town adjacent. Over the centuries, Zug's Old Town has regularly suffered from landslides which have deposited buildings and people into the lake, most recently in 1887; today, with the addition of modern retaining lake walls, the danger has receded.

The town's location on the crystal-blue Zugersee is very attractive, framed by the high wooded plateau of the Zugerberg rising 600m to the east and the peak of the Rigi (see above) on its southwest shores.

Arrival, information and lake transport

The town is clustered around the northeast corner of the small Zugersee, with the station about 400m north of the lakeshore, and the same amount again north of the Old Town, which ranges down the eastern shore of the lake. Zug is a rail junction, situated at the point where a line from Luzern in the west meets the main north–south route running from Zürich through Flüelen and the Gotthard Tunnel to Ticino. By **road**, Zug is on the A4 between Luzern and Zürich, and is easily accessible from the Gotthard routes, detouring via Schwyz. **Parking** is not a problem in the modern part of town around the station, but it's tricky and expensive trying to park in or near the Old Town.

The station has all the usual services, including a change office (daily 7am–8.30pm) and bike rental (daily 7am–7.30pm). You emerge from the station at a little roundabout at the head of Alpenstrasse, leading down (south) to the lake. Less than 50m away on the left is the **tourist office** (Mon–Fri 8.30am–6pm, Sat 8.30am–3pm; hours slightly truncated in winter; ☎041/711 00 78, *www.zug.ch*), from where you can get a free city map and plenty of guidance. Zug's main **post office** is on Postplatz, and inside the Zuger Kantonalbank on Postplatz are three terminals giving **Internet access** free for fifteen minutes (Mon–Fri 9am–5pm).

Lake transport

Boats ply the Zugersee from top to bottom. Departures for a two- or three-hour tour around the lake leave from the Bahnhofsteg, at the foot of Alpenstrasse (mid-April to May Sun only; June–Sept daily; Oct Sat & Sun only). Note that some of the summer Sunday boats are short one-hour round trips. Contact Zugersee Schifffahrt, Alpenstrasse 14 (☎041/726 24 24, *www.zugersee-info.ch*), for more, and also for details of their numerous eat-aboard trips – everything from winter brunches to Glenn Miller-accompanied starlit dinners.

Accommodation

Zug's hoteliers – like most business people in the city – fairly glow with financial health: the combination of Zug's high business profile, its proximity to both Luzern and Zürich, and its chronic shortage of **accommodation** means that they can overcharge and still be rewarded with enviously high occupancy rates. Booking ahead is vital.

The nearest **campsite** is 2km west of town on the lakeshore at Chamer Fussweg 36 (☎041/741 84 22) – take bus #4 from Bundesplatz to Brüggli (direction Hünenberg). An HI **hostel** is at Allmendstrasse 8 (☎041/711 53 54, fax 710 51 21; ①; closed mid-Jan to mid-March); walk west along the lakefront Chamerstrasse, follow Allmendstrasse north under a railway bridge, and the hostel is to the right behind a petrol station. Dorm beds are Fr.27.

Of the **hotels**, best value in the Old Town was formerly *Hotel Löwen*, a stone's throw from the water on Landsgemeindeplatz (☎041/711 77 22, fax 711 67 41), closed for renovation work at the time of writing but likely to remain in the ③ category after reopening in 2000.

Central, Grabenstrasse 9 (☎041/710 39 60, fax 711 21 65). Pleasant family hotel on the main road just above the Old Town, with smallish but comfortable rooms. ③.

Guggital, Zugerbergstrasse 46 (☎041/711 28 21, fax 710 14 43). Up on the slopes overlooking the town from the south and – for the views and the service – the best mid-range choice. All rooms are modern and renovated, and virtually all face the lake for gorgeous sunsets (pay more for a balcony). Bus #11 from Metalli (cross under the station, and wait outside the Zuger Kantonalbank) stops outside. ③–④.

Ochsen, Kolinplatz 11 (☎041/729 32 32, fax 729 32 22). A sixteenth-century gabled exterior and plush reception belie the rooms, which are less characterful than you might expect for a house venerable enough to have once hosted Goethe – the best are high up at the back overlooking rooftops and an internal courtyard. Weekdays you can barely move for suits. ⑤.

Pension Bahnhof, Alpenstrasse 6 (☎041/711 00 89, fax 710 85 27). Zug's cheapest rooms (without shower), though shabby and not particularly welcoming. Reception open Mon–Fri 8.30–11.30am & 5–7pm. ①.

The Town

Alpenstrasse leads from the station past Bundesplatz straight down to the lakeshore jetty from where boats depart all around the Zugersee. Views of the Rigi and, to the west, the Pilatus and Bernese Alps are terrific. Vorstadt follows the eastern lakeshore to **Postplatz**, on the the edge of Zug's tiny Old Town.

From Postplatz, Neugasse, lined with shops, leads south to **Kolinplatz** and the striped-roof **Zytturm**, at 52m the Old Town's tallest building but these days tucked into a corner beside a busy traffic road and largely forgotten. Built in the mid-thirteenth century as a watchtower, it was renovated to its present shape in 1557, and endowed with a clock in 1574. The shields below the clock face are those of the eight Swiss cantons at the time of the tower's construction (from left to right, Zürich, Bern, Luzern, Uri, Schwyz, Unterwalden, Glarus and Zug). As well as the astronomical clock, there's a host of tiny details on the tower, including, under the archway, a beautiful late-Gothic wavy-haired angel. Just above the upper ledge, you'll spot a painting of a rat with an interesting history (see box below).

Opposite the Zytturm, Kolinplatz features a fountain dedicated to Wolfgang Kolin, standard-bearer of the Swiss army at their 1422 defeat by the Duke of Milan. Heading beneath the Zytturm brings you into the most atmospheric part of the Old Town, cobbled lanes lined with medieval gabled and balconied (and often frescoed) houses. Just behind the Zytturm is Zug's **Rathaus**, dating from 1509 and retaining much of its original woodwork, and a few steps north is the waterside **Landsgemeindeplatz**. From the Rathaus, Unteraltstadt and Oberaltstadt both lead south to the tiny **Liebfrauenkapelle**, dating from 1266 but boasting a marvellous Baroque interior.

If you follow the alleys uphill from the chapel, and cross the main Grabenstrasse, you'll spot St Oswaldsgasse leading left to the **Kirche St Oswald**, built between 1478 and 1545 and dedicated to St Oswald of Northumbria (605–642). Inside you'll find another lavish Baroque interior and a nineteenth-century mural above the choir of Christ poised above several romantically depicted scenes from the Bible. As you leave, look above the double portal to see a beautiful carved statue of Mary flanked by St Oswald and St Michael. It's a short walk from here up Kirchenstrasse to the **Burg**, a circular, top-heavy construction that was once the headquarters of the Kyburg and Habsburg governors, and now houses the town's **museum** (Tues–Fri 2–5pm, Sat & Sun 10am–noon & 2–5pm; Fr.5, free on Sun; SMP), worth a look for its historical and archeological bits and bobs and for its model of medieval Zug. A few metres further up the hill is the **Kunsthaus**, with usually very good temporary art exhibitions. If you head along Dorfstrasse, and across the main Ägeristrasse, you'll spot a set of quiet, concealed steps leading up to the **chapel** of a Capuchin convent (1597), with an adjacent, well-tended walled cemetery. Tranquil covered steps bring you down to opposite the old **mint**, with Postplatz to the right.

Eating and drinking

The best concentration of places to **eat and drink** is in and around Landsgemeindeplatz – on sunny days, cafés and restaurants lay tables out on the waterfront square, but there's also plenty of choice in the alleys all around. The lakefront road Vorstadt is shoulder to shoulder with restaurants, most offering fish of one kind or another. Best low-budget dining is in the *Coop* restaurant in the mall on Bundesplatz.

THE TALE OF A RAT

An apocryphal story tells of how the Zytturm – once the town's watchtower – came to acquire a painting of a **rat**. Watchmen holed up in the tower night after night used to complain of the fat, long-tailed rats that scampered around them and stole their food. No way was found to keep the rats away, until a foreign scholar, passing through Zug on his way to Salerno, heard of the problem and advised the watchmen to paint a big, fat rat on the wall where the creatures got into the watchrooms. They did so, and the following night, when the rats appeared again, the watchmen saw them catch sight of the painting, sniff around it, and flee in fear. The painting stayed, and rats have never plagued the Zytturm again.

> ### CHERRY PIE . . . BUT NOT AS WE KNOW IT
>
> Zug is famous around Switzerland for its cherries, which give rise both to many varieties of local **Kirsch** (cherry brandy) and to **Zuger Kirschtorte**, a delectably buttery almond tart saturated with Kirsch that breathes cherry fumes but, oddly, has not a single fruit adorning it. *Kirschtorte* is on offer all over town – the best is made fresh daily at Konditorei Meier, Alpenstrasse 16. Aside from coffee and a slice, they can box up a whole *Torte* for you to take away in any of six sizes (Fr.19–47).

Balou, Kirchenstrasse 7. Hip little local bar away from the lake, open daily until late.

Chaotikum, Chamerstrasse 41. A shack beside the main road 1km west of town painted "CHAOS" where you can enjoy a good, solid meal for less than Fr.15, if you don't mind the rough-edged crowd, wafting cannabis smoke and loud jangly music. Cheap beer too. Closed Mon.

Fischmärt, Fischmarkt 15. Comfy Old Town bar with booths and a range of malt whiskies. Closed Sun.

Hecht, Fischmarkt 2 (☎041/729 81 30, *www.hecht.ch*). *The* place for fish – an elegant, historic lakefront building featuring refined lake-fresh cuisine at Fr.60 and up. Closed Wed & Thurs.

Rathauskeller, Oberaltstadt 1 (☎041/711 00 58). Top restaurant in the canton, housed in the historic Rathaus. Upstairs is the highest of *haute cuisine*, with a six-course evening *menu* currently Fr.146, but the ground-floor bistro serves simpler, more affordable dishes from the same kitchen. Closed Sun & Mon.

Schiffbar, Graben 2. Two different bars with the same name: much preferable is the upstairs one (self-dubbed the *Panorama*), with an elevated terrace aiding peaceful contemplation of the lake below.

Speck, Alpenstrasse, corner Gotthardstrasse. Simple *menus* in the pasta-and-salad vein are around Fr.13, plus good *Kirschtorte*. Closed Sun.

Syrtaki, Vorstadt 26 (☎041/711 40 41). Lakefront Greek restaurant with *moussaka* (Fr.22) and good fish options (Fr.30).

Widder, Landsgemeindeplatz 12 (☎041/711 03 16). Excellent Old Town choice, with hot meals all day and terrace seating in summer. Relaxed South African ownership not only means the staff speak English, but also adds ostrich and springbok steaks to the already full menu of Swiss specialities, quality pizzas and super-fresh lake fish.

Schwyzerland

Occupying the picturesque northeastern corner of the lake and extending north to the wild hills bordering the Zürichsee, unsung **Schwyzerland** takes in a series of broad, lush valleys enclosed between Alpine foothills and overlooked by the massive twin peaks of the Mythen. The gentle resort of **Brunnen** lies on the lake, while a short distance inland is the cantonal capital **Schwyz**, an old and graceful town with plenty of history. To the north, the ancient monastery church at **Einsiedeln** draws pilgrims from around the world to pay homage to the icon of the Black Madonna.

Brunnen

Of all the resort towns on the lake, **BRUNNEN** is perhaps most dramatically located, snug in a right-angled corner of the shore between the crests of the Rigi and the scarps of the Fronalpstock. Vistas from its jetty are stupendous, looking the length of the Urnersee south to the snowy peaks around the Gotthard; directly across to the misty cliffs of Seelisberg, with the Uri-Rotstock and Titlis behind; and east the length of the Vierwaldstättersee to far-distant Luzern. Brunnen basks at the head of a wind tunnel which draws the warm Föhn wind north from the Mediterranean, frequently turning

THE RÜTLI MEADOW

On the western shore of the Urnersee, and visible from Brunnen, is a flapping Swiss flag planted in the **Rütli meadow**, a sloping patch of grass above the shoreline that holds unique, almost mystical, significance for the Swiss. Legend and national pride says that it was here on August 1, 1291, that representatives from the three forest cantons around the lake – Uri, Schwyz and Nidwalden – met amidst continuing Habsburg repression to sign a pact of eternal mutual defence, thereby laying the foundation of the Swiss Confederation as it stands today. Nowadays, 1291 is taken as the birthdate of the nation, and August 1 is the official Swiss national holiday. Rütli gained contemporary significance when on July 25, 1940, under threat of a Nazi invasion, the Swiss commander in chief, General Guisan, conducted a ceremony at this most resonant spot at which the entire Swiss officer corps – several hundred men – reaffirmed their allegiance to the Confederation and to Swiss neutrality (see p.521).

And yet, despite the proud flag which stands on the meadow today, and the crowds of parents who bring their children here to tell them the story of William Tell (see box pp.364–5) and the birth of Switzerland, many historians doubt that anything very much happened at Rütli at all. Some pour scorn on the idea that such an obviously important document in formal Latin – now on display in a Schwyz museum – would have been written and signed in a meadow (although this is countered by the signing of England's Magna Carta at Runnymede meadow in 1215), and claim that the three representatives met at Rütli on November 7, 1307, simply in order to renew their formal written pledge of 16 years before. Other historians, yet more controversially, suggest that the Swiss Confederation developed organically, and that there was either no movement of resistance against the Habsburgs in 1291 at all, or that the Rütli oath was merely one in an array of other equally "eternal" or "perpetual" alliances between valley communities that came and went over the centuries. Nothing is certain, but most ordinary people have little truck with such trifling details anyway: over the years the story has come to represent much more than its bare facts might suggest. The **Charter of Confederation**, as the document came to be known, has become as potently symbolic for the Swiss as the Declaration of Independence is for Americans, and the Rütli itself has become a place of nationalistic pilgrimage, focus of the country's national celebrations every August.

the Urnersee choppy and stormy – rapidly fluctuating weather conditions mean that it's not unknown to look south to glorious sunshine on the high Alps and east to pelting rain over Luzern. Mad King Ludwig of Bavaria took a real shine to Brunnen in 1865 during a stay, and would reputedly order his boatmen to row him out at midnight into the middle of the glassy lake with a team of alphorn-blowers, to then spend the small hours revelling in the mournful, ethereal sound of the alphorn echoing beneath the silhouetted mountains all around.

The easiest excursion from Brunnen is to the **Urmiberg** peak nearby (1140m; *www.marktkreisel.ch/urmiberg*) – this is one not to be missed, with stunning views both on the way up in the tiny cable-car and from the summit itself. Hiking trails from the top include a steep path back down to Brunnen (an hour and a half; a gentler descent adds an hour), and other trails down to Gersau or Goldau (both three hours). There's a summit restaurant, and also the opportunity (for Fr.150) to leap off into space on a tandem paragliding flight, courtesy of the Brunnen-based adventure operator Touch And Go, Parkstrasse 14 (☎041/820 54 31, *www.paragliding.ch*).

Practicalities

Brunnen's **train station** is set back from the lakeshore jetty, about ten minutes' walk inland on the main Bahnhofstrasse – you should allow plenty of time if you're switching from a boat to a train, or vice versa. Before you get to the station, you'll pass the

tourist office, 150m from the jetty at Bahnhofstrasse 32 (Mon–Fri 8.30am–noon & 1.30–6pm; April–Sept also Sat 9am–noon; ☎041/825 00 40) – they can help you out with information for the whole area, including Schwyz (which only has a tiny information counter).

There are plenty of places to **stay**. Two **campsites** are on the western side of the Muota river, near the Urmiberg cable-car: *Hopfreben* (☎041/820 18 73) and *Urmiberg* (☎041/820 33 27). The best value of the lakeview **hotels** is *Bellevue* (☎041/820 13 18, fax 820 38 89; ③), with stylishly modern rooms behind their ornate wrought-iron balconies. On the main street in the village is the charming seventeenth-century *Weisses Rössli* (☎041/820 10 22, fax 820 11 22; ②–③), Ludwig's old haunt, with comfortably traditional rooms, an excellent **restaurant** – with quality Swiss cuisine for Fr.25 or so – and a truly splendid Royal Chamber decked out in the Bavarian colours of white and blue with plenty of gold trim. On a quiet road beside the stream is the *Gotthard* (☎041/825 40 60, fax 825 40 61; ②), a simple place set in its own gardens, while the *National* is an old roadhouse close to the station (☎041/820 18 78; ①), with a choice of spartan en-suite and shared-bath rooms. The *Brunnerhof* on Kapellplatz in the centre, as well as offering some rooms, has stomach-filling *menus* for under Fr.20; both it and the *Park* restaurant further back inland offer veggie dishes. There's a handful of lively **café-bars** in the village, including the popular *Dodo* on Bahnhofstrasse, and *Mezcalito* on the lakefront Axenstrasse, with a page of different cocktails and pricey food at Fr.30 and up.

Schwyz

A small but characterful town 5km northeast of Brunnen, **SCHWYZ** (pronounced *shveets*) is capital of its canton. First mentioned in a document dated August 14, 972, Schwyz was associated culturally and militarily with its neighbours Uri and Nidwalden from as early as 1144. After the combined confederate forces won a famous victory against the Habsburgs at nearby Morgarten in 1315, they all became collectively dubbed "Schwyzers" and the land of Helvetia became known instead as Schweiz, or Switzerland. The men of Schwyz were sought after as particularly accomplished mercenaries throughout the Middle Ages and after, and many were able to return to their home town with fat wallets to build for themselves the fine townhouses which characterize the old centre today.

The Town

Schwyz is best known for being the repository of the ancient documents embodying the history of the Confederation, on display in the **Bundesbriefarchiv**, Bahnhofstrasse 20 in the town centre (Museum of Federal Charters; May–Oct Tues–Fri 9–11.30am & 1.30–5pm, Sat & Sun 9am–5pm; Nov–April Tues–Fri 9–11.30am & 1.30–5pm, Sat & Sun 1.30–5pm; Fr.4; SMP). This small, beautifully simple 1936 building, with a garden and a cloister of attractive arches, houses a wealth of banners, flags, coins and venerable parchments recording events in Swiss history – ask for the excellent English notes at the desk. The main treasure is upstairs, in a great hall lined with huge flags and banners taken from various battlefields over the centuries. At the far end, lying alone in its own display case, is a small rectangular piece of parchment covered in close lines of text. This is the original **Charter of Confederation**, reputedly signed and sealed on the Rütli meadow on August 1, 1291; the wax seals of Uri and Nidwalden still dangle from it, but the seal of Schwyz was lost long ago.

The historical theme is continued in the inventive **Forum of Swiss History**, a branch of the Swiss National Museum, in the town centre beside the bus station (Tues–Sun 10am–5pm; Fr.5; SMP). The ground floor is devoted to investigations of how people in both the countryside and the city used environmental resources throughout history; the

---

CUTTING A DASH

In 1884, an impoverished young Swiss, Carl Elsener, believed he had spotted a gap in the market for dependable pocket knives, and founded the Swiss Cutlers' Association in order to supply knives and blades to the army. But times were hard: by 1893 his venture had collapsed, and a German competitor had started making knives more cheaply. His colleagues departed, leaving him to be bailed out by his family. Elsener persevered, making lighter and more elegant version of his knives, which he patented in 1897. By word of mouth, the knives grew in popularity, and even without an official seal of approval, Swiss army officers began to ask for them specifically. Elsener had originally named his factory – located in Ibach, just south of Schwyz – after his mother Victoria, but when stainless steel was invented in 1921 and given the international designation INOX, Elsener combined the two into one. **Victorinox** knives gained official backing from the Swiss Army and, after World War II, from the US Army too. Today, in myriad varieties, they are the best-known brand of Swiss army knife in the world, and the only ones permitted to use the Swiss cross as their logo. Some 34,000 are still churned out every day by the same factory in Ibach, some ten minutes' walk south of Schwyz town centre at Schmiedgasse 57. Its on-site **shop** sells the complete range of knives at discount factory prices (Mon–Fri 7.30am–noon & 1.15–6pm, Sat 8am–3pm).

---

middle floor concentrates on social history, with assessments of power structures and relations between the church and the state; and the top floor concentrates on why and how Switzerland survived in the way that it did. Plenty of videos and interactive displays keep you interested throughout – some of the background details, like audio panels letting you hear eye-witness accounts of the great fires of Lausanne in 1219 and 1235, or the dramatization of a 1528 witch trial, are the most memorable of all.

The central Hauptplatz square is a few steps east of the museum, dominated by two great buildings, both rebuilt after a town fire in 1642: on a terrace above is the large **Parish Church of St Martin**, with an extraordinarily ornate interior; while the foursquare **Rathaus** sits on the square itself, its facade decorated with frescoes painted in 1891 to celebrate the 600th anniversary of the Rütli oath. Alleys to the northwest bring you to the **Ital-Reding Haus** (May–Oct Tues–Fri 2–5pm, Sat & Sun 10am–noon & 2–5pm; Fr.4; SMP), a splendid, early seventeenth-century manor house set in its own gardens and with a magnificent interior, its upper rooms bedecked with skilfully carved panelling on wall and ceiling. Across the garden – and within the same complex – is the ancient **Haus Bethlehem**, dating from 1287 and thus the oldest wooden house in the country. Squeezing through its minuscule rooms with their extra-low ceilings makes you feel a bit like Alice.

Practicalities

Schwyz is rather awkward both to get to and to stay in, and you'd probably do better spending the night in Brunnen down the road. Schwyz is a **bus**-oriented town, with the main central bus station ("Schwyz-Post") handling arrivals from Brunnen. The **train station** is in the suburb of Seewen, some 2km west of Schwyz centre – buses run from outside to Schwyz-Post. The **tourist office** is a counter within the central post office off Schmiedgasse, down the hill from Hauptplatz (Mon–Fri 7.30am–noon & 1.30–6.30pm, Sat 8–11am; ☎041/810 19 91).

Places to **stay** are limited to the *Hirschen*, Hinterdorfstrasse 14 (☎041/811 12 76, *h.elmiger.schwyz@swissonline.ch*; ①), a cosy old place with rooms both en suite and not; and the *Wysses Rössli*, Hauptplatz 3 (☎041/811 19 22, fax 811 10 46; ③), with large pleasant rooms and an excellent **restaurant**, especially strong on fish specialities (*menus* Fr.23). *Ratskeller*, Strehlgasse 3 (closed Sun & Mon), is another quality restaurant, with a less expensive bistro area to one side (*menus* Fr.18).

Einsiedeln

The small village of **EINSIEDELN**, in the hills of northern Schwyz 25km northeast of Brunnen, has been Switzerland's most important site of pilgrimage for a thousand years, and still draws a quarter of a million devout believers every year. The village itself is utterly unremarkable, but the mighty Benedictine **Kloster** (monastery) which dominates it is exceptional, and worth a detour whether you're drawn by faith or curiosity.

Some history

"Einsiedeln" means hermitage, and is named for **St Meginrat**, who withdrew to what was then wild forest in about 828 AD, where he lived and prayed, kept alive by food brought to him by two wild ravens. On January 21, 861, two bandits named Richard the Aleman and Peter the Rhaetian visited Meginrat with the intention of robbing him of the treasures they imagined he possessed; he received them with food and drink, only to be murdered in return. Meginrat's two ravens pursued the criminals to Zürich and flew above their heads, screaming, until the two confessed to their crime and were executed. Hermits continued to come to Meginrat's dark forest, and although his cell fell into ruin, the self-built altar at which he prayed was maintained, and a small **chapel** built around it. In 934, a provost of Strasbourg cathedral came to the forest, and persuaded the hermits living there to form a **Benedictine** community. He built a church on the site, and invited the Bishop of Konstanz to perform the consecration – the bishop was about to do so, when a voice was heard ringing through the church, insisting three times over that Christ himself had already consecrated the church. The Pope declared this to be a **miracle**, and issued a papal bull blessing the pilgrimage to Einsiedeln.

From then on, the monastery enjoyed special privilege, with large royal grants, positions of honour for the abbots, and protection afforded by the noble lords of the area. By 1286 a Chapel of Our Lady, built over the remains of St Meginrat's cell, was already a focal point. This originally held a Romanesque figure of Mary, but after a destructive fire in 1468, a different statuette of Mary with the infant Christ, carved in wood sometime before 1440, replaced it. It is this figure, blackened by smoke from the candles of centuries, which became the focus for pilgrimage, and which has retained its numinous power to this day as the Black Madonna.

The church

The monastery complex was entirely rebuilt from 1704 to 1726 in the most lavish of late-Baroque styles. As you emerge from the cluster of the village centre, the vast **Klosterplatz** opens out in front. The rather plain sandstone front of the church, with its twin towers rising from an immense 140m-long facade, is framed by unusual semi-circular sunken arcades. The ornate **Well of Our Lady** in the square taps the water of Meginrat's spring – pilgrims traditionally drink from each of the 14 spouts in turn on their approach to the church.

The **interior**, designed by Kaspar Moosbrugger, one of the monks, is immediately breathtaking, although with the regular cycle of services continuing daily you may not get a chance to wander round admiring it. The nave is decorated with gorgeously detailed **frescoes** by Cosmas Damian Asam, and every part of the lofty white interior is detailed in lavish gold. An intricate wrought-iron choir screen gives into the stunning pink Rococo **choir**, its ceiling bedecked with animated sculptures of angels. However, the focus of all the pilgrims' attention is the black marble **Chapel of Our Lady**, positioned in a huge octagonal bay just inside the main portal. The invading French destroyed the chapel in 1798 (although the monks had already removed the Black Madonna to the Tyrol for safekeeping), and the present chapel building dates from a Neoclassical reconstruction in 1817. The **Black Madonna** itself, a little over a metre tall and usually dressed in a jewelled and tasselled golden dress donated by Canton Uri in 1734, stands illuminated within at the centre of attention.

Practicalities

Trains run every hour from Luzern to Biberbrugg, where you have to change for the climb to Einsiedeln; hourly trains from Brunnen require an extra change at Arth-Goldau. Einsiedeln's **train station** is a ten-minute walk from the church: from Dorfplatz out front, head east along Hauptstrasse. The **tourist office** is just off Klosterplatz at Hauptstrasse 85 (Tues–Fri 10am–noon & 1.30–5pm, Sat & Sun 10am–4pm; ☎055/418 44 88). Almost every building in sight of the church is a **hotel**: *Sonne*, Hauptstrasse 82 (☎055/412 28 21, fax 412 41 45; ①), has basic, spartan rooms; *Storchen*, Hauptstrasse 79 (☎055/412 37 60, fax 412 61 04; ②), is a comfortable place with a good restaurant, while *Rot-Hut*, Hauptstrasse 80 (☎055/412 22 41, fax 412 71 37; ②), is smaller and not so characterful. There are plenty of places to **eat** – ranging from the simple *Pizzeria Zia Teresa*, Hauptstrasse 21 (closed Mon & Tues), up to the quality restaurants with their Fr.20-ish *menus* on and near Klosterplatz, including the *Katharinahof*, *Bären* and *St Georg*.

Every three years or so, the monastery stages a massed **open-air production** of the *Great World Theatre* – a religious drama by Pedro Calderón de la Barca premièred at the Spanish court in 1685. Some 600 villagers take part, coached by the monks themselves. The next production will take place from June 23 to September 9, 2000; for information and tickets (Fr.33–92), contact Welttheater Gesellschaft, Postfach 523, CH-8840 Einsiedeln (☎055/422 16 92). Einsiedeln is a fully functioning monastic community, with around a hundred priests and brothers. **Mass** is celebrated several times a day, most notably with Gregorian chanting at 7.30am and choral accompaniment for Vespers at 4pm. Of the many annual **pilgrimage festivals**, the most colourful is the Feast of the Miraculous Dedication on September 14, which culminates in a candlelit procession around the square.

Uri and the Alpine passes

The mountainous **Canton Uri** occupies the land between the lake and the barrier of the high Alps. Although Uri shares borders with Bern, Valais, Ticino, Graubünden and Glarus, it is cut off from them all by 2000m-plus mountain passes, and the only cantons with which it has easy exchange of influence are its old partners from the 1291 Rütli oath, Schwyz and Nidwalden. It's no coincidence that Uri is the setting for the medieval legend of **William Tell** (see box pp.364–5), absorbed into Swiss consciousness as near fact and serving to define the essence of Swissness to the rest of the world. The small cantonal capital **Altdorf** was where Tell did his apple shooting.

Uri also holds the keys to the great trans-Alpine **Gotthard** route, one of the main Alpine passes. For centuries, people and traffic have followed the ancient road up and over the mountains, although these days massively long tunnels draw trains and most of the cars swiftly to and from Ticino and Italy. **Andermatt**, on the south side of the Gotthard, is uniquely located at an Alpine crossroads, with six high-level routes passing through or near the town.

Flüelen and around

FLÜELEN is the farthest point of the lake from Luzern, a picturesque little place with the train station right beside the landing stage. This is the southern terminus of the **Axenstrasse**, the narrow road which clings below the cliffs of the eastern shore of the Urnersee south from Brunnen. The road was only completed in 1865, and enabled travellers to approach the Gotthard for the first time by land, instead of forcing them to take a ship from Luzern or Brunnen. Some 3km north of Flüelen – and accessible only by car, boat or walking (no buses use the Axenstrasse) – is the **Tellsplatte**, a flat rock onto which William Tell is purported to have leapt to escape the clutches of Gessler (see box overleaf). Beside it is a restaurant and, beautifully framed amidst the trees, the **Tellskapelle**, a tiny monument built in 1880 with arched loggia featuring vivid frescoes depicting the story of Tell. Boats serving this point from Brunnen also pass the **Schillerstein**, a 25m high natural obelisk near the Rütli which was inscribed in 1859: "To Friedrich Schiller, the Chronicler of Tell".

Buses from Flüelen station run into central **ALTDORF**, some 3km south (Altdorf's own train station is inconveniently located 1km west of the centre). The heart of Altdorf is the Rathausplatz, dominated by the impressive **Telldenkmal** (Tell Monument) – a much-photographed icon erected in 1895 and depicting a sturdy, bearded Tell raising his eyes fearlessly to the horizon, while his son, embodiment of the Swiss people themselves, accepts his father's protecting arm and gazes trustingly upwards at him. This square is reputedly the scene of the apple-shooting event commemorated in the legend. Alleys around and about have retained plenty of character, but if the Tell bug has bitten you, grab a bus bound for **BÜRGLEN**, a village 2km northeast on the Klausen road, which is celebrated as Tell's birthplace. The **chapel** which sits beside the village church on the site of Tell's house was dedicated as early as 1582, with interior frescoes depicting the legend dating from the 1750s. Around the corner from the 1786 Tell fountain out front is the **Tell Museum** (daily: July & Aug 9.30am–5.30pm; May, June, Sept & Oct 10–11.30am & 1.30–5pm; Fr.4; SMP), a worthwhile little place crammed with Tell curiosities; ask them to set up the informative and watchable twenty-minute slide-show (in English) on the history of the legend.

What's remarkable about the Altdorf area is the understatedness of its Tellmania – you get the feeling that Tell, although something of a caricature to non-Swiss, is far too important to the locals to start a whole tourist circus. Tellsplatte, Altdorf and Bürglen are all out-of-the-way places, little visited by foreigners, and you may well find that the only tourists who you come across are Swiss families, spending a weekend in the area to give the kids a glimpse of their heritage.

Practicalities

Uri is light on tourist information – the main **tourist office** is in the Gotthard motorway service area on the N2, 10km south of Flüelen, and Altdorf's little branch, just off the main square at Rathausplatz 7, has only a few bits and bobs (July & Aug Mon–Fri 9am–6pm, Sat 9–11.30am; Easter–June & Sept–Oct Mon–Fri 9.30–11.30am & 1.30–5.30pm, Sat 9.30–11.30am; Nov–Easter Mon–Fri 1.30–5pm; ☎041/872 04 50).

For accommodation in **Flüelen**, aim for the *Tell & Post* hotel, Axenstrasse 12 (☎041/874 11 30, fax 874 11 35; ②), with serviceable rooms, en suite and not; or the more elegant *Weisses Kreuz*, opposite the landing stage at Axenstrasse 2 (☎041/870 17 17, fax 870 17 75; ②). Trains from Flüelen serve both Luzern and Zürich (with alternate services requiring a change at Arth-Goldau), as well as heading south through the Gotthard to Ticino. Buses depart from Flüelen train station forecourt for Altdorf-Post or Altdorf-Telldenkmal and, in summer, due east over the Klausen Pass (1948m) into Canton Glarus.

The best-value hotel in **Altdorf** is the *Schwarzen Löwen*, Tellsgasse 8 (☎041/874 80 80, fax 874 80 70; ②), which has renovated rooms, all clean and pleasant (choose one off the street) – one room has retained the original furniture from when Goethe stopped by in the 1770s. Rathausplatz has plenty of terrace cafés and restaurants, as do the surrounding streets. Buses to Bürglen depart from the square, or from Altdorf-Post, 100m south on Bahnhofstrasse.

The most characterful accommodation choice of the lot, though, is the *Gasthaus Adler* in the centre of **Bürglen** (☎041/870 11 33, fax 870 71 55; ①), a fine old sixteenth-

THE LEGEND OF WILLIAM TELL

The legend of **William Tell** is the central defining myth in Swiss national consciousness. Most schoolchildren, whether in Switzerland or elsewhere in the West, know at least the bare bones of the story, but whereas in most cultures it is little more than one folktale among many, in Switzerland, it has come to embody the very essence of Swissness.

THE STORY

At a time soon after the opening of the Gotthard Pass, when the Habsburg emperors of Vienna sought to control Uri and thus control trans-Alpine trade, a new bailiff, **Hermann Gessler**, was despatched to Altdorf. The proud mountain folk of Uri had already joined with their Schwyzer and Nidwaldner neighbours at Rütli in pledging to resist the Austrians' cruel oppression, and when Gessler raised a pole in the central square of Altdorf and perched his hat on the top, commanding all who passed before it to bow in respect, it was the last straw. **William Tell**, a countryman from nearby Bürglen, either hadn't heard about Gessler's command or chose to ignore it; whichever, he walked past the hat without bowing. Gessler seized Tell, who was well known as a marksman, and set him a challenge. He ordered him to shoot an apple off his son's head with his crossbow; if Tell was successful, he would be released, but if he failed or refused, both he and his son would die.

The boy's hands were tied. Tell put one arrow in his quiver and another in his crossbow, took aim, and shot the apple clean off his son's head. Gessler was impressed and infuriated – and then asked what the second arrow was for. Tell looked the tyrant in the eye and replied that if the first arrow had struck the child, the second would have been for Gessler. For such impertinence, Tell was arrested and sentenced to lifelong imprisonment in the dungeons of Gessler's castle at Küssnacht, northeast of Luzern. During the long boat journey a violent storm arose on the lake, and the oarsmen – unfamiliar with the lake – begged with Gessler to release Tell so that he could steer them to safety. Gessler acceded, and Tell cannily manoeuvred the boat close to the shore, then leapt to freedom, landing on a flat rock (the **Tellsplatte**) and simultaneously pushing the boat back into the stormy waters.

Determined to see his task through and use the second arrow, Tell hurried to Küssnacht. As Gessler and his party walked along on a dark lane called Hohlegasse on their way to the castle, Tell leapt out, shot a bolt into the tyrant's heart and melted back into the woods to return to Uri. His comrades were inspired by Tell's act of bravery to throw off the yoke of Habsburg oppression in their homeland, and to remain forever free.

century roadhouse inn, with wooden eaves bedecked in ivy and a handful of alluringly creaky guest rooms above a *gutbürgerliche* restaurant.

Andermatt and around

If you're travelling south by train, you're likely to miss the small town of **ANDERMATT**, surrounded by the high Alps on all sides, since it lies beyond the entrance to the Gotthard Tunnel at Göschenen (see p.366). This once-great staging post for four major Alpine crossings is now even bypassed by the motorway, which plunges into its own tunnel, also at Göschenen. However, as the hub of many long-distance hiking routes, Andermatt still sees plenty of visitors in the short Alpine summer (June–Sept), and equal numbers in the winter skiing season, with red and black runs galore off the nearby **Gemsstock** summit (2963m), and an abundance of cross-country routes. The Gemsstock is also the best summer viewpoint in the area, since the town is too close to the valley sides to offer any panoramas of its own. Beware that Andermatt also serves as the Swiss Army's principal Alpine training centre – you may find an over-preponderance of military types around and about, and it's prudent to check with the

THE LEGEND

Walter Dettwiler, in his book *William Tell: Portrait of a Legend* (1991), outlines the impact of the Tell legend over the centuries. The basis of the story – a marksman forced by an overlord to shoot an object from the head of a loved one – first appears in **Scandinavian sagas** written centuries before the Swiss version was first committed to paper in the fifteenth century. It was an epic song, however, composed in 1477 about the founding of the Swiss Confederation and including a section on the story of Tell, which accounted for the widespread circulation of the legend. During the **French Revolution**, the popularity of William Tell rose to a peak: he was viewed as a freedom fighter in the noblest of traditions and the tale was held up as a justification for the killing of Louis XVI – all the more so because Tell and the French revolutionary armies shared a common enemy, the Austrian Habsburgs. In the 1770s and 1780s, the German poet Goethe had travelled extensively throughout Switzerland, later telling his friend, the playwright **Friedrich Schiller**, of his journeyings. Schiller's famous play *Wilhelm Tell* (1804) drew from Goethe's first-hand accounts as well as from ancient Swiss chronicles to set the Tell legend in stone, and over subsequent decades, to broadcast the story to a wide European public. **Rossini**'s opera *Guillaume Tell*, which premièred in Paris in 1829, did for the Romance-language countries of Europe what Schiller's play had done for the Teutonic.

With the final unification of Switzerland in 1848 after half-a-century of war, a mood of national liberation and communal purpose became crystallized around the enduring significance of William Tell, who began to be portrayed with increasing idealism, notably in the **Tell monument** in Altdorf, which was unveiled in 1895. **Ferdinand Hodler**, most famous of Swiss artists, drew directly on this monument for his seminal portrait of Tell as a godlike figure, emerging from a gap in the clouds with arm outstretched (see p.238). Throughout **World War II**, the image and notion of a deeply moral, fervently nationalistic Tell hardened the resolve of ordinary Swiss to resist domination by Nazi Germany, and contributed to Switzerland's self-imposed exclusion from the co-operative international organizations – specifically the United Nations and the European Union – which arose after 1945.

However, the **700th anniversary** of the Confederation, celebrated in 1991, brought dissenting voices to the fore for the first time, with revisionist historians searching for more pragmatic reasons for the survival of Swiss culture than the doings of a single male hero. The annual retelling of Schiller's drama on an open stage in touristic Interlaken (see p.253) to an audience increasingly made up of foreigners is, too, beginning to ring hollow, and as the millennium turns, popular perception has become increasingly cynical over the continuing appropriateness of William Tell as an icon for a 21st-century Switzerland.

tourist office that your chosen route is open to civilians before you set off on any long-distance hikes.

The high passes all round offer possibilities for spectacular round-trip **driving tours** – you can follow the route from Andermatt over the Gotthard, Nufenen and Furka passes by postbus twice a day in summer (see p.266); or it's equally possible to strike out with your own transport over the Susten, Grimsel and Furka passes, with an intermediate stop for lunch in Meiringen (see p.264). To the east, the Oberalp Pass leads on to Disentis/Mustér in Graubünden (see p.459).

Andermatt practicalities

Andermatt's train station is 400m north of the town centre; turn left outside for the **tourist office**, in the same building as the postbus booking centre (July–Sept & Dec–March Mon–Sat 9am–noon & 2–5.30pm; rest of year Mon–Fri same times; ☎041/887 14 54, *www.andermatt.ch*). Aside from *Lager Zgraggen* (☎041/887 16 58, fax 872 02 41, *wapimmo@tic.ch* – turn right from the station), with dorms from Fr.18, Andermatt's rather pricey **accommodation** is clustered around the picturesque main

Gotthardstrasse, which can get nastily crowded in summer: *Sonne*, at no. 76 (☎041/887 12 26, fax 887 06 26; ②), is a cosy old wooden place, while the *Drei Könige & Post*, at no. 69 (☎041/887 00 01, fax 887 16 66, *hotel@3koenige.ch*, *www.3koenige.ch*; ③), has modern, comfortable rooms. **Eating and drinking** is a hotel affair, with plenty of choice up and down the main street.

The Gotthard Pass and Tunnel

The most famous of all the Alpine passes, the **St Gotthard** or **San Gottardo** (2108m), is also the most memorable. The turbulent Schöllenen Gorge, a few kilometres north of Andermatt, was first bridged in the thirteenth century, allowing traffic to penetrate up the full length of the Reuss valley from Flüelen to the pass itself, from where a continuation road followed the valley of the River Ticino all the way south to Bellinzona and Milan. Today, three daily buses (July–Sept only) follow the new road from Andermatt up to the pass and on down to Airolo. The old cobbled road, which branches off partway up, is much quieter and more picturesque. Both meet on top, where you'll find a wild windswept spot with a handful of buildings clustered around a small lake that's become an unfortunately popular picnicking spot for day-tripping families. The pass is one of Europe's watersheds: rain or snowmelt on the north side ultimately ends up in the Rhine and the North Sea, while moisture on the south side flows into the Po and the Mediterranean.

The old **hospice** beside the road now houses the engaging **Museo Nazionale del San Gottardo** (May–Oct daily 9am–6pm; Fr.8; SMP), which outlines the history of the pass with models, reliefs, paintings and audiovisual slide-shows. Across the road, there are simple modern rooms available at the often-busy *Albergo San Gottardo* (☎091/869 12 35, fax 869 18 11, *hotel@gotthard-hospiz.ch*, *www.gotthard-hospiz.ch*; ②; May–Oct). From the pass, most traffic follows the new road down to Airolo, but the old cobbled road that snakes down behind the *albergo* off the back of the pass into Ticino is truly spectacular, with terrific vistas all the way down into the Val Tremolo ("Valley of Trembling"). If you're **hiking**, it's a three-hour walk to Airolo this way, or six hours by an off-road route through Val Canaria; on the north side, Andermatt is three hours away via the small village of Hospental, or six by a more scenic route through the deserted valleys around Maighels.

Foot traffic had used the pass since about 1200, and the first carriage crossed in 1775. Less than a century later in 1872, after decades of debate over routes and costs, work began on a **rail tunnel** beneath the pass. Over seven years and 277 lives later, the bores which had begun simultaneously from Göschenen and Airolo met midway on February 29, 1880. The first trains ran through the 15km-long tunnel in 1882. This line is still a vital north–south artery, carrying at peak times an average of one train every six minutes – with five million passengers and 25 million tonnes of freight carried to and fro each year. The Gotthard journey is one of Switzerland's great train rides, not so much for the long stretch of blackness as you swoosh beneath the Alps, but for the spectacular approach. South of Flüelen, you climb slowly and dramatically up the wild valley, passing through dozens of straight tunnels and, around **Wassen**, a series of tightly spiralled tunnels, which gain maximum altitude at minimum gradients. Wassen's little onion-domed church, prominent on its rock, is a famous landmark: you'll pass it three times, first high above you, then on a level, and finally far below you before you're plunged into darkness shortly afterwards at **Göschenen**. Trains emerge at Airolo (see p.493) for the long journey down to Bellinzona.

The Gotthard **road tunnel**, completed in 1980 after eleven years of construction, is – at 16.3km – the longest road tunnel in the world, and although prone to hideous kilometres-long jams on both approaches, it remains open year-round, while the pass road above is impassable in winter.

The Furka Pass

Two buses a day from Andermatt (July–Sept) cross the **Furka Pass** (2431m) west into Canton Valais, while mainline passenger and car-carrying trains use the year-round Furka-Basis Tunnel beneath the pass. Buses aside, the main draw on the Uri side is a volunteer-run antique mountain **steam train**, the DFB, which puffs its way from Realp – a hamlet an easy hour-and-three-quarter walk from Andermatt – up to a station near the pass (mid-July to mid-Aug 4 daily; mid-June to mid-July & mid-Aug to Sept Fri–Sun 2–4 daily; *www.net4u.ch/dfbfurka*). In 1999, test trains successfully continued on into the old Muttbach tunnel beneath the pass, a short ride ending up in **Gletsch** (see p.325); old-time passenger services are slated to run between Realp and Gletsch in 2000 or 2001, with a projected run along the length of the line from Realp to **Oberwald** to follow.

Between Realp and the pass is *Hotel Tiefenbach* (☎041/887 13 22, fax 887 00 70; ②), with quality dorms from Fr.30, also open in winter as base camp for some of the best cross-country skiing in the country.

The Oberalp Pass

Directly east of Andermatt is the **Oberalp Pass** (2044m) into Canton Graubünden, passable to trains year-round. This is the route of the famous Glacier Express (see p.38) between Zermatt and St Moritz, which runs via the Furka-Basis Tunnel, Andermatt and the Oberalp on its way to Chur. Local trains from Andermatt to Disentis/Mustér can drop you on the pass itself, trailhead for a host of high-country summer hikes. Two scenic routes run through the bleak and invigorating high country down to Andermatt, one via the Lolenpass (5hr 30min), the other via the Maighelspass (6hr 30min), while an easier one heads out to Fellilücke, and from there to Nätschen and Andermatt (5hr).

travel details

TRAINS

Altdorf to: Brunnen (hourly; 10min); Schwyz (hourly 15min).

Andermatt to: Brig (hourly; 2hr); Disentis/Mustér (hourly; 1hr 10min); Flüelen (twice hourly; 1hr – change at Göschenen); Oberalppass (at least hourly; 25min).

Arth-Goldau to: Lugano (hourly; 2hr 10min); Luzern (3 hourly; 30min); Rigi Kulm (hourly; 35min); Zürich (hourly; 40min).

Brunnen to: Altdorf (hourly; 10min); Flüelen (twice hourly; 10min); Luzern (twice hourly; 45min – some change at Arth-Goldau); Zug (hourly; 35min – some change at Arth-Goldau).

Einsiedeln to: Brünnen (hourly; 50min – change at Biberbrugg & Arth-Goldau); Luzern (hourly; 1hr – change at Biberbrugg); Zürich (every 30min; 45min – change at Wädenswil).

Engelberg to: Luzern (hourly; 1hr).

Flüelen to: Andermatt (twice hourly; 1hr – change at Göschenen); Brunnen (twice hourly; 10min); Lugano (hourly; 2hr 5min); Luzern (twice hourly; 55min – some change at Arth-Goldau); Schwyz (twice hourly; 15min); Zürich (hourly; 1hr 15min – some change at Arth-Goldau).

Hergiswil to: Engelberg (hourly; 50min); Luzern (hourly; 10min); Stans (hourly; 10min).

Luzern to: Basel (twice hourly; 1hr 5min); Bellinzona (hourly; 2hr 15min); Bern (twice hourly; 1hr 20–30min); Brienz (hourly; 1hr 15min); Brunnen (twice hourly; 45min – some change at Arth-Goldau); Einsiedeln (hourly; 1hr – change at Biberbrugg); Engelberg (hourly; 1hr); Flüelen (twice hourly; 55min – some change at Arth-Goldau); Hergiswil (hourly; 10min); Interlaken Ost (hourly; 1hr 55min); Lugano (hourly; 2hr 45min); Stans (hourly; 20min); Zug (twice hourly; 20min); Zürich (twice hourly; 50min).

Rigi Kulm to: Arth-Goldau (hourly; 45min); Vitznau (hourly; 40min).

Schwyz to: Altdorf (hourly; 15min); Flüelen (twice hourly; 15min).

Stans to: Engelberg (hourly; 40min); Hergiswil (hourly; 10min); Luzern (hourly; 20min).

Vitznau to: Rigi Kulm (hourly; 30min).

Zug to: Bellinzona (hourly; 2hr); Brunnen (hourly; 35min – some change at Arth-Goldau); Lugano (hourly; 2hr 30min); Luzern (twice hourly; 20min); Zürich (twice hourly; 25min).

BUSES

Altdorf to: Bürglen (hourly; 5min); Flüelen (hourly; 10min).

Andermatt to: Airolo via Gotthardpass (July–Sept 3 daily; 50min); Oberwald via Furkapass (July–Sept 2 daily; 1hr 30min);

Brunnen to: Schwyz (every 10–20min; 10min).

Flüelen to: Altdorf (hourly; 10min); Linthal via Klausenpass (July–Sept 4 daily; 2hr 20min).

Gersau to: Schwyz (hourly; 25min); Weggis (hourly; 25min).

Göschenen to: Meiringen via Sustenpass (July–Sept 2 daily; 1hr 45min).

Schwyz to: Brunnen (every 10–20min; 10min).

Stans to: Beckenried (twice hourly; 20min); Seelisberg (hourly; 45min).

Weggis to: Gersau (hourly; 25min); Vitznau (hourly; 10min).

BOATS

(following is a summary of April–Oct services; fewer boats run in other months, quite often only on Sun if at all)

Brunnen to: Luzern (approx hourly; 1hr 50min–2hr 40min); Vitznau (approx hourly; 1hr–1hr 15min).

Flüelen to: Luzern (approx 7 daily; 2hr 50min–3hr 40min).

Luzern to: Alpnachstad (6 daily; 1hr 30–45min); Beckenried (approx hourly; 1hr 20min–2hr); Brunnen (approx hourly; 1hr 50min–2hr 40min); Flüelen (approx 7 daily; 2hr 50min–3hr 40min); Kehrsiten-Bürgenstock (6 daily; 35min); Vitznau (approx hourly; 40min–1hr 10min); Weggis (approx hourly; 35-50min).

Vitznau to: Brunnen (approx hourly; 1hr–1hr 15min); Luzern (approx hourly; 40min–1hr 10min).

Zug to: Arth-am-See (3–6 daily; 45min–2hr).

INTERNATIONAL TRAINS

Arth-Goldau to: Milan (hourly; 3hr 45min).

Luzern to: Milan (hourly; 4hr 15min – some change at Arth-Goldau).

Zug to: Milan (hourly; 4hr – some change at Arth-Goldau).

PLACE NAMES IN THIS CHAPTER

German	French	Italian
Gotthard	Gothard	Gottardo
Luzern	Lucerne	Lucerna
Nidwalden	Nidwald	Nidvaldo
Obwalden	Obwald	Obvaldo
Schwyz	Schwytz	Svitto
Vierwaldstättersee	Lac des Quatre-Cantons	Lago dei Quattro Cantoni
Zug	Zoug	Zugo
Zugersee	Lac de Zoug	Lago di Zugo
Zürich	Zurich	Zurigo

Guilds procession, Zürich Spring Festival

Grossmünster, Zürich

View of the Monte Rosa massif from Gornergrat, above Zermatt

Piz Corvatsch, above St Moritz

Alphorns, Klosters

The Matterhorn

Winter festivities in Davos

Sciora aiguilles, Graubünden

Ski-joring, St Moritz

Madonna del Sasso, above Locarno, Ticino

Verscio, Ticino

CHAPTER NINE

ZÜRICH AND AROUND

Zürich's relationship to the world is not of the spirit, but of commerce.

C.G. Jung

Not so long ago, **ZÜRICH** was famed for being the cleanest, most icily calm and efficient city in Europe: apocryphal stories abound from the 1960s and 1970s of the gentle tranquillity of the midweek lunch hour in the financial district, of tourists embarking on efforts to find a cigarette butt or an empty crisp packet discarded on the streets – and drawing a blank every time. No more. If you live in a big city yourself and are tiring of Switzerland's picture-perfect country towns, visiting Zürich will be like coming home – finally you can walk on crowded, multi-ethnic streets, buy a kebab, get a drink after midnight, feel a lived-in urban buzz. There's been a massive explosion in the city's arts and popular culture over the last two years, expressing itself most tangibly in a host of clubs and a thriving underground dance scene. Wry Zürchers like to make much of how apt it is that you have to tut, purse your lips and clear your throat to say the city's name (*tsoorikh* in dialect), but this stereotype no longer conveys the essence of what is now a dynamic, exciting city.

You're likely to find that this most beautiful of Swiss cities, astride a river and turned towards a crystal-clear lake and distant snowy peaks, has plenty to keep you amused. The medieval Old Town, characterized by steep, cobbled alleys and attractive, small-scale architecture, comprises a substantial part of the city centre and is perfect for exploratory wanderings. With a handful of medieval churches to take in, a spectacular art gallery, the most engaging café culture in German-speaking Switzerland and a wealth of nightlife, you could easily spend days here. To do so, however, you'll have to marry up the appeal of the place with its expense – prohibitive even by Swiss standards. Alternatively, you could base yourself in either of two towns near Zürich – **Winterthur** or **Baden** – both of which have museums and galleries of their own, and much more affordable accommodation than you'll find in Zürich itself.

Some history

Although there's evidence of settlement around Zürich from the Bronze Age and before, the **Romans** were the first to fortify the site, turning the Lindenhof into a

---

ACCOMMODATION PRICE CODES

All the hostels, pensions and hotels in this book have been graded according to the following price codes, which indicate the price for the cheapest double room available during the high season. Single rooms can cost anything between sixty and eighty percent of the double-room rate. For hostels with dormitories, the price per bed has been quoted. See p.45 for more details.

① under Fr.100	④ Fr.200–250	⑦ Fr.350–400
② Fr.100–150	⑤ Fr.250–300	⑧ Fr.400–500
③ Fr.150–200	⑥ Fr.300–350	⑨ over Fr.500

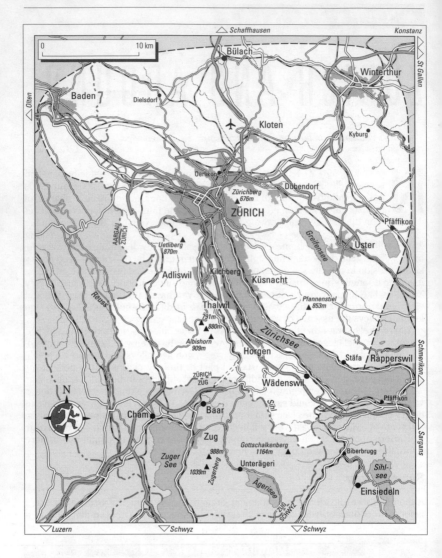

customs post in the first century BC and naming it *Turicum*. The legend of the city's foundation dates from the martyrdom of **Felix and Regula** (see box, p.389), deserters from a Roman legion based in Valais. During the eleventh and twelfth centuries, Zürich's traders built up fabulous wealth, mainly from textiles such as wool and silk. In 1336, however, a visionary burgomaster, **Rudolf Brun**, shuffled the merchant nobility out of power, handing control instead to workers' guilds (which were to keep a hold on the city until the nineteenth century). Shortly after, still under Brun's direction, Zürich joined the nascent Swiss Confederation.

TOO RICH!

Political activism within Zürich's youth movement during the 1970s culminated in major riots in 1980–81 and the police closure of the city's autonomous youth centre. The counterculture regrouped around two large community **squats**, the activities of which have passed into the city's collective memory. The first, known as **Wohlgroth**, took over an empty commercial building next to the train tracks on Zollstrasse; the squatters immediately erected a placard on the roof to greet trains rolling into the city with a huge imitation SBB station sign reading not "Zürich" but *"Zu reich"* ("Too rich"). At a stroke, this guaranteed them fame. The Wohlgroth developed into a thriving centre for arts, music and alternative culture, and such was its popularity that, after some years of hand-wringing at the loss of rent on such a prime site, the chief executive of the corporation which owned the building personally came visiting with the offer to donate another less embarrassingly visible building to the collective. His offer, needless to say, was rejected, and shortly afterwards the police evicted the place with tear gas and water cannon. Perhaps the greatest legacy of the Wohlgroth, aside from their classic *Zu reich* prank, is that the neighbourhood has now become the heart of the city's new subculture.

The second big squat of the early 1980s was of the **Rote Fabrik**, a former silk mill in a beautiful lakeside location south of the city, owned by the municipality. Whereas similar city-owned places squatted in Bern and Geneva have remained illegal and on the radical fringes of city life to this day, it's a mark of discreet Zürcher pragmatism that in 1987 the Rote Fabrik collective voted to apply for legal status and an arts subsidy from the city council. This was granted, millions of francs flowing into their coffers shortly after. These days, although its alternative heart still beats, the Rote Fabrik is able to develop and stage avant-garde dance and drama that gets taken seriously by the *Neue Zürcher Zeitung*, the city's most conservative newspaper. The flipside, of course, is that a mere mention of the place makes the committed radicals in Bern roll their eyes and start muttering about a sell out.

The thriving city experienced its zenith of power and prestige in the sixteenth century, when it became the first Swiss city to embrace the **Reformation**. The city's spiritual father, Huldrych **Zwingli** (see box p.385), preached in the Grossmünster from 1519 until his death in 1531. With the abolition of the Catholic Mass in 1525, Zürich became a centre for dissident intellectuals from all over Europe. After 1549, when Calvinist doctrine was adopted over Zwinglian, the city experienced a slow fading in its fortunes. The French Revolution of 1789 sparked **pro-libertarian** demonstrations at Stäfa, south of Zürich, but the city itself remained a backwater. A city councillor, **Alfred Escher**, is credited with reinventing Zürich as the economic capital of Switzerland, by his legislative innovations boosting tourism, banking and local manufacturing industry in the late nineteenth century. Strict neutrality during World War I again made Zürich a refuge for dissidents, and for some months in 1916 and 1917, the city was home to **Lenin**, mulling over the future Russian Revolution, **James Joyce**, holed up near the university writing *Ulysses*, and a band of emigré artists calling themselves "Dada", who spent their evenings lampooning Western culture at the famous **Cabaret Voltaire**.

With the recent revelations about Switzerland's economic and material complicity with the Nazis, Zürich's exact role during and after World War II hasn't yet been pinpointed, but the city emerged post-war to flourish, becoming one of the world's leading financial centres; by the 1960s its foreign exchange speculators had become so powerful and secretive that they were dubbed "the gnomes of Zürich" by British Labour Ministers during the 1964 sterling crisis. Today, Zürich is the single most important market for **gold** and precious metals, and boasts the world's fourth-largest **stock market** after New York, London and Tokyo. This exceptional affluence tends to define the city these days and yet, despite its wealth, Zürich is not a flashy place at all. The ghost of Zwingli still stands at the shoulder of the super-discreet bankers, industrialists and business people who live and breathe the city's ingrained Protestant work ethic, but it's in fact the individualism that Zwingli encouraged which continually bubbles to the surface.

Most recently, following a relaxation of licensing laws, Zürich is discovering a new will to party. Alongside all its sights and its breathtaking lakeside beauty, Zürich is re-inventing itself again, and a gritty and engaging subculture has begun to flow beneath its slick, monied surface.

Arrival

Zürich is one of the principal gateways for international arrivals **by air** into Switzerland. The pocket-sized airport (*www.zurich-airport.com*), about 11km northeast in Kloten, is regularly voted to be one of the best in the world – baggage often turns up at the carousels before you do, and you can be sitting on a train heading for the city within an easy 45 minutes of touching down.

There are two adjacent terminals: A (serving Swissair, Crossair, Austrian, Sabena, Delta and Singapore) and B (all other carriers). Both terminals' arrivals halls have **tourist information** desks (A: daily 5.30am–midnight; B: daily 5.45am–10.30pm), both with free maps, advice, hotel reservations boards, and surprisingly useful touch-screen information systems. There are ATMs nearby, but you'll get the best deals on changing money in the train station downstairs (see below).

For transport on from the airport, the most obvious way to go is by **train**. The sub-terranean train station is directly beneath Terminal B. Trains depart 4–7 times hourly all day to the city's main station, Zürich Hauptbahnhof (10min; Fr.5.40; last 12.20am). Departures are also frequent to points all over the country, so if you're heading else-where you can generally get a train directly from the airport, avoiding a change at Zürich. You may prefer the pricey convenience of the **hotel bus** service (daily: half-hourly 6.30am–noon & 5–8pm, hourly 1–4pm & 9–10pm; ☎01/300 14 10), which leaves from the arrivals level between the two terminals, and can drop you twenty minutes later at the door of any of around thirty hotels in the centre. The fare – Fr.22 for one person, Fr.30 for two people, and so on – is substantially higher than the train but undercuts the **taxis**, which charge the earth for the short ride into the city (about Fr.60).

By train

Zürich's **Hauptbahnhof** (HB) has trains arriving continuously from all corners of Switzerland and around Europe. It's a massive beehive of a place located in the heart of the city, extending three storeys below ground and taking in a shopping mall, super-market, post office and a fair sprinkling of restaurants.

Most trains arrive at **street level**, where the echoing station hall is home to the change office (daily 6.30am–10.45pm), a scattering of fast-food stalls and cafés, a post office, a free hotel reservations board and, at the far end under artist Niki de St-Phalle's flying blue "Guardian Angel" (installed in 1997 to celebrate the 150th anniversary of Swiss railways), the city **tourist office** (see opposite). Out of sight behind the travel bureau are the bike rental office and left-luggage counter.

One level **down** you'll find luggage lockers, while going down again brings you to the **shopping level**, with a warren of echoing subterranean passageways stretching off in all directions. **S-Bahn** suburban trains leave from the lowest level to local destinations such as Uetliberg and Adliswil. Trains from these platforms to nearby towns such as Winterthur and Baden are slower than the intercity trains that leave from the main platforms above, but depart far more frequently.

By bus

Zürich is served by a few international **buses**. Most arrive from points east such as Vienna, Budapest, Prague and Zagreb, but once-weekly Eurolines buses make the seventeen-hour trek to Zürich from London, via Rheims and Strasbourg. All terminate at the open bus park on Sihlquai opposite the *Walhalla* hotel, 50m behind the station. Domestic Swiss postbuses all terminate in the suburbs.

By car

Roads feed into Zürich from all points of the compass. The N1 brings traffic from Bern and Basel in the west, and Konstanz, St Gallen and Winterthur in the east; the N3 and N4 feed in from Luzern, the Gotthard and Chur in the south, and Schaffhausen in the north.

Parking in Zürich is more difficult, and much more expensive, than in most other Swiss cities. All of the Old Town, plus chunks of the central commercial district, are off limits, and although there are half-a-dozen parking garages in the centre – the one on Uraniastrasse is big (☎01/211 47 38) – they can be prohibitively expensive, sometimes more than Fr.25 per day. If you know you'll be arriving by car, it's a good idea to ask your hotel in advance about parking spaces: some offer free, or discounted, spaces to guests. If you're only staying a day or two, ask at any police station for a Fr.10 **day permit** allowing you to park on the street in blue zones – though even then you'll have to find a space. Otherwise, the easiest option is to head for the **airport**: secure parking managed by Sprenger Garages is nearby at Flughafenstrasse 8 in Kloten (☎01/814 37 70, fax 813 18 32; outdoor parking Fr.30 first day, Fr.10/day thereafter; covered parking Fr.115 first week). You can reserve a space here by phone or fax – quote your name, the make of car and its licence plate.

Information

The main **tourist office** is in the station's main hall, on street level beneath the flying blue angel (April–Oct Mon–Fri 8.30am–8.30pm, Sat & Sun 8.30am–6.30pm; Nov–March Mon–Fri 8.30am–7pm, Sat & Sun 9am–6.30pm; ☎01/215 40 00, *www.zurichtourism.ch*). They have a welter of brochures from hotels and service companies all over the city and the country, and can give you an adequate map of the city centre for free, or sell you one covering the whole city, including a transport map, for Fr.3. Staff can also book you onto one of the two-to-three-hour **city tours** by bus, cable-car and/or boat, which take in various parts of the city and surrounding area for Fr.30–40. They also offer a two-hour **guided walk** through the old town in English (May–Oct Mon–Fri 2.30pm, Sat & Sun 10am & 2.30pm; Nov–April Wed & Sat 10am; Fr.18), and can sell tickets for the various trips by boat around the lake (see box p.377).

If you're planning to be in Zürich for three days or more, you'd do well to check out the **Zürich Night Card**. This costs Fr.20 and gives you free city transport on three consecutive nights from 5pm until the last (ordinary) bus, tram or train, as well as various offers at an OK selection of bars, restaurants and clubs. You can pick up information and the card itself from the tourist office and most hotels.

Zürich News, a German/English booklet published fortnightly (*www.zuerich.ch*), is a useful source of information on sightseeing, the latest exhibitions and other bits and bobs, also available widely.

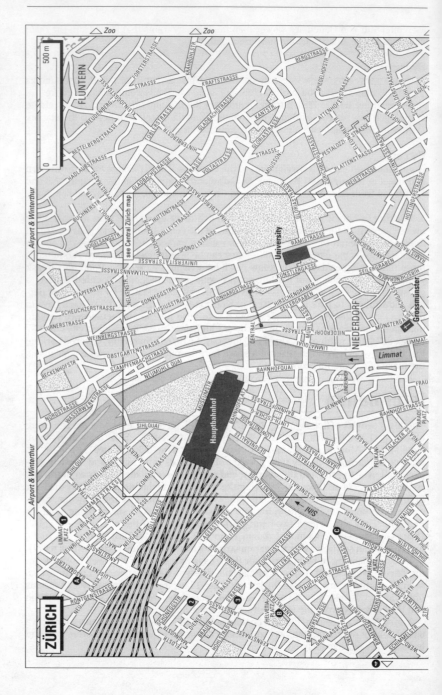

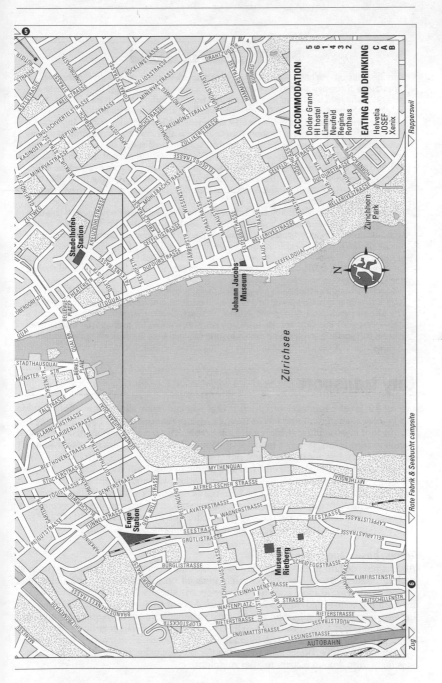

ACCOMMODATION
Dolder Grand 5
HI hostel 6
Limmat 1
Neufeld 4
Regina 3
Rothaus 2

EATING AND DRINKING
Helvetia C
JOSEF A
Xenix B

Zürichsee

Zürichhorn Park

Stadelhofen Station

Johann Jacobs Museum

Bellevue Platz

Stadthausquai

Bürkli Platz

Enge Station

Museum Rietberg

N

▽ Rapperswil

▽ Rate Fabrik & Seebucht campsite

▽ Zug

▽

ZÜRICH'S FESTIVALS

Zürich's biggest party is August's massive **Street-Parade** (*www.street-parade.ch*), a tumultuous three-day techno weekend of floats, costumes, dancing in the streets and general hedonism, second in size and energy only to Berlin's Love Parade held a week or two beforehand; if you're in the city, you won't be able to miss it.

On a more traditional note, the **Sechseläuten** is Zürich's spring festival, held on the third Monday in April, and is the only time in the year that Zürich's establishment preens its feathers in public: a highlight of the festival is a parade through the city centre by the city's traditional guilds, dressed in costume. The festival culminates at 6pm precisely with the burning of the Böögg – an effigy stuffed with fireworks – on Sechseläutenplatz next to Bellevue, to symbolize the end of winter. Throughout the evening the guilds take turns to visit each other in their respective guildhalls, most of which have happily become rather good restaurants.

One evening in the week before Christmas sees the **Lichterschwimmen**, a tradition of launching floating candles from the Rathausbrücke onto the River Limmat, to the accompaniment of gingerbread and *glühwein*. Zürich's **Fasnacht** (Carnival) is a boisterous affair, fun if you happen to be in the city, but it's still small fry compared with those of Luzern and Basel. However, the summertime **Züri Fäscht** – held every three years (next on July 6–8, 2001) – is worth making a diversion for, with the whole city throwing itself into fairground revelry.

Zürich's annual **Festspiele** is a festival of theatre, opera, music and art, held from late June to mid-July, with special productions, concerts and exhibitions all over the city. The **Theaterspektakel**, during late August and early September, also packs out the city's stages and sees lakeside marquees set up on Mythenquai for avant-garde drama from around the world. There's also a citywide international **jazz festival** every November.

City transport

One of the great advantages of Zürich is that you can enjoy all the buzz of big city life in a compact setting that's no larger than a single *arrondissement* of Paris: covering the city **on foot** is perfectly feasible, even pleasurable. The main Bahnhofstrasse, from the station to Bürkliplatz, is only a bit over 1km long. Nonetheless, Zürich's **city transport** system is legendary for its efficiency, punctuality and convenience, with the city centre and surrounding suburbs linked by a cat's cradle of bus, tram and S-Bahn routes joining every point of interest to just about every other with minimum hassle. You could even take advantage of the city's free bike-rental scheme. Taxis, in a place where even millionaire bankers use the tram, are an extravagance; aside from the numerous public ranks, you can hail a cab in the street, or order one from Züri Taxi (☎01/222 22 22), Taxi 2000 (☎01/444 44 44), or Taxis for the Disabled (☎01/272 42 42).

Trams, buses and trains

After a referendum in the 1970s, in which Zürchers rejected a proposal to build an underground metro system, the city has focused on its eco-friendly and ubiquitous **trams**, while easing most cars off the city-centre streets. A dozen tram lines weave through the centre, and dozens of **bus** routes fan out from suburban termini to outlying districts. **S-Bahn** suburban trains, most originating from or passing through the main station, add a third dimension, linking to Zug and Einsiedeln in the south and Winterthur, Schaffhausen and Stein-am-Rhein in the north, as well as serving the nearby Uetliberg summit. **Boats** are covered in the box opposite. All public transport operates daily from around 5.30am to after midnight.

TAKING TO THE WATER

One of the most pleasurable ways of seeing Zürich and the surrounding countryside is from the **water**, and there's no shortage of options for rides long and short. However, you should note that almost all the boat trips mentioned below only operate during the summer months (April–Oct); in winter, service is drastically reduced, and is dependent on good weather. For all **enquiries**, contact either the tourist office or the Zürichsee Schifffahrtsgesellschaft (ZSG, or Lake Zürich Shipping Company; ☎01/487 13 33, *www.zsg.ch*). Full timetables are posted at the company office at **Bürkliplatz**, from where almost all boats depart. Swiss Pass and Eurail pass holders travel free, while InterRailers go for half-price.

One of the best short trips is on the **Limmatschiff**, which departs from the Landesmuseum for the scenic river journey through the heart of the city, including a short trip on the lake and the return journey up the Limmat again. The round trip takes about 55 minutes, and departures are every half-hour (July & Aug daily 10am–9pm; May, June & early Sept Mon–Fri 1–9pm, Sat & Sun 10am–9pm; April & mid-Sept to mid-Oct Mon–Fri 1–6pm, Sat & Sun 10am–6pm).

Regular boats also ply the length of the Zürichsee, from Zürich to **Rapperswil** (2hr), and beyond to Schmerikon (another 1hr 30min), stopping at just about every shoreside town on the way. Another possibility for relaxed exploration is in **Stäfa** village about an hour and a half from Zürich, clustered on the shore at the foot of the Pfannenstiel in the largest vinegrowing region in the canton. The S-Bahn lines running along both shores of the lake can make the return journey to Zürich a picturesque one in itself.

The ZSG also runs a host of **pleasure cruises** on the lake, including circular sightseeing trips from and to Zürich without stopping (1hr 30min or 2hr 45min), nostalgia trips to Rapperswil by steamship (1hr 45min), and full 7-hour day cruises. Eat-aboard cruises – in daylight and after dark – are some of the most popular with the locals and, although prices vary (Fr.15–50), are not prohibitively expensive.

Ticketing is organized by zone, with the city centre (but not Uetliberg or the airport) covered by Zone 10. Tickets bought from the machines at all stops can be used for all transport – both land- and water-based – within each zone, with unlimited changes permitted. The most useful Zone 10 ticket is the Fr.7.20 **Tageskarte** (press the green button), valid for 24 hours; the blue "Stadt Zürich" button gives a Zone 10 ticket valid for an hour (Fr.3.60); while the yellow "Kurzstrecke" button gives a short-hop one-way ticket (Fr.2.10) good for up to five stops – the black panel lists the stations for which it is valid. Swiss Pass holders travel free, but Eurailers and InterRailers must pay full price.

On Friday and Saturday nights only (roughly 1–2.30am), a handful of **night buses** depart from Bellevue for various suburban destinations, for a flat Fr.5 – other tickets and passes are not valid.

Bikes, mopeds and motorbikes

The station has the usual **bike-rental** facilities (daily 6am–10.50pm), but, if there is high demand, you might have to resort to the other SBB rental facility at Oerlikon station, in a northern suburb. Zürich is also one of the cities offering **free bikes** for a Fr.20 returnable deposit on production of ID. There are six locations dotted throughout the city (all daily 7.30am–9.30pm): the main one is on Zollstrasse next to platform 18 of the station (open year-round), and the most accessible others are at the Globus department store on Usteristrasse, at Theaterplatz, and outside Bahnhof Enge (all May–Oct only).

Erne's Euromotos, Sihlquai 67 (☎01/272 77 72) can rent you motorized two-wheel transport – anything from a 50cc scooter (Fr.50/day) to a monster 955cc Triumph Daytona (Fr.170/day). Staff speak English, and offer weekend discounts.

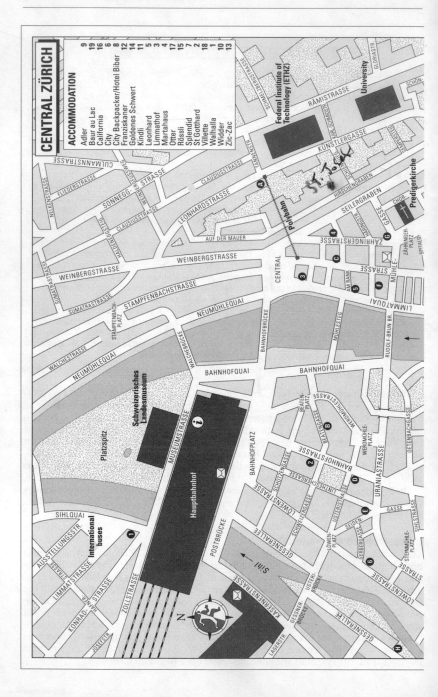

CENTRAL ZÜRICH

ACCOMMODATION

Adler	9
Baur au Lac	19
California	16
City	6
City Backpacker/Hotel Biber	8
Franziskaner	12
Goldenes Schwert	14
Kindli	11
Leonhard	5
Limmathof	3
Martahaus	4
Otter	17
Rössli	15
Splendid	7
St Gotthard	2
Villette	18
Walhalla	1
Widder	10
Zic-Zac	13

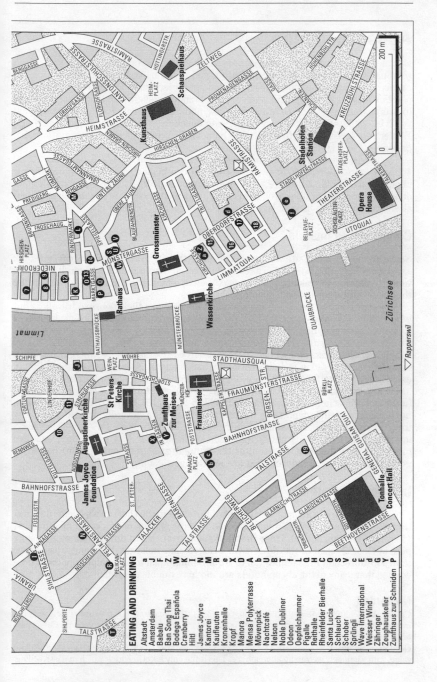

EATING AND DRINKING

Altstadt	a
Amsterdam	J
Babalu	F
Ban Song Thai	Z
Bodega Española	W
Cranberry	K
Hitl	I
James Joyce	N
Kantorei	M
Kaufleuten	R
Kronenhalle	e
Kropf	X
Manora	D
Mensa Polyterrasse	A
Mövenpick	b
Nachtcafé	U
Nelson	B
Noble Dubliner	T
Odeon	f
Oepfelchammer	L
Pigalle	Q
Reithalle	H
Rheinfelder Bierhalle	C
Santa Lucia	O
Schlauch	S
Schober	V
Sprüngli	c
Wave International	E
Weisser Wind	d
Zähringer	G
Zeughauskeller	Y
Zunfthaus zur Schmiden	P

Accommodation

Despite its being one of the most expensive cities in the world, Zürich can still offer a reasonably full range of **accommodation**, and if you book ahead you'll have a good chance of finding something pleasant within your price range. Prices at the higher-end places, though, can be frightful, and some mid-range hoteliers take this as *carte blanche* to overcharge: you'd be well advised to take nothing for granted and investigate what you'll be getting for your money before you check in. Nearby Baden (see p.403) and Winterthur (see p.398) offer equally characterful accomodation at more affordable prices.

The tourist office's dedicated **hotel reservation service** (☎01/215 40 40, fax 215 40 44, *hotel@zurichtourism.ch*, or over-the-counter) can book a room in the hotel of your choice for free within Zürich, or Fr.10 elsewhere in Switzerland. Make sure to ask them about any weekend or off-season deals the city happens to be running, which can often slash walk-in rates to bargain levels.

Camping and hostels

Seebucht, the one **campsite** within easy reach of the city, is at Seestrasse 559 (☎01/482 16 12, fax 482 16 60; May–Oct). Take bus #161 or #165 from Bürkliplatz south along the western shore of the lake to Stadtgrenze, the city boundary; the campsite is down by the water, with good and well-maintained facilities.

Although many of the university's student dorms open their doors to travellers out of term-time (ask at the tourist office for details), there are very few ordinary **hostels** in the city, meaning that booking ahead is strongly advised. Best place in town is the excellent *City Backpacker/Hotel Biber*, Niederdorfstrasse 5 (☎01/251 90 15, fax 251 90 24, *backpacker@access.ch, www.backpacker.ch/city-backpacker*, ①). Newly refurbished, it enjoys a central location and super-friendly management. A dorm bed is around Fr.30 excluding breakfast, plus Fr.20 key deposit. Some singles and doubles are available, along with free kitchen use, laundry service (Fr.9), and Internet access. The city's HI hostel is at Mutschellenstrasse 114 (☎01/482 35 44, fax 480 17 27; ①). Its prices are low, but it reeks of a rather depressing institutionalism and is awkwardly situated a long way from the city in a humdrum southwestern suburb. Dorm beds are Fr.30, and a few parking spaces are free. Take tram #7 (direction Wollishofen) to Morgental, then walk five minutes (follow the signs). As well as these, the *Martahaus* (see opposite) has some good-quality, partitioned dorms that are worth investigating.

Inexpensive hotels

The greatest concentration of **inexpensive hotels** is in the Old Town's Niederdorf district. None is more than ten minutes' walk from the station, or you could take tram #4 (direction Tiefenbrunnen), from Bahnhofquai: it runs south down Limmatquai, stopping at Central, each of the three river bridges, and Bellevue. For Langstrasse, take tram #13 (direction Frankental) north from Bahnhofquai to Limmatplatz, although be warned that many of the cheap hotels around here double as brothels.

Niederdorf
California, Schifflände 18 (☎01/262 40 50, fax 262 43 67). A case of style over substance, with the innovation of desert murals and vaguely Aztec decor accompanied by a distinctly un-Californian brusqueness of service. The sizeable rooms are comfortable nonetheless. ③.

Goldenes Schwert, Marktgasse 14 (☎01/266 18 18, fax 266 18 88, *hotel@rainbow.ch*). Excellent value, with a uniquely easygoing atmosphere. This is the only hotel in Zürich which makes a selling-point of its gay- and lesbian-friendliness. Comfortable rooms are large, bright, individually decorated and inexpensive, but you should insist on the fifth floor to avoid noise from the bars and nightclub. They also have quality apartments for Fr.200 or less. ③.

Leonhard, Limmatquai 136 (☎01/251 30 80, fax 252 38 70, *www.access.ch/hotel-leonhard*). Small, super-friendly family-run place, with big, clean rooms that are good value despite the street noise. ③.

Limmathof, Limmatquai 142 (☎01/261 42 30, fax 262 02 17). Although it's one of the only cheapies overlooking the river, you'd do well to eschew the noisy river-view rooms for the newer, quieter ones at the back. Front or back, though, you'll have problems swinging a cat. ②.

Martahaus, Zähringerstrasse 36 (☎01/251 45 50, fax 251 45 40, *info@martahaus.ch*, *www. martahaus.ch*). Basic hotel in a rather dodgy area, but a safe and thoroughly respectable place to rest your head for minimal franc outlay. No en-suite facilities, and you should go for a back room to avoid street noise. ①.

Otter, Oberdorfstrasse 7 (☎01/251 22 07, fax 251 22 75). Best in this bracket by miles, relaxed, friendly and great value, with an unconventional clientele of students and artists. Uniquely colourful rooms, all with big, comfy beds, are decked in murals, drapes and plants, ones higher up with lovely rooftop views. Shower and toilet are shared between the three rooms on each floor. A good indication of the mood of the place is that breakfast only happens from 9am (11am weekend). The top-floor apartment, for Fr.180, feels like home. ②.

Splendid, Rosengasse 5 (☎01/252 58 50, fax 262 61 40). Gloomy unrenovated small hotel, with no TVs, no en-suite facilities, no decoration and no lift. Quiet, ordinary and honestly cheap. Locked daily 2.30–5am. ①.

Villette, Kruggasse 4 (☎01/251 23 35, fax 251 23 39). Homely little place above an award-winning fondue restaurant just off Bellevue. Plain rooms are clean enough and adequate for simple tastes – the breakfast is notably good – and the owner of the place (who also does the fondues) is full of jolly stories and banter. ②–③.

Zic-Zac, Marktgasse 17 (☎01/261 21 81, fax 261 21 75, *rockhotel@bluewin.ch*, *www.ziczac.ch*). Ordinary cheapie, which has taken some marketing advice and reinvented itself as a "rock hotel", dubbing their poky and rather depressing rooms the "Bryan Adams" or the "Pink Floyd" in an attempt to attract business. But don't imagine you'll get something special for your money: the theming stops at the door. ②.

Around Langstrasse and west

Limmat, Limmatstrasse 118 (☎01/448 15 95, fax 448 15 96). In the same building as the popular *X-tra* bar and nightclub, just off the Limmatplatz in a young and trendy part of town. Pricey rooms are small, with postmodern decor and all facilities; the non-en-suite ones are much better value. ③.

Neufeld, Goldbrunnenplatz (☎01/463 74 00, fax 463 78 13). Thoroughly respectable good-value family hotel west of the centre, with spotless rooms and a reputation to uphold. Set in Wiedikon, a neighbourhood with many Jewish residents, it even offers kosher breakfasts. Trams #9 or #14 (direction Triemli) to Goldbrunnenplatz. ③.

Regina, Hohlstrasse 18 (☎01/298 55 55, fax 298 56 00). The least dodgy of Langstrasse's many dodgy hotels, although the prevalence of over-friendly single women in the hotel bar tells its own story. Nonetheless, the rooms are perfectly fine, clean but smallish, and a good Fr.20–30 cheaper than similar places elsewhere. ③.

Rothaus, Sihlhallenstrasse 1 (☎01/241 24 51, fax 291 09 95). On the honky-tonk Langstrasse. Next-door is a sex cinema and the bar downstairs is a pick-up joint, but if you can overlook that, you can save Fr.30–40 on perfectly adequate en-suite rooms, equipped with all facilities and soundproofed windows. ①–②.

Walhalla, Limmatstrasse 5 (☎01/446 54 00, fax 446 54 54, *walhalla-hotel@bluewin.ch*). Good value in an unromantic location 50m behind the station, with large, pleasantly decorated rooms. Cheaper rooms available in a nearby annexe. ②–③.

Mid-range hotels

Mid-range options abound across the city. Those in Niederdorf are generally quiet and characterful, although universally pricey and often renovated, while those elsewhere in the city tend to offer better value at the expense of noisier or more mundane surroundings. Don't be deceived by the invariably plush lobbies, which often precede less-than-plush rooms, although all places mentioned below offer TV, phone and minibar.

Adler, Rosengasse 10 (☎01/266 96 96, fax 266 96 69, *hoteladler@swissonline.ch*). Very clean, light and pleasant hand-decorated rooms set amidst the old town buzz above a famous fondue restaurant. Service is good, the pastel interior is modern, and rates undercut similar places on the west bank. ④.

City, Löwenstrasse 34 (☎01/217 17 17, fax 217 18 18, *hotelcity@bluewin.ch*). A comfortable, quiet, unremarkable choice in the shopping district, reasonably priced and efficiently staffed, with many more singles than doubles. ④.

Franziskaner, Niederdorfstrasse 1 (☎01/250 53 00, fax 250 53 01, *service@hotel-franziskaner.ch*, *www.hotel-franziskaner.ch*). Charming small hotel in classic style, with dark-wood decor and a popular outdoor terrace on a square in the heart of the old town. A little pricey for what you get, but the top-floor rooms, sharing a spacious rooftop terrace, are delightful. ③–⑤.

Kindli, Pfalzgasse 1 (☎01/211 59 17, fax 211 65 28). A building dating from the sixteenth century, a hostel since (at least) 1774. These days it's one of Zürich's most charming hotels, renovated throughout in florid Laura Ashley style, and with a tranquil location in the steep cobbled lanes below the Lindenhof. Rooms are not spacious, but are elegant and characterful. ⑤.

Rössli, Rössligasse 7 (☎01/252 21 21, fax 252 21 31, *hotelroessli@reconline.ch*). Super-chic choice, the spartan wood-and-stone rooms with crisp white styling are spotlessly clean. ⑤.

Expensive hotels

Top-end, extremely **expensive** accommodation is what Zürich does best, and there's any number of chain- and private-owned palaces catering for executives and the brand of international glitterati willing to sign away Fr.1200 or more for a night in one of the many absurdly luxurious suites on offer. Ordinary mortals could get away with half that for a standard double in these places, but be aware that if you're willing to part with such stratospheric amounts, you'd probably have a more memorable time in, say, St Moritz or on Lake Luzern.

Baur au Lac, Talstrasse 1 (☎01/220 50 20, fax 220 50 44, *info@bauraulac.ch*, *www.bauraulac.ch*). One of Zürich's oldest hotels, in the same family since 1844, now luxuriating in top-to-bottom renovations completed in 1997. Set in a private park on the lakeshore adjacent to Bahnhofstrasse, it fairly shimmers with opulent grandeur; touches such as in-room hi-fi systems, jacuzzis and ISDN connections make all the difference. ⑨.

Dolder Grand, Kurhausstrasse 65 (☎01/269 30 00, fax 269 30 01, *reservations@doldergrand.ch*). An extraordinary nineteenth-century palace perched atop a hill overlooking the city and accessible only by private funicular. Towers, cupolas, spires and turrets sprout from all sides of the elegant building; inside, the high-ceilinged rooms are unsurpassable. Completing the picture are a private nine-hole golf course, a full-size pool with wave machine, one of Switzerland's top *haute cuisine* restaurants, and plenty of walking trails into the parks and forest all around. ⑨.

St Gotthard, Bahnhofstrasse 87 (☎01/227 77 00, fax 227 77 50, *hotelstgotthard@bluewin.ch*). *Grande dame* of the city-centre hotels, in the same family since 1889, with a perfect location and bags of charm. The understated elegance of the dark-wood-and-leather lobby, however, isn't matched in the rooms, which are spacious and comfortable but have been done up in a rather cloying chintzy style. A bargain, considering the competition. ⑦–⑧.

Widder, Rennweg 7 (☎01/224 25 26, fax 224 24 24, *widder@active.ch*). On a quiet Old Town street, a row of eight medieval houses has been gutted to make this stylish and innovative modern hotel, reeking of super-smooth class but without the merest whiff of *hauteur*. The bar's array of several hundred single malts adds to the appeal. ⑨.

The City

Because the River Limmat divides the **Old Town** into two distinct halves, it's easier to consider the two banks of the river as separate entities rather than to concentrate on a New Town/Old Town split. The alleys of the east bank – known as **Niederdorf** or the

"Dörfli" – are full of cafés and small shops, with the enormous twin towers of the **Grossmünster** as a centrepiece. The slender spire to the north belongs to the Predigerkirche with, above it on a hill to the east, the grandiose architecture of the university.

Opposite, the **west bank** is the oldest part of the city, centred around the raised platform of the **Lindenhof** and characterized by expensive fashion outlets and offices. Nearby rise the graceful spires both of **St Peter's**, featuring the largest clock face in Europe, and the **Fraumünster**, a medieval church decorated in this century with beautiful stained glass by Marc Chagall. The long, curving **Bahnhofstrasse** follows the ancient course of the western city wall, and is now one of Europe's most prestigious shopping streets, packed with jewellers and designer boutiques.

The best of the city's thirty-odd **museums** are the marvellous Kunsthaus on the fringes of the Niederdorf, and the Schweizerisches Landesmuseum (Swiss National Museum) in a park on the west bank.

The east bank

It's a walk of only 100m from the station across the Bahnhofbrücke to the east bank of the Limmat and a large square bedecked with tram wires, known as **Central**. From here, the **Niederdorf** district stretches south along the riverside for about 1km, but a more engaging walk than the busy riverside Limmatquai is to fork onto the narrow pedestrianized **Niederdorfstrasse** one block east. The tackiness of the initial stretches – replete with fast-food stalls and lowlife beerhalls – soon mellows, and

DADA IN ZÜRICH

At the same time as both a pre-Revolution Lenin and a *Ulysses*-obsessed Joyce were staying in Zürich, a group of maverick European intellectuals was also seeking refuge in the city from the bloodshed and misery of World War I. In 1915, Hugo Ball, a writer and theatre-director, had arrived from Munich with his partner Emmy Hennings, a dancer and singer. It seemed to them, as to many horrified by the brutality of war, that Western civilization had finally lost all reason; with a group of like-minded friends, they made an arrangement with the owner of the *Meierei* tavern at Spiegelgasse 1 to use the pub's backroom for a "literary cabaret" to demonstrate to the people of Zürich and the world the moral bankruptcy of Western culture. On Saturday, February 3, 1916, Ball, Hennings, the Romanian poet Tristan Tzara, Hans Arp (an artist from Franco-German Alsace), and a handful of other emigrés inaugurated the **Cabaret Voltaire** with a night of wild music, poetry and dance, intended to satirize art and literature by placing unreason against reason, anti-art against art. On June 15, they published a magazine with contributions from Kandinsky, Modigliani and others, and presented themselves as "**Dada**", the most significantly meaningless name they could find, picked at random out of a dictionary (*dada* is French for "hobby-horse").

Dada's poignant absurdities aptly expressed the mood of dislocation and crisis seizing Western society, and the movement spread rapidly. In New York, Dada was centred at Alfred Stieglitz's gallery "291", meeting point for Man Ray, Marcel Duchamp and others. In Berlin, Dadaists such as George Grosz relentlessly lampooned high society, and were the initiators of the brand-new technique of photomontage. In the Netherlands, Dada became *De Stijl*, led by Mondrian. In 1920, some of the Zürich Dadaists moved to Paris and there formed the Surrealist movement, which later attracted artists such as Dalí and Miró. The greatest legacy of Dada was its liberating influence in overturning previously unquestioned strictures of style and order, not only in art and writing but across society as a whole. What is both appropriate and extraordinary is that such a movement should have emerged from – of all places – neutral, bourgeois Zürich.

there are plenty of opportunities for random exploration of atmospheric little cobbled alleys, many of which open onto secluded courtyards adorned with medieval fountains.

A short way down on the left is **Rindermarkt**, where Gottfried Keller – generally thought of as Switzerland's national poet – lived (at no. 9) and drank (at the *Oepfelchammer* opposite, see p.391). A little further along, **Spiegelgasse** enjoyed a burst of fame during World War I: Lenin and Krupskaja stayed for fourteen months at no. 14, in the home of Titus Kammerer, a cobbler, before returning to Russia in April 1917 to lead the revolution; while diagonally opposite, a pub at no. 1 (long since renovated) housed the original *Cabaret Voltaire*, birthplace of the Dada art movement (see box p.383).

Niederdorfstrasse, which becomes **Münstergasse**, leads on to the **Grossmünster church** (see below) and beyond, as Oberdorfstrasse, out to the open **Bellevue** plaza, dominated on its south side by the lavish opera house. A short distance up the hill to the left – by the main Rämistrasse or any of the back alleys (tiny **Trittligasse** is the most beautiful) – lies the **Kunsthaus** (see below), while a pleasant riverside walk south along the quay will bring you after 1km to the Zürichhorn park.

The Grossmünster

With its distinctive twin sugar-loafed towers, and a venerable history at the heart of the Swiss-German Reformation, the **Grossmünster** – or Great Minster – dominates Zürich's skyline. In a tight-packed city of generally modest, small-scale architecture, it is dauntingly gigantic; and yet, caught half a millennium ago in the eye of a tight-lipped theological hurricane, it has been denuded of virtually all its interior decorative grandeur. Today it's as bare as a cellar inside, but its beauty – as the Reformers would have wanted – is all in its lofty austerity, and its associations. In twelve years preaching from the Grossmünster's pulpit in the sixteenth century, **Huldrych Zwingli**, a contemporary of Luther's and the initiator of the Reformation in Switzerland (see box opposite), transformed Zürich from a sparsely populated hinterland town into a renowned religious centre attracting students and theologians from around Europe. Quite aside from the architecture, the sense of history in the church is compelling.

After its foundation by **Charlemagne** in the ninth century on a site of long-established religious significance (recent excavations below the church suggest the existence of a **Roman** cemetery), the church was constructed in its present form between 1100 and 1230. At that time, the north tower was higher than its twin, since it held, and still holds, the bells. In the late fifteenth century, the south tower was brought up to the same height and adorned on its south side with a grotesque statue of a seated Charlemagne. After a disastrous **fire** in 1763, the spires and upper sections of the towers were demolished, and reconstruction shortly after produced the Gothic belfries, watchrooms and octagonal cupolae which survive today. The fire also gave impetus to much **Baroque** alteration to the church interior, and the nineteenth and twentieth centuries saw a continuous programme of restoration of its original Romanesque character.

The building is skewed from the river bank, its broad front facing northwest. The most impressive approach is across paved Zwingliplatz, with the main North Portal featuring capitals adorned with animals, birds and, on the extreme left, a fiddle player. To the right, at the base of the North Tower, is a modern statue of Heinrich Bullinger, Zwingli's successor. **Inside** (March–Oct Mon–Sat 9am–6pm; Nov–Feb Mon–Sat 10am–4pm; free), the overriding impression is of the loftiness of the galleried space and its austerity; aside from some **capitals** decorated with battle scenes – and, on the third pillar on the north side, Charlemagne's discovery of the graves of Felix and Regula – almost no decoration survives. The altar paintings were removed in 1524 at Zwingli's behest, as were the church treasures. Most decorative elements which survive today

HULDRYCH ZWINGLI (1484–1531)

At the vanguard of the Reformation, **Huldrych** (or Ulrich) **Zwingli** is one of the most radical anti-establishment figures in the whole history of Europe, a dedicated and eloquent humanist who developed a passion for the liberty of individuals to decide the course of their lives free from the strictures of the past. An archetypal "red under the bed" fifth columnist, he used his position of authority in the church to undermine and reinvent the power structures of the church itself. He died at 47 fighting for his cause.

Whereas Zwingli's contemporary Martin Luther was poorly educated and underwent his internal religious crisis in social isolation, Zwingli came to his personal revolution through education, studying in Basel, Bern, Vienna and possibly Paris, and absorbing the humanist ideas of the Dutch philosopher Erasmus. After ten years as a pastor, his study of scripture led Zwingli to begin questioning the teachings of the Catholic Church; in 1518 he was appointed to the Grossmünster, and began to develop his deeply controversial ideas from the pulpit, proclaiming the sole authority of the word of God as revealed in the Bible, and preaching against church practices. Zürich's congregation, democratically inclined and politically autonomous, was receptive. Barely a year had passed since Luther had nailed his 95 theses to the door of the Wittenberg church.

In 1523, with mounting tension fuelled by an increasingly vocal opposition to clerical celibacy, monasticism, the observance of Lent and the whole structure of papal control, Zwingli was summoned to a public disputation in Zürich with a papal representative. It says a great deal for Zwingli's powers of persuasion and the city of Zürich's courage that, in the historic disputation at a time of religious and political turbulence, the city council came down on the side of their preacher. The papal representative returned to Rome the loser, and mass was celebrated at the Grossmünster for the last time in 1525.

Zwingli's ideas spread rapidly, and by 1529 Bern, Basel and St Gallen had all embraced the Reformation. Opposition came from two sides: the Anabaptists, who wanted even more radical reform, and the Swiss "Forest Cantons" around Lake Luzern that had taken up arms in loyalty to Rome. War broke out in 1531; Zwingli went into battle but was killed at Kappel. His lead in Zürich was followed by his son-in-law Heinrich Bullinger, but after 1536 the impetus for reform in Switzerland passed to Jean Calvin, a young preacher working in Geneva. Calvin initially followed Zwingli's doctrine, but soon departed from most of Zwingli's more radical teachings to develop his own strict theology. Today, thanks in no small measure to the voyages of Calvinist Puritans to the New World, Calvin is much more familiar than his predecessor, but it was the little-known Zwingli who paved the way, forging ideas of personal liberty, and using them to strike at the very heart of the institutionalized hierarchy that had been taken for granted throughout Europe for centuries.

are replacements, including the pulpit (1851) and the organ (1960). The windows of gorgeously colourful **stained glass** were made in 1933 by Augusto Giacometti and stand alone for their artistic accomplishment. It's worth ducking into the **crypt**, a long triple-aisled hall, the largest of its kind in Switzerland, dominated by the fifteenth-century statue of Charlemagne taken from the South Tower (the one up there now is a replica) and also featuring some well-preserved brush wall drawings dating from 1500. You can **climb** the South Tower for a spectacular view over the city, but normally only by appointment (☎01/252 59 49).

To the right as you leave the Grossmünster onto Zwingliplatz is a door set into the wall of what was once the chapterhouse, now the university's Theological Institute. This gives into the atmospheric **cloister**, originally built in 1170–80, partly demolished in 1848 and renovated in the 1960s. Aside from enjoying the tranquillity of strolling through the vaulted bays around a central garden, it's worth visiting to see the twelfth-century capitals and spandrels of the arched windows, decorated with grotesque faces, monkeys, dragons, centaurs and other fabulous creatures.

The Kunsthaus

Five minutes' walk east up the hill from Bellevue is a square formally dubbed Heimplatz but known to every Zürcher as **"Pfauen"** (Peacocks), after the peacock statue over the famous Schauspielhaus theatre. The adjacent café, now a *Mövenpick*, was for decades known as the Pfauen Café, and was James Joyce's favourite watering hole – it still has a peacock as its inn sign.

Dominating the square is Zürich's **Kunsthaus**, Switzerland's best gallery (Tues–Thurs 10am–9pm, Fri–Sun 10am–5pm; Fr.6 for the permanent collection only, or Fr.8–14 to include temporary exhibits; free on Sundays). As well as an expansive permanent collection, the Kunsthaus hosts a continuous flow of top-flight temporary exhibitions, advertised widely around town. If you visit just one art museum in the country, this should be it. You can pick up a handheld audioguide to the collections for Fr.6.

The collection begins even before you get inside: beside the main door is **Rodin's** vivid *Gate of Hell*, while sculptures by **Moore**, Maillol and others dot the grounds. Inside, the ground-floor galleries house whatever temporary exhibit is on; for the permanent collection (*"Sammlung"*), head left up the stairs next to the ticket booth and double back on yourself at the top to begin with the medieval Masters of the Carnation, the leading Swiss painters of around 1500. **Dutch and Flemish** painting is represented by Rubens, Rembrandt, Hals and others. A narrow corridor leads through to the massive **Graphics Collection** (80,000 works, of which only a tiny fraction can be exhibited), but to keep the thread head left into the Venetian room, for **Canaletto** and **El Greco**. To one side of the Venetians are more canvasas from the Italian and Dutch Baroque. Head back to the Venetians and turn right for a complex of rooms devoted mainly to Swiss artists of the nineteenth century, including many works from Anker, Böcklin, Segantini (see p.474) and **Füssli**, who lived and worked for many years in London.

Back at the head of the stairs, turning left brings you into the new wing, housing a stunning collection of twentieth-century art. A broad selection of pop, concrete and abstract expressionist art is headed by a number of **Warhol**s, a **Rothko** and a gigantic wall-sized installation by Baselitz. Up the stairs here, past some geometric constructivist sculpture and a mezzanine with works by Bacon and Twombly, you'll come to an area devoted to Alberto **Giacometti**, with the widest array of his sculpture in the world. This connects to the uppermost floor of the old wing which houses the best parts of the collection. A collection of French sculpture since Rodin is here dominated, unusually, by **Matisse**. Cubism, Fauvism and **Dada** are all represented, and works by Miró, Dalí and De Chirico head an impressive **Surrealist** overview. **Picasso**, Chagall, Klee and Kandinsky all have whole rooms to themselves, there are two of **Monet's** most beautiful water-lily canvases, while **Van Gogh**, Gauguin, Cézanne and the largest **Munch** collection outside Scandinavia top an extraordinary journey. Last but not least is the rare chance to revel in the powerful, mystical landscapes of Alps and lakes by the Swiss painter **Hodler**.

University museums

If you follow Rämistrasse uphill from the Kunsthaus, you'll soon come to the university quarter. At Rämistrasse 73 is the **Archeological Collection** (Tues–Fri 1–6pm, Sat & Sun 11am–5pm; free), with a range of impressive pieces, but no English notes. Aside from the wealth of Etruscan ware, the most interesting artefacts come from the Middle East: outstanding are an entire case devoted to the stunning Egyptian Fayoum portraits from the first centuries BC–AD; wall-sized steles from ninth-century BC Nimrud (modern Iraq); a complete mummy, and dozens of statuettes of ancient Egyptian deities (including some memorable cats); and many Roman and Hellenic pieces.

Close by, the **ETH Graphics Collection**, Rämistrasse 101 (entrance on Karl Schmid-Strasse; Mon–Fri 10am–5pm, Wed until 8pm; free), houses thousands of woodcuts, etchings and engravings from all periods, particularly strong on Dürer, Rembrandt, Goya and Picasso.

The university buildings are connected to Central in the city centre 40m below by the **Polybahn funicular** (daily 6.45am–7.15pm), an institution in Zürich since 1889. Normal city transport tickets are valid for the two-minute ride.

South from Bellevue

The lakeside promenades running south from Bellevue are crowded with people all summer long, blading, strolling and chatting in the sunshine. On the easy walk south to the lush Zürichhorn park, you'll pass the **Johann Jacobs Museum** at Seefeldquai 17 (Fri & Sat 2–5pm, Sun 10am–5pm; free), a small, mildly diverting place in an elegant lakeside villa that is devoted entirely to the cultural history of coffee. Selections of Rococo and Neoclassical porcelain ware, silver coffeepots, painting, prints and drawings all show the impact of coffee on European society, while videos of TV ads for coffee from the 1950s onwards will make you grin. Needless to say, you can help yourself to free coffee throughout.

Well south of the Zürichhorn park is the small but extremely high-quality private fine-art collection of **E.G. Bührle**, at Zollikerstrasse 172 (Tues & Fri 2–5pm, Wed 5–8pm; Fr.9; tram #2, #4 to Wildbachstrasse, then walk 10min). The paintings are mostly by French Impressionists and Post-Impressionists, displayed in a tastefully furnished private mansion. Manet, Van Gogh (including an 1887 self-portrait) and Cézanne's landscapes form the centrepiece of the collection, but there are dozens of other artists represented, including Monet, Renoir, Sisley, Degas, Toulouse-Lautrec, Seurat, Matisse, Braque and Picasso. Filling out this extraordinary collection are works by Rembrandt, including *Portrait of Saskia*, a rare painting of his wife.

The west bank

Emerging on the south side of the station into hectic Bahnhofplatz, you're met by a statue of Alfred Escher, a prominent nineteenth-century politician and industrialist who is credited with single-handedly leading Zürich into the modern business age. In an inspired piece of statue placement, he gazes down **Bahnhofstrasse**, one of the most prestigious shopping streets in Europe, an enduring symbol of Zürich's wealth and a fascinating counterpoint to the quaintness of the Niederdorf alleys. This is the gateway into the modern city, and is where all of Zürich comes to walk, snack and shop, whether to browse at the inexpensive department stores that crowd the first third of the street, or to sign away Fr.25,000 on a Rolex watch or a Vuitton handbag at the understated super-chic boutiques further south.

Two-thirds of the way along the boulevard is **Paradeplatz**, a tram-packed little square offering some of the best people-watching in the city. It's around here that the frippery retreats and Zürich's serious money begins: the streets off Paradeplatz are home to more **banks**, insurance companies and top-name designer outlets than you could shake a stick at. Most major Swiss banks are headquartered around here – no small matter, when you consider that just one of them, UBS, has assets of around $600 billion, roughly the same as the Swiss gross national product. With Zürich being the world's largest **gold** market, it's a sobering thought to consider that Bahnhofstrasse, if not paved with gold, is at least founded on the stuff, countless ingots piled high in well-protected vaults beneath your feet.

Bahnhofstrasse ends at the hectic and unromantic paved **Bürkliplatz**, departure point for all boat trips on the lake and boasting a fabulous view of the Zürichsee and its eastern "Gold Coast", named for the mansions and grandiose public buildings lining the shore that bask all summer long in the afternoon sunshine.

Around the Lindenhof

Between Bahnhofstrasse and the river lies the western portion of the Old Town, and there are many picturesque alleys to explore here. Rennweg branches off the Bahnhofstrasse, and a short walk left from it up the hill will bring you to the **Lindenhof**, the oldest part of Zürich and site of the original Roman customs post. The broad space is quiet now, occupied mostly by chess-playing old-timers, and gives a wonderful panorama over the rooftops on both sides of the river. Descending on steep **Pfalzgasse** into a dense network of cobbled lanes, **Augustinergasse**, with its romantic oriel-windowed houses, leads to tiny Münzplatz overlooked by the beautiful **Augustinerkirche**, dating from 1274. Spare and simple inside, the church was secularized during the Reformation in 1524 and became the town's mint, but it was renovated and re-dedicated in the nineteenth century and is now used by the Christ Catholics (see p.220). Nearby, the **James Joyce Foundation**, Augustinergasse 9 (Tues, Wed & Fri noon–6pm, Thurs noon–9pm, Sat & Sun 11am–6pm; free), has a creaking library and reading room crammed with research materials and Joyceana of all kinds. Joyce wrote *Ulysses* during his wartime exile in Zürich (1915–19); he returned in 1940, and died on January 13, 1941, laid to rest in Fluntern cemetery next to the Zoo, where there is now a statue to him. The Foundation can direct you to his various haunts around town, and they also hold weekly open readings from *Ulysses* (Thurs 4.30–6pm) and *Finnegans Wake* (Thurs 7–9pm). On the opposite side of Bahnhofstrasse, at Pelikanstrasse 8, is the preserved *James Joyce* pub (see p.392).

Augustinergasse leads on to the **St Peters Kirche** (Mon–Fri 8am–6pm, Sat 8am–4pm), dating from the thirteenth century but much altered in 1705. The fact that it boasts the largest clock face in Europe (8.7m in diameter; 1534) is considerably less interesting than the unusual sight, above the pulpit amidst Baroque bas-relief, of the name of God in Hebrew lettering. A tiny stepped alley adjacent to the church, **Thermengasse**, has a catwalk taking you over an excavated Roman baths. A short distance south is the Münsterhof, with the grand Baroque **Zunfthaus zur Meisen** housing the National Museum's impressive ceramics collection (Tues–Sun 10.30am–5pm; free), including some gorgeous eighteenth-century porcelain and faience.

The Fraumünster

The Münsterhof is dominated by the graceful, slender-spired **Fraumünster**, a beautiful church that boasts a breathtaking series of stained-glass windows by Marc Chagall and Augusto Giacometti that should not be missed.

It's not known when the church was founded, but on July 21, 853, King Ludwig the German signed over to his daughter Hildegard a convent which already stood on the site. In 874, Hildegard's sister Bertha consecrated what was probably a simple, towerless basilica, and built a crypt beneath to house the relics of **Felix and Regula** (see box opposite). During the eleventh century, the abbesses of the convent gained the title of imperial princesses and considerable rights in the town, and the present structure was built during the thirteenth century. The convent was suppressed under Zwingli's Reformation, and in 1524 all the icons, ornaments and the organ were destroyed. During the following centuries, the minster became the place of worship for Veltliner and Huguenot refugees, was temporarily a Russian Orthodox church, and – between 1833 and 1844 – hosted both Catholic and Protestant services. There was much renovation around the turn of the century, and again in 1960, when the Romanesque choir was reopened as an integral part of the building. In 1967, **Marc Chagall** – then 80 – accepted the commission to make new stained glass for the five 10m-high choir windows. The stunning artistry of the windows he produced makes them one of the highlights of Zürich.

Entrance (Mon–Sat: May–Sept 9am–6pm; March, April & Oct 10am–5pm; Nov–Feb 10am–4pm) is into the transept through the small east door beneath the spire, and

---

FELIX AND REGULA

Legend has it that **Felix and Regula**, Roman Christians and the patron saints of Zürich, fled to the city from the massacre of their legion in Valais in the third century AD. They were martyred by decapitation on the site of today's **Wasserkirche** for refusing to pray to Roman gods, whereupon they picked up their heads and carried them up the hill to the spot where they wished to be buried. Over the next centuries, pilgrims came from all over the region to pray at the graves of the saints, even though the legend of their martyrdom was probably one which survived by word of mouth only. By the eighth century the story had been written down, in conjunction with another tale in which **Charlemagne** arrived at the same spot having hunted a stag all the way from Aachen near Köln, when his horse suddenly went down on its knees in deference to the saints buried beneath. Charlemagne proceeded to found a church and adjacent chapterhouse in their honour, the forerunner of the **Grossmünster**. In the late ninth century, relics of the saints were transferred to the newly rebuilt Fraumünster, the women's convent just across the Limmat, forming a **pilgrimage trail** through the city: the Grossmünster as the site of burial, the Wasserkirche as the site of execution, and the Fraumünster as the repository of the saints' remains. A bridge – the Münsterbrücke – was built to link all three in about 1220.

---

attention is so concentrated on the choir that you may well find the rest of the church has been roped off. Staff inside sell an excellent colour brochure (Fr.5) on the Chagall windows.

The Romanesque **choir** dates from 1250–70; it is extremely high (18m) and has a wonderful simplicity of design that would make it a magical place even without its Chagall windows. The blood-red **"Prophets"** window, on the north wall (left), features Elisha at the bottom watching Elijah mount to heaven in a chariot of fire; above, drenched in a divine blue, sits Jeremiah. The **"Law"** window, on the opposite, south, wall, has Moses looking down upon the disobedience and suffering of the people, who are following a horseman into war. Below is Isaiah in the arms of a seraph, preparing to proclaim his message of peace to the world. Of the three main windows, the left, known as the **"Jacob"**, window, shows the patriarch's struggle with the angel and his dream of a ladder to heaven. The yellow **"Zion"** window on the right shows an angel trumpeting the beginning of eternity and the descent of New Jerusalem from the heavens; below are a radiant King David and Bathsheba. Finally, the central **"Christ"** window shows Joseph, standing at the bottom beside a huge tree – the tree of life, and the family tree of Christ – with, floating in its upper branches, a vision of Mary holding the baby Jesus with the Lamb of God at her feet. Scenes from Jesus' life and parables culminate in an associative depiction of the crucifixion; a cross is barely visible, and Christ is already floating free of the world towards the source of luminescence above.

Giacometti's 1940s work in the 9m-high window in the north transept, visible as you head out, is equally stunning. Were it not for the Chagall windows, this vision of God and Christ, with eight prophets below, and Matthew, Mark, Luke and John framed by ten angels, would take pride of place; as it is, it's doomed to play second fiddle.

Emerging from the Fraumünster, the Münsterbrücke leads across the river to the beautiful late-Gothic **Wasserkirche**, site of Felix and Regula's martyrdom (see box above) and still used mostly for services (visiting hours Wed 9–11am & 2–5pm), the Baroque **Helmhaus** (guildhall) and the Grossmünster beyond. It's an equally short walk south to Bürkliplatz.

The Schweizerisches Landesmuseum

Behind the main station, and unmistakeable in its mock-Gothic, purpose-built castle, is the **Schweizerisches Landesmuseum**, Museumstrasse 2 (Swiss National Museum;

Tues–Sun 10.30am–5pm; free; *www.slmnet.ch*). This massive building has a wide and varied collection covering the range of Swiss history, and is well worth investigation, though some of its displays are rather sterile. The collection is so vast, and the layout of the place so labyrinthine, that you may find it more satisfying to consult a (free) floor-plan and then head straight for those areas which interest you rather than to try and absorb the whole thing. Staff give regular guided tours of the whole collection in English (June–Sept Thurs 10.30am; free).

The museum begins with a series of rooms devoted to **sacred art** from the ninth to the sixteenth centuries, displaying medieval wood carvings, painted altar pieces, a wheelable model of Christ on an ass (used in Palm Sunday processions), and 65 copies of the 153 panels adorning the ceiling of the church at Zillis (see p.456). Fifteenth-century **stained glass** has been installed in a room which also displays a sequence of images of some less well-known saints (including St Vitus, patron saint of bedwetting). Rooms lead you past a reconstruction of an eighteenth-century **apothecary** and a intricately detailed sixteenth-century bestiary; up some stairs are several watches and clocks, and a display on **exploration** crowned by a spectacular two-metre-high globe dating from 1570. Pieces showing the life of the Swiss **nobility** include a decorated gentleman's sleigh from seventeenth-century Luzern. Stairs lead up again to a tower, with dozens of cases of **costumes**, some pieces of silver and eighteenth- and nineteenth-century **toys**. Returning back down the same stairs brings you to a sequence of **Baroque** and Rococo rooms, including a ceremonial hall from a Zürich house of 1660. There's also a section on **military history**, as well as an **archeological collection**, comprising a wealth of finds from Roman Zürich. Pick of the Iron Age collection is a stunning

---

ABOVE ZÜRICH

One of the best short trips out of the city is to the hill of **Uetliberg**, a twenty-minute train ride away and a favoured getaway for the locals to do a spot of sledding (winter) or picnicking (summer). Uetliberg is also one end of a popular hiking route, running about two hours south along a forested ridge overlooking the lake to Felsenegg, from where a cable-car can deliver you 300m down to Adliswil village to catch a train back to Zürich. If you're doing the whole circular journey, press *131 on the ticket machine; otherwise press 8138 for Uetliberg only.

From Zürich HB, S-Bahn **trains** depart at least every half-hour to Uetliberg. At the tiny end station, where an information hut can give you a free hiking map of the area identifying plenty of short and long trails, you'll find the *Gmüetliberg* restaurant (Mon–Sat 8am–midnight, Sun 8am–10pm; *www.gmuetliberg.ch*), a basic affair offering a self-service buffet for an above-average Fr.16 (daily 8am–6pm only). The trail which begins at Uetliberg station is tagged the *Planetenweg* (Planet Path), and features models of the planets on a scale of 1:1 billion, with the distances between them also to scale. From the station, it's about a ten-minute walk uphill to the **summit**, passing the Sun, Mercury, Venus, Earth and Mars on the way – Pluto is about 5km away at Felsenegg.

From the top of the summit's 30m viewing tower, which boosts your altitude to 900m, there are terrific 360-degree views over Zürich, the whole curve of the lake and, on a clear day, east into Austria and as far southwest as the Jungfrau. Also on the summit is the *Uto Kulm* **hotel** and restaurant (☎01/457 66 66, fax 457 66 99, *utokulm@uetliberg.ch*, *www.uetliberg.ch*; ④), a handy place for refreshment. Its clean, modern rooms offer considerably better value for money than similar city-centre hotels, especially when you throw in the tranquillity, the alpine vistas and free 4WD pickups to and from the station (also ask about their Fr.222 lovers' package, which comprises dinner, an en-suite room and breakfast for two). The panoramic walking route from *Uto Kulm* to Felsenegg and beyond passes another couple of restaurants. The **cable-car** runs every fifteen minutes between Felsenegg and Adliswil (daily: May–Sept 8am–10pm; Oct–April 9am–8pm), from where it's less than ten minutes' walk to Adliswil S-Bahn station.

embossed golden bowl from 600 BC; Neolithic and Bronze Age artefacts bring you back round to the entrance again.

Museum Rietberg

The impressive **Museum Rietberg** (*www.rietberg.ch*) comprises two villas set in a lush park southwest of the centre, which together house a spectacular collection of non-European art. Signs from the Rietberg stop on tram #7 direct you up into the park; a right-hand fork takes you to the Villa Wesendonck, a left-hand fork to the Park-Villa Rieter. The main collection is housed in the grandiose **Villa Wesendonck** (Tues–Sun 10am–5pm; Fr.6 for both buildings, plus about Fr.6 for any special exhibits), where the composer Richard Wagner lived for a time in 1857. Once inside, head left for a chronological tour, through rooms of Indian and Chinese Buddhist art and sculpture from between the third and sixteenth centuries – look out for the blissfully serene lovers' faces, in glorious contrast to the mournfulness on display in the Landesmuseum's European art of roughly the same period. A four-armed dancing Shiva in bronze, surrounded by a ring of fire, is particularly stunning. Upstairs are some intricate Tibetan bronzes, Chinese ceramics, and a host of American, African and Australasian pieces. The smaller **Park-Villa Rieter** (Tues–Sat 1–5pm, Sun 10am–5pm) houses on two floors changing selections from the museum's enormous collection of exquisite Asian painting: Indian art on ground level, Chinese and Japanese art upstairs.

Eating and drinking

As you might expect from a city like Zürich, there's a wealth of variety in **eating and drinking** possibilities, with as much available at the bottom end of the market as at the top.

Cafés and café-bars

There's an enormous variety of both **cafés** and **café-bars** in Zürich and, as ever, the difference between them, and between a café and a restaurant, is blurred. The most characterful places tend to be crowded on the alleys of Niederdorf, but the shopping streets around Bahnhofstrasse also shelter a handful of quality watering-holes. Exclusively gay bars, and Zürich's sole women-only bar, are listed in the box on p.396.

Niederdorf

Altstadt, Kirchgasse 4. Cool jazzy bar, open from breakfast time onwards, that's gaining a reputation as an old-town meeting point away from the sleaze.

Babalu, Schmidgasse 6. Tiny postmodern-style bar, its chic denizens quaffing bottled beers and cocktails amidst an onslaught of jungle beats.

Cranberry, Metzgergasse 3. Strange combination of a cosy bar – predominantly gay – and what the management call a "smoking lounge" for dispersing cigar smoke and other fragrant aromas into the night air.

Nachtcafé, Münstergasse 26. An upstairs members-only restaurant, bar and dancefloor (no aftershave, no entry) with a chic basement bar open to all. Handy for late-night liquor, but still so hip it hurts. Closed Sun.

Odeon, Limmatquai 2. Compact café-bar on Bellevue, where Lenin once sat and watched the world go by. There's little sign of revolutionary activity these days – although the bar prices would spark a popular uprising in any city other than Zürich.

Oepfelchammer, Rindermarkt 12. A 200-year-old building, all creaking timbers and lop-sided ceilings, famous for its association with the city's literary son, Gottfried Keller. The reason to visit is for beer in the tiny low-beamed upper front room, consistently packed. Legend has it that if you can swing up and wriggle your way through the gap between beam and ceiling, your beers are on the house: Keller may have done it, but few have braved the waiters since. Closed Sun & Mon.

Pigalle, Marktgasse 14. Legendary little bar filled with the elegantly wasted, or at least those who are aspiring.

Rheinfelder Bierhalle, Niederdorfstrasse 76. Best of the many Central-end beerhalls. With wooden benches, zero decoration and bright lights, this is a place to get shamelessly, sociably drunk, laugh loudly and clap strangers on the back. The food is cheap and hearty: daily specials for around Fr.13 are padded out by their infamous "Jumbo Jumbo Cordon Bleu", at Fr.22 – a slab of deep-fried cheese-slathered meat so big it dangles off the plate on both sides. Closed Sun.

Schlauch, Münstergasse 20 (upstairs). Quiet, friendly and relaxed diner-bar, perfect to catch your breath from the Niederdorf scrum. Sizeable plates of health-conscious food (veggie and not), and a snooker hall adjacent attract a young, vaguely alternative crowd. Closed Mon & Tues.

Schober, Napfgasse 4. A memorable old confectioner's and café that's straight out of Mary Poppins – a riot of frothy white lace, flowers and choice treats – but head through to the capacious interior for quite simply the best mug of hot chocolate (with whipped cream) you will ever have tasted. It's even a shame to spoil it with a slice of home-made apple strudel … but then again.

Wüste, Oberdorfstrasse 7. Mellow, comfortable café-bar below the *Otter* hotel, decorated in ethnic style and dotted with candles.

Zähringer, Spitalgasse at Zähringerplatz. Long-standing co-operative-run bastion of Zürcher counterculture, attracting an alternative clientele for snacks, herbal teas and beer. Dawn opening on the weekends makes it a mecca for clubbed-out sleepyheads. Mon 6pm–midnight, Tues–Fri 8am–midnight, Sat & Sun 5am–midnight.

Around Bahnhofstrasse

Amsterdam, Schwanengasse 4. Tiny, dark old town café for fresh juices and healthy snacks.

Helvetia, Stauffacherquai 1. Loud and jovial locals' haunt just across the Sihl – the only bar in town where you can get full table service after midnight (closes 1am weekdays, 2am weekends). A little pricey for everyday consumption, but very civilized for a nightcap or three.

James Joyce, Pelikanstrasse 8. The ultimate memorial to one of Zürich's best-known visitors. The pub comprises the original nineteenth-century interior of the Jury Hotel's "Antique Bar", saved from the developers in the 1970s, transported piece by piece from Dame Street, Dublin, and reassembled here to stand as a relic of a bygone age. Closed from 7pm on Sat, and all day Sun.

Kaufleuten, Pelikanstrasse 18. Modish venue for mixing with Zürich's burgeoning "in" scene. Designers, musicians, bankers and the idle rich flock here, and to the club next door (see below) – a pricey *stange* is worth it for the buzz.

Mövenpick, Paradeplatz. Perfect people-watching café, with a great selection of teas and coffees from around the world, plus snacks and full meals all day long.

Nelson, Beatengasse 11. Massive, noisy pub seconds from the station, crammed on weekend nights with Zürich's sizeable contingent of teenage au pairs and exchange students on the pull. Cheap beer, late opening, live music, DJs, and TV sport make for a heady, if predictable, brew.

Noble Dubliner, Talstrasse 82. Good beer and a talkative atmosphere make this cosy, comfy pub hugely popular with locals and expats alike.

Sprüngli, Bahnhofstrasse 21. Main branch of the world-famous confectioner's, displaying cabinets full of the most exquisite chocolates and cakes imaginable, plus their own speciality, *Luxemburgli*, cream-filled bites that you'd have to be made of stone not to drool over. Enjoy it all in the upstairs café-patisserie overlooking Paradeplatz. A free choc with every espresso.

West and south

Xenix, Kanzleistrasse 56 at Helvetiaplatz. Wooden shack-bar just off Langstrasse, part of the city's leading art-house cinema and crammed most nights with a fascinating bunch of artists, filmmakers and wannabes lubricating their vocal chords at each other. On Thursdays, *Xenix* becomes *Xenia*, the bar and cinema both strictly women-only.

Ziegel oh Lac, at the Rote Fabrik arts centre (see p.395), Seestrasse 395. One of the most appealing bar/restaurant-spaces in the city, with a light, open interior and waterside seating in summer but way south of the city, far from the crush. Signs declare "Smoking Cannabis is Illegal", but to little effect. The food is quality, balanced stuff (Fr.12–22). Closed Mon.

Inexpensive and mid-range restaurants

There's a host of good-quality **affordable restaurants** in every corner of the city that can do you a filling lunch for Fr.15–20, or a full evening meal for roughly twice that; Niederdorf is shoulder to shoulder with them. Traditional Zürich cuisine is rich and heavy with meat, epitomized in the city's trademark *Züri Gschnetzlets* – diced veal in a creamy mushroom sauce, generally served alongside *Rösti*. As a general rule, at lunch time the area around Bahnhofstrasse is livelier than Niederdorf, while in the evening the reverse is true.

Niederdorf

Adler's Swiss Chuchi, Rosengasse 10 (☎01/266 96 66). Landmark Swiss den below the *Adler* hotel, freshly renovated in bright, modern style amidst ranks of sleazy sex shops. Good-value fondue or raclette (Fr.25–30) are what to go for; the bargain lunch specials have a careful, home-cooked touch as well, but cheese is the thing.

Ban Song Thai, Kirchgasse 6 (☎01/252 33 31). One of the city's better Thais, small and pleasant with a varied menu. Lunch specials start from Fr.15, evening meals more than twice that. Closed Sun.

Bodega Española, Münstergasse 15 (☎01/251 23 10). Small, dark-wood place, concealed from the street behind a wine shop and dripping with atmosphere. Upstairs is the restaurant, with a long menu ranging from *tortilla catalana* to an unmissable *paella* (Fr.37 for two). The buzzing tapas bar downstairs is also outstanding, with a huge range from Fr.4.60 (or Fr.10.50 for a large plate).

Kantorei, Neumarkt 2 (☎01/252 27 27). Warm and pleasant young restaurant in a little-visited part of the Old Town serving unpretentious modern Swiss cuisine and doubling as a tranquil café between mealtimes.

Pinte Vaudoise, in *Hotel Villette*, Kruggasse 4 (☎01/251 23 35). Traditional dark-wood den serving what has been regularly voted as the best fondue in Zürich. The jovial owner/manager/chef is used to tourists and can explain the range of fondues on offer (around Fr.22). Closed Sat in summer, & Sun.

Santa Lucia, Marktgasse 21. Simple Niederdorf Italian with a wide selection of good-value pasta and pizza, plus the bonus of late-night service until 2am.

Weisser Wind, Oberdorfstrasse 20. Comfortable, traditional Niederdorf setting for Italian and Swiss specialities, with plenty of vegetarian options, for around Fr.20–30. A beerhall in all but name. Closed Sun.

Around Bahnhofstrasse

Hiltl, Sihlstrasse 28 (☎01/227 70 00; *www.hiltl.ch*). Top-quality vegetarian celebrating its 100th-plus birthday but updated with bright decor, calm, friendly service and excellent fare. Spurn the à la

---

CHEAP EATS

Zürich offers a wealth of places to **eat cheaply** and reasonably well. The self-service *Manora*, on the fifth floor of the Manor department store at Bahnhofstrasse 75, has good, balanced meals of all kinds for Fr.10–15. You'll find plenty of falafel, sausage, noodle and chip stalls all along Niederdorf, but you can often do better with the daily special (around Fr.12) at one of the beerhalls. In the station you're spoiled for choice but, in addition to the handy *Rösti Bar* up on street level (from Fr.12), check out the stand-up *Suan Long*, on the lower shopping level (daily 10.30am–9.30pm), which does filling Asian dishes for Fr.12–15. Another stand-up place is *Wave International*, in the Jelmoli department store on Seidengasse, with excellent Italian, Swiss, Asian, Turkish and Arabic nosh for Fr.8–13. The *Mensa Polyterrasse*, on Künstlergasse at the university – turn right out of the Polybahn – has full meals, including veggie, for Fr.10.50, less for students (Mon–Fri & every other Sat 11.15am–1.30pm, also Mon–Thurs & every other Fri 5.30–7.15pm).

carte options for the expansive and great-value hot and cold buffet – by night featuring delectable Indian dishes. At Fr.4.60 for 100g, you can put together a sizeable meal for Fr.20, much less if you take it out and picnic on the nearby Lindenhof instead.

JOSEF, Gasometerstrasse 24 at Josefstrasse (☎01/271 65 95). Young, trendy hangout in an up-and-coming area: a jazzy candle-lit bar attached to a semi-formal restaurant that gets rave reviews from local hipsters and is well worth a splash (Fr.30–40).

Reithalle, Gessnerallee 8 (☎01/212 07 66). Formerly the military riding school, this complex of buildings along the Sihl has been turned into a theatre and centre for performing arts, with one long, stone-floored hall serving as a combination bar and restaurant. It attracts a lively and eclectic crowd of twenty-somethings with a varied menu of light, modern dishes (many vegetarian), and a relaxed, share-a-table attitude. Saturday nights they crank up the music for late-night dancing.

Zeughauskeller, Bahnhofstrasse 28a at Paradeplatz (☎01/211 26 90). A wood-ceilinged chamber dating from the fifteenth century that's now the city's top beerhall, a sometimes chaotic place serving hearty meat dishes and plenty of the amber nectar. One of the most extensive sausage menus around – over a dozen different varieties – is crowned by a one-metre giant that should keep four people occupied for some time. Although the menu is in English (and ten other languages), this is very popular with Zürchers of a certain bank balance – a long way from the rough-and-ready beerhalls of Niederdorf.

Expensive restaurants

There's no shortage of **expensive restaurants** in Zürich, places where you'd be lucky to come away with change from Fr.50 per person, and are probably looking at almost twice that for a full meal. The following are a handful of the more characterful and accessible places among the city's wealth of formal *haute cuisine* outlets.

Hummerbar, in *Hotel St Gotthard*, Bahnhofstrasse 87 (☎01/227 76 21). Of the three restaurants in the hotel, this is the most appealing, a wonderfully romantic place for *Hummer* (lobster) and a host of other seafood, all flown in fresh daily and prepared in pristine style for consumption amidst a formal, *fin-de-siècle* setting. Prices – compared with others under this heading – are reasonable, but who's counting when you're contemplating fresh oysters?

Kronenhalle, Rämistrasse 4 (☎01/251 02 56). One of Zürich's best restaurants. An impressive array of the twentieth century's great and good have licked their chops appreciatively here, but the ambience of the place, bedecked with original Picassos, Matisses and Braques, remains amiable rather than stiff. Then again, with at least one hors d'oeuvre over Fr.100, they can afford to be amiable. The cuisine is outstanding but undramatic – there's little on the menu that you won't have seen before – but where the place scores is in its down-to-earth attitude to those who decide to spurn the champagne and truffles in favour of enjoying the atmosphere over a sausage and a glass of beer instead.

Kropf, In Gassen 16 (☎01/221 18 05). An atmospheric listed building, boasting a frescoed interior which dates from its conversion into a restaurant in 1888, and which stands a little askance with the solid *bürgerliche* cooking on offer: Bacchic revels may be erupting all around, but only in picture form on the ceiling. Meat, potatoes and dumplings in various forms, along with tripe, are staples, and yet standards are high and the food is never dull. Closed Sun.

Zunfthaus zur Schmiden, Marktgasse 20 (☎01/251 52 87). The guildhall of the smiths, dating from 1520, and now a spectacular setting in which to linger over the richest of Swiss-German cuisine, meat-heavy platters and top Zürcher specialities such as *geschnetzeltes Kalbfleisch* (veal in a white wine and cream sauce), everything in mighty portions. Closed Sun.

Nightlife and entertainment

For a city that's a minnow in world terms, Zürich has a surprisingly wide range of **nightlife and entertainment**. Live rock and jazz – although easy to find most nights of the week – take second place to the city's amazingly dynamic club scene, which covers the gamut from techno to salsa. The city is also home to a top-flight orchestra, a world-famous opera company, and one of the German-speaking world's premier theatres.

You can find complete what's-on **listings** for the week ahead in *ZüriTipp*, the Friday supplement to the *Tages Anzeiger* newspaper (English Web version at *www.zueritipp.ch/essentials*). The tourist booklet *Zürich News* covers major events, but nothing out of the mainstream. The clubbers' bible, with full listings, is *Forecast* (Fr.3 monthly). **Tickets** for almost any event can be had from Billetzentrale Zürich (BiZZ), a city-run organization housed in a hut on Werdmühleplatz (Mon–Fri 10am–6.30pm, Sat 10am–2pm; ☎01/221 22 83), which mirrors the larger, mainstream venues by closing down for July and August. Prices are high: Fr.10–15 for ordinary live bands and clubs, Fr.20–25 for big-name shows, Fr.15–60 for classical concerts, and Fr.16–270 for the opera.

Rock music and jazz

Zürich is a minor stop on the European tour circuit for big-name stars, but a burgeoning local scene gives rich pickings for **live music** at a spread of venues around town, headed by the Rote Fabrik. Many people make the short trip to Winterthur to see bands at the Albani (see p.403).

Abart, Manessestrasse 170. Regular eclectic choice of local and foreign bands.

Casa Bar, Münstergasse 20. Zürich's longest-running jazz venue, still featuring live music nightly.

Dynamo, Wasserwerkstrasse 21. Bills itself as a "youth culture centre" and, as well as a disco and jazz school, hosts live bands with an alternative, punkish bias.

Moods, Sihlamtstrasse 5. The city's premier jazz club, with good restuarant attached, pulling in top-flight names.

Rohstofflager, Josefstrasse 224. Lively mix of DJs and live bands.

Rote Fabrik, Seestrasse 395 (*www.rotefabrik.ch*). Alternative-style arts complex, in old graffitied industrial buildings on the lakeshore some 5km southwest of town, hosting a continuous flow of bands famous and unknown from all musical genres. Bus #161 or #165 from Bürkliplatz (last bus returns after midnight).

Widder Bar, Widdergasse 6. Chic city-centre hotel bar featuring quality weekly (Wed) jazz nights.

Clubs

Zürich's **club** scene has skyrocketed recently, helped by legislation permitting some all-night opening: you'll find the city's dance venues heaving with a new-found energy lacking in most European cities. Heart of the new subculture is **Langstrasse**, formerly the red-light district, which these days is undergoing a transformation into an eclectic and exciting neighbourhood – music stores and clubwear boutiques cheek by jowl with the biker bars and sex cinemas of old. Its cafés are full of artists and young people, and you'll come across cosmopolitan bars, chic bistros and crowded alternative hangouts. The northern half of **Niederdorf** has some of the same vibe. The **industrial quarter** northwest of Langstrasse is where the best underground clubs hide themselves, but new ones open every month: you could either head out there and follow your ears (Thurs, Fri or Sat after midnight), or chat and check flyers in Zap Records at Zähringerstrasse 47. There's something happening every night of the week, but Friday and Saturday are busiest. Most places open 10–11pm and close by about 3 or 4am, although a few stay open until 6am or later on the weekend. Entry is usually Fr.10–15.

Dynamo, Wasserwerkstrasse 21. Alternative sounds, everything from guitar-based pop to the deepest drum'n'bass.

El Cubanito, Bleicherweg 5. Salsa and funk.

Inkognito, Hardturmstrasse 122. Atmospheric cutting-edge styles out in the industrial quarter.

Kaufleuten, Pelikanstrasse 18. Plush city-centre mecca, mainstream housey beats drawing a curious blend of clubbers and bankers.

Klinik, Freigutstrasse. Best and most innovative club in the city, with a drum'n'bassy tilt and dynamic feel.

GAY AND LESBIAN ZÜRICH

Zürich has a thriving **gay and lesbian** scene, probably the best established and most diverse in the country. Although no hotel will turn a gay or lesbian couple away, the *Goldenes Schwert* is the only one to make a selling point of its gay- and lesbian-friendliness; handily enough, it occupies the same building as *T&M*, one of the best gay bar/cabaret/disco venues in the city, dark, campy and cruisey. The huge *Barfüsser*, Spitalgasse 14, is Europe's longest-running gay bar, established in 1956 and embracing all scenes, while *Cranberry* (see p.391) is a more relaxed, talkative meeting place for non-scene types. The "Bermuda Triangle" is a cruisey area around Mühlegasse, epitomized by *Emilio's Bagpiper* ("where you meet the right people") at Zähringerstrasse 11. *Labyrinth*, Pfingstweidstrasse 70, is a hugely popular gay/straight techno club. **Lesbians** must rely on a smaller scene, focused around the *Venus* women-only bar (see "Women's contacts", p.398), and the Thursday women-only nights at the *Xenix* bar and cinema (see "Film" below). *Tabu*, Josefstrasse 142, is a lesbian-owned café-bar that attracts a lot of lesbian and gay customers (closed Sun & Mon).

For more **information**, contact HAZ (Homosexuelle Arbeitsgruppen Zürich), at Sihlquai 67 (Tues–Fri 7.30–11pm, Sun 11am–2pm). Zürich's magazine for gays is *Cruiser* (☎01/450 19 89; *www.cruiser.ch*), for lesbians *BOA* (☎01/291 26 01), and you can pick up the *Columbia Fun-Map*, pinpointing gay-owned and gay-friendly businesses in Zürich and eastern Switzerland, at all the bars above. The gay helpline is ☎01/271 70 11 (Tues & Thurs 8–10pm); the lesbian one ☎01/272 73 71 (Thurs 6–8pm).

Labyrinth, Pfingstweidstrasse 70. Hard house firing up an energetic mixed gay/straight crowd.

Oxa, Andreasstrasse 70. Premier venue for techno and house; famous for its after-hours parties (Sat & Sun 5am–noon).

Rohstofflager, Josefstrasse 224. Techno nights interspersed with live bands.

Rote Fabrik, Seestrasse 395. Subculture venue with changing nights and big-name DJs.

X-tra, Limmatstrasse 118. Hugely popular multipurpose venue just off Limmatplatz, with triphop and funky sounds entertaining a youngish crowd. Bar and restaurant adjacent, and *Hotel Limmat* upstairs.

Film

Zürich's **cinemas** are mostly two- or three-screen houses showing the latest releases, almost always in their original language, although afternoon shows are sometimes dubbed. Check in the listings for "E/d/f", which means English spoken with German and French subtitles. Non-English-language films are rarely given English subtitles. Prices are universally high (Fr.15–17) but every cinema in the city has cut-price Fr.11 tickets for all shows on Mondays.

City-centre cinemas showing Hollywood releases abound. There are two art-house cinemas with daily changing programmes of retrospectives and experimental movies from around the world: Xenix Filmclub, Kanzleistrasse 56 at Helvetiaplatz; and Filmpodium im Studio 4, Nüschelerstrasse 11.

Classical music, opera and theatre

The acoustically superb Tonhalle concert hall, Claridenstrasse 7 (☎01/206 34 34), inaugurated by Brahms in 1895, has a programme of world-class **classical music** of all kinds from both the resident Tonhalle and Zürich Chamber orchestras and guest performers. Many of Zürich's churches – principally the Grossmünster, Fraumünster, Predigerkirche and St Peter's – host regular concerts of organ, choral and chamber music, as does the Conservatory (Florhofgasse 6), the *Dolder Grand Hotel* (see p.382) and the Kunsthaus. The city's large Opernhaus (☎01/268 66 66) has an impressive programme of both **opera and ballet**: performances sell out quickly, but you can check on the season's schedule at *www.operabase.com* and write for tickets, which go on sale a month ahead of time, to: Opernhaus Billetkasse, Falkenstrasse 1, CH-8008 Zürich.

The Schauspielhaus **theatre**, Rämistrasse 34 (☎01/265 58 58), is one of the German-speaking world's finest: during World War II, it was Europe's only German-language theatre that continued to stage productions independent of Nazi censorship. The main stage remains Zürich's most prestigious, while the cellar-studio hosts avant-garde productions. Zürich also has more than a dozen other theatres, big and small, presenting everything from tragedy to puppetry, but all in German. Perhaps the most accessible performances for non-German speakers are the top-quality **cabaret** shows at the Hcchtplatz Theatre (☎01/216 31 26).

Listings

Books Zürich's best general source of books in English is Stäheli, Bahnhofstrasse 70. For travel books – including Rough Guides – head for the Travel Bookshop, Rindermarkt 20.

Car rental Avis, Gartenhofstrasse 17 (☎01/296 87 87) and airport (☎01/800 77 33); Budget, Steinstrasse 21 (☎01/450 75 35) and airport (☎01/813 31 31); Europcar, Josefstrasse 53 (☎01/271 56 56) and airport (☎01/813 20 44); Hertz, Morgartenstrasse 5 (☎01/242 84 84) and airport (☎01/814 05 11).

Changing money Best is the change bureau in the station (daily 6.30am–10.45pm). This is also the place to pick up money wired by Western Union.

Consulates Republic of Ireland, Claridenstrasse 25 (☎01/289 25 15); UK, Minervastrasse 117 (☎01/383 65 60); USA, Dufourstrasse 101 (☎01/422 25 66). New Zealand has a consulate in Geneva (see p.105); other English-speaking countries are represented by their embassies in Bern (see p.231).

Email and Internet access For neon-lit surfing, swing along to Stars ("US of A") Bistro in the station; one corner is known as Cybergate (daily 11.30am–11.30pm; Fr.15/hr). Café Urania, at Uraniastrasse 9 (Sun–Thurs 10am–11pm, Fri & Sat 10am–midnight; Fr.15/hr) lets you pay by the minute. The stand-up coin-or-credit-card terminal at the station's change bureau costs Fr.3 for 10min.

Flights For all domestic and international flight enquiries from Zürich-Kloten airport, call ☎157 10 60. For a train ticket to the airport, press 8058 on the ticket machines. MFGZ Rundflug, based at the airport (☎01/814 26 20), offers sightseeing flights long and short (April–Oct only).

Laundry Mühlegasse 11, Niederdorf (Mon–Fri 7.30am–noon & 1–6.30pm).

Libraries The central municipal library is at Zähringerplatz 6 (Mon–Fri 8am–8pm, Sat 8am–4pm).

Lost property The city office is at Werdmühlestrasse 10 (Mon–Fri 7.30am–5.30pm; ☎01/211 25 51). The station office is near the head of platform 17 (daily 7am–6pm).

Medical facilities Most convenient is the Permanence Medical Centre at Bahnhofplatz 15 (daily 7am–11pm, but with a 24-hour emergency room; ☎01/215 44 44). Dial ☎01/269 69 69 if you need a doctor or dentist. There's a pharmacy beside the Permanence clinic (daily 7am–midnight); and Pharmacy Bellevue, Theaterstrasse 14, is open daily 24 hours.

Parks and gardens The small Platzspitz park (daily 6am–9pm), where the Sihl meets the Limmat, was once known as Needle Park, crunching underfoot with used syringes from the flaked-out junkies all around. These days it's been entirely cleaned up, and is good for a short wander framed by the two rivers. The Zürichhorn park on the lakefront is a popular place for soaking up some sunshine and has an exquisite Chinese garden (Fr.7), and there's a waterside Arboretum a few minutes west of Bürkliplatz. Further afield, the pleasant, open Botanischer Garten, Zollikerstrasse 107 (March–Sept Mon–Fri 7am–7pm, Sat & Sun 8am–6pm; hours slightly curtailed in winter; tram #2 or #4 to Höschgasse), is a riot of colour in spring and summer, and has three tropical planthouses. You'll find luscious orchids and a steamy little tropical forest complete with birds and turtles in the fragrant Schauhäuser der Stadtgärtnerei, Sackzelgasse 25 (daily 9–11.30am & 1.30–4.30pm; tram #3 to Hubertus). There's also a huge succulents collection at Mythenquai 88 (same times), and a 150-species-strong aviary at Mythenquai 1 (Tues–Sun 10am–noon & 2–4pm).

Police Headquarters is at Bahnhofquai 3 (☎01/216 71 11).

Post Zürich's main post office is the Sihlpost, an unmissable behemoth poised over the Sihl next to the main station on Kasernenstrasse (Mon–Fri 6.30am–10.30pm, Sat 6.30am–8pm, Sun 11am–10.30pm). You can collect mail sent to you at Poste Restante, Schalter 8, Sihlpost, CH-8021 Zürich, from counter 8. There's also a post office within the station.

Smart drugs For all kinds of weird and wonderful (and legal) party-boosting substances, check out Smart Stuff, Badenerstrasse 129 (Tues–Fri noon–7pm, Sat noon–4pm). A full range of smoking paraphernalia can be had from various Niederdorf headshops; the best is Paradise, Brunngasse 3.

Spectator sport The famous Grasshoppers (☎01/447 46 46; *www.gcz.ch*) are one of Europe's top football (soccer) teams, and supply many players to the Swiss national outfit. With FC Zürich, the city's other club (☎01/492 74 74; *www.fcz.ch*) too, your chance of catching a high-quality game is high. Grasshoppers' ice-hockey team (☎01/317 20 72) is also pre-eminent, and there's a host of other Zürich teams involved in the national sport.

Supermarkets Largest and most convenient central supermarket is the Coop, on Bahnhofbrücke (Mon–Fri 7am–8pm, Sat 7am–4pm).

Travel agents Most central office of discount flight agents SSR Reisen is Leonhardstrasse 10 (Mon noon–6pm, Tues, Wed & Fri 10am–6pm, Thurs 10am–8pm, Sat 10am–1pm; ☎01/261 97 57).

Women's contacts First stop is the FIZ (Fraueninformationszentrum; Quellenstrasse 25; Mon–Fri 9am–1pm; ☎01/271 82 82). *Venus*, Badenerstrasse 219, is Zürich's sole women-only bar (daily 5pm–midnight; accompanied men welcome Thursdays; tram #2 or #3 to Lochergut). The *Xenix* bar and cinema are women-only on Thursdays. Schema F, Mattengasse 27 (Tues–Fri 6–8pm; Oct–May also Sun 4–6pm; ☎01/271 96 88), is a library devoted to women's and lesbian fiction and non-fiction, although it's of limited use to non-German speakers.

Around Zürich

The countryside around Zürich holds a couple of small-scale gems, mostly ignored by visitors either absorbed in the city or hurrying to the mountains. This is a shame, since **Winterthur** is easily accessible from Zürich, and serves as a refreshing small-town counterpoint to the place, while still coming up with a full deck of museums and galleries that easily hold their own in comparison. Fifteen minutes west of Zürich, **Baden** is a genteel and comfortable spa town that has an impressive gallery of its own. Accommodation prices in both Winterthur and Baden can undercut Zürich's by quite a long way, and with transport to and from Zürich fast and easy, you could save yourself significant sums – and be guaranteed a peaceful night's sleep – by basing yourself in either town instead of their bigger neighbour.

Winterthur

A peaceful town of almost 100,000, set in rolling countryside on the River Töss 25km northeast of Zürich, **WINTERTHUR** makes for a useful overnight stop on the way to Stein-am-Rhein and Schaffhausen, and also has a volley of impressive museums – fifteen in all – that are worth making some time for.

Evidence of a nearby settlement called *Vitudurum* goes back to the first century AD, but the city dates its history from 1264, when it was granted status by the Habsburg king Rudolf. In 1467, the Habsburgs sold Winterthur to Zürich, ensuring it remained subject to its neighbour until the Napoleonic invasion in 1798. The Industrial Revolution powered the city's meteoric growth during the nineteenth century, and after 1848 it also became the centre of the democratic movement in Switzerland, with political theorists and activists basing themselves in the city. Winterthurer architects and engineers visited England in mid-century to study building-design for factories and workers' housing, and so brought back English ideas for the huge new factories going up to serve Winterthur's booming textile and railway engineering industries. Most Swiss today still indelibly associate Winterthur – the country's sixth-largest city – with industry: it has managed successfully to pull off the transition into hi-tech, and remains an energetic place, boosted by a thriving cultural scene and its own university and vocational college. It's also surprisingly green, and the combination of students, bicycles, green hills and world-class art galleries can make for a pleasant day or two.

Arrival and orientation

Winterthur is well connected to Zürich by both mainline trains and the S-Bahn. The **station** is centrally located at the western edge of the small Old Town, no more than a

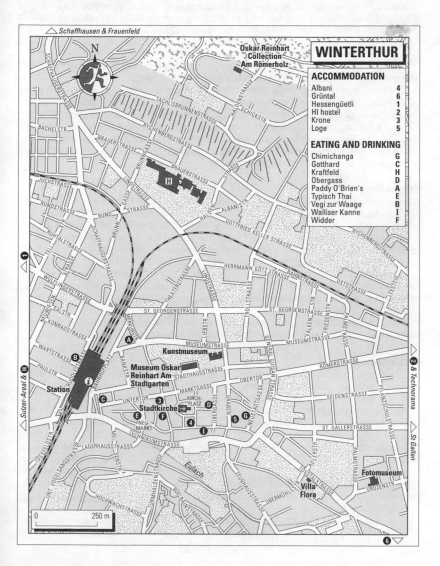

△ Schaffhausen & Frauenfeld

WINTERTHUR

Oskar Reinhart Collection Am Römerholz

ACCOMMODATION

Albani	4
Grüntal	6
Hessengüetli	1
HI hostel	2
Krone	3
Loge	5

EATING AND DRINKING

Chimichanga	G
Gotthard	C
Kraftfeld	H
Obergass	D
Paddy O'Brien's	A
Typisch Thai	E
Vegi zur Waage	B
Walliser Kanne	I
Widder	F

Kunstmuseum

Museum Oskar Reinhart Am Stadtgarten

Station

Stadtkirche

Villa Flora

Fotomuseum

Eulach

0   250 m

WINTERTHUR'S FESTIVALS

The best and most popular of the town's annual events is the **Albanifäscht**, a weekend of live rock music and jazz held in late June. The **Kyburgiade** is a week-long series of chamber music concerts held in early August in the romantic setting of Kyburg castle. The **Musikfestwochen**, in late August and early September, see Winterthur's Old Town taken over for live music of all kinds, in the street and bars. If you're around in May, ask at the tourist office about the **Eschenberg-Schwinget**, a folksy festival of traditional wrestling held in a nearby meadow, and **Jodlersonntag**, Yodelling Sunday. Also sometime in May, Whitsun is celebrated in Winterthur in an unusual fashion as **Afro-Pfingsten**, a kind of mini-carnival of African music and food.

---

short stroll from all the city-centre sights. The parallel streets Stadthausstrasse and Untertor lead due east from Bahnhofplatz into the Old Town.

The pedestrianized Old Town itself is roughly triangular, spreading east from a point at Bahnhofplatz. The main east–west street begins as **Untertor**, continues east as **Marktgasse**, and changes its name again to **Obertor** as it crosses **Graben**. Obertor ends at a traffic junction, some 500m east of the starting point at the station. The network of Old Town alleys lies south of the Untertor–Obertor line; parallel one street north runs **Stadthausstrasse** bordered by the Stadtgarten, and one street north again is **Museumstrasse**, with the Kunstmuseum.

Information

The helpful **tourist office** is in the train station (Mon–Fri 8.30am–6.30pm, Sat 8.30am–4pm; ☎052/269 26 66, fax 269 26 60, *www.winterthur-city.ch*), with maps and stacks of information on the city, including pamphlets detailing bike routes around town and into the surrounding countryside (the station has the usual bike rental facilities). The most useful item on sale is a **Museumspass**, which gives free entry to all the city museums for one/two/three days (Fr.20/25/28). Ask, too, about the **Kunstweekend** offer, comprising accommodation and free museum entry over two weekend days (from Fr.104) or three (Fr.184). You can join a ninety-minute guided **tour** of the town, beginning from the tourist office at 10am on the first and third Saturdays of each month (May–Oct only; Fr.15).

The Stadtbibliothek, in the same building as the Kunstmuseum, has **Internet access** (Mon 10am–6pm, Tues–Fri 8am–6pm, Sat 8am–4pm; Fr.12/hr).

Accommodation

Winterthur's range of **accommodation** is geared largely towards the business trade, though prices are still generally lower than in Zürich. You should bear in mind that hotels in town are often booked solid, and definitely need reserving ahead.

The nearest **campsite** is *Am Schützenweiher*, Eichliwaldstrasse 4 (☎052/212 52 60), 1.5km north of town, some 300m south of the N1 (Ohringen exit). Open year-round, it has good facilities, and access onto the forested Wolfensberg nearby; take bus #3 to Seuzacherstrasse, then walk 300m north. The basic **HI hostel** is in Schloss Hegi, Hegifeldstrasse 125 (☎052/242 38 40, fax 242 58 30; ①; March–Oct), a fifteenth-century stately home; take bus #10 or #680 to Schlossacker. Large dorms come without breakfast (Fr.16 first night, Fr.14 thereafter). At the time of writing, it was uncertain whether the hostel would abandon the castle for new premises in town; check with the tourist office for the latest news.

Albani, Steinberggasse 16 (☎052/212 69 96, fax 212 69 86). Best budget hotel, above the famous Old Town club and music venue just south of Kirchplatz. The OK rooms are big and well kept, but aren't en suite and there's no breakfast. Free entry for gigs downstairs. ①.

Grüntal, Im Grüntal 1 (☎052/232 25 52, fax 232 25 33). Solid country inn at a quiet crossroads 4.5km southeast of town, with hospitality, good service and pleasant rooms making up for the journey to and from. Bus #6 to Grüntal. ②.

Hessengüetli, Oberfeldstrasse 10 (☎052/222 33 53, fax 222 01 02). A tiny, family-run hotel above a Chinese–Vietnamese restaurant in a quiet area 1.5km northwest of the centre, with a stream on one side and the wooded Brüelberg rising behind. Their en-suite rooms are good value, and you'll have no trouble with car or bike parking. Bus #2 to Feldtal. ②.

Krone, Marktgasse 49 (☎052/213 25 21, fax 213 48 08). Historic renovated Old Town building, stylish and super-comfortable. ③.

Loge, Graben 6 (☎052/213 91 21, fax 212 09 59, *hotelloge@access.ch*, *www.hotelloge.ch*). Modern and very quiet hotel in the heart of the Old Town – go for the light, top-floor rooms with panoramic balcony. On-site parking. ③.

The Town

Winterthur's main draw are its excellent **museums**; these aside, the pedestrianized Old Town has some charm once you get off the main shopping streets – the elegant medieval Stadtkirche, for example, with its luridly kitschy modern murals, is worth a look – but other than enjoying the atmosphere at one of the many street cafés there's not much to aim for.

If you have extra time, or if Victorian industrial architecture lights your fire, you should head southwest under the tracks into the **Sulzer-Areal** district, where hulking disused brick-built factories are slowly being reclaimed as atmospheric theatre spaces, bars and skating arenas.

THE MUSEUMS

Winterthur's best **museums** are the two separate Oskar Reinhart art collections – one housed in the town centre ("am Stadtgarten"), the other on a hill near the town ("am Römerholz") – and the Kunstmuseum. The Fotomuseum and Villa Flora are close runners-up. Note that they're all closed on Mondays. If you don't have a Museumspass (see opposite), ask at either of the two Reinhart museums for their combined entry ticket of Fr.12.

The **Oskar Reinhart Collection am Römerholz**, Haldenstrasse 95 (Tues–Sun 10am–5pm; Fr.8; SMP), is one of the leading private art collections assembled in Europe in the twentieth century. Born in 1885, Reinhart came from a local trading family, but aged 41 withdrew from business and moved into the villa Am Römerholz to devote himself to his passion for art. When he died in 1965, part of his collection passed to the municipality (and is now housed in the Stadtgarten museum), and the remaining 200 paintings and his villa at Römerholz were bequeathed to the nation. This latter half of his collection is an idiosyncratic mingling of styles and periods, brought together more for each piece's artistic qualities than as an attempt to form a representative

---

MUSEUMSBUS

The city and Heidi Taxi (☎052/202 22 22) jointly run a **Museumsbus**, unnecessary for the town-centre Stadtgarten collection and the Kunstmuseum, but very handy for getting to and from the Römerholz collection, some distance from town on a hilltop. Minibuses depart from the station (Tues–Sun hourly 9.45am–4.45pm), picking up at the Stadtgarten and the Kunstmuseum a few minutes later, and dropping off at the gates of the Römerholz gallery. Departures from there back to town are on the hour 10am to 5pm. The Fr.5 fare is valid all day. On Sundays the bus makes extra stops at the Villa Flora and the Fotomuseum.

Otherwise, reaching the Römerholz collection involves city bus #3 to Spital and a stiff ten- or fifteen-minute climb.

CASTLES AROUND WINTERTHUR

There are four castles near the town, of which three are visitable. The best is **Schloss Kyburg**, some 7km south of Winterthur (March–Oct Tues–Sun 9am–noon & 1–5.30pm; Nov, Jan & Feb Tues–Sun 10am–noon & 2–4pm; Fr.4). Dating from the tenth and eleventh centuries, it's majestically sited on a hilltop above the Töss river and offers plenty of opportunity for exploration, both inside the castle walls and in the countryside around. The castle plays host in early August to a week of chamber music. Postbus #655 from the SBB station in Effretikon (a suburb of Winterthur) runs to Kyburg.

Schloss Mörsburg is 6km northeast of town, near Stadel (March–Oct Tues–Sun 10am–noon & 1.30–5pm; Nov–Feb Sun 10am–noon & 1.30–5pm; free), although it's only accessible by car (via Sulz). With a lovely Romanesque chapel and excavated ramparts, the thirteenth-century castle also contains a museum of the Historical Society of Winterthur, with ceramics, handicrafts and weapons on show. **Schloss Hegi** (March–Oct Tues–Thurs & Sat 2–5pm, Sun 10am–noon & 2–5pm; free; bus #10 or #680 to Schlossacker) is easiest to get to, 3km east of town, but is less engaging; more of a moated mansion than a castle, it dates from the fifteenth century and has much of its interior preserved. It also currently houses the city's hostel.

The fourth stately home is **Schloss Wülflingen**, a stout sixteenth-century country house 4km northwest of town, now a conference centre and pricey traditional restaurant (closed Mon & Tues).

overview of any one artist or genre. There are works from fifteenth- and sixteenth-century German masters, including Matthias Grünewald, Lukas Cranach the Elder and Hans Holbein the Younger; a small group of Italian and Spanish works, including some by El Greco and Goya; and fifteenth- to seventeenth-century Dutch and Flemish painting dominated by Breughel, Rubens, Hals and Rembrandt. Many works from French Baroque, Neoclassicist and Romantic artists – including some of Delacroix's best portraits – lead on to Reinhart's marvellous Impressionist collection with a range of works by Renoir, Manet, Degas, and many more. The museum has a lovely sunny café to help you catch your breath.

Back in the town, the **Museum Oskar Reinhart am Stadtgarten**, Stadthausstrasse 6 (Tues 10am–8pm, Wed–Sun 10am–5pm; Fr.8; SMP), is of less general interest, concentrating on German, Swiss and Austrian artists from the eighteenth to the twentieth centuries. On the ground floor are a few rooms of portraits by local artists including Graff and Füssli. On the floor above are Romantic landscapes from all over Switzerland, and up another floor are some marvellous studies of children by the Swiss artist Albert Anker, and works by Hodler, Segantini and Giovanni Giacometti. The new top-floor extension features changing exhibitions.

Just across the gardens behind lies the **Kunstmuseum**, Museumstrasse 52 (Tues 10am–8pm, Wed–Sun 10am–5pm; Fr.8 for the permanent collection, more for temporary exhibits; SMP), with a spectacular collection covering international art over the last century. The tour begins upstairs, with a room devoted to Van Gogh, Monet, Rousseau and sculpture by Picasso and Rodin. Hodler and a Cubist room lead on to a Surrealist selection topped by Miró and a rare self-portrait by De Chirico. Works by Brancusi lead into the high-ceilinged, white-walled extension, dominated by Mondrian, American artists and sculpture by Alberto Giacometti, with rooms to one side devoted to temporary exhibits.

The critic Paul Graham has called Winterthur's **Fotomuseum**, Grüzenstrasse 44 (Tues–Fri noon–6pm, Sat & Sun 11am–5pm; Fr.8; SMP), "the most beautiful museum of photography in Europe", and it's easy to see why. Housed in a brick-built renovated former warehouse, it's light, bright and open, and benefits further from its policy of staging five or six top-drawer annual exhibitions each year. The museum is a walkable

400m southeast from the Old Town, off Tösstalstrasse (or bus #2 to Schleife). Very nearby, at Tösstalstrasse 44, is the **Villa Flora** (Tues–Sat 2–5pm, Sun 11am–3pm; Fr.6), with a small but high-quality French Post-Impressionist art collection, Fauvist and Nabi works (Matisse, Vallotton, and more) fleshed out with earlier works by Cézanne, Van Gogh and others.

The **Technorama**, Technoramastrasse 1 (Tues–Sun 10am–5pm; Fr.15; *www.technorama.ch*; bus #5), will keep you occupied on a wet afternoon, but despite the brochure-led hype it doesn't really justify the shelling out of such a hefty entrance fee. Spread over three floors of a renovated warehouse, it's packed with physics experiments of all kinds to demonstrate water and flow patterns, acoustics, magnetism, light waves, and everything else you've forgotten from misspent afternoons in the school lab. Where the place scores is with its fancier displays – making water seem to flow upwards with strobe lights, for instance, or puffing giant smoke rings and then whisking up a tornado out of nowhere. It's a shame that all accompanying notes are in German or French. Kids, obviously, won't care a hoot and will have a great time.

Eating, drinking and nightlife
You'll have no trouble finding places to **eat and drink**. If you're watching every penny, nosh in the *EVA* department store beside the station, or at the *Widder* (see below). **Nightlife** can be surprisingly good, with all-night bars around the station, lively music bars on Neumarkt, some rougher student/biker dives along Technikumstrasse and a handful of weekend dance clubs.

Albani, Steinberggasse 16. Smallish Old Town bar and venue well able to draw Zürchers out into the sticks with a quality programme of DJs and live music – previous headliners include Pearl Jam and Sheryl Crow. Weekend nights are packed. Fr.15 or so for bands.

Chimichanga, Neustadtgasse 19. Attractive dark low-ceilinged *Stübli* converted into a quality Tex-Mex restaurant and bar, boasting especially chunky burritos. Eat well for Fr.30.

Gotthard, Untertor opposite station. Switzerland's first-ever 24-hour bar, a young, friendly joint that's a peaceful café during the day; at night it attracts a few lowlifes but avoids the sleaze of its Bahnhofplatz neighbours.

Kraftfeld, off Tössfeldstrasse in Sulzer-Areal industrial quarter, 100m beyond Brockenhalle junk shop. Alternative artists' community which lays on hectic DJ nights featuring experimental drum'n'bass, plus occasional concerts, films and happenings. Tues & Fri 11pm–6am.

Obergass, Obergasse corner Schulgasse. Quiet easy-going café to eat, read and drink in, with a wide range of food, veggie and not, for Fr.14–25. Closed Sun.

Paddy O'Brien's, Merkurstrasse 25. Quality Irish pub five minutes north of the station to warm your jaded cockles, with 12 beers on tap, TV football and enough of a reputation to pull in The Dubliners for a gig now and again.

Typisch Thai, Neumarkt 3. Full range of Thai dishes, with friendly service and plenty for veggies. Fr.12–15 for lunch, double in the evenings. Closed Mon.

Vegi zur Waage, Rudolfstrasse 15. Behind the station, an excellent value café and all-day restaurant, cosy and bright. *Menus* can be Fr.15, or all you can eat for Fr.21, with a Sri Lankan buffet every evening. Mon–Fri 6am–11pm.

Walliser Kanne, Steinberggasse 25. Quality Swiss specialities, served in classic style, with subdued decor and a calm atmosphere. Around Fr.35. Closed Sun.

Widder, Metzggasse 9. Subculture Old Town café-bar, with long wooden tables and loud music. Exceptionally good food, well prepared and in massive portions for under Fr.15.

Baden and around

A pleasant, relaxing spa town on the River Limmat, 24km downstream from Zürich in Canton Aargau, **BADEN** (German for "baths") makes for a peaceful stopover on a journey across the north of the country, and could easily serve as a base from which to explore Zürich without suffering that city's stratospheric accommodation prices.

There's not an awful lot to do, other than enjoy the ancient Old Town, take in a fine collection of Impressionist art, and enjoy a soothing dip in the warm, sulphurous spring waters ... but that's the point. People have been coming to Baden for centuries to sit around doing absolutely nothing, and there are few more genteel and stately towns in the country in which to follow suit.

Arrival, orientation and information

The town is divided into two, with the **station** in the middle. South (right) of the station is the centre, focused around the **Old Town** with the ruined Stein castle above. North (left) of the station, in a bend of the Limmat, is the low-lying **Kurgebiet**, or Cure District, with the thermal baths and a handful of venerable old hotels clustered around Kurplatz. The main Badstrasse, which becomes Bäderstrasse, connects the two neighbourhoods, running along a terrace above the Limmat valley.

Baden's friendly and helpful **tourist office** is 100m north of the station, at Bahnhofstrasse 50 (Mon–Fri 8.30am–noon & 2–6pm, Sat 10am–noon; ☎056/222 53 18, *www.baden-schweiz.ch*). They offer excellent free guided tours of the town (Mon 2pm).

Accommodation

On the east side of the Limmat, about 200m south of the wooden bridge, you'll find an HI **hostel**, Kanalstrasse 7 (☎056/221 67 36, fax 221 76 60; ①; mid-March to Christmas), clean and safe, with dorms from Fr.25; and on the busy riverside street in Ennetbaden, also on the eastern bank of the Limmat but directly opposite the Kurgebiet, is *Hirschen* (☎056/222 69 66; ①) with plenty of dead-simple rooms. Baden's **hotels** are good value compared with those in Zürich nearby, but they're geared towards monied long-stayers and you'll need deepish pockets. Aim if you can for one of the Belle Epoque Kurhotels in the spa district, all of which exude bags of period charm: choice is *Blume*, Kurplatz 4 (☎056/222 55 69, fax 222 42 98; ③–④), dating back to 1421 and built around an amazing interior atrium space, with classically grand public areas and a range of elegant rooms. Romantic *Verenahof*, Kurplatz 1 (☎056/203 93 93, fax 203 93 94, *verenahof@bluewin.ch*; ③–⑤) is a more upmarket, renovated version of the same.

The Town

At Schlossbergplatz at the southern end of Badstrasse is the turreted fifteenth-century **Stadtturm**, gateway into the Old Town. On a hill above to the west, and visible from all over town, is the **Stein castle**, for three centuries the meeting place of the Confederate Diet (Switzerland's parliament of the day), but partially destroyed in 1712 by the Protestant forces of Bern, Basel and Zürich during a battle against the Catholic cantons of Solothurn, Luzern and Zug. Rathausgasse runs east from the Stadtturm just inside the walls, and partway along you'll find the **Stadthaus** (Town Hall): take a look inside at the whimsical modern ceiling murals of clouds and sky, and then head two floors up to the old **Tagsatzungssaal** (meeting hall), a gorgeously restored interior dating from 1497, complete with full wood panelling and original stained glass showing the Swiss cantonal flags. (You'll have to ask in one of the offices on the same floor for the key, since the anonymous modern door to the hall is kept locked). An alley from Rathausgasse leads through to Kirchplatz, with its atmospheric **church**, built in 1420 (and retaining its Gothic arches) but later renovated in a surprisingly frill-free Baroque style. Stairways and steep alleys head down to a picturesque covered **wooden bridge** of 1813, leading to the stout bailiff's castle on the other bank. If the rock nearby looks oddly flat, it's because after the rainy night of June 25, 1899, the whole top of the crag sheared off and crashed into the river – such a momentous event that it is still talked about today.

It's a short but pleasant walk north along the banks of the Limmat, on a footpath fragrant with wild garlic, to the tranquil **Kurgebiet**. Kurplatz, a peaceful little square, is

surrounded on all sides by Belle Epoque hotel architecture that is the height of dignified elegance, and is worth exploring in itself. Baden's nineteen **springs** were well
known to the Romans, who called the place *Aquae Helveticae* and built a lavish baths
complex to exploit the hot water, a million litres of which emerges every day at a toasty
47°C, having spent the last 30,000 years rising from 3km down. All through the Middle
Ages, and well into the nineteenth century, Baden was infamous for the high jinks that
took place in its pools: the combination of deliciously hot water, naked bodies, and four-
to-six-week residential "cures" seems to have loosened inhibitions a treat.

Things are somewhat more subdued in these more prudish times, and these days
your flesh is more likely to receive attention from a no-nonsense white-coated masseur
than from an amorous wooer. In the Baden tradition, all the Kurhotels (see opposite) are
built over their own **springs** which serve their own thermal pools; the **public pools**
(Mon–Fri 7.30am–9pm, Sat & Sun 7.30am–8pm; ☎056/203 91 12; Fr.15) are on Kurplatz,
beside the *Verenahof* hotel, with a drinking fountain outside – although you may have
trouble keeping the warm smelly water down long enough for it to do any internal good.
As an extra, you can enjoy an hour and three-quarters in your own private tub (one/two
person) for Fr.15/30. Saunas start from Fr.16.50, full massages from Fr.41 for 25min.

THE LANGMATT FOUNDATION

At Römerstrasse 30, 150m west of the Kurgebiet, you'll find the **Langmatt Foundation**
(April–Oct Tues–Fri 2–5pm, Sat & Sun 11am–5pm; Fr.10; SMP) housing a small but
excellent collection of French Impressionist art. The charming house, dating from
1900–05 and resplendent in its own gardens, belonged to one Sidney Brown, a founder
of the engineering multinational ABB, headquartered in Baden. Off the reception area,
the **Venetian salon** (room 3), with Louis XV and XVI furniture, is hung with views of
the city painted by an unknown artist around 1745; next door you'll find work by
Cézanne, Renoir and Pissarro. A wonderful Degas nude, and several small Renoir portraits, are curiously hung in a corridor (room 7) opposite the toilets. The atmospheric
library (room 8) has several shining landscapes by Corot and Degas, while the purpose-built **gallery** (room 9) is hung with several Cézannes, works by Van Gogh, Monet,
Gauguin and the beautiful *Portrait of Suzanne Valadon plaiting her hair* by Renoir.
Upstairs rooms are mostly devoted to the history of the family.

Eating and drinking

For **eating**, there are plenty of pavement cafés and restaurants along Badstrasse and in
the Old Town. The *Schwyzerhüsli*, Badstrasse 38 (☎056/222 62 63; closed Sun) is a popular place to sit and watch the world go by, and has plenty of healthy salads as well as
substantial Swiss fare, with *menus* from Fr.17. *Rose*, Weitegasse 23, is a bright, modern,
friendly little place with good food that's open until 1.30am Friday and Saturday nights.
Round the corner, *Bar Spuntino*, Vordere Metzggasse 4, is a *paninoteca* with a huge
range of hot and cold *paninis* for Fr.5–8, as well as pasta dishes for Fr.12. Up on the east
bank of the Limmat is the *Schloss Schartenfels* (☎056/426 19 27; closed Tues), an 1894
folly now housing a gourmet restaurant with terrace overlooking the town. For **drinking**, check out *Stadttor* on Schlossbergplatz, a cosy local watering hole. *Gasthof zum
Wilden Mann*, Oberegasse 33, has a super-hip bar replete with candles, sofas and more
than its fair share of floppy haircuts.

Around Baden

The gentle Aargauer countryside around Baden holds a succession of quiet farming villages with little to mark them out as special, other than **LENGNAU**, 8km north of
Baden, and **ENDINGEN**, 3km further on. These two villages, for centuries up to about
100 years ago, were almost exclusively Jewish. Since the early thirteenth century Jews

WALKING THE JURA HÖHENWEG

The **Jura Höhenweg** (or High Route) makes for a multi-day hiking tour through a region unlike any other in Switzerland, stretching 199km along the length of the Swiss Jura from Dielsdorf, 12km east of Baden, to Borex near Geneva. End to end it takes about fourteen days to complete. Small villages and isolated farms point to a scant population throughout the region, and you can often find yourself walking for long distances without signs of habitation. In this limestone country there's a rich flora in summer, and long views across the *Mittelland* from open ridge crests show either the abrupt wall of the Bernese Alps or the snowy Mont Blanc range.

The notes below are meant as a guideline only: you shouldn't set off without a good **map** (those covering the route are LS 5005, 5019, 5016, 241, 242, 5020 and 260 – all at 1:50,000). The essential accompaniment to any part of the walk is *The Jura* by Kev Reynolds and R. Brian Evans (see "Books", p.530), which gives details of accommodation to be had along the route in modest inns or mountain farms with outhouse dormitories, and also includes winter ski traverses. Local tourist offices can also supply information on hiking short stretches. See p.71 for the basics.

Reached by S-Bahn train from Zürich, **Dielsdorf** slumbers in a countryside of farms and market gardens, but within an hour of setting out the way goes through **Regensburg** which, with its thirteenth-century castle turret, stone-walled houses and cobbled square, is the finest village of the whole route. You'll also pass through **Baden** and **Brugg** on the first day, but thereafter the true nature of the Jura becomes evident, with the well-marked trail undulating to the horizon through steep green hills and charming farmland basins. From Brugg the route takes to high ground north of the River Aare, and beyond **Staffelegg** it almost reaches 1000m on the wooded summit of the Geissflue with views between the trees to the Black Forest. Edging above **Olten**, on day four the route joins a track engineered by Swiss soldiers during World War I across the flank of the 1098m Belchenflue, adorned with large regimental insignia carved and painted on the steep rock walls. Later the same day hundreds of reinforced timber steps take the path up towards the Roggenflue to emerge on a prominent limestone cliff with more expansive views before descending to **Balsthal**. Day five ends on the Weissenstein (1284m), whose panorama was immortalized in *The Path to Rome* by Hilaire Belloc: "One saw the sky beyond the edge of the world getting purer as the vault rose. But right up ... ran peak and field and needle of intense ice, remote from the world."

On reaching **Frinvillier** on day six the Höhenweg passes suddenly from German-speaking to French-speaking Switzerland, to become known as the **Chemin des Crêtes**. Architectural styles change too, as though you've crossed an international frontier. Above Frinvillier you'll gain the 1607m **Chasseral** (see p.182); ribs of limestone project through the turf, and a hotel just below (☎032/751 24 51) gazes out to Lac de Neuchâtel with the Eiger, Mönch and Jungfrau floating on the horizon. On day nine the trail edges a huge limestone cauldron, the Creux du Van, the most dramatic feature on the long walk. A farm nearby offers a mattress in an outhouse for the simplest of overnight lodgings, and next day the path leads down to **Sainte-Croix**, home of the Swiss musical-box industry (see p.173). A steady climb then gains an open plateau close to the French border with military defences in evidence, before a sharp pull culminates on the summit of Le Suchet at 1588m. Passing through **Vallorbe** on day twelve (see p.174) the route investigates the Source de l'Orbe in a woodland whose glades are soggy with newborn streams. Mont Tendre, crossed on the same day, marks the highest point of the Jura at 1679m. From it, you can absorb a panorama of Lake Geneva and the snowcapped Alps. The last two days are spent mostly along the ridge among flowers – from the final high point of La Dôle, walkers can share Rousseau's pleasure: "The moment when from the very top of the Jura mountains I discovered Lake Geneva, was a moment of ecstasy and delight." From there, 1200m of descent through woodland, meadows and an open plain of wheatfields, brings the wanderer at last to **Borex** above Lake Geneva itself.

had lived in Basel and Zürich: Jewish financing, for instance, made it possible for Basel's bishops to buy Kleinbasel outright in the 1220s and to build the first Rhine bridge shortly afterwards. On January 16, 1349, the Basel government decided to pack the town's Jews into a wooden house on an island in the Rhine and burn it to the ground; those who escaped were expelled six months later when plague arrived, accused of poisoning the city's water supply. Jews were allowed back to the city after the 1356 earthquake in order to finance rebuilding work, but in 1397 they were again expelled, this time for good. They took refuge in the Baden countryside, settling at Lengnau and Endingen, where Jewish life in Switzerland was concentrated for more than four centuries. In 1805, a Jewish community was refounded in Basel, but it was only in 1874, after extreme pressure was brought to bear by the US and France, that Switzerland finally guaranteed full religious and civil rights to all religious denominations in its constitution, one of the last European states to do so.

Today, Lengnau and Endingen – despite being largely depopulated of their Jews – still bear many traces of the past. Lengnau's little village square is overlooked not by a church, but by a large **synagogue**, and the village has many characteristic old double-doored houses, not seen elsewhere in the country. The great **domed synagogue** in the middle of Endingen is currently undergoing renovation work. Between the two villages, in a quiet location off the road, is an overgrown **Israelitischer Friedhof** (Jewish Cemetery), with graves dating back to 1750. All these sites are kept locked, but the Baden tourist office can put you in touch with guides from the local Jewish community, who will take you round and explain some more of the history.

travel details

TRAINS

Baden to: Basel (hourly; 50min), Bern (hourly; 1hr 20min); Zürich (every 30min; 15min).

Winterthur to: Baden (every 30min; 50min); Bern (every 30min; 1hr 50min); Schaffhausen (hourly; 35min); St Gallen (every 30min; 45min); Stein-am-Rhein (hourly; 40min); Zürich (4 hourly; 20min).

Zürich HB to: Adliswil (every 20min; 15min); airport (4–7 hourly; 10min); Baden (every 30min; 15min); Basel (every 30min; 1hr); Bellinzona (hourly; 2hr 30min); Bern (every 30min; 1hr 10min); Biel/Bienne (hourly; 1hr 30min); Chur (hourly; 1hr 35min); Einsiedeln (every 30min; 45min – change at Wädenswil); Flughafen (airport; 4–7 hourly; 10min); Fribourg (every 30min; 1hr 40min); Geneva (every 30min; 3hr); Interlaken Ost (hourly; 2hr 15min); Lausanne (every 30min; 2hr 30min); Lugano (hourly; 3hr); Luzern (hourly; 50min); Neuchâtel (hourly; 1hr 50min); St Gallen (every 30min; 1hr 10min); Sargans (hourly; 1hr 10min); Schaffhausen (hourly; 40min); Solothurn (hourly; 1hr 5min); Uetliberg (every 30min; 25min); Winterthur (4 hourly; 20min); Zug (twice hourly; 25min).

BUSES

Baden to: Endingen (hourly; 25min); Lengnau AG (hourly; 18min).

BOATS

(following is a summary of April–Oct services; fewer boats run in other months, quite often only on Sun if at all)

Zürich (Bürkliplatz) to: Rapperswil (hourly; 1hr 45min); Schmerikon (twice daily; 3hr 20min).

INTERNATIONAL TRAINS

Zürich HB to: Amsterdam (7 daily; 9hr); Berlin (8 daily; 8hr 20min); Budapest (1 daily; 13hr); Frankfurt (hourly; 4hr); Hamburg (8 daily; 7–8hr); Innsbruck (6 daily; 3hr 50min); Köln (hourly; 6hr); Milan (hourly; 4hr 30min); München (4 daily; 4hr 20min); Paris (7 daily; 6hr 20min); Prague (1 daily; 10hr 30min); Stuttgart (every 2hr; 2hr 50min); Vienna (3 daily; 9hr 15min); Zagreb (1 daily; 14hr).

PLACE NAMES IN THIS CHAPTER		
German	**French**	**Italian**
Winterthur	Winterthour	Winterthur
Zürich	Zurich	Zurigo
Zürichsee	Lac de Zurich	Lago di Zurigo

CHAPTER TEN

THE NORTHEAST AND LIECHTENSTEIN

S witzerland's rural **NORTHEAST** – known as *Ostschweiz* – is one of the least celebrated areas of the country, and is often sidelined by tourists anxious to get to the household names further south. Which, of course, means that you can enjoy the mountains and lakes, medieval town centres and rolling verdant countryside, in relative peace, free from hard-sell tourism and the glitz and glamour of big-name resorts. Most visitors haven't even heard of the main city of the northeast, **St Gallen**, and yet its magnificent Baroque cathedral and well-preserved medieval town-centre make it a major cultural landmark. Immediately to the south lies the hilly backcountry of **Appenzell**, sheltering a close-knit, still largely isolated community of farmers and crafts people occupying the foothills of the Alpstein range. The highest mountain in the region is the Säntis, which tops 2500m – mediocre in Swiss terms, but still tall enough to enjoy plenty of snow, vistas stretching to the horizon and quality hiking in the web of valleys beneath it.

The River Rhine, which bulges out into the huge **Bodensee** (often anglicized to Lake Constance) in Switzerland's northeast corner, throws a protective loop around this part of Switzerland, forming international frontiers with Germany to the north, and Austria and the tiny independent statelet of **Liechtenstein** to the east. At the westernmost tip of the lake, the cosmopolitan shoreside German city of **Konstanz** is divided from its Swiss twin of **Kreuzlingen** only by an arbitrary dividing line between buildings. The beautiful river journey west from Kreuzlingen runs past **Stein-am-Rhein**, an almost perfectly preserved medieval village boasting spectacular sixteenth- and seventeenth-century frescoes and one of the country's best small historical museums, and ends at the atmospheric medieval town of **Schaffhausen**, dubbed "Rheinfallstadt" for its proximity to the mighty **Rhine falls**, the largest waterfall in Europe.

ACCOMMODATION PRICE CODES

All the hostels, pensions and hotels in this book have been graded according to the following price codes, which indicate the price for the cheapest double room available during the high season. Single rooms can cost anything between sixty and eighty percent of the double-room rate. For hostels with dormitories, the price per bed has been quoted. See p.45 for more details.

① under Fr.100	④ Fr.200–250	⑦ Fr.350–400
② Fr.100–150	⑤ Fr.250–300	⑧ Fr.400–500
③ Fr.150–200	⑥ Fr.300–350	⑨ over Fr.500

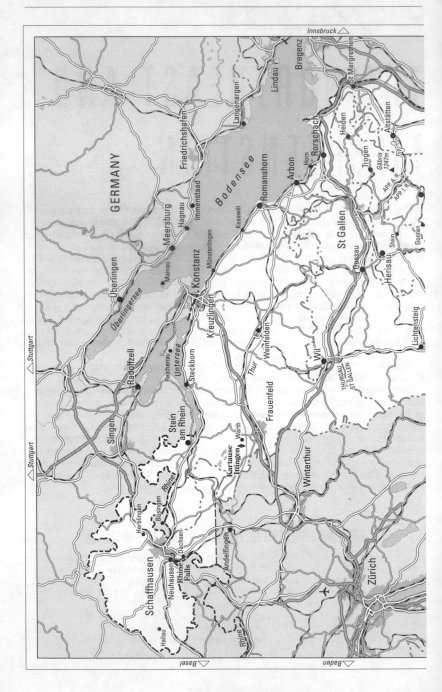

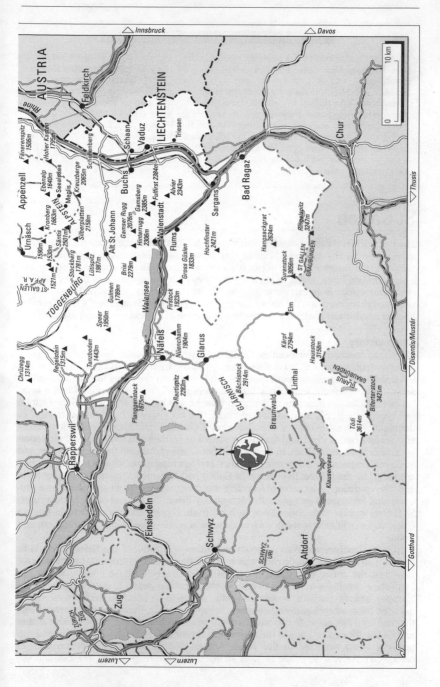

EXPLORING THE NORTHEAST

There are a couple of **travel passes** covering different areas of the Ostschweiz region. The **Thurgau Day Pass** (Fr.27.50) is best value, covering all transport within Canton Thurgau as well as journeys to and from Konstanz, St Gallen, Winterthur and Schaffhausen. If you're planning a boat trip along the Swiss shore of the lake or down the Rhine from Kreuzlingen to Schaffhausen, this will save you plenty. The **Appenzell-Toggenburg Regional Pass** (May–Oct only) takes in St Gallen's city buses, all the mountain railway and cable-car journeys around the Alpstein including the Säntis, and trains and postbuses from Buchs to Rorschach and Romanshorn: for three days' free travel in seven, the pass costs Fr.78; for five in fifteen it's Fr.98.

For information and brochures on the whole region, contact the Ostschweiz Tourist Association, Postfach, CH-9001 St Gallen (☎071/227 37 37, *www.ostschweiz-i.ch*).

St Gallen

The main urban centre of eastern Switzerland, **ST GALLEN** is a relaxed and conservative provincial city set amidst rolling countryside between the Appenzell hills to the south and the Bodensee to the north. It's a gentle place, with a busy modern centre and a beautiful Old Town, and is worth a night or two on a journey through the region. The city's centrepiece is an extraordinarily lavish Baroque abbey: the cathedral is impressive enough by itself, but the abbey library is celebrated as Switzerland's finest secular Rococo interior and contains a world-class collection of ancient books and manuscripts.

Some history

More than most other Swiss cities, St Gallen's owes its existence to the religious community which remains at its core. In around 612, the Irish monk **Gallus** – a follower of Columba – was travelling south from the Bodensee into the valley forests. Depending on who you speak to, legend has it that he either fell over, or stumbled into a briar patch, or spoke to a bear who understood what he was saying; whichever, Gallus felt he had received a sign from God, and so chose that very spot to build his hermitage. In the eighth century, a follower of Gallus named **Otmar** established a monastic community around Gallus's cell, and founded a school of scribes and translators, which soon became famous throughout. In the 830s, Abbot Gozbert founded the great **library**, and St Gallen's reputation as a centre of culture and learning grew, while a town flourished around it. By the thirteenth century, St Gallen had become an important market town and it's reputation as a centre of learning was being ousted by its reputation as a producer and exporter of exceptionally high-quality **linen**. By the end of the Middle Ages, St Gallen was the only Swiss town to have trade representatives resident in foreign cities, and was linked by stagecoach to centres of textile processing in Nuremberg and Lyon.

In 1529, Joachim von Watt – known as **Vadian** – introduced the Reformation to St Gallen, sparking iconoclastic riots which forced the monks temporarily to flee the city. However, the abbey survived as a walled, independent Catholic enclave within the Protestant city. Early in the eighteenth century, **cotton** began to outsell linen around Europe, and St Gallen's weavers rapidly switched production techniques. Some decades later, when **hand-embroidery** became popular, the weavers embraced this too, and by 1790, some 40,000 women were working from home to embroider cotton and muslin for export. Early in the nineteenth century, St Gallen hand-embroidered cotton was being exported to the young United States. Meanwhile, the creation of Napoleon's Helvetic Republic in 1798 stripped the sovereign abbey, the city and the region of real power – when St Gallen joined the Swiss Confederation in 1803 as a new, Protestant canton, one of its first actions was to **dissolve the abbey**.

The invention of embroidery machines in the 1820s and 1830s brought a golden age to St Gallen. A few decades later, the region boasted some 100,000 machines, with production still centred in the home. By 1913, embroidery was Switzerland's largest export industry, with St Gallen accounting for around half of the entire world production of textiles. These days, that figure is down to just 0.5 percent, but Swiss embroidery remains a highly valued, luxury commodity and production continues in the hands of small, highly specialized companies that supply designs and finished products to *haute couture* fashion houses: Lacoste's famous crocodile logo, for instance, is Swiss embroidered. St Gallen's now almost entirely computerized embroidery industry still relies on some two thousand local women working from home on fine hand-sewn detailing impossible to achieve by machine.

Arrival, orientation and information

St Gallen's **train station** is 200m southwest of the Old Town, with the **tourist office** opposite at Bahnhofplatz 1a, on the far side of the square as you emerge (Mon–Fri 9am–noon & 1–6pm, Sat 9am–noon; ☎071/227 37 37, *www.stgallen-i.ch*). As well as providing maps and guidance for the city, staff can supply information on the whole Ostschweiz region. In their *Tourist Information* booklet you'll find various discount vouchers for, amongst other things, the Appenzeller Volkskunde Museum in Stein (see p.422), and the Säntis cable-car (see p.421). The two-hour guided **city walking tour** starts from the tourist office, and takes in the Textilmuseum, cathedral, abbey library and bits of the Old Town (June–Sept Mon, Wed & Fri 2.30pm; Fr.15).

St Gallen is a stop on the summer rock-festival circuit, with the **Open Air festival** taking place over the last weekend in June and pulling in a varied range of musical attractions – 1999 attendees included Van Morrison, Blondie, the Asian Dub Foundation and Metallica. Information and tickets can be had from the tourist office, or from a dedicated hotline (☎071/222 21 21, *www.openairsg.ch*).

Accommodation

In keeping with the atmosphere of the Old Town, St Gallen has some characterful **accommodation** on offer. The tourist office **hotel reservations line** (☎071/227 37 47) can take bookings for St Gallen as well as the surrounding area, and has a **package** including bed and breakfast in a hotel of your choice, free admission to all city museums, half-price travel on Bodensee boats and a discount on the Säntis cable-car, starting at just Fr.110 for two people.

The nearest **campsite** is *Leebrücke*, in Bernhardzell a couple of kilometres to the north of town (☎071/298 49 69; May–Sept). St Gallen's HI **hostel** is at Jüchstrasse 25 (☎071/245 47 77, fax 245 49 83; ①; March to mid-Dec) – take the Trogenerbahn narrow-gauge train from outside the main station to the Schülerhaus stop, and walk up the hill. Dorms are Fr.24.

Einstein, Berneggstrasse 2 (☎071/227 55 55, fax 227 55 77, *hotel@einstein.ch*, *www.einstein.ch*). The city's top choice, a grand old hotel housed in a former textile factory that boasts generously appointed rooms and quality service. ⑤.

Elite, Metzgergasse 9 (☎071/222 12 36, fax 222 21 77). Plain and serviceable rooms near Marktplatz, both en suite and not. ②.

Im Portner & Pförtnerhof, Bankgasse 12 (☎071/222 97 44, fax 222 98 56). Warm, characterful Old Town hotel, with the comfortable *Im Portner* original entirely upstaged by the antique-style, half-timbered *Pförtnerhof* annexe across the street, boasting leaded-light windows, wood panelling and modern bathrooms. ④.

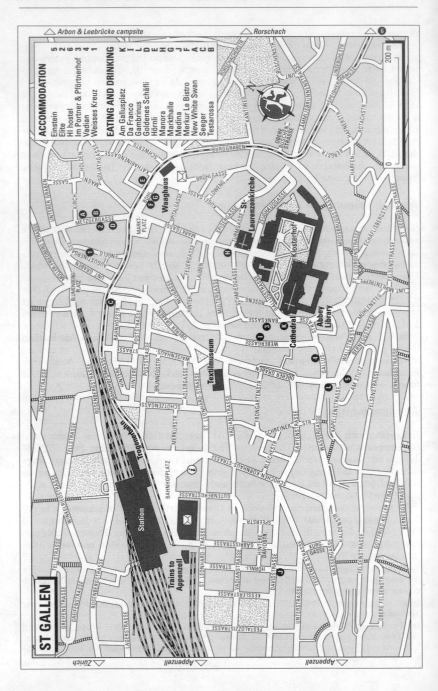

Vadian, Gallusstrasse 36 (☎071/223 60 80, fax 222 47 48). House-proud little hotel on a quiet street steps from the cathedral, with pleasantly renovated rooms, some en suite. ②.

Weisses Kreuz, Engelgasse 9 (☎ & fax 071/223 28 43). Cheapest place in town, although rooms are shabby. Some are en suite. ①.

The City

St Gallen's Old Town is roughly circular, crossed by the main pedestrian streets of **Vadianstrasse/Multergasse** leading east from the station, and **Marktgasse** running south from Marktplatz, a hub for buses and shoppers. Dominating the town is the **cathedral**, its twin towers visible from most points. The attractive alleys and streets all around are characterized by exactly 111 elaborate **oriels**, or small projecting bay windows, most of which are younger than the houses to which they're attached – a fashion for them in the early eighteenth century meant that many were carved from wood, painted, and then stuck onto the stone facade to satisfy the whim of the nouveau-riche merchant who lived within. Some of the most remarkable can be found at Schmiedgasse 15 (House of the Pelican) and 21 (House of Strength); Kugelgasse 8 (House of the Ball) and 10 (House of the Swan); Hinterlauben 10 (House of the Deep Cellar); and Spisergasse 22 (the Camel Oriel). Along **Gallusstrasse** you'll also come across a wealth of architectural styles in the space of a few metres: half-timbered cottages from the Middle Ages rub shoulders with Baroque townhouses and grand dwellings put up during St Gallen's golden age of textile production in the nineteenth and early twentieth centuries. The **Textilmuseum**, Vadianstrasse 2 (April–Oct Mon–Sat 10am–noon & 2–5pm; Nov–March Mon–Fri 10am–noon & 2–5pm; Fr.5; SMP), has an interesting and well-presented collection, focusing on hand-made embroidery and lace from St Gallen and around the world, along with useful explanations of the growth and decline in the industry.

The tall, steepled **St-Laurenzenkirche** on Marktgasse (Mon–Fri 9.30–11.30am & 2–4pm) dates from the ninth century, and originally stood within the monastic enclosure of the cathedral and abbey. Entirely renovated in Neo-Gothic style in the mid-nineteenth century, and restored in the 1970s according to the 1845 plans, it has a narrow but lofty nave flanked by Gothic pointed side arches.

The Cathedral

St Gallen's giant Baroque **cathedral** is unmissable. Designed by one Peter Thumb from Bregenz, it was completed in 1767 after just twelve years' construction work. Easiest access is through the west door on Gallusstrasse, although it's worth making your way through the church and out into the enclosed Klosterhof, at the heart of the complex, where you can see the full height of the extraordinary soaring **east facade**, dating from the 1760s. The convex facade of the apse rises above the formal lawns of the abbey, and is flanked by the two huge, concave towers rising in three sections. To the left is the palace wing, still the residence of the Bishop of St Gallen.

The **interior** of the cathedral (Mon–Fri 9am–6.30pm, Sat 9am–5pm, Sun noon–7pm) is vast, a broad, brightly lit white basilica with three naves and a central cupola. Although not especially high, the interior has a sense of huge depth and breadth thanks to its accomplished architecture: from the sandstone of the floor and wood of the pews, fanciful light-green stuccowork – characteristic of churches in the Konstanz region – draws your eye up the massive double-width pillars to the array of frescoes on the ceiling. The frescoes (1757–66) are almost entirely the work of one artist: Josef Wannenmacher, from Tomerdingen in southern Germany. Above the western end of the nave is a panel showing Mary sitting on a cloud surrounded by angels. The huge central cupola shows paradise, with the Holy Trinity in the centre surrounded by concentric rings of cloud on which are arrayed apostles and saints. Details throughout the rest of the cathedral are splendid: the lavish, mock-tasselled pulpit; the ornate choir screen; the richly carved walnut-wood confessionals; the intricate choir stalls; and, far away at the back of the choir, the high altar flanked by black marble columns with gold trim. The south altar features a bell brought by Gallus on his seventh-century journey from Ireland, one of the three oldest surviving bells in Europe.

The abbey library

Within the same complex of buildings as the cathedral, and just adjacent to it, is the famous **abbey library**, or Stiftsbibliothek, one of the oldest libraries in Europe and classified by UNESCO as a World Heritage Site both for its stunning interior and for its huge collection of rare and unique medieval books and manuscripts. You enter the library beneath a sign reading, in Greek, *psyches iatreion*, or "Pharmacy of the Soul". Ranged beside are dozens of pairs of oversized felt slippers – slip your shoed feet into a pair, to save the gorgeous inlaid wooden floor of the library from scuffing. The 28-by-10-metre room (April–Oct Mon–Sat 9am–noon & 1.30–5pm, Sun 10am–noon & 1.30–4pm; Dec–March Mon–Sat 9am–noon & 1.30–4pm; Fr.7; SMP) is acclaimed as Switzerland's finest surviving example of a Baroque secular interior, and the first glimpse of it as you enter is dizzying. Designed by the same Peter Thumb who worked on the cathedral, the library dates from slightly later, so its orthodox Baroque architecture is overlaid with the opulent decoration of the Rococo period which then held sway. The four **ceiling frescoes** by Josef Wannenmacher depict with bold *trompe l'oeil* perspectives the early Christian theological councils of Nicaea, Constantinople, Ephesus and Chalcedon. Amongst the wealth of smaller frescoes set amongst the ceiling stucco, in the far southeast corner you'll spot **The Venerable Bede**, a seventh-century English monk from Northumbria who wrote one of the first histories of England: he is shown as a scholar, with, beside him, a magic number square. This four-by-four sequence, where the numbers add up to 34 horizontally, vertically, diagonally and from the four corners, is thought to have been invented by Pythagoras in ancient Greece, but took on a new mystical power for early Christians who understood Christ to have died at 34 years of age.

The **books** are ranged on floor-to-ceiling shelves all around. You're free to wander around and examine the spines – books were originally organized by subject, indicated by the cherubs at the head of capitals around the library, but are now arranged alphabetically. If you open the recessed panels between each bookcase, inside you'll find registers of books in the nearby shelves with space to leave your name: the library still operates as an ordinary lending library and study centre, with some 140,000 volumes focused on the Middle Ages. Its list of cultural treasures is extraordinary – for a start, there are more **Irish manuscripts** in St Gallen than there are in Dublin, some fifteen handwritten examples from the seventh century and after, including a Latin manuscript of the Gospels dating from 750. Other works include an astronomical textbook written in 300 BC; copies made in the fifth century of works by Virgil, Horace and other classical authors; texts written by the Venerable Bede in his original Northumbrian language; the oldest book to have survived in German, dating from the eighth century; and a **plan of St Gallen monastery** drawn on parchment in the early ninth century to serve as a blueprint for construction of new buildings. Various of these and other treasures of the library's upstairs manuscript room (no public access) are put on display in glass cases dotted around the main library area. An ancient Egyptian **mummy** in the library dates from 700 BC and was a gift to the mayor of St Gallen at the beginning of the nineteenth century; unsure of what to do with the thing, he plonked it in this corner, where it has sat incongruously ever since.

Eating and drinking

St Gallen has a good range of **eating and drinking** places to cover all price ranges. For standard self-service fare, head for the *Manora* on Marktgasse, but look out also for stalls all over the centre selling St Gallen's famous Olma sausage, eaten ketchup- and mustard-free in a *Bürli*, or bread roll. A feature of St Gallen dining is the handful of traditional tavern-restaurants housed on the upper floor of old townhouses dotted around the centre.

Am Gallusplatz, Gallusstrasse 24 (☎071/223 33 30). The city's best restaurant, where you can enjoy high-quality French cuisine amidst suitably stout decor. Your best option is to come for lunch, when *menus* are lighter in tone and cost less (around Fr.25) – otherwise, you're looking at Fr.50-plus. Closed Sat lunch & Mon.

Da Franco, Webergasse 23. Pasta and pizza galore, with a choice of 25 different risottos. Eat well for Fr.18.

Gambrinus, Wassergasse 5 (☎071/222 47 71). Comfortable, low-lit den for standard brasserie-type *menus* (around Fr.20), plus veggie options, with the added attraction of live jazz every night – top-name artists on Wed and Sat nights command entrance fees of Fr.25–30, but otherwise entry is free to the house band. Closed Sun & Mon.

Goldenes Schäfli, Metzgergasse 5 (☎071/223 37 37). Best known of St Gallen's upper-floor restaurants, with low ceilings, wood panelling all around and creaking floors. The food is all hearty local fare, with plenty of offal on the menu – the house speciality is calf's liver – and other local dishes such as sautéed lake fish. *Menus* start from a very reasonable Fr.15. Closed Sun in summer.

Hörnli, Marktplatz (☎071/222 66 86). Easy-going restaurant specializing in delicious *Rösti*, also with some *menus* under Fr.15. A main attraction is its open-all-hours policy (Mon–Thurs 6.30am–12.30am, then continuously Fri 6.30am until Mon 4am).

Markthalle, Marktplatz. Cool modern interior churning out quality deli-type snacks and meals to local office types – prices are lower in the stand-up section, with perch stools, than in the table-and-chair bit in the back, although you can get a meal at either for less than Fr.17. After 6pm, it turns into a bar-style "night café", with more limited food options. Closed Sun.

Medina, Davidstrasse 11 (☎071/223 22 37). Quiet Tunisian bar-plus-restaurant, serving authentic Arabic/North African cuisine to the musical accompaniment of Umm Kalthoum's classic ballads. Especially good kebabs are fleshed out by quality *harira* tomato-and-chickpea soup and other specialities, and the fact that the place draws a clientele of expat Arabs speaks volumes.

Merkur Le Bistro, Marktplatz. Rock-bottom prices in this upstairs all-day diner, with *menus* from Fr.13. Closed Sun in summer.

New White Swan, Metzgergasse 24. Fast-paced little diner serving up huge portions of steaming Asian-style stomach fillers to students and others on tight budgets.

Seeger, Oberer Graben 2. Elegant big-windowed café with inexpensive food, playing classical music during the day to a twenty-something crowd relaxing on the leather sofas inside, or at tables on the pavement terrace.

Testarossa, Metzgergasse 20. Pretty good pizzas for around Fr.16. Closed Mon.

Nightlife and entertainment

Students attending the University of St Gallen, on a hillside campus north of town, feed what passes for the **nightlife**, although locals have no compunction about jumping on a train to Zürich for a better choice. Supplementing the clutch of first-run **cinemas** around Marktplatz, Kinok, at Grossackerstrasse 3, shows arthouse films from around the world, with cut-price tickets on Mondays. There's live **jazz** nightly at *Gambrinus* (see above). **Clubs** abound: *Ozon*, Goliathgasse 28, is best known, with a varied range of sounds from drum'n'bass to disco, but it can get a bit rough. *Jib*, upstairs at Löwengasse 1, plays Latin and salsa, while *Baracca*, Teufenerstrasse 2, is a hugely popular all-day late-opening DJ bar. *Seeger*, a café at Oberer Graben 2, hosts pumping Friday and Saturday night dance parties for a youthful crowd.

Listings

Bike rental In the station (Mon–Fri 7.30am–7.45pm, Sat & Sun 7.30am–noon & 2–6.45pm).
Books Ribaux, Webergasse 22, has a hefty stock of second-hand books in English.

Car rental Avis, Zürcherstrasse 207a (☎071/279 30 30); Budget, Zilstrasse 57 (☎071/282 30 40); Europcar, Parkgarage Neumarkt (☎071/222 11 14); Hertz, Zürcherstrasse 63 (☎071/278 84 74).

Changing money In the station (Mon–Fri 8am–7.30pm, Sat 8am–6pm, Sun 10am–6pm).

Email and Internet Media Lounge, Katharinengasse 10 (Mon–Fri 9am–9pm, Sat 10am–5pm) charge Fr.2 for the first ten minutes, then Fr.0.20/min after that.

Lost property The city office is at Vadianstrasse 57 (☎071/224 60 15).

Medical facilities 24-hour emergency room at the Kantonsspital, Rorschacherstrasse 95 (☎071/494 11 11).

Post Main office is opposite the station (Bahnhofplatz, CH-9001).

Travel agents Discount flight agents SSR Reisen are at Frongartenstrasse 15 (Mon 1–6pm, Tues–Fri 9am–6pm, Sat 9am–noon; ☎071/223 43 47).

Appenzellerland

Regarded by cosmopolitan urbanites as the epitome of country bumpkin-ness and mercilessly mocked for its folksy ways, **Appenzellerland** is the stuff of jokes in Switzerland. Yet although a sophisticated Lausannois or Basler might chortle to hear it, the region is actually something of a sensuous delight: as you cross the verdant hills south from St Gallen, the pungent smells of cows and cheese assault your nose; on a

---

APPENZELL TRADITIONS

More than most other areas of the country, Appenzell has clung on to its many rural **traditions** as modern, living elements of local culture: although you may be tempted to dismiss demonstrations of local crafts or evenings of folkloric music as phoney touristic kitsch, in fact such events are put on as much for the benefit of locals as for visitors. Weddings, dances and celebrations of all kinds count as excuses for locals to don **traditional dress**, with the women in stiff-winged caps and lace-edged dresses, and the men in elaborate embroidered scarlet waistcoats, with tight black trousers and a silver earring dangling from their right ear.

It seems as if everything Appenzell does is just plain different: up until 1988, the Appenzell **school year** began in the spring, instead of in the autumn as everywhere else. The village of **Urnäsch**, 10km west of Appenzell, celebrates New Year's Eve twice, once on December 31 and again, in order to keep faith with the long-abandoned Julian calendar, on January 13. Even the ornate silver **pipes** smoked by Appenzeller old-timers are idiosyncratic, curving down at the end instead of up, with the tobacco kept in place by a little sliding lid.

In politics, too, Appenzell stands alone. It was only in 1990 that the men of Ausserrhoden finally, and reluctantly, allowed **women** to have the vote in cantonal affairs. Innerrhoden held out for another year until the federal supreme court ruled its exclusion of women to be unconstitutional. (Curiously, it was a substantial proportion of Innerrhoden's women who were siding with the men to exclude themselves: in a poll on whether to extend suffrage, it was only those women aged roughly thirty to fifty who overwhelmingly voted in favour.)

Then, in 1998, Ausserrhoden controversially voted to end centuries of tradition by abolishing the **Landsgemeinde** – the ancient embodiment of Swiss direct democracy in which citizens gathered in traditional dress once a year in the town square of the cantonal capital to vote by brandishing a short sword (the badge of citizenship) in response to a series of shouted yay-or-nay questions – in favour of introducing a secret written ballot. Innerrhoden, though, will have none of this, and remains one of the last Swiss cantons, along with Glarus, to use the Landsgemeinde, which takes place on the last Sunday in April and is a nationally televised event. What the Eurocentric city-types of Geneva or Basel think of it all is anyone's guess.

wander through the villages, busy embroidery and the fussily net-curtained windows of wooden houses delight the eye; and local cooking, particularly rich with butter and cream, has a delicious silkiness.

Encircled by rolling hills, with the looming snowy peaks of the Alpstein ridges to the south, Appenzell has for centuries been a land apart. Monks from St Gallen colonized the area in the tenth century, calling it *Abtszell* or Abbey Cell, but the local fiercely independent peasantry threw off ecclesiastical control in a series of wars in the fourteenth century. Although surrounded by St Gallen's territory, Appenzell joined the Swiss Confederation in 1513, long before its more powerful neighbour. Shortly afterwards it split into two tiny autonomous half-cantons – Protestant **Ausserrhoden**, and Catholic **Innerrhoden**. For touristic purposes, the two half-cantons are together dubbed **Appenzellerland**, but the divisions between them remain to this day, with Ausserrhoden's dynamic economy based on manufacturing industry and Innerrhoden's more languorous one based on tourism and the preservation of traditional culture and crafts.

Appenzell village, 20km south of St Gallen and the capital of Innerrhoden, the least populous of all Swiss cantons, is the main draw of the area for its quaint, traditional air – preserved even amidst the hordes of high-season day-trippers. Previously accessible via a series of winding backcountry lanes, the village was only recently connected by train to the national network. Other than **Stein**'s excellent museum and show dairy, surrounding villages hold few attractions, but there's plenty of excellent **hill walking**, with routes crossing the velvety green hills around Appenzell and south to the higher, rocky peaks of the Alpstein and its highest point, the snowy **Säntis** (2502m).

Appenzell

The main street of **APPENZELL** is car-free Hauptgasse, running from a bridge over the River Sitter at the entrance to the village west for 300m or so to the broad, open Landsgemeindeplatz; it's worth a wander along to admire the intricately painted old wooden houses with their rows of small, closely packed windows – *Löwen Drogerie*, a pharmacy at no. 20, has a particularly gorgeous facade with depictions of herbs and flowers. During the eighteenth and nineteenth centuries, the embroidery industry of nearby St Gallen relied upon thousands of women working by hand from home, with the intricate embroidery of Appenzell particularly highly prized: the upstairs rooms in these buildings, flooded by daylight through the lines of windows, were used as workshops. Hand-embroidery flourished into the first half of the twentieth century, and is still carried on by a few specialists here and there, with workshops often located on atmospheric and characterful back alleys.

In the same building as the tourist office you'll find the **Appenzell Museum**, Hauptgasse 4 (April–Oct daily 10am–noon & 2–5pm; Nov–March Tues–Sun 2–4pm; Fr.5; SMP). The collection of interesting examples of local carpentry and crafts is spread out over six floors, spilling over onto the upper floors of the arcaded Rathaus next door: highlights include many pieces of nineteenth-century Appenzell hand-embroidery, religious art, and militaria from Claux Castle, the ruins of which are visible on a nearby hilltop. Don't miss the short videos shown on demand in a viewing room on the ground floor – the one on local musical traditions is especially good. A few steps to the east of the museum is the **Church of St Mauritius**, much more ornate than you would expect for a relatively small country village. Its Baroque interior, the high altar flanked by gold figures, is oddly asymmetrical, with the choir off kilter and the southern half of the church broader than the northern half.

Often overlooked by visitors, but worth sniffing out, is the **Museum Liner**, on the edge of the village at Unterrainstrasse 5 (April–Oct Thurs & Fri 2–5pm, Sat & Sun 11am–5pm; Fr.8; *www.museumliner.ch*). This gallery, devoted to the work of father-and-son local artists Carl August Liner and Carl Walter Liner, is interesting mainly for its boldly conceived, postmodern design in steel by the Zürich partnership of Annette Gigon and Mike Guyer. Exhibitions of the Liners' uninspiring modernistic art are made more appealing by the addition of changing exhibits of mainly Swiss contemporary works.

Practicalities

Appenzell is served by two narrow-gauge **train** lines (both free to Eurail and Swiss Pass holders, half-price to InterRailers). The first runs direct from outside St Gallen station via Gais; the second runs from Herisau, which itself has easy connections to and from St Gallen. Appenzell's **station**, with bike rental and a change counter, is 200m south of the centre, with the **post office** (CH-9050) opposite. The friendly and helpful **tourist office** is on the main street, at Hauptgasse 4 (June–Oct Mon–Fri 9am–noon & 2–6pm, Sat 9am–noon & 2–5pm; Nov–May closes one hour earlier; ☎071/788 96 41, *www.ktai.ch*), and has material covering the whole Appenzellerland region. They also offer a host of **package deals**, including one that covers dinner, bed and breakfast in Appenzell and entry to the museum and dairy in Stein, for Fr.160 for two people. Watch out for the raft of Catholic festivals kept as **public holidays** in Appenzell, including Corpus Christi, Assumption Day (Aug 15), St Maurice's Day (Sept 22), All Saints' Day (Nov 1) and the Immaculate Conception (Dec 8). Every Friday at 7pm (June–Sept), the central *Hotel Säntis* plays host to an evening of traditional folkloric **music**.

ACCOMMODATION

On the whole, Appenzell's **accommodation** is neat, quiet and characterful, to suit the village. Not many people seem to stay, but it's definitely worth doing so, not least because the village is set on a sloping patch of meadow tipped westwards towards low hills, and on clear summer evenings the tranquil streets are filled with lingering twilight until after 10pm. There's a central hotel **reservations hotline** for the Appenzellerland region, toll-free within Switzerland – ☎0800/801 887.

Landgasthof Eischen in Kau, 4km west (☎071/787 50 30, fax 787 56 60; ③; closed Feb), is a comfortable country inn with good **dorms** for Fr.35 and a **campsite**; dorms (Fr.25) are also available at *Gasthaus Hof*, a small **hotel** with cosy rooms just off Landsgemeindeplatz in Appenzell village (☎071/787 22 10, fax 787 58 83; ②). Pretty *Gasthaus Traube* at Marktgasse 7 (☎071/787 14 07, fax 787 24 19; ②; closed Feb) has newly renovated rooms that are small but attractive, but it's worth making your way up the hill behind the station to find the *Freudenberg* (☎ & fax 071/787 12 40; ②; closed Nov), not so much for the rooms, which are plain and unremarkable, but for the views from the balconies over the village and surrounding countryside. At Hauptgasse 1 is the attractive and well-run *Adler* (☎071/787 13 89, fax 787 13 65, *adlerhotel@bluewin.ch*; ②–③), overlooking the River Sitter and with a range of quality rooms both modern and traditionally styled. The two most characterful places in town are at opposite sides of Landsgemeindeplatz. On the south side is the heavily gabled *Appenzell* (☎071/787 42 11, fax 787 42 84, *info@hotel-appenzell.ch*, *www.hotel-appenzell.ch*; ③–④), with chunky wooden beds in spacious and comfortable rooms, while on the north side is the luxury *Säntis* (☎071/788 11 11, fax 788 11 10, *romantikhotelsaentis@bluewin.ch*, *www.romantikhotels.com/rhappen*; ④), with some canopied or four-poster beds and polished wood everywhere; smaller attic rooms are priced attractively.

EATING AND DRINKING

Many hotels in the village offer quality **eating and drinking** to service the tide of visitors in season. Of all the local specialities – including *Chäshörnli*, cheese-and-potato mini-dumplings, *Birnebrot* or pear bread, a sweet liqueur named *Alpenbitter*, and a fragrant herb-based Schnapps dubbed *Kräuter* – the one you won't be able to avoid is Appenzeller cheese (see p.52), advertised widely around Switzerland with endearingly rustic images of gap-toothed kids and fresh-faced milkmaids. If you choose to buy some, take the advice of the shopkeepers and have it vacuum-sealed, otherwise you'll find the pong seeping its way into everything else in your bag.

The best-value eatery by a long streak is *Hotel Appenzell* on Landsgemeindeplatz (closed Tues lunchtime): go through the *confiserie* shop into the restaurant behind. *Menus* are from Fr.17, excellently prepared with a light touch; the house speciality, rare enough in Swiss cities let alone in a country town, is a range of fresh vegetarian and health-conscious food. Elsewhere, it's not hard to find more traditional fare, mostly relying heavily on pork, potatoes and creamy sauces. *Gasthaus Traube* is one of the better choices, generally with *menus* around Fr.20, while the bustling old-style restaurant in *Gasthaus Hof* concentrates on a host of excellent cheese dishes, including snack-worthy *Käseschnitte* (cheese-on-toast). Unsurprisingly, the luxury *Hotel Säntis* on Landsgemeindeplatz has the swankiest dining in town, although the ground-floor *Stübli* and terrace is considerably cheaper and much less formal than the upstairs restaurant with its Gallic-accented menu.

Around Appenzell

Walking in the pretty countryside **around Appenzell** can be rewarding, with inns and guesthouses galore dotting the landscape – so many that you could walk for days in any direction from inn to inn without encountering a town, and without having to carry food. Trails are well signposted, as usual, and the signposts even carry a little goblet to show which places have an inn. The tourist office in Appenzell has plenty of maps and trail guides, as well as mountain-bike routes and the brochure *Barfuss durchs Appenzellerland*, outlining a trail which you can follow barefoot through grassy meadows from Appenzell village up to **Gonten**, a couple of hours west. Gonten is also the scene of the cantonal *Schwingen* (traditional wrestling) championships, held in late June.

Most hiking trails are crammed into and around the narrow valleys sandwiched between the three great rock walls of the Alpstein range. The small village of **Wasserauen**, a short train ride or a couple of hours' walk south of Appenzell, is the base station for a cable-car running up to **Ebenalp** (1640m), from where a high-level route takes you five hours along the ridge crest to the Säntis (see below). Another route from Wasserauen runs up for an hour into the narrow valley of the beautiful **Seealpsee**. This isolated tarn is the site of a celebrated annual folkloric festival which culminates in a yodelling of Mass on Assumption Day morning (August 15). The attractive *Berggasthaus Forelle* on the lakeshore (☎071/799 11 88, fax 799 15 96; ③; April–Oct) has comfortable, traditional-style rooms as well as dorms for Fr.25, while on a different side of the lake is the simpler *Berggasthaus Seealpsee* (☎071/799 11 40, fax 799 18 20; ③; April–Oct). Both have terrace tables at which to enjoy succulently prepared lake fish. Beyond Seealpsee, a two-hour trail hairpins its way steeply up to **Meglisalp**, with its own rustic *Berggasthaus* (☎ & fax 071/799 11 28; ③; dorms Fr.26; May–Oct), and a festival of folkloric dancing on a weekend in late July.

Appenzell's most famous peak is the **Säntis**, at 2502m well below the mighty proportions of the Alps but nonetheless the highest point for miles around. Trains run from Appenzell to the small town of Urnäsch, departure point for hourly buses which follow a winding road up to **Schwägalp**, from where a cable-car rises to the Säntis summit, marked by a giant striped TV tower. This is a popular day trip, especially in summer, and if you're staying for lunch, you'd do best to aim for the older, more atmospheric *Berggasthaus* on top, rather than the newer canteen-style diner – both, though, have terraces offering spectacular panoramas over the Bodensee and into Austria one way, and over the Toggenburg valley and towards Zürich the other. From the Säntis summit, it's an easy three-and-a-half hour hike along to Ebenalp, from where you can pick up transport connections back to Appenzell.

Stein

Herisau, capital of the half-canton Appenzell Ausserrhoden, and connected to Appenzell village by train, is a workaday town with much less character than its neighbour, but is nonetheless handy as a departure point for an hourly bus to St Gallen via the backcountry village of **STEIN**; you'll often see the village's name suffixed "AR" (the cantonal abbreviation for Ausserrhoden) to distinguish it from Stein-am-Rhein and other Steins. Stein's main draw is the engaging **Appenzeller Volkskunde Museum** (Folklore Museum; April–Oct Mon 1.30–5pm, Tues–Sat 10am–noon & 1.30–5pm, Sun 10am–6pm; Nov–March Sun 10am–5pm; Fr.7). Make sure you pick up the English notes from the desk, and you could also ask about the displays of weaving or traditional musical instruments which take place regularly in the museum. The ground floor has an introduction to Appenzell and its people, along with displays devoted to cowbells, ornamental beltmaking, carpentry and other folk crafts. Upstairs is a reconstructed traditional wooden bedroom, complete with painted furniture, as well as displays of embroidery, weaving and jewellery. The best part of the museum, though, is on the top floor, which is devoted to Appenzell's **folk art**, made by nineteenth-century farmers who decorated furniture, milk pails and other implements with ornate designs and who took to painting scenes from daily life on canvas and wood. Johannes Müller is the most prolific of these uncelebrated artists; he lived all his 91 years in Stein as a clockmaker and artist, and his wonderfully simple, almost childlike landscapes are characterized by vibrantly green hills crisscrossed by long lines of cattle led by traditionally dressed herders.

Next door is the **Appenzeller Schaukäserei** (Show Dairy; March–Oct Mon–Fri 9am–7pm, Sat & Sun 8am–7pm; Nov–Feb daily 9am–6pm; free), where you can watch the various processes of cheesemaking from a gallery above the huge vats and churns – try to time your visit to coincide with the main cheesemaking procedures (daily 9–11am).

The Bodensee

Forming a natural border between Switzerland and Germany, the long **Bodensee** – often anglicized to Lake Constance – is a huge bulge in the course of the Rhine, some 67km from end to end. Unlike most of the Swiss lakes, it doesn't have the benefit of shoreline mountains, and so is exposed to winds year-round and experiences particularly rough weather in the winter. During spring 1999, when the combination of heavy rain and an unusually large quantity of snowmelt in the Alps led to major flooding throughout the country, the lake rose to its highest level for more than a century – many coastal towns were flooded, and even as late as August the harbour fronts at Rorschach and Stein-am-Rhein remained underwater.

Three countries border the lake. The head of the lake, at the extreme southeastern corner, is **Austrian**, focused around the genteel town of Bregenz. The northern and northeastern shore are lined with **German** towns, largest of which is the cosmopolitan city of **Konstanz**, separated from its contiguous **Swiss** suburb of **Kreuzlingen** only by an arbitrary international frontier. Haze and lingering fog can often mask the views across the water, but this hasn't stopped the lakeshore becoming one of Germany's main summer-holiday destinations; this rubs off on the southwestern, Swiss shore, too, where the scattering of soporific little resorts such as **Rorschach** and **Arbon** have a strong Teutonic air about them.

TAKING TO THE WATER

All three countries have their own **boat operators** on the lake. The main Swiss one, covering journeys between Rorschach and Kreuzlingen, is the Schweizerische Bodensee-Schifffahrtsgesellschaft, based at Romanshorn harbour (☎071/463 34 35, *www.sbsag.ch*). Journeys west up the River Rhine from Kreuzlingen to Stein-am-Rhein and Schaffhausen are operated by the Schweizerische Schifffahrtsgesellschaft Untersee und Rhein, based at Freier Platz 7 in Schaffhausen (☎052/625 42 82, *www.urh.ch*).

There are dozens of **excursion cruises** all round the lake during the summer season (April–Oct), in addition to the regular summer ferry routings which, on the Swiss side, hop their way from Rorschach to Kreuzlingen. In the peak season (June to mid-Sept), it's possible to spend **a day on the lake**, leaving Rorschach at 10.55am for the two-hour cruise to Kreuzlingen, where you have an hour or so for lunch before departing at 2.05pm on the gorgeous journey on the Untersee and down the Rhine to Schaffhausen, arriving at 5.25pm; the other way, going against the current, takes from 10.30am to 6.25pm. Some boats cross from the Swiss shore to the German side, stopping at Friedrichshafen, Langenargen or Lindau, as well as Bregenz in Austria. From Kreuzlingen, boats also shuttle over to Konstanz, and to other German destinations such as Meersburg, Überlingen and Radolfzell. Year-round **car ferries** run between Romanshorn and Friedrichshafen, and between Konstanz and Meersburg.

While InterRailers pay half-price on journeys along the Swiss shore, Eurail and Swiss Pass holders travel free. The **Thurgau Day Pass** (see p.412) covers free journeys along the Swiss shore and from Romanshorn to Friedrichshafen. The **Bodensee Pass** (Fr.40 for 15 days) gives half-price travel on boats, trains and buses all around the lake; holders can buy **Bodensee Day Passes** (Fr.28 per set of three), valid for free boat travel on the whole lake and the Rhine as far as Schaffhausen.

Rorschach

Only about 9km northeast of St Gallen, the little lakeside resort of **RORSCHACH** lies on a bay below the grassy Rorschacherberg, and is one of the more pleasant stops along the Swiss shore. It has two train stations: the main Hauptbahnhof is 1km east of the town centre, which is focused around the more useful **Hafenbahnhof** (harbour station). Rorschach suffered particularly badly during the 1999 floods, when the Hafenbahnhof was under a metre or two of water, and the main street **Hauptstrasse** was lined with sandbags; fortunately, the fine sixteenth-to-eighteenth century houses along the street, with their attractive oriel windows, survived. The **Kolumbanskirche** just off the street is a rather lovely broad white late-Baroque church dedicated to the Irish monk Columba, with much gilded glitter inside, an enormous oval ceiling fresco and, unusually, an interior clock. Down on the harbour front is the old **Kornhaus**, emblem of a once-thriving grain trade between St Gallen and Germany across the water. Near it, in an old warehouse in front of the Hafenbahnhof, is a **museum** devoted to vintage cars (July & Aug daily 10am–6pm, March–June & Sept–Oct Sun 10am–6pm; Fr.7). A rack railway winds up from the Hafenbahnhof beside the Rorschacherberg to the tranquil health resort of **Heiden**, with plenty of leg-stretching hiking trails around and about.

The famous **Rorschach Ink-Blot Test**, in which a subject is asked to describe the images that they see in the random shape of a blot, was invented by one Hermann Rorschach, a Swiss psychologist born in 1884 in Arbon down the road who, as far as records show, never actually set foot in Rorschach itself.

Practicalities

Rorschach's **tourist office** is opposite Hafenbahnhof at Hauptstrasse 63 (April–Oct Mon 2–5.30pm, Tues–Fri 9.30am–noon & 2–5.30pm; June–Sept also Sat 9.30am–noon;

Nov–March Mon–Fri 2–5pm; ☎071/841 70 34, *www.tourist-rorschach.ch*). There's a pleasant lakeside HI **hostel** at Churerstrasse 4 (☎071/844 97 12, fax 844 97 13; ①; April–Oct), with dorms costing a steep Fr.32. Otherwise, the best-value **hotel** is *Löwen*, Hauptstrasse 92 (☎071/841 38 87, fax 841 49 32; ①), with a choice of en-suite and shared-bath rooms. The comfortable *Hotel Mozart* is on the lakefront 150m west of the Hafenbahnhof (☎071/841 06 32, fax 841 99 38; ③), with quality renovated rooms.

For **eating and drinking**, *Wirtschaft Pöstli*, at Signalstrasse 2, is beside the post office outside the Hafenbahnhof and has serviceable *menus* of standard Swiss fare from Fr.13, and seven kinds of *Rösti* to choose from. *Pizzeria Roma*, Hauptstrasse 54, offers pasta and a range of 25 pizzas for around Fr.15, with the benefit of a lakeview terrace as well. There's a *Coop* self-service restaurant in the pedestrianized shopping area on Poststrasse.

From Arbon to Münsterlingen

A couple of hours' walk northwest of Rorschach – or a short hop by train or boat – is the ancient village of **ARBON**, reputedly the point at which Columba and Gallus stepped ashore. Walk left from the train station for about ten minutes to reach the tranquil village centre, marked by the spire of the **Kirche St Martin**, with, in its grounds, the tiny eleventh-century **Galluskapelle**. Adjacent is the sixteenth-century **Schloss Arbon**, now housing a small historical museum devoted to the town, of only passing interest (May–Sept daily 2–5pm; March, April, Oct & Nov Sun 2–5pm; Fr.2). The old streets nearby hold a number of interesting half-timbered buildings, most seventeenth- or eighteenth-century. The little disused chapel on Kapellgasse was built in 1390, but deconsecrated in 1777 and is now daubed with graffiti.

Some 7km further along the shore is **ROMANSHORN**, a run-of-the-mill lakeside resort with nothing much to see or do other than take the car ferry across to Friedrichshafen on the German shore. Continuing along the lakeshore, a couple of kilometres before Kreuzlingen lies the village of **MÜNSTERLINGEN**, worth stopping in to visit its extraordinary sixteenth-century Baroque church, originally part of a Benedictine convent (*Münster*). The interior is beautifully decorated, with a spectacularly lavish altarpiece flanked by twisted gilt and turquoise columns, and a cupola overhead painted with a *trompe l'oeil* fresco: the abbess of the convent in the 1680s was related to master sculptor Christof Daniel Schenck from Konstanz, and brought him in to do some of the decoration and to sculpt the wood figures still on display in the

AN ICY TALE

The most interesting story of **Münsterlingen church** begins in the sixteenth century when the climate was considerably chillier than it is today; during that century, it is said, the lake froze solid six or seven times. One winter, as the Reformation was taking hold in Münsterlingen, a church official from **Hagnau**, a town on the German bank opposite, walked across the frozen lake to Münsterlingen, where the church was being emptied of its decoration. He managed to save a single statuette of John the Baptist from the depradations of the Protestant iconoclasts, and took it back to Hagnau for safekeeping. When the lake froze again some years later, he remembered his journey, and brought the statuette back. Ever since then, a freezing of the lake has been the sign for a solemn procession to be made across the ice to take the statuette back to the opposite shore. In 1830, Münsterlingen's clergy and villagers delivered the figurine to Hagnau, where it remained until the harsh winter of 1963, when the ice was solid enough to return it to Münsterlingen church. There it still sits, awaiting the next icy spell – although the statuette on display is a copy of the original, which is kept under lock and key in the crypt.

church. A particularly striking altar curtain dating from 1565, used during Lent to hide the glory of the altar, hangs to one side, with an image of Christ on the cross surrounded by depictions of highly symbolic objects connected with the Passion – a rooster clutching a key, the head of Judas, a hammer and nails, three dice, and so on.

Kreuzlingen and Konstanz

At the northwestern corner of the Bodensee, the small town of **KREUZLINGEN** is an anomaly, nothing more than a southern suburb of the cosmopolitan city of **Konstanz** – it just happens that Kreuzlingen is on the Swiss side of the international frontier, whereas Konstanz is on the German side. Kreuzlingen is like border towns everywhere, full of traffic streaming through without stopping and imbued with a feeling that the exciting stuff is happening elsewhere, just out of sight. It has little history of its own, but is nonetheless worth stopping in, both as a base from which to spend a day or two exploring Konstanz, and for its own **Kirche St Ulrich**, 150m south of the centre on Hauptstrasse. This Baroque church houses the remarkable Ölbergkapelle, containing a 1780 **wood carving** of the Passion comprising around 300 individual figures; the sculpture is teeming with intricate detail, and is surmounted by a fifteenth-century cross (*Kreuz* in German) which has survived three major fires. The church itself is no less dazzling, with a stunningly ornate choir screen in green and gilt.

Kreuzlingen's main station, the **Hauptbahnhof**, is 150m south of the international border; head east (left) out of the station to reach the traffic lights on Hauptstrasse. The **tourist office** is more or less opposite, in the TCS travel agency at no. 39 (Mon–Fri 8.30am–noon & 1.45–6pm; ☎071/672 38 40). From here, Hafenstrasse continues east to the lakeshore, where you'll find both the landing stage for boats and the **Hafenbahnhof**. Nearby is the old Villa Hörnliberg, housing an HI **hostel**, Promenadenstrasse 7 (☎071/688 26 63, fax 688 47 61; ①; March–Nov) – dorms are Fr.23 and they also have bikes to rent. A little further south along the lakeshore brings you to the *Fischerhaus* **campsite** (☎071/688 49 03, fax 688 17 76; April–Oct). The best of the **hotels** is the *Bahnhof-Post*, directly opposite the Hauptbahnhof at Nationalstrasse 2 (☎071/672 79 72, fax 672 49 82; ②), a serviceable place with friendly staff managing en-suite and shared-bath rooms. *Park Kafi*, Hauptstrasse 82, is the **restaurant** of choice, with a huge and affordable menu taking in pasta, meaty mains, veggie options and summer salads, for Fr.15–20. It's also open daily until midnight for savouring a beer or two. In the same vein, *Zapfenzieler*, Hauptstrasse 44, is an amiable bar with pavement terrace. The giant *Coop* supermarket on Alleestrasse has a quality self-service diner attached.

Konstanz (Constance)

The real point of coming to Kreuzlingen is to visit the German city of **KONSTANZ** just over the frontier. This ancient city straddling the Rhine at its outflow from the Bodensee has, despite occupying the "Swiss" bank of the river, never been a part of Switzerland, but – thanks to its giant cathedral – has remained an important ecclesiastical hub for centuries. Between 1414 and 1418, Konstanz was the focus of world attention, as it hosted an ecumenical council which attempted to heal divisions within the Church that had left three popes, based in Rome, Avignon and Pisa, competing for supremacy. Kings, princes, cardinals and other decision makers, religious and secular, came to Konstanz from all over Europe – along with more than 70,000 hangers-on – to take part in the deliberations, which eventually agreed on the necessity of papering over the cracks. The permanent schism of the Reformation followed exactly a century later. The council sat in Konstanz's huge **Münster** at the heart of the Old Town, originally a Romanesque basilica which continued to be added to until 1856, when a spire was placed atop the tower. The alleys and streets all around are attractive and characterful, and the town is given extra dynamism by the presence of students from the local university. It's worth dropping into the super-efficient **tourist office** beside the station (May–Sept Mon–Fri 9am–6.30pm, Sat 9am–1pm; Oct–April Mon–Fri 9am–noon & 2–6pm) to pick up their English booklet detailing a self-guided **walking tour** of the Old Town. **Trains** take three minutes to run between Kreuzlingen's main station and Konstanz, but it's really no hardship to walk the fifteen minutes or so between the two – whichever way you choose, you'll need to show your **passport**. You can **change money** into Deutschmarks at the counter in the Swiss half of Konstanz's station without commission.

Schaffhausen

Capital of the northernmost Swiss canton that shares its name, **SCHAFFHAUSEN** has one of the most captivating medieval town centres in the whole of Switzerland. In addition, just 3km down river are the mighty **Rhine falls**, a blockage to shipping on the otherwise navigable river that to this day forces boats making the journey from the Bodensee to unload their goods (or passengers), and then load up again beyond the falls for the journey on towards Basel. Almost as if too far north to be of concern to most visitors to Switzerland, Schaffhausen is nonetheless an unsung, uncelebrated gem.

A bankside docking point had already developed into the thriving market town of **Scafusun** by 1045. (The name of the town probably derives from its many riverside boathouses – boat is *Schiff* in German.) During the thirteenth and fourteenth centuries, Schaffhausen grew rapidly, handling salt and cereals from Bavaria and the Tyrol for sale at the town market and for transport on beyond the falls. Granted the status of a free city in 1415 during the Council of Konstanz, Schaffhausen joined the Swiss Confederation in 1501. With an expansion of trade, the town maintained steady growth, its eighteenth-century merchants indulging in the fashion for adding ornate **oriel** windows to the pre-existing Gothic or Renaissance buildings. Hydroelectric works built in the nineteenth century to exploit the flow of the Rhine brought the area into the industrial age.

During **World War II**, Schaffhausen was the only Swiss town to be **bombed** by Allied aircraft: about 100 civilians were killed during a raid by American bombers on April 1, 1944. The US claimed that pilots had mistakenly identified Schaffhausen – the only sizeable chunk of Swiss territory on the north bank of the Rhine – as a German target. They apologized profusely and paid out compensation ... only to make the same mistake again on February 22, 1945, this time killing sixteen in Schaffhausen and nine in Stein-am-Rhein (also on the "wrong" side of the river). Records that could possibly throw light onto the allegation that the bombings were in fact an Allied response to Schaffhausen's munitions industries supplying arms to the Nazis in breach of Swiss neutrality are, as yet, still classified.

In recent years, Schaffhausen has developed into a busy modern town, now expanded well beyond its medieval centre, and capitalizing on its position on the fulcrum between Germany and Switzerland to act as a commercial and cultural bridge between the two. It has also absorbed a high number of **Sri Lankan** immigrants and asylum seekers, leading to an unusually broad ethnic mix on the streets and plenty of local advertising posters in Tamil.

Arrival, orientation and information

Schaffhausen's **train station** is at the northwestern edge of the compact Old Town, served by both Swiss SBB and German DB trains (the latter running along the north-

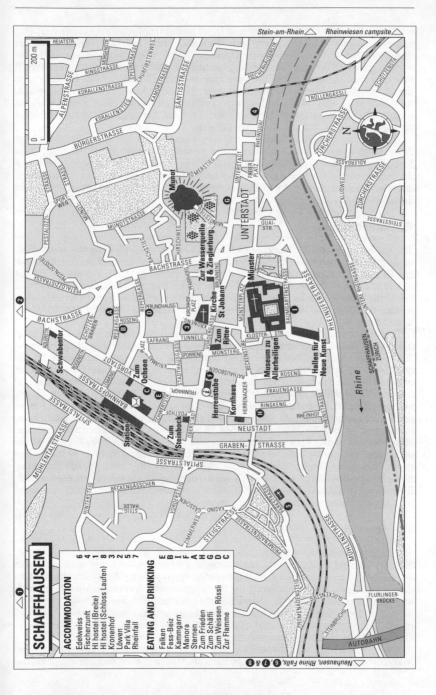

SCHAFFHAUSEN

ACCOMMODATION

Edelweiss	6
Fischerzunft	4
HI hostel (Breite)	1
HI hostel (Schloss Laufen)	8
Kronenhof	3
Löwen	2
Park Villa	5
Rheinfall	7

EATING AND DRINKING

Falken	E
Fass-Beiz	B
Kammgarn	I
Manora	F
Sternen	A
Zum Frieden	H
Zum Schäfli	G
Zum Weissen Rössli	D
Zur Flamme	C

Stein-am-Rhein △   Rheinwiesen campsite △

Neuhausen, Rhine Falls, 6, 7 & 8 △

ern bank of the Rhine and terminating at Basel Bad. station). Counters inside deal with money changing (Mon–Sat 7am–7pm, Sun 9am–7pm) and bike rental (Mon–Fri 6am–8pm, Sat & Sun 8am–8pm). Opposite is the main **post office** (CH-8201 Schaffhausen 1). One block east from the station is bustling Fronwagplatz, where you'll find, under the big clock tower, the main **tourist office** (July–Sept Mon–Fri 9am–5pm, Sat 10am–4pm, Sun 10am–1pm; Oct–June Mon–Fri 9am–5pm, Sat 10am–noon; ☎052/625 51 41, *www.sh.ch*), with plenty of information and excellent guided **walking tours** of the Old Town (May–Oct Tues, Wed, Fri & Sat 2.15pm; Fr.10), which include a tasting of five wines in a vintner's after the walk.

The best way to arrive at Schaffhausen is **by boat** from further up the Rhine. At least three boats a day (May–Sept) make the beautiful journey along the river from Kreuzlingen via Stein-am-Rhein, a peaceful ride between wooded banks on just about the only stretch of the Rhine to be free of heavy industry. Boats dock in Schaffhausen at Freier Platz, just beside the main road bridge at the southeastern corner of the Old Town.

Accommodation

The quality **campsite** *Rheinwiesen* (☎052/659 33 00; May–Sept) is on the south bank of the river at Langwiesen, 2km southeast of the centre. Dorms cost Fr.23 in the modern HI **hostel** at Randenstrasse 65, in the suburb of Breite, 1km northwest of the station (☎052/625 88 00, fax 624 59 54; ①; March–Oct; bike rental available), or you can spend the same for dorms in another, older HI hostel in Schloss Laufen, a castle overlooking the Rhine falls 3km west of town (☎052/659 61 52, fax 659 60 39; ①; mid-March to mid-Nov).

There's not a big choice of **hotels** in the centre, and the best budget deals are to be found in surrounding suburbs. The least expensive is the comfortable old guesthouse *Löwen*, at Im Hösli 2 in Herblingen, 3km north of the centre and reachable on bus #5 (☎052/643 22 08; ②), although its rooms are all modern and renovated. In the centre of run-of-the-mill Neuhausen, ten minutes' walk from both Schaffhausen and the Rhine falls, you'll find the *Edelweiss*, Pestalozzistrasse 20 (☎052/672 34 34, fax 672 34 35; ②), and the *Rheinfall*, Zentralstrasse 60 (☎052/672 13 21, fax 672 14 29; ②), both of them simple and serviceable. On the edge of Schaffhausen's Old Town is *Park Villa*, Parkstrasse 18 (☎052/625 27 37, fax 624 12 53; ②–③), an atmospheric old mansion complete with chandeliers and Persian carpets: one lovely shared-bath room which opens onto the garden can undercut the other, en-suite rooms by Fr.40 or more. The central *Kronenhof*, Kirchhofplatz 7 (☎052/625 66 31, fax 624 45 89; ③), has slick business-class rooms, but Schaffhausen's most characterful choice is the *Fischerzunft*, Rheinquai 8 (☎052/625 32 81, fax 625 32 85; ④), a super-modern hotel on the riverfront with just ten rooms – not all with Rhine views.

The Town

Schaffhausen's beautiful riverside Old Town is crammed full of well-preserved architecture, which lend the narrow, cobbled streets a charm to rival any town centre in Switzerland. A good place to begin is the central **Fronwagplatz**, the town's marketplace during the Middle Ages. Dominating the long square is the **Fronwagturm**, within which originally hung the market's massive scales; the clock and astronomical device on the top dates from 1564. Beside it is the late-Baroque **Herrenstube**, one of the town's most distinguished townhouses, although the facade of the **Zum Steinbock** house, 100m west at Oberstadt 16, is even more impressive, covered in stucco Rococo curlicues.

If you stroll north on Fronwagplatz, past the square's two medieval fountains – the **Metzgerbrunnen** (1524), topped by a statue of a Swiss mercenary, and the

Mohrenbrunnen (1535), with a Moorish king – you'll come to the **Zum Ochsen** house, one of the most grandiose in the city, at Vorstadt 17. The late-Gothic facade of this former inn was remodelled in 1608 and decorated with striking Renaissance frescoes of classical heroes. The oriel window is especially graceful: it shows, in five panels, a woman embodying each of the five senses – holding a mirror (sight), a glove (touch), a flower (smell), a stringed instrument (hearing) and a cake (taste). These oriels were often tacked on to existing buildings during renovation work in the seventeenth and eighteenth centuries, both to demonstrate the houseowner's wealth and good taste, and also to give people inside a clear view up and down the street. Goethe visited Schaffhausen three times – in 1775, 1779 and 1797 – and apocryphally remarked that the locals must be very curious folk, not least because as well as 170-odd proper oriels dotted around the Old Town, there are dozens of half-oriels, often with spyholes in the floor to allow people within to look directly down on the heads of callers. Suitably enough, one of Schaffhausen's many nicknames is **Erkerstadt**, or the City of Oriel Windows.

North of the Zum Ochsen, a short detour past the frescoes of the Zum Grossen Käfig house at Vorstadt 43, showing the triumphal parade of the medieval Mongol king Tamerlane, brings you to the northern gate of the city, the **Schwabentor**. The tower itself dates from 1370, but on the outer face, just above the arch, is a small panel added during renovations in 1933, which shows a boy with a pig under his arm dodging the traffic. The dialect inscription *Lappi tue d'Augen uf* translates as "Silly people should keep their eyes open" – a reference to the increasingly heavy motorized traffic of the 1930s.

Vordergasse and the Munot

Karstgässchen leads from opposite the Zum Ochsen house into **Platz**, its fountain sporting another grim-faced mercenary. From here, alleys bring you south onto the main **Vordergasse**, a shopping street sloping downhill to the east. On the corner of Münstergasse is Schaffhausen's most celebrated house, the **Zum Ritter**, its facade covered in a spectacularly intricate design acclaimed as the most significant Renaissance fresco to survive north of the Alps (although the original is now preserved in the town's Museum zu Allerheiligen and this is a 1930s copy). Originally dating from 1570, the fresco depicts, over three storeys, various elements of knightly virtues (*Ritter* means "knight"): the central panel shows Odysseus in the Land of the Lotus-Eaters, tempted by a voluptuous woman, while above is a Roman knight who sacrificed himself for the glory of his country. Below is a trusting girl, symbolizing virtue, protected by a king (the government) and a woman holding a mitre (the church). From the Zum Ritter, alleys head southwest to another of Schaffhausen's broad open squares, **Herrenacker**, surrounded by tall, dignified facades, with, on the west side, the town's massive **Kornhaus** (1679).

From the Zum Ritter house, Vordergasse continues east to the Gothic, five-naved **Kirche St Johann** (Mon–Sat: April–Sept 9am–6pm; Oct–March 10am–5pm), expanded six times since it was begun in the eleventh century. In a niche on the south side of the tower is a small statue of the Madonna and Child without any feet: they were removed during the Reformation when a wall was built to hide the image. A few steps east, in front of a fountain statue of William Tell, is the magnificent double-fronted Rococo mansion **Zur Wasserquelle und Zieglerburg.**

Some 50m north of the Zur Wasserquelle is a footbridge over the main Bachstrasse road, which brings you onto steps climbing the hill to the **Munot**. This is Schaffhausen's trademark circular fortress, built by forced labour in 1564 after the religious wars of the Reformation. The interior (daily: May–Sept 8am–8pm; Oct–April 9am–5pm) is dark and gloomy, with massive stone vaulting strong enough to support the 40,000-tonne superstructure. An internal spiral ramp – one of only three such designs in Europe (see also p.93) – brings you out onto the circular roof of the bastion, with good views over the town. A different door exits onto stairs running through the vines planted on the Munot hill, down to the small riverside quarter known as **Unterstadt**; Schaffhausen's annual Old Town shindig, held on a weekend in late June, still passes on alternate years between the salt-of-the-earth folk of the Unterstadt and their toffee-nosed neighbours of the town centre further west.

The Münster and the museums

Schaffhausen's lofty **Münster zu Allerheiligen** (Cathedral of All Saints) is the focus of the Old Town. The first church on the site dated from 1049, very soon after the founding of the town itself, and was replaced in 1103 by the building which still stands today. The beautifully restored Romanesque church tower gives a hint as to the interior (Tues–Sun 10am–noon & 2–5pm), in which twelve huge columns of Rorschach sandstone line the austere, mostly unadorned, Romanesque nave. Beside the cathedral, the Romanesque-Gothic **cloister** is the largest in Switzerland, a lovely broad walkway circling the Junkernfriedhof, or noblemen's cemetery, many of whose inhabitants are commemorated on plaques set into the wall. In the cathedral courtyard sits the gigantic **Schiller Bell**, cast in 1486: its Latin inscription of *vivos–voco/mortuos–plango/fulgura–frango* ("I call on the living, lament the dead, halt the lightning") is supposed to have inspired German poet Friedrich Schiller to compose his *Song of the Clock* ... despite the fact that Schiller never set foot in Schaffhausen. Just beyond is the atmospheric little **herb garden**, precisely recreated according to medieval records.

In the same complex as the Münster is Schaffhausen's principal historical museum, the **Museum zu Allerheiligen** (May–Oct Tues–Fri 10am–noon & 2–5pm, Sat & Sun 10am–5pm; Nov–April Tues–Sun 10am–noon & 2–5pm; free; *www.allerheiligen.ch*). Unfortunately, although the collections are interesting, the desk can't help out with recent English notes and there's also been so much reorganization in recent years that the museum's own plan is out of date. The ground floor is mostly given over to the vast archeological collection but, as with the rambling historical collections spread over this and the upper floors, there's little coherence. The place is like a labyrinth, and you could either wander, enjoying the surprise of coming across a roomful of early medieval religious art, or a restored Gothic chapel, or a display on Schaffhausen's military history, or instead cut your losses and head for the topmost floor, which holds an engaging collection of **art** by Swiss painters and sculptors of the last five hundred years.

Baumgartenstrasse marks the southern boundary of the cathedral quarter. In an old textile factory metres from the river at no. 23 is the **Hallen für Neue Kunst** (Contemporary Art Spaces; May–Oct Sat 2–5pm, Sun 11am–5pm; Fr.14; *www.modern-art.ch*). Pricier than it need be, and with awkwardly limited opening hours, this impressive gallery is still well worth a visit, with work by artists, known and unknown, from the 1960s to the present spread over several vast floors. Particularly striking in such airy surroundings are the geometrical games in two and three dimensions of Robert Mangold, and Sol LeWitt's dazzling cube installations.

The Rhine falls

Schaffhausen's best excursion is the short trip westwards to the **Rhine falls**, Europe's largest waterfall. They are truly magnificent, not so much for their height (a mere 23m) as for their impressive breadth (150m) and the sheer drama of the place, with the spray rising in a cloud of rainbows above the forested banks. The turreted castle Schloss Laufen on a cliff directly above the falls to the south completes the spectacle. August 1 – the Swiss National Day – is particularly impressive, with a huge fireworks display mounted on the riverside.

Getting to the falls is simplicity itself: the 3km riverside **walk** from Schaffhausen to the suburban town of Neuhausen, where the falls are located, takes about 45 minutes;

or you could take city **bus** #1 or #6 to Neuhausen Zentrum, from where the well-sign-posted falls are five minutes' walk away. Schloss Laufen even has a **train** station (April–Oct only), served by hourly trains on the line between Schaffhausen and Winterthur. (Neuhausen's own station is awkwardly far from the falls.)

Once you're within sight of the falls, though, you're inevitably brought down to earth with a bump by the hordes of tourists crowding both banks in search of the best camera angle, and by the circus of souvenir stalls and dismal restaurants all around. The worst of it is on the north bank; crossing by the arched footbridge over to the south bank – which can still get unpleasantly overrun – at least means you can experience the power of the falls at close quarters. Damp steps (Fr.1) lead from the souvenir shop at Schloss Laufen down to various platforms at the very edge, from where the roaring waters tumble inches from your nose.

The best way to see the falls is from one of the daredevil **boats** which scurry around in the spray; Rhyfall-Mändli (☎052/672 48 11) is the best-known operator, running a host of very popular trips continuously throughout the day (June–Aug 10am–6pm; May & Sept 11am–5pm; Fr.5–6.50). Boats depart from easy-to-spot jetties on both banks.

Eating and drinking

Schaffhausen has a good range of places to **eat**, from the self-service *Manora* diner just off Fronwagplatz upwards. The best budget dining is to be done at the cosy *Fass-Beiz*, Webergasse 13 (closed Sun), a co-operative-run café-bar which offers plenty of wholesome, home-cooked veggie dishes for under Fr.15. Unterstadt is lined with cheerful, inexpensive places in which to join the locals for some hearty nosh: typical among them is *Zum Schäfli* at no. 21, with *menus* of standard Swiss fare from Fr.14. *Zur Flamme*, above a WWF shop at Vorstadt 9 (☎052/624 09 05; closed Mon eve and Sun) is an informal veggie restaurant, offering excellent food for well under Fr.20 – or go for the five-course evening *menu* for Fr.45. Pizza and pasta dishes are available for Fr.20 or so at the bright, funky *Sternen*, Webergasse 38, while *Falken*, Vorstadt 5, has quality Swiss food for roughly the same price. Moving up the scale is *Zum Frieden*, Herrenacker 11 (☎052/625 47 15), an atmospheric tavern-style place with a good-value *Stübli* at ground-floor level and a pricier formal restaurant upstairs serving Frenchified mains for around Fr.40. Top of the heap is the spectacular *Fischerzunft*, Rheinquai 8 (see "Accommodation"), rated in the top half-dozen restaurants in the country and offering a unique cuisine blending French and East Asian elements: don't expect change from Fr.100 per head.

There's any number of places at which to **drink**: café-bars line all the Old Town squares, with those on Fronwagplatz particularly well placed for people-watching. *Fass-Beiz* (see above) is a quiet little nook to savour a beer or three, while there's a lively café-bar (closed Mon & Tues) attached to the *Kammgarn* cultural centre at Baumgartenstrasse 19. *Zum Weissen Rössli*, Repfergasse 28, is the loudest, smokiest bar in town.

Stein-am-Rhein and around

Positioned at the point where the Untersee arm of the Bodensee narrows into the Rhine 20km east of Schaffhausen, little **STEIN-AM-RHEIN** is an almost perfectly preserved medieval village, famed throughout Switzerland for the intricacy of the sixteenth-century **frescoes** which adorn an array of houses in the village. It's well worth a visit, but sees so many tour buses during the frantic summer season – about a million people pass through annually – that the best way to enjoy the place is to stop overnight: it's only after 5pm and before 10am that you'll find much peace.

If you're not pressed for time, it's worth a detour to the museum complex at **Kartause Ittingen**, a former monastery set amidst hop fields and open, rolling farmland beyond the hills south of Stein-am-Rhein.

Arrival, information and accommodation

At least six **boats** a day in summer arrive at Stein-am-Rhein, three from Kreuzlingen upriver and three from Schaffhausen downriver. Otherwise, Stein-am-Rhein's **train station** – connected to Schaffhausen and Winterthur, Kreuzlingen and St Gallen – is on the southern bank of the Rhine, a couple of minutes' walk from the bridge. The tiny **tourist office** is at Oberstadt 9 (Mon–Fri 9–11am & 2–5pm; ☎052/741 28 35); opposite, the *Kiosk Charregass* (see "Eating and Drinking" below), offers **Internet** access (Fr.1.25 for 5min).

There are three riverside **campsites** within a few kilometres of the village: the nearest is *Grenzstein*, about 1km east (☎052/741 51 44, fax 741 45 52) and open year-round; sites at Wagenhausen, 2km west (☎052/741 42 71, fax 741 41 57; April–Oct), and the *Hüttenberg* at Eschenz, 2km east (☎052/741 23 37; year-round), are both rated with five stars. The HI **hostel** at Hemishoferstrasse 87, about fifteen minutes' walk due east from Understadt (☎052/741 12 55, fax 741 51 40; ①; March–Oct), has dorms from Fr.23. The least expensive **hotel** is the *Mühlethal* on Öhningerstrasse 250m east of Rathausplatz (☎052/741 27 25, fax 741 33 63; ②), with a good **restaurant** serving inexpensive wood-fired pizza (closed Mon). There are a few beds above the *Schiff* restaurant beside the quay (☎052/741 22 73, fax 741 45 52; ②), which also has a pleasant garden for riverside dining, while 100m east along the waterfront is the *Rheingerbe* (☎052/741 29 91, fax 741 21 66; ②), an old wood-beamed house with some rooms overlooking the Rhine. The *Adler* is directly on Rathausplatz (☎052/742 61 61, fax 741 44 40; ③), its brilliantly decorated facade sheltering pine-decor rooms which are surprisingly plain and ordinary, though comfortable enough.

The Town

The best way to arrive at Stein-am-Rhein is **by boat**. If you head east along the Schiffländi quay, and then cut north on tiny Schwarzhorngasse, you'll come in a minute's stroll to the breathtaking **Rathausplatz**. This square at the heart of the village is often acclaimed as the most picturesque in the country, ringed by medieval half-timbered buildings vying with each other for the lavishness of their frescoes and the gracefulness of their oriels. Standing alone at the head of the square is the Rathaus, built in 1539–42: the half-timbered top storeys are original, the middle floor dates from a 1745 renovation, and the ground floor facade and entranceway were added in 1865. The line of facades along the south side of the square is dazzling, each one sporting a fresco illustrating the house name: from left to right are the *Hirschen* (stag); *Krone* (crown); *Vordere Krone* (foremost crown), sporting an especially lofty gable; *Roter Ochsen* (red ox), the town's oldest tavern, with a Gothic facade; *Steinerner Trauben* (stony grapes); *Sonne* (sun), the oldest hotel in the village with new frescoes dating from 1900; and the *Schwarzer Horn* (black horn). Opposite, on the north side, are the *Adler* (eagle); and, most impressive of all, the *Weisser Adler* (white eagle), bedecked in the town's oldest frescoes, a Holbein-esque series of Renaissance-style scenes painted in 1520–25.

Inevitably, the rest of the village pales in comparison, but there are plenty of picturesque narrow lanes and alleys to explore off to each side, ignored by most visitors who, after a quick circuit of Rathausplatz, content themselves with a five-minute glance at the main Understadt–Oberstadt street running through the square, and the quayside.

A manor house at Understadt 18, originally dating from 1279 but entirely renovated in 1819, has been converted into the **Museum Lindwurm** (March–Oct Mon &

Wed–Sun 10am–5pm; Fr.5; SMP), with surprisingly interesting and informative displays outlining Stein-am-Rhein's bourgeois and agricultural life in the nineteenth century. The desk keeps English translations of the extensive notes which are posted alongside each section. A great deal of work has been done in the museum to recreate the living conditions of the wealthy upper-class family who owned the house and the servants and farmworkers who also lived there. Walking through the cobbled stables, the Empire-style drawing room, and the spartan servants' quarters under the eaves, feels like stepping back in time.

Eating and drinking

The village is crammed with **eating** places of various descriptions: a five-minute stroll will turn up something to fill a gap. Snacks and inexpensive pizzas can be had at *Kiosk Charregass*, at Oberstadt 10 (closed Mon); there's a *Migros* self-service diner two minutes north of the Untertor gate at the western end of Understadt; and an inexpensive *crêperie* at Understadt 10. Otherwise, you're looking at more formal, expensive dining. Beside the bridge at Rhigasse 8 is the *Rheinfels* (☎052/741 21 44; closed Wed), with an atmospheric all-wood dining room specializing in excellent fish, *menus* costing around Fr.35. The gorgeous interior of the *Roten Ochsen* on Rathausplatz (☎052/741 23 28; closed Mon) is dripping with atmosphere to suit the outstanding food, purely local ingredients going into their Swiss specialities. Top choice is the *Sonne*, also on Rathausplatz (☎052/741 21 28; closed Tues & Wed), with the ground-floor *Weinstube* serving excellent daily *menus* for around Fr.25 prepared in the same kitchen as the gourmet delights which might set you back Fr.60 or more in the restaurant upstairs. Prominent on a hill above the town is Schloss Hohenklingen, formerly the residence of the feudal lords of the area and now converted into a restaurant (☎052/741 21 37; closed Mon & Jan–Feb), boasting views at least as good as the food.

Kartause Ittingen

A short distance south of Stein-am-Rhein and well worth a visit is **Kartause Ittingen**, a former Charterhouse (Carthusian monastery) out in the countryside near **Warth**, some 6km south over a ridge from Stein-am-Rhein. From 1461 until 1868, the old buildings were home to a community of between twelve and fifteen Carthusian monks; recently restored after decades of neglect, the complex today houses the **Ittinger Museum** (Mon–Fri 2–5pm, Sat & Sun 11am–5pm; Fr.5), which sheds light on the life of the Carthusian order. The monks lived a life of extreme austerity, taking all meals except Sunday lunch alone in their cell, having each day divided into strict periods of work, rest and prayer (including a three-hour service every night from 11.30pm, and never more than four-and-a-half hours' sleep at a stretch), and remaining committed by oath to silence at all times. The restored rooms of the monastery begin directly opposite the museum entrance with the stunning Rococo **church**, its long nave divided into four and flanked by extraordinarily intricate choir stalls, carved around 1700. The dramatic high altar depicts St Bruno, founder of the Carthusian order. There's no organ, since the Carthusian Mass is sung according to its medieval foundations, without accompaniment. Beside the church is the **Little Cloister**, prelude to a series of decorated and partly furnished rooms once used by the monks, including the Refectory (room 4), with seventeenth-century portraits ringing the walls. The **Great Cloister**, off which are the fifteen monks' cells, leads around an internal garden with summerhouse. More rooms upstairs, some with original decoration, include a tiny **prison** with barred window, and an unusual upper-level gallery in the church, looking the length of the nave.

Some rooms in the museum are also given over to the cantonal **Kunstmuseum** (same times and ticket), which houses a collection of twentieth-century Swiss art;

highlights include a penetrating self-portrait by Helen Dahm and the playful Yellow Submarine-like canvases of Josef Wittlich. The ticket desk sells a short English guide on the whole museum complex for a few francs.

Practicalities

Unless you have a car, it's difficult to reach Kartause Ittingen. Hourly **buses** run from Stein-am-Rhein to Warth, leaving you fifteen minutes' walk away. Transport from the modern town of Frauenfeld, 4km south of the monastery and connected to St Gallen and Winterthur by train – is slightly more convenient; two buses a day (10am & 2pm) depart from Frauenfeld station for the Kartause itself, and there are also hourly buses to Warth. You'd do just as well renting **bikes** from Frauenfeld station (daily 5.30am–8.30pm) and cycling. The tourist office in Frauenfeld station (Mon–Fri 9am–noon & 2–6pm, Sat 9am–noon; ☎052/721 31 28, *www.stadt-frauenfeld.ch*) can help with maps and information.

Part of the complex of old buildings at Ittingen, which are arrayed around a peaceful large internal courtyard area, has been renovated as a modern conference-style **hotel** (☎052/748 44 11, fax 747 26 57, *kartause@bluewin.ch*, *www.kartause.ch*; ③) – all exposed brick and bright, functional comforts. The *Herberge* section adjacent has spotless, spartan shared-bath rooms (②). The on-site **restaurant**, *Zur Mühle*, has quality modern cuisine and is not drastically expensive (*menus* Fr.20–25), but the open farmland all around is prime picnic territory – it's worth dropping into the little **shop** to nose around in all kinds of choice home-made goodies, including fresh-baked bread, fragrant *eaux-de-vie* and cider distilled on site, home-grown vegetables and, most appealing of all, the lip-smacking Klosterbräu beer, brewed from hand-picked hops grown just outside the monastery walls and sold by the bottle.

Liechtenstein

Only slightly larger than Manhattan island, **LIECHTENSTEIN** is the world's fourth-smallest country, a chip of green squeezed between the Rhine and the Austrian Alps. It's a quiet, unassuming place, home to some 30,000 overwhelmingly Catholic Liechtensteiners, who sing their own German words to "God Save the Queen" as the national anthem and regard themselves as entirely separate from the Swiss, with whom neighbourly relations only began in 1923. This said, you won't notice many obvious differences between Liechtenstein and its neighbour and, inevitably, the main reason to visit is the novelty value, but there are also some peaceful, rustic spots to enjoy outside the toytown capital **Vaduz**.

Some history

Liechtenstein is the only country in the world to be named after the people who own it. The Romans came through after their conquest of the area in 15 BC, following which the area of Liechtenstein was passed from pillar to post until the sixteenth century, when it formed two domains ruled from afar by noble German dynasties. In 1699, Johann Adam Andreas of the **Von Liechtenstein** family of Vienna bought the Lordship

---

EXPLORING LIECHTENSTEIN

Regular postbuses serve all villages in Liechtenstein. Swiss **transport passes** are valid for journeys into and around Liechtenstein, as is the Appenzell–Toggenburg Regional Pass (see box p.412), but neither are valid for the Austrian trains from Buchs to Schaan. Liechtenstein has its own transport pass, an excellent-value deal offering a week's unlimited bus rides throughout the principality for just Fr.10.

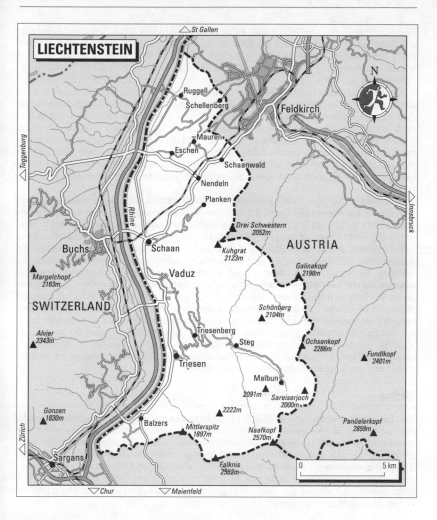

of Schellenberg, and then in 1712 the County of Vaduz, in order to get a seat in the imperial German Diet of Princes. Shortly after, his little patch was renamed the Principality of Liechtenstein.

In 1815, after Napoleon's international politicking, Liechtenstein formed part of the German Confederation. When that collapsed in 1866, Liechtenstein became entirely independent under a so-called **democratic monarchy**, in which the Prince takes an active political role. Until 1919, the principality had a customs union with Austria–Hungary, but following that empire's defeat in World War I, Liechtenstein negotiated a customs treaty with Switzerland in 1923, since when borders have been open and unmarked between the two neighbours.

The current head of state, a direct descendant of the country's founders, is His Serene Highness **Prince Hans Adam II** von und zu Liechtenstein, who – unlike most

European monarchs – wields considerable power and in fact makes a point of regularly speaking his mind on political matters. He has guided and overseen Liechtenstein's entry into the UN (1990) and the sub-EU European Economic Area (1995), both of which controversially created a gulf in relations with more reticent Switzerland. Almost as if in return, Liechtenstein was landed in December 1997 with the surprise announcement from Rome that the Pope had decreed the creation of a new Archdiocese of Liechtenstein, with the extremely controversial **Wolfgang Haas** as the new bishop. Parliamentarians and even the Prince claimed to have been left in the dark about the announcement, catching the news on television four days before Christmas. Haas – a Liechtensteiner by birth – had spent years raising hackles in nearby Chur with his attacks on the role of women in the church and society, and his dismissive attitude towards lay workers; many Liechtensteiners wondered if they were being foisted with such a turbulent priest in recompense for snubbing their neighbours.

Meanwhile, the principality gets on with doing what it does best: making money. Despite the big players all around it, Liechtenstein has managed to carve a unique modern identity by playing big itself. Its low-tax, ask-me-no-questions **banks** haven't been under the kind of international scrutiny that has been focused on Swiss banks throughout the 1990s, and so have escaped demands for liberalization – the tiny principality nurses some Fr.80 billion from global clients in anonymous numbered accounts. In addition, the country has made a mint from producing highly collectable **postage stamps** for the best part of a century, and is now so rich that it is even able to entice guest workers in from Switzerland. Its industries – including the making of sausage skins and false teeth – sound wonderfully quirky (and there's a noticeable lack of heavy industry throughout the principality's green countryside), but they nonetheless manage to bring in almost Fr.4 billion annually. Most locals are well aware of the benefits of material comfort, and Liechtensteiner villages have a neat, bourgeois atmosphere about them, rather disappointing if you've come expecting to see signs of an ancient monarchy stuck somewhere in the Middle Ages.

Vaduz

You have to feel sorry for **VADUZ**. It could have been a quiet and pleasant Rhineside provincial town like Sargans on the Swiss bank opposite; instead, it labours under the unreasonable weight of being capital of an historical oddity. The little town bulges with glass-plated banks and squadrons of whistle-stop foreigners aimless with anticlimax. The tiny town centre is modern, not especially attractive, and there's not much to see or do that's different from what can be seen or done in any other small town in the area, aside from enjoying the Prince's impressive art collection or depositing a million or two in a numbered account.

Arrival and information

Regular **postbuses** run to Vaduz from Sargans and Buchs, both of them on the main SBB train line between St Gallen and Chur. Austrian Railways (ÖBB, or OeBB) operates six daily **trains** between Buchs and Feldkirch (Austria) which stop at Schaan, 3km north of Vaduz, from where buses shuttle into Vaduz.

The **tourist office** is 50m east of the post office at Städtle 37 (Mon–Fri 8am–noon & 1.30–5.30pm; June–Aug also Sat 9am–noon & 1–5pm, Sun 10am–noon & 1–5pm; April, May, Sept & Oct also Sat 10am–noon & 1–4pm; May & Sept also Sun 10am–noon & 1–4pm; ☎232 14 43, *touristinfo@lie-net.li, www.searchlink.li/tourist*). They have information on the whole country, but their principal service is to bang an official Liechtenstein stamp into your passport to prove to your friends that you've visited the place – an entirely unnecessary novelty that nonetheless comes at a price (Fr.2).

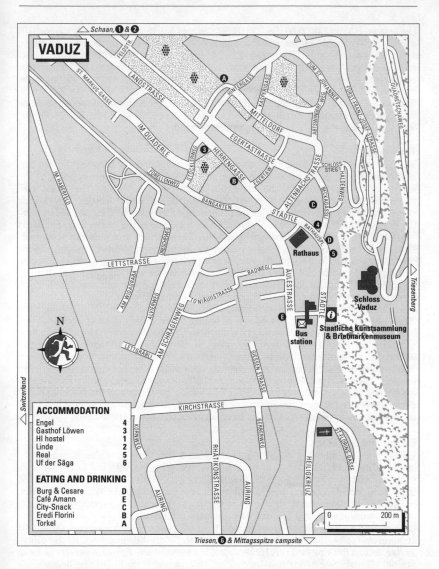

△ *Schaan,* ❶ & ❷

VADUZ

Rathaus

Schloss Vaduz

Staatliche Kunstsammlung & Briefmarkenmuseum

Bus station

ACCOMMODATION

Engel	4
Gasthof Löwen	3
HI hostel	1
Linde	2
Real	5
Uf der Säga	6

EATING AND DRINKING

Burg & Cesare	D
Café Amann	E
City-Snack	C
Eredi Florini	B
Torkel	A

N

△ *Switzerland*

△ *Triesenberg*

0   200 m

Triesen, ❻ & *Mittagsspitze campsite* ▽

Accommodation

The nearest **campsite** to Vaduz is the quiet and pleasant *Mittagsspitze*, about 6km south beyond Triesen (☎392 36 77, fax 392 36 80). Liechtenstein's HI **hostel** is at Untere Rüttigasse 6, 2km or so north of Vaduz near Schaan (☎232 50 22, fax 232 58 56; ①; March–Nov) – it's about a half-hour walk from Buchs, or take the bus from Buchs or Vaduz to Mühleholz. Otherwise, **hotel** accommodation in Vaduz is expensive – the cheapest deal is *Engel*, Städtle 13 (☎236 17 17, fax 233 11 59; ③), a boxy place in the centre with modern, comfortable rooms. More upmarket options are *Gasthof Löwen*,

Herrengasse 35 (☎232 00 66, fax 232 04 58, *loewen@hotels.li*, *www.hotels.li/loewen*; ④), a lovely 600-year-old inn, renovated throughout but with period furniture and fittings, and the *Real*, Städtle 21 (☎232 22 22, fax 232 08 91, *real@hotels.li*, *www.relaischateaux.ch/real*; ④), with ten super-comfortable modern rooms and a gourmet restaurant. A handful of less expensive places are within easy reach of Vaduz: *Hotel Linde* is at Feldkircherstrasse 1 in the middle of Schaan (☎232 17 04, fax 232 09 29, *linde@rooms.ch*; ②), on the main road but with pleasant, soundproofed rooms; while *Uf der Säga* is an excellent, family-run hotel near Triesen (☎392 43 77, fax 392 34 41; ②), with spotless rooms and a quiet countryside location.

The Town

The hub of town is the post office, where all buses stop, midway between the two parallel main streets, Äulestrasse and pedestrianized Städtle. In the same building as the tourist office on Städtle is the chief reason to come to Vaduz, the **Staatliche Kunstsammlung** (State Art Collection; daily 10am–noon & 1.30–5.30pm; Nov–March closes 5pm; Fr.5). This is the world-famous private collection inherited and added to by the Prince himself, with space for currently only a fraction of the works to be exhibited – by late 2000, the entire collection will be on display in a huge new museum being built 100m to the north. Until then, the floor above the tourist office shows changing exhibits of modern art, while on the top floor is the main collection, including works by Rubens, Rembrandt, Jordaens and more. Look out in particular for a striking series of enamels on copper by Courteys, including the gorgeous *Urteil des Paris*, and exquisite late-sixteenth century ivory panels carved in bas-relief by Ignaz Elhafen.

In the same building is the **Briefmarkenmuseum** (Postage Stamp Museum; daily 10am–noon & 1.30–5.30pm; Nov–March closes 5pm; free), likely to be of interest to philatelists only. The **Landesmuseum** (Liechtenstein National Museum), closed at the time of writing for extensive long-term renovation, is 100m south on Städtle. Perched picturesquely on the forested hillside above Vaduz is the Prince's restored sixteenth-century **Schloss Vaduz**, but this particular Liechtensteiner's castle is his home, and is off limits to the public. Knots of people nonetheless gather at the castle gates to admire the doughty towers and turrets. Groups of ten or more can book a guided tour of the Hofkellerei des Fürsten von Liechtenstein, the Prince's own **vineyard**, covering a patch of land just north of Vaduz at Feldstrasse 4 (☎232 10 18; Fr.20, includes tastings of five wines).

Eating and drinking

Unless you can afford to splash out, **eating and drinking** in Vaduz is unlikely to inspire. *City-Snack*, Städtle 5, is as basic as Liechtenstein gets, with fast-food-style dishes from Fr.10. Nearby at Städtle 15, *Cesare* offers good Italian *menus* for Fr.20 (closed Sat & Sun), while *Burg* next door has all-you-can-eat salads for Fr.15, and pizzas for less. Incognito *Café Amann*, Äulestrasse 56, is worth a look for its value meals and a breath of local atmosphere. *Eredi Florini*, Herrengasse 9 (closed Sun), is a gourmet deli – bankers and suited business-types munch their simple but delicious meals (Fr.12–20) at stand-up tables, then sloosh down an espresso before heading back to the office. *Torkel*, amidst the vineyards off Hintergasse, is owned by the Prince, a perfect place to sample old-style Swiss/Austrian specialities, with *menus* from Fr.30. The best restaurant in the country is *Au Premier* in *Hotel Real*, its vast 20,000-bottle wine cellar complementing the heavy, unreconstructed French cuisine emanating from the kitchen (*menus* Fr.50 and above).

Listings

Bike rental Melliger AG, Das Zweirad-Center, Kirchstrasse 10 (Mon & Wed–Fri 8am–noon & 1.30–6.30pm, Tues 8am–noon, Sat 8am–2pm); or at the train stations in Buchs or Sargans (both daily 6am–8.30pm).

Car rental Avis, Im alten Riet 23, Schaan (☎232 59 44); Budget, Landstrasse 221, Triesen (☎392 13 88); Europcar, St Gallerstrasse 100, Buchs, Switzerland (☎081/750 08 10); Hertz, Waldteilstrasse 298, Nendeln (☎373 12 88).

Changing money Liechtensteiner banks charge commission, unlike the counters in the stations at Buchs or Sargans (both daily 6am–8.30pm).

Consulates The only English-speaking country represented in Liechtenstein is the UK, at Städtle 7 (☎236 14 38).

Paragliding Tandem paragliding flights over the Rhine valley (Fr.150) are organized by Hang Loose, Gewerbeweg 10 (☎230 07 07).

Post Main office is in the centre of Vaduz (FL-9490).

Around Liechtenstein

Attractions around the principality are low key, and aside from the skiing/hiking resort of Malbun, almost entirely untouristed.

North of Schaan is the Unterland region, with a handful of small villages and some pleasant walks through the rolling countryside and dark woods between the Rhine and the mountains. From **Nendeln**, a path climbs for an hour through the forest to Liechtenstein's smallest community, **Planken** (population 337), from where a steep 2hr route takes you up to the **Gafadurahütte** at 1428m (☎373 24 42), with dorms for around Fr.30 and spectacular views back into Switzerland. In the north of the country alongside the Austrian border is tiny **SCHELLENBERG**, overlooked by the ruins of the medieval Obere Burg castle set amidst lush forest. Schellenberg's sole hotel is the simple *Krone* (☎373 11 68, fax 373 21 22; ①), run by the same family for 120 years and offering a choice of en-suite and shared-bath rooms.

South of Vaduz is the Liechtensteiner Oberland, with the workaday village of Triesen overshadowed by pretty **TRIESENBERG**, perched on a sunny hillside above the Rhine valley. Triesenberg is best known as the adopted home of a community of Walser people, who left their homes in Wallis (German-speaking Valais) in the thirteenth century to spread out across central Europe. Many of the houses in Triesenberg are old wooden chalets built in the Walser style, and the modern, well-presented **Walser Heimatmuseum** in the village centre (Tues–Fri 1.30–5.30pm, Sat 1.30–5pm; June–Aug also Sun 2–5pm; Fr.2) documents and celebrates Walser history and culture. A scenic three-hour round trip path leads you from Triesenberg through Gnalp and Masescha and back to the village. The most attractive **hotel** in Triesenberg is *Nürnberger's* (☎237 47 77, fax 237 47 70, *mampfis@home.lol.li*, *www.nuernbergers-hotel.li*; ②), a modern place with characterful en-suite rooms; prices drop for stays over one night.

Malbun

From Triesenberg, Liechtenstein's sole back-country road climbs through a long tunnel beneath an Alpine ridge to **STEG** and on to **MALBUN**. This quiet hamlet at 1600m is Liechtenstein's only ski resort, with half-a-dozen little lifts and a handful of gentle runs. Boosting the principality's blue-blooded connections, Malbun was where Prince Charles and Princess Anne learned their snowploughing technique, back in the days before Klosters became the resort of choice. Steg is the trailhead for a web of **cross-country ski** routes through the Valüna valley to the south. In summer, the area has a wealth of lonesome high-country **hikes**: a classic full-day mountain trek from Steg rises south through the Valüna valley up to the Naafkopf (2570m), before returning via the Augstenberg and Malbun. From Malbun, a rewarding three- or four-hour hike begins with a journey up the Sareis chairlift and then heads south along the Austrian border to the scenically positioned **Pfalzerhütte** at 2111m (☎263 36 79; ①), with a few beds and dorms from Fr.30.

Malbun's **tourist office** is beside the bus stop from Vaduz (Mon–Fri 9am–noon & 1.30–5pm, Sat 9am–noon & 1–4pm; ☎263 65 77), and can give details of winter ski and snowboard packages, such as seven nights half board with a lift pass for Fr.535. Summer hiking deals include a four-night package of guided day- and night-time hikes on old smuggling routes across the mountains into Austria for Fr.475. The most congenial **place to stay** is the pleasant *Berggasthaus Sücka* near Steg (☎263 25 79, fax 263 25 77, *suecka@bluewin.ch*; ①), with dorms from Fr.27 and good food. The tiny *Walserhof* is Malbun's budget deal (☎264 43 23; ②), but the *Alpen* is a more attractive place (☎263 11 81, fax 263 96 46; ②), with some en-suite rooms. The chalet-style *Malbunerhof* (☎263 29 44, fax 263 95 61, *malbunerhof@supra.net*, *www.schwaerzler-hotels.vol.at*; ③) is the most upmarket place in the village, its balconied rooms luxuriously appointed and very comfortable. **Eating and drinking** is in the handful of hotel restaurants, or up at the *Berggasthof Sareiserjoch* – the top station of the Sareis chairlift, or an hour's hike up from Malbun – with a scenic terrace and hearty, warming Swiss dishes that rely heavily on the local Malbuner smoked ham. All these places close in April and November.

travel details

TRAINS

Appenzell to: Herisau (hourly; 35min); St Gallen (every 30min; 45min); Urnäsch (hourly; 15min); Wasserauen (hourly; 15min).

Arbon to: Romanshorn (every 30min; 10min); Rorschach Hafen (every 30min; 7min); Rorschach (every 30min; 10min).

Buchs to: Bad Ragaz (hourly; 20min); Chur (hourly; 35min); Landquart (hourly; 25min); Rorschach (hourly; 40min); St Gallen (hourly; 55min); Sargans (hourly; 10min); Schaan (6 daily; 5min).

Frauenfeld to: Romanshorn (hourly; 30min); St Gallen (twice hourly; 1hr – change in Weinfelden or Wil); Winterthur (twice hourly; 15min); Zürich (hourly; 40min).

Herisau to: Appenzell (hourly; 35min); St Gallen (3 hourly; 10min).

Kreuzlingen to: Romanshorn (every 30min; 25min); Rorschach (every 30min; 50min); Rorschach Hafen (every 30min; 45min); Schaffhausen (hourly; 55min).

Romanshorn to: Arbon (every 30min; 10min); Frauenfeld (hourly; 30min); Kreuzlingen (every 30min; 25min); Rorschach (every 30min; 15min); Rorschach Hafen (every 30min; 20min); St Gallen (hourly; 25min); Schaffhausen (hourly; 1hr 25min); Stein-am-Rhein (hourly; 55min).

Rorschach to: Arbon (every 30min; 10min); Chur (hourly; 1hr 20min); Kreuzlingen (every 30min;

50min); Romanshorn (every 30min; 15min); Rorschach Hafen (3 hourly; 3min); St Gallen (twice hourly; 15min).

Rorschach Hafen to: Arbon (every 30min; 7min); Heiden (hourly; 25min); Kreuzlingen (every 30min; 45min); Romanshorn (every 30min; 20min); Rorschach (3 hourly; 3min).

St Gallen to: Appenzell (every 30min; 45min); Bern (every 30min; 2hr 30min); Buchs (hourly; 55min); Chur (hourly; 1hr 35min); Frauenfeld (twice hourly; 1hr); Geneva (twice hourly; 4hr 20min); Herisau (3 hourly; 10min); Romanshorn (hourly; 25min); Rorschach (twice hourly; 15min); Sargans (hourly; 1hr 10min); Schaffhausen (hourly; 1hr 30min; some change in Winterthur); Stein-am-Rhein (hourly; 1hr 25min); Winterthur (twice hourly; 45min); Zürich (twice hourly; 1hr 10min).

Sargans to: Bad Ragaz (3 hourly; 5min); Buchs (hourly; 10min); Chur (3 hourly; 20min); Rorschach (hourly; 50min); St Gallen (hourly; 1hr 10min); Zürich (hourly; 1hr 10min).

Schaffhausen to: Kreuzlingen (hourly; 55min); Lugano (hourly; 4hr 15min); Romanshorn (hourly; 1hr 25min); Stein-am-Rhein (every 30min; 20min); Schloss Laufen (hourly; 5min); Winterthur (hourly; 35min); Zug (hourly; 1hr 20min); Zürich (hourly; 35min).

Stein-am-Rhein to: Kreuzlingen (hourly; 30min); Romanshorn (hourly; 55min); St Gallen (hourly; 1hr 35min).

BUSES

Buchs to: Vaduz (every 20min; 15min).

Frauenfeld to: Kartause Ittingen (2 daily; 10min); Stein-am-Rhein (hourly; 30min).

Herisau to: Stein AR (hourly; 20min).

St Gallen to: Stein AR (hourly; 15min).

Sargans to: Vaduz (every 20min; 30min).

Schaan to: Schellenberg (hourly; 20min).

Stein AR to: Herisau (hourly; 20min); St Gallen (hourly; 15min).

Stein-am-Rhein to: Frauenfeld (hourly; 30min); Warth (hourly; 20min).

Urnäsch to: Schwägalp (hourly; 25min).

Vaduz to: Buchs (every 20min; 15min); Malbun (hourly; 30min); Sargans (every 20min; 30min); Schaan (every 20min; 10min); Steg (hourly; 25min); Triesen (every 20min; 5min); Triesenberg (every 20min; 15min).

BOATS

(following is a summary of May–Sept services)

Kreuzlingen to: Romanshorn (at least 2 daily; 1hr 15min); Schaffhausen (at least 3 daily; 3hr 45min); Stein-am-Rhein (at least 3 daily; 2hr 25min).

Romanshorn to: Arbon (at least 3 daily; 30min); Kreuzlingen (at least 2 daily; 1hr 5min); Rorschach (at least 3 daily; 55min).

Rorschach (Hafen) to: Romanshorn (at least 3 daily; 55min).

Schaffhausen to: Kreuzlingen (at least 3 daily; 4hr 45min); Stein-am-Rhein (at least 3 daily; 2hr).

INTERNATIONAL TRAINS

Buchs to: Feldkirch, Austria (every 2hr; 20min).

Konstanz to: Frankfurt (every 2hr; 4hr 30min); Hamburg (every 2hr; 8hr).

Kreuzlingen to: Konstanz, Germany (every 30min; 3min).

St Gallen to: Innsbruck (4 daily; 4hr 15min; change at Buchs); München (4 daily; 4hr 30min); Prague (1 daily; 9hr 30min).

St Margrethen to: Bregenz, Austria (hourly; 20min).

Schaffhausen to: Basel Bad. via Germany (hourly; 1hr 10min); Stuttgart (every 2hr; 2hr 10min).

INTERNATIONAL BUSES

Buchs to: Feldkirch, Austria (every 20min; 30min).

Vaduz to: Feldkirch, Austria (every 20min; 40min).

INTERNATIONAL BOATS

(following is a summary of May–Sept services)

Romanshorn (Autoquai) to: Friedrichshafen, Germany (at least hourly; 40min).

Rorschach (Hafen) to: Friedrichshafen, Germany (daily; 1hr 20min); Lindau, Germany (at least 2 daily; 1hr 15min).

PLACE NAMES IN THIS CHAPTER

German	French	Italian
Appenzell Ausserrhoden	Appenzell Rhodes-Extérieures	Appenzello esterno
Appenzell Innerrhoden	Appenzell Rhodes-Intérieures	Appenzello interno
Bodensee	Lac de Constance	Lago di Constanza
Deutschland	Allemagne	Germania
Glarus	Glaris	Glarona
Konstanz	Constance	Constanza
Österreich	Autriche	Austria
Rhein	Rhin	Reno
St Gallen	St-Gall	San Gallo
Säntis	Säntis	Sentis
Schaffhausen	Schaffhouse	Sciaffusa
Thurgau	Thurgovie	Turgovia

CHAPTER ELEVEN

GRAUBÜNDEN

S witzerland's largest canton, **GRAUBÜNDEN**, occupies the entire southeast of the country and takes in a huge but sparsely populated area that's the most culturally diverse in Switzerland, bordering on Liechtenstein and Austria to the north, and Italy to the east and south. Its folded landscape of deep, isolated valleys (well over a hundred of them), sheer rocky summits and thick pine forests makes it the wildest and loneliest part of Switzerland, more difficult than most to get around in, but also more rewarding, with some of the finest scenery in the Alps. Glaciers oozing from between the high mountains launch two of Europe's great rivers – the Rhine and the Inn – on their long journeys to the North Sea and the Black Sea respectively, while two smaller rivers water pomegranates, figs and chestnuts in secluded southern valleys en route to the Po and the Gulf of Venice.

The canton – once the Roman province of Rhaetia Prima – is officially **trilingual**, known as *Graubünden* in German, *Grigioni* in Italian and *Grischun* in **Romansh**, the last of these a direct descendant of Latin which has survived locked away in the mountain fastnesses far from the cantonal capital **Chur** since the legions departed 1500 years ago. You'll also come across the canton's French name of *Grisons*, although there are no French-speaking communities.

Until the nineteenth century, **Rhaetia** was entirely separate from its western neighbour of Helvetia. As Helvetia began to experience stirrings towards independence in the thirteenth and fourteenth centuries, the population of Rhaetia also began to organize themselves, with the ideal of throwing off the feudal oppression of the bishops and lords who nominally ruled the area. The impenetrable landscape of the hinterland was on their side: as one historian of the region, Benjamin Barber, accurately noted, "an army occupying Chur no more controls Graubünden than does one in Milan or Vienna." The 1367 **League of the House of God** was the first of these popular associations, soon followed by the **Grey League** in 1395 (formed by a band of highland shepherds dubbed "the grey farmers" for their trademark grey wool cloth) and, in 1436, the **League of the Ten Jurisdictions**. The three loose groupings came together in 1471 to pledge mutual assistance, and were soon able – with the spur of the Reformation – to seize political power from the nobles. Since then the people have been free, and they relish the fact more than most other Swiss. It was only in 1803 that the

---

ACCOMMODATION PRICE CODES

All the hostels, pensions and hotels in this book have been graded according to the following price codes, which indicate the price for the cheapest double room available during the high season. Single rooms can cost anything between sixty and eighty percent of the double-room rate. For hostels with dormitories, the price per bed has been quoted. See p.45 for more details.

① under Fr.100	④ Fr.200–250	⑦ Fr.350–400
② Fr.100–150	⑤ Fr.250–300	⑧ Fr.400–500
③ Fr.150–200	⑥ Fr.300–350	⑨ over Fr.500

EXPLORING GRAUBÜNDEN

Graubünden's **Rhätische Bahn** (RhB) has one of the most scenic train networks in the world and, to take advantage, a host of all-in **package deals** exist which enable you to experience the most dramatic journeys (see p.38) without worrying about where to eat during the trip or booking hotels at either end. The classiest of these runs over a single weekend in mid-July, taking in a vintage **Orient Express** train from Zürich to Lugano, and continuing the next day on the Bernina Express train from Lugano to Chur via Tirano (or the whole route in reverse); included in the Fr.510 fare are all train tickets, B&B in an upmarket hotel in Lugano, meals on board the Orient Express, a lunch in Tirano, plus a return ticket to Zürich from anywhere in Switzerland. The **Bernina Express** route from Chur, Davos or St Moritz to Lugano (or reverse), with two nights' B&B (one in your Graubünden starting-point city and one in Lugano) plus a return ticket from anywhere in Switzerland costs Fr.330. Fr.279 buys you a reservation on the classic **Glacier Express** from Chur or St Moritz to Zermatt, with one night's B&B (either in St Moritz or Zermatt). The RhB also runs its own **Pullman** coaches on various scenic full-day routes, on selected days in summer only (June–Sept) – from Chur/St Moritz to Tirano and back (Fr.136/98); St Moritz to Scuol and back (Fr.98); a circular trip to and from Chur via Davos (Fr.98); and from Chur over the Albula Pass to St Moritz and back (Fr.113). The same routes in ordinary carriages but pulled by **steam-engines** cost roughly half. Finally, the Rail Rider is a **roofless train** completely open to the elements, which shuttles the forty minutes between Filisur and Preda on the dramatic Albula route two or three times daily on weekends in July and August (Fr.15/25 one-way/return; no reservation needed). Needless to say, you can travel on ordinary scheduled trains covering all these routes for much less than these all-in prices; seats in standard, non-panoramic carriages on all RhB trains are free to InterRail, Eurail and Swiss Pass holders (except Glacier Express trains between Disentis/Mustér and Brig, which are free to Swiss Pass holders but full price to Eurailers and InterRailers).

Gilt-edged packages aside, if you're planning to cover a lot of ground independently, Graubünden – more than most Swiss cantons – merits **renting a car**. Buses penetrate to the most remote valleys and hamlets, but often only every two hours or so, and journeys can be long and tortuous. Because of the mountainous nature of the terrain, train coverage is less than universal, and long-distance cycling routes tend to trace the main valleys only or require you to tackle steep gradients. Your own car lets you explore to your heart's content, and investigate outlying corners such as Val Bregaglia or the Lower Engadine that might otherwise take up a full and frustrating day on the bus.

If you do opt for public transport, you'd do well to take advantage of the **Regional Pass**. It costs Fr.140/105 for fifteen/seven days, and covers unlimited journeys over five/three days on all RhB trains, the SBB line between Chur and Bad Ragaz, and the RhB bus between Tirano and Lugano, with half-price reductions on these lines the rest of the time. All postbuses, most cable-cars and funiculars, the Furka–Oberalp line between Disentis/Mustér and Brig, and Davos city buses are half-price throughout the pass's validity. The **Regional Pass Plus**, for Fr.190/135, gives free unlimited journeys on all trains, buses, cable-cars and funiculars throughout the canton for five/three days as above, with half-price the rest of the time, and the Furka–Oberalp trains and Davos city buses half-price the whole time. Both are only issued between May and October, and are available from train stations in the region. For more information, contact Rhätische Bahn, Bahnhofstrasse 25, CH-7002 Chur (☎081/254 91 04, fax 254 91 05, *contact@rhb.ch*, *www.rhb.ch*).

For complete information on travel and package deals throughout the whole canton, contact the **Graubünden Tourist Office**. They have administrative offices at Alexanderstrasse 24, CH-7001 Chur (☎081/254 24 24, fax 254 24 00, *contact@graubuenden.ch*, *www.graubuenden.ch*).

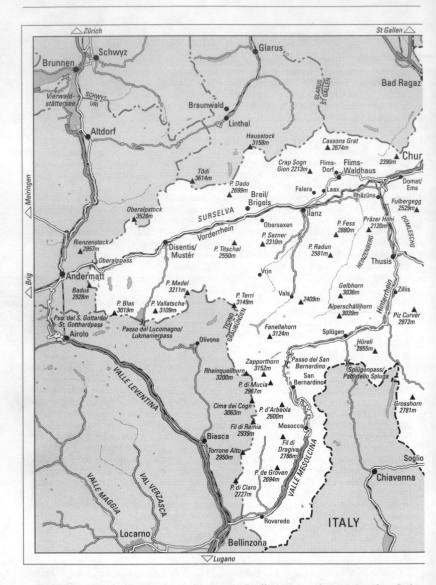

united "Graubünden", or Grey Leagues, finally assented to join the Swiss Confederation, and to this day Bündners consistently vote in large numbers against joining the EU.

The canton's resorts – headed by **St Moritz**, **Klosters** and **Davos** – are some of the most famous names in the Alps and offer world-class skiing and top-quality hiking, but they're far from the whole story. The beautiful **Engadine valley** runs for almost 100km along a southern terrace of the Alps, bathed in glittering sunlight that

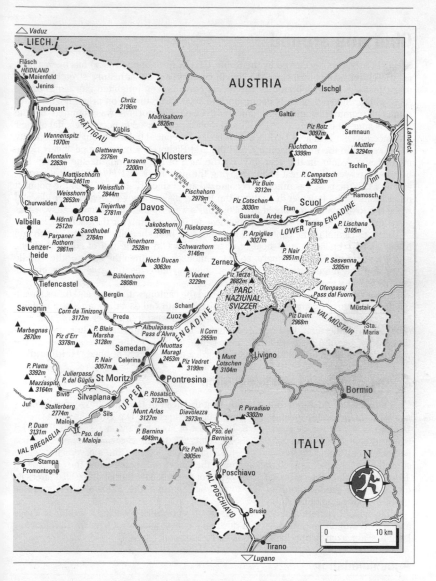

pours from blue skies for well over 300 days a year. This is the heartland of Romansh culture, and once you get out of the main German-speaking resorts, Romansh language, style and architecture pervade Graubünden's far-flung corners. South of the Alps, three of the canton's most enticing valleys – **Bregaglia** and **Poschiavo** in particular – are entirely Italian speaking, filled with a Mediterranean lushness in their flora and cuisine that could easily tempt you to leave the mountains behind and just keep heading south.

Chur and around

Sitting in a deep valley carved by the Rhine, **CHUR** (pronounced *koor*) has been a powerful ecclesiastical centre since the fourth century, but has a history stretching back much further: it is celebrated as the oldest continuously inhabited city north of the Alps, with archeological finds dating back to 3000 BC. Situated on prime north–south routes of commerce and communication, Curia Rhaetorium was founded by the Romans after their conquest of 15 BC, and rapidly progressed to become capital of their province Rhaetia Prima. St Luzius, a missionary, is reputed to have brought Christianity to the region in the fourth century, and the first Bishop of Chur to be positively documented was Asinio, in the year 451. By the turn of the millennium, the bishop had become a powerful political ruler, enjoying the patronage of Holy Roman Emperors, and by 1170, the post was officially recognized as a Prince-Bishopric. With the populist movements of the fourteenth century, the Prince-Bishop's power began to erode, and when the Reformation took hold in 1526, Chur's wealthy merchants and craftsworkers were able to take over all significant political decision making for themselves.

Today, as capital of the canton and boasting "the best shopping between Zürich and Milan", Chur retains a great deal of character. Its Old Town, full of cobbled alleys, secret courtyards and foursquare, solid townhouses, breathes the spirit of the Middle Ages, and the huge **cathedral** towering above symbolizes the rule of the bishop-princes of years gone by.

Chur serves as the linchpin of routes around the canton, with buses and trains sneaking their way through high, narrow valleys to the south and east through the mountains of Central Graubünden to Davos and St Moritz, and west into Surselva up to the high Alps around Andermatt. In a remote mountain fastness southeast of Chur sits the picturesque resort of **Arosa**, while the more gentle foothills to the northeast, around the village of Maienfeld on the Liechtenstein border, are cloyingly dubbed **"Heidiland"**.

Arrival, orientation and information

Chur's **train** and huge **postbus station** is at the head of Bahnhofstrasse, five minutes northwest of the central Postplatz, on the northern edge of the Old Town. As well as maps, the **tourist office** at Grabenstrasse 5, 100m east of Postplatz (Mon 1.30–6pm, Tues–Fri 8.30am–noon & 1.30–6pm, Sat 9am–noon; ☎081/252 18 18, *www.churtourismus.ch*), has pamphlets explaining the red and green footprints painted on Chur's pavements, which show the routes of self-guided walking tours: the longer red route around the eastern Old Town and south to the cathedral is the better of the two. The tourist office also offers its own excellent **guided tour** of the town, starting from the Rathaus on Poststrasse (April–Oct Wed 2pm; Fr.6).

All overnight visitors get a book of **discount vouchers** covering a wealth of shops and services, including money off a postbus journey, and a free return train journey back to Chur from Arosa, Ilanz, Küblis or Tiefencastel.

Accommodation

Chur has a good, affordable range of **accommodation**, concentrated in a handful of historic inns in the heart of the Old Town.

The **campsite** *Au* is 1km northwest of the centre at Felsenaustrasse 61 (☎081/284 22 83, fax 284 56 83, *info@camping-chur.ch*, *www.camping-chur.ch*), and is open year-round. The nearest HI **hostel** is some 12km south in the resort town of Valbella, at Voa Sartons 41 (☎081/384 12 08, fax 384 45 58; ①; mid-June to Oct & mid-Dec to April), with dorms at Fr.24.

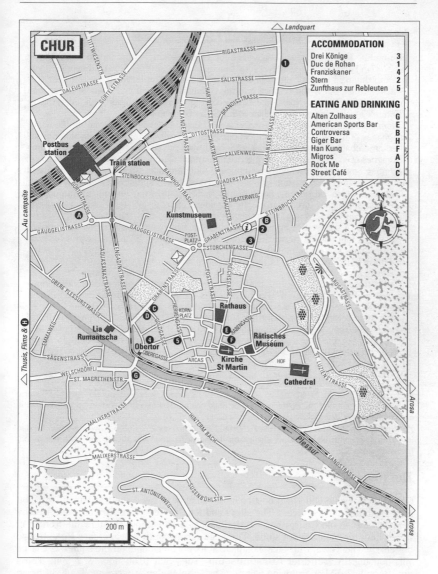

CHUR

△ Landquart

ACCOMMODATION

Drei Könige	3
Duc de Rohan	1
Franziskaner	4
Stern	2
Zunfthaus zur Rebleuten	5

EATING AND DRINKING

Alten Zollhaus	G
American Sports Bar	E
Controversa	B
Giger Bar	H
Han Kung	F
Migros	A
Rock Me	D
Street Café	C

Postbus station

Train station

△ Au campsite

Kunstmuseum

◁ Thusis, Films & H

Lia Rumantscha

Obertor

Rathaus

Rätisches Museum

Kirche St Martin

Cathedral

▷ Arosa

▷ Arosa

Plessur

0   200 m

Drei Könige, Reichsgasse 18 (☎081/252 17 25, fax 252 17 26, *dreikoenige@churtourismus.ch*, *www.forum.ch/drei-koenige-chur*). A 200-year-old inn steps from the tourist office in the Old Town, characterful and welcoming. ②.

Duc de Rohan, Masanserstrasse 44 (☎081/252 10 22, fax 252 45 37, *ducderohan@gr-net.ch*). Comfortable old manor house 400m north of the centre, with renovated rooms, quality service and a pleasant, sophisticated atmosphere. ③.

Franziskaner, Kupfergasse 18 (☎081/252 12 61). Plain, inexpensive rooms in the Old Town, with both en-suite and shared-bath choices. ②.

ROMANSH

Romansh, the third official language of Graubünden, is the fourth language of Switzerland and the principal everyday tongue of some seventy thousand people. If you stick to the main tourist centres of Chur, Davos and St Moritz, you'll see and hear only Swiss-German, but if you venture into the countryside, you'll find signs to the *staziun* pointing along Via Principala, and hear people greeting each other with "Allegra!" or "Bun di!" in what sounds like Italian with a Swiss-German accent.

Romansh can trace its roots directly back to Latin, fountainhead for all the Romance languages of Europe. After the Roman conquests, so-called Vulgar Latin, spoken by soldiers, merchants and officials, slowly merged over the centuries with the pre-existing langagues of conquered areas, giving rise to four main linguistic groups: Ibero-Romance, including Spanish, Catalan and Portuguese; Gallo-Romance, mainly French; Italian; and Rhaeto-Romance, comprising Friulian and Ladin, two languages spoken by around 750,000 people in the extreme north of Italy, and Romansh, spoken only in Graubünden. The first significant inroads made by outsiders into the isolated Romansh-speaking mountain communities was in the thirteenth century, when German-speaking Walsers from Canton Valais settled in some of the high valleys; their legacy survives to this day, with Davos (once called Tavau, the Romansh word for "alp") still majority Swiss-German, and German-speaking communities clustered together in otherwise Romansh Surselva. In 1464, a huge fire destroyed Chur, and crafts people arrived from the north to rebuild the town, in the process erasing virtually all its Romansh culture and language.

In the middle of the nineteenth century Romansh was still counted as the native tongue of over half the population of Graubünden, but the development of roads and railways penetrating otherwise remote valleys led to greater and greater erosion, as the Romansh people themselves realized that their language was an impediment to getting well-paid work outside their traditional communities. With schools, churches and communes slowly switching over to German, a conscious effort began with the turn of the century to nurture Romansh: cultural **pressure groups** and writers' organizations began to promote the language both in Graubünden and nationwide. In 1938, an amendment to the Swiss

Stern, Reichsgasse 11 (☎081/252 35 55, fax 252 19 15, *stern@churtourismus.ch*). Another historic inn with quality service and modern, wood-beamed rooms. The excellent restaurant (see below) is a particular asset. ③.

Zunfthaus zur Rebleuten, Pfisterplatz 1 (☎081/257 13 57, fax 257 13 58). Lovely guildhouse dating from 1483, with elaborate scrollwork on its facade, a good restaurant and attractive wood-beamed rooms. ②.

The Town

Chur's picturesque Old Town nestles in the shadow of the cathedral, which looms on high ground to the southeast. The alleys and fountained squares are characterized by their terraces of old Churer houses, traditionally built without shutters and fronted in rather dour, greyish Scalära stone. The main north–south thoroughfare **Poststrasse** bisects the Old Town, with busy Postplatz at its northern end; on the square is a large villa housing the **Bündner Kunstmuseum** (Tues–Sun 10am–noon & 2–5pm, Thurs until 8pm; Fr.7; SMP), featuring paintings by Graubünden artists Angelika Kauffmann and Giovanni and Alberto Giacometti. Something of an iconic feminist heroine during her lifetime and afterwards, Kauffmann was born in Chur on October 30, 1741, and moved to London at the age of 25. She quickly estabished a solid reputation there, becoming one of the most popular artists of the time, and was one of the founding members of the Royal Academy in 1768. Although she was best known in her day for the kind of dramatic narrative painting exemplified in *Hector and Paris* (1770), on permanent display in the museum, today's art historians tend to reject these works as overly

Constitution confirmed the status of Romansh as a **national language**, a halfway-house proposal which still required Romansh-speakers to use German, French or Italian. In 1996 a second constitutional amendment elevated Romansh to the status of a semi-official language of the Confederation, thereby preserving its status amongst Romansh communities, guaranteeing its appearance on official documents such as passports and in legislation affecting Romansh areas, and eliminating the requirement for Romansh-speakers to use any other language.

Romansh itself, however, is not a unified whole: there is a welter of different **dialects**, each of which can vary dramatically from the others. The word for "cup", for example, in German is *Tasse*, in Italian *tazza*, but in the Sursilvan dialect of Romansh, spoken west of Chur, it is *scadiola*; in the Sutsilvan of the Hinterrhein valley, *scariola*; in the Surmeiran of the Julier and Albula valleys, *cuppegn*; and in Putèr and Vallader, spoken in the Upper and Lower Engadine respectively, *cupina*. In 1980, the Lia Rumantscha, a leading Romansh cultural organization, put forward a proposal to regularize this mishmash. The result was the creation of **Rumantsch Grischun** (Graubünden Romansh), a composite written language formed by averaging out words across all five dialects; under this new system, "cup" became *cuppina*. Nonetheless, despite the lack of a Romansh capital city able to provide a cultural and linguistic focus for the language, and the consequent reliance of Romansh-speakers on German-language companies and media for work and information respectively, there was still some resistance to forming a hybrid in this way; today, local communities still stick to their own dialect in everyday life, and presenters on Radio Grischa and Radio Piz Corvatsch, the two Graubünden stations, speak their own local idiom. Rumantsch Grischun has become a unifying tool in those situations where Romansh speakers are currently forced to default into German for ease of communication, and yet many proposals such as a Romansh daily newspaper haven't got off the drawing board.

The Lia Rumantscha, with federal funding, has already published a German–Romansh dictionary, and has an English–Romansh one currently in production. For booklets and more information, you can either drop into their offices at Obere Plessurstrasse 47 in Chur, consult their excellent Web site (*www.liarumantscha.ch*), or contact them at Chascha Postala 1, Via da la Plessur 47, CH-7001 Cuira (☎081/252 44 22, fax 252 84 26, *liarum@spin.ch*).

sentimental and favour instead her portraits, of which there are also plenty on display, not least a graceful self-portrait (1780).

Following Poststrasse 100m south will bring you to the arcaded courtyard of the fifteenth-century **Rathaus**. One street to the east is Reichsgasse, an atmospheric old alley with, at no. 57, a plaque commemorating the birthplace of Angelika Kauffmann. Reichsgasse ends in the attractive open square of Arcas, dominated by the Gothic **Kirche St Martin**, dating from 1491 and now sporting three beautiful stained-glass windows by Alberto Giacometti. Opposite the church, bustling Oberegasse runs west to the **Obertor**, a city gate and remnant of Chur's medieval fortifications. Immediately behind the church rises the hill upon which the cathedral sits; just to the left, in a quiet courtyard at Hofstrasse 1, is the impressive **Rätisches Museum** (Rhaetian Museum; Tues–Sun 10am–noon & 2–5pm; Fr.5), housing the canton's historical collections on six floors. The basement offers a standard trot through the archeology of the area, while upper floors have generally engaging displays on the history of Chur and of Graubünden as a whole. Unfortunately, everything is organized thematically and not chronologically, so the fine old decorated wooden chests and ornately carved wardrobes from various parts of the canton are scattered over different floors, in between bits of arts and crafts, pottery, textiles and more.

The Cathedral

Chur is dominated physically and spiritually by its huge **cathedral**, constructed between 1151 and 1272 in late-Romanesque and Gothic styles. Still hived off from the workaday town by a thick gated wall, which reflects the bitterness of the disputes between bishop-princes and local population which flared around the Reformation, the cathedral is the focus of the **Hof**, a complex of eighteenth-century buildings in the heart of the city protecting Chur's religious elite from contact with the mob. Today, from his palace beside the cathedral, the Bishop of Chur still controls a diocese covering Graubünden, all the central Swiss cantons and Zürich, and students flock to the adjacent St Luzi theological seminary to train for the priesthood. In 1997, responding to years of rancour sparked by ultra-conservative bishop Wolfgang Haas, the Vatican decreed the splitting away of Liechtenstein from the ancient Diocese of Chur; Haas was transferred to Vaduz, and Chur was finally granted a more moderate bishop who could set about reuniting the diocese.

The atmospheric **interior** of the cathedral (daily 8am–7pm) is huge and gloomy, with Romanesque capitals above the massive columns showing grotesque creatures and gargoyle-like demons. To the left of the main nave is a blank space where once stood the **altar of St Laurentius**: thieves broke into the cathedral through the crypt a few years back and looted both the altar and its paintings. The altar was destroyed, but the paintings were later recovered and are now under restoration. Looking back from the **choir steps**, it becomes apparent that the ground plan of the church is asymmetrical: the nave is out of alignment with the choir. Many stories are put about as to why this should be, the most fanciful of which is that, from the perspective of the choir, the nave is tilted to the right, to match the tilt of Christ's drooping head on the cross. What's more likely is that the twelfth-century architects, following the ground plan of previous buildings, were restricted by the bedrock, which peeps through at the base of the northern and northeastern walls. High up opposite the Baroque **pulpit** is a tiny gallery – this is one end of a "secret" passage from the bishop's palace next door, allowing the bishop to enter the House of God at a suitably lofty altitude and without soiling his shoes on the courtyard outside. The elaborate winged **high altar**, carved in 1486–92 by Jakob Russ, is well worth a close look, although these days it's kept locked and protected by alarms: you might want to wait for one of the many tour groups and tag along behind as they're led into the choir. The intricate depiction of the crucifixion, with Christ stumbling under the weight of the cross, rises from the floor to a mere 5cm below the ceiling – evidence that it was carved *in situ*. The artist thoughtfully incorporated a tiny, whimsical self-portrait into a crescent moon just behind the crucifix at eyelevel, and also devoted much attention to the unseen rear of the altarpiece, covering it with detailed portraits. Below the choir, the **crypt** holds four carved stone figures of the Apostles dating from around 1200.

ABOVE CHUR

Chur is proud of the fact that it's the only Swiss city with its own hiking and winter-sports area accessible from the city centre. The **Brambrüesch** mountain rises to 2174m immediately southwest of the Old Town (*www.brambruesch.ch*) and its affordability and ease of access are the main draws – the cable-car station is just off Kasernenstrasse, five minutes' walk west of the Obertor. The journey to Brambrüesch itself, a platform at 1600m, is in two sections, with a midway change at **Känzeli**, and if you're staying overnight in Chur, you qualify for a fifty-percent discount on the ride. In summer, there are plenty of hiking routes, as well as paragliding over the town (contact the tourist office for details). In winter a low-priced ski pass (Fr.27 for a full day; Fr.14 after 1pm) covers chairlifts from Brambrüesch up to the **Dreibündenstein** peak (2174m), giving access to 25km of undemanding pistes, a 6km toboggan run from Brambrüesch to Känzeli and such diversions as night-time skiing and snow hikes.

Eating and drinking

Chur's Old Town has a fair range of places to **eat**, many of them offering the classic regional dish of *Bündnerfleisch*, prime beef air dried in an open attic or under the eaves of a barn and sliced paper-thin in an aromatic *Bündnerteller* – a carefully presented plate of cold meats. You'll also find *Bündnerfleisch* taking centre-stage in *Bündner Gerstensuppe*, a creamy barley soup with vegetables. With hunting still very popular in the countryside all around, you'll also see plenty of **game** on autumn menus, including stews of deer or chamois. Another local speciality is Passugger **mineral water**, bottled in Passugg a couple of kilometres south; however, at least while staying in Chur itself, Passugger is not worth paying for, since it flows from every tap and street fountain in the town.

There's a big self-service *Migros* diner behind the station at Gäuggelistrasse 28 (closed Sun). *Controversa*, Steinbruckstrasse 1 (closed Sun lunch), is a bright, modern restaurant with an excellent salad buffet and plenty of light pasta meals with veggie options (Fr.15–20), while the Chinese *Han Kung*, Rabengasse 6 (closed Mon), has three-course lunch *menus* for well under Fr.20. Two excellent places for top-quality regional cooking are the *Rebleuten* (see "Accommodation"; closed Sat lunch & Sun), with *menus* from Fr.15 served in its atmospheric wood-panelled restaurant; and the *Stern* (also see "Accommodation"), probably slightly the better of the two, with *menus* around Fr.20. Right beside the Obertor at the southwestern corner of the Old Town is the *Alten Zollhaus*, Malixerstrasse 1 (☎081/252 33 98), with plain, hearty meals served downstairs in its cosy *Stübli* from Fr.11, and more formal dining in the upstairs restaurant, from Fr.20 or so.

As the location of the canton's only matriculation college, Chur has loads of pre-university students packing the dozens of **bars** around the Obertor: *Street Café*, Grabenstrasse 47, is most popular, but *Rock Me*, Goldgasse 3, runs a close second. The convivial *American Sports Bar* is at Rabengasse 7, with – as you'd expect – TVs showing ice hockey and American football. Some 1.5km west of the Old Town, in a business-park area of furniture showrooms and petrol stations (bus #1 to Agip), is the much-vaunted *Giger Bar*, Comercialstrasse 23 (closed Sun). Owned by Swiss-born Hollywood special-effects designer H.R. Giger (see p.129), the bar is kitted out in the style of his greatest creation, *Alien*, with sleek, skeletal chairs, black decor, and a limbless, writhing female torso hoisted above the bar like a flag. Oddly enough, though, if you go expecting to plug into an exciting cutting-edge subculture, you'll be disappointed: despite the decor, it's an utterly ordinary after-work bar for local business folk with its radio tuned to a light-melodies channel.

Listings

Bike rental In the station (daily 6am–8.50pm).

Car rental Avis, Kalchbühlstrasse 12 (☎081/252 39 73); Budget, Kasernenstrasse 30 (☎081/252 29 04); Europcar, Kasernenstrasse 67 (☎081/254 22 22); Hertz, Kasernenstrasse 88 (☎081/252 32 22).

Changing money In the station (daily 6am–9pm).

Laundry Grabenstrasse, beside the Obertor (Mon–Sat 9am–midnight, Sun noon–midnight; Fr.6 per wash).

Markets The Gänggelimarkt is a flea market held every first Saturday of the month on Arcas, while nearby on Oberegasse is Chur's weekly fresh food market (May–Oct Sat morning).

Medical facilities 24-hour emergency room at the Kantonsspital, Loestrasse 170 (☎081/256 61 11).

Post Main office is beside the station (Hauptpost, CH-7000 Chur 1), with another big office on Postplatz (CH-7000 Chur 2).

Travel agents Discount flight agents SSR Reisen are on Unteregasse (Mon–Fri 10am–6.30pm, Sat 10am–1pm; ☎081/252 97 76).

Arosa

AROSA was discovered by the outside world in 1883 when Dr Otto Herwig-Hold, on a skiing tour of the remote mountains south of Chur, came across the little community – a perfect spot to build his new tuberculosis sanatorium. The chest patients of old have long since given way to winter- and summer-sports enthusiasts, and the little isolated village has developed into one of Graubünden's most acclaimed resorts, yet it's still small enough to have retained its atmosphere and lacks even a trace of the hotshot swagger of Davos or St Moritz.

Arosa lies at the end of a single, spectacular road which cuts its way up into a sheer and narrow valley southeast of Chur, passing on the way through a succession of idyllic terraced villages and offering vistas breathtaking enough to make you want to stop and gape every three minutes – which you could do, but for the fact that in the 32km journey, there's a total of 244 switchbacks. It's easier, and no less spectacular, to take the narrow-gauge RhB **train** direct to Arosa, which departs from the forecourt of Chur station and shadows the road all the way up.

Arosa occupies the broad sunny bowl of the Schanfigg, surrounded on all sides by snowy peaks – the Weisshorn (2653m) is the main focus due west of the resort, along with the Hörnli (2512m) to the south and the Brüggerhorn (2401m) to the north. The town itself consists of two areas: the main resort is Ausserarosa, clustered around the train station and the Obersee lakelet; while the older village at the upper end of the valley is dubbed Innerarosa. Arosa's **skiing** is excellent, with over 70km of mostly blue and red pistes sidewinding down the gentle sunny slopes around the resort; beginners will feel especially at home. There's also 25km of cross-country pistes in and around the resort. Lifts and a gondola rise from the Obersee to the Weisshorn (with a chairlift from halfway up branching over to the Brüggerhorn), and at the very end of the road in Innerarosa there's another gondola connecting to the Hörnli.

There are several good high-altitude summer **hikes**: from the Weisshorn summit, a scenic and easygoing four-hour trail heads over the Carmennapass and through the lonely Urden valley to **Tschiertschen**, connected to Chur by postbus; or you could head across the meadows from the Weisshorn middle station to Alpenblick and the tranquil Schwellisee before returning to Arosa (3hr). Another dramatic route leads off the back of the Hörnli summit and across the peaks to the **Parpaner Rothorn** (2861m), from where cable-cars run down to Lenzerheide, near Valbella 12km south of Chur, and connected to Chur by bus.

Practicalities

Trains arrive at the Obersee amidst resort bustle, and the **tourist office** is five minutes' walk away, uphill on Arosa's only proper road, Poststrasse (May–Nov Mon–Fri 8am–noon & 2–6pm, Sat 9am–1pm; July & Aug also Sat 2–4pm; Dec–April Mon–Fri 9am–6pm, Sat 9am–5.30pm, Sun 10am–noon & 4–5.30pm; ☎081/378 70 20, *www.arosa.ch*). All buses within the village are free, and private cars are banned between midnight and 6am (except to arrive or depart). **Ski passes** cost from Fr.52 for a day, or Fr.239 for a week, and the **ski school** (☎081/377 11 50) is beside the train station. In summer, you can rent **mountain bikes** from the station, from Bootshaus on the Obersee (☎081/377 23 77) and from Carmenna Sport in the centre (☎081/377 12 05), and carry them on the first stage of the Weisshorn cable-car for free. Note that most hotels and services close in the between-seasons of April–May and November–December.

The tranquil **campsite** is below the main resort, on a path winding down from the tourist office (☎081/377 17 45); partway down is a branch off to the HI **hostel** on Seewaldweg (☎ & fax 081/377 13 97; ①; mid-June to Oct & mid-Dec to mid-April), with good dorms for Fr.26. There are dozens of **hotels**, almost all of which charge extra if you stay less than three nights, especially in the winter season. Note too that summer prices can be up to fifty percent cheaper than the high-season winter rates listed below. Location can make all the difference to your stay: the busy main street, with its cluster of shops, restaurants and hotels, is easy to avoid, with peaceful places dotted around on all sides. *The Lindemann's*, on Postplatz (☎081/377 50 79, fax 377 34 39; ②), is a convenient, family-run little pension in the centre, while *Suveran*, above the Catholic church (☎081/377 19 69, fax 377 19 75; ②), is a quieter, simpler place with shared-bath rooms. *Sonnenhalde* (☎081/377 15 31, fax 377 44 55; ②) is in Innerarosa, near the skating rink, excellently located for the winter-only Carmenna draglift and Tschuggen chairlift, with super-friendly service and surprisingly well-appointed rooms. The *Isla*, Neubachstrasse 30 (☎081/377 12 13, fax 377 44 42; ④), is a pleasant, efficient place on a quiet street between the Obersee and its lower twin, the Untersee. There's any number of places to splash out, including the super-luxurious *Arosa Kulm* (☎081/378 88 88, fax 378 88 89, *www.arosakulm.ch*; ⑨) at the top of Innerarosa, but if you're here to relish the winter snows, the place to be is the romantic *Prätschli*, in a unique location on the slopes high above the Obersee (☎081/377 18 61, fax 377 11 48; ⑦; mid-Dec to mid-April only), with road access but truly out in the wilds.

Eating and drinking options are down-to-earth to suit the clientele, with a handful of simple diners around the Obersee and the lower reaches of Poststrasse, including the landmark *Orelli's*, where you can fill up on fish dishes, *Röschti* or salad for under Fr.15 (also with veggie meals). *Pizzeria Grottino*, just down the road from it, has quality pizza/pasta staples for Fr.13–18. Otherwise you're looking at hotel dining: *Hold*, up near the Hörnli cable-car, is a popular place offering raclette *a-gogo* every week, while *Quellenhof*, near the tourist office, has good *menus* for under Fr.20. The *Anita* (☎081/377 11 09), above the main street near the church, harbours an excellent gourmet restaurant, with multicourse dinners coming in at well over Fr.50.

Heidiland

The Rhine valley north of Chur winds through lush meadowland to the small industrial town of **Landquart** – an important rail junction for the line to Davos – and on to **BAD RAGAZ**, a rather graceful spa resort full of cheery elderly folk strolling happily along the neat boulevards feeling much better than they used to, thanks to the town's thermal springs which rise at a cosy 34°C to soothe away rheumatic and circulatory problems. Take a dip at the Tamina Therme baths (daily 7.30am–9pm; Fr.16), located behind the luxurious *Grand Hotel Quellenhof* or at the simpler Dorfbad, in the town centre (May–Sept Mon–Fri 8.30–11am & 2.30–5pm, Sat 8.30–11am), 1km or so southwest of the train station.

The hills above Bad Ragaz are where the Heidiland region got its name: the Swiss author Johanna Spyri set her wholesome classic of children's literature *Heidi* in and around the village of **MAIENFELD**, and the place milks its claim to fame mercilessly. Local trains between Chur and Bad Ragaz stop at Maienfeld station, starting point for a gentle half-day amble up into the lush pastureland on the mountain slopes. The trail leads first past Maienfeld's pretty central square and the **tourist office** (Mon–Fri 10am–noon & 1.30–5pm, Sat closes 4pm; ☎081/302 58 58), which has maps and swathes of Heidi kitsch, and then on up the hill to the hamlet of Oberrofels, now cruelly renamed **Heididorf**. Regardless of the lack of firm evidence linking Spyri's story with any particular house, one old wooden chalet near the execrable *Heidihof Hotel* has been seized upon as being "the original **Heidi's House**", and converted into a museum to show how Heidi would have lived a hundred years ago (April–Oct daily 10am–5pm; Fr.5). A trail – which, thankfully, most people don't seem to bother with – leads from Heididorf further up into the high pastures, past another lone chalet designated **Peter the Goatherd's Hut** and up to Heidi Alp, supposed home to Heidi's wise

Alm-Uncle. The trail is actually very scenic, winding back down through lush meadows filled with spring wildflowers to the village of Jenins, and back to Heididorf.

The Bündner Herrschaft

The east bank of the Rhine around Maienfeld, taking in the adjacent villages of Fläsch, Jenins and Malans, is one of Switzerland's more unusual winemaking areas, dubbed the **Bündner Herrschaft**. In what would otherwise be far too inhospitable a climate, luscious red Pinot Noir grapes – introduced in the seventeenth century by the French Duc de Rohan – are nurtured by the warm southerly Föhn wind, which can sometimes raise summer temperatures well above 25°C. The villages are linked by footpaths, generally quiet once you're out of the range of Heidi-seekers, and have a handful of rustic inns at which to enjoy a carafe of local wine alongside a square meal. Schloss Brandis, a medieval castle on the edge of Maienfeld (☎081/302 24 23), has a renowned restaurant

---

CHILDREN OF THE ROAD

The story of the Swiss gypsy people, known as the **Jenisch** (or Yenish), and how they have been treated over the last century by the Swiss authorities, is shocking, and exposes a calculated policy of Nazi-style eugenics carried out in Switzerland behind closed doors well into the 1970s. For almost fifty years, the Swiss government advocated and funded the wholesale kidnapping of Jenisch children, separating more than six hundred babies and toddlers from their families in what was nothing less than a determined attempt to completely wipe out Jenisch culture. Ghosts have still not been put to rest almost thirty years on, and the scandal remains a source of national shame and anger.

The Jenisch are one of the three main groups of central European gypsies, along with the Sinti and the Roma. During and after the great waves of gypsy migration in the seventeenth and eighteenth century, they travelled all over the continent, many arriving in Switzerland and specifically in Graubünden, where they lived a generally quiet, if socially ostracized, life. Amidst the tide of nationalism that swept through Europe after World War I, the science of **eugenics** gained widespread credibility, with its notion of state-sponsored "cleansing" of the racial gene pool by the forced removal from society of those with mental illnesses, physical disabilities and other characteristics seen as socially aberrant. Along with Jews and homosexuals, people with a lifestyle centred on travelling were singled out for special treatment. In 1926, the Swiss government approved a project set up by the children's charity Pro Juventute intended to eliminate vagrancy. Entitled **Kinder der Landstrasse** ("Children of the Road"), it effectively sanctioned child abduction: police seized Jenisch newborns and infants from their mothers without warning and carted them off to orphanages run by Pro Juventute. Some children were handed on to foster parents, effectively to vanish into society; others ended up shunted from pillar to post until their adulthood. Controlling committees brought in psychologists to deliver lengthy personality assessments and, as a result, large numbers of children were consigned to mental institutions, one of the most notorious of which was the Waldhaus clinic in Chur. Parents were not only not informed of their children's whereabouts, but were actively barred from making inquiries.

Kinder der Landstrasse was founded and directed by Alfred Siegfried. One of the aims of the project, according to Siegfried's own admission, was effectively to eliminate the Jenisch people altogether: "We must say that we have already achieved much if these people do not start a family, do not reproduce without restraint and bring new generations of degenerate and abnormal children into the world." As late as 1964 Siegfried was writing: "Nomadism, like certain dangerous diseases, is primarily transmitted by women... Anyone wishing to combat nomadism efficiently must aim to destroy the travellers' communal existence. Hard as it may seem, we must put an end to their family community. There is no other way." Under Siegfried's guidance, boys were forced into

for gourmet regional specialities, and an impressive cellar, and the *Landhaus* in Fläsch (☎081/302 14 36; closed Mon & Tues), *Traube* in Jenins (closed Thurs), and *Zum Ochsen* in Malans (closed Mon) all concentrate as much on their wines as on their generally very affordable *menus*.

Central Graubünden

The **Central Graubünden** region south of Chur is perhaps the canton's wildest area, characterized by deep, narrow valleys, ancient forests, tumbling mountain torrents and a succession of quiet old villages that feel as if they've seen few visitors since the Roman legions – who are known to have crossed the two main Alpine passes of the area, the Splügen and the Julier. Aside from simple inns in most villages, there are few facilities for tourists anywhere, and not even many side routes by which you can escape into the

apprenticeships or onto farms as cheap labour, and girls were often either sent to convents, or simply kept under lock and key: Uschi Waser, chair of Naschet Jenische, foundation recently set up to campaign for Jenisch rights, was placed in 23 different institutions in 18 years. Jenisch were not just forbidden from marrying other Jenisch, they were imprisoned for attempting it. Mariella Mehr, a Jenisch writer who has campaigned to expose the Kinder der Landstrasse project, described her treatment at the hands of the scientists: "When I was three years old [1953], they realised I didn't want to talk. They decided to force me. They used a kind of bath-tub... The patients were made to lie in the tub and covered with a plank so they couldn't get out. Only their heads were above water. They were kept there in freezing-cold water for up to twenty hours."

In 1972, the Swiss weekly *Der Schweizerischer Beobachter* exposed the Kinder der Landstrasse project, to universal public outrage. Pro Juventute closed the operation down a year later, and yet, according to official reports, there were about a hundred victims of Kinder der Landstrasse still incarcerated in clinics and institutions in 1988, after the Swiss state had formally acknowledged its moral, political and financial responsibility for the abductions and apologized to the Jenisch. Although Pro Juventute's own summations of individual cases remain under a 100-year embargo, the findings of an **official report** into the whole affair were published in June 1998. Ruth Dreyfuss, President of the Swiss Confederation, was led to comment that "the conclusions of the historians leave no room for doubt. Kinder der Landstrasse is a tragic example of discrimination and persecution of a minority that does not share the way of life of the majority." The effects of the revelations on Swiss society have been devastating: along with the Nazi gold scandal, accusations of collaboration with the Nazis before and during World War II, and continuing evidence from historians undermining the treasured notion of Swiss neutrality, Kinder der Landstrasse – and specifically its cruelty and systematic inhumanity – has delivered a body blow to the generally accepted image of a wholesome, morally upright Switzerland, an image that has been held both by the Swiss themselves and by outsiders for a century or more.

The Jenisch, meanwhile, have begun to gain a new appreciation of their own culture. About five thousand of Switzerland's 35,000 Jenisch still head out on the road each summer, working as antique dealers or crafts people, handing on their skills and the Jenisch language to new generations. They have been assigned caravan grounds all over the country, and their children can even study while on the road with correspondence courses offered by many Swiss schools for the purpose. The majority of Jenisch however – often light-skinned and fluent in Swiss-German – live a settled life in mostly low-income housing on the edge of many Swiss cities, completely cut off from their culture. Meanwhile, Pro Juventute (*www.projuventute.ch*), though it dissociates itself from the Kinder der Landstrasse project these days, is still working to "protect children in danger of abandonment and vagrancy".

wilderness: the most convenient way to experience the area is through the window of a train or a postbus, both of which offer spectacularly scenic rides through different valleys.

The train from Chur to St Moritz heads west to the road and rail junction of Reichenau before cutting south into the Hinterrhein valley to the village of **Rhäzüns**. On a forested rise down by the river, ten minutes' walk north of the village, is the isolated **chapel of Sogn Gieri** (St George), the building dating from Carolingian times, its interior covered with amazingly fresh and colourful frescoes made in the sixteenth century (chapel kept locked; key and map available at Rhäzüns station). South of Rhäzüns, the valley sides close in, opening out again south of Rothenbrunnen below the sharp ridges of the **Domleschg** to the east, cresting 2500m, and the rounded gentler slopes of the **Heinzenberg** to the west.

Some 12km south of Rhäzüns is the main town of the region, **THUSIS**, loomed over on all sides by precipitous mountains and thick forest. From here, the main road continues south to Bellinzona (see below) – another road swings east, shadowed by the train line which coils into the deep ravine of the Albula for a memorably dramatic journey passing below sheer cliffs, through 16 tunnels and over 27 bridges, including one viaduct which carries the line 89m above the yawning valley. Both road and rail line arrive after 12km at **Tiefencastel**, a small valley-bottom crossroads town, its prominent white church saving it from being lost altogether in the thick pine forests on all sides. Every route from Tiefencastel is up, and although trains continue east on their circuitous route to St Moritz, buses follow a more dramatic road climbing steeply south towards the Julierpass, passing on the way through the hamlet of **BIVIO**. This tiny place is the only commune north of the Alps with an Italian-speaking majority – although in true Swiss style it also has a long-standing Romansh minority and some German speakers as well. Most Italian speakers use Lombardic Italian, broadly similar to the dialect of the Val Bregaglia, although linguists have picked up use of the Bergamasco dialect, brought over the mountains from Italy, as well as formal, written "High" Italian. Just to complete the jigsaw, the hamlet has both a Catholic and a Protestant church, each with a multilingual pastor. Bivio's cosy *Hotel Solaria* (☎081/684 51 07, fax 684 12 90; ②), in the same family for three generations, offers summer horse-riding and walking packages: a two-day horse ride over the isolated, pedestrian-only Septimer Pass (2310m), including full board in the hotel and a guide, costs from Fr.400; while five half-board overnights, plus guided half-day rides or hikes is Fr.650. Contact Bivio's tourist office (☎081/684 53 23, fax 684 55 58, *kurverein@bivio.ch*) for more details. Ten kilometres or so south of Bivio is the **Julierpass** or **Pass dal Güglia** (2284m), the heights of which are still marked by the column stumps of a long-demolished Roman temple. The Upper Engadine, and St Moritz, lie just over the pass.

From Thusis to Bellinzona

Some 5km south of Thusis, the main road – followed by postbuses on their way to Bellinzona – plunges into another extraordinary ravine, with sheer rock walls barely 10m apart rising some 500m from the bed of the foaming Hinterrhein. This **Via Mala** (Evil Road) was first constructed in 1473, various improvements since then resulting in a web of bridges spanning the gorge. At one point, you can descend 321 steps to the valley floor to see both the ancient original road and the bridges lined up way overhead (April–Oct daily 8am–sunset; Fr.3).

The gorge opens up 8km south of Thusis at the small farming village of **ZILLIS** (Ziràn in Romansh), worth a stop to investigate the painted wooden ceiling in its small **St Martinskirche** (Baselgia Sontg Martegn). Located on what was formerly the main route between Konstanz and Milan, the first village church dated from the sixth century, but it was later overbuilt by the current Romanesque building, which still sports a huge external **mural of St Christopher**, patron saint of travellers. The polygonal choir dates from 1509, but complete renovation in 1940 means that the interior is today brand shiny new, in stark contrast to the painted wood-panelled ceiling which is original twelfth-century but almost perfectly preserved.

The **ceiling** is divided into 153 square panels, each of which sports a different, remarkably clear image (there's a handy stack of mirrors by the door to save you cricking your neck). Running all the way around the edge is the sea, with angels in all four corners representing the four winds. The interior panels are devoted to stories from the life of Christ, which start at the east (choir) end and run from north to south row by row until you reach the west (door). The sixth row from the choir, for instance, shows the Three Wise Men and the Holy Family's flight into Egypt on a donkey; the ninth row begins with Christ's baptism in the Jordan and ends with the miracle of turning water into wine at Cana; four rows below it is Jesus entering Jerusalem on a donkey; two rows below that is the kiss of Judas. Christ crowned with thorns is the last of the biblical scenes, since the final row, instead of depicting the Crucifixion and Resurrection, is instead inexplicably devoted to scenes from the life of St Martin, implying that the unknown artist was, for some reason, unable to complete his intended story-cycle.

Some 6km south of Zillis, the main road bends westwards, but if you have your own transport (or take the bus from Andeer, a few kilometres south of Zillis), you might want to detour up the remote **Val Ferrera**, laced with waterfalls and flanked by 3000m-plus peaks. The lonely road penetrates for some 25km through barely half-a-dozen widely spaced hamlets, ending up at **Juf**, a cluster of farmhouses which, at 2126m, claims the title of the highest permanently occupied village in Europe.

The main road from Zillis continues through the deep Rheinwald forest to the dourly picturesque village of **SPLÜGEN**, with a jumble of traditional slate-roofed houses, a **tourist office** (☎081/650 90 30, *www.splugen.ch*), a year-round **campsite** (☎081/664 14 76) and four **hotels**, including the *Pratigiana*, an old smugglers' haunt (☎081/664 11 10, fax 664 12 88; ②). The **Splügenpass** (2113m), 10km south of the village and reached via a twisting minor road, marks the Italian border; postbuses use this road to reach the town of Chiavenna, 30km south, from where postbuses run back into Switzerland up the Val Bregaglia (see p.476) to St Moritz. From Splügen itself, the main road climbs west in the shadow of the giant Zapportgletscher, one of the sources of the Rhine, to the **San Bernadino Pass**. These days the pass route is undercut by a long road tunnel open year-round, which feeds down into the long **Valle Mesolcina** on the south side of the Alps, completely Italian speaking but still in the territory of Graubünden. The main road coils down out of the mountain air, becoming a fully fledged motorway alongside the hilltop Castello di Misox, at roughly the point where vines, fig trees and chestnut forests spring up all around, giving a hint of the lushness of the gorgeous Canton Ticino spreading out to the west. The Ticinese capital, Bellinzona (see p.484), lies 24km further south.

Surselva

A long straight road west from Chur leads you up into the big, broad wooded valley of the River Vorderrhein (the *Rein Anteriur* in Romansh), a patch of countryside known in Romansh as **Surselva**, the High Forests. The little-known ski and sports resort of **Flims** is within easy reach of Chur, but west of Flims the only access is along the valley floor by a single road or rail line. The handful of quiet towns along the way is capped at the extreme western end of the valley by a huge Benedictine abbey at **Disentis/Mustér**, staging post for journeys south over the Lukmanier (Lucomagno) Pass into Canton Ticino, and west via the Oberalppass and Andermatt into Canton Valais.

Along with most of the Romansh-speaking areas of Graubünden, Surselva has kept hold of many ancient **customs** rooted in pagan, Roman or early Christian seasonal rites. These are often hard to come across, and generally hold a great deal more significance for those taking part than for outside observers, but there are some rituals – most notably winter ones – which are worth looking out for. At Epiphany (January 6), the village of **Breil/Brigels** 12km west of Ilanz resounds to traditional songs as groups representing the Three Wise Men deliver the Christmas message to all and sundry. After nightfall on Easter Sunday, young men gather on the hillside above two hamlets beside Breil/Brigels, **Dardin** and **Danis-Tavanasa**, and ceremonially fling discs of burning wood known as **trer schibettas** down into the valley while simultaneously pledging their love to a particular woman – tradition has it that it's possible to predict the success or failure of the match depending on the flight of the disc. Carnival in **Domat/Ems**, 6km west of Chur, is celebrated as **Tschaiver** with masked festivities on both Mardi Gras (*margis bel*, or Beautiful Tuesday) and the Thursday after (*gievgia grassa*, or Fat Thursday).

Flims

On a hillside above the river some 18km west of Chur, the winter and summer resort of **FLIMS** is well known to the Swiss, who consistently pack the place out every season, but is virtually unknown outside the country. There are two parts to Flims – **Flims-Dorf** is the older, original village with most amenities and the base station for the ski lifts, while **Flims-Waldhaus** is a newer resort, with most of the hotels, set amidst beech and larch woods on a slightly higher elevation 1km south. Some 5km south of Waldhaus – across the German–Romansh language border – is the quiet village of **Laax**, with tiny **Falera** up a 3km branch road completing the picture. Flims, Laax and Falera all share the extensive "Alpine Arena" ski region, centred on the **Crap Sogn Gion** mountain (2228m), accessed by a cable-car from Laax-Murschetg on the edge of Laax village, and the **Cassons Grat** (2634m), served by a combination of chairlifts and a cable-car from Flims-Dorf. Falera has a chairlift to Curnius, halfway up the Crap Sogn Gion. Beginners and intermediates are best served, with plenty of nursery slopes and practice areas around Waldhaus, and a host of blues and reasonably testing reds all over the mountain. Ski passes cost Fr.55/59 for a weekday/weekend day, with discounts outside peak season. In summer, the **hiking** network is extensive, plenty of trails winding their way through the forest on the cliffs above the River Vorderrhein. Alternatively, take the chairlift up to the broad, level plateau atop the Cassons Grat, where there's a pleasant three-hour circular walk offering Alpine panoramas. The three-hour trek from Falera up to Crap Sogn Gion, and along the crest to Crap Masegn is especially beautiful too. Swissraft in Flims-Waldhaus (☎081/911 52 50; *www.swissraft.ch*) offer summer-only **white-water rafting** on the Vorderrhein between Ilanz and Reichenau (Fr.99/143 for a half/full day).

Practicalities

Flims is served by regular postbuses from Chur. The main **tourist office** is in Flims-Waldhaus (Mon–Fri 9am–noon & 2–6pm, Sat 9am–noon; Dec–April Sat also 2–5pm; ☎081/920 92 00, *www.alpenarena.ch*), beside both the post office (CH-7018) and the postbus stop. Buses from Chur first run through Flims-Dorf, stopping outside the post office (CH-7017). The local Guest Card covers buses to and from the lift stations.

The least expensive **accommodation** is also handily close to the Dorf lifts: *Alte Säge*, at Sulten 187 just down from the main road (☎081/911 28 07, fax 911 28 41), has dorms for Fr.27 as well as use of a kitchen. Also convenient for the Dorf lifts is the *Curtgin*

(☎081/911 35 56, fax 911 34 55; ②–③), a cosy family-run hotel. The tiny, modern *Uaul Pign* in Waldhaus (☎081/911 13 39, fax 911 56 39; ②) is in a tranquil location well away from the road, with only ten rooms, all with balconies looking into the forest. In Laax, the *Bellaval*, Via Falera 112 (☎081/921 47 00, fax 921 48 55, *bellaval@bluewin.ch*; ③–④), offers peace and quiet, with pleasant, well-appointed rooms. Skiers could do a lot worse than stay right on the slopes, at the *Berghotel Crap Sogn Gion* (☎081/921 22 70, fax 921 22 73, *thersche@whitearena.ch*; ④) – overpriced for the quality of rooms, but good value considering the unbeatable location.

Eating and drinking is largely a hotel affair, with a handful of restaurants in Flims-Dorf, including the *Central*, with *menus* of solid regional fare from Fr.14. *Pomodoro* is an inexpensive pizzeria in Waldhaus, while the restaurant in the *Hotel Bellevue* beside the Dorf lifts has great food, including local specialities and plenty of veggie options, for Fr.20 and upwards. Locals also favour the *Meiler* opposite, with much the same style.

West to Disentis/Mustér

Some 5km west of Laax is the town of **ILANZ**, known in Romansh as **Glion**. These days it's a lively commercial and cultural centre for the Surselva region, but in times gone by this was one of the most important towns in the whole of Graubünden. From the train station, which holds a tourist information counter (Mon–Fri 8–11.30am & 1.30–6pm; ☎081/925 20 70), a short wander through the town centre, spanning the River Vorderrhein, will turn up a surprising number of stately sixteenth- and seventeenth-century townhouses. The town has a couple of unassuming hotels, including the *Rätia*, on Via Centrala by the bridge (☎081/925 23 93, fax 925 32 93; ②), with an excellent, local-style restaurant serving regional cuisine. From Ilanz, a couple of minor roads penetrate two beautiful side valleys famed for their broad meadows and cherry trees: the **Valser valley** (named for its thirteenth-century Walser colonizers, and still German speaking today), which ends at the village of Vals; and, to its west, the lush, Romansh-speaking **Val Lumnezia** rising to tiny Vrin.

There's little to stop for further west up the valley of the Vorderrhein until, after 28km, the huge white abbey of **DISENTIS** (also known by its Romansh name of **MUSTÉR**) hoves into view. A Benedictine community was founded here in the eighth century, only to be sacked by a marauding Saracen army in 940. Later churches were replaced in the late seventeenth century by the current Baroque building – itself badly damaged by the French in 1799 and by a fire in 1861. Nonetheless, the community survived and today numbers about forty priests and novices. The white interior of the great **abbey church** is immediately impressive, not least because of the startling contrast of such lavish ornament with the wild, open countryside all about. Built in 1712 by Kaspar Moosbrugger, architect of the church at Einsiedeln (see p.361), it is covered in gilt and ornate stucco, with light flooding in from high windows and a deep choir. An internal passageway in the west wall signposts the way through the corridors of the monastery and up some stairs to the still and silent **Marienkirche**, its triple apse surviving as the only remnant of the tenth-century church sacked by the Saracens.

Davos and Klosters

At the southern end of the **Prättigau**, or Meadow Valley, which meanders a path south from the junction point of Landquart north of Chur, lie the twin resorts of **Davos** and **Klosters**, two of the most famous names in the Alps enjoying some of the best skiing in the world. Walser migrants arrived in the valley in the thirteenth century, and the area – surrounded on three sides by Romansh – is still German speaking to this day. The focus is fair and square on outdoorsiness, whether that means skiing and snowboarding in the winter, or long-distance hiking in the summer. There's not a lot else to grab your attention.

Winter sports in Davos and Klosters

The main reason to come to either Davos or Klosters is for the outstanding **skiing**. Although both resorts are quite far apart, they share the same ski area and lift pass – indeed, the prime attraction of skiing here is the sense of openness you get from swooshing down broad well-tended pistes which go on and on, for more than 10km in many cases from mountaintop to valley bottom.

The big focus of everyone's attention is the **Parsenn** ski area on the north side of Davos and the west side of Klosters (*www.parsenn.ch*), with the Weissfluh summit as its centrepiece. However, there are just three methods of access from the valley floor, all of which suffer from queues aplenty in peak season. The **Parsennbahn** funicular starts from Davos-Dorf and rises to the Weissfluhjoch saddle just below the summit; the little **Schatzalpbahn** funicular from Davos-Platz takes you to a broad snow shelf, from where you must switch to chairlifts and gondolas for the journey further up; while the **Gotschnagrat** cable-car (*www.gotschna.ch*) rises from Klosters-Platz station to a ridge just east of the Weissfluh. Once you've arrived on the mountain, there are plenty of draglifts serving dozens of blue and red runs, including giant, weaving pistes from the top of the Weissfluh all the way down through the trees to hamlets such as Küblis, Saas and Serneus north of Klosters. For more testing runs, you could attempt the notorious Gotschnawang, scene of an avalanche in 1988 which killed Prince Charles's equerry and which is now regularly off limits, or a handful of black runs on the lower, steep slopes above Davos-Dorf and Wolfgang.

Moving onto one of the four other ski sectors in the Davos/Klosters area can take you away from the crowds. From Davos-Platz station, cable-cars rises to Ischalp, and from there to the **Jakobshorn** summit (*www.fun-mountain.ch*), with a hatful of scenic blues and reds. Bus #1 from Davos-Dorf serves Dörfji, the base station of the cable-car up to **Pischa** (2483m), while a gondola from Davos-Glaris (bus #7 from Davos centre) rises to the **Rinerhorn** (2053m), which has lifts going higher to access blues, reds and a testing black run down to the valley. A gondola rises from Klosters-Dorf to the east side of its valley and the ski area of **Madrisa**, also with plenty of long, exciting reds on pistes which hug the Austrian border.

Passes, considering the range of skiing on offer, are excellent value. A comprehensive REGA pass costs Fr.160 for three days, Fr.268 for six days. A day pass for the Parsenn is Fr.54, for the Jakobshorn Fr.50; while a Parsenn-Plus gives you access to all the mountains around Davos for Fr.107 for two days. Week-long passes benefit from twenty percent discounts before mid-December, during most of January, and from mid-March until the end of the season.

Snowboarders should aim principally for the Parsenn, although the Jakobshorn is the favourite of many and there's some limited scope for experimentation on the Madrisa as well. Both Davos and Klosters have plenty of other diversions, including indoor swimming, ice-skating, tobogganing (especially on Schatzalp) and **paragliding**: a number of operators in both resorts offer tandem flights for around Fr.160–180, including Paragliding Davos (☎079/236 39 49), Spina (☎081/401 14 14) and Hans Guler (☎081/413 60 43) in Davos, and Flugcenter Grischa (☎081/422 20 70) in Klosters.

Davos

Twinned in a touristic masterstroke with Aspen, Colorado, **DAVOS** isn't so much a resort as a full-blown town, way up at 1560m. The antithesis of a peaceful Alpine ski village, it's a bustling honky-tonk of a place, famous for its toothpaste-fresh air and its consistently excellent snow cover. The town has been attracting **skiers** for generations and recently gained new life (and hipness) with the seal of approval of Switzerland's **snow-boarding** cognoscenti. Originally a health resort, Davos's high altitude and long hours of sunshine eased the suffering of tuberculosis patients from around the world: by 1900, there were almost three-quarters of a million overnight visitors every year, long before winter sports were even thought of. The consumptive Robert Louis Stevenson completed *Treasure Island* while resident at a Davos sanatorium in 1882; three decades later, in 1912, German novelist Thomas Mann visited Davos and was inspired to write his celebrated *The Magic Mountain*. The funicular lines serving the slopes above Davos were constructed around 1930, since when the town has blossomed into one of the world's best-known winter-sports destinations. In summer, the snows recede to reveal a surrounding of lush countryside and Davos takes on a new lease of life – not least because hotel prices plummet.

Yet another hat worn by the town is that of a major international **conference venue**: in the last week of January each year, presidents, prime ministers and assorted mega-suits of the World Economic Forum meet at Davos under the gaze of the world's media to discuss global cashflow and set the financial agenda for the year ahead, regularly sparking anti-capitalist demonstrations in the process.

Arrival, orientation and information

The two contiguous halves of the town, **Davos-Platz** and **Davos-Dorf**, are strung along a four-kilometre ribbon of low-key development on the floor of the Landwasser valley. Bustling Platz is where most hotels and amenities are; low-key Dorf is generally where locals take refuge; and the giant Congress Centre is between the two. The main street, **Promenade**, lined with shops and hotels, feeds traffic one-way from Dorf to Platz; parallel one block to the south is quieter **Talstrasse**, which is one-way from Platz to Dorf. The town is dominated by the giant **Weissfluh** (2844m), which rises immediately to the north, flanked by various smaller peaks such as the Strelagrat (2545m) and Schwarzhorn (2670m). On the other, south, side of the town looms the **Jakobshorn** (2590m), framed by parallel side valleys. There are outlying suburbs on both sides, linked to Davos proper by bus or train – east of Dorf, beyond the pretty Davosersee lake, is Davos-Wolfgang; west of Platz is Davos-Glaris – but these are quiet hamlets with few facilities.

Davos lies at the far end of a circular **train** line from Chur, the eastern half of which runs via Landquart and Klosters, the western half of which runs via Filisur: there are some direct trains as well as plenty of one-stop connections. All trains stop at both Davos-Dorf and Davos-Platz, although the latter is the main terminus. Postbuses run direct from Chur.

There are two branches of the **tourist office** – one opposite Dorf station, the other at Promenade 67 in the middle of Platz (both mid-June to mid-Oct Mon–Fri 8.30am–6pm, Sat 8.30am–4pm; April to mid-June & mid-Oct to Nov Mon–Fri 8.30am–6pm, Sat 8.30am–12.30pm, Dorf closes Mon–Fri noon–1.45pm; Dec–March Mon–Fri 8.30am–6pm, Sat 8.30am–5pm, Sun 10am–noon; ☎081/415 21 21, *www.davos.ch*). Both have stacks of English information about the town and the surrounding area, and can also provide information on services such as transporting your baggage from hotel to hotel while you hike or cycle some of the multi-day mountain routes between Davos, Arosa and Lenzerheide. A **Guest Card** gives free unlimited use of Davos's excellent public transport, covering buses and trains between Platz and Dorf, and along 15km of the valley floor; the city buses stop at all points of interest in the town, and also run out to Wolfgang, Glaris and up the Flüela road to the base station of the Pischa ski area.

Accommodation

As you might expect, Davos is packed with **accommodation** options, but none could be called a bargain. Prices get hiked ruthlessly across the board in the winter season.

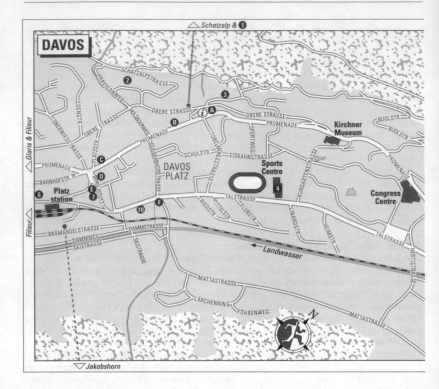

Beware, too, that virtually all facilities and services are closed in the between-seasons, from mid-April until June and mid-October until mid-December.

There's a **campsite**, *Färich*, about 1km south of Dorf on the road towards the Flüela Pass (☎081/416 10 43; May–Sept). A bus stops outside. The HI **hostel**, *Höhwald*, is in Wolfgang, pleasantly situated in the trees on the east side of the Davosersee lake (☎081/416 14 84, fax 416 50 55; ①), with dorms for Fr.21; take bus #6 or #11 to Seebühl, from where it's a five-minute walk. Otherwise, there's a fistful of places both in Platz and Dorf and the surrounding area which offer dormitory places: the huge *Sportzentrum*, at Talstrasse 41 in the middle of Platz (☎081/415 36 36, fax 415 36 37), is one of the most convenient, with simple, brand-new lino-and-plastic-style four-bed rooms for Fr.48 per bed – but check with the tourist office, who keep a complete list.

Alte Post, Berglistutz 4, Platz (☎ & fax 081/413 54 03, *jakobshorn@spin.ch*, *www.fun-mountain.ch*). Serviceable little place beside Platz station that offers winter weekend deals of two nights' B&B in a double room plus a two day lift pass for the Jakobshorn for Fr.160 per person. ③.

Bahnhof-Terminus, Talstrasse 3, Platz (☎081/413 25 25, fax 413 71 77, *bahnhof-terminus@bluewin.ch*, *www.bestwestern.com*). Large, airy rooms and private parking directly opposite Platz station. ⑤.

Berghotel Schatzalp, on Schatzalp above Platz (☎081/413 83 31, fax 413 13 44, *berghotel schatzalp@bluewin.ch*). Although there's any number of five-star palaces in Davos, this old Jugendstil sanatorium is the most characterful top-end accommodation by a long streak, perched on a tranquil terrace 300m above the town and only accessible by funicular. Views from the ranks of balconied rooms – which boast up to four more hours of sunshine per day than the town – over the Jakobshorn and beyond are worth paying for. ④–⑦.

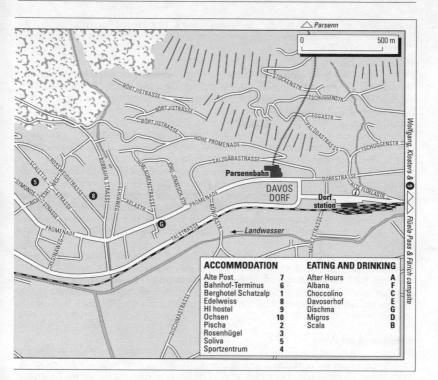

ACCOMMODATION		EATING AND DRINKING	
Alte Post	7	After Hours	A
Bahnhof-Terminus	6	Albana	F
Berghotel Schatzalp	1	Choccolino	C
Edelweiss	8	Davoserhof	E
HI hostel	9	Dischma	G
Ochsen	10	Migros	D
Pischa	2	Scala	B
Rosenhügel	3		
Soliva	5		
Sportzentrum	4		

Edelweiss, Rossweidstrasse 9, Platz (☎081/416 10 33, fax 416 11 30, *edelweiss-davos@gr-net.ch*). The best in this price range, with private parking and a pleasant, comfortable atmosphere. ③.

Ochsen, Talstrasse 10, Platz (☎081/413 52 22, fax 413 76 71). Bright, cosy rooms, many with balconies, close to Platz station. ③–④.

Pischa, Strelastrasse 2, Platz (☎081/413 55 13, fax 413 16 19, *pischa@bluewin.ch*). Pleasant, cosy and quiet, way up above Platz (with a free shuttle bus up and down the hill). Relatively small price-hike makes it good value in winter. ④.

Rosenhügel, Rosenhügelweg 5, Platz (☎081/413 54 25, fax 413 12 31). Perched on a terrace above the Platz tourist office, this friendly place has a choice of en-suite and shared-bath rooms, some with good views over the town. ②–③.

Soliva, Symondsstrasse 7, Platz (☎081/416 57 27, fax 416 71 67). Very small, quiet family-run B&B opposite the Kongresszentrum. ②.

The Kirchner Museum

Sole attraction for non-sports fans in Davos is the **Kirchner Museum**, 600m east of the Platz tourist office on Promenade (Tues–Sun: July–Sept & Christmas–Easter 10am–noon & 2–6pm; rest of year 2–6pm; Fr.8; SMP). This impressively airy structure houses a vibrant collection of artworks by the German Expressionist painter Ernst Ludwig Kirchner. Born in 1880, Kirchner moved to Berlin in 1911, but after an intensive period of work which produced a host of starkly stylish woodcuts and sketches, his health deteriorated rapidly. He emigrated to Davos in 1917 following a nervous breakdown, and lived in a number of small shacks out in the countryside, where he produced a constant flow of expressive, highly colourful paintings, including the celebrated, luminous *Davos im Sommer*. In 1936, Kirchner's work was tagged "degenerate" by the Nazis and, in a deep depression, the artist committed suicide in Davos two years later.

Hiking and biking

Davos's famously good **skiing** and snowboarding is covered on p.460, and in summer the opportunities for **hiking and biking** are equally good. From the Weissfluhjoch, accessed by the Parsennbahn funicular from Dorf (or a testing three- or four-hour walk up), the views of Piz Buin and the Austrian and Italian Alps are spectacular, even better from the summit itself, the Weissfluhgipfel, served by a cable-car from the funicular top-station. The invigorating walk back down from the Weissfluhjoch takes a couple of hours, while the tough hike over the back of the mountain to Arosa takes about six hours. The route down to Klosters is about four hours.

There's almost limitless possibilities for easier walks, especially in the meadows and woods around the small Davosersee lake, a short distance beyond Dorf. A short stroll from the top of the Schatzalpbahn, beyond the grand old *Berghotel* and into the fragrant woods brings you to the **Alpinum**, a botanical garden of Alpine flora covering the hillside (mid-May to Sept daily 9am–5pm; Fr.3). On the other side of the valley, there are some leg-stretching trails from the Pischa and Jakobshorn summits back to Davos (2–3hr).

There are plenty of **mountain bike** routes around Davos, including several routes along the valley floor west as far as Wiesen (31km round trip), and a classic 20km run from the Weissfluhjoch down to Küblis, 8km northwest of Klosters. For Fr.21.50, you can load your bike onto the Parsennbahn up to the Weissfluhjoch and follow a testing 14km trail down to Klosters, then transport yourself and your bike back to Davos by train.

Eating and drinking

Unless you're taking advantage of half-board deals in your hotel, you'll need a plenty of cash to be able to **eat and drink** well in Davos. Budget options include a *Migros* super-market and takeaway just above Platz station, or if you're catering for yourself, the *After Hours* convenience store, at Promenade 69, is open 24 hours daily. The ultra-swish *Choccolino*, Promenade 45, is a *confiserie* and café, with classical music on Sunday brunch time and a proper cup of tea.

There's a handful of simple pizza/pasta restaurants around town where you can eat for under Fr.20: *Hotel Albana*, Talstrasse 18, is one of the cosier options; *Hotel Dischma*, Promenade 128, is another, in addition offering good *Rösti* and fondues; while *Hotel Ochsen*'s atmospheric dining room and *Stübli* (see "Accommodation") also have quality Graubünden cooking at reasonable prices. The large *Hotel Europe*, Promenade 63, shelters the bright and modern *Scala* restaurant, with inexpensive pizzas and daily *menus* for around Fr.20. The Chinese restaurant in *Hotel Bahnhof-Terminus* (see "Accommodation") is the best in town, authentic cuisine coming in at around Fr.25. If you have a spare Fr.100 or so, you might experiment with the spectacular cooking on display at the *Hotel Davoserhof*, Berglistutz 2 (☎081/415 66 66), which also offers the finest terrace views in town.

Focus of Platz's buzzing **nightlife** is the all-night *Ex-Bar*, alongside the tourist office, which only really gets going after 3am. The *Chämi*, 200m east, is another very popular choice. There are pool tables in the *Hotel Montana*'s lively bar, and cocktail pianists in the *Hotel Europa*, which also hosts the *Cabanna* disco and the canton's swankiest casino.

Listings

Bike rental Dorf station (☎081/416 24 44), Ettinger sports shops at Promenade 153 and Talstrasse 6 (☎081/410 12 12), Flüela Sport opposite Dorf station (☎081/416 73 73), and a handful of other places rent mountain bikes for around Fr.30/day (all May–Sept).

Car rental Avis, Talstrasse 22, Platz (☎081/413 75 43); Hertz, Flüelastrasse 2, Dorf (☎081/416 57 90).

Changing money In Platz station (daily 6am–9pm), or Dorf station (daily 7am–8pm).

Email and Internet Roro, Promenade 123, Platz (Mon–Fri 8.30am–noon & 2–6.30pm, Sat 8.30am–4pm) charge Fr.5 for 20min, or Fr.12/hr.

Laundry Self-service laundry at Promenade 102, Platz (Mon–Sat 8am–8pm).

Post Main office is opposite Platz station (CH-7270), with a smaller office next to Dorf station (CH-7260).

Klosters

Instantly recognizable to Britons as the favoured winter getaway of Prince Charles, little **KLOSTERS** – about 9km northeast of Davos – steals quite a march on its neighbour in terms of ambience. Where Davos has traffic, bright lights, street bustle and concrete multistorey hotels, Klosters has peace and quiet, an appealing huddle of dark-wood chalets and a village atmosphere. Furthermore, Klosters is linked to Davos's famous Parsenn ski slopes (see p.460), and the two share a lift pass covering each other's pistes and mountain transport: in choosing a base in the area, you could do worse than shun Davos altogether.

Practicalities

Klosters also has a Platz and a Dorf, with the usual division between the two: Platz is the centre of things, while 2km to the north sits the smaller, quieter Dorf. Both are on the Landquart–Davos train line, and are also linked by town buses, which are free with the resort's Guest Card. The main **tourist office** is in Platz, to the right of the station (Mon–Sat 8.30am–noon & 2.30–6pm; June–Oct Sat closes 5pm; Dec–April also Sun 9–11.30am & 3.30–6.30pm; ☎081/410 20 20, *www.klosters.ch*), and there's a branch office in Dorf, also to the right of the station (mid-June to Oct & Dec to mid-April Mon–Sat 8.30am–noon). The Platz post office (CH-7250) is opposite the station. As in Davos, almost everything is closed in the between-seasons, but unlike in Davos, the winter price hikes won't break the bank.

The cosy HI **hostel** *Soldanella* is at Talstrasse 73, a fifteen-minute climb above Platz (☎081/422 13 16, fax 422 52 09; ①), with dorms from Fr.26. The weathered-wood *Sonne*, Hauptstrasse 155 (☎081/422 13 49, fax 422 19 48; ②), is the best low-end deal, with small and simple shared-bath rooms, some with balcony, while the *Madrals*, Monbielerstrasse 4 (☎081/422 12 78, fax 422 49 60; ②), is in a slightly elevated location, all its rooms with south-facing balcony. The *Chesa Grischuna*, Bahnhofstrasse 12

THE VEREINA TUNNEL

In the first expansion of the Rhätische Bahn train network in 85 years, work was completed in November 1999 on a tunnel beneath the Alps linking Klosters and Sagliains (just west of Scuol in the Lower Engadine). The new **Vereina Tunnel** (*www.rhb.ch*), as it's been called, is over 19km long, the longest narrow-gauge rail tunnel in the world, and will considerably ease both road and rail traffic in the region. The Flüela Pass road will now remain closed all winter (roughly Nov–May), replaced by the car-carrying shuttle trains which run every half-hour during the day, year-round (Fr.27/35 per car plus nine passengers summer/winter, with a small surcharge during the winter peak). Ordinary trains will also run on a new routing using the tunnel from Chur and Landquart through to Scuol or St Moritz. The flipside of this – that the rustic and once-tranquil Lower Engadine and Val Müstair may have to deal with some overflow tourism from Davos and St Moritz – has yet to be assessed.

(☎081/422 22 22, fax 422 22 25, *chesagrischuna@bluewin.ch*; ⑤), may look like a tumbledown old chalet from the outside, but is in fact one of the liveliest and chic-est places in town. Prince Charles's establishment of choice is the dignified *Walserhof*, Landstrasse 141 (☎081/422 42 42, fax 422 14 37; ⑤). Moving away from Platz, the rustic, peaceful *Malein*, at Landstrasse 120 halfway to Dorf (☎081/422 10 88; ①), has a handful of en-suite or shared-bath rooms, while in Dorf itself, you'll find comfortable, peaceful rooms at the logwood-style *Rätia* (☎081/422 47 47, fax 422 47 49, *hotelraetiak-losters@bluewin.ch*, *www.hotelraetia.ch*; ③).

There's less choice for **eating and drinking** than in Davos. Most of the hotels listed above also have restaurants attached: the *Sonne* (closed Mon & Tues) is especially well thought of, with good regional *menus* starting from Fr.16, and the *Walserhof* was recently awarded two Michelin stars for the first time. The *Vereina* restaurant in the heart of Platz serves quality pizzas. *Wynegg*, Landstrasse 205 (☎081/422 13 40; winter only) enjoys royal patronage, serving beer and hearty meals that are surprisingly affordable; while to eat at chichi *Chesa Grischuna* (see above), you should book a week or so in advance and expect to lose a fistful of francs.

The Lower Engadine

Beyond the mountains, in the farthest corner of Switzerland – and requiring some dedication to reach – is the **Lower Engadine** (Engiadina Bassa in Romansh, Unterengadin in German). Remote from Chur, let alone from the rest of the country, this attractive valley nurtures a quite distinct, thoroughly Romansh culture that has been allowed to flourish in isolation for centuries. Although the Austrian Tyrol is just a few kilometres away on the north side of the impassable Piz Buin range, it might just as well be on the other side of the continent. The succession of hamlets which cling to the banks of the

---

CUSTOMS IN THE LOWER ENGADINE

Even more than in Surselva, the communities of the Lower Engadine keep alive the ancient local **customs** as an expression of their Romansh heritage. In Ramosch and Tschlin, two hamlets 10km east of Scuol, the **Mattinadas** tend to overshadow even Christmas and New Year. On January 2, the local children organize a parade through the village dragging a decorated sledge behind them and collecting bucketsful of home-made sweets and candy (*mattinadas*); after a communal feast, everyone then embarks on an evening of dancing until midnight, whereupon the kids sit down to another banquet, this time of traditional butter biscuits smothered in whipped cream. The whole procedure is then repeated either the next day, or on the Saturday following, by the young men of the village.

Epiphany celebrations (January 6) in the Lower Engadine communities take the form of **Bavania**, or **Buania**. In the afternoon, the village girls gather together and draw lots to choose a lover; they then visit their allotted man and, to mark their conquest and Fate's irrevocable decision, they tie a red ribbon round his neck. Later that night, at the village dance, the girls are waited on and chaperoned by their ribboned partner … presumably, happily ever after.

In Scuol, the first Saturday in February sees the ceremonial torching of the **Hom d'strom**, or Man of Straw, in front of the town's court building, probably as a symbolic banishment of the winter. Perhaps the biggest celebration of the lot, though, takes place in many villages on March 1 – the children's festival of **Chalandamarz** or **Calonda mars**. This originates in the Roman New Year celebration *Calendae Martii*, and these days takes the form of a colourful spring parade, with cowbell-ringing and traditional songs.

foaming River Inn (or En in Romansh), tumbling its way towards Innsbruck, the Danube and eventually the Black Sea, show their Latin origins as much as does the language of their inhabitants: thick-walled houses stuccoed in cream abound, complete with small, deep-set windows and scarlet geraniums sprouting from every windowbox, reminiscent of Mediterranean village architecture found much further south. Everywhere you'll see the characteristic *sgraffiti* decoration – ornate, curlicued designs, pictures and even mottoes or dedications studiously etched into the white stuccoed facade of a house to reveal a darker, coloured layer beneath. The beautifully decorated little cottages and quaint cobbled squares, set against a tremendous backdrop of dark pine forests and looming mountains, combine to give the fairy-tale valley a uniquely romantic air.

Scuol is the main town of the valley, prefaced by a succession of charming cliffside villages such as Guarda and Ftan. **Zernez** serves as the gateway for exploration of the **Parc Naziunal Svizzer**, Switzerland's only national park, a vast chunk of highland wilderness. Beyond the park in tiny **Müstair** village is one of Switzerland's greatest cultural treasures – a Carolingian church sporting perfectly preserved medieval frescoes.

Transport in the valley isn't easy. Trains from St Moritz and, with the opening of the Vereina Tunnel, also from Klosters, serve both Zernez and Scuol, while postbuses run northeast to the Austrian border and southeast to Müstair. Timetables, though, can leave you waiting a couple of hours between buses and unless you're on an extended walking tour of the valley (see p.470), driving is really the transport of choice, allowing you to detour to hamlets which take your fancy, or enjoy the sunset in Müstair and still make it to St Moritz well before bedtime.

Scuol and around

The road from Davos over the dramatic, icy Flüela Pass drops down into the Engadine at the gateway village of **SUSCH**, a perfect introduction to the valley, its cobbled alleys filled with the rushing noise of the River Inn. Set picturesquely amidst the *sgraffitied* houses, the **Baselgia San Jon** boasts two towers – one Romanesque, the other late Gothic. To the east, beyond the ruined castle of Chaschinas on its hill, rears the giant Piz Arpiglias (3027m). The road to Scuol continues from Susch through tremendous scenery between the high, wooded valley walls; along the way is a string of alluring little villages, most positioned slightly above the valley-floor road and rail line. Some 7km northeast of Susch on a lofty perch above the river, **GUARDA** is especially gorgeous, its architecture and traditional *sgraffiti* meriting a federal order of protection. Just beyond, **Ardez** and **Ftan** are both equally worthy of a stop.

Some 22km east of Susch, the lively town of **SCUOL** (pronounced *sh-kwol*), known as Schuls in German, is beautifully located in a sunny, open part of the Inn valley at the end of the train line. Its reputation is built on its history as a spa town, a reputation shared by its neighbours across the river, **Vulpera** and **Tarasp**. In the centre of Scuol, the huge new **Bogn Engiadina** complex (Engadine Baths; daily 10am–10pm; ☎081/861 20 00) offers a range of pools and treatments, including saunas and both indoor and outdoor Finnish baths (Fr.23), as well as a heavenly two-hour session in the Roman-Irish baths (reserve one day ahead; Fr.54) which takes in the whole works: warm and hot rooms, vapour baths, massages, mineral plunge pools and more. Little-used streets behind the baths head down the hill into Scuol's picture-pretty Old Town, filled with traditional houses, tinkling fountains and an especially photogenic village square. The view of **Chaste Tarasp** (Tarasp Castle) on the opposite bank is now overshadowed a little by a modern hotel – the panorama from Ftan is better – but the castle is still worth a closer look; buses or a ninety-minute walk bring you to the gates. Parts of the restored seventeenth-century castle survive from its construction in 1040, and it was the seat of Austrian bailiffs of the region until Graubünden joined the

Confederation in 1803. Guided tours of the interior are in German only (June–Sept daily; contact tourist office for times and prices; SMP). The Motta Naluns **ski** area (2146m, with lifts up to 2800m) offers plenty of easy and intermediate runs, including long, thrilling reds from Piz Champatsch 12km back down to Scuol. Scuol's **snowboarding** school is the oldest in Europe. A one-day lift pass is Fr.43, or Fr.57 to include a session at the Bogn Engiadina afterwards.

East of Scuol, postbuses penetrate the wilder reaches of the valley up to the Austrian border and on to the Tyrolean hub of Landeck. Just before the frontier, a minor road curls back to climb into a cramped, isolated valley, at the very end of which sits **SAMNAUN** (*www.samnaun.ch*), the only German-speaking community in the region and, for some bizarre reason, a duty-free area. The whole place is crammed with banks, shops and cut-price petrol stations, all open long hours including Sundays. A tough, multi-day hiking trail leads from Samnaun over the Zeblasjoch pass to the famous Austrian resort of Ischgl.

Practicalities

Scuol has no monopoly on **places to stay** in the valley. Ftan has a couple of hotels – the charming, traditionally styled *La Tschuetta* stands out (☎081/864 12 30, fax 864 80 68; ③) – while the *Piz Buin*, at the edge of Guarda village (☎081/862 24 24, fax 862 24 04, *hotel.pizbuin@bluewin.ch*, *www.pizbuin.ch*; ②), is also remarkably good value. Both villages have excellent restaurants. Cross the river from Ardez on a covered wooden bridge to reach the ultimate in tranquil campsites, *Sur En* (☎081/866 35 44, fax 866 32 37), open year-round.

Scuol's **train station** is over 1km west of the centre, which is a bus ride or a ten-minute downhill walk away. The helpful **tourist office** is beside the post office (CH-7550) on Stradun (Mon–Fri 8am–noon & 2–6.30pm; June–Oct & Dec–April also Sat 10am–noon & 2–6pm, Sun 4–6pm; ☎081/861 22 22, *www.scuol.ch*). Head over the bridge below the Old Town to reach the **campsite** *Gurlaina* (☎081/864 15 01, fax 864 07 60; June to mid-Oct & mid-Dec to mid-April). Although Scuol's main drag has plenty of more or less ordinary **hotels**, there are a couple of traditional *sgraffitied* gems clustered around Plaz, the old village square: *Gabriel*, Rablüzza 159a (☎081/864 11 52, fax 864 83 58, *hotel.gabriel.scuol@bluewin.ch*; ②), is the best value, a rambling old house with terraces, roof gardens and spotless rooms; *Engiadina*, Rablüzza 152 (☎081/864 14 21, fax 864 12 45; ③), retains its attractive, oriel-windowed exterior, and also has comfortably renovated guest rooms, some of which are panelled in light, knotty pine. There are inexpensive **restaurants** along Stradun, including *Traube*, which serves quality regional fare (*menus* from Fr.25).

Zernez and around

Some 6km south of Susch sits the graceful little town of **ZERNEZ**, the slender white steeple of its church marking a junction of valleys: north is the Lower Engadine, south is the Upper Engadine, while to the east, a road leads through the vast **Parc Naziunal Svizzer** to the Ofenpass/Pass dal Fuorn and on into the Val Müstair. Although attractive enough in its own right, Zernez comes into its own as a staging post for hikes into the park. The village **tourist office** on the main street can help with maps and some guidance (Mon–Fri 8.30am–noon & 2–5.30pm; June–Oct also Sat 8.30am–noon & 2–4pm; ☎081/856 13 00), but the park office (see below) has more detailed information. The **campsite** *Cul* is 500m behind Zernez station (☎081/856 14 62; May to mid-Oct), while the town itself has plenty of **hotels**. *Piz Terza* (☎081/856 14 14, fax 856 14 15; ①) has modern, generic rooms near the church, while *Spöl* just behind it (☎081/856 12 79, fax 856 19 48; ②) is a more characterful choice; both are within ten minutes' walk of the park entrance. *Bettini* (☎081/856 11 35, fax 856 15 10; ②) is slightly further away in the town centre, but a definite step up in quality and ambience.

Parc Naziunal Svizzer

Zernez lies on the doorstep of the **Parc Naziunal Svizzer**, a swathe of Alpine wilderness stretching for 169 square kilometres either side of the Ofen/Fuorn road. Established in 1914, the park's credo is to leave nature well alone: absolutely everything, from the tiniest lichen to the six pairs of golden eagles that breed in the park, is protected. Forest fires are monitored but allowed to burn unchecked; injured animals are left to their own devices; and roaming wardens can and will impose fines should you so much as pick a flower. People are allowed to walk in the park (provided they don't step off the marked trails), but prominent notice boards publish stringent regulations prohibiting everything from littering to making loud noises. This being Switzerland, everyone takes the rules seriously, with the result that the park remains pristine, an entirely undeveloped natural environment where flora and fauna of all kinds thrive. Red and roe deer, ibex and chamois roam freely, as do hares, foxes and huge numbers of marmots. Aside from the golden eagles, there are also bearded vultures, kestrels, ravens, various woodpeckers, grouse, partridge and skylarks. The venomous northern viper or adder is also around, but you'd have to tiptoe to come upon one unawares. Pine and larch forests grow as high as 2300m, beyond which Alpine meadows are carpeted in springtime with edelweiss, gentians and a host of other high-altitude flowers. Further up still are bare rocky areas and permafrost.

About 1km east of Zernez is the National Park House, the main **information office**, open the same hours as the park itself (June–Oct daily 8.30am–6pm, Tues until 10pm; ☎081/856 13 78, *www.nationalpark.ch*). The office is overflowing with maps, trail guides (including coverage of two-, three- and four-day hikes) and useful information on animal sightings, all of it available in English. Entry to the park is free, and there are plenty of stunning **trails** through it, but it can get uncomfortably crowded on summer weekends in particular. If you're **driving**, head on the main road to any one of nine free parking areas within the park boundaries, from all of which long and short trails twist out to north and south. **Postbuses** running every two hours between Zernez and Müstair also stop at each parking area. Note that cycling in the park is prohibited. There are only two **places to stay** within the park, both of which need reserving in advance. *Hotel Il Fuorn*, beside Parking 6 (☎081/856 12 26, fax 856 18 01; ②–③), is a comfortable old lodge with shared-bath rooms, and has a newer wing with en-suite rooms. A four-hour circuit beginning and ending at the hotel takes you on a self-guided nature trail, with informative notice boards along the way outlining the park's ecology. Alternatively, a three-hour walk south from the National Park House, or a four-hour trail from Parking 3, brings you to *Chamanna/Blockhaus Cluozza* (☎081/856 12 35; ①–②), a simple Alpine hut with spartan rooms and Fr.25 dorm beds.

Val Müstair

As you crest the Ofenpass/Pass dal Fuorn 20km south of Zernez, spread out in front is the idyllic **Val Müstair**, a lush, peaceful valley pointing the way south into Italy. This finger of Switzerland is cut off by the mountains from the rest of Graubünden and is entirely surrounded by Italian territory, but nonetheless remains determinedly Romansh in language and culture. Half-a-dozen hamlets dot the green slopes on the 8km descent to picturesque **SANTA MARIA**, the main village of the valley, with a Gothic church just off its narrow main street. However, the chief reason for visiting the valley, its scenery aside, is to reach **MÜSTAIR**, the border village (pronounced *mooshtire*), some 4km further on. Virtually the last buildings before the Italian frontier are a

HIKING IN THE ENGADINE VALLEY

The 94km **Engadine valley**, with its numerous tributaries and adjacent valleys, offers a wealth of opportunities for walks of all degrees of seriousness, as well as the modest ascent of several peaks with commanding summit viewpoints. Maps which cover the area are the LS 249, 259, 268, and 269, all of them 1:50,000. Valuable reading are two books by Kev Reynolds: *Walking in the Alps* and *Walks in the Engadine* (see "Books", p.531).

Starting in the south in **Val Bregaglia**, one of the most notable villages is **Soglio** (see p.476), which sits on the right-hand hillside gazing south to Val Bondasca, Piz Badile and the blade-like Sciora aiguilles. Paths leading out of Soglio climb the hillside to Alp Tombal, to Pass da Cam and Pass Düana for the most breathtaking views. These are steep trails, while a slightly less severe path (of 4hr) entices the walker from **Promontogno** below Soglio into Val Bondasca and up to its inner recesses where the *Sciora Hut* (☎081/822 11 38) stands immediately below the pinnacles after which it is named, with Piz Badile towering above to the southwest. Experienced mountain walkers could continue for four hours over the exposed Colle Vial below Badile to the *Sasc Furä Hut* (☎081/822 12 52), or cross the high Cacciabella Pass in the east to reach the *Albigna Hut* (☎081/822 14 05) in 4hr 30min.

In the Upper Engadine, **Maloja** offers several rewarding walks, especially up to the lovely alp hamlets of Grevasalvas and Blaunca (1hr). Above them lies Lägh da Lunghin, birthplace of the River Inn, and a path which climbs to Piz Lunghin (2780m) in 3hr 30min from Maloja. From that elevated point both Engadine and Bregaglia are spread out below. Across the valley, Val Fex gives gentle walking in idyllic surroundings, while a belvedere path above its entrance makes a high traverse round to **St Moritz-Bad** (up to 5hr from Sils Maria). From St Moritz a classic walk crosses the 2755m Fuorcla Surlej for a stimulating view of Piz Bernina and Piz Roseg (*Berghaus Fuorcla Surlej*; ☎081/842 63 03), then descends into Val Roseg and continues to **Pontresina** (up to 6hr). Walkers staying in Pontresina should visit the *Coaz Hut* (☎081/842 62 78) and neighbouring *Tschierva Hut* (☎081/842 63 91), the first in 4hr 30min, the second in an hour less: both give close views of glaciers and their icefalls. The *Boval Hut* (☎081/842 64 03) is another unmissable 3hr 30min walk, giving stupendous high mountain and glacier scenery for much of the way, while the easy but steep ascent of the 3262m Piz Languard directly above Pontresina (up to 4hr) is the best place to enjoy an alpine sunrise or sunset.

The **Parc Naziunal Svizzer** in the Lower Engadine (see p.469) has any number of walks from which red and roe deer, marmots, chamois and ibex may be seen. The best base for an exploration is the *Blockhaus Cluozza* (see p.469), reached in 3hr from **Zernez**, since an overnight there enables you to cross into neighbouring valleys by a number of passes. Further down-valley, the charming village of **Guarda** (see p.467) gives access to Val Tuoi, near the head of which stands the *Tuoi Hut/Chamanna Tuoi* (☎081/862 23 22) below Piz Buin. This is gained in about 2hr 30min from Guarda, while strong walkers could continue across the right-hand ridge at the 2735m Furcletta and descend through Val Tasna to **Ardez** – a total of 7hr 30min.

Scuol (see p.467) is the main resort in the Lower Engadine. Behind it to the south, Val S-charl leads to **S-charl**, a tiny summer-only hamlet at a confluence of glens. From here, walkers could cross Fuorcla Funtana da S-charl to the Ofen Pass/Pass dal Fuorn (3hr 30min); the Pass da Costainas to Santa Maria in Val Müstair (5hr; see p.469); or take an easy 1hr stroll to Alp Sesvenna among streams and pastures that are full of Alpine flowers in early summer.

Carolingian monastery and church, the **Baselgia San Jon**, or Klosterkirche St Johann, reputedly founded by Charlemagne himself around 800 and still a functioning Benedictine convent today. The site has been deemed by UNESCO to be a cultural heritage site of world importance for the array of brilliantly coloured **Romanesque frescoes** adorning the interior of its monastery church (free entry). The style and detail of the frescoes, which depict stories such as the stoning of St Stephen and the Dance of

Salome, are breathtaking, and the atmosphere of the church, its adjacent cemetery and cobbled courtyard make the journey well worth while. A small **museum** off the court-yard has chunks of Carolingian carving and Baroque statues and icons (June–Oct Mon–Sat 9–11am & 2–5pm; Feb–May Mon 2–5pm, Sun 3–5pm; Fr.3).

A **tourist office** in Müstair has information on the whole valley (Mon–Fri 9–11am & 2–6pm; ☎081/858 50 00, *www.muestair.ch*). Santa Maria has a quiet and characterful HI **hostel**, *Chasa Plaz* (☎081/858 50 52, fax 858 54 96; ①; June–Oct & mid-Dec to April), with dorms from Fr.23, while in Müstair there's the good-value *Landgasthof Münsterhof* (☎081/858 55 41, fax 858 50 58, *muensterhof@swissonline.ch*; ③), its characterful old rooms filled with antiques. Behind the border petrol station – which offers Internet access – is Müstair's **campsite** (☎081/858 54 10), in a peaceful spot on the riverside.

The Upper Engadine

The **Upper Engadine** (Engiadin'Ota in Romansh, Oberengadin in German), is justly celebrated as one of the most scenic valleys in Switzerland, a heart-stoppingly beautiful array of forests, snowy mountains and silvery lakes, raised high at 1800m and looking southwest directly into the crispest and clearest sunshine in the Alps. The long, straight 55km run southwest from Zernez takes in a handful of attractive little resorts, all of them entirely overshadowed by **St Moritz**, which holds court in mid-valley. In point of fact, many of the smaller fry – such as **Pontresina** and **Celerina** – that tug on St Moritz's skirts have more to offer than their mentor, but for a century past and proba-bly for a century to come, the Moritz name is the one that sells.

Crossing the two major mountain passes that lead on from St Moritz delivers you into small fingers of territory entirely unlike the rest of Graubünden. To the southwest, the Maloja Pass feeds into the deep and lush **Val Bregaglia**, while to the southeast, a road and rail line crosses the Bernina Pass into the equally idyllic **Val Poschiavo**. Both are thoroughly Italian, in language, culture and flora, and both offer a taste of Mediterranean-style living that's like a revelation after the high mountain valleys.

St Moritz

ST MORITZ sticks out like a sore thumb. Seemingly plopped down unceremoniously amidst the quiet villages of the Engadine – although, of course, it was here long before they were, a spa as far back as the Bronze Age – St Moritz is a brassy, in-your-face reminder of the world beyond the high valley walls, the kind of place that gives money a bad name. For a century or more, it's been the prime winter retreat of the interna-tional jetset, who over the years have created a mini-Manhattan of Vuitton and Armani in this stunningly romantic setting of forest, lake and mountains. When the tourist office trumpets St Moritz's "champagne climate", they don't necessarily mean the sparkling sunshine – although there's plenty of that as well, 322 days of it a year on aver-age. And yet the town itself is neither cosmopolitan, attractive nor graceful; its ski-slopes engaging but – compared with Davos or the Jungfrau – generally undemanding. What St Moritz has that no other resort has is the name, and that glisters better than gold, enough for the tourist board to make it a patented registered trademark so that no one else can touch it. Presidents and princes, Hollywood starlets, nobility and nou-veaux riches clamour to be associated with St Moritz, and the place gladly responds, turning on the razzle all winter long with a endless round of banquets, celebrations and spectacles centred around the frozen Lej da San Murezzan lake, including horse racing, polo and even cricket on ice. Summer is downtime, when the hoi polloi arrive to hike and relax in the sunshine. The range of sports and activities on offer both in winter and summer is vast, but despite the hype there's not much sense of adventure – all that money tends to get in the way. The final, mortal blow is that the Swiss themselves turn their backs on St Moritz: less than a third of the town's visitors are locals. Like Leicester Square in London or Fisherman's Wharf in San Francisco, it's good to see St Moritz … but it's a relief to get away.

Arrival, orientation and information

The town spans two villages: when people refer to St Moritz, they're talking about **St Moritz-Dorf**, a cluster of hotels, restaurants and boutiques on the hillside above the lake. **St Moritz-Bad**, far removed from the glitz 2km southwest down on the lakeshore, is a distinctly unattractive mini-sprawl of concrete apartment blocks and sports halls. Via dal Bagn connects the two. The **train station** (also the main postbus terminus, and the place to reserve for the Palm Express postbus to Lugano) is awkwardly placed below Dorf, on the opposite side of the lake from Bad; it has a money-changing counter (daily 6.50am–8.10pm).

Via Serlas winds up from the station past the main post office (CH-7500) to the central square of Dorf. The **tourist office** is 100m east at Via Maistra 12 (July–Aug & Dec–April Mon–Sat 9am–6pm; Christmas–March also Sun 4–6pm; rest of year Mon–Fri 8am–noon & 2–6pm, Sat 9am–noon; ☎081/837 33 33, *www.stmoritz.ch*).

Accommodation

Few bargains come wrapped with the St Moritz name, and **accommodation** is no exception: prices are high across the board, and during the winter season they go stratospheric. The **campsite** – *Olympiaschanze* – is about 1km southwest of Bad (☎081/833 40 90; June–Sept), and there's a modern, good quality HI **hostel**, the *Stille*, at Via Surpunt 60 in Bad (☎081/833 39 69, fax 833 80 46; ②), with dorm beds, including obligatory half board, costing a moritzy Fr.43 (bike rental available). There are dozens of **hotels** scattered through Dorf and Bad, virtually all of which are closed in the April and November between-seasons.

Badrutt's Palace, Via Serlas 27, Dorf (☎081/837 10 00, fax 837 29 99, *palace@palace-st-moritz.ch*, *www.palace-st-moritz.ch*). Legendary five-star palace that started the whole St Moritz tale back in 1864, when Johannes Badrutt lay down a challenge to a party of English summer regulars: spend a winter here, he said, and I'll foot the bill. They came, then their friends came the year after, and since then Badrutt has been quids in. These days, unless you're willing to toss zeros around like confetti, you probably won't even get past the flunkey on the door: men must wear a jacket and tie just to stand in the lobby. If you do get in, make the most of it – this is the haunt of filmstars, princesses (real and wannabe) and more fur than you'll find walking around in the forest. You'd like a room in Christmas week? That'll be Fr.1700. ⑨.

Bellaval, Via Grevas 55, Dorf (☎081/833 32 45, fax 833 04 06). The cheapest rooms in Dorf, right beside the station, spartan and not especially well taken care of. ②.

Bernina, Via dal Bagn 5, Bad (☎081/833 60 22, fax 833 19 40). Quality low-end option that avoids excessive winter price-hikes and has a range of shared-bath and en-suite rooms – all of them small, but then so are the prices (relatively speaking). ②.

Languard, Via Veglia 14, Dorf (☎081/833 31 37, fax 833 45 46, *languard@bluewin.ch*). Comfortable, friendly little family hotel in the middle of Dorf that keeps a tighter lid on its winter surcharges than its near neighbours. ③.

National, Via da l'Ova Cotschna 1, Bad (☎081/833 32 74, fax 833 32 75; mid-June to mid-Oct only). Well out of the crush, behind the Bad post office, with serviceable – and affordable – en-suite and shared-bath rooms. ②.

Nolda, Via Crasta 3, Bad (☎081/833 05 75, fax 833 87 51, *info@nolda.ch*, *www.nolda.ch*). Pleasant enough pack-'em-in hotel next to the Signal cable-car, with pine-clad rooms that do the job. ④.

Sporthotel Stille, beside the hostel in Bad (☎081/833 69 48, fax 833 07 08). Popular with skiers and snowboarders, who crowd out its no-frills rooms. ①.

Steffani, Plazza da la Posta Veglia 1, Dorf (☎081/832 21 01, fax 833 40 97). Comfortable, business-class hotel on the central square, with a few airs and graces but efficient and welcoming. ⑦.

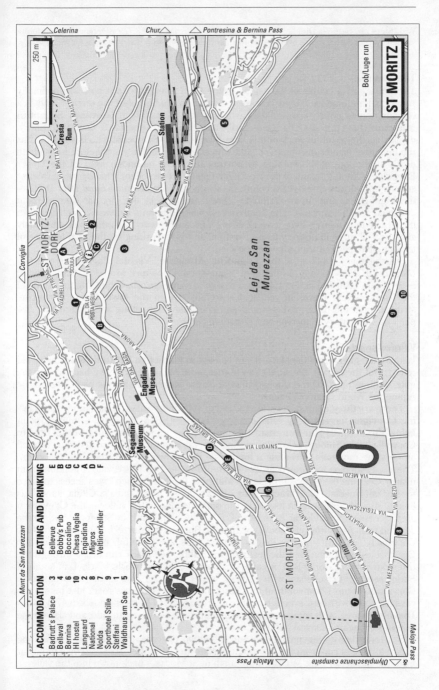

ST MORITZ

----- Bob/Luge run

△ Celerina

Chur △ △ Pontresina & Bernina Pass

0   250 m

Cresta Run

△ Corviglia

ST MORITZ DORF

Station

VIA MAISTRA

VIA BRATTAS

VIA SERLAS

VIA VEGLIA

PL. DA SCOULA

VIA MAISTRA

VIA QUADRELLAS

VIA STREDA

PL. DA LA POSTA VEGLIA

VIA ARONA

VIA SOMPLAZ

VIA DA BASN

Engadine Museum

Segantini Museum

VIA GREVAS

VIA GREVAS

Lej da San Murezzan

VIA GREVAS

VIA DAL BAGN

VIA LUDAINS

VIA SALET

VIA SELA

VIA SURPUN

VIA MEZDI

VIA TEGIAITSCHA

VIA ROSATSCH

VIA GIOVANNI SEGANTINI

VIA SAN GIAN

VIA MEZDI

VIA MEZDI

ST MORITZ-BAD

△ Munt da San Murezzan

△ Munt da San Murezzan

ACCOMMODATION	
Badrutt's Palace	3
Bellaval	4
Bernina	6
HI hostel	10
Languard	2
National	8
Nolda	7
Sporthotel Stille	9
Steffani	1
Waldhaus am See	5

EATING AND DRINKING	
Bellevue	E
Bobby's Pub	B
Boccalino	G
Chesa Veglia	C
Engiadina	A
Migros	D
Veltlinerkeller	F

△ Olympiaschanze campsite

Maloja Pass △

Maloja Pass

Maloja Pass △

Waldhaus am See, Via Dim Lej 6, Dorf (☎081/833 76 76, fax 833 88 77). Big, quiet lodge offering inoffensive, renovated rooms overlooking the lake below Dorf, with discount rates for weekly stays. ⑤.

The Town

There are only a couple of diversions in the town to explore, but both are definitely worth making time for. About 1km west of Dorf on Via Somplaz, the terrace road, is a curious domed church-like building which holds the excellent **Giovanni Segantini Museum** (June to mid-Oct & Dec–April Tues–Sun 10am–noon & 3–6pm; Fr.7; SMP), displaying the beautiful work of this largely self-taught Symbolist who is acclaimed as the definitive painter of Alpine life, and who spent the twelve years before his sudden death at the age of 41 working to portray the clear mountain light of the Upper Engadine. Although many of the works on display are excellent – including an intense self-portrait, drawn three years before his death, and the poignant *Dead Deer* (1892) – the highlight is the Alpine Triptych, shown upstairs in the circular domed room designed for the purpose. The sequence of vast, luminous canvases, each between three and four metres long, covers *Birth*, *Life* and *Death*. Segantini had studiously sketched all three in entirety as preparation, and was working on the final touches of the complete painted triptych when he died.

On the terrace below is the **Engadine Museum**, Via dal Bagn 39 (June–Oct Mon–Fri 9.30am–noon & 2–5pm, Sun 10am–noon; Dec–April Mon–Fri 10am–noon & 2–5pm, Sun 10am–noon; Fr.5), housed in a solid stone *sgraffitied* building that's one of the few surviving pieces of vernacular architecture in the town. Inside are reconstructed interiors of farmhouses and patrician mansions, along with interesting displays on the history of the spa and Engadine culture.

Winter sports

With all the glamour of the place, it can be easy to forget that St Moritz is actually a ski resort. But then again, the skiing (*www.skiengadin.ch*) is really only a backdrop to the glitz, although in 2003 the slopes will take centre stage as St Moritz plays host to the Alpine Ski World Championships.

There are three main sectors. On the north side of the valley is the sunny, south-facing **Corviglia**, accessed by cable-car from St Moritz-Bad to Signal, a midway point below the Munt da San Murezzan (2659m), and by funicular from St Moritz-Dorf to Corviglia itself (2468m), below the soaring Piz Nair summit at 3057m. Red runs abound all over the mountain, including a long piste down through the trees into the valley. There's a half-pipe for snowboarders on the Munt da San Murezzan. A gondola from nearby Celerina (see opposite) rises to Marguns (2278m), which gives access to more testing intermediate and difficult runs off Las Trais Fluors and Piz Glüna, as well as linking directly to Corviglia itself. On the opposite side of the valley is the **Corvatsch** area, accessed by cable-car from Surlej, a hamlet 3km south of St Moritz-Bad, and a chairlift from Alp Surlej, just above the hamlet. Both serve Murtèl below the peak of Piz Corvatsch (3451m) – again, long sweeping reds are plentiful, especially from the Corvatsch Bergstation, and the testing 8km Hahnensee black run drops through the trees down to St Moritz-Bad. A cable-car from the village of Sils Maria 4km south of Surlej serves Furtschellas, with its own welter of blues and scenic reds linked to Corvatsch. Some 12km south of St Moritz on the Bernina Pass road, just before the pass itself and with easy access from the nearby resort of Pontresina (see p.476), is the **Diavolezza** area, with some long, steep difficult runs on the south side, and also off the face of Piz Lagalb (2959m) opposite.

St Moritz boasts legendary bob and toboggan courses, including an exhilarating 4.2km toboggan run from the viewpoint of **Muottas Muragl** – accessed by a funicular from the hamlet of Punt Muragl, 4km north of St Moritz – back down into the valley, a vertical drop of 700m (you can rent a sled at the top). The death-defying **Cresta Run** is for pros only, but the 1.6km **Olympic bob-run** (*www.olympia-bobrun.ch*) is open to amateurs, with advance registration required (contact the St Moritz tourist office). There's also the famous five-kilometre **Preda–Bergün toboggan run** (*www.berguen.ch*): wooden sleds can be rented to make the winter run from Preda station, just over the Albula Pass, and the specially modified track run takes you down through the scenic Albula valley to Bergün, from where RhB trains will cart you back to the beginning (Fr.29 for a day ticket). Trains run late, so you can sled the illuminated route by night.

There's a range of different **passes**. A one-day pass for Corvatsch and Furtschellas, or for Corviglia, Piz Nair and Marguns, is Fr.50, for Diavolezza Fr.44. Three consecutive days for all areas costs Fr.144, or Fr.150 for three days in any four. Similarly, six consecutive days comes to Fr.258, or Fr.232 for five days in any six. For the well heeled, there's a **season ticket** which also covers the lifts in Gstaad for Fr.800, as well as a TOP-Skipass season ticket taking in the Upper Engadine, Davos/Klosters, Arosa, Flims/Laax and Gstaad – a snip at Fr.930. All these cover **free transport** on city buses between Dorf and Bad, RhB trains to the Bernina Pass and between Samedan and Pontresina, as well as postbuses from Silvaplana to Surlej, Sils Maria to the Furtschellas station, and St Moritz all the way through the Val Bregaglia to Castasegna and Soglio.

Eating and drinking

You'll find no bargains **eating and drinking** in St Moritz. The best place to look is Via dal Bagn down towards Bad – down here are a giant new *Migros*, the inexpensive *Bellevue* with self-service meals (closed Sun), and *Boccalino* at Via dal Bagn 6 (☎081/832 11 11), a lively, bustling place with a range of quality wood-fired pizzas for under Fr.15, as well as pasta staples. The *Veltlinerkeller*, Via dal Bagn 11 (☎081/833 40 09), is a perennial favourite; ignore the hunting trophies on the walls, and concentrate on the quality, lightly prepared food in front of you – excellent pastas, fish dishes and grilled meats with *menus* starting at around Fr.22. *Engiadina*, on Plazza da Scuola 10 in the middle of Dorf (☎081/833 32 65; closed Sun), is another popular place, this time concentrating on fondue – pay about Fr.26 for the ordinary version, or considerably more for the house special with extra champagne. The famous *Chesa Veglia*, Via Veglia 2 in the middle of Dorf (☎081/837 28 00), is one of St Moritz's swankier restaurants, with three separate dining areas, all of them exclusive, expensive and cloying. If you're looking for a meal to remember, spurn the array of top-end restaurants in town and reserve well ahead for the *Marmite* at the top station of the Corviglia funicular (☎081/833 63 55) – if caviar and truffles at 2500m are to your liking, that is.

St Moritz has a plethora of exclusive **bars**, discos, nightclubs and drinking dens – most of which are either for members only, shielded by sky-high entry fees, or simply dull and expensive. Cut your losses and have a pint at *Bobby's Pub*, Via dal Bagn 52, instead.

Around St Moritz

A handful of resorts cluster around St Moritz, all of them characterful places to stay and offering easy access to skiing and hiking facilities throughout the area. Just 2km – or a half-hour walk – east of St Moritz is **CELERINA**, also known by its Romansh name of **Schlarigna**. This pleasant small town on the banks of the Inn has an atmospheric old cobbled quarter of traditional Engadine architecture, and it's also the base station for a gondola rising to the ski slopes of Corviglia (see opposite). On a grassy knoll about 1km east of the centre is the isolated **Baselgia San Gian**, with a Romanesque choir and a painted wooden ceiling dating from 1478 (mid-June to mid-Oct Mon 2–4pm, Wed 4–5.30pm, Fri 10.30am–noon; Dec–March Wed 2–4pm; free). The **tourist office** is in the centre on Via Maistra (Mon–Fri 8.30am–noon & 2–6pm, Sat 10am–noon & 3–5pm;

☎081/830 00 11, *www.celerina.ch*). There's a handful of inexpensive hotels in the centre, but the most characterful choice is the *Chesa Rosatsch*, a 350-year-old inn on the riverbank (☎081/837 01 01, fax 837 01 00, *hotel@rosatsch.ch*, *www.rosatsch.ch*; ④).

On the other side of the valley from Celerina rises the ridge of **Muottas Muragl** (2455m), starting point for a 4.2km toboggan run (see p.474). The view from the top, some 700m above the valley, is one of the highlights of a visit to the region, offering a clear, uninterrupted gaze southwest up the length of the Engadine, its string of lakes glittering in the sunlight. The plain, shared-bath rooms of the *Berghotel* on the top (☎081/842 82 32, fax 842 82 90, *hotelmmb@skiengadin.ch*; ②) are a rare bargain.

Less than 2km up the Bernina Pass road from Punt Muragl is the swish resort of **PONTRESINA**, lying in a privileged, wind-sheltered position on a southwest-facing terrace amidst meadows and fragrant woods. Access to the Diavolezza slopes is easy from here (see p.474), and the scenery of high rocky peaks to east and west interspersed with glaciers – most notably the huge Morteratsch Glacier, sidling down from Piz Bernina (4049m) – is impressive. The small village has St-Moritzy aspirations, with fully half-a-dozen luxury palace hotels and a glitteringly modern main street. The **tourist office** is in the centre on Via Maistra (Mon–Fri 8.30am–noon & 2–6pm, Sat 8.30am–noon & 3–6pm; ☎081/838 83 00, *www.pontresina.com*). *Pensione Valtellina*, also on Via Maistra (☎081/842 64 06; ①), is a cosy little **hotel** with simple rooms and a shower down the corridor, while the *Bahnhof* is across the river by the station (☎081/838 80 00, fax 838 80 09; ②). Next door there are dorms for Fr.30 and bikes for rent at the HI **hostel** *Tolais* (☎081/842 72 23, fax 842 70 31; ①), trailhead for routes into the deep and dramatic Val Roseg (see box p.470).

Val Bregaglia

The Engadine continues to rise gently for 16km beyond St Moritz, past the little resort villages of Silvaplana and Sils on their own lakes, to the **Maloja Pass** (1815m). Tough hiking trails to the north climb into the mountains up to the Lunghin Pass, a rare triple watershed: from this point, the Inn flows to the Danube, and from there to the Black Sea; the Julier flows via the Rhine to the North Sea; and the Maira flows into the Po, and then into the Mediterranean.

From Maloja, the road suddenly tumbles off the cliff edge and down in a series of concertina switchbacks into the beautiful **Val Bregaglia** (Bergell in German), one of Graubünden's three Italian-speaking valleys – the others are Mesolcina (see opposite) and Poschiavo (see below). Suddenly, everything is different: the crisp air of the Alps is replaced by the warm breezes of the south, pine forests and rocky, snowy crags by lush, green vegetation, and *sgraffitied* bungalows by flinty, slate-roofed cottages.

Roughly 14km from the pass is the main village of the valley, **Vicosoprano**, an attractive, quiet place bypassed by the main road which heads on south through tiny **STAMPA**, birthplace of the painter Augusto Giacometti and his son, the sculptor Alberto, and home to the valley's **tourist office** (Mon–Fri 9–11.30am & 3–5.30pm; July–Sept also Sat 9–11.30am; ☎081/822 15 55). The road shadows the river, coiling on down the valley past ruined hilltop castles and isolated, crumbling roadside churches.

From the hamlet of **Promontogno**, 3km west of Stampa and about the same distance east of the border village Castasegna, postbuses follow a narrow branch road which climbs the north wall of the valley to **SOGLIO**. This eyrie of a hamlet, narrow, cobbled alleys lined with close-set stone buildings, offers tremendous panoramic views over the valley: its lofty terrace sits opposite the 3300-metre Pizzo Badile, and is backed by the equally lofty Piz dal Märc and Piz Duan. The village is the focus of a wealth of mountain walks, easy ones following a valley-side route down to Stampa (2hr), as well as longer high-level hikes back to Vicosoprano, or up through the treeline behind the village (see box p.470). But there are lazier reasons to spend a day or three in Soglio: the

Palazzo Salis in the village (☎081/822 12 08, fax 822 16 00; ②; Easter–Oct) is one of Switzerland's more extraordinary hotels. Soglio was the seat of the Von Salis family long before 1630, when the *palazzo* was constructed, and the hotel is still owned by the same family today. The whole place is an eye-opening experience, from the echoing vaulted hall, crammed with antique furniture, chaise longues, open fireplaces and suits of armour, to its grand guest rooms (none en suite), stone-floored down below, wood-floored above, complete with four-poster beds and antique stoves.

Val Poschiavo

From Pontresina, the **Bernina Pass** (2328m) is about 15km southeast. This route is part of the Bernina Express, one of the packaged train rides which carry panorama carriages from Chur, Davos and St Moritz into the idyllic **Val Poschiavo** and down to the Italian border town of Tirano, from where postbuses skirt the shores of Lake Como, ending up back in Switzerland at Lugano (see p.38). Ordinary trains also run on regular schedules between St Moritz, Pontresina and Tirano: however you travel in the valley, it's still gorgeous. A classic vantage point from which to look over the whole area is **Alp Grüm**, on the train line but not the road (reachable after a two-hour walk from the car park at the *Ospizio Bernina* inn on the pass): from 2091m on a bright day you can see clear down to the Lago di Poschiavo and beyond. The *Belvedere* hotel and restaurant (mid-May to Oct) provides refreshment while you're up there.

After a series of hairpins, the railway joins the road again at the little village of **San Carlo**, watched over by its ancient church tower, and heads on a couple of kilometres further to **POSCHIAVO**. The difference between this laid-back, photogenic Italianate town, and, the Alpine resort of Pontresina the same distance the other side of the pass, couldn't be more striking. Poschiavo's tranquil old quarter, just across the river from the train station, is filled with tall, foursquare eighteenth-century shuttered mansions in various shades of pastel, their windowboxes overflowing with local carnations, overlooking sunny plazas that are stone-paved in swirling patterns and ringed with terrace cafés. The place is perfect for soaking up some sunshine – of which there's plenty – filling up on risotto instead of fondue, and savouring a carafe of Valtellina wine from the Italian regions bordering. On the north side of the central Piazza Comunale, also labelled with its Romansh name of Plazza da Cumün, is the seventeenth-century Protestant **Chiesa di Sant'Ignazio**, which holds an inscription stating that the town was *riformata da gli errori e superstizioni* in 1520. Despite this claim, the Catholic **Chiesa San Vittore**, dating from the late fifteenth century, remains a powerful presence 200m away on the south side of the square. The same square holds the **tourist office** (Mon–Fri 8am–noon & 2–6pm; July & Aug also Sat 9am–noon & 2–5pm; ☎081/844 05 71, *www.valposchiavo.ch*). Of the **hotels**, *Croce Bianca*, a five-minute walk south near a row of graceful old townhouses (☎081/844 01 44, fax 844 12 70, *croce. bianca@swissonline.ch*; ②), and *Suisse*, on Via da Mez southwest of the square (☎081/844 07 88, fax 844 19 67, *hotel.suisse@bluewin.ch*, *www.forum.ch/suisse*; ②–③), are both long-standing fixtures in the town but with newly renovated rooms.

South to Tirano

Beyond the Lago di Poschiavo and the village of **Brusio** – with its famous, and much-photographed, circular viaduct bringing trains gently down to the valley floor – is the Italian border at tiny Campocologno, 16km south of Poschiavo. Some 4km further is the Italian town of **TIRANO**, terminus of Swiss trains. The Swiss station (with a money-changing counter) and its Italian counterpart (with trains to Milan roughly every two hours) sit adjacent to each other, with passport control between the two. Swiss postbuses to Lugano – the second leg of the Bernina Express – depart from round the corner (signposted). To reach Tirano's **tourist office**, walk ahead to the traffic lights – it's beside the "Viale 44" shop (Tues & Wed 10am–noon, Thurs 9.30–10.30am & 3–5pm, Fri 9.30–10.30am, Sat 10am–noon & 3–5pm; ☎0039-0342/706.066). The Old Town, dead ahead on the west bank of the river, is extremely picturesque and almost entirely residential, with cobbled, arcaded courtyards, and tiny sloping lanes leading up to the medieval Porta Bormina at the top of the town, beyond which lie open meadows. Just off a busy roundabout 1km northwest of the centre is the pilgrimage church of **Madonna di Tirano**, commemorating an appearance of the Virgin on September 29, 1504. Its fantastically lavish interior boasts an especially ornately carved organ case, while the shrine is focused around a statue of Mary – proclaimed by Pope Pius XII the patron saint of the Valtellina valley, where Tirano sits – dressed in a silk and gold robe donated in 1746 by the people of the valley.

travel details

TRAINS

Arosa to: Chur (hourly; 1hr).

Chur to: Arosa (hourly; 1hr); Buchs (hourly; 35min); Davos Dorf & Platz (hourly; 1hr 30min; summer change in Landquart); Disentis/Mustér (hourly; 1hr 20min); Ilanz (hourly; 40min); Klosters (hourly; 1hr 10min); Maienfeld (hourly; 15min); Rhäzüns (hourly; 20min); St Gallen (hourly; 1hr 35min); St Moritz (hourly; 2hr); Sargans (hourly; 25min); Thusis (twice hourly; 30–45min); Tiefencastel (hourly; 50min); Tirano via Bernina Pass (June–Oct 1 daily; 4hr 30min); Zermatt via Andermatt & Brig (1–3 daily; 5hr 45min); Zürich (hourly; 1hr 35min).

Davos (Platz & Dorf) to: Chur (hourly; 1hr 30min); Klosters (twice hourly; 25min); Tirano via Bernina Pass (June–Oct 1 daily; 3hr 30min).

Disentis/Mustér to: Andermatt via Oberalppass (hourly; 1hr 10min); Chur (hourly; 1hr 20min); Ilanz (hourly; 40min).

Ilanz to: Chur (hourly; 40min); Disentis/Mustér (hourly; 40min).

Klosters to: Chur (hourly; 1hr 10min); Davos Dorf & Platz (twice hourly; 25min); Scuol (hourly; 45min).

Maienfeld to: Chur (hourly; 15min).

Pontresina to: St Moritz (hourly; 10min).

Poschiavo to: St Moritz (hourly; 1hr 40min); Tirano (hourly; 45min).

St Moritz to: Pontresina (hourly; 10min); Poschiavo (hourly; 1hr 40min); Tirano via Bernina Pass (hourly; 2hr 30min); Zermatt via Andermatt & Brig (1–2 daily; 8hr); Zernez (hourly; 55min; change at Samedan).

Thusis to: Chur (twice hourly; 30–45min); St Moritz (hourly; 1hr 35min).

Zernez to: St Moritz (hourly; 50min; change at Samedan).

BUSES

Andeer to: Juf (5 daily; 55min).

Chur to: Bellinzona via San Bernadino Tunnel (every 2hr; 2hr 15min); Flims (twice hourly; 45min); St Moritz via Julier Pass (1–2 daily; 2hr 40min); Splügen (every 2hr; 1hr); Zillis (every 2hr; 40min).

Davos (Platz & Dorf) to: Zernez via Flüela Pass (July–Oct every 2hr; 1hr).

Disentis/Mustér to: Biasca via Lukmanier/Lucomagno Pass (June–Sept 2 daily; 1hr 55min).

Flims to: Chur (twice hourly; 45min); Laax (twice hourly; 10min).

Laax to: Flims (twice hourly; 10min); Ilanz (hourly; 25min).

Müstair to: Zernez (every 2hr; 1hr 10min).

St Moritz to: Lugano via Chiavenna, Italy (1–2 daily; 4hr); Soglio (every 2hr; 1hr 25min; change at Promontogno).

Soglio to: St Moritz (every 2hr; 1hr 40min; change at Promontogno).

Splügen to: Bellinzona (every 2hr; 1hr 20min); Chur (every 2hr; 1hr); Thusis (hourly; 35min).

Thusis to: Bellinzona (every 2hr; 1hr 50min); Splügen (hourly; 35min).

Tiefencastel to: Bivio (hourly; 55min).

Zernez to: Davos Dorf & Platz via Flüela Pass (July–Oct every 2hr; 1hr); Müstair via Pass dal Fuorn (every 2hr; 1hr 10min).

Zillis to: Chur (every 2hr; 40min); Thusis (hourly; 15min).

INTERNATIONAL TRAINS

Chur to: Amsterdam (1 daily; 10hr 40min); Brussels (2 daily; 9hr 30min); Hamburg (1 daily; 12hr 30min); Frankfurt (2 daily; 5hr 50min); Köln (2 daily; 7hr 50min); Paris (1 daily; 9hr 30min).

Tirano (Switzerland/Italy) to: Milan (at least 5 daily; 2hr 30min).

INTERNATIONAL BUSES

St Moritz to: Chiavenna, Italy, via Maloja Pass (every 2hr; 1hr 40min).

Scuol to: Landeck, Austria (every 2hr; 2hr).

Thusis to: Chiavenna, Italy, via Splügen Pass (2 daily; 2hr 40min; change at Splügen).

Tirano (Switzerland/Italy) to: Lugano via Italy (June–Oct 1 daily; 3hr 15min).

PLACE NAMES IN THIS CHAPTER		
German	**French**	**Italian**
Chur	Coire	Coira
Graubünden	Grisons	Grigioni
Hinterrhein	Rhin Postérieur	Reno Posteriore
Lukmanier	Lukmanier	Lucomagno
Ofen	Ofen	Fuorn
Österreich	Autriche	Austria
Rhein	Rhin	Reno
Tessin	Tessin	Ticino
Vorderrhein	Rhin Antérieur	Reno Anteriore

CHAPTER TWELVE

TICINO

It is strange how different the sun-dried, ancient, southern slopes of the world are, from the northern slopes. It is as if the god Pan really had his home among these sunbleached stones and tough, sun-dark trees. So I was content, coming down into Airolo . . .

D.H. Lawrence

The Italian-speaking canton of **TICINO** (*Tessin* in German and French) occupies the balmy, lake-laced southern foothills of the Alps. It's radically different from the rest of the country in almost every way: culture, food, architecture, attitude and driving style owe more to Milan than Zürich, and the famously sunny skies even draw in fog-bound Milanese for a breath of air. Every Swiss has their own favourite bit of the country – the mountain panorama above Interlaken, morning mist on Lake Luzern, perhaps the waterfront promenade at Vevey – but everybody loves the Ticino. The place is simply irresistible: a short train ride under the Alps and you can emerge in glittering sunshine to a tiny corner of the Italian Mediterranean that is forever Switzerland, peopled by expressive, stylish, hot-blooded folk as different from the stolid farmers of the north as they could possibly be. And it's no wonder they're hot-blooded. As an ethnic and linguistic minority of eight percent in their own country and nothing more than a quaint irrelevance to the city hotshots of Milan and Turin next door, the Ticinesi consistently have to struggle to get their voices heard in the corridors of power.

The glamour of their canton, and its stunning natural beauty – lushly wooded hills rising from azure water, date palms swaying against deep blue skies, red roofs framed by purple bougainvillea – often seem to blind outsiders with romance. And the German-speaking Swiss in particular fall head over heels for the Latin paradise on their doorstep. It takes just three hours from the grey streets of suburban Zürich to reach the fragrant subtropical gardens of Lugano, and from March till November German Swiss come in their thousands to sit beneath vine-shaded outdoor terraces of simple *grotti* or *osterie* (rustic local taverns) and choose polenta, risotto or herb-scented salads from bilingual Italian-German menus, sample a carafe of one of the dozens of varieties of Ticinese merlot, and still pay with francs at the end.

ACCOMMODATION PRICE CODES

All the hostels, pensions and hotels in this book have been graded according to the following price codes, which indicate the price for the cheapest double room available during the high season. Single rooms can cost anything between sixty and eighty percent of the double-room rate. For hostels with dormitories, the price per bed has been quoted. See p.45 for more details.

① under Fr.100	④ Fr.200–250	⑦ Fr.350–400
② Fr.100–150	⑤ Fr.250–300	⑧ Fr.400–500
③ Fr.150–200	⑥ Fr.300–350	⑨ over Fr.500

The best way to **get around** in Ticino depends on what you're planning to see and do. **Train** services, either run by **FFS** (the Italian abbreviation for SBB, the federal railway company) or by one or two local operators, are perfectly fine for accessing the three major towns, Bellinzona, Locarno and Lugano, with **local buses** from each of them serving points close at hand. However, if you want to explore the hinterland but your time is at all pressed, relying on public transport alone can be frustrating: **postbuses** penetrate to even the remotest valley and hamlet, but tend to run on schedules that leave a two-hour gap between services. **Renting a car** would be a better option, but you should bear in mind that all three major towns, and the roads between them, are choked with **cars**, and it can be quite literally impossible to find a parking space in the town centres.

Oddly, there's no cantonal transport pass, only two regional offerings which overlap on coverage: you should check the exact terms at a tourist office before you buy, and match the right one with your travel plans. The **Lugano Regional Pass** gives free travel on trains and boats on and around Lago di Lugano (including the funiculars up to San Salvatore and Monte Brè), with half-price discounts on transport around Locarno, for three days within seven (Fr.70) or seven consecutive days (Fr.92). Similarly, the **Locarno/Ascona Regional Pass** gives free travel on trains and boats in the Swiss basin of Lago Maggiore, plus half-price on funiculars, chairlifts and transport in and around Lugano, for three days in seven (Fr.50) or seven consecutive days (Fr.76). Both are offered in the summer only (April–Oct), and both are given at a discount to Swiss Pass holders.

Ticino Turismo are the most professional and efficient of all the Swiss tourist organizations, and have libraries full of excellent brochures and leaflets publicizing the canton. Contact them at Villa Turrita, CP 1441, CH-6501 Bellinzona (☎091/825 70 56, fax 825 36 14, *ett@tourism-ticino.ch*, *www.tourism-ticino.ch*).

Although linguistically, culturally and temperamentally Italian, the Ticino has been controlled by the Swiss since the early 1500s, when Uri, Schwyz and Unterwalden moved to secure the southern approaches of the Gotthard Pass against the Dukes of Milan. For three centuries the Ticinesi remained under the thumb of the tyrannical northerners, until **Napoleon** arrived in 1798 to reorganize the area under his new Cisalpine Republic. But faced with a mere exchange of overlords, the Ticinisi held out for independence, and under the banner "Liberi e Svizzeri!", "Free and Swiss!", the **Republic of Ticino** joined the Confederation as a new canton in 1803.

Since then, the Ticinesi – appearances notwithstanding – remain resolutely Swiss, and have little truck with foreigners calling them Italian, although it's also almost impossible for an outsider to tell the locals apart from the 36,000 Italian *frontalieri* who cross into Ticino daily to work for salaries well below the Swiss average. A cruel irony of life here is that Ticino suffers Switzerland's highest **unemployment** rates, even while its service industries thrive – staffed by Italians and paid for by thousands of Swiss-German tourists and second-homeowners. Similarly, young Ticinesi, who would naturally gravitate towards universities or jobs in nearby Milan, are forced by their lack of an EU passport to go north into culturally and linguistically "foreign" Switzerland instead. The reality behind Ticino's glamorous front is a tale of fifty years or more of social dislocation and a draining, deep-rooted frustration with chiefly Swiss-German-inspired isolationism.

Architecture and design have been taken seriously for centuries past, with a string of world-class architects emanating from the Ticino from the Middle Ages onwards – among the contemporary crop, **Mario Botta** stands out (his most famous building is perhaps the new San Francisco Museum of Modern Art), along with Luigi Snozzi and Aurelio Galfetti. The tradition is now augmented by an Academy of Architecture, affili-

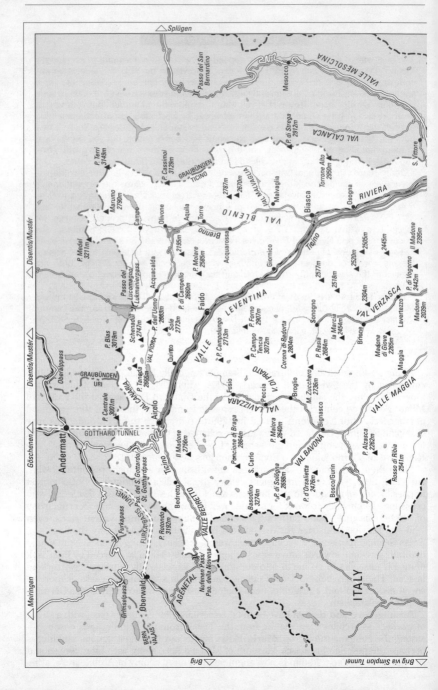

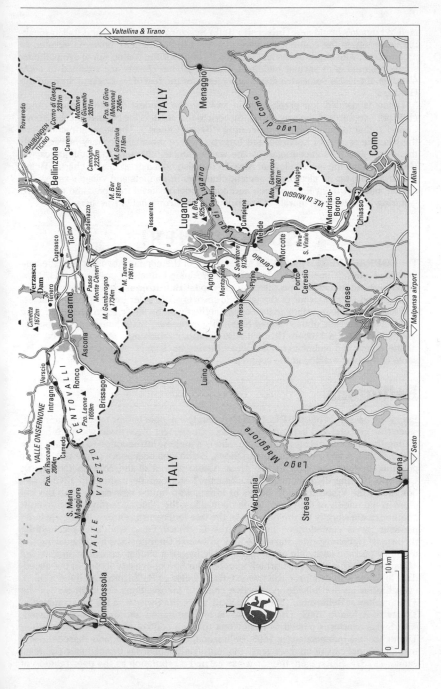

△ Valtellina & Tirano

ITALY

GRAUBÜNDEN
TICINO

Roveredo

Corno di Gesero 2231m
Mottone di Giumello 2031m
Pzo. di Gino (Menone) 2245m

Menaggio

Lago di Como

Como

Carena

Camoghe 2233m
M. Garzirola 2116m

Bellinzona

Milan

Cadenazzo

Cugnasco
Ticino

Tesserete

Lugano
M. Brè 925m
M. Boglia
Lago di Gandria

Mte. Generoso 1601m

Muggio

VALLE DI MUGGIO

Mendrisio-Borgo

Chiasso

Campione

Melide

Morcote

Riva S. Vitale

Verzasca Dam

Tenero
Passo Monte Cèneri
M. Tamaro 1961m
M. Gambarogno 1734m

Cimetta 1672m

Locarno

Agno

Montagnola

S. Salvatore 912m

Figino

Porto Ceresio

Ceresio

Malpensa airport

Ascona

Varese

Verscio

Intragna

Ronco

CENTOVALLI

Pzo. Leone 1659m

Brissago

Luino

Ponte Tresa

VALLE ONSERNONE

Camedo

Pzo. di Ruscada 2004m

VALLE VIGEZZO

ITALY

Lago Maggiore

Verbania

Stresa

Arona

Sesto

S. Maria Maggiore

Domodossola

N

0   10 km

ated to Lugano's brand-new **Università della Svizzera Italiana**, the first Italian-speaking university in the country, founded in 1996. Much time and money is devoted to architecture, with cities, towns and villages throughout the canton full of sympathetic, subtle restoration of ancient buildings. Kitschy Alpine chalets are confined to *Oltre Gottardo*, the locals' somewhat disparaging term for the rest of Switzerland "beyond the Gotthard".

Ticino is divided topographically in two by the modest **Monte Ceneri** range (1961m), two-thirds of the way down: the area to the north is the **Sopraceneri** ("Above Ceneri"), that to the south is **Sottoceneri** ("Below Ceneri"). The main attractions are the lakeside resorts of **Locarno** and **Lugano**, where mountain scenery merges with the subtropical flora encouraged by the warm climate, although the cantonal capital **Bellinzona** and the quiet valleys of **Alto Ticino** also hold a great deal of charm. Ticino is known, too, for its plethora of ancient churches in hamlets and villages across the canton, many of them Romanesque and containing medieval frescoes, and most also featuring huge external murals of St Christopher, patron saint of travellers.

SOPRACENERI

The **SOPRACENERI** region takes in the whole of the northern two-thirds of the canton. Road and rail lines stream down from the Alpine tunnels, bypassing the Ticinese hinterland and funnelling into the cantonal capital **Bellinzona**, a quietly elegant place often passed over in favour of the lakeside resorts – the latter exemplified by shades-and-*gelati* **Locarno**, revelling in its location at the tip of the idyllic **Lago Maggiore**. The real beauty, however, of this rugged region lies in the very hinterland that most people see hurtling past at 110kph. Unspoilt **Alto Ticino**, comprising a network of wild, pre-Alpine valleys and mountain-top lakelets glittering in clear, crystalline sunshine, holds some of the best walking in the country.

Bellinzona

Everyone passes through **BELLINZONA**, but few people bother to stop – their loss, since this graceful and beautiful old town is the perfect place to draw breath before hitting the lakeside glitz further south, and is a mellow introduction to the easy pace of the Ticino. A fortress since Roman times, Bellinzona occupies a prime valley-floor position, holding the keys to the great Alpine passes of the Novena (Nufenen), Gottardo (Gotthard), Lucomagno (Lukmanier) and San Bernadino. In 1242 it was bought by the Visconti family, dukes of Milan, who built a new **castle** atop the hill plum in the middle of the valley, while their allies, the Rusconi family of Como, built another castle slightly up the hillside. In the late fourteenth century, the newly independent Swiss confederates north of the Gotthard Pass, who had successfully thrown off Habsburg rule, started to look to secure their position by conquering the territory on the south side of the pass. They began a violent campaign against the Milanese forces in the 1420s, which spurred the Sforza dynasty – then in the ascendant in Milan – to reinforce the two existing castles at Bellinzona and build a third, even higher up the hillside. A massive chain of fortifications cut right across the Ticino valley at Bellinzona ... but to no avail, since the Swiss won the town under the Treaty of Arona in 1503. Three centuries of domination and oppression followed, with Swiss overlords posted to Bellinzona to keep control of the peasantry. When Ticino became independent in 1803, Bellinzona, Locarno and Lugano shared the status of cantonal capital on a six-year rota, until Bellinzona was handed sole rights as capital in 1878. Since then, the town has earned a reputation as the poor relation of

BELLINZONA'S FESTIVALS

Bellinzona's February carnival, known as **Rabadan**, takes in a huge masked parade and festivities in and around the Old Town, starting on the Thursday before Mardi Gras and continuing all weekend. The town also hosts an array of music festivals, including a **piano** competition in late April and May; "**Piazza Blues**", drawing some big-name performers to play open air on a weekend in late June (*www.piazzablues.ch*); and an **opera** festival in late July, with performances held in the open courtyard of Castelgrande – *Carmen* is slated for 2000, and *Aida* for 2001. Tickets for the blues festival (free or Fr.10), and the piano and opera festivals (Fr.50–130) can be had from the tourist office.

Locarno and Lugano – undeserved, since it might lack a lake, but it also lacks the hectic pace, the crowds and the touristic sheen of its bigger neighbours. Gentle Bellinzona is blessed with medieval architecture and picturesque churches galore, and also serves as the main access point for excursions into the wild and little-known Alto Ticino region.

Arrival, orientation and information

Bellinzona's **train station** is 500m northeast of the Old Town. The **tourist office** is in the heart of the Old Town, under the arcades of the Palazzo Civico at Via Camminata 2, off Piazza Nosetto (Mon–Fri 8am–6.30pm, Sat 9am–noon; April–Sept also Sat noon–5pm; ☎091/825 21 31, *www.bellinzona.ch*). They have plenty of maps, information and walking suggestions for the city and the Alto Ticino area, and can make free hotel reservations. The *Benvenuti a Bellinzona* brochure has a complete rundown of the city's sights with a city map on the back, or you could pick up *Alto Ticino Weekend* – a series of interesting essays (in four languages) on architecture ancient and modern in the city, and some simple walking routes and driving itineraries in the higher valleys. The official **guided walking tour** takes advantage of the bustling Saturday market to offer an unusual full-day itinerary, taking in all the castles and their museums as well as a walk around the Old Town (July–Oct Sat 10am–5pm; Fr.30 includes a quality grotto lunch, museum entry fees and bus rides in between walks); book before noon one day in advance.

Note that the cobbled streets of Bellinzona's Old Town, from the post office south to Piazza Indipendenza, are banned to private vehicles from 7.30pm to 6am.

Accommodation

Bellinzona doesn't have a wide choice of **accommodation**, and what there is wins no prizes for style or imagination. The **campsite** nearest town is *Bosco di Molinazzo*, by the river in Molinazzo, a northern suburb (☎091/829 11 18, fax 829 23 55; April–Sept), but there are no hostels within reach.

Of the **hotels**, *Tsui-Fok,* 150m southeast of Indipendenza at Via Nocca 20 (☎ & fax 091/825 13 32; ①), is a pretty simple Chinese restaurant with four inexpensive rooms upstairs. *San Giovanni* is more convenient at Via San Giovanni 7 (☎ & fax 825 19 19; ②), another restaurant (this time Ticinese) with upstairs rooms, though they're better kept and more pleasant. Both of these have shared-bath rooms only. *Croce Federale*, Viale Stazione 12 (☎091/825 16 67, fax 826 25 50; ②), is the most pleasant of four hotels on this street by the station, well located on the edge of the pedestrian zone and with comfortable, unremarkable rooms. *Unione*, Via Generale Guisan 1 (☎091/825 55 77, fax 825 94 60; ③; closed Christmas to mid-January), is Bellinzona's best, with efficient service but rooms that don't make it above ordinary.

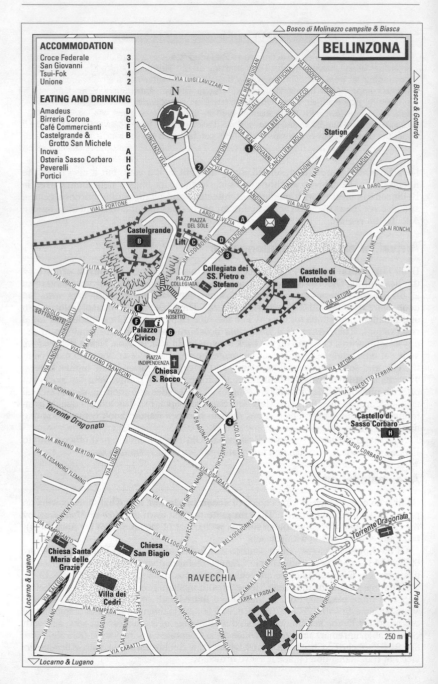

The Town

High on Bellinzona's central rock rise the massive towers and walls of **Castelgrande** (Tues–Sun 9am–midnight; free), most impressive of the town's three medieval castles. Known to have been occupied as far back as the Neolithic age, the hill was fortified first by the Romans, and then again in the thirteenth century by Milanese forces to protect the valley routes to and from the great Alpine passes. For three centuries between the Swiss conquest and Ticinese independence, Castelgrande was known as the **Castello d'Uri** after its trans-Alpine occupiers (Montebello was the Castello di Svitto (Schwyz), while Sasso Corbaro was the Castello di Untervaldo). Just to confuse things further, the rock on which the castle sits is known as **Monte San Michele**. The whole hilltop complex has been imaginatively and sympathetically restored by local architect Aurelio Galfetti – he added a **lift**, one of the highlights of Bellinzona's modern architecture, that is dramatically recessed deep into the bedrock of the hill behind the central Piazza del Sole and emerges at a purpose-built modern fortification on an upper terrace of the castle. The castle grounds are serene, overlooked by the slender thirteenth-century **White Tower**, with two upper windows on all four faces, and the fourteenth-century **Black Tower**, with three windows on its longer side. Despite their names, both, like the castle itself, are grey granite, and between them run lines of distinctive Lombard-style **winged battlements**, which you'll see on castles all over Ticino. Off the central lawns you'll find the **historical museum** (Feb–Dec Tues–Sun 10am–12.30pm & 1.30–5.30pm; Fr.4, or combination ticket for museums in all three castles Fr.8; SMP), divided into two sections. The archeology side offers a tour through Bellinzona's ancient past, including an excellent audiovisual show (in English) presenting the history of the town. The museum's pride and joy, though, is a set of murals made in 1470 to decorate the wooden ceiling of a villa in the town, depicting a complex set of allegorical themes dealing with love, faith and virtue.

Atmospheric steps wind down from Castelgrande to the elegant Renaissance buildings of **Piazza Collegiata** in the centre of the Old Town, dominated by the lavish Collegiata church, built by the same architect who worked on Como's cathedral and decorated with Baroque frescoes and stucco. Narrow, shaded lanes branch out all around: arcaded **Piazza Nosetto** is just south, with the Cà Rossa house on the way featuring a striking red terracotta facade – a style fashionable in early nineteenth-century Milan. From Nosetto, a gateway leads into the courtyard of the **Palazzo Civico**, a magnificent Renaissance building rebuilt in the 1920s but still retaining its loggias which wind attractively around both upper floors.

Behind the Collegiata, on the eastern side of the piazza, a path rises to the picturesque **Castello di Montebello** (Tues–Sun 8am–6pm; free), some ninety metres higher in elevation than Castelgrande, with suitably impressive views of the town. From a vantage point on the lofty ramparts, it's easy to trace the line of defensive fortifications which link the two castles across the width of the Ticino valley. The castle itself is impressive, with a fifteenth-century courtyard and residential palace surrounding an older central portion dating from the thirteenth century, the latter now housing a modern **museum** of Gothic and Renaissance architecture (Tues–Sun 10am–12.30pm & 1.30–5.30pm; Fr.4, or combination ticket for museums in all three castles Fr.8). A stiff 45-minute climb further up will bring you to **Castello di Sasso Corbaro** (April–Oct Tues–Sun 8am–6pm; free), some 230m above Bellinzona, designed and built in six months in 1479 by a military engineer brought in from Florence after the Swiss defeat of Milanese troops at the Battle of Giornico. It shelters a particularly welcome vine-shaded courtyard *osteria* and has a spectacular rampart panorama. A **museum** of local crafts and traditions is currently under renovation, and the castle keep has a gallery showing changing exhibits by contemporary Ticinese artists and sculptors (combination ticket valid). To save your legs, catch bus #4 from the centre to Artore near Castello di Sasso Corbaro, and wend your own path back down the hillside.

WALKS AROUND BELLINZONA

WALKS AROUND BELLINZONA

There are plenty of quiet, picturesque **walks** near Bellinzona which could fill a pleasant afternoon. One of the best begins in nearby **Roveredo** (in Graubünden's Val Mesolcina and served by postbuses from Bellinzona), from where an old cart track on the "quiet" side of the river heads through tiny San Giulio and into the woods opposite San Vittore, before crossing the river at a little bridge in Lumino and heading on through the forest to Arbedo on the outskirts of Bellinzona. You'll come across plenty of peaceful shady *grotti* on the way. Side roads off the main Via San Gottardo lead through Arbedo and under the tracks to the picturesque Chiesa Rossa, an ancient red-washed church sitting lost and forgotten beside industrial warehouses on Via del Carmagnola backing onto the tracks (total 2hr walking). Buses can run you the final 1.5km south into Bellinzona centre.

The walk to **Prada** begins in the car park of the hospital in Ravecchia, a southern suburb (city bus #5) – cobbled alleys lead you alongside vineyards to a mule track which climbs gently beneath the looming Castello di Sasso Corbaro to the tiny isolated Chiesa di San Girolamo di Prada, set amidst the ruins of Prada village (45min). Tougher paths lead on from Prada through forests into the secluded Val Morobbia, an old smugglers' route; two or three postbuses a day from Bellinzona to the last village in the valley, **Carena**, bring you to the trailhead of a tough, but deserted, five-hour hike up to the Passo di San Jorio (2014m), marking the Italian frontier, and back.

South of Piazza Indipendenza

Peaceful **Piazza Indipendenza** is 100m south of the tourist office and sports a 1903 obelisk commemorating the first century of Ticinese independence. Half hidden behind a tree on the east side of the square is the **Chiesa di San Rocco**, a small but atmospheric church built in 1330 and renovated in 1478. Following Via Lugano south from Indipendenza for 600m brings you to Piazza San Biagio, and the gates of the **Villa dei Cedri**, home of Bellinzona's art collection. It's worth having a wander in the lush and beautiful grounds (daily: April–Sept 8am–8pm, Oct–March 9am–5pm; free) before heading in to the museum (Tues–Sat 10am–noon & 2–6pm, Sun 10am–6pm; Fr.8; SMP), which focuses on nineteenth- and twentieth-century Swiss and Lombard art. The frescoed **Chiesa di San Biagio** beside the villa dates from the twelfth century, and has a huge mural of St Christopher beside the door, but was undergoing extensive renovation at the time of writing, as was the beautiful **Chiesa di Santa Maria delle Grazie** attached to a disused convent 100m west across the tracks – this was severely damaged by fire after a nativity scene caught alight on New Year's Eve 1997, but although some frescoes were entirely lost and the altars have now been removed for safekeeping, attempts are being made to restore its enormous late-fifteenth-century interior fresco of the crucifixion.

Eating and drinking

Like administrative capitals everywhere, Bellinzona suffers from a stunted entertainment scene – it has plenty of places to **eat and drink**, but none really stands out. Cheap self-service nosh is at *Inova*, Ticino's version of *Manora*, in the Innovazione department store on Viale Stazione. Castelgrande houses two eateries (both closed Mon): the *Grotto San Michele* spreads itself over the panoramic terrace, where you can eat well for Fr.14–20, whereas the interior *Castelgrande* restaurant, full of postmodern black leather and tubular steel furniture, is a much snootier affair (☎091/826 23 53, *www.castelgrande.ch*) – you'll get little change from Fr.60 for its modern, Ticino-inspired cuisine. The atmospheric *Osteria Sasso Corbaro*, in Bellinzona's topmost castle (☎091/825 55 32; closed Mon & Nov–March), serves up authentic Ticinese fare – accompanied by plenty of wine – at stone tables in the shady castle courtyard, or in a great hall within; *menus* are Fr.25 or so. *Portici*, a pleasant *osteria*/pizzeria in the Old Town on Vicolo Muggiasca (closed Sun lunch & Mon), serves palatable food in its shady courtyard to a young, easy crowd of regulars for Fr.20 or less. *Birreria Corona*, Via Camminata 5 (closed Sun), is an atmospheric café-bar fronting quite a good restaurant in the back, with *menus* also around Fr.20. Pavement café-bars abound, including *Café Commercianti*, Via Teatro 5, a popular place that doubles as a *gelateria*, and especially around Via Codeborgo, where you'll see (or hear) the jumping *Amadeus Pub* on Vicolo Torre (closed Sun) and the equally lively *Peverelli* at Codeborgo 12 (closed Mon).

Listings

Adventure sports Swissraft has an office in Gorduno, a village northwest of Bellinzona (☎091/921 00 71, *www.swissraft.ch*), and offers a half-day of rafting from Cama to Bellinzona (Fr.85), mountain bike tours from Fr.75, plenty of canyoning options (Fr.95–175) and tons more.

Bike rental In the station (daily 6am–6.30pm).

Car rental Europcar, Via San Gottardo 71 (☎091/820 60 40); Hertz, Via Zorzi 40 (☎091/826 10 33).

Changing money In the station (daily 6am–8.40pm).

Markets There's a colourful, friendly weekly market of breads, local cheeses, wines, fruit and veg, and handicrafts held in the alleys of the Old Town every Saturday (7am–noon). Restaurants in the Old Town take the opportunity to offer local specialities of polenta or risotto for Saturday lunch *al fresco*. Also don't miss the annual cheese market in early October, where all the Ticinese Alpine producers parade their mountain cheeses for sale.

Post Main office is 200m southwest of the station, Viale Stazione 18 (CH-6500 Bellinzona 1).

Alto Ticino

By far the most pristine part of this sometimes tiresomely touristic canton, the region of **ALTO TICINO** (Upper Ticino) north of Bellinzona is a haven of wild, lonesome valleys cutting deep into the landscape on the approach to the high Alps, dotted with rustic stone-built hamlets teetering on steep slopes. As throughout the rest of the canton – though less obtrusively here – many of the original Ticinese communities, which laboured so long to scrape a living from the land, are now financially enriched, if culturally challenged, by the presence of many German and Swiss-German second-homeowners seeking refuge from the pressures of city life. The villages and the scenery nonetheless survive unscathed, and if getting off the beaten path is your aim, you're likely to find greater satisfaction in Alto Ticino than in most other parts of the country, let alone the canton. **Biasca** is the gateway to the region, a small town at the junction of the scenic **Val Blenio** – which heads north from Biasca up to **Olivone**, then cuts over to the Lucomagno Pass – and the main **Valle Leventina**, which bends northwest up to the foot of the Gottardo Pass and the quiet town of Airolo, where the rural Val Bedretto splits off west to the Novena Pass.

You'd do well to check your planned itinerary with the tourist office in Bellinzona before you set off: although information and maps are much the same wherever you go, staff in the regional tourist offices in Biasca, Acquarossa and Airolo are less likely to be fluent in English. The brochures *Alto Ticino Weekend* and *Itinerari in Alto Ticino* – the latter more informative but dating from 1993 – give acres of cultural and hiking background to the area, or you could opt for a **guided tour**, run on a fixed weekly schedule by the Bellinzona tourist office (July–Oct only): every Monday there's a nature tour from Biasca up into the Val Blenio and back (8.30am–6pm; Fr.40); on Tuesdays, a round-trip hike from Biasca into the Leventina (8.30am–6.30pm; Fr.30); on Wednesdays, a tour of Romanesque churches in Biasca, Giornico and Negrentino

(10am–5pm; Fr.30); and on Fridays, a stiff climb from Biasca (304m) to the hut on Alpe di Cava (2256m) and back (8.30am–6pm; Fr.40 includes lunch). All these tours start from Biasca train station, but must be booked with tourist offices either in Bellinzona or Biasca before noon one day in advance.

Biasca

The small town of **BIASCA** sits in a grand location at the junction of three valleys: the Valle Leventina, the Val Blenio and to the south towards Bellinzona a part of the River Ticino called the **Riviera**, which crams in side by side a motorway, a main road, a minor road, a train line and several footpaths, all snaking between wooded mountain sides rising 1500m above your head. High above the town to the southeast, commanding an eagle's-eye view of all routes in and out, is the imposing thirteenth-century **Chiesa di San Pietro e Paolo**, with a sixteenth-century portico tacked on to its simple, Romanesque facade. Collect the key from the newer parish church halfway up the hillside. Inside, the irregular Romanesque floor plan – architects seem to have struggled with the sloping bedrock – is unchanged, and the interior walls are covered in an array of medieval frescoes.

Biasca's **train station** is 750m south of the centre. The **tourist office** is just off Piazza Centrale on the tiny Piazzetta Cavalier Pellanda (Mon–Fri 8.30–11.30am & 2–6pm; May–Oct also Sat 8.30–11.30am; ☎091/862 33 27, *www.biasca.ch*). Stairs up to the church rise directly behind the tourist office. Of the **hotels**, the *Posta* (☎ & fax 091/862 21 21; ③), directly opposite the station, has adequate rooms above a goodish restaurant, while the modern *Al Giardinetto* is better placed, in the centre, at Via Pini 21 (☎091/862 17 71, fax 862 23 59, *info@algiardinetto.ch*, *www.algiardinetto.ch*; ①–②), with a ten-percent walkers' discount for stays over three days. Look out for the regular Saturday market, showcasing fresh produce from the upper valleys.

Val Blenio

Quiet **Val Blenio** cuts north from Biasca, off the main Leventina routes, a broad open valley that basks in generous sunshine and has limitless opportunities for walking exploration. The valley floor is dotted with villages, themselves marked by *rustici*, stone-built peasant dwellings, sometimes little more than shacks, that are topped with rough slate roofs. A lot of these are now holiday cottages, renovated and rented out for tidy sums to nature-starved northerners, but the valley has nonetheless made sure to protect its most valuable assets – peace, quiet and unspoilt natural beauty. Oddly enough, the Bleniesi have been known throughout Europe for centuries as foodie entrepreneurs, a skill probably picked up in Milan sometime in the Middle Ages and passed on through the generations. In 1600 one Signor Bianchini from the valley was no less than head chef to the King of Spain; in 1849, a Signor Baggi won an award for selling the best ice cream in France; while the Gatti family – also from the Blenio – owned and managed 230 restaurants and cafés throughout late-Victorian England. Locals will have you believe that fully three-quarters of all chestnut sellers in Switzerland today are from the Val Blenio.

The Sentiero Basso is the main valley-floor path: the walk from Biasca to **ACQUAROSSA** on the west bank of the river is a gently rising 13km, taking a little under four hours. Acquarossa is also home to the valley's **tourist office** on Via Lucomagno, open limited weekday hours only (☎091/871 17 65). On the east bank just north of Biasca is **Malvaglia**, whose village church boasts a gigantic fresco of St Christopher; from here a tortuous branch road climbs in a series of hairpins into the

A WALKING TOUR OF ALTO TICINO

A two-week walking **Tour of Ticino** explores the finest valleys and most remote land-scapes in the upper part of the canton. The granite massifs of the Lepontine Alps, as these mountains are known, are among the least visited of any in Switzerland. You can wander for hours on end, even in the height of summer, and see no one, even while the lower valleys and the lakes of Maggiore and Lugano are thronged with holiday-makers. The scenery is charming: clear streams tumble through the valleys, numerous tarns flecked among the high plateaux add a sparkle to the crags, and deep green pools in hidden corners invite walkers to pause for a well-deserved midsummer bathe. Accommodation is sometimes sparse in the small villages of the upper valleys, but there are plenty of mountain huts (*capanne*). As ever, it's easy to pick out **shorter walks** if you prefer something less taxing: from the Valle Santa Maria through Val Piora to Airolo, for instance, or from Bignasco to Fusio. **Maps** to pack are the LS 265, 266, 275 and 276 (all 1:50,000), and *Walking in the Alps* and *Walking in Ticino*, both by Kev Reynolds (see "Books", p.531), are essential reading.

The tour begins either in **Torre** or **Dangio**, two adjacent villages in the upper Valle di Blenio 4km south of Olivone. The route heads through Val Soi on a path which climbs to **Capanna Adula** (☎091/872 15 32) at the southern end of Val Carassina. Day two takes the walker through Val Carassina to a small dammed lake, then descends to **Olivone** (see p.492) before following a mule track through a defile into Val Camadra. On the western hillside the path leads to **Capanna Boverina** (☎091/872 15 29). Next day you continue up to Passo di Gana Negra, cross Valle Santa Maria and make a steady ascent to Passo Colombe. An enjoyable descent from there takes the route into the gentle tarn-glistening Val Piora where overnight accommodation is found in **Capanna Cadagno** (☎091/868 13 23). Day five is a short one, but there's plenty of opportunity to divert to mountain lakes and big views. The route crosses Bochetta di Cadlimo to Pian Bornengo at the head of Val Canaria, then descends this glen to **Airolo** at the foot of the Gottardo Pass. On the south side of Valle Leventina the way resumes on a belvedere trail known as the Strada degli alpi Bedretto, but on reaching the alp hutments of Piano di Pesciüm it cuts into Val Torta and climbs to **Capanna Cristallina** (☎091/869 23 30). The following stage makes a crossing of the Cristallina massif to **Capanna Basòdino** (☎091/753 27 97) by one of two routes, both of which notch up several tarns, crossing rocky passes amid wild country.

On day eight, an easy downhill walk leaves the big mountains and descends through the woods and pastures of Val Bavona to **Bignasco** at the head of the Valle Maggia. It's a glorious walk leading past tiny hamlets and feathery waterfalls to a confluence of valleys. Leaving Bignasco on day ten the suggested route goes through Val Cocco and over Passo del Cocco at its head, before dropping to the remote and simple **Capanna Alpe d'Osola**. Although open from April to November this hut is unstaffed, so you'll need to carry food (cooking facilities are provided). The way now negotiates Bochetta di Mugaia in the south ridge of Monte Zucchero, before descending 1600m to **Sonogno**. Day eleven crosses Passo di Redorta (2181m) to Val di Pertüs whose stark walls plunge into the depths of a gorge. Val di Pertüs feeds into Val di Prato, and this in turn spills into Val Lavizzara where you spend the night in **Prato-Sornico**. The tour heads north to **Fusio**, a short journey on linking trails that avoids most of the road between the two villages. On such a short stage it would be worth diverting up to Lago di Mognola high on the eastern hillside, at the northern end of which an airy path makes a traverse before plunging steeply to the valley near Fusio. The final (thirteenth) day's walk leads back to Valle Leventina via Passo Campolungo. The pass is more than 1000m above Fusio, while the descent to **Rodi-Fiesso**, 10km south of Airolo, is a steep 1300m, but the path is mostly good and there are consistently fine views on both sides to make this a fitting conclusion to the route.

lonesome gorge of the **Val Malvaglia** amidst tremendous scenery of steep wooded slopes dropping away into a seemingly bottomless ravine. From a point on the road, it's possible to park and walk across a bridge spanning the valley, on the other side of which a dramatic mule track penetrates for a couple of hours' walk to **Dagro**, a hamlet on the northern side of the valley with broad views.

As you rise into the Blenio, the lush green slopes begin to close in. The main town at the head of the valley, below the sharp-peaked Sosto on one side and the Töira on the other, is **OLIVONE**, an utterly tranquil little place some 24km north of Biasca that reflects the valley's once-noble pretensions in its array of grandiose, if worn, eighteenth- and nineteenth-century mansions and villas – rather out of place amidst the orchards and increasingly wild high-valley scenery. Up in the village is the *Osteria Centrale* (☎091/872 11 07; ①), meeting place for the locals, which serves tasty home-cooked fare and has a few simple rooms. Down a short hill beside the main road is the post office and bus stop with, alongside, the *Albergo San Martino* (☎091/872 15 21, fax 872 26 62; ①), a slightly more upmarket proposition, also with excellent traditional food and pizzas plus a choice of en-suite or shared-bath rooms. A five-hour walk from Olivone climbs to the **Lucomagno Pass** (1914m); the road over the pass to Disentis/Mustér in Graubünden (see p.459) is perhaps the most scenic route in and out of Ticino.

Valle Leventina

From Biasca, the motorway, the main road and the train all blaze a trail northwest into the **Valle Leventina**, heading for the Gottardo Pass and tunnels at the end. There's no doubt that this is a spectacular route, whether heading north or south, but its heavy usage is its downfall – hemmed in by the high valley walls, the hiss and rumble of traffic noise from the motorway can seem obtrusively loud to valley-floor walkers and cyclists. Unless you're planning high-altitude hikes in the tranquil mountains flanking the valley (see box p.491), it's best to use the bus or train to scoot along the valley floor.

Make time, though, for **GIORNICO**, a small town 9km northwest of Biasca. It was here in 1478 that a Swiss force numbering six hundred defeated a 10,000-strong Milanese army, thereby linking Ticino's subsequent history to Switzerland instead of to Italy. Giornico is lovely, a typical Ticinese village built on the gentle slopes either side of the tumbling River Ticino, with cobbled alleys running picturesquely between old stone-roofed houses, and a photogenic hump-backed bridge crossing to a wooded island mid-river, and from there to the west bank, where rises the campanile of the **Chiesa di San Nicolao**, one of the most impressive and atmospheric of Ticino's many Romanesque churches. Its external walls are decorated with Lombardic designs, while inside is a fresco-decorated choir placed above a beautiful triple-apsed half-sunken crypt. Down an alley below the church is the Casa Stanga, an old house converted into the small **Museo di Leventina** (April–Oct Tues–Sun 2–5pm; Fr.2), with a few rooms of diverting historical bits and bobs. More interesting is the concrete hangar in the fields 300m north of Giornico's little train station. This vast, blank structure is in fact an art gallery, **La Congiunta**, dedicated to the sculpture of Zürich artist Hans Josephsohn – though you'd never know from the outside. Pick up the keys at the *Osteria Giornico* on the main road (closed Wed). Inside are three rooms of lumpy metal reliefs and a few seemingly half-finished sculptures in bronze dating from 1950 to 1991. Peter Märkli's deserted, deconstructed gallery setting suits Josephsohn's stark, brutal art perfectly, making the museum one of the oddest, and most striking, you'll come across.

Giornico has a couple of terrific *grotti*, both of them dripping with atmosphere and serving up the kind of simple, lovingly prepared food you wouldn't expect to be able to buy. The *Grotto dei Due Ponti* is the one everyone goes to, perfectly located on the mid-river island, its shaded terrace overlooking the rushing water. *Grotto Pergola*, tucked away on the west bank of the river and south of San Nicolao, serves even better food, although their garden is less alluring.

Some 28km north of Giornico is **AIROLO**, first town in the Ticino for the millions who pour out of the Gottardo train and road tunnels each year heading south. Thankfully bypassed by the main routes, it's a quiet town with a handful of hotels serving as staging post for summer journeys up to the Gottardo (Gotthard Pass; see p.366), or into the Val Bedretto and from there to the Novena (Nufenen Pass; see p.325). The town is also the trailhead for plenty of high-altitude walks, especially into the stunning **Val Piora** outlined in the box on p.491. Winter sees Airolo transformed into a small-scale ski resort. The town is also home to the Leventina's **tourist office** on Via San Gottardo, open limited weekday hours (☎091/869 15 33, *www.leventinanet.ch*).

Locarno

Mainline trains and fast cars speed south from Bellinzona to Lugano and Milan, while a branch line and often packed minor roads head west for some 15km to **Lago Maggiore** and its principal Swiss resort, **LOCARNO**. This characterful old town enjoys the most glorious of locations, on a broad sweeping curve of a bay in the lake, and also clocks up the most sunshine hours of anywhere in Switzerland. The arcades and piazzas of the town centre are overlooked by subtropical gardens of palms, camellias, bougainvillea, cypress, oleanders and magnolias, which flourish on the lakeside promenades and cover the wooded slopes which crowd in above the town centre.

Locarno slumbered under Swiss occupation after 1503, but with independence in the nineteenth century it found its feet as the most elegant of the country's lakeside resorts. In 1925 its backdrop of Belle Epoque hotels and piazza cafés served as the setting for the **Treaty of Locarno**, signed by the European powers in a failed effort to secure peace following World War I. The seeds planted at Locarno exploded into war again in 1939, but the town went from strength to strength during the 1950s and after, growing in chic-ness year on year. These days, Locarno focuses all its considerable resources on tourism, and draws in two very different sets of customers: one, from the German-speaking north, arrive to test out their hiking boots, while the other, from fog- and smog-bound Milan, come to test out their sunglasses. The cobbled alleys of Locarno's Old Town, lined with Renaissance facades, can get entirely overrun by the rich and wannabe-famous on summer weekends, yet still – in the midst of the hubbub – the place manages to retain its sun-drenched cool.

Arrival, orientation and information

Locarno's **train station** is 100m north of the lakeshore landing stage and 150m northeast of the main central square, Piazza Grande. Postbuses and local buses depart from the front of the station. The municipality of Locarno itself is quite small, and the city takes in the neighbouring contiguous districts of **Muralto**, just east of the station, and **Minusio**, further east still, both of which pop up regularly in listings as if they were separate towns.

The efficient but often crowded **tourist office** is in the Casino complex on Via Largo Zorzi, 100m southwest of the station (March–Oct Mon–Fri 9am–6pm, Sat 10am–4pm, Sun 10am–2pm; Oct–March Mon–Fri 9am–12.30pm & 2–6pm; ☎091/751 03 33, *www.lagomaggiore.org*), and has information on the city and the whole region; they can also make hotel bookings for you. Their **guided walking tour** starts from the office and takes in a tour of the churches of the Old Town and the Castello Visconteo (April–Oct Mon 9.45am; Fr.5).

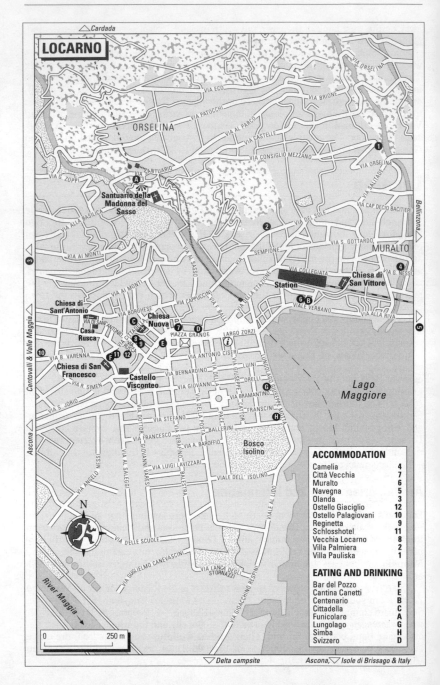

LOCARNO

ACCOMMODATION

Camelia	4
Città Vecchia	7
Muralto	6
Navegna	5
Olanda	3
Ostello Giaciglio	12
Ostello Palagiovani	10
Reginetta	9
Schlosshotel	11
Vecchia Locarno	8
Villa Palmiera	2
Villa Pauliska	1

EATING AND DRINKING

Bar del Pozzo	F
Cantina Canetti	E
Centenario	B
Cittadella	C
Funicolare	A
Lungolago	G
Simba	H
Svizzero	D

LOCARNO'S FESTIVALS

Most events and festivities take place on Piazza Grande in the summer – the tourist office can give full details and sell tickets. The season kicks off in late May with the "Back Home Again" **American music festival**, followed in mid-June by a weekend devoted to "I Feel Good", the **Locarno Funk Festival**. A couple of weeks later is the popular **New Orleans Jazz Festival** just 3km down the road in and around the Old Town of Ascona, followed in mid-July by a competition and display of **beach volleyball** in Piazza Grande.

The world-class **Locarno International Film Festival**, held over ten days in early August, is stealing a march on Cannes for both movie quality and star appeal, and is now rated among the top five film festivals in the world. Catch major offerings on the huge open-air screen in Piazza Grande, playing to 7500 people nightly (Fr.20), or one of the 12 daily screenings in the city's cinemas (Fr.14). Fr.200 buys a universal festival pass. For information and listings ahead of time, contact the Festival internazionale del film Locarno, Via della Posta 6, CH-6600 Locarno (☎091/756 21 21, *www.pardo.ch*).

Over three weeks in late August and September, Ascona presents its **Settimane Musicali** ("Music Weeks"), a series of prestigious classical concerts held in various locations around the region.

Accommodation

Swarming as it is with tourists, Locarno is also crammed with **accommodation** of all kinds. The tourist office has a leaflet "Hotels Special", advertising six nights en-suite B&B for two in any one of a handful of two-star hotels for Fr.780.

The pricey *Delta* **campsite** (☎091/751 60 81, fax 751 22 43; March–Oct) is a fifteen-minute walk south along the lakeshore. The modern **HI hostel** *Ostello Palagiovani*, Via Varenna 18 (☎091/756 15 00, fax 756 15 01; ①), has dorms from Fr.31 and bike rental, but it's in an awkward western location – take bus #31 or #36 (direction Centovalli) to Cinque Vie. Two other places offer dorms, both in the heart of the Old Town: the small *Ostello Giaciglio*, Via Rusca 7 (☎091/751 30 64, fax 752 38 37), charges Fr.30 but gives no breakfast, while the much better *Città Vecchia* (see below) has good all-in dorms for Fr.31.

Camelia, Via Nessi 9, Muralto (☎091/743 00 21, fax 743 00 22, *hotel@camelia.ch*, *www.camelia.ch*; March–Oct). Elegant, eager-to-please family hotel set in fragrant floral gardens and offering spacious rooms, some with balcony and lake view. ③.

Città Vecchia, Via Torretta 13 (☎ & fax 091/751 45 54; March–Oct). Centrally placed "garni" hotel, with dorms and simple, shared-bath rooms. ①.

Muralto, Piazza Stazione 8 (☎091/743 01 81, fax 743 43 15, *info@hotelmuralto.com*, *www.hotelmuralto.com*). Huge place directly opposite the station offering solid business-class quality on all but the uppermost floors, where light, vastly spacious rooms have picture-perfect lake views from on high and all creature comforts. ④–⑥.

Navegna, Via alla Riva 2, Minusio (☎091/743 22 22, fax 743 31 50, *hotelnavegna@bluewin.ch*; March–Nov). About 1.5km east of the centre, directly on the waterfront, with modern, stylishly renovated rooms, private parking and an excellent restaurant. ③.

Olanda, Via ai Monti 139a (☎ & fax 091/751 47 27; March–Oct). Small family-style pension high up on the hill road to Madonna del Sasso, set amidst lush palms and camellias. Most rooms – simple but appealing – have balconies with romantic lake views. Discounts for stays over three days. Private parking. ②.

Reginetta, Via Motta 8 (☎ & fax 091/752 35 53, *reginetta.locarno@bluewin.ch*, *www.reginetta-locarno.ch*; March–Oct). A prime location in the heart of the Old Town's web of alleys, offering fresh, renovated rooms, some with balcony but all shared-bath. ①.

Schlosshotel, Via San Francesco 7a (☎091/751 23 61, fax 751 73 23, *schlosshotel@ticino.com*, *www.ticino.com/schlosshotel*; March–Nov). Large, slightly old-fashioned rooms in a well-kept Old Town pile. ③.

Vecchia Locarno, Via Motta 10 (☎ & fax 091/751 65 02). Scruffily characterful Old Town gem, with both shared-bath and en-suite rooms above a courtyard restaurant and winebar. ②.

Villa Palmiera, Via del Sole 1, Muralto (☎091/743 14 41, fax 743 03 20; March–Nov). Stylish and comfortable villa-style hotel on a hill just above the centre, with private parking. ②–③.

Villa Pauliska, Via Orselina 6, Muralto (☎091/743 05 41). Handsome townhouse on a hill above the town, with just four nicely furnished en-suite rooms. ②.

The Town

The focus of town is **Piazza Grande**, an attractive arcaded square just off the lakefront that is lined with pavement cafés and serves as the town's meeting point, social club and public catwalk. Warm summer nights serve up some great people-watching, as exquisitely groomed locals parade to and fro beneath the street lights neck high in nonchalance, all the cafés a-buzz and fragrant breezes bringing in the scent of flowers from the lakeside gardens. The palm-fringed lakefront promenade runs south from the east edge of the Piazza to the **Bosco Isolino** park, five minutes away, but most interest lies in the narrow streets of Locarno's **Old Town**, ranged on gently rising ground behind the piazza: spending an afternoon wandering through the sixteenth- and seventeenth-century alleys with an ice cream is the best way to blend in with Locarno life.

From the west end of Piazza Grande, lanes run up to Via Cittadella and the richly Baroque **Chiesa Nuova**, decorated with a huge statue of St Christopher outside. Its sumptuously stuccoed ceiling is crawling with detail, featuring gilded scallops and scrollwork, and hosts of fleshy cherubs. The tiny arcaded courtyard, reached through a side door, is a charming, tranquil spot entirely removed from the bustle of the alleys. Following the atmospheric Via di Sant'Antonio brings you to the huge and rather sombre **Chiesa di Sant'Antonio**, dating from the seventeenth century but rebuilt following a fatal roof collapse in 1863. Beside the church is **Casa Rusca** (Tues–Sun 10am–noon & 2–5pm; Fr.5; SMP), a worthwhile art museum housed in a grand white eighteenth-century building with an internal open-air atrium surrounded by arcades on three levels; the exhibitions are temporary, drawn from the museum's mainly modernist collections, principally a donation by the twentieth-century Swiss artist Jean Arp of a wealth of his paintings and sculptures.

Alleys lead south downhill to the tall **Chiesa di San Francesco**, consecrated as part of a monastery in the fourteenth century over an earlier church that had been founded by wandering Franciscans either during St Francis of Assisi's lifetime or shortly after his death in 1226. In 1480, a member of the order established a hermitage on the hillside above Locarno, which is now the Madonna del Sasso pilgrimage site (see below). Renovation of the church in the sixteenth century included frescoes, most of which are now fading badly. Further down sits the stout thirteenth-century **Castello Visconteo**, built by the dukes of Milan and badly damaged by the attacking Swiss army in 1513. It now houses the town's **Museo Archeologico** (April–Oct Tues–Sun 10am–noon & 2–5pm; Fr.5; SMP), worth visiting if only for its collection of stunningly beautiful Roman glassware and ceramics, near intact brightly coloured pieces all with distinctively designed high-arched handles.

On the other side of town in Muralto, 100m east of the station, is the austere and atmospheric twelfth-century Romanesque basilica of **San Vittore**, built over a church first mentioned in the tenth century and now surrounded by generic suburban housing redevelopments firmly rooted in the late-twentieth. Medieval fresco-fragments inside and the Renaissance relief of St Victor on the bell tower are a diverting contrast to the uninspiring views over the train station.

Madonna del Sasso

Most striking of all Locarno's sights is the Franciscan **Santuario della Madonna del Sasso** church (daily 6.30am–7pm), an impressive ochre vision floating above the town

---

WALKS AROUND LOCARNO

From the top station of the Madonna del Sasso funicular in Orselina, a cable-car rises to **Cardada** (1350m), and a spectacular chairlift whisks you even higher up to **Cimetta** (1672m) – both offer plenty of walking routes on the flower-strewn meadows above Locarno and the lake.

The tourist office has a brochure, *Sentieri della Collina*, pinpointing the route of two pleasant walking paths on the hillside just above the town. The Sentiera Collina Bassa is 5.4km long, and takes you from the Madonna del Sasso funicular east through Orselina and onto the Via Panoramica through the suburb of **Brione** above Minusio, before gently coming down to the lakeshore in **Tenero** (1hr 40min), from where buses and trains return you to Locarno. The Sentiera Collina Alta runs for 6.3km from **Monte Brè**, the next hill west of Orselina (bus #32), on a scenic, winding path through the foothills to **Contra**, and down to Tenero (2hr).

---

on a wooded crag – *sasso* means rock – and consecrated in 1487 on the spot where, seven years earlier, the Virgin had appeared to Brother Bartholomeo da Ivrea from the San Francesco monastery in the town. The twenty-minute walk up through the lush ravine of the Torrente Ramogno and past a handful of decaying shrines, is atmospheric enough in itself; or you could take the half-hourly funicular from just west of the station to Ticino's greatest photo-op, looking down through the palms to the sunlit arcaded main front of the church and glittering blue lake behind.

Within the complex is a small **museum** of icons (Easter–Oct Sun–Fri 2–5pm; Fr.2.50), but the church **sanctuary** is the focus of all the pilgrims' attention. On the way through the complex you'll pass several striking terracotta sculpture groups of biblical scenes. The low, Baroque interior of the church features a number of paintings, two of which stand out: Bramartino's emotionally charged *Fuga in Egitto* (Flight to Egypt, 1522) and local artist Antonio Ciseri's *Trasporto di Cristo al Sepolcro* (1870). The statue of the Virgin on the high altar was sculpted for the church's consecration by an unknown artist. By the doorway are dozens of votive offerings from pilgrims giving thanks for the intervention of Mary in their daily lives.

Eating and drinking

Piazza Grande is full of cafés and pizzerias buzzing from morning until after midnight, but **eating** and **drinking** is more atmospheric in the old town alleys. Fresh fish plucked from the lake is Locarno's speciality – look out for trout (*trota*), perch (*persico*), pike (*luccio*) and whitefish (*coregone*). Simple self-service fare can be had at the *Inova* across from the station.

Bar del Pozzo, Piazza Sant'Antonio. Friendly local café-bar on a quiet Old Town square, a little out of the tourist crush.

Cantina Canetti off Piazza Grande. Plain local cooking (Fr.15) in a noisy diner, with the added bonus of live accordion on Friday and Saturday nights.

Centenario, Lungolago 13, Muralto (☎091/743 82 22). Best restaurant in Locarno, serving internationally acclaimed *nouvelle cuisine* in an appealing blend of French and Italian styles. A lakeside terrace and three-figure bills come as standard. Closed Sun & Mon.

Cittadella, Via Cittadella 18 (☎091/751 58 85). The popular trattoria section at ground level is excellent, serving pizzas, pasta and simple fish dishes for Fr.20 or less, while upstairs the formal restaurant concentrates on fish alone – and does it well (*menus* Fr.30–35). Closed Mon.

Funicolare, beside funicular top station. Quiet, simple place that benefits from a spectacular secluded terrace garden overlooking Madonna del Sasso at which to savour their fish specialities. Closed Thurs & Nov–Jan.

Lungolago, Via Bramantino 1. Classy pizzeria, *paninoteca* and pub where locals go to flee the invasion of white-knee'd northerners.

Navegna (see "Accommodation"). A little east of town in Minusio, but right on the lakefront and highly acclaimed for its delicately prepared and presented Ticinese cuisine (*menus* Fr.35). Closed Nov–March.

Simba, Lungolago 3a. Lively DJ bar that's one of the more popular places in town.

Svizzero, Piazza Grande. Best of the many pizzerias and diners on the square, with affordable fresh-made pasta, wood-fired pizza and plenty of Italian staples. Bustling from breakfast till the small hours.

Listings

Adventure sports Trekking Team, Breitistrasse 1, CH-8335 Hittnau (☎01/950 33 88, *www.trekking.ch*), organize plenty of adventure sports in the valleys around Locarno: their classic canyoning adventure in the Centovalli costs Fr.125, while others in the Verzasca, Onsernone and Malvaglia cost up to Fr.185. However, they're best known as bungee specialists, with the jewel in their crown being the death-defying 220m leap off the Verzasca Dam by day or floodlit night (Fr.255, includes training), as performed by James Bond in the opening scene of *Goldeneye*. Jumping off the Intragna railway bridge (70m; Fr.125) pales by comparison, but you could do both for Fr.345. All these need to be reserved in advance, as do their various rock-climbing, parachuting and other activity packages.

Bike rental In the station (daily 6am–7pm) and at the HI hostel.

Car rental Avis, c/o Aral, Via Locarno, Ascona (☎091/791 44 55); Europcar, Garage Nessi, Via Cantonale, Cadenazzo (☎091/858 15 10); Hertz, Via Sempione 12 (☎091/743 50 50).

Changing money In the station (daily 6am–8.40pm).

Email and Internet Computer World in Cinecentro Rialto, Via San Gottardo 1 (50m from the station), charges Fr.3 to start with, then Fr.0.20/min thereafter.

Medical facilities Ospedale La Carità, Via all'Ospedale 1 (☎091/756 71 11) has a 24-hour emergency room.

Post Main office is on Piazza Grande (CH-6600 Locarno 1).

Around Locarno

The valleys around Locarno are groaning with hiking possibilities, and offer some of the most beautiful scenery in the whole canton – which means that trails can get a little overcrowded in the summer season. **Val Verzasca** and **Valle Maggia** both lead north from Locarno, while the gorgeous **Centovalli** runs west on one of the most scenic and dramatic train rides in the country. The small resort of **Ascona** lies a little southwest of Locarno, with the beautiful **Isole di Brissago** just offshore.

About 1.5km east of Locarno is the suburb of **Tenero**, standing at the head of the **VAL VERZASCA**, the southern end of which is blocked by the gigantic Verzasca Dam, scene of one of the world's highest bungee-jumps (see "Listings" above). Buses run past the dam to **Corippo**, at the end of the lake behind, a beautiful cluster of old stone cottages crowned by a tall campanile; 3km north is **Lavertezzo**, whose claim to fame is perhaps the most-photographed bridge in Switzerland, a graceful seventeenth-century double arch that leaps from bank to island to bank. Many quieter trails head off into side valleys from Lavertezzo, while Verzasca itself cuts deeper and deeper for another 14km to **Sonogno** at the valley's end, passing on the way through **Brione**, whose church boasts fourteenth-century Giotto-style frescoes.

The deeper, even more rugged gorge of the **VALLE MAGGIA** runs north from Locarno, very narrow in its initial stretches and only opening out further along around **Gordevio**. You'd do best to take a bus to **Bignasco**, 30km north of Locarno, where the valley divides into the **Val Lavizzara** leading northeast and the completely isolated **Val Bavona** heading northwest. Bignasco and Lavizzara link in with the walking tour of Alto Ticino described in the box on p.491. Bavona is truly wild, a strip of valley floor

---

BOATS ON LAGO MAGGIORE

Boats crisscross the Swiss shores of the exceptionally beautiful **Lago Maggiore**, as well as running way down the lake into Italy (all boats run April–Oct only). Service is provided by the NLM, with their main Swiss office at the Locarno landing stage (☎091/751 18 65, *www.navlaghi.it*). Note that Maggiore is the only major lake in the country to be **excluded** from the Swiss Pass and European train passes.

For **fare** purposes, the Swiss basin of the lake is divided into two: a **day pass** for the area either north or south of Ascona is Fr.11, or for the whole Swiss basin is Fr.20 (seven days Fr.50). Otherwise a **Lago Maggiore Holiday Card** gives free transport on the whole of Lago Maggiore and half-price on Lago di Lugano; one/three/seven days cost Fr.33/54/72. Rapid hydrofoils, which run on routes into Italy, command a Fr.3 each-way reservation fee. You'll need your **passport** if you're catching boats into Italy.

The **Lago Maggiore Express** train and boat journey (see p.500), can also run in reverse: a 9.15am boat from Locarno (not Wed) meanders down two-thirds of the lake to the Italian resort of Stresa, from where trains connect to Domodossola for the Centovalli line back to Locarno, arriving at 5.15pm (Fr.42). Various other **excursion** tickets take in visits to the Italian islands of Isole Madre and Isole Bella.

10km long that rises 500m over its length and is hemmed in by sheer scarps on both sides. There are twelve rustic, crumbling hamlets in the valley, all without electricity save **San Carlo**, the last community of all, characterized by tall, narrow stone houses built by the valley's sixteenth-century inhabitants.

Ascona

Just 3km southwest of Locarno, on the other, south-facing side of the Maggia delta, is the small village of **ASCONA**, a magnet for idealistic, sun-starved northerners for a century or more. The place was nothing more than a fishing hamlet until the end of the nineteenth century, when a slow but steady influx began of philosophers, theosophists, spiritualists, pacifists and artists, most of whom were responding to the growing belief that a return to nature was the best remedy for the moral disintegration of Western capitalist society. The Russian anarchist Mikhail Bakunin was the first, living in Locarno in the 1870s, and at the turn of the century the artists Henri Oedenkoven and Uda Hofmann established an esoteric, vegetarian artists' colony on the hill of **Monte Verità** beside the village. An array of European fringe intellectuals followed, including the famous anarchist Kropotkin, and various practitioners of the new arts of psychology and psychoanalysis. In 1913, Rudolf von Laban set up his nudist School of Natural and Expressive Dance within the Monte Verità community, attracting Isadora Duncan among others, and during and after World War I artists and pacifists flocked to Ascona from all over Europe. The buildings atop the peaceful wooded hill are now used mostly for conferences, but a few have been preserved as a **museum** of the movement (April–June & Sept–Oct Tues–Sun 2.30–6pm; July & Aug Tues–Sun 3–7pm; Fr.6). It's a short walk up the hill from the bus stop (bus #33) to the **Casa Anatta**, with two floors of the original wooden house given over to papers and photos commemorating the artists' exploits. A walk past the main Bauhaus conference centre and into the woods brings you to the tiny **Casa Selma**, used as the community's retreat, and on further to the **Elisarion**, housing a vast circular painting by Elisar von Kupffer, an artist from a noble Baltic family who spent many years at Monte Verità, depicting the freedoms and spiritual liberations of communal life.

Ascona village itself is well worth a stroll, with a huge open lakefront piazza crammed with terrace cafés and restaurants, and attractive cobbled lanes leading back into the older quarter, full of artisans' galleries and diverting little craft shops. The **Museo**

Comunale d'Arte Moderna, in a sixteenth-century *palazzo* at Via Borgo 34 (Tues–Sat 10am–noon & 3–6pm, Sun 10am–noon; Fr.3), has a high-quality collection focused on Marianne von Werefkin, one of the many artists attracted to Ascona in its heyday and joint founder of Munich's expressionist *Blaue Reiter* movement. One of her best canvases on display is the terrifying Munch-like *Il Cenciaiolo* (The Rag-Man, 1920), but there are dozens more. Ascona's **tourist office**, near the waterfront in Casa Serodine (Mon–Fri 9am–6.30pm; June–Sept also Sat 9am–6pm, Sun 9am–2pm; ☎091/791 00 90, *www.ascona.ch*), run a gentle walking tour of the old village (April–Oct Tues 10am; Fr.5).

One of the best excursions in the area is to the lovely botanic park on the **Isole di Brissago** (April–Oct daily 8.45am–6pm; Fr.6 in addition to boat ticket or pass), twin islands situated opposite the resort of Brissago, 4km south of Ascona, and accessible by hourly boats from Locarno and Ascona, or by more regular shuttles from **Porto Ronco**, the nearest point on the mainland. These tiny dots of green in the shimmering lake overflow with luxuriant subtropical flora basking in the hot sun (this is also the lowest point in Switzerland, 193m above sea level). The main island – about ten minutes' stroll end to end – has an attractive 1929 villa at one end, now a conference centre and quality restaurant (☎091/791 43 62). Only groups can stay overnight; everyone else must leave on the last boat (around 6pm).

The Centovalli railway

Locarno is the eastern terminus of the wonderful **Centovalli railway**, one of Switzerland's most scenic rides. Little, clanky trains depart from beneath Locarno station into the spectacular Centovalli – so named for its "hundred" side valleys – most of the time winding slowly on precarious bridges and viaducts above ravine-like depths (sit on the left for the best views). The area is renowned for its natural beauty, and – with a walking map from Locarno tourist office – you could get out at any of the villages en route, pick up a trail and head off into the hills. There's no lack of *grotti*, cafés and simple budget accommodation. One neat way to see the route is with the **Lago Maggiore Express** ticket, which combines the Centovalli line with a train at Domodossola south to the Maggiore resort of Stresa, then a boat back north to Locarno (Fr.42; 9hr total).

Tiny **VERSCIO**, 4km northwest of Locarno, is a lovely, utterly tranquil stone-built village which also houses the **Teatro Dimitri**, a highly acclaimed international mime school founded by Asconan local "Clown Dimitri", a protégé of Marcel Marceau. The small theatre in a cobbled lane off the village square (☎091/796 15 44, *www.teatrodimitri.ch*), stages regular budget performances by students and professionals all summer long, and is also the training ground for the excellent Circus Monti, which tours Swiss towns and cities every year.

Some 3km down the line is **Intragna** – the graceful 70m bridge just before the village was the scene of Switzerland's first-ever bungee jump, and remains a choice spot for leaping (see "Listings", p.498). After the border at **Camedo** (passport needed), trains roll through rustic villages of the Italian **Valle Vigezzo** and ease down into bustling **DOMODOSSOLA** – in Italy, but effectively a terminus of the Swiss train network. Fast Swiss trains from here run west through the Simplon/Sempione Tunnel to Brig and on to Bern, while equally fast Italian trains head south to Milan. If you have time to kill between trains, head 200m west from the station into the old part of town, set around a series of attractively crumbling arcaded piazzas.

SOTTOCENERI

The **SOTTOCENERI** region south of Bellinzona and Locarno is much more developed than the Sopraceneri, with dozens of neat, prosperous towns crammed in between the

narrowing international borders to east and west. The principal draw is the sophisticated and stylish city of **Lugano**, sited on a bay of the glorious **Lago di Lugano**, which
twists out into Italy on both sides. Jutting out into the lake just a stone's throw from the
city is the sun-drenched **Ceresio peninsula**, dotted with idyllic Italianate country villages and crisscrossed by some of the loveliest easy walks in the canton.

Lugano

With its compact cluster of Italianate piazzas and extensive tree-lined promenades,
LUGANO is far and away the most alluring of Ticino's lake resorts, much less touristic than Locarno but with, if anything, double the chic. Even Milanese style-junkies,
who give very little quarter even to their own provincial towns, bring friends over to
Lugano for some shopping, a lakeside *apéro* and a good meal. The ever-aspiring
Luganesi return the compliment by dropping in to Milan – just 50km south – for a taste
of big city highlife and to pick a good dance club. Their home town is nonetheless an
exciting place, full of energy and style. Set on a south-facing bay of the cerulean blue
Lago di Lugano, its lake vistas are astonishing – the city is framed on all sides by
wooded, sugar-loaf hills rising from the water that have led to its being dubbed the "Rio
of the Old World". Both **Monte Brè** to the northeast and **San Salvatore** to the south
are served by funiculars, and both give spectacular views over to the snow-capped Alps.

Lugano is third behind Zürich and Geneva as a Swiss banking centre, and the city
centre reflects this, with none of Locarno's Belle-Epoque stuffiness – its old alleys and
winding lanes are full of commerce, whether in the form of enticing delicatessens and
boutiques or graceful, villa-style hotels and apartment buildings. Ancient churches and
a clutch of world-class art galleries, including the famous **Thyssen-Bornemisza
Collection**, are draws in themselves, quite aside from the simpler pleasures of a stroll
under the lakeside palms alongside the shimmering lake. If there is a drawback to
Lugano, it's the **traffic** – unpleasantly heavy most of the time, especially along the lakefront corniche, and marked by alarming Italian-style driving. But at night, looking down
from the summit of Brè amidst a warm southerly breeze, with the toot and rumble of
cars rising from a bed of twinkling lights, you could feel yourself a long, long way from
Switzerland.

Arrival, orientation and information

Lugano's **train station** overlooks the town from the west, and is linked to the centre by
a short-run funicular or by steps down to Via Cattedrale, from where lanes run through
to the main **Piazza della Riforma**, one block back from the waterfront. The station is
also the arrival and reservations point for the daily Palm Express **postbuses** direct to
St Moritz through Italy; all other postbuses depart from Piazza Rezzonico, adjacent to
Riforma in the centre. (If you're travelling on to Milan by train, ask for a free city-trans-
port pass with your ticket.) Like Locarno, Lugano takes in a number of adjacent districts which often appear in listings as if they were separate towns. The modestly
named **Paradiso** is just around the lakeshore south of the city centre; **Cassarate** is just
east of the centre at the foot of Brè, the slopes of which are covered by the mansions
and private palaces of the seriously wealthy **Castagnola** district. To complicate things
further, locals – and some maps – refer to the Lago di Lugano simply as **Ceresio**.

Lugano's little **airport** is 4km west of the city in Agno, served by internal flights and
some European routings. Shuttle buses into the city wait for flight arrivals. The driver
will drop you at your hotel (Fr.10 one-way including luggage), and on departure you can
book a pick-up from your hotel back to the airport (☎079/221 42 43). If you're arriving
at **Milan Malpensa** airport, 40km southwest of Lugano in Italy, Bus Express

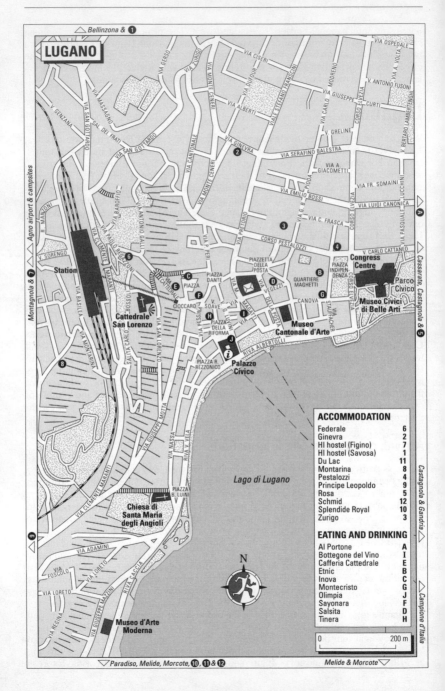

LUGANO

Station

Cattedrale San Lorenzo

Congress Centre

Parco Civico

Museo Civici di Belle Arti

Museo Cantonale d'Arte

Palazzo Civico

Chiesa di Santa Maria degli Angioli

Lago di Lugano

Museo d'Arte Moderna

N

ACCOMMODATION

Federale	6
Ginevra	2
HI hostel (Figino)	7
HI hostel (Savosa)	1
Du Lac	11
Montarina	8
Pestalozzi	4
Principe Leopoldo	9
Rosa	5
Schmid	12
Splendide Royal	10
Zurigo	3

EATING AND DRINKING

Al Portone	A
Bottegone del Vino	I
Cafferia Cattedrale	E
Etnic	B
Inova	C
Montecristo	G
Olimpia	J
Sayonara	F
Salsita	D
Tinera	H

0   200 m

LUGANO'S FESTIVALS

Music of various kinds tops the agenda at festivals in and around Lugano. The season opens in mid-April with eight or nine weeks of the **Primavera Concertistica**, a classical programme of renowned soloists and orchestras performing in the main Congress Centre; tickets (Fr.20–100) and schedules can be had from the tourist office. In early July, **Estival Jazz** (Summer Jazz) covers a series of free concerts in Mendrisio, Tesserete and Lugano that have been running for decades: in the 1950s, Dexter Gordon, Max Roach and Ornette Coleman all played at Lugano, and in the 1960s the festival featured some of Keith Jarrett's earliest performances.

The end of July sees two huge **firework** displays over the lake, with the Italian enclave of Campione throwing down the gauntlet on July 24 and Lugano itself responding a week later for Swiss National Day on August 1. The **Blues to Bop and World Music Festival** in early September is another free event.

(☎091/682 88 20, *www.busexpress.com*) operate four daily shuttles at 8.30am, 11.30am, 4.30pm and 7pm direct from Malpensa airport to the border town of Chiasso (40min) and Lugano (1hr); a one-way fare, including luggage, is Fr.30.

Lugano's **tourist office** is in the Palazzo Civico on Riva Albertolli, directly opposite the main landing stage (April–Oct Mon–Fri 9am–6.30pm, Sat 9am–12.30pm & 1.30–5pm, Sun 10am–2pm; Nov–March Mon–Fri 9am–12.30pm & 1.30–5.30pm; ☎091/913 32 32, *www.lugano-tourism.ch*). They have the usual piles of information on the city, including a useful pocket Official Guide in four languages, as well as informative brochures on the region around Lugano. Their excellent **guided walking tour** of the city, starting from the Chiesa degli Angioli on Piazza Luini, is free (April–Oct Mon 9.30am). **City buses** are free to Swiss Pass, Lugano Regional Pass and InterRail holders, but full price to Eurailers (Fr.1.20–1.90 per trip, or Fr.5 for a day pass).

Accommodation

Lugano has plenty of **accommodation** to suit all budgets. There's a five-star **campsite**, *La Piodella*, by the lakeshore in Muzzano, 3km west of town near Agno airport (☎091/994 77 88, fax 994 67 08; closed Nov), with four more campsites in close proximity to it – cheapest is *Molinazzo* (☎091/605 17 57, fax 605 14 01; April–Oct). One of Switzerland's best-value **HI hostels** (complete with swimming pool), is at Via Cantonale 13, Savosa (☎091/966 27 28, fax 968 23 63; ①; mid-March to Oct), with dorms for Fr.26 – take bus #5 to Crocifisso from the stop 200m left out of the train station. Another option is the HI hostel in an idyllic location at **Figino** on the Ceresio peninsula (☎091/995 11 51, fax 995 10 70; March to mid-Oct), offering dorms for Fr.25 and bike rental – hourly postbuses from outside the Lugano tourist office go to Casoro, a stop beside the hostel (20min). The well-located *Hotel Montarina* (see below) has quality modern dorms within the city centre for Fr.35, with discounts for stays over two nights.

Inexpensive hotels

Ginevra, Via Ginevra 7 (☎091/923 61 70, fax 923 61 75). Rather grotty from the outside, but balconied rooms on the upper floors at the back aren't bad for the price. Shared-bath rooms are a steal, considering the central location. ①–②.

Montarina, Via Montarina 1 (☎091/966 72 72, fax 966 12 13, *asbest@tinet.ch*; closed Jan). Efficient little place in a nice garden just behind the station, with clean, all-new rooms and helpful management. ①.

Pestalozzi, Piazza Indipendenza 9 (☎091/921 46 46, fax 922 20 45). Quality choice bang in the centre, 150m from the lakeshore, with serviceable rooms in an Art Nouveau-style building. ②.

Rosa, Via Landriani 2 (☎091/922 92 86, fax 923 42 70). A small B&B hotel overlooking the civic park just east of the centre, with shared-bath and en-suite rooms. ②.

Schmid, Via delle Scuole 9 (☎091/994 91 21, fax 994 18 13). Clean, pleasant family-run place beside the Salvatore funicular in Paradiso; the rooms aren't modern, but are atmospheric, and some bigger ones with double balconies are a bargain. ②–③.

Zurigo, Corso Pestalozzi 13 (☎091/923 43 43, fax 923 92 68). Central, very clean and well-kept place, with modern rooms, private parking and a trace of style as well. ②.

Mid-range and expensive hotels

Federale, Via Regazzoni 8 (☎091/922 05 51, fax 923 29 88, *reservation@hotel-federale.ch*, *www.hotel-federale.ch*). Impressive townhouse set in the quiet leafy district immediately below the station, well away from traffic and with lake views from upper floors; quality modern rooms are characterful and good value. ③–④.

Du Lac, Riva Paradiso 3 (☎091/994 19 21, fax 994 11 22, *dulac@dial.eunet.ch*, *tivi.eunet.ch/dulac*). Modern lakefront hotel, something of an eyesore but nonetheless with comfortable, balconied rooms looking onto the lake; those without a lake view cost much less. Go for the upper floors. ④–⑤.

Principe Leopoldo, Via Montalbano 5 (☎091/985 88 55, fax 985 88 25, *info@leopoldo.ch*, *www.leopoldo.ch*). Disconcertingly lavish palace way up on a hill overlooking the lake, dripping in traditional elegance and luxury, with guest facilities to match. ⑧–⑨.

Splendide Royal, Riva Caccia 7 (☎091/985 77 11, fax 985 77 22, *info@splendide.ch*, *www.splendide.ch*). Lugano's best and most expensive establishment, with public and guest room interiors that live up to the hotel's name. Accept nothing less than one of the vast new rooms on the top floor, offering some of the best views in the city. ⑨.

The Town

Centre of Lugano is the broad, spacious **Piazza della Riforma**, a huge café-lined square perfect for eyeballing passers-by over a cappuccino. The lake is a few metres away behind the Neoclassical **Palazzo Civico**, as are the characterful steep lanes of the Old Town on the opposite side of the square. Wandering through the dense maze of shopping alleys northwest of Riforma, you're bound to stumble on the extraordinary Gabbani delicatessen, whose fame spreads far beyond the borders of the canton – the interior is an Aladdin's Cave of fine *salsiccia* made especially for the shop, cabinets full of Alpine cheeses from the farmers of Alto Ticino, pastries and foodie delights galore. From bustling Piazza Cioccaro just past the deli, the atmospheric stepped Via Cattedrale doglegs steeply up to **Cattedrale San Lorenzo**, characterized by an impressive Renaissance portal, fragments of fourteenth- to sixteenth-century interior frescoes, and spectacular views from its terrace.

The narrow, unassuming **Via Nassa** – which nonetheless rivals Zürich's Bahnhofstrasse for international designer-label chic – heads southwest from Riforma through a string of picturesque little squares to the medieval **Chiesa di Santa Maria degli Angioli** on Piazza Luini. This plain little church beside a disused funicular track was founded in 1490 as part of a Franciscan monastery (suppressed in 1848 during Switzerland's civil war). Inside, the wall separating the nave from the chancel is entirely covered with a monumental fresco painted in 1529 by Bernadino Luini that depicts, in intricate and gory fashion, the Passion and Crucifixion; up above is St Sebastian, graphically pierced by arrows. Frescoes of unnamed towns cover the three arches through to the chancel: beneath the left-hand arch is a depiction of Jerusalem. On the left-hand wall is another fresco by Luini, this time of the Last Supper.

A wander across to the lakefront park opposite the church reveals a bust of one **"Giorgio" Washington** set in a position of honour. Needless to say, Washington never set foot in Lugano; a nineteenth-century Swiss entrepreneur who had made his fortune in the United States donated the sculpture as a mark of honour towards the land of

Lugano boasts two vantage points, both accessible from within the city limits. A funicular rises from Cassarate, ten minutes' walk east of the centre, to the summit of **Monte Brè**, a sheer 660m directly above the city (also accessible by car), offering spectacular views from the summit café over the lake, the curve of Lugano's bay and due west to the snowy Monte Rosa massif, behind which lurks the Matterhorn. Bracing walks lead off all over the mountain, including a four-hour circuit out to Monte Boglia and back.

From Paradiso, ten minutes south of the centre, a funicular rises to **San Salvatore**, a rugged rock pinnacle offering especially good 360° panoramas from the roof of the little church on the summit, a short climb from the funicular station. A terrace café by the top station attends to refreshment needs. This is also the starting point for a number of walks south into the Ceresio peninsula: it's about an hour and twenty minutes through Carona village to Morcote (see p.508) on the tip of the peninsula.

opportunity across the ocean. Some 100m south of the Chiesa degli Angioli on the lakefront is the **Museo d'Arte Moderna**, Riva Caccia 5 (Tues–Sun 9am–7pm; entry varies), which puts on one or two fine-art exhibitions a year of world-class quality; watch for the posters around town.

East of Piazza della Riforma

Five minutes walk east from Riforma brings you to the **Museo Cantonale d'Arte**, a fine old villa at Via Canova 10 (Tues 2–5pm, Wed–Sun 10am–5pm; Fr.7 for the permanent collection, Fr.10 to include temporary shows; SMP). Inside you'll find some paintings by Klee and Renoir amongst local depictions of peasant life by Swiss and Italian artists of the nineteenth and twentieth centuries. Another 100m east is the attractive waterfront Parco Civico. Within the park, the nineteenth-century Villa Ciani – with some sumptuously decorated ceilings – houses the **Museo Civici di Belle Arti** (Tues–Sun 10am–noon & 2–6pm; Fr.5), showing works by Cranach, Giovanni Serodine and Henri Rousseau among plenty of Impressionist and Modernist canvases.

A pleasant thirty-minute lakeside walk east along the shore leads you to the undramatic gates of **Villa Favorita**, also with its own bus stop (bus #1). This is the home of part of the famous **Thyssen-Bornemisza art collection**, the world's second-greatest in private hands, after the Queen's (Easter–Oct Fri–Sun 10am–5pm; Fr.10). The Old Masters were shipped to Madrid in 1992 on a ten-year loan, and what's left are excellent nineteenth- and twentieth-century European and American works, many of them by relative unknowns but all the more eye-opening for that. But the art is only part of the story: the villa can only be approached via a long cypress-lined path through lavishly beautiful exotic **waterside gardens**, a dreamy wander almost worth the entrance fee by itself. Once you arrive at the villa, the collection begins upstairs with some remnants of antique furniture and sculpture from the original, complete collection. Upstairs again is the **main gallery**, with works by Schiele and Munch standing out, as does the set of realist, poster-like works by artists working in the Soviet Union immediately post-Revolution. Perhaps the most startling work of all, though, is a photorealist New York street scene, painted in 1976 by Richard Estes with astonishing detail. The roomful of Toulouse-Lautrec lithographs, although the jewel of the collection, are somehow less impressive by comparison.

Once you emerge from the villa gates, you could continue your stroll east around the base of Monte Brè, joining the Sentiero di Gandria footpath through the gorgeous **Parco degli Ulivi**, a Mediterranean-style lakefront park shaded by olive trees, cypress, laurels, oleander and deliciously fragrant rosemary. This whole south-facing horn of Monte Brè is protected as an area of special scientific interest, revelling in a semitropical microclimate of near-continuous sunshine and just a handful of rainy days a year. After about an hour's wandering, you come around to the picturesque village of **GANDRIA**, rising straight from the water a few kilometres west of the international border, and inaccessible by road (although still swamped with day-trippers). Right beside the landing stage on the opposite shore, served by plenty of boats from Gandria itself as well as Lugano centre, is the **Museo delle Dogane Svizzere** (Customs Museum; April–Oct daily 1.30–5.30pm; free), with a moderately interesting collection of customs-related bits and bobs that lack decent English notes, although the displays relating to smuggling methods speak for themselves.

Eating and drinking

Lugano is blessed with any amount of pleasant, atmospheric places to **eat**, and you'll have no difficulty finding somewhere to suit your mood and your budget. Those on a tight budget should aim for the self-service diner within the big Inova department store just off Piazza Cioccaro, the lower terminus of the station funicular. The many bars and cafés around Riforma all offer good, inexpensive food at lunch and dinner – yet although they get packed with evening **drinkers**, hip, bar-hopping Luganesi prefer to tuck themselves away elsewhere, filling out a handful of vibrant bars off the main streets of the centre.

Al Portone, Viale Cassarate 3 (☎091/923 55 11). Gourmet restaurant that manages to keep a pleasantly relaxed ambience alongside its spectacular, inventive new Italian cuisine. Top quality commands top prices. Closed Sun & Mon.

Bottegone del Vino, Via Magatti 1. Old-style wine bar beside the post office, with waiters in proper white aprons and a huge range of wines on offer by the glass or bottle. Closed Sun.

Cafferia Cattedrale, Via Cattedrale 6. Small, friendly café dispensing espresso as it should be.

Etnic, Quartiere Maghetti, east of the post office. A superb, inexpensive bamboo-and-candlelight diner tucked away in an unlikely looking purpose-built warren of shops and pharmacies. The menu is all Mediterranean, with Greek and Lebanese specialities around Fr.15, or you could plump for a beer or a banana daiquiri from the bar instead. Either way, the atmosphere is happy, studentish and relaxed. Closed Sun eve.

Montecristo, Via Canova, junction Stauffacher. Painfully hip new café-bar, reasonably laid-back during the day but crammed to the rafters most nights, when even the sound system fails to drown the conversation.

Olimpia, Piazza della Riforma. Venerable old institution housed in one wing of the Palazzo Civico, and best of the many cafés around the square for its surprisingly good, inexpensive food. *Menus* of Italian staples, steaks and a few more interesting dishes rarely go for more than Fr.20.

Salsita, Via Vegezzi. Pumping evening and late-night place doubling as a cool drinking-den and mid-priced Mexican eatery (*menus* Fr.25 or so), filled with a sharp-dressing, easy crowd of youthful regulars. Closed Mon.

Sayonara, Via Soave 10. Fast-paced central diner offering inexpensive pizza and pasta options, along with filling staples like polenta for around Fr.15.

Tinera, Via dei Gorini 2. Very popular rustic *grotto*-style restaurant, specializing in Ticinese and Lombard dishes such as *pollo alla cacciatora* (spicy chicken stew) and home-made pasta, along with an array of excellent local merlots. *Menus* around Fr.20. Closed Sun & Aug.

Listings

Adventure sports As-Best, Via Basilea 28, CP 9, CH-6903 Lugano (☎091/966 11 44, *www.asbest.ch*), have a full range of adventure sports on offer in and around Lugano, including canyoning (from Fr.90), rap jumps (Fr.90), freeclimbing (Fr.90), paragliding (Fr.150), mountain biking and more.

Ballooning Balloon Team, Via delle Scuole 18 in Pregassona (☎091/940 47 16, *www.hats.ch/balloons*) offer year-round hot-air balloon trips, depending on the weather, for Fr.380 per person.

Bike rental In the station (daily 7am–8pm), at the Figino hostel (see "Accommodation") and at various sports shops around town.

Car rental Avis, Hotel Albatro, Via Clemente Maraini 8 (☎091/913 41 51) and airport (☎091/605 54 59); Europcar, Via Monte Boglia 24 (☎091/971 01 01) and airport (☎091/605 12 11); Hertz, Via San Gottardo 13 (☎091/923 46 75) and airport (☎091/605 58 93). Best deal by far, though, are the two-person Smart cars from Smart Rent, Riva Paradiso 26 (☎091/993 13 13, *www.smartrent.ch*).

Changing money In the station (Mon–Sat 7.10am–7.45pm, Sun 8am–7.45pm).

Consulates The only English-speaking country with representation in Lugano is the UK, at Via Motta 19 (☎091/923 86 06).

Email and Internet City-Disc on Piazza Dante charge Fr.4 for 20min, or Fr.10/hr.

Flights For flight enquiries for Lugano-Agno airport, call ☎091/610 12 12.

Gay and lesbian Spazio Gay, Via Stazio 10 in Massagno (☎091/968 17 17), is the main information centre for Ticino's gay scene.

Lost property Check with the police office on Piazza Riforma (☎091/800 71 10), or at the train station.

Markets There's a picturesque flower, fruit and veg market on Piazza Riforma, with antiques and handicrafts alongside on Via Canova (Tues & Fri 7am–noon). On Saturdays (8am–5pm), the Quartier Canova is again given over to antiques, with Via Vegezzi and Via Soave hosting the fruit and veg market.

Medical facilities Ospedale Civico, Via Tesserete 46 (☎091/805 61 11), has a 24-hour emergency room.

Post Main office is in the centre on Via della Posta (CH-6900 Lugano 1).

Around Lugano

The possibilities for getting out into the countryside around Lugano and the lake are plentiful – the tourist office has individual sheets on 21 cycling routes and 28 walking trails out of the city, both long and short, taxing and easy. The best area to head for is the hilly countryside of the **Ceresio peninsula**, extending directly behind the San Salvatore mountain opposite Lugano, with lake views to east, south and west that are continually captivating. Postbuses and/or boats from Lugano serve all villages on the peninsula.

The only draw on the opposite shore of the lake is the tiny Italian enclave of **Campione d'Italia**, which opted out of the campaign for independence in 1798 and so formed a part of Italy when all around it became Swiss. The village – for that's all it is,

---

BOATS ON LAGO DI LUGANO

More even than other Swiss lakes, the idyllic **Lago di Lugano** merits taking to the water simply for the pleasure of it. The Società Navigazione del Lago di Lugano, or **SNL**, provide the service; their ticket booth is at the main Lugano landing stage opposite the tourist office (daily 7.30am–6.30pm; ☎091/971 52 23). This stage is known as **Lugano-Centrale**; there are also jetties at Lugano-Giardino and Castagnola to the east, and Lugano-Paradiso to the south. Boats run between April and October roughly every 45min over to **Gandria** and **Campione** on the eastern arm of the lake; while others depart every two hours south to **Morcote** and on around the Ceresio peninsula to Ponte Tresa, stopping at most places on the way. A panoramic two-and-a-half-hour cruise around the lake, with commentary in English, runs daily (April–Oct) at 2.40pm, and there are also a hatful of cruises throughout the day offering on-board meals, drinks and/or music. In **winter**, a skeleton service operates three boats daily to Morcote, and a few each week over to Campione and Gandria.

A **day pass** on the lake is Fr.32; any three days' unlimited travel costs Fr.48; while seven consecutive days cost Fr.58. All SNL boats are free to Swiss Pass and Lugano Regional Pass holders, but Eurail and InterRail bring no discounts.

even though it's very swish – has Italian police driving around in Swiss-registered cars, and a noticeable lack of either lire or passport controls. Where the place has made a mint is in benefiting from Italian gaming law, considerably more liberal – at least until recent changes in the law – than in Switzerland: Campione's massive lakeside **casino**, with unlimited stakes, is where Lugano's many high rollers come to dally after dark.

The Ceresio peninsula

Although San Salvatore is the most obvious landmark on the **Ceresio peninsula**, just 4km southwest of central Lugano rises a lower hill dubbed the **Collina d'Oro** or Hill of Gold, not for its minerals but for its sun-drenched tranquillity. On the top sits the village of **MONTAGNOLA**, home for 43 years to the writer Hermann Hesse. Hesse was born in Germany in 1877, and came to Montagnola in 1919 following traumatic separation from his family after World War I. He rented the **Casa Camuzzi**, an ornate villa, where he lived for twelve years, and where, in an extraordinary outpouring of creativity, he wrote his classic works *Klingsor's Last Summer*, *Siddhartha* and *Steppenwolf*, among many others. In 1924, he was granted Swiss citizenship, and then, in 1931, he moved to the Casa Bodmer, also in Montagnola, where he wrote *The Glass Bead Game*, which won him the Nobel Prize for Literature in 1946. Hesse died in Montagnola in 1962.

In 1997, the Casa Camuzzi in the village was opened as the **Museo Hermann Hesse** (March–Oct Tues–Sun 10am–12.30pm & 2–6.30pm; Nov–Feb Sat & Sun same times; Fr.5; SMP). There are no signs to the museum from the Montagnola bus stop; with the village post office behind you, walk down the slope and aim through a narrow passage leading ahead off the square. The house is five minutes further on the right. Walking around the old villa is interesting in itself, although the modest displays – Hesse's umbrella, Hesse's table – are labelled in Italian and German only. What makes the entry fee worthwhile, however, is an excellent 45-minute video in English on the writer's life in Montagnola that the staff can set up for you in a basement room; aside from interviews, readings and tales of Hesse's many illustrious visitors, the documentary features trenchant observations made by Hesse on the inexorable rise of tourism in Lugano during the 1940s and 1950s. The museum staff can also direct you onto a scenic **walking trail** around the village dotted with eight points of interest related to Hesse.

On the eastern side of the peninsula, exactly at the point where the train tracks, main road and motorway all cross the lake on a low bridge, sits the village of **MELIDE**, home to the kitschy but rather fun **Swissminiatur** (mid-March to Oct daily 9am–6pm; Fr.10.50; *www.swissminiatur.ch*). This small park features 1:25 scale models of just about every attraction in Switzerland, from Geneva's cathedral to Appenzell's main street, as well as some more idiosyncratic choices (Burgdorf train station, Zürich airport circa 1958). The reproductions are excellent, whether you've seen the real thing or are wondering if it would be worthwhile to make the journey, and moving model boats, trains and cable-cars of all shapes and sizes liven the static models up no end. A wander through the whole place, with 113 exhibits, might take an entertaining hour or two – buy the English leaflet (Fr.2) for a brief rundown of each model.

Morcote and Vico Morcote

The best of the Ceresio lies at the peninsula's southern tip. Here you'll find the captivating village of **MORCOTE**, once a fishing community and now eking out a living as a lakeside attraction. Its photogenic arcaded houses – and slightly tacky antique shops – are strung along the shoreline road, with a web of tranquil, stepped lanes leading up the hill behind to the beautiful **Chiesa di Santa Maria del Sasso**, a fifteen-minute climb (April–Oct Mon–Fri 8am–6pm, Sat & Sun 9am–6pm; Nov–March Mon–Fri 1.30–6pm, Sat & Sun 9am–6pm). The atmospheric hillside church has well-preserved sixteenth-century frescoes inside, and boasts views from its terrace over the lake and hills beyond that are stunning. Several walks explore the lush woodlands nearby, including a long trail back up to San Salvatore (2hr 30min).

Morcote has a handful of hotels, but also suffers from a great deal of tourist attention, and very many feet tramping its alleys. One way to escape is to aim for the even tinier village of **VICO MORCOTE**, on the hard-to-reach hillside above and 1km north of Morcote. Here, although the church is just as picturesque and the tiny village piazzas are lined with old stone-built houses that are just as beautiful, unlike in Morcote you can actually hear the fountains tinkle, smell the camellias and stand alone in the middle of the street to absorb the atmosphere. On a junction within the village beside the rustic *Osteria al Böcc* (gnocchi or spaghetti Fr.14), you'll find the tranquil *Bellavista* (☎091/996 11 43, fax 996 12 88; ③–⑥). Its impressive restaurant is run by a young, highly accomplished team, who serve exquisite, lightly prepared local cuisine on a beautiful terrace high above the lake; *menus* are around Fr.70. The hotel rooms to one side are outstanding, the bargain of the region – fresh and flooded with light. Their top-floor luxury suite, huge and spotless, with billowing curtains and a private terrace, is utterly romantic, and half the price of those in the more mundane surroundings of Lugano.

South to Italy

South of Lugano, main roads and trains shoot through the hot, dry region known as the Mendrisiotto, after **Mendrisio**, largest town in the area and a major wine-growing centre. Six kilometres on, and 23km south of Lugano, the Italian frontier is marked by **Chiasso**, a particularly unprepossessing border town, with a gigantic train station on the edge of a desultory town centre and swarms of motorized and foot traffic passing through during the morning and evening rush hours. The Italian city of **Como** is 5km beyond the border; **Milan** is 30km further.

travel details

TRAINS

Bellinzona to: Airolo (hourly; 50min); Basel (twice hourly; 3hr 20min); Biasca (hourly; 10min); Brunnen (hourly; 1hr 45min); Locarno (every 30min; 20min); Lugano (twice hourly; 25min); Luzern (twice hourly; 2hr 10min); Zürich (twice hourly; 2hr 30min).

Biasca to: Airolo (hourly; 40min); Bellinzona (hourly; 10min).

Locarno to: Bellinzona (every 30min; 20min); Intragna (twice hourly; 20min); Verscio (hourly; 15min).

Lugano to: Basel (twice hourly; 3hr 50min); Bellinzona (twice hourly; 25min); Brunnen (hourly; 2hr 10min); Luzern (twice hourly; 2hr 40min); Zürich (twice hourly; 3hr).

BUSES

Airolo to: Andermatt via Gottardo (July–Sept 3 daily; 50min); Oberwald via Novena/Nufenen Pass (July–Sept 2 daily; 2hr 45min).

Ascona to: Brissago (every 30min; 10min); Locarno (every 15min; 15min).

Bellinzona to: Biasca (hourly; 25min); Chur (every 2hr; 2hr 15min); Giornico (hourly; 40min); Locarno (hourly; 50min).

Biasca to: Bellinzona (hourly; 25min); Disentis/Mustér (June–Sept 2–3 daily; 1hr 20min; change at Lucomagno/Lukmanier Pass); Giornico (hourly; 10min); Olivone (every 2hr; 40min).

Locarno to: Ascona (every 15min; 15min); Bellinzona (hourly; 50min); Brissago (every 30min; 30min); Tenero (at least hourly; 15min).

Lugano to: Casoro (approx. hourly; 20min); Melide (approx. hourly; 15min); Montagnola (hourly; 20min); Morcote (approx. hourly; 30min); Vico Morcote (every 2hr; 35min; change at Olivella).

BOATS

(following is a summary of April–Oct services)

Ascona to: Isole di Brissago (hourly; 15min); Locarno (approx twice hourly; 20–30min).

Locarno to: Ascona (approx twice hourly; 20–30min); Isole di Brissago (hourly; 45min–1hr).

Lugano to: Gandria (approx. every 45min; 35min); Melide (every 2hr; 35min); Morcote (every 2hr; 1hr).

Porto Ronco to: Isole di Brissago (every 40min; 5–10min).

INTERNATIONAL TRAINS

Locarno to: Domodossola (approx. hourly; 1hr 45min).

Lugano to: Como (hourly; 40min); Florence (3 daily; 4hr 20min); Genoa (2 daily; 3hr 40min); Milan (hourly; 1hr 30min); Rome (1 daily; 8hr); Turin (3 daily; 3hr 20min; change at Milan); Venice (1–2 daily; 5hr).

INTERNATIONAL BUSES

Lugano to: Chiavenna (1–3 daily; 2hr 30min); Chur, Davos & St Moritz via Italy (Bernina Express; July–Sept 1 daily; 6–9hr; change at Tirano); St Moritz via Italy (Palm Express; 1–3 daily; 4hr).

INTERNATIONAL BOATS

Locarno to: Stresa (April–Oct 1–2 daily; 1hr 20min–3hr 30min).

PLACE NAMES IN THIS CHAPTER		
German	**French**	**Italian**
Brig	Brigue	Briga
Gotthard	Gothard	Gottardo
Graubünden	Grisons	Grigioni
Italien	Italie	Italia
Langensee	Lac Majeur	Lago Maggiore
Lukmanier	Lukmanier	Lucomagno
Mailand	Milan	Milano
Nufenen	Nufenen	Novena
Simplon	Simplon	Sempione
Tessin	Tessin	Ticino
Wallis	Valais	Vallese

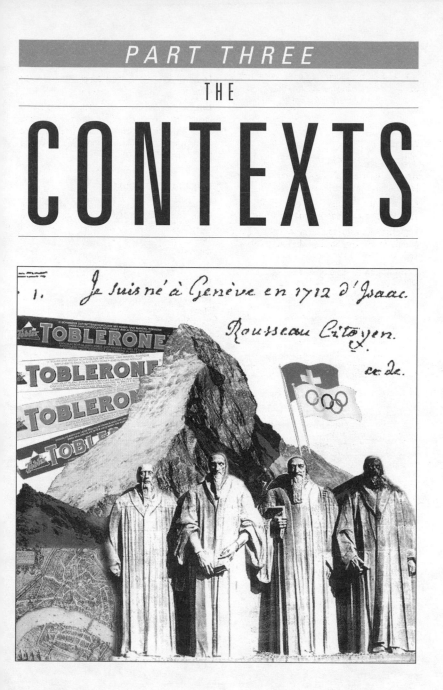

THE HISTORICAL FRAMEWORK

Switzerland is often dismissed as an irrelevance in the broader picture of European history: because the country is peaceful today, the underlying suspicion is that it either wasn't subject to the same tide of events as elsewhere, or that the place is just somehow inherently tranquil. Both ideas are false.

The Swiss difference came in solving the same problems that everyone else had in entirely different, co-operative ways. Decentralization, consultation and co-operation are still key Swiss attributes, as they were in 1291 at the start of the country's history, when a group of mountain farmers decided to band together to defy their foreign occupiers. And stability didn't come easily: up until 150 years ago, Switzerland was the most unstable country in Europe, with a history spanning centuries of internecine conflict. The Alpine calm that is notorious – or notoriously boring – today came at the price of almost a millennium of war.

EARLY CIVILIZATIONS

In Appenzell and near the Rhine in Schaffhausen are scattered remains of the **Paleolithic** civilizations that occupied the area of Switzerland in between the long periods of prehistoric glaciation. Around 10,000 years ago, at the end of the last major Ice Age, hunter-fisherfolk moved in to occupy the Mittelland, soon afterwards building permanent villages on piles on the shores of the lakes of Zürich, Neuchâtel, Geneva and others. During the **Bronze Age** and early **Iron Age**, the settled villagers began both to make contact with neighbouring populated regions, and to make war on them. In the first millennium BC, the **Celts** advanced into Switzerland from the west, bringing with them a new culture and new sophistication, as exemplified in the fortified Celtic township discovered at **La Tène**, near Neuchâtel, and others near Basel, Bern and Zürich.

THE ROMANS: 58 BC–400 AD

In 58 BC at Bibracte in modern France, a **Roman** army under Julius Caesar defeated the **Helvetii** – a group of Celtic tribes resident in the fertile area between the Alps and the Jura – and forced them to move en masse to the western part of Switzerland to serve as an irregular frontier force. Over the next hundred years or so, after also conquering **Rhaetia** (modern Graubünden), the Romans gradually opened up the country, building the first roads over the major Alpine passes – most significantly the **Grand-St-Bernard**, as well as the Julier and Splügen further east – and founding provincial towns at Nyon, Augst near Basel, and Avenches, the last of which became the Roman capital, with more than fifty thousand inhabitants in its heyday. For two centuries or more under the Romans, Switzerland enjoyed peace and prosperity, with towns established at Geneva, Lausanne, Martigny, Baden (a huge spa), Zürich, Chur and elsewhere. Agriculture flourished, and the region's settlements were populated by a cosmopolitan cultural mix of native Celts and settled Roman officials. The peace was shattered in 260, when the **Alemanii** – a group of Celtic tribes from the area of modern Germany – broke through the Romans' fortified northern border and pushed southwards. Amidst increasing turmoil and confusion, embattled Roman Helvetia and Rhaetia were reduced to impoverished frontier regions.

THE ROOTS OF FREEDOM: 400–1516

Around 400, Rome withdrew its legions from the area of Switzerland, and Germanic tribes moved in to take control. In the western regions, the originally Germanic **Burgundians** settled and adopted both the Christianity and the Latin language of the local Gallo-Roman tribes. On the south side of the mountains, and in the closed Alpine valleys of Rhaetia, Lombardic and **Romansh** peoples retained close cultural links with their former Roman overlords, the latter adapting Vulgar Latin into their own unique language. Elsewhere, **Aleman** tribes slowly trickled down from the north into the less hospitable thick forests of the central and northeastern parts of Helvetia to build new villages and agricultural settlements, generally doing so without displacing previous inhabitants and halting their advances at points where the land was already populated by Burgundians. Unlike their Latin-speaking neighbours, the Germanic Alemans had had little contact with Rome and Christianity, and so continued to use their own native language and follow their own customs. In this way, a **border** of language and culture slowly developed along a line running roughly north–south through the area, marking the easternmost limit of Latinate Burgundian territory and the western-most limit of Alemanic territory. This language border survives today as the frontier between French- and German-speaking Switzerland.

Around 600, both the Alemans and the Burgundians were conquered by the **Franks**, who absorbed them into their empire under first **Merovingian** and then **Carolingian** kings. The Frankish Empire greatly expanded Latin Christianity throughout Switzerland – and especially into the pagan Alemanic areas – with a network of **monasteries** spreading into the countryside. Ecclesiastical complexes which have survived from this time still flourish at Romainmôtier, Einsiedeln, Engelberg and St Gallen. **Feudalism** also spread, and the once-great Roman towns fell into decline as local warrior nobles took control over an agrarian society of lords, vassals and a vast, impoverished peasantry. In 870, **Charlemagne**'s empire was split, with the dividing line running right through the middle of modern Switzerland. Chaos and conflict erupted, and it wasn't until around 1050 that peace and order returned to the region, nominally under the control of the Holy Roman Empire.

THE BIRTH OF THE CONFEDERATION

During the twelfth century, about a third of the dense forests of central Switzerland were cleared for ploughing and settlement, and the noble dynasties who had emerged from the conflicts of previous centuries – among them the houses of **Habsburg**, **Zähringen**, **Savoy** and Kyburg – established towns such as Bern, Fribourg, Murten and Winterthur from which to assert their control over the increasingly prosperous countryside..

Around 1220, the road over the great **St Gotthard Pass** was opened up for traffic, and those communities lying on the northern approaches to the pass – specifically Uri and Schwyz – suddenly took on massive importance to the imperial rulers further north. A resurgence in **trade** with the Mediterranean world, and especially Byzantium and the Arab east, after almost a millennium of isolation led to luxury goods making their way across the Alpine passes into northern Europe. Local lords, merchants, princes and the valley communes squabbled with each other for control of the lucrative pass routes. The situation needed resolution, and the Holy Roman Emperor himself stepped in, granting to Uri in 1231 and to Schwyz in 1240 the privilege of freedom from feudal overlordship. With the dying out of the Zähringen and Kyburg lines, the Austrian house of **Habsburg** had seized the chance to extend its influence over much of Switzerland, but the proud, independent people farming the remote, high valleys of Uri and Schwyz, and their neighbours in forested Unterwalden, remained self-reliant and more or less free.

Rudolf of Habsburg, who had ruled since 1273, died in 1291, thus pitching the region into uncertainty. Popular revolts arose all across the Habsburg realm, especially directed against entrenched power bases such as the monastery at Einsiedeln. In response, a number of Swiss communities forged new partnerships, or renewed old ones, to give themselves a degree of protection against an uncertain future. The legendary **founding of the Swiss Confederation** on the Rütli meadow on August 1, 1291, by representatives of Uri, Schwyz and Unterwalden (see p.358), was just one of these alliances, and is thought to have been a renewal of an earlier agreement of unknown date declaring that an attack on any one of the partners was an attack on them all. The legend of **William Tell** (see p.364), which is first documented more than two centuries after the signing at Rütli, probably arose both as a justification of the sporadic rebellions against authority that followed the death of Rudolf, and as a neat way to embody the concept of Swiss liberty in a single heroic figure – there is no mention either of Tell or of any organized resistance to the Habsburgs in contemporary thirteenth-century chronicles. The Rütli document is no Declaration of Independence: it has no vision of founding a lasting political entity, and enshrines no basic human rights or privileges. It is expedient, but it nonetheless came to symbolize freedom to the Swiss. The name they gave themselves after 1291 – **Eidgenossen** – is untranslatable in English (approximating to "comrades bound by oath into a co-operative"), but has a special significance even today. Switzerland still calls itself the *Eidgenossenschaft*, and the word *Eidgenosse* is listed in dictionaries as a synonym for "Swiss".

CONSOLIDATION AND GROWTH

During the 1290s and into the 1300s, while the imperial throne remained vacant, revolts continued against symbols of Habsburg power. In 1315, at **Morgarten** near Schwyz, an army of peasants from the newly formed Confederation clashed with and defeated a force of Austrian knights sent to quell the trouble. Ludwig of Habsburg, the new emperor, was forced to concede yet more privileges to the three cantons, this time guaranteeing them freedom from any threat of imperial intervention. Instead, the Habsburgs shifted their attention to the rapidly growing market town of **Luzern**, transport hub for the journey to and from the Gotthard, and tried to force it to take up arms against its lakeside neighbours. Rather than submit to Habsburg domination, Luzern instead threw in its lot with the self-dubbed "Schwyzers", and joined the Confederation in 1332. Unable to bring the Swiss to heel, Habsburg bailiffs withdrew altogether from the region after about 1350 and left the hard-nosed peasants to their own devices. The local economy flourished, centred on the Gotthard Pass.

The feudal system that had been instituted by the Franks gradually began to collapse under pressure from an increasingly prosperous and ambitious free peasantry, who formed an array of democratic rural communes. This form of direct rural democracy went hand in hand with the rise in the power of urban workers: **Zürich**, which had already experienced a revolution by

its guilds that had overthrown the city's ruling nobility, joined the Confederation in 1351 to protect its trade interests against a resurgence in power of the nobles. Very soon afterwards, tiny **Glarus** and **Zug** were roped into the Confederation in order to secure overland transport routes; and then **Bern**, which was looking to expand its territory westwards, joined in 1353 to defuse the possibility of attack from by the east by the increasingly powerful Confederation.

Suddenly, in a little over sixty years, the insignificant Schwyzers – born out of a pact of farming folk – were able to call on an army of over 100,000, and had control of a large swathe of former Habsburg territory across the northern foothills of the Alps. Similar leagues of alliance among ordinary farmers in impenetrable Rhaetia to the east were coalescing into an organized opposition to noble Habsburg rule. While blue-blooded Habsburg armies swept victorious through the great cities of Swabia, in southern Germany, the very same armies experienced crushing defeats in Switzerland in the face of the increasingly sophisticated Confederate soldiery, most notably at **Sempach** in 1386 and **Näfels** in 1388 – both names resonant even today for the patriotic Swiss. Following their successes, the eight cantons formed an independent state within the Habsburg empire that was ruled – uniquely – by city-based burghers and merchants and founded on the principles of tight-knit social co-operation … this at a time when elsewhere across Europe kings, princes and noble dynasties held unchallenged sway.

MILITARY CONQUEST

The fifteenth century saw continued expansion by the Confederation. Forces from Uri and Obwalden crossed the Gotthard to seize the **Valle Leventina** south to Bellinzona, in order to secure their trade route (crushing the armies of the Dukes of Milan as they did so), while Confederate forces took advantage both of popular uprisings against the abbot of **St Gallen** to extend their influence further eastwards, and of a dispute between Austria and Luxembourg to seize control of the fertile northern lands of **Aargau**.

After 1460, Swiss **mercenaries** became known and feared throughout Europe for their bravery and military skill, tested on battlefields in the west of the country fighting Charles the Bold of **Burgundy**. Celebrated victories at Grandson, Murten and Nancy in the years 1476–77 effectively wiped Burgundy from the map as a regional power, but nonetheless led to the first of many subsequent disputes within the Confederation over the balance of power between towns and countryside. Rural cantons were loath to see Bern – principal victor against Charles – become any more powerful, and only accepted the entry of **Fribourg** and **Solothurn** to the Confederation in 1481 on the condition that they took a role of arbitration between the cities and the countryside to moderate urban expansionism. Following Zürich's victory in the **Swabian War** of 1499 – which won final and complete freedom for the cantons from the German Empire – both **Basel** and **Schaffhausen** joined the Confederation (1501), followed by tiny **Appenzell** in 1513. By then, the thirteen cantons possessed extensive subject territories, including Aargau, Thurgau and a swathe of Ticino. The first Swiss parliament, the **Diet**, met regularly in Baden as a forum to bring Confederate opinion together, both by discussion and – even at this early date – by majority voting.

REFORMATION AND RELIGIOUS CONFLICT: 1516–1798

The **Reformation**, which began in Germany in the early sixteenth century and spread across Europe, was sparked in Switzerland by **Huldrych Zwingli**, a lay priest in Zürich (see p.385). City after city overthrew its ecclesiastical overlords in favour of the new **Protestantism**: St Gallen, Basel, Biel/Bienne, Schaffhausen and, in 1528, Bern. In each place, the urban guilds were the motive force behind the overthrow, and once Catholicism had been ejected, each city government gained new power and authority over the countryside surrounding it, fuelling rural resentment. With the Church's land around Zürich merely parcelled out to the city authorities, the rural peasantry saw no benefit from the change, and many switched support to the extreme, but largely ineffectual, **Anabaptist** movement, which sought the abolition of serfdom altogether. When Zwingli promulgated the controversial notion of reorganizing the Confederacy under the twin **city** leadership of Zürich and Bern, many Catholics from small towns and villages in central Switzerland in particular resisted strongly, feeling both their religious faith and their political voice to be under threat. Conflict broke out in 1531, in which Zwingli was killed and the Catholic forces won the right to veto in the Diet what they considered anti-rural policies.

Nonetheless, the Reformation continued to spread: with the help of Bernese forces, Geneva won its independence from Savoy in 1530, and shortly afterwards – along with Neuchâtel, Lausanne and the Vaud countryside – accepted the Reformation. In 1536, the French priest **Jean Calvin** settled in Geneva, establishing a rigid Protestant theocracy that spread the city's reputation for religious zeal and tolerance Europe-wide.

The situation became further entrenched in the 1550s and 1560s, with the coalescing of the Reformation around Calvinist doctrine, and the consequent launch of the **Counter-Reformation** in a bid to preserve Catholic territory and reassert Catholic rights. With the support of Spain – a major world power – the Catholic cantons retained their religious identity within the Confederation (although in 1597 Appenzell split into two half-cantons, one Protestant and one Catholic), but they increasingly nurtured an inferiority complex towards the Protestant cities, which held a grip on political authority and the economy. The latter had started to take on new vitality, boosted by the presence of skilled Huguenot and Veltliner craftspeople, **Protestant refugees** from Catholic regimes in France and Italy.

THE SEVENTEENTH CENTURY

Throughout the tense seventeenth century, it was only shared economic interests that kept the Confederation together: a lucrative system of **textile processing** developed, in which merchants in the cities (generally Protestant) supplied raw materials to peasants in the countryside (generally Catholic), who worked up the finished product and delivered it back to the city merchants for trading on or export. Politics, however, remained in deadlock. No new regions could be admitted to the Confederation, since to do so would upset the delicate balance between Catholic and Protestant cantons. Mistrust on the part of Catholics of a perceived Protestant agenda for domination of the Confederation prevented reorganization or redistribution of jointly administered subject territories, which included Graubünden and Valais.

This wariness filtered over into foreign policy, with the continuing traffic in mercenaries entangling the Confederation in a complex web of **armed neutrality**. All the cantons had pledged to supply France with manpower; in addition, the Catholic ones had links with Spain and Savoy, the Protestant ones with various German principalities and the Netherlands. (The Battle of Malplaquet in 1709 between France and Holland is the most famous example of Swiss mercenaries taking to the battlefield against each other.) The Confederation stayed out of the **Thirty Years' War** (1618–48) – the first significant test of its neutrality – but still imposed new taxes to strengthen its frontier defences and assumed state control of trade in staple foodstuffs. In 1645, a peasants' rebellion in the east of the country against the new austerities was suppressed with violence and executions. In 1653, after the currency was devalued without warning, wiping out the meagre savings of the rural peasantry overnight, a full-scale **Peasants' Revolt** set out to reclaim ancient rights enshrined in agreements from the early days of the Confederation. Without any ado, the urban patricians of Bern and Luzern called in the army to crush the revolt with ruthlessness, and then launched a campaign to reform the Confederate charter in favour of themselves. This was blocked by the rural cantons, who then went to war to safeguard their interests. In a mark of the turbulence of the period, Protestant urban aristocrats and Catholic rural aristocrats first combined to crush the peasantry, then within a few years turned to face each other in bloody conflict. After two separate battles at **Villmergen**, in 1656 and 1712, Catholics conceded Protestant rights both in confederal matters and in administering the joint dependencies.

THE BUILD-UP TO REVOLUTION

The Protestant victory in 1712 – which ended Catholic hegemony in confederal affairs – also ended two centuries of religious conflict, and resulted in a **social and economic shift** in favour of the largely Protestant cities. Catholic regions of the country, which had remained free from the dour influence of Calvin, enjoyed relative freedom in personal conduct but were industrially backward, while Protestant areas benefited from a better-educated populace and the presence of Protestant artisans from around Europe. French Huguenots in particular, their name a corruption of *Eidgenosse*, were the motive force behind a growth in urban manufacturing industries such as **watchmaking** in the northwest and **textiles** in the east (cotton, calico, silk and embroidery). During the Swiss industrial revolution of the eighteenth century, **commercial farming** also began to take hold in the rural cantons.

The second half of the century saw the liberal **Enlightenment** replacing the rigours of Calvinism country-wide, with writers and thinkers such as Jean-Jacques Rousseau and Heinrich Pestalozzi feeding a new spirit of Helvetic nationalism which brought Catholics and Protestants together in their patriotic concern for the nation.

However, political life became increasingly ossified, with the swing away from the tumultuous religious conflict of the recent past demonstrating itself in profound **conservatism**. Fearful of a repetition of the peasants' uprising, urban patrician dynasties asserted their traditional prerogatives in a series of measures designed to concentrate power in their own hands. Increasing prosperity and the influence of liberal Enlightenment philosophies in towns and countryside alike led to growing intolerance of patrician rule on the part of ordinary people: in Lausanne in 1723, in Geneva in 1737, in Bern in 1749, in Ticino in 1755, and in Geneva again throughout the 1760s, popular insurrections against entrenched systemic injustice demonstrated a grass-roots desire for change.

REVOLUTION AND CIVIL WAR: 1798–1848

The impact in Switzerland of the **French Revolution** of 1789 was enormous. The Confederation itself remained neutral in the battles that followed, but popular revolutionary demonstrations throughout Vaud – at that time a Bernese colony – and at Stäfa near Zürich acted as a prelude and a spur to a full-scale **French invasion** in 1798 by armies under Napoleon. Revolution swept through the country. In Ticino, Aargau and the lower Valais, the old patrician establishment was swept away; urban residents of Basel, Zürich and

Schaffhausen at a stroke won equality before the law; Vaud declared itself independent from Bern; and the brief burst of resistance to the French mounted in central areas was violently suppressed. On March 5, French forces entered Bern, marking the fall of the *ancien régime* in Switzerland.

Within weeks, Napoleon promulgated a new constitution intended to replace the archaic patchwork of communities and privileges, decentralized authority and internecine mistrust that had prevailed since the Middle Ages. His brave new **Helvetic Republic**, "unitary and indivisible", did away with cantons altogether and instead vested centralized power, French-style, nominally in the people but actually in a five-man executive. This showed just how drastically Napoleon underestimated the Swiss, who broke the habit of centuries by coming together – liberal and conservative, Catholic and Protestant alike – in unanimous rejection of his imposed new order. A series of *coup d'états* attempting to end French domination prompted Napoleon to withdraw his troops from the country in short order in 1802. Civil war immediately broke out, and Napoleon stepped in as arbitrator, this time prudently urging the Swiss themselves to come up with a constitution. This shortlived **Mediation**, as it was called, restored the notion of autonomous cantons, and in addition conferred full cantonal status on six areas previously under joint administration – St Gallen, Graubünden, Aargau, Thurgau, Ticino and Vaud – meanwhile giving the country the new title of the **Swiss Confederation**, a name it bears today.

AFTER NAPOLEON

The calm was shortlived: once Napoleon himself was defeated at Waterloo in 1815, the democratic, federal balance in Switzerland collapsed. The 1815 **Congress of Vienna** reasserted old patrician privileges throughout Europe, not least in Switzerland, where aristocratic families regained control over local and federal politics. Geneva, Neuchâtel and Valais entered the Swiss Confederation as **new cantons**, and Bern was granted the Jura as compensation for its losses in Aargau and Vaud. For fifteen years, the political situation simmered, until street fighting in Paris in 1830 sparked in Switzerland the **Regeneration**, a similar movement of liberalization. This led to seizures of

power around the country by united bands of peasants, urban merchants, and craftspeople, who drew up cantonal constitutions enshrining equality and political rights for all – rural and urban alike – and instituted democratic elections to the cantonal governments. In 1831, the patricians of **Basel** condoned a localized civil war, and the division of the formerly unified canton into two antagonistic half-cantons, rather than surrender any of their powers to radical activists.

Despite ongoing political conflict, Switzerland was nonetheless enjoying an **economic** boom. Manufacturing industry had slowly been mechanized from the turn of the century but, unlike in Britain – the only country in Europe to be more industrially advanced – Switzerland experienced no rush to the cities by an impoverished proletariat. Swiss factories, where they existed, were in rural areas, and drew their labour from the local peasantry, who often came to work after tending to their herds in the fields. Cottage industry, where textiles were processed or watches assembled by individuals working in their own homes under contract from urban suppliers, remained a mainstay of Swiss economic development. The piecemeal, individual-driven Swiss textile industry was efficient enough to stave off competition from Britain's "dark satanic mills" throughout the first half of the century. In addition, new – and diverse – fields of expertise in chemical production, chocolatemaking and tourism boosted national confidence and the image of the country in the eyes of the world. Internal religious conflict, however, was again rearing its head.

THE SONDERBUND WAR

After the upheavals of the early 1830s, conflict between **radical** liberals and **conservative** – generally Catholic – activists led to increasingly bitter squabbles. After Aargau overturned the constitutional equality of Protestantism and Catholicism in 1841 and ordered all religious buildings in the canton to be shut down, outraged Catholics in neighbouring Luzern nullified that canton's newly drafted liberal constitution and – in a move intended to provoke – invited the **Jesuit** order to run the canton's schools. This, in turn, outraged radical opinion, which valued liberal education highly and viewed Jesuit control of the schools as nothing less than a backward step into superstition.

Violent, radical-led scuffles soon broke out, aimed at Luzern's Catholics. In response, the Catholic cantons – Luzern, Zug, Schwyz, Uri, Obwalden, Nidwalden, Fribourg and Valais – formed an illegal resistance force, dubbed the **Sonderbund** (Separatist League), which threatened to destabilize the country. During 1846, a series of localized revolutions put radicals in control of more and more cantons nationwide until, by 1847, with a majority in the Diet, they demanded the expulsion of the Jesuits from the country, the drafting of a new democratic constitution, and the forced dissolution of the Sonderbund. **Civil war** was inevitable, and – as much to head off potentially disastrous intervention by the great European powers as anything else – the federal commander in chief General Henri Dufour took the opportunity to strike rapidly and effectively. In a month-long campaign during November 1847 he easily took Fribourg and Zug, and then Luzern, crushing the heartland of the Sonderbund with casualties barely in three figures. The remaining Catholic cantons capitulated following the decisive **Battle of Gislikon** at the end of November.

RECONCILIATION: 1848–1918

The postwar **Federal Constitution of 1848** – still in effect today – marked the birth of the modern Swiss state. It enshrined a host of liberal measures designed to limit severely conservative, patrician power and to permit continued expansion of industry and the economy. For the first time, Switzerland had a **central government**, with a parliament comprising two directly elected houses. With the background of revolutions breaking out alarmingly all over Europe during 1848, the radical liberals – conscious of the centuries of Swiss conflict behind them – devised a constitution that was able to defuse the age-old Catholic fears of Protestant domination. They did so principally by **dividing power** between the centre and the cantons, thereby allowing the majority Protestants and the minority Catholics to engage in democratic debate together, in the knowledge that each needed the other to survive. Devolution of power to self-governing cantons – **federalism** – allowed the retention of strong Catholic communities at the cantonal level and the creation of strong Protestant-led institutions at the national level. And, following 25 years of continued peace and consolidation, the formal

adoption in 1874 of the **referendum** as the prime tool for consultation of the people – on matters of local, cantonal and national interest alike – ensured that politicians remained directly accountable to the electorate. Amidst steady economic growth, in railways, tourism, chemicals, engineering and heavy industry, **national reconciliation** was allowed to develop organically over the second half of the century, and with it came further democratization, with the adoption of proportional representation in cantonal elections and the growth of consultation and compromise at executive level in the federal government.

With the mood of reconciliation after 1848, plus an ever-increasing flow of tourists exploring the newly fashionable Alps, the huge national celebrations of six hundred years of Swiss history in 1891, and the unveiling of the idealistic monument to William Tell in Altdorf in 1895, a new, specifically **Swiss national identity** began to develop. However, although the appeal of Swiss national unity was strong, the new mood of European **nationalism** threatened – paradoxically – to split the country apart again. The alluringly woolly ideas that developed at this time of race, social darwinism and the mystical destiny shared by all people who shared a particular language (exemplified in the concept of uniting Europe's German-speaking *Volk*), held a far more romantic, supranational appeal. German Swiss looked towards the achievements of Germany, with its booming economy, military prowess and advanced social-welfare policies, and felt themselves to be part of it, distanced from their French-speaking compatriots. Similarly, French Swiss looked towards the cultural achievements of *fin-de-siècle* France, and saw their Swiss-German neighbours as foreign. Italian-speaking Swiss in particular felt the arbitrary international border between them and the "rest" of Italy, its culture and literature, to be increasingly absurd. More even than at the height of religious conflict in centuries past, at the dawn of the twentieth the Swiss had stopped talking to each other.

WORLD WAR I AND AFTER

Officially, Switzerland stayed out of **World War I**. In practice, the army had been "thoroughly Prussianized", as Jonathan Steinberg puts it, and its commanders saw no reason not to support Germany. As soon as war broke out in the summer of 1914, Switzerland began passing military intelligence to Berlin. The mood within the country soured, as German and French Swiss retreated from each other, both backing opposite sides in the war. In an echo of the trenches of northern France, a *Graben*, or trench, opened up along the language border between the two. French Swiss were increasingly outraged by their army's pro-German bias, and in 1917 the Swiss foreign minister was forced to resign after secretly trying to negotiate a European peace between Germany and the new revolutionary regime in Russia.

Economic conditions were also hard, compounded by the need to maintain hundreds of thousands of soldiers guarding the frontiers, and to support a growing number of refugees and asylum seekers. In 1915 and 1916, Lenin, Trotsky and Zinoviev were all resident in Switzerland, and the influence of their revolutionary socialist agitations, as well as subsequent news of the successful Russian Revolution, spurred impoverished Swiss workers on to a **General Strike** in November 1918. For three days the Federal Council dithered, then called in the army. The strikers capitulated soon afterwards and went back to work, but had made their point: in a referendum in 1919 on whether to adopt proportional representation in national elections – a major plank of the workers' concerns, since majority voting had effectively excluded the Socialist Party from real power – the Swiss people voted overwhelmingly in favour. The Federal Council acknowledged the benefits of compromise, and met the strike committee face to face to address their concerns. Soon after, policies on welfare expansion and a 48 hour working week became law.

NEUTRALITY AND WORLD WAR II: 1918–1945

The rise in power of a socialist-minded proletariat immediately after the war prompted a correspondent rise in the old forces of Catholic conservatism, as well as in rural farmers, who quickly won a place on the Federal Council alongside the urban Radicals. At the same time, Switzerland began to take the first overt steps away from its traditional absolute neutrality, voting in 1920 to join the **League of Nations** – which was headquartered in Geneva, lending both the city and the country a sheen of international prestige that it retains to this day – and yet insisting on an exclusion clause that permitted Swiss adherence to an ill-defined partisan neutrality. The contradiction remained untested until 1935, when the League imposed economic sanctions on fascist Italy after the invasion of Abyssinia: Switzerland (or, more accurately, its right-leaning Ticinese foreign minister, Giuseppe Motta) could not bring itself to punish Italy, and withdrew from the League in favour of a return to absolute neutrality.

As elsewhere, the economic bubble of the 1920s burst in the early 1930s, with a crippling **depression** halving output, decimating incomes and causing huge unemployment. At the same time, cosy domestic political coalitions were breaking down under the influence of proportional representation, which brought a myriad of economic and political interest groups into parliament. After **Hitler**'s rise to power in Germany in 1933, sympathetic Nazi "fronts" emerged, gathering support nationwide from right-wing conservatives and hard-hit petty bourgeois merchants who together proposed a root-and-branch revision of the Federal Constitution. But both a devaluation of the franc in 1936 (which boosted Swiss industry in the run-up to war) and a new partnership of liberals and social democrats – who, in the face of spreading fascism, had together consciously abandoned the ideal of class war that had served them so well in the General Strike – were effectively able to sideline these authoritarian movements in favour of continued democratic debate. As war became more and more likely during the late 1930s, the country bolstered its own national institutions, affirming the status of **Romansh** as a national language, authorizing widespread official usage of **Swiss-German** as a distancing measure from the High German of the Third Reich, and showcasing homegrown achievements at a **National Exhibition** in 1939. In addition, it readied its economy and industry for war, passing a series of laws to protect individual earnings should mobilization become necessary, and introducing anonymous **numbered bank accounts** to protect the savings of German Jews from seizure by the Nazis.

SWITZERLAND AND THE JEWS

As across Europe, **anti-Semitism** worked its way into official Swiss policy over decades. Freedom of residence and civic and legal equality had been granted to Jews in Switzerland only in 1866, and even in the glow of pan-Helvetic pride in national diversity around 1891, a referendum was passed in 1893 banning Jewish ritual slaughter of animals on ostensibly compassionate grounds (ritual slaughter remains illegal in Switzerland today). Russian pogroms in the 1880s resulted in floods of destitute Jews heading west across Europe, and subsequent concerns about **Überfremdung**, or foreign infiltration, of Switzerland showed themselves in discriminatory immigration policies that required complete assimilation and social absorption before civic protection could be conferred: in virtually all cases, Jews who applied for refugee status were deemed to be alien to Swiss society and unassimilable.

As the European situation worsened during the 1930s, Switzerland searched for a way to keep the Jews out – as did many European governments – without being seen to compromise their reputation for neutrality and tradition of providing asylum. In 1938, in response to a specific request to the Gestapo made by Switzerland's police chief, Germany ordered that the passports of all "non-Aryan" Germans – that is, Jews – be stamped with a "J" to identify them to border guards, who were then instructed to turn them back. After August 1942, racial persecution alone was deemed to be not sufficient grounds for emergency admission to the country, and the borders were effectively closed. Only twelve Jews in each year of the war were granted Swiss naturalization papers, and of some 300,000 refugees who were accepted into Switzerland, just ten percent were Jewish. Surviving records testify to 25,000 Jews being turned back at the borders, but the real figure must have been vastly higher.

By autumn 1942, the Red Cross in Geneva knew unequivocally of the systematic murder of Jews in Nazi death camps. Under pressure from the Swiss government, it did and said nothing. The borders remained closed. A few individuals within Switzerland were working against the policies of the government, but the official line was that – in the notorious words of Federal Councillor Eduard von Steiger – "the lifeboat is full".

WORLD WAR II

In the summer of 1939, Switzerland mobilized between ten and twenty percent of its entire population in preparation for **war**. Germany had already invaded Austria in 1938 under the pretext of "union" (*Anschluss*), and by June 1940, Denmark, Norway, Holland, Belgium, Luxembourg and France had all succumbed to the Nazi tanks. Mussolini's fascist Italy lay to the south. Switzerland was surrounded. An invasion by the Axis powers seemed imminent, and on July 25, 1940, following an extremely controversial speech hinting at advantages to be gained by collusion with Berlin, the Swiss commander in chief **General Guisan**, along with the entire Swiss officer corps, took ship in Luzern for the **Rütli** meadow, semi-mythical scene of the founding of the Confederation in 1291. There, at this most resonant spot, Guisan reaffirmed the Swiss commitment to resistance and neutrality, and conducted a ceremony at which all officers did the same. Rumblings of discontent among junior officers at the hints of collaboration in the upper echelons of command were quelled.

And yet it is now clear that collaboration continued apace. Unlike in the previous war, this time the flouting of Swiss neutrality was usefully concealed beneath a glow of national pride and unity, fuelled by the Rütli declaration. The role of Switzerland in World War II is still extremely controversial today, but historians now accept that the country escaped Nazi invasion not simply through the doggedness and tenacity of its troops. Both the Allied and the Axis powers were very well served by having an ostensibly neutral, stable Switzerland at the heart of war-torn Europe. The country's role as a **banking and financial centre** was pivotal: both sides needed to buy war *materiel* and resources, and the only truly convertible currency accepted for payment worldwide for the duration of the war was the Swiss franc. Basel's Bank of International Settlements – a bank of national banks, with board members drawn from the US, Britain, France, Germany and elsewhere – kept the wheels of international capitalism turning throughout the war, and was the only place where **high-level meetings** continued in extreme secrecy between Allied and Axis officials, meetings that were treasonous by the standards of both. Right up until the fall of Berlin in 1945, the Swiss National Bank accepted **gold** from Germany in exchange for Swiss francs, in the full and certain knowledge that Berlin would then use the money to keep the Axis war machine supplied, and that the ingots being shipped into Switzerland by the ton had been looted from the banks of invaded countries and/or melted down from the possessions and even the teeth of dead Jews. Hitler also needed to keep the **Alpine passes** that linked Germany and Italy open, and benefited from Swiss **industry**, which continued to supply the Third Reich with guns, ammunition and heavy artillery, in exchange for essential raw materials and food.

After the Rütli gathering – at the height of the threat of invasion – General Guisan ordered Swiss frontier defence positions to withdraw from the national borders in order to fortify positions within the high Alpine chain. The *réduit national* ("Fortress Switzerland") took shape: at almost any point after 1940, Hitler could have crossed the frontier and taken the entire populated lowlands – Basel, Zürich, Bern, Geneva and the countryside – without a fight, and reduced independent Switzerland to a scattering of snowbound bunkers in the high Alps. But such an invasion would have impoverished the Reich and, in reality, Switzerland was safe: the military kudos to be gained by Hitler's having a subdued, occupied Switzerland subject to Allied bombing was vastly outweighed by the material benefit of his nurturing a nominally neutral, independent Switzerland that remained enthusiastically open for business.

SONDERFALL SCHWEIZ: 1945–2000

Patrick Kury, an historian at the University of Basel, has written in *Images of Switzerland* (see "Books", p.530): "After World War II, the lack of experience of war made Swiss people believe that they were a kind of chosen people living outside history. This strange belief goes together with the misconception that between 1933 and 1945 Switzerland had followed a humanitarian tradition, and had never practised an anti-Jewish [policy]. In the postwar period, neutrality – the number one state maxim – also helped to neutralize analysis and discussion." The glow of national pride in having reached war's end unscathed – despite the fact that Switzerland's citizen army had merely sat tight and kept its head down – was intoxicating, and the Swiss felt themselves to be special: the term **Sonderfall Schweiz**, or "Switzerland as a Special Case", is often used to describe the period. The extent of official collaboration with both warring parties was widely known by foreign governments – who shunned Switzerland immediately postwar – but was generally not even suspected by ordinary Swiss.

However, whereas war swept away old social and political habits across Europe, in Switzerland things continued after the war much as they had done before: while the new world order expressed itself in the establishment of the **United Nations** in 1945, Switzerland stuck tight to its neutrality and stayed out. By 1946 international diplomatic relations had been repaired, and the country – with its intact industry, low taxes, and sociopolitical stability – took on the role of catalyst to European reconstruction. At a time of austerity, Swiss banks were able to draw on large capital reserves (although the provenance of part of this was later to be called into question in connection with the Nazi gold affair). With the **Cold War**, fear of the spread of communism took over from fear of the spread of fascism. Political parties that were already rooted in concordance moved together into a rock-solid national consensus. Dubbed after 1959 the **"magic formula"**, this ensured two seats on the Federal Council went to the moderate-left Liberals, two to the moderate-right Christian Democrats, two to the leftwing Social Democrats and one to the rightwing People's Party.

Along with most of the rest of Western Europe, Switzerland experienced a cycle of economic fortunes – consolidation in the 1950s, boom in the 1960s, recession in the 1970s, entrenchment and readjustment in the 1980s, streamlined growth in the 1990s. However, despite massive advances in personal and national wealth, and success in adapting traditional industries to the new era – exemplified by the launch of **Swatch**, a slick, new company that dragged the Swiss watch industry out of its fustiness – it took until the 1990s for Switzerland to bring itself fully into line with European conceptions of social modernity. **Women** only got the vote in national elections in 1971, decades behind most other European countries, and even as late as 1991, one canton (Appenzell Inner-Rhodes) had to be legally forced to accept women onto the cantonal electoral roll by the Federal Supreme Court. Switzerland is now also the only European country with **universal male conscription**; in November 1989 a petition-led initiative resulted in a 36-percent national vote in favour of immediate abolition of the Swiss army. The number was sizeable enough to leave the generals shaken and to prompt a major rethink of Switzerland's citizen-soldiery, which introduced in 1992 – for the first time – conscientious objection, by which conscripts could opt for civilian service. Before this, otherwise law-abiding Swiss 20-year-olds could be jailed by military courts for refusing army duty. The magic formula also had its detractors: student-led agitation in the late 1960s led to the formation shortly afterwards both of an active **Green Party** and an active rightwing **conservative** bloc. In the 1970s the Greens halted Switzerland's nuclear industry in its tracks and violent separatist agitation led to the formation of a new **Canton Jura** (see p.185), while the conservatives set alarm bells ringing in the minds of honest hardworking folk about the quantity of foreigners in the country.

As the Western European powers drew together in the 1950s in a **common market**, the insular Swiss looked on, the national mood still one of "Fortress Switzerland". Consistently throughout the postwar period, the Swiss people have voted against joining international bodies of political co-operation. In 1986, a proposal for **United Nations** membership received a resounding "no" from 76 percent of Swiss voters, and today Switzerland – along with a couple of Pacific islands – remains virtually the only country in the world without a voting presence in the UN.

Switzerland had been a member of the European Free Trade Area (EFTA), a purely commercial body without political ambitions, since 1960; when its EFTA partners Sweden, Finland and Austria applied to join the **European Union** in 1992, Switzerland was forced to follow suit. Put to the vote, the national margin of defeat was narrow, but analysis of the figures showed that 70 percent had voted yes in francophone Romandie, but just 44 percent had voted yes in German-speaking areas; roughly similar figures taken as a national whole split pro-EU urban voters away from anti-EU rural voters. The figures reignited national soul-searching over the age-old social and linguistic divide, and Switzerland shelved its application.

The reverberations of the 1992 vote still resound around the country today, exploited by a new bloc of strident, rightwing opinion shaped and led by the notorious **Christoph Blocher**, leader of the Zürich section of the SVP (Swiss People's Party). Campaigning throughout the 1990s on a platform of anti-EU, anti-immigration rhetoric – wrapped up in a cloak of pro-Swiss, pro-neutrality platitudes – Blocher's SVP won the largest share of the vote in the October 1999 **general elections**, putting the "magic formula" under intense pressure. To drive home his advantage, in January 2000 Blocher began calling for an extra seat to be reserved for the People's Party on the Federal Council, to be occupied by himself.

It is debatable whether Blocher would have made such gains had it not been for a series of **scandals** throughout the 1990s that sent the country reeling. Suddenly, as if from nowhere, the squeaky-clean image that postwar generations had of themselves and their country was shown to have been an illusion. In 1989, **Elizabeth Kopp**, the first woman to serve as a Federal Councillor – and something of an icon of the new Switzerland – had to resign when it was revealed that she had tipped off her husband about ongoing investigations into his financial dealings. The same year it emerged that the Swiss **secret police** had been keeping hundreds of thousands of files on individuals under the guise of monitoring anti-patriotic activity. In 1999, an accountant in the defence department under investigation in a multimillion-franc **fraud** case – the largest in Swiss history – turned out to be an intelligence agent, and claimed he had withdrawn the money on the orders of his boss to fund the secret training of a shady battalion of highly armed agents for purposes unknown.

But the story that hit the international headlines, and brought Switzerland into the uncomfortable glare of global attention, concerned its **wartime** record (documented at *www. giussani.com* and elsewhere).

WARTIME REAPPRAISAL

With the end of the Cold War in 1989, former Communist countries in Eastern Europe opened their borders and their state archives. **Jews** who had survived the Holocaust began petitioning the governments in Warsaw, Budapest, Prague and elsewhere – often with the help of international Jewish organizations such as the New York-based **World Jewish Congress** (WJC) – for return of property that had been seized by the Nazis. In summer 1995, the **fiftieth anniversary** of the end of World War II prompted apologies from many Western governments for their activities during wartime. Swiss President **Kaspar Villiger** officially apologized for the introduction of the "J" stamp in the passports of German Jews and for Switzerland's closing its borders to Jewish refugees at the height of the Final Solution. Meanwhile, WJC researchers had been recording case after case of Holocaust survivors being refused access to their dead relatives' accounts in Swiss banks, often on spurious grounds such as not providing a death certificate. They began to smell a rat, and turned to the US National Archives, which held official wartime government records tracking the flow of money through Switzerland. They uncovered records showing that the Swiss banks were not just sitting on the assets of dead Jews, but that they had also accepted vast quantities of obviously looted **gold** as part of a hitherto only guessed-at secret, semi-official network of economic collusion with the Third Reich.

The story rapidly hit the headlines, and pressure built for official investigations to begin. In early 1996, the **Swiss Bankers' Association** disingenuously announced it had uncovered a mere Fr.39m in heirless accounts. Pressure built throughout the year, with the WJC and other organizations – Jewish and not – demanding full access to banks' archives to get to the bottom of the story. In January 1997, a security guard working at UBS, **Christoph Meili**, made public the fact that the bank was secretly shredding large quantities of prewar documents. Meili was fired for violating the bank's secrecy and prosecuted shortly afterwards, but became something of a folk hero, not least to liberal-minded Swiss who were getting increasingly uncomfortable with the banks' attitude. It was becoming clear to the Swiss establishment that the game was up: in March, the President, **Arnold Koller**, attempted to head off the oncoming onslaught by proposing the financing of a Fr.7 billion fund from the gold reserves of the Swiss National Bank to support Swiss and foreign victims of oppression and natural disaster – the so-called **Swiss Solidarity Foundation**. Then a local newspaper revealed that **Credit Suisse** – another major Swiss bank – had opened an account for the Nazi SS during the war and that the **Bank for International**

Settlements in Basel had acted as a safe conduit for much of the Reich's looted gold, and the WJC publicized documents from the US National Archive stating that **Japan**, wartime ally of the Nazis, had also used Swiss banks. Meanwhile, the banks themselves were scrabbling to prove their good faith: by July, Fr.17m that had lain in dormant accounts since the war had been returned to the descendants of account holders, but 24 hours after the publication of a new list of 2000 accounts supposedly opened by non-Swiss citizens before 1945 – which the banks claimed to have been unable to trace – it transpired that many of the names appeared in current phonebooks in Switzerland and elsewhere, and would have been traceable with minimal effort.

The affair was souring international relations. Switzerland made official complaints to the BBC over a documentary entitled "Nazi Gold", which it claimed was inaccurate and inflammatory. Canada was forced to admit that it had laundered at least six tons of Nazi gold via Switzerland and Portugal. Bill Clinton and the US Congress granted the bank security guard Christoph Meili asylum, and UBS dropped the case against him in the Swiss courts and apologized. Amidst the tide of accusation and counter-accusation, the **Red Cross** issued an unprecedented statement admitting a "moral failure" in not having spoken out during the war against the ongoing genocide of the Jews.

In October 1997, the Swiss Bankers' Association released a new list of 14,000 dormant accounts opened before 1945. Shortly after, a committee of historians chaired by **Jean-François Bergier** reported that, in addition to the $389m of gold purchased from Nazi Germany by the Swiss National Bank (approximately $4 billion in modern-day terms), some $61m of Nazi gold had been bought by the Swiss commercial banks (among which were UBS and Credit Suisse), three times more than previously thought. In mid-1998, the Bergier commission confirmed that the Swiss National Bank had known that much of the gold they were buying had been looted from occupied countries, and also that officials had been aware that the Nazis were robbing Jews and other persecuted groups before exterminating them.

With an array of lawsuits brought by tens of thousands of Holocaust survivors making their way slowly through the US courts, and escalating threats of a Swiss–US trade war, the international pressure on the Swiss banks to acknowledge culpability for their wartime activities and their subsequent attempts to block investigation was inexorable. In June 1998, after two months of negotiations with lawyers acting for Holocaust survivors, the three largest banks, Credit Suisse, UBS and SBC, offered $600m as a universal sum to settle all claims connected with Holocaust-era assets, and declared it to be their final, top offer. Two months later, desperate to see an end to the story, they agreed to settle for twice as much – $1.25 billion, the so-called **global settlement sum**, to be paid in four instalments into a bank account in the US each November (1998–2001), awaiting final negotiations on distribution of the money. According to a poll, less than half the Swiss population declared itself content with the outcome, most of them believing $1.25 billion to be too high a settlement figure. Meanwhile, the damaging revelations continued to emerge, most notably in February 1999, when the Red Cross was forced to acknowledge deep regret over the fact that in 1949 it issued **Josef Mengele**, the infamous doctor at the Auschwitz death camp, with a permit to travel through Switzerland.

In December 1999, after three years' research, two official commissions set up to look into the whole affair issued their final reports. The **Volcker Commission**, which examined Swiss bank accounts from the Nazi era, found almost 54,000 accounts that had been opened between 1933 and 1945, and, in addition to the thousands of names already declared, advised the banks to publish a further 25,000 names of account holders suspected to have been victims of the Nazis. It estimated that, at current prices, these accounts totalled between $200m and $440m. The report of the **Bergier Commission**, set up to investigate Switzerland's wartime treatment of refugees, merely confirmed what many already

knew, that Switzerland had deliberately blocked the entry of refugees, condemning Jews and others to certain death at the hands of the Nazis. It identified a strain of "cultural, social and political" anti-Semitism that ran through the country at the time. The report prompted Swiss President **Ruth Dreifuss** – the only Jewish woman to have served in the post – to reiterate the government's official apology of 1995 and to acknowledge the major flaws in Swiss asylum policy before and during the war. Final plans to allocate the global settlement sum were delayed until mid-2000 in order to give time to absorb the reports of both commissions.

The whole sorry saga of the 1990s struck deep at the heart of Swiss self-confidence. Statements like those issued by the Bergier Commission that "Switzerland declined to help people in mortal danger" ran counter to all the notions of ethical behaviour that postwar Swiss generations learned from their parents, from each other and from their history books. For some, it has been almost too much to bear: the anger and frustration that has been stirred up in the proudly nationalistic working people of the inner heart of the country in particular, has coincided with the rise of the rightwing demagogue Christoph Blocher, who has channelled it into a coherent, extremist political strategy directed against foreigners of all kinds, embodied in the EU, the UN and the many asylum seekers and guest workers resident in Switzerland. In the mood of the late 1990s, Blocher is able to accuse organizations such as the WJC of blackmail with impunity. The proposal to establish the **Swiss Solidarity Foundation** (see opposite), backed by liberal-minded Swiss, has also been stymied by Blocher, who wants to put the millions into a scheme to bolster state pensions instead. A referendum on the issue, set for March 2000, could go either way. What is clear at the turn of the millennium is that the idea of *Sonderfall Schweiz*, Switzerland as a "Special Case", is dead.

ALPINE FLORA AND FAUNA

From valley floor to mountain summit Switzerland enjoys a wide range of wildlife and botanical habitats. Thanks to the huge difference in altitude, climate and vegetation zones, there's nearly always something of interest to see, whether you're a dedicated naturalist, expert botanist or just a visitor with an interest in the overall mountain environment.

FAUNA

In the distant past the Swiss Alps were inhabited by such creatures as the cave bear, cave lion and panther, and not more than a few hundred years ago the most prolific animals found in the Alpine valleys included the lynx and wildcat, and the wolf. Periods of glaciation drove the first group from the mountains, while hunters reduced the numbers of the latter: the last wolf in Switzerland was thought to have been shot in 1947, but a handful of suspected sightings of wolves during 1999 in the Valais are under current investigation by naturalists. Hunting is still popular today, but is generally under strict controls. The **Parc Naziunal Svizzer** in the Lower Engadine (Swiss National Park; see p.469) is a haven for numerous resident and migratory animals, and is perhaps the country's most rewarding location for the casual wildlife observer,

since something like half of the seventy species of mammals found in Switzerland can be seen there.

Alpine fauna is noted for its extreme shyness, which is why observation can be difficult, but many animals that inhabit the more remote regions of the high Alps also descend to lower altitudes. The following survey, though by no means comprehensive, picks out the highlights.

MAMMALS

The **red deer** (*Cervus elaphus*) had disappeared from much of the country before the National Park was established in 1914, but natural migration from neighbouring regions of Austria saw a steady repopulation in the forested valleys of Graubünden. The adult male dominates a harem of several hinds, and vigorously defends them against all challengers. Fawns are born in May or June and are suckled for three or four months, remaining within easy reach of forest shelter. In summer the adult coat is reddish brown, turning grey-brown in winter. The much smaller **roe deer** (*Capreolus capreolus*) has similar colouring, is timid but also very inquisitive, and can be found roaming around the upper timber line. The best time to observe roe deer is in the early morning, or towards dusk when they stray from tree cover to open meadows and favoured drinking pools. The adult male sprouts slender horns, which are shed during the autumn, at the end of the rut.

The **red squirrel** (*Sciurus vulgaris*), like its American grey cousin in England, favours a woodland habitat and is fairly common throughout Switzerland. Despite the name its coat is dark brown, or almost black, and the female produces up to seven young, born naked and blind in a spherical drey.

The **European lynx** (*Lynx lynx*) was reintroduced into the Swiss Alps in 1970. Weighing 20–30kg it lives in the forests where it preys on birds and mammals up to the size of a roe deer, which it kills with a bite through the neck. Casual sightings are extremely rare. The **wildcat** (*Felis silvestris*) is another elusive forest animal. Larger than the domestic cat, it nevertheless has a purr not unlike that of an ordinary moggie, but a miaow that is deeper and more powerful. A few specimens were released into the wild near Interlaken, and others in the Jura, but it is still by no means common.

The **Alpine hare** (*Lepus timidus*) has a wide distribution in northern Europe and is found in open country both below and above the tree line, to about 3000m. In winter its coat is white; in summer, brown with white patches. Thanks to the production of two, and sometimes three, litters a year, the hare manages to maintain its numbers against the ravages of a variety of carnivores.

Throughout the Alps the shrill, high-pitched alarm whistle of the **marmot** (*Marmota marmota* – or *Murmeltier* in German) will be heard from late spring until early autumn. One of the most widespread of all Alpine rodents, it is ever wary of such predators as the fox and eagle, for which it forms the chief food source. Living in burrows, mostly above the tree line, the marmot hibernates in a "nest" of dried grasses for as many as seven months a year in the upper regions around 3000m, or five to six months at lower altitudes. At the end of hibernation pairing occurs almost at once, and after a 33-day gestation period the young are born, naked and with eyes closed. The young do not emerge from their burrows much before the end of July, by which time they've grown a covering of fur, and are able to attack the coarse meadow grasses with their razor-like teeth. An adult grows to a length of 48–56cm, with a 16–20cm tail, and by September weighs around 4–6kg, although some males can weigh up to 9kg. They live to approximately ten years, although some have been known to reach twenty.

The **chamois** (*Rupicapra rupicapra* – or *Gemse* in German) is found not only in the Alpine regions, but also in the lower Jura mountains of the west and northwest of Switzerland. Although sought by hunters in the autumn, in select areas it has enjoyed protected status since the sixteenth century. The Engadine is thought to have one of Europe's largest populations of this handsome antelope-like ruminant with short hooked horns and a russet coat sometimes lightening to fawn-grey in summer. Noted for its agility, it is also prone to disease, especially the notorious chamois-blindness that occasionally devastates complete herds. The rut finishes in November and the young are born between mid-May and mid-June after a gestation of 160–180 days. A fully grown chamois reaches 1.10–1.30m in length and weighs up to 50kg (male) or 30–35kg (female). Longevity is about twenty years. They can be seen, either singly or in herds, throughout the Swiss Alps – but rarely at close quarters.

While the chamois has short but graceful horns, the stockier male **ibex** (*Capra ibex* – or *Steinbock* in German) has large, knobbly, scimitar-shaped horns which are used as weapons during the battles for dominance that accompany the autumn rut. Defeated males must then wait their turn for sexual maturity until they are able to defend a harem of their own. Although the chamois ranges high in the mountains, the ibex zone is even higher – some have been sighted at over 4000m. For the greater part of the year it lives above the tree line, often roaming to the high snows in summer, but occasionally descending to the forests in winter. Weighing up to 100kg, the ibex negotiates narrow rock ledges with confidence and precision despite its stocky body and comparatively short legs, and apparently displays great care when crossing slopes threatened by avalanche. A sizeable herd roams the upper slopes of Piz Albris near Pontresina in Val Bernina, another can be seen high above Val de Bagnes in the Valais, often grazing close to the Sentier de Chamois hiking trail.

BIRDS

In woodlands of the Alpine foothills, and in the Jura, the bizarre call of the **capercaillie** (*Tetrao urogallus*) rattles in the early hours of a spring dawn: first a pop, then another, followed by a quickening succession that precedes what can only be described as a cork being drawn from a bottle. The capercaillie is scarce enough in the Alps to create a thrill of excitement when heard or seen – its dark shape has easy camouflage in a beech, larch or pine wood where it can feed on assorted berries, buds and needles, but where it can also fall prey to such predators as the fox and marten, while the young are sometimes taken by a goshawk or golden eagle.

Game birds of the forest regions are notoriously difficult to observe except, perhaps, when accidentally flushed out of cover. The hazel hen (*Tetrastes bonasia*), black grouse (*Lyrurus tetrix*), ptarmigan (*Lagopus mutus*) and rock partridge (*Alectoris graeca*) are all found in the National Park, as is the long-billed woodcock (*Scolopax rusticola*), in marshy ground near the tree line.

Other woodland birds found in various parts of Switzerland include a number of **owls**: the eagle owl, tawny, long-eared, pygmy, and small, golden-eyed tengmalm's owl (*Aegolius funereus*), which takes over the abandoned nests of woodpeckers. There are several species of **woodpecker** too, notably the green, great-spotted, black, and rare three-toed woodpecker (*Picoides tridactylus*), all of which are found at some time or other in the forests of the National Park.

There's no shortage of songbirds, most of which are widely distributed throughout Europe, but it is the mountain specialists that are notable in the high Alpine regions and whose presence adds an extra dimension to the climber's day – the **alpine accentor** (*Prunella collaris*), for example, whose nest has been discovered above 3000m and whose song resembles that of the lark, as does its mating flight. Another is the brightly coloured **rock thrush** (*Monticola saxitilis*) that returns to the Alps in mid-May after wintering in tropical Africa. Then there's the **alpine chough** (*Pyrrhocorax graculus*), whose aerial acrobatics, yellow beak and strident call are familiar to all who visit the hikers' huts in the high mountains, where this gregarious bird comes as a scavenger after leftover scraps of food.

The **golden eagle** (*Aquila chrysaetus*) builds its eyrie on inaccessible rock ledges high in the mountains, and with no shortage of sites to choose from, and no shortage of prey either, there's a fair chance of spotting one of these graceful predators sailing over the high pastures in search of food. The golden eagle has a broad appetite: although its basic diet in the summer consists of marmot, it will also strike grouse and mountain hare, and may even try to take the young of chamois and red deer. Since it makes short work of sick and weak animals, its contribution to the maintenance of strong, healthy species is significant.

FLORA

The range of **plants** found in Switzerland is enormous, as one might expect in a country whose soil, habitat, climate and altitude varies from region to region and, in some cases, from one valley to the next. Igneous rocks may dominate in one district, with more plant-friendly limestone in another. Habitats vary from damp grassland to semi-arctic rockface, from desert-like scree to shady woodland, from glacial moraine to the marshy fringe of a mountain lake, from a sunny cliff or stretch of limestone pavement to an acid valley bog. Each has its own specific flora.

Mountains create their own microclimate. One side may be damp, the other protected in a rain shadow. A south-facing hillside will be different from the opposite, north-facing slope, and on a mountainside the seasons change, not by the calendar, but by altitude. All these factors have an effect on the plant life, as do grazing and cultivation of the soil.

In the lower valleys **soldanellas**, **primulas**, **crocus**, **anemones** and others come into flower early in the year as the snow melts, and having bloomed they wither and all but disappear, with only their leaves remaining hidden beneath the new grass of the meadowlands. But as the season advances and the snow recedes, so the same flowers appear higher up the hillside. By mid-June or July, alongside many other plants, they colour the "alps" – the upper pastures – before cattle are brought up for summer grazing. Before the end of July most of the pasture flowers will have gone, but it is then that the screes, moraine walls and rockfaces display their own special Alpine flora.

Of the early pasture and meadowland flowers the **pasque flower** comes in several forms. *Pulsatilla vernalis*, or the spring pasque flower, has its white petals often flushed a pale violet on the outside, while the alpine pasque flower (*Pulsatilla alpina*) is protected from the cold by a coating of tiny hairs. The tiny **alpine snowbell** (*Soldanella alpina*) on the other hand has no apparent protection, even though it often pushes its way through the melting snowfields. Its tassled petals vary from violet to pink-blue depending on habitat, for it may be found on sites as diverse as shallow pockets of limestone, and damp pastures up to 3000m.

The **lily** family is another pasture and meadowland favourite that comes in a great variety of forms, including asphodel, crocus, fritillary and scilla. The claret-headed martagon lily (*Lilium martagon*) appears in shady woodland glades of the Jura, while the extravagant, showy orange lily (*Lilium bulbiferum*) adorns grassy terraces above Urnerboden, east of Altdorf in Canton Uri.

If the lily family has spawned a variety of species, the **gentian** is even more numerous, and in Switzerland is represented by such extremes as the tall, multi-flowered great yellow gentian (*Gentiana lutea*), whose starry flowers burst from an upright stem, to the tiny, delicate blue favourite, the spring gentian (*Gentiana verna*), and deep royal blue – almost navy – of the trumpet gentian (*Gentiana kochiana*), that sometimes appears to have practically no stem at all, but produces flowers almost as it emerges from the turf.

The low-growing, evergreen **alpenrose** shrub (*Rhododendron ferrugineum*) has a remarkably wide range throughout the Alps, flowering pink to deep red on hillsides up to 3200m between June and August, and where it forms a carpet the summer display can be extremely attractive. The **creeping azalea** (*Loiseleuria procumbens*) is a member of the same family, has similar colouring and, at first glance, looks like a much-reduced version of the alpenrose. But this plant prefers exposed peaty sites, and is often found on acid soils, growing at altitudes of 1500–3000m.

Forming cushions over rocks and screes the **moss campion** (*Silene acaulis*) is a mass of pink in a bed of deep green, an eye-catching beauty, while the rosettes of the **common houseleek** (*Sempervivum tectorum*) can decorate otherwise drab moraines when they produce their stalk of bright pink flower heads in summer.

And of course there's the **edelweiss** (*Leontopodium alpinum*), whose woolly grey flowers have for some reason become prized above all other mountain plants. Found usually, but not exclusively, on limestone, it may be seen clustered in short grass overlooking a glacier, or thrusting from a cliff face. Its distribution in Switzerland ranges from the Engadine to the Bernese and Pennine Alps, flourishing between 1700 and 3400m.

Kev Reynolds

BOOKS

It's surprisingly hard to find books about Switzerland. Go to any large bookstore, and you'll see plenty of shelves devoted to the history and politics of Germany, France, Italy and the rest of Europe, but you'll be lucky to find a single work on Switzerland. Literature is the same, with Swiss authors rarely reaching audiences in their native languages outside the borders of their own country, let alone getting translated into English for a wider market.

The best places to hunt are the large **Internet** bookstores: try *barnesandnoble.com*, *bol.com*, *bookshop.co.uk*, *amazon.com* or *amazon.co.uk*. In Britain, Daunt Books, 81 Marylebone High St, London W1M 3DE (☎020/7224 2295), handily organizes its stock of travel books, fiction and non-fiction by country instead of by author or theme, making it easy to riffle through their Swiss titles. The Alpine Club Library, 55 Charlotte Rd, London EC2A 3QF (☎020/7613 0755, *www.alpine-club.org.uk*), has one of the most comprehensive collections of **mountaineering** literature in the world, over 25,000 books, plus journals, guidebooks and expedition reports, including several thousand works on Switzerland alone. Non-members may visit by appointment (Wed–Fri 2–5pm), but no borrowing is allowed.

Pro Helvetia, the federally funded Arts Council of Switzerland, publishes a range of slim paperbacks giving erudite background to the country and its culture in English – subjects covered include music, theatre, the four literatures of Switzerland, Swiss composers, dance and ballet, media, cinema, architecture, philosophy, politics, social structure, refugees, multilingualism, and more. You can get any or all of them for free by contacting your nearest Swiss embassy, or Pro Helvetia at Hirschengraben 22, CH-8024 Zürich (☎01/267 71 71, fax 267 71 06, *phmail@pro-helvetia.ch*).

Publishers are listed below in the form of UK publisher/US publisher, where both exist. Where books are published in only one of these countries we have specified which one; when the same company publishes the book in both, its name appears just once. "UP" stands for University Press, "o/p" signifies out of print. "Bergli" refers to Bergli Books, a small English-language Swiss publisher which produces and distributes a range of books on Switzerland. For details, contact them at Eptingerstrasse 5, CH-4052 Basel (☎061/373 27 77, fax 373 27 78, *www.bergli.ch*).

TRAVEL

EARLY TRAVELLERS

When the first *Murray's Handbook* to Switzerland appeared in 1838, there had already been a couple of centuries or more of travelogues telling of adventures had while on long crossings of the Alps; throughout the nineteenth century, the trickle of memoirs became a flood. Most of these venerable tomes are now long out of print, and the list below is a small selection of more widely available works.

Peter Arengo-Jones, *Queen Victoria in Switzerland* (Robert Hale). Absorbing transcript of Victoria's diaries from her incognito stay in Luzern in August 1868, along with a commentary weaving events into the context of historical and political events of the day.

Mavis Coulson, *Southwards to Geneva* (Alan Sutton). Well-researched survey of two centuries of English travellers' musings on Geneva and the Swiss, including excerpts from the writings of Boswell, Maria Edgeworth, Byron, Shelley and more, along with plenty of pictures, engravings and sketches.

Elma Dangerfield, *Byron & the Romantics in Switzerland 1816* (Thomas Lyster). Slim account of the travels, passions and writings of Byron, Shelley *et al* on their famous visit to Lake Geneva.

Alexandre Dumas, *Travels in Switzerland* (Owen o/p). Entertaining tales of Dumas's journeyings around Switzerland in 1832, at the age of 25.

Heinrich Harrer, *The White Spider* (Flamingo). Classic mountaineer's tale of the first ascent of the North Face of the Eiger in July 1938 by a four-man team from Germany. Full of thrills, spills and remarkably evocative writing.

Mark Twain, *A Tramp Abroad* (Oxford UP) and *Climbing the Rigi* (Hürlimann). Wry, witty and hugely enjoyable tales of mountain climbing and exploration in the Alps when such a thing was the height of fashion.

Edward Whymper, *Scrambles Amongst the Alps* (Dover). Modern reprint of the nineteenth-century mountaineer's original account of the conquest of the Matterhorn, amongst many other epic tales of adventure.

MODERN TRAVELLERS AND EXPAT LIFE

Paul N. Bilton, *The Perpetual Tourist: In Search of a Swiss Role* (Bergli). A diary of an Englishman living in Switzerland, documenting the author's various attempts to bridge the cultural divide. The author quote on the back says it all: "The British look for humour in everything; the Swiss are brought up not to expect it."

Dianne Dicks (ed), *Ticking Along With the Swiss* and *Ticking Along Too* (Bergli). Entertaining collections of personal stories from travellers to Switzerland and various expats living and working there – light reading that offers a sidelong glance at the people and the culture.

Shirley Eu-Wong, *Culture Shock! Switzerland* (Kuperard). Slim, chatty trawl through the idiosyncracies of Swiss society, written more for arriving expats than tourists, though with handy bits and pieces for all.

David Hampshire, *Living and Working in Switzerland* (Survival). A complete rundown of rules and regulations for those planning to emigrate, either permanently or just for the winter ski-bum season, along with a raft of useful tips on how to avoid the worst of the bureaucracy.

Susan Tuttle, *Inside Outlandish* (Bergli). Brief little book that playfully tries to bridge the expat gap, explaining the Swiss to outsiders and outsiders to the Swiss.

Vitali Vitaliev, *Little is the Light* (Simon & Schuster). Subtitled "Nostalgic travels in the mini-states of Europe", this is a trail through Luxembourg, San Marino, the Isle of Man, and various other statelets by an award-winning Russian journalist – the chapter on Liechtenstein is an especially witty and engaging portrait of the country, and one of the few to take the place at least halfway seriously.

GUIDEBOOKS

Marcia & Philip Lieberman, *Switzerland's Mountain Inns* (Countryman, US). Lovingly folksy walking tour of many isolated *Berghäuser* tucked away in the remote Alps, along with plenty of tried and trusted advice for hikers looking to get away from it all.

Marcia & Philip Lieberman, *Walking Switzerland The Swiss Way* (Mountaineers, US). Quality guide to walks throughout the country, with full background, plus plenty of trail information and practical guidelines.

Kev Reynolds, *Walking in the Alps*, *The Valais*, *Central Switzerland*, *The Jura* (with R. Brian Evans), *The Engadine*, *Ticino*, *The Alpine Pass Route*, and *Chamonix to Zermatt: The Walker's Haute Route* (all Cicerone, UK; some Hunter, US, others Interlink, US). The classic Swiss walking guides, vividly and knowledgeably written, containing detailed route descriptions and sketch-maps. *Walking in the Alps* is the largest, an amalgam of several long-distance routes with new trails; all the others are neat little volumes concentrating on particular areas or hikes.

Ian Robertson, *Blue Guide: Switzerland* (A&C Black/Norton). Encyclopedic historical and architectural tour of the whole country, packed with detail on virtually every historical building and a wealth of sketched-out mountain walks and climbs, but lacking any practical information on how to get around or where to stay.

Elisabeth Upton-Eichenberger, *Vaud* and *Zermatt* (Upton-Eichenberger, UK). Excellent self-published guides to two of the country's most celebrated corners, full of tales, historical odds and ends, and other delightfully long-winded material that gets edited out of most ordinary guidebooks.

HISTORY AND SOCIETY

Nicolas Bouvier, Gordon A. Craig & Lionel Gossman, *Geneva, Zürich, Basel* (Princeton UP). Learned modern-day portrait of the three biggest and most important Swiss cities, pulling in strands of history, culture and national identity to paint a picture of present-day Swiss urbanism.

Tom Bower, *Blood Money* (Pan) and *Nazi Gold* (Harperperennial, US). Two recent exposés of the Nazi gold scandal, both sensational airport-style paperbacks full of shocked prose, but both nonetheless getting down to the nitty-gritty.

Joy Charnley & Malcolm Pender (eds), *Images of Switzerland: Challenges from the Margins* (Peter Lang, Bern). Slender collection of essays published by the Centre for Swiss Cultural Studies at Glasgow University, including a review of historical attitudes towards the Jews before World War II, and assessments of themes of marginalization in recent Swiss-German, -French and -Italian literature.

Walter Dettwiler, *William Tell: Portrait of a Legend* (Swiss National Museum). Fascinating little study of the web of tales surrounding the Swiss national hero, and the many different ways the story has been told over the centuries to suit the concerns of each particular age.

Dieter Fahrni, *An Outline History of Switzerland* (Pro Helvetia). Compact 130-page overview of the main events in Swiss history from Julius Caesar to the Nazi gold scandal, a little gushing on recent events and accomplishments (this is, after all, published by the official Arts Council of Switzerland) but nonetheless valuable for its clarity and simplicity of approach. Available free from Swiss embassies worldwide.

Stephen P. Halbrook, *Target Switzerland: Swiss Armed Neutrality in World War II* (Sarpedon). Controversial work putting forward the thesis that it was the mobilization of Switzerland's citizen army, and not high-level politicking and collaboration, that kept the Third Reich at bay during World War II. Lambasted for being naive, it nonetheless brings some interesting facts to light, although remains ultimately unconvincing.

Rolf Kieser & Kurt R. Spillmann (eds), *The New Switzerland: Problems and Policies* (Society for the Promotion of Science and Scholarship, Palo Alto, US). Twenty-eight essays by political and historical specialists on aspects of Swiss culture and society at the end of the century, universal in approach and coverage.

Adam LeBor, *Hitler's Secret Bankers* (Simon & Schuster). Cool, clear uncovering of the role Switzerland – and particularly Basel's Bank of International Settlements – played in laundering Nazi assets and funding both the Nazi and Allied war machines.

Caroline Moorhead, *Dunant's Dream* (HarperCollins). Subtitled "War, Switzerland and the History of the Red Cross", this is a massively detailed trawl through the previously closed archives of the Red Cross, documenting the history of the organization and the sometimes hesitant entanglements of its well-intentioned bureaucrats in the nastiest wars of the twentieth century.

Mitya New, *Switzerland Unwrapped* (I.B. Tauris). Fascinating delve into the country's skeleton-rich cupboards, presenting eye-witness accounts of Swiss treatment of Jews and gypsies, attempts to solve Zürich's drug problems, traditional Swiss culture and how it fits into modern society, and more, well written by a Reuters journalist with an eye for a story.

Joachim Remak, *A Very Civil War* (Westview Press). Illustrated chronicle of the Sonderbund war of 1847 that draws many parallels with the events of the American civil war that followed within fifteen years.

Jonathan Steinberg, *Why Switzerland?* (Cambridge UP). Outstanding overview of Swiss society, history and culture, a learned yet anecdotal account of the country that is rich with detail but maintains a superb grasp of the wider picture. Manages to give profound insight into how Switzerland works, and why it is the way it is, while remaining easily readable and digestible. Perfect train-journey reading: if you buy only one book about the country, buy this one.

John Wraight, *The Swiss and the British* (Michael Russell o/p). Comprehensive study of relations between the two countries – political, cultural, sporting, military and more – in the form of an exhaustive chronology from the earliest times until the present day. Currently out of print, but scheduled for a new edition by 2001.

Jean Ziegler, *The Swiss, The Gold and the Dead* (Harcourt Trade/Penguin). Of all the flood of books that jumped onto the bandwagon of the Nazi gold scandal once the depth of Swiss collaboration became clear, this was the most devastating, written by a highly qualified academic at the University of Geneva and former

Federal Council member – hounded and now politically ostracized for remaining uncowed by the storm of protest his revelations unleashed. His calm condemnation of the entire Swiss establishment for their role in funding the Nazis, perpetuating the war and refusing to come to the help of the Jews endeared him to no one, but he is nonetheless sticking to his guns from the political wilderness. For that if nothing else, this is the cream of the "Nazi Gold" crop.

LITERATURE

SWITZERLAND IN FOREIGN FICTION

This is necessarily a tiny bite at a very large apple, a handful of personal selections that omits much more than it includes.

Anita Brookner, *Hotel du Lac* (Penguin). A romantic novelist runs away from her impending marriage to spend a season at a grand hotel in a genteel lakeside resort (Vevey in all but name), and there finds what seems to be the start of a new life of freedom. Beautifully crafted prose, the best of Brookner's usually rather dry offerings, and winner of the 1984 Booker Prize.

Robert Edric, *In Desolate Heaven* (Random House). Complex and touching story of post-World War I trauma revolving around two former British officers and the woman who befriends them, set in a Swiss spa town.

Graham Greene, *Dr Fischer of Geneva* (Penguin). Apocalyptic novella set in and around the lakeside residence of a rich misanthrope who decides to take his revenge on the fawning socialites who crave his money. A fluent and compelling read, published when Greene was 76.

Patricia Highsmith, *Small g: a Summer Idyll* (Penguin). Highsmith – who spent her last years living in a Ticinese village – is best known for *Strangers on a Train* (made into a film by Alfred Hitchcock in 1951), along with her many works of crime fiction centred on the character of Tom Ripley. *Small g* is focused on the characters who frequent a Zürich bar during one summer, with a story of love, sexuality and generosity expertly plotted around them. She died a month before its publication in 1995.

Henry James, *Daisy Miller* (Penguin). The novella that made James's name, a witty, insightful portrait of a young American tourist visiting Lake Geneva who flirts and teases, and then travels to the Château de Chillon unchaperoned and so gets her comeuppance.

Thomas Mann, *The Magic Mountain* (Minerva/Random House). Seminal World War I novel of ideas that employs a group of patients in a Davos sanatorium to discuss ideas of love, war and death, the characters' ongoing tuberculosis symbolizing the sickness of European society as a whole. Although this novel is acclaimed as the author's greatest, it was received less than favourably in Davos itself, whose residents objected to the town's portrayal as a place of neglect where sufferers stood little chance of being cured. This and Mann's other books were later burned by the Nazis in his native Germany.

Mary Shelley, *Frankenstein* (Penguin). The famous tale of an idealistic doctor's dabblings with the elemental forces of life, inspired by "a half-waking nightmare" and written near Geneva in the summer of 1816 as Mary Shelley's offering in a ghost-story-writing competition dreamt up by Lord Byron.

SWISS AUTHORS

This is a choice of the handful of Swiss authors, classic and modern, whose works have been translated into English. Almost all are German-Swiss. The couple of 1930s novels by the Lausannois writer Charles-Ferdinand Ramuz that have been translated into English – *Terror on the Mountain* and *When the Mountain Fell*, virtually the only works by any French-Swiss authors to be published in English – are now out of print. The array of writings by the great Ticinese poet and novelist Francesco Chiesa, who died in 1973 at the age of 102, have yet to find an English translator, as do any by Romansh writers (bar a single out-of-print anthology).

Reto R. Bezzola, *The Curly-Horned Cow: Anthology of Swiss-Romansh Literature* (o/p). The sole translation into English of any Romansh writing, now out of print.

Michael Butler & Malcolm Pender (eds), *Rejection and Emancipation* (Berg). Study of writing in German-speaking Switzerland between 1945 and 1991, with lit-crit essays on

Frisch and Dürrenmatt, as well as Meyer, Loetscher, Schriber and others.

Max Frisch, *Man in the Holocene* (Harcourt Brace). The most striking of the six novels by Frisch, who was born in Zürich in 1911 and is acclaimed as one of the century's greatest writers. This is a haunting but moving meditation on mortality, illuminating the slow decay of an old man's thought processes as he approaches death. Frisch's other novels are *Bluebeard*, *Gantenbein*, *Homo Faber*, his acclaimed masterpiece *I'm Not Stiller*, and *Montauk*.

Jeremias Gotthelf, *The Black Spider* (Knightscross). Stories, tales and morality pieces from the nineteenth-century Emmental, as told by Gotthelf, a cleric turned author.

Hermann Hesse, *Steppenwolf* (Penguin). Hesse's best-known work, profound social deconstruction wrapped up as fantasy, which weaves strands of eastern religion and mysticism into the compelling tale of a middle-aged misanthrope's progress towards social and spiritual maturity, "violently misunderstood" according to Hesse. Of his dozens of other works, *Siddhartha* is a graceful retelling of the legend of the Buddha; *Narziss and Goldmund* is a picaresque portrait of two monks, one a scholar, the other a bohemian; and *The Glass Bead Game* is a monumental utopian novel, set in a future where an elite group develops a game that resolves the world's conflicts.

Zoë Jenny, *The Pollen Room* (Bloomsbury). An understated, mesmeric novel, translated from the German, poetically chronicling a marriage breakup through the eyes of a child. This is the first novel by Jenny, who was born in Basel in 1974.

Gottfried Keller, *Green Henry* (John Calder). Massive tome of a novel, and a highly celebrated *Bildungsroman*, charting the Zürich-born author's country, youth and philosophy, written between 1846 and 1855 to a backdrop of unrequited love in Berlin.

Johanna Spyri, *Heidi* (Penguin). Perhaps the most famous book ever written about

Switzerland, but a hopelessly moralistic, cloying tale for all that. Spyri nonetheless expertly evokes the folksiness and stolid culture of the Swiss alpine farmers and effortlessly pulls heartstrings for her cheese-munching, milk-quaffing heroine.

Beat Sterchi, *The Cow* (Faber, UK). Newly translated epic first novel set in a dairy farm and an abattoir, focusing on the experiences of a Spanish guest worker in Switzerland. *The Guardian* praised its "uncompromising magnificence as a work of art".

Robert Walser, *Masquerade and other stories* (Quartet). Improvised prose poems and poetic short stories from Walser's life in four cities (Zürich, Berlin, Biel/Bienne and Bern) over the period 1899–1933, tracing influences on and similarities with Kafka and other avant-garde modernists of the time. Walser, born in Biel in 1878, published seven novels, of which three dating from his years in Berlin showcase to best effect his fluent, ironic social observation (*The Tanner Siblings*, 1907; *The Handyman*, 1908; *Jakob von Gunten*, 1909). All remain untranslated. After 1933, Walser spent his last 22 years in an asylum near Appenzell. "I wrote nothing more," he said. "What for? My world had been obliterated by the Nazis."

FOOD AND DRINK

Marianne Kaltenbach, *Cooking in Switzerland* (Wolfgang Hölker, Münster, Germany). Friendly trot through some unreconstructed traditional Swiss recipes, heavy on the meat and cream. Available at the Bider & Tanner bookshop in Basel and elsewhere.

John C. Sloan, *The Surprising Wines of Switzerland* (Bergli). Best book by far on the variety of Swiss wines and viticulture, exploring each area – and virtually each vineyard – with enthusiasm and expertise.

Sue Style, *A Taste of Switzerland* (Bergli). Best of the handful of cookery books devoted to Switzerland, with informed, interesting cultural background to local festivals and food celebrations dotted in amongst the recipes.

LANGUAGE

For a relatively small country bang in the heart of Western Europe, Switzerland has an astonishingly complicated array of languages to have to come to terms with. The one crumb of comfort is that almost everyone you'll come across will speak at least a smattering of English, and some Swiss are disconcertingly multilingual: fluency in six or seven languages isn't as rare as you might assume.

There are four national languages in Switzerland. Broadly, **German** is spoken in the centre and the east; **French** in the west; **Italian** in the south; and **Romansh** in a few small areas of the southeast. The dividing lines between them (see map) mostly stem from the movements of tribal peoples in medieval times, and generally have nothing to do with the cantonal boundaries, which were drawn up much later. Cantons Bern, Fribourg and Valais are all bilingual German/French, while Graubünden is trilingual German/Italian/Romansh.

All the spoken languages of Switzerland have differences from the orthodox standard versions used elsewhere that you may already have a grasp of. The German spoken in Switzerland, for instance, is completely different from that spoken in Germany or Austria, and has its own unique vocabulary, grammar and syntax. Its umbrella title "Swiss-German" covers a multitude of regional **dialects** with marked differences both from each other and from standard German: the dialect of Basel is different from that of Zürich, which is different again from that spoken in the high valleys of Oberwallis. In addition, both the French and Italian of Switzerland have small but noticeable

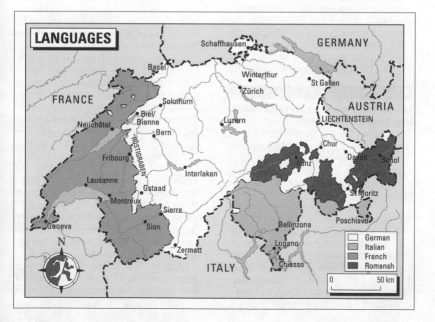

LANGUAGES

Schaffhausen — GERMANY

Basel

Winterthur
Zürich — St Gallen

FRANCE

Solothurn
AUSTRIA
LIECHTENSTEIN

Biel/
Bienne
Neuchâtel
Bern
Luzern

Chur

Fribourg
Ilanz
Davos
Scuol

Lausanne
Interlaken

Gstaad
St Moritz

Montreux
Sierre
Poschiavo

Geneva
Sion
Bellinzona

N
Zermatt
Lugano

ITALY
Chiasso

	German
	Italian
	French
	Romansh

0   50 km

FACTS AND FIGURES

According to census figures, about 64 percent of the Swiss population calls itself German speaking, 19 percent French speaking, 7.5 percent Italian speaking and 0.7 percent Romansh speaking (the rest are "others", principally English-speaking expats and international officials). However, a different census asked which languages people used every day. Taking multiple responses into account, the percentages became 72 German, 33 French, 14.5 Italian, 11 English, 1 Romansh and 11 other – good news for English-speaking visitors, since this shows that more than one in ten of the Swiss population use English regularly every day alongside their own mother tongue.

differences from the "pure" languages spoken over the borders. Romansh (see p.448) has detectably the same Latin roots as French and Italian, but is different from both of them.

As for **phrasebooks**, Rough Guides' own *French, Italian* and *German* are handy (though you'll earn extra respect for attempting Swiss-German where possible), with dictionary-style listings both from and to English, as well as menu readers and grammar sections. The first Romansh-English/English-Romansh dictionary and phrasebook, by Manfred Gross & Daniel Telli, appeared in September 1999 (Hippocrene). Most useful of the lot is an invaluable little phrasebook of **all four Swiss languages** entitled *Schweizer Sprachen, Langues suisses, Lingue svizzere, Linguas svizras*, produced by Dynamicha, a Swiss publisher (CP 421, CH-2001 Neuchâtel; ☎ & fax 032/721 36 06, *www.dynamicha.ch*; ISBN 3952132314). Unfortunately, there's not a word of English in it, so you'll need to be already grounded in at least one of the four in order to make sense of the rest.

GERMAN

Two forms of German are used in Switzerland. **High German**, or *Hochdeutsch* (also known as *Schriftdeutsch*, "Written German") is the same language used throughout German-speaking Europe. **Swiss-German**, or *Schwyzertütsch*, comprises dozens of regional dialects unique to Switzerland, and is unrecognizable to speakers of High German.

No one speaks High German in everyday situations in Switzerland – oral use of High German is restricted to school education, the mass media and public speaking. In all other situations, everyone naturally uses their own local dialect of Swiss-German. And unlike in Britain or France, no one in German-speaking Switzerland strives to copy a Zürich accent or a Basel accent in order to gain greater credibility.

Using the dialect of your home town is a source of pride.

However, Swiss-German is hardly ever written. It's only relatively recently that a dictionary laying down agreed spellings has been compiled, and it's still open to some controversy: ask a Swiss person to write something in Swiss-German and they'll probably struggle to think of how to spell the words. Everybody writes in High German (which is also the language of all signs and public notices) – but when reading out loud, they mentally transcribe the High German text into their own dialect of Swiss-German as they're going along. People see the written word *Dienstag* (Tuesday), and say *tseeschtig*, or *Abend* (evening), and say *obik*. Many High German words simply aren't used: *guten Tag* (hello) is *grüezi* in Swiss-German; *Straßenbahn* (tram) is *Tram*; *Fahrrad* (bicycle) is *Velo*; while regional differences mean that *Wiese* (meadow) is *Wise* in St Gallen but *Matte* in Bern. Add in a range of idiosyncratic regional **accents**, much greater than the accent difference between, say, Munich and Hamburg; a tendency to stick the coy **diminutive** *-li* onto the end of nouns, and to use the throat-rasping **ch** (as in the Scottish *loch*) wherever possible; and a **stress pattern** that lays emphasis in unfamiliar places (usually on the first syllable of a word); and the gulf from High German becomes unbridgeable. To a speaker of *Hochdeutsch*, Swiss-German sounds archaic and singsong ... and this seems to delight the Swiss, who get their own back when they ask Germans to say the Swiss word for "kitchen cupboard": transliterated as *chuchichäschtli*, it sounds, when spoken correctly, like a cat coughing up a hairball. Even the Swiss affectionately dub their own language *Mundart*, or "mouth skill".

Much has been written about the role of Swiss-German as an emblem and symbol of Swissness, and how the accent of each region reflects that region's character: the taut, stretched vowels of *Baseldytsch*; the slow, loping tone of *Berntütsch*; the clipped efficiency of *Züridütsch*; and so on. No Swiss would dream of erasing these differences beneath a unified norm – and no such norm exists. We've picked a rough transliteration of **Bernese dialect** to use here, which will be universally understood, even if they do say things slightly differently elsewhere. Even if you stumble and splutter, the very fact that you're attempting to get your tongue around Swiss-German pronunciation at all will prove a winner with the locals – very much more so than if you were to launch without warning into the slick, snooty language of the "big canton", Germany.

SWISS-GERMAN PRONUNCIATION

Any attempt to lay down rules for Swiss-German **pronunciation** is doomed to failure, since pronunciation of vowels in particular varies from district to district, and even from village to village. The following is only the loosest of guidelines.

In written German, note that all nouns begin with a capital letter, and that an umlaut (¨) over a vowel is sometimes replaced by an "e": Graubünden can be written as Graubuenden. In Switzerland, the German letter ß is always written out as "ss".

VOWELS

Most of the time, pronounce all vowels: *grüezi* has a definite "eh" in the middle, and *Grossbrittanie* has two vowel sounds at the end. In our transliteration, *eis* has only one vowel sound. In our transliteration a double vowel, such as in *Määntig* or *Ziischtig*, doubles the length of the sound.

a as in f**a**ther

ä is sometimes pronounced as in b**ea**r (eg Bärn) and sometimes as in p**ai**d (eg spät)

ai as in l**ie**

au as in h**ou**se

äu as in **oi**l

e as in d**ay** or w**e**t

ee roughly as in d**ay**

ei as in h**ei**ght or sometimes as in fr**ee**

eu approximates to an *ü* sound

i as in l**ee**k

ie as in fr**ee**

o as in b**o**ttom or r**o**se

ö is like the French eu, or the "urgh" in the middle of "colonel"

u as in b**oo**t

ü is like the French u, or a tight-lipped version of tr**ue**

y is a double-length **ee** – Schwyz is pronounced *shveets*

CONSONANTS

There are no silent **consonants**. Differences from English include the following:

ch is a strong throaty rasp, as in the Scottish *loch*

gg is pronounced "ck": "Egg" is *eck*, and may even be written as Eck

j is like an English *y*: "Jura" is *yoora*

k has a throaty rasp attached to it: *danke* is transliterated as *dunkcha*

s is like a softened English *z*

sp at the start of a word is pronounced *shp*

st is always pronounced *sht*

w is like an English *v*

z is always pronounced *ts*

FRENCH

Swiss-**French** is much less fraught with idiosyncracies than Swiss-German. Dialect, though still used in the hinterlands of the Jura, has virtually died out. Differences do remain from standard French – principally in accent and inflection – but the Gallic aspirations of most locals mean that you can speak whatever French you know and be both understood and respected. Indeed, in sharp contrast to France, in Romandie you can even speak English with impunity. The surprising thing is that very few French Swiss speak or understand German. High German – dubbed, with a Gallic disdain for the messy *patois* of their compatriots, *le bon allemand* – is taught in some schools beyond elementary level, but generally only as an optional subject. (On the other hand, schools in German-speaking Switzerland almost always teach French as a compulsory subject until leaving age.) French Swiss have virtually no opportunity to learn anything of spoken Swiss-German without going to live and work on the other side of the language border and picking it up bit by bit.

The most noticeable differences between Swiss-French and standard French are in just a

WORDS AND PHRASES

	SWISS-GERMAN	FRENCH	ITALIAN
THE BASICS			
good morning	guete Morge	bonjour	buongiorno
good evening	guete Obig	bonsoir	buona sera
hello/hi!	grüezi! (grüssech in Bern; grüess Gott in the east)	salut!	salve!/ciao!
cheers! (toast)	proscht!	santé!	salute!
enjoy your meal	enguete	bon appétit	buon appetito
goodbye	of Widerluege	au revoir	arrivederci
bye!	tschüss!/ciao!	salut!	ciao!
yes	jo	oui	si
no	nei	non	no
OK	OK	ça marche	va bene
please	bitte	s'il vous plaît	per favore
thank you (very much)	merci/dunkcha (vielmol)	merci (beaucoup)	(molte) grazie
you're welcome	bitte	je vous en prie	prego
excuse me	entscholdigong	excusez-moi	mi scusi
I'm sorry	es tued mer leid	je suis désolé	mi dispiace
do you speak English?	reded Sii Änglisch?	parlez-vous anglais?	parla inglese?
I come from...	ich be vo...	je viens de...	vengo da...
Britain	Grossbritannie	Grande-Bretagne	Gran Bretagna
Ireland	Irland	Irlande	Irlanda
the US/Canada	d'Schtaate/Kanada	États-Unis/Canada	Stati Uniti/Canada
Australia	Auschtralie	Australie	Australia
New Zealand	Neuseeland	Nouvelle Zélande	Nuova Zelanda
I (don't) speak...	ich rede (ned)...	je (ne) parle (pas)...	io (non) parlo...
High German	Hochdütsch	allemand	tedesco
Swiss-German	Schwyzertütsch	suisse allemand	svizzero-tedesco
French	Französisch	français	francese
Italian	Italiänisch	italienne	italiana
I (don't) understand	ich verschtoh (ned)	je (ne) comprends (pas)	(non) capisco
DIRECTIONS AND TRAVEL			
here/there	hier/dött	ici/là(-bas)	qui/li
left/right	links/rächts	gauche/droite	sinistra/destra
straight on	graduus	tout droit	sempre diritto
near/far	noch/wiit	près/loin	vicino/lontano
quick/slow	schnell/langsam	rapide/lent	rapido/lento
broad/narrow	breit/schmal	large/étroit	largo/stretto
train	Zug	train	treno
station	Bahnhof	gare	stazione
information	Auskunft	renseignements	informazioni
ticket office	Schalter	guichet	sportello
ticket	Billet	billet	biglietto
day card	Tageskarte	carte journalière	carta giornaliera
departure	Abfahrt	départ	partenza
arrival	Ankunft	arrivée	arrivo
which platform for the train to Zürich?	uf welem Gleis fahrt de Zog noch Züri?	sur quel quai part le train pour Zurich?	da quale binario parte il treno per Zurigo?
when does the train arrive in Geneva?	wenn chond de Zog z'Genf aa?	à quelle heure le train arrive t-il à Genève?	quando arriva il treno a Ginevra?

change at Olten	umsteigen in Olten	changer à Olten	cambiare a Olten
lost-property office	Fundbüro	objets trouvés	oggetti smarriti
toilets	Toiletten/WC (spoken: vaytsay)	toilettes	gabinetti
women's toilet	Frauen/Damen	dames	signore
men's toilet	Männer/Herren	hommes	signori
postbus	Postauto	car postal	autopostale
bus stop	Haltestelle	arrêt	fermata
when does the bus to Chur leave?	wenn fahrt de Bus noch Chur?	à quelle heure part le bus pour Coire?	quando parte il autobus per Coira?
supplement	Zuschlag	supplément	sovratassa
tourist bus/coach	Car	autocar	pullman
(rental) car	(Miet)Auto	voiture (de location)	automobile (a noleggio)
parking area	Parkplatz	place de parc	parcheggio
covered car park	Parkhaus	parking	autosilo
available/full	frei/besetzt	libre/occupé	libero/occupato
breakdown	Panne	panne	panna
(steam-)boat	(Dampf)Schiff	bateau (à vapeur)	battello (a vapore)
boat travel	Schifffahrt	navigation	navigazione
(rental) bike	(Miet)Velo	vélo (de location)	bicicletta (a noleggio)
mountain bike	Mountainbike	vélo tout terrain (VTT)	rampichino
airport	Flughafen	aéroport	aeroporto
police	Polizei	police	polizia
fire brigade	Feuerwehr	pompiers	pompieri
ambulance	Ambulance	ambulance	ambulanza

TELLING THE TIME

what time is it?	was isch för Ziit?	quelle heure est-il?	che ora sono?
it's nine o'clock	es isch nüüni	il est neuf heures	sono le nove
1.05	füüf ab eis	une heure cinq	l'una e cinque
2.15	Viertel ab zwöi	deux heures et quart	le due e un quarto
5.45	Viertel vor sächsi	six heures moins quart	le sei meno un quarto
9.40	zwänzg vor zääni	dix heures moins vingt	le dieci meno venti
10.30	halbi elfi (ie half to 11)	dix heures et demie	le dieci e mezza
noon	Mettag	midi	mezzogiorno
midnight	Metternacht	minuit	mezzanotte
an hour	e Schtond	une heure	un'ora
half-an-hour	e Halbschtond	une demi-heure	mezz'ora

HOTELS AND SHOPS

entrance/exit	Eingang/Ausgang	entrée/sortie	entrata/uscita
emergency exit	Notausgang	sortie de secours	uscita di sicurezza
push/pull	drücken/ziehen	poussez/tirez	spingere/tirare
reception	Empfang	réception	ricezione
do you have any rooms available?	händ Sii noh freii Zimmer?	avez-vous des chambres libres?	ha camere libere?
I reserved a room.	ich ha es Zimmer reserviert	j'ai réservé une chambre	ho riservato una camera.
have you got...?	händ Sii...?	avez-vous...?	avete...?
I'd like...	ich hätt gärn...	j'aimerais...	vorrei...
a single room	Einzelzimmer	chambre simple	camera singola
a double room	Doppelzimmer	chambre double	camera doppia
with a shower	mit Dusche	avec douche	con doccia

CONTINUES OVER . . .

HOTELS AND SHOPS (continued)

with a bath	*mit Bad*	*avec bain*	*con bagno*
with a balcony	*mit Balkon*	*avec balcon*	*con balcone*
with a mountain/	*mit Blick uf d'Berge/*	*avec vue sur les*	*con vista sulle*
lake view	*uf de See*	*montagnes/sur le lac*	*montagne/sul lago*
without	*ohne/oni*	*sans*	*senza*
how much is the room...	*was choschtet ...*	*combien coûte*	*quanto costa*
	s'Zimmer	*a chambre...*	*la camera...*
with breakfast	*mit Frühstück*	*avec petit-déjeuner*	*con prima colazione*
with half board	*mit Halbpension*	*en demi-pension*	*mezza pensione*
dormitory	*Massenlager*	*dortoir*	*dormitorio*
campsite	*Campingplatz*	*camping*	*campeggio*
fully booked	*voll/besetzt*	*complet*	*completo*
big/small	*gross/chli*	*grand/petit*	*grande/piccolo*
new/old	*neu/alt*	*nouveau/vieux*	*nuovo/vecchio*
hot/cold	*warm/chalt*	*chaud/froid*	*caldo/freddo*
clean/dirty	*suber/dräckig*	*propre/sale*	*pulito/sporco*
quiet/noisy	*ruhig/lärmig*	*silencieux/bruyant*	*silenzioso/rumoroso*
open/closed	*offen/geschlossen*	*ouvert/fermé*	*aperto/chiuso*
opening hours	*Öffnungszeiten*	*heures d'ouverture*	*orari d'apertura*
day off	*Ruhetag*	*jour de repos*	*giorno di riposo*
VAT (sales tax)	*MWST*	*TVA*	*IVA*

NUMBERS

0	*null*	*zéro*	*zero*
half	*halb*	*demi*	*mezzo*
1	*eis*	*un*	*uno*
2	*zwöi*	*deux*	*due*
3	*drü*	*trois*	*tre*
4	*vier*	*quatre*	*quattro*
5	*füüf*	*cinq*	*cinque*
6	*sächs*	*six*	*sei*
7	*sibe*	*sept*	*sette*
8	*acht*	*huit*	*otto*
9	*nüün*	*neuf*	*nove*
10	*zää*	*dix*	*dieci*
11	*elf*	*onze*	*undici*
12	*zwölf*	*douze*	*dodici*
13	*drizää*	*treize*	*tredici*
14	*vierzää*	*quatorze*	*quattordici*
15	*föfzää*	*quinze*	*quindici*
16	*sächzää*	*seize*	*sedici*
17	*sibezää*	*dix-sept*	*diciasette*
18	*achzää*	*dix-huit*	*diciotto*
19	*nüünzää*	*dix-neuf*	*diciannove*
20	*zwänzg*	*vingt*	*venti*
21	*einezwänzg*	*vingt et un*	*ventuno*
22	*zwöiezwänzg*	*vingt-deux*	*ventidue*
30	*driisg*	*trente*	*trenta*
40	*vierzg*	*quarante*	*quaranta*
50	*föfzg*	*cinquante*	*cinquanta*
60	*sächzg*	*soixante*	*sessanta*
70	*sibezg*	*septante*	*settanta*
80	*achzg*	*huitante*	*ottanta*

90	*nüünzg*	*nonante*	*novanta*
100	*hondert*	*cent*	*cento*
101	*honderteis*	*cent un*	*centouno*
200	*zwöihondert*	*deux cents*	*duecento*
1000	*tuusig*	*mille*	*mille*
2000	*zwöituusig*	*deux mille*	*duemila*
2001	*zwöituusigundeis*	*deux mille un*	*duemila uno*
first	*erscht (1.)*	*premier (1er)*	*primo (1º)*
second	*zwöit (2.)*	*deuxième (2e)*	*secondo (2º)*
third	*dret (3.)*	*troisième (3e)*	*terzo (3º)*
fourth	*viert (4.)*	*quatrième (4e)*	*quarto (4º)*
fifth	*füüft (5.)*	*cinquième (5e)*	*quinto (5º)*
once	*einisch*	*une fois*	*una volta*
twice	*zwöimol*	*deux fois*	*due volte*
three times	*drümol*	*trois fois*	*tre volte*

DAYS AND MONTHS

Beware that abbreviations of the days (for opening hours posted outside museums or shops) can be confusing: "Di" in French-speaking areas means Sunday, but in German-speaking areas means Tuesday. Similarly, "Do" is Thursday in German, but Sunday in Italian.

Monday	*Määntig (Mo)*	*lundi (lu)*	*lunedì (lu)*
Tuesday	*Ziischtig (Di)*	*mardi (ma)*	*martedì (ma)*
Wednesday	*Mettwoch (Mi)*	*mercredi (me)*	*mercoledì (me)*
Thursday	*Donnschtig (Do)*	*jeudi (je)*	*giovedì (gi)*
Friday	*Friitig (Fr)*	*vendredi (ve)*	*venerdì (ve)*
Saturday	*Samschtig (Sa)*	*samedi (sa)*	*sabato (sa)*
Sunday	*Sonntig (So)*	*dimanche (di)*	*domenica (do)*
day	*Tag*	*jour*	*giorno*
in the morning	*am Morge*	*le matin*	*la mattina*
in the afternoon	*am Nomitag*	*l'après-midi*	*di pomeriggio*
in the evening	*am Obig*	*le soir*	*di sera*
at night	*i de Nacht*	*la nuit*	*di notte*
yesterday	*geschter*	*hier*	*ieri*
today	*höt*	*aujourd'hui*	*oggi*
tomorrow	*morn*	*demain*	*domani*
week	*Woche*	*semaine*	*settimana*
month	*Monet*	*mois*	*mese*
year	*Johr*	*année*	*anno*
spring	*Früelig*	*printemps*	*primavera*
summer	*Sommer*	*été*	*estate*
autumn	*Herbscht*	*automne*	*autunno*
winter	*Wenter*	*hiver*	*inverno*
January	*Januar*	*janvier*	*gennaio*
February	*Februar*	*février*	*febbraio*
March	*März*	*mars*	*marzo*
April	*Aprel*	*avril*	*aprile*
May	*Mai*	*mai*	*maggio*
June	*Juni*	*juin*	*giugno*
July	*Juli*	*juillet*	*luglio*
August	*Auguscht*	*août*	*agosto*
September	*September*	*septembre*	*settembre*
October	*Oktober*	*octobre*	*ottobre*
November	*Novämber*	*novembre*	*novembre*
December	*Dezämber*	*décembre*	*dicembre*

handful of words: instead of *soixante-dix, qua-tre-vingts* and *quatre-vingt-dix*, "seventy", "eighty" and "ninety" are *septante, huitante* and *nonante* respectively (although in recent years the influence of international banking in Geneva has encouraged the adoption there of the orthodox French usage of *quatre-vingts* instead of *huitante*). A PO box is a *boîte postale* in France but a *case postale*, or CP, in Switzerland. And in the Fribourgeois country-side, the *–ens* ending of place names such as Vuadens is pronounced in full (*voo-a-donce*) instead of the final *s* remaining silent.

FRENCH PRONUNCIATION

French **pronunciation** can be hard to master, not least because of the tight-lipped precision of many of the sounds compared with slack-jawed English, as well as the lack of any marked stress patterns – in French, equal stress is given to all syllables in a word.

VOWELS

a as in h**a**t

au as in **o**ver

e as in g**e**t

é between g**e**t and g**a**te

è between g**e**t and g**u**t

eu as in h**u**rt

i as in mach**i**ne

o as in h**o**t

ô as in **o**ver

ou as in f**oo**d

u is a tight-lipped version of the English tr**ue**

The following are extra-tricky nasal sounds:

in/im like **a**nxious

an/am and *en/em* like D**on**caster said through your nose

on/om like D**on**caster said with a heavy cold

un/um like **u**nderstand

CONSONANTS

Consonants at the ends of words are usually silent: *pas plus tard* ("not later") is thus pro-nounced *pa-ploo-tarr*. However, when the fol-lowing word begins with a vowel, you should run the consonant over: *pas après* ("not after") is *pazapray*. There are a few differences from English:

ch is an English *sh*

ç is an English *s*

j as in plea**s**ure: "Jura" is *zhoora*

h is silent

ll as in ba**y**onet: "billet" is *bee-yay*

r is growled rather than trilled

th is like an English *t*: "thé" is *tay*

ITALIAN

In **Italian**-speaking Switzerland, written or High Italian is used less than the **Lombardic** dialect common to most of northern Italy. There are also about seven **local** Ticinese dialects, differ-ent again from each other and from Lombardic. Almost all Ticinesi are effectively **quadrilin-gual**: to friends and family, the language of inti-macy is the home dialect; on the street, the lan-guage of friendly conversation is Lombardic; to strangers and where there's any element of reserve, the language of formality is High Italian; and, in addition, most Ticinesi are also proficient in German and/or Swiss-German in order to communicate with the vast numbers of tourists from the north. English, although spo-ken by some, remains well down the list.

The upshot of this is that, even if you hap-pened to be fluent in Lombardic dialect, every-one you met in Ticino would anyway instinctive-ly speak to you – a stranger and a foreigner – in standard Italian, which fortunately is not exces-sively hard for English-speakers to master.

ITALIAN PRONUNCIATION

Pronunciation of Italian is easy, since every word is spoken exactly as it is written and usu-ally enunciated with exaggerated, open-mouthed clarity. The only slight difficulties come in the following **consonants**, which dif-fer from English:

c before e or i is an English *ch*: "cioccolata" is *chokolata*

ch is an English *k*: "chiesa" is *kee-ay-za*

g before e or i is an English *j*: "Maggiore" is *madge-or-eh*, "giorno" is *jorno*

g before h as in **g**un

gli as in mil**li**on: "figlia" is *fil-ya*

gn as in o**ni**on: "bagno" is *ban-yo*

h is silent

sci as in **shi**p

sce as in **she**d

z as in ba**ts**

ROMANSH

There's a survey of the various dialects of Romansh on p.448. Some similarities exist with Italian as regards pronunciation, but there are a few significant differences:

c before e or i is pronounced as in ba**ts**

ch before a or o is a palatal sneeze-like *tya* sound lost in the middle of sta**tu**te, almost an English *ch* but not quite; if there's a preceding *s*, Romansh separates the two with a hyphen – the Engadine town of Chamues-ch is pronounced something like *tyamwesh-tyuh*

ch before e or i is pronounced as in **c**at

g before e or i is pronounced as in **g**eranium

g before h is pronounced as in **g**arlic

gl before i and at the end of a word is like sta**lli**on: Muragl is *moo-rye-el*

gn as in o**ni**on

h is silent

j is like an English y

qu before a, e or i as in **qu**ack

s before any consonant is an English sh

tg is like an English *ch*: "notg" is like *notch*

THE BASICS

hello	*bun di*	no	*na*	I'm sorry	*i ma displascha*
hi!	*allegra!*	OK	*va bain*	I (don't) speak	*jau (na) discur*
cheers! (toast)	*viva!*	please	*anzi*	Romansh	*(betg) rumantsch*
goodbye	*a revair*	thank you	*grazia (fitg)*	I (don't)	*jau (na) chap-*
bye!	*ciao!*	(very much)		understand	*esch (betg)*
yes	*gea*	excuse me	*stgisai*		

TRAVEL

train	*tren*	information	*infurmaziuns*	postbus	*auto postal*
station	*staziun*	ticket	*bigliet*	bus stop	*fermada*

HOTELS AND SHOPS

I'd like…	*jau avess gugent…*	how much is the	*quant custa la chombra…*	
a single room	*chombra singula*	room…		
a double room	*chombra dubla*	with breakfast	*cun ensolver*	
with a basin	*cun aua currenta*	with half board	*mesa pensiun*	
with a shower	*cun duscha*	dormitory	*champ da massa*	
with a bath	*cun bogn*	campsite	*plazza de campar*	
		open/closed	*avert/serrà*	
		day off	*di da repaus*	

EATING AND DRINKING

bread	*paun*	pork	*portg*	vegetables	*verdura*
butter	*paintg*	chicken	*pulaster*	fruit	*fritgs*
cheese	*chaschiel*	game	*selvaschina*	white/	*vin alv/*
soup	*schuppa*	sausage	*liongia*	red wine	*cotschen*
beef	*bov*	fish	*pesch*	a beer	*ina biera*
veal	*vadè*	potato	*tartuffel*	water	*aua*

DAYS AND NUMBERS

Monday	*glindesdi*	in the afternoon	*il suenter-*	2	*dus*
Tuesday	*mardi*		*mezdi*	3	*trais*
Wednesday	*mesemna*	in the evening	*la saira*	4	*quatter*
Thursday	*gievgia*	at night	*la notg*	5	*tschintg*
Friday	*venderdi*	yesterday	*ier*	6	*sis*
Saturday	*sonda*	today	*oz*	7	*set*
Sunday	*dumengia*	tomorrow	*damaun*	8	*otg*
day	*di*	0	*nulla*	9	*nov*
in the morning	*la damaun*	1	*in*	10	*diesch*

GLOSSARY

GERMAN

ABFAHRT departure

ACHTUNG! Beware!

ALTSTADT Old Town

ANKUNFT arrival

AUSKUNFT information

BACH stream

BAHNHOF station

BERG mountain

BERGFÜHRER mountain guide

BERGWEG mountain path

BILLETS tickets

BLAUE ZONE blue zone (city parking)

BRÜCKE bridge

DEUTSCHSCHWEIZ German-speaking Switzerland

DORF village

DURCHGANG passageway

FLUSS river

FUSSGÄNGERZONE pedestrian zone

GASSE alley

GEFAHR! Danger!

GEPÄCK baggage

GIPFEL summit

GLETSCHER glacier

GUTBÜRGERLICHE traditional, solidly bourgeois

HAFEN harbour

HAUPTBAHNHOF main station

HOCHSAISON high season

HOF court or courtyard

HORN peak

JASS (*yass*) extremely complicated card game played in taverns by young and old using nonstandard Swiss playing cards which feature Rosen (roses), Schilden (shields), Eicheln (acorns) and Schellen (bells)

JUGENDHERBERGE youth hostel

KANTÖNLIGEIST literally "little cantonal spirit": describes a stubborn Swiss parochialism, a blinkered pride in the attributes and culture of one's own town or canton above all others (with the same overtones as "Little Englander")

KIRCHE church

KLOSTER monastery or convent

KUNST art

KURVEREIN tourist office

MASSENLAGER dormitory

MATRATZENLAGER dormitory

MITENAND friendly welcoming Swiss-German term for everyone in a group, with the same disarming overtones as "folks" in English: a hotel receptionist or maitre d' will greet a party with *grüezi mitenand* ("hello everyone"), a waiter will say *enguete mitenand* ("enjoy your meal, folks"), and so on

MÜNSTER minster or cathedral

NACHSAISON low season

NORD north

OBER upper

OST east

PLATZ town square

RATHAUS town hall

RÖSTIGRABEN informal name for the language border – a *Graben* is a military trench – between French-speaking Switzerland (where they don't eat the traditional potato dish *Rösti*) and German-speaking Switzerland (where they do)

SAMMLUNG collection

SBB Swiss Federal Railways

SCHLOSS castle or stately home

SCHLUCHT gorge

SCHWEIZ Switzerland

SEE lake

STRASSE street

SUD south

TAL valley

TESSIN Ticino

TOR gate

TOURISMUS tourist office

TOURISTENLAGER dormitory

TURM tower

VERBOTEN! Prohibited!

VERKEHRSVEREIN tourist office

VORSAISON low season

WALD forest

WANDERWEG footpath

WELSCHLAND informal name for French-speaking Switzerland (the Swiss-German word *Choderwelsch* means "gobbledy-gook")

WESTSCHWEIZ formal name for French-speaking Switzerland

ZEUGHAUS arsenal

FRENCH

AUBERGE DE JEUNESSE youth hostel

BASSE-SAISON low season

BILLETTES tickets

BOIS woods

CFF Swiss Federal Railways

CHÂTEAU castle or stately home

CHEMIN PÉDESTRE footpath

COL mountain pass

ÉGLISE church

EST east

FORÊT forest

GARE station

HAUTE-SAISON high season

HÔTEL DE VILLE town hall

INTERDIT! Prohibited!

NORD north

OFFICE DU TOURISME tourist office

OUEST west

PONT bridge

RANDONNÉE hike

RENSEIGNEMENTS information

ROMANDIE French-speaking Switzerland

RUE street

RUELLE alley

SUD south

SUISSE Switzerland

SUISSE ALÉMANIQUE German-speaking Switzerland

SUISSE ROMANDE French-speaking Switzerland

TESSIN Ticino

TOUR tower

VIEILLE VILLE Old Town

ZONE POUR PIÉTONS pedestrian zone

ITALIAN

ALBERGO hotel or inn

ALLOGGIO accommodation

ALTA STAGIONE high season

ARRIVO arrival

BASSA STAGIONE low season

BIGLIETTI tickets

BOSCO forest or woodland

CAPANNA alpine hut

CASTELLO castle

CENTRO STORICO Old Town

CHIESA church

ENTE TURISTICO tourist office

EST east

FFS Swiss Federal Railways

FIUME river

GHIACCIAIO glacier

GROTTO rustic country tavern

LAGO lake

NORD north

OSTELLO PER LA GIOVENTÙ youth hostel

OSTERIA rustic country tavern

OVEST west

PALAZZO CIVICO city hall

PARTENZA departure

PERICOLO! Danger!

PIANO floor or storey (in a building)

PIZ peak

PONTE bridge

RIFUGIO alpine hut

SENTIERO footpath

SUD south

SVIZZERA Switzerland

SVIZZERA ROMANDA French-speaking Switzerland

SVIZZERA TEDESCA German-speaking Switzerland

TORRE tower

VIA street

VICOLO alley

VIETATO! Prohibited!

ZONA PEDONALE pedestrian zone

ART AND ARCHITECTURE

APSE semi-circular termination at the east (altar) end of a church

BAROQUE exuberant architectural style of the seventeenth and early eighteenth centuries, characterized by ornate decoration, complex spatial arrangements and grand vistas. The term is also applied to the sumptuous style of painting of the same period

BIEDERMEIER simple, bourgeois style of painting and decoration practised throughout the first half of the nineteenth century in German-speaking Europe

CAPITAL the top of a column, usually ornate

CAROLINGIAN mid eighth to early tenth century style of art and architecture named after Charlemagne

CHANCEL part of a church in which the altar is located

CHOIR part of a church where the service is sung, usually beside the altar

FRESCO mural painting applied to wet plaster, so that the colours immediately soak in

GOTHIC architectural style of the thirteenth and fourteenth centuries, with an emphasis on verticality, characterized by pointed arches, ribbed vaulting and flying buttresses

NEOCLASSICAL late-eighteenth and early nineteenth-century style of art and architecture which returned to Classical styles as a reaction against Baroque and Rococo excesses

ORIEL projecting bay window

RENAISSANCE fifteenth- and sixteenth-century Italian-originated movement in art and architecture, inspired by the rediscovery of Classical ideals

ROCOCO highly florid, light and graceful eighteenth-century style of architecture, painting and interior design, forming the last phase of Baroque

ROMANESQUE solid architectural style of the late tenth to mid-thirteenth centuries, characterized by round-headed arches and a penchant for horizontality and geometrical precision

ROOD SCREEN screen in a Catholic church dividing the nave from the chancel (and thus separating worshippers from clergy)

SGRAFFITI exterior house decoration of the Romansh-speaking Engadine Valley of Graubünden whereby designs or mottoes are etched into a white layer of plaster to reveal a darker-coloured layer beneath

SPANDREL the underside of an arch

STUCCO plaster used for decorative effects

TROMPE L'OEIL painting designed to fool the viewer into believing it is three-dimensional.

INDEX

barnes & Noble, Inc
5303 FM 1960 West
Houston, TX 77069
281-631-0681
281-631-0681 01-19-01 S02947 R002

Rough Guide to Switzerla   18.95
1858285380

SUB TOTAL   18.95
SALES TAX   1.37
TOTAL   20.32
AMOUNT TENDERED

CASH   2.75
GIFT CARD REDEEM   17.57
Card # 349010198686643
AUTH CODE: #818032
BALANCE REMAINING   .00

TOTAL PAYMENT   20.57
CHANGE   .25
Thanks for shopping at Barnes & Noble!
#125387 01-19-01 03148P 012
Booksellers Since 1873

ROUGH GUIDES: Travel

Amsterdam
Andalucia
Australia

Austria
Bali & Lombok
Barcelona
Belgium &
  Luxembourg
Belize
Berlin
Brazil
Britain
Brittany &
  Normandy
Bulgaria
California
Canada
Central America
Chile
China
Corfu & the
  Ionian Islands
Corsica
Costa Rica
Crete
Croatia
Cyprus
Czech & Slovak
  Republics
Dodecanese &
  the East Aegean

Dominican
  Republic
Ecuador
Egypt
England
Europe
Florida
France
French Hotels &
  Restaurants
  1999
Germany
Goa
Greece
Greek Islands
Guatemala
Hawaii
Holland
Hong Kong &
  Macau
Hungary
India
Indonesia
Ireland
Israel & the
  Palestinian
  Territories
Italy
Jamaica
Japan
Jordan

Kenya
Lake District
Laos
London
Los Angeles
Malaysia,
  Singapore &
  Brunei
Mallorca &
  Menorca
Maya World
Mexico
Morocco
Moscow
Nepal
New England
New York
New Zealand
Norway
Pacific
  Northwest
Paris
Peru
Poland
Portugal
Prague
Provence & the
  Côte d'Azur
The Pyrenees
Rhodes & the
  Dodecanese

Romania
St Petersburg
San Francisco
Sardinia
Scandinavia
Scotland
Scottish
  highlands and
  Islands
Sicily
Singapore
South Africa
South India
Southwest USA
Spain
Sweden
Syria

Thailand
Trinidad &
  Tobago
Tunisia
Turkey
Tuscany &
  Umbria
USA
Venice
Vienna
Vietnam
Wales
Washington DC
West Africa
Zimbabwe &
  Botswana

AVAILABLE AT ALL GOOD BOOKSHOPS

WHEN WAS THE LAST TIME YOU FELT THIS GOOD IN THE AIR?

swissair
1-800-221-4750

Partner in the Delta Air Lines, Midwest Express Airlines
and US Airways frequent flyer programs.